DISCARD

INTERNATIONAL BIBLIOGRAPHY
OF THE SOCIAL SCIENCES
BIBLIOGRAPHIE INTERNATIONALE
DES SCIENCES SOCIALES

Publications of the ICSSD / Publications du CIDSS

INTERNATIONAL BIBLIOGRAPHY OF THE SOCIAL SCIENCES / BIBLIOGRAPHIE INTERNATIONALE DES SCIENCES SOCIALES

[published annually in four parts / paraissant chaque année en quatre parties, since 1961 / Jusqu'en 1961: UNESCO, Paris].

International bibliography of sociology / Bibliographie internationale de sociologie [red cover/couverture rouge]. Vol. 1: 1951 (Publ. 1952).

International bibliography of political science / Bibliographie internationale de science politique [grey cover/couverture grise]. Vol. 1: 1952 (Publ. 1954).

International bibliography of economics / Bibliographie internationale de science économique [yellow cover/couverture jaune]. Vol. 1: 1952 (Publ. 1955).

International bibliography of social and cultural anthropology / Bibliographie internationale d'anthropologie sociale et culturelle [green cover/couverture verte]. Vol. 1: 1955 (Publ. 1958).

Prepared by / Etablie par

THE INTERNATIONAL COMMITTEE FOR SOCIAL SCIENCE INFORMATION AND DOCUMENTATION
LE COMITÉ INTERNATIONAL POUR L'INFORMATION ET LA DOCUMENTATION EN SCIENCES SOCIALES

27, rue Saint-Guillaume, 75007 Paris

Members / Membres, 1985

Dominique Babini, *Fundación José María Aragón, Buenos Aires*
Djamchid Behnam, *Conseil International des Sciences Sociales, Paris*
Russell Bernard, *University of Florida, Gainesville*
John B. Black, *University of Guelph*
Bernardo Colombo, *Facoltà die Scienze statistiche demografiche ed attuariali, Padova*
Azuka Dike, *University of Nigeria, Nsukka*
Géry d'Ydewalle, *Universiteit te Leuven*
Jean-E. Humblet, *University of British Columbia, Vancouver*
Jean Laponce, *University of British Columbia, Vancouver*
Yoshiro Matsuda, *Hitotsubashi University, Tokyo*
Kyllikki Ruokonen, *Helsinki School of Economics Library, Helsinki*
Janusz Sach, *Centre d'information scientifique de l'Académie polonaise des Sciences, Varsovie*
William A. Steiner, *Squire Law Library, Cambridge*
Daniel Vitry, *Université de droit, d'économie et des sciences sociales, Paris*

General Secretary / Secrétaire Général

JEAN MEYRIAT

École des hautes études en sciences sociales, Paris

Assistant General Secretary and Managing Editor
Secrétaire Général Adjoint et Secrétaire de Rédaction

JEAN VIET

Maison des sciences de l'homme, Paris

Associate Editor / Co-rédacteur

JOHN B. BLACK

University of Guelph, Ontario

INTERNATIONAL BIBLIOGRAPHY OF THE SOCIAL SCIENCES

BIBLIOGRAPHIE INTERNATIONALE DES SCIENCES SOCIALES

1984

International Bibliography of SOCIOLOGY

Bibliographie internationale de SOCIOLOGIE

VOL. XXXIV

Prepared by the
International Committee for Social Science Information and
Documentation

Établie par le
Comité international pour l'information et la documentation
en sciences sociales

TAVISTOCK PUBLICATIONS
LONDON AND NEW YORK

Manuscript prepared under the auspices of the International Sociological Association by the ICSSD with the financial support of Unesco (Subvention — 1984-1985, DG/7.6.2/SUB. 15 (SHS))

Manuscrit préparé sous les auspices de l'Association Internationale de Sociologie par le CIDSS avec le concours financier de l'Unesco (Subvention — 1984-1985, DG/7.6.2/SUB. 15 (SHS))

Published in 1987 by
Tavistock Publications Ltd.
11 New Fetter Lane,
London EC4P 4EE

Published in the USA by
Tavistock Publications
in association with Methuen, Inc.
29 West 35th Street, New York, NY 10001

British Library Cataloguing in Publication Data

International bibliography of sociology. —
(International bibliography of the social
sciences) Vol. 34

1. Sociology — Bibliography
I. International Committee for Social Science
Information and Documentation II. Series
016.301   Z7164.S68

ISBN 0-422 81120 3
ISSN 0085-2066

Printed in Great Britain
by Richard Clay & Co. Ltd
Bungay, Suffolk

TABLE OF CONTENTS
TABLE DES MATIÈRES

Preface VII

Préface VIII

Criteria for the selection of items IX

Critères pour la sélection des références XI

Annex / Annexe : Other bibliographical journals /
Autres revues bibliographiques XIII

Acknowledgements / Remerciements XV

List of Periodicals consulted / Liste des périodiques consultés XVII

Classification scheme / Plan de classification XXXIII

Bibliography for 1984 / Bibliographie pour 1984 1

Author Index / Index des auteurs 227

Subject Index 275

Index des matières 352

PREFACE

This issue takes its place in the annual four volume series of the *International Bibliography of the Social Sciences,* regularly published since 1952. These volumes are respectively dedicated to Sociology, Economics, Political Science and Social and Cultural Anthropology.

Each of these volumes is intended to index the main primary publications of a given year pertaining to one social science discipline; in addition, some publications not covered by the previous volumes are also mentioned. So a cumulative but at the same time selective memory is enriched with a new stratum. It is intended to make possible retrospective search rather than current awareness. Our criteria for selection are explained on page IX.

Each volume is expected to satisfy in most cases the requirements of people working in a given discipline. For this purpose some citations of publications related to several disciplines are duplicated in two or even three of our volumes.

However, it will be often useful, in order to collect more information, to search not only this volume but also one of the three others in the same series, or a bibliography published by another organization pertaining to a neighbouring field : a list of the main bibliographical journals is given as an annex.

For some years the edition of our Bibliography has been computerized. In this way we are developing a database which is already available on-line and will be soon made publicly accessible. The published volumes are therefore a product of this base.

PRÉFACE

Ce nouveau tome prend place dans la série annuelle en quatre volumes, désormais bien connue, de la *Bibliographie Internationale des Sciences Sociales*, régulièrement publiée depuis 1952. Ces volumes sont respectivement consacrés à la Sociologie, à la Science Economique, à la Science Politique et à l'Anthropologie Sociale et Culturelle.

Chacun de ces volumes a pour objet de recenser les principales publications originales parues pendant un an dans la discipline qu'il couvre. Il signale en outre les titres qui n'avaient pas pu l'être l'année précédente. Il enrichit d'une nouvelle strate une mémoire cumulative mais sélective destinée à permettre la recherche rétrospective plus encore que l'information courante. Nos critères de sélection sont expliqués ci-après.

Chaque volume doit pouvoir suffire dans la plupart des cas aux spécialistes de la discipline couverte; c'est pourquoi certaines des références à des publications intéressant plusieurs disciplines sont répétées dans deux ou même trois de ces volumes.

Néanmoins, on aura souvent intérêt, pour obtenir davantage d'informations, à compléter l'utilisation du présent volume par celle de l'un des trois autres de notre série, ou encore d'une bibliographie publiée par une autre organisation et couvrant un domaine voisin : quelques-unes des plus importantes parmi ces dernières sont indiquées en annexe.

Depuis plusieurs années la préparation de notre Bibliographie est informatisée. Nous constituons ainsi une banque de données qui est d'ores et déjà consultable, et dont l'accès va bientôt être rendu public. Les volumes imprimés représentent ainsi un produit de cette banque.

CRITERIA FOR THE SELECTION OF ITEMS

	Included	**Left out**
Subject	Documents relevant to one of the main social sciences : political science, economics, sociology, social and cultural anthropology; or to an interdisciplinary field, e.g. political philosophy, history of ideas, economic history, constitutional law, public international law, social psychology, demography, urban planning...	general philosophy, general or political history, law and jurisprudence, experimental or clinical psychology, humanities, human biology, physical anthropology, archaeology...
Nature of Items	Writings of a scientific nature, i.e. intending to communicate new knowledge on a subject, with a theoretical component	
	Up-to-date writings, bringing new ideas or making use of new materials	Purely informative or popular papers, presentation of primary data, legislative or judicial texts, description of a current situation without general implications
		Monographs on a topic of a parochial relevance only (Exception : in *Anthropology*, even local monographs may have a general significance and deserve inclusion)
Type of Documents *Books*	Scholarly books Advanced level textbooks (but with discretion) Collections of original articles	Popular books elementary textbooks
	First edition, or new and completely revised edition	2nd, 3rd ... editions

	Included	Left out
	Translation into a more known language of a book originally published in a language known by few people	Translation into languages with a limited area of utilization
Articles	Scholarly articles published in specialised journals (monthly or less frequent)	Articles in newspapers or journals published several times each month
	Authored articles	Unsigned articles
	Articles of relevance to one of the social sciences pub-lished in a journal of some other speciality	
	Review articles, significant book reviews	
		Redundant articles (by the same author on the same topic in several journals)
		Partisan or polemical articles
		Very short articles, brief communications (unless of major significance)
Serials	First issue only of a new specialised journal or yearbook	
Research reports, theses, dissertations	If published, or if publicly available from a known repository	
Unpublished governmental documents	If containing analysis with general significance, and if easily available for loan or photocopy	If purely administrative per nature, or containing only data
Microforms	If micro-edition of works not available under other form	If reproduction of documents previously published
Bibliographic materials	Specialised (social science) bibliographies, progress reports, specialised glossaries or dictionaries	

CRITÈRES POUR LA SÉLECTION DES RÉFÉRENCES

	Sont retenus	Sont exclus
Sujet	Les documents concernant l'une des principales sciences sociales : science politique, science économique, sociologie, anthropologie sociale et culturelle; ou un domaine interdisciplinaire, ex. : philosophie politique, histoire des idées, histoire économique, droit constitutionnel, droit international public, psychologie sociale, démographie, planification urbaine...	philosophie générale, histoire générale ou politique, législation et droit, psychologie expérimentale ou clinique, humanités, biologie humaine, anthropologie physique, archéologie...
Nature des Références	Ecrits de nature scientifique, c'est à dire destinés à communiquer des connaissances nouvelles sur un sujet avec une composante théorique	
	Ecrits à jour, apportant des idées nouvelles ou utilisant des données nouvelles	Ecrits uniquement informatifs ou destinés au grand public, recueils de données primaires, textes législatifs ou juridiques, description d'une situation ne présentant pas d'implication de portée générale
		Etudes monographiques d'un sujet d'intérêt purement local (Exception : en *Anthropologie*, même des monographies locales peuvent être pertinentes et méritent d'être retenues)
Type de Documents *Livres*	Ouvrages de recherche Manuels de niveau post-universitaire (avec modération) Recueils d'articles originaux	Livres pour grand public, manuels élémentaires
	1ère édition, ou alors édition entièrement revue et complétée	2ème, 3ème ... éditions

	Sont retenus	Sont exclus
	Traduction en une langue largement diffusée d'un livre originellement publié dans une langue de faible diffusion	Traduction dans des langues de faible diffusion
Articles	Articles ''savants'' publiés dans des revues spécialisées (mensuelles ou paraissant moins fréquemment)	Articles de journaux ou de périodiques paraissant plusieurs fois par mois
	Articles signés	Articles anonymes
	Articles relevant d'une des sciences sociales publiés dans une revue de spécialisation différente	
	Articles critiques, comptes rendus critiques substantiels	Articles répétitifs (publiés par le même auteur sur le même sujet dans des revues différentes)
		Articles de nature partisane ou polémique
		Articles très courts, communications brèves (sauf si elles sont d'une portée exceptionnelle)
Publications en séries	La première livraison seulement d'un nouveau périodique spécialisé ou annuaire	
Rapports de recherche, thèses	S'ils ont été publiés, ou s'ils sont à la disposition du public dans un dépôt bien identifié	
Documents officiels inédits	S'ils contiennent des analyses de valeur générale, et si l'on peut facilement les emprunter ou les photocopier	S'ils sont de nature purement administrative ou contiennent seulement des données
Microformes	Les éditions sur microforme de livres qui ne seraient pas disponibles autrement	Les reproductions de documents antérieurement publiés
Matériaux bibliographiques	Les bibliographies spécialisées en sciences sociales, les rapports sur l'avancement de recherches, les glossaires ou dictionnaires spécialisés	

ANNEX/ANNEXE
OTHER BIBLIOGRAPHICAL JOURNALS
AUTRES REVUES BIBLIOGRAPHIQUES

I.   ABSTRACTING JOURNALS (covering the same fields as the *International Bibliography of the Social Sciences*)
RECUEILS DE RÉSUMÉS ANALYTIQUES (couvrant les mêmes disciplines que la *Bibliographie internationale des sciences sociales.*)

Economics / Science économique:
Economic Titles / Abstracts. The Hague, Nijhoff, 1974 — . 24 x (per year/par an)
Journal of Economic Literature. Pittsburgh, American Economic Association, 1962 — . 4 x (per year/par an)

Political Science / Science politique:
International Political Science Abstracts / Documentation politique internationale. Paris, International Political Science Association, 1951 — . 6 x (per year/par an)

Social and Cultural Anthropology / Anthropologie sociale et culturelle:
Abstracts in Anthropology. New York, Baywood Publishing Co., 1970 — . 4 x (per year/par an)

Sociology / Sociologie:
Bulletin signaletique — Centre national de la recherche scientifique. Section 521. Sociologie, ethnologie. Paris, CNRS, 1969 — . 4 x (per year/par an)
Sociological Abstracts. San Diego, CA, Sociological Abstracts Inc., 1952 — . 8 x (per year/par an)

II.   CURRENT BIBLIOGRAPHIES (in related fields)
BIBLIOGRAPHIES COURANTES (dans des disciplines voisines)

Social Sciences in general / Sciences sociales en général:
London Bibliography of the Social Sciences. London, Mansell, 1975 — . 1 x (per year/par an)
Novaja Inostrannaja Literatura po Obscestvennym Naukam. Moskva, INION, 1947 — . (7 series) 12 x (per year/par an)
Social Sciences Citation Index. Philadelphia, Institute for Scientific Information, 1973 — . 2 x (per year/par an)
Social Sciences Index. New York, Wilson Co., 1974 — . 4 x (per year/par an)

Biological Sciences / Sciences biologiques:
Biological Abstracts. Philadelphia, BioSciences Information Service of Biological Abstracts, 1927 — . 24 x (per year/par an)

Business Economics / Économie d'entreprise:
Business Periodicals Index. New York, Wilson Co., 1958 — . 12 x (per year/par an)

Demography / Démographie:
Population Index. Princeton, Office of Population Research, 1935 — . 4 x (per year/par an)

Economics / Science économique:
Bibliographie der Wirtschaftswissenschaften. Göttingen, Vandenhoeck und Ruprecht, 1968 — . 2 x (per year/par an)

Geography / Géographie:

Bibliographie géographique internationale. Paris, Centre National de la Recherche Scientifique, 1891 — 1976 : 1 x; 1977 — . 4 x (per year/per an)

Geo-abstracts. Norwich, University of East Anglia, 1960 — . (7 series) 6 x (per year/par an)

History / Histoire:

Bibliographie internationale des sciences historiques. Paris, Colin, 1926 — . 1 x (per year/par an)

Historical Abstracts. Santa Barbara, CA, American Bibliographical Center-Clio Press, 1955 — . 4 x (per year/par an)

Law / Droit:

Index to Foreign Legal Periodicals. London, Institute of Advanced Legal Studies, 1960 — . 4 x (per year/par an)

Linguistics / Linguistique:

Bibliographie linguistique. Utrecht, Spectrum, 1949 — .1 x (per year/par an)

Philosophy / Philosophie:

Bibliographie de la philosophie. Paris, Vrin, 1937 — . 4 x (per year/par an)

Psychology / Psychologie:

Psychological Abstracts. Washington, DC, American Psychological Association, 1927 — . 12 x (per year/par an)

ACKNOWLEDGEMENTS

The data contained in this Bibliography were compiled by combining the work of our editorial office, which uses all possible sources, and the communications of our foreign contributors who give us first-hand knowledge of their country's publications.

We acknowledge with many thanks the contributions made : for *Argentina* by Fundación José María Aragón, Buenos Aires, and Ms Dominique BABINI and Ms Corina T. de SEOANE; for *France* by Fondation nationale des sciences politiques et Maison des sciences de l'homme, Paris; for *Hungary* by Fővárosi Szabó Ervin Könyvtár, Budapest, and Mrs Mária VÁGH and Katalin GÁL; for *India* by National Social Science Documentation Centre, Indian Council of Social Science Research, New Delhi, and Dr S.P. AGRAWAL; for *Jamaica* by Institute of Social and Economic Research, University of the West Indies, Kingston and Miss Laura Ann MUNRO; for *Japan* by Japan Sociological Society, Tokyo; for *Poland* by Ośrodek Informacji Naukowej, Polska Akademia Nauk, Warszawa and Dr Kazimierz MARDOŃ; for *Spain* by Instituto Balmés de Sociología, Madrid, and Mrs Valentina FERNÁNDEZ VARGAS; for the *USSR* by Institut Naučnoj Informacii po Obščestvennym Naukam, Moskva, and Prof. V. VINOGRADOV and Dr Robert MDIVANI.

We also thank Agnès MAJOROS and Marie FERRAZZINI who helped the editors for collecting and classifying the bibliographical data; and the data creation and production staff located in Guelph, Canada : Audrey KITCHING, Dorothy KARL, Elizabeth SMITH, Ruth JOHNSTON, Linda DAEHN.

REMERCIEMENTS

Les données bibliographiques contenues dans ce volume ont été réunies en combinant le travail de notre bureau de rédaction, qui exploite toutes les sources possibles, et les contributions de divers correspondants étrangers qui nous font connaître de première main les publications de leur pays respectif.

Nous sommes heureux de remercier particulièrement les institutions et les personnalités qui nous ont aidés cette année, et dont les noms sont donnés ci-dessus.

Nous remercions aussi Agnès MAJOROS et Marie FERRAZZINI qui ont assisté les responsables de la publication pour rassembler et classer les données; et les membres de l'équipe de création et de production des données informatisées à Guelph, Canada : Audrey KITCHING, Dorothy KARL, Elizabeth SMITII, Ruth JOIINSTON, Linda DAEIIN.

Acta Juridica	Budapest
Acta Sociologica	København
Actes de la Recherche en Sciences Sociales	Paris
Actions et Recherches Sociales	Evry
Actualité Économique	Montréal, PQ
Administration (Dublin)	Dublin
Administration and Society	Beverly Hills, CA
Administrative Science Quarterly	Ithaca, NY
Advances in Librarianship	New York, NY
Affari Sociali Internazionali	Milano
Africa (London)	London
Africa (Roma)	Roma
Africa Development / Afrique et Développement	Dakar
Africa Today	Denver, CO
African Affairs	London
Afrique et Asie Modernes	Paris
Afrique Littéraire	Paris
Ageing and Society	Cambridge, MA
Aggiornamenti Sociali	Milano
Agrártörténeti Szemle / Agricultural History Review	Budapest
Agricultura y Sociedad	Madrid
Aikoku Gakuen Junior College Kiyo	
Ajia Keizai	Tokyo
Aktual'nye Problemy Istorii Marksistsko-Leninskoj Filosofii	Moskva
Állam-és Jogtudomány	Budapest
Allemagnes d'Aujourd'hui	Paris
Alternatives	New York, NY-Peterborough, ON
América Indígena	México
American Behavioral Scientist	Beverly Hills, CA
American Economic Review	Nashville, TN
American Economist	New York, NY
American Journal of Economics and Sociology	New York, NY
American Journal of International Law	Washington, DC
American Journal of Political Science	Austin, TX
American Journal of Sociology	Chicago, IL
American Political Science Review	Washington, DC
American Politics Quarterly	Beverly Hills, CA
American Psychologist	Lancaster, PA
American Sociological Review	Washington, DC
Amérique Latine	Paris
Análise Social	Lisbon
Annales de Géographie	Paris
Annales de l'INSEE	Paris
Annales de l'Institut de Sociologie	Bruxelles
Annales de la Recherche Urbaine	Montreuil
Annales des Pays de l'Amérique Centrale et des Caraïbes	Aix en Provence
Annales du Centre de Recherches sur l'Amérique Anglophone	Talence
Annales Internationales de Criminologie	Paris
Annales-Économies, Sociétés, Civilisations	Paris
Annals of the American Academy of Political and Social Science	Philadelphia, PA
Année Sociologique	Paris
Annual Report for Women's Studies	
Annual Report of Women's Studies Society	
Annual Review of Information Science and Technology	New York, NY
Annual Review of Sociology	Palo Alto, CA
Applied Economics	London
Archiv des Öffentlichen Rechts	Tübingen

Archiv für Kommunalwissenschaften	Stuttgart
Archiv für Sozialgeschichte	Bonn
Archives de Politique Criminelle	France
Archives de Sciences Sociales des Religions	Paris
Archives Européennes de Sociologie	Paris
Argument	Berlin
Armed Forces and Society	Chicago, IL
Asia Pacific Community	Tokyo
Asian Affairs (London)	London
Asian and Pacific Quarterly of Cultural and Social Affairs	Seoul
Asian Economies	Seoul
Asian Profile	Hong Kong
Asian Studies	Quezon City
Asian Survey	Berkeley, CA
Aussenwirtschaft	Zurich
Australian and New Zealand Journal of Sociology	Melbourne
Australian Journal of Public Administration	Sydney
Australian Quarterly	Sydney
Autrement. Série Monde	Paris
Autrement. Série Mutations	Paris
AWR Bulletin	Wien
Bangladesh Development Studies	Dacca
Berkeley Journal of Sociology	Berkeley, CA
Betriebswirtschaft (Die)	Stuttgart
Blätter für Deutsche und Internationale Politik	Köln
Boletín de Estudios Latinoamericanos y del Caribe	Amsterdam
BRISES	Paris
British Journal of Industrial Relations	London
British Journal of Political Science	London
British Journal of Sociology	London
Brookings Papers on Economic Activity	Washington, DC
Bulletin d'Information du CENADDOM	Talence
Bulletin de l'Institut d'Histoire du Temps Présent	Paris
Bulletin de Psychologie	Paris
Bulletin du Centre de Documentation et d'Études Juridiques, Économiques et Sociales	Cairo
Bulletin du Crédit National	Paris
Bulletin of Aichi University of Education	
Bulletin of Concerned Asian Scholars	San Francisco, CA
Bulletin of Indonesian Economic Studies	Canberra
Bulletin of Kohriyama Women's College	
Bulletin of Peace Proposals	Oslo
Bulletin of St. Luke's College of Nursing	
Bulletin of the Faculty of School Education Hiroshima University	Hiroshima
Bunka	
Buraku Mondai Ronkyu	
Cadmos	Genève
Cahier — Centre de Recherche sur les Mutations des Sociétés Industrielles	Paris
Cahiers d'Anthropologie	Paris
Cahiers d'Études Africaines	Paris
Cahiers d'Outre-Mer	Talence
Cahiers de la Communication	Paris
Cahiers de Sociologie et de Démographie Médicales	Paris
Cahiers du Centre d'Études de l'Emploi	Paris
Cahiers du Monde Hispanique et Luso-brésilien	Toulouse
Cahiers Français	Paris
Cahiers Internationaux de Sociologie	Paris
Cahiers ORSTOM. Série Sciences Humaines	Paris
Cahiers Québécois de Démographie	Québec, PQ
Cajanus	Kingston

California Management Review	Los Angeles, CA
Cambridge Journal of Economics	London
Canadian Journal of African Studies	Ottawa
Canadian Journal of Political and Social Theory	Winnipeg, MB
Canadian Journal of Political Science	Waterloo, ON
Canadian Journal of Sociology / Cahiers Canadiens de Sociologie	Edmonton, AB
Canadian Public Policy	Guelph, ON
Canadian Review of Sociology and Anthropology / Revue Canadienne de Sociologie et d'Anthropologie	Calgary, AB
Carnets de l'Enfance	Geneva
China Quarterly	London
China Report	New Delhi
Chinese Economic Studies	Armonk, NY
Chukyo Junior College Ronso	
Chuo Law Review	Tokyo
Chuo University Journal of the Faculty of Literature	
Chuo-gakuin University Bulletin of the Research Institute	
Civilisations	Bruxelles
CLES	Paris
Columbia Journal of World Business	New York, NY
Commentary	New York, NY
Commerce et Coopération	Paris
Communautés	Paris
Communications (Paris)	Paris
Communications (Sankt Augustin)	Sankt Augustin
Community Development Journal	London
Comparative Education Review	Chicago, IL
Comparative Political Studies	Beverly Hills, CA
Comparative Politics	New Brunswick, NJ
Comparative Social Research	Greenwich, CT
Comparative Studies in Society and History	Cambridge
Comparative Urban Research	New Brunswick, NJ
Comunicación	Buenos Aires
Comunicación y Cultura	Buenos Aires
Conflict	New York, NY
Connaissance Politique	Paris
Connexions	Paris
Conscience et Liberté	Berne
Consommation	Paris
Contemporary Crises	Amsterdam
Contemporary French Civilization	Bozeman, MT
Contemporary Review	London
Contradictions	Paris
Contrepoint	Paris
Contributions to Indian Sociology	New Delhi
Convergence	Fribourg-Toronto, ON
Courrier des Pays de l'Est	Paris
Cristianismo y Sociedad	Argentina
Critica Marxista	Roma
Critica Sociologica	Roma
Critique	Paris
Cuadernos Americanos	Mexico
Cuadernos Hispanoamericanos	Madrid
Cuadernos Médico-Sociales	Rosario
Culture Technique	Neuilly-sur-Seine
Current	Washington, DC
Current Sociology / Sociologie Contemporaine	London
Cybernetica	Namur
Człowiek i Światopogląd	Warsaw
Dados	Rio de Janeiro
Daedalus (Cambridge)	Cambridge, MA
Débat	Paris

Demográfia	Budapest
Demografía y Economía	México
Demografie	Praha
Demography	Ann Arbor, MI
Demosta'	Praha
Deutsche Studien	Berlin
Deutsche Zeitschrift für Philosophie	Berlin
Deutschland Archiv	Köln
Development and Change	London
Déviance et Société	Genève
Dialectics and Humanism	Florence
Difesa Sociale	Roma
Diogène	Paris
Documentation Européenne	Bruxelles
Documents CEPESS	Bruxelles
Droit Social	Paris
East Asia	Frankfurt-am-Main
East European Quarterly	Boulder, CO
Eastern Anthropologist	Lucknow
Econometrica	New Haven, CT
Economia e Lavoro	Padova
Economic and Industrial Democracy	London
Economic and Social Review	Dublin
Economic Development and Cultural Change	Chicago, IL
Economic Inquiry	Los Angeles, CA
Economic Journal	London
Economic Record	Melbourne
Economics of Education Review	Cambridge, MA
Économie et Humanisme	Lyon
Économie et Statistique	Paris
Économies et Sociétés	Paris-Geneva
Economisch en Sociaal Tijdschrift	Antwerpen
Economy and Society	London
Einheit	Berlin
Ekistics	Athens
Ekonomický Časopis	Bratislava
Ekonomska Revija	Ljubljana
Enfance	Paris
Equal Opportunities International	Hull [UK]
Erde	Berlin
Espace Géographique	Paris
Espace, Populations, Sociétés	Lille
Espaces et Sociétés	Paris
Esprit	Paris
Estudios Sociales	Santo Domingo
Ethics	Chicago, IL
Ethnic and Racial Studies	Henley-on-Thames
Ethnology	Pittsburgh, PA
Études (Paris)	Paris
Études Canadiennes / Canadian Studies	Talence
Études Foncières	Paris
Études Helléniques	Montréal, PQ
Études Internationales	Québec, PQ
Études Rurales	Paris
Europäische Rundschau	Vienna
Europe (Paris)	Paris
European Journal of Political Research	Amsterdam
European Journal of Social Psychology	The Hague
Evaluation Studies	Beverly Hills, CA
Ežegodnik — Sovetskaja Associacija Političeskih Nauk	Moskva
Family Planning Perspectives	New York, NY

Filosofskie Nauki	Alma-Ata
Filosofskie Voprosy Mediciny i Biologii	Kiev
For New Sociology	
Formation Emploi	Paris
Frankfurter Hefte	Frankfurt-am-Main
Futures	Guildford-East
	Lansing, MI
Futuribles	Paris
Gaifu	
Gakushuin Daigaku Hogakubu Kenkyū Nenpo	[Nihon]
Gegenwartskunde	Opladen
Gendai no Riron	
Gendai to Shiso	Tokyo
Genève-Afrique	Genève
Genus	Roma
Geographical Journal	London
Geographical Review	New York, NY
Geographische Rundschau	Braunschweig
Gérontologie et Société	Paris
Geschichte und Gesellschaft	Göttingen
Gewerkschaftliche Monatshefte	Köln
Giornale degli Economisti e Annali di Economia	Milano
Gledišta	Beograd
Government and Opposition	London
Growth and Change	Lexington, KY
Gunma Journal of Liberal Arts and Sciences	
Hamburger Jahrbuch für Wirtschafts- und Gesellschaftspolitik	Hamburg
Harvard Educational Review	Cambridge, MA
Harvard Law Review	Cambridge, MA
Hauswirtschaft und Wissenschaft	München
Heiwa Kyoiku Kenkyū	
Hermes	Santa Barbara, CA-
	Stuttgart
Higher Education	Amsterdam
Hiroshima Shudai Ronshu	Hiroshima
Historical Social Research / Historische Sozialforschung	Köln
History and Theory	Middletown, CT
History of European Ideas	Elmsford, NY-Oxford
Hitotsubashi Journal of Social Sciences	Tokyo
Hitotsubashi Journal of Social Studies	Tokyo
Hogaku Kenkyū	Tokyo
Hokkaido Daigaku Jinbunkagaku Ronshu	
Hokkaido University Journal of the Graduate School of Environmental Science	
Hokkaido University Reports on Cultural Science	
Homme	Paris
Homme et Société	Paris
Human Organization	New York, NY
Human Relations	London
Human Rights Quarterly	Baltimore, MD
Human Systems Management	Amsterdam
Humanisme et Entreprise	Paris
Humanizacja Pracy	Warszawa
Hyogo University of Teacher Education Journal	
IBLA	Tunis
Ideas en Ciencias Sociales	Buenos Aires
Ideologia i Polityka	Warszawa
IDS Bulletin	Brighton
IFO Studien	Berlin
Ikkyo Kenkyū	

Immigrants and Minorities	London
Indian Journal of Economics	Allahabad
Indian Journal of Politics	Aligarh [Uttar Pradesh]
Indian Journal of Social Research	New Delhi
Indian Journal of Social Work	Maharashtra
Indian Labour Journal	Simla
Indonesian Quarterly	Djakarta
Industrial and Labor Relations Review	Ithaca, NY
Industrial Relations	Berkeley, CA
Industry of Free China	Taiwan
Information Economics and Policy	Amsterdam
Inquiry	Oslo
Insurgent Sociologist	Eugene, OR
Integration	Bonn
Inter-American Economic Affairs	Washington, DC
Interchange	Toronto, ON
Internasjonal Politikk	Bergen
International and Comparative Law Quarterly	London
International·Journal of Comparative Sociology	Leiden
International Journal of Lifelong Education	Lewes [UK]
International Journal of Middle East Studies	Cambridge-New York, NY
International Journal of Political Education	Amsterdam
International Journal of Public Administration	New York, NY
International Journal of Social Economics	Bradford
International Journal of Sociology	Armonk, NY
International Journal of Sociology and Social Policy	Humberside
International Journal of the Sociology of Language	The Hague
International Journal of the Sociology of Law	London
International Journal of Urban and Regional Research	London
International Lawyer	Chicago, IL
International Library Review	London
International Migration / Migrations Internationales	Geneva
International Migration Review	New York, NY
International Political Science Review	Beverly Hills, CA
International Review of History and Political Science	Meerut
International Review of Industrial Property and Copyright Law	Weinheim-Deerfield Beach, FL
International Social·Science Journal / Revue Internationale des Sciences Sociales	Paris
International Social Science Review	Toledo, OH
International Socialism	London
International Studies Quarterly	Detroit, MI
International Yearbook of Organizational Democracy	London
Internationale Spectator	The Hague
Internationales Asienforum	Cologne
Investigación Económica	México
Israel Law Review	Jerusalem
Istorija SSSR	Moskva
Items	New York, NY
Izvestija Akademii Nauk Gruzinskoj SSR. Serija Filosofii i Psihologii	Tbilisi
Izvestija Akademii Nauk Kazahskoj SSR. Serija Obščestvennyh Nauk	Alma-Ata
Izvestija Akademii Nauk SSSR. Serija Ėkonomičeskaja	Moskva
Izvestija Akademii Nauk Tadžikskoj SSR. Otdelenie Obščestvennyh Nauk	Dušǎnbe
Izvestija Severo-Kavkazskogo Naučnogo Centra Vysšej Školy. Obščestvennye Nauki	Rostov
Izvestija Sibirskogo Otdelenija Akademii Nauk SSSR. Serija Ėkonomiki i Prikladnoj Sociologii	Novosibirsk
Jahrbuch für Christliche Sozialwissenschaften	Münster-Göttingen
Jahrbuch für Sozialwissenschaft	Göttingen

Jahrbuch für Volkskunde und Kulturgeschichte	Berlin
Japanese Journal of Sociological Criminology	Tokyo
Jb. Soziol. u. Sozialpol.	
Jel-Kép	Budapest
Jerusalem Journal of International Relations	Jerusalem
Jerusalem Quarterly	Jerusalem
Jewish Journal of Sociology	London
Jinbun Ronso : Bulletin of the Faculty of Humanities and Social Sciences	Tsu
Jinmonronkyu	
Journal de la Société de Statistique de Paris	Paris
Journal for the Theory of Social Behaviour	Oxford
Journal für Sozialforschung	Vienna
Journal of African Law	London
Journal of American Studies	Cambridge [UK]
Journal of Applied Behavioral Science	New York, NY
Journal of Arab Affairs	Fresno, CA
Journal of Asian Studies	Ann Arbor, MI
Journal of Biosocial Science	Oxford
Journal of Black Studies	Los Angeles, CA
Journal of Broadcasting	Philadelphia, PA
Journal of Communication	Austin, TX
Journal of Comparative Economics	New York, NY
Journal of Conflict Resolution	Ann Arbor, MI
Journal of Consumer Affairs	Columbia, MO
Journal of Contemporary Asia	Stockholm
Journal of Contemporary History	London
Journal of Developing Areas	Macomb, IL
Journal of Development Economics	Amsterdam
Journal of Development Studies	London
Journal of Eastern African Research and Development	Nairobi
Journal of Economic Issues	Lincoln, NE
Journal of Economic Theory	Philadelphia, PA
Journal of Educational Sociology	Washington, DC
Journal of Family History	Minneapolis, MN
Journal of Health, Politics Policy and Law	Durham, NC
Journal of Human Resources	Madison, WI
Journal of Information Science	London
Journal of Interamerican Studies and World Affairs	Beverly Hills, CA- London
Journal of Jewish Communal Service	New York, NY
Journal of Labor Research	Fairfax, VA
Journal of Law and Society	Oxford
Journal of Management Studies	Oxford
Journal of Marriage and the Family	Minneapolis, MN
Journal of Mathematical Sociology	London
Journal of Military Sociology	
Journal of Okinawa Christian Junior College	
Journal of Peasant Studies	London
Journal of Personality and Social Psychology	Washington, DC
Journal of Political and Military Sociology	Dekalb, IL
Journal of Political Economy	Chicago, IL
Journal of Political Studies	Jullundur
Journal of Politics	Gainesville, FL
Journal of Population Problems	Tokyo
Journal of Public Economics	Lausanne
Journal of Public Policy	Cambridge [UK]
Journal of Ryukoku University	
Journal of Social Issues	New York, NY
Journal of Social Policy	Cambridge
Journal of Social Psychology	Provincetown, MA
Journal of Social, Political and Economic Studies	Washington, DC
Journal of Southeast Asian Studies	Singapore

Journal of Southern African Studies	London
Journal of the Faculty of Liberal Arts, Yamaguchi University	
Journal of the Institute for Socioeconomic Studies	White Plains, NY
Journal of the Market Research Society	London
Journal of Vocational Behavior	Ann Arbor, MI
Journalism Quarterly	Minneapolis, MN
Jugoslovenski Pregled	Beograd
Kagaku to Shiso	Tokyo
Kagawa Daigaku Ippan Kyoiku Kenkyū	Kagawa
Kagoshima Keizai Daigaku Shakaigakubu Ronshu	[Nihon]
Kaigai Shakaihosho	
Kansai Gaikokugo Daigaku Kenkyū Ronshu	Osaka
Kansai University Bulletin of the Faculty of Sociology	Osaka
Keio Journal of Politics	Tokyo
Keizai Hyoron	Tokyo
Keizaigaku-ronshu of Kagoshima University	Kagoshima
Kenkyū Kiyo	
Khamsin	London
Kidma	Jerusalem
Kinjo Gakuin Daigaku Ronshū	[Nihon]
Kinjo Gakuin Daigaku Ronshū, Social Science Series	
Kinjo Gakuin University Bulletin, Social Sciences Series	
Kōbe Daigaku Ronshu	Kōbe
Kōbe University Bulletin of the Faculty of Letters	Kōbe
Kokumin Seikatsu Kenkyū	Tokyo
Kölner Zeitschrift für Soziologie und Sozialpsychologie	Wiesbaden
Kommunist (Moskva)	Moskva
Kommunist Gruzii	Tbilisi
Kommunist Moldavii	Kišinev
Kommunist Sovetskoj Latvii	Riga
Korea and World Affairs	Seoul
Korea Journal	Seoul
Közgazdasági Szemle	Budapest
Kultúra és Közösség	Budapest
Kultura i Społeczeństwo	Warszawa
Kumamoto Journal of Culture and Humanities	
Kumamoto Tandai Ronshu	
Kursbuch	Berlin
Kwansaigakuin Sociology Department Studies	
Kwartalnik Opolski	Warszawa
Kwartalnik Pedagogiczny	Warszawa
Kyklos	Basel
Kyoiku Shakaigaku Kenkyū	[Nihon]
Kyoikugaku Ronshu	
Labour Annual 1984	
Langages	Paris
Language Problems and Language Planning	Austin, TX
Latin American Perspectives	Riverside, CA
Latin American Research Review	Austin, TX
Latinskaja Amerika	Moskva
Law and Policy Quarterly	Beverly Hills, CA
Law and Society Review	New York, NY
Leviathan	Wiesbaden
Library Trends	Champaign, IL
Magyar Pszichológiai Szemle	Budapest
Magyar Tudomány	Budapest
Majalah Demografi Indonesia	Djakarta
Manchester School of Economic and Social Studies	Manchester
Mass Communication Review Yearbook	Beverly Hills, CA
Masses Ouvrières	Paris

Media, Culture and Society	London
Méditerranée	Aix-en-Provence
Medvetánc	Budapest
Meisei University Bulletin of Sociology	
MEMO	London
Memoirs of Kanazawa Technical College	
Memoirs of Osaka Kyoiku University	
Mens en Maatschappij	Deventer
Metodologičeskie Voprosy Nauki	Saratov
Micropolitics	New York, NY
Middle Eastern Studies	London
Milbank Memorial Fund Quarterly	Cambridge, MA
Minerva	London
Mita Journal of Economics	Tokyo
Mitarbeit (Die)	Göttingen
Mitteilungen aus der Arbeitsmarkt- und Berufsforchung	Stuttgart
Miyagi Gakuin Kenkyū Ronbunshu	Tokyo
Modern China	Beverly Hills, CA-
	London
Modern Law Review	London
Mois en Afrique	Paris
Molodoj Kommunist	Moskva
Montalbán	Caracas
Monthly Review	New York, NY
Mots	Paris
Mouvement Social	Paris
Mulino	Bologna
Narody Azii i Afriki	Moskva
Nationalities Papers	Omaha, NB
Nationaløkonomisk Tidsskrift	København
Naučnoe Upravlenie Obščestvom	Moskva
Naučnye Doklady vysšej Školy. Naučnyj Kommunizm	Moskva
Nekotorye Filosofskie Problemy Gosudarstva i Prava	Saratov
Netherlands Journal of Sociology	Amsterdam
Neue Politische Literatur	Stuttgart
Neue Praxis	Neuwied
New German Critique	Milwaukee, WI
New Hungarian Quarterly	Budapest
New Left Review	London
NHK Annual Bulletin of Broadcasting Culture Research	
Nieuwe West Indische Gids	Bussum
Nihon Minzokugaku	Tokyo
Nihon University Journal of Sociology	
Niigata University Studies in Humanities	
Nord e Sud	Naples
Nordisk Administrativt Tidsskrift	København
Norois	Poitiers
Notas de Población	Santiago
Nouvelle Revue Internationale	Paris
Nouvelles Campagnes	Toulouse
Nouvelles Questions Féministes	Paris
Novaja i Novejšaja Istorija	Moskva
Novos Estudos CEBRAP	São Paulo
Nowe Drogi	Warszawa
Nueva Sociedad	Caracas
Obščestvennye Nauki (Moskva)	Moskva
Observations et Diagnostics Économiques	Paris
Öffentliche Verwaltung	Stuttgart
Okinawa Kokusai University Bulletin of the Department of Sociology	
Okinawa L + E	
Økonomi og Politik	København

Oktjabr	Kraljevo
Opinion Publique	Paris
Optima	Johannesburg
Orbis	Louvain
Organization Studies	New York, NY-Berlin
Orient	Opladen
Orientation Scolaire et Professionnelle	Paris
Osaka Daigaku Nenpo Ningen Kagaku	Osaka
Osaka Shiritsu Daigaku Seikatsu Kagakubu Kiyō	Osaka
Osaka Studies in Sociology of Education	
Osaka University Annals of Human Sciences	
Österreichische Zeitschrift für Politikwissenschaft	Wien
Osteuropa	Stuttgart
Pacific Affairs	New York, NY
Pacific Viewpoint	Wellington
Papers of the Regional Science Association	Philadelphia, PA
Parole et Société	Paris
Pártélet	Prague
Patterns of Prejudice	London
Pensée	Paris
Perspectives (UNESCO)	Paris
Perspectives Universitaires	Montreal, PQ
Peuples Méditerranéens / Mediterranean Peoples	Paris
Peuples Noirs — Peuples Africains	Paris
Philosophy and Public Affairs	Princeton, NJ
Philosophy of the Social Sciences	Aberdeen
Phylon	Atlanta, GA
Planning and Administration	The Hague
Planning Outlook	Newcastle
Plural Societies	The Hague
Pluriel	Paris
Policy Studies Journal	Urbana, IL
Policy Studies Review	Urbana, IL
Political Anthropology Yearbook	New Brunswick, NJ
Political Behavior	New York, NY
Political Methodology	Los Altos, CA
Political Psychology	Los Angeles, CA
Political Quarterly	London
Political Science	Wellington
Political Studies	Oxford
Politico	Pavia
Politics and Society	Washington, DC
Politique	Paris
Politique Africaine	Paris
Politique Internationale	Paris
Politiques et Management Public	Paris
Polity	Amherst, MA
Polityka Spofeczna	Warszawa
Population	Paris
Population and Development Review	New York, NY
Population Bulletin of the United Nations	New York, NY
Population Research and Policy Review	Wilmington, DE
Population Studies	London
Populi	New York, NY
Pouvoirs	Paris
Praca i Zabezpieczenie Spofeczne	Warszawa
Présence Africaine	Paris
Priroda	Moskva-Sofîa
Problemi del Socialismo	Milan
Problems of Communism	Washington, DC
Problemy Filosofii	Kiev
Problemy Marksizmu-Leninizmu	Warszawa

Problemy Naučnogo Kommunizma	Moskva
Projet	Paris
Przegląd Statystyczny	Warszawa
Psihologičeskij Žurnal	Moscow
Psychologie Française	Paris
Pszichológia	Budapest
Public Choice	The Hague
Public Interest	New York, NY
Public Opinion	Washington, DC
Public Opinion Quarterly	New York, NY
Quaderni di Sociologia	Torino
Quality and Quantity	Amsterdam
Quarterly of Social Security Research	Tokyo
Quarterly Review of Economics and Business	Champaign, IL
Queen's Quarterly	Kingston, ON
Questions Actuelles du Socialisme	Belgrade
Rabočij Klass i Sovremennyj Mir	Moskva
Race and Class	London
Radical Humanist	New Delhi
Raison Présente	Paris
Rassegna Economica (Napoli)	Napoli
Rassegna Italiana di Sociologia	Bologna
Rassegna Sindacale. Quaderni	Roma
Rasselenie i Demografičeskie Processy	
Raumforschung und Raumordnung	Cologne
Razón y Fe	Madrid
Readings on Women's Studies	
Recherche Sociale	Paris
Recherches Internationales	Paris
Recherches Sociographiques	Québec, PQ
Recherches Sociologiques	Louvain
Recht der Jugend und des Bildungswesens	Neuwied
Reflets et Perspectives de la Vie Économique	Bruxelles
Regards sur l'Actualité	Paris
Regional Studies	Cambridge [UK]
Relations Industrielles	Québec, PQ
Reports of National Institute of Police Science	
Reports of the University of Electro-Communications	
Research in Corporate Social Performance and Policy	Greenwich, CT
Research in Economic Anthropology	Evanston, IL
Research in Human Capital and Development	Baltimore, MD
Research in Law, Deviance and Social Control	Greenwich, CT
Research in Organizational Behavior	Greenwich, CT
Research in Population Economics	Greenwich, CT
Research in Social Problems and Public Policy	Amherst, MA
Research Policy	Amsterdam
Review (F. Braudel Center)	Beverly Hills, CA
Review of African Political Economy	London
Review of Contemporary Sociology	
Revija za Sociologiju	Zagreb
Revista de Administração de Empresas	Rio de Janeiro
Revista de Administração Pública	Rio de Janeiro
Revista de Ciencias Sociales de la Universidad de Costa Rica	San José
Revista de Estudios de Juventud	
Revista de Filozofie	București
Revista de Istorie	București
Revista de Planeación y Desarrollo	Bogotá
Revista de Política Social	Madrid
Revista Española de Investigaciones Sociológicas	Madrid
Revista Geográfica	Mexico
Revista Interamericana de Planificación	Bogotá

Revista Internacional de Sociología	Madrid
Revista Javeriana	Bogotá
Revista Latinoamericana de Psicología	Bogotá
Revista Mexicana de Sociología	México
Revue Algérienne des Sciences Juridiques, Économiques et Politiques	Algiers
Revue Belge de Sécurité Sociale	Bruxelles
Revue Canadienne d'Études du Développement	Ottawa
Revue d'Allemagne	Strasbourg
Revue d'Économie Régionale et Urbaine	Paris
Revue d'Études Comparatives Est-Ouest	Paris
Revue de Corée	Seoul
Revue de Droit Rural	Paris
Revue de Géographie Alpine	Paris
Revue de Géographie de Lyon	Lyon
Revue de l'Institut de Sociologie	Bruxelles
Revue de l'Unesco pour la Science de l'Information, la Bibliothéconomie et l'Archivistique	Paris
Revue des Pays de l'Est	Bruxelles
Revue des Sciences Morales et Politiques	Paris
Revue du Marché Commun	Paris
Revue Économique et Sociale	Lausanne-Dorigny
Revue Européenne des Sciences Sociales	Genève
Revue Européenne des Sciences Sociales. Cahiers Vilfredo Pareto	Genève
Revue Française d'Études Américaines	Paris
Revue Française de Civilisation Britannique	Paris
Revue Française de Science Politique	Paris
Revue Française de Sociologie	Paris
Revue Française des Affaires Sociales	Paris
Revue Hospitalière de France	Lyon
Revue Internationale d'Action Communautaire	Montreal, PQ
Revue Internationale de Sécurité Sociale	Genève
Revue Internationale de Sociologie / International Review of Sociology	Rome
Revue Internationale du Travail	Genève
Revue Nouvelle	Tournai
Revue Politique et Parlementaire	Paris
Revue Roumaine	Bucharest
Revue Roumaine d'Études Internationales	Bucharest
Revue Roumaine des Sciences Sociales. Série de Sociologie	Bucharest
Revue Tunisienne de Communication	Tunis
Ritsumeikan Review of Industrial Society	
Rivista di Studi Politici Internazionali	Firenze
Rivista Internazionale di Scienze Economiche e Commerciali	Milano
Rivista Internazionale di Scienze Sociali	Milano
Rivista Italiana di Scienza Politica	Bologna
Roczniki Socjologii Wsi	Warszawa
Round Table	London
RS. Cuadernos de Realidades Sociales	Madrid
Ruch Prawniczy, Ekonomiczny i Socjologiczny	Poznań
Rundfunk und Fernsehen	Hamburg
Rural Sociology	Lexington, KY-Knoxville, TN
Sage Annual Review of Studies in Deviance	Beverly Hills, CA
Sage Yearbook in Women's Policy Studies	Beverly Hills, CA
Sbornik Prací Filosofické Fakulty Brnenské University	Brno
Scandinavian Political Studies	Helsinki
Schweizer Monatshefte	Zürich
Schweizerische Zeitschrift für Soziologie	St-Saphorin
Science and Public Policy	London
Sciences Sociales — Académie des Sciences de l'URSS	Moscou
Sciences Sociales du Japon Contemporain	[Nihon]
Scientific American	New York, NY

Scientometrics	Budapest
Search	Miami, FL
Seikei University Bulletin of the Faculty of Humanities	
Seishonen Mondai Kenkyū	
Seminar	New Delhi
Senri Ethnological Studies	Osaka
Sensyu Keieigaku Ronsyu	
Service Social	Quebec, PQ
Shakaigaku Hyoron	Tokyo
Shakaigaku Kenkyū	Tokyo
Shakaigaku Kenkyū Nenpo	Tokyo
Shakaigaku Nenpo	Tokyo
Shakaigaku Nenshi	Tokyo
Shakaigaku Ronso	Tokyo
Shakaigaku Zasshi	
Shakaigaku-shi Kenkyū	[Nihon]
Shakaikagaku Tokyu	
Signs	New York, NY
Sistema	Madrid
Social Action	New Delhi
Social Compass	Louvain-la-Neuve
Social Dynamics	Capetown
Social Forces	Chapel Hill, NC
Social Gerontology	
Social Indicators Research	Dordrecht
Social Networks	Bethlehem, PA
Social Philosophy and Policy	Oxford
Social Policy	New York, NY
Social Problems	Buffalo, NY
Social Psychology Quarterly	Washington, DC
Social Research	New York, NY
Social Science Information / Information sur les Sciences Sociales	London
Social Science Journal (Fort Collins)	Fort Collins, CO
Social Science Quarterly	Austin, TX-Baton Rouge, LA
Social Science Research	New York, NY
Social Sciences in China	Beijing
Social Service Delivery Systems	Beverly Hills, CA
Social Service Review	Chicago, IL
Social Theory and Practice	Tallahassee, FL
Socialismo y Participación	Lima
Socialist Register	London
Socialist Review	San Francisco, CA
Society	New Brunswick, NJ
Socijalizam	Beograd
Socio-Economic Planning Sciences	Oxford-Elmsford, NY
Sociologia (Roma)	Roma
Sociologia Internationalis	Berlin
Sociologia Ruralis	Assen
Sociologica	
SOCIOLOGICA — Revista Argentina de Ciencias Sociales	
Sociological Analysis	San Antonio, TX
Sociological Focus	Akron, OH
Sociological Inquiry	Austin, TX
Sociological Methods and Research	Beverly Hills, CA
Sociological Perspectives	Beverley Hills, CA-London
Sociological Quarterly	Carbondale, IL
Sociological Review	Keele
Sociologičeskie Issledovanija	Moskva
Sociologicus	
Sociologie du Travail	Paris
Sociologie et Sociétés	Montréal, PQ

Sociologija	Beograd
Sociologija Sela	Zagreb
Sociologische Gids	Meppel
Sociologos	[Nihon]
Sociologus	Berlin
Sociology (London)	London
Sociology and Social Research	Los Angeles, CA
Sociology of Education	Washington, DC
Sociology of the Sciences	Dordrecht
Sociološki Pregled	Belgrade
Sogo Toshi Kenkyū	
Sophia University Studies in Sociology	[Nihon]
Soshioroji	Kyoto
South Africa International	Johannesburg
South African Labour Bulletin	Braamfontein
Southern Economic Journal	Chapel Hill, NC
Southern Quarterly	Hattiesburg, MS
Sovetskaja Arheologija	Moskva
Sovetskaja Ètnografija	Moskva
Sovetskoe Gosudarstvo i Pravo	Moskva
Soviet Geography	New York, NY
Soviet Jewish Affairs	London
Soviet Studies	Glasgow
Soziale Welt	Göttingen
Sozialer Fortschritt	Bonn
SŠA	Moskva
St. Andrew's University Sociological Review	
Staat (Der)	Berlin
Statistika	Praha
Statisztikai Szemle	Budapest
Stato e Mercato	Bologna
Statsvetenskaplig Tidskrift	Lund
Studi di Sociologia	Milano
Studi Emigrazione	Roma
Studia Demograficzne	Warszawa
Studia Filozoficzne	Warszawa
Studia nad Ekonomiką Regionu	Katowice
Studia Socjologiczne	Wrocław
Studies in Family Planning	New York, NY
Studies in Humanities and Sciences	
Studies in Modern Manners and Customs	
Studies of Broadcasting	Tokyo
Studies of Sociological History	
Study Reports of Baika Junior College	
Study Reports of Fukuoka Junior College of Social Work and Child Education	
Südosteuropa — Zeitschrift für Gegenwartsforschung	München
Supreme Court Review	Chicago, IL
Szociológia	Budapest
Tamagawa Daigaku Ronso	
Társadalmi Szemle	Budapest
Társadalomkutatás	Budapest
Társadalomtudományi Közlemények	Budapest
Teachers College Record	New York, NY
Teaching Political Science	Beverly Hills, CA
Teaching Politics (London)	London
Teaching Sociology	Beverly Hills, CA
Technological Forecasting and Social Change	New York, NY
Telos	St. Louis, MO
Temps Modernes	Paris
Teorija in Praksa	Ljubljana
Theologia Diakonia	

Theory and Decision	Dordrecht
Theory and Society	Amsterdam
Third World Planning Review	Liverpool
Tiers-Monde	Paris
Tocqueville Review	Charlottesville, VA
Tohoku Fukushi Kiyo	
Toshi Mondai	Tokyo
Toyo University Bulletin of Faculty of Sociology	
Toyo University Bulletin of the Graduate School	
Travail et Société	Genève
Travaux de l'Association Henri Capitant	Paris
Trudy Akademii Nauk Litovskoj SSR. Obščestvennye Nauki	Vil'njus
Ufahamu	Los Angeles, CA
Universitas	Stuttgart
Universitas (Colombia)	Colombia
Urban Affairs Annual Reviews	Beverly Hills, CA
Urban Affairs Quarterly	Beverly Hills, CA
Urban and Social Change Review	Boston, MA
Urban Geography	Silver Spring, MD
Urban Law and Policy	Amsterdam
Urban Studies	Edinburgh
Uzbekistonda Ižtimoij Fanlar	Taškent
Valóság	Budapest
Verfassung und Recht in Übersee	Hamburg
Vestnik Akademii Medicinskih Nauk SSSR	USSR
Vestnik Akademii Nauk Kazahskoj SSR	Alma-Ata
Vestnik Harkovskogo Politehničeskogo Instituta	Harkov
Vestnik Harkovskogo Universiteta	Harkov
Vestnik Moskovskogo Universiteta. Serija Filosofija	Moskva
Vestnik Moskovskogo Universiteta. Teorija Naučnogo Kommunizma	Moskva
Vestnik Obščestvennyh Nauk. Akademija Nauk Armjanskoj SSR	Erevan
Vierteljahresschrift für Sozialrecht	München
Vierteljahrschrift für Sozial- und Wirtschaftsgeschichte	Stuttgart
Viitorul Social	Bucarest
Világosság	Budapest
Vingtième Siècle. Revue d'Histoire	Paris
Vita e Pensiero	Milan
Voprosy Ēkonomiki	Moskva
Voprosy Filosofii	Moskva
Voprosy Istorii	Moskva
Voprosy Istorii KPSS	Moskva
Voprosy Naučnogo Kommunizma (Erevan)	Erevan
Voprosy Naučnogo Kommunizma (Kiev)	Kiev
Voprosy Obščestvennyh Nauk (Kiev)	Kiev
Voprosy Teorii i Metodov Ideologičeskoj Raboty	Moskva
Vorgänge	Hamburg
Vozes	Petropolis [Brazil]
Wallonie	Namur
Waseda Daigaku Bungakubu Kenkyū Kiyo	
Waseda University Social Sciences Review	
West European Politics	London
Western Political Quarterly	Salt Lake City, UT
Wiadomości Statystyczne	Warszawa
Wieś i Rolnictwo	Warszawa
Wieś Współczesna	Warszawa
Wilson Quarterly	Boulder, CO
WIST. Wirtschaftswissenschaftliches Studium	München-Frankfurt-am-Main
Women and Politics	New York, NY
World Affairs	Washington, DC

World Development	Elmsford, NY
World Economy	Princeton, NJ
World Politics	Princeton, NJ
Yale Law Journal	New Haven, CT
Yearbook of Population Research in Finland	Helsinki
Yugoslav Survey	Belgrade
Zagadnienia Ekonomiki Rolnej	Warszawa
Zaïre-Afrique	Kinshasa
Zeitschrift der Gesellschaft für Kanada-Studien	Bochum-Neumünster
Zeitschrift für Agrargeschichte und Agrarsoziologie	Frankfurt-am-Main
Zeitschrift für Betriebswirtschaft	Wiesbaden
Zeitschrift für Bevölkerungswissenschaft	Wiesbaden
Zeitschrift für Politik	Cologne
Zeitschrift für Sozialökonomie	Hamburg
Zeitschrift für Soziologie	Stuttgart

CLASSIFICATION SCHEME
PLAN DE CLASSIFICATION

10   **Social Sciences. Research. Documentation**
Sciences sociales. Recherche. Documentation

10100   Social sciences. Sociology / Sciences sociales. Sociologie   1-72

10200   Research workers. Sociologists / Chercheurs. Sociologues   73-91

10300   Organization of research. Research policy / Organisation de la recherche. Politique de recherche
10310   Current research / Recherche en cours   92-109
10320   Applied research. Interdisciplinary research / Recherche appliquée. Recherche interdisciplinaire   110-115
10330   Research centres / Centres de research
10340   Organization of research. Research policy / Organisation de la recherche. Politique de la recherche   116-130
10350   Research equipment / Équipement de la recherche   131-139
10360   Sociological associations / Associations de sociologie

10400   Congresses. Meetings / Congrès. Réunions

10500   Documents. Information processing / Documents. Traitement de l'information
10510   Documentation / Documentation   140-149
10520   Documentary analysis. Reference works / Analyse documentaire. Ouvrages de référence   150-152
10530   Information services / Services d'information   153-165
10540   Documentalists / Documentalistes
10550   Terminology / Terminologie   166-168
10560   Biographies / Biographies   169-183
10570   Articles. Periodicals / Articles. Périodiques   184-186
10580   Proceedings. Reports / Actes. Rapports
10590   Textbooks. Theses / Manuels. Thèses   187-191

11   **Methodology. Theory**
Méthodologie. Théorie

11100   Epistemology. Research methods. Theory / Épistémologie. Méthodes de recherche. Théorie
11110   Philosophy. Theory / Philosophie. Théorie   192-269
11120   Epistemology. Explanation. Understanding / Epistémologie. Explication. Compréhension   270-296
11130   Research techniques. Sociological analysis / Techniques de recherche. Analyse sociologique   297-360

11200   Data collection. Experiments / Rassemblement des données. Expériences
11210   Experimentation. Observation / Expérimentation. Observation   361-373
11220   Sampling. Surveys / Échantillonnage. Enquêtes   374-379
11230   Interviews. Questionnaires / Entretiens. Questionnaires   380-389
11240   Personality measurement. Tests / Mesure de la personnalité. Tests . .   390
11250   Sociodrama / Sociodrame

11300   Mathematical analysis. Statistical analysis / Analyse mathématique. Analyse statistique
11310   Algebra. Calculus. Logic / Algèbre. Calcul. Logique   391-406
11320   Statistical analysis / Analyse statistique   407-438
11330   Cybernetics. Information theory / Cybernétique. Théorie de l'information   439-440
11340   Graph theory / Théorie des graphes
11350   Stochastic processes. Statistical decision. Game theory / Processus stochastiques. Décision statistique. Théorie des jeux   441-446
11360   Attitude scales / Échelles d'attitude   447-449

12   Individuals. Groups. Organizations
              Individus. Groupes. Organisations

12100   Psychology. Social psychology. Sociometry / Psychologie. Psychologie
           sociale. Sociométrie
12110   Psychoanalysis. Social psychology / Psychanalyse. Psychologie sociale   450-479
12120   Psychological factors / Facteurs psychologiques

12200   Individuals. Personality / Individus. Personnalité
12210   Ego. Identity / Ego. Identité   480-487
12220   Egocentrism. Self-concept / Égocentrisme. Conception de soi   488-513
12230   Personality / Personnalité   514-535
12240   Cognition. Emotion. Motivation / Cognition. Émotion. Motivation . .   536-574

12300   Interpersonal relations / Relations interpersonnelles
12310   Human relations. Sociability / Relations humaines. Sociabilité   575-592
12320   Social perception / Perception sociale   593-612
12330   Interpersonal attraction / Attraction interpersonnelle   613-627
12340   Interpersonal influence / Influence interpersonnelle   628
12350   Interpersonal conflicts / Conflits interpersonnels   629-637
12360   Intergroup relations / Relations intergroupes   638-660

12400   Groups / Groupes
12410   Group dynamics / Dynamique de groupe   661-671
12420   Primary groups. Training groups / Groupes primaires. Groupes de
           formation   672-681
12430   Group size / Dimension du groupe   682-698
12440   Group integration / Intégration du groupe   699-703
12450   Group membership / Appartenance au groupe   704-707
12460   Group performance / Performance du groupe   708

12500   Bureaucracy. Organization / Bureaucratie. Organisation
12510   Sociology of organization / Sociologie des organisations   709-720
12520   Complex organizations / Organisations complexes   721-736
12530   Bureaucracy / Bureaucratie   737-780

12600   Leadership. Role / Commandement. Rôle
12610   Authority / Autorité   781-793
12620   Leadership / Commandement   794-799
12630   Role / Rôle   800-805

12700   Attitudes. Opinion / Attitudes. Opinion
12710   Behaviour / Comportement   806-818
12720   Cognitive dissonance. Prejudice / Dissonance cognitive. Préjugé   819-825
12730   Dogmatism. F Scale / Dogmatisme. Échelle F   826-831
12740   Opinion / Opinion   832-840
12750   Ideology / Idéologie   841-860
12760   Collective behaviour / Comportement collectif   861-870

13   Culture. Socialization. Social life
              Culture. Socialisation. Vie sociale

13100   Culture. Social environment. Value / Culture. Milieu social. Valeur
13110   Social and cultural anthropology / Ethnologie   871-882
13120   Civilization. Culture. Society / Civilisation. Culture. Société   883-1008
13130   Cultural dynamics. Cultural relations / Dynamique culturelle. Relations
           culturelles   1009-1045
13140   Social norms. Social control. Value systems / Normes sociales. Régulation
           sociale. Systèmes de valeurs   1046-1082
13150   Alienation. Socialization. Social conformity / Aliénation. Socialisation.
           Conformité sociale   1083-1186

13200   Customs. Traditions / Coutumes. Traditions   1187-1208

13300   Ethics. Morals / Éthique. Morale   1209-1230

13400   Law. Regulation / Loi. Réglementation   1231-1263

13500   Magic. Mythology. Religion / Magie. Mythologie. Religion
13510   Religion. Sociology of religion / Religion. Sociologie religieuse   1264-1315

13520	Magic. Primitive religion / Magie. Religion primitive	1316-1322
13530	Buddhism. Christianity / Bouddhisme. Christianisme	1323-1402
13540	Churches. Religious communities. Sects / Églises. Communautés religieuses. Sectes	1403-1439
13550	Clergy. Religious authority / Clergé. Autorité religieuse	
13560	Cults. Rites / Cultes. Rites	1440-1448
13570	Myths. Religious doctrines / Mythes. Doctrines religieuses	1449-1470
13580	Religious behaviour / Comportement religieux	1471-1487
13590	Church and State. Religious practice / Église et État. Pratique religieuse	1488-1501
13600	Science. Sociology of knowledge / Science. Sociologie de la connaissance	1502-1524
13700	Communication. Language / Communication. Langage	
13710	Linguistics. Semiotics / Linguistique. Sémiotique	1525-1536
13720	Communication. Signs / Communication. Signes	1537-1582
13730	Language / Langage	1583-1630
13740	Audience / Public	1631
13750	Advertising. Propaganda / Publicité. Propagande	1632-1637
13760	Mass communication / Communication de masse	1638-1763
13800	Art / Art	
13810	Aesthetics. Artists. Museums / Esthétique. Artistes. Musées	1764-1787
13820	Literature / Littérature	1788-1832
13830	Fine arts / Beaux-arts	1833-1839
13840	Music / Musique	1840-1848
13850	Dramatic art / Art dramatique	1849-1857
13860	Folk art / Art populaire	
13900	Education / Éducation	
13910	Educational sociology / Sociologie de l'éducation	1858-1919
13920	Educational systems. Educational policy / Systèmes d'enseignement. Politique de l'éducation	1920-1989
13930	Primary education. Secondary education / Enseignement primaire. Enseignement secondaire	1990-2018
13940	School environment / Milieu scolaire	2019-2024
13950	Higher education / Enseignement supérieur	2025-2079
13960	Adult education / Éducation des adultes	2080-2107
13970	Civic education. Technical education / Instruction civique. Enseignement technique	2108-2112
13980	Academic success. School failure / Réussite dans les études. Échec scolaire	2113-2122
13990	Pedagogy. Teaching. Teachers / Pédagogie. Enseignement. Enseignants	2123-2153
14	**Social structure** **Structure sociale**	
14100	Social system / Système social	2154-2182
14200	Social stratification / Stratification sociale	
14210	Social differentiation / Différenciation sociale	2183-2232
14220	Castes. Slavery / Castes. Esclavage	2233-2244
14230	Social classes / Classes sociale	2245-2328
14240	Social status / Statut social	2329-2338
14250	Elite. Intellectuals / Élite. Intellectuels	2339-2367
14260	Social mobility / Mobilité sociale	2368-2388
14300	Social change / Changement social	
14310	History / Histoire	2389-2407
14320	Future / Futur	2408-2411
14330	Social change / Changement social	2412-2482
14340	Changing society / Société en transformation	2483-2501
15	**Population. Family. Ethnic group** **Population. Famille. Groupe ethnique**	
15100	Demography. Genetics / Démographie. Génétique	
15110	Population research / Recherche démographique	2502-2557

15120	Households. Men. Women / Ménages. Hommes. Femmes	2558-2633
15130	Eugenism. Heredity / Eugénisme. Hérédité	2634
15200	Age groups / Groupes d'âge	
15210	Age. Cohorts. Generations / Âge. Cohortes. Générations	2635-2642
15220	Childhood / Enfance	2643-2663
15230	Youth / Jeunesse	2664-2707
15240	Adulthood / Âge adulte	2708-2710
15250	Old age / Vieillesse	2711-2762
15300	Population evolution. Population policy / Évolution de la population. Politique démographique	
15310	Population growth / Accroissement de la population	2763-2821
15320	Morbidity / Morbidité	2822-2845
15330	Mortality / Mortalité	2846-2900
15340	Fertility. Natality / Fécondité. Natalité	2901-2960
15350	Family planning / Planification de la famille	2961-3019
15400	Marriage. Family / Mariage. Famille	
15410	Sexual behaviour / Comportement sexuel	3020-3053
15420	Marriage. Nuptiality / Mariage. Nuptialité	3054-3102
15430	Family / Famille	3103-3201
15440	Women's status / Statut de la femme	3202-3280
15500	Ethnic groups / Groupes ethniques	
15510	Ethnicity. Tribes / Ethnicité. Tribus	3281-3357
15520	Interethnic relations. Racism / Relations interethniques. Racisme	3358-3432
15600	Migration / Migration	
15610	Migrants. Migration policy / Migrants. Politique migratoire	3433-3453
15620	External migration / Migration externe	3454-3536
15630	Internal migration / Migration interne	3537-3571
16	**Environment. Community. Rural. Urban** **Environment. Communauté. Rural. Urbain**	
16100	Ecology. Geography. Human settlements / Écologie. Géographie. Établissements humains	
16110	Human geography / Géographie humaine	3572-3595
16120	Nature. Soils. Water / Nature. Sols. Eau	3596-3608
16130	Citizens. Inhabitants / Citoyens. Habitants	3609-3615
16200	Community / Communauté	3616-3646
16300	Rural. Urban / Rural. Urbain	
16310	Rural sociology / Sociologie rurale	3647-3743
16320	Urban sociology / Sociologie urbaine	3744-3930
17	**Economic Life** **Vie économique**	
17100	Economic sociology / Sociologie économique	3931
17200	Economic systems / Systèmes économiques	
17210	Economic doctrines / Doctrines économiques	3932-3939
17220	Capitalism. Collectivism / Capitalisme. Collectivisme	3940-3960
17300	Economic situation. Standard of living / Situation économique. Niveau de vie	
17310	Economy. Economic development / Économie. Développement économique	3961-3966
17320	Income. Living conditions / Revenu. Conditions de vie	3967-3989
17400	Enterprises. Production / Entreprises. Production	
17410	Business economics. Management / Économie de l'entreprise. Gestion	3990-4013
17420	Productivity. Technology / Productivité. Technologie	4014-4065
17430	Agriculture. Trade. Industry / Agriculture. Commerce. Industrie	4066-4098
17500	Consumption. Market. Prices / Consommation. Marché. Prix	
17510	Consumer behaviour / Comportement du consommateur	4099-4109

17520	Demand. Supply / Demande. Offre	4110-4114
17600	Credit. Financing. Money / Crédit. Financement. Monnaie	4115-4123
17700	Economic policy. Planning / Politique économique. Planification	4124-4136

18   **Labour**
        Travail

18100	Industrial sociology. Sociology of work / Sociologie industrielle. Sociologie du travail	4137-4148
18200	Employment. Labour market / Emploi. Marché du travail	
18210	Labour. Manpower / Travail. Main-d'oeuvre	4149-4177
18220	Employment. Unemployment / Emploi. Chômage	4178-4219
18230	Employment services. Job evaluation / Services d'emploi. Évaluation des emplois	4220-4229
18240	Women workers. Young workers / Travailleuses. Jeunes travailleurs .	4230-4323
18300	Personnel management. Working conditions / Administration du personnel. Conditions de travail	
18310	Work standards. Work study / Normes de travail. Étude du travail .	4324-4347
18320	Working conditions / Conditions du travail	4348-4442
18330	Labour turnover / Renouvellement de la main-d'oeuvre	4443-4451
18400	Occupations. Vocational training / Professions. Formation professionnelle	
18410	Occupational sociology / Sociologie de la profession	4452-4458
18420	Occupational life. Vocational guidance / Vie professionnelle. Orientation professionnelle	4459-4505
18500	Employees. Technicians. Workers / Employés. Techniciens. Travailleurs	
18510	Workers / Travailleurs	4506-4522
18520	Employees / Employés	4523-4526
18530	Managers. Technicians / Cadres. Techniciens	4527-4534
18540	Liberal professions / Professions libérales	4535-4537
18600	Labour relations / Relations du travail	4538-4567
18610	Labour law / Droit du travail	4568-4577
18620	Employers' organizations / Organisations patronales	4578
18630	Trade unions / Syndicats	4579-4669
18640	Labour disputes / Conflits du travail	4670-4689
18650	Arbitration. Mediation / Arbitrage. Médiation	4690-4704
18660	Collective agreements. Workers' participation / Conventions collectives. Participation des travailleurs	4705-4727
18700	Leisure / Loisir	4728-4730
18710	Leisure time / Temps de loisir	4731-4736
18720	Leisure utilization / Utilisation des loisirs	4737-4759

19   **Politics. State. International relations**
        Politique. État. Relations internationales

19100	Political science. Political sociology / Science politique. Sociologie politique	4760-4768
19200	Political doctrines. Political thought / Doctrines politiques. Pensée politique	
19210	Political philosophy / Philosophie politique	4769-4770
19220	Political power / Pouvoir politique	4771
19230	Communism. Nationalism / Communisme. Nationalisme	4772-4807
19240	Democracy. Dictatorship / Démocratie. Dictature	4808-4821
19300	Constitution. State / Constitution. État	
19310	Political systems / Systèmes politiques	4822-4847
19320	Human rights / Droits de l'homme	4848-4870
19330	Political representation / Représentation politique	
19340	Government / Gouvernement	4871-4881
19350	Parliament / Parlement	
19360	Judiciary power / Pouvoir judiciaire	4882-4884
19400	Public administration / Administration publique	
19410	Civil service. Technocracy / Fonction publique. Technocratie	4885-4894
19420	Central government. Local government / Administration centrale. Administration locale	4895-4906

19500	Political parties. Pressure groups / Partis politiques. Groupes de pression	
19510	Party systems. Political parties / Systèmes de parti. Partis politiques .	4907-4918
19520	Pressure groups. Protest movements / Groupes de pression. Mouvements contestataires	4919-4956
19530	Political majority. Political opposition / Majorité politique. Opposition politique	4957-4958
19600	Political behaviour. Elections. Politics / Comportement politique. Élections. Politique	
19610	Political leaders. Political society / Leaders politiques. Société politique	4959-4961
19620	Political attitudes. Political participation / Attitudes politiques. Participation politique	4962-4991
19630	Elections / Élections	4992-5021
19640	Politics / Politique	5022-5027
19700	Army. Military sociology / Armée. Sociologie militaire	5028-5038
19800	International relations / Relations internationales	
19810	International law. International organizations / Droit international. Organisations internationales	5039-5044
19820	Foreign policy. Sovereignty / Politique étrangère. Souveraineté	5045-5048
19830	International cooperation. War / Coopération internationale. Guerre	5049-5055
19840	Disarmament. Weapons / Désarmement. Armes	
20	**Social problem. Social service. Social work** **Problème social. Service social. Travail social**	
20100	Social problems / Problèmes sociaux	
20110	Applied sociology / Sociologie appliquée	5056-5067
20120	Social pathology / Pathologie sociale	5068-5077
20130	Disasters / Catastrophes	5078-5080
20140	Poverty / Pauvreté	5081-5117
20150	Alcoholism. Drugs of abuse / Alcoolisme. Drogue	5118-5143
20160	Crime. Delinquency / Délit. Délinquance	5144-5252
20200	Social policy / Politique sociale	
20210	Social action. Social planning / Action sociale. Planification sociale . .	5253-5340
20220	Social security / Sécurité sociale	5341-5379
20300	Social work / Travail social	5380-5392
20400	Social services / Services sociaux	
20410	Medical sociology. Medicine / Sociologie médicale. Médecine	5393-5402
20420	Public health / Santé publique	5403-5436
20430	Hospitals / Hôpitaux	5437-5458
20440	Social workers / Travailleurs sociaux	5459-5482

10100   SOCIAL SCIENCES. SOCIOLOGY
SCIENCES SOCIALES. SOCIOLOGIE

1   "Modèle économique et sciences sociales. Marx-Keynes", *Économies et Sociétés* 18(10), oct 84 : 3-150.

2   "Sedanji trenutek jugoslovanske sociologije" (Current Yugoslavian sociology), *Teorija in Praksa* 21(1-2), feb 84 : 83-107. [With a contribution by Frane ADAM]

3   AGULLA, J. C. "La experiencia generacional de la sociología en la República Argentina" (Sociology's generational experience in the Argentine Republic), *Ideas en Ciencias Sociales* 1(1), 1984 : 17-39.

4   AKIMOTO, Ritsuo. "Chicago gakuha no keisei to sono daiici sedai" (The first generation of Chicago school and its formation), *Shakaikagaku Tokyu* 29, 1984 : 437-470.

5   AKIMOTO, Ritsuo. "W. I. Thomas no Chicago jidai" (W. I. Thomas and the Chicago school of sociology), *Shakaigaku Nenshi* 25, 1984 : 23-44.

6   ALEKSANDROWICZ, Dariusz. "Spór o obiektywizm w socjologii niemieckiej jako konflikt modeli racjonalności" (Controversy on objectivism in German sociology as a conflict of rationality models), *Studia Filozoficzne* 4, 1984 : 157-165.

7   ALO, Oladimej I. "Contemporary convergence in sociological theories : the relevance of the African thought-system in theory formation", *Présence Africaine* (126), trim. 2, 83 : 34-57. [Nigeria]

8   AMIOT, Michel. "L'enseignement de la sociologie en France. Résumé et conclusions d'une enquête conduite à l'initiative de la Société française de sociologie", *Revue Française de Sociologie* 25(2), apr-jun 84 : 281-291.

9   ANDERSON, R. J.; HUGHES, J. A.; SHARROCK, W. W. "Wittgenstein and comparative sociology", *Inquiry* 27(2-3), jul 84 : 268-276.

10   ANTONETTI, Nicola. "Luigi Sturzo : istituzioni, classe dirigente e società civile (gli scritti dal 1923 al 1926)" (Luigi Sturzo : institutions, ruling classes and civil society (writings from 1923 to 1926)), *Sociologia* 18(3), sep-dec 84 : 23-45.

11   ATOYI, Yoshio. *Sociology at the turn of the century.* Tokyo : Dobunkan, 1984, 176 p.

12   AUSTIN, Diane J. *Australian sociologies.* Sydney; Boston, MA : G. Allen and Unwin, 1984, viii-202 p.

13   BADESCU, Ilie. "Echoes of the Bucharest School of Sociology in America", *Revue Roumaine des Sciences Sociales. Série de Sociologie* 28(1), jan-jun 84 : 29-37.

14   BAÑO, Rodrigo. *Nuevos estilos y nuevos temas en los análisis de ciencias sociales en la última década* (New styles and new themes in Chilean social sciences analyses of the last decade). Santiago de Chile : FLACSO, 1984, 15 p.

15   BARNETT, Homer Garner. *Qualitative science.* New York, NY : Vantage Press, 1983, ix-267 p. ill., bibl., ind.

16   BASH, Harry H. "Sociology as discipline and as profession : a sociological scratch for every social itch?", *International Journal of Sociology and Social Policy* 4(1), 1984 : 15-28. [USA]

17   BOTTOMORE, T. *Sociology and socialism.* Brighton : Wheatsheaf Books, 1984, 212 p.

18   BRUNNER, José Joaquín. *Las cambiantes funciones de la sociología en Chile hasta 1950 : intelectuales, discursos, intereses* (The changing functions of Chilean sociology until 1950 : intellectuals, speeches, interests). Santiago de Chile : Facultad Latinoamericana de Ciencias Sociales, 1984, 52 p.

19   BRUNNER, José Joaquín. *Estudios del campo científico : la sociología chilena antes de su fase de profesionaliezación plena* (Studies on the scientific field : Chilean sociology before its full professionalization step). Santiago de Chile : Facultad Latinoamericana de Ciencias Sociales, 1984, 200 p.

20   BRYANT, Christopher G. A. "Development and direction in sociology : the American way and others", *British Journal of Sociology* 35(4), dec 84 : 608-618. [A review article]

21   BULMER, Martin. *The Chicago School of Sociology : institutionalization, diversity, and the rise of sociological research.* Chicago, IL : University of Chicago Press, 1984, xx-204 p.

22   BURKE, Edmund III. "The institutionalization of sociology in France : its social and political significance", *International Social Science Journal / Revue Internationale des Sciences Sociales* 36(4), 1984 : 643-655.

23   BUSINO, Giovanni. "Sociologie di ieri e sociologie di oggi" (Sociology of yesterday and
          sociology of today), *Revue Européenne des Sciences Sociales. Cahiers Vilfredo Pareto* 22(66),
          1984 : 41-53.

24   DROUARD, Alain; [ed.]. *Le développement des sciences sociales en France : au tournant des années
          soixante; table ronde réunie les 8-9 janvier 1981 à l'Institut d'histoire du temps présent.* Paris : Édi-
          tions du Centre National de la Recherche Scientifique, 1983, 186 p. bibl.

25   FICHTER, Joseph H. "Sociology of our times", *Social Forces* 62(3), mar 84 : 573-584.

26   FIGUEROA NAVARRO, Alfredo; [comp.]. *El desarrollo de las ciencias sociales en Panamá*
          (The development of social sciences in Panama). Panamá : Universidad de Panamá,
          1983, lxii-535 p. ill., bibl.

27   GAREAU, Frederick H. "An empirical analysis of the international structure of American
          social science", *Social Science Journal (Fort Collins)* 21(3), jul 84 : 23-36.

28   GAREAU, Frederick H. "The United States as a center of social science", *Social Science
          Quarterly* 65(3), sep 84 : 840-847.

29   GEDDES, Patric. "Sociology : early evolutionary perspective", *Indian Journal of Social Research*
          25(3), dec 84 : 243-280.

30   GELLNER, Ernest. "The scientific status of the social sciences", *International Social Science
          Journal / Revue Internationale des Sciences Sociales* 36(4), 1984 : 567-586.

31   GHEORGHIU, Mihai Dinu. "La sociologie roumaine conteporaine", *Actes de la Recherche
          en Sciences Sociales* 55, nov 84 : 68-70.

32   GLENN, Norval D. "An alternative view of sectarianism in the social sciences", *Social
          Science Quarterly* 65(3), sep 84 : 848-853. [USA]

33   GOLDSTEIN, Jan. "Foucault among the sociologists : the 'disciplines' and the history
          of the professions", *History and Theory* 23(2), 84 : 170-192. [France]

34   GUILLÉ-ESCURET, Georges. "Le fait social contre nature", *Temps Modernes* 40(451),
          feb 84 : 1497-1517.

35   HALLEN, G. C. "Sociology in India : antecedents, beginnings and progress", *Indian Journal
          of Social Research* 25(3), dec 84 : 227-242.

36   HAMAGUCHI, Haruhiko. "1920-nendai no nihon shakaigaku no dohkoh" (Some
          movements of Japanese sociology in 1920s), *Studies of Sociological History* 6, 1984 : 1-13.

37   HICKOX, M. S. "The problem of early English sociology", *Sociological Review* 32(1),
          feb 84 : 1-17.

38   JACOBY, Joseph E.; [et al.]. "There 'is' life (and work) after sociology : implications for
          curriculum design", *Teaching Sociology* 11(4), jul 84 : 399-417. [USA]

39   KANTOWSKY, D. "Max Weber's contributions to Indian sociology", *Contributions to Indian
          Sociology* 18(2), jul-dec 84 : 307-317.

40   KAWAMURA, Nozomu. "Katayama Sen to Meiji shakaigaku" (Katayama Sen and Meiji
          sociology), *Kagaku to Shiso* 51, 1984 : 32-48.

41   KAY, Susan Ann; MEIKLE, Douglas B. "Political ideology, socio- biology and the US
          women's rights movement", *Women and Politics* 3(2-3), aut 83 : 67-95. [USA]

42   KÖNIG, René. "Über das vermeintliche Ende der deutschen Soziologie vor der Machter-
          greifung des Nationalsozialismus" (On the supposed end of the German Sociology before
          the seizure of power of the national socialism), *Kölner Zeitschrift für Soziologie und Sozial-
          psychologie* 36(1), mar 84 : 1-42.

43   KRAŚKO, Nina. "Historia instytucjonalizacji socjologii w Polsce : 1918-1939" (The history
          of institutionalization of sociology in Poland : 1918-1939), *Studia Socjologiczne* 92(1),
          1984 : 231-249.

44   KUIPERS, Theo. A. F. "Olson, Lindenberg en reductie in de sociologie" (Olson, Lindenberg
          and reductions in sociology), *Mens en Maatschappij* 59(1), jan 84 : 45-67.

45   LANTZ, Herman R. "Continuities and discontinuities in American sociology", *Sociological
          Quarterly* 25(4), 1984 : 581-596.

46   LEPEHIN, A. V. "K voprosu o sootnošenii sociologii i social'nogo upravlenija" (Question
          on correlation between sociology and social management), *Vestnik Moskovskogo Universiteta.
          Teorija Naučnogo Kommunizma* (5), 1983 : 72-75.

47   LYON, David. "The idea of a Christian sociology : some historical precedents and current
          concerns", *Sociological Analysis* 44(3), 1983 : 227-242.

48   MATTICK, P. Jr. "Marx and ideas of a social science", *Économies et Sociétés* 18(7-8),
          jul-aug 84 : 147-181.

49   MAYRL, William W.; [ed.]. "Recognizing and rewarding teaching", *Teaching Sociology*
          12(1), oct 84 : 3-127. [USA]

50   MOKRZYCKI, Edmind; [ed.]. *Kryzys i schizma. Antyscjentystyczne tendencja w socjologii współczesnej*
          (Crisis and schism. Antiscientific tendencies in contemporary sociology. 2 vols.).
          Warszawa : Państwowy Instytut Wydawniczy, 1984, 389; 245 p. bibl.

51   MORI, Mototaka. "Ninshiki hihan to tohitsu kagaku — 1920 nendai no Austria shakaigaku" (Austro-Marxism and sociology), *Shakaigakushi Kenkyu* 6, 1984 : 48-61.
52   MOTWANI, Kewal. "Sociology : synoptic and integral approach to social life", *Indian Journal of Social Research* 25(3), dec 84 : 281-292.
53   PATIÑO AVILA, J. Ernesto. *Kant y las ciencias sociales* (Kant and the social sciences). Tunja : Ediciones 'La rana y el Aguila', 1984, 122 p. bibl.
54   PERSELL, Caroline Hodges. "An interview with Robert K. Merton", *Teaching Sociology* 11(4), jul 84 : 355-386. [On Robert K. Merton's teaching ideas and practices as well as his personal and institutional rewards for teaching]
55   PITTENDRIGH, Adele S.; JOBES, Patrick C. "Teaching across the curriculum : critical communication in the sociology classroom", *Teaching Sociology* 11(3), apr 84 : 281-296.
56   RE, Anna da. "Naissance et développement de la sociologie en Italie", *Annales de l'Institut de Sociologie*, 1983 : 219-227.
57   SABERWAL, Satish. "For a sociology of India : uncertain transplants; anthropology and sociology in India", *Contributions to Indian Sociology* 17(2), jul-dec 83 : 301-315.
58   SAINT-ARNAUD, Pierre. *William Graham Sumner et les débuts de la sociologie américaine.* Québec : Presses de l'Université Laval, 1984, 235 p. bibl., ind.
59   SARKAR, Benoy Kumar. "Comparative-historical approach to sociology under the Calcutta School", *Indian Journal of Social Research* 25(3), dec 84 : 293-303. [Followed by 'Additional observations' by Santosh K. NANDY, ibid. : 304-318]
60   SHOJI, Kohkichi. "Kaku-jidai no sekai-shakaigaku" (World sociology in the nuclear age), *Shakaigaku Kenkyu Nenpo* 8, 1984 : 29-59.
61   SINGH, Yogendra. *Image of man : ideology and theory in Indian sociology.* Delhi : Chanakya Publications, 1984, vi-194 p. bibl., ind.
62   SWATOS, William H. Jr. "The faith of the fathers : on the Christianity of early American sociology", *Sociological Analysis* 44(1), 1983 : 33-52.
63   SWINGEWOOD, Alan. *A short history of sociological thought.* London : Macmillan, 1984, x-355 p.
64   SZÁNTÓ, Tibor; ZSOLNAI, László. "Önmagát kereső társadalomtudomány" (Social science : searching its identity), *Valóság* 27(4), 1984 : 1-14.
65   SZTOMPKA, Piotr; [ed.]. *Masters of Polish sociology.* Wrocław : Ossolineum, 1984, 250 p.
66   TILMAN, Rick; SIMICH, J. L. "On the use and abuse of Thorstein Veblen in modern American sociology. II. Daniel Bell and the 'Utopianizing' of Veblen's contribution and its integration by Robert Merton and C. W. Mills", *American Journal of Economics and Sociology* 43(1), jan 84 : 103-114. [See for the first part, ibid. 42(2), oct 83]
67   VIEHOFF, Ludger. "Zur Entwicklung der Soziologie an den Hochschulen der Bundesrepublik Deutschland von 1960-1981" (On the development of sociology in West German higher education between 1960-1981), *Zeitschrift für Soziologie* 13(3), jul 84 : 264-272.
68   VINCK, Dominique. "Sociobiologie et néo-libéralisme", *Revue Nouvelle* 40(3), mar 84 : 291-297.
69   WEYER, Johannes. *Westdeutsche Soziologie 1945-1960 . deutsche Kontinuitäten und nordamerikanischer Einfluss* (West German sociology 1945-1960 : German continuities and North American influence). Berlin : Duncker und Humblot, 1984, 447 p. bibl., ind.
70   WOZNIAK, Paul R. "Making sociobiological sense out of sociology", *Sociological Quarterly* 25(2), 1984 : 191-204.
71   YAZAWA, Shujiro. *Gendai America shakaigaku-shi kenkyu* (A history of modern American sociology). Tokyo : University of Tokyo Press, 1984, 317 p.
72   ZSIGMOND, László. *August Comte : a XIX. század politikai gondolkodásának történetéből* (Auguste Comte : from the XIXth century history of political thought). Budapest : Akadémiai Kiadó, 1984, 457-1-3 p. ill., bibl.

10200   RESEARCH WORKERS. SOCIOLOGISTS
CHERCHEURS. SOCIOLOGUES

73   "Modern masters of science", *Social Research* 51(3), 1984 : 583-835.
74   CARO, Jean-Yves. "Scientificité et rapports sociaux", *Sociologie du Travail* 26(1), jan-mar 84 : 4-24.
75   COLLECTIF 'RÉVOLTES LOGIQUES'. *L'empire du sociologue.* Paris : La Découverte, 1984, 164 p.
76   DEWS, Peter. "Power and subjectivity in Foucault", *New Left Review* (144), apr 84 : 72-95.
77   EVANS, Arthur S. "Role relations of black sociologists with the black community : perceptions of sociologists", *Journal of Black Studies* 13(4), jun 83 : 477-487. [USA]
78   GERČIKOV, V. I. "Metody raboty zavodskogo sociologa" (The methods of a factory sociologist's activity), *Izvestija Sibirskogo Otdelenija Akademii Nauk SSSR. Serija Ėkonomiki i Prikladnoj Sociologii* (2), 1984 : 56-65.

79   GOĆKOWSKI, Janusz. *Autorytety świata uczonych* (Authorities in the world scolars). Warszawa : Państwowy Instytut Wydawniczy, 1984, 291 p.
80   KALETA, Andrzej; [ed.]. *Józef Chałasiński — socjolog i humanista. Materiały z konferencji naukowej* (Józef Chałasiński as sociologist and humanist. Materials from an Academic Conference). Toruń : Uniwersytet im. Mikołaja Kopernika, 1984, 169 p.
81   KHANNA, Durga Prasad Singh. *Dr. Bhagwan Das as a social thinker.* Delhi : Shree Publishing House, Jain Book Depot, 1983, vi-iv-244 p. bibl.
82   LE DOEUFF, Michelle. "Sartre, l'unique sujet parlant", *Esprit* (5), mai 84 : 181-191.
83   LYSON, Thomas A.; SQUIRES, Gregory D. "The promise and perils of applied sociology : a survey of non-academic employers", *Sociological Inquiry* 54(1), wint 84 : 1-15.
84   RICHARDS, J. M. "Structure of specialization among American population scientists", *Scientometrics* 6(6), 1984 : 425-432.
85   SAINT-SERNIN, Bertrand. "Michel Serres à mi-parcours", *Études*, mar 84 : 369-381.
86   SAINT-SERNIN, Bertrand. "Raymond Aron", *Études*, aug 84 : 7-17.
87   SELVIN, Hanan C.; WILSON, Everett K. "On shaping sociologists' prose", *Sociological Quarterly* 25(2), 1984 : 205-222.
88   SUPEK, Rudi. "Sociolog kao istraživač i kao odgajatelj" (Sociologist as a researcher and as an educator), *Revija za Sociologiju* 14(1-2), 1984 : 3-10.
89   TOREN, Nina. "National cultures of science : a study of Soviet and American immigrant scientists in Israël", *Science and Public Policy* 11(3), jun 84 : 125-160.
90   WATTS, W. David; JOHNSON, Roland H. III. "Employment of sociology graduates, 1982", *Teaching Sociology* 11(2), jan 84 : 183-204. [USA]
91   ZUPANOV, Josip; ŠPORER, Željka. "Profesija sociolog" (The profession of sociologist), *Revija za Sociologiju* 14(1-2), 1984 : 11-46. [Yugoslavia]

10300   ORGANIZATION OF RESEARCH. RESEARCH POLICY
ORGANISATION DE LA RECHERCHE. POLITIQUE DE RECHERCHE

10310   Current research
Recherche en cours

92   "Social science and public policy : research support in social science", *Society* 21(4), jun 84 : 76-91. [USA] [With contributions by Marshall ROBINSON, Harvey BROOKS]
93   AKIMOTO, Ritsuo. "Chicago gakuha daini sedai to shakaigaku no kohsoh" (The second generation of Chicago school and the scope of sociology), *Waseda Daigaku Bungakubu Kenkyu Kiyo* 30, 1984 : 45-60.
94   BAR-HAIM, Gabriel. "Styles of research and research self-images of academics in four socio-behavioral fields", *Social Science Information / Information sur les Sciences Sociales* 23(6), 1984 : 1009-1028.
95   BOOTH, David B. "Studying research methods by examining changing research strategies", *Teaching Sociology* 11(2), jan 84 : 205-212.
96   BRAUN, Hans; ARTICUS, Stephan. "Sozialwissenschaftliche Forschung im Rahmen der amerikanischen Besatzungspolitik 1945-1949" (Social science research in the framework of the American occupation policy 1945-1949), *Kölner Zeitschrift für Soziologie und Sozialpsychologie* 36(4), dec 84 : 703-737. [Germany FR]
97   BROADHEAD, Robert S. "Human rights and human subjects : ethics and strategies in social science research", *Sociological Inquiry* 54(2), 1984 : 107-123. [USA]
98   BRYMAN, Alan. "The debate about quantitative and qualitative research : a question of method of epistemology?", *British Journal of Sociology* 35(1), mar 84 : 75-92.
99   COOK, Judith A.; FONOW, Mary M. "Methoden feministischer Soziologie in den Vereinigten Staaten" (Feminist sociology methods in the United States), *Argument* 26(143), feb 84 : 57-69.
100   FEDOTOVA, V. G. "Issledovanija specifiki obščestvennyh nauk" (Research on the social science specificity), *Voprosy Filosofii* (1), 1984 : 165-172.
101   HAMAGUCHI, Haruhiko. "Rumania shakaigaku no kenkyukatsudo no shindohkoh" (New tendencies in Rumanian sociological research), *Shakaigaku Nenshi* 25, 1984 : 43-61.
102   KIM, Jae-On. "An approach to sensitivity analysis in sociological research", *American Sociological Review* 49(2), apr 84 : 272-282. [USA]
103   LISLE, Edmond; MACHIN, Howard; YASIN, Sy; [eds.]. *Traversing the crisis : the social sciences in Britain and France.* London : Economic and Social Research Council, 1984, 297 p. bibl.
104   MCCARTNEY, James L. "Setting priorities for research : new politics for the social sciences", *Sociological Quarterly* 25(4), 1984 : 437-455. [USA]

105   MURRAY, Linda A.; RICHARDSON, T. E. *Intelligent knowledge-bases systems : UK social science research inputs.* London : Economic and Social Research Council Education and Human Development Committee; Merstham, Redhill, Surrey : School Government Publishing Co., 1984, 26-14 p.

106   NICHOLSON, Michael. *The scientific analysis of social behaviour : a defence of empiricism in social science.* London : F. Pinter, 1983, xii-252 p. bibl., ind.

107   PACE, Enzo. "Le langage sociologique et son laboratoire. À propos du Bulletin bibliographique et des Notes de lecture dans les Archives de Sciences Sociales des Religions", *Archives de Sciences Sociales des Religions* 58(1), jul-sep 84 : 5-27.

108   REYES, Román. *La voluntad de fragmento : para una filosofía de las ciencias sociales* (The will of fragment : for a philosophy of the social sciences). Madrid : Akal, 1983, 159 p. bibl.

109   TURIEL, Elliot. *The development of social knowledge morality and convention.* Cambridge : Cambridge University Press, 1983, viii-240 p. ind., tabl., ill.

10320   Applied research. Interdisciplinary research
Recherche appliquée. Recherche interdisciplinaire

110   BLUMBERG, Melvin; PRINGLE, Charles D. "How control groups can cause loss of control in action research : the case of Rushton Coal Mine", *Journal of Applied Behavioral Science* 19(4), 1983 : 409-425. [USA]

111   DUBOST, J.; [et al.]. "Recherche-action et expérimentations sociales", *Connexions* 43, 1984 : 5-115.

112   LYNCH, Frederick R. "Totem and taboo in sociology : the politics of affirmative action research", *Sociological Inquiry* 54(2), spr 84 : 124-141.

113   PETERS, Michael; ROBINSON, Viviane. "The origins and status of action research", *Journal of Applied Behavioral Science* 20(2), 1984 : 113-124.

114   SOMMER, Robert. "Action research is formative : research at the Saskatchewan Hospital, 1957-61", *Journal of Applied Behavioral Science* 19(4), 1983 : 427-438. [Canada]

115   WINKIN, Yves. "La Fondation Macy et l'interdisciplinarité", *Actes de la Recherche en Sciences Sociales* 54, sep 84 : 87-90. [USA]

10330   Research centres
Centres de research

10340   Organization of research. Research policy
Organisation de la recherche. Politique de la recherche

116   "Research support and intellectual advance in the social sciences", *Items* 37(2-3), sep 83 : 33-49. [USA] [With contributions by Marshall ROBINSON, Henry W. RIECKEN, Harvey BROOKS, Thomas F. JUSTER, Roberta BALSTAD MILLER]

117   BENACHENHOU, A. "Politiques technologiques et politiques éducatives", *Travail et Société* 9(4), oct-dec 84 : 355-366.

118   CHIBA, Masashi. "Kyodo kenkyu no koka o ageru tame ni -kojin teki keiken ni yoru kyodo kenkyu ron" (A methodological examination of joint research), *Sogo Toshi Kenkyu* 21, 1984 : 111-128.

119   CUMMINGS, Scott. "The political economy of social science funding", *Sociological Inquiry* 54(2), 1984 : 154-170. [USA]

120   DAVIS, Charles H. "L'UNESCO et la promotion des politiques scientifiques nationales en Afrique sub-saharienne, 1960-1979", *Études Internationales* 14(4), dec 83 : 621-638.

121   DYNES, Russell R. "The institutionalization of COSSA : an innovative response to crises by American social science", *Sociological Inquiry* 54(2), 1984 : 211-229. [Consortium of Social Science Associations]

122   GOLDBERG, Albert I.; KATS, Rachel. "Migration and research commitments : long term effects of national socialization", *International Migration / Migrations Internationales* 22(2), 1984 : 129-143. [Israel]

123   HIMMELSTEIN, Jerome L.; ZALD, Mayer. "American conservatism and government funding of the social sciences and the arts", *Sociological Inquiry* 54(2), 1984 : 171-187.

124   JAIRATH, Vinod K. "In search of roots — the Indian scientific community", *Contributions to Indian Sociology* 18(1), jan-jun 84 : 109-130.

125   JONES, Lyle V.; LINDZEY, Gardner; COGGES-HALL, Porter E.; [eds.]. *An assessment of research doctorate programs in the United States : social and behavioral sciences.* Washington, DC : National Academy Press, 1982, xii-249 p.

126   MEHEU, Louis; [et al.]. "La science au Québec francophone : aperçus sur son
         institutionnalisation et sur les conditions d'accès à sa pratique", *Canadian Review of Sociology
         and Anthropology / Revue Canadienne de Sociologie et d'Anthropologie* 21(3), aug 84 : 247-274.
127   ORGANISATION DE COOPÉRATION ET DE DÉVELOPPEMENT ÉCONOMIQUE.
         Politiques nationales de la science : Grèce. Paris : OCDE, 1984, 123 p. bibl.
128   PFETSCH, Frank R. "Die Säkulare Entwicklung der Staatlichen Wissenschafts-Ausgaben
         in Deutschland 1870-1975" (State's scientific functions evolution in Germany,
         1870-1975), *Historical Social Research / Historische Sozialforschung* (28), oct 83 : 3-29.
129   SNELLEN, I. T. M. "Social merit as a criterion of scientific choice : its application in
         Dutch science policy", *Minerva* 21(1), spr 83 : 16-36.
130   ZUICHES, James J. "The organization and funding of social science in the NSF", *Sociological
         Inquiry* 54(2), 1984 : 188-210. [USA] [National Science Foundation]

**10350   Research equipment
             Équipement de la recherche**

131   "Computerkultur" (Computer culture), *Kursbuch* (75), mar 84 : 1-179. [With contributions
         by Wolfgang COY, Oswald WEINER, Grand JOHN]
132   BERTASIO, Danila. "Expert systems e 'intelligenza quotidiana'" (Expert systems and
         'everyday intelligence'), *Studi di Sociologia* 22(2), apr-jun 84 : 160-163.
133   BODEN, Margaret A. "Artificial intelligence and social forecasting", *Journal of Mathematical
         Sociology* 9(4), 1984 : 341-356.
134   BORILLO, Mario. *Informatique pour les sciences de l'homme : limites de la formalisation du
         raisonnement.* Bruxelles : Mardaga, 1984, 210 p. bibl.
135   CENTRE DE COORDINATION POUR LA RECHERCHE ET L'ENSEIGNEMENT
         EN INFORMATIQUE ET SOCIÉT61E. *Société et informatique.* Paris : Delagrave, 1984,
         190 p. bibl.
136   FILENI, Franco. "Per un'analisis sistematica del rapporto fra informatica e cultura" (For a
         systematic analysis of the relation between informatics and culture), *Sociologia* 18(3),
         sep-dec 84 : 95-112.
137   FLECK, James. "Artificial intelligence and industrial robots : an automatic end for
         utopian thought?", *Sociology of the Sciences* 8, 1984 : 189-231.
138   SALVADORI, Mario. "Il fascino del computer" (Computer's fascination), *Critica Sociologica*
         69, 1984 : 64-71.
139   WARNIER, Jean-Dominique. *L'homme face à l'intelligence artificielle.* Paris : Éditions
         d'Organisation, 1984, 140 p. bibl.

**10360   Sociological associations
             Associations de sociologie**

**10400   CONGRESSES. MEETINGS
             CONGRÈS. RÉUNIONS**

**10500   DOCUMENTS. INFORMATION PROCESSING
             DOCUMENTS. TRAITEMENT DE L'INFORMATION**

**10510   Documentation
             Documentation**

140   "Internasjonal nyhetsformidling" (International information dissemination), *Internasjonal
         Politikk* (3), 1983 : 309-357. [With contributions by Torstein SANDØ, Nils Morten
         UDGAARD, Knut FRYDENLUD]
141   HUBER, Wolfgang. *Vom quantitativen zum qualitativen Begriff der Information* (From quantitative
         to qualitative concept of information). Regensburg : F. Pustet, 1984, 106 p. ill., bibl.
142   HUSSAIN, Donna. *Information resource management.* Homewood, IL : R. D. Irwin, 1984,
         xiii-645 p. ill., bibl., ind.
143   JANSEN, Torben Bo. "Information technology : the need for social experiments",
         Technological Forecasting and Social Change 23(4), aug 83 : 325-352.
144   POWERS, Michael J.; ADAMS, David Robert; MILLS, Harlan D. *Computer information
         systems development : analysis and design.* Cincinnati, OH : South-Western Publishing Co.,
         1984, xiv-686 p. ill., ind.
145   ROMNEY, A. Kimball; WELLER, Susan C. "Predicting informant accuracy from patterns
         of recall among individuals", *Social Networks* 6(1), mar 84 : 59-77.
146   SIMONDS, A. P. "On being informed", *Theory and Society* 11(5), sep 82 : 587-616.

147   SZOSTAK, Władysław. *Rola systemów informacyjnych w procesach sterowania społeczeństwem socjalistycznym. Analiza modelowa* (Role of information systems in the processes of governing of socialist society. Model analysis). Kraków : Uniwersytet Jagielloński, 1984, 151 p.

148   THIERAUF, Robert J. *Effective management information systems : accent on current practices.* Columbus, OH : C. E. Merrill, 1984, v-558 p. ill., bibl., ind.

149   TOMASETTA, Leonardo. "I servo-meccanismi del potere informatico" (The servo-mechanisms of informative power), *Rassegna Italiana di Sociologia* 25(2), apr-jun 84 : 177-219.

10520   Documentary analysis. Reference works
Analyse documentaire. Ouvrages de référence

150   CASTRO DE SALMERÓN, Alicia; SAUCEDO LUGO, María Elena; ALVAREZ DE PÉREZ, María Graciela. *Bibliografía sobre educación superior en América Latina* (Bibliography on higher education in Latin America). México : Universidad Nacional Autónoma de México, 1983, 197 p. ind.

151   KALIA, Narendra Nath. "The sociological book review : a substitute for the standard term paper", *Teaching Sociology* 11(2), jan 84 : 213-218.

152   VARET, Gilbert; [ed.]. *Bibliographie et informatique : les disciplines humanistes et leurs bibliographies à l'âge de l'informatique.* Paris : Éditions de la Maison des Sciences de l'Homme, 1984, 178 p.

10530   Information services
Services d'information

153   "Genealogy and libraries", *Library Trends* 32(1), sum 83 : 3-159. [USA] [With contributions by Bill R. LINDER, Samuel M. ANDRUSKO]

154   ADIMORAH, E. N. O. "Analyse des progrès économiques accomplis par les bibliothèques publiques au Nigéria, en tant qu'institutions sociales", *Revue de l'Unesco pour la Science de l'Information, la Bibliothéconomie et l'Archivistique* 5(3), sep 83 : 173-181 & 210.

155   BEZZUBOV, A. N.; KLEPOV, V. N. "O strukture i funkcijah informacionnogo banka dannyh po problemam molodeži" (On the structure and functions of the information data bank on youth problems), *in : Social'naja informacija v sisteme naučnyh issledovanij problem molodeži* Moskva, 1983 : 76-93.

156   BLACK, Donald V.; FUNG, Margaret C. "Information systems and services in China and Japan", *Annual Review of Information Science and Technology*, 1983 : 307-354.

157   CACALY, Serge. *Les banques de données des sciences de l'homme et la société.* Paris : A Jour, 1984, 71 p. bibl.

158   CHANDLER, G. "The West German national library and information system : a broad comparative survey of its evolution and structure, 1946-83", *International Library Review* 16(3), jul 84 : 323-339.

159   DANIELS SHEPARD, Marietta. "Information systems and library automation in Latin America", *Advances in Librarianship* 13, 1984 : 152-184.

160   KHAN, M. H. "Public libraries in Bangladesh", *International Library Review* 16(2), apr 84 : 125-141.

161   KIRATSOV, P. "Développement d'un service centralisé et automatisé d'information scientifique et technique en République populaire de Bulgarie", *Revue de l'Unesco pour la Science de l'Information, la Bibliothéconomie et l'Archivistique* 5(3), sep 83 : 165-172.

162   LUNDU, Maurice C. "The National Information System (NATIS) concept and the development of libraries in Zambia : some underlying critical issues", *International Library Review* 16(4), oct 84 : 373-385.

163   MCCARTHY, C. M. "Problems of library and information system automation in Brazil", *Journal of Information Science* 7(4-5), dec 83 : 149-158.

164   PIŠTORA, Ladislav. "Retrospektivní vývoj a současný stav sítě lidových knihoven v ČSSR" (Retrospective evolution and actual condition of popular libraries network in Czechoslovakia), *Statistika* (6), 1984 : 272-282.

165   WHITE, Lawrence J. *The public library in the 1980s : the problem of choice.* Lexington, MA; Toronto, ON : Heath, Lexington Books, 1983, xiii-208 p. [USA]

10540   Documentalists
Documentalistes

10550   Terminology
Terminologie

166   ABERCROMBIE, Nicholas; HILL, Stephen; TURNER, Bryan S. *The Penguin dictionary of sociology.* London : A. Lane, 1984, 266 p. bibl.
167   AITCHISON, Jean; ALLEN, C. G.; [eds.]. *Bibliography of mono- and multilingual vocabularies, thesauri subject headings, and classification schemes in the social sciences.* Paris : UNESCO, 1982-83, 101 p. ind.
168   MANN, M. *International encyclopedia of sociology.* New York, NY : Continuum, 1984, xi-434 p.

10560   Biographies
Biographies

169   "In memory of Alvin W. Gouldner", *Theory and Society* 11(6), nov 82 : 731-944.
170   "On Erving Goffman", *Theory and Society* 13(5), sep 84 : 621-695.
171   "Pour Raymond Aron (1905-1983)", *Revue Européenne des Sciences Sociales* 22(66), 1984 : 5-40. [With contributions by Raymond BOUDON, Franciszek DRAUS]
172   BERTAUX, Daniel; KOHLI, Martin. "The life story approach : a continental view", *Annual Review of Sociology* 10, 1984 : 215-237.
173   BUCHMANN, Marlis; GURNY, Ruth. "Wenn Subjektivität zur Subjetivismus wird... Methodische Probleme der neueren soziologischen Biographieforschung" (When subjectivity becomes subjectivism... Methodical problems of the new sociological biography research), *Kölner Zeitschrift für Soziologie und Sozialpsychologie* 36(4), dec 84 : 773-782.
174   CAMARGO, Aspásia. "Os usos da histórica oral e da história de vida : trabalhando com elites políticas" (The uses of oral history and life history : studying political elites), *Dados* 27(1), 1984 : 5-28.
175   DENZIN, Norman K. "Interpretando as vidas de pessoas comuns : Sartre, Heidegger e Faulkner" (Interpreting the life of ordinary people : Sartre, Heidegger and Faulkner), *Dados* 27(1), 1984 : 29-43.
176   DUMAZEDIER, Joffre. "À propos de l'étude de Michael Pollak sur 'Paul Lazarsfeld, fondateur d'une multinationale scientifique' ", *Actes de la Recherche en Sciences Sociales* 55, nov 84 : 49-53. [Voir aussi ibid. : 25, 1979 : 45-59]
177   HALSEY, A. H. "T. H. Marshall : past and present 1893-1981, President of the British Sociological Association 1964-1969", *Sociology (London)* 18(1), feb 84 : 1-18.
178   KÖNIG, René. "In memoriam Raymond Aron (15. März 1905 bis 17. Oktober 1983)" (In memoriam Raymond Aron (15th March, 1905 to 17th October 1983)), *Kölner Zeitschrift für Soziologie und Sozialpsychologie* 36(1), mar 84 : 209-210.
179   LAUTMAN, Jacques. "Raymond Aron (1905-1983)", *Sociologie du Travail* 26(1), jan-mar 84 : 1-3.
180   LEVY, René. "Per una ricerca biografica integrata dal punto di vista strutturale-teoretico" (For an integrated biographical research from the structural theoretical point of view), *Critica Sociologica* 70, 1984 : 6-40.
181   OHYAMA, Nobuyoshi. "Aru shiage-ko no seikatsu-shi to zohsen-gyo rohshi kankei : mensetsu no kiroku to kaisetsu" (A finisher's life history and industrial relations in a shipyard : a personal interview and explanatory notes), *Hokkaido Daigaku Jinbunkagaku Ronshu* 21, 1984 : 59-126. [Japan]
182   OSWALD, Hans. "In memoriam Erving Goffman (11. July 1922 bis 20. November 1982)" (In memoriam Erving Goffman (11th July 1922 to 20th November 1982)), *Kölner Zeitschrift für Soziologie und Sozialpsychologie* 36(1), mar 84 : 210-213.
183   SCHRAMM, Wilbur. "In memoriam Ithiel de Sola Pool, 1917-1984", *Public Opinion Quarterly* 48(2), 1984 : 525-526.

10570   Articles. Periodicals
Articles. Périodiques

184   BOVONE, Laura; GASPARINI, Giovanni. "Vent'anni di 'Studi di Sociologia' : alcune considerazioni d'insieme" (Twenty years of 'Studi di Sociologia' : some global considerations), *Studi di Sociologia* 22(3), jul-sep 84 : 220-235.
185   FISCHER, Werner. "Les 10 ans de la Revue suisse de Sociologie", *Schweizerische Zeitschrift für Soziologie / Revue Suisse de Sociologie* 10(3), 1984 : 643-646.
186   GREENBAUM, Joseph; MACK, Arien; [eds.]. "Fifty years of Social Research : Continental and Anglo-American perspectives", *Social Research* 51(1-2), 1984 : 1-578. [Contains a selection of articles of today's interest published in the journal]

10580   **Proceedings. Reports**
             Actes. Rapports

10590   **Textbooks. Theses**
             Manuels. Thèses

187   HARA, Junsuke; UMINO, Michio. *Shakai chosa enshu* (Social research : a practical manual).
       Tokyo : University of Tokyo Press, 1984, 191 p.
188   MORIN, Edgar. *Sociologie.* Paris : Fayard, 1984, 465 p. bibl.
189   MOSCOVICI, Serge; [ed.]. *Psychologie sociale.* Paris : Presses Universitaires de France,
       1984, 596 p. bibl.
190   SAITO, Yoshio; IGARASHI, Yoshio; [eds.]. *Shakaigaku no riron to ohyoh* (Sociology :
       theoretical and applied). Tokyo : Fukumura Shuppan, 1984, 220 p.
191   STOKES, Randall. *Introduction to sociology.* Dubuque, IA : W. C. Brown Publishers,
       1984, xviii-542 p. ill., bibl., ind.

11100   EPISTEMOLOGY. RESEARCH METHODS. THEORY
         EPISTÉMOLOGIE. MÉTHODES DE RECHERCHE. THÉORIE

11110   Philosophy. Theory
         Philosophie. Théorie

192   "Filosofija-čelovek-kul'tura : k itogam XVII Vsemirnogo filosofskogo kongressa" (Philosophy — man — culture : in connection with the philosophers world congress), *Voprosy Filosofii* 37(5), 1984 : 30-62.

193   "Marx : au lendemain d'un centenaire. I. Critique de la politique et de l'économie politique", *Économies et Sociétés* 18(7-8), jul-aug 84 : 3-332.

194   "Studi su Erving Goffman" (Studies on Erving Goffman), *Rassegna Italiana di Sociologia* 25(3), apr-jun 84 : 349-442.

195   "Tendances actuelles de la philosophie", *Diogène* 128, oct-dec 84 : 77-141.

196   ARNAULT, France. "Frédéric Le Play, de la métallurgie à la science sociale", *Revue Française de Sociologie* 25(3), jul-sep 84 : 437-457.

197   ASSITER, Alison. "Althusser and structuralism", *British Journal of Sociology* 35(2), jun 84 : 272-296.

198   BAILEY, Kenneth. "Beyond functionalism : towards a nonequilibrium analysis of complex social systems", *British Journal of Sociology* 35(1), mar 84 : 1-18.

199   BECHER, Heribert J. "Georg Simmel in Strassburg" (Georg Simmel in Strasburg), *Sociologia Internationalis* 22(1), 1984 : 3-42.

200   BERTILSSON, Margareta. "The theory of structuration : prospects and problems", *Acta Sociologica* 27(4), 1984 : 339-353.

201   BESSONOV, B. N.; STOLJAROV, V. V.; [eds.]. *Filosofija i kul'tura : k XVII vsemirnomu filosofskomu kongressu* (Philosophy and culture : to the XVIIth World Philosophical Congress). Moskva : Akademija Obščestvennyh Nauk pri CK KPSS, 1983, 167 p.

202   BOUDON, Raymond; BOURRICAUD, François. "Herbert Spencer ou l'oublié", *Revue Française de Sociologie* 25(3), jul-sep 84 : 343-351.

203   BROWN, Harold I. "Pour un retour à l'empirisme", *Diogène* 126, apr-jun 84 : 56-78.

204   BUDD, Richard J.; NORTH, Derek; SPENCER, Christopher. "Understanding seat-belt use : a test of Bentler and Speckart's extension of the 'theory of reasoned action'", *European Journal of Social Psychology* 14(1), jan-mar 84 : 69-78. [UK]

205   COLLIOT-THÉLÈNE, Catherine. "Le matérialisme historique a aussi une histoire", *Actes de la Recherche en Sciences Sociales* 55, nov 84 : 15-21.

206   CRAIB, Ian. *Modern social theory : from Parsons to Habermas*. Brighton, Sussex : Wheatsheaf Books, Harvester, 1984, viii-230 p. bibl., ind.

207   DIENELT, Karl. *Tiefenpsychologie und Marxismus : eine kritische Analyse ihrer Beziehungen* (Deep psychology and marxism : a critical analysis of their relations). Wien : Böhlau, 1983, 133 p. bibl., ind.

208   DZIEWULSKI, Henryk. "Alfred Schütz : uspołecznienie pojmowania świata" (Alfred Schütz : a social approach to the world), *Studia Socjologiczne* 94(3), 1984 : 129-154.

209   DŽIOEV, O. I. "Ob osobennostjah filosofskogo znanija i o predmete filosofii" (Characteristics of philosophical knowledge and on the philosophy object), *Izvestija Akademii Nauk Gruzinskoj SSR. Serija Filosofii i Psihologii* (1), 1983 : 103-112.

210   FENTON, Steve. *Durkheim and modern sociology*. Cambridge : Cambridge University Press, 1984, 276 p.

211   FETISOV, V. Ja. *Naučnyj kommunizm kak sociologičeskaja teorija* (Scientific communism as a sociological theory). Leningrad : Izdatel'stvo Leningradskogo Universiteta, 1983, 167 p.

212   FILIPOVIĆ, Mileva. "Strukturalna dijalektika kao metod istraživanja društvenih pojava" (Structural dialectics as a method for research into social trends), *Sociologija* 26(1-2), jan-jun 84 : 111-124.

213   FLIS, Andrzej. "Myśl społeczno-polityczna Edwarda Abramowskiego" (Social and political thought of Edward Abramowski), *Studia Socjologiczne* 93(2), 1984 : 151-175.

214   FLIS, Janusz. "Wiodące idee strukturalizmu oxfordzkiego" (Leading ideas of the Oxford structuralism), *Studia Socjologiczne* 94(3), 1984 : 105-128.

215   FRASER, Nancy. "'Postestructuralismo y política'. Los discípulos franceses de Jacques Derrida" ('Post-structuralism and politics'. Jacques Derrida's French disciples), *Revista Mexicana de Sociología* 45(4), oct-dec 83 : 1209-1229.

216   FREUND, Julien. "Karl Marx et la sociologie dite révolutionnaire", *Revue Européenne des Sciences Sociales. Cahiers Vilfredo Pareto* 22(66), 1984 : 91-110.

217   FRISBY, David. *Georg Simmel.* Chichester : E. Horwood; London... Tavistock Publications, 1984, 161 p. bibl., ind.

218   GEDE, A. "Antinomija postistorizma i neistorizma v sovremennom buržuaznom soznanii" (Antinomy of post-historicism and neo-historicism in contemporary bourgeois consciousness), *in : Filosofija, politika, kul'tura* Moskva : s.n., 1983 : 52-61.

219   GRATHOFF, Richard; WALDENFELS, Bernhard; [eds.]. *Sozialität und Intersubjektivität : phänomenologische Perspektiven der Sozialwissenschaften im Umkreis von Aron Gurwitsch und Alfred Schütz* (Sociality and intersubjectivity : phenomenological perspectives of social sciences as defined by Aron Gurwitsch and Alfred Schütz). München : W. Fink, 1983, 410 p. bibl., ind.

220   HAFERKAMP, Hans. "Interaktionsaspekte, Handlungszusammenhänge und die Rolle des Wissenstransfers. Eine handlungstheoretische Kritik der Theorie des kommunikativen Handelns" (Aspects of interaction, coherences of action and the role of knowledge transfer. An action-theoretical critique of the theory of communicative action), *Kölner Zeitschrift für Soziologie und Sozialpsychologie* 36(4), dec 84 : 783-798. [Discussion of Jürgen Habermas' theory of communicative action]

221   HITT, Michael A.; KEATS, Barbara W. "Empirical identification of the criteria for effective action programs", *Journal of Applied Behavioral Science* 20(3), 1984 : 203-222.

222   JOAS, Hans. "Durkheim et le pragmatisme. La psychologie de la conscience et la constitution sociale des catégories", *Revue Française de Sociologie* 25(4), oct-dec 84 : 560-581.

223   JOHNSTON, Les. "Marxism and capitalist possession", *Sociological Review* 32(1), feb 84 : 18-37.

224   KALOMALOS, Thanassis. *La science du matérialisme social : théorie générale.* Paris : Anthropos; Athènes : EKKE, 1984, 196 p.

225   KANTOR, K. M. "Filosofija i kul'tura v istoričeskom razvitii čelovečestva" (Philosophy and culture in the historical development of the humanity), *Voprosy Filosofii* (7), 1983 : 86-99.

226   KELLY, Robert F. "The legalization of the Kantian tradition in moral philosophy and sociology : an analysis of Rawls and Parsons", *Sociological Focus* 17(1), jan 84 : 45-58.

227   KNAPP, Peter. "Domains of applicability of social-scientific theories : problems of the empirical falsifiability of bounded generalizations", *Journal for the Theory of Social Behaviour* 14(1), mar 84 : 25-41.

228   KOBAYASHI, Kazuho. "Dodai-jyobu kouzou ron no sai-kento" (Rethinking of the theory of base and superstructure), *Shakaigaku Nenpo* 13, 1984 : 57-77.

229   KOLM, Serge Christophe. "Marxisme et bouddhisme", *Cahiers Internationaux de Sociologie* 77, 1984 : 339-360.

230   KOZYR-KOWALSKI, Stanisław. "Marksizm a scholastyka pojęciowa" (Marxism and conceptual scholasticism), *Studia Socjologiczne* 92(1), 1984 : 11-37.

231   LANGANEY, André. "La nouvelle démographie de l'évolution", *Population* 39(3), mai-jun 84 : 587-606.

232   LLOYD, Genevieve. "Reason, gender, and morality in the history of philosophy", *Social Research* 50(3), 1983 : 491-513.

233   MAEDA, Yutaka. "Schutz to Weber ni okeru kohi gainen" (Concepts of action in Alfred Schutz and Max Weber), *Kenkyu Kiyo* 6(3), 1984 : 1-25.

234   MALININ, V. "Konkretnyj istorizm protiv abstraknogo antropologizma" (Concrete historicism against abstract anthropologism), *Kommunist (Moskva)* (2), 1984 : 65-74.

235   MANN, Ram Singh. *Anthropological and sociological theory : approaches and applications.* Jaipur : Rawat Publications, 1984, 375 p. bibl., ind.

236   MCCARTHY, Thomas A. "Cambios en la relación de la teoría con la práctica en la obra de Jürgen Habermas" (Change in the theory and practice relationship in Jürgen Habermas' works), *Revista Mexicana de Sociología* 45(4), oct-dec 83 : 1179-1207.

237   MCNALL, Scott G. "The Marxian project", *Sociological Quarterly* 25(4), 1984 : 473-495.

238   MICCOLI, Paolo. *E. Husserl e la fenomenologia : il senso umano del mondo della vita* (E. Husserl and the phenomenology : the human measuring of the life world). Roma : Città Nuova, 1983, 120 p. bibl., ind.

239   MILLER, R. W. *Analyzing Marx.* Princeton, NJ : Princeton University Press, 1984, xii-319 p.

240   MISZTAL, Bronisław; MISZTAL, Barbara A. "The explanatory utility of major sociological theories developed in Poland, 1970-1980", *Sociology (London)* 18(2), mai 84 : 239-252.

241   MOUZELIS, Nicos. "On the crisis of Marxist theory", *British Journal of Sociology* 35(1), mar 84 : 112-121.

242   NISHIHARA, Kazuhisa. "Genshogaku-teki shakaigaku no kohzu to hoko -sono kigogaku teki tenkai ni mukete" (The fundamentals and direction of phenomenological sociology), *Gunma Journal of Liberal Arts and Sciences* 18, 1984 : 1-24.

243   OKRENT, Mark B. "Hermeneutics, transcendental philosophy and social science", *Inquiry* 27(1), mar 84 : 23-49.

244   ONO, Michikuni. "Kouzou to symbol : kozo shugi no shiten" (Structure and symbol : the structuralist perspective), *Shakaigaku Zasshi* 1, 1984 : 15-31.

245   OOSTEN, Jarich; RUIJTER, Arie de; [eds.]. *The future of structuralism. Papers of the IUAES-Intercongress, Amsterdam, 1981.* Göttingen : Edition Herodot, 1983, 452 p. ill.

246   PAUL, Jean-Louis. *Le principe ouvrier dans la théorie de Marx : contre l'économie de la critique, en réponse à la 'Critique de l'économie' de M. Voyer.* Sant-Eloy-les-Mines, Puy-de-Dôme : Ressouvenances, 1983, xxviii-98 p. bibl.

247   PIPPING, Knut. "'Who reads Westermarck today?'", *British Journal of Sociology* 35(3), sep 84 : 315-332. [Edvard Westermarck, 1862-1939]

248   POSTONE, Moishe; BRICK, Barbara. "Critical pessimism and the limits of traditional Marxism", *Theory and Society* 11(5), sep 82 : 617-658.

249   POTTER, Jonathan. "Testability, flexibility : Kuhnian values in scientists' discourse concerning theory choice", *Philosophy of the Social Sciences / Philosophie des Sciences Sociales* 14(3), sep 84 : 303-330.

250   RUBIO CARRACEDO, José. *Positivismo, hermenéutica y teoría crítica en las ciencias sociales* (Positivism, hermeneutics and critical theory in the social sciences). Barcelona : Editorial Humanitas, 1984, 335 p. bibl.

251   SATO, Yasuyuki. "Aruga shakaigaku to kouzou shugi -Aruga no ruikei ron no saikaishaku" (Aruga's sociological theory and structuralism : reinterpretation of Aruga's 'Type theory'), *Niigata University Studies in Humanities* 66, 1984 : 17-41.

252   SCAFF, Lawrence A. "Weber before Weberian sociology", *British Journal of Sociology* 35(2), jun 84 : 190-215.

253   SEIDMAN, Steven. "The main aims and thematic structures of Max Weber's sociology", *Canadian Journal of Sociology / Cahiers Canadiens de Sociologie* 9(4), 1984 : 381-404.

254   ŠEVČENKO, V. "Plodotvornaja razrabotka social'no-filosofskoj teorii marksizma" (The successful elaboration of the socio-philosophical theory of marxism), *Kommunist (Moskva)* (10), 1983 : 105-109.

255   SÈVE, Lucien. *Structuralisme et dialectique.* Paris : Messidor-Éditions Sociales, 1984, 261 p. bibl.

256   SEWART, John J. "Is a critical sociology possible : Alvin Gouldner and the 'Dark side of the dialectic'", *Sociological Inquiry* 54(3), 1984 : 231-259.

257   SHIOBARA, Tsutomu; [eds.]. *Shakaigaku no riron* (Sociological theories). Tokyo : Hoso-Daigaku-Kyoiku-Shinkokai, 1984, 141 p.

258   SIEBERT, R. J. *The critical theory of religion : the Frankfurt School.* Berlin; New York, NY . . . Mouton, 1984, 360 p.

259   SMITH, A. Anthony. "Two theories of historical materialism : G. A. Dohen and Jürgen Habermas", *Theory and Society* 13(4), jul 84 : 513-540.

260   TEPLOV, F. "Marksovoe učenie i buržuaznye fal'sifikacii" (Marx's teaching and bourgeois falsifications), *Kommunist (Moskva)* (18), 1983 : 7-18.

261   TITTENBRUN, Jacek. "Strukturalny funkcjonalizm Talcotta Parsonsa a materialism historyczny" (Talcott Parsons' structural functionalism and historical materialism), *Problemy Marksizmu-Leninizmu* 2, 1984 : 203-213.

262   TOMINAGA, Ken'ichi. *Gendai no shakai kagakusha — gendai shakai kagaku ni okeru jissho shugi to rinen shugi* (Positivism and idealism in social sciences today). Tokyo : Kodansha, 1984, 454 p.

263   VACCARINI, Italo. "La parabola delle teoria sociologiche" (Parable of sociological theory), *Studi di Sociologia* 22(3), jul-sep 84 : 327-343.

264   VAN DIJK, Jan. *Westers marxisme als sociale wetenschap : object, methode en praktijk van een onderzoekstraditie* (Western Marxism as social science : the subject, method and practice of a special tradition). Nijmegen : SUN, 1984, 392 p. bibl.

265   VOGEL, Lise. *Marxism and the oppression of women.* New Brunswick, NJ : Rutgers University Press, 1983, 253 p. bibl., ind.

266   WILKES, K. V. "Pragmatics in science and theory in common sense", *Inquiry* 27(4), dec 84 : 339-361.

267   YMONET, Marie. "Les héritiers du 'Capital'. L'invention du marxisme en France au lendemain de la Commune", *Actes de la Recherche en Sciences Sociales* 55, nov 84 : 3-14.

268   YOKOYAMA, Yasuo. *Shakaigaku riron to shakai shiso* (Sociological theory and social thought). Tokyo : Keio Tsushin, 1984, 263 p.
269   ZAKRZEWSKA, Elżbieta. "Psychologia konstruktów osobistych a socjologia życia codziennego — podobieństwa i różnice" (Psychology of personal constructs and sociology of everyday life — similarities and differences), *Studia Socjologiczne* 93(2), 1984 : 209-225.

11120   Epistemology. Explanation. Understanding
Epistémologie. Explication. Compréhension

270   ADAMEK, Wojciech. "Przewidywanie w naukach społecznych : analiza metodologiczna" (Forecasting in the social sciences : methodological analysis), *Studia Socjologiczne* 92(1), 1984 : 97-111.
271   APARICIO, Miriam de Santander. "La crisis de la sociología en su relación con modelos epistemológicos actuales" (Crisis of the sociology in relation to present epistemological patterns), *SOCIOLOGICA — Revista Argentina de Ciencias Sociales* 9, 1984 : 37-52.
272   BREEN, Richard. "Fitting nonhierarchical and association log-linear models using GLIM", *Sociological Methods and Research* 13(1), aug 84 : 77-107.
273   CORTESE, Anthony J. "Moral judgment in Chicano, black, and white young adults", *Sociological Focus* 17(3), aug 84 : 189-199. [USA]
274   DOMENACH, Jean-Marie. "Epistemologia e autonomia" (Epistemology and autonomy), *Rivista Internazionale di Scienze Economiche e Commerciali* 31(1), jan 84 : 6-13.
275   ERINA, É. B. "Istinnost' i točnost' social'nogo predvidenija" (Truth and accuracy of social forecast), *in : Kategorii filosofii i razvitie naučnogo poznanija* Saratov, 1983 : 133-135.
276   FARARO, Thomas J. "Neoclassical theorizing and formalization in sociology", *Journal of Mathematical Sociology* 10(3-4), 1984 : 361-393.
277   FENYÖ, Stefano. *Teoria, osservazione ed esperienza nella discussione epistemologica contemporanea* (Theory, observation and experience in the contemporary epistemological discussion). Roma : Ateneo, 1983, 238 p. bibl.
278   FUNATSU, Mamoru. "'Kaishaku' to shakai katei" ('Interpretation' and social process), *Shakaigaku Hyoron* 35(1), 1984 : 49-57.
279   GALAVOTTI, Maria Carla; GAMBETTA, Guido; [eds.]. *Causalità e modelli probabilistica* (Causality and stochastic models). Bologna : CLUEB, 1983, 151 p. bibl., ind.
280   HICKS, Lou E. "Conceptual and empirical analysis of some assumptions of an explicity typological theory", *Journal of Personality and Social Psychology* 46(5), mai 84 : 1118-1131. [USA]
281   JILEK, Miroslav. "Da li je moguće istraživati moguće" (Is it possible to investigate possible?), *Revija za Sociologiju* 13(1-4), 1983 : 63-79.
282   JOHN, Robert. "Max Weber's epistemology of the cultural sciences : presupposition of 'interpretive sociology'", *Social Science Journal (Fort Collins)* 21(3), jul 84 : 91-109.
283   JUDD, Charles M.; LUSK, Cynthia M. "Knowledge structures and evaluative judgments : effects of structural variables on judgmental extremity", *Journal of Personality and Social Psychology* 46(6), jun 84 : 1193-1207. [USA]
284   KAČAJNOVA, N. B. "Soderžanie kategorij sub'ekta i ob'ekta naučnogo social'nogo prognozirovanija" (Content of the subject and object of scientific social forecast categories), *in : Kategorii filosofii i razvitie naučnogo poznanija* Saratov, 1983 : 135-136.
285   KHOURY, Joseph. "Un cas d'invariance de modèles en sciences sociales : les modèles de revenu proposés par Jean Stoetzel", *Revue Française de Sociologie* 25(1), jan-mar 84 : 100-109.
286   LATOUCHE, Serge. *Le procès de la science sociale : introduction à une théorie critique de la connaissance.* Paris : Anthropos, 1984, 219 p. ind.
287   LEVINSEN, Jørn. *Rationalitet og beslutninger* (Rationality and decision). Roskilde : Institut for Samfundsøkonomi og Planlaegning, 1983, 268 p. bibl.
288   LONG, J. Scott. "Estimable functions in log-linear models", *Sociological Methods and Research* 12(4), mai 84 : 399-432.
289   MCCLURE, John. "On necessity and commonsense : a discussion of central axioms in new approaches to lay explanation", *European Journal of Social Psychology* 14(2), apr-jun 84 : 123-149.
290   POCHE, Bernard. "Paradigmes sociologiques et pratiques sociales", *Revue de l'Institut de Sociologie* (1-2), 1984 : 35-53.
291   TACQ, J. J. A. *Causaliteit in sociologisch onderzoek* (Causality in sociological research). Deventer : Van Loghum Slaterus, 1984, 337 p. ill., bibl., ind.
292   TODOROV, Tzvetan. "Epistemology of the human sciences", *Economy and Society* 13(1), feb 84 : 25-42. [Original translation from the French by Elizabeth KINGDOM]

13

293   VENUTI, Maria Caterina. *Epistemologia e filosofia dell'educazione* (Epistemology and philosophy of education). Palermo : S. F. Flaccovio, 1983, 140 p. bibl.

294   VORONOVIČ, B. A. "Ob'ektivnoe i sub'ektivnoe v social'nyh processah" (The objective and the subjective in social processes), *Filosofskie Nauki* (3), 1984 : 39-47.

295   YOSHIZAWA, Natsuko. "Shakaigaku to kan-shukan sei mondai -'shukan shugi' hihan saiko" (Sociology and the problem of 'intersubjectivity'), *Shakaigaku Hyoron* 35(2), 1984 : 135-144.

296   ZUKIER, Henri; PEPITONE, Albert. "Social roles and strategies in prediction : some determinants of the use of base-rate information", *Journal of Personality and Social Psychology* 47(2), aug 84 : 349-360. [USA]

11130   Research techniques. Sociological analysis
Techniques de recherche. Analyse sociologique

297   ALDENDERFER, Mark S.; BLASHFIELD, Roger K. *Cluster analysis.* Beverly Hills, CA : Sage Publications, 1984, 88 p. bibl., ill.

298   ALEXANDER, Jeffrey C. "Social-structural analysis : some notes on its history and prospects", *Sociological Quarterly* 25(1), 1984 : 5-26.

299   ALLERBECK, Klaus R.; HOAG, Wendy J. "Umfragereplikation als Messung sozialen Wandels. Jugend 1962-1983" (Survey reply as measurement of social change. The youth 1962-1983), *Kölner Zeitschrift für Soziologie und Sozialpsychologie* 36(4), dec 84 : 755-772. [Germany FR]

300   BALÁZS, János. *A hasítás adatcsoportosító eljárás leírása, bemutatása országos naturális gazdasági mutatók segítségével* (Description, presentation of the splitting method of data distribution with the help of national natural economic indicators). Budapest : Magyar Tudományos Akadémia Szociológiai Kutatóintézete, 1982, 71 p.

301   BATEMAN, N. *Data construction in social surveys.* London : Allen and Unwin, 1984, xii-147 p.

302   BERRY, William Dale. *Nonrecursive causal models.* Beverly Hills, CA : Sage Publications, 1984, 95 p.

303   BEYNIER, Dominique; LE GALL, Didier. *Analyse du social : théorie et méthodes.* Paris : Anthropos, 1984, 140 p.

304   BLALOCK, Hubert M. "Contextual-effects models : theoretical and methodological issues", *Annual Review of Sociology* 10, 1984 : 353-372.

305   BORTAZ, V. "Mehanizmy realizacii metodologičeskoj funkcii" (Mechanisms of the methodological function realization), *Obščestvennye Nauki (Moskva)* (6), 1983 : 65-77.

306   CIBOIS, Philippe. *L'analyse des données en sociologie.* Paris : Presses Universitaires de France, 1984, 218 p. bibl.

307   COHEN, Ayala. "Exploratory data analysis methods : a study of industrial workers' work role centrality", *Sociological Methods and Research* 12(4), mai 84 : 433-452. [Israel]

308   CROOK, Anne. "Data protection in the United Kingdom", *Journal of Information Science* 7(1), aug 83 : 15-22. [Continued in ibid. : 7(2), sep 83 : 41-57]

309   DICKIE-CLARKE, H. F. "Anthony Gidden's theory of structuration", *Canadian Journal of Political and Social Theory* 8(1-2), spr 84 : 92-110.

310   DOREIAN, Patrick; TEUTER, Klaus; WANG, Chi-Hsien. "Network autocorrelation models : some Monte Carlo results", *Sociological Methods and Research* 13(2), nov 84 : 155-200.

311   DOSKAČ, A. G. "Predposylki sistemnogo issledovanija o kružajuščej sredy" (Premises of the systemic approach to the environment), *in : Dialektika v naukah o prirode i čeloveke : trudy III Vsesojuznogo Soveščanija po filosofskim voprosam sovremennogo estestvoznanija. IV. Čelovek, obščestvo i priroda v vek NTR* Moskva, 1983 : 266-270.

312   DOW, Malcolm M. "A biparametric approach to network autocorrelation : Galton's Problem", *Sociological Methods and Research* 13(2), nov 84 : 201-217.

313   ESSER, Hartmut. "Figurationssoziologie und methodologischer Individualismus. Zur Methodologie des Ansatzes von Norbert Elias" (Figurational sociology and methodological individualism. On the methodology of Norbert Elias' approach), *Kölner Zeitschrift für Soziologie und Sozialpsychologie* 36(4), dec 84 : 667-702.

314   FARARO, Thomas J.; DOREIAN, Patrick. "Tripartite structural analysis : generalizing the Breiger-Wilson formalism", *Social Networks* 6(2), jun 84 : 141-175.

315   FEGER, Hubert; DROGE, Ulfert. "Repräsentation von Ordinaldaten durch Graphen : ordinale Netzwerkskalierung" (Representation of ordinal data through graphs : ordinal network scaling), *Kölner Zeitschrift für Soziologie und Sozialpsychologie* 36(3), sep 84 : 494-510.

316   FLIS, Mariola. "Czas historyczny a struktura społeczna" (Time and social structure), *Studia Socjologiczne* 92(1), 1984 : 37-45.

317   FOX, James Alan; TRACY, Paul E. "Measuring associations with randomized response", *Social Science Research* 13(2), jun 84 : 188-197.

318   FOX, John. "Detecting changes of level and slope in repeated-measures data", *Sociological Methods and Research* 12(3), feb 84 : 263-277.

319   GRAS, Alain. "Le mystère du temps : nouvelle approche sociologique", *Diogène* 128, oct-dec 84 : 103-124.

320   GVIŠIANI, D. M. "K. Marks i metodologičeskie problemy sistemnyh issledovanij" (K. Marx and methodological problems of systemic research), *in : Sistemnye issledovanija : metodologičeskie problemy. Ežegodnik* Moskva, 1983 : 7-10.

321   GVIŠIANI, D. M. "Sistemnyj podhod k issledovaniju global'nyh problem" (The systemic approach to research of global problems), *in : Nauka i čelovečestvo : dostupno i točno o glavnom v mirovoj nauke. Mezdunarodnyj ežegodnik* Moskva, 1983 : 237-249.

322   HASHIZUME, Daisaburo; SHIDA, Kiyoshi; TSUNEMATSU, Naoyuki. "Kiki ni tatsu kozo-kino shugi -waga kuni ni okeru tenkai to sono mondai-ten" (Structural-functional analysis at a crisis : its developments in Japan, problems and some conclusions), *Shakaigaku Hyoron* 35(1), 1984 : 2-18.

323   HITZLER, Ronald. "Existenzialer Skeptizismus. Vorschläge zu einem protosoziologischen Orientierungsrahmen" (Existential scepticism. Proposals for a protosociological orientation frame), *Sociologia Internationalis* 22(2), 1984 : 197-215.

324   HOLTMANN, Dieter. "Interpretation der Effekte in der multivariaten Modellbildung" (Interpretation of effects in the multivariate model formation), *Zeitschrift für Soziologie* 13(1), jan 84 : 60-71.

325   HUMMEL, Hans J.; SODEUR, Wolfgang. "Interpersonelle Beziehungen und Netzstruktur. Bericht über ein Projekt zur Analyse der Strukturentwicklung unter Studienanfängern" (Interpersonal relations and network structure. Report on a project for the analysis of structure development among beginning students), *Kölner Zeitschrift für Soziologie und Sozialpsychologie* 36(3), sep 84 : 511-556.

326   JAGODZINSKI, Wolfgang. "Identification of parameters in cohort models", *Sociological Methods and Research* 12(4), mai 84 : 375-398.

327   KAPPELHOFF, Peter. "Strukturelle Äquivalenz in Netzwerken : algebraische und topologische Modelle" (Structural equivalence in networks : algebraic and topological models), *Kölner Zeitschrift für Soziologie und Sozialpsychologie* 36(3), sep 84 : 464-493.

328   KARSON, Marvin J. *Multivariate statistical methods : an introduction.* Ames, IA : Iowa State University Press, 1982, x-307 p.

329   KEMEROV, V. E. "Metodologija obščestvoznanija : perspektivy i problemy" (Methodology of knowledge on society : prospects and problems), *Voprosy Filosofii* (12), 1983 : 80-86.

330   KUJI, Toshitake. *Kokan riron to shakaigaku no houhou* (Exchange theory and sociological method). Tokyo : Shinsensha, s.d., 263 p.

331   LANDES, David S. *Revolution in time : clocks and the making of the modern world.* Cambridge, MA . Harvard University Press; London : Belknap Press, 1983, xviii-482 p.

332   LEDOUX, Yves. "Espaces et appropriation spatiale", *Annales de l'Institut de Sociologie*, 1983 : 143-160.

333   LEDRUT, Raymond. *La forme et le sens dans la société.* Paris : Méridiens, 1984, 192 p.

334   LISS, L. F. "Nekotorye metodologičeskie problemy programmirovanija sociologičeskogo issledovanija vypusknikov vysšej školy" (Some methodological problems of the sociological research planning for the high schools students), *in : Metodologiceskie problemy naucno-issledovatel'skih programm* Novosibirsk, 1983 : 126-134.

335   LIVEANU, Vasile. "Matematica si istoria social-economică" (Mathematics and socio-economic history), *Revista de Istorie* 37(4), apr 84 : 365-372.

336   MANDELL, Myrna. "Application of network analysis to the implementation of a complex project", *Human Relations* 37(8), aug 84 : 659-679.

337   MARGOLIS, Joseph. "Relativism, history and objectivity in the human studies", *Journal for the Theory of Social Behaviour* 14(1), mar 84 : 1-23.

338   MILES, Matthew B.; HUBERMAN, A. Michael. *Qualitative data analysis : a sourcebook of new methods.* Beverly Hills, CA : Sage Publications, 1984, 262 p. ind.

339   MULKAY, Michael. "The ultimate compliment : a sociological analysis of ceremonial discourse", *Sociology (London)* 18(4), nov 84 : 531-549. [Nobel Ceremonies]

340   NIELSEN, Greg N.; JACKSON, John B. "Toward a research strategy for the analysis of CBC English-language radio drama and Canadian social structure", *Canadian Journal of Sociology / Cahiers Canadiens de Sociologie* 9(1), 1984 : 21-45.

341   OKUDA, Kazuhiko. "Jissho kenkyu ni okeru kihon teki mondai no kento : chosa kyohi keiko no bunseki" (On basic problems of survey : a analysis on refusal trends), *Sensyu Keieigaku Ronsyu* 37, 1984 : 45-74.

342 PORTNJAGIN, A. P. "Metodologičeskie problemy determinacii antroposociogeneza" (Methodological problems of determination of anthroposociogenesis), *Metodologičeskie Voprosy Nauki* (9), 1983 : 91-109.

343 PUŠKIN, V. G. "Sistemno-kibernetičeskij podhod v social'nom poznanii" (Systemic and cybernetical approach in social knowledge), *in : Determinacija social'nogo poznanija* Leningrad, 1983 : 3-16.

344 ŠATALOVA, O. A. "Metodologičeskie problemy sistemnogo podhoda v issledovanii social'noj struktury" (Methodological problems of systemic approach in research on social structure), *in : Metodologičeskaja funkcija materialističeskoj dialektiki* Moskva, 1983 : 53-59.

345 SCHRODT, Philip A. *Microcomputer methods for social scientists.* Beverly Hills, CA : Sage Publications, 1984, 96 p. ill., bibl.

346 SCHUTT, Russell K.; BLALOCK, Hubert Jr.; WAGENAAR, Theodore C. "Goals and means for research methods courses", *Teaching Sociology* 11(3), apr 84 : 235-258.

347 SCHWARTZ, Joseph E.; SPRINZEN, Merle. "Structures of connectivity", *Social Networks* 6(2), jun 84 : 103-140.

348 SHIDA, Kiyoshi. "Fuku kino yoken riron no fukano sei : kouzou bunka kasetsu no baai" (The impossibility of multi-functional-requisite theory : the case of structural differentiation hypothesis), *Sociologos* 8, 1984 : 96-107.

349 SINGLY, François de. "Les manoeuvres de séduction : une analyse des annonces matrimoniales", *Revue Française de Sociologie* 25(4), oct-dec 84 : 523-559. [France]

350 SRIVASTAVA, R. N. "Some fatal methodological issues confronting the modern sociologist", *Indian Journal of Social Research* 25(1), apr 84 : 32-48.

351 STUDER, K. E.; BARBONI, E. J.; NUMAN, K. B. "Structural analysis using the input-output model : with special reference to networks of science", *Scientometrics* 6(6), 1984 : 401-423.

352 SZMATKA, Jacek. "Struktury bliskiego i dalekiego dystansu" (Structures of the near and far distance), *Studia Socjologiczne* 93(2), 1984 : 227-237.

353 TJULIN, I. G.; [et al.]. "Analytical methods and research methods in international relations", *in : Analitičeskie metody i metodiki v issledovanii meždunarodnyh otnošenij* Moskva, 1982 : 160.

354 TURNER, Stephen P. "Durkheim as a methodologist. II. Collective forces, causation, and probability", *Philosophy of the Social Sciences / Philosophie des Sciences Sociales* 14(1), mar 84 : 51-71. [See for the first part, ibid. : 13, 1983 : 425-450]

355 TURUK, G. P. "Izmerenie odnorodnosti sociologičeskoj informacii" (Measurement of the sociological information homogeneity), *Vestnik Moskovskogo Universiteta. Serija Filosofija* (1), 1984 : 19-26.

356 VELING, Kars. *Methodologie en de grondslagen van een pluriforme sociologie* (Methodology and basic problems of a pluriform sociology). Assen : Van Gorcum, 1983, 245 p. ill., bibl., ind.

357 VORONOV, A. A. "Modeli sravnenija v sistemnoj dinamike" (Models of comparison in systemic dynamics), *in : Filosofsko-metodologičeskie osnovanija sistemnyh issledovanij : sistemnyj analiz i sistemnoe modelirovanie* Moskva, 1983 : 180-187.

358 WASSERMAN, Stanley; GALASKIEWICZ, Joseph. "Some generalizations of p1 : external constraints, interactions and non-binary relations", *Social Networks* 6(2), jun 84 : 177-192.

359 WOODRUM, Eric. "'Mainstreaming' content analysis in social science : methodological advantages, obstacles, and solutions", *Social Science Research* 13(1), mar 84 : 1-19.

360 ZIEGLER, Rolf; [ed.]. "Analyse sozialer Netzwerke" (Analyses of social networks), *Kölner Zeitschrift für Soziologie und Sozialpsychologie* 36(3), sep 84 : 433-618.

11200 DATA COLLECTION. EXPERIMENTS
RASSEMBLEMENT DES DONNÉES. EXPÉRIENCE

11210 Experimentation. Observation
Expérimentation. Observation

361 "Legal aspects of census", *Öffentliche Verwaltung* 37(11), jun 84 : 453-459. [Germany FR] [With contributions by Sigmund WIMMER, Monika GÜNTHER]

362 ANDEZIAN, S. "L'observation participante et l'identité de l'anthropologue", *Recherches Sociologiques* 15(2-3), 1984 : 165-180.

363 ARARAGI, Shinzo. "Buraku kyogi-hi ni yoru chiiki shakai kenkyu" (A local community study method approached by Burakukyogikai), *Kumamoto Journal of Culture and Humanities* 12, 1984 : 25-52.

364 ARISUE, Ken. "Chiiki shakai kenkyu to chiiki bunka ron : gendai toshi-shakaigaku no tenkai" (Community studies and community culture : a revolution of contemporary urban sociology), *Hogaku Kenkyu* 57(8), 1984 : 1-27.

365 BERNER, Hermann. *Die Entstehung der empirischen Sozialforschung : zum Apriori und zur Sozialgeschichte der quantifizierenden Sozialanalyse* (The formation of empirical social research : on the a priori and social history of quantifying social analysis). Giessen : Focus, 1983, 222 p. bibl.

366 CHAPOULIE, Jean-Michel. "Everett C. Hughes et le développement du travail de terrain en sociologie", *Revue Française de Sociologie* 25(4), oct-dec 84 : 582-608.

367 COENEN-HUTHER, Jacques. "Observation et conceptualisation en sociologie : pour une épistémologie positive", *Revue de l'Institut de Sociologie* (1-2), 1984 : 167-198.

368 GELAŠVILI, N. M. "Kritika empiričeskoj sociologii" (Critics of empirical sociology), *in : Aktual'nye problemy filosofii* Tbilisi, 1983 : 140-157.

369 HAYASHI, Masataka. "Ushi-jima no shakai kouzou to jyumin no seikatsu kouzou -toku ni rekishi katei to keizai, seisan, rodo no kouzou ni tsuite" (Social structure and life of inhabitants in Ushijima island), *Journal of the Faculty of Liberal Arts, Yamaguchi University* 18, 1984 : 13-31.

370 MCCALL, George J. "Systematic field observation", *Annual Review of Sociology* 10, 1984 : 263-282.

371 MERLER, Alberto. "Evoluzione dell'analisi sociologica e 'realtà nazionale' in Brasile" (Evolution of sociological analisis and 'national reality' in Brazil), *Studi di Sociologia* 22(1), jan-mar 84 : 75-89.

372 ROBERTS, Fred S. *Measurement theory with applications to decision making, utility, and the social sciences.* Cambridge, Cambridgeshire; New York, NY : Cambridge University Press, 1984, xxii-420 p. ill., bibl.

373 TADEJ, Perla. "Mogućnosti i perspektive promatranja sa sudjelovanjem" (Possibilities and perspectives of participant's observation), *Revija za Sociologiju* 13(1-4), 1983 : 81-94.

11220   Sampling. Surveys
Échantillonnage. Enquêtes

374 ANTOINE, Jacques. "Les sondages d'opinion en France : évolution récente et rôle dans la société", *Journal de la Société de Statistique de Paris* 125(2), trim. 2, 84 : 63-73.

375 BARROW, Christine. *Guidelines for the conduct of social surveys in the Caribbean : the experience of a five-island, interdisciplinary questionnaire survey.* Cave Hill : Institute of Social and Economic Research (Eastern Caribbean), University of the West Indies, 1983, viii-117 p. bibl., ill.

376 DAVIS, James Allan; SMITH, Tom William. *General social survey cumulative file, 1972-1982.* Ann Arbor, MI : Inter-University Consortium for Political and Social Research, 1983, ca. 900 p.

377 LANCELOT, Alain. "Sondages et démocratie", *Opinion Publique* (1), 1984 : 257-266. [France]

378 OGRYZKO-WIEWIÓRSKI, Henryk. "Rozwój metodologii badań surveyowych : artykuł przeglądowy" (Development of the methodology of survey research : a cross-sectional paper), *Studia Socjologiczne* 92(1), 1984 : 139-160.

379 STONE, Linda; CAMPBELL, J. Gabriel. "The use and misuse of surveys in international development : an experiment from Nepal", *Human Organization* 43(1), 1984 : 27-37. [Fertility surveys]

11230   Interviews. Questionnaires
Entretiens. Questionnaires

380 DALESSIO, Anthony; IMADA, Andrew S. "Relationships between interview selection decisions and perceptions of applicant similarity to an ideal employee and self : a field study", *Human Relations* 37(1), jan 84 : 67-80.

381 DELIENS, L.; VAN GOOR, H. "Retrospectieve vertekening in interviews. Een empirische onderzoek naar het gebruik van interviews bij het opsporen ven beleidsprocessen uit het recente verleden" (Retrospective bias in survey-interviews. An empirical study of the use of survey-interviews in tracking down recent policy processes), *Sociologische Gids* 31(5), 1984 : 390-411.

382 GROVES, Robert M.; MATHIOWETZ, Nancy A. "Computer assisted telephone interviewing : effects on interviewers and respondents", *Public Opinion Quarterly* 48(1b), 1984 : 356-369. [USA]

383 GRUNDHÖFER, Horst. "Einmal mehr : Ähnlichkeit von Interviewer- und Befragten-einstellung — unbewusste Angleichung im Interviewprozess oder blosser Scheineffekt?" (Once more : interviewer-respondent resemblance — unconscious adaptation during the process of interview or only an illusory effect?), *Zeitschrift für Soziologie* 13(3), jul 84 : 260-263.

384 HOX, J. J.; DE LEEUW, E. D.; DUIJX, A. W. M. "The postman rings thrice. Een onderzoek naar twee kenmerken van Dillman's Total Design Method voor postenquêtes" (The postman rings thrice. A research on two characteristics of Dillman's Total Design Method for mail surveys), *Mens en Maatschappij* 59(2), mai 84 : 189-194.

385 JOBBER, David; SANDERSON, Stuart. "The effects of a prior letter and coloured questionnaire paper on mail survey response rates", *Journal of the Market Research Society* 25(4), oct 83 : 339-349. [UK]

386 LUTYŃSKA, Krystyna. *Wywiad kwestionariuszowy. Przygotowanie i sprawdzanie narzędzia badawczego* (The questionnaire interview. Preparation and verification of the research instrument). Warszawa : Ossolineum, 1984, 221 p.

387 MEERTENS, Roel W.; [et al.]. "Effects of hypothesis and assigned task on question selection strategies", *European Journal of Social Psychology* 14(4), oct-dec 84 : 369-378.

388 OWSLEY, Heidi H.; SCOTTON, Carol Myers. "The conversational expression of power by television interviewers", *Journal of Social Psychology* 123(2), aug 84 : 261-271.

389 RABOW, Jerome; NEUMAN, Carole A. "Garbaeology as a method of cross-validating interview data on sensitive topics", *Sociology and Social Research* 68(4), jul 84 : 480-497.

11240   Personality measurement. Tests
Mesure de la personnalité. Tests

390 SHARROCK, W. W.; WATSON, D. R. "What's the point of 'rescuing motives'?", *British Journal of Sociology* 35(3), sep 84 : 435-451. [See S. BRUCE and R. WALLIS, 'Rescuing motives', ibid. : 34(1), mar 83]

11250   Sociodrama
Sociodrame

11300   MATHEMATICAL ANALYSIS. STATISTICAL ANALYSIS
ANALYSE MATHÉMATIQUE. ANALYSE STATISTIQUE

11310   Algebra. Calculus. Logic
Algèbre. Calcul. Logique

391 FARARO, Thomas J.; [ed.]. "Mathematical ideas and sociological theory. Current state and prospects", *Journal of Mathematical Sociology* 10(3-4), 1984 : 219-393.

392 FREEMAN, Linton C. "Turning a profit from mathematics : the case of social networks", *Journal of Mathematical Sociology* 10(3-4), 1984 : 343-360.

393 FÜSTÖS, László. *Lineáris egyenletrendszerek általános modelljei* (General models of linear equation systems). Budapest : Magyar Tudományos Akadémia Szociológiai Kutatóintézete, 1983, 161 p.

394 GIBSON, Roland. "Marx and logic as social function", *International Journal of Social Economics* 11(6), 1984 : 3-43.

395 HAYES, Adrian C. "Formal model building and theoretical interests in sociology", *Journal of Mathematical Sociology* 10(3-4), 1984 : 325-341.

396 HECKATHORN, Douglas D. "Mathematical theory construction in sociology : analytic power, scope, and descriptive accuracy as trade-offs", *Journal of Mathematical Sociology* 10(3-4), 1984 : 295-323.

397 MARSDEN, Peter V.; LAUMANN, Edward O. "Mathematical ideas in social structural analysis", *Journal of Mathematical Sociology* 10(3-4), 1984 : 271-294.

398 MARTENS, Bernd. *Differentialgleichungen und dynamische Systeme in der Sozialwissenschaften : Stabilität, Katastrophen und Komplexität dynamischer Modelle* (Differential equations and dynamic systems in the social sciences : stability, catastrophes and complexity of dynamic models). München : Profil, 1984, 209 p. ill., bibl.

399 MAYHEW, Bruce H. "Baseline models of sociological phenomena", *Journal of Mathematical Sociology* 9(4), 1984 : 259-281. [With discussions by Jonathan H. TURNER; [et al.] ibid. : 283-304 and a response by the author : 305-339]

400 PAPOZJAN, S. S. *Matematičeskie metody v social'noj psihologii* (Mathematical methods in social psychology). Moskva : Nauka, 1983, 343 p.

401   RINDSKOPF, David. "Structural equation models : empirical identification, Heywood cases, and related problems", *Sociological Methods and Research* 13(1), aug 84 : 109-119.

402   SCHMUTZ, Georges. "La logique théorique en sociologie", *Revue Européenne des Sciences Sociales. Cahiers Vilfredo Pareto* 22(66), 1984 : 203-207.

403   TATE, Richard L. "Limitations of centering for interactive models", *Sociological Methods and Research* 13(2), nov 84 : 251-271.

404   WALLING, Derald; HOTCHKISS, H. Lawrence; CURRY, Evans W. "Power models and error terms", *Sociological Methods and Research* 13(1), aug 84 : 121-126.

405   WILLER, David. "Analysis and composition as theoretic procedures", *Journal of Mathematical Sociology* 10(3-4), 1984 : 241-269.

406   WILSON, Thomas P. "On the role of mathematics in the social sciences", *Journal of Mathematical Sociology* 10(3-4), 1984 : 221-239.

       11320   Statistical analysis
                  Analyse statistique

407   "Ratio (The) correlation dilemma", *Social Forces* 62(4), jun 84 : 1040-1058.

408   "Sociologie et statistique", *Économie et Statistique* 168, jul-aug 84 : 3-105. [With contributions by Yannick LEMEL, François de SINGLY, Nicolas HERPIN]

409   ACKERMANN, Werner. "Journée d'étude : 'Sociologie et Statistique' ", *Année Sociologique* 34, 1984 : 227-232. [Paris, le 15 octobre 1982]

410   AMBURGEY, Terry L.; CARROLL, Glenn R. "Time-series models for event counts", *Social Science Research* 13(1), mar 84 : 38-54.

411   ANDORKA, Rudolf. "A system of social indicators for the CMEA countries and for Hungary", *Social Indicators Research* 14(3), apr 84 : 241-261.

412   ANDORKA, Rudolf. "Társadalomstatisztika az 1930-as években" (Social statistics in the 1930s), *Statisztikai Szemle* 62(4), apr 84 : 397-413.

413   BALEVSKI, Dano. "Problémy a perspektivy rozvoje statistiky BLR" (Problems and development prospects of Bulgarian statistics), *Statistika* (2), 1984 : 49-55.

414   BARTÓK, János. *Faktoranalízis a gyakorlatban* (Factor analysis in practice). Budapest : MRT Tömegkommunikációs Kutatóközpont, 1983, 19 p.

415   CIECHOCIŃSKA, Maria. "Regional indicators in social planning", *Social Indicators Research* 14(3), apr 84 : 333-349. [Poland]

416   CUTRIGHT, Phillips; HARGENS, Lowell. "The Threshold Hypothesis : evidence from less developed Latin American countries, 1950-1980", *Demography* 21(4), nov 84 : 428-473.

417   DAVIS, James A. "Extending Rosenberg's technique for standardizing percentage tables", *Social Forces* 62(3), mar 84 : 679-708.

418   DINITTO, Diana. "Time-series analysis : an application to social welfare policy", *Journal of Applied Behavioral Science* 19(4), 1983 . 507-518. [USA]

419   DOBRIANOV, Velichko. "Social indicators and social management", *Social Indicators Research* 14(3), apr 84 : 313-331.

420   GINGERICH, Wallace J. "Meta-analysis of applied time-series data", *Journal of Applied Behavioral Science* 20(1), 1984 : 71-79.

421   GRÉMY, Jean-Paul. "Sur les différences entre pourcentages et leur interprétation", *Revue Française de Sociologie* 25(3), jul-sep 84 : 396-420.

422   HÉRAN, François. "L'assise statistique de la sociologie", *Économie et Statistique* (168), jul-aug 84 : 23-35.

423   ILLNER, M. "On functional types of indicators in social planning", *Social Indicators Research* 14(3), apr 84 : 275-285. [Czechoslovakia]

424   KARUNATILAKE, H. N. S. "Main socio-economic statistical series of South Asian countries : a critical survey", *International Social Science Journal / Revue Internationale des Sciences Sociales* 36(2), 1984 : 369-402.

425   KHAKHULINA, L. A. "Indicators for interrelated study of living standard and life style", *Social Indicators Research* 14(3), apr 84 : 287-293. [USSR]

426   KOVACSICS, Jozsef; [et al.]. "Az informatika fejlödésének hatása a statisztika elméletére és gyakorlatára" (Influence of computer science development on statistics theory and practice), *Statisztikai Szemle* 62(8-9), sep 84 : 831-861. [Hungary]

427   LISSOWSKI, Grzegorz. "Zastosowanie modeli logarytmiczno-liniowych do analizy związków między wieloma zmiennymi jakosciowymi" (Application of logarithmic-linear models in the analysis of relations between many qualitative variables), *Studia Socjologiczne* 93(2), 1984 : 239-263.

428   PENDLETON, Brian F. "Correcting for ratio variable correlation : examples using models of mortality", *Social Science Research* 13(3), sep 84 : 268-286. [USA]

429   PENEFF, Jean. "La fabrication statistique ou le métier du père", *Sociologie du Travail* 26(2), jun 84 : 195-211.

430   PERRY, Charles S. "Economic activity and social indicators : a rural-urban discontinuum?", *American Journal of Economics and Sociology* 43(1), jan 84 : 61-74. [USA]

431   SCHOENBERG, Ronald; RICHTAND, Carol. "Application of the EM method : a study of maximum likelihood estimation of multiple indicator and factor analysis models", *Sociological Methods and Research* 13(1), aug 84 : 127-150.

432   SHEN, Cynthia H.; YOUNG, Frank W. "The structural context of social indicator differentials in Japanese prefectures 1965-1975", *Social Indicators Research* 15(1), jul 84 : 17-42.

433   SINGLY, François de. "Les bons usages de la statistique dans la recherche sociologique", *Économie et Statistique* (168), jul-aug 84 : 18-21.

434   SPIRER, Herbert F.; JAFFÉ, A. J. "Misuses of statistics : lessons from statisticians, non-statisticians, students and teachers", *American Journal of Economics and Sociology* 43(2), apr 84 : 205-216. [USA]

435   STRAHL, Danuta. "Ścieżka proporcjonalnego rozwoju w ujęciu dynamicznym" (Path of proportional development : the dynamic approach), *Przegląd Statystyczny* 29(3-4), 1982 : 465-476.

436   SWANSON, David A.; TEDROW, Lucky M. "Improving the measurement of temporal change in regression models used for County Population Estimates", *Demography* 21(3), aug 84 : 373-381.

437   VERWAYEN, Henri. "Social indicators : actual and potential uses", *Social Indicators Research* 14(1), jan 84 : 1-27.

438   WINSHIP, Christopher; MARE, Robert D. "Regression models with ordinal variables", *American Sociological Review* 49(4), aug 84 : 512-525.

11330   Cybernetics. Information theory
Cybernétique. Théorie de l'information

439   GLASER, S. "Once more unto the system", *Human Relations* 37(6), jun 84 : 473-490.
440   PANDOLFI, Alessandro. "L'evoluzione dell'illuminismo e la teoria sistemica" (The evolution of the enlightenment and the systemic theory), *Studi di Sociologia* 22(2), apr-jun 84 : 144-159.

11340   Graph theory
Théorie des graphes

11350   Stochastic processes. Statistical decision. Game theory
Processus stochastiques. Décision statistique. Théorie des jeux

441   ALLO, Eliane. "L'émergence des probabilités", *Actes de la Recherche en Sciences Sociales* 54, sep 84 : 77-81.

442   CHICHILNISKY, Graciela; HEAL, Geoffrey. "Patterns of power : bargaining and incentives in two-person games", *Journal of Public Economics* 23(3), apr 84 : 333-349.

443   LIEBRAND, Wim B. G. "The effect of social motives, communication and group size on behaviour in an N-person multi-stage mixed-motive game", *European Journal of Social Psychology* 14(3), jul-sep 84 : 239-264.

444   MAUSKOPF, Joséphine; WALLACE, T. Dudley. "Fertility and replacement : some alternative stochastic models and results for Brazil", *Demography* 21(4), nov 84 : 519-536.

445   RAPOPORT, Amnon. "Variability in payoff disbursement in coalition formation experiments", *European Journal of Social Psychology* 14(3), jul-sep 84 : 265-280.

446   ZAGARE, Frank C. *Game theory : concepts and applications.* Beverly Hills, CA : Sage Publications, 1984, 96 p. ill., bibl.

11360   Attitude scales
Échelles d'attitude

447   JOE, Victor C. "Factor analysis of the conservatism scale", *Journal of Social Psychology* 124(2), dec 84 : 175-178.

448   MILLER, Peter V. "Alternative question forms for attitude scale questions in telephone interviews", *Public Opinion Quarterly* 48(4), 1984 : 766-778. [USA]

449   SZABÓ, Márton. "A hierarchikus tudatról" (On hierarchic awareness), *Valóság* 27(2), 1984 : 28-37.

12100   PSYCHOLOGY. SOCIAL PSYCHOLOGY. SOCIOMETRY
         PSYCHOLOGIE. PSYCHOLOGIE SOCIALE. SOCIOMÉTRIE

12110   Psychoanalysis. Social psychology
         Psychanalyse. Psychologie sociale

450   "Aspects actuels de la psychologie soviétique", *Sciences Sociales — Académie des Sciences de l'URSS* (3), 1984 : 24-96. [With contributions by B. LOMOV, E. CHOROKHOVA, Y. ZABRODINE]

451   "Exercice (L') de la psychanalyse aujourd'hui", *Débat* (30), mai 84 : 167-189. [With contributions by Robert CASTEL, Serge LEBOVICI, Jacques-Alain MILLER]

452   "International education in psychology", *American Psychologist* 39(9), sep 84 : 996-1042. [USA] [With contributions by Michael COLE, Harry C. TRIANDIS, Richard W. BRISLIN, Virginia STAUDT SEXTON, Henryk MISIAK]

453   "Introductory social psychology : concept and content", *Teaching Sociology* 11(2), jan 84 : 115-150.

454   "Psychologie clinique et psychanalyse", *Connexions* 40, 1984 : 3-114.

455   "Psychologist (The) and organized labor", *American Psychologist* 39(4), apr 84 : 428-445. [USA] [With contributions by Gregory E. HUSZCZO]

456   AIT-SAHALIA, Rachid. "Quelques réflexions sur la recherche et l'enseignement de la psychologie en Algérie", *Enfance* (4), trim. 4, 83 : 351-362.

457   BLASS, Thomas. "Social psychology and personality : toward a convergence", *Journal of Personality and Social Psychology* 47(5), nov 84 : 1013-1027.

458   CLAUSEN, John A.; [et al.]. "'The American soldier' and social psychology", *Social Psychology Quarterly* 47(2), jun 84 : 184-213. [STOUFFER, S. A.; [et al.], 'The American soldier : combat and its aftermath.' Princeton, NJ : Princeton University Press, 1949, first two volumes of the four-volume series 'Studies in Social Psychology in World War II']

459   DOISE, Willem. "Tensions et niveaux d'analyse en psychologie sociale expérimentale", *Connexions* 42, 1983 : 57-72.

460   DUBOST, Jean; [et al.]. "Psychologie sociale et psychosociologie", *Connexions* 42, 1983 : 5-157.

461   DUCRET, Jean-Jacques. *Jean Piaget, savant et philosophe : les années de formation, 1907-1924; étude sur la formation des connaissances et du sujet de la connaissance. 2 vols.* Genève : Droz, 1984, xix-997 p. bibl., ind.

462   DUNCAN, Otis Dudley. *Notes on social measurement : historical and critical.* New York, NY : Russell Sage Foundation, 1984, xi-256 p. bibl., ind.

463   ENRIQUEZ, Eugène. "Éloge de la psychosociologie", *Connexions* 42, 1983 : 113-133.

464   FASSIN, Didier. "Anthropologie de la folie", *Cahiers Internationaux de Sociologie* 77, 1984 : 237-271.

465   FORRESTER, John. "Who is in analysis with whom? Freud, Lacan, Derrida", *Economy and Society* 13(2), 1984 : 153-177.

466   FORSYTH, Donelson R.; POPE, William Ray. "Ethical ideology and judgments of social psychological research : multidimensional analysis", *Journal of Personality and Social Psychology* 46(6), jun 84 : 1365-1375. [USA]

467   GRANERO, Mirta. "La psicología comunitaria : orígenes, principios y fundamentos teóricos" (Community psychology : origins, principles and theoretical basis), *Revista Latinoamericana de Psicología* 16(3), 1984 : 387-400.

468   KOSOLAPOV, N. A. *Social'naja psichologija i meždunarodnye otnošenija* (Social psychology and international relations). Moskva : Nauka, 1983, 271 p.

469   KRISHNA, Shyam. *A study of personality differences between normal and problem children.* Gorakhpur : Pustaksthan, 1983, 12-159 p. bibl.

470   LOMOV, B. F.; [et al.]. *Psihologičeskaja nauka i obščestvennaja praktika* (Psychological science and social practice). Moskva : Nauka, 1983, 169 p.

471   MCMAHON, A. M. "The two social psychologies : postcrises directions", *Annual Review of Sociology* 10, 1984 : 121-140.

472   PETIT, François. "La psychosociologie des organisations. Des théories au terrain : une discipline systémique?", *Connexions* 42, 1983 : 73-95.

473   SHORTER, Edward. "Les désordres psychosomatiques sont-ils 'hystériques'? Notes pour une recherche historique", *Cahiers Internationaux de Sociologie* 76, 1984 : 201-224.

474   ŠIHIRIEV, P. N. "Tendencii razvitija sovremennoj zapadno-êvropejskoj social'noj
       psihologii" (Tendencies of development of the contemporary Western European social
       psychology), *Psihologičeskij Žurnal* (4), 1983 : 146-153.
475   SMITH, Leslie. "Genetic epistemology and the child's understanding of logic", *Philosophy
       of the Social Sciences / Philosophie des Sciences Sociales* 14(3), sep 84 : 367-376. [With a discussion
       by P. J. LOPTSON and I. W. KELLY, ibid. : 377-383 and an answer by the author,
       ibid. : 385-391]
476   THRYSØE, Willy. *Marxisme og psykoanalyse* (Marxism and psychoanalysis). Roskilde :
       Roskilde Universitetscenter, Institut for Socialvidenskab, 1983, ii-194 p. bibl.
477   UESUGI, Takamichi; FUKAYA, Masashi; [ed.]. *Kodomo to seinen no keisei* (Character
       building in childhood and youth). Tokyo : Dai'ichi Hoki, 1984, 265 p.
478   VEEN, P.; WILKE, H. A. M. *De kern van de sociale psychologie* (The core of social psychology).
       Deventer : Van Loghum Slaterus, 1984, 254 p. bibl., ill., ind.
479   ZEIGARNIK, B. V. "Kurt Lewin and Soviet psychology", *Journal of Social Issues* 40(2),
       1984 : 181-192.

       12120   Psychological factors
                Facteurs psychologiques

       12200   **INDIVIDUALS. PERSONALITY**
                INDIVIDUS. PERSONNALITÉ

       12210   Ego. Identity
                Ego. Identité

480   BRZEZINSKI, Jerzy; NOWAK, Leszek; [eds.]. *Świadomość jednostkowa a świadomość społeczna*
       (Individual consciousness and social consciousness). Warszawa : Państwowe Wydawnictwo
       Naukowe, 1984, 251 p.
481   CARROLL, William K. "The individual, class, and corporate power in Canada", *Canadian
       Journal of Sociology / Cahiers Canadiens de Sociologie* 9(3), 1984 : 245-268.
482   GUDYMENKO, A. V.; STAROSTIN, B. S. "Obščestvo i individ" (Society and the
       individual), *in : Razvivajuščiesja strany : êkonomičeskij rost i social'nyj progress* Moskva,
       1983 : 462-497.
483   HOŁDA-RÓZIEWICZ, Henryka. "Jednostka w koncepcjach Augusta Comte'a" (The
       individual in the concepts of Auguste Comte), *Studia Socjologiczne* 92(1), 1984 : 251-269.
484   LEONARD, Peter. *Personality and ideology : toward a materialist understanding of the individual.*
       London : Macmillan, 1984, xii-228 p.
485   READ, Doris; ADAMS, Gerald R.; DOBSON, William R. "Ego-identity status, personality,
       and social-influence style", *Journal of Personality and Social Psychology* 46(1), jan 84 : 169-177.
486   SPANO, Ivano. *Individuo e società : elementi per una sociologia marxista* (Individual and society :
       elements for a Marxist sociology). Abano Terme; Padova : Francisci, 1983, 155 p. bibl.
487   YASUKAWA, Hazime. "G. H. Mead ni okeru kohi to perspective -self gainen no sai-kosei
       ni mukete" (Act and perspective in G. H. Mead : toward a reconstruction of the concept
       of self), *Hitotsubashi Journal of Social Sciences* 9(1), 1984 : 119-135.

       12220   Egocentrism. Self concept
                Égocentrisme. Conception de soi

488   ANDERSEN, Susan M.; ROSS, Lee. "Self-knowledge and social inference : I. The
       impact of cognitive/affective and behavioral data : II. The diagnosticity of cognitive/affective
       and behavioral data", *Journal of Personality and Social Psychology* 46(2), feb 84 : 280-307.
489   APFELBAUM, Erika; VASQUEZ, Ana. "Les réalités changeantes de l'identité", *Peuples
       Méditerranéens / Mediterranean Peoples* (24), sep 83 : 83-101. [France]
490   BOKSZAŃSKI, Zbigniew. "Koncepcja siebie a obraz innego" (Self-concept and the image
       of the other), *Kultura i Społeczeństwo* 28(3), 1984 : 169-178.
491   CHASSIN, Laurie; STAGER, Susan F. "Determinants of self-esteem among incarcerated
       delinquents", *Social Psychology Quarterly* 47(4), dec 84 : 382-390.
492   ESPOSITO, Elena. "N. Luhmann e la portata sociologica dell' 'autopoiesis' " (N. Luhmann
       and the sociological meaning of 'autopoiesis'), *Sociologia* 18(3), sep-dec 84 : 83-93.
493   FAZIO, Russell H.; HERR, Paul M.; OLNEY, Timothy J. "Attitude accessibility following
       a self-perception process", *Journal of Personality and Social Psychology* 47(2), aug 84 : 277-286.
       [USA]
494   FISHER, D. V. "A conceptual analysis of self-disclosure", *Journal for the Theory of Social
       Behaviour* 14(3), oct 84 : 277-296.

495   FOURIE, David P. "Self-attribution theory and the sun-sign", *Journal of Social Psychology* 122(1), feb 84 : 121-126.

496   GARAI, L. "Vers une théorie psycho-économique de l'identité sociale", *Recherches Sociologiques* 15(2-3), 1984 : 313-335.

497   HOELTER, Jon W. "Relative effects of significant others on self-evaluation", *Social Psychology Quarterly* 47(3), sep 84 : 255-262. [USA]

498   HOGE, Dean R.; MCCARTHY, John D. "Influence of individual and group identity salience in the global self-esteem of youth", *Journal of Personality and Social Psychology* 47(2), aug 84 : 403-414.

499   IGONET-FASTINGER, P. "Approche socio-anthropologique et socio-historique de l'identité", *Recherches Sociologiques* 15(2-3), 1984 : 233-240.

500   KEARL, Michael C.; HOAG, Lisbeth J. "The social construction of the midlife crisis : a case study in the temporalities of identity", *Sociological Inquiry* 54(3), 1984 : 279-300.

501   KUJI, Toshitake. "Houhou ron teki kojin shugi, shinrigaku teki kangen shugi hihan no kento" (On critiques of methodological individualism or psychological reductionism), *Jinbun Ronso : Bulletin of the Faculty of Humanities and Social Sciences* 1, 1984 : 17-31.

502   LAPIERRE, J. W. "L'identité collective, objet paradoxal : d'où nous vient-il?", *Recherches Sociologiques* 15(2-3), 1984 : 195-206.

503   LICHTENSTEIN, Heinz. *The dilemma of human identity.* New York, NY : J. Aronson, Scribner Bk. Co., 1983, xiv-399 p. bibl., ind.

504   LISÓN, Carmelo. "Vagad o la identidad aragonesa en el siglo XV" (Vagad or the Aragonese identity in the XVth century), *Revista Española de Investigaciones Sociológicas* 25, jan-mar 84 : 95-136.

505   MASCIE-TAYLOR, C. G. N.; LASKER, G. W. "Geographic distribution of surnames in Britain : the Smiths and Joneses", *Journal of Biosocial Science* 16(3), jul 84 : 301-308.

506   MOYA, Carlos. "Identidad colectiva : un programa de investigación científica" (Collective identity : a programme of scientific research), *Revista Española de Investigaciones Sociológicas* 25, jan-mar 84 : 7-35.

507   NTANOMBAYE, P. *Des noms et des hommes : aspects psychologiques et sociologiques du nom au Burundi.* Paris : Karthala, 1983, 281 p.

508   ORIOL, M. "De l'identité organique au gestionnaire de l'identité", *Recherches Sociologiques* 15(2-3), 1984 : 181-194.

509   ORIOL, M.; IGONET-FASTINGER, P. "Recherches sur les identités : le retour paradoxal du sujet dans les sciences sociales", *Recherches Sociologiques* 15(2-3), 1984 : 155-164.

510   PIAZZI, Giuliano. "Identità, socializzazione, cultura" (Identity, socialization, culture), *Studi di Sociologia* 22(2), apr-jun 84 : 176-190.

511   PÖRN, Ingmar. "Kierkegaard and the study of the self", *Inquiry* 27(2-3), jul 84 : 199-205.

512   SCHLEGEL, Jean-Louis. "Ah, je risle culte du corps dans la société contemporaine", *Projet* (181), jan 84 . 74-07.

513   SHIN, Eui-Hang; YU, Eui-Young. "Use of surnames in ethnological research : the case of Kim's in the Korean-American population", *Demography* 21(3), aug 84 : 347-360.

12230   Personality
        Personnalité

514   BODALEV, A. A. *Ličnost' i obščenie : izbrannye trudy* (Personality and communication : selected works). Moskva : Pedagogika, 1983, 271 p.

515   BOGDANOV, V. A. *Social'no-psihologičeskie svojstva ličnosti* (Socio-psychological characteristics of the personality). Leningrad : Izdatel'stvo Leningradskogo Universiteta, 1983, 89 p.

516   BUEVA, L. "Čelovek kak samocel' obščestvennogo razvitija" (Man as the supreme objective of social development), *in : Ličnost' v sovremennom mire : doklady sovetskih učenyh k XVII v semirnomu filosofskomu kongressu 'Filosofija i kul'tura'* [Montreal, Canada, 21-27 august 1983] Moskva, 1983 : 1-7.

517   CEHARIN, É. M. "Socializm i razvitie ličnosti" (Socialism and the personality development), *Voprosy Filosofii* (7), 1983 : 108-115.

518   COCHRAN, Larry. "On the categorization of traits", *Journal for the Theory of Social Behaviour* 14(2), jul 84 : 183-209.

519   DAŠDAMIROV, A. F. *Problema ličnosti v marksistko-leninskoj teorii nacii i nacional'nyh otnošenij* (The personality problem in the Marxist-Leninist theory of nation and national relations). Baku : Azerneŝr, 1984, 155 p.

520   ÉREMENKO, V. A.; STRELEC, S. N. "Dialektika social'no-tipičeskogo i individual'nogo v svete dejatel'nostnogo podhoda k ličnosti" (Dialectics of the socio-typical and the

individual at the light of the activity approach to personality), Filosofskie Voprosy Mediciny i Biologii 15, 1983 : 23-30.

521   GABUZJAN, K. S. "K voprosu o ponjatii i strukture social'noj aktivnosti ličnosti" (Question on the concept and structure of the personality social activity), *Voprosy Naucnogo Kommunizma (Érevan)* (2), 1982 : 211-221.

522   GOULD, Carol C. "Self-development and self-management : a response to Doppelt", *Inquiry* 27(1), mar 84 : 87-103.

523   HENNIS, Wilhelm. "Max Webers Thema. 'Die Persönlichkeit und die Lebensordnungen'" (Max Weber's subject. 'Personality and rules of life'), *Zeitschrift für Politik* 31(1), 1984 : 11-52.

524   IOFFE, S. F.; HLEBNIKOV, I. B. "Social'noe planirovanie i razvitie ličnosti" (Social planning and the personality development), *in : Trudovoj kollektiv i formirovanie ličnosti* Moskva, 1983 : 38-51.

525   KUČENKO, V. I.; [ed.]. *Social'naja aktivnost' licnosti v uslovijah razvitogo socializma* (Social activity of the personality under conditions of developed socialism). Kiev : Naukova Dumka, 1983, 343 p.

526   LJANCEV, P. P. *Formirovanie čeloveka kak ličnosti : social'no-filosofskij aspekt* (Formation of man as a personality : the socio-philosophical aspect). Leningrad : Izdatel'stvo Leningradskogo Universiteta, 1984, 119 p.

527   MAGUN, V. S. *Potrebnosti i psihologija social'noj dejatel'nosti ličnosti* (Needs and psychology of the personality social activity). Leningrad : Nauka, 1983, 176 p.

528   MIHEEV, A. I.; SAVČENKO, T. M. "Faktory formirovanija aktivnoj žiznennoj pozicii ličnosti v trudovom kollektive" (Factors of formation of a personality active vital position in a labour collectivity), *in : Trudovoj kollektiv v razvitom socialističeskom obščestve* Petrozavodsk, 1983 : 79-95.

529   PHARES, E. Jerry. *Introduction to personality.* Columbus, OH : C. E. Merrill, 1984, xvii-740 p. ill., bibl., ind.

530   SADYKOV, M. B.; [ed.]. *Ličnost' v obščestvennyh otnošenijah : social'no-filosofskij aspekt ličnostnyh otnosenij* (Personality in social relations : the social and philosophical aspects of personal relations). Kazan' : Izdatel'stvo Kazanskogo Universiteta, 1983, 78 p.

531   SOKOLOVA, É. I. "Problema kriterija progressa ličnosti" (The problem of criteria of the personality progress), *in : Filosofskie problemy obščestvennogo progressa* Gor'kij, 1983 : 149-154.

532   TITARENKO, L. G. "Potrebnosti ličnosti kak ob'ekt ideologičeskoj bor'by" (The personality needs as an object of ideological struggle), *Naučnye Doklady Vysšej Školy. Naučnyj Kommunizm* (6), 1983 : 84-92.

533   VELIKIJ, P. P.; [ed.]. *Metodologičeskie problemy issledovanija duhovnogo mira ličnosti* (Methodological problems of research on the personality spiritual world). Krasnojarsk : Krasnojarskij Gosudarstvennyj Universitet, 1983, 133 p.

534   VIL'ČKO, Ja. A. "Ličnost' kak sub'ekt duhovnyh otnošenij" (Personality as a subject of spiritual relations), *in : Ličnost' kak sub'ekt i ob'ekt obščestvennyh otnošenij v uslovijah razvitogo socializma* Rjazan', 1984 : 73-90.

535   VORONCOV, B. N. "O razumnyh potrebnostjah ličnosti i ih kriterii" (On the personality reasonable needs and their criteria), *Filosofskie Nauki* (3), 1983 : 20-27.

12240   Cognition. Emotion. Motivation
Cognition. Émotion. Motivation

536   "Intelligence, intelligences", *Autrement. Série Mutations* (57), feb 84 : 1-184.

537   ABELL, Peter. "Comparative narratives : some rules for the study of action", *Journal for the Theory of Social Behaviour* 14(3), oct 84 : 309-331.

538   AGNEW, Robert. "Goal achievement and delinquency", *Sociology and Social Research* 68(4), jul 84 : 435-451. [USA]

539   ALEKSANDROVA, É.; FEDOROVSKAJA, É. "Mehanizm formirovanija i vozvyšenija potrebnostej" (The mechanism of formation and elevation of needs), *Voprosy Ékonomiki* (1), 1984 : 15-25.

540   BAJLUK, V. V.; JADYKINA, N. V. "Mehanizm dejstvija i mehanizm ispol'zovanija zakonov obščestva" (Mechanism of action and mechanism of utilization of the society laws), *in : Kategorii dialektiki. Dialektika zakonomernoj svjazi* Sverdlovsk, 1982 : 93-100.

541   BEN-ZEEV, Aaron. "The Kantian revolution in perception", *Journal for the Theory of Social Behaviour* 14(1), mar 84 : 69-84.

542   BENNER, Jeffrey. *Structure of decision : the Indian foreign policy bureaucracy.* Delhi : South Asia, 1984, xii-214 p.

543   CRANDALL, James E. "Social interest as a moderator of life stress", *Journal of Personality and Social Psychology* 47(1), jul 84 : 164-174.

544   DE RIVERA, Joseph; [ed.]. "The analysis of emotional experience", *American Behavioral Scientist* 27(6), jul-aug 84 : 675-828.

545   ECCLES (PARSONS), Jacqueline; ADLER, Terry; MEECE, Judith L. "Sex differences in achievement : a test of alternate theories", *Journal of Personality and Social Psychology* 46(1), jan 84 : 26-43. [USA]

546   EFIMOVA, N. Ju.; ZAIKA, N. F. "O specifike duhovnyh potrebnostej" (On the specificity of spiritual needs), *Problemy Filosofii* (61), 1984 : 16-22.

547   GAMBETTA, Diego. "Decision mechanisms : educational choices in Italy", *Social Science Information / Information sur les Sciences Sociales* 23(2), 1984 : 275-323.

548   GEREBEN, Ferenc; NAGY, Attila. "Nemi szerepek és olvasási szokások" (Sex roles and reading habits), *Kultúra és Közösség* 11(3), 1984 : 7-22.

549   GLADWYN, Christina H. "Frontiers in hierarchical decision modeling", *Human Organization* 43(3), 1984 : 198-276.

550   GRAY, Louis N.; TALLMAN, Irving. "A satisfaction balance model of decision making and choice behavior", *Social Psychology Quarterly* 47(2), jun 84 : 146-159.

551   HANSEN, Pierre; [ed.]. *Essays and surveys on multiple criteria decision making : proceedings of the Vth International Conference on Multiple Criteria Decision Making, Mons, August 9-13, 1982.* New York, NY; Berlin : Springer, 1983, vii-441 p.

552   HATTORI, Toru. "Karl Korsch no jissen gainen to tetsugaku no shiyo o megutte" (On Karl Korsch's concept of practice and the abolition of philosophy), *Ritsumeikan Review of Industrial Society* 38, 1984 : 63-86.

553   HEKMAN, Susan. "Action as a text : Gadamer's hermeneutics and the social scientific analysis of action", *Journal for the Theory of Social Behaviour* 14(3), oct 84 : 333-354.

554   HINDESS, Barry. "Rational choice theory and the analysis of political action", *Economy and Society* 13(3), 1984 : 255-277.

555   INGLEHART, Ronald; RABIER, Jacques-René. "Du bonheur ... les aspirations s'adaptent aux situations", *Futuribles* (80), sep 84 : 29-58. [Europe] [Continued in ibid. : (81), oct 84 : 3-29]

556   JEEVES, Malcolm A.; GREER, G. Brian. *Analysis of structural learning.* London; New York, NY : Academic Press, 1983, ix-269 p. ill., bibl., ind.

557   KAMMAN, Richard; FARRY, Marcelle; HERBISON, Peter. "The analysis and measurement of happiness as a sense of well-being", *Social Indicators Research* 15(2), aug 84 : 91-115. [New Zealand]

558   KELLEY, David; KRUEGER, Janet. "The psychology of abstraction", *Journal for the Theory of Social Behaviour* 14(1), mar 84 : 43-67.

559   KURMANBAEVA, N. M. "O roli potrebnostej v formirovanii interesov" (On the role of needs in the formation of interests), *Izvestija Akademii Nauk Kazahskoj SSR. Serija Obščestvennyh Nauk* (5), 1983 : 11-16.

560   MANI, A. *Determinants of educational aspirations among Indonesian youth.* Singapore . Maruzen Asia, 1983, vii-51 p. bibl.

561   MASCIE-TAYLOR, C. G. N. "Assortative mating for IQ : a multivariate approach", *Journal of Biosocial Science* 16(1), jan 84 : 109-117.

562   PEIL, Margaret. "African urban life : components of satisfaction in Sierra Leone", *Social Indicators Research* 14(3), apr 84 : 363-384.

563   PRAMLING, Ingrid. *The child's conception of learning.* Göteborg : Acta Universitatis Gothoburgensis, 1983, 194 p. ill., bibl.

564   RAY, John J. "Achievement motivation as a source of racism, conservatism, and authoritarianism", *Journal of Social Psychology* 123(1), jun 84 : 21-28.

565   ROMANOW, Allyn L. "A Brownian motion model for decision making", *Journal of Mathematical Sociology* 10(1), 1984 : 1-28.

566   ROŽKO, K. G. *Princip dejatel'nosti* (The principle of activity). Tomsk : Izdatel'stvo Tomskogo Universiteta, 1983, 211 p.

567   SANFORD, Stephanie; EDER, Donna. "Adolescent humor during peer interaction", *Social Psychology Quarterly* 47(3), sep 84 : 235-243. [USA]

568   SAYLES, Marnie L. "Relative deprivation and collective protest : an impoverished theory?", *Sociological Inquiry* 54(4), 1984 : 449-465.

569   SELVIN, Hanan C.; WILSON, Everett K. "Cases in point : a limited glossary of stumblebum usage", *Sociological Quarterly* 25(3), 1984 : 417-427. [On good and correct writing]

570   SOLES, Deborah Hansen. "On the indeterminacy of action", *Philosophy of the Social Sciences / Philosophie des Sciences Sociales* 14(4), dec 84 : 475-488.

571   SZOCKI, Józef. "Wiejska zbiorowość czytelnicza i jej preferencje" (The countryside reading community and its priorities), *Wieś Współczesna* 8, 1984 : 149-154.

572 TABAČKOVSKIJ, V. G.; TACENKO, A. I.; [eds.]. *Dialektika dejatel'nosti i kul'tura* (Dialectics of activity and culture). Kiev : Naukova Dumka, 1983, 296 p.

573 WEGNER, Daniel M.; [et al.]. "The emergence of action", *Journal of Personality and Social Psychology* 46(2), feb 84 : 269-279.

574 WILSON, John P.; PETRUSKA, Richard. "Motivation, model attributes, and prosocial behavior", *Journal of Personality and Social Psychology* 46(2), feb 84 : 458-468.

12300 INTERPERSONAL RELATIONS
RELATIONS INTERPERSONNELLES

12310 Human relations. Sociability
Relations humaines. Sociabilité

575 "Socialité (La)", *Actions et Recherches Sociales* (1), mar 84 : 7-104. [France] [With contributions by Michel MAFFESOLI, Jacques BEAUCHARD, Patrick BAUDRY, Pierre TAMINIAUX, Henri-Pierre JEUDY]

576 ANDERSSON, Lars. "Intervention against loneliness in a group of elderly women : a process evaluation", *Human Relations* 37(4), apr 84 : 295-310.

577 BARALDI, Claudio. "Interpenetrazione e complessità" (Interpenetration and complexity), *Sociologia* 18(3), sep-dec 84 : 61-81.

578 DONATI, Pierpaolo. "Le trasformazioni del rapporto comunicativo nella relazione interpersonale medico-paziente" (Changes in the social structure of physician-patient interpersonal relationships), *Rassegna Italiana di Sociologia* 25(4), oct-dec 84 : 547-571.

579 EDWARDS, David J. "The experience of interpersonal touch during a personal growth program : a factor analytic approcah", *Human Relations* 37(9), sep 84 : 769-780.

580 JØRGENSEN, Per Schultz. *Den sociale relation : kvalitative analyser* (The social relation : qualitative analysis. 2 vols.). Copenhagen : Akademisk Forlag, 1983.

581 KITTSTEINER, Heinz-Dieter. "From grace to virtue : concerning a change in the presentation of the parable of the prodigal son in the XVIIIth and early XIXth centuries", *Social Science Information / Information sur les Sciences Sociales* 23(6), 1984 : 955-975.

582 KOLLER, Karl; GOSEN, Sylvia. "On living alone, social isolation and psychological disorder", *Australian and New Zealand Journal of Sociology* 20(1), mar 84 : 81-92. [Australia]

583 LAUBIER, Patrick de. "Aspects sociologiques de la solitude dans les sociétés industrielles avancées", *Travail et Société* 9(1), mar 84 : 85-95.

584 LILGE, Hans-Georg. *Zielkonflikte : betriebswirtschaftliche und sozialpsychologische Probleme einer interpersonalen Konflikthandhabung* (Conflicts of aims : management and sociopsychological problems in handling interpersonal conflicts). Berlin : V. Spiess, 1984, 468 p. ill., bibl.

585 MEEKER, Barbara F. "Cooperative orientation, trust, and reciprocity", *Human Relations* 37(3), mar 84 : 225-243.

586 NAGATA, Eriko. "Goshu-sei no kojin gori teki na kiso" (Individualistic and rationalistic foundation of reciprocity), *Sociologos* 8, 1984 : 108-118.

587 O'MALLEY, Michael N.; SCHUBARTH, Glena. "Fairness and appeasement : achievement and affiliation motives in interpersonal relations", *Social Psychology Quarterly* 47(4), dec 84 : 364-371.

588 POWER, Richard. "Mutual intention", *Journal for the Theory of Social Behaviour* 14(1), mar 84 : 85-102.

589 RUSSELL, Dan; [et al.]. "Social and emotional loneliness : an examination of Weiss's typology of loneliness", *Journal of Personality and Social Psychology* 46(6), jun 84 : 1313-1321. [USA]

590 TAMAMIZU, Toshiaki. "Gendai no ishiki jyokyo ni okeru 'koritsu-ka' to 'maibotsu-sei' : jiritsu to rentai eno mosaku o komete" ('Isolation' and 'confined self' in the consciousness of today : toward a grouping identity and solidarity), *Kagaku to Shiso* 53, 1984 : 67-83.

591 VERDIER, R. "Le désir, le devoir et l'interdit : masques et visages de la vengeance", *Déviance et Société* 8(2), jun 84 : 181-193.

592 VERQUERRE, Régis. "Etude des relations interpersonnelles dans des classes mixtes de premier cycle", *Bulletin de Psychologie* 37(366), aug 84 : 733-742. [France]

12320 Social perception
Perception sociale

593 CUTRONA, Carolyn E.; RUSSELL, Dan; JONES, R. Dallas. "Cross-situationa consistency in causal attributions : does attributional style exist?", *Journal of Personality and Social Psychology* 47(5), nov 84 : 1043-1058.

594 EFFLER, Manfred. "Attribution theories of lay epistemology", *European Journal of Social Psychology* 14(4), oct-dec 84 : 431-437. [With a reply by Arie W. KRUGLANSKI, ibid. : 439-446]

595 HASTIE, Reid. "Causes and effects of causal attribution", *Journal of Personality and Social Psychology* 46(1), jan 84 : 44-56. [USA]

596 HEWSTONE, Miles; [eds.]. *Attribution theory : social and functional extensions.* Oxford : Basil Blackwell, 1983, xii-256 p. ill., bibl., ind.

597 JAIN, Uday; MAL, Suraj. "Effect of prolonged deprivation on attribution of causes of success and failure", *Journal of Social Psychology* 124(2), dec 84 : 143-149.

598 JONES, Sue. "The politics of problems : intersubjectivity in defining powerful others", *Human Relations* 37(11), nov 84 : 881-894.

599 LAU, Richard R. "Dynamics of the attribution process", *Journal of Personality and Social Psychology* 46(5), mai 84 : 1017-1028.

600 LEWICKI, Pawel. "Birth order and person perception dispositions", *European Journal of Social Psychology* 14(2), apr-jun 84 : 183-190.

601 MELBURG, Valerie; [et al.]. "A reexamination of the empathic observers paradigm for the study of divergent attributions", *Journal of Social Psychology* 124(2), dec 84 : 201-208.

602 MORRISON, Thomas L.; GREENE, Les R.; TISCHLER, Nancy G. "Member perceptions in small and large Tavistock groups", *Journal of Social Psychology* 124(2), dec 84 : 209-217.

603 READ, Stephen J. "Analogical reasoning in social judgment : the importance of causal theories", *Journal of Personality and Social Psychology* 46(1), jan 84 : 14-25. [USA]

604 SANO, Masahiko. "Labelling ron ni kansuru genshogaku-teki hihan -Warren = Johnson no baai" (A phenomenological critique of labelling theory : the case of Warren & Johnson), *Toyo University Bulletin of the Graduate School* 20, 1984 : 61-72.

605 TORIS, Carol; DE PAULO, Bella M. "Effects of actual deception and suspiciousness of deception on interpersonal perceptions", *Journal of Personality and Social Psychology* 47(5), nov 84 : 1063-1073.

606 TYLER, Tom R.; RASINSKI, Kenneth. "Comparing psychological images of the social perceiver : role of perceived informativeness, memorability, and affect in mediating the impact of crime victimization", *Journal of Personality and Social Psychology* 46(2), feb 84 : 308-329.

607 VAN DER PLIGT, Joop; TAYLOR, Colin. "Trait attribution : evaluation, description and attitude extremity", *European Journal of Social Psychology* 14(2), apr-jun 84 : 211-221.

608 VISCUSI, W. Kip; O'CONNOR, Charles J. "Adaptive responses to chemical labeling : are workers Bayesian decision makers?", *American Economic Review* 74(5), dec 84 : 942-956.

609 WATKINS, David; ASTILLA, Estela. "The dimensionality, antecedents, and study method correlates of the causal attribution of Filipino children", *Journal of Social Psychology* 124(2), dec 84 : 191-199.

610 WINTER, Laraine; ULEMAN, James S. "When are social judgments made? : evidence for the spontaneousness of trait inferences", *Journal of Personality and Social Psychology* 47(2), aug 84 : 237-252.

611 YUNKER, James A. "Objective information and social consensus : some empirical evidence on the relative importance of objective and subjective determinants of social judgment", *American Journal of Economics and Sociology* 43(4), oct 84 : 413-425. [USA]

612 ZUCKERMAN, Miron; FELDMAN, Lauren S. "Actions and occurrences in attribution theory", *Journal of Personality and Social Psychology* 46(3), mar 84 : 541-550.

12330 Interpersonal attraction
Attraction interpersonnelle

613 "Courtship, love and marriage in contemporary China", *Pacific Affairs* 57(2), sum 84 : 209-266. [With contributions by Marilyn B. YOUNG, Margery WOLF, Gail HERSHATTER, Emily HONIG]

614 "Solidarités traditionnelles et développements mutualistes", *Communautés* (65), sep 83 : 6-248. [Africa]

615 ARABIE, Phipps. "Validation of sociometric structure by data on individuals' attributes", *Social Networks* 6(4), dec 86 : 373-403.

616 BERG, John H. "Development of friendship between roommates", *Journal of Personality and Social Psychology* 46(2), feb 84 : 346-356.

617 BLAU, Peter M.; BEEKER, Carolyn; FITZPATRICK, Kevin M. "Intersecting social affiliations and intermarriage", *Social Forces* 62(3), mar 84 : 585-606. [USA]

618   DUMONT, Louis. *Affinity as a value : marriage alliance in south India, with comparative essays on Australia.* Chicago, IL; London : University of Chicago Press, 1983, x-230 p. ill., bibl.
619   FUJITA, Kunihiko. "Ai no sho-so" (Aspects of romantic love), *Kagawa Daigaku Ippan Kyoiku Kenkyu* 26, 1984 : 17-31.
620   JERROME, Dorothy. "Good company : the sociological implications of friendship", *Sociological Review* 32(4), nov 84 : 696-718.
621   KALLIOPUSKA, Mirja. *Empatia* (Empathy). Helsinki : Kirjayhtymä, 1983, 204-1 p. bibl.
622   KOSTECKI, Marian; MRELA, Krzysztof. "Collective solidarity in Poland's powdered society", *Insurgent Sociologist* 12(1-2), 1984 : 131-141.
623   MCADAMS, Dan P.; HEALY, Sheila; KRAUSE, Steven. "Social motives and patterns of friendship", *Journal of Personality and Social Psychology* 47(4), oct 84 : 828-838.
624   REES, C. Roger; SEGAL, Mady Wechsler. "Intragroup composition, equity, and interpersonal attraction", *Social Psychology Quarterly* 47(4), dec 84 : 328-336. [USA]
625   STERNBERG, Robert J.; GRAJEK, Susan. "The nature of love", *Journal of Personality and Social Psychology* 47(2), aug 84 : 312-329.
626   TESSER, Abraham; CAMPBELL, Jennifer; SMITH, Monte. "Friendship choice and performance : self-evaluation maintenance in children", *Journal of Personality and Social Psychology* 46(3), mar 84 : 561-574.
627   TÖRNBLOM, Kjell Y.; FREDHOLM, Eva M. "Attribution of friendship : the influence of the nature and comparability of resources given and received", *Social Psychology Quarterly* 47(1), mar 84 : 50-61.

12340   Interpersonal influence
Influence interpersonnelle

628   WEISS, Johannes. "Stillvertretung. Überlegungen zu einer vernachlässigten soziologischen Kategorie" (Silent representation. Considerations on a neglected sociological category), *Kölner Zeitschrift für Soziologie und Sozialpsychologie* 36(1), mar 84 : 43-55.

12350   Interpersonal conflicts
Conflits interpersonnels

629   BHAN, Kiran Sumbali. *Psychology of human aggression : a comparative study of age groups and sexes.* New Delhi : Northern Book Centre, 1984, xv-98 p. bibl., ind., ill.
630   CAPRARA, G. V.; [et al.]. "The eliciting cue value of aggressive slides reconsidered in a personological perspective : the weapons effect and irritability", *European Journal of Social Psychology* 14(3), jul-sep 84 : 313-322.
631   CUATRECASAS, Juan. *Psicogenia de la agresión* (Psychogenesis of aggression). Buenos Aires : Ediciones Tres Tiempos, 1983, 184 p. bibl.
632   DUNDE, Siegfried Rudolf. "Symptom oder Destruktivkraft : zur Funktion des Neides in der Gesellschaft" (Symptom of destructive force : on the function of envy in society), *Sociologia Internationalis* 22(2), 1984 : 217-233.
633   LINNEWEBER, Volker; [et al.]. "Classification of situations specific to field and behaviour : the context of aggressive interactions in schools", *European Journal of Social Psychology* 14(3), jul-sep 84 : 281-295.
634   LÖSCHPER, Gabi; [et al.]. "The judgment of behaviour as aggressive and sanctionable", *European Journal of Social Psychology* 14(4), oct-dec 84 : 391-404.
635   MARGALIT, Baruch A.; MAUGER, Paul A. "Cross-cultural demonstration of orthogonality of assertiveness and aggressiveness : comparison between Israel and the United States", *Journal of Personality and Social Psychology* 46(6), jun 84 : 1414-1421.
636   MUMMENDEY, Amélie; LINNEWEBER, Volker; LÖSCHPER, Gabi. "Actor or victim of aggression : divergent perspectives — divergent evaluations", *European Journal of Social Psychology* 14(3), jul-sep 84 : 297-311.
637   MUMMENDEY, Amélie; [et al.]. "Social-consensual conceptions concerning the progress of aggressive interactions", *European Journal of Social Psychology* 14(4), oct-dec 84 : 379-389.

12360   Intergroup relations
Relations intergroupes

638   BARTMANN, Hermann; JOHN, Klaus-Dieter. "Aspekte eines dynamischen Konfliktmodells" (Aspects of a dynamic conflict model), *Jahrbuch für Sozialwissenschaft* 34(3), 1983 : 267-289. [Germany FR]

639   BOVA, Vincenzo. *Conflittualità sociale e lotte operaie in Polonia, 1956-1980* (Social conflicts and workers struggle in Poland, 1956-1980). Bologna : Centro Studi Europa Orientale, 1983, 191 p. bibl.

640   BÜHL, Walter L. "Die Dynamik sozialer Konflikte in katastrophentheoretischer Darstellung" (The dynamics of social conflicts in catastrophe-theoretical representation), *Kölner Zeitschrift für Soziologie und Sozialpsychologie* 36(4), dec 84 : 641-666.

641   DIANI, Maro; BAGNARA, Sebastiano. "Les tracts comme indicateurs de tensions conflictuelles", *Revue Française de Sociologie* 25(3), jul-sep 84 : 376-395. [Italie]

642   DISTEFANO, Thomas. "Interorganizational conflict : a review of an emerging field", *Human Relations* 37(5), apr 84 : 351-366.

643   GALESKI, Boguslaw. "Current explanations of social conflicts in Poland", *Politico* 49(2), jun 84 : 193-221.

644   GORDON, Michael E.; SCHMITT, Neal; SCHNEIDER, Walter G. "Laboratory research on bargaining and negotiations : an evaluation", *Industrial Relations* 23(2), 1984 : 218-233.

645   JOHNSON, David W.; JOHNSON, Roger T. "The effects of intergroup cooperation and intergroup competition on ingroup and outgroup cross-handicap relationships", *Journal of Social Psychology* 124(1), oct 84 : 85-94.

646   KRAUSS, Ellis S.; ROHLEN, Thomas P.; STEINHOFF, Patricia G.; [eds.]. *Conflict in Japan.* Honolulu, HI : University of Hawaii Press, 1984, 417 p.

647   KRAVITZ, David A.; IWANISZEK, John. "Number of coalitions and resources as sources of power in coalition bargaining", *Journal of Personality and Social Psychology* 47(3), sep 84 : 534-548.

648   LEBEL, Pierre. *L'art de la négociation.* Paris : Éditions d'Organisation, 1984, 197 p.

649   PALOHEIMO, Heikki. "Pluralism, corporatism and the distributive conflict in developed capitalist countries", *Scandinavian Political Studies* 7(1), mar 84 : 17-38.

650   REYKOWSKI, Janusz. *Logika walki. Szkice z psychologii konfliktu społecznego w Polsce* (The logic of struggle. Essays on psychology of social conflict in Poland). Warszawa : Książka i Wiedza, 1984, 159 p.

651   REZNIKOV, V. B. "Social'nye konflikty v brazil'skoj derevne" (Social conflicts in Brazilian countryside), *Latinskaja Amerika* (3), mar 84 : 31-42.

652   RUBIN, Jeffrey Z.; [ed.]. "Negotiation : issues and themes", *American Behavioral Scientist* 27(2), nov-dec 83 : 135-279.

653   SALIPANTE, Paul F.; ARAM, John D. "The role of organizational procedures in the resolution of social conflict", *Human Organization* 43(1), 1984 : 9-15. [USA] [In three urban hospitals]

654   SIERRA POP, Oscar Rolando. "The Church and social conflict in Guatemala", *Social Compass* 30(2-3), 1983 : 317-348.

655   SPREAD, Patrick. "Blau's exchange theory, support and the macrostructure", *British Journal of Sociology* 35(2), jun 84 : 157-173.

656   STERNBERG, Robert J.; SORIANO, Lawrence J. "Styles of conflict resolution", *Journal of Personality and Social Psychology* 47(1), jul 84 : 115-126.

657   SUSSKIND, Lawrence; RUBIN, Jeffrey Z.; [eds.]. "Negotiation : behavioral perspectives", *American Behavioral Scientist* 27(2), nov-dec 83 : 131-279.

658   SZTUMSKI, Janusz; WÓDZ, Jacek. *Z problematyki konfliktów społecznych i dezorganizacji społecznej. Na przykładzie badań empirycznych w Polsce południowej* (Of the problems of social conflicts and social disorganisation. Based on empirical study in Southern Poland). Wrocław : Ossolineum, 1984, 150 p.

659   TADAO TSUKASHIMA, Ronald. "Chronological cognitive and political effects in the study of interminority group prejudice", *Phylon* 44(3), sep 83 : 217-231. [USA]

660   WEEKS, Dudley. *Conflict partnership.* Orange, CA : Trans World Productions; Great Cacapon, WV : Conflict management Workshop, 1984, 128 p.

12400   GROUPS
GROUPES

12410   Group dynamics
Dynamique de groupe

661   BURT, Ronald S. "Network items and the General Social Survey", *Social Networks* 6(4), dec 86 : 293-339. [USA]

662   FARARO, Thomas J.; SKVORETZ, John. "Based networks and social structure theorems", *Social Networks* 6(3), sep 84 : 223-258. [Peter BLAU's theory of social structure. See for the first part ibid. : 3(3), sep 81 : 137-159]

663   FREEMAN, Linton C. "The impact of computer based communication on the social structure of an emerging scientific specialty", *Social Networks* 6(3), sep 84 : 201-221.
664   HAMMER, Muriel. "Explorations into the meaning of social network interview data", *Social Networks* 6(4), dec 86 : 341-371. [USA]
665   HANSEN, Erik Jørgen. *Socialgrupper i Danmark* (Social groups in Denmark). København : Socialforskningsinstituttet, 1984, 189 p. bibl.
666   JONES, F. L.; KELLEY, Jonathan. "Decomposing differences between groups : a cautionary note on measuring discrimination", *Sociological Methods and Research* 12(3), feb 84 : 323-343.
667   LENK, Peter J. "The structure of a random relation with an application to a nomination network", *Social Networks* 6(1), mar 84 : 1-30.
668   MAYER, Thomas F. "Parties and networks : stochastic models for relationship networks", *Journal of Mathematical Sociology* 10(1), 1984 : 51-103.
669   NISHIYAMA, Misako. "Shokuba 'sho-shudan' ni kansuru ta-jigen kaiseki" (Multi-dimensional analysis of small group activities in factories), *Kwansaigakuin Sociology Department Studies* 48, 1984 : 101-125. [Continued in ibid. : 49, 1984 : 153-178]
670   SCHENK, Michael. *Soziale Netzwerke und Kommunikation* (Social networks and communication). Tübingen : J. C. B. Mohr, 1984, xii-366 p. bibl., ind.
671   ZACHARY, Wayne W. "Modeling social network processes using constrained flow representations", *Social Networks* 6(3), sep 84 : 259-292.

12420   Primary groups. Training groups
Groupes primaires. Groupes de formation

672   "Analyse de groupe : formation et psychothérapie", *Connexions* 41, 1984 : 1-124.
673   "Théorie, pratique et recherche sur le petit groupe", *Service Social* 32(1-2), jun 83 : 11-295. [With contributions by Lise DARVEAU-FOURNIER, Alice HOME, Michèle CARDIN, Sheilagh, HODGINS, Pauline MORISSETTE]
674   BOALT BOËTHIUS, Siv. *Autonomy, coping, and defense in small work groups : an analysis of psychological processes within and between individual group members.* Stockholm : Department of Psychology, University of Stockholm, 1983, 184 p. ill., bibl.
675   HANSELL, Stephen. "Cooperative groups, weak ties, and the integration of peer friendships", *Social Psychology Quarterly* 47(4), dec 84 : 316-328. [USA]
676   KLEVORICK, Alvin K.; ROTHSCHILD, Michael; WINSHIP, Christopher. "Information processing and jury decisionmaking", *Journal of Public Economics* 23(3), apr 84 : 245-278. [USA]
677   MCKEGANEY, Neil. "'No doubt she's really a little princess' : a case study of trouble in a therapeutic community", *Sociological Review* 32(2), mai 84 : 328-348.
678   POUSSET, André. "Comportement de résolution de problème en petit groupe sans leader", *Revue de l'Institut de Sociologie* (1-2), 1984 : 133-165.
679   SANDLER, Todd; TSCHIRHART, John T. "Mixed clubs : further observations", *Journal of Public Economics* 23(3), apr 84 : 381-389.
680   SMITH, Karl A.; JOHNSON, David W.; JOHNSON, Roger T. "Effects of controversy on learning in cooperative groups", *Journal of Social Psychology* 122(2), apr 84 : 199-209.
681   YAMAGISHI, Toshio. "Development of distribution rules in small groups", *Journal of Personality and Social Psychology* 46(5), mai 84 : 1069-1078.

12430   Group size
Dimension du groupe

682   AEBISCHER, Verena; HEWSTONE, Miles. "Minority influence and musical preference : innovation by conversion not coercion", *European Journal of Social Psychology* 14(1), jan-mar 84 : 23-33.
683   AUSTER, Donald. "Mentors and protégés : power-dependent dyads", *Sociological Inquiry* 54(2), 1984 : 142-153.
684   BHACHU, Parminder. "East African Sikhs in Britain : experienced settlers with traditionalistic values", *Immigrants and Minorities* 3(3), nov 84 : 276-296.
685   CHABRY, Laurent; CHABRY, Annie. *Politique et minorités au Proche-Orient : les raisons d'une explosion.* Paris : Maisonneuve et Larose, 1984, 359 p. bibl., cartes.
686   KEDOURIE, Elie. "Minorities and majorities in the Middle East", *Archives Européennes de Sociologie* 25(2), 1984 : 276-282.
687   KIRKLAND, James Ray. "Armenian migration, settlement and adjustment in Australia", *International Migration / Migrations Internationales* 22(2), 1984 : 101-128.

688   LACROIX, Jean-Michel. "Tchèques et Slovaques au Canada : intégration et survie", *Annales du Centre de Recherches sur l'Amérique Anglophone* 9, 1983 : 75-93.
689   LINCOLN, James R. "Analyzing relations in dyads : problems, models, and an application to interorganizational research", *Sociological Methods and Research* 13(1), aug 84 : 45-76.
690   MASON, David. "The concept of minority and intergroup conflict in Africa", *Patterns of Prejudice* 18(4), oct 84 : 3-15.
691   PONTING, J. Rick. "Conflict and change in Indian / non-Indian relations in Canada : a comparison of 1976 and 1979 national attitude surveys", *Canadian Journal of Sociology / Cahiers Canadiens de Sociologie* 9(2), spr 84 : 137-177.
692   ROY, W. T. "A note on the role of Maoris in New Zealand politics", *Plural Societies* 14(3-4), wint 83 : 69-76.
693   SACHDEV, Itesh; BOURHIS, Richard Y. "Minimal majorities and minorities", *European Journal of Social Psychology* 14(1), jan-mar 84 : 35-52.
694   SAMPSON, Robert J. "Group size, heterogeneity, and intergroup conflict : a test of Blau's 'Inequality and heterogeneity'", *Social Forces* 62(3), mar 84 : 618-639.
695   SANDIS, Eva. "The socio-economic integration of Puerto Ricans in the continentual United States", *Annales du Centre de Recherches sur l'Amérique Anglophone* 9, 1983 : 155-176.
696   SEGURA, Denise. "Labor market stratification : the Chicana experience", *Berkeley Journal of Sociology* 29, 1984 : 57-91. [USA]
697   SELIKTAR, Ofira. "The Arabs in Israel : some observations on the psychology of the system of controls", *Journal of Conflict Resolution* 28(2), jun 84 : 247-269.
698   SIMON, Rita J. "Refugee families' adjustment and aspirations : a comparison of Soviet Jewish and Vietnamese immigrants", *Ethnic and Racial Studies* 6(4), oct 83 : 492-504. [USA]

12440   Group integration
Intégration du groupe

699   FRIEDKIN, Noah E. "Structural cohesion and equivalence explanations of social homogeneity", *Sociological Methods and Research* 12(3), feb 84 : 235-261. [USA]
700   GRUENFELD, Leopold W.; LIN, Thung-Rung. "Social behavior of field independents and dependents in an organic group", *Human Relations* 37(9), sep 84 : 721-741.
701   LONG, Susan. "Early integration in groups : 'a group to join, and a group to create'", *Human Relations* 37(4), apr 84 : 311-332.
702   NARAYAN, V. K.; NATH, Raghu. "The influence of group cohesiveness on some changes induced by flexitime : a quasi-experiment", *Journal of Applied Behavioral Science* 20(3), 1984 : 265-276. [USA]
703   ULMAN, Richard Barrett; ABSE, D. Wilfred. "The group psychology of mass madness : Jonestown", *Political Psychology* 4(4), dec 83 : 637-661. [Guyana]

12450   Group membership
Appartenance au groupe

704   BROWN, Rupert; WILLIAMS, Jennifer. "Group identification : the same thing to all people?", *Human Relations* 37(7), jul 84 : 547-564.
705   FELMLEE, Diane; EDER, Donna. "Contextual effects in the classroom : the impact of ability groups on student attention", *Sociology of Education* 56(2), apr 83 : 77-87. [USA]
706   LEITER, Jeffrey. "Classroom composition and achievement gains", *Sociology of Education* 56(3), jul 83 : 126-132.
707   MACKIE, Diane; COOPER, Joel. "Attitude polarization : effects of group membership", *Journal of Personality and Social Psychology* 46(3), mar 84 : 575-585. [USA]

12460   Group performance
Performance du groupe

708   MANZ, Charles C.; SIMS, Henry P. Jr. "Searching for the 'unleader' : organizational member views on leading self-managed groups", *Human Relations* 37(5), apr 84 : 409-424.

12500   BUREAUCRACY. ORGANIZATION
BUREAUCRATIE. ORGANISATION

12510   Sociology of organization
Sociologie des organisations

709   BACHARACH, Samuel B.; [ed.]. *Research in the sociology of organizations.* Greenwich, CT;
        London : JAI Press, 1983, ix-276 p.
710   GRUNOW, Dieter; WOHLFAHRTH, Norbert. "Methodenanwendung in der empirischen
        Organisationsforschung. Ergebnisse einer empirischen Reanalyse" (Methods utilization
        in empirical organizational research. Results of an empirical reanalysis), *Zeitschrift für
        Soziologie* 13(3), jul 84 : 243-259.
711   KARASAWA, Kazuyoshi. "Nihon no kigyo no soshiki-shakaigaku teki bunseki" (The
        approach to organizational sociology of business enterprise in Japan), *Mita Journal of
        Economics* 77(2), 1984 : 117-133.
712   KIMURA, Kiyoshi. "Soshiki kaihatsu ron no ichi kenkyu" (A study on the theory of
        organization development), *Aikoku Gakuen Junior College Kiyo* 4(1), 1984 : 75-86.
713   MASUCH, Michael. "Rationaliteit en irrationaliteit in organisaties : vicieuze cirkels als
        probleem" (Rationality and irrationality in organizations : the case of vicious circles),
        Sociologische Gids 31(5), 1984 : 442-461.
714   MILLS, Edgar; HARRIS, Richard J.; BRISCHETTO, Robert. "Internships in an instant
        bureaucracy : some organizational lessons", *Journal of Applied Behavioral Science* 19(4),
        1983 : 483-495. [USA]
715   POND, Samuel B, III; ARMENAKIS, Achilles A.; GREEN, Samuel B. "The importance
        of employee expectations in organizational diagnosis", *Journal of Applied Behavioral Science*
        20(2), 1984 : 167-180.
716   RAISER, Harald. *Systemtheoretische Untersuchung bürokratischer und partizipativer Organisationen*
        (System theoretical research on bureaucratic and participative Organizations). Spardorf :
        Wilfer, 1983, v-385 p. ill., bibl.
717   RUBINSTEIN, David; WOODMAN, Richard W. "Spiderman and the Burma raiders :
        collateral organization theory in action", *Journal of Applied Behavioral Science* 20(1),
        1984 : 1-16. [With a comment by William R. SHADISH Jr. ibid. : 17-18, and a reply
        by the author : 19-21]
718   SHRIVASTAVA, Paul; SCHNEIDER, Susan. "Organizational frames of reference",
        Human Relations 37(10), oct 84 : 795-809.
719   VREDENBURGH, Donald J.; MAURER, John G. "A process framework of organizational
        politics", *Human Relations* 37(1), jan 84 : 47-66.
720   WEINERT, Ansfried B. "Menschenbilder in Organisations- und Führungstheorien. Erste
        Ergebnisse einer empirischen Überprüfung" (Man's images in the theories of organization
        and management. The first results of an empirical examination), *Zeitschrift für Betriebswirt-
        schaft* 54(1), 1984 : 30-62.

12520   Complex organizations
Organisations complexes

721   BADELT, Christoph. "Freiwilligengruppen als Problem der ökonomischen Klubtheorie"
        (Volunteer groups as a problem of the economic club theory), *Kyklos* 37(1), 1984 : 59-81.
722   BATE, Paul. "The impact of organizational culture on approaches to organizational problem-
        solving", *Organization Studies* 5(1), 1984 : 43-66. [In collaboration with the European
        Group for Organizational Studies, Berlin, New York]
723   FERRAND-BECHMANN, Dan. "Voluntary action in the welfare state : two examples",
        Social Service Delivery Systems 6, 1983 : 183-201. [France]
724   FORSÉ, Michel. "Les créations d'associations : un indicateur de changement social",
        Observations et Diagnostics Économiques (6), jan 84 : 125-145. [France]
725   GLAUSER, Michael J. "Upward information flow in organizations : review and conceptual
        analysis", *Human Relations* 37(8), aug 84 : 613-643.
726   GREIL, Arthur L.; RUDY, David R. "Social cocoons : encapsulation and identity trans-
        formation organizations", *Sociological Inquiry* 54(3), 1984 : 260-278.
727   GRUNDELACH, Peter. "Social transformation and new forms of voluntary associations",
        Social Science Information / Information sur les Sciences Sociales 23(6), 1984 : 1049-1081.
        [Denmark]
728   KNOKE, David; PRENSKY, David. "What relevance do organization theories have for
        voluntary associations?", *Social Science Quarterly* 65(1), mar 84 : 3-20.
729   MATEJKO, Alexander J. *Beyond bureaucracy? A sociotechnical approach to the dialectics of complex
        organizations.* Köln : Verlag für Gesellschaftsarchitektur, 1984, xviii-468 p. bibl., ind.
730   ODEYE, Michèle. "Le phénomène associatif en villes africaines (Dakar, Brazzaville)",
        Communautés (66), dec 83 : 41-55. [Senegal; Congo]
731   PASSARIS, Solange; RAFFI, Guy. *Les associations.* Paris : La Découverte, 1984, 125 p.
        bibl.

732 SATO, Yoshiyuki. "Association no chihei" (The horizon of association), *Review of Contemporary Sociology* 18, 1984 : 112-128.

733 TJOSVODL, Dean. "Cooperation theory and organizations", *Human Relations* 37(9), sep 84 : 743-767.

734 VAN MAANEN, John; BARLEY, Stephen R. "Occupational communities : culture and control in organizations", *Research in Organizational Behaviour* 6, 1984 : 287-365.

735 WESTRUM, Ron; SAMAHA, Khalil; DES HARNAIS, Gaston. *Complex organizations : growth, struggle, and change.* Englewood Cliffs, NJ : Prentice-Hall, 1984, viii-344 p. bibl., ind., ill.

736 WILPERT, Bernhard. "Participation in organizations : evidence from international comparative research", *International Social Science Journal / Revue Internationale des Sciences Sociales* 36(2), 1984 : 355-366.

12530   Bureaucracy
Bureaucratie

737 "Critical perspectives on management studies and management science", *Journal of Management Studies* 21(3), jul 84 : 253-368. [With contributions by M. I. REDD, Michael ROSEN, Rosemary STEWART]

738 BARLING, Julian; [ed.]. *Behaviour in organizations : South African perspectives.* Johannesburg; New York, NY : McGraw-Hill, 1983, 553 p. ill., bibl., ind.

739 BERG, Bruce. "Public choice, pluralism and scarcity : implications for bureaucratic behavior", *Administration and Society* 16(1), mai 84 : 71-82.

740 CASEY, Neil. "An early organizational hegemony : methods of control in a Victorian naval dockyard", *Social Science Information / Information sur les Sciences Sociales* 23(4-5), 1984 : 677-700.

741 CHENG, Joseph L. C. "Organizational coordination, uncertainty, and performance : an integrative study", *Human Relations* 37(10), oct 84 : 829-851.

742 CIBORRA, C.; MIGLIARESE, P.; ROMANO, P. "A methodological inquiry of organizational noise in sociotechnical systems", *Human Relations* 37(8), aug 84 : 565-588.

743 DALEY, Dennis. "Controlling the bureaucracy among the States : an examination of administrative, executive, and legislative attitudes", *Administration and Society* 15(4), feb 84 : 475-488. [USA]

744 DONATI, Paolo R. "Organization between movement and institution", *Social Science Information / Information sur les Sciences Sociales* 23(4-5), 1984 : 837-859.

745 DUNHAM, Randall B. *Organizational behavior : people and processes in management.* Homewood, IL : Irwin, 1984, xvii-547 p. ill., bibl., ind.

746 ENRIQUEZ, Eugène. "Structures d'organisation et contrôle social", *Connexions* 41, 1984 : 97-124. [Organisation industrielle]

747 FERGUSON, Kathy E. "Bureaucracy and public life : the feminization of the policy", *Administration and Society* 15(3), nov 83 : 295-322. [USA]

748 FINE, Gary Alan. "Negotiated orders and organizational cultures", *Annual Review of Sociology* 10, 1984 : 239-262.

749 FITZROY, Felix R.; MUELLER, Dennis C. "Cooperation and conflict in contractual organizations", *Quarterly Review of Economics and Business* 24(4), 1984 : 24-49. [Followed by a rejoinder by Oliver E. WILLIAMSON, ibid. : 64-71]

750 FOMBRUN, Charles J. "Structures of organizational governance", *Human Relations* 37(3), mar 84 : 207-223.

751 GLASSMAN, Robert B. "A sociobiological examination of management theory Z", *Human Relations* 37(5), apr 84 : 367-392. [William OUCHI's Management Theory Z]

752 GÖPEL-GRUNER, Dagmar. *Organization development : theoretischer Überblick und praktischer Einsatz in einer Diensleistungsunternehmung* (Organization development : theoretical perspective and practical action in a service industry). Spardorf : Verlag R. F. Wilfer, 1983, 309 p. ill., bibl.

753 HANNAN, Michael T.; FREEMAN, John. "Structural inertia and organizational change", *American Sociological Review* 49(2), apr 84 : 149-164.

754 HARRIS, Barry C. *Organization : the effect on large corporations.* Ann Arbor, MI : University of Michigan Research Press, 1983, x-126 p.

755 HEYDERBRAND, Wolf V. "Strategie innovative nelle organizzazioni complesse" (Innovative strategy in complex organizations), *Critica Sociologica* 69, 1984 : 23-47.

756 KETS DE VRIES, Manfred F. R.; MILLER, Danny. "Group fantasies and organizational functioning", *Human Relations* 37(2), feb 84 : 111-134.

757 KIESER, Alfred. "Konflikte in Organisationen. Organisationsstruktur und Bedürfnisse des Individuums" (Conflicts in organizations. The organization structure and the individual's needs), *WIST. Wirtschaftswissenschaftliches Studium* 12(8), 1983 : 381-388.

758   KŐHEGYI, Kálmán. "Szervezeti változások végrehajtásának érdek- és hatalmi viszonyai"
       (Interest and power relations of the implementation of organizational changes), *Szociológia*
       12(1-2), 1983 : 79-115.
759   LEBLICI, Huseyin; WHETTEN, David A. "The concept of horizontal hierarchy and
       the organization of interorganizational networks : a comparative analysis", *Social Net-
       works* 6(1), mar 84 : 31-58. [USA]
760   LEDVINKA, James; HILDRETH, W. Bartley. "Integrating planned-change intervention
       and computer simulation technology : the case of affirmative action", *Journal of Applied
       Behavioral Science* 20(2), 1984 : 125-140.
761   LEGGE, Karen. *Evaluating planned organizational change.* London; Orlando, FL : Academic
       Press, 1984, x-243 p. bibl., ind.
762   MARKHAM, William T.; BONJEAN, Charles M.; CORDER, Judy. "Measuring
       organizational control : the reliability and validity of the control graph approach", *Human
       Relations* 37(4), apr 84 : 263-294.
763   MELUCCI, Alberto. "An end to social movements? Introductory paper to the sessions
       on 'new movements and change in organizational forms'", *Social Science Information /
       Information sur les Sciences Sociales* 23(4-5), 1984 : 819-835.
764   MONTJARDET, Dominique; BENGUIGUI, Georges. "Utopie gestionnaire, utopie
       sociologique? Réflexions sur un débat", *Revue Française de Sociologie* 25(1), jan-mar
       84 : 91-99. [France] [Voir D. MONTJARDET; G. BENGUIGUI, 'L'utopie gestion-
       naire. Les couches moyennes entre l'État et les rapports de classe', ibid. : 23(4),
       oct-dec 82 : 605-638]
765   NYSTROM, Paul C.; STARBUCK, William H. "Managing beliefs in organizations",
       Journal of Applied Behavioral Science 20(3), 1984 : 277-287. [USA]
766   OVALLE, Nestor K. II. "Organizational/managerial control processes : a reconceptualization
       of the linkage between technology and performance", *Human Relations* 37(12),
       dec 84 : 1047-1062.
767   PATERIA, A. K. "Developmental role of bureaucracy in post-independence India",
       Indian Journal of Social Research 25(1), apr 84 : 49-57.
768   PRIGOZIN, A. I. "Cel' organizacij : suščnost', problemy, razvitie" (The objective of
       organizations : nature, problems, development), *in : Aktual'nye problemy social'nogo
       upravlenija v regione* Vladivostok, 1982 : 137-245.
769   SASSOON, Joseph. "Ideology, symbolic action and rituality in social movements : the
       effects on organizational forms", *Social Science Information / Information sur les Sciences Sociales*
       23(4-5), 1984 : 861-873.
770   SCURRAH, Martin J. "The sector and firm in self-management", *Economic and Industrial
       Democracy* 5(3), aug 84 : 325-340. [Peru; Chile]
771   SHENKAR, Oded. "Is bureaucracy inevitable? : the Chinese experience", *Organization
       Studies* 5(4), 1984 : 289-307.
772   SJOBERG, Gideon; VAUGHAN, Ted R.; WILLIAMS, Norma. "Bureaucracy as a moral
       issue", *Journal of Applied Behavioral Science* 20(4), 1984 : 441-453. [USA]
773   TAINIO, Risto; SANTALAINEN, Timo. "Some evidence for the cultural relativity of
       organizational development programs", *Journal of Applied Behavioral Science* 20(2), 1984 : 93-111.
774   ULRICH, Dave. "Specifying external relations : definition of and actors in an organization's
       environment", *Human Relations* 37(3), mar 84 : 245-262.
775   VANCE, Charles M. "Integration of organizational behavior within higher education : four
       levels of needed involvement for upperclass and graduate curricula", *Human Relations*
       37(3), mar 84 : 191-205. [USA]
776   VAUGHAN, Ted R.; SJOBERG, Gideon. "The individual and bureaucracy : an alternative
       Meadian interpretation", *Journal of Applied Behavioral Science* 20(1), 1984 : 57-69.
777   WALTER, Gordon A. "Organizational development and individual rights", *Journal of
       Applied Behavioral Science* 20(4), 1984 : 423-439.
778   WEXLEY, Kenneth N.; YUKL, Gary A. *Organizational behavior and personnel psychology.*
       Homewood, IL : R. D. Irwin, 1984, xv-570 p. bibl., ind.; ill.
779   WHITLEY, Richard. "The development of management studies as a fragmented
       adhocracy", *Social Science Information / Information sur les Sciences Sociales* 23(4-5), 1984 : 775-818.
       [USA]
780   ZEITZ, Gerald. "Bureaucratic role characteristics and member affective response in
       organizations", *Sociological Quarterly* 25(3), 1984 : 301-318.

12600   **LEADERSHIP. ROLE**
         COMMANDEMENT. RÔLE

12610   Authority
         Autorité

781   BIAGI, Marta C.; FERNÁNDEZ, Marta E. "Tipos de dominación Weberianos a la luz de la lógica de la autoridad de Bochenski" (Weber's types of domination enlightened by Bochenski's logic of authority), *SOCIOLOGICA — Revista Argentina de Ciencias Sociales* 9, 1984 : 11-22.

782   EGASHIRA, Seigo. "Charisma to kindai" (Charisma and modernity), *Ikkyo Kenkyu* 8(4), 1984 : 141-154.

783   KIMURA, Kunihiro. "Eikyo ryoku kohshi to sougo sayo chitsujyo -E. Goffman no eikyo ryoku ron" (The exercise of power and the interaction order : Erving Goffman on power), *Shakaigaku Kenkyu* 47, 1984 : 131-150.

784   LABOURDETTE, Sergio Daniel. *El poder : hacia una teoría sistemática* (Power : towards a systematic theory). Buenos Aires : Editorial de Belgrano, 1984, 196 p. ill., bibl.

785   MIYAMOTO, Kohji. "Power gainen no bunseki teki yukosei : Barry Hindess no teigen o tegakari ni" (The analytical effectiveness of the concept of 'power' : a critical examination of Barry Hindess' propositions), *Soshioroji* 28(3), 1984 : 23-39.

786   MIYAMOTO, Kohji. "Shakai riron ni okeru power ron no ichi -Anthony Giddens no baai" (The role of power theory in Anthony Giddens' social theory), *Osaka University Annals of Human Sciences* 5, 1984 : 61-77.

787   MURPHY, Raymond. "The structure of closure : a critique and development of the theories of Weber, Collins, and Parkin", *British Journal of Sociology* 35(4), dec 84 : 547-567.

788   NUMATA, Kenya. "Shin-shukyo kenkyu ni karisuma ron" (Arguments on charisma in the studies of new religions), *St. Andrew's University Sociological Review* 18(1), 1984 : 29-59.

789   POWELL, Brian; JACOBS, Jerry. "Gender differences in the evaluation of prestige", *Sociological Quarterly* 25(2), 1984 : 173-190. [USA]

790   SÉGUY, Jean. "Charisme, prophétie, religion populaire", *Archives de Sciences Sociales des Religions* 57(2), apr-jun 84 : 153-168.

791   SERINO, Vinicio. *Aspetti e problemi del potere in Max Weber* (Aspects and problems of power in Max Weber). Lecce : Milella, 1983, 173 p. bibl., ind.

792   TAKASHIMA, Hideki. "M. Weber ni okeru 'shihai' to kyoiku" (M. Weber's 'Herrschaft' and education), *Meisei University Bulletin of Sociology* 4, 1984 : 46-61.

793   WEJLAND, Andrzej P. *Prestiż. Analiza struktur pojęciowych* (Prestige. Concept structure analysis). Warszawa : Polska Akademia Nauk Instytut Filozofii i Socjologii, 1983, 139 p. bibl.

12620   Leadership
         Commandement

794   BROWNE, Ray B.; FISHWICK, Marshall W.; [eds.]. *The hero in transition*. Bowling Green, OH : Bowling Green University Popular Press, 1983, 324 p. ill., bibl. [Heroes in motion pictures, USA]

795   DAVIS, Tim R.; LUTHANS, Fred. "Defining and researching leadership as a behavioral construct : an idiographic approach", *Journal of Applied Behavioral Science* 20(3), 1984 : 237-251.

796   MORRISON, Thomas L. "Member reactions to a group leader in varying leadership roles", *Journal of Social Psychology* 122(1), feb 84 : 49-53.

797   NORRIS, William P. "Coping with poverty in urban Brazil : the contribution of patron-client relationships", *Sociological Focus* 17(4), oct 84 : 259-273.

798   RUTTE, C. G.; WILKE, H. A. M. "Social dilemmas and leadership", *European Journal of Social Psychology* 14(1), mar 84 : 105-121.

799   WOOD, James R. "Leaders, values, and societal change", *Sociological Analysis* 45(1), 1984 : 1-10.

12630   Role
         Rôle

800   COYNE, Margaret Urban. "Role and rational action", *Journal for the Theory of Social Behaviour* 14(3), oct 84 : 259-275.

801   EAGLY, Alice H.; STEFFEN, Valerie J. "Gender stereotypes stem from the distribution of women and men into social roles", *Journal of Personality and Social Psychology* 46(4), apr 84 : 735-754.

802   GRADEV, Doncho. *Socialnite roli na lichnostta* (Social role and personality). Sofiá :
        Partizdat, 1984, 165 p. bibl.
803   KERBER, Kenneth W.; SINGLETON, Royce Jr. "Effects of role dominance on trait
        and situation attributions", *Journal of Social Psychology* 122(1), feb 84 : 59-66.
804   MARTIN, Thomas N. "Role stress and inability to leave as predictors of mental health",
        Human Relations 37(11), nov 84 : 969-983.
805   WATANABE, Hideki. "Yakuwari bunseki no kihon wakugumi -yakuwari kenkyu no tame
        no ichi kosatsu" (Fundamental frameworks of role analysis : systematization of role
        research), *Reports of the University of Electro-Communications* 35(1), 1984 : 111-125.

12700   ATTITUDES. OPINION
ATTITUDES. OPINION

12710   Behaviour
Comportement

806   BRECKLER, Steven J. "Empirical validation of affect, behavior, and cognition as distinct
        components of attitude", *Journal of Personality and Social Psychology* 47(6), dec 84 : 1191-1205.
807   CLARK, Alfred W.; POWELL, Robert J. "Changing drivers' attitudes through peer group
        decision", *Human Relations* 37(2), feb 84 : 155-162.
808   DECONCHY, Jean-Pierre. "La résistance à la validation expérimentale d'une connaissance
        portant sur les comportements 'idéologiques' ", *Archives de Sciences Sociales des Religions*
        58(1), jul-sep 84 : 117-138. [Comportement animal — Comportement humain]
809   JEFFERY, Ina A. "Conceptualization of a systems-based interdisciplinary approach to
        human behavior", *International Social Science Review* 59(4), 1984 : 33-36.
810   KLEINKE, Chris L. "Two models for conceptualizing the attitude-behavior relationship",
        Human Relations 37(4), apr 84 : 333-350.
811   LISKA, Allen E. "A critical examination of the causal structure of the Fishbein/Ajzen
        attitude-behavior model", *Social Psychology Quarterly* 47(1), mar 84 : 61-74.
812   LISKA, Allen E. "Estimating attitude-behavior reciprocal effects within a theoretical
        specification", *Social Psychology Quarterly* 47(1), mar 84 : 15-23.
813   LORD, Charles G.; LEPPER, Mark R.; MACKIE, Diane. "Attitude prototypes as
        determinants of attitude-behavior consistency", *Journal of Personality and Social Psychology*
        46(6), jun 84 : 1254-1266. [USA]
814   OLSON, James M.; CAL, A. Victoria. "Source credibility, attitudes, and the recall of
        past behaviours", *European Journal of Social Psychology* 14(2), apr-jun 84 : 203-210.
815   PAGEL, Mark D.; DAVIDSON, Andrew R. "A comparison of three social-psychological
        models of attitude and behavioral plan : prediction of contraceptive behavior", *Journal
        of Personality and Social Psychology* 47(3), sep 84 : 517-533. [USA]
816   RAY, J. J. "Attitude to abortion, attitude to life and conservatism in Australia", *Sociology
        and Social Research* 68(2), jan 84 : 236-246.
817   SIX, Bernd; KRAHÉ, Barbara. "Implicit psychologists' estimates of attitude-behaviour
        consistencies", *European Journal of Social Psychology* 14(1), jan-mar 84 : 79-86.
818   WILSON, Timothy D.; [et al.]. "Effects of analyzing reasons on attitude-behavior
        consistency", *Journal of Personality and Social Psychology* 47(1), jul 84 : 5-16. [USA]

12720   Cognitive dissonance. Prejudice
Dissonance cognitive. Préjugé

819   "Representation", *Social Research* 51(4), 1984 : 841-1097.
820   DEAUX, Kay; LEWIS, Laurie L. "Structure of gender stereotypes : interrelationships
        among components and gender label", *Journal of Personality and Social Psychology* 46(5),
        mai 84 : 991-1004. [USA]
821   ISOMURA, Ei'ichi; FUKUOKA, Yasunori; [eds.]. *Masu komi to sabetsu-go mondai* (The
        problem of discriminative words in Japanese journalism). Tokyo : Akashi Shoten,
        1984, 252 p.
822   KAWAMURA, Nozomu. "Shihon shugi shakai to sabetsu mondai" (Capitalist society
        and the discrimination problems), *Buraku Mondai Ronkyu* 9, 1984 : 101-127.
823   NICHOLS, Keith R.; MCANDREW, Francis T. "Stereotyping and autostereotyping in
        Spanish, Malaysian, and American college students", *Journal of Social Psychology* 124(2),
        dec 84 : 179-189.
824   OPP, Karl-Dieter. "Balance theory : progress and stagnation of a social psychological
        theory", *Philosophy of the Social Sciences / Philosophie des Sciences Sociales* 14(1), mar 84 : 27-49.

825   REQUENA Y DÍEZ DE REVENGA, Miguel. "Las representaciones colectivas de los
      pueblos indoeuropeos" (Collective representations of Indoeuropean peoples), *Revista
      Española de Investigaciones Sociológicas* 25, jan-mar 84 : 181-195.

12730   Dogmatism. F Scale
Dogmatisme. Échelle F

826   CAMPBELL, Colin. "Romanticism and the consumer ethic : intimations of a Weber-style
      thesis", *Sociological Analysis* 44(4), 1983 : 279-295.
827   RAY, John J. "Alternatives to the F scale in the measurement of authoritarianism : a
      catalog", *Journal of Social Psychology* 122(1), feb 84 : 105-119.
828   RAY, John J.; KIEFL, Walter. "Authoritarianism and achievement motivation in
      contemporary West Germany", *Journal of Social Psychology* 122(1), feb 84 : 3-19.
829   RIGBY, K. "Acceptance of authority and directivness as indicators of authoritarianism : a
      new framework", *Journal of Social Psychology* 122(2), apr 84 : 171-180.
830   SHAMIR, Michal; SULLIVAN, John. "The political context of tolerance : the United
      States and Israel", *American Political Science Review* 77(4), dec 83 : 911-928.
831   SHERNOCK, Stanley Kent. "Continuous violent conflict as a system of authority",
      Sociological Inquiry 54(3), sum 84 : 301-329.

12740   Opinion.
Opinion

832   "Ce qui divise les Français. Histoire et actualité", *Débat* (30), mai 84 : 3-43. [With contri-
      butions by Alain DUHAMEL, Maurice AGULHON, François FURET]
833   BRUNNER, José Joaquín. *Entrevistas, discursos, identidades* (Interviews, speeches, identities).
      Santiago de Chile : Facultad Latinoamericana de Ciencias Sociales, 1983, 352 p. bibl. [Chile]
834   CHAUDHRY, Kiren Aziz; MCDONOUGH, Peter. "State, society and sin : the political
      beliefs of university students in Pakistan", *Economic Development and Cultural Change* 32(1),
      oct 83 : 11-44.
835   FEDORIK, V. M. "Rol' obščestvennyh potrebnostej i interesov v processe formirovanija
      obščestvennogo mnenija v razvitom socialističeskom obščestve" (Role of social needs
      and interests in the process of the public opinion formation in the developed socialist
      society), *Problemy Filosofii* (61), 1984 : 9-16.
836   GLYNN, Carroll J.; MCLEOD, Jack M. "Public opinion du jour : an examination of the
      spiral of silence", *Public Opinion Quarterly* 48(4), 1984 : 731-740.
837   LIPSET, Seymour Martin; SCHNEIDER, William. *The confidence gap : business, labor and
      government in the public mind.* New York, NY : Macmillan, Free Press; London : Collier
      Macmillan, 1983, xii-434 p.
838   RAMBAUDI, Daniele. "Nemico del popolo. Analisi di un espediente retorico nella strategia
      del consenso" (Economy of the people. Analysis of a rhetoric expedient in the strategy
      of consensus), *Sociologia* 18(3), sep-dec 84 : 157-171.
839   ŠAGULIDZE, T. G. "Obščestvennoe mnenie : kak sredstvo obespečenija social'nogo i
      pravovogo kontrolja" (Public opinion as a mean of guarantee of social and legal control),
      in : Obščestvennoe mnenie : opyt ego izučenija Tbilisi, 1984 : 107-119.
840   SMITH, Brian H.; TURNER, Frederick C. "Zur Qualität von Meinungsforschung in
      autoritären Regimes : Latein- und Südamerika in den siebziger Jahren" (Opinion studies
      value under authoritarianist regimes : Latin and South America in the Seventies), *Journal
      für Sozialforschung* 24(1), 84 : 17-46.

12750   Ideology
Idéologie

841   "Idéologies, magies et religions", *Actions et Recherches Sociales* (3), nov 83 : 5-117. [With
      contributions by Guillaume RACCA-SERRA, Henri-Pierre JEUDY, Claude RIVIERE,
      Jean-Marie BROHM]
842   ALEXANDER, Peter; GILLI, Roger; [eds.]. *Utopias.* London : Duckworth, 1984, xx-218-9 p.
      ill., bibl., ind.
843   BLINOVA, L. N. "Nekotorye voprosy leninskogo analiza social'nyh kornej utopij" (Some
      questions on the Leninist analysis of utopian social roots), *in : Aktual'nye problemy istorii
      i teorii naučnogo kommunizma* Moskva, 1983 : 51-56.
844   BOUDON, Raymond. "Le phénomène idéologique : en marge d'une lecture de Pareto",
      Année Sociologique 34, 1984 : 87-125.

845 CARLTON, Eric. "Ideologies as belief systems", *International Journal of Sociology and Social Policy* 4(2), 1984 : 17-29.

846 CLAVEL, Maïté. "La haine de l'utopie", *Cahiers Internationaux de Sociologie* 77, 1984 : 361-382.

847 DEL AGUILA, Rafael. "Crítica y reivindicación de la utopía : la racionalidad del pensa-miento utópico" (Criticism and claiming of utopia : the rationality of utopian thought), *Revista Española de Investigaciones Sociológicas* 25, jan-mar 84 : 37-70.

848 MATJAŠ, T. P.; ÊRFURT, U. "Problema bessoznatel'nogo v buržuaznoj 'teorii ideologii'" (The problem of unconscious in the bourgeois 'theory of ideology'), *Izvestija Severo-Kavkazskogo Naučnogo Centra Vysšej Školy. Obščestvennye Nauki* (2), 1983 : 46-52.

849 MIKAMI, Takeshi. "Utopianism to millennialism" (Utopianism and millennialism), *Soshioroji* 29(2), 1984 : 45-63.

850 MONJARDET, Dominique. "La pensée utopique et les couches moyennes : quelques hypothèses", *Sociologie du Travail* 26(1), mar 84 : 50-63.

851 MURAV'EV, V. I. "Principy utočnenija specifiki kategorii 'ideologija' v istoričeskom materializme" (Definition principles of specificity of the 'ideology' category in historical materialism), *in : Problemy obščestvennogo soznanija* Tomsk, 1983 : 15-25.

852 PARDO, Isaac J. *Fuegos bajo el agua : la invención de utopía.* Caracas : Fundación la Casa de Bello, 1983, 800 p. bibl.

853 SIERRA ALVAREZ, José. "De las utopìas socialistas a las utopías patronales : para una genealogía de las disciplinas industriales paternalistas" (From socialist utopia to employers' utopia : for a genealogy of paternalistic industrial disciplines), *Revista Española de Investigaciones Sociológicas* 26, apr-jun 84 : 19-44.

854 ŠUL'GOVSKIJ, A. F.; [ed.]. *Sovremennye ideologičeskie tečenija v Latinskoj Amerike* (Contemporary ideological trends in Latin America). Moskva : Nauka, 1983, 352 p.

855 THOMPSON, John B. "Ideology and the social imaginary : an appraisal of Castoriadis and Lefort", *Theory and Society* 11(5), sep 82 : 659-681.

856 THOMPSON, John B. *Studies in the theory of ideology.* Cambridge, Cambridgeshire : Polity Press, 1984, viii-347 p. ill., bibl., ind.

857 TOŠČENKO, Ž. T. "K voprosu o naučnyh osnovah ideologičeskoj dejatel'nosti v uslovijah razvitogo socializma" (Question on scientific bases of ideological activity under conditions of developed socialism), *Voprosy Teorii i Praktiki Ideologiceskoj Raboty* (14), 1983 : 115-169.

858 TOŠČENKO, Ž. T. "O soderžanii ideologičeskoj dejatel'nosti i eĕ meste v obščestvennoj žizni" (On the content of ideological activity and its place in social life), *in : Voprosy teorii ideologičeskoj raboty : o sušcnosti zadačah i osnovnyh ponjatijah* Moskva, 1982 : 18-28.

859 VOROPAEV, Ju. F. "Genezis Marksovyh vzgladov na ideologiju i ih otraženie v buržuaznoj literature" (Genesis of Marx's views on ideology and their reflection in bourgeois literature), *in : Metodologija i metodika prepodavanija istorii filosofii* Sverdlovsk, 1983 : 49-64.

860 WARREN, Mark. "Nietzsche's concept of ideology", *Theory and Society* 13(4), jul 84 : 541-565.

12760 Collective behaviour
Comportement collectif

861 AGUIRRE, B. E. "The conventionalization of collective behavior in Cuba", *American Journal of Sociology* 90(3), nov 84 : 541-566.

862 BACZKO, Bronisław. *Les imaginaires sociaux : mémoires et espoirs collectifs.* Paris : Payot, 1984, 242 p. bibl.

863 BANDYOPADHYAY, Tradas. "On the frontier between possibility and impossibility theorems in social choice", *Journal of Economic Theory* 32(1), feb 84 : 52-66.

864 BOOTH, Alison. "A public choice model of trade union behaviour and membership", *Economic Journal* 94(376), dec 84 : 883-898. [UK]

865 CHAMBERLIN, John R.; [et al.]. "Social choice observed : five presidential elections of the American Psychological Association", *Journal of Politics* 46(2), mai 84 : 479-502.

866 CHAMPAGNE, Patrick. "La manifestation. La production de l'évènement politique", *Actes de la Recherche en Sciences Sociales* 52-53, jun 84 : 18-41.

867 FRANK, J. A. "La dynamique des manifestations violentes", *Canadian Journal of Political Science* 17(2), jun 84 : 325-349. [ENG]

868 LASH, Scott; URRY, John. "'The new Marxism of collective action : a critical analysis'", *Sociology (London)* 18(1), feb 84 : 33-50.

869 SHIOBARA, Tsutomu. "Undo no shakaigaku no kaiko to tenbo" (Thinking over theories of collective behavior and social movements), *in : The tenth anniversary collected papers* Osaka : Osaka University, Faculty of Human Sciences, 1984 : 207-237.

870 TILLY, Charles. "Les origines du répertoire de l'action collective contemporaine en France et en Grande-Bretagne", *Vingtième Siècle. Revue d'Histoire* (4), oct 84 : 89-104.

13 CULTURE. SOCIALIZATION. SOCIAL LIFE
CULTURE. SOCIALISATION. VIE SOCIALE

13100 CULTURE. SOCIAL ENVIRONMENT. VALUE
CULTURE. MILIEU SOCIAL. VALEUR

13110 Social and cultural anthropology
Ethnologie

871 AKIMOTO, Ritsuo. "R. E. Park ni okeru jinshu to bunka" (Contribution of Robert E. Park to the sociology of race and culture), *Shakaikagaku Tokyu* 30, 1984 : 41-78.

872 BROMLEJ, Ju. V.; KUZ'MINA, L. "Ėtnologija i obščestvo" (Ethnology and society), *Obscestvennye Nauki (Moskva)* (1), 1984 : 183-191.

873 CZERWIŃSKI, Marcin. "Kryzys poznawczy socjologii kultury" (Cognitive crisis in the sociology of culture), *Kultura i Społeczeństwo* 28(3), 1984 : 61-71.

874 HONNETH, Axel. "Die zerrissene Welt der symbolischen Formen. Zum kultursoziologischen Werk Pierre Bourdieus" (The torn world of symbolic forms. The sociology of culture developed by Pierre Bourdieu), *Kölner Zeitschrift für Soziologie und Sozialpsychologie* 36(1), mar 84 : 147-164.

875 HOPKINS, Frances L. "New causal theory and ethnomethodology : cocitation patterns across a decade", *Scientometrics* 6(1), 1984 : 33-53.

876 IKONNIKOVA, S. N. "Sociologija kul'tury kak special'naja otrasl'znanija" (Sociology of culture as a special department of learning), *in : Sociologija kul'tury metodologija i praktika kul'turno-prosvetitel'noj dejatel'nosti* Leningrad, 1982 : 3-14.

877 INOUE, Shun; [ed.]. *Chiiki bunka no shakaigaku* (A sociology of regional culture). Kyoto : Sekaishisosha, 1984, 221 p. [Japan]

878 KITAZAWA, Yutaka. "Parsons riron to ethnomethodology — shukan-sei mondai ni kansuru houhou bunseki o megutte" (Parsons' theories and ethnomethodology : theoretical perspectives for method analysis on the problem of subjectivity), *Shakaigaku Hyoron* 35(1), 1984 : 58-76.

879 LATOUCHE, Serge. "L'anthropologie et la clef du paradis perdu", *Homme et Société* 71-72, jan-jun 84 : 65-79.

880 LUQUE, Enrique. "Sobre antropología política (diálogo polémico con un viejo discurso)" (About political anthropology (controversial dialogue with an old discourse)), *Revista Española de Investigaciones Sociológicas* 25, jan-mar 84 : 71-93.

881 WINKIN, Yves. "Travail ethnographique et objectivation", *Actes de la Recherche en Sciences Sociales* 55, nov 84 : 41-45.

882 ZIJDERVELD, Anton C. *Sociologie als cultuurwetenschap : een beknopte methodologie van de cultuursociologie* (Sociology as cultural science : a concise methodology of sociology of culture). 's-Gravenhage : VUGA, 1983, 107 p.

13120 Civilization. Culture. Society
Civilisation. Culture. Société

883 *Approches sociologiques des modes de vie*. Paris : Copédith, 1983. [France] [2 vols.]

884 "Aventure Australie", *Autrement. Série Monde* (7), apr 84 : 1-294. [With contributions by Michèle DECOUST, François MISSEN, Barbara GLOWCZEWSKI, Dominique FRETARD, Pierre GRUNDMANN]

885 "Cultura y contracultura" (Culture and counterculture), *Nueva Sociedad* (73), aug 84 : 23-106. [Latin America] [With contributions by Darcy AIBEIRO, Luis BRITTO GARCIA, Fernando ALEGRIA, Fernando MIRES, Oscar LANDI, Beatriz SARLO]

886 "Culture et développement", *Tiers-Monde* 25(97), mar 84 : 5-204. [With contributions by LÉ Thanh KHÔI, Carmel CAMILLERI, Serge LATOUCHE]

887 "E l'Italia va..." (And Italy goes on...), *Critique* 40(447-448), sep 84 : 569-754. [With contributions by Alberto CAPATTI, Philippe RENARD, Giovanna ANGELI, Georges BANU, Eric DARRAGON]

888 "Évolution (L') de la société française", *Opinion Publique* (1), 1984 : 133-198. [With contributions by Olivier DUHAMEL, François de CLOSETS]

889 "How multicultural?", *Australian Quarterly* 55(2), wint 83 : 136-233. [Australia] [With contributions by Brian BULLIVANT, James JUPP, Russel WARD, Don AITKIN]

890   "Nation (La) en 1984'', *Cadmos* 7(25), spr 84 : 3-87. [With contributions by Georges
        NIVAT, Sergio ROMANO, Elemer HANKISS, Fabrizio FRIGERIO, Jean Marie
        ARRIGHI]
891   "Nation et liberté'', *Diogène* 124, oct-dec 83 : 3-82.
893   "Organizational culture'', *Administrative Science Quarterly* 28(3), sep 83 : 331-502. [With
        contributions by Mariann JELINEK, Linda SMIRCICH, Kathleen L. GREGORY,
        Kenwyn K. SMITH, Valerie M. SIMMONS]
894   "Pétrole et société'', *Peuples Méditerranéens / Mediterranean Peoples* (26), mar 84 : 3-209. [Algeria;
        Norway] [With contributions by Paul VIEILLE, Nirou EFTEKHARI, Fatima
        BENTALEB]
895   "Polonais (Les) malgré tout'', *Critique* 40(440-441), feb 84 : 1-156. [With contributions by
        Marie-Anne LESCOURRET, Krzysztof POMIAN, Jean-Paul COUCHOUD, Jan
        KLOSSOWICZ]
896   "Revendications (Les) à vivre autrement'', *Contradictions* (38), wint 84 : 1-160. [With
        contributions by Christian MAROY, Gérard MAUGER, Claude FOSSE-POLIAK,
        Alphonse ALVAREZ, E. LEGRAIN, J. DUPONT]
897   "Società (La) italiana negli anni '50'' (The Italian society in the 50s), *Sociologia (Roma)*
        18(1-2), jan-aug 84 : 1-372-ii.
898   "Sozialistische Lebensweise'' (Socialist way of life), *Einheit* 39(8), 1984 : 681-697.
        [German DR] [With contributions by Toni HAHN, Gunnar WINKLER, Helmut
        HANKE, Gottfried STIEHLER]
899   "Vie privée, travail, espace public au Japon'', *Sciences Sociales du Japon Contemporain* (4),
        oct 83 : 1-124. [With contributions by Takashi MIYAJIMA, Patrick BEILLEVAIRE]
900   AGRAWALA, Vasudeva Sharana. *India, a nation.* Varanasi : Prithivi Prakashan,
        1983, vi-179 p.
901   AGULLA, Juan C. *Estudios sobre la sociedad argentina* (Studies on Argentine society).
        Buenos Aires : Ediciones de Belgrano, 1984, 248 p.
902   ALNOL'DOV, A. I.; ORLOVA, É. A.; [eds.]. *Socialističeskij obraz žizni i novyj čelovek* (The
        socialist way of life and the new man). Moskva : Politizdat, 1984, 176 p.
903   ASANOVIC, Sreten. "La création culturelle dans la société socialiste autogestionnaire'',
        Questions Actuelles du Socialisme 34(5), mai 84 : 95-106. [Yugoslavia]
904   BAGES, Robert; [et al.]. "Modes de vie et arbitrages entre les activités dans les familles
        rurales et urbaines'', *Année Sociologique* 34, 1984 : 61-86. [France]
905   BAWIN-LEGROS, Bernadette. "Produire sa vie — histoire de quelques tentations?'',
        Revue de l'Institut de Sociologie (1-2), 1984 : 71-87.
906   BEYHAUT, Gustavo. *Raíces contemporáneas de América latina* (Contemporary roots of Latin
        America). Buenos Aires : Editorial Universitaria de Buenos Aires, 1984, 168 p. bibl.
907   BROMLEJ, N. Ta. "Usilenie social'noj odnotipnosti obraz žizni v pbščestve real'nogo
        socializma'' (Strengthening of the social homogeneity of way of life in real socialism
        society), *Istorija SSSR* 27(1), feb 84 : 28-42.
908   BROWNE, Eric C.; VERTZ, Laura L. "An old people in a new state : the problem of
        national integration in West Germany'', *Comparative Politics* 16(1), oct 83 : 85-95.
909   BRÜNNER, José Joaquín. *Cultura autoritaria y cultura escolar* (Authoritarian culture and the
        culture of the school). Santiago de Chile : Facultad Latinoamericana de Ciencias Sociales,
        1984, 68 p.
910   BRŮŽEK, Miloslav. *Teorie kultury* (Theory of culture). Praha : Státní Pedagogické Nakl.,
        1984, 343 p. bibl., ind.
911   BULLIVANT, Brian Milton. *Pluralism, cultural maintenance and evolution.* Clevedon, Avon :
        Multilingual Matters, 1984, xi-126 p. bibl., ind.
912   BURAKOWSKI, Stanisław. "Florian Znaniecki jako przedstawiciel refleksji cywilizacyjnej''
        (Florian Znaniecki's reflection on civilization), *Kultura i Społeczeństwo* 28(2), 1984 : 177-190.
913   CALINESCU, Matei. "Comment peut-on être Roumain?'', *Cadmos* 6(23-24), wint 83 : 30-44.
914   CAMILLERI, Carmel. "Images de l'identité et ajustements culturels au Maghreb'',
        Peuples Méditerranéens / Mediterranean Peoples (24), sep 83 : 127-152.
915   CARDUNER, Jean; [comp.]. *Pratiques culturelles.* Ann Arbor, MI : Michigan Romance
        Studies, 1983, 188 p. bibl. [France]
916   CATTELL, Raymond B.; BRENNAN, Jerry. "The cultural types of modern nations,
        by two quantitative classification methods'', *Sociology and Social Research* 68(2), jan 84 : 208-235.
917   ČEHARIN, É. M. "Nekotorye voprosy razvitija sovetskogo obsčestva i gosudarstva''
        (Some questions on Soviet society and State development), *Ežegodnik — Sovetskaja Associacija
        Političeskih Nauk*, 1981 : 78-86.
918   CLAPIER-VALLADON, S.; [ed.]. *Vie quotidienne hier et aujourd'hui dans les Alpes-Maritimes.*
        Nice : Centre de la Méditerranée Moderne et Contemporaine, 1983, 142 p. bibl.

919   CSEH-SZOMBATHY, László; [ed.]. *Egy korosztály életútja : az 1928-34ben született férfiakról.* *Kutatási beszámoló* (Life path of a generation : on men born between 1928-34. Research report). Budapest : Magyar Tudományos Akadémia Szociológiai Kutató Intézete, 1984, 395 p.

920   DURHAM, Eunice R. "Cultura e ideologia" (Culture and ideology), *Dados* 27(1), 1984 : 71-89.

921   EGOROV, A. G. "O socialističeskom, kommunističeskom progresse na sovremennom etape razvitija sovetskogo obščestva" (Socialist and communist progress at the actual stage of Soviet society's development), *Voprosy Istorii KPSS* (3), mar 84 : 23-50.

922   FELLING, Albert; PETERS, Jan; SCHREUDER, Osmund. "National Identität : die fünf Niederlande" (National identity : the five Netherlands), *Kölner Zeitschrift für Soziologie und Sozialpsychologie* 36(4), dec 84 : 738-754.

923   FRÉDÉRIC, Louis. *La vie quotidienne au Japon au début de l'ère moderne : 1868-1912.* Paris : Hachette, 1984, 404 p. ind.

924   FUCHS, Victor R. *How we live.* Cambridge, MA; London : Harvard University Press, 1983, 293 p. [USA]

925   FURTER, Pierre. "Cultures minoritaires et mal développement", *Tiers-Monde* 25(97), mar 84 : 59-74. [Western Europe]

926   GAZAR'JAN, V. G. "Ponjatie social'nogo faktora" (The social factor concept), *Izvestija Akademii Nauk Tadžikskoj SSR. Otdelenie Obščestvennyh Nauk* (1), 1983 : 24-31.

927   GHEORGHE, Elena; MISCOL, Oltea. "Socialismul si cultura" (Socialism and culture), *Revista de Filozofie* 31(1), feb 84 : 5-10. [Romania]

928   GIZATOV, K. T.; [et al.]. *Aktual'nye problemy socialističeskoj kul'tury : tezisy dokladov naučnoj konferencii* (Topical problems of the socialist culture : reports of a scientific conference). Kazan', 1983, 74 p.

929   GLEZERMAN, G. E.; [et al.]. *Socialističeskij obraz žizni* (The socialist way of life). Moskva : Politizdat, 80, 316 p.

930   GOŁEBIOWSKI, Bronisław. "Kultura i naród w twórczości Józefa Chałasińskiego" (The culture and the nation in the works of Józef Chałasiński), *Kultura i Społeczeństwo* 28(4), 1984 : 65-85.

931   GOŁEBIOWSKI, Bronisław. "Spór o kulturę robotniczą : refleksje i znaki zapytania" (The debate on the working class culture : reflections and question marks), *Kultura i Społeczeństwo* 28(1), 1984 : 55-70.

932   GONČARENKO, N. V. "Problemy rašcveta i upadka duhovnoj kul'tury" (Problems of the blooming and decline of intellectual culture), *Voprosy Filosofii* (7), 1983 : 99-107.

933   GOUDSBLOM, J. "De civilisatietheorie in het geding" (The civilization theory at stake), *Sociologische Gids* 31(2), 1984 : 138-163.

934   GOUROU, Pierre. *Riz et civilisation.* Paris : Fayard, 1984, 299 p. bibl., ind.

935   HAGENDIJK, R. P. "Changes in Dutch student culture", *Netherlands' Journal of Sociology* 20(1), apr 84 : 59-75.

936   HANKISS, Elemér. "'Második társadalom'? Kísérlet egy fogalom meghatározására és egy valóságtartomány leírására" ('Second society'? An attempt to describe reality unit and to determine a concept), *Valóság* 27(11), 1984 : 25-44.

937   HANOVA, O. V. "Dialektika kul'tury" (Dialectics of culture), *in : Kategorii filosofii i razvitie naučnogo poznanija* Saratov, 1983 : 143-145.

938   HARCSA, István. "A munkásfiatalok életkörülményeiről" (Life conditions of young workers), *Társadalmi Szemle* 39(7-8), 1984 : 68-78. [Hungary]

939   HASHIMOTO, Kazuta. "Seikatsu yohshiki o meguru ninshiki to tenkan" (Analysis and social plan for way of life), *Kokumin Seikatsu Kenkyu* 24(3), 1984 : 20-42.

940   HOMENKO, A. I. *Obščee i osobennoe v razvitii socialističeskogo obraza žizni* (The general and the particular in the socialist way of life development). Kiev : Naukova Dumka, 1983, 143 p.

941   IMAIZUMI, Reisuke. "Taishu shakai no kouzou" (Structure of mass society), *Bulletin of Kohriyama Women's College* 20, 1984 : 135-149.

942   JACENKO, A. I. "Filosofskoe ponjatie kul'tury" (Philosophical concept of culture), *in : Aktual'nye metodologičeskie voprosy sovremennoj nauki* Kiev, 1983 : 124-127.

943   JAGODZINSKI, Wolfgang. "Materialism in Japan reconsidered : toward a synthesis of generational and life-cycle explanations", *American Political Science Review* 77(4), dec 83 : 887-894.

944   JAVEAU, Claude. "Prolégomènes prétendument méthodologiques à une sociologie du quotidien", *Revue de l'Institut de Sociologie* (1-2), 1984 : 89-99.

945   JONSSON, Britta. *Alternative livsformer i sjuttiotalets Sverige* (Alternative ways of life and collective settlements in Sweden). Uppsala : Uppsala Universitet, Sociologiska Institutionen, 1983, 186 p. ill., bibl.

946   JUHÁSZ, Júlia. "Old habits in new surroundings", *New Hungarian Quarterly* 25(93), 1984 : 142-148. [Hungary]

947   KACI, Djamel; KENDILLEN, Leila. "L'Algérie, privée de son quotidien", *Peuples Méditerranéens / Mediterranean Peoples* (26), mar 84 : 127-145.

948   KALINA, V. F.; TOHT, A. "Nravstvennoe i pravovoe vospitanie kak sredstvo utverždenija socialistiĉeskogo obraza žizni" (Moral and legal formation as a mean of reinforcement of the socialist way of life), *Naučnye Doklady Vysšej Školy. Naučnyj Kommunizm* (3), 1983 : 77-82.

949   KAMLER, Howard. "Life philosophy and life style", *Social Indicators Research* 14(1), jan 84 : 69-81.

950   KIERSCH, Gerhard. "Une nouvelle identité allemande?", *Études*, feb 84 : 161-169.

951   KŁOSKOWSKA, Antonina. "Jakościowa i ilościowa analiza kultury symbolicznej" (Qualitative and quantitative approach to symbolic culture), *Kultura i Społeczeństwo* 28(2), 1984 : 39-52.

952   KON, I. "Kul'tura i obraz ĉeloveka" (Culture and the man's model), *in : Ličnost' v sovremennom mire : doklady sovetskih učenyh k XVII v semirnomu filosofskomu kongressu 'Filosofija i kul'tura'* [Canada, Montreal', 21-27 avgust 1983 g] Moskva, 1983 : 19-24.

953   KONEV, V. A.; [ed.]. *Dialektika kul'tury* (Dialectics of culture). Kujbyšev : Kujbyševskij Gosudarstvennyj Universitet, 1982, 133 p.

954   KÖPECZI, Bela. "Culture and national identity", *New Hungarian Quarterly* 25(94), sum 84 : 21-25. [Hungary]

955   KRZEMIEŃ-OJAK, Sław. "Problem kultury robotników w ujęciu Antonia Gramsciego" (Antonio Gramsci on the problems of working class culture), *Kultura i Społeczeństwo* 28(1), 1984 : 71-82.

956   KULCSÁR, Kálmán. *Contemporary Hungarian society*. Budapest : Corvina, 1984, 291 p.

957   KULIĈENKO, M. I. *Nacija i social'nyj progress* (Nation and social progress). Moskva : Nauka, 1983, 317 p.

958   KUTRZEBA-POJNAROWA, Anna. "Przyszłość kultury wsi w świetle jej przeszłości" (The future of peasant culture in the light of its past), *Kultura i Społeczeństwo* 28(4), 1984 : 97-107.

959   LAUTMAN, Jacques. "Les modes de vie dans les sociétés contemporaines", *Revue des Sciences Morales et Politiques* 138(4), 1983 : 611-625.

960   LECHNER, Norbert. *El estudio de la vida cotidiana* (The study of everyday life). Santiago de Chile : FLACSO, 1984, 210 p. [Chile]

961   LEMEL, Yannick. "Le sociologue des pratiques du quotidien entre l'approche ethnographique et l'enquête statistique", *Économie et Statistique* (168), jul-aug 84 : 5-11.

962   LIVSIĈ, Ju.; [ed.]. *Socialistiĉeskij obraz žizni : dialektika razvitija i problemy soveršenstvovanija* (The socialist way of life : dialectics of development and problems of improvement). Tallin : Tallinskij Politehniĉeskij Institut, 1983, 124 p.

963   LUHMANN, Niklas. "The self-description of society : crisis fashion and sociological theory", *International Journal of Comparative Sociology* 25(1-2), 1984 : 59-72.

964   MACHADO PAIS, José. "Fontes documentais em sociologia da vida quotodiana" (Documentary sources in the sociology of daily life), *Análise Social* 20(4), 1984 : 507-519.

965   MÁRMORA, Leopoldo. "Limites y ambigüedades de la concepción marxista de nación" (Limitations and ambiguities of the Marxist concept of nation), *Revista Mexicana de Sociología* 45(4), oct-dec 83 : 1105-1113.

966   MATEJKO, Alexander J. "Is the West in a real trouble?", *Revue Internationale de Sociologie / International Review of Sociology* 19(1-2-3), apr-aug-dec 83 : 27-60.

967   MATSUMOTO, Kazuyoshi. "'Societas' to 'communitas' -ryosha no ippan gainen zushiki eno kanren ni tsuite" ('Societas' and 'communitas' : on their relevance to a generalized conceptual scheme), *Niigata University Studies in Humanities* 65, 1984 : 71-97.

968   MCFATE, Patricia A.; [ed.]. "Paying for culture", *Annals of the American Academy of Political and Social Science* 471, jan 84 : 9-157. [USA]

969   METCALF, William J. "A classification of alternative lifestyle groups", *Australian and New Zealand Journal of Sociology* 20(1), mar 84 : 66-80. [Australia; New Zealand]

970   MEŽVEV, V. "Kul'tura — ĉelovek — obšĉestvo" (Culture — man — society), *Obšĉestvennye Nauki (Moskva)* (3), 1984 : 107-120.

971   MILLER, Joan G. "Culture and the development of everyday social explanation", *Journal of Personality and Social Psychology* 46(4), apr 84 : 961-978.

972   MILLER, Lawrence M. *American spirit : visions of a new corporate culture*. New York, NY : W. Morrow, 1984, 188 p. ill., bibl.

973   MILLER, William C. *Life, stress, and values*. Menlo Park, CA : SRI International, Values and Lifestyles Program, 1983, 95 p. ill., bibl.

974 MILOGOLOV, S. V. "Civilizacija kak uslovie obščestvennogo suščestvovanija čeloveka" (Civilization as a condition of the man's social existence), *in : Kul'tura i civilizacija. Sbornik* Moskva, 1984 : 39-53.

975 MOORHOUSE, H. F. "Professional football and working class culture : English theories and Scottish evidence", *Sociological Review* 32(2), mai 84 : 285-315.

976 MORRIS, Raymond N. "Canada as a family : Ontario responses to the Québec in dependence movement", *Canadian Review of Sociology and Anthropology / Revue Canadienne de Sociologie et d'Anthropologie* 21(2), mai 84 : 181-201.

977 MOTT, Frank L.; MOTT, Susan H. "Prospective life style congruence among American adolescents : variations in the association between fertility expectations and ideas regarding women's roles", *Social Forces* 63(1), sep 84 : 184-208.

978 NAGY, Katalin S. *A mindennapi vizuális kultúráról — a lakberendezési szokások alapján* (On every-day visual culture — based on the furnishing customs). Budapest : MRT Tömegkom-munikációs Kutatóközpont, 1982, 228 p. [Hungary]

979 OL'ŠANSKIJ, D. V. "Ponjatie 'kul'tura' v psihologičeskoj traktovke : grani sub'ektivnogo rassmotrenija kul'tury kak dejatel'nosti" (The 'culture' concept in the psychological interpretation : borders of the subjective examination of culture as an activity), *in : Kul'tura i civilizacija. Sbornik* Moskva, 1984 : 111-122.

980 OSSOWSKI, Stanisław. *O ojczyźnie i narodzie* (On fatherland and nation). Warszawa : Państwowe Wydawnictwo Naukowe, 1984, 152 p.

981 PÁL, László. "Kísérlet a 'helyi társadalom'" (An attempt to approach the dimensions of 'local society'), *Társadalomkutatás* 2(3-4), 1984 : 85-97.

982 PALLOTTINI, Michele. *Cronica e critica di una cultura : la Spagna di Francisco Franco* (Chronicle and criticism of a culture : Francisco Franco's Spain). Bologna : Pàtron, 1983, 167 p. bibl., ind.

983 PARK, Han S. "Belief systems, culture, and national integration of Korea", *Asian Profile* 11(5), oct 83 : 487-496.

984 PELOILLE, Bernard. "Jalons pour une sociologie de la nation française", *Revue Internationale de Sociologie / International Review of Sociology* 19(1-2-3), apr-aug-dec 83 : 88-114.

985 PLATKOVSKIJ, V. V. "Istoričeskie predposylki civilizacii" (Historical premises of civilization), *in : Kul'tura i civilizacija. Sbornik* Moskva, 1984 : 65-84.

986 RADNITZKY, Gerard. "Die ungeplante Gesellschaft. Friedrich von Hayeks Theorie der Evolution spontaner Ordnungen und selbstorganisierender Systeme" (Unequal society. Friedrich von Hayek's theory on spontaneous order evolution and self-organizing system), *Hamburger Jahrbuch für Wirtschafts- und Gesellschaftspolitik* 29, 1984 : 9-33.

987 RAMÍREZ GOICOECHEA, Eugenia. "Cuadrillas en el País Vasco : identidad local y revitalización étnica" (Friendship groups in Euskadi : local identity and ethnic revival), *Revista Española de Investigaciones Sociológicas* 25, jan-mar 84 : 213-220.

988 RAŠKOVA, R. T. "Kritika sovremennoj katoličeskoj interpretacii marksistskoj teorii kul'tury" (Critics of the contemporary Catholic interpretation of the marxist theory of culture), *in : Problemy ateizma i kritiki religii v trudah K. Marksa i F. Èngel'sa* Leningrad, 1983 : 61-76.

989 SAURMA, Adalbert. "Der Alltag als soziologisches Thema. Ein Bericht über deutsch-sprachige Beiträge" (Everyday life as a sociological topic. A report on contributions in German language), *Schweizerische Zeitschrift für Soziologie / Revue Suisse de Sociologie* 10(1), 1984 : 7-35.

990 SCHWEDER, Richard A.; LEVINE, Robert A.; [eds.]. *Culture theory : essays on mind, self and emotion.* Cambridge : University Press, 1984, viii-359 p. tabl., bibl.

991 SMITH, Dennis. "Norbert Elias — established or outsider?", *Sociological Review* 32(2), mai 84 : 367-389. [A review article on two books of Norbert ELIAS : The civilizing process. II. State formation and civilization. Oxford, Blackwell, 1982, 376 p., and The court society. Oxford, Blackwell, 83, 301 p.]

992 SMITH, Robert J. *Japanese society. Tradition, self, and the social order.* London; New York, NY... Cambridge University Press, 1983, x-176 p. bibl., ind.

993 ŠPILJUK, V. A.; [ed.]. *Obščestvo zrelogo socializma : obraz žizni i social'noe edinstvo* (The society of mature socialism : the way of life and social unity). L'vov : Izdatel'stvo pri L'vovskom Universiteta, 1983, 179 p.

994 STEVENSON, John. *British society, 1914-1945.* London : A. Lane, 1984, 503 p. bibl., ind.

995 SUHODOB, T. D. "Kul'tura kak universal'no-predmetnaja harakteristika obščestvennoj praktiki : k postanovke problemy raspredmečivanija kul'tury" (Culture as an universal-object characteristic of social practice : statement of the problem of the culture diffusion), *Problemy Filosofii* (59), 1983 : 74-79.

996 TANAKA, Yasumasa. "Culture and advanced technologies", *Gakushuin Daigaku Hogakubu Kenkyu Nempo* 19, 1984 : 35-124.

997 THODEN VAN VELZEN, H. U. E. "The Djuka civilization", *Netherlands' Journal of Sociology* 20(2), oct 84 : 85-97. [Suriname]

998 TIRYAKIAN, Edward A.; [ed.]. "The global crisis. Sociological analyses and responses", *International Journal of Comparative Sociology* 25(1-2), apr 84 : 130 p. [With contributions by Johan GALTUNG, Alain TOURAINE, Tom R. BURNS, Gary GEREFFI]

999 TORRES, Félix. "Post modernisme et histoire", *Esprit* 86(2), feb 84 : 98-112.

1000 ULIN, Robert C. *Understanding cultures : perspectives in anthropology and social theory.* Austin, TX : University of Texas Press, 1984, 200 p. bibl., ind.

1001 UTASI, Ágnes. "Életsílusok, fogyasztás. Egy kutatás résztanulmánya" (Life styles and consumption. Part study of a research), *Társadalomtudományi Közlemények* 14(1), 1984 : 48-68.

1002 VERRET, Michel. "Mémoire ouvrière, mémoire communiste", *Revue Française de Science Politique* 34(3), jun 84 : 413-427. [France]

1003 WAGNER DE REYNA, Alberto. "Amérique latine : culture et pauvreté", *Diogène* 126, apr-jun 84 : 43-55.

1004 WIERUSZEWSKA, Maria. "Horyzonty badń kultury wsi" (Horizons of studies on culture in the countryside), *Wieś i Rolnictwo* 44(3), 1984 : 95-101.

1005 WILBERT, Gerd. "Ökonomische Aspekte kultureller Dienstleistungen in der UdSSR" (Economic aspects of cultural services in USSR), *Osteuropa* 33(11-12), dec 83 : 882-891.

1006 ZAGLADIN, V. V.; FROLOV, I. T. "Global'nye problemy i sud'by civilizacii" (Aggregate problems and the destiny of the civilization), *Oktjabr'* (5), 1984 : 156-166.

1007 ŽARNIKOV, A. È. "Nekotorye problemy teorii nacii v trudah K. Marksa i sovremennost'" (Some problems of the theory of nation in K. Marx's works and the contemporary era), *Naučnye Doklady Vysšej Školy. Naučnyj Kommunizm* (5), 1983 : 21-30.

1008 ŽURAVLEV, V. V. "O progresse hudožestvennoj kul'tury" (On the progress of artistic culture), *Voprosy Filosofii* (7), 1983 : 126-132.

13130 Cultural dynamics. Cultural relations
Dynamique culturelle. Relations culturelles

1009 "Main-mise sur la culture", *Esprit* (3), mar 84 : 45-110. [France] [Suite d'articles par Pierre-Michel MENGER, Erhard FRIEDBERG, Philippe URFALINO, Jacques DARRAS, Claude GILBERT]

1010 AMATYA, Sãphalya. *Some aspects of cultural policy in Nepal.* Paris : UNESCO, 1983, 67 p.

1011 ARNOL'DOV, A. O.; [ed.]. *Kul'turnyj progress : filosofskie problemy* (The cultural progress : philosophical problems). Moskva : Nauka, 1984, 326 p.

1012 BASKER, Eileen; DOMINGUEZ, Virginia R. "Limits of cultural awareness : the immigrant as therapist", *Human Relations* 37(9), sep 84 : 693-719. [Israel]

1013 BIERNACKA, Maria. *Oświata w rozwoju kulturowym polskiej wsi* (Education in cultural development of the Polish country). Wrocław : Ossolineum, 1984, 208 p.

1014 CHATTERJI, Probhat Chandra. *Secular values for secular India.* New Delhi : Lola Chatterji, 1984, xvii-348 p. bibl., ind.

1015 CLUZEL, Jean. *Les pouvoirs publics et la transmission de la culture.* Paris : LGDJ, 1984, 183 p. ind. [France]

1016 FREUND, Wolfgang Slim. "Die universitäre Zusammenarbeit im Bereich von Geistes- und Sozialwissenschaften zwischen der Bundesrepublik Deutschland und den Maghreb-Staaten" (Universitary cooperation for arts and social sciences between Germany Federal Republic and Maghreb States), *Orient* 24(4), dec 83 : 677-692.

1017 GIRENKO, N. "K voprosu o dinamike kul'tury" (Question on the dynamics of culture), *in : Tradicii i sovremennost' : materialy vyezdnoj sessii naučnogo Soveta po problemam Afriki* [Leningrad, 16-18 fevrualja 1981 g] Moskva, 1983 : 9-21.

1018 GREGOIRE, Robert. "La Communauté et la culture", *Revue du Marché Commun* (274), feb 84 : 56-62.

1019 GRUNER, Roger. "Des Maghrébins à la recherche de leur identité culturelle", *Afrique et Asie Modernes* (142), aut 84 : 63-86.

1020 HAMANN, Rudolf. "Tradition als kulturelle Identität" (Tradition as cultural identity), *Hamburger Jahrbuch für Wirtschafts- und Gesellschaftspolitik* 29, 1984 : 275-291.

1021 HAY, Henry F. "Europe and the American mind", *History of European Ideas* 5(2), 84 : 137-148.

1022 IBRAGIMOV, R. I. *Aktual'nye problemy kul'turnogo stroitel'stva na sovremennom ètape* (Topical problems of culture edification in the contemporary stage). Krasnojarsk : Knižnoe Izdatel'stvo, 1984, 103 p.

1023   JACHER, Władysław. "Integracja kulturowa ludności na Śląsku" (Cultural integration of Silesia population), *Kwartalnik Opolski* 1, 1984 : 5-17.

1024   MBUNDA, D.; [et al.]. *Problems of culture and cultural values in the contemporary world.* Paris : UNESCO, 1983, 80 p. bibl.

1025   MCCORMACK, Thelma. "Culture and the State", *Canadian Public Policy* 10(3), sep 84 : 267-277. [Canada]

1026   MÉNDEZ DOMINGUEZ, Alfredo. *El cambio cultural y las diferencias de fecundidad en Guatemala* (Cultural changes and fertility variations in Guatemala). Guatemala : Ministry of Education, 1984, 219 p. bibl., ill., tabl.

1027   MICELI, Sergio. "Teoria e prática da política cultural oficial no Brasil" (Theory and practice of official cultural policy in Brazil), *Revista de Administração de Empresas* 24(1), mar 84 : 27-31.

1028   MOROT-SIR, Edouard. "Vers une conscience et une politique nouvelles de la culture en France", *Contemporary French Civilization* 8(1-2), wint 84 : 263-293.

1029   PASCALLON, Pierre. "Le développement culturel et les pays du Tiers-Monde", *Tiers-Monde* 24(95), sep 83 : 497-512.

1030   PIAZOLO, Paul Harro. "Europäische Kulturgemeinschaft : notwendige Schritte auf ein grosses Ziel" (The European cultural community : necessary steps towards a big aim), *Integration* (2), apr 84 : 79-90.

1031   PREISWERK, Roy A. *À contre-courants : l'enjeu des relations interculturelles.* Lausanne : Éditions d'En Bas, 1984, 256 p. bibl.

1032   REILLY, Charles A. "Cultural movements in Latin America : sources of political change and surrogates for participation", *Political Anthropology Yearbook* 2, 1983 : 127-153.

1033   SANSON, Henri. *Christianisme au miroir de l'Islam : essai sur la rencontre des cultures en Algérie.* Paris : Éditions du Cerf, 1984, 195 p.

1034   SEOANE PASCUAL, Luis. "En torno a la identidad cultural de la segunda generación de emigrantes españoles en Holanda y Suiza" (On the cultural identity of the second generation of Spanish emigrants in Holland and Switzerland), *Revista Española de Investigaciones Sociológicas* 26, apr-jun 84 : 113-127.

1035   SKOT-HANSEN, Dorte. *Kulturpolitik og folkekultur : en kultursociologisk undersøgelse af folke-kulturens stilling i lokalsamfundet og i kulturpolitikken* (Cultural policy and folk culture : a cultural sociological examination of the folk culture situation in the legal communities and in cultural policies). Copenhagen : Akademisk Forlag, 1984, 307-ix p. ill., bibl. [Norway]

1036   STEFĂNESCU, Ion T. "Dimensiuni ale politici-culturale in etapa actuală" (The cultural policy dimensions), *Viitorul Social* 76(4), aug 83 : 289-294. [Romania]

1037   TEWARI, Vishwa Nath. *Punjab : a cultural profile.* Delhi : Vikas, 1984, 90 p.

1038   TWENHÖFEL, Ralf. "Kulturkonflikt und Integration. Zur Kritik der Kulturkonfliktthese" (Culture conflict and integration. Critique of the thesis of culture conflict), *Schweizerische Zeitschrift für Soziologie / Revue Suisse de Sociologie* 10(2)(3pel. No), 1904 : 405-131. [Switzerland]

1039   UNIVERSITÉ DE SAINT-ÉTIENNE. CENTRE INTERDISCIPLINAIRE D'ÉTUDES ET DE RECHERCHES SUR L'EXPRESSION CONTEMPORAINE. *Cultures en conflit?* Saint-Étienne : CIEREC, 1984, 204 p. bibl., ind.

1040   VACCARINI, Italo. "Potere culturale, mass media e dinamica storico-sociale" (Cultural power, mass media and socio-historical dynamics), *Studi di Sociologia* 22(4), oct-dec 84 : 428-441.

1041   VAN NIEUWENHUIJZE, C. A. O. "Culture and development : the prospects of an after-thought", *Civilisations* 33(2), 1983 : 5-70.

1042   WIERUSZEWSKA, Maria. "Tożsamość kulturowa w badaniu społeczeństwa wiejskiego" (Cultural identity in the studies on rural community), *Wieś i Rolnictwo* 43(2), 1984 : 133-138.

1043   WILLIAMS, Raymond. *Culture and society, 1780-1950.* New York, NY : Columbia University Press, 1983, 365 p. [UK]

1044   WONDJI, Christophe. "Yves Person et la renaissance des cultures et des sociétés africaines", *Présence Africaine* 129, trim. 1, 84 : 38-52.

1045   ZIEMILSKI, Andrzej. "Trzy modele doświadczenia kulturalnego" (Three models of cultural experience), *Kultura i Społeczeństwo* 28(3), 1984 : 103-123.

13140   Social norms. Social control. Value systems
Normes sociales. Régulation sociale. Systèmes de valeurs

1046   "Crise (La) de l'éducation aux valeurs dans la société zaïroise", *Zaïre-Afrique* 24(183), mar 84 : 131-187. [With contributions by Kaita KADIAMBIYE, Esan-Akus EBUN-E-NKEN, NDUMU-NZIZIDI, Mata Lingume MAWEYA]

1047   "Papers on the crisis of institutions in India", *Contributions to Indian Sociology* 18(2), jul-dec 84 : 219-292.

1048   "Technologie und sociale Kontrolle" (Technology and social control), *Österreichische Zeitschrift für Politikwissenschaft* 12(4), 1983 : 339-476. [Austria] [With contributions by Hermann FRITZL, Roman HUMMEL]

1049   ARHANGEL'SKIJ, L. M. "Moral'nye cennosti i sovremennost'" (Ethical values and the contemporary era), *Voprosy Filosofii* (11), 1983 : 88-93.

1050   BAER, Douglas E.; CURTIS, James E. "French Canadian-English Canadian differences in values : national survey findings", *Canadian Journal of Sociology / Cahiers Canadiens de Sociologie* 9(4), 1984 : 405-427.

1051   BECKER, J. W.; NAUTA, A. P. N. "Verandering van normen en waarden : een nieuw terrein van studie" (Change and norms and values : a new field of study), *Mens en Maatschappij* 59(2), mai 84 : 195-201.

1052   CALISTA, Donald J. "Postmaterialism and value convergence : value priorities of Japanese compared with their perceptions of American values", *Comparative Political Studies* 16(4), jan 84 : 529-555.

1053   CAMILLERI, Carmel. "Les usagers de l'identité : l'exemple du Maghreb", *Tiers-Monde* 25(97), mar 84 : 29-42.

1054   CAPLOW, Theodore. "Rule enforcement without visible means : Christmas gift giving in Middletown", *American Journal of Sociology* 89(6), mai 84 : 1306-1323.

1055   CARTOCCI, Roberto. "I valori postmaterialisti dieci anni dopo" (Post materialist values ten years after), *Rivista Italiana di Scienza Politica* 13(3), dec 83 : 413-443.

1056   CHRISTENSON, James A.; [et al.]. "Value orientations of organized religious groups", *Sociology and Social Research* 68(2), jan 84 : 194-207. [USA]

1057   DARRÉ, Jean-Pierre. "La production des normes au sein d'un réseau professionnel : l'exemple d'un groupe d'éleveurs", *Sociologie du Travail* 26(2), apr-jun 84 : 141-156. [France]

1058   DJAÏT, Hichem. "Une quête pour les valeurs en Islam", *Diogène* 124, oct-dec 83 : 95-111.

1059   DUCZKOWSKA-MAŁYSZ, Katarzyna. "Ziemia w systemie wartości rodzin rolniczych" (Land in the system of values in farming families), *Wieś i Rolnictwo* 44(3), 1984 : 41-52.

1060   FARARO, Thomas J.; SKVORETZ, John. "Institutions as production systems", *Journal of Mathematical Sociology* 10(2), 1984 : 117-182. [With a discussion by Morris ZELDITCH Jr.; [et al.], ibid. : 183-210 and a reply by the authors, ibid. : 211-218]

1061   FINCKENSTEIN, Christiane. "Patriotismus und Höflichkeit : das gegenwärtige chinesische Wertesystem" (Patriotism and politeness : actual Chinese value system), *Zeitschrift für Politik* 30(4), dec 83 : 409-414.

1062   FORTES, Meyer. *Rules and the emergence of society.* London : Royal Anthropological Institute, 1983, iv-52 p. bibl.

1063   FREIDSON, Eliot. "The changing nature of professional control", *Annual Review of Sociology* 10, 1984 : 1-20. [USA]

1064   HECHTER, Michael. "Quando gli attori si adequano alle regole. I costi del controllo e la produzione dell'ordine sociale" (When actors comply. Monitoring costs and the production of social order), *Rassegna Italiana di Sociologia* 25(2), apr-jun 84 : 221-257.

1065   HOGE, Dean R.; HOGE, Jann L. "Period effects and specific age effects influencing values of alumni in the decade after college", *Social Forces* 62(4), jun 84 : 941-962. [USA]

1066   JAGODZINSKI, Wolfgang. "Wie transformiert man Labile In Stabile RELationen? Zur Persistenz postmaterialistischer Wertorientierungen" (How can we transform Labile into Stable RELations? On the persistency of postmaterialistic value orientations), *Zeitschrift für Soziologie* 13(3), jul 84 : 225-242.

1067   JUNUSOV, A. M. "Internacional'noe i nacional'noe v duhovnyh cennostjah socialističeskoj nacii" (International and national trends in the Socialist nation's spiritual values), *Uzbekistonda Ižtimoij Fanlar* (6), 1984 : 28-34. [USSR]

1068   KILBOURNE, Brock K.; KILBOURNE, Maria T. "Norms of social conduct and the foot-in-the-door", *Journal of Social Psychology* 123(1), jun 84 : 13-20.

1069   KITAMURA, Kazuo. "Kindai shakai teki kachi kan to hensa-chi" (Values in modern society and 'Hensachi'), *Journal of Educational Sociology* 39, 1984 : 187-199.

1070   KLIMOV, V. A.; LISTVIN, V. F. *Naučnoe upravlenie socialističeskim obščerstvom i social'nyj kontrol'* (Scientific management of the socialist society and social control). Saratov : Izdatel'stvo Saratovskogo Universiteta, 1983, 70 p.

1071   KLOCKARS, Carl B.; [ed.]. "Lies, secrets, and social control", *American Behavioral Scientist* 27(4), apr 84 : 411-544. [With contributions by David T. LYKKEN, Fred MONTANINO]

1072 KORNIENKO, É. V.; PEDAN, V. P. "K voprosu o suščnosti i strukture cennostnyh orientacij ličnosti" (Question on the nature and structure of valuable orientations of the personality), *Vestnik Har'kovskogo Universiteta* (244), 1983 : 108-112.

1073 LISTHAUG, Ola. "Confidence in institutions : findings from the Norwegian values study", *Acta Sociologica* 27(2), 1984 : 111-122.

1074 MEIER, Robert F.; BURKETT, Steven R,; HICKMAN, Carol A. "Sanctions, peers, and deviance : preliminary models of a social control process", *Sociological Quarterly* 25(1), wint 84 : 67-82.

1075 MURAMATSU, Yasuko; AKIYAMA, Toyoko; YOKOYAMA, Shigeru. "Nihon jin no ishiki henka no shoso -danjyo betsu, danjyo nenso betsu ni mita 10 nenkan no henka" (Changing values of the Japanese : comparison of trends classified by sex and age over a ten-year period), *NHK Annual Bulletin of Broadcasting Culture Research* 29, 1984 : 1-50.

1076 NAKAJIMA, Michio. "Durkheim ni okeru keizai, shakai, doutoku : 'seido' no riron" (Economy, society and morality in Durkheim's sociology : a theory of institution), *Soshioroji* 29(1), 1984 : 1-20.

1077 NÉMEDI, Dénes. "Az értékmentesség elve a szociológiában. Kísérlet a probléma felvázolására" (The principle of value absence in sociology. An attempt to outline the question), *Valóság* 27(1), 1984 : 30-43.

1078 OPP, Karl-Dieter. *Die Entstehung sozialer Normen : ein Integrationsversuch soziologischer, sozial-psychologischer und ökonomischer Erklärungen* (The origin of social norms : an attempt to integrate sociological, sociopsychological and economic explanations). Tübingen : Mohr, 1983, ix-240 p. ill., bibl., ind.

1079 ROSS, H. Laurence. "Social control through deterrence : drinking-and-driving laws", *Annual Review of Sociology* 10, 1984 : 21-35. [USA]

1080 RUTTAN, Vernon W.; HAYAMI, Yujiro. "Toward a theory of induced institutional innovation", *Journal of Development Studies* 20(4), jul 84 : 203-223.

1081 THÉVENOT, Laurent. "Rules and implements : investment in forms", *Social Science Information / Information sur les Sciences Sociales* 23(1), 1984 : 1-45.

1082 ZIEGLER, Rolf. "Norm, Sanktion, Rolle. Eine strukturale Rekonstruktion soziologischer Begriffe" (Norm, sanction, role. Structural reconstruction of sociological concepts), *Kölner Zeitschrift für Soziologie und Sozialpsychologie* 36(3), sep 84 : 433-463.

13150   Alienation. Socialization. Social conformity
Aliénation. Socialisation. Conformité sociale

1083 "Ethnographie de la violence", *Études Rurales* 95-96, jul-dec 84 : 9-129.

1084 "Into and out of deviant careers", *Social Problems* 31(2), dec 83 : 182-221. [USA] [With contributions by Joan MOORE, Patricia A. ADLER, Peter ADLER, Neal SHOVER, Barry GLASSNER]

1085 "Isolement et solitude", *Gérontologie et Société* 27, dec 83 : 3-127. [France]

1086 "Siècle (Le) de tous les terrorismes", *Esprit* (10-11), nov 84 : 1-272. [Suite d'articles par Paul HENZE, Stanislas LEN]

1087 "Terrorism", *World Affairs* 146(1), sum 83 : 3-116. [With contributions by Harvey J. McGEORGE II, Susan MORRISEY LIVINGSTONE, Samuel T. FRANCIS]

1088 "X naučni skup sociologa Jugoslavije (9-12.XI.1983) na temu : integrativni i dezintegrativni procesi u jugoslovenskom društvu" (Xth Scientific meeting of the Yugoslav sociologists (9th-12th November 1983) on the subject : integration and disintegration processes of Yugoslav society), *Sociologija* 26(1-2), jan-jun 84 : 1-110. [Yugoslavia]

1089 AITOV, N. "Kak dostigaetsja social'naja odnorodnost'" (How is obtained social homogeneity?), *Molodoj Kommunist* (1), 1984 : 7-14.

1090 ARCHER, D.; GARTNER, R. *Violence and crime in cross-national perspective.* New Haven, CT : Yale University Press, 1984, x-341 p.

1091 BEAUD, Paul. *La société de connivence : média, médiations et classes sociales.* Paris : Aubier-Montaigne, 1984, 382 p. bibl.

1092 BICHOT, Jacques. "Les nouveaux partenaires sociaux", *Humanisme et Entreprise* (142), dec 83 : 1-14. [France]

1093 BUBNOVIČ, A. V. "Nekotorye metodologičeskie problemy issledovanija socialističeskogo obščestvennogo soznanija" (Some methodological problems of research on socialist social consciousness), *Vestnik Akademii Nauk Kazahskoj SSR* (4), 1983 : 65-68.

1094 BUSS, Arnold H.; BRIGGS, Stephen R. "Drama and the self in social interaction", *Journal of Personality and Social Psychology* 47(6), dec 84 : 1310-1324.

1095 CHAUDHURI, K. K. "Participation in Indian society", *International Social Science Journal / Revue Internationale des Sciences Sociales* 36(2), 1984 : 255-269.

1096   COLLINS, Randall. "Alienazione : micro o macro?" (Alienation : micro or macro?), _Studi di Sociologia_ 22(2), apr-jun 84 : 109-126.

1097   DASGUPTA, Hoimanti. "Determinants of Social distance", _Indian Journal of Social Research_ 25(2), aug 84 : 193-209. [India]

1098   DECLEVE, H.; [et al.]. _La violence sociale._ Louvain-la-Neuve : Ciaco, 1983, 149 p.

1099   DEJEMEPPE, Benôit; RIGAUX, Marie-Françoise. "Violence et justice : les choses telles qu'elles sont", _Revue Nouvelle_ 80(10), oct 84 : 271-281. [Belgium]

1100   DOGALOV, A. G. "Social'no-filosofskij analiz prirody massovogo soznanija" (A socio-philosophical analysis of mass consciousness), _Vestnik Akademii Nauk Kazahskoj SSR_ (11), 1983 : 66-68.

1101   DRAKE, Richard. "The Red and the Black : terrorism in contemporary Italy", _International Political Science Review_ 5(3), 84 : 279-298.

1102   EGAN, Kieran. "Educating and socializing : a proper distinction?", _Teachers College Record_ 85(1), aut 83 : 27-42.

1103   EJIMA, Shusaku. "'Mondai kohdo' eno shakaigaku teki sekkin -chugakusei no ishiki to kohdo o meggute" (A sociological approach to the deviant behavior in junior high school), _Heiwa Kyoiku Kenkyu_ 11, 1984 : 73-114. [Japan]

1104   ENGINEER, Asghar Ali. "A theory of communal riots", _Seminar_ (291), nov 83 : 14-19. [India]

1105   ENRIQUEZ, Eugène. _De la horde à l'État : essai de psychanalyse du lien social._ Paris : Gallimard, 1983, 460 p. bibl., ind.

1106   EYRE, L. Alan. "Political violence and urban geography in Kingston, Jamaica", _Geographical Review_ 74(1), jan 84 : 24-37.

1107   FALK, Gerhard. "Terror as politics : the German case", _International Review of History and Political Science_ 20(4), nov 83 : 22-32.

1108   FECTEAU, J. M. "Transition au capitalisme et régulation de la déviance. Quelques réflexions à partir du cas bas-canadien", _Déviance et Société_ 8(4), dec 84 : 345-356.

1109   FERGE, Zsuzsa. "The reproduction of social relations", _New Hungarian Quarterly_ 25(94), 1984 : 137-148. [Hungary]

1110   FORSYTH, Craig J.; BANKSTON, William B.; JONES, J. H. "Organizational and extra-organizational determinants of occupationally induced social marginality : a study of merchant seamen", _Sociological Focus_ 17(4), oct 84 : 325-336. [USA]

1111   GABEL, Joseph. "Durkheimianism and political alienation : Durkheim and Marx", _Canadian Journal of Sociology / Cahiers Canadiens de Sociologie_ 9(2), 1984 : 179-189.

1112   GOŁEBIOWSKI, Bronisław. "Problemy świadomości społecznej mieszkańców wsi (w listach do redakcji 'Gromady-Rolnika Polskiego' z 1983 r.)" (Problems of social consciousness of the countryside population (based on letters to 'Gromada-Rolnik Polski' magazine in 1983)), _Wieś Współczesna_ 12, 1984 : 31-39.

1113   GUILLEMIN, Alain. "'Doucement, c'est tout de même une femme'. Remarques sur le statut de la violence dans les manifestations paysannes", _Actes de la Recherche en Sciences Sociales_ 52-53, jun 84 : 42-48.

1114   GUPTA, K. C. "Political alienation in India", _Indian Journal of Social Research_ 25(2), aug 84 : 105-114.

1115   HAMPSON, Robert B. "Adolescent prosocial behavior : peer-group and situational factors associated with helping", _Journal of Personality and Social Psychology_ 46(1), jan 84 : 153-162. [USA]

1116   HAWLEY, Willis; [et al.]. _Strategies for effective desegregation : lessons from research._ Lexington, MA : Lexington Books, 1983, x-210 p. bibl., ind.

1117   HELSON, Ravenna; MITCHELL, Valory; MOANE, Geraldine. "Personality and patterns of adherence and nonadherence to the social clock", _Journal of Personality and Social Psychology_ 46(5), mai 84 : 1079-1096. [USA]

1118   HOFFMAN, Bruce. "Right-wing terrorism in Europe", _Orbis_ 28(1), spr 84 : 16-27.

1119   HOFFMAN, Bruce. "Right-wing terrorism in Europe", _Conflict_ 5(3), 1984 : 185-210. [Voir aussi : pp. 233-244 : by Gordon R. BRAINERD Jr.]

1120   INOUE, Jun'ichi. "Shakai ishiki kenkyu to gensho-gaku teki apurohchi" (Studies of social consciousness and phenomenological approach), _For New Sociology_ 10(2/3), 1984 : 66-74.

1121   INOUE, Shun. "Bohryoku ni tsuite" (On violence), _Studies in Modern Manners and Customs_ 8, 1984 : 37-55.

1122   IWAMI, Kazuhiko. "Chugaku-sei no tai-kyoshi bohryoku ishiki : 'gakko kan' bunseki o baikai ni" (A background of social violence : on students' consciousness of school life), _Seishonen Mondai Kenkyu_ 33, 1984 : 1-16.

1123   JACQUES, Jeffrey M.; HALL, Robert L. "Desegregation of higher education : an examination of traditionally black and white institutions", _Sociological Inquiry_ 54(4), 1984 : 382-407. [USA]

1124 JAGUARIBE, Hélio. "Raça, cultura e classe, na integração das sociedades" (Race, culture and class in the integration of societies), *Dados* 27(2), 1984 : 125-143.

1125 KAES, René; [et al.]. "Perspectives psychanalytiques sur les conduites sociales", *Connexions* 44, 1984 : 7-186.

1126 KEŠELAVA, V. "Problema otčuždenija i materialističeskoe ponimanie istorii" (The problem of alienation and the materialist understanding of history), *Kommunist Gruzii* (2), 1983 : 55-62.

1127 KETHUDOV, R. G. "Otčuždenie i ideologija" (Alienation and ideology), in : *Aktual'nye problemy filosofii* Tbilisi, 1983 : 11-26.

1128 KLÜVER, Hartmut. "Die 'Brot-Revolten' in Tunesien und Marokko im Winter 1983/84" ('Bread revolts' in Tunisia and Morocco during winter 1983/84), *Orient* 25(1), 1984 : 123-130.

1129 KOZAKIEWICZ, Mikołaj. "Kryzys społeczno-ekonomiczny a socjalizacja młodzieży" (Socio-economic crisis and socialization of young people), *Wieś Współczesna* 7, 1984 : 47-56.

1130 KRASIN, Ju.; LEJBZON, B. "Kommunisty i novye dviženija obščestvennogo protesta" (The communists and the new movements of social contestation), *Kommunist (Moskva)* (5), 1984 : 105-115.

1131 KRJAŽKOV, P. Ė.; [ed.]. *Obščestvennoe soznanie i social'naja praktika* (Social consciousness and social practice). Moskva : Moskovskoj Oblastnoj Pedagogičeskij Institut imeni N. K. Krupskoj, 1982, 121 p.

1132 KROHN, Marvin D.; LANZA-KADUCE, Lonn; AKERS, Ronald L. "Community context and theories of deviant behavior : an examination of social learning and social bonding theories", *Sociological Quarterly* 25(3), 1984 : 353-371. [USA]

1133 KUŽEL'NAJA, I. P. "Formirovanie socialističeskogo soznanija u studenčeskoj molodeži" (Formation of the social consciousness among the young students), *Vestnik Har'kovskogo Politehničeskogo Instituta* (201-202), 1983 : 15-22.

1134 LAGRANGE, H. "Perceptions de la violence et sentiment d'insécurité", *Déviance et Société* 8(4), dec 84 : 321-344. [France]

1135 LAGRANGE, Hugues. "La perception de la violence par l'opinion publique", *Revue Française de Sociologie* 25(4), oct-dec 84 : 636-657. [France]

1136 LANDAU, Simha F. "Trends in violence and aggression : a cross cultural analysis", *International Journal of Comparative Sociology* 25(3-4), sep-dec 84 : 133-158.

1137 LAUDERDALE, Pat; [et al.]. "External threat and the definition of deviance", *Journal of Personality and Social Psychology* 46(5), mai 84 : 1058-1068.

1138 LEGAULT, Albert. "La dynamique du terrorisme : le cas des Brigades rouges", *Études Internationales* 14(4), dec 83 : 639-681. [Italy]

1139 LEGOWICZ, Jan. "Zrodla i przejawy nihilizmu spolecznego" (Sources and symptons of social nihilism), *Nowe Drogi* 417(2), feb 84 : 24-39. [Poland]

1140 LEWIS, Glen. *Real men like violence : Australian men, media, and violence.* Kenhurst, New South Wales : Kangaroo Press, 1983, 176 p. ill., bibl., ind.

1141 MARSDEN, Peter V.; CAMPBELL, Karen E. "Measuring tie strength", *Social Forces* 63(2), dec 84 : 482-501.

1142 MASTERS, Roger D. "Ostracism, voice, and exit : the biology of social participation", *Social Science Information / Information sur les Sciences Sociales* 23(6), 1984 : 877-893.

1143 MAYNARD, Douglas W.; ZIMMERMAN, Don H. "Topical talk, ritual and the social organization of relationships", *Social Psychology Quarterly* 47(4), dec 84 : 301-316.

1144 MIGUENS, José Enrique. "Le discours magique du terrorisme politique", *Diogène* 126, apr-jun 84 : 114-134.

1145 MISHRA, L. N. "A study of political alienation among professional groups", *Indian Journal of Social Research* 25(2), aug 84 : 162-170. [India]

1146 MITCHELL, Richard G. Jr. "Alienation and deviance : strain theory reconsidered", *Sociological Inquiry* 54(3), 1984 : 330-345.

1147 MUIR, Donald E.; MCGLAMERY, C. Donald. "Trends in integration attitudes on a Deep-South campus during the first two decades of desegregation", *Social Forces* 62(4), jun 84 : 963-972. [USA]

1148 NIELSEN, Kurt Aagaard. *Sociologi og socialisation* (Sociology and socialization). København : Institutionen Sociologi, 1983, 197 p. bibl.

1149 OLENIČEVA, G. V. "Specifika genezisa nekotoryh cennostnyh form obščestvennogo soznanija" (Specificity of genesis of some valuable forms of social consciousness), in : *Problemy obščestvennogo soznanija* Tomsk, 1983 : 53-59.

1150 PERRY, Elizabeth. "Collective violence in China, 1880-1980", *Theory and Society* 13(3), mai 84 : 427-454.

1151   PODGORNYH, N. I. "Problemy issledovanija ob'ektivnyh osnov obščestvennogo soznanija" (Problems of research on the objective bases of social consciousness), *in : Problemy obščestvennogo soznanija* Tomsk, 1983 : 3-14.

1152   POITEVIN, Guy. *Inde : les marginaux de l'éternel; idéologies de la pauvreté et identité culturelle chez les étudiants marginaux en Inde.* Paris : L'Harmattan, 1984, 211 p.

1153   RADU, Michael S. "Terror, terrorism, and insurgency in Latin America", *Orbis* 28(1), spr 84 : 27-41.

1154   REICHER, S. D. "The St. Paul's riot : an explanation of the limits of crowd action in terms of a social identity model", *European Journal of Social Psychology* 14(1), mar 84 : 1-21. [UK]

1156   RIBOLZI, Luisa. "Processi di socializzazione e sociologia dell'educazione" (Socialization process and sociology of education), *Studi di Sociologia* 22(3), jul-sep 84 : 271-288.

1157   RIORDAN, Catherine A.; [et al.]. "Prosocial behavior following transgression : evidence for intrapsychic and interpersonal motives", *Journal of Social Psychology* 124(1), oct 84 : 51-55.

1158   ROHRMOSER, Günter. "Terroristische Gewalt oder das Ende des Dialog" (Terrorist violence at the end of the dialogue), *Staat (Der)* 23(3), 1984 : 321-336. [Germany FR]

1159   ROOK, Karen S. "The negative side of social interaction : impact on psychological well-being", *Journal of Personality and Social Psychology* 46(5), mai 84 : 1097-1108. [USA]

1160   ROSIECKI, Wojciech. "Wokót problemu świadomości młodzieży" (Around the problem of youth consciousness), *Ideologia i Polityka* 3, 1984 : 89-98.

1161   RUBEL, M. "Pour une étiologie de l'aliénation politique : Marx à l'école de Spinoza", *Économies et Sociétés* 18(7-8), jul-aug 84 : 223-241.

1162   SANDELANDS, Lloyd E.; CALDER, Bobby J. "Referencing and bias in social interaction", *Journal of Personality and Social Psychology* 46(4), apr 84 : 755-762.

1163   SATO, Tomio. "Datsu-bussho-ka to sogai : sogai ron no sai-hyoka no tame ni" (De-reification and alienation : an approach to revaluate to the theory of alienation), *Shakaigaku Nenshi* 25, 1984 : 197-213.

1164   SCIULLI, David. "Talcott Parsons's analytical critique of Marxism's concept of alienation", *American Journal of Sociology* 90(3), nov 84 : 514-540.

1165   SCOTT, William A.; STUMPF, John. "Personal satisfaction and role performance : subjective and social aspects of adaptation", *Journal of Personality and Social Psychology* 47(4), oct 84 : 812-827. [Australia]

1166   ŠEJNIS, V. L. "Osnovny sfery social'noj žizni i tendencii i osobennosti razvitija" (Main spheres of social life : tendencies and characteristics of development), *in : Razvivajuščiesja strany·: ėkonomičeskij rost i social'nyj progress* Moskva, 1983 : 498-542.

1167   SHERMAN, Lawrence W.; [et al.]. "The specific deterrent effects of arrest for domestic assault", *American Sociological Review* 49(2), apr 84 : 261-272. [USA]

1168   SILVER, Charles. "Utilitarian participation", *Social Science Information / Information sur les Sciences Sociales* 23(4-5), 1984 : 701-729.

1169   SINGH, Bhudev. "Alienation among factory workers", *Indian Journal of Social Research* 25(2), aug 84 : 133-150. [India]

1170   SINHA, R. K. "Alienation among schedule castes in an urban setting", *Indian Journal of Social Research* 25(2), aug 84 : 151-161. [India]

1171   SLABY, Andrew Edmund; TANCREDI, Laurence R. *Collusion for conformity.* New York, NY : J. Aronson, distributed by Scribner, 1983, xii-209 p. bibl., ind.

1172   STOCKHAMMER, Helmut. *Sozialisation und Kreativität : Theorien, Techniken, Materialien* (Socialization and creativity : theories, techniques, materials). Wien : Im Verlag des Verbandes der Wissenschaftlichen Gesellschaften Österreichs, 1983, 224 p. bibl.

1173   SULIMOV, E. F. "O proizvodstve i vosproizvodstve obščestvennoj žizni v uslovijah razvitogo socializma" (Social life production and reproduction in developed socialist society), *Voprosy Filosofii* 37(6), 1984 : 40-51. [USSR]

1174   SWARUP, Anand. "Sources of student alienation", *Indian Journal of Social Research* 25(2), aug 84 : 115-132. [India]

1175   TACUSSEL, Patrick. *L'attraction soiale : le dynamisme de l'imaginaire dans la société monocéphale.* Paris : Méridiens, 1984, 204 p.

1176   TIHUN, S. V. "O soderžanie ponjatija 'internacionalizacija obščestvennoj žizni'" (On the content of the 'internationalization of social life' concept), *Naučnye Doklady Vysšej Školy. Naučnyj Kommunizm* (3), 1983 : 115-120.

1177   TOURAINE, Alain. "The waning sociological image of social life", *International Journal of Comparative Sociology* 25(1-2), 1984 : 33-44.

1178   TRIANDIS, Harry C.; [et al.]. "Individual models of social behavior", *Journal of Personality and Social Psychology* 46(6), jun 84 : 1389-1404.

1179   VALADIER, Paul. "Le terrorisme, défi à la démocratie", *Études*, mai 84 : 581-595.

1180 WELZ, Rainer. *Drogen, Alkohol und Suizid : strukturelle und individuelle Aspekte abweichenden Verhaltens* (Drugs, alcohol and suicide : structural and individual aspects of deviant behaviour). Stuttgart : F. Enke, 1983, 166 p. ill., bibl., ind. [Germany FR]

1181 WHALEN, Jack; FLACKS, Richard. "Echoes of rebellion : the liberated generation grows up", *Journal of Military Sociology* 12(1), 1984 : 61-78. [USA] [Student protest at the University of California]

1182 WODZ, Jacek. "La déviance normale dans le quotidien", *Revue de l'Institut de Sociologie* (1-2), 1984 : 22-34.

1183 WRIGHT, James D.; ROSSI, Peter H.; DALY, Kathleen. *Under the gun : weapons, crime, and violence in America.* New York, NY : Aldine Publishing House, 1983, 360 p. bibl., ind.

1184 ZANARDO, Aldo. "Cultura e violenza politica" (Culture and political violence), *Critica Marxista* 21(5), oct 83 : 23-44. [Italy]

1185 ZEITLIN, June H. "Domestic violence : perspectives from Washington", *Sage Yearbooks in Women's Policy Studies* 7, 1983 : 263-275. [USA]

1186 ZELDIN, R. Shepherd; SAVIN-WILLIAMS, Ritch C.; SMALL, Stephen A. "Dimensions of prosocial behavior in adolescent males", *Journal of Social Psychology* 123(2), aug 84 : 159-168.

13200 CUSTOMS. TRADITIONS
COUTUMES. TRADITIONS

1187 "Humeur de mode", *Autrement. Série Mutations* (62), sep 84 : 1-232. [With contributions by Janet KERR, Brigitte OUVRY-VIAL, Bernard TURLE]

1188 AZOVCEVA, S. G. "Sootnošenie gnoseologičeskih i social'no-èkonomičeskih aspektov vospitatel'no-reguljativnyh funkcij tradicij" (Correlation of the gnoseological and socio-economic aspects of educational regulating functions of traditions), *in : Vzaimodejstvie èkonomičeskoj i social'noj storon žizni obščestva v uslovijah razvitogo socializma* Smolensk, 1983 : 100-107.

1189 BARBICHON, Guy. "Un colloque sur les cultures populaires", *Année Sociologique* 34, 1984 : 233-237. [Nantes, 9-10 juin 1983]

1190 BASTENIER, Albert; [et al.]. *Culture mosaïque : approche sociologique des cultures populaires.* Lyon : Chronique Sociale; Bruxelles : Vie Ouvrière, 1984, 239 p.

1191 COMBS, James E. *Polpop : politics and popular culture in America.* Bowling Green, OH : Bowling Green University Popular Press, 1984, 172 p. bibl.

1192 DE FRIEDEMANN, Nina S. "Perfiles sociales del carnaval en Barranquilla" (Social aspects of carnival in Barranquilla), *Montalbán* 15, 1984 : 127-151. [Colombia]

1193 DEBRAY, Quentin. *L'esprit des moeurs : structures et significations des comportements quotidiens.* Lausanne : Éditions P.-M. Favre, 1983, 185 p. bibl.

1194 GORDON, Pierre. *Les fêtes à travers les âges : leur unité, l'origine du calendrier.* Neuilly-sur-Seine, Hauts-de-Seine . Arma Artis, 1983, 102 p. bibl.

1195 HOBSBAWM, Eric; RANGER, Terence; [eds.]. *The invention of tradition.* Cambridge : Cambridge University Press, 1983, 320 p. ind.

1196 KAPLAN, Steven L.; [ed.]. *Understanding popular culture; Europe from the Middle Ages to the XIXth century.* Berlin; New York, NY... Mouton, 1984, 380 p.

1197 LOMBARD, Jacques. "Fêtes et carnavals du Nord. Rites de survivance ou exaltation communale?", *CLES* (2), sem. 2, 83 : 3-12. [France]

1198 MACKERRAS, Colin. "Folksongs and dances of China's minority nationalities : policy, tradition and professionalization", *Modern China* 10(2), apr 84 : 187-226.

1199 NAKAGAWA, Hideki. "Ryuko to personal influence : taishu sosa no kanousei" (Fashion and personal influence : possibility of mass manipulation), *Sociologicus* 7, 1984 : 79-90.

1200 OSIEL, Mark. "O debate atual sobre a cultura popular" (Current debate on popular culture), *Novos Estudos CEBRAP* 2(3), nov 83 : 16-24. [Brazil]

1201 OSIEL, Mark J. "Going to the people : popular culture and the intellectuals in Brazil", *Archives Européennes de Sociologie* 25(2), 1984 : 245-275.

1202 PIOTROWSKI, Marcin. "Zespoły folklorystyczne jako forma aktywności kulturalnej mieszkańców wsi" (Folk groups as a form of rural population's cultural activity), *Roczniki Socjologii Wsi* 18, 1980-81 : 123-128.

1203 POLLAK-ELTZ, Angelina. "Folklore y cultura en los pueblos negros de Yaracuy" (Folklore and culture of Yaracuy Black peoples), *Montalbán* 15, 1984 : 23-125.

1204 SOCIÉTÉ D'ETHNOLOGIE FRANÇAISE; SOCIÉTÉ FRANÇAISE DE SOCIOLOGIE. *Les cultures populaires : introductions et synthèses; colloque tenu à l'Université de Nantes, 9-10 juin 1983.* Paris : SEF, SFS, 1984, 112 p.

1205 VIKTORIN, V. M. "Obyčai i zakon kak reguljatory dejatel'nosti" (Customs and laws as the activity regulators), *Nekotorye Filosofskie Problemy Gosudarstva i Prava* (4), 1983 : 65-80.

1206   VLASOVA, V. B. "Tradicija kak forma preemstvennosti kul'tury" (Tradition as a form of
        the continuity of culture), *in : Kul'tura i civilizacija. Sbornik* Moskva, 1984 : 123-139.
1207   WEBER, Silke. "Política e educação o movimento de cultura popular no Recife" (Politics
        and education : the popular culture movement of Recife), *Dados* 27(2), 1984 : 233-262.
1208   ZOC, V. A.; [ed.]. *Tradicii, obrjady, sovremennost'* (Traditions, rites, contemporary era).
        Kiev : Politizdat Kieva, 1983, 292 p.

13300   ETHICS. MORALS
ÉTHIQUE. MORALE

1209   ARDIGÒ, Achille. "Dimensioni etiche, trasformazioni sociali e problemi della democrazia"
        (Ethical dimensions, social transformations and problems of democracy), *Sociologia* 18(3),
        sep-dec 84 : 3-22.
1210   BROUGHTON, John M. "Women's rationality and men's virtues : a critique of gender
        dualism in Gilligan's theory of moral development", *Social Research* 50(3), 1983 : 597-542.
1211   FINNIS, John. *Fundamentals of ethics.* Oxford : Clarendon Press, 1983, x-163 p. bibl., ind.
1212   FONSECA, Claudia. "La violence et la rumeur : le code d'honneur dans un bidonville
        brésilien", *Temps Modernes* 40(455), jun 84 : 2193-2235.
1213   FUMUNI, Bikuri. "Les textes d'éthique ou de morale africaine au Zaïre : de 1970 à nos
        jours", *Zaïre-Afrique* 24(184), apr 84 : 197-206.
1214   GREER, J. E. "Moral cultures in Northern Ireland", *Journal of Social Psychology* 123(1),
        jun 84 : 63-70. [Between Roman Catholics and Protestants]
1215   HARU, Terry T. "Moral obligation and conceptions of world hunger : on the need to
        justify correct action", *Journal of Applied Behavioral Science* 20(4), 1984 : 363-382.
1216   HELIN, E.; KELLENS, G. "Quételet, la morale et la statistique", *Déviance et Société* 8(1),
        mar 84 : 1-12. [Belgique]
1217   KATASE, Kazuo. "Dotoku teki shakai-ka eno ninchi hattatsu ron teki approach jyosetsu :
        L. Kohlberg ni okeru 'hattatsu' no ronri" (The cognitive-developmental approach to
        moral socialization : an introductory essay), *Bunka* 48(1-2), 1984 : 1-20.
1218   KĘDELSKI, Mieczysław. *Szacowanie relacji między umieralnością i trwaniem zycia a środowiskiem
        społeczno-ekonomicznym w Polsce* (Estimation of the relations between morality, life
        expectancy and socio-economic environment in Poland). Warszawa : Szkoła Główna
        Planowania i Statystyki, 1983, 154 p.
1219   LYONS, David. *Ethics and the rule of law.* Cambridge : University of Cambridge, 1984, x-229 p.
1220   MURPHY, Peter. "Moralities, rule choice, and the universal legislator", *Social Research*
        50(4), 1983 : 757-801.
1221   MUSGRAVE, P. W. "The moral values of some Australian adolescents : a report and
        discussion", *Australian and New Zealand Journal of Sociology* 20(2), jul 84 : 197-217.
1222   NUMATA, Kenya. "Shumo dantai narabi ni shin-shukyo kyodan ni okeru kazoku rinri"
        (The family ethics of ethical society and new religions), *St. Andrew's University Sociological
        Review* 18(2), 1984 : 63-92.
1223   ROTH, Guenther. "Maz Weber's ethics and the peace movement today", *Theory and Society*
        13(4), jul 84 : 491-511.
1224   SJOBERG, Gideon; VAUGHAN, Ted R.; SJOBERG, Andrée F.; [eds.]. "Ethics, values,
        and human rights : 1984", *Journal of Applied Behavioral Science* 20(4), 1984 : 311-489.
1225   SJOBERG, Gideon; VAUGHAN, Ted R.; SJOBERG, Andrée F. "Morals and Applied
        Behavioral research : a prefatory essay", *Journal of Applied Behavioral Science* 20(4),
        1984 : 311-321.
1226   SMITH, Dennis. "Morality and method in the work of Barrington Moore", *Theory and
        Society* 13(2), mar 84 : 151-176.
1227   SOSA, Nicolás M. "Ética y Ciencia : la responsabilidad del científico" (Ethics and science :
        the scientist's responsibility), *RS Cuadernos de Realidades Sociales* (23-24), jan 84 : 5-20.
1228   STER, Joze. "Kriza morala" (Moral crisis), *Teorija in Praksa* 21(4), apr 84 : 363-376. [Yugoslavia]
1229   VAN DER LINDEN, Harry. "Marx and morality : an impossible synthesis?", *Theory and
        Society* 13(1), jan 84 : 119-135.
1230   WAISMANN, Friedrich. *Wille und Motiv : zwei Abhandlungen über Ethik und Handlungstheorie*
        (Will and motive : two essays on ethics and action theory. Ed. by Joachim Schulte).
        Stuttgart : Reclam, 1983, 195 p. bibl.

13400   LAW. REGULATION
LOI. RÉGLEMENTATION

1231   "Dénonciation (La)", *Actes de la Recherche en Sciences Sociales* 51, mar 84 : 3-79.

1232 BEGAUX-FRANCOTTE, Colette. "Quelques particularités du droit pénal soviétique : le houliganisme", *Revue des Pays de l'Est* 25(1), 1984 : 97-144.

1233 BOASSO, Camilo A. "Derecho y Sociedad" (Law and Society), *SOCIOLOGICA — Revista Argentina de Ciencias Sociales* 9, 1984 : 23-36.

1234 BREUER, Stefan. *Sozialgeschichte des Naturrechts* (Social history of natural law). Opladen : Westdeutscher Verlag, 1983, vi-702 p. bibl.

1235 CLARK, Malcolm. *The legal enterprise : questions in the philosophy of law*. Baltimore, MD : the Author, 1984, viii-299 p. bibl., ind.

1236 FARIA, José Eduardo. *Sociologia jurídica : (crise do direito e práxis política)* (Sociology of law : (crisis of law and political praxis)). Rio de Janeiro : Forense, 1984, xii-194 p. bibl.

1237 FAUGERON, Claude; JAKUBOWICZ, Patrick. "Les magistrats et la loi pénale", *Revue Française de Sociologie* 25(4), oct-dec 84 : 658-683.

1238 GEDDERT, Heinrich. *Recht und Moral : zum Sinn eines alten Problems* (Law and morals : to the meaning of an old problem). Berlin : Duncker und Humblot, 1984, 339 p. bibl., ind.

1239 GORDON, Robert J.; MEGGITT, Mervyn J. *Law and order in the New Guinea highlands : encounters with Enga*. Hanover, NH : University Press of New England, 1984, 266 p. bibl., ind.

1240 GREČIN, A. S. "Opyt sociologičeskogo izučenija pravosoznanija" (An essay of sociological study on legal consciousness), *Sociologičeskie Issledovanija (Moskva)* (2), 1983 : 121-126.

1241 GRIFFITHS, J. "Heeft de rechtssociologie een toegevoegde waarde?" (Has the sociology of law an admitted value?), *Mens en Maatschappij* 59(1), jan 84 : 82-97.

1242 HERZOG, Felix. "La ballade d'un vieil habit rapiécé. Sur l'histoire de la réforme du droit pénal allemand", *Déviance et Société* 8(3), sep 84 : 233-250.

1243 HUND, John. "Legal and sociological approaches to indigenous law in South Africa", *Social Dynamics* 8(1), jun 82 : 29-40.

1244 IRELAND, P. W. "The rise of the limited liability company", *International Journal of the Sociology of Law* 12(3), aug 84 : 239-260.

1245 KAY, Geoffrey; MOTT, James. "Notes on the law of capital", *International Journal of the Sociology of Law* 12(3), aug 84 : 261-270.

1246 KISSLER, Leo. *Recht und Gesellschaft : Einführung in die Rechtssoziologie* (Law and society : introduction to the sociology of law). Opladen : Leske + Budrich, 1984, 167 p. bibl., ind.

1247 KISSLER, Leo. *Rechtssoziologie für die Rechtspraxis* (Sociology of law for the practice of law). Neuwied : Luchterhand, 1984, ix-130 p. bibl.

1248 KRAWIETZ, Werner. *Recht als Regelsystem* (Law as rule system). Wiesbaden : F. Steiner, 1984, xix-231 p. bibl., ind.

1249 KYNTÄJÄ, Timo. *Oikeussosiologia* (Sociology of law). Porvoo : Söderström, 1983, 340 p. ill., bibl.

1250 LE ROY, Étienne. "Legal paradigm and legal discourse : the case of the laws of French-speaking Black Africa", *International Journal of the Sociology of Law* 12(1), feb 84 : 1-22. [Original translation by Iain STEWART]

1251 LEVI, Michael. "Giving creditors the business : the criminal law in inaction", *International Journal of the Sociology of Law* 12(3), aug 84 : 321-333.

1252 MACHAN, Tibor R.; JOHNSON, M. Bruce; [eds.]. *Rights and regulation : ethical, political, and economic issues*. San Francisco, CA : Pacific Institute for Public Policy; Cambridge, MA : Harper and Row, Ballinger, 1983, xxv-309 p.

1253 O'MALLEY, Pat. "Trends in the sociology of the Australian legal order", *Journal of Law and Society* 11(1), spr 84 : 91-103.

1254 PAUCHET, Catherine. "Justice pénale et politique criminelle en Albanie", *Archives de Politique Criminelle* (7), 84 : 243-261.

1255 PECES-BARBA MARTÍNEZ, Gregorio. *Introduction to the philosophy of law*. Madrid : Debate, 1983, 370 p. bibl., ind.

1256 RÁCZ, Attila. "A jog forrásai a szocialista országokban" (Sources of law in socialist countries), *Állam-és Jogtudomány* 27(1), 1984 : 53-73.

1257 ROBERT, Philippe. *La question pénale*. Genève : Droz, 1984, 249 p. bibl.

1258 ROSENFIELD, Denis L. *Politique et liberté : une étude sur la structure logique de la philosophie du droit de Hegel*. Paris : Aubier, 1984, 342 p. bibl.

1259 RULE, James B. "Law and strategy in sociological explanation", *Archives Européennes de Sociologie* 25(1), 1984 : 167-182.

1260 SHARLET, Robert; BEIRNE, Piers. "In search of Vyshinsky : the paradox of law and terror", *International Journal of the Sociology of Law* 12(2), mai 84 : 153-177. [USSR]

1261 SHARMA, Ram Avtar; [ed.]. *Justice and social order in India*. Delhi : Intellectual, 1984, xv-432 p.

1262 TEUBNER, Gunther. "After legal instrumentalism? Strategic models of post-regulatory law", *International Journal of the Sociology of Law* 12(4), nov 84 : 375-400.

1263   VOGLER, Richard. "The law as a nuclear-free zone : legality and the peace movement", *International Journal of the Sociology of Law* 12(2), mai 84 : 195-203.

13500   MAGIC. MYTHOLOGY. RELIGION
MAGIE. MYTHOLOGIE. RELIGION

13510   Religion. Sociology of religion
Religion. Sociologie religieuse

1264   "Aspects de la sociologie de la religion aux Pays Bas", *Social Compass* 30(4), 1983 : 398-524. [With contributions by Walter GODDIJN, H. D. DE LOOR, Leo SPRUIT, Martien VAN HEMERT, Gerard VAN TILLO]

1265   "Rationalisme et religions", *Raison Présente* (72), trim. 4, 84 : 3-165. [With contributions by Jean BOUSSINESQ, Joël MARTINE, Claude H. BRETEAU, Nello ZAGNOLI, Marion AUBREE, Maxime RODINSON]

1266   "Religion (La) aux Etats-Unis", *Conscience et Liberté* (26), sem. 2, 83 : 69-96. [With contributions by E. S. GAUSTAD, J. R. WOOD, G. M. ROSS, R. W. NIXON, M. A. TYNER, P. LANARES, A. J. MENANDEZ]

1267   "Religion et politique dans la culture française", *Parole et Société* 9(3-4), 1983 : 145-296. [With contributions by René REMOND, Jean CARBONNIER, Guy MICHELAT, Michel SIMON, Jean-Paul WILLAIME]

1268   "Religion, éthique et théorie sociologique. Bilan et perspectives", *Archives de Sciences Sociales des Religions* 57(2), apr-jun 84 : 181-182. [Colloque international tenu à l'Université Catholique de Louvain, Louvain-la-Neuve, 8-10 décembre 1983]

1269   "Secularization patterns and the Westward spread of the Welfare State, 1883-1983 : two dialogues about how and why Britain, the Netherlands, and the United States have differed", *Comparative Social Research* 6, 83 : 3-65. [With contributions by Richard K. FENN, John T. S. MADELEY]

1270   "Symposium on scholarship and sponsorship", *Sociological Analysis* 44(3), 1983 : 177-225. [In sociology of religion]

1271   "Symposium on the work of Guy E. Swanson", *Sociological Analysis* 45(3), 1984 : 177-222. [A neo-Durkheimian contemporary American sociologist of religion]

1272   "Symposium on the work of Harvey Cox", *Sociological Analysis* 45(2), 1984 : 77-113. [American contemporary sociologist of religion]

1273   "Vie (La) religieuse en Hongrie", *Conscience et Liberté* (28), 84 : 44-134.

1274   "Women and religion", *Signs* 9(1), aut 83 : 1-58. [With contributions by P. Steven SANGREN, Mary Ellen ROSS, Cheryl Lynn ROSS, David HOLMBERG; see also pp. 59-72 by Gayle Graham YATES]

1275   AGARWAL, G. K. "Role of religion in India's economic development", *Indian Journal of Social Research* 25(1), apr 84 : 79-84.

1276   AUGER, Iván. *Estados Unidos : el renacimiento de la religión civil* (The revival of civil religion in the United States). Santiago de Chile : FLACSO, 1984, 35 p.

1277   AZRIA, Régine; ABBRUZZESE, Salvatore; [et al.]. "Bulletin bibliographique", *Archives de Sciences Sociales des Religions* 56(2), oct-dec 83 : 199-326. [Périodiques et ouvrages récents de sociologie des religions]

1278   BAINBRIDGE, William Sims; STARK, Rodney. "Formal explanation of religion : a progress report", *Sociological Analysis* 45(2), 1984 : 145-158.

1279   BELLAH, Robert N. "La religion civile aux États-Unis", *Débat* (30), mai 84 : 95-111.

1280   BERTRAND, Michèle. "Symposium 'Psychanalyse et sciences sociales des religions'", *Archives de Sciences Sociales des Religions* 57(2), apr-jun 84 : 177-179. [Paris, 7-9 décembre 1983]

1281   BURGALASSI, Silvano; GIUZZARDI, Gustavo; [eds.]. *Il fattore religione nella società contemporanea* (The religious factor in contemporary society). Milano : Franco Angeli, 1983, 240 p. ill., bibl.

1282   CARROLL, Terrance G. "Secularization and States of modernity", *World Politics* 36(3), apr 84 : 362-382.

1283   COLOMER, Fernando. "Religión y crítica religiosa en el pensamiento de E. Levinas" (Religion and religious critics in E. Levinas' thought), *RS Cuadernos de Realidades Sociales* (23-24), jan 84 : 169-182.

1284   DUMAIS, Alfred. "Théoriser la religion : expliquer ou comprendre", *Archives de Sciences Sociales des Religions* 58(1), jul-sep 84 : 53-65.

1285   EARHART, H. Byron. *Religions of Japan : many traditions within one.* San Francisco, CA : Harper and Row, 1984, 160 p. bibl., ind.

1286   FLOWERS, Ronald Bruce. *Religion in strange times : the 1960s and 1970s.* Macon, GA : Mercer University Press, 1984, 275 p. bibl., ind. [USA]

1287   FOJGEL', A. M. "Social'nye korni religii : ih priroda i mehanizm funkcionirovanija" (Social roots of religion : their nature and mechanism of functioning), *in : Problemy obščestvennogo soznanija* Tomsk, 1983 : 105-122.

1288   FUKADA, Hiroshi. "J. S. Mill ni okeru shakaikagaku to shukyo" (J. S. Mill's reconciliation of social science and religion), *Studies in Humanities and Sciences* 29, 1984 : 101-118.

1289   GAUCHET, Marcel. "Fin de la religion?", *Débat* (28), jan 84 : 155-175.

1290   HADDEN, Jeffrey K.; LONG, Theodore E.; [eds.]. *Religion and religiosity in America : studies in honor of Joseph H. Fichter.* New York, NY : Crossroad, 1983, 192 p.

1291   HAND, Carl M.; VAN LIERE, Kent D. "Religion, mastery-over-nature, and environmental concern", *Social Forces* 63(2), dec 84 : 555-570.

1292   HERVIEU-LEGER, Danièle. "Les sociologues et le christianisme", *Projet* (183), mar 84 : 331-347. [France]

1293   HINNELS, John R.; [ed.]. *The Penguin dictionary of religions.* Harmondsworth, IL : Penguin, 1984, 550 p. bibl., ind.

1294   KENNEDY, Richard. *The dictionary of beliefs : an illustrated guide to world religions and beliefs.* s.l., Sussex : Ward Lock Educational, 1984, 256 p. ill., bibl.

1295   KOŽURIN, Ja. Ja.; [ed.]. *Social'no-filosofskie aspekty kritiki religii* (Socio-philosophical aspects of critics of the religion). Leningrad : Gosudarstvennyj Muzej Istorii, Religii i Ateizma, 1982, 300 p.

1296   KRZEPKOWSKI, Stanisław. "Socjologia europejska wobec religii : Max Weber i Emil Durkheim" (European sociology against religion : Max Weber and Emile Durkheim), *Człowiek i Światopoglad* 3, 1984 : 50-59.

1297   LANE, Dermot A. *Foundations for a social theology : praxis, process and salvation.* New York, NY : Paulist Press, 1984, 192 p. bibl., ind.

1298   LANZETTI, Clemente. "Sociologia della religione" (Sociology of religion), *Studi di Sociologia* 22(3), jul-sep 84 : 261-270.

1299   LIEBMAN, Charles S.; DON-YEHIYA, Eliezer. "The dilemma of reconciling traditional culture and political needs : civil religion in Israel", *Comparative Politics* 16(1), oct 83 : 53-66.

1300   LIPSITZ, George. "'The drum major instinct' : American religion since 1945", *Telos* (58), wint 84 : 95-107.

1301   MCEDLOV, M. P. "O sovremennyh processah v religii" (Current processes in religion), *Voprosy Filosofii* 37(2), feb 84 : 141-155.

1302   MINERBI BELGRADO, Anna. *Paura e ignoranza : studio sulla teoria della religione in d'Holbach* (Fear and ignorance : study on d'Holbach's theory of religion). Firenze : L. S. Olschki, 1983, 275 p. bibl., ind.

1303   MOLTMANN, Jürgen. *Politische Theologie, politische Ethik* (Political theology, political ethics). München : Kaiser; Mainz : Grünewald, 1984, 195-1 p. bibl.

1304   MOSHER, William D.; HENDERSHOT, Gerry E. "Religion and fertility : a replication", *Demography* 21(2), mai 84 : 185-191. [USA]

1305   NIKOL'SKIJ, L. B. "Religija i jazyk v stranah zarubežnogo vostoka" (Religion and language in Eastern countries), *Narody Azii i Afriki* (3), 1984 : 35-44.

1306   O'TOOLE, Roger. *Religion : classic sociological approaches.* Toronto, ON; New York, NY : McGraw-Hill Ryerson, 1984, 268 p. bibl., ind.

1307   PRUDHOMME, Claude. *Histoire religieuse de la Réunion.* Paris : Karthala, 1984, 369 p. bibl., cartes.

1308   ROBERTS, Keith A. *Religion in sociological perspective.* Homewood, IL : Dorsey Press, 1984, xv-450 p. ill., bibl., ind.

1309   SEGUNDO, Juan-Luis. "Les deux théologies de la libération en Amérique latine", *Études*, sep 84 : 149-161.

1310   SÉGUY, Jean. "Le temps des bilans? Dictionnaire et encyclopédies", *Archives de Sciences Sociales des Religions* 58(2), oct-dec 84 : 205-210.

1311   SMITH, Michael E. "The special place of religion in the Constitution", *Supreme Court Review*, 1983 : 83-123. [USA]

1312   SWATOS, William H. Jr. "Enchantment and disenchantment in modernity : the significance of 'religion' as a sociological category", *Sociological Analysis* 44(4), 1983 : 321-337.

1313   UTSUNOMIYA, Teruo. "Genshogakuteki shakaigaku to sono shukyo ron" (Phenomenological sociology and its theory of religion), *Hokkaido University Reports on Cultural Science* 21, 1984 : 1-22.

1314   WALLIS, Roy; BRUCE, Steve. "The Stark-Bainbridge theory of religion : a critical analysis and counter proposals", *Sociological Analysis* 45(1), 1984 : 11-27.

1315   WHALING, Frank; [ed.]. *Contemporary approaches to the study of religion. I. The humanities. II. The social sciences.* Berlin; New York, NY... s.n., 1984, 520; 318 p.

13520   Magic. Primitive religion
Magie. Religion primitive

1316   DEAN, John. "Magic and mystery in the fiction of Ursula K. Le Guin", *Social Science Information / Information sur les Sciences Sociales* 23(1), 1984 : 143-153.
1317   DOVE, Janine; MARÇAIS, Dominique. "The senses and the hidden meaning", *Social Science Information / Information sur les Sciences Sociales* 23(1), 1984 : 195-210.
1318   HOLMBERG, David. "Shamanic soundings : femaleness in the Tamang ritual structure", *Signs* 9(1), aut 83 . 40-58. [Nepal]
1319   MÜNSTER, Arno. "Messianisme juif et pensée utopique dans l'oeuvre d'Ernest Bloch", *Archives de Sciences Sociales des Religions* 57(1), jan-mar 84 : 15-28.
1320   O'KEEFE, Daniel Lawrence. *Stolen lightning : the social theory of magic.* New York, NY : Vintage Books, 1983, xxii-598 p.
1321   SACHS, Viola. "The occult language and scripture of the New World", *Social Science Information / Information sur les Sciences Sociales* 23(1), 1984 : 129-141.
1322   VIVAN, Itala. "The scar in the letter : an eye into the occult in Hawthorne's text", *Social Science Information / Information sur les Sciences Sociales* 23(1), 1984 : 155-193. [Colloquium on the 'Uses of the occult, magic and witchcraft in American culture', held at the Maison des Sciences de l'Homme, Paris, in March 1982]

13530   Buddhism. Christianity
Bouddhisme. Christianisme

1323   "Catholicisme (Le) en Corée", *Revue de Corée* 16(2), sum 84 : 3-62 & 71-88. [With contributions by Sok-U CH'OE, Ki-Bok CH'OE, Kwang CHO, Oik-Hui KIM]
1324   "Islam : a symposium on a contemporary resurgence", *Seminar* (290), oct 83 : 11-48. [With contributions by Syed BARAKAT AHMED, A. R. SAIYED, A. H. H. ABIDI, Ashgar Ali ENGINEER, Godfrey JANSEN]
1325   "Islam, economy and political power : the Indonesian case", *Social Compass* 31(1), 1984 : 2-89. [With contributions by Cees VAN DIJK, Ernst UTRECHT, Susan RODGERS, Hiroko HORIKOSHI]
1326   "Resettlement (The) of Soviet Jews in Australia : a note", *Soviet Jewish Affairs* 14(1), feb 84 : 47-55.
1327   AHMAD, Imtiaz; [ed.]. *Modernization and social change among Muslims in India.* New Delhi : Manohar, 1983, xlix-281 p.
1328   AHMED, Akbar S. "Islam and the district paradigm : emergent trends in contemporary Muslim society", *Contributions to Indian Sociology* 17(2), jul-dec 83 : 155-183.
1329   AITKEN, Robert. *The mind of clover : essays in Zen Buddhist ethics.* San Francisco, CA : North Point Press, 1984, xiv-199 p. bibl.
1330   AOI, Kazuo. "Zen to shakaigaku" (Zen and sociology), *Shakaigaku Hyoron* 35(3), 1984 : 2-13.
1331   AUZA, Néstor T. *Los católicos argentinos : su experiencia política y social* (Argentine Catholics : their political and social experience). Buenos Aires : Claretiana, 1984, 128 p.
1332   AZRIA, Régine. "Réflexions autour d'un colloque", *Archives de Sciences Sociales des Religions* 57(2), apr-jun 84 : 183-188. [Colloque national 'Judaïsme, judaïcités : récits, narrations, actes de langage' (Paris, 23-26 janvier 1984)]
1333   BÄTZ, Kurt. *Judentum : Wege und Stationen seiner Geschichte* (Judaism : ways and phases of its history). Stuttgart : Calwer Verlag, 1984, 173 p. ill., maps, bibl., ind.
1334   BAUBÉROT, Jean. "Le protestantisme français et son historiographie", *Archives de Sciences Sociales des Religions* 58(2), oct-dec 84 : 175-186.
1335   BECKER, George. "Pietism and science : a critique of Robert K. Merton's hypothesis", *American Journal of Sociology* 89(5), mar 84 : 1065-1090.
1336   BEER, Patrice de. "L'Islam en Malaisie", *Afrique et Asie Modernes* (139), wint 84 : 43-55.
1337   BERQUE, Jacques. *L'Islam au temps du monde.* Paris : Sindbad, 1984, 277 p.
1338   BIERSCHENK, Thomas. *Religion and political structure : remarks on Ibadism in Oman and the Mzab (Algeria).* Bielefeld : University of Bielefeld, Faculty of Sociology, Sociology of Development Research Centre, 1983, 27 p. bibl.
1339   BOCIURKIW, Bohdan R. "The changing Soviet image of Islam", *Search* 4(3-4), wint 83 : 59-80.
1340   BORGGREFE, Friedhelm. *Polens Protestanten zwischen rotem Bruder und schwarzer Schwester* (Poland's protestants between red brother and black sister). Kassel : Verlag des Gustav-Adolf-Werkes; Erlangen : Verlag der Evangelisch-Lutheranischen Mission, 1983, 144-8 p. ill.
1341   BOWEN, Kurt Derek. *Protestants in a Catholic state : Ireland's privileged minority.* Kingston : McGill-Queen's University Press; Dublin... Gill and Macmillan, 1983, x-237 p. bibl., ind.

1342   BRECHON, Pierre; DENNI, Bernard. *Attitudes religieuses et politiques des catholiques pratiquants.*
       Enquête par questionnaire dans huit assemblées dominicales grenobloises. Grenoble : BDSP-Institut
       d'Études Politiques, 1982, 204 p. CR: Michelat, Guy, *Archives de Sciences Sociales des*
       Religions, 57(1), jan-mar 84 : 141-147. [France]
1343   BUBIS, Gerald B. "Strengthening of the Jewish family as an instrument of Jewish
       continuity", *Journal of Jewish Communal Service* 59(4), sum 83 : 306-317.
1344   BUCKLEY, Anthony D. "Walls within walls : religion and rough behavior in an Ulster
       community", *Sociology (London)* 18(1), feb 84 : 19-32.
1345   BURGHART, Richard. "For a sociology of Indias : an intracultural approach to the study
       of Hindu society", *Contributions to Indian Sociology* 17(2), jul-dec 83 : 275-299.
1346   CARROLL, Lucy. "The Muslim family in India : law, custom, and empirical research",
       Contributions to Indian Sociology 17(2), jul-dec 83 : 205-222.
1347   CHANDON-MOET, Bernard. "Christianisme et différenciation ethnique : les catholiques
       de la Basse-Betsiboka (Madagascar)", *Archives de Sciences Sociales des Religions* 57(1),
       jan-mar 84 : 103-113.
1348   CIPRIANI, Roberto. "Religion and politics. The Italian case : diffused religion", *Archives*
       de Sciences Sociales des Religions 58(1), jul-sep 84 : 29-51. [Catholic religion]
1349   COLORNI, Vittore. *Judaica minora : saggi sulla storia dell'ebraismo italiano dall'antichità all'età*
       moderna (Jewish minority : essays on Italian Jewish history from Antiquity to the modern
       age). Milano, A. Giuffrè, 1983, xii-825-5 p. bibl., ill.
1350   DARCZEWSKA, Krystyna. "O podstawowych cechach społecznych katolicyzmu w
       Polsce" (On basic social attributes of Catholicism in Poland), *Problemy Marksizmu-*
       Leninizmu 2, 1984 : 270-279.
1351   DAS, Veena. "For a folk-theology and theological anthropology of Islam", *Contributions to*
       Indian Sociology 18(2), jul-dec 84 : 293-300. [India]
1352   DASSETTO, Felice; BASTENIER, Albert. *L'Islam transplanté : vie et organisation des minorités*
       musulmanes de Belgique. Berchem : EPO; Bruxelles : Vie Ouvrière, 1984, 200 p. bibl.
1353   DONEGANI, Jean-Marie. "L'appartenance au catholicisme français. Point de vue
       sociologique", *Revue Française de Science Politique* 34(2), apr 84 : 197-228.
1354   DU PASQUIER, Roger. *Découverte de l'Islam.* Genève : Éditions des Trois Continents;
       Paris : Éditions du Seuil, 1984, 177 p. ind.
1355   DUMONT, Paul. "L'Islam en Turquie, facteur de renouveau?", *Temps Modernes* 41(456-457),
       aug 84 : 352-376.
1356   ELBOUDRARI, Hassan. "Islams, politiques et idéologies au Maghreb : études récentes",
       Archives de Sciences Sociales des Religions 56(2), dec 83 : 177-189.
1358   FALLDING, Harold. "How Christian can a sociology be?", *Canadian Journal of Sociology /*
       Cahiers Canadiens de Sociologie 9(1), wint 84 : 1-19.
1359   FINESTEIN, Israel. "Jews in British society; a review article", *Jewish Journal of Sociology*
       26(1), jun 84 : 53-59. [Since the seventeenth century]
1360   FREND, W. H. C. *The rise of Christianity.* Philadelphia, PA : Fortress Press, 1984, 1042 p.
       bibl., ind.
1361   FRY, C. George; [et al.]. *Great Asian religions.* Grand Rapids, MI : Baker Book House,
       1984, 227 p. ill., bibl., ind.
1362   FUJII, Masao. "Founder worship in Kamakura Buddhism", *Senri Ethnological Studies* 11,
       1984 : 155-167.
1363   GLUCKLICH, Ariel. "Karma and pollution in Hindu dharma : distinguishing law from
       nature", *Contributions to Indian Sociology* 17(1), jan-jul 84 : 25-43. [India]
1364   GUTIÉRREZ ESTÉVEZ, Manuel. "En torno al estudio comparativo de la pluralidad
       católica" (On the comparative study of the catholic plurality), *Revista Española de*
       Investigaciones Sociológicas 27, jul-sep 84 : 137-174. [Peru; Mexico; Spain]
1365   HAYES, Louis D. "Islamization and education in Pakistan", *Asia Pacific Community* (23),
       wint 84 : 96-105.
1366   HORNSBY-SMITH, M. P.; LEE, Raymond N.; REILLY, Peter A. "Social and religious
       change in four English Roman Catholic parishes", *Sociology (London)* 18(3), aug 84 : 353-365.
1367   IRVING, Thomas Ballantine. *Islam resurgent : the Islamic world today.* Lahore : Suhail
       Academy, 1983, 300 p. ill.; maps.
1368   KELLY, James R. "Catholicism and modern memory : some sociological reflections on the
       symbolic foundations of the rhetorical force of the pastoral letter, 'The challenge of
       peace'", *Sociological Analysis* 45(2), 1984 : 131-144. [USA]
1369   KEPEL, Gilles. "L'Egypte aujourd'hui : mouvement islamiste et société savante", *Annales-*
       Économies, Sociétés, Civilisations 39(4), aug 84 : 667-680.
1370   KOLACK, Shirley. "A note on the Georgian Jews of Tbilisi", *Jewish Journal of Sociology*
       26(1), jun 84 : 47-52. [USSR]

1371 KRIEGEL, Annie. *Réflexion sur les questions juives.* Paris : Hachette, 1984, 633 p.

1372 LADOR-LEDERER, Joseph. "The terms of Jewry's international identity", *Jerusalem Journal of International Relations* 6(4), 83 : 30-46.

1373 LANGLOIS, Claude. "Le catholicisme au féminin", *Archives de Sciences Sociales des Religions* 57(1), jan-mar 84 : 29-53. [France, XIXe s.]

1374 LEVIN, Nora. "Soviet Jewish immigrants in Philadephia, 1972-82", *Soviet Jewish Affairs* 14(3), nov 84 : 15-29.

1375 LEWIS, Bernard. *The Jews of Islam.* Princeton, NJ : Princeton University Press, 1984, 240 p. ind.

1376 MACEOIN, Denis; AL-SHAHI, Ahmed; [eds.]. *Islam in the modern world.* New York, NY : St. Martin's Press; London : Croom Helm, 1983, xv-148 p. ind.

1377 MERTON, Robert K. "The fallacy of the latest word : the case of 'pietism and science' ", *American Journal of Sociology* 89(5), mar 84 : 1091-1121.

1378 MILLER, Jack; [ed.]. *Jews in Soviet culture.* New Brunswick, NJ : Transaction Books, 1983, 325 p. ind.

1379 MINAULT, Gail. "Some reflections on Islamic revivalism vs. assimilation among Muslims in India", *Contributions to Indian Sociology* 18(2), jul-dec 84 : 301-305.

1380 MONTERO GARCÍA, Feliciano. *El primer catolicismo social y la Rerum novarum en España, 1889-1902* (The early social Catholicism and 'Rerum novarum' in Spain, 1889-1902). Madrid : CSIC, 1983, 495 p. bibl., ind.

1381 MUHIĆ, Fuad. "O muslimanskem nacionalizmu" (Muslim nationalism), *Teorija in Praksa* 21(1-2), feb 84 : 44-54. [Yugoslavia]

1382 NAZIR-ALI, Michael. *Islam, a Christian perspective.* Philadelphia, PA : Westminster Press, 1984, 192 p. ind.

1383 OSCHLIES, Wolf. "The Jews in Bulgaria since 1944", *Soviet Jewish Affairs* 14(2), mai 84 : 41-54.

1384 PIJNENBURG, Bert. "Ketholieken en protestanten in hegendaags Nederland : een herwaardering van de deconfessionalisering" (Catholics and Protestants in today's Netherlands : an assessment of deconfessionalisation), *Sociologische Gids* 31(6), 1984 : 487-506.

1385 PINKUS, Benjamin. *The Soviet government and the Jews, 1948-1967.* Cambridge, Cambridgeshire; New York, NY : Cambridge University Press, 1984, xiv-612 p. ind., bibl.

1386 PRANDI, Carlo. "Le catholicisme italien à l'époque de l'unité : apocalypse et compromis", *Archives de Sciences Sociales des Religions* 58(1), jul-sep 84 : 67-83.

1387 RO'I, Yaacov. "The task of creating the new Soviet man : 'atheistic propaganda' in the soviet muslim areas", *Soviet Studies* 36(1), jan 84 : 25-44.

1388 ROBINSON, Francis. "Islam and Muslim society in South Asia", *Contributions to Indian Sociology* 17(2), jul-dec 83 : 185-203.

1389 ROSEN, Lawrence. *Bargaining for reality : the construction of social relations in a Muslim community.* London; Chicago, IL : University of Chicago Press, 1984, xii-210 p. bibl.

1390 RÜRUP, Reinhard; [ed.]. "Juden in Deutschland zwischen Assimilation und Verfolgung" (The Jews in Germany between assimilation and persecution), *Geschichte und Gesellschaft* 9(3), 1983 : 331-478.

1391 RUTHVEN, Malise. *Islam in the world.* New York, NY : Oxford University Press, 1984, 400 p. bibl.

1392 SCHWARTZ, Michael. *The persistent prejudice : anti-Catholicism in America.* Huntington, IN : Our Sunday Visitor, 1984, 277 p.

1393 SHANKARI, Uma. "Brahmin, king and bhakta in a temple in Tamil Nadu", *Contributions to Indian Sociology* 18(2), jul-dec 84 : 169-187. [India] [Aruḷmiku Tyāgarājasvāmi Kōyil temple dedicated to Shiva]

1394 SHINAR, Pessah. *Essai de bibliographie sélective et annotée sur l'Islam maghrébin contemporain : Maroc, Algérie, Tunisie, Libye : 1830-1978.* Paris : Éditions du Centre National de la Recherche Scientifique, 1983, xxi-506 p. ind., bibl.

1395 SILBERMANN, Alphons. *Was ist jüdischer Geist? Zur Identität der Juden* (What is Jewish spirit? On the identity of Jews). Zürich : Interfrom; Osnabrück : Fromm, 1984, 121 p. bibl.

1396 STEEMAN, Théodore M. "Troeltsch and modern American religion", *Archives de Sciences Sociales des Religions* 58(1), jul-sep 84 : 85-116.

1397 TANALSKI, Dionizy. "Przemiany i perspektywy katolicyzmu w socjalizmie" (Transformations and perspectives of Catholicism in socialism), *Problemy Marksizmu-Leninizmu* 1, 1984 : 100-115.

1398 TOMKA, Miklós. "Társadalmi változás — vallási változás. A mai magyar katolicizmus szerkezeti transzformációi" (Social change — religious change. Structural transformations of Hungarian Catholicism today), *Szociológia* 12(3), 1983 : 253-272.

1399 TRIAUD, Jean-Louis. "Hommes de religion et confréries islamiques dans une société en crise, l'Aïr aux XIX^c et XX^c siècles. Le cas de la Khalwatiyya", *Cahiers d'Études Africaines* 23(3), 1983 : 239-280. [Niger]

1400 WALTZ, Susan E. "The islamist challenge in Tunisia", *Journal of Arab Affairs* 3(1), spr 84 : 99-113.

1401 WILSON, Stephen R. "Becoming a yogi : resocialization and deconditioning as conversion processes", *Sociological Analysis* 45(4), 1984 : 301-314.

1402 WIXMAN, Ronald. "Demographic trends among Soviet Moslems (1959-79)", *Soviet Geography* 25(1), jan 84 : 46-60.

13540   Churches. Religious communities. Sects
Églises. Communautés religieuses. Sectes

1403 ARNOLD, Odile. *Le corps et l'âme : la vie des religieuses au XIXe siècle.* Paris : Éditions du Seuil, 1984, 373-10 p. bibl.

1404 ASCH, Susan. *L'Église du prophète Kimbangu : de ses origines à son rôle actuel au Zaïre, 1921-1981.* Paris : Karthala, 1984, 342 p. bibl., cartes.

1405 ASKEW, Thomas A.; SPELLMAN, Peter W. *The churches and the American experience : ideals and institutions.* Grand Rapids, MI : Baker Book House, 1984, 260 p. ill., bibl., ind.

1406 AUBERY, Pierre. "Immuable et changeante Église, vue des États-Unis", *Temps Modernes* 40(451), feb 84 : 1479-1496.

1407 BECKFORD, James A. "Religious organisation : a survey of some recent publications", *Archives de Sciences Sociales des Religions* 57(1), jan-mar 84 : 83-102.

1408 BUMGARNER, George William; CARROLL, James Elwood. *The flowering of Methodism in western North Carolina.* Charlotte, NC : Commission on Archives and History of the Western North Carolina Conference of the United Methodist Church, 1984, viii-175 p. ill., bibl., ind.

1409 CARLSON, Elwood. "Penetration of a conventional religious hierarchy by media evangelism", *Sociology and Social Research* 68(4), jul 84 : 498-509. [USA]

1410 COFFY, Robert. *L'Église.* Paris : Desclée, 1984, 208 p. bibl.

1411 DÄHN, Horst. "Die Kirchen im Spannungsfeld von Loyalität und Opposition in der DDR" (Churches in GDR between loyalism and opposition), *Deutsche Studien* 22(88), dec 84 : 321-341.

1412 DENZLER, Georg; FABRICIUS, Volker. *Die Kirchen im Dritten Reich : Christen und Nazis Hand in Hand?* (Churches under Third Reich : Christians and Nazis hand in hand?). Frankfurt-am-Main : Fischer Taschenbuch Verlag, 1984. [2 vols.]

1413 FOSTER, Thomas W. "Separation and survival in Amish society", *Sociological Focus* 17(1), jan 84 : 1-15. [USA]

1414 GALENSON, Walter. *The United Brotherhood of Carpenters : the first hundred years.* Cambridge, MA; London : Harvard University Press, 1983, vii-440 p

1415 GREELEY, Andrew M. *Angry Catholic women.* Chicago, IL : Thomas More Press, 1984, 213 p. ill., bibl.

1416 GUZMAN GARCIA, Luis; PUENTE DE GUZMAN, Maria Alicia. "Formation des classes, luttes populaires et discours religieux au Nicaragua", *Social Compass* 30(2-3), 1983 : 211-231.

1417 HALEVI, Ran. *Les loges maçonniques dans la France d'Ancien régime : aux origines de la sociabilité.* Paris : Colin, 1984, 118 p. cartes, bibl.

1418 HEMPTON, David. *Methodism and politics in British society, 1750-1850.* Stanford, CA : Stanford University Press, 1984, 276 p. bibl., ind.

1419 IKOR, Roger. "Les sectes et la liberté", *Revue des Sciences Morales et Politiques* 139(2), 1984 : 235-246. [France]

1420 KELLER, Thomas. "Politique et deuil : le nouvel irrationalisme allemand", *Allemagnes d'Aujourd'hui* (87), mar 84 : 39-54.

1421 KELLEY, Jonathan; MCALLISTER, Ian. "The genesis of conflict : religion and status attainment in Ulster, 1968", *Sociology (London)* 18(2), mai 84 : 171-190.

1422 KOHN, Rachael L. E. "Praising the Lord and penetrating the community : transition and dual leadership functions in a contemporary Hebrew Christian group", *Sociological Analysis* 45(1), 1984 : 29-39.

1423 KRAMER, Fred. "Cult members as victimizers and victims", *Sage Annual Review of Studies in Deviance* 7, 1983 : 169-102.

1424 LAITIN, David D. "Conversion and political change : a study of (Anglican) Christianity and Islam among the Yorubas of Ile-Ife", *Political Anthropology Yearbook* 2, 1983 : 155-188. [Nigeria]

1425   LANGLOIS, Claude. *Le catholicisme au féminin : les congrégations françaises à supérieure générale au XIXᵉ siècle.* Paris : Éditions du Cerf, 1984, 776 p. bibl., ind.
1426   LAUBIER, Patrick de. *La pensée sociale de l'Église catholique : un idéal historique de Léon XIII à Jean Paul II.* Fribourg : Éditions Universitaires, 1984, 212 p. bibl., ind.
1427   MAINWARING, Scott. "The Catholic Church, popular education and political change in Brazil", *Journal of Inter-American Studies and World Affairs* 26(1), feb 84 : 97-124.
1428   MAIR, Nathan H. "The Québec protestant churches and the question of nationalism", *Social Compass* 31(4), 1984 : 379-390.
1429   MAUSS, Armand L. "Sociological perspectives on the Mormon subculture", *Annual Review of Sociology* 10, 1984 : 437-460.
1430   PIERRARD, Pierre. *L'Église et les ouvriers en France : 1840-1940.* Paris : Hachette, 1984, 599 p. bibl., ind.
1431   PIRET, Jean-Marc; DECONCHY, Jean-Pierre. "Le paradigme 'franc-maçonnerie' : émancipation-initiation", *Archives de Sciences Sociales des Religions* 57(2), apr-jun 84 : 169-175.
1432   POULAT, Émile. "Paroisses et communes de France", *Archives de Sciences Sociales des Religions* 56(2), oct-dec 83 : 191-193.
1433   RICHARD, Pablo. "La Iglesia que nace en América central" (Birth of the Church in Central America), *Cristianismo y Sociedad* 22(1), 1984 : 71-94.
1434   SÉGUY, Jean. "Pour une sociologie de l'ordre religieux", *Archives de Sciences Sociales des Religions* 57(1), jan-mar 84 : 55-68.
1435   SINDA, Martial. "L'État africain post-colonial : les forces sociales et les communautés religieuses dans l'État postcolonial en Afrique", *Présence Africaine* (127-128), trim. 3-4, 83 : 240-260.
1436   THADDEN, Rudolf von. "Kirchengeschichte als Gesellschaftsgeschichte. Diskussionsforum" (Church history as history of society. A discussion forum), *Geschichte und Gesellschaft* 9(4), 1983 : 598-614.
1437   TURCOTTE, Paul-André. "Éducation catholique et nationalisme dans l'ensignement secondaire quécécois", *Social Compass* 31(4), 1984 : 365-377.
1438   VARACALLI, Joseph A. *Toward the establishment of liberal Catholicism in America.* Washington, DC : University Press of America, 1983, 326 p. bibl.
1439   YOSHITANI, Hiroya. "Chiho shugen to minzoku shakai -sekido shugen to kannon shinko no jirei" (Regional sect of Shugendo and folk society), *Memoirs of Kanazawa Technical College* 9, 1984 : 69-84.

        13550   **Clergy. Religious authority**
                 Clergé. Autorité religieuse

        13560   **Cults. Rites**
                 Cultes. Rites

1440   DA SILVA, José Ariovaldo. *O movimento litúrgico no Brasil : estudo histórico* (Liturgical movement in Brazil : historical study). Ptrópolis : Vozes, 1983, 399 p. bibl.
1441   EJIMA, Shusaku. "'Sosen suhai' gainen eno shukyo-shakaigaku teki sai-kento" (A re-examination to the concept of 'ancestor cult' in sociology of religion), *Hiroshima Shudo Ronshu* 24(2), 1984 : 379-407.
1442   FERGUSON, Douglas W. "The changing social meanings of sacrifices in Jewish worship : an historical overview", *Sociological Focus* 17(3), aug 84 : 211-221.
1443   HEGLAND, Mary. "Ritual and revolution in Iran", *Political Anthropology Yearbook* 2, 1983 : 75-100.
1444   MORINIS, E. Allan. *Pilgrimage in the Hindu tradition : a case study of West Bengal.* Delhi : Oxford University Press, 1984, viii-346 p.
1445   NELSON, G. K. "Cults and new religions : towards a sociology of religious creativity", *Sociology and Social Research* 68(3), apr 84 : 300-325.
1446   RAJ, Lajpat. "The cult and magic politics in China", *China Report* 20(2), apr 84 : 17-27.
1447   SANGREN, P. Steven. "Female gender in Chinese religious symbols : Kuan Yin, Ma Tsu, and the 'eternal mother'", *Signs* 9(1), aut 83 : 4-25.
1448   SUZUKI, Masataka. "Tsushima, Nii no saishi to sonraku kukan" (Rituals and village cosmology in Nii, Tsushima island), *Nihon Minzokugaku* 151, 1984 : 1-24.

        13570   **Myths. Religious doctrines**
                 Mythes. Doctrines religieuses

1449   AYROOKUZHIEL, A. M. Abraham. *The sacred in popular Hinduism : an empirical study in Chirakkal, north Malabar.* Madras : Christian Literature Society, 1983, x-198 p.

1450   CHAMPION, Françoise. "La 'fable mystique' et la modernité", *Archives de Sciences Sociales des Religions* 58(2), oct-dec 84 : 195-202.

1451   CROIX, Alain. *Les Bretons, la mort et Dieu : de 1600 à nos jours.* Paris : Messidor-Temps Actuels, 1984, 264 p. bibl., ill.

1452   ĐORĐEVIĆ, Dragoljub B. "Religijski simboli" (Religious symbols), *Sociologija* 26(3-4), jul-dec 84 : 305-316. [Yugoslavia]

1453   FERRAROTTI, Franco. "The paradox of the sacred", *International Journal of Sociology* 14(2), 1984 : 2-108. [Translation by the author of his book entitled 'Il paradosso del sacro' (Roma, Laterza, 1983)]

1454   GARELLI, Franco. *Il volto di Dio : l'esperienza del sacro nella società contemporanea* (The God's will : experience of the sacred in contemporary society). Bari : De Donato, 1983, 267 p. bibl. [Italy]

1455   GILLEN, Otto. *Der Mensch in Gottes Hand : religiöse und mystische Erfahrungen unserer Zeit* (The man in God's hand : religious and mystical experiences of our time). Stein-am-Rhein : Christiana-Verlag, 1984, 160 p. ill., bibl.

1456   GITWORTH, Jacques. "Une entreprise de relativisation socio-culturelle", *Archives de Sciences Sociales des Religions* 56(2), oct-dec 83 : 163-168. [À propos du livre Marc AUGÉ, Le génie du paganisme. Paris : Gallimard, 1982, 336 p.]

1457   HERZBERG, Max John. *Myths and their meaning.* Boston, MA : Allyn and Bacon, 1984, ix-357-16 p. ill., bibl., ind.

1458   HINZ, Eike. "Kanjòbal Maya divination : an outline of a native psycho-sociotherapy", *Sociologus* 34(2), 1984 : 162-184.

1459   JACKSON, N. V.; CARTER, P. "The attenuating function of myth in human understanding", *Human Relations* 37(7), jul 84 : 515-533.

1460   LADRIÈRE, Paul. "Le sens du sacré et le métier de sociologue", *Archives de Sciences Sociales des Religions* 57(1), jan-mar 84 : 115-139.

1461   LÖWY, Michaël. "Pour une sociologie de la mystique juive : à propos et autour du 'Sabbataï Sevi' de Gerschom Scholem", *Archives de Sciences Sociales des Religions* 57(1), jan-mar 84 : 5-13.

1462   MIRESCU, Adriana. "Mircea Eliade e il mito come vita spirituale totale" (Mircea Eliade and the myth as total spiritial life), *Critica Sociologica* 69, 1984 : 85-92.

1463   NOWICKA, Ewa. "Sporne problemy w badaniach nad mite" (Controversial problem of the studies on the myth), *Kultura i Społeczeństwo* 28(3), 1984 : 87-101.

1464   STOVER, Ronald G.; HOPE, Christine A. "Monotheism and gender status : a cross-societal study", *Social Forces* 63(2), dec 84 : 335-348.

1465   VIDAL, Daniel. "Un livre deux voix. Figures de la mystique : le dit de Michel de Certeau", *Archives de Sciences Sociales des Religions* 58(2), oct-dec 84 : 187-194.

1466   WALLIS, Roy. *The elementary forms of the new religious life.* London : Routledge and Kegan Paul, 1984, x-156 p. bibl., ind.

1167   WESTLEY, Frances. *The complex forms of the religious life : a Durkheimian view of new religious movements.* Chico, CA : Scholars Press, 1983, 199 p. bibl.

1468   WILSON, Stephen; [ed.]. *Saints and their cults. Studies in religious sociology, folklore and history.* Cambridge; London... Cammbridge University Press, 1983, xii-435 p. ill., maps, bibl.

1469   YOSHITANI, Hiroya. "Noto chiho no kannon reijyo -chiiki teki reijyo no hassei to sanjyusan ka sho seiritsu no shuhen" (Sacred places of the 'Kannon' in the Noto area), *Nihon Minzokugaku* 154, 1984 : 74-90. [Japan]

1470   ZITO, George V. "Toward a sociology of heresy", *Sociological Analysis* 44(2), 1983 : 123-130.

13580   Religious behaviour
Comportement religieux

1471   BAINBRIDGE, William Sims. "Religious insanity in America : the official nineteenth-century theory", *Sociological Analysis* 45(3), 1984 : 223-239.

1472   CHLEWIŃSKI, Zdzisław. "Religijność a neurotyzm i ekstrawersja : badania mieszkańców wsi Zacisze" (Religiousness versus neurotism and extraversion : studies on the inhabitants of Zacisze), *Studia Socjologiczne* 94(3), 1984 : 179-197.

1473   CIUPAK, Edward. *Religijność młodego Polaka* (Religiosity of Polish youth). Warszawa : Książka i Wiedza, 1984, 239 p.

1474   FEATHER, N. T. "Protestant ethic, conservatism, and values", *Journal of Personality and Social Psychology* 46(5), mai 84 : 1132-1141. [Australia]

1475   FURNHAM, A. "The protestant work ethic : a review of the psychological literature", *European Journal of Social Psychology* 14(1), jan-mar 84 : 87-104. [Max Weber's thesis]

1476   FURNHAM, Adrian; MUHIUDEEN, Clare. "The Protestant work ethic in Britain and Malaysia", *Journal of Social Psychology* 122(2), apr 84 : 157-161.

1477 GORDON, David F. "Dying to self : self-control through self-abandonment", *Sociological Analysis* 45(1), 1984 : 41-55. [Process of self-abandonment in two Jesus People groups]

1478 KENT, Stephen A. "Weber, Goethe, and the Nietzschean allusion : capturing the source of the 'iron cage' metaphor", *Sociological Analysis* 44(4), 1983 : 297-319.

1479 MARIAŃSKI, Janusz. "Współzależność postaw wobec religii i postaw godnościowych" (Interdependence of religiosity and personal dignity), *Kultura i Społeczeństwo* 28(3), 1984 : 43-60.

1480 MILLER, Arthur H.; WATTENBERG, Martin P. "Politics from the pulpit : religiosity and the 1980 elections", *Public Opinion Quarterly* 48(1b), spr 84 : 301-317. [USA]

1481 NISHIYAMA, Toshihiko. *Shukyo teki personality no shinrigaku teki kenkyu* (Psychological study of religious personality). Tokyo : Taimeido, 1984, 326 p.

1482 PETERSEN, Larry R.; TAKAYAMA, K. Peter. "Religious commitment and conservatism : toward understanding an elusive relationship", *Sociological Analysis* 45(4), 1984 : 355-369. [USA]

1483 PIWOWARSKI, Władysław. "Przemiany religijności ludowej w środowisku wiejskim" (Evolution of folk religiosity in rural social settings), *Kultura i Społeczeństwo* 28(3), 1984 : 27-41.

1484 STARK, Rodney. "Religion and conformity : reaffirming a 'sociology' of religion", *Sociological Analysis* 45(4), 1984 : 273-282. [USA]

1485 TIER, Akolda M. "Freedom of religion under the Sudan Constitution and laws", *Journal of African Law* 26(2), aut 82 : 133-151.

1486 WHALING, Frank; [ed.]. *The world's religious traditions : current perspectives in religious studies; essays in honour of Wilfred Cantwell Smith.* Edinburgh : T. & T. Clark, 1984, viii-311 p. bibl., ind.

1487 YATES, Gayle Graham. "Spirituality and the American feminist experience", *Signs* 9(1), aut 83 : 59-72.

13590 Church and State. Religious practice
Église et État. Pratique religieuse

1488 "Pratiques de la religion catholique : permanences et détachements", *Opinion Publique* (1), 1984 : 186-198. [France]

1489 ARKOUN, Mohammed. "Positivisme et tradition dans une perspective islamique : le kémalisme", *Diogène* 127, jul-sep 84 : 89-107.

1490 BARKER, Eileen. "The British right to discriminate", *Society* 21(4), jun 84 : 35-41.

1491 BAUBÉROT, Jean. "Religion diffuse et sécularisation. XVIIe Conférence Internationale de Sociologie des Religions (Londres, 28 août-1er septembre 1983)", *Archives de Sciences Sociales des Religions* 56(2), oct-dec 83 : 195-198.

1492 CASANOVA, José. "The politics of the religious revival", *Telos* (59), spr 84 : 3-33.

1493 FERRAROTTI, Franco. "Il mito della secolarizzazione" (The myth of secularization), *Critica Sociologica* 69, 1984 : 11-22.

1494 HARPER, Charles L.; LEICHT, Kevin. "Religious awakenings and status politics : sources of support for the New Religious Right", *Sociological Analysis* 45(4), 1984 : 339-353. [USA]

1495 JACQUEMET, Gérard. "Déchristianisation, structures familiales et anticléricalisme : Belleville au XIXᵉ siècle", *Archives de Sciences Sociales des Religions* 57(1), jan-mar 84 : 69-82. [France]

1496 OLIVER, Ivan. "Current revivals of interest in religion : some sociological observations", *Archives de Sciences Sociales des Religions* 58(2), oct-dec 84 : 159-174.

1497 PÉTRUSSON, Pétur. *Church and social change : a study of the secularization process in Iceland, 1830-1930.* Helsingborg : Plus Ultra, 1983, 199 p. ill., bibl.

1498 PIRES, José Maria. "Relações Igreja-Estado no Brasil pós-64" (Church-State relationships in Brazil after 1964), *Vozes* 77(10), dec 83 : 53-57.

1499 ROBBINS, Thomas. "Constructing cultist 'mind control'", *Sociological Analysis* 45(3), 1984 : 241-256. [USA]

1500 STUMP, Roger W. "Regional divergence in religious affiliation in the United States", *Sociological Analysis* 45(4), 1984 : 283-299.

1501 SUTTER, Jacques. *La vie religieuse des Français à travers les sondages d'opinion : 1944-1976. 2 vols.* Paris : Éditions du Centre National de la Recherche Scientifique, 1984, 1350 p. bibl., ind.

13600 SCIENCE. SOCIOLOGY OF KNOWLEDGE
SCIENCE. SOCIOLOGIE DE LA CONNAISSANCE

1502 "Science, technique, société aux États-Unis aujourd'hui", *Culture Technique* (10), jun 83 : 197-333. [With contributions by Jean-Paul MOATTI, Dorothy NELKIN, Melvin KRANSBERG, Loren GRAHAM]

1503   AHMAD, Aqueil. "Toward closer links between science and society in India : a futuristic formula", *Technological Forecasting and Social Change* 25(3), mai 84 : 209-223.

1504   ARIMOTO, Akira. "Merton ni okeru 'kagaku no housho taikei' ron" (The theory of 'reward system of science' in R. K. Merton), *Kyoikugaku Ronshu* 13, 1984 : 1-16.

1505   BAČEŠKINA, T. I. "Bazis i nadstrojka kak social'no-filosofskie kategorii" (Basis and superstructure as socio-philosophical categories), *Vestnik Moskovskogo Universiteta. Serija Filosofija* (1), 1984 : 10-18.

1506   BERNER, Karl-Heinz. *Wissen, Wirklichkeit und Wahrheit : strukturalistische Überlegungen zur Entwicklung von Wissen und Wissenschaft aus der Erfahrung* (Knowledge, reality and truth : structuralist considerations on the development of knowledge and science from the experience). Pfaffenweiler : Centaurus-Verlagsgesellschaft, 1983, 270 p. bibl.

1507   BRUNNER, José Joaquín. *Estudios del campo científico : el paradigma mertoniano* (Studies on the scientific field : the Mertonian paradigm). Santiago de Chile : Facultad Latinoamericana de Ciencias Sociales, 1984, 92 p.

1508   BRUNNER, José Joaquín. *Estudios del campo científico : teoría y práctica científica según Kuhn* (Studies on the scientific field : scientific theory and practice according to Kuhn). Santiago de Chile : Facultad Latinoamericana de Ciencias Sociales, 1984, 70 p.

1509   CIPRIANI, Roberto; [et al.]. *Verità, conoscenza e ligittimazione* (Truth, knowledge and legitimation). Roma : Ianua, 1983, 215 p. bibl.

1510   FUHRMAN, Ellsworth R. "Alvin Gouldner and the sociology of knowledge : three significant problem shifts", *Sociological Quarterly* 25(3), 1984 : 287-300.

1511   HARMS, John B. "Mannheim's sociology of knowledge and the interpretation of 'Weltanschauungen' ", *Social Science Journal (Fort Collins)* 21(2), apr 84 : 33-48.

1512   KAPLAN, Morton A. *Science, language and the human condition.* New York, NY : Paragon House, 1984, 394 p.

1513   LALLEMENT, J. "Histoire de la pensée ou archéologie du savoir?", *Économies et Sociétés* 18(10), oct 84 : 61-93.

1514   LARIONESCU, Maria. "Contributions of the Bucharest School of Sociology to the development of the sociology of science", *Revue Roumaine des Sciences Sociales. Série de Sociologie* 28(1), jan-jun 84 : 39-47.

1515   MAIRE, Jean-Claude. "La science, l'homme et la société", *Humanisme et Entreprise* (144), apr 84 : 29-48.

1516   MENDELSOHN, Everett; NOWOTNY, Helga; [eds.]. "Nineteen eighty-four : science between utopia and dystopia", *Sociology of the Sciences* 8, 1984 : v-xv-3-303. [With contributions by Aant ELZINGA, Andrew JAMISON, James FLECK, Yarom EZRAHI.]

1517   MILIĆ, Vojin. "Sociology of knowledge and sociology of science", *Social Science Information / Information sur les Sciences Sociales* 23(2), 1984 : 213-273.

1518   PAPADOPOULOS, Jean. *Popper, philosophe politique et sociologuqe de la science.* Genève : Département de Science Politique, Université de Genève, 1984, 62 p. bibl.

1519   RIEDLE, Klaus. *Wissenschaft und Kernenergie : eine wissenschaftssoziologische Untersuchung zur Kontroverse um Kernenergie* (Science and nuclear energy : a sociology of science research on the nuclear energy controversy). Opladen : Leske + Budrich, 1984, x-233 p. ill., bibl.

1520   SATO, Naoyoshi. "Meiji shoki ni okeru gakuchi no sentaku" (The selection of knowledge in early Meiji era), *Shakaigaku Kenkyu* 47, 1984 : 17-42.

1521   SCHROYER, Trent. "On finalization in science", *Theory and Society* 13(5), sep 84 : 715-723. [Review essay]

1522   SHEKHAWAT, Virenda. "De quelques tendances épistémologiques en philosophie des sciences", *Diogène* 128, oct-dec 84 : 77-102.

1523   TRUBNIKOV, M. "Poznanie i problema čeloveka" (Knowledge and problem of man), *Obščestvennye Nauki (Moskva)* (6), 1983 : 78-88.

1524   ZANKER, Karin. "Biologie — Technik — humanistische Verantwortung" (Biology — technics — humanist responsibility), *Deutsche Zeitschrift für Philosophie* 32(5), 1984 : 447-456.

13700   COMMUNICATION. LANGUAGE
COMMUNICATION. LANGAGE

13710   Linguistics. Semiotics
Linguistique. Sémiotique

1525   "Lingüística y revalorización cultural en la Amazonia" (Linguistics and cultural revalorization in Amazonia), *América Indígena* 43(4), dec 83 : 693-892. [With contributions by Harriet E. Melanis KLEIN, Louisa STARK, Ernest C. MIGLIAZZA, Arthur P. SORENSEN Jr., Mary Ruth WISE]

1526   DAS GUPTA, Amitabha. "An ambiguity in the paradigm : a critique of Cartesian
        linguistics", *Philosophy of the Social Sciences / Philosophie des Sciences Sociales* 14(3), sep 84 : 351-366.
1527   FISHMAN, Joshua A.; [ed.]. "The decade past, the decade to come", *International Journal of
        the Sociology of Language* 45, 1984 : 5-160. [For the 10th anniversary of the International
        Journal of the Sociology of Language]
1528   FISHMAN, Joshua A.; [ed.]. "International sociolinguistic perspectives", *International Journal
        of Sociology of Language* 50, 1984 : 5-179.
1529   FOUQUIER, Éric. "Les effets du sémiologue. Notions opératoires pour une sémiologie
        des effets dus aux mass media", *Diogène* 127, jul-sep 84 : 121-143.
1530   HAGENDIJK, R. P.; PRINS, A. A. M. "Referenties en revérences. Onzekerheid,
        afhankelijkheid en citeernetwerken in de Nederlandse sociologie" (References and
        reverences. Uncertainty, dependence and ciration networks in the Dutch sociology),
        Mens en Maatschappij 59(3), aug 84 : 226-250.
1531   HARRIS, Peter Richard. "Shyness and psychological imperialism : on the dangers of
        ignoring the ordinary language roots of the terms we deal with", *European Journal of
        Social Psychology* 14(2), apr-jun 84 : 169-181.
1532   KEARNEY, Mary-Louise. "Sociolinguistics and language teaching", *International Social
        Science Journal / Revue Internationale des Sciences Sociales* 36(1), 1984 : 157-167.
1533   RADOVANOVIC, Milorad. "Linguistic theory and sociolinguistics in Yugoslavia",
        International Journal of the Sociology of Language 44, 1983 : 55-70.
1534   ROS I GARCIA, María; STRUBELL I TRUETA, Miquel; [eds.]. "Catalan sociolinguistics",
        International Journal of Sociology of Language 47, 1984 : 5-121.
1535   THASS-THIENEMANN, Theodore. *Understanding the unconscious meaning of language.* New
        York, NY : J. Aronson, 1983, viii-437 p. bibl., ind.
1536   TRUDGILL, Peter; [ed.]. *Applied sociolinguistics.* London; Orlando, FL : Academic Press,
        1984, xii-271 p. bibl., ind.

        13720   Communication. Signs
        Communication. Signes

1537   "Critical communications research in North America", *Media, Culture and Society* 6(3),
        jul 84 : 332. [With contributions by Dallas W. SMYTHE, Sarah DOUGLAS, Thomas
        GUBACK, Jennifer Daryl SLACK, Eileen R. MEEHAN]
1538   "Después del año mundial de la comunicación : nuevo orden informativo o nuevo des-
        equilibrio mundial" (After the communication world year : new information order or
        new world disequilbrium), *Comunicación y Cultura* (11), mar 84 : 3-185. [With contributions
        by Héctor SCHMUCLER, Fernando REYES MATTA, Eduardo RIVERA PORTO,
        Lilia BRICENO, Raquel SALINAS BASCUR]
1539   "Ferment in the field : communications scholars address critical issues and research talks of
        the discipline", *Journal of Communication* 33(3), sum 83 : 4-368. [With contributions by
        Wilbin SCHRAMM, Everett M. ROGERS, Steven H. CHAFFEE, Robert GRANDI,
        Armand MATTELART]
1540   "Guide des technologies de l'information", *Autrement. Série Mutations* (63-64), nov 84 : 1-464.
1541   AMBRESTER, Marcus L.; STRAUSE, Glynis Holm. *A rhetoric of interpersonal communication.*
        Prospect Heights, IL : Waveland Press, 1984, xiii-337 p. ill., bibl., ind.
1542   ANGELUSZ, Róbert; [et al.]. *A társadalmi kommunikáció kutatása Magyarországon. A tömeg-
        kommunikációs és közvéleménykutatások stratégiai terve* (Social communication research in
        Hungary. The strategic plan of mass communication and public opinion researches).
        Budapest : MRT Tömegkommunikációs Kutatóközpont, 1982, 62 p.
1543   BENYAMIN, Isabelle; [et al.]. "Pratiques de communication et modèles de développement",
        Recherche Sociale (92), dec 84 : 1-84.
1544   BOHNEN, Alfred. "Handlung, Lebenswelt und System in der soziologischen Theoriebildung :
        zur Kritik der Theorie des kommunikativen Handelns von Jürgen Habermas" (Action,
        life-world and system in sociological theory formation : critics of Jürgen Habermas'
        theory of communication), *Zeitschrift für Soziologie* 13(3), jul 84 : 191-203.
1545   BORDENAVE, Juan E. Díaz. "A comunicação e o fortalecimento da organização popular"
        (Communication and popular organization strengthening), *Vozes* 78(1), feb 84 : 46-54.
        [Brazil]
1546   BOREV, V. Ju. "Kul'tura i kommunikacija : k ponjatiju 'kul'turno-kommunikativnogo
        sistema'" (Culture and communication : to the 'cultural-communicative system'
        concept), *in : Dialektika kul'tury* Kujbyšev, 1982 : 87-90.

1547   BRETON, Raymond. "The production and allocation of symbolic resources : an analysis of the linguistic and ethnocultural fields in Canada", *Canadian Review of Sociology and Anthropology / Revue Canadienne de Sociologie et d'Anthropologie* 21(2), mai 84 : 123-144.

1548   CHEBEL, Malek. *Le corps dans la tradition au Maghreb.* Paris : Presses Universitaires de France, 1984, 207 p. bibl.

1549   CIVIKLY, Jean M.; SCHUETZ, Janice E. *Participating in the communication process.* Dubuque, IO : Kendall/Hunt Publishing Co., 1984, i-145 p. ill.

1550   CRESPI, Pietro. "Narrazione e ascolto. Aspetti e problemi dell'approccio orale in sociologia" (Narration and listening. Aspects and problems of the oral approach in sociology), *Critica Sociologica* 70, 1984 : 41-52.

1551   CUSHMAN, Donald P.; CAHN, Dudley D. *Communication in interpersonal relationships.* Albany, NY : State University of New York Press, 1984, 170 p. bibl., ind.

1552   EDGAR, Patricia; RAHIM, Syed A.; [eds.]. *Communication policy in developed countries.* London; Boston, MA : Kegan Paul International, 1983, v-297 p. bibl.

1553   EHRLICH, Konrad; REHBEIN, Jochen; [eds.]. *Kommunikation in Schule und Hochschule : linguistische und ethnomethodologische Analysen* (Communiation in schools and universities : linguistic and ethnomethodological analyses). Tübingen : G. Narr, 1983, 533 p. ill., bibl.

1554   FEKETEKUTY, Geza; ARONSON, Jonathan D. "Meeting the challenges of the world information economy", *World Economy* 7(1), mar 84 : 63-86.

1555   FODDY, W. H. "A critical evaluation of Altman's definition of privacy as a dialectical process", *Journal for the Theory of Social Behaviour* 14(3), oct 84 : 297-307.

1556   FØNS-JØRGENSEN, Eva; POULSEN, Jørgen. *Massekommunikationsforskning in Danmark 1980-1985* (Mass communication research in Denmark 1980-1985). Århus : Statsbiblioteket, 1983, 49 p. bibl.

1557   GOBAN-KLAS, Tomasz. "Information at the time of sociopolitical crisis : Poland in the Summer of 1980", *Mass Communication Review Yearbook* 4, 1983 : 489-500.

1558   GONSALES, R. F. "Obščenie i ègo značenie v razrabotke problemy ličnosti" (Communication and its meaning in the personality problems study), *Psihologičeskij Žurnal* (4), 1983 : 40-47.

1559   GOOD, Anthony. "A symbolic type and its transformations : the case of South Indian Poṅkal", *Contributions to Indian Sociology* 17(2), jul-dec 83 : 223-244.

1560   GUSFIELD, Joseph R.; MICHALOWICZ, Jerzy. "Secular symbolism : studies of ritual, ceremony, and the symbolic order in modern life", *Annual Review of Sociology* 10, 1984 : 417-435.

1561   HARAYAMA, Tetsu. "Seiso-ka no katei to smbolic sogo sayo" (Symbolic interaction in the process of stratification), *Bulletin of St. Luke's College of Nursing* 9, 1984 : 49-55.

1562   LA HAYE, Yves de. *Dissonances : critique de la communication.* Grenoble : Pensée Sauvage, 1984, 191 p. ill., bibl., ind. [France]

1563   LEONARD-BARTON, Dorothy. "Interpersonal communication patterns among Swedish and Boston area entrepreneurs", *Research Policy* 13(2), apr 84 : 101-114.

1564   MARHUENDA, Jean-Pierre. "À propos de quelques bilans de la recherche française en communicaiton", *Cahiers de la Communication* 3(5), 1983 : 427-448.

1565   MUNIZAGA, Giselle; RIVERA, Anny. *La investigación social en Chile* (Social communication research in Chile). Lima : Centro de Estudios y Promoción del Desarrollo, 1983, 228 p.

1566   NAGAI, Michio. "Cultural lag and international communication : the case of Japan", *Information, Economics and Policy* 1(1), 1983 : 69-73.

1567   OKWESA, B. A. "Perspectives on communication problems in the English-speaking Caribbean", *Cajanus* 17(4), 1984 : 215-222.

1568   ONO, Michikuni. "Comte no kigo riron -hi-ito teki kigo kara ito-teki kigo eno iko" (Comte's theory of signs : the passage from involuntary signs to voluntary signs), *Kobe Daigaku Ronshu* 33, 1984 : 61-92.

1569   PEARSON, Judy Cornelia. *Gender and communication.* Dubuque, IA : W. C. Brown Publishers, 1984, xviii-386 p. ill., bibl., ind.

1570   REUILLARD, J. P.; OUDOT, J.; MORGON, A. *Les effets pervers dans la communication humaine.* Lyon : Presses Universitaires de Lyon, 1984, 166 p. bibl.

1571   SATO, Yoshiyuki. "Taiwa teki kohi to seikatsu sekai -Habermas riron no rikai no tame ni" (Communicative action and lifeworld : in order to understand J. Habermas' theory), *Waseda University Social Sciences Review* 30(2), 1984 : 83-115.

1572   SCHENK, Michael. "Meinungsführer und Netzwerke persönlicher Kommunikation" (Opinion leader and personal communication network), *Rundfunk und Fernsehen* 31(3-4), 1983 : 326-336.

1573   SERVAES, Jan. *Communication and development : some theoretical remarks.* Leuven : Acco, 1983, 77 p. ill., bibl.

1574   SONDHI, Krishan. *Communication, growth, and public policy : the Indian experience.* New Delhi :
          Breakthrough Publications, 1983, x-228 p. bibl.
1575   SPYBEY, Tony. "Frames of meaning : the rationality in organizational cultures", *Acta
          Sociologica* 27(4), 1984 : 311-322.
1576   STEPHEN, Timothy D. "A symbolic exchange framework for the development of intimate
          relationships", *Human Relations* 37(5), apr 84 : 393-408.
1577   SWANBORN, P. G.; VAN ZIJL, P. J. M. "Interactionists do it only symbolically. Een
          inhoudsanalyse van symbolische interactionistisch onderzoek" (Interactionists do it only
          symbolically. A content analysis of symbolic interactionist research), *Mens en Maatschappij*
          59(2), mai 84 : 142-164.
1578   TAKASAKI, Nozomu; OZAWA, Takahiro. "Analysis of information flow in Japan",
          Information, Economics and Policy 1(2), 1983 : 177-193.
1579   VAN OUTRIVE, L.; VAN NULAND, J.; LENOIR, N. "Le contrôle de la protection de
          la vie privée", *Déviance et Société* 8(3), sep 84 : 295-313.
1580   VINOGRADOV, V. A. "Informacija i global'nye problemy sovremennosti" (Information
          and global problems at the present time), *Voprosy Filosofii* 36(12), dec 83 : 95-106.
1581   WANG, Georgette; DISSANAYAKE, Wimal. *Continuity and change in communication systems : a
          croos-cultural perspective.* Norwood, NJ : Ablex Publishing Corporation, 1984, 368 p. bibl.,
          ind.
1582   ZOLLER, Michael. "Öffentliche Kontrolle und öffentliches Interesse. Die Diskussion um
          Binnenpluralismus und Aussenpluralismus in der amerikanischen Medienpolitik" (Public
          control and public interest. The debate on internal and external pluralism in American
          media policy), *Hamburger Jahrbuch für Wirtschafts- und Gesellschaftspolitik* 29, 1984 : 257-273.

          **13730   Language
                     Langage**

1583   "Français (Le), langue internationale de la communication scientifique et technique?",
          Perspectives Universitaires 2(1), 1984 : 5-277. [With contributions by J. CANTACUZENE,
          J.-C. CORBEIL, S. HAMEL, G. de SAINT MAUR]
1584   "Langue maternelle et rendement scolaire", *Perspectives (UNESCO)* 14(1), 1984 : 37-154.
          [With contributions by William Francis MACKEY, Joshua A. FISHMAN, György
          SZEPE, Chadly FITOURI, Ayo BAMGBOSE_]
1585   "Neurolinguistique (La) du bilinguisme", *Langages* 18(72), dec 83 : 5-123. [With contributions
          by Michel PARADIS, Yvan LEBRUN, R. L. RAPPORT, Linda M. GALLOWAY]
1586   ABUHAMDIA, Zakaria A. "English departments at Arab universities : toward a 'planning
          based model'", *Language Problems and Language Planning* 8(1), spr 84 : 21-34.
1587   ADAIR, Philippe. "La sociologie phagocytée par l'économique : remarques critiques à
          propos de 'ce que parler veut dire' de P. Bourdieu", *Sociologie du Travail* 26(1), jan-mar
          84 : 105-114. [BOURDIEU, Pierre. Ce que parler veut dire : l'économie des échanges
          linguistiques. Paris, Fayard, 1982]
1588   BACHMANN, Christian; BASIER, Luc. "Le verlan : argot d'école ou langue des
          Keums?", *Mots* (8), mar 84 : 169-185. [France]
1589   BAETENS BEARDSMORE, Hugo; [ed.]. "Language and television", *International Journal
          of Sociology of Language* 48, 1984 : 5-113.
1590   BLANKOFF-SCARR, G. "Le bilinguisme en Union soviétique : aggression linguistique
          ou phénomène naturel?", *Revue des Pays de l'Est* 24(1-2), 1983 : 161-181.
1591   BOGUO, Makeli. "La promotion de la langue maternelle en tant qu'instrument de
          l'éducation et de la culture", *Mois en Afrique* 19(215-216), jan 84 : 101-116. [Africa]
1592   BOIS, Pierre du. "Welsch, Deutsch, Schweizerdeutsch. Der 'Unterschied des Idioms'"
          (Welsh, German and German Swiss. Differences between dialects), *Schweizer Monatshefte*
          64(10), oct 84 : 793-804.
1593   BRUCHIS, Michael. "The language policy of the CPSU and the linguistic situation in
          Soviet Moldavia", *Soviet Studies* 36(1), jan 84 : 108-126.
1594   CABRAL, Nelson E. "Portuguese Creole dialects in West Africa", *International Social Science
          Journal / Revue Internationale des Sciences Sociales* 36(1), 1984 : 77-85.
1595   COLEMAN, Hywel; [ed.]. "Language and work. I. Law, industry, education", *International
          Journal of Sociology of Language* 49, 1984 : 5-133.
1596   COOPER, Robert L. "A framework for the description of language spread : the case of
          modern Hebrew", *International Social Science Journal / Revue Internationale des Sciences Sociales*
          36(1), 1984 : 87-112.
1597   CORRAZE, Jacques. *Les communications non-verbales.* Paris : Presses Universitaires de France,
          1983, 2e rev., 206 p. ill., bibl.

1598 CORVALAN, Graziella. "El bilingüismo en la educacion en el Paraguay" (Bilingualism in education in Paraguay), *Latin American Research Review* 18(3), 1983 : 109-126.

1599 DEPREZ, K.; [et al.]. "Les non-néerlandophones dans l'enseignement de la langue néerlandaise à Bruxelles. Qui et pourquoi?", *Recherches Sociologiques* 15(1), 1984 : 117-146.

1600 DUDLEY, Edward J.; HELLER, Peter; [eds.]. *American attitudes toward foreign languages and foreign cultures.* Bonn : Bouvier, 1983, 146 p. ill., bibl.

1601 FISHMAN, Joshua A. "Mother tongue claiming in the United States since 1960 : trends and correlates related to the 'revival of ethnicity'", *International Journal of Sociology of Language* 50, 1984 : 21-99.

1602 FISHMAN, Joshua A.; [ed.]. "Language choice and language control", *International Journal of Sociology of Language* 44, 1983 : 5-166.

1603 GILES, Howard; [ed.]. "The dynamics of speech accomodation", *International Journal of Sociology of Language* 46, 1984 : 5-146.

1604 GINGRAS, Yves. "La valeur d'une langue dans un champ scientifique", *Recherches Sociographiques* 25(2), mai-aug 84 : 285-296. [Canada]

1605 GRENIER, Gilles. "Une analyse microéconomique des déterminants des transferts linguistiques des minorités hors-Québec en 1971", *Actualité Économique* 60(2), jun 84 : 149-163.

1606 GRIZE, Jean-Blaise. "Langues naturelles et langages formels", *Revue Européenne des Sciences Sociales. Cahiers Vilfredo Pareto* 22(66), 1984 : 231-286.

1607 HAARMANN, Harold. "The role of ethnocultural stereotypes and foreign languages in Japanese commercials", *International Journal of Sociology of Language* 50, 1984 : 101-121.

1608 HARTUNG, Wolfdietrich. "Some aspects of linguistic variation in one-language societies", *International Social Science Journal / Revue Internationale des Sciences Sociales* 36(1), 1984 : 129-142.

1609 HUMBLET, Jean-E. "The language problem in international organizations", *International Social Science Journal / Revue Internationale des Sciences Sociales* 36(1), 1984 : 143-155.

1610 HUNTER, Ian. "After representation : recent discussions of the relation between language and literature", *Economy and Society* 13(4), 1984 : 397-430.

1611 KHUBCHANDANI, Lachman M. "Language modernization in the developing world", *International Social Science Journal / Revue Internationale des Sciences Sociales* 36(1), 1984 : 169-188. [India]

1612 KRAMARAE, Cheris; SCHULZ, Muriel; O'BARR, William M.; [eds.]. *Language and power.* Berkeley, CA : Sage, 1984, 320 p.

1613 KUO, Eddie C. Y. "Mass media and language planning : Singapore's 'speak mandarin' campaign", *Journal of Communication* 34(2), spr 84 : 24-35.

1614 LANDRY, R.; ALLARD, R. "Bilinguisme additif, bilinguisme soustractif et vitalité ethnolinguistique", *Recherches Sociologiques* 15(2-3), 1984 : 337-358. [Canada]

1615 LOKOMBE KITETE, Ndew'Okongo. "Évaluation de l'enseignement du français en Afrique centrale : une étude critique des manuels scolaires de l'enseignement primaire : le cas du Zaïre", *Tiers-Monde* 25(97), mar 84 : 169-188.

1616 LUCKMANN, Thomas. "Language in society", *International Social Science Journal / Revue Internationale des Sciences Sociales* 36(1), 1984 : 5-20.

1617 MCKIRNAN, David J. "Speech norms and perception of ethno-linguistic group differences : toward a conceptual and research framework", *European Journal of Social Psychology* 14(2), apr-jun 84 : 151-168.

1618 MIRACLE, Andrew W. Jr.; [ed.]. *Bilingualism, social issues and policy implications.* Athens, GA : University of Georgia Press, 1983, x-188 p. bibl.

1619 NDOMA, Ungina. "National language policy in education in Zaire", *Language Problems and Language Planning* 8(2), sum 84 : 173-184.

1620 NELDE, Peter Hans. "Deutsche Munderheiten und ihre Sprache in Europa" (German minorities and their language in Europe), *Language Problems and Language Planning* 8(1), spr 84 : 1-20.

1621 OWENS, Robert E. Jr. *Language development : an introduction.* Columbus, OH : Merrill, 1984, xiv-394 p. ill., bibl., ind.

1622 PEUKERT, Reinhard. *Gesprächshermeneutik* (Speech hermeneutics). Frankfurt-am-Main : Extrabuch Verlag, 1984, xviii-350 p. bibl.

1623 RAFFERTY, Ellen. "Languages of the Chinese of Java : an historical review", *Journal of Asian Studies* 43(2), feb 84 : 247-272.

1624 SAINT-OUEN, François. "De la matérialité du discours aux espaces discursifs", *Revue Française de Science Politique* 34(3), jun 84 : 428-448. [France]

1625 SHEARMAN, Peter. "Language, sovietization and ethnic integration in the USSR", *Journal of Social, Political and Economic Studies* 8(3), aut 83 : 227-256.

1626 SHORISH, M. Mobin. "Planning by decree : the Soviet language policy in Central Asia", *Language Problems and Language Planning* 8(1), spr 84 : 35-49.

1627   SIGAL, Silvia. "Sur le discours militaire : Argentine 1976-1978 et un déjà vu", Homme et
        Société (71-72), jun 84 : 33-53.
1628   VAN DEN EEDEN, P.; SARIS, W. E. "Empirische onderzoek naar multilevel uitspraken"
        (Empirical research on multilevel speeches), Mens en Maatschappij 59(2), mai 84 : 164-178.
1629   VAN LIER, Leo A. W. "Discourse analysis and classroom research : a methodological
        perspective", International Journal of Sociology of Language 49, 1984 : 111-133.
1630   WANDRUSZKA, Mario. Das Leben der Sprachen : vom menschlichen Sprechen und Gespräch (The
        life of languages : on human language and speech). Stuttgart : Deutsche Verlagsanstalt,
        1984, 292 p. bibl.

        13740   Audience
                 Public

1631   ALBRECHT, Richard. "Dem Leser auf der Spur? Bedenken gegen alte und neue
        empirische Buchmarkt-, Buch- und Leser-Forschung und ihre Resultate in der BRD"
        (Following the reader? Thoughts on research on the book market, books and the readers
        in GFR), Communications (Sankt Augustin) 9(1), 1983 : 3-19.

        13750   Advertising. Propaganda
                 Publicité. Propagande

1632   BERRIO, Jordi. Teoría social de la persuasión (Social theory of persuasion). Barcelona : Editorial
        Mitre, 1983, 287 p. bibl.
1633   CAMPOS MANZO, José Maria. A tragédia da propaganda no Brasil (The tragedy of
        propaganda in Brazil). Rio de Janeiro : Collector's Editora, 1983, 238 p.
1634   IVANOV, V. N. "Sociologija propagandy : nekotorye aspekty soderžanija" (Sociology of
        propaganda : some aspects of its content), Sociologičeskie Issledovanija (Moskva) (3), 1983 : 36-44.
1635   KANEHISA, Tching. La publicité au Japon : image de la société. Paris : Maisonneuve et Larose,
        1984, 166 p. bibl.
1636   NETTER, Jeffry M. "Political competition and advertising as a barrier to entry", Southern
        Economic Journal 50(2), oct 83 : 510-520. [USA]
1637   PFLAUM, Dieter; BÄUERLE, Ferdinand; [eds.]. Lexikon der Werbung (Lexicon of advertising).
        Landsberg-am-Lech : Verlag Moderne Industrie, 1983, 383 p. ill., ind.

        13760   Mass communication
                 Communication de masse

1638   "Audiovisuel et développement", Tiers-Monde 24(95), sep 83 : 557-588. [With contributions
        by Yvonne MIGNOT-LEFEBVRE, Martha STUART, Yves CABANNES, Ayi-
        Francisco d' ALMEIDA]
1639   "Bandes (Les) dessinées", Communications (Sankt Augustin) 9(2-3), 1983 : 149-240. [With
        contributions by F. KNILLI, Hervé FISCHER, Demosthenes SAVRAMIS]
1640   "Children and television", Journal of Broadcasting 28(4), aut 84 : 431-476. [USA] [With
        contributions by Joanne CANTOR, Barbara J. WILSON, Mable L. RICE, Ronald J.
        FABER]
1641   "Cinéma (Le) français, entre l'argent, le pouvoir et la télévision", Études sep 84 : 197-211.
        [Table ronde avec Claude CHABROL, Eric ROHMER, Marie-Claude TRAILHOU,
        Jean-Claude GUIGET, Jean-Claude BRISSEAU]
1642   "Cinémas noirs d'Afrique", Afrique Littéraire (68-69), trim. 3, 83 : 5-204. [With contribu-
        tions by Victor BACHY, Ferid BOUGHEDIR, Jacques BINET, Alain RICARD]
1643   "Communications with and without technology", Ekistics 50(302), oct 83 : 318-425. [With
        contributions by Arthur C. CLARKE, P. BARTHOLEME, Pier-Giovanni D'AYALA,
        Richard L. MEIER, Benjamin D. SINGER]
1644   "Competition and diversity among radio formats : legal and structural issues", Journal of
        Broadcasting 28(2), spr 84 : 127-145. [With contributions by Theodore L. GLASSER,
        Erwin G. KRASNOW, William E. KENNARD]
1645   "Comunicadores y participación" (Communicators and participation), Comunicación (43),
        oct 83 : 4-93. [Venezuela] [With contributions by José I. REY, Jorge A. RICHARDS,
        Marcelino BISBAL, Berta BRITO]
1646   "Controversies : television at the crossroads", Society 21(6), oct 84 : 6-40. [USA] [With
        contributions by Bert BRILLER, Steven MILLER, Susan B. NEUMAN, David
        PEARL]

1647   "Historians and movies : the state of the art", *Journal of Contemporary History* 19(1), jan 84 : 1-187. [With contributions by Richard GRENIER, Clive COULTASS, Peter B. HIGH, Daniel J. LEAB, Douglas GOMERY, David WEINBERG]

1648   "Information (The) age", *Political Quarterly* 54(2), jun 83 : 111-195. [With contributions by William GOSLING, Anthony SMITH, Tom STONIER, Carolyn HAYMAN, Jeremy MITCHELL]

1649   "Kritische Presse? Pressekritik" (Critical press? press critics), *Vorgänge* 23(2), 1983 : 49-101. [Germany FR] [With contributions by Anton Andreas GUHA, Harry PROSS, Eckart SPOO]

1650   "Media (The) in the margins", *Media, Culture and Society* 6(2), apr 84 : 93-189. [With contributions by COMEDIA, David BEVAN, Rohan SAMARAJIWA, Peter M. LEWIS, David KUNZLE]

1651   "Media effects", *Mass Communication Review Yearbook* 4, 1983 : 21-125. [USA] [With contributions by Mabel L. RICE, Robert P. HAWKINS, Suzanne PINGREE]

1652   "Messy (The) media. A symposium on the state of radio and television", *Seminar* (292), dec 83 : 11-42. [India] [With contributions by Dilip BOBB, A. G. NOORANI, Yash PAL]

1653   "Paysage (Le) des média écrits et audio-visuels", *Documents CEPESS* 24(3-4), 1983 : 1-176.

1654   AKIYAMA, Takashiro. "Teletext and TV programs for the deaf and hard of hearing in Japan", *Studies of Broadcasting* (20), mar 84 : 17-38.

1655   ALMEIDA, Ayi-Francisco d'. "Les politiques de communication sociale au moyen du cinéma : le cas des pays africains", *Tiers-Monde* 24(95), sep 83 : 583-588.

1656   ALONSO ERAUSQUIN, Manuel. "Televisión y público infantil" (Television and youth audience), *Razón y Fe* 209(1026), mar 84 : 238-247. [Spain]

1657   ALTHEIDE, David L. "Media hegemony : a failure of perspective", *Public Opinion Quarterly* 48(2), 1984 : 476-490.

1658   BACQUET, Alexis. *Médias et christianisme.* Paris : Éditions du Centurion, 1984, 173 p. bibl.

1659   BALLE, Francis. "Mythes et réalités de la démocratie électronique", *Connaissance Politique* 2, mai 83 : 106-112.

1660   BENNETT, W. Lance. "Culture, communication and political control", *Political Anthropology Yearbook* 2, 1983 : 39-52. [USA]

1661   BERRY, Colin. "Learning from television news : a critique of the research", *Journal of Broadcasting* 27(4), aut 83 : 359-370. [USA]

1662   BOEMER, Marilyn Laurence. "An analysis of the violence content of the radio thriller dramas — and some comparisons with television", *Journal of Broadcasting* 28(3), sum 84 : 341-353. [USA]

1663   BOGART, Leo. "The public's use and perception of newspapers", *Public Opinion Quarterly* 48(4), 1984 : 709-719. [USA]

1664   BONNEY, Bill. "Australian broadcasting, professionalism and 'national reconciliation'", *Media, Culture and Society* 5(3-4), oct 83 : 263-274.

1665   BOYLE, Harry J. "Television's failures and its non-commercial promise", *Queen's Quarterly* 90(4), wint 83 : 1015-1025. [North America]

1666   BULLINGER, Martin. "Elektronische Medien als Marktplatz der Meinungen" (Electronic media as a market place of opinions), *Archiv des Öffentlichen Rechts* 108(2), 1983 : 161-215.

1667   CARROLL, Glenn R. "Dynamics of publisher succession in newspaper organizations", *Administrative Science Quarterly* 29(1), mar 84 : 93-113. [USA]

1668   CESAREO, Giovanni; [et al.]. "Dibattito sul best-seller", *Critica Sociologica* 70, 1984 : 61-82.

1669   CHAIGNEAU, Pascal. "La presse à Madagascar", *Cahiers de la Communication* 3(4), 1983 : 283-319.

1670   CHAM, Mbye Baboucar. "Art and ideology in the work of Sembene Ousmane and Haile Gerima", *Présence Africaine* (129), trim. 1, 84 : 79-91. [Africa]

1671   CHERKI, Eddy; CLAVAUD, Richard. "L'Amérique du Nord face aux nouveaux médias", *Futuribles* (77), mai 84 : 39-58.

1672   CLEMENT, Jérôme. "Un projet de loi pour garantir le pluralisme", *Revue Politique et Parlementaire* 85(907), dec 83 : 29-47. [France]

1673   CURIEN, Nicolas; GENSOLLEN, Michel. "Les nouvelles techniques des télécommunications : le domaine de la décision et celui de l'invention", *Cybernetica* 26(4), 1983 : 247-264.

1674   DE BARROS, José Tavares. "O Ensino do cinema no Brasil", *Vozes* 78(5), jul 84 : 43-57.

1675   DRÜKE, Helmut. *Journalisten und Gewerkschaft : Probleme und Perspektiven der gewerkschaftlichen Organisierung der Tageszeitungsjournalisten in der Bundesrepublik Deutschland* (Journalists and trade union : problems and prospects of trade union organization of daily press journalists in the Federal Republic of Germany). Frankfurt-am-Main : Haag + Herchen, 1984, 202 p. ill., bibl.

1676   DURAND, Jacques. "La consommation des médias : recherche d'un modèle", *Cahiers de la Communication* 3(5), 1983 : 403-426.

1677   DZINIC, Firdus. "Radio and television", *Yugoslav Survey* 25(2), mai 84 : 87-106. [Yugoslavia]

1678   DZINIC, Kirdus. "Radio-televizija" (Radio-television), *Jugoslovenski Pregled* 28(2), feb 84 : 65-74. [Yugoslavia]

1679   FABRE-ROSANE, Gilles. "Les réformes de l'audiovisuel", *Revue Politique et Parlementaire* 85(907), dec 83 : 48-57. [France]

1680   FERRAROTTI, Franco. "Considerazioni conclusive circa il rapporto autori-editori : limiti e prospettive future di questa ricerca" (Final considerations about authors-publishers relationship : limitations and future prospects of this research), *Critica Sociologica* 70, 1984 : 53-60.

1681   FOMIN, A. V. "Sociologičeskij analiz nekotoryh aspektov vospitatel'nogo vozdejstvija kinematografa na molodež'" (Sociological analysis of some aspects of educational influence of cinema on youth), *in : Sociologija vysšej školy* Gor'kij, 1983 : 61-72.

1682   FORGE, Simon. "Cablevision — the other services", *Futures* 16(5), oct 84 : 520-532.

1683   GARDES, Jean-Claude. "La presse satirique allemande de 1945 à nos jours", *Allemagnes d'Aujourd'hui* (87), mar 84 : 88-107.

1684   GEIBEL, Karl. *Mediendschungel : eine kritische Bestandsaufnahme* (Media jungle : a critical statement). Gerlingen : Bleicher, 1983, 423 p. ill., bibl., ind.

1685   GIFREU, Josep. *Sistema i polítiques de la comunicació a Catalunya : (premsa, ràdio, televisió i cinema, 1970-1980)* (Communication system and policies in Catalonia : (press, radio, television and cinema, 1970-1980)). Barcelona : Avenç, 1983, xvii-572 p. bibl., ind.

1686   GLASMAN, Monique. "L'information dans un pays en développement : la Côte d'Ivoire", *Projet* (182), feb 84 : 147-158.

1687   GLOVER, David. *The sociology of the mass media*. Ormskirk, Lancashire : Causeway Books, 1984, 74 p. bibl., ind.

1688   GOTO, Kazuhiko. "Japanese project for direct broadcasting satellite service", *Studies of Broadcasting* (19), mar 83 : 9-47.

1689   GUSTAFSSON, Karl Erik. "Medienstruktur und Medienpolitik in Schweden am Anfang der achtziger Jahre" (Media structure and media policy in Sweden in the early eighties), *Universitas* 39(1), 1984 : 81-92.

1690   GUTIÉRREZ, Francisco. "Las radios comunitarias. Una experiencia de comunicación alternativa" (Community radio. An alternative communication experience), *Nueva Sociedad* (71), feb 84 : 87-92. [Costa Rica]

1691   HAARMANN, Harold. "The role of German in modern Japanese mass media : aspects of ethnocultural stereotypes and prestige functions of language in Japanese society", *Hitotsubashi Journal of Social Studies* 16(1), apr 84 : 31-41.

1692   HANÁK, Katalin. "Férfi és nő kommunikátorok a televízióban" (Male and female communicators on the screen), *Jel-Kép* 5(1), 1984 : 55-65. [Hungary]

1693   HARMAN, Chris. "The revolutionary press", *International Socialism* (24), sum 84 : 3-44.

1694   HENNINGHAM, J. P. "Comparisons between Australian and US broadcast journalists' professional values", *Journal of Broadcasting* 28(3), sum 84 : 323-331.

1695   HIRSCH, Helga. "Unabhängiges Publikationswesen in Polen 1976-1983" (Independant publications in Poland, 1976-1983), *Osteuropa* 34(7), jul 84 : 515-531.

1696   HIZAOUI, Abdelkrim. "La presse tunisienne à l'ère du pluralisme : liberté ou institution-nalisation?", *Revue Tunisienne de Communication* (3), jun 83 : 61-70.

1697   HOFSTETTER, C. Richard; STRAND, Paul J. "Mass media and political issue per-ceptions", *Journal of Broadcasting* 27(4), aut 83 : 345-358. [USA]

1698   INOUE, Teruko. "Masu komi to jyosei no gendai" (Women's magazines in recent Japan), *Readings on Women's Studies* 1, 1984 : 42-73.

1699   JENDOUBI, Mehdi. "La formation des journalistes", *Revue Tunisienne de Communication* (3), jun 83 : 29-40.

1700   JENDOUBI, Mehdi. *Journalisme d'agence, journalisme de base*. Tunis : Institut de Presse et des Sciences de l'Information, 1984, vi-111 p. bibl., ind.

1701   JENSEN, Stefan. "Aspekte der Medien-Theorie : welche Funktionen haben die Medien in Handlungssystemen?" (Aspects of media-theory : which are the functions of media in action systems?), *Zeitschrift für Soziologie* 13(2), apr 84 : 145-164.

1702   JOHNSSON-SMARAGDI, Ulla. *TV use and social interaction in adolescence : a longitudinal study*. Stockholm : Almqvist and Wiksell Insternational, 1983, vii-239 p. ill., bibl.

1703   JOOSSENS, Luc; [ed.]. *Les enfants et la publicité télévisée : enquête d'influence*. Bruxelles : CRIOC, Vie Ouvrière, 1984, 153 p.

1704   KAZIN, A. L. "Hudožestvennyj obraz i dokument (O meste kinoiskusstva v kul'ture)"
        (Artistic image and document : the role of cinema in cultural life), *Voprosy Filosofii* 37(7),
        1984 : 53-62. [USSR]
1705   KNILLI, Friedrich; NICKOLAUS, Barbara. "Programming for direct satellite television",
        Communications (Sankt Augustin) 9(1), 1983 : 29-59.
1706   KUNCZIK, Michael. *Kommunikation und Gesellschaft : Theorien zur Massenkommunikation*
        (Communication and society : mass communication theories). Köln : Böhlau, 1984,
        vi-284 p. ill., bibl., ind.
1707   KUO, Eddie C. Y. "Television and language planning in Singapore", *International Journal of
        the Sociology of Language* 48, 1984 : 49-64.
1708   LOWE, Philip; MORRISON, David. "Bad news or good news : environmental politics
        and the mass media", *Sociological Review* 32(1), feb 84 : 75-90. [UK]
1709   LUGER, Kurt. "Die Zukunft der Massenmedien in Österreich" (The future of mass media
        in Austria), *Rundfunk und Fernsehen* 31(2), 1983 : 143-158.
1710   MEYER, Manfred; [ed.]. *Children and the formal features of television : approaches and findings of
        experimental and formative research.* München; New York, NY : K. G. Saur, 1983, 333 p.
        ill., bibl.
1711   MEYER, Philip; WEARDEN, Stanley T. "The effects of public ownership on newspaper
        companies : a preliminary inquiry", *Public Opinion Quarterly* 48(3), 1984 : 564-577. [USA]
1712   MILO, Daniel. "La bourse mondiale de la traduction : un baromètre culturel?", *Annales-
        Économies, Sociétés, Civilisations* 39(1), feb 84 : 92-115.
1713   MIQUEL, Pierre. *Histoire de la radio et de la télévision.* Paris : Librairie Académique Perrin,
        1984, 393 p. bibl., ind.
1714   MITROPOULOS, Mit. "Public participation, as access in cable television in the USA",
        Ekistics 50(302), oct 83 : 385-397.
1715   MIURA, Shigeji; TAMURA, Norio; OCHI, Noboru; [eds.]. *Gendai new media ron* (On new
        media today). Tokyo : Gakubunsha, 1984, 249 p.
1716   MORAGAS SPA, Miguel de. "Mass communication and political change in Spain,
        1975-1980", *Mass Communication Review Yearbook* 4, 1983 : 501-520.
1717   MORIN, Violette. "Le présent actif dans le feuilleton télévisé", *Communications (Paris)* 39,
        1984 : 239-246. [France]
1718   MOROZOV, B. M.; [ed.]. *Éffektivnost' sredstv massovoj informacii i propagandy* (Efficiency of
        mass information and propaganda means). Moskva : Akademija Obščestvennyh Nauk
        pri CK KPSS, 1983, 138 p.
1719   MOSLEY, Paul. " 'Popularity functions' and the role of the media : a pilot study of the
        popular press", *British Journal of Political Science* 14(1), jan 84 : 117-129. [UK]
1720   MURAMATSU, Yasuko. "Mass communication naiyo to sono jyuyo ni kansuru jyosei-gaku
        teki kosatsu" (Contents of mass communication and audience response : from a viewpoint
        of women's studies), *Studies of Broadcasting* 34, 1984 : 57-79.
1721   OEPEN, Manfred. "Media, migrants and marginalization : the situation in the Federal
        Republic of Germany", *International Migration Review* 18(65), 1984 : 111-121.
1722   OHASHI, Terue. "Mass media ni yoru jyosei no ishiki keisei" (How does mass media
        affect women's consciousness formation), *Soshioroji* 28(3), 1984 : 117-137.
1723   OKADA, Naoyuki. "Mass communication kenkyu no tenkai to genjyo -mass media no
        koka, eikyo o megutte" (Development of mass communication studies and an overview
        of present state : the effects and influences of the mass media), *Studies of Broadcasting*
        34, 1984 : 9-37.
1724   ORGANISATION INTERNATIONALE DU TRAVAIL. *Profession : journaliste; étude sur
        la condition du journaliste en tant que travailleur.* Genève : BIT, 1984, ix-180 p. bibl.
1725   ORY, Pascal. "Mickey go home! La désaméricanisation de la bande dessinée (1945-1950)",
        Vingtième Siècle. Revue d'Histoire (4), oct 84 : 49-60. [France]
1726   PALMER, Michael Beaussenat. *Des petits journaux aux grandes agences : naissance du journalisme
        moderne 1863-1914.* Paris : Aubier-Montaigne, 1983, 350 p. bibl.
1727   PEREZ GOMEZ, Angel A. "Cine español en auge" (Growth of Spanish cinema), *Razón y
        Fe* 209(1027), apr 84 : 378-390.
1728   PEREZ, María. "¿Es la historieta comunicación y cultura de masas?" (Do cartoons constitute
        communication and mass culture?), *Revista de Ciencias Sociales de la Universidad de Costa
        Rica* 27-28(1-2), 1984 : 107-115.
1729   PETROV, L. V. "O zakonomernostjah istoričeskogo razvitija massovoj kommunikacii"
        (On the laws of historical development of mass communication), *in : Sociologija kul'tury :
        metodologija i praktika kul'turno-prosvetitel'noj dejatel'nosti* Leningrad, 1982 : 25-34.
1730   PIVETEAU, Jacques. *L'extase de la télévision.* Paris : Insep Éditions, 1984, 255 p. ill., bibl.

1731   PORRO, Renato. *Infanzia e mass-media* (Childhood and mass media). Milano : Franco Angeli, 1984, 169 p. ill., bibl.

1732   QUERE, Mireille. "Presse, élite, pouvoir", *Revue Française de Civilisation Britannique* 2(2), sep 83 : 87-104. [UK]

1733   QUESTER, George H. "Transboundary television", *Problems of Communism* 33(5), oct 84 : 76-87. [Eastern Europe]

1734   RABOY, Marc. "Media and politics in Socialist France", *Media, Culture and Society* 5(3-4), oct 83 : 303-320.

1735   RAPPING, Elayne. "The magic world of nonfiction television", *Monthly Review* 35(7), dec 83 : 28-43. [USA]

1736   RENCKSTORF, Karsten. *Menschen und Medien in der postindustriellen Gesellschaft : neuere Beiträge zur Begründung eines alternative Forschungsatzes* (Men and media in the post-industrial society : latest contributions to justify an alternative research approach). Berlin : V. Spiess, 1984, 225 p. ill., bibl. [Continues : Neue Perspectiven in der Massenkommunikationsforschung (New perspectives in mass communication research), 1977]

1737   RENTSCHLER, Eric. "Kluge, film history, and Eigensinn : a taking of stock from the distance", *New German Critique* (31), wint 84 : 109-124. [Germany FR]

1738   RIEFFEL, Rémy. *L'élite des jouranlistes : les hérauts de l'information.* Paris : Presses Universitaires de France, 1984, 220 p.

1739   SAEZ, José Luis. "Tres décadas de cultura dominicana" (Three decades of Dominican culture), *Estudios Sociales (Santo Domingo)* 17(55), mar 84 : 69-84.

1740   SALMON, Charles T.; LEE, Jung-Sokk. "Perceptions of newspapers fairness : a structural approach", *Journalism Quarterly* 60(4), wint 83 : 663-671. [USA]

1741   SAMARAJIWA, Rohan. "Third-World entry to the world market in news : problems and possible solutions", *Media, Culture and Society* 6(2), apr 84 : 119-136.

1742   SATO, Takeshi. "Igirisu ni okeru mass communication kenkyu" (Mass communication research in Britain), *Studies of Broadcasting* 34, 1984 : 167-199.

1743   SATO, Takeshi. "Shimin seikarsu to new media" (Citizen's life and 'new media'), *Toshi Mondai* 75(6), 1984 : 3-13.

1744   SCHUDSON, Michael. "News media and democratic processing", *Society* 21(2), feb 84 : 45-53. [USA]

1745   SCHUWER, Philippe. "L'édition de demain sera-t-elle programmée?", *Revue des Sciences Morales et Politiques* 139(1), 1984 : 99-115.

1746   SHIMIZU, Mikio. "30 years of Japanese TV in figures and tables", *Studies of Broadcasting* (19), mar 83 : 120-129.

1747   SNIZEK, W. E. "Casting the first rock : some observations on the bestowers and recipients of journal article comments in sociology", *Scientometrics* 6(4), 1984 : 215-222.

1748   STREETER, Thomas. "Policy discourse and broadcast practice : the FCC, the US broadcast networks and the discourse of the market-place", *Media, Culture and Society* 5(3-4), oct 83 : 247-262.

1749   SZECSKÖ, Tamás. "A tömegkommunikáció és az élet új algoritmusai" (Mass communication and the new algorithms of life), *Valóság* 27(10), 1984 : 7-13.

1750   SZEKFÜ, András. *A tömegkommunikáció új útjai* (New paths of mass communication). Budapest : Kossuth Könyvkiadó, 1984, 102 p.

1751   TAKASHINA, Susumu. "The role of broadcasting in regional Japan. From the report on the local broadcasting research project", *Studies of Broadcasting* (20), mar 84 : 91-131.

1752   TAKESHITA, Toshio. "Gidai settei kenkyu no shikaku -masukomi koka kenkyu ni okeru riron to jissho" (The perspective of agenda-setting research : theory and verification in mass communication effect studies), *Studies of Broadcasting* 34, 1984 : 81-116.

1753   TAMURA, Norio. *New media no America* (New media in America). Tokyo : Nippon Kogyo Shimbunsha, 1984, 276 p.

1754   TAMURA, Norio; [ed.]. *New media gyosei* (New media and local government). Tokyo : Sogo-rodo Kenkyusho, 1984, 418 p.

1755   TAYLOR, Henry; DOZIER, Carol. "Television violence, African-Americans, and social control : 1950-1976", *Journal of Black Studies* 14(2), dec 83 : 107-136.

1756   TIERNEY, Joan D. "A study of the influence of television heroes on adolescents", *Communications (Sankt Augustin)* 9(1), 1983 : 113-141.

1757   TONNON, Philippe. "Aspects de la librairie en Belgique en 1984", *Wallonie* 11(4), 1984 : 239-248.

1758   TOUSSAINT, Nadine. "Presse : pluralisme et concentration", *Regards sur l'Actualité* (97), jan 84 : 3-15. [France]

1759   VEITH, Richard H. "Videotex and teletext", *Annual Review of Information Science and Technology* 18, 1983 : 3-28.

1760   WATARI, Akeshi. "Media to ko teki kuhkan" (The media and the individual space), *Gendai no Riron* 21(3), 1984 : 35-44.
1761   WILEY, Richard E. "Competition and deregulation in telecommunications : the American experience", *Mass Communication Review Yearbook* 4, 1983 : 697-719.
1762   WILLIAMS, Patricia E.; [et al.]. "The impact of leisure-time television on school learning", *Evaluation Studies* 8, 1983 : 327-358.
1763   WILLOT, Didier. "Les nouveaux médias", *Revue Politique et Parlementaire* 85(907), dec 83 : 59-64. [France]

13800   ART
ART

13810   Aesthetics. Artists. Museums
Esthétique. Artistes. Musées

1764   "Création (La) luxuriante", *Autrement. Série Monde* (9), oct 84 : 268-311. [Southern Africa] [With contributions by Pierre HAFFNER, Jacques SOULILLOU, Christian GIRARD, Jean-Jacques MANDEL]
1765   "New York creation", *Autrement. Série Monde* (10), nov 84 : 1-340.
1766   "Points de vue sur l'art", *Diogène* 128, oct-dec 84 : 3-76.
1767   DAIX, Pierre. *L'ordre et l'aventure : peinture, modernité et répression totalitaire.* Paris : Arthaud, 1984, 286 p. bibl., ind.
1768   GABÁS PALLÁS, Raúl. *Estética : el arte como fundamento de la sociedad* (Aesthetics : the art as basis of society). Barcelona : Humanitas, 1984, 132 p. bibl.
1769   GREENFELD, Liah. "The role of the public in the success of artistic styles", *Archives Européennes de Sociologie* 25(1), 1984 : 83-98. [Israel]
1770   JASPER, James M. "Art and audiences : do politics matter?", *Berkeley Journal of Sociology* 29, 1984 : 153-180.
1771   JIMENEZ, Marc. *Vers une esthétique négative : Adorno et la modernité.* Paris : Le Sycomore, 1983, 421 p. bibl., ind.
1772   KWAŚNIEWSKI, Krzysztof. "Społeczna tożsamość sztuki, jej dziedzin i środków ich transmisji" (Social identity of the arts), *Kultura i Społeczeństwo* 28(3), 1984 : 73-85.
1773   LABKOVSKAJA, G. S.; [ed.]. *Èstetičeskaja kul'tura i èstetičeskoe vospitanie* (Aesthetic culture and aesthetic education). Moskva : Prosveščenie, 1983, 303 p.
1774   MAZEPA, V. I.; [ed.]. *Èstetičeskoe soznanie i hudožestvennaja kul'tura : problema vzaimodejstvija* (Aesthetic consciousness and artistic culture : problems of their interaction). Kiev : Naukova Dumka, 1983, 279 p.
1775   NAGY, Endre. *A magyar esztétika történetéből : felvilágosodás és reformkor* (From the history of Hungarian aesthetics : enlightenment and reformation). Budapest : Kossuth Kiadó, 1983, 534 p. bibl.
1776   OVSJANNIKOV, M. F. "Kapitalizm i hudožestvennoe tvorčestco" (Capitalism and artistic creation), *in : Iskusstvo i ideologičeskaja bor'ba* Moskva, 1983 : 38-49.
1777   PULLEGA, Paolo. *La comprensione estetica del mondo : saggio sul giovane Lukács* (The aesthetic understanding of the world : essay on the young Lukács). Bologna : Cappelli, 1983, 141 p. bibl.
1778   SEIGUERMAN, Osvaldo. *Arte e ideología* (Art and ideology). Buenos Aires : Editorial Stilcograf, 1984, 134 p. ill., bibl.
1779   SHIBATA, Singo. *Geijutsu teki rodo no riron — geijutsu teki souzou no riron* (Theory of artistic labour : theory of artistic creation). Tokyo : Aoiki Shoten, 1984, 318 p.
1780   SIMONTON, Dean Keith. "Artistic creativity and interpersonal relationships across and within generations", *Journal of Personality and Social Psychology* 46(6), jun 84 : 1273-1286.
1781   STANLEY-BAKER, Joan. *Japanese art.* New York, NY : Thames and Hudson, 1984, 216 p. ill., ind., bibl.
1782   STEINKRAUS, Warren E. *Philosophy of art.* Lanham, MD : University Press of America, 1984, rev., xii-246-22 p. bibl., ind., ill.
1783   SUŁKOWSKI, Bogusław. "Postawy emocjonalne i skłonności interpretacyjne robotników wobec sztuki" (Emotional and intellectual reactions of the workers on the works of art), *Kultura i Społeczeństwo* 28(1), 1984 : 83-89.
1784   WARD, Daniel Franklin. *Personal places : perspectives on informal art environments.* Bowling Green, OH : Bowling Green State University Popular Press, 1984, 177 p. ill., bibl. [USA]
1785   WOJNAR, Irena. "Społeczna obecność sztuki a wychowanie człowieka" (The social presence of the art and the education of man), *Kultura i Społeczeństwo* 28(2), 1984 : 25-38.

1786   ZIS', A. Ja.; [ed.]. *Socialističeskij obraz žizni i iskusstvo* (The socialist way of life and art). Moskva : Iskusstvo, 1983, 296 p.

1787   ZOLBERG, Vera L. "American art museums : sanctuary or free-for-all?", *Social Forces* 63(2), dec 84 : 377-392.

13820   Literature
          Littérature

1788   "African fiction", *Présence Africaine* (130), trim. 2, 84 : 71-131. [With contributions by J. A. ONKONKWO, A.-S. MALANDA, C. DAILLY]

1789   "Comment parler de la littérature?", *Débat* (29), mar 84 : 139-166. [With contributions by Marc FUNMAROLI, Gérard GENETTE, Tzvetan TODOROV]

1790   "Création (La) littéraire et l'imaginaire", *Diogène* 127, jul-sep 84 : 3-88.

1791   "Écrivains de RDA", *Allemagnes d'Aujourd'hui* (86), dec 83 : 67-127. [With contributions by Gérard RAULET, Rudolf WOLFF, Christine KOLB]

1792   "Literatur in Bewegung" (Literature on the move), *Argument* 25(142), dec 83 : 802-849. [Germany FR; German DR] [With contributions by Karen RUOFF, Klaus-Michael BOGDAL]

1793   "Littérature de Turquie", *Europe (Paris)* (655-656), dec 83 : 3-148.

1794   "Littérature et politique", *Homme et Société* 73-74, jul-dec 84 : 3-208.

1795   "Littérature et société", *Politique Africaine* (13), mar 84 : 3-78. [Africa] [With contributions by Alain RICARD, Albert GERARD, Bernard MOURALIS, J. V. SINGLER, Wole SOYINKA, Femi OSOFISAN]

1796   "Littérature et société en Amérique latine", *Cahiers du Monde Hispanique et Luso-brésilien* (42), 1984 : 5-180. [With contributions by Jacques LEENHARDT, Alejandro LOSADA, Ole OSTERGAARD, Jacques GILARD]

1797   "Neue Lyrik der DDR" (New poetic literature in GDR), *Deutsche Studien* 22(85), mar 84 : 3-64. [With contributions by Anneli HARTMANN, Theo MECHTENBERG]

1798   AMUTA, Chidi. "The Nigerian civil war and the evolution of Nigerian literature", *Canadian Journal of African Studies* 17(1), 1983 : 85-99.

1799   BARKER, Francis; [ed.]. *The politics of theory : proceedings of the Essex Conference on the Sociology of Literature, July 1982.* Colchester : University of Essex, 1983, 264-245-4 p. bibl., ill.

1800   BEN CHEIKH, Abdelkader. "Écrivains et édition dans les pays arabes", *Revue Tunisienne de Communication* (3), jun 83 : 7-27.

1801   BERNSTEIN, J. M. *The philosophy of the novel : Lukács, Marxism, and the dialectics of form.* Minneapolis, MN : University of Minnesota Press, 1984, xxiii-296 p.

1802   CAESAR, Michael; HAINSWORTH, Peter; [eds.]. *Writers and society in contemporary Italy : a collection of essays.* New York, NY : St. Martin's Press, 1984, xii-289 p. bibl., ind.

1803   CARROLL, Michael P. "Alligators in the sewer, dragons in the well and Freud in the toilet. Some contributions to the psychoanalytic study of urban legends", *Sociological Review* 32(1), feb 84 : 57-74.

1804   CHERNI, Zeineb. "La pensée de l'amour. Essai sur la littérature féminine tunisienne", *IBLA* 46(152), sem. 2, 83 : 279-298.

1805   CONDÉ, Maryse. "De l'autre bord, un autre pays. L'Afrique vue par les écrivains afro-américains", *Politique Africaine* (15), sep 84 : 34-47.

1806   DINO, Gusine. "Soixante ans de roman turc", *Temps Modernes* 41(456-457), aug 84 : 396-417.

1807   HARLOW, Barbara. "Palestine or Andalusia : the literary response to the Israeli invasion of Lebanon", *Race and Class* 26(2), aut 84 : 33-43.

1808   HEATH, Shirley Brice. "Oral and literate traditions", *International Social Science Journal / Revue Internationale des Sciences Sociales* 36(1), 1984 : 43-57. [Developing countries]

1809   HEINRICH, Nathalie. "Les traducteurs littéraires : l'art et la profession", *Revue Française de Sociologie* 25(2), apr-jun 84 : 264-280. [France]

1810   HOMANS, Margaret. " 'Her very own howl' : the ambiguities of representation in recent women's fiction", *Signs* 9(2), win 83 : 186-205.

1811   HUMBERT, Geneviève. "Prosateurs et politiques. Les grandes lignes de l'évolution de la vie littéraire en RDA (1973-1983)", *Revue d'Allemagne* 16(1), mar 84 : 60-76.

1812   JAY, Salim. "Romans maghrébins (1967-1983)", *Afrique Littéraire* (70), trim. 4, 83 : 1-128.

1813   KNIGHT, Stephen; MUKHERJEE, S. N.; [eds.]. *Words and worlds : studies in the social role of verbal culture.* Sydney : Sydney Association for Studies in Society and Culture, 1983, 197-4 p. ill., bibl.

1814   KOFFLER, Judith S.; [et al.]. "Terror in the Modern Age : the vision of literature, the response of law", *Human Rights Quarterly* 5(2), mai 83 : 109-213. [With contributions by R. WEISBERG, R. SZULKIN, G. HARTMAN, T. DES PRES, S. TOUSTER, D. A. J. RICHARDS, D. ORLOW, G. GIBIAN, N. M. NAIMARK, N. TUMARKIN] [Abstract 34-365]

1815 LAFARGE, Claude. *La valeur littéraire : figuration littéraire et usages sociaux des fictions.* Paris : Fayard, 1983, 354 p. bibl., ind.

1816 LAMBERECHTS, Luc. "Modèles et modalités de la représentation de la société dans le roman allemand moderne : un aperçu sélectif et synthétique", *Revue de l'Institut de Sociologie* (1-2), 1984 : 121-131.

1817 LEUNG, Angela K. "Sexualité et sociabilité dans le Jin Ping Mei, roman érotique chinois de la fin du XVIᵉᵐᵉ siècle", *Social Science Information / Information sur les Sciences Sociales* 23(4-5), 1984 : 653-676.

1818 LIEHM, Antonin J. "La littérature centre-européenne aujourd'hui", *Cadmos* 6(23-24), wint 83 : 45-51.

1819 MECHLING, Jay. "Peter L. Berger's novels of precarious vision", *Sociological Inquiry* 54(4), 1984 : 359-381.

1820 MULLINS, Lynn S.; KOPELMAN, Richard E. "The best seller as an indicator of societal narcissism : is there a trend?", *Public Opinion Quarterly* 48(4), 1984 : 720-730. [USA]

1821 MUNTEAN, George. "Littérature roumaine : repères et tendances", *Revue Roumaine* 38(7-8), 1984 : 184-199.

1822 RADWAY, Janice. "Interpretative communities and variable literacies : the function of romance reading", *Daedalus* 113(3), sum 84 : 49-73. [USA]

1823 ROBIN, Régine. "La littérature yiddish soviétique : minorité nationale et polyphonisme", *Temps Modernes* 41(458), sep 84 : 539-556. [With contributions by Mariana SAUBER]

1824 SAKUTA, Kei'ichi; TOMINAGA, Shigeki; [eds.]. *Jison to kaigi* (Pride and doubt : toward a sociology of literature). Tokyo : Chikuma Shobo, 1984, 248 p.

1825 SANDERS, Ivan. "Sequels and revisions : the Hungarian Jewish experience in recent Hungarian literature", *Soviet Jewish Affairs* 14(1), feb 84 : 31-45.

1826 SCHLOTT, Wolfgang. "Leser und Lesekultur im sowjetischen Literaturunterricht" (Reader and culture by reading in Soviet literature education), *Osteuropa* 34(4), apr 84 : 246-255.

1827 TUCHMAN, Gaye; FORTIN, Nina E. "Fame and misfortune : edging women out of the great literary tradition", *American Journal of Sociology* 90(1), jul 84 : 72-96. [UK]

1828 UENO, Chizuko. "Ijin, marebito, gairai-sha mata wa yasei no kenryoku riron" (A visiting God legend : a quest for the legitimation of the rule), *Gendai-shiso* 12(4), 1984 : 76-98.

1829 VÖRÖS, Gizella B. *Népszerű művek világképe. I. Krimielemzések. II. Lektürelemzések* (World image of best-sellers. I. Crime stories analyses. II. Light fiction analyses). Budapest : Művelődéskutató Intézet, 1982, 188 p. [Hungary] [Part II : published 1983, 219 p.]

1830 WEIGEL, Sigrid. "Women begins relating to herself : contemporary German women's literature", *New German Critique* (31), wint 84 : 53-94. [See also pp. 95-108 by Miriam HANSEN]

1831 YU, Shiao-Ling. "Voice of protest : political poetry in the post-Mao era", *China Quarterly* (96), dec 83 : 703-719.

1832 ZIPES, Jack David. *Fairy tales and the art of subversion : the classical genre for children and the process of civilization.* New York, NY : Wildman Press, 1983, 214 p. bibl., ind.

13830 Fine arts
Beaux-arts

1833 "Architecture and public spaces", *Public Interest* (74), wint 84 : 3-157. [USA] [With contributions by R. SCRUTON, W. HUBBARD, N. GLAZER, J. B. JACKSON, R. STARR, D. LYNDON, M. A. SCULLY]

1834 DAMUS, Martin. "Veränderungen in Form und Inhalt der Malerei der DDR" (Painting evolution in German Democratic Republic), *Deutschland Archiv* 16(10), oct 83 : 1072-1084.

1835 KAIN, Roger. "Conservation du patrimoine architectural et des villes historiques en Grande Bretagne", *Norois* 31(123), sep 84 : 379-392.

1836 NAHOUM-GRAPPE, Véronique. "La ligne : un dessin de l'esthétique contemporaine", *Social Science Information / Information sur les Sciences Sociales* 23(2), 1984 : 369-379.

1837 RICCI, Giacomo. "Le tortuose strade dell' architettura italiana contemporanea" (Tortuous way of actual Italian architecture), *Nord e Sud* 30(4), dec 83 : 177-189.

1838 SIMMS, L. Moody Jr. "Toward norms : the fine arts in the American South, 1900-1960", *Southern Quarterly* 21(2), wint 83 : 39-67.

1839 STĂNCIULESCU, Traian Dinorel. "Valorile culturale în arhitectura satului românesc" (Cultural values in Romanian village architecture), *Viitorul Social* 76(4), aug 83 : 311-321.

13840   Music
Musique

1840   "Country music : tradition and the individual talent", *Southern Quarterly* 22(3), spr 84 : 1-174.
[USA] [With contributions by Charles R. TOWNSEND, Patrick B. MULLEN, Stephen
B. TUCKER, Mary BUFWACK]

1841   "Show-biz : les stars, les pros, les fans", *Autrement. Série Mutations* (58), mar 84 : 1-264.
[France]

1842   CERULO, Karen A. "Social disruption and its effects on music : an empirical analysis",
Social Forces 62(4), jun 84 : 885-9O4.

1843   GOJOWY, Detlef. "Neue Musik und Musikwissenschaft in der Sowjetunion" (Music in
Soviet Union), *Osteuropa* 33(11-12), dec 83 : 870-881.

1844   MENGER, Pierre-Michel. "Création et consommation musicales : le grand écart", *Esprit*
(3), mar 84 : 51-62. [France]

1845   SERI, Dedy. "Musique traditionnelle et développement national en Côte d'Ivoire",
Tiers-Monde 25(97), mar 84 : 109-124.

1846   STARR, S. Frederick. "The rock inundation", *Wilson Quarterly* 7(4), aut 83 : 58-67. [USSR]

1847   TIBORI, Timea. *Bartók zenéjének fogadtatása a 80-as években. Egy zenesociológiai vizsgálat eredményei*
(The reception of Bartók's music in the 80-ies. Results of a music-sociological research).
Budapest : Művelődéskutató Intézet, 1984, 66 p.

1848   ZHORDANIA, Josif. "Georgian folk-singing : its source, emergence and modern development", *International Social Science Journal / Revue Internationale des Sciences Sociales* 36(3),
1984 : 537-549. [USSR]

13850   Dramatic art
Art dramatique

1849   "Théâtre (Le) à la Réunion", *Bulletin d'Information du CENADDOM* 14(73), trim. 1, 84 : 39-48.

1850   "Théâtre (Le) au Canada", *Études Canadiennes / Canadian Studies* 9(15), dec 83 : 3-127. [With
contributions by Josette FERAL, Elaine F. NARDOCCHIO, Marie-Lyne PICCIONE,
Brian POCKNELL]

1851   DELDIME, Roger. "Évolution de l'éthique et de l'esthétique du Théâtre de l'Atelier rue
Sainte-Anne", *Revue de l'Institut de Sociologie* (1-2), 1984 : 277-286. [Bruxelles]

1852   EDEBIRI, U. "L'utilisation du pidgin français dans le théâtre africain", *Peuples Noirs —
Peuples Africains* 7(40), sep 84 : 97-114.

1853   EPSKAMP, Kees. "Going 'popular' with culture : theatre as a small-scale medium in
developing countries", *Development and Change* 15(1), jan 84 : 43-64.

1854   GEORGE, Vincent. "Community theatre as a strategy in rural community development :
the case of New Market, Jamaica", *Community Development Journal* 19(3), jul 84 : 142-150.

1855   KIDD, Ross; RASHID, Mamunur. "Theatre by the people for the people and of the people :
people's theatre and landless organizing in Bangladesh", *Bulletin of Concerned Asian Scholars*
16(1), mar 84 : 30-45.

1856   KOWALEWICZ, Kazimierz. "Pomysły do badań nad krytyką teatralną" (Some suggestions
for the study on theatrical criticism), *Kultura i Społeczeństwo* 28(2), 1984 : 97-110.

1857   POUPEYE, Camille. *Le théâtre chinois.* Bruxelles : Éditions Labor, 1984, 239 p. ill., bibl.

13860   Folk art
Art populaire

13900   EDUCATION
ÉDUCATION

13910   Educational sociology
Sociologie de l'éducation

1858   "École (L')", *Pouvoirs* (30), 1984 : 117 p. [France] [With contributions by R. GIROD,
A. PERCHERON, N. GLAZER, J.-J. VESTRE, P. RAYNAUD]

1859   "Educational research : issues in cross-national collaboration", *IDS Bulletin* 15(4), oct 84 : 1-91.
[Developing countries] [With contributions by Dietrich GOLDSCHMIDT, Kenneth
KING, John OXENHAM; ENG; SPA; FRE]

1860   "Pédagogie, espoirs et désillusions", *Raison Présente* (71), trim. 3, 84 : 23-133. [France]
[With contributions by Daniel ZIMMERMANN, Jacqueline MARCHAND]

1861   "Sociologie de l'éducation", *Recherches Sociologiques* 15(1), 1984 : 3-149. [With contributions
by C. DUBAR, D. PATY, J. NIZET, J. L. GOUVEIA]

1862   "Symposium on the year of the reports : responses from the educational community",
    Harvard Educational Review 54(1), 1984 : 1-87. [USA] [With contributions by David
    IYACK, Elisabeth HANSOT]

1863   "Teaching in America", *Wilson Quarterly* 8(1), 1984 : 47-105. [With contributions by Patricia
    ALBJERG GRAHAM, Gary SYKES, Val R. RUST, Denis P. DOYLE]

1864   ARRUDA, Marcos. "O desafio da educação popular na Nicaragua" (The challenge of
    popular education in Nicaragua), *Vozes* 77(8), oct 83 : 16-31.

1865   BAYCE, Rafael. *La investigación contemporánea en educación : una evaluación epistemológica de teoría
    y métodos* (Educational research today : an epistemological evaluation of theory and
    methods). Montevideo : Centro de Informaciones y Estudios del Uruguay, Acali
    Editorial, 1983, 179 p. ill., bibl.

1866   BENEDIKTOV, B. A.; BENEDIKTOV, S. B. *Psihologija obučenija i vospitanija v vysšej škole*
    (Psychology of teaching and education in high schools). Minsk : Vyšějšaja Škola, 1983, 224 p.

1867   BERTHELOT, Jean-Michel. *Le piège scolaire*. Paris : Presses Universitaires de France,
    1983, 297 p. bibl.

1868   BOLSTER, Arthur S. Jr. "Toward a more effective model of research on teaching",
    Harvard Educational Review 53(3), 1983 : 294-308.

1869   BRUNNER, José Joaquín. *Algunas consideraciones sobre la investigación educacional en América
    Latina* (Some considerations on educational research in Latin America). Santiago de
    Chile : Facultad Latinoamericana de Ciencias Sociales, 1984, 35 p.

1870   BUCKLAND, Peter. "The education crisis in South Africa : restructuring the policy
    discourse", *Social Dynamics* 8(1), jun 82 : 14-28.

1871   BURGESS, Robert G. "Exploring frontiers and settling territory : shaping the sociology
    of education", *British Journal of Sociology* 35(1), mar 84 : 122-137.

1872   CARIDE, José Antonio. "Educación y desarrollo social" (Education and social development),
    RS Cuadernos de Realidades Sociales (23-24), jan 84 : 95-113.

1873   CASPARD, Pierre; [ed.]. *La presse d'éducation et d'enseignement : XVIIIᵉ siècle-1940; répertoire
    analytique. I. A-C. II. D-J.* Paris : Institut National de la Recherche Pédagogique, CNRS,
    81-84, 558; 685 p.

1874   CLAUSSE, Arnould. *Évolution des doctrines et des méthodes pédagogiques : du conditionnement à
    la liberté.* Fribourg : Éditions Universitaires, 1983, 200 p. bibl., ind.

1875   COBALTI, Antonio. *Sociologia dell'educazione : teorie e ricerche sul sistema scolastico* (Sociology of
    education : theories and researches on the school system). Milano : Franco Angeli, 1983,
    146 p. bibl., ind.

1876   COBBE, James H. "The educational system, wage and salary structures, and income
    distribution : Lesotho as a case study circa 1975", *Journal of Developing Areas* 17(2),
    jan 83 : 227-242.

1877   DATLER, Wilfried. *Was leistet die Psychoanalyse für die Pädagogik? Ein systematischer Aufriss*
    (What does psychoanalysis for pedagogy? A systematical design) Wien · Jugend und
    Volk, 1983, 175 p. bibl.

1878   DEAN, E.; HARTMANN, P.; KATZEN, M.; [eds.]. *History in Black and White : an analysis
    of South African school history text-books.* Paris : UNESCO, 1983, 137 p. bibl., tabl.

1879   DELCOURT, J. "Vers une nouvelle sociologie de l'éducation", *Recherches Sociologiques* 15(1),
    1984 : 11-27.

1881   FRANCO ARBELAEZ, Augusto. "50 años de educación en Colombia" (50 years of
    education in Colombia), *Revista Javeriana* 100(500), dec 83 : 359-376.

1882   FROESE, Leonhard. *Ausgewählte Studien zur vergleichenden Erziehungswissenschaft : Positionen
    und Probleme* (Selected studies on comparative educational sciences : positions and
    problems). München : Minerva Publikation, 1983, viii-158 p. bibl.

1883   GARCÍA GUADILLA, Carmen. "Production et transferts théoriques dans la recherche
    éducative : le cas de l'Amérique latine", *Tiers-Monde* 25(97), mar 84 : 75-93.

1884   GASPERINI, Lavinia. "Direction culturelle, éducation et développement au Mozambique",
    Tiers-Monde 25(97), mar 84 : 189-204.

1885   GIROUX, Henry A. "Theories of reproduction and resistance in the new sociology of
    education. A critical analysis", *Harvard Educational Review* 53(3), 1983 : 257-293.

1886   GIROUX, Henry A. *Theory and resistance in education : a pedagogy for the opposition.* London;
    Exeter, NH : Heinemann Educational Books, 1983, xiv-280 p. bibl., ind.

1887   GROSPERRIN, Bernard. *Les petites écoles sous l'Ancien Régime.* Rennes : Ouest France, 1984,
    175 p. ill., bibl.

1888   HAMMERSLEY, Martyn. "Some reflections upon the macro-micro problem in the
    sociology of education", *Sociological Review* 32(2), mai 84 : 316-324.

1889   HERNÁNDEZ DÍAZ, José María. *Educación y sociedad en Béjar durante el siglo XIX* (Education and society in Béjar during the XIXth century). Salamanca : Ediciones Universidad de Salamnca, Instituto de Ciencias de la Educación, 1983, 356 p. ill., bibl.

1890   KECKEISEN, Wolfgang. *Pädagogik zwischen Kritik und Praxis : Studien zur Entwicklung und Aufgabe kritischer Erziehungswissenschaft* (Pedagogy between criticism and practice : studies on the development and tasks of critical educational science). Weinheim : Beltz, 1984, 298 p. bibl.

1891   KONDO, Motoo; ARIMOTO, Akira; [eds.]. *Gendai shakai to kyoiku* (Modern society and education). Tokyo : Fukumura Shuppan, 1984, 229 p.

1892   LING, Peter. *Education policy in Australia, 1880-1914.* Melbourne : Centre for Youth and Community Studies, Phillip Institute of Technology, 1984, 282 p.

1893   MARCEL, Odile. *Une éducation française.* Paris : Presses Universitaires de France, 1984, 198 p.

1894   MILLER, Errol. *Educational research : the English-speaking Caribbean.* Ottawa : International Development Research Centre, 1984, 199 p. bibl.

1895   MONCADA, Alberto. *Más allá de la educación* (Beyond the education). Madrid : Tecnos, 1983, 125 p. bibl. [Spain]

1896   NG'ANG'A, James Mwangi. *Education in Kenya since independence : a bibliography, 1963-1983.* Nairobi : Kenyatta University College Library, 1983, ii-145 p. ind.

1897   NISHINE, Kazuo. "M. Weber no kyoiku shakaigaku : shoki Weber no kyoiku kankyo" (Sociology of education in Max Weber : the educational environment of Max Weber in his youth), *Bulletin of the Faculty of School Education Hiroshima University* 1(7), 1984 : 1-14.

1898   OSBORNE, Robert D. "Scrutinising education in Northern Ireland", *Administration (Dublin)* 31(4), 1984 : 443-454.

1899   POWERS, Richard H. *The dilemma of education in a democracy.* Chicago, IL : Regnery Gateway, 1984, 253 p. [USA]

1900   QAYSI, Māhir. *Youth education in Iraq and Egypt, 1920-1980 : a contribution to comparative education within the Arab region = Tarbiyat al-shabab fi al-'Iraq wa-Misr, 1920-1980.* Leuven : Helicon, 1983, liii-638 p. ill., bibl.

1901   RAILLON, Louis. *L'enseignement ou la contre-éducation : essai de pédagogie fondamentale.* Paris : Presses Universitaires de France, 1984, 206 p. bibl.

1902   RAJ, Lajpat. "Education in China", *China Report* 19(5), oct 83 : 3-12.

1903   REXING, Heinz-Peter. *Bildung und Beschäftigung* (Education and employment). Bochum : Studienverlag N. Brockmeyer, 1983, viii-207 p. ill., bibl. [Germany FR]

1904   RIBOLZI, Luisa. "La sociologia dell'educazione come sociologia dei processi di socializzazione" (The sociology of education as sociology of educational processes), *Studi di Sociologia* 22(4), oct-dec 84 : 422-427.

1905   SALOMÉ, Bernard. *Éducation et développement : le cas de Haïti.* Paris : OECD Centre de Développement, 1984, 139 p.

1906   SCHIZZEROTTO, Antonio. "I collegamenti della sociologia dell'educazione italiana con la riflessione scientifica in ambito internazionale : alcuni appunti" (The links between Italian sociology of education and international research : some remarks), *Studi di Sociologia* 22(1), jan-mar 84 : 90-98.

1907   SZCZEPAŃSKI, Jan. "Oświata — system czy dramat?" (Education — system or drama), *Człowiek i Światopogląd* 9, 1984 : 4-12.

1908   TAVEL, David; [ed.]. *Modern educational controversies.* Lanham, MD : University Press of America, 1984, 336 p. bibl. [USA]

1909   TAYLOR, Gerald D. "Community education : agent of social change or guardian of the status quo ?", *Interchange* 15(2), 84 : 23-42. [USA]

1910   TAYLOR, W. H. "Missionary education in Africa reconsidered : the Presbyterian educational impact in Eastern Nigeria, 1846-1974", *African Affairs* 83(331), apr 84 : 189-205.

1911   TRIGUEIRO MENDES, Durmeval; [ed.]. *Filosofia da educação brasileira* (Philosophy of Brazilian education). Rio de Janeiro, RJ : Civilização Brasileira, 1983, 239 p. bibl., ill.

1912   VAN HAECHT, Anne. "Modèles pédagogiques et réformes structurelles dans l'enseignement belge", *Annales de l'Institut de Sociologie*, 1983 : 201-218.

1913   VERMA, G. C. *Modern education, its growth and development in Rajasthan, 1818-1983.* Jaipur : Publication Scheme; Sharan Book Depot, 1984, xvi-464 p. bibl., maps, ind.

1914   VIET, Jean; VAN SLYPE, Georges. *EUDISED. Thesaurus multilingue pour le traitement de l'information en éducation. Version française.* Berlin; New York, NY... Mouton, 1984, nouv., xx-302 p. [Nouvelle édition préparée en 1984 pour le Conseil de l'Europe et la Commission des Communautés Européennes. Également publié en anglais, allemand, néerlandais, danois, italien, portugais, espagnol et grec]

1915   WHITE, F. C. *Knowledge and relativism : an essay in the philosophy of education.* Assen : Van Gorcum, 1983, ix-148 p. bibl.

1916   WHITE, Merry I. "Japanese education : how do they do it?", *Public Interest* (76), sum 84 : 87-101.

1917   WIN, Kanwza. "Education in the Socialist Republic of the Union of Burma", *Asian and Pacific Quarterly of Cultural and Social Affairs* 16(1), spr 84 : 52-59.

1918   WINCŁAWSKI, Włodzimierz. "Józefa Chałasińskiego socjologia wychowania" (Józef Chałasiński as a theoretician of the sociology of education), *Kultura i Społeczeństwo* 28(4), 1984 : 87-96.

1919   ZAMBELLI, Franco. *L'osservazione e l'analisi del comportamento : problemi e tendenze metodologiche nella ricerca in educazione* (Observation and analysis of behaviour : methodological problems and trends in educational research). Bologna : Pàtron, 1983, 327 p. ill., bibl.

13920   **Educational systems. Educational policy**
         Systèmes d'enseignement. Politique de l'éducation

1920   "Mountain (The) States Legal Foundation Conference on private education and the law", *Journal of Social, Political and Economic Studies* 9(1), spr 84 : 1-128. [USA] [With contributions by Maxwell A. MILLER, Bruce HAFEN]

1921   "Stratégies d'aide et développement de l'éducation", *Perspectives (UNESCO)* 13(4), 1983 : 465-560. [With contributions by Paul HURST, Hyung-Ki KIM, Ananda W. P. GURUGE, Aklilu HAB-TE]

1922   BASTID, Marianne. "Chinese educational policies in the 1980's and economic development", *China Quarterly* (98), jun 84 : 189-219.

1923   BLOCK, A. de; MARTENS, L. *Moderne schoolsystemen* (Modern school systems). Antwerpen : Standaard Educatieve Uitgeverij, 1983, 305 p. ill., bibl.

1924   BLOSSFELD, Hans-Peter. "Bildungsreform und Beschäftigung der jungen Generation im öffentlichen und privaten Sektor : eine empirisch vergleichende Analyse" (Educational reform and youth employment in public and private sectors : an empirical comparative analysis), *Soziale Welt* 35(1-2), 1984 : 159-189. [Germany FR]

1925   BOTOAS, B. P. *Struktura processa vospitanija : metodologičeskie aspekty* (Structure of the educational process : methodological aspects). Kaunas : Šviesa, 1984, 190 p. [USSR]

1926   BRAVO, Héctor Félix. *El estado y la enseñanza privada* (State and private education). Buenos Aires : Editorial de Belgrano, 1984, 98 p. bibl. [Argentina]

1927   CASTIGLIONE, Laurence V. "Educating the gifted and the talented", *Journal of the Institute for Socioeconomic Studies* 8(4), wint 84 : 79-92. [USA]

1928   CONLISK, John. "Four invalid propositions about equality, efficiency and intergenerational transfers through schooling", *Journal of Human Resources* 19(1), wint 84 : 3-21. [USA]

1929   COOPER, Bruce S.; [et al.]. "The latest word on private-school growth", *Teachers College Record* 85(1), aut 83 : 88-99. [USA]

1930   COSTIN, Lela B., RAAB, Erich. *Schulsozialarbeit in den USA* (School social work in the USA). München : Deutsches Jugendinstitut, 1983, 178 p. bibl.

1931   CREEMERS, Bert P. M.; HOEBEN, W.; KOOPS, K. *De kwaliteit van het onderwijs* (The quality of education). Haren : Research Instituut voor het Onderwijs in het Noorden; Groningen : Wolters-Noordhoff, 1983, iv-243 p. bibl.

1932   CURTIS, Bruce. "Capitalist development and educational reform. Comparative material from England, Ireland and Upper Canada to 1850", *Theory and Society* 13(1), jan 84 : 41-68.

1933   DE TEZANOS, Araceli; MUÑOZ, Guillermo; ROMERO, Emiliano. *Escuela y comunidad : un problema de sentido* (School and community : a problem of feeling). Bogotá : Universidad Pedagógica Nacional, Centro de Investigaciones, 1983, 240 p. ill., bibl. [Colombia]

1934   DERMUTZ, Susanne. *Der österreichische Weg : Schulreform und Bildungspolitik in der Zweiten Republik* (The Austrian way : school reform and educational policy under the Second Republic). Wien : Verlag für Gesellschaftskritik, 1983, 259 p. ill., bibl.

1935   DIEZ HOCHLEITNER, Ricardo; TENA ARTIGAS, Joaquin; GARCÍA CUERPO, Marcelino. *Éducation et travail dans la réforme éducative espagnole*. Paris : UNESCO, 1984, 64 p. bibl.

1936   DOBLES, Ricardo R. *Escuela y comunidad* (School and commuinity). San José : Editorial Universidad Estatal a Distancia, 1983, 414-5 p. ill., maps, bibl. [Costa Rica]

1937   DODGE, Peter. "Sociological realism and educational achievement", *International Social Science Review* 59(3), sum 84 : 134-138.

1938   DURAND, Yves; [et al.]. *L'enjeu éducatif : situation, comparaisons, propositions.* Paris : CLC, 1984, 186 p.

1939   ENDERWITZ, Herbert. *Weltweite Bildungsreform : Möglichkeiten einer realen Utopie* (Worldwide educational reform : opportunities of a real utopia). Köln : Bund-Verlag, 1983, 139 p. ill.

1940   ESCOTET, Miguel Angel. "La planificación educativa para Iberoamérica : utopismo y realismo" (Educational planning for Latin America : utopia and realism), *Cuadernos Hispanoamericanos* (406), apr 84 : 53-70.

1941   FANDIÑO, Graciela. *Tendencias actuales en la educación colombiana* (Present trends in Colombian education). Bogotá : Universidad Santo Tomás, Centro de Enseñanza Desescolarizada, 1984, 508 p. ill., bibl.

1942   FILONOV, G. N. "Metody kommunističeskogo vospitanija v uslovijah razvitogo socializma, problemy teorii i praktiki" (Methods of communist education under conditions of developed socialism, theoretical and practical problems), *in : Sovetskaja obščeobrazovatel'naja škola k 60-letiju SSSR* Moskva, 1983 : 221-234.

1943   FRANKLIN, Richard K. "Elite conflict over educational enrollment and school management policy in the People's Republic of China, 1957-1979", *Asian Profile* 11(5), oct 83 : 423-446.

1944   FULLAT GENÍS, Octavio. *Escuela pública, escuela privada* (Public school, private school). Barcelona : Humanitas, 1983, 185 p. ill., bibl. [Spain]

1945   GEORGEON, François. "La politique de l'enseignement en Turquie", *Temps Modernes* 41(456-457), aug 84 : 378-395.

1946   GOUVEIA, J. L. "Quelques écueils à la démocratisation de l'éducation : à partir de l'expérience québécoise", *Recherches Sociologiques* 15(1), 1984 : 93-116.

1948   HARDING, Robert R. "Housing discrimination as a basis for interdistrict school desegregation remedies", *Yale Law Journal* 93(2), dec 83 : 340-361. [USA]

1949   HARRISON-MATTLEY, Peter. "Obstacles to educational reform", *Australian Quarterly* 55(2), wint 83 : 219-233. [Australia]

1950   HEPBURN, Mary A. "Democratic schooling : five perspectives from research in the United States", *International Journal of Political Education* 6(3), nov 83 : 245-262.

1951   HERRIMAN, Michael. "Academic freedom in Australia", *Interchange* 15(1), 84 : 82-93.

1952   INSTITUT INTERNATIONAL DE PLANIFICATION DE L'ÉDUCATION. *La planification de l'éducation dans le contexte des problèmes actuels du développement.* Paris : UNESCO, l'Institut, 1984, 168 p.

1953   JUNGBLUTH, Paul. "Covert sex-role socialization in Dutch education. A survey among teachers", *Netherlands Journal of Sociology* 20(1), apr 84 : 43-57.

1954   KORTE, Elke. "Der Numerus Clausus im Prozess gesellschaftlicher Entwicklungen" (Numerous clauses in the social development process), *Gegenwartskunde* 33(1), trim. 1, 84 : 25-37. [Germany FR]

1955   LECLERCQ, Jean Michel. *Le Japon et son système éducatif.* Paris : La Documentation Française, 1984, 120 p. ill., bibl.

1956   LEVIN, Henry M.; [et al.]. *Educação e desigualdade no Brasil* (Education and inequality in Brazil). Petrópolis : Vozes, 1984, 291 p. ill., bibl.

1957   LUCAS, Madeleine. "Étude de différents déterminants de l'orientation en classes de cinquième et de troisième", *Orientation Scolaire et Professionnelle* 13(2), jun 84 : 139-158. [France]

1958   MARSHNER, Connaught; [ed.]. *A blueprint for education reform.* Chicago, IL : Regnery/ Gateway, 1984, vi-303 p. bibl.

1959   MASCHINO, Maurice Tarik. *Savez-vous qu'ils détruisent l'université?* Paris : Hachette, 1984, 226 p. [France]

1960   MATTHEWS, P. W. "Multiculturalism and multicultural education in Australia. II. Multicultural education", *Plural Societies* 14(3-4), wint 83 : 3-43.

1961   MISZTAL, Maria. "Społeczno-psychologiczne aspekty reprodukcji struktury edukacyjnej w Polsce" (Social and psychological aspects of reproduction of the educational structure in Poland), *Studia Socjologiczne* 93(2), 1984 : 87-106.

1962   MOITEL, Pierre. *Éducation, mission impossible?* Paris : Cerf, 1984, 115 p. bibl. [France]

1963   MONCHAMBERT, Sabine. *La liberté de l'enseignement.* Paris : Presses Universitaires de France, 1983, 431 p. bibl.

1964   MULLIGAN, James G. "A classroom production function", *Economic Inquiry* 22(2), apr 84 : 218-226.

1965   MUSHABEN, Joyce Marie. "Reform in three phases : judicial action and the German federal framework law for higher education of 1976", *Higher Education* 13(4), aug 84 : 423-438.

1966   NEIDERT, Lisa J.; TIENDA, Marta. "Converting education into earnings : the patterns among Hispanic origin men", *Social Science Research* 13(4), dec 84 : 303-320. [USA]

1967   OJIMA, Fumiaki. "Koko kyoiku kan no kouzou -koko kyoshi no koko kyoiku kaikaku ni taisuru ishiki o chushin to shite" (Teachers' attitudes towards high school reform), *Osaka Studies in Sociology of Education* 5, 1984 : 31-62.

1968   OLLMAN, Bertell. "Academic freedom in America today : a marxist view", *Monthly Review* 35(10), mar 84 : 24-46.

1969 ORGANISATION DE COOPÉRATION ET DE DÉVELOPPEMENT ÉCONOMIQUE. *Examens des politiques nationales d'éducation : Portugal.* Paris : OCDE, 1984, 124 p. bibl.

1970 OSIPOV, V. "Social'nye funkcii sistemy obrazovanija" (Social functions of the educational system), *Vestnik Obscestvennyh Nauk (Akademija Nauk Armjanskoj SSR)* (6), 1983 : 29-36.

1971 PELED, Elad. "Equality in Israel's educational policy", *Jerusalem Quarterly* (30), wint 84 : 17-28.

1972 PETERS, Heinz. *Das paraguayische Erziehungswesen von 1811 bis 1865 : Schule und Staat in einem Modell autozentrierter Entwicklung* (The Paraguayan educational system from 1811 to 1865 : school and State in a self-centred development model). Frankfurt-am-Main : P. Lang, 1984, 397 p. bibl.

1973 POGLIA, Edo. *Politique et planification de l'éducation en Suisse : un essai de systématisation.* Berne : Lang, 1983, mult. p. bibl.

1974 PORTO, A. J. "Propuesta para una ley de ciencia y educación superior" (Proposal for a law in science and higher education), *Ideas en Ciencias Sociales* 1(1), 1984 : 95-99.

1975 RAMA, Germán W.; [ed.]. *Mudanças educacionais na América Latina : situações e condições* (Educational changes in Latin America : situations and conditions). Fortaleza, Ce : Edições Universidade Federal do Ceará, 1983, 358 p. bibl.

1976 ROMILLY, Jacqueline de. *L'enseignement en détresse.* Paris : Julliard, 1984, 218 p. ind.

1977 SANTOS HERNÁNDEZ, Roberto. *Pasado, presente y perspectivas de la educación nacional institucionalizada* (Past, present and prospects of the institutionalized national education). Santo Domingo : Editora Alfa y Omega, 1983, 232 p. ill., bibl. [Dominican Republic]

1978 SAQIB, Ghulam Nabi. *Modernization of Muslim education in Egypt, Pakistan, and Turkey : a comparative study.* Lahore : Islamic Book Service, 1983, rev., xi-385 p. bibl., tabl.

1979 SAXE, Richard W.; ROSENBERGER, David S.; SOMMERVILLE, Joseph C. *School-community relations in transition.* Berkeley, CA : McCutchan Publishing Corporation, 1984, v-361 p. bibl., ind., ill.

1980 SCHMIDA, Leslie C.; KEENUM, Deborah G.; [eds.]. *Education in the Middle East.* Washington, DC : AMIDEAST, 1983, iv-143 p. bibl.

1981 SOKÓLSKA, Joanna. "Asiracje edukacyjne młodzieży robotniczej i chłopskiej" (Educational aspirations of worker and peasant youth), *Kwartalnik Pedagogiczny* 3, 1984 : 120-127.

1982 SRB, Vladimír. "Le niveau d'éducation de la population de la République Socialiste Tchécoslovaque au cours des années 1950-1980", *Demosta* 16(3-4), 1983 : 21-25.

1983 TERRAIL, Jean-Paul. "Familles ouvrières, école, destin social (1880-1980)", *Revue Française de Sociologie* 25(3), jul-sep 84 : 421-436. [France]

1984 VELÁZQUEZ GUZMÁN, María Guadalupe. "Política educativa y estructura agraria : una visión campesina" (Educational policy and agrarian structure : a peasant view), *Revista Mexicana de Sociología* 45(3), jul-sep 83 : 781-795. [Mexico]

1985 WESTERGÅRD-NIELSEN, N. "En søgemodel for overgangen fra uddannelse til erhverv : Teori og empiri" (A search model of the transition from education to work : theory and empirical findings), *Nationaløkonomisk Tidsskrift* 121(2), 1983 : 181-199.

1986 WOLFE, Barbara L.; BEHRMAN, Jere R. "Who is schooled in developing countries? The roles of income, parental schooling, sex, residence and family size", *Economics of Education Review* 3(3), 1984 : 231-245. [Nicaragua]

1987 WROBEL, Vera. "Escolas públicas e privadas : uma leitura sociológica de sua dinâmica organizacional" (Public and private schools : a sociological interpretation of their organizational dynamics), *Dados* 27(2), 1984 : 215-232. [Brazil]

1988 WYCKOFF, James H. "The nonexcludable publicness of primary and secondary public education", *Journal of Public Economics* 24(2), aug 84 : 331-351. [USA]

13930 Primary education. Secondary education
Enseignement primaire. Enseignement secondaire

1990 ALEXANDER, Karl L.; PALLAS, Aaron M. "Private schools and public policy : new evidence on cognitive achievement in public and private schools", *Sociology of Education* 56(4), oct 83 : 170-182. [USA] [With a response by Sally B. KILGORE, ibid. : 182-186]

1991 CAIN, Glen G.; GOLDBERGER, Arthur S. "Public and private schools revisited", *Sociology of Education* 56(4), oct 83 : 208-218. [USA] [With a response by James S. COLEMAN and Thomas HOFFER, ibid. : 219-234]

1992 CLARAMUNT, Ana N.; FERRA, Coloma. *Rentabilidad de la educación primaria en Mendoza* (Primary education output in Mendoza). Mendoza . Universidad Nacional de Cuyo, 1984, 75 p. [Argentina]

1993 CORKE, Michael. "What future for South Africa's private schools?", *Optima* 32(1), mar 84 : 26-37.

1994   CUBAN, Larry. "Transforming the frog into a prince : effective schools research, policy, and practice at the district level'', *Harvard Educational Review* 54(2), 1984 : 129-151. [USA]

1995   FINCH, Janet. "The deceit of self help : preschool playgroups and working class mothers", *Journal of Social Policy* 13(1), jan 84 : 1-20.

1996   GONTARD, Maurice. *L'enseignement secondaire en France de la fin de l'Ancien Régime à la loi Falloux : 1750-1850.* Aix-en-Provence : Edisud, 1984, 254-2 p. ill., bibl.

1997   HANNAN, Damian; [et al.]. *Schooling and sex roles : sex differences in subject provision and student choice in Irish post-primary schools.* Dublin : Economic and Social Research Institute, 1983, xxviii-446 p. ill., bibl.

1998   HOPE, Keith. "Are high schools really heteronomous?", *Sociology of Education* 56(3), jul 83 : 111-125.

1999   ISAMBERT-JAMATI, Viviane. *Culture technique et critique sociale à l'école élémentaire.* Paris : Presses Universitaires de France, 1984, 156 p. bibl.

2000   KOJIMA, Masaru. "Manila nihon jin shogakko no shakai teki seikaku" (Social characters of the Japanese primary school in Manila), *Journal of Ryukoku University* 242, 1984 : 169-206.

2001   LEVASSEUR, Jacqueline; CHASSAING, Françoise. "Évaluation de l'enseignement à l'école élémentaire. Présentation générale du dispositif'', *Orientation Scolaire et Profession-nelle* 13(1), mar 84 : 5-16. [France]

2002   MAJUMDAR, Prabhat Kumara; CHAUDHURI, Buddhadeb. *Faltering first step : reasons for disparity of sex-ratio in primary education level; a sociological analysis.* New Delhi : Cosmo, 1983, xii-227 p. bibl., ind.

2003   MAUPAS, Didier; [et al.]. *L'école en accusation.* Paris : Albin Michel, 1984, 242 p. bibl. [France]

2004   MILNER, Jean Claude. *De l'école.* Paris : Éditions du Seuil, 1984, 152 p. bibl.

2005   MOBE-FANSIAMA, Anicet. "L'expression culturelle dans les écoles du Zaïre", *Mois en Afrique* 19(215-216), jan 84 : 117-126.

2006   MORGAN, William R. "Learning and student life quality of public and private school youth", *Sociology of Education* 56(4), oct 83 : 187-202. [USA] [With a response by James S. COLEMAN and Thomas HOFFER, ibid. : 219-234]

2007   NOWACKI, Grzegorz. "Młodzież szkolna a socjalizm" (School youth and socialism), *Studia Socjologiczne* 94(3), 1984 : 199-222.

2008   OKUDA, Shinjo; HISHIMURA, Yukihiko. "The development of secondary education in Japan after World War II'', *Higher Education* 12(5), nov 83 : 567-578.

2009   PATY, D. "Socialisation des adolescents et organisation scolaire. Étude du fonctionnement des collèges français", *Recherches Sociologiques* 15(1), 1984 : 58-66.

2010   PINEDA ARROYO, José María; INFESTAS GIL, Angel; HERRERO CASTRO, Santos. *La innovación en educacipreescolar : expectatives y problemas* (The innovation in preschool education : expectancies and problems). Salamanca : Ediciones Universidad de Salamanca, Instituto de Ciencias de la Educación, 1984, 218 p. ill., bibl. [Spain]

2011   PURKAIT, Biswa Ranjan. *Administration of primary education under Mont-Ford reforms and its impact in West Bengal.* Calcutta : Firma KLM, 1984, xiv-265 p. bibl., ind.

2012   REYER, Jürgen. "Die Schule : eine ursprünglich sozialpädagogische Einrichtung?" (School : primarily a socio-pedagogical institution?), *Neue Praxis* (2), 1984 : 140-153. [Germany FR]

2013   ROSARIO, Fe María; PÉREZ DE ZAPATA, Amarilis. *Estado del arte de la educación pre-escolar en la República Dominicana* (State of the art on preschool education in the Dominican Republic). Santiago de los Caballeros : Centro de Documentación e Investigación Educativa; Centro de Investigaciones, Universidad Católica Madre y Maestra, 1983, 232 p. ill., bibl.

2014   SAUL, Mahir. "The Quaranic school farm and child labour in Upper Volta", *Africa (London)* 54(2), 1984 : 71-87.

2015   SHAVIT, Yossi. "Tracking and ethnicity in Israeli secondary education", *American Sociological Review* 49(2), apr 84 : 210-220.

2016   SMOLICZ, J. J.; LEAN, R. "A cultural and social profile of catholic schools : a parent study", *Australian Quarterly* 56(1), aut 84 : 86-103.

2017   SOMMER, Carl. *Schools in crisis : training for success or failure?* Houston, TX : Cahill Publishing Co., 1984, xiii-335 p. bibl. [USA]

2018   TAEUBER, Karl E.; JAMES, David R. "Racial segregation among public and private schools : a response", *Sociology of Education* 56(4), oct 83 : 204-207. [USA] [With a response by James S. COLEMAN and Thomas HOFFER, ibid. : 219-234]

13940   School environment
Milieu scolaire

2019   CIANO, Jane. *Causes and effects of secondary school drop-out in Nairobi, Kenya.* Nairobi : ACO
         Project, 1983, iii-71-14 p. bibl.
2020   CROZIER, Michel; PATY, Dominique. "Analyse stratégique et organisation scolaire.
         I. Questions d'éducation et stratégie du changement. II. Socialisation des adolescents
         et organisation scolaire : étude du fonctionnement et collèges français", *Recherches
         Sociologiques* 15(1), 1984 : 55-66.
2021   EVÊQUOZ, Grégoire. *Le contexte scolaire et ses otages : vers une approceh systématique des difficultés
         scolaires.* Paris : Éditions ESF, 1984, 142 p. bibl. [France]
2022   HOLLINGSWORTH, Ellen Jane; LUFLER, Henry S. Jr.; CLUNE, William H. III.
         School discipline : order and autonomy. New York, NY : Praeger, 1984, 176 p. bibl., ind.
         [USA]
2023   NIZET, J. "L'exercice du contrôle dans les écoles secondaires", *Recherches Sociologiques* 15(1),
         1984 : 67-91. [Belgique]
2024   POPKEWITZ, Thomas S. *Change and stability in schooling : the dual quality of educational reform.*
         Victoria : Deakin University Press, 1983, 112 p. bibl.

13950   Higher education
Enseignement supérieur

2025   "Foreign students in comparative perspective", *Comparative Education Review* 28(2),
         mai 84 : 163-339. [With contributions by Hans N. WEILER, Gerald W. FRY, Joyce
         LEWINGER MOOCK, William K. CUMMINGS, Peter WILLIAMS]
2026   "Future (The) of higher education in Britain", *Higher Education* 13(2), apr 84 : 115-224.
         [With contributions by Gary RHOADES, Jean-Claude CASTAGNOS, Claude
         ECHEVIN, Olivier FULTON]
2027   "Independence (The) of the University and the funding of the State : essays on academic
         freedom in Canada", *Interchange* 15(1), 84 : 1-160. [With contributions by Michel
         HORN, John GRANT, Michael HERRIMAN, Ed. MONAHAN]
2028   "Modern Korean higher education", *Korea Journal* 23(10), oct 83 : 4-48. [With contributions
         by Jongchol KIM, Sin-Bok KIM, Uchang KIM]
2029   "Student and alumni attitudes", *Social Forces* 62(4), jun 84 : 941-972. [With contributions
         by Dean R. HOGE, Jann L. HOGE, Donald E. MUIR, Donald C. McGLAMERY]
2030   "Universität und Gesellschaft" (University and society), *Geschichte und Gesellschaft* 10(1),
         1984 : 5-121. [Germany FR]
2031   ALTBACH, Philip G. "Student politics in the Third World", *Higher Education* 13(6),
         dec 84 : 635-655.
2032   ARATA, Silvia; FERNÁNDEZ, Marta E. *Educación y estratificación social : reflexiones acerca
         del origen social de los estudiantes universitarios* (Education and social stratification : reflections
         on the social origin of university students). Buenos Aires : FADES Ediciones, 1984,
         29 p. [Argentina]
2033   AVETISJAN, É. H. "Studenčeskij kollektiv, harakternye osobennosti i social'naja rol'"
         (The students collectivity : characteristics and the social role), *Voprosy Naučnogo
         Kommunizma (Érevan)* (2), 1982 : 189-199.
2034   BRUNNER, José Joaquín. *Informe sobre el desarrollo y el estado actual del sistema universitario
         en Chile* (Report on the development and present state of the higher education system in
         Chile). Santiago de Chile : Facultad Latinoamericana de Ciencias Sociales, 1984, 244 p.
2035   CAMILLERI, C. "Les étudiants étrangers en France et leur discours sur l'identité
         culturelle'", *Bulletin de Psychologie* 37(364), feb 84 : 287-297.
2036   CIRIA, Alberto; SANGUINETTI, Horacio J. *La reforma universitaria : 1918-1983* (The
         university reform : 1918-1983. 2 vols.). Buenos Aires : Centro Editor de América Latina,
         1983, 377 p. bibl. [Argentina]
2037   CLARKE, Alex M.; [et al.]. "University autonomy and public policies : a system theory
         perspective", *Higher Education* 13(1), feb 84 : 23-48. [Australia]
2038   COHEN, Yolande. "Student protest in the Welfare State : France and West Germany
         in the 1960's", *Comparative Social Research* 6, 83 : 299-312.
2039   CRAVEN, B. M ; [et al.] "Resource reallocation in higher education in Britain", *Higher
         Education* 12(5), nov 83 : 579-589.
2040   CROSSON, Patricia H. *Public service in higher education : practices and priorities.* Washington, DC :
         Association for the Study of Higher Education, 1983, 130 p. ill., bibl.

2041   DE MARTINI, Joseph R. "Student unrest in the nineteenth century : a sociological case study", *Sociological Inquiry* 54(4), 1984 : 408-431. [USA] [University of Illinois]

2042   DEVADOSS, Mudiappasamy; [et al.]. "Power, involvement and organizational effectiveness in higher education", *Higher Education* 13(4), aug 84 : 379-391.

2043   EHARA, Takekazu. *Gendai koto kyoiku no kouzou* (Mass higher education in contemporary Japan). Tokyo : University of Tokyo Press, 1984, 297 p.

2044   ESCALA, Alberto. *Universidad, crisis y perspectivas* (University, crisis and prospects). Buenos Aires : Editorial Anteo, 1983, 106 p. [Argentina]

2045   FRAILE, Eduardo A. "Estudio sociológico : Universitarios y Ancianos. Análisis comparativo" (Sociological study : graduates and aged. A comparative analysis), *RS Cuadernos de Realidades Sociales* (23-24), jan 84 : 249-263.

2046   FREDRIKSEN, Birger. *Main trends in Norwegian higher education since 1960*. Oslo : Norsk Utenrikspolitisk Institutt, 1984, 41-1 p. ill., bibl.

2047   FROOMKIN, Joseph; [ed.]. *The crisis in higher education*. New York, NY : Academy of Political Science, 1983, x-177 p. [USA]

2048   GRUSON, Pascale; MARKIEWICZ-LAGNEAU, Janina. *L'enseignant supérieur et son efficacité : France, États-Unis, URSS, Pologne*. Paris : Documentation Française, 1983, 240 p. ill., bibl.

2049   HARMAN, Grant. "The erosion of university independence : recent Australian experience", *Higher Education* 12(5), nov 83 : 501-518.

2050   HARVEY, Edward B. "The changing relationship between university education and inter-enerational social mobility", *Canadian Review of Sociology and Anthropology / Revue Canadienne-de Sociologie et d'Anthropologie* 21(3), aug 84 : 275-284.

2051   JARAUSCH, Konrad Hugo. *Deutsche Studenten 1800-1970* (German students 1800-1970). Frankfurt-am-Main : Suhrkamp, 1984, 254-1 p. bibl.

2052   JAROUSSE, Jean-Pierre. "Les contradictions de l'Université de masse dix ans après (1973-1983)", *Revue Française de Sociologie* 25(2), apr-jun 84 : 191-210. [France]

2053   KOGAN, Maurice; KOGAN, David. *The attack on higher education*. London : Kegan Page, 1983, 160 p. bibl. [UK]

2054   KOZAKIEWICZ, Mikołaj. "Kryzys społeczno-ekonomiczny — przemiany wartości a perspektywy kształcenia wyższego" (A socio-economic crisis — changes in the values and perspectives of higher education), *Wieś i Rolnictwo* 42(1), 1984 : 55-66.

2055   LANE, Jan-Erik. "Higher education regionalization", *Higher Education* 13(4), aug 84 : 347-368. [Sweden]

2056   LEVITT, Cyril. *Children of privilege : student revolt in the sixties; a study of student movements in Canada, the United States, and West Germany*. Toronto, ON; Buffalo, NY : University of Toronto Press, 1984, xiii-266 p. ill., bibl., ind.

2057   LINARES VALDIVIA, Edmundo. *La rebelión de la universidad contra el régimen militar : (ensayos sociológicas y políticos)* (The revolt of the university against military regime : (sociological and political essays)). La Paz : Ediciones Galaxia, 1983, 221 p.

2058   MARINI, Margaret Mooney. "Women's educational attainment and the timing of entry into parenthood", *American Sociological Review* 49(4), aug 84 : 491-511. [USA]

2059   MARTA SOSA, Joaquin. *El estado y la educación superior en Venezuela* (The state and higher education in Venezuela). Caracas : Equinoccio, 1984, ix-205 p. bibl.

2060   MARUYAMA, Tetsuo; NEGI, Akira. "Koto kyoiku kikan to shite no senshu gakko" (The special training school as a higher education system in Japan), *Kinjyo Gakuin Daigaku Ronshu, Social Science Series* 26, 1984 : 45-69.

2061   NAVLAKHA, Suren. "Self-legitimacy of Indian higher education", *Contributions to Indian Sociology* 18(2), jul-dec 84 : 245-265.

2062   NEAVE, Guy R.; JENKINSON, Sally. *Research on higher education in Sweden : an analysis and an evaluation*. Stockholm : Almqvist och Wiksell International, 1983, 112 p. bibl.

2063   OLESEN LARSEN, Peder. "Medindflydelsen på universiteterne, forbillede eller problembarn" (Influence in the universities, a model or a problem?), *Økonomi og Politik* 57(2), 1983 : 107-121. [Denmark]

2064   PALMER, Monte; NEDELCOVYCH, Mima. "The political behavior of Moroccan students", *Journal of Arab Affairs* 3(1), spr 84 : 115-130.

2065   PINTO, Marina. *Federalism and higher education : the Indian experience*. Bombay : Orient Longman, 1984, xiii-250 p. bibl., ind.

2066   POPOV, Nebojša. "Prilozi proučavanju studentskih pokreta u Jugoslaviji" (Contributions to the study of student movements in Yugoslavia), *Socioloski Pregled* 18(1-2), aug 84 : 19-42.

2067   PREMFORS, Rune. "Analysis in politics : the regionalization of Swedish higher education", *Comparative Education Review* 28(1), feb 84 : 85-104.

2068   RAILLON, François. *Les étudiants indonésiens et l'Ordre nouveau : politique et idéologie du 'Mahasiswa indonésia', 1966-1974.* Paris : Éditions de la Maison des Sciences de l'Homme, 1984, 351 p. bibl., ind.

2069   RITTER, Robert L. *Higher education : the initial step.* Dubuque, IA : Kendall/Hunt Publishing Co., 1984, 108 p. ill.

2070   SELVARATNAM, V.; GOPINATHAN, S. "Higher education in ASEAN towards the year 2000", *Higher Education* 13(1), feb 84 : 67-83.

2071   SHATTOCK, Michael L.; BERDAHL, Robert O. "The British University Grants Committee 1919-83 : changing relationships with government and the universities", *Higher Education* 13(5), oct 84 : 471-499.

2072   SNIZEK, William E.; MAYER, Lawrence. "Cosmopolitanism and localism among undergraduate students : a study in anticipatory socialization", *Acta Sociologica* 27(1), 1984 : 19-29. [USA]

2073   SPINKS, J. A.; HO, D. Y. F. "Chinese students at an English language university : prediction of academic performance", *Higher Education* 13(6), dec 84 : 657-674.

2074   ST. JOHN, Edward P.; MCCRIG, Robert. "Management development in Australian colleges and universities", *Higher Education* 13(6), dec 84 : 619-634.

2075   TYGART, C. E. "Moral autonomy and social-political activism among the faculty and staff of a West Coast University", *Sociological Inquiry* 54(1), 1984 : 16-25. [USA]

2076   WILSON, Brian. "Problems of University adjustment experienced by undergraduates in a developing country", *Higher Education* 13(1), feb 84 : 1-22. [Zambia]

2077   WINDOLF, Paul. "Formale Bildungsabschlüsse als Selektionskriterium am Arbeitsmarkt" (Formal educational qualifications as selective factors in the job market), *Kölner Zeitschrift für Soziologie und Sozialpsychologie* 36(1), mar 84 : 75-106. [Western Europe]

2078   WINKLER, Donald R. "The costs and benefits of foreign students in United States higher education", *Journal of Public Policy* 4(2), mai 84 : 115-138.

2079   YANIV, Avner. "Jews and Arabs on campus", *Jerusalem Quarterly* (30), wint 84 : 29-42.

13960   Adult education
Éducation des adultes

2080   "Alphabétisation, santé, nutrition et revenu", *Carnets de l'Enfance* (61-62), 1983 : 11-214. [With contributions by Arthur GILLETTE, John RYAN, Michael V. D. BOGAERT, Nadia YOUSSEF, Mary Racelis HOLLN-STEINER, Nyi NYI]

2081   "International Council for adult education", *Convergence* 17(2), 1984 : 3-64. [With contributions by Chris DUKE, Francisco VIO GROSSI, Emilia ROJO, Mark BRAY, Patrick KEANE]

2082   "Literacy and numeracy : understanding words and numbers", *Journal of the Market Research Society* 26(2), apr 84 : 89-169. [UK] [With contributions by John O'BRIEN, Norman WEBB, Peter BILLINS, Peter ROBINSON]

2083   BORSTOW, B. "Adult education : a Sartreran-based perspective", *International Journal of Lifelong Education* 3(3), jun 84 : 193-202.

2084   CÁMARA, Gabriel. *Impacto y relevancia de la educación básica : panorámica sobre el estado de la investigación* (Impact and relevance of the basic education : panorama of the state of the research). México, DF : CEE, GEFE, 1983, 100-1 p. bibl.

2085   CROMBIE, Alastair D.; HERRIES-JENKINS, Gwyn. *The demise of the liberal tradition : two essays on the future of British university adult education.* Leeds : University of Leeds, Department of Adult and Continuing Education, 1983, 105 p. ill., bibl.

2086   CROSS, Kathryn Patricia; MCCARTAN, Anne-Marie. *Adult learning : state policies and institutional practices.* Washington, DC : Association for the study of Higher Education, 1984, 152 p.

2087   DARKENWALD, Gordon G.; KNOX, Alan Boyd; [eds.]. *Meeting educational needs of young adults.* San Francisco, CA : Jossey-Bass, 1984, 110 p. bibl., ind.

2088   DE MOURA CASTRO, Cláudio; GUSSO, Divonzir Arthur. *O ensino básico : necessidades, prioridades e dúvidas* (The basic education : needs, priorities and duties). Brasília : CNRH, 1983, 27 p. [Brazil]

2089   DUBAR, C. "Les fonctions de la formation continue en France : interprétations et confrontations théoriques", *Recherches Sociologiques* 15(1), 1984 : 29-36.

2090   ESPÉRANDIEU, Véronique; LION, Antoine; BÉNICHOU, Pierre. *Des illetrés en France . rapport au Premier ministre.* Paris : La Documentation Française, 1984, 157 p. ill., bibl.

2091   FALLENSTEIN, Klaus. *Sozial-kognitive Determinanten der Weiterbildungsbeteiligung* (Socio-cognitive determinants of further education involvement). München : Profil, 1984, 226 p. ill., bibl. [Germany FR]

2092   FORDHAM, Paul. "A view from the wall : commitment and purpose in university adult
          education", *International Journal of Lifelong Education* 2(4), 1983 : 341-354. [UK]
2093   GELPI, Ettore. "Lifelong education : opportunities and obstacles", *International Journal of
          Lifelong Education* 3(2), jun 84 : 79-87.
2094   HAMEL, Rainer Enrique. "Socio-cultural conflict and bilingual education : the case of the
          Otomí Indians in Mexico", *International Social Science Journal / Revue Internationale des Sciences
          Sociales* 36(1), 1984 : 113-128.
2095   KULICH, Jindra. *Adult education in continental Europe : an annotated bibliography of English-
          language materials, 1980-1982.* Vancouver, BC : Centre for Continuing Education, Univer-
          sity of British Columbia, International Council for Adult Education, 1984, ii-173 p. ind.
2096   LOVETT, Tom; CLARKE, Chris; KILMURRAY, Avila. *Adult education and community
          action : adult education and popular social movements.* London : Croom Helm, 1983, 163 p.
          bibl., ind. [UK]
2097   MALI, M. G. *Adult education in India.* New Delhi : Deep and Deep, 1984, viii-239 p. bibl.,
          ind.
2098   ONUSHKIN, Victor G.; TONKONOGAYA, E. P. *Adult education in the USSR.* Prague :
          European Centre for Leisure and Education, 1984, 107 p. bibl.
2099   SHERMAN SWING, Elizabeth. "Flemings and Puerto Ricans : two applications of a
          conflict paradigm in bilingual education", *International Journal of the Sociology of Language*
          44, 1983 : 27-42.
2100   SJÖSTRÖM, Margareta; SJÖSTRÖM, Rolf. *How do you spell development? A study of a literacy
          campaign in Ethiopia.* Uppsala : Almqvist and Wiksell International, 1983, 196 p. ill., bibl.
2101   STREET, Brian V. *Literacy in theory and practice.* Cambridge : University Press, 1984, x-243 p.
2102   TERROT, Noël. *Histoire de l'éducation des adultes en France : la part de l'éducation des adultes
          dans la formation des travailleurs, 1789-1971.* Paris : Edilig, 1983, 307 p. bibl.
2103   TIETGENS, Hans. "Institutionelle Strukturen der Erwachsenenbildung" (Institutional
          structure of adult education), *Recht der Jugend und des Bildungswesens* 31(2), 1983 : 98-107.
          [Germany FR]
2104   TORRES, Carlos A. *La educación de adultos en México 1976-1981* (Adult education in Mexico
          1976-1981). México : FLACSO, 1984, 51 p.
2105   VLADISLAVLEV, A. P.; [ed.]. *Aktual'nye problemy nepreryvnogo obrazovanija* (Actual problems
          of continuing education). Moskva : APN SSSR, 1982, 158 p. [USSR]
2106   WANDERLEY, Luiz Eduardo W. *Educar para transformar : educação popular, Igreja Católica
          e política no Movimento de Educação de Base* (Educating to change : popular education, the
          Catholic Church and politics in the Basic Education Movement). Petrópolis : Vozes,
          1984, 524-36 p. bibl. [Brazil]
2107   WATANABE, Hiroshi. *Shakai kyoiku chosa ho* (Method of social research for adult education).
          Tokyo : Zennihon Shakai Kyoiku Rengokai, 1984, 540 p.

          **13970   Civic education. Technical education
          Instruction civique. Enseignement technique**

2108   LADNER, Benjamin; [ed.]. *The humanities in precollegiate education.* Chicago, IL : University
          of Chicago Press, 1984, x-198 p. bibl., ind.
2109   SŁOMIŃSKA, Janina. *Wychowanie religijne w rodzinie : typy postaw rodziców w zakresie
          wychowania religijnego* (Religious education within family : types of parental attitudes
          towards religious education). Warszawa : Akademia Teologii Katolickiej, 1984, 176 p.
          [Poland]
2110   TAWNEY, James W.; GAST, David L. *Single subject research in special education.* Columbus, OH :
          C. E. Merrill Publishing Co., 1984, xii-433 p. bibl., ind.
2111   THIESSEN, Elmer J. "Indoctrination and religious education", *Interchange* 15(3), 84 : 27-43.
2112   YSSELDYKE, James E.; ALGOZZINE, Bob. *Introduction to special education.* Boston, MA :
          Houghton Mifflin, 1984, xix-498 p. ill., bibl., ind.

          **13980   Academic success. School failure
          Réussite dans les études. Échec scolaire**

2113   "Réussir à l'école", *Perspectives (UNESCO)* 14(3), 1984 : 371-438. [With contributions by
          Beryl LEVINGER, Pierre LADERRIERE, V. M. MONAKHOV, A.M. PYSKALO,
          Miroslav MACH]
2114   AMBERT, Anne-Marie; SAUCIER, Jean-François. "Adolescents' academic success and
          aspirations by parental marital status", *Canadian Review of Sociology and Anthropology /
          Revue Canadienne de Sociologie et d'Anthropologie* 21(1), feb 84 : 62-74. [Canada]

2115   BOULOT, Serge; BOYSON-FRADET, Danielle. "L'échec scolaire des enfants de travailleurs
        immigrés : un problème mal posé", *Temps Modernes* 40(452-453-454), mai 84 : 1902-1914.
        [France]
2116   DANON-BOILEAU, Henri. *Les études et l'échec : de l'adolescence à l'âge adulte.* Paris : Payot,
        1984, 235 p.
2117   EKERWALD, Hedvig. *Den intelligenta medelklassen : en litteraturstudie över social bakgrund och
        studieresultat* (The intelligent middle classes : a study of literature on social background
        and academic achievement). Uppsala : Uppsala Universitet; Stockholm : Almqvist och
        Wiksell International, 1983, ix-183 p. ill., bibl., ind.
2118   FAUNCE, William A. "School achievement, social status, and self-esteem", *Social Psychology
        Quarterly* 47(1), mar 84 : 3-14. [USA]
2119   HAWKINS, M. J. "Comte's theory of mental development", *Revue Européenne des Sciences
        Sociales. Cahiers Vilfredo Pareto* 22(66), 1984 : 71-90.
2120   ROSENFELD, Gerry. *Shut those thick lips ! A study of slum schoolfailure.* Prospect Heights, IL :
        Waveland Press, 1984, 120 p. [USA]
2121   ROWAN, Brian; MIRACLE, Andrew W. Jr. "Systems of ability grouping and the
        stratification of achievement in elementary schools", *Sociology of Education* 56(3),
        jul 83 : 133-144.
2122   WHITE, Karl R. "The relation between socioeconomic status and academic achievement",
        Evaluation Studies 8, 1983 : 602-622.

        13990   Pedagogy. Teaching. Teachers
        Pédagogie. Enseignement. Enseignants

2123   "Computer (The) in education in critical perspective", *Teachers College Record* 85(4),
        sum 84 : 59-639. [With contributions by Harriet K. CUFFARO, Arthur G. ZAJONC,
        Douglas NOBLE, Robert J. SARDELLO]
2124   "Teaching public administration", *Teaching Political Science* 11(2), wint 84 : 54-83. [USA]
        [With contributions by George M. GUESS, Tim DE YOUNG, Bruce J. Perlman, Brack
        BROWN, Ronald SCHMIDT]
2125   ALWIN, Duane F. "Trends in parental socialization values : Detroit (1958-1983)", *American
        Journal of Sociology* 90(2), sep 84 : 359-382. [USA]
2126   BÖLLING, Rainer. *Sozialgeschichte der deutschen Lehrer : ein Überblick von 1800 bis zur Gegenwart*
        (Social history of German teachers : an overview from 1800 to the present time). Göttingen :
        Vandenhoeck und Ruprecht, 1983, 193 p. ill., bibl., ind.
2127   BOURDIEU, Pierre. *Homo academicus.* Paris : Éditions de Minuit, 1984, 302 p. ind.
2128   BOUTIN, André. *Formation et développements.* Bruxelles : P. Mardaga, 1983, 232 p. bibl.
2129   DOW, Gwyneth. "Viewpoint : sponsored and contest mobility revisited : tensions for
        teachers", *Sociological Review* 32(2), mai 84 : 349-366.
2130   DUBORGEL, Bruno. *Imaginaire et pédagogie : de l'iconoclasme scolaire à la culture des songes.*
        Paris : Sourire Qui Mord, 1983, iv-480 p. ill., bibl., ind.
2131   EBERTS, Randall W. "Union effects on teacher productivity", *Industrial and Labor Relations
        Review* 37(3), apr 84 : 346-358. [USA]
2132   FORQUIN, Jean-Claude. "La sociologie du curriculum en Grande-Bretagne : une nouvelle
        approche des enjeux sociaux de la scolarisation", *Revue Française de Sociologie* 25(2), apr-jun
        84 : 211-232.
2133   GINSBURG, Mark B.; ARIAS-GODINEZ, Beatriz. "Nonformal education and social
        reproduction/transformation : educational radio in Mexico", *Comparative Education Review*
        28(1), feb 84 : 116-127.
2134   GOODSON, Ivor F.; BALL, Stephen J.; [eds.]. *Defining the curriculum : histories and ethno-
        graphies of school subjects.* London; New York, NY : Falmer Press, 1984, 305 p. bibl., ind.
2135   HERZBERG, Irene; NISSEN, Ursula. *Erzieherausbildung in sechs europäischen Ländern :
        Dänemark, England, Frankreich, Italien, Niederlande, Schweden* (Teacher-training in six
        European countries : Denmark, England, France, Italy, Netherlands, Sweden).
        München : Verlag Deutsches Jugendinstitut, 1983, 120 p. bibl.
2136   IKEDA, Hideo; ASOH, Makoto; [eds.]. *Kyoiku kakushin to kyoiku keikaku* (Educational
        innovation and educational planning). Tokyo : Daiichihohki, 1984, 286 p.
2137   KUCZI, Tibor. "A pedagógusszerep néhány szociológiai jellemzője" (Some sociological
        characteristics of schoolteachers' role), *Valóság* 27(6), 1984 : 53-64.
2138   LA GARANDERIE, Antoine de. *Le dialogue pédagogique avec l'élève.* Paris : Centurion, 1984,
        124 p. bibl.
2139   LAPRÉVOTE, Gilles. *Les écoles normales primaires en France, 1879-1979 : splendeurs et misères de
        la formation des maîtres.* Lyon : Presses Universitaires de Lyon, 1984, 250 p. ill., bibl.

2140   LEGER, Alain. "A quel type social d'élèves vont les préférences des professeurs?", *Bulletin de Psychologie* 37(366), aug 84 : 749-756. [France]

2141   LOCATIS, Craig; ATKINSON, Francis D. *Media and technology for education and training.* Columbus, OH : C. E. Merrill Publishing Co., 1984, ix-354 p. bibl., ind., ill.

2142   MOORE JOHNSON, Susan. "Teacher unions in schools : authority and accommodation", *Harvard Educational Review* 53(3), 1983 : 309-326. [USA]

2143   MUEL-DREYFUS, Francine. *Le métier d'éducateur : les instituteurs de 1900, les éducateurs spécialisés de 1968.* Paris : Éditions de Minuit, 1983, 269 p. bibl., ind.

2144   NIZET, J. "L'exercice du contrôle dans les écoles secondaires", *Recherches Sociologiques* 15(1), 1984 : 67-91.

2145   NIZET, Jean; [et al.]. *Violence et ennui : malaise au quotidien dans les relations professeurs-élèves.* Paris : L'Éducateur, 1984, 184 p.

2146   RANJARD, Patrice. *Les enseignants persécutés.* Paris : R. Jauze, Alternative, 1984, 248 p. bibl.

2147   SAINT-GEORGES, P. de. "Le geste quotidien d'enseigner. Quelques apports de l'analyse systèmique de la communication", *Recherches Sociologiques* 15(1), 1984 : 37-54.

2148   SHEINGOLD, Karen; [et al.]. "Microcomputer use in schools : developing a research agenda", *Harvard Educational Review* 53(4), nov 83 : 412-432.

2149   SMITH, Thomas Ewin. "School grades and responsibility for younger siblings : an empirical study of the 'teaching function'", *American Sociological Review* 49(2), apr 84 : 248-260. [USA]

2150   SNYDER, Eldon E.; SPREITZER, Elmer. "Identity and commitment to the teacher role", *Teaching Sociology* 11(2), jan 84 : 151-166.

2151   SOŁOMA, Luba. *Nauczyciele o swojej pracy i pozycji społecznej* (Teachers on their work and social position). Olsztyn : Wydawnictwa Wyższej Szkoły Pedagogicznej, 1984, 203 p.

2152   UNRUH, Glenys G.; UNRUH, Adolph. *Curriculum development : problems, processes, and progress.* Berkeley, CA : McCutchan Publishing Corporation, 1984, xii-340 p. ill., bibl., ind.

2153   WAARDENBURG, Jean-Jacques. *L'enseignement dans le monde arabe.* Louvain : Université Catholique de Louvain, Institut des Pays en Développement, Centre d'Études et de Recherches sur le Monde Arabe Contemporain, 1983, 77 p. bibl.

14100   SOCIAL SYSTEM
SYSTÈME SOCIAL

2154   "Sistem i ponašanje društvenih subjekata" (Social subjects system and behaviour), *Socijalizam* 26(10), 1983 : 1369-1474. [Yugoslavia] [With contributions by Stipe ŠUVAR]

2155   "Testing Blau's theory", *Social Forces* 62(3), mar 84 : 585-639. [With contributions by Peter M. BLAU, Terry C. BLUM, Robert J. SAMPSON]

2156   AITOV, N. A.; [ed.]. *Upravlenie social'nymi processami : upravlenie razvitiem social'noj struktury* (Management of social processes : management of the social structure development). Ufa : s.n., 1983, 134 p.

2157   BOOKMAN, John T. "Locke's contract : would people consent to it?", *American Journal of Economics and Sociology* 43(3), jul 84 : 357-368.

2158   COLOMBIS, Alessio. "Amoral familism and social organisation in Montegrano : a critique of Banfield's thesis", *Peuples Méditerranéens / Mediterranean Peoples* (25), dec 83 : 11-34. [Italy]

2159   DRIC, V. I.; [ed.]. *Social'naja infrastruktura i socialističeskij obraz žizni* (Social infrastructure and the socialist way of life). Minsk : Nauka i Tehnika, 1983, 216 p.

2160   DRUDY, Sheelagh. "Education, class and labour force entry", *International Journal of Sociology and Social Policy* 4(1), 1984 : 63-79. [UK]

2161   FILIPPOV, F. R.; [et al.]. *Social'nye peremeščenija kak faktor vosproizvodstva i izmenenija social'noj struktury razvitogo socialističeskogo obščestva* (Social displacements as a factor of reproduction and change of social structure of the developed socialist society). Moskva : s.n., 1982, 55 p.

2162   HECHTER, Michael. "When actors comply : monitoring costs and the production of social order", *Acta Sociologica* 27(3), 1984 : 161-183.

2163   IGITHANJAN, É. D.; GAFT, L. G. "Iz opyta provedenija regional'nogo sociologičeskogo issledovanija dinamiki social'noj struktury sovetskogo obščestva" (An essay of carrying out a regional sociological research on dynamics of the Soviet society social structure), *in : Regional'nye osobennosti social'nyh peremeščenij v razvitom socialističeskom obščestve* Moskva, 1983 : 9-19.

2164   KATUNARIĆ, Vjeran. "Socijalna fragmentacija" (Social fragmentation), *Revija za Sociologiju* 13(1-4), 1983 : 3-22.

2165   KOLOSI, Tamás. *Struktúra és egyenlőtlenség* (Structure and inequality). Budapest : Kossuth Kiadó, 1983, 265 p. bibl. [Hungary]

2166   LASSMAN, Peter. "Social structure, history and evolution", *Economy and Society* 13(1), feb 84 : 1-19.

2167   LIM, Hy-Sop. "South Korean social structure and its effects on unification", *Korea and World Affairs* 8(1), spr 84 : 62-71.

2168   MARRA, Ezio. "Struttura sociale e voto a Torino : un'applicazione delle techniche esplorative dei dati" (Social structure and voting behaviour in Torino : an application of data analysis techniques), *Quaderni di Sociologia* 30(2-3-4), 1982 : 309-354.

2169   MEILLASSOUX, Claude. "La reproduction sociale", *Cahiers Internationaux de Sociologie* 77, 1984 : 393-395.

2170   MLECZKO, Franciszek Wiktor. "Struktura nieformalna wsi w 40-leciu PRL" (The countryside informal social structure during forty years of People's Poland), *Wieś Współczesna* 8, 1984 : 76-91.

2171   MURNIEK, É. "Soveršenstvovanie social'noj struktury i social'nye aspekty nacional'nyh otnošenij" (Improvement of the social structure and social aspects of national relations), *Kommunist Sovetskoj Latvii* (10), 1983 : 69-77.

2172   NAGLA, B. K. *Factionalism, politics and social structure.* Jaipur : Rawat, 1984, 246 p.

2173   OCHIAI, Emiko. "Shussan no shakai-shi ni okeru futatsu no kindai : kazoku hendo ron no kokoromi" (Two modern phases in social history of reproduction : toward a theory of family change), *Sociologos* 8, 1984 : 78-94.

2174   SATO, Yasuyuki. "Kokan riron no keitai to ronri Aruga kizaemon to Levi-Strauss no kokan riron o hikaku shite" (Forms and logics of exchange theories : the comparison of exchange theories between Aruga's and Levi-Strauss), *Shakaigaku Hyoron* 34(4), 1984 : 37-51.

2175   SCHOFIELD, Norman. "Social equilibrium and cycles on compact sets", *Journal of Economic Theory* 33(1), jun 84 : 59-71.

2176   SMITH, Dorothy E. "Textually mediated social organization", *International Social Science Journal / Revue Internationale des Sciences Sociales* 36(1), 1984 : 59-75.

2177   STEINER, H.; WINKLER, G. "Das soziologische Erbe von Karl Marx in seiner Bedeutung für die Erforschung der Sozialstruktur und Lebensweise in der Gegenwart (Thesen)" (The sociological inheritance of Karl Marx in its meaning for the research of the social structure and way of life of the present time), *Jb. Soziol. u. Sozialpol.*, 1983 : 19-34.

2178   SUNESSON, June. "Organizing and discipline", *Acta Sociologica* 27(3), 1984 : 199-213.

2179   SUSATO, Shigeru. *Gendai France no shakai kohzoh — shakaigaku teki shiza* (The social structure in modern France). Tokyo : University of Tokyo Press, 1984, 378 p.

2180   SZTOMPKA, Piotr. "The global crisis and the reflexiveness of the social system", *International Journal of Comparative Sociology* 25(1-2), 1984 : 45-58.

2181   TSUTSUI, Kiyotada. *Showa-ki nihon no kouzou* (Political and social structure of Japan in Showa era). Tokyo : Yuhikaku, 1984, 313 p.

2182   TUDOR, Gheorghe. "Evolutia structurii sociale a Romaniei" (Romania's social structure evolution), *Revista de Istorie* 37(6), jun 84 : 507-516.

14200   SOCIAL STRATIFICATION
STRATIFICATION SOCIALE

14210   Social differentiation
Différenciation sociale

2183   "Arbeitsteilung und Frauenpolitik" (Division of labour and women policy), *Argument* 26(144), apr 84 : 185-232. [With contributions by Hilary ROSE, Cynthia COCKBURN, Kornelia HAUSER, Regine MEYER]

2184   "Différenciation (La) sociale", *Bulletin de Psychologie* 37(365), jun 84 : 467-532. [With contributions by S. S. BREHM, G. LEMAINE, J. Cl. DESCHAMPS, J. KASTERSZTEIN]

2185   "Health, violence, race and class", *Latin American Perspectives* 10(4), aut 83 : 5-126. [Latin America] [With contributions by Anna RUBBO, Michael TAUSSIG, James J. HORN, Anne FERGUSON, Trevor SUDAMA]

2186   BARBUT, Marc. "Note sur quelques indicateurs globaux de l'inégalité : C. Gini, V. Pareto, P. Lévy", *Revue Française de Sociologie* 25(4), oct-dec 84 : 609-622.

2187   BARON, James N. "Organizational perspectives on stratification", *Annual Review of Sociology* 10, 1984 : 37-69.

2188   BEER, Ursula. *Theorien geschlechtlicher Arbeitsteilung* (Theories of the sexual division of labour). Frankfurt-am-Main; New York, NY : Campus, 1984, 255 p. bibl.

2189   BÉTEILLE, A. *The idea of natural inequality and other essays.* Delhi : Oxford University Press, 1984, x-190 p.

2190   BORNSCHIER, Volker. "Zur sozialen Schichtung in der Schweiz" (Social stratification in Switzerland), *Schweizerische Zeitschrift für Soziologie / Revue Suisse de Sociologie* 10(3), 1984 : 647-688.

2191   BRIAND, Jean-Pierre. "Sur quelques conséquences des différents emplois du code des catégories socio-professionnelles", *Économie et Statistique* 168, jul-aug 84 : 45-58. [France]

2192   BRONFMAN, Mario; TUIRAN, Rodolfo A. "La desigualdad social ante la muerte : clases sociales y mortalidad en la niñez" (Social inequality before death : social classes and infantile death rate), *Cuadernos Médico Sociales* 29-30, nov 84 : 53-76.

2193   BUCHNER-JEZIORSKA, Anna. "O równości i sprawiedliwości społecznej" (On social equality and inequality), *Studia Socjologiczne* 92(1), 1984 : 179-191.

2194   COMBESSIE, Jean-Claude. "L'évolution comparée des inégalités : problèmes statistiques", *Revue Française de Sociologie* 25(2), apr-jun 84 : 233-254. [France]

2195   CRABB, Edward G. *Social inequality : classical and contemporary theorists.* Toronto, ON : Holt, Rinehart and Winston of Canada, 1984, xiv-199 p. ill., bibl., ind.

2196   DURAN HERAS, María Angeles. *Desigualdad social y enfermedad* (Social inequality and illness). Madrid : Editorial Técnos, 1982, 180 p.

2197   EVANGELISTI, Valerio. "Punks : nuove forme di antagonismo sociale" (Punks : new form of social antagonism), *Mulino* 33(291), feb 84 : 77-110. [UK]

2198   FERREIRA DE ALMEIDA, João. "Temas e conceitos nas teorias da estratificação social" (Subjects and concepts in the theories of social stratification), *Análise Social* 20(2-3), 1984 : 167-190.

2199   FLORENS, Jean-Pierre. "Inégalité et dépendance statistique", *Revue Française de Sociologie* 25(2), apr-jun 84 : 255-263. [France]

2200   GONTAREV, G. A. "Leninskij princip social'noj differenciacii v idejno-političeskom razvitii obščestva" (The Leninist principle of social differentiation in ideological and political development of the society), *in : Problemy idejno-nravstvennogo vospitanija v leninskom teoretičeskom nasledii posleoktjabr'skogo perioda* Tambov, 1984 : 150-169.

2201 GREENHALGH, Susan. *Is inequality demographically induced? The family cycle and the distribution of income in Taiwan, 1954-1978.* New York, NY : Population Council, 1983, i-66 p. ill., bibl.

2202 GUPTA, Shiva K. "The significance of social stratification in Harijan community", *Indian Journal of Social Work* 45(2), jul 84 : 175-187. [India]

2203 HANDL, Johann. "Chancengleichheit und Segregation : ein Vorschlag zur Messung ungleicher Chancenstrukturen und ihrer zeitlichen Entwicklung" (Equal opportunity and segregation : a proposal to measure unequal opportunity structures and their evolution), *Zeitschrift für Soziologie* 13(4), oct 84 : 328-345.

2204 HAROUEL, Jean-Louis. *Essai sur l'inégalité.* Paris : Presses Universitaires de France, 1984, 287 p. bibl.

2205 HAUSER, Robert M.; TSAI, Shu-Ling; SEWELL, William H. "A model of stratification with response error in social and psychological variables", *Sociology of Education* 56(1), jan 83 : 20-46. [USA]

2206 ISHIKAWA, Akihiro. "Shakai kaiso to kenko jyotai" (Social stratification and health conditions), *Chuo University Journal of the Faculty of Literature* 117, 1984 : 141-159. [Japan]

2207 JAROSZ, Maria. *Nierówności społeczne* (Social inequalities). Warszawa : Książka i Wiedza, 1984, 269 p. [Poland]

2208 JOÓ, Rudolf. *Nemzeti és nemzetiségi önrendelkezés, önkormányzat, egyenjogúság* (National and minority self-determination, autonomy, equality in rights). Budapest : Kossuth, 1984, 280 p.

2209 KENDE, Pierre; [et al.]. *Égalité et inégalités en Europe de l'Est.* Paris : Presses de la Fondation Nationale des Sciences Politiques, 1984, 455 p. bibl.

2210 KOLOSI, Tamás; WNUK-LIPIŃSKI, Edmund; [eds.]. *Equality and inequality under socialism : Poland and Hungary compared.* London; Beverly Hills, CA : Sage Publications, 1983, 201 p. ill., bibl.

2211 KOLOSI, Tamás; WNUK-LIPIŃSKI, Edmund; [eds.]. *Nierówności społeczne w Polsce i na Węgrzech* (Social inequalities in Poland and Hungary). Wrocław : Ossolineum, 1984, 204 p.

2212 KOLOSI, Tamás; [ed.]. *Rétegződés-modell vizsgálat* (Stratification-model research. 3 vols.). Budapest : Magyar Szocialista Munkáspárt KB Társadalomtudományi Intézete, 82-84, 310;396;280 p.

2213 KORALEWICZ-ZĘBIK, Jadwiga. "The perception of inequality in Poland, 1956-1980", *Sociology (London)* 18(2), mai 84 : 225-238.

2214 KRISHNA IYER, V. R. *Justice in words and injustice in deeds for the depressed classes.* Delhi : Indian Social Institute, 1984, iv-19 p. [India]

2215 KUDRIN, V. "Buržuaznye teorii 'social'noj stratifikacii' i 'social'noj mobil'nosti' na službe antikommunizma" (Bourgeois theories of 'social stratification' and social mobility' in attendance on anticommunism), *Problemy Naučnogo Kommunizma* (17), 1983 : 212-226.

2216 LAUTARD, E. Hugh; LOREE, Donald J. "Ethnic stratification in Canada, 1931-1971", *Canadian Journal of Sociology / Cahiers Canadiens de Sociologie* 9(3), 1984 : 333-344.

2217 MARION, Marie-Odile. "Desigualdad social y minorías étnicas de México" (Social inequality and ethnic minorities of Mexico), *Cuadernos Americanos* 42(5), oct 83 : 43-54.

2218 NELSON, William. "Equal opportunity", *Social Theory and Practice* 10(2), sum 84 : 157-184.

2219 PAHL, R. E. *Divisions of labour.* Oxford : Basil Blackwell, 1984, x-362 p.

2220 PANDY, Riajendra. "Max Weber's theory of social stratification : controversies, contexts and correctives", *Indian Journal of Social Research* 25(1), apr 84 : 1-15.

2221 PLACE, Helen. "Equal opportunity in New Zealand legislation and implementation", *Equal Opportunities International* 3(1), 1984 : 1-10.

2222 POPOVIĆ, Mihailo V. "Klasno-slojne nejednakosti u jugoslovenskom društvu" (Class-layer inequalities in Yugoslav society), *Sociologija* 26(3-4), jul-dec 84 : 265-292.

2223 RASMUSSEN, Erik. "Lighedsbegreber" (Equality concept), *Økonomi og Politik* 56(1), 1982 : 28-39.

2224 RENAUD, Jean; BERNARD, Paul. "Places et agents : les divisions ethnique et sexuelle du travail au Québec de 1931 à 1981", *Cahiers Québécois de Démographie* 13(1), apr 84 : 87-100.

2225 ROSENFELD, Rachel A.; NIELSEN, François. "Inequality and careers : a dynamic model of socioeconomic achievement", *Sociological Methods and Research* 12(3), feb 84 : 279-321.

2226 SIRIANNI, Carmen J. "Justice and the division of labour : a consideration of Durkheim's 'Division of labour in society'", *Sociological Review* 32(3), aug 84 : 449-470.

2227 ŚWIĄTKIEWICZ, Wojciech. *Zróznicowanie społeczne a uczestnictwo w kulturze* (Social differentiation and participation in culture). Katowice : Uniwersytet Śląski, 1984, 196 p.

2228 SZEGŐ, Andrea. "Gazdaság és politika — érdek és struktúra. Történetszociológiai-struktúraelméleti vázlat társadalmunk érdektagozódásáról" (Economy and politics —

interest and structure. Historic-sociological outline on interest stratification of the Hungarian society from a structure-theoretic viewpoint), *Medvetánc* 3(2-3), 1983 : 49-92.

2229   WALOSIK, Jerzy. "Rozumienie zjawiska nierówności społecznej w marksistowskim nurcie polskiej myśli społecznej lat 1884-1939" (Understanding of social inequality phenomenon in the Marxist trend of the Polish social thought, 1884-1939), *Studia Filozoficzne* 4, 1984 : 147-156.

2230   WILLIAMS, Kirk R.; TIMBERLAKE, Michael. "Structural inequality, conflict, and control : a cross-national test of the threat hypothesis", *Social Forces* 63(2), dec 84 : 414-432.

2231   WOŹNIAK, Robert. "Wizja społeczeństwa egalitarnego w myśli teoretycznej V. I. Lenina" (Vision of egalitarian society in V. I. Lenin's theoretical thought), *Problemy Marksizmu-Leninizmu* 2, 1984 : 67-80.

2232   YAMAMOTO, Noboru. *Dain toshi shakai no kaiso kosei to shakai idou* (Social stratification and social mobility in metropolitan community). Tokyo : Akashi Shoten, 1984, 380 p. [Japan]

14220   Castes. Slavery
Castes. Esclavage

2233   DEV, Bimal J. *Cosmogony of caste and social mobility in Assam.* Delhi : Mittal, 1984, 182 p.

2234   GUPTA, A. R. *Caste hierarchy and social change : a study of myth and reality.* Delhi : Jyotsana, 1984, 208 p.

2235   KOLENDA, Pauline. *Caste in contemporary India : beyond organic solidarity.* Jaipur : Rawat, 1984, 181 p.

2236   KUMAR, Vijay; RAI, Ramesh Chandra. "Social background of schedule caste and schedule tribe legislators in Bihar", *Indian Journal of Politics* 17(2), jun 83 : 37-47. [India]

2237   LOVEJOY, Paul E. *Transformations in slavery : a history of slavery in Africa.* Cambridge, Cambridgeshire; New York, NY : Cambridge University Press, 1983, 336 p. bibl., ind.

2238   PARVATHAMMA, C. *Scheduled castes and tribes : a socio-economic survey.* Delhi : Ashish, 1984, 310 p.

2239   PARVATHAMMA, C.; SATYANARAYANAN. *New horizons and scheduled castes.* Delhi : Ashish, 1984, 384 p. [India]

2240   RANGARI, A. D. *Indian caste system and education.* Delhi : Deep and Deep, 1984, 275 p.

2241   ROBERTS, Michael. "'Caste feudalism' in Sri Lanka? A critique through the Asokan Persona and European contrasts", *Contributions to Indian Sociology* 18(2), jul-dec 84 : 189-217.

2242   ROSS, Robert. *Cape of torments. Slavery and resistance in South Africa.* London; Boston, MA... Routledge and Kegan Paul, 1983, xi-160 p. bibl., ind., maps.

2243   SARKAR, J. *Caste occupation and change.* Delhi : B. R. Publishers, 1984, 112 p. [India]

2244   SRINIVAS, M. N. "Some reflections on the nature of caste hierarchy", *Contributions to Indian Sociology* 18(2), jul-dec 84 : 151-167. [India]

14230   Social classes
Classes sociale

2245   "Making (The) of the Chinese working class", *Modern China* 9(4), oct 83 : 387-499. [With contributions by Emily HONIG; Lynda Norene SHAFFER, Sulamith HEINS POTTER]

2246   ADAMSON, David. "Social class and ethnicity in nineteenth century rural Wales", *Sociologia Ruralis* 24(3-4), 1984 : 202-215.

2247   ALLEN, P. T. "The class imagery of 'traditional proletarians'", *British Journal of Sociology* 35(1), mar 84 : 93-111. [UK]

2248   ANYANG'NYONG'O, Pater. "The economic foundations of the State in contemporary Africa : a stratification and social classes", *Présence Africaine* (127-128), trim. 3-4, 83 : 187-196.

2249   BEREZINA, Ju-I. "Rabocij klass Japonii 70-x godov tehnologičeskie sdvigi : zanjatost" (The working class in Japan during the seventies : technological changes and employment), *Rabocij Klass i Sovremennyj Mir* 12(4), aug 83 : 93-100.

2250   BIDOU, Catherine. *Les aventuriers du quotidien : essai sur les nouvelles classes moyennes.* Paris : Presses Universitaires de France, 1984, 200 p. [France]

2251   BIHR, Alain. "Le champ aveugle de la lutte de classe", *Homme et Société* 71-72, jan-jun 84 : 99-124.

2252   BLOM, Raimo. *Classes and the state.* Tampere : Department of Sociology and Social Psychology, University of Tampere, 1983, 204 p. ill., bibl.

2253   BOURDIEU, Pierre. "Espace social et genèse des 'classes'", *Actes de la Recherche en Sciences Sociales* 52-53, jun 84 : 3-15.

2254 BRITTEN, Nicky. "Class imagery in a national sample of women and men", *British Journal of Sociology* 35(3), sep 84 : 406-434. [UK]

2255 BRUNEAU, Michel. "Class formation in the Northern Thai peasantry", *Journal of Contemporary Asia* 14(3), 84 : 343-359.

2256 CANNON, Lynn Weber. "Trends in class identifications among Black Americans from 1952 to 1978", *Social Science Quarterly* 65(1), mar 84 : 112-126.

2257 CARBONI, Carlo. "Observaciones comparativas sobre la estructura de clase de los países capitalistas avanzados" (Comparative observations on the class structure of developed capitalist countries), *Revista Española de Investigaciones Sociológicas* 26, apr-jun 84 : 129-149.

2258 CATANZARO, Raimondo; TIMPANARO, Daniela. "Las capas medias en Italia" (Middle classes in Italy), *Revista Española de Investigaciones Sociológicas* 26, apr-jun 84 : 167-198.

2259 CONNEL, R. W. "Class formation on a world scale", *Review (F. Braudel Center)* 7(3), wint 84 : 407-440.

2260 CUNEO, Carl J. "Has the traditional petite bourgeoisie persisted?", *Canadian Journal of Sociology / Cahiers Canadiens de Sociologie* 9(3), 1984 : 269-301. [Canada]

2261 CURTIS, James; [ed.]. "Class and social stratification", *Canadian Journal of Sociology / Cahiers Canadiens de Sociologie* 9(3), 1984 : v-vii-245-344. [Canada]

2262 DILIGENSKIJ, G. G. "Massovoe obščestvenno-političeskoe soznanie rabočego klassa kapitalističeskih stran : problemy tipologii i dinamiki" (The working class socio-political mass consciousness in the capitalist countries), *Rabočij Klass i Sovremennyj Mir* (1), 1984 : 33-48. [Continued in ibid. (2), 1984 : 26-43]

2263 DOBRATZ, Betty A.; KOURVETARIS, George A. "Class consciousness and political attitudes among Athenians", *Sociological Inquiry* 54(4), 1984 : 432-448. [Greece] [1977]

2264 ERIKSON, Robert. "Social class of men, women and families", *Sociology (London)* 18(4), nov 84 : 500-514. [Sweden]

2265 GARRON, Robert. *Le manifeste de la classe moyenne.* Paris : Economica, 1984, 174 p.

2266 GLENDAY, Daniel. "Le domaine colonial : class formation in a natural resource enclave", *Canadian Journal of Sociology / Cahiers Canadiens de Sociologie* 9(2), 1984 : 159-177. [Canada]

2267 GOŁĘBIOWSKI, Bronisław. "Klasa robotnicza a przemiany kultury polskiej — wybrane problemy" (Working class and transformations of Polish culture — selected problems), *Nowe Drogi* 10, 1984 : 167-175.

2268 GORDON, L. A.; NAZIMOVA, A. K. "Tehniko-tehnologičeskij progress i social'noe razvitie sovetskogo rabočego klassa" (Technical and technological progress and Soviet working class social development), *Voprosy Filosofii* 37(7), 1984 : 18-38.

2269 GÜZEL, Sehmus. "Etre ouvrier en Turquie", *Temps Modernes* 41(456-457), aug 84 : 267-298.

2270 HALLER, Max. *Theorie der Klassenbildung und sozialen Schichtung* (Theory of class formation and social stratification). Frankfurt-am-Main; New York, NY : Campus, 1983, 223 p. bibl., ind.

2271 HAMANA, Atsushi. "Shakai-so to shite no shizoku -sono shokugyo seikatsu to nichijyo teki seikatsu youshiki o chushin to shite" (Shizoku as a social class : concerning their occupational life and their daily life style), *Sophia University Studies in Sociology* 8, 1984 : 24-53. [Japan]

2272 HRYNIEWICZ, Janusz T. "Sosunki produkcji, klasy i ruchliwość społeczna w Polsce" (Production relations, classes and social mobility in Poland), *Studia Socjologiczne* 92(1), 1984 : 47-78.

2273 IKEDA, Kanji. "Gouldner no 'atarashii kaikyu ron' to hihan teki dango bunka" (Gouldner's theory of the new class and culture of critical discourse), *Hyogo University of Teacher Education Journal* 4(2), 1984 : 49-62.

2274 ISLAM, Rizwanul. "Non-farm employment in rural Asia : dynamic growth or proletariani-sation", *Journal of Contemporary Asia* 14(3), 84 : 306-324.

2275 JAYADEVA DAS, D. *Working class politics in Kerala : a study of coir workers.* Thundathil, Kariavattom : T. C. Lilly Grace, 1983, vi-288-xvi p. bibl., ind.

2276 JURIČIĆ, Živka. "Pokušaj marksističkog utemeljenja pitanja mjesta i uloge radničke klase u jugoslovenskom socijalističkom društvu" (Attempt to lay Marxist foundation of the question of working class' place and role in Yugoslav socialist society), *Sociologija* 26(1-2), jan-jun 84 : 125-137.

2277 KEREMECKIJ, Ja. N. "Evoljucija političeskogo soznanija rabočego klassa" (The evolution of working class political consciousness), *SSA* 14(5), mai 84 : 15-27. [USA]

2278 KERSTHOLT, Frans. "De grenzen van de arbeidersklasse : een theoretische kritiek op enkele recente marxistische theorieën" (The limites of the working class : a theoretical critique of some recent Marxist theories), *Mens en Maatschappij* 59(1), jan 84 : 27-44.

2279 KISSISSOU-BOMA, J. R. *Classes sociales et idéologies en Afrique centrale.* Brazzaville : École Supérieure du Parti, 1983, 157 p. bibl.

2280 KOSOLAPOV, R. I. "Istoričeskaja missija rabočego klassa" (Historical mission of the working class), *Problemy Naučnogo Kommunizma* (17), 1983 : 3-16.

2281 KOZYR-KOWALSKI, Stanisław. "Klasy społeczeństwa a ekonomiczno-socjologiczne pojmowanie własności" (Social classes and the socio-economic conception of property), *Kultura i Społeczeństwo* 28(1), 1984 : 15-36. [Continued in ibid. : 28(2), 1984 : 129-153]

2282 KUMAR GHOSH, Suniti. "The Indian bourgeoisie and imperialism", *Bulletin of Concerned Asian Scholars* 15(3), aug 83 : 2-16.

2283 LISLE-WILLIAMS, Michael. "Merchant banking dynasties in the English class structure : ownership, solidarity and kinship in the City of London, 1850-1960", *British Journal of Sociology* 35(3), sep 84 : 333-362.

2284 LIVINGSTONE, D. W. *Class ideologies and educational futures*. Barcombe; Lewes, Sussex : Falmer Press, 1983, xiii-251 p. ill., bibl., ind.

2285 LOJKINE, Jean; VIET-DEPAULE, Nathalie. *Classe ouvrière, société locale et municipalités en région parisienne. Éléments pour une analyse régionale et une approche monographique : le cas d'Ivry-sur-Seine*. Paris : Centre d'Étude des Mouvements Sociaux, 1984, 308 p.

2286 LONGUENESSE, Elisabeth. "Rente pétrolière et structure de classe dans les pays du Golfe", *Peuples Méditerranéens / Mediterranean Peoples* (26), mar 84 : 147-161.

2287 LUČINVA, S. M. "Srednie sloi i perehodnye revoljucionnye processy" (Middle classes and transitional revolutionary processes), *Vestnik Moskovskogo Universiteta. Teorija Naučnogo Kommunizma* (4), 1983 : 71-80.

2288 MADOR, Ju. P.; MEREMINSKIJ, G. M. "Kul'tura rabočego klassa v buržuaznom obščestve i idejnaja bor'ba" (Culture of the working class in the bourgeois society and the ideological struggle), *in : Rabočij klass v mirovom revoljucionnom processe* Moskva, 1984 : 278-199.

2289 MARIANELLI, Alessandro. *Proletariato di fabbrica e organizzazione sindacale in Italia all'inizio del secolo : il caso dei lavoratori del vetro* (Factory's proletariat and trade unions in Italy at the beginning of the century : the case of the glass workers). Milano : Franco Angeli, 1983, 317 p. bibl. [Italy]

2290 MASSEY, David. "Class struggle and migrant labor in South African gold mines", *Canadian Journal of African Studies* 17(3), 1983 : 429-448.

2291 MOOSER, Josef. *Arbeiterleben in Deutschland 1900-1970 : Klassenlagen, Kultur und Politik* (Workers' life in Germany 1900-1970 : class positions, culture and politics). Frankfurt-am-Main : Suhrkamp, 1984, 303 p. bibl.

2292 MUNSLOW, Barry. *Proletarianisation in the Third World*. London; Dover, NH : Croom Helm, 1984, 336 p. bibl., ind.

2293 NAKAMURA, Masato. "Gendai shihon shugi ni okeru rodo to kaikyu" (Labour process and class structure in contemporary capitalism), *Sociologos* 8, 1984 : 120-137.

2294 NEVESELY, Karel. "K revizionisticke sociologicke koncepci P. Machonina o ceskoslovenske Tridni a socialni strukture v druhé polovine sedesatych let" (P. Machonin's revisionist thought on Czechoslovakian class structure in the second half of the sixties), *Sbornik Prací Filosofické Fakulty Brnenske University* 32(27), 1983 : 95-108.

2295 NIOSI, Jorge. "The Canadian bourgeoisie : towards a synthetical approach", *Canadian Journal of Political and Social Theory* 7(3), aut 83 : 128-149.

2296 NOVIKOV, A. I. "Kritika V. I. Leninym melkoburžuaznoj ideologii" (V. I. Lenin's critics on the petty bourgeois ideology), *Aktual'nye Problemy Istorii Marksistsko-Leninskoj Filosofii* (1), 1983 : 68-80.

2297 NOWAKOWSKI, Stefan. "Awans społeczny robotnika w pracach Józefa Chałasińskiego" (The problem of the social promotion of workers in the works of Józef Chałasiński), *Kultura i Społeczeństwo* 28(4), 1984 : 51-64.

2298 OKAJI, Toshio. "Kaikyu kouzou-ka to kaikyu hi-kouzou-ka : N. Poulantzas 'koritsu-ka sayo' o chushin ni" (Class structuration and class destructuration : with reference to N. Poulantzas' 'effet d'isolement'), *Sociologica* 8(2), 1984 : 49-66.

2299 OKAJI, Toshio. "Rodo katei ni okeru kaikyu hi-kouzou-ka : Taylor system to taishu no ronri" (Class destructuration in the labor process : Taylor system and logic of mass), *Sociologica* 9(1), 1984 : 53-70.

2300 OLOGOUDOU, Emile. "Les fondements économiques de l'État : la stratification et les classes sociales en Afrique indépendante", *Présence Africaine* (127-128), trim. 3-4, 83 : 215-239. [Benin]

2301 OSTAPENKO, I. P. "Voztrastanie roli rabočego klassa SSSR v upravlenii proizvdostvom v 70-e gody" (USSR's working class increasing role in production management in the seventies), *Voprosy Istorii* 52(2), feb 84 : 3-18.

2302 PARPART, Jane L.; SHAW, Timothy M. "Contradiction and coalition : class fractions in Zambia 1964-1984", *Africa Today* 30(3), 1983 : 23-51.

2303   PETERSEN, Trond. "Class and exploitation : description and ethics. Notes on John Roemer's 'A general theory of exploitation and class'", *Acta Sociologica* 27(4), 1984 : 323-337.

2304   PLETNEV, É. "Mesto naemnogo truda v teorii K. Marksa i rabočij klass segodnja" (Place of the salaried labour in the K. Marx's theory and the working class today), *Kommunist (Moskva)* (17), 1983 : 33-42.

2305   REYNA, S. P. "Dual class formation and agrarian underdevelopment : an analysis of the articulation of production relations in Upper Volta", *Canadian Journal of African Studies* 17(2), 1983 : 211-233.

2306   ROBINSON, Robert V. "Reproducing class relations in industrial capitalism", *American Sociological Review* 49(2), apr 84 : 192-196.

2307   ROY, William G. "Class conflict and social change in historical perspective", *Annual Review of Sociology* 10, 1984 : 483-506.

2308   RUSZKOWSKI, Pawel. "Mannheima koncepcja klas" (Mannheim's concept of classes), *Studia Socjologiczne* 93(2), 1984 : 187-207.

2309   SANDOVAL, Salvador Antonio M.; AVELAR, Sonia María. "Conciencia obrera y negociación colectiva en Brasil" (Working class consciousness and collective bargaining in Brazil), *Revista Mexicana de Sociología* 45(3), jul-sep 83 : 1027-1047.

2310   SAUŚ, Jan. "Kapitalizm i socjalizm a klasy według Stanisława Ossowskiego" (Capitalism and socialism and classes according to Stanislaw Ossowski), *Studia Socjologiczne* 94(3), 1984 : 47-67.

2311   SELLIER, François. *La confrontation sociale en France : 1936-1981.* Paris : Presses Universitaires de France, 1984, 240 p. bibl., ind.

2312   SHOLK, Richard. "The national bourgeoisie in post-revolutionary Nicaragua", *Comparative Politics* 16(3), apr 84 : 253-276.

2313   SPAULDING, Marc; MCQUARIE, Donald. "Recent development in the Marxist theory of classes : considerations on the 'new middle class' ", *Social Science Journal (Fort Collins)* 21(2), apr 84 : 83-98.

2314   SUDAMA, Trevor. "Class, race and the State in Trinidad and Tobago", *Latin American Perspectives* 10(4), aut 83 : 75-96.

2315   SZCZUPACZYŃSKI, Jerzy. "Klasa robotnicza w procesie przemian stosunków panowania klasowego formacji kapitalistycznej" (The working class in the process of the changing relations of class power in the capitalist formation), *Kultura i Społeczeństwo* 28(1), 1984 : 31-54.

2316   SZYMANSKI, Albert. *Class structure : a critical perspective.* New York, NY : Praeger, 1983, xx-674 p.

2317   SZYMANSKI, Albert. "Class struggle in socialist Poland", *Insurgent Sociologist* 12(1-2), 1984 : 115-130.

2318   TANAKA, Hidetaka. "Saint-Simon no kaikyu ron" (A basic structure of Saint-Simon's class theory), *Sociologos* 8, 1984 : 12-26.

2319   TEDESCHI, Piero. "Una prima formalizzazione geometrica della teoria economica delle classi sociali" (Toward a first geometrical formalization of the economic theory of social classes), *Rassegna Italiana di Sociologia* 25(2), apr-jun 84 : 259-298.

2320   TEN NAPEL, Henk. *Aspecten van de ontwikkeling van de Curaçaose arbeidersklasse* (Aspects of the working class development in Curaçao). Willemstad : Universiteit van de Nederlandse Antillen, 1983, vi-161 p. ill., bibl.

2321   TERWEY, Michael. "Klassenlagen als Determinanten von Einkommensungleichheit" (Class conditions as determinants of income inequality), *Zeitschrift für Soziologie* 13(2), apr 84 : 134-144.

2322   TSUDA, Masumi. "Class consciousness of Japanese workers", *Hitotsubashi Journal of Social Studies* 16(1), apr 84 : 5-18.

2323   VAN ZANDT WINN, Stephen. "Social class and income returns to education in Sweden : a research note", *Social Forces* 62(4), jun 84 : 1026-1034.

2324   WATSON, James L.; [ed.]. *Class and social stratification in post-revolution China.* New York, NY : Cambridge University Press, 1984, vii-289 p. tabl., ill., ind.

2325   YAMAMOTO, Noboru. *Shakai kaikyu to shakai seiso* (Social class and social stratification). Tokyo : Akashi Shoten, 1984, 356 p. [Japan]

2326   YEN, Ch'ing-huang. *Class structure and social mobility in the Chinese community in Singapore and Malaya, 1800-1911.* Adelaide : University of Adelaide, Centre for Asian Studies, 1983, 24 p. bibl.

2327   ZAMOGIL'NYJ, S. I. "Stanovlenie kategorii 'klass' v istorii filosofsko-sociologičeskoj mysli" (Future of the 'class' category in history of the philosophical and sociological thought), *in : Kategorii filosofii i razvitie naučnogo poznanija* Saratov, 1983 : 130-132.

2328   ZINGRAFF, Rhonda; SCHULMAN, Michael D. "Social bases of class consciousness : a
         study of Southern textile workers with a comparison by race", *Social Forces* 63(1),
         sep 84 : 98-116.

14240   Social status
Statut social

2329   FERNÁNDEZ, Marta E.; ARATA, Silvia. *Educación y estratificación social : reflexiones acerca
         del origen social de los estudiantes universitarios* (Education and social stratification : reflections
         on the social origin of university students). Buenos Aires : FADES Ediciones, 1984, 29 p.
2330   FÖLDESI-SZABÓ, Gyöngyi. *Az élsportolói státusz Magyarországon* (The social status of top
         athletes in Hungary). Budapest : Sportpropaganda Vállalat, 1983, 242 p.
2331   HAWKES, Glenn R.; [et al.]. "Status inconsistency and job satisfaction : general population
         and Mexican-American subpopulation analyses", *Sociology and Social Research* 68(3),
         apr 84 : 378-389. [USA]
2332   HEMBROFF, Larry A.; MYERS, David E. "Status characteristics : degrees of task
         relevance and decision processes", *Social Psychology Quarterly* 47(4), dec 84 : 337-346.
2333   HICKS, Alexander; FLIGSTEIN, Neil. "Reevaluating the uses of status : the case of
         earnings determination", *Social Science Research* 13(1), mar 84 : 90-110. [USA]
2334   HIRSCHMAN, Charles; WONG, Morrison G. "Socioeconomic gains of Asian Americans,
         Blacks, and Hispanics : 1960-1976", *American Journal of Sociology* 90(3), nov 84 : 584-607.
         [USA]
2335   MOLNAR, Joseph J.; LAWSON, William D. "Perceptions of barriers to black political
         and economic progress in rural areas", *Rural Sociology* 49(2), sum 84 : 261-283.
2336   NAP, Charles B.; POWERS, Mary G. *The socioeconomic approach to status measurement : with
         a guide to occupational and socioeconomic status scores.* Houston, TX : Cap and Gown Press,
         1983, xiii-149 p. ill., bibl., ind.
2337   POHOSKI, Michał. "Kariery szkolne i kariery społeczno-zawodowe a pochodzenie społeczne"
         (School career, vocational career and social origin), *Kultura i Społeczeństwo* 28(2), 1984 : 155-171.
2338   SELL, Jane; FREESE, Lee. "The process of eliminating status generalization", *Social Forces*
         63(2), dec 84 : 538-554.

14250   Elite. Intellectuals
Élite. Intellectuels

2339   "Élites (Les) en Grande-Bretagne", *Revue Française de Civilisation Britannique* 2(2), sep
         83 : 1-121. [With contributions by Paul BRENNAN, Evelyne GINESTET, Michel
         LEMOSSE, Claire CHARLOT, Richard SIBLEY, Mireille QUERE]
2340   "Intellectuels, travail intellectuel", *Pensée* (240), aug 84 : 5-75. [France] [With contributions
         by D. BLEITRACH, A. CHENU, J. CHAMBAZ, D. MONTEUX]
2341   ARAB-OGLY, E. "Rajmon Aron v zerkale i 'zazerkale' svoih memuarov" (Raymond
         Aron visible and invisible in his Memoirs), *MEMO* (8), 1984 : 114-132.
2342   BLANCHOT, Maurice. "Les intellectuels en question", *Débat* (29), mar 84 : 3-28. [France]
2343   BLEITRACH, Danielle. *Le music-hall des âmes nobles : essai sur les intellectuels.* Paris : Éditions
         Sociales, 1984, 190 p.
2344   BURTON, Michael G. "Elite and collective protest", *Sociological Quarterly* 25(1),
         wint 84 : 45-66.
2345   ČERNEGA, V. N. "Évoljucija politiko-administrativnoj elity vo Francii" (Political and
         administrative elite evolution in France), *Ežegodnik — Sovetskaja Associacija Političeskih
         Nauk*, 1981 : 118-127.
2346   DILCHEV, Konstantin. *Klasa-rŭkovoditel* (The ruling class). Sofia : Profizdat, 1983, 171 p.
         bibl.
2347   DJORKJEVIĆ, Živorad. "Le Parti et les intellectuels", *Questions Actuelles du Socialisme* 34(6),
         jun 84 : 82-89. [Yugoslavia]
2348   GLOECKNER, Edward. "Die Intelligenzia in der sowjetischen Gesellschaft" (Intelligentsia
         in Soviet society), *Osteuropa* 34(7), jul 84 : 477-499.
2349   HALL, J. A. "Aron's principles", *Government and Opposition* 19(4), aut 84 : 423-437.
2350   HOFFMANN, Stanley. "Raymond Aron 1905-1983", *Journal für Sozialforschung* 24(2),
         84 : 185-193.
2351   KNOPP, András; RADICS, Katalin. "A fiatal értelmiség helyzetéről" (The situation of
         young intellectuals), *Társadalmi Szemle* 39(7-8), 1984 : 52-67. [Hungary]

2352 KOZYREV, Ju. N.; [ed.]. *Sociologičeskie issledovanija intelligencii* (Sociological researches of intelligentsia). Moskva : Institut Sociologičeskih Issledovanij Akademija Nauk SSSR, 1982, 195 p.

2353 LÖNNROTH, Lars. "The intellectual civil servant : the role of the writer and the scholar in Nordic culture", *Daedalus* 113(2), spr 84 : 107-136.

2354 MCCONNELL, Scott. "Homage to Raymond Aron", *Commentary* 77(5), mai 84 : 39-46.

2355 MURTHY, Sheela. "The role of intellectuals : a reappraisal", *China Report* 19(2), apr 83 : 3-6. [China]

2356 NYQUIST, Thomas E. *African middle class elite*. Grahamstown : Institute of Social and Economic Research, Rhodes University, 1983, 303 p. ill., bibl., ind.

2357 PAPPI, Franz Urban. "Boundary specification and structural models of elite systems : social circles revisited", *Social Networks* 6(1), mar 84 : 79-95.

2358 PINTO, Louis. "La vocation de l'universel. La formation de la représentation de l'intellectuel vers 1900", *Actes de la Recherche en Sciences Sociales* 55, nov 84 : 23-32.

2359 PRIDATKINA, L. P. "Kritika nemarksistskih koncepcij o meste i roli sovetskoj intelligencii v uslovijah razvitogo socialističeskogo obščestva" (Critics of the non-marxist conception on the place and role of Soviet intelligentsia under conditions of the developed socialist society), *in : XXVI s'ezd KPSS o dostiženii social'noj odnorodnosti sovetskogo obščestva* Moskva, 1983 : 156-171.

2360 PRIEST, T. B. "Elite and upper class in Philadelphia, 1914", *Sociological Quarterly* 25(3), 1984 : 319-331.

2361 SABOUR, M'hammed. *The cultural identification and alienation of the Arab intelligentsia : a theoretical background and typological outline*. Joensuu : University of Joensuu, Faculty of Education, 1984, 76 p. ill., bibl.

2362 SIRINELLI, Jean-François. "Raymond Aron avant Raymond Aron (1923-1933)", *Vingtième Siècle. Revue d'Histoire* (2), apr 84 : 15-30.

2363 STEPANJAN, C. A.; [ed.]. *Sovetskaja intelligencija i eё rol' v stroitel'stve kommunizma* (Soviet intelligentsia and its role in the building of communism). Moskva : Nauka, 1983, 383 p.

2364 TEITELBOIM, Volodia. "L'intellectuel latino-américain et la défense de l'identité culturelle", *Nouvelle Revue Internationale* 26(12), dec 83 : 46-60.

2365 TÓTH, Pál Péter. *A magyar értelmiség két vilagháború közötti történetéhez* (History of the Hungarian intelligentsia between the two world wars). Budapest : Oktatási Minisztérium, Marxismus-Leninizmus Oktatási Főosztály,, 1983, 92 p.

2366 WINOCK, Michel. "Les intellectuels dans le siècle", *Vingtième Siècle. Revue d'Histoire* (2), apr 84 : 3-14. [France]

2367 YOUXIN, Cheng; KEJING, Li. "Intellectuals : their class and social role", *Social Sciences in China* 2(3), 1984 : 27-54. [China]

14260 Social mobility
Mobilité sociale

2368 ADAM, Barry D.; BAER, Douglas E. "The social mobility of women and men in the Ontario legal profession", *Canadian Review of Sociology and Anthropology / Revue Canadienne de Sociologie et d'Anthropologie* 21(1), feb 84 : 21-46.

2369 ANDRESS, Hans-Jürgen. "Deskription intragenerationeller Mobilitätsprozesse mit Verlaufsdaten. Richtung, Ausmass und Abfolge von Tätigkeitswechseln in einer Kohorte von Berufsanfängern" (Description of intragenerational mobility processes with running data. Direction, extent and succession of activity change in a cohort of career-beginners), *Kölner Zeitschrift für Soziologie und Sozialpsychologie* 36(2), jun 84 : 252-276. [Germany FR]

2370 CAMPBELL, Richard T. "Status attainment research : end of the beginning or beginning of the end", *Sociology of Education* 56(1), jan 83 : 47-62.

2371 FLERE, Sergej. "Međungeneracijska vertikalna pokretljivost u vojvodini" (Intergeneration vertical mobility in Vojvodina), *Sociologija* 26(1-2), jan-jun 84 : 159-172. [Yugoslavia]

2372 GOLDMAN, Robert; TICKAMYER, Ann. "Status attainment and the commodity form : stratification in historical perspective", *American Sociological Review* 49(2), apr 84 : 196-209.

2373 GRUSKY, David B.; HAUSER, Robert M. "Comparative social mobility revisited : models of convergence and divergence in 16 countries", *American Sociological Review* 49(1), feb 84 : 19-38.

2374 HARCSA, István. "Social mobility in rural Hungary", *East European Quarterly* 17(4), jan 84 : 493-502.

2375 HAUSER, Robert M. "Vertical class mobility in England, France and Sweden", *Acta Sociologica* 27(2), 1984 : 87-109.

2376   JENCKS, Christopher; CROUSE, James; MUESER, Peter. "The Wisconsin model of status attainment : a national replication with improved measures of ability and aspiration", *Sociology of Education* 56(1), jan 83 : 3-19.

2377   KAELBLE, Hartmut. *Soziale Mobilität und Chancengleichheit im XIX. und XX. Jahrhundert : Deutschland im internationalen Vergleich* (Social mobility and equal opportunity in the XIXth and XXth centuries : Germany in international comparison). Göttingen : Vandenhoeck und Ruprecht, 1983, 322 p. ill., bibl., ind.

2378   KANOMATA, Nobuo. "Chii tassei bunseki no seika to kadai" (The results and tasks of status attainment research), *Shakaigaku Hyoron* 35(2), 1984 : 17-33.

2379   KAWAI, Takao. "Studies on social mobility in postwar Japan : their development and problems", *Keio Journal of Politics* 5, 1984 : 27-51.

2380   KERCKHOFF, Alan. "The current state of social mobility research", *Sociological Quarterly* 25(2), spr 84 : 139-153.

2381   LEQUIN, Yves-Claude. "Mobilité sociale et classe ouvrière dans les pays arabes (colloque, Alger — 24/29 mars, 1984)", *Recherches Internationales* (12), jun 84 : 54-72.

2382   ROBINSON, Robert V. "Structural change and class mobility in capitalist societies", *Social Forces* 63(1), sep 84 : 51-71.

2383   RUSSELL, Peter A. "The development of popular attitudes to social mobility in English Canada", *Zeitschrift der Gesellschaft für Kanada-Studien* 4(1), 1984 : 33-43.

2384   SIMKUS, Albert. "Structural transformations and social mobility : Hungary, 1938-1973", *American Sociological Review* 49(3), jun 84 : 291-307.

2385   SKVORETZ, John. "The logic of opportunity and mobility", *Social Forces* 63(1), sep 84 : 72-97. [USA]

2386   SRIVASTAVA, K. C. "Intergenerational mobility among scheduled castes", *Indian Journal of Social Research* 25(1), apr 84 : 24-31. [India]

2387   TABARD, Nicole. "Mobilité sociale, fratrie et descendance", *Consommation* 31(3), sep 84 : 19-50. [France] [ENG]

2388   THÉLOT, Claude. "L'évolution de la mobilité sociale dans chaque génération", *Économie et Statistique* 161, dec 83 : 3-22. [France]

14300   **SOCIAL CHANGE**
         CHANGEMENT SOCIAL

14310   **History**
         Histoire

2389   "Histoire et sciences sociales", *Annales-Économies, Sociétés, Civilisations* 38(6), dec 83 : 1217-1303. [With contributions by Claude LEVI-STRAUSS, Samuel N. EISENSTADT, François HARTOG]

2390   "Philosophy (The) of history teaching", *History and Theory* 22(4), 83 : 1-121. [With contributions by Denis SHEMILT, P. J. LEE, David STOCKLEY, Kieran EGAN, James FITZGERALD, M. B. BOOTH]

2391   "Sozialgeschichte und Kulturanthropoligie" (Social history and cultural anthropology), *Geschichte und Gesellschaft* 10(3), 1984 : 293-424.

2392   BALLHATCHET, Kenneth. "The rewriting of South Asian history by South Asian historians after 1947", *Asian Affairs (London)* 15(1), feb 84 : 27-38.

2393   BENDIX, Reinhard. *Force and freedom : on historical sociology.* Berkeley, CA : University of California Press, 1984, xviii-143 p.

2394   BOSWORTH, Edmund; HILLENBRAND, Carole; [eds.]. *Qajar Iran : political, social, and cultural change, 1800-1925.* Edinburgh : Edinburgh University Press, 1983, xxv-414 p. ill., bibl., ind.

2395   GONZALEZ, Luis. "L'historiographie mexicaine aujourd'hui", *Diogène* 125, jan-mar 84 : 78-92.

2396   KETTLER, David; MEJA, Volker; STEHR, Nico. "Karl Mannheim and conservatism : the ancestry of historical thinking", *American Sociological Review* 49(1), feb 84 : 71-85.

2397   KONSTANTINOV, F. R.; [ed.]. *Marksistsko-leninskaja teorija istoričeskogo processa : istoričeskij process : celostnost', ëdinstvo i mnogoobrazie, formacionnye stupeni* (The Marxist-Leninist theory of historical process : historical process, integrity unity and variety, formational stages). Moskva : Nauka, 1983, 535 p.

2398   KUMAR, Ravinder. *Essays in the social history of modern India.* Delhi : Oxford, 1983, viii-306 p. bibl., ind.

2399   LEE, Clive Howard. *Social science and history : an investigation into the application of theory and quantification in British economic and social history.* London : Social Science Research Council; Merstham, Redhill, Surrey : School Government Publishing Co., 1983, v-69 p. bibl.

2400 MÜNKLER, Herfried. "Gesellschaft und Kultur im Italien der Renaissance. Ein Literatur-bericht" (Society and culture in Renaissance Italy. A review of literature), *Kölner Zeitschrift für Soziologie und Sozialpsychologie* 36(1), mar 84 : 126-146.

2401 REULECKE, Jürgen. *Sozialer Frieden durch soziale Reform : der Centralverein für das Wohl der Arbeitenden Klassen in der Frühindustrialisierung* (Social peace through social reform : the Central Union for the Welfare of Working Classes in the early industrialization). Wuppertal : P. Hammer, 1983, 307 p. bibl., ind.

2402 ROUCH, Jean-Louis. *Prolétaire en veston : une approche de Maurice Dommanget, instituteur, syndicaliste, historien social et libre penseur, 1888-1976.* Treignac, Corrèze : Les Monédières, 1984, 231 p. bibl.

2403 SKVORCOV, L. V. *Sub'ekt istorii i social'noe samosoznanie* (The subject of history and social consciousness). Moskva : Politizdat, 1983, 264 p.

2404 SOGRINE, Vladimir. "La politique des États-Unis dans le miroir de l'historiographie radicale américaine", *Sciences Sociales — Académie des Sciences de l'URSS* (3), 1984 : 137-151.

2405 SOKOLOVA, M. N. "Žurnal 'Annaly' i ego ėvoljucija" ('Annales' review and its evolution), *Novaja i Novejšaja Istorija* 27(6), 1984 : 76-87. [France]

2406 VACCARINI, Italo. "Sistemi simbolico-religiosi e dinamica storico-sociale" (Symbolic-religious systems and historical-social dynamics), *Studi di Sociologia* 22(1), jan-mar 84 : 37-60.

2407 VACULIK, Jaroslav. "Ke krizi nasi historiografie ve druhe polovine sedesatych let" (On our historiography's crisis in the second half of the sixties), *Sbornik Prací Filosofické Fakulty Brnenske University* 32(27), 1983 : 87-93. [Czechoslovakia]

14320 Future
Futur

2408 "Status of futures research", *Futures* 16(4), aug 84 : 382-417. [With contributions by Roy AMARA, Harold S. BECKER]

2409 IUPIN, A. A. "Prognoz i predvidenie v strukture znanij o buduščem" (Forecast and previzion in the structure of knowledge on future), *in : Filosofskie problemy obščestvennogo progressa* Gor'kij, 1983 : 115-122.

2410 KAČANOVSKIJ, Ju. V. "Istorija i prognozirovanie v rabotah futurologov Gudzonovskogo Instituta; kritičeskij analiz" (History and forecast in the Hudson Institute futurologists works : a critical analysis), *in : Filosofskie problemy obščestvennogo progressa* Gor'kij, 1983 : 123-136.

2411 SPENCER, Martin E. "Social science and the consciousness of the future", *Theory and Society* 11(5), sep 82 : 683-712.

14330 Social change
Changement social

2412 "Aspects du développement", *Diogène* 126, apr-jun 84 : 3-55.

2413 "Studi sulla teoria dello scambio" (Studies on the theory of change), *Rassegna Italiana di Sociologia* 25(1), jan-mar 84 : 3-172.

2414 BADEEVA, G. V. "Metodologičeskie problemy upravlenija social'nym razvitiem kollektiva" (Methodological problems of management of the collectivity social development), *Naučnoe Upravlenie Obščestvom* (16), 1983 : 121-160.

2415 BAUMANN, Roland. *Sozialer Wandel : Ansätze zur Gesellschaftsveränderung am Beispiel der Entwicklung von Stadt und Land* (Social change : essays on the evolution of society by the example of town and country development). Köln : Pahl-Rugenstein, 1983, 109 p. bibl.

2416 BÉJIN, André. "Les darwinistes sociaux et Malthus", *Social Science Information / Information sur les Sciences Sociales* 23(1), 1984 : 79-94.

2417 BENEDIKTOV, N. A.; [ed.]. *Filosofskie problemy obščestvennogo progressa* (Philosophical problems of social progress). Gor'kij : Gor'kovskij Universitet imeni N. I. Lobačesvskogo, 1982, 164 p.

2418 BENOIST, Jean. *Un développement ambigu. Structure et changement de la société réunionnaise.* Paris : Fondation pour la Recherche et le Développement dans l'Océan Indien, 1983, 200 p.

2419 BERTHOUD, Gérald; BUSINO, Giovanni; [eds.]. "L'exploration de la modernité. La démarche de Louis Dumont", *Revue Européenne des Sciences Sociales. Cahiers Vilfredo Pareto* 22(68), 1984 : 5-206.

2420 BOJKO, P. N.; [et al.]. *Brazilija : tendencii ėkonomičeskogo i social'no-političeskogo razvitija* (Brazil : tendencies of its economic and socio-political development). Moskva : Nauka, 1983, 367 p.

2421 BOKAN', Ju. I. "Social'noe novatorstvo : suščnost', problemy" (Social innovation : nature, problems), *Naučnye Doklady Vysšej Školy. Naučnyj Kommunizm* (6), 1983 : 46-54.

2422   BOUDON, Raymond. *La place du désordre : critique des théories du changement social.* Paris :
        Presses Universitaires de France, 1984, 245 p. ind.
2423   BRANCH, Kristi; [et al.]. *Guide to social assessment : a framework for assessing social change.*
        Boulder, CO : Westview Press, 1984, xv-322 p. ill., bibl., ind.
2424   BÜHL, Walter L. "Gibt es eine soziale Evolution?" (Is there a social evolution?), *Zeitschrift
        für Politik* 31(3), sep 84 : 302-332.
2425   BUTURLOV, R. V.; SLAVIN, B. F. "O metodologičeskih problemah social'nogo
        razvitija i upravlenija trudovym proizvodstvennym kollektivom" (On the methodological
        problems of social development and management of a labour production collectivity),
        in : Trudovoj kollektiv i formirovanie ličnosti Moskva, 1983 : 3-24.
2426   CAMPBELL, Susan M. *Earth community : living experiments in cultural transformation.* San
        Francisco, CA : Evolutionary Press, 1983, xii-242 p. ill., bibl.
2427   CESAREO, Vincenzo. "Verso una società più flessibile?" (Towards a more flexible society?),
        Studi di Sociologia 22(1), jan-mar 84 : 3-21.
2428   CORMACK, Ian R. N. *Towards self-reliance : urban social development in Zimbabwe.* Gweru :
        Mambo Press, 1983, xxiv-280 p. bibl.
2429   DESHERIEV, Yunus D. "Social progress and sociolinguistics", *International Social Science
        Journal / Revue Internationale des Sciences Sociales* 36(1), 1984 : 21-39.
2430   DJIWANDONO, A. Sudiharto. "Expectations and prospect of development in the socio-
        cultural field during Pelita IV", *Indonesian Quarterly* 12(3), jul 84 : 340-353. [Indonesia]
2431   DŽUNUSOV, M. S. "Koncepcija proletarskogo internacionalizma K. Marksa i sovremennaja
        praktika obščestvennogo razvitija" (The K. Marx's conception of proletarian inter-
        nationalism and contemporary practice of social development), *Naučnye Doklady Vysšej
        Školy. Naučnyj Kommunizm* (6), 1983 : 19-26.
2432   FERRAND, Dominique J. "Problématique des méthodes de la rationalisation dans les
        organisations", *Philosophy of the Social Sciences / Philosophie des Sciences Sociales* 14(3),
        sep 84 : 289-302.
2433   FRANCO, R. "Significados y contenidos del desarrollo social de las políticas sociales"
        (Meaning and contents of social development and social policies), *Ideas en Ciencias Sociales*
        1(1), 1984 : 41-54.
2434   FÜRER-HAIMENDORF, Christoph von. *The Sherpas transformed : social change in a Buddhist
        society of Nepal.* New Delhi : Sterling, 1984, 197 p.
2435   FURUKI, Toshiaki. "Nihon shakai to sono bunka -tajyo teki shakai hatten ron tono kanran
        de" (Society and culture in Japan : a study based on the multilineal social development
        theory), *Chuo Law Review* 91(1-2), 1984 : 205-231.
2436   GAILLARD, Jean-Michel. *Les mutations économiques et sociales au XIXᵉ siècle : 1780-1880.*
        Paris : Nathan, 1984, 191 p. bibl. [France]
2437   GOLENKOVA, Z. "Social'noe razvitie socialističeskogo obščestva" (Social development
        of the socialist society), *Obščestvennye Nauki (Moskva)* (6), 1983 : 176-179.
2438   GORIELY, Georges. "Georges Sorel et l'idée de révolution", *Revue de l'Institut de Sociologie*
        (1-2), 1984 : 7-22.
2439   HARCSA, István. "Társadalmi folyamatok Magyarországon és Csehszlovákiában" (Social
        processes in Hungary and in Czechoslovakia), *Statisztikai Szemle* 62(4), apr 84 : 370-388.
2440   HOFFMAN, O. "Cultúrá si schimbare socialǎ in tǎrile in curs de dezvoltare" (Culture
        and social change in developing countries), *Viitorul Social* 76(2), apr 83 : 151-155.
2441   HUYSSEN, Andreas. "From counter-culture to neo-conservatism and beyond : stages of the
        postmodern", *Social Science Information / Information sur les Sciences Sociales* 23(3), 1984 : 611-624.
2442   KAPLAN, A. B.; [ed.]. *Social'nyj progress i ideologičeskaja bor'ba* (Social progress and the
        ideological struggle). Moskva : INION Akademija Nauk SSSR, 1983, 174 p.
2443   KARAKSEEV, T. D. *Dialektika razvitija duhovnogo potenciala sovetskogo obščestva* (Dialectics
        of development of the Soviet society spiritual potentialities). Frunze : Ilim, 1984, 201 p.
2444   KODJO, Edem. "La dimension sociale du développement en Afrique", *Travail et Société*
        9(4), oct-dec 84 : 385-395.
2445   KRYSINSKI, Wladimir. "Fragments et fragmentation : le destin de la modernité et les
        pratiques romanesques", *Social Science Information / Information sur les Sciences Sociales* 23(3),
        1984 : 577-587.
2446   KULCSÁR, Kálmán. *Social changes and modernization in Hungary.* Budapest : Institute of
        Sociology of the Hungarian Academy of Sciences, 1983, 42 p. bibl.
2447   LAEYENDECKER, L. *Sociale verandering : problemen en theorieën* (Social change : problems
        and theories). Meppel : Boom, 1984, 404 p. bibl., ind.
2448   LYSENKO, A. A.; [ed.]. *Dialektika social'nyh processov* (Dialectics of social processes).
        Kiev : Višča Škola, 1983, 216 p.

2449 MAHAROV, V. G.; [ed.]. *Dialektika obščestvennogo razvitija* (Dialectics of social development). Moskva : Mysl', 1984, 320 p.

2450 MALYŠKO, L. N. *Konkretno-istoričeskaja obuslovlennost' čelovečeskoj dejatel'nosti : problemy ob'ektivnogo i sub'ektivnogo v obščestvennom razvitii* (The concrete historical determination of the human activity : problems of the objective and the subjective in social development). Kiev : Višča Škola, 1983, 176 p.

2451 MAYHEW, Leon. "In defense of modernity : Talcott Parsons and the utilitarian tradition", *American Journal of Sociology* 89(6), mai 84 : 1273-1305.

2452 MENDRAS, Henri; FORSÉ, Michel. *Le changement social : tendances et paradigmes.* Paris : Armand Colin, 1983, 284 p. ill., bibl., ind.

2453 MINOR, W. William. "Neutralization as a hardening process : considerations in the modeling of change", *Social Forces* 62(4), jun 84 : 995-1019.

2454 MORGAN, Gareth; RAMIREZ, Rafael. "Action learning : a holographic metaphor for guiding social change", *Human Relations* 37(1), jan 84 : 1-28.

2455 MURILLO FERROL, Francisco; [et al.]. *Informe sociológico sobre el cambio social en España, 1975-1983* (Sociological report on social change in Spain, 1975-1983). Madrid : EURAMERICA, 1983, xxv-979 p. ill., bibl.

2456 NAMIHIRA, Isao. "Okinawa no kindai-ka to shakai kousei no hendo" (Modernization of Okinawa and changes in the social composition), *Okinawa Kokusai University Bulletin of the Department of Sociology* 12(1), 1984 : 1-21.

2457 OSIPOV, N. É.; BELOV, N. I. "K probleme obščestvennogo progressa. Égo suščnost' i kriterii" (The problem of social progress. Its nature and criteria), *in : Kategorri dialektiki i ih metodologičeskaja i mirovozzrenčeskaja funkcija* Čeboksary, 1983 : 61-70.

2458 PACEWICZ, Piotr. "Socjopsychologiczne teorie zachowań rewolucyjnych paradygmat zbiorowej choroby i paradygmat racjonalnego uzdrawiania świata" (Socio-psychological theories of revolutionary behaviours : paradigm of collective disease and paradigm of rational healing of the world), *Studia Socjologiczne* 94(3), 1984 : 155-177.

2459 PALIWAL, M. R. *Social change and education : present and future.* Delhi : Uppal, 1984, x-354 p. [India]

2460 PAŠKOV, A. S.; [ed.]. *Trud i social'noe razvitie socialističeskogo obščestva* (Labour and social development of the socialist society). Leningrad : Izdatel'stvo Leningradskogo Universiteta, 1983, 207 p.

2461 PLIMAK, É. G. *Revoljucionnyj process i revoljucionnoe soznanie* (The revolutionary process and revolutionary consciousness). Moskva : Politizdat, 1983, 240 p.

2462 POLE, D. Graham. *India in transition.* Delhi : Durga, 1984, xii-395 p.

2463 RAULET, Gérard. "La fin de la 'raison dans l'histoire'?", *Social Science Information / Information sur les Sciences Sociales* 23(3), 1984 : 559-576.

2464 ROIZ CÉLIX, Miguel. "Los limites de la modernización en la estructura social de Cataluña y Euskadi" (The limits of modernization in the social structure of Catalonia and Euskadi), *Revista Española de Investigaciones Sociológicas* 25, jan-mar 84 : 199-212.

2465 ROVATI, Giancarlo. "Trasformazioni sociali e processi politici" (Social change and political processes), *Studi di Sociologia* 22(3), jul-sep 84 : 301-316.

2466 SABERWAL, Satish. "On the social crisis in India : political traditions", *Contributions to Indian Sociology* 17(1), jan-jul 84 : 63-84.

2467 SAJÓ, András. "A társadalmi-jogi változás folyamata" (The process of social and legal change), *Állam-és Jogtudomány* 26(2), 1983 : 181-218.

2468 SCHIRMACHER, Wolfgang. "The end of metaphysics : what does this mean?", *Social Science Information / Information sur les Sciences Sociales* 23(3), 1984 : 603-609. [Original translation]

2469 SCHMIDT, Burghart. "Postmodernism as aggressive and conflict-avoiding dialectics", *Social Science Information / Information sur les Sciences Sociales* 23(3), 1984 : 589-602.

2470 SECRETAN, Philibert. "Éléments pour une théorie de la modernité", *Diogène* 126, apr-jun 84 : 79-98.

2471 SEIDMAN, Steven. "Modernity, meaning, and cultural pessimism in Max Weber", *Sociological Analysis* 44(4), 1983 : 267-278.

2472 ŠEJNIS, V. L. "Social'noe razvitie i social'nyj progress" (Social development and social progress), *in : Razvivajuščiesja strany : ěkonomičeskij rost i social'nyj progress* Moskva, 1983 : 543-589.

2473 SMIRNOV, G. L. "Nekotorye zadači filosofskogo osmyslenija novogo ětapa razvitija sovetskogo obščestva" (Some objectives of a philosophical understanding of a new stage of the Soviet society development), *Voprosy Filosofii* (5), 1984 : 3-19.

2474 SNOW, David A.; MACHALEK, Richard. "The sociology of conversion", *Annual Review of Sociology* 10, 1984 : 167-190.

2475   SOLOPOV, Ě. F.; [ed.]. *Vozrastanie roli nauki v social'no-ěkonomičeskom razvitii sovetskogo obščestva* (Elevation of the science role in socio-economic development of the Soviet society). Moskva : s.n., 1983, 58 p.

2476   SUMMERS, Gene F.; BRANCH, Kristi. "Economic development and community social change", *Annual Review of Sociology* 10, 1984 : 141-166. [USA]

2477   TEZANOS, José Félix. "Cambio social y modernización en la España actual" (Social change and modernization in Spain today), *Revista Española de Investigaciones Sociológicas* 28, oct-dec 84 : 19-61.

2478   TIRYAKIAN, Edward A. "The global crisis as an interregnum of modernity", *International Journal of Comparative Sociology* 25(1-2), 1984 : 123-130.

2479   UNGUREANU, Ion. "L'évolutionnisme social et les perspectives du développement", *Revue Roumaine des Sciences Sociales. Série de Sociologie* 28(1), jan-jun 84 : 49-55.

2480   VAN REE, Erik. "De tweede revolutie" (The second revolution), *Sociologische Gids* 31(6), 1984 : 474-486.

2481   ZAGHAL, Ali S. "Social change in Jordan", *Middle Eastern Studies* 20(4), oct 84 : 53-75.

2482   ZUBKOV, M. F.; ANIŠIN, V. A.; [eds.]. *Revoljucija i kontrrevoljucija v Latinskoj Amrike : kritika nemarksitskih koncepcij* (Revolution and counterrevolution in Latin America : critics of the non-Marxist conceptions). Moskva : Universitet Družby Narodov imeni P. Lumumby, 1983, 119 p.

**14340   Changing society
Société en transformation**

2483   *Dynamics of nation-building with particular reference to the role of communication : country profiles in historical perspective.* Bangkok : UNESCO Regional Office for Education in Asia and the Pacific, 1983, 201 p. tabl.

2484   BADHAM, Richard. "The sociology of industrial and post-industrial societies", *Current Sociology* 32(1), 1984 : vi-1-141.

2485   BLISS, Frank. "Traditionelle Gesellschaft, Regionalentwicklung und nationaler Rahmen in Ägypten" (Traditional society, regional development, and the national context in Egypt), *Sociologus* 34(2), 1984 : 97-120.

2486   BROMLEJ, Ju. V.; [ed.]. *Istorija pervobytnogo obščestva : obščie voprosy. Problemy antroposociogeneza* (History of the primitive society : general questions. Problems of anthropo-sociogenesis). Moskva : Nauka, 1983, 432 p.

2487   BUNKER, Stephen G. "Modes of extraction, unequal exchange, and the progressive underdevelopment of an extreme periphery : the Brazilian Amazon, 1600-1980", *American Journal of Sociology* 89(5), mar 84 : 1017-1064.

2488   KALDATE, Sudha; [ed.]. *Contemporary India : a sociological perspective; essays in honour of M. G. Kulkarni.* Delhi : Ajanta, 1984, 272 p.

2489   LAPONCE, Jean. "Nation-building as body-building : a comparative study of the personalization of city, province and state by anglophone and francophone Canadians", *Social Science Information / Information sur les Sciences Sociales* 23(6), 1984 : 977-991.

2490   LAURENT, Philippe. "Les tiers mondismes contestés", *Études*, feb 84 : 171-181.

2491   LENSKI, Gerhard; NOLAN, Patrick D. "Trajectories of development : a test of ecological evolutionary theory", *Social Forces* 63(1), sep 84 : 1-23.

2492   LISÝ, Ján. "Globálne problémy v buržoáznych koncepciách postindustriálnej spoločnosti" (Global problems in bourgeois conceptions of post-industrial society), *Ekonomický Časopis* 32(1), 1984 : 54-65.

2493   LONG, Norman. "Creating space for change : a perspective on the sociology of development", *Sociologia Ruralis* 24(3-4), 1984 : 168-184.

2494   NACER, Bourenane. "La crise et la théorie du développement : quelles fonctions sociales?", *Africa Development* 8(2), jun 83 : 60-73.

2495   RIOUX, Marcel. "Remarks on emancipatory practices and industrial societies in crisis", *Canadian Review of Sociology and Anthropology / Revue Canadienne de Sociologie et d'Anthropologie* 21(1), feb 84 : 1-20.

2496   SATHYAMURTHY, T. V. "Development research and the social sciences in India", *International Social Science Journal / Revue Internationale des Sciences Sociales* 36(4), 1984 : 673-697.

2497   TER-AKOPJAN, N. B. "Razvitie vzgljadov Karla Marksa na pervobytnoe obščestvo" (Development of Karl Marx's views on the primitive society), *Sovetskaja Arheologija* (4), 1983 : 13-21.

2498   TOKEI, Ferenc. "On the historical basis of the problems of development of the 'Third World'", *Journal of Contemporary Asia* 13(3), 83 : 314-323.

2499   TURNER, Bryan S. "State, civil society and national development : the Scottish problem", *Australian and New Zealand Journal of Sociology* 20(2), jul 84 : 161-182.

2500   WIEDEMANN, Paul; MÜLLER, Karl. "Le développement socio-économique des pays nouvellement industrialisés", *Travail et Société* 9(3), sep 84 : 285-312.

2501   WOHLFARTH, Karl Anton. *Leistung und Ethos : Überlegungen zu Entstehung und Kritik der industriellen Gesellschaft* (Programme and ethos : reflexions on the origin and critique of the industrial society). Paderborn : Schöningh, 1984, 267 p. bibl., ind.

15100 DEMOGRAPHY. GENETICS
DÉMOGRAPHIE. GÉNÉTIQUE

15110 Population research
Recherche démographique

2502 "Démogéographie (La) en question", *Espace, Population, Sociétés* (2), 1984 : 13-126. [France]
[With contributions by Catherine RHEIN, Pierre Jean THUMERELLE, Nadir
BOUMAZA, Jean René BERTRAND]

2503 "Forecasting regional population change and its economic determinants and consequences",
Socio-Economic Planning Sciences 17(5-6), 1983 : 235-380. [With contributions by Ann VAN
DER VEEN, Gerard EVERS, David A. PLANE, Andrew M. ISSERMAN]

2504 "Mezinárodní demografická konference Smolenice 1983" (International demographic
conference, Smolenice 1983), *Demografie* 26(1), 1984 : 1-12.

2505 *Modele i prognozy demograficzne* (Demographic models and projections). Warszawa : Szkoła
Główna Planowania i Statystyki, 1983, 215 p.

2506 "Población y desarrollo en América Latina" (Population and development in Latin America),
Notas de Población 12(34), apr 84 : 9-77.

2507 "Population : social cultural and health perspectives", *Social Action* 34(3), jul-sep 84 : 229-306.
[India]

2508 "Population analysis group : census office, State Council, and Department of vital statistics,
State statistical bureau : a few analyses of China's population", *Chinese Economic Studies*
17(3), spr 84 : 33-41.

2509 "Rapport (13e) sur la situation démographique de la France", *Population* 39(4-5),
jul-oct 84 : 669-732.

2510 ARTHUR, W. Brian. "The analysis of linkages in demographic theory", *Demography* 21(1),
feb 84 : 109-128.

2511 BILLET, Jean; GUIBOURDENCHE, Henri. "L'évolution récente de la population dans
les pays de l'arc alpin (sans l'Italie)", *Revue de Géographie Alpine* 72(1), 1984 : 5-114.
[With contributions by Jean BILLET, Henri ROUGIER, Jacky HERVIN, Johannes
REMMER, Claude MEYZENQ]

2512 BOLDYREV, V. A. *Narodonaselenie v razvitom socialističeskom obščestve : teorija i politika*
(Population in the developed socialist society : theory and policy). Moskva : Finansy
i Statistika, 1983, 231 p.

2513 CALOT, Gérard. *La mesure des taux en démographie : âge en années révolues ou âge atteint dans
l'année, incidence du choix de la définition, application à la fécondité, application à la fécondité
génerale.* Paris : Presses Universitaires de France, 1984, vii-321 p.

2514 CARTIER, Michel. "Les leçons du troisième recensement chinois", *Courrier des Pays de
l'Est* (282), mar 84 : 31-51.

2515 CATSIAPIS, Jean. "La population de la Grèce en 1983", *Études Helléniques* 1(2), 1983 : 13-20.

2516 CONDRAN, Gretchen A. "An evaluation of estimates of underenumeration in the census
and the age pattern of mortality, Philadelphia, 1880", *Demography* 21(1), feb 84 : 53-70.

2517 DE MESQUITA SAMARA, Eni; DEL NERO DA COSTA, Iraci. *Demografia histórica :
bibliografia brasileira* (Historical demography : Brazilian bibliography). São Paulo :
Instituto de Pesquisas Econômicas, 1984, 75 p. ind.

2518 DE OLIVEIRA, Zuleica Lopes Cavalcanti. "Conceitos e definições para um atlas de
populacção da América latina" (Concepts and definitions for a population atlas of Latin
America), *Revista Geográfica* (97), jun 83 : 113-129.

2519 DREIFELDS, Juris. "Demographic trends in Latvia", *Nationalities Papers* 12(1),
spr 84 : 49-84. [USSR]

2520 DUMONT, Gérard-François. "L'Europe face à sa démographie", *Contrepoint* (48), 1984 : 13-22.

2521 DUPÂQUIER, Jacques. *Pour la démographie historique.* Paris : Presses Universitaires de
France, 1984, 188 p. bibl., ind.

2522 DUPÂQUIER, Michel. "William Farr, démographe", *Population* 39(2), mar-apr 84 : 339-356.
[UK]

2523 DUPONT, Véronique. "Grandes lignes de l'évolution de la population française depuis la
deuxième guerre mondiale", *Revue Française des Affaires Sociales* 38(suppl.), jun 84 : 3-14.

2524   DUSSAULT, Georges. "Israël : l'enjeu démographique", *Afrique et Asie Modernes* (143), wint 85 : 85-98.

2525   EARNHARDT, Kent C. *Population research, policy, and related studies in Puerto Rico : an inventory.* Río Piedras : Editorial de la Universidad de Puerto Rico, 1984, vii-132 p. ind.

2526   ÉGLITE, P.; [ed.]. *Aktual'nye problemy demografii* (Topical problems of demography). Riga : Zinatne, 1983, 217 p.

2527   FESTY, Patrick. "Effets et répercussions de la première guerre mondiale sur la fécondité française", *Population* 39(6), nov-dec 84 : 977-1010.

2528   FRĄTCZAK, Ewa; [et al.]. "Prognoza demograficzna dla Polski na lata 1983-1990 oraz 1995" (Demographic forecast for Poland 1983-1990 and 1995), *Studia Demograficzne* 21(4), 1983 : 29-51.

2529   GHOSH, Pradip K.; [ed.]. *Population, environment and resources, and Third World development.* Westport, CT : Greenwood Press, 1984, xx-634 p.

2530   HENRY, Louis. *Démographie : analyse et modèles.* Paris : Institut National d'Études Démographiques, 1984, 2e, 341 p. ind.

2531   ISSERMAN, Andrew M.; FISHER, Peter S. "Population forecasting and local economic planning : the limits on community control over uncertainty", *Population Research and Policy Review* 3(1), jan 84 : 27-50. [USA] [See also Elizabeth W. MOEN : Population forecasting and planning : some philosophical issues]

2532   JOWETT, A. J. "The growth of China's population, 1949-1982", *Geographical Journal* 150(2), jul 84 : 155-170.

2533   KEYFITZ, Nathan. "Impact of trends in resources, environment and development on demographic prospects", *Population Bulletin of the United Nations* 16, 1984 : 1-15.

2534   KEYFITZ, Nathan. "The population of China", *Scientific American* 250(2), feb 84 : 22-31.

2535   KIM, Young J.; STROBINO, Donna M. "Decomposition of the difference between two rates with hierarchical factors", *Demography* 21(3), aug 84 : 361-372.

2536   KIRK, Maurice. "The return of Malthus? The global demographic future, 2000-2050", *Futures* 16(2), apr 84 : 124-138.

2537   KULCSÁR, Kálmán; [ed.]. *A népesedés és a népesedéspolitika : tanulmányok* (Population and population policy : studies). Budapest : Kossuth Kiadó, 1983, 235 p. ill., bibl.

2538   LACHIVER, Marcel. "Trente années de démographie historique en France", *Année Sociologique* 34, 1984 : 165-199.

2539   LAROSE, André. "Les démographes et la population du Canada sous le régime français (1934-1966)", *Cahiers Québécois de Démographie* 13(1), apr 84 : 41-58.

2540   MATTHIESSEN, P. C. "Befolkningssituationen i Europa" (The demographic situation in Europe), *Nationaløkonomisk Tidsskrift* 121(2), 1983 : 215-229.

2541   MIELKE, James H.; [et al.]. "Historical epidemiology of smallpox in Aland, Finland : 1751-1890", *Demography* 21(3), aug 84 : 271-295.

2542   NEW ZEALAND PLANNING COUNCIL. MONITORING GROUP. *The New Zealand population : patterns of change.* Wellington : the Council, 1984, v-64 p. ill., bibl.

2543   NOIN, Daniel. "La population de la France au début des années 80", *Annales de Géographie* 93(517), jun 84 : 290-302.

2544   POULALION, Gabriel. *La science de la population.* Paris : Librairies Techniques, 1984, viii-333 p. ill., bibl.

2545   PRESSAT, Roland. "Vues historiques sur la population de l'U.R.S.S.", *Population* 39(3), mai-jun 84 : 541-562.

2546   PUSHKA, Asllan. "Odnosi između razmještaja stanovništva, reljefa i stupnja društveno-gospodarskog razvitka u SAP Kosovu" (The relationship between population distribution, relief and level of socio-economic development in the SAP Kosovo), *Sociologija Sela* (82), 1983 : 221-231. [Yugoslavia]

2547   REHER, David-Sven. "La importancia del análisis dinámico ante el análisis estático del hogar y la familia. Algunos ejemplos de la ciudad de Cuenca en el siglo XIX" (The importance of the dynamic analysis before the statistical analysis of household and family. Some examples from the city of Cuenca in the XIXth century), *Revista Española de Investigaciones Sociológicas* 27, jul-sep 84 : 107-135. [Spain]

2548   SAHLI, Anne-Marie. "La population du bassin méditerranéen", *Politico* 49(1), mar 84 : 121-132.

2549   SCHMID, Josef. *Bevölkerungsveränderungen in der Bundesrepublik Deutschland : eine Revolution auf leisen Sohlen* (Population changes in the Federal Republic of Germany : a revolution from a low level). Stuttgart : W. Kohlhammer, 1984, 127 p. ill., bibl.

2550   ŠUBRTOVÁ, Alena. "Teorie demografické revoluce : příspěvek ke genezi" (Theory of demographic revolution : contribution to genesis), *Demografie* 26(3), 1984 : 193-200.

2551   TOLNAY, Stewart E.; GUEST, Avery M. "American family building strategies in 1900 : stopping or spacing", *Demography* 21(1), feb 84 : 9-18.

2552   TURPEINEN, Oiva. "The percentage of deaths under one year of age of all deaths in Finland in 1749-1865", *Yearbook of Population Research in Finland* 22, 1984 : 46-54.
2553   UNITED NATIONS. SECRETARIAT. "Techniques for integrating population variables into development planning : a preview of a forthcoming manual of the Population Division of the United Nations", *Population Bulletin of the United Nations* 16, 1984 : 77-89.
2554   VUKOVICH, György. "Népesség — urbanizáció — környezet" (Population — urbanization — environment), *Statisztikai Szemle* 62(6), jun 84 : 573-583. [Hungary]
2555   WILLIAMSON, J. G. "British mortality and the value of life, 1781-1931", *Population Studies* 38(1), mar 84 : 157-172.
2556   WUNSCH, Guillaume J. "Theories, models and knowledge. The logic of demographic discovery", *Genus* 40(1-2), jan-jun 84 : 1-17.
2557   ZHONGSHEN, Zhang. "Kína népesedése és a népességtudomány fejlődése a felsőoktatási intézményekben" (Population and Chinese demographic science development in high schools), *Demográfia* 26(4), 1983 : 562-571.

15120   Households. Men. Women
Ménages. Hommes. Femmes

2558   "Animal, mon amour !", *Autrement. Série Mutations* (56), jan 84 : 1-214. [France]
2559   "Corps (Le)", *Cahiers Internationaux de Sociologie* 77, 1984 : 237-395.
2560   "Femmes (Les) dans la Communauté européenne", *Documentation Européenne* (4), 1984 : 1-35.
2561   "Sexuel (Le)", *Cahiers Internationaux de Sociologie* 76, 1984 : 3-224. [With contributions by Georges BALANDIER, André BEJÍN, Naty GARCÍA GUADILLA, André PADOUX, Claude BAUHAIN, Kenji TOKITSU, Abdelwahab BOUHDIBA, Michel MAFFESOLI]
2562   AMANO, Masako. "Reisai kouri gyo shufu no rohdo to ishiki -reisai kouri gyo no sonritsu jyoken" (Working life and opinion of housewives in small retail shops), *Kinjogakuin Daigaku Ronshu* 105, 1984 : 71-108. [Japan]
2563   ANDORKA, Rudolf. "Household structure and work on household or auxiliary plots in the contemporary Hungarian village", *East European Quarterly* 17(4), jan 84 : 469-489.
2564   BARRÈRE-MAURISSON, M.-A.; [et al.]. *Le sexe du travail : structures familiales et système productif.* Grenoble : Presses Universitaires de Grenoble, 1984, 320 p.
2565   BEJÍN, André; GARCÍA GUADILLA, Naty. "Sept thèses erronées sur le machisme latino-américain", *Cahiers Internationaux de Sociologie* 76, 1984 : 21-28.
2566   BORCHORST, Anette; SIIM, Birte. *Kvinder i velfaerdsstaten* (Women in welfare state). Aalborg : Aalborg Universitetsforlag, 1984, 263 p. ill., bibl. [Denmark]
2567   BUECHLER, Steve. "Sex and class : a critical overview of some recent theoretical work and some modest proposals", *Insurgent Sociologist* 12(3), 1984 : 19-32.
2568   BUJRA, Janet M. "Class, gender and capitalist transformation in Africa", *Africa Development* 8(3), sep 83 : 17-42.
2569   BUTTEL, Frederick H.; GILLESPIE, Gilbert W. Jr. "The sexual division of farm household labor : an exploratory study of the structure of on-farm and off-farm labor allocation among farm men and women", *Rural Sociology* 49(2), sum 84 : 183-209.
2570   CHABAUD, Danielle. "Problématiques de sexes dans les recherches sur le travail et la famille", *Sociologie du Travail* 26(2), jul-sep 84 : 346-359.
2571   CODE, Lorraine B. "Responsibility and the epistemic community : woman's place", *Social Research* 50(3), 1983 : 537-555.
2572   DHAVERNAS, Marie-Jo; [et al.]. "Cave Canem : à propos de la 'libération animale'", *Temps Modernes* 40(450), jan 84 : 1331-1340.
2573   DOLTON, Peter J. "Testing for sex discrimination in maximum likelihood models", *Applied Economics* 16(2), apr 84 : 225-235.
2574   EHARA, Yumiko; YOSHII, Hiroaki; YAMASAKI, Keiichi. "Sei-sabetsu no ethno-methodology — taimen teki communication jyokyo ni okeru kenryoku souchi" (Ethnomethodology of sexism : from the perspective of conversational analysis), *Review of Contemporary Sociology* 18, 1984 : 143-176.
2575   EICKELMAN, Christine. *Women and community in Oman.* New York, NY : New York University Press, 1984, 251 p. ind., bibl., ill.
2576   ENGLAND, Paula. "Wage appreciation and depreciation : a test of neo-classical economic explanations of occupational sex segregation", *Social Forces* 62(3), mar 84 : 726-749.
2577   ERMISCH, J. F.; OVERTON, Elizabeth. "Minimal household units : a new approach to the analysis of household formation", *Population Studies* 39(1), mar 85 : 33-54.
2578   ERVIN, Delbert; THOMAS, Barbara J.; ZEY-FERRELL, Mary. "Sex discrimination and rewards in a public comprehensive university", *Human Relations* 37(12), dec 84 : 1005-1028. [USA]

2579   FERGE, Zsuzsa. "Biologikum és nemek közötti egyenlőség. A politika és a biológikum" (Biological being and gender equality. Politics and biological character), *Magyar Tudomány* 29(2), 1984 : 111-119.

2580   FILGUEIRA, Nea; [et al.]. *La mujer en el Uruguay : ayer y hoy* (The woman in Uruguay : yesterday and today). Montevideo : Ediciones de la Banda Oriental, 1983, 142 p. bibl.

2581   FLANAGAN, Owen J. Jr.; ADLER, Jonathan E. "Impartiality and particularity", *Social Research* 50(3), 1983 : 576-596. [Women's conception of morality]

2582   FREEDMAN, Ann E. "Sex equality, sex differences, and the Supreme Court", *Yale Law Journal* 92(6), mai 83 : 913-968. [USA]

2583   GHOSH, S. K. *Women in a changing society.* Delhi : Ashish, 1984, 188 p.

2584   GIDDINGS, Paula. *When and where I enter : the impact of Black women on race and sex in America.* New York, NY : W. Morrow, 1984, 408 p. bibl., ind.

2585   GLENN, Norval D.; TAYLOR, Patricia Ann. "Education and family income : a comparison of white married men and women in the US", *Social Forces* 63(1), sep 84 : 169-183.

2586   GLICK, Paul C. "American household structure in transition", *Family Planning Perspectives* 16(5), sep-oct 84 : 205-211.

2587   GLICK, Paul C. "Les ménages aux États-Unis, 1960-1970-1982", *Population* 39(4-5), jul-oct 84 : 787-806.

2588   HANÁK, Katalin. *A nő képe a televízióban* (The image of the women in television). Budapest : Magyar Rádió Televízió Tömegkommunikációs Kutatóközpontja, 1984, 92 p.

2589   HAY, Margaret Jean; STICHTER, Sharon; [eds.]. *African women south of the Sahara.* London; New York, NY : Longman, 1983, xiv-225 p. bibl., ind.

2590   HELD, Thomas; MURRAY, Barbara; [et al.]. "Bilder von Mann und Frau / Images de l'homme et de la femme", *Schweizerische Zeitschrift für Soziologie / Revue Suisse de Sociologie* 10(3), 1984 : 723-812.

2591   HUNT, Jennifer. "The development of rapport through the negotiation of gender in field work among police", *Human Organization* 43(4), 1984 : 283-296. [USA]

2592   IRIGARY, Luce. *Éthique de la différence sexuelle.* Paris : Éditions de Minuit, 1984, 198 p.

2593   JANMAN, Karen. "Gender dependency of occupational deviance and role overload as determinants of fear of success imagery", *European Journal of Social Psychology* 14(4), oct-dec 84 : 421-429.

2594   JURICH, Joan. "The relationship of modernity of sex roles to pregnancy planning", *Sociological Focus* 17(3), aug 84 : 223-242.

2595   KOMAROVSKY, Mirra; MAYER, Ellen R. "Consistency of female gender attitudes : a research note", *Social Forces* 62(4), jun 84 : 1020-1025. [USA]

2596   KRAMAR, Robin. "Economic theory and the sexual segregation of the labour market", *Australian Quarterly* 55(4), sum 83 : 388-404. [Australia]

2597   LE BRETON, David. "L'effacement ritualisé du corps", *Cahiers Internationaux de Sociologie* 77, 1984 : 273-286.

2598   MAGUIRE, Patricia. *Women in development : an alternative analysis.* Amherst, MA : Center for International Education, University of Massachusetts, 1984, v-68 p. bibl.

2599   MANDERSON, Lenore; [ed.]. *Women's work and women's roles : economics and everyday life in Indonesia, Malaysia, and Singapore.* Canberra; New York, NY : Australian National University Press, 1983, x-265 p. ill., bibl., ind.

2600   MASCARENHAS, Ophelia; MBILINYI, Marjorie J. *Women in Tanzania : an analytical bibliography.* Uppsala : Scandinavian Institute of African Studies; Stockholm : Swedish International Development Authority, 1983, 256 p. ind.

2601   MILLSAP, Mary Ann. "Sex equity in education", *Sage Yearbooks in Women's Policy Studies* 7, 1983 : 91-119. [USA]

2602   MORGAN, S. P.; RINDFUSS, R. R. "Household structure and the tempo of family formation in comparative perspective", *Population Studies* 38(1), mar 84 : 129-139.

2603   MUKHOPADHYAY, Carol Chapnick. "Testing a decision process model of the sexual division of labor in the family", *Human Organization* 43(3), 1984 : 226-242. [USA]

2604   NAILS, Debra. "Social-scientific sexism : Gilligan's mismeasure of man", *Social Research* 50(3), 1983 : 643-664. [See C. GILLIGAN, 'In a different voice : psychological theory and women's development.' Cambridge, MA-London : Harvard University Press, 1982]

2605   NAILS, Debra; O'LOUGHLIN, Mary-Ann; WALKER, James C.; [eds.]. "Women and morality", *Social Research* 50(3), aut 83 : 487-695. [With contributions by Linda J. NICHOLSON, John M. BROUGHTON]

2606   NICHOLSON, Linda J. "Women, morality, and history", *Social Research* 50(3), 1983 : 514-536.

2607   O'BRIEN, Denise; TIFFANY, Sharon W.; [eds.]. *Rethinking women's roles : perspectives from the Pacific.* London; Berkeley, CA : University of California Press, 1984, xiv-237 p. map, bibl.

2608   PADOUX, André. "Le monde hindou et le sexe : symbolisme, attitudes, pratiques", *Cahiers Internationaux de Sociologie* 76, 1984 : 29-49.

2609   PETERSON, Abby. "The gender-sex dimension in Swedish politics", *Acta Sociologica* 27(1), 1984 : 3-17.

2610   POWELL, Gary N.; POSNER, Barry Z.; SCHMIDT, Warren H. "Sex effects on managerial value systems", *Human Relations* 37(11), nov 84 : 909-921.

2611   RAWALT, Marguerite. "The Equal Rights Amendment", *Sage Yearbooks in Women's Policy Studies* 7, 1983 : 49-78. [USA]

2612   RAY, John J.; LOVEJOY, F. H. "The great androgyny myth : sex roles and mental health in the community at large", *Journal of Social Psychology* 124(2), dec 84 : 237-246.

2613   RICHER, Stephen. "Sexual inequality and children's play", *Canadian Review of Sociology and Anthropology / Revue Canadienne de Sociologie et d'Anthropologie* 21(2), mai 84 : 166-180.

2614   ROBERTSON, Claire C. *Sharing the same bowl : a socioeconomic history of women and class in Accra, Ghana.* Bloomington, IN : Indiana University Press, 1984, 299 p. bibl., ind.

2615   SAS, Judit H. *Nőies nők és férfias férfiak. A nőkkel és a férfiakkal kapcsolatos társadalmi sztereotípiák élete, eredete és szocializációja* (Woman-like women and man-like men. The life, origin and socialization of women and men related social stereotypes). Budapest : Akadémiai Kiadó, 1984, 251 p.

2616   SAVOY-CLOT, Isabelle. "Quelle égalité pour les femmes? L'expérience suisse", *Travail et Société* 9(1), mar 84 : 97-116.

2617   SCHEIRER, Mary Ann. "Household structure among welfare families : correlates and consequences", *Journal of Marriage and the Family* 45(4), nov 83 : 761-771. [USA]

2618   SIEGERS, Jacques. "L'égalité des sexes dans la répartition du travail : le but est-il en vue? Le cas des Pays-Bas", *Travail et Société* 9(2), jun 84 : 165-178.

2619   SILTANEN, Janet; STANWORTH, Michelle. "The politics of private woman and public man", *Theory and Society* 13(1), jan 84 : 91-118.

2620   STANWORTH, Michelle. "Women and class analysis : a reply to John Goldthorpe", *Sociology (London)* 18(2), mai 84 : 159-170. [UK] [Reply to John H. GOLTHORPE's article on the same subject, ibid. : 17(4), nov 83; see also Anthony HEATH and Nicky BRITTEN, ibid. : 18(4), nov 84 : 476-490, and John H. GOLDTHORPE's final reply, ibid. : 18(4), nov 84 : 491-499]

2621   SWEET, James A. "Components of change in the number of households, 1970-1980", *Demography* 21(2), mai 84 : 129-140. [USA]

2622   TOMEH, Aida K.; GALLANT, Clifford J. "French men's and women's sex role attitudes", *International Journal of Comparative Sociology* 25(3-4), sep-dec 84 : 226-242.

2623   TZURIEL, David. "Sex role typing and ego identity in Israeli, oriental, and Western adolescents", *Journal of Personality and Social Psychology* 46(2), feb 84 : 440-457. [Israel]

2624   UENO, Chizuko. "Gender no bunka jinruigaku" (A cultural anthropology on gender), *Hermes* 1, 1984 : 138-151.

2625   UNESCO. *Social science research and women in the Arab world.* London : Frances Pinter, 1984, x-175 p.

2626   VAN DOORNE-HUISKES, J. "Vrouwen in mobiliteits- en stratificatieonderzoek" (Women in mobility and stratification research), *Mens en Maatschappij* 59(3), aug 84 : 269-291.

2627   VOYDANOFF, Patricia; [ed.]. *Work and family : changing roles of men and women.* Palo Alto, CA : Mayfield Publishing Co., 1984, viii-383 p. ill., bibl.

2628   WALDAUER, Charles. "The non-comparability of the 'comparable worth' doctrine : an inappropriate standard for determining sex discrimination in pay", *Population Research and Policy Review* 3(2), jun 84 : 141-166.

2629   WEILER, Antonius Gerardus; [et al.]. *Vrouwen en maatschappij : wetenschappelijke reflexies over de rol van vrouwen in de opbouw van cultuur en samenleving* (Women and society : scientific considerations on the women's role in the development of cultural and social life). Baarn : Ambo, 1984, 144 p. bibl.

2630   WESTLANDER, Gunnela. "Equality of the sexes in an organizational perspective : a Swedish experiment", *Organization Studies* 5(3), 1984 : 243-259.

2631   YAO, Esther Shun-shin Lee. *Chinese women, past and present.* Mesquite, TX : Ide House, 1983, 271 p. bibl., ind.

2632   ZENT, Michael R. "Sex and mental disorder : a reappraisal", *Sociological Focus* 17(2), apr 84 : 121-136.

2633   ZUBENKO, L. A. "Stanovlenie ličnosti sovetskoj ženščiny v uslovijah socializma" (The future of the Soviet woman's personality under conditions of socialism), *in : XXVI s'ezd KPSS i formirovanie ličnosti v razvitom socialističeskom obščestve* Moskva, 1982 : 39-45.

15130   Eugenism. Heredity
Eugénisme. Hérédité

2634   DUMONT, Martine. "Le succès mondain d'une fausse science : la physiognomonie de Johann Kaspar Lavater", *Actes de la Recherche en Sciences Sociales* 54, sep 84 : 2-30. [Switzerland]

15200   AGE GROUPS
GROUPES D'ÂGE

15210   Age. Cohorts. Generations
Âge. Cohortes. Générations

2635   BRAUNGART, Richard G. "Historical generations and generation units : a global pattern of youth movements", *Journal of Military Sociology* 12(1), 1984 : 113-135.

2636   CALOT, Gérard. "La mesure des taux en démographie : taux par âge en années révolues et taux par âge atteint dans l'année", *Population* 39(1), jan-feb 84 : 107-146.

2637   ESLER, Anthony. *The generation gap in society and history : a select bibliography. 2 vols.* Monticello, IL : Vance Bibliographies, 1984, 219 p. ind., bibl.

2638   ESLER, Anthony. " 'The truest community' : social generations as collective mentalities", *Journal of Military Sociology* 12(1), 1984 : 99-112.

2639   FONER, Nancy. *Ages in conflict : a cross-cultural perspective on inequality between old and young.* New York, NY : Columbia University Press, 1984, 305 p. ind.

2640   SUGAYA, Yoshiko. "Raifu kohsu no sedai, cohort hikaku" (Intergenerational differences and intercohort changes in the female life course), *Miyagi Gakuin Kenkyu Ronbunshu* 60, 1984 : 19-38.

2641   THORNTON, Arland; CHANG, Ming-Cheng; SUN, Te-Hsiung. "Social and economic change, intergenerational relationships, and family formation in Taiwan", *Demography* 21(4), nov 84 : 475-499.

2642   THUMERELLE, P. J. "Structure par âge : pays d'Europe, régions françaises", *Espace, Populations, Sociétés* (2), 1984 : 127-144.

15220   Childhood
Enfance

2643   ANDERSON, Kathryn H. "The effect of health programs on breast-feeding and child mortality in peninsular Malaysia", *Research in Population Economics* 5, 1984 : 87-112.

2644   CALLAN, Victor J.; WILKS, Jeffrey. "Perceptions about the value and cost of children : Australian and Papua New Guinean high school youth", *Journal of Biosocial Science* 16(1), jan 84 : 35-44.

2645   DAVID, Marie-Gabrielle; GOKALP, Catherine. "La semaine d'un enfant scolarisé", *Consommation* 31(1), mar 84 : 59-88. [France] [ENG]

2646   GOODMAN, Gail S.; [ed.]. "The child witness", *Journal of Social Issues* 40(2), 1984 : 1-176. [With contributions by Marcia K. JOHNSON, Mary Ann FOLEY, Robert S. PYNOOS, Spencer ETH]

2647   HEGAR, Rebecca L. "Foster children and parents' right to a family", *Social Service Review* 57(3), sep 83 : 429-447. [USA]

2648   HUFFMAN, Sandra L. "Determinants of breastfeeding in developing countries : overview and policy implication", *Studies in Family Planning* 15(4), jul-aug 84 : 170-183.

2649   IGLESIAS DE USSEL, Julio. "La relación infancia y familia en España" (Childhood and family relationship in Spain), *Revista Española de Investigaciones Sociológicas* 27, jul-sep 84 : 7-39.

2650   KIRK, H. David; MCDANIEL, Susan A. "Adoption policy in Great Britain and North America", *Journal of Social Policy* 13(1), jan 84 : 75-84.

2651   LAJEUNESSE-PILLARD, Nicole. *Regard sur l'abandonnisme : les adolescents sans images en autrui.* Toulouse : Erès, 1984, 107 p. bibl., ind.

2652   LAMBERT, Wallace E. "Cross-cultural perspectives on children's development and identity", *Teachers College Record* 85(3), spr 84 : 349-364.

2653   MASSARD, Josiane. "Le don d'enfants dans la société malaise", *Homme* 23(3), sep 83 : 101-114.

2654   MENSAH, Ebow. "Children as beggars : a case study from Zaria/Nigeria", *Sociologus* 34(1), 1984 : 30-46.

2655   MEYROWITZ, Joshua. "The adultlike child and the childlike adult : socialization in an electronic age", *Daedalus* 113(3), sum 84 : 19-48.

2656   PASSOW, A. Harry. "Éducation (L') des surdoués", *Perspectives (UNESCO)* 14(2), 1984 : 183-194.

2657   POWELL, Fred. "Adoption policy in Northern Ireland 1929-82", *Administration (Dublin)* 32(2), 1984 : 201-230.

2658   RYAN, Judy; DENT, Owen. "An introduction to survival analysis : factors influencing the duration of breast feeding", *Australian and New Zealand Journal of Sociology* 20(2), jul 84 : 183-196. [Australia]

2659   SHAND, Nancy. "Breastfeeding as cultural or personal decision : sources of information and actual success in Japan and the United States", *Journal of Biosocial Science* 16(1), jan 84 : 65-80.

2660   STRATHMAN, Terry. "From the quotidian to the utopian : child rearing literature in America, 1926-1946", *Berkeley Journal of Sociology* 29, 1984 : 1-34.

2661   TEASDALE, T. W.; OWEN, David R. "Social class and mobility in male adoptees and non-adoptees", *Journal of Biosocial Science* 16(4), oct 84 : 521-530.

2662   TITKOW, Anna. *Child and values.* Warszawa : Polish Academy of Sciences Institute of Philosophy and Sociology, University of Warsaw Institute of Sociology, 1984, 171 p.

2663   WETHERALL, Charles F. *The gifted kids guide to creative thinking.* Minneapolis, MN : Wetherall Publishing Co., 1984, 143 p. ill., bibl.

15230   Youth
Jeunesse

2664   "1985, année internationale de la jeunesse", *Perspectives (UNESCO)* 14(2), 1984 : 221-304. [With contributions by Christopher MURRAY, Sibylle HUBNER-FUNK, Werner SCHEFOLD, Edgar MONTIEL, Ivan Dmitriyevich ZVEREV, Julia SZALAI]

2665   "Jeunes et société", *Contradictions* (40-41), 1984 : 1-170. [France] [With contributions by O. GALLAND, A. TAROZZI, P. FACCIOLI, J. P. BARTLOLOME, B. FRANCQ, F. GOFFINET]

2666   "Jeunesse (La) et le monde d'aujourd'hui", *Revue Roumaine* 37(7), 1983 : 1-115. [With contributions by Mihail STOICA, Aculin CAZACU, Aurel GHIBITIU, Catalin ZAMFIR, Petre DATCULESCU]

2667   "Juventud (La) espanola hoy" (Spanish youth today), *Razón y Fe* 210(1030-31), aug 84 : 3-144. [With contributions by José Miguel MARINAS, Andrés TORNOS, Cristóbal SARRIAS, Juan ARRIBAS, Pedro FERRER PI, Enrique SANCHEZ, Santiago GARCIA ECHEVARRIA]

2668   "L'insertion sociale et professionnelle des jeunes à la Martinique et à la Réunion", *Bulletin d'Information du CENADDOM* 14(74), trim. 2, 84 : 18-48. [With contributions by J. P. CESAIRE, Y. NAGOU, Hector SAE]

2669   "Mouvements de jeunes en Suisse : thèses et antithèses", *Schweizerische Zeitschrift für Soziologie / Revue Suisse de Sociologie* 10(1), 1984 : 125-286.

2670   ADAMS, Gerald R.; [et al.]. "Ego identity status, conformity behavior, and personality in late adolescence", *Journal of Personality and Social Psychology* 47(5), nov 84 : 1091-1104.

2671   ALLARDT, Erik; UUSITALO, Ritva. *Youth in modern society : problems in the transition to adulthood.* Helsinki : University of Helsinki, Department of Sociology, 1984, 32-2 p. bibl.

2672   BAETHGE, Martin; SCHOMBURG, Harald; VOSKAMP, Ulrich. *Jugend und Krise : Krise aktueller Jugendforschung* (Youth and crisis : crisis of the present youth research). Frankfurt-am-Main : Campus-Verlag, 1983, viii-250 p. bibl.

2673   BLANCPAIN, Robert; ZEUGIN, Peter; HÄUSELMANN, Erich. *Erwachsen werden : Ergebnisse und Folgerungen aus einer Repräsentativbefragung* (Becoming adult : results and conclusions of a representative survey). Bern : P. Haupt, 1983, vii-306 p. ill. [Switzerland]

2674   BOROWICZ, Ryszard. "Subiektywna ocena własnej sytuacji życiowej przez młodziez" (A subjective appraisal by young people of their own life situation), *Wieś i Rolnictwo* 42(1), 1984 : 185-200.

2675   BOUILLIN-DARTEVELLE, Roselyne. *La génération éclatée : loisirs et communication des adolescents.* Bruxelles : Éditions de l'Université de Bruxelles, 1984, 272 p. bibl.

2676   BRAGA DE CRUZ, Manuel; [et al.]. "A condição social da juventude portuguesa" (Social condition of the Portuguese youth), *Análise Social* 20(2-3), 1984 : 285-308.

2677   CANOVAS SANCHEZ, Francisco. "La información y la orientación en la política de juventud" (Information and orientation in youth policy), *Revista de Estudios de Juventud* (16), dec 84 : 11-24. [Spain]

2678   CAVALLI, Alessandro. "Giovani, politica sociale e 'Welfare State'" (Young people, social policy and 'Welfare State'), *Giornale degli Economisti e Annali di Economia* 43(11-12), nov-dec 84 : 861-966. [UK; USA; France]

2679 DELLA SELVA, Patricia C.; DUSEK, Jerome B. "Sex role orientation and resolution of Eriksonian crises during the late adolescent years", *Journal of Personality and Social Psychology* 47(1), jul 84 : 204-212.

2680 DEUTSCHES JUGENDINSTITUT. *Lebenslage Jugend : Problemzonen und Perspektiven alltäglicher Lebensbewältigung* (Youth life problems : areas and daily prospects of daily life achievement). München : Das Institut, 1983, 198 p. bibl. [Germany FR]

2681 DI GIORGI, Piero. "L'adolescenza : fase naturale o storico-culturale dello sviluppo psichico?" (Adolescence : natural of historico-cultural phase of the psychic development?), *Critica Sociologica* 70, 1984 : 83-93.

2682 DILLON, Michele. "Youth culture in Ireland", *Economic and Social Review* 15(3), apr 84 : 153-172.

2683 EMNA, Ben-Miled; [et al.]. *Étude sur les jeunes.* Tunis : Université de Tunis, Centre d'Études et de Recherches Économiques et Sociales, 1984, 219 p. bibl. [Tunisia]

2684 FERRER, Julio. *Punkare och skinheads : socialisering i gäng* (Punk and skinheads : socializing the gangs). Stockholm : Norstedt, 1983, 224-1 p. ill., bibl. [Sweden]

2685 FRITH, Simon. *The sociology of youth.* Ormskirk, Lancashire : Causeway Books, 1984, 68 p. bibl., ind. [UK]

2686 GARELLI, Franco. *La generazione della vita quotidiana : i giovani in una società differenziata* (Everyday life generation : young people in a differentiated society). Bologna : Il Mulino, 1984, 329 p.

2687 GOLDBERG, Harvey E. *Green Town's youth : disadvantaged youth in a development town in Israel.* Assen : Van Gorcum, 1984, 158 p.

2688 HAVELKA, J.; OTTOMANSKÝ, J. "La situation de la jeune génération en République Socialiste Tchécoslovaque", *Demosta* 16(3-4), 1983 : 13-17.

2689 HELWIG, Gisela. *Jugend und Familie in der DDR* (Youth and family in the GDR). Köln : Deutschland Archiv Verlag, 1984, 126 p. bibl., ind.

2690 IWAMA, Tsuyoshi. "Sienen nyushoku keikaku no genjyo Ceylon no yattapata keikaku no jirei" (Youth settlement scheme in Ceylon), *Tamagawa Daigaku Ronso* 24, 1984 : 1-11.

2691 IWAMI, Kazuhiko; TATSUMOTO, Yoshifumi. "Nijussai seinen no ishiki to taiken -seinen kenkyu ni okeru zokusei teki approach no igi" (Twenty-year-old youths' consciousness and experiences), *Kansai University Bulletin of the Faculty of Sociology* 16(1), 1984 : 247-275. [Japan]

2692 JOHNSTON, W. Lee. "A modified Piagetian cognitive development model : political impulsiveness in American youths", *International Journal of Political Education* 6(3), nov 83 : 203-221.

2693 KOZAKIEWICZ, Mikołaj. *Młodziez w okresie przełomów* (Young people in a turning-point period). Warszawa : Ludowa Spółdzielnia Wydawnicza, 1984, 290 p. [Poland]

2694 LEMKE, Christiane. "Jugendliche in der DDR — Freizeitpolitik und Freizeitverhalten" (Youth in GDR : policy and leisure behaviour), *Deutschland Archiv* 17(2), feb 84 : 166-182.

2695 MIGNON, Jean-Marie. *Afrique : jeunesses uniques, jeunesse encadrée; institutions de jeunesse d'éducation populaire et de sports dans onze pays d'Afrique francophone.* Paris : L'Harmattan, 1984, 260 p.

2696 MLONEK, Krystyna. "Przeobrażenia w populacji młodzieży w Polsce w latach 1950-1980 i ich konsekwencje dla polityki społecznej" (Changes in the young population in Poland 1950-1980 and their consequences for social policy), *Studia Demograficzne* 22(3), 1984 : 17-40.

2697 MUSHABEN, Joyce Marie. "Anti-politics and successor generations : the role of youth in the West and East German peace movements", *Journal of Political and Military Sociology* 12(1), spr 84 : 171-190.

2698 NÉMETH, Károly. "Ifjúságpolitikánk néhány kérdése" (Some questions of our policy toward youth), *Pártélet* 29(6), 1984 : 3-11. [Hungary]

2699 RAGHUVANSHI, M. S. *Modernising rural youth : on the role of formal education.* Delhi : Ajanta, 1984, xx-306 p. [India]

2700 RALIC, Prvoslav. "Savez komunista i 'omladinsko pitanje' danas" (Communist League and 'youth question'), *Socijalizam* 27(5), 1984 : 703-718. [Yugoslavia]

2701 ROŠKA, S. "Nesostojatel'nost' buržuaznyh koncepcij o molodeži" (Inconsistency of the bourgeois conceptions on youth), *Kommunist Moldavii* (2), 1983 : 83-90.

2702 SPECHT, Walter. "Jugendliche Banden und Präventionsprogramme in den USA" (Youth bands and prevention programs in the USA), *Neue Praxis* (?), 1984 : 124-139.

2703 TERESTYÉNI, Tamás. "Többféle ifjúságkép. Az ifjúság a politikai napilapokban" (Various images of the youth in the Hungarian political dailies), *Jel-Kép* 5(4), 1984 : 68-73.

2704 TRYFAN, Barbara. "Socjalno-bytowe warunki dziecka w rodzinie wiejskiej" (Social and living conditions of the rural child), *Roczniki Socjologii Wsi* 18, 1980-81 : 165-177.

2705   UNIVERSITÉ DE TUNIS. CENTRE D'ÉTUDES ET DE RECHERCHES ÉCONOMI-
        QUES ET SOCIALES. *Jeunesse et changement social; actes du colloque organisé à Tunis,
        8-13 novembre 1982.* Tunis : CERES, 1984, 265-71 p.
2706   WILLENER, Alfred. *L'avenir instantané : mouvement des jeunes à Zurich.* Lausanne : Éditions
        P.-M. Favre, 1984, 205-4 p. ill., bibl.
2707   YAMAGUCHI, Tohru; MORITA, Yohji; IMAZU, Kohjiro. *Seishonen shakaigaku* (Sociology
        of youth). Tokyo : Kohbundo-Shuppansha, 1984, 233 p.

        15240   Adulthood
        Âge adulte

2708   DANNEFER, Dale. "Adult development and social theory : a paradigmatic reappraisal",
        American Sociological Review 49(1), feb 84 : 100-116. [USA]
2709   MARINI, Margaret Mooney. "Age and sequencing norms in the transition to adulthood",
        Social Forces 63(1), sep 84 : 229-244. [USA]
2710   SARACENO, Chiara. "Per una analisi della condizione di adulto" (For an analysis of
        adulthood), *Rassegna Italiana di Sociologia* 25(4), oct-dec 84 : 517-546.

        15250   Old age
        Vieillesse

2711   "Ageing and public policy : the politics of agenda-setting", *Policy Studies Journal* 13(1),
        sep 84 : 111-203. [With contributions by Charles D. ELDER, Robert W. COBB, Erick
        KINGSON, David C. SCHWARTZ, Jon PYNOOS]
2712   "Santé (La) : connaître pour agir", *Gérontologie et Société* 28, apr-mai 84 : 3-174. [3e âge.
        With contributions by Jean BASSALER, A. COLVEZ, A. SVANBORG, Janine
        VALLERY-MASSON]
2713   "Vie (La) associative des plus de 50 ans", *Gérontologie et Société* 26, oct 83 : 5-158.
2714   ABU-LABAN, Sharon McIrvin. "Les femmes âgées : problèmes et perspectives", *Sociologie
        et Sociétés* 16(2), oct 84 : 69-78. [Amérique du Nord]
2715   ANOHIN, A. M. "Étiko-psihologičeskie problemy v gerontologii" (Ethical and psychological
        problems in gerontology), *Vestnik Akademii Medicinskih Nauk* (6), 1984 : 77-84.
2716   BÉLAND, François. "The family and adults 65 years of age and over : co-residency and
        availability of help", *Canadian Review of Sociology and Anthropology / Revue Canadienne de
        Sociologie et d'Anthropologie* 21(3), aug 84 : 302-317. [Canada]
2717   BERMAN, Yitzhak. "Growing old in Israel", *Kidma* 7(4), 1984 : 30-40.
2718   BOURDELAIS, Patrice. "L'émergence d'un nouveau savoir médical sur la vieillesse en
        France : au XIXᵉ et début du XXᵉ siècles", *Gérontologie et Société* 28, apr-mai 84 : 5-18.
2719   BRAAM, G. P. A. "Social stratification and the aged in the Netherlands; the aged as a
        minority category", *Netherlands' Journal of Sociology* 20(2), oct 84 : 98-114.
2720   BRAUNGART, Margaret M. "Aging and politics", *Journal of Military Sociology* 12(1),
        1984 : 79-98. [USA]
2721   BURGALASSI, Silvano. "La condizione anziana ad una svolta : oggetto e soggetto del
        proprio futuro?" (Old age at a turning point : object or subject of its future?), *Giornale
        degli Economisti e Annali di Economia* 43(11-12), nov-dec 84 : 743-758. [Italy]
2722   COLLOT, Claudette. "Une vie plus longue, mais une vie plus solitaire", *Gérontologie et
        Société* 27, jan 84 : 75-86. [France]
2723   DESJARDINS, Bertrand; LÉGARÉ, Jacques. "Le seuil de la vieillesse. Quelques réflexions
        de démographes", *Sociologie et Sociétés* 16(2), oct 84 : 37-48. [DC; LDC]
2724   DIRN, Louis; MENORAS, Henri. "Le troisième âge animera la société française", *Futuribles*
        (80), sep 84 : 3-28.
2725   DOKUČAEVA, T. N. "Obščestvennaja gruppa pensionerov v social'noj strukture sovetskogo
        obščestva" (The pensioners social group in the social structure of the Soviet society),
        in : XXVI s'ezd KPSS o dostiženii social'noj odnorodnosti sovetskogo obščestva Moskva,
        1983 : 132-142.
2726   ENOMOTO, Kazuko. "Rojin fukushi no igi to rinen ni tsuite" (An essay on idea and
        definition of welfare for the aged), *Kumamoto Tandai Ronshu* 35(2), 1984 : 1-20.
2727   FISCHER, Lucy Rose; HOFFMAN, Carol. "Who cares for the elderly : the dilemma
        of family support", *Research in Social Problems and Public Policy* 3, 1984 : 169-215. [USA]
2728   GIORI, Danilo. "Deterioramento fisiologico e desocializzazione : note su un modello atto
        a promuovere una interpretazione della vecchiaia come fenomeno collettivo" (Physiological
        deterioration and desocialization : notes on a model surveying to promote an interpretation

of old-age as a collective phenomenon), *Giornale degli Economisti e Annali di Economia* 43(11-12), nov-dec 84 : 783-793. [Italy]

2729 GOVAERTS, France. "Temps social, personnes âgées et identité", *Gérontologie et Société* 25, jun 83 : 123-139.

2730 HAZAN, Haim. "Religion in an old age home : symbolic adaptation as a survival strategy", *Ageing and Society* 4(3), jun 84 : 137-156. [Israel]

2731 HEISEL, Marsel A. "Aging and the developing world", *Populi* 11(2), 1984 : 13-20.

2732 KANERKO, Isamu. *Kourei-ka no shakai sekkei* (Social design for aging society). Kyoto : Academic Press, 1984, 237 p. [Japan]

2733 KASAHARA, Masanari. "Kourei-ka shakai to rojin mondai" (An aged society and the problem of the old), *Nihon University Journal of Sociology* 90, 1984 : 64-76.

2734 KNAPP, Martin. "The outputs of old people's homes in the post-war period", *International Journal of Sociology and Social Policy* 3(3), 1983 : 55-85. [UK]

2735 KOO, Ja-Soon. "Ageing in Korean society", *Korea Journal* 24(5), mai 84 : 32-48.

2736 KOYANO, Wataru. "Shakai-ronengaku ni okeru successful aging no sokutei" (Measurement of successful aging in social gerontology), *Theologia Diakonia* 16, 1984 : 105-121.

2737 LENOIR, Rémi. "Une bonne cause. Les Assises de retraités et des personnes âgées", *Actes de la Recherche en Sciences Sociales* 52-53, jun 84 : 80-87. [France]

2738 LOCKETT, Betty A. "Setting the Federal Agenda for health research : the case of the National Institute on Aging", *Journal of Health, Politics Policy and Law* 9(1), spr 84 : 63-80. [USA]

2739 MAKI, Masahide. "Kourei-ka shakai to rodo mondai -karei to shokugyo nouryoku" (An ageing society and labour problems : ageing and career development in the Japanese business organizations), *Kwansaigakuin Sociology Department Studies* 49, 1984 : 133-151.

2740 MASSÉ, Jacqueline; T.-BRAULT, Marie-Marthe. "Sociétés, vieillissement et stratification des âges", *Sociologie et Sociétés* 16(2), oct 84 : 3-14.

2741 MIDWINTER, Eric. "The exclusion of elderly people from everyday life", *Administration (Dublin)* 32(1), 1984 : 15-36. [UK]

2742 MIETHE, Terance D.; LEE, Gary R. "Fear of crime among older people : a reassessment of the predictive power of crime-related factors", *Sociological Quarterly* 25(3), 1984 : 397-415.

2743 MUNNICHS, J. M. A. "L'enseignement scientifique des aspects psychologiques et sociaux de la gérontologie", *Gérontologie et Société* 25, jun 83 : 117-122.

2744 MUTRAN, Elizabeth; REITZES, Donald G. "Inter-generational support activities and well-being among the elderly : a convergence of exchange and symbolic interaction perspectives", *American Sociological Review* 49(1), feb 84 : 117-130. [USA]

2745 NISHISHITA, Akitoshi. "San sedai no jyosei ni okeru do, bekkyo ishiki no kenkyu" (Preferred living arrangements in old age of three generations of Japanese women), *Social Gerontology* 19, 1984 : 43-57.

2746 OBIDZINSKI, Stanisław. "Starość na wsi — rzeczywistość a oczekiwania" (Old age in the countryside — reality and expectations), *Wieś Współczesna* 8, 1984 : 101-110.

2747 OHATA, Hiroshi; [et al.]. "'Rojin ikoi no ie' riyou-sha no ruikei to riyou jyokyo" (A study on the use of the 'Rest home for the aged'), *Social Gerontology* 20, 1984 : 65-77. [With contributions by Hiroshi TAKAHASHI, Shogo TAKEGAWA, Koichi HIRAOKA]

2748 PAILLAT, Paul. "Âge et isolement", *Gérontologie et Société* 27, jan 84 : 5-10. [France]

2749 PAILLAT, Paul. "La population âgée dans le recensement de 1982", *Gérontologie et Société* 30, oct 84 : 132-140.

2750 PHILIBERT, Michel. "Le statut de la personne âgée dans les sociétés antiques et préindustrielles", *Sociologie et Sociétés* 16(2), oct 84 : 15-27.

2751 ROOT, Laurence S.; TROPMAN, John E. "Income sources of the elderly", *Social Service Review* 58(3), sep 84 : 384-403. [USA]

2752 ROSENMAYR, Leopold. "Dix points sur la gérontologie sociale de demain ou à la recherche d'une 'liberté sur le tard'", *Sociologie et Sociétés* 16(2), oct 84 : 29-35.

2753 ROSSI, Giovanna. "Dal benessere eterodiretto all'autodiretta qualitá della vita : per una analisi della condizione anziana" (From externality defined well-being to self-determined quality of life : suggestions for an analysis of the condition of old people), *Studi di Sociologia* 22(4), oct-dec 84 : 374-393.

2754 ROWLAND, D. T. "Old age and the demographic transition", *Population Studies* 38(1), mar 84 : 73-87. [Australia]

2755 ŠAPIRO, V. D. *Social'naja aktivnost' požilyh ljudej v SSSR* (Social activity of the aged people in the USSR). Moskva : Nauka, 1983, 129 p.

2756 SHER, Ada Elizabeth. *Aging in post-Mao China : the politics of veneration.* Boulder, CO : Westview Press, 1984, xv-211 p. ill., bibl.

2757   SHIBATA, Hiroshi; KOYANO, Wataru; HAGA, Hiroshi. "ADL kenkyu no saikin no dohkoh — chiiki rojin o chushin to shite" (A review of recent research on everyday life activities : especially in the community elderly), *Social Gerontology* 21, 1984 : 70-83. [Japan]
2758   SZWARC, Halina. *Les personnes âgées dans le monde : Pologne / The elderly all over the world : Poland.* Paris : Centre International de Géographie Sociale, 1983, 120 p. bibl.
2759   TRYFAN, Barbara. "Aktualne problemy wiejskiej starości" (Current problems of old age in rural areas), *Wieś Współczesna* 4, 1984 : 47-58.
2760   VAN DER BURGH, C.; [et al.]. *White elderly persons living in the inner-city area of Pretoria : an exploratory study.* Pretoria : Human Sciences Research Council, 1983, xii-85 p. bibl.
2761   WATANABE, Yuko. "Rojin no shukan teki kohfuku shakudo no hohoron teki kento" (A methodological consideration on the measures of subjective welfare of the elderly), *Quarterly of Social Security Research* 20(1), 1984 : 81-91.
2762   YAGUCHI, Kazue; [et al.]. "Kourei sha no morale ni mirareru seisa to sono yoin bunseki" (Sex differences in the morale among the community elderly), *Social Gerontology* 20, 1984 : 46-58. [With contributions by Daisaku MAEDA, Hitoshi ASANO, Akitoshi NISHISHITA]

15300   **POPULATION EVOLUTION. POPULATION POLICY**
         ÉVOLUTION DE LA POPULATION. POLITIQUE DÉMOGRAPHIQUE

15310   **Population growth**
         Accroissement de la population

2763   "Dynamique spatiale de la population dans les pays méditerranéens", *Méditerranée* 50(4), 1983 : 3-93. [With contributions by Jorge GASPAR, Georges REYNE, Yves PECHOUX, Michel ROUX, Michel SIVIGNON]
2764   "Políticas de redistribución de la población de América latina" (Population redistribution policy in Latin America), *Notas de Población* 12(34), apr 84 : 79-114.
2765   "Research on rural women : feminist methodological questions", *IDS Bulletin* 15(1), jan 84 : 1-63. [With contributions by Magdalena LEON, Elisabeth CROLL; SPA; FRA]
2766   "Situación demográfica de América Latina evaluada en 1983 : estimaciones para 1960-1980 y proyecciones para 1980-2025" (Demographic situation of Latin America in 1983 : estimates for 1960-1980 and projections for 1980-2025), *Notas de Población* 11(33), dec 83 : 9-65.
2767   "Symposium (A) on local growth control", *Population Research and Policy Review* 3(1), jan 84 : 1-95. [With contributions by Elizabeth W. MOEN, Andrew M. ISSERMAN, Peter S. FISHER, Kingsley DAVIS]
2768   AIRD, John S. "The preliminary results of China's 1982 census", *China Quarterly* (96), dec 83 : 613-640.
2769   ANDĚL, Jiří. "K problematice 'měření' diferenciace vybraných demografických struktur (na příkladě krajů ČSR)" (Problems of differentiation 'measuring' of selected demographic structures (on example of regions of the Czech Socialist Republic)), *Demografie* 26(3), 1984 : 217-228.
2770   ARCHETTI, Eduardo. "Rural families and demographic behaviour : some Latin American analogies", *Comparative Studies in Society and History* 26(2), apr 84 : 251-279.
2771   BANISTER, Judith. "An analysis of recent data on the population of China", *Population and Development Review* 10(2), jun 84 : 241-271.
2772   BARRAN, José P.; [et al.]. *Sectores populares y vida urbana* (Poor people and urban life). Buenos Aires : Consejo Latinoamericano de Ciencias Sociales, 1984, 283 p.
2773   BILLIG, Wilhelm. "Transformacja demograficzna w epoce uprzemysłowienia" (Demographic transformation at the epoch of indusrialization), *Studia Demograficzne* 22(1), 1984 : 27-42. [Poland]
2774   BRONSZTEJN, Szyja. "Oblicze demograficzne państwa Izrael" (Demographic picture of Israel), *Studia Demograficzne* 22(3), 1984 : 101-117.
2775   CALOT, Gérard. "Données nouvelles sur l'évolution démograhique chinoise : I. Les recensements de 1953, 1964 et 1982 et l'évolution des taux bruts depuis 1950", *Population* 39(4-5), jul-oct 84 : 807-835. [Continued in ibid. : 39(6), nov-dec 84 : 1045-1062; II. L'évolution de la fécondité, de la nuptialité, de l'espérance de vie à la naissance et de la répartition urbaine/rurale de la population]
2776   CHARBONNEAU, Hubert. "Essai sur l'évolution démographique du Québec de 1534 à 2034", *Cahiers Québécois de Démographie* 13(1), apr 84 : 5-22.
2777   COALE, Ansley J. *Rapid population change in China, 1952-1982.* Washington, DC : National Academy Press, 1984, xiii-89 p. ill., bibl.

2778   CRIMMINS, Eileen M.; [et al.]. "New perspectives on the demographic transition : a theoretical and empirical analysis of an Indian State, 1951-1975", *Economic Development and Cultural Change* 32(2), jan 84 : 227-253.

2779   DE COLA, Lee. "Statistical determinants of the population of a nation's largest city", *Economic Development and Cultural Change* 33(1), oct 84 : 71-98.

2780   DEMENY, Paul. "A perspective on long-term population growth", *Population and Development Review* 10(1), mar 84 : 104-128.

2781   EVANS, Jeremy. "The growth of urban centres in Java since 1961", *Bulletin of Indonesian Economic Studies* 20(1), apr 83 : 44-57.

2782   FRĄTCZAK, Ewa. "Kohortowa ocena zmian w liczbie ludności miejskiej w okresach międzyspisowych" (Cohort estimation of changes in the size of the urban population in intercensal periods), *Studia Demograficzne* 22(1), 1984 : 87-92. [Poland]

2783   GASSON, Ruth. "Farm women in Europe : their need for off farm employment", *Sociologia Ruralis* 24(3-4), 1984 : 216-228.

2784   GIRARD, Alain. *L'homme et le nombre des hommes : essais sur les conséquences de la révolution démographique.* Paris : Presses Universitaires de France, 1984, 359 p. ind.

2785   GOSAL, Gurdev Singh. "Spatial dimensions of recent population growth in India", *Social Science Information / Information sur les Sciences Sociales* 23(4-5), 1984 : 627-652.

2786   HULL, Terence H.; HULL, Valerie J. "Population change in Indonesia : findings in the 1980 census", *Bulletin of Indonesian Economic Studies* 20(3), dec 84 : 95-119.

2787   HUTCHISON, Ray. "Miscounting the Spanish origin population in the United States : corrections to the 1970 census and their implications", *International Migration / Migrations Internationales* 22(2), 1984 : 73-89.

2788   IONČAR, Ana. "Kretanje ukupnog stanovništva SR Hrvatske" (Changes in the total population of the Socialist Republic of Croatia), *Sociologija Sela* 21(79-81), 1983 : 9-24.

2789   JAGIELSKI, Andrzej. "Rozmieszczenie ludności, migracje a rozwój społeczno-gospodarczy : doświadczenia Polski" (Spatial distribution of the population, migration and socio-economic development : Poland's experience), *Studia Demograficzne* 22(4), 1984 : 35-53.

2790   KELLEY, Allen C.; WILLIAMSON, Jeffrey G. "Population growth, industrial revolutions, and the urban transition", *Population and Development Review* 10(3), sep 84 : 419-441.

2791   KŁODZIŃSKI, Marek. "Dwuzawodowość ludności rolniczej" (Biprofessionalism of the rural population), *Roczniki Socjologii Wsi* 18, 80-81 : 23-39.

2792   KOŚCIAŃSKI, Tadeusz. "Kilka uwag o ludności wsi Aglomeracji Lubelskiego Zagłębia Węglowego : doniesienie z badań naukowych" (Some remarks on the population of villages in the Lublin Coal Basin Agglomeration : scientific research communiqué), *Roczniki Socjologii Wsi* 18, 80-81 : 69-79.

2793   KOWALSKI, Mieczysław. "Postawy ludności wiejskiej wobec wsi i miasta jako środowiska zamieszkania" (Rural population's attitudes towards living in town or village), *Roczniki Socjologii Wsi* 18, 80-81 : 81-93.

2794   KUČERA, Milan. "Reprodukce obyvatelstva ČSSR v letech 1961-1980 podle výsledků sčítání" (Reproduction of Czechoslovak population during 1961-1980 by census results), *Demografie* 26(1), 1984 : 19-32.

2795   LAND, Kenneth C.; HOUGH, George C. Jr.; MCMILLAN, Marilyn M. "New midyear age-sex-color-specific estimates of the U.S. population for the 1940s and 1950s : including a revision of coverage estimates for the 1940 and 1950 censuses", *Demography* 21(4), nov 84 : 623-645. [USA]

2796   LANGE, Norbert de. "Das Bevölkerungswachstum der USA in den siebziger Jahren : sechs demographische Überraschungen" (The US-American population growth in the 70s : six demographic surprises), *Zeitschrift für Bevölkerungswissenschaft* 10(1), 1984 : 53-73.

2797   LI, K. T. "Population distribution and quality of life in the Taiwan area", *Industry of Free China* 60(3), sep 83 : 1-24.

2798   LIVADA, Svetozar. "Vitalni pokazatelji o seoskom i poljoprivrednom stanovništvu SR Hrvatske ili demografski slom" (Vital indicators of the rural and agricultural population in the Socialist Republic of Croatia — demographical breakdown), *Sociologija Sela* 21(79-81), 1983 : 39-57.

2799   MAJER, Andrzej. "Postawy wobec zabudowy w lokalnym środowisku" (Attitudes towards buildings in a local environment), *Roczniki Socjologii Wsi* 18, 80-81 : 95-103.

2800   MARTORELLI, Horacio. *La lucha por la supervivencia : vida y trabajo de las mujeres en el medio rural* (Struggle for survival : women's life and work in rural environment). Montevideo : Fundación de Cultura Universitaria, Centro Interdisciplinario de Estudios sobre el Desarrollo Uruguay, 1984, 108 p. ill., map, bibl. [Uruguay]

2801   MCNICOLL, Geoffrey. "Consequences of rapid population growth : an overview and assessment", *Population and Development Review* 10(2), jun 84 : 177-240.

2802   MIKOV, Ė. G.; MOTRIČ, Ė. L. "Demografičeskie processy kak funkcija urovnja
        social'no-ėkonomičeskogo razvitija regiona" (Demographic processes as a function of
        the socio-economic development level of a region), *in : Aktual'nye problemy social'nogo
        upravlenija v regione* Vladivostok, 1982 : 3-14.
2803   MOKYR, Joel. "Three centuries of population change", *Economic Development and Cultural
        Change* 32(1), oct 83 : 183-192. [UK] [Review article on E. A. WRIGLEY and R. S.
        SCHOFIELD's book, 'The population history of England, 1541-1871 : a reconstruction.'
        Cambridge, MA : Harvard University Press, 1981, 779 p.]
2804   NATALE, Marcello. "La recente evoluzione demografica in Italia e le principali implicazioni
        economiche e sociali" (Recent demographic evolution in Italy and the main economic
        and social implications), *Difesa Sociale* 63(2), apr 84 : 5-17.
2805   NAZARETH, J. Manuel. "Conjuntura demográfica da população portuguesa no período
        de 1970-1980 : aspectos globais" (Demographic conjuncture of Portuguese population
        in the 1970-1980 period : global aspects), *Análise Social* 20(2-3), 1984 : 237-262.
2806   ORLEANS, Leo A.; BURNHAM, Ly. "The enigma of China's urban population", *Asian
        Survey* 24(7), jul 84 : 788-804.
2807   PAI PANANDIKER, V. A.; CHAUDHURI, P. N. *Demographic transition in Goa and its
        policy implications.* New Delhi : Uppal Publishing House, 1983, viii-46 p.
2808   PARTHASARATHI, J. *Rural population.* Delhi : B. R. Publishers, 1984, 272 p. [India]
2809   PEREZ, Lisandro. "The political contexts of Cuban population censuses, 1899-1981",
        Latin American Research Review 19(2), 1984 : 143-161.
2810   PRESSAT, Roland. "Les prévisions de population urbaine : examen critique des
        méthodes", *Giornale degli Economisti e Annali di Economia* 43(7-8), jul-aug 84 : 452-469.
2811   RANCIC, Miroljub. "The population of urban and other localities", *Yugoslav Survey* 25(2),
        mai 84 : 11-20. [Yugoslavia]
2812   RANČIĆ, Miroljub. "Stanovništvo gradskih i ostalih naselja" (The population of urban
        agglomerations), *Jugoslovenski Pregled* 27(6), jun 83 : 235-242. [Yugoslavia]
2813   SAGAZA, Haruo; OTOMO, Atsushi; [ed.]. *Ajia sho-koku no jinko toshi-ka* (Urban concentration
        of population in Asian countries). Tokyo : IDE, 1984, 298 p.
2814   SAHLI, Anne Marie. "Quelques aspects particuliers de la situation démographique en
        Algérie", *Genus* 40(3-4), jul-dec 84 : 173-184.
2815   SOLOMONESCU, Olimpia. "Recent and long-term trends in the evolution of Romania's
        population", *Revue Roumaine des Sciences Sociales. Série de Sociologie* 28(1), jan-jun 84 : 3-10.
2816   ŠTAMBUK, Maja. "Promjene u sociodemografskoj strukturi seoskog stanovništva"
        (Changes in the socio-demographic structure of rural population), *Sociologija Sela* 21(79-81),
        1983 : 25-37.
2817   STEHLÍK, Jiří. "Příspěvek k určení maximálního počtu světového obyvatelstva" (Contri-
        bution to determination of maximum number of world population), *Demografie* 26(1),
        1984 : 40-54.
2818   STEPHAN, G. Edward; STEPHAN, Karen H. "Population redistribution and changes
        in the size-density slope", *Demography* 21(1), feb 84 : 35-40.
2819   TABAH, Léon. "A turning point", *Populi* 11(4), 1984 : 13-20.
2820   UNITED NATIONS. SECRETARIAT. "Population distribution, migration and
        development : main issues for the 1980s", *Population Bulletin of the United Nations* 16,
        1984 : 26-39.
2821   VOLGYES, Ivan. "Vom Bauern zum sozialistischen Agrarproduzenten. Modernisierung
        und sozialpsychologischer Wandel in Ungarns Landbevölkerung" (From peasant to
        socialist agricultural producer. Socio-psychological change and modernization of rural
        population in Hungary), *Osteuropa* 33(11-12), dec 83 : 911-927.

        **15320   Morbidity
                   Morbidité**

2822   "Perspectives on persons with disabilities", *American Psychologist* 39(5), mai 84 : 516-552.
        [USA] [With contributions by Arnold WEICKER, Douglas A. FENDERSON, Adrienne
        ASCH]
2823   BLONDEAU, Danielle. "Raison de la folie, folie de la raison", *Revue de l'Institut de Sociologie*
        (1-2), 1984 : 55-70.
2824   BROW, Phil. "Mental patients as victimisers and victims", *Sage Annual Review of Studies
        in Deviance* 7, 1983 : 183-217. [USA]
2825   CORNES, Paul. *The future of work for people with disabilities : a view from Great Britain.* New
        York, NY : International Exchange of Experts and Information in Rehabilitation, World
        Rehabilitation Fund, 1984, 80 p. bibl.

2826 DUCKWORTH, Derek. *The classification and measurement of disablement.* London : HMSO, 1983, xv-120 p. ill., bibl., ind. [UK]

2827 FERAGUS, Jacques. "L'évaluation de l'action sociale. La velorisation du handicapé", *Revue Française des Affaires Sociales* 38(1), mar 84 : 103-129. [France]

2828 GOLDIN, Carol S. "The community of the blind : social organization, advocacy and cultural redefinition", *Human Organization* 43(2), 1984 : 121-131. [USA]

2829 GUPTA, Kuntesh. "Problem of family relationships of the disabled", *Indian Journal of Social Research* 25(1), apr 84 : 99-102. [India]

2830 HALE, Ronald J.; SCHMITT, Raymon L.; LEONARD, Wilbert M. II. "Social value of the age of the dying patient : systematization, validation, and direction", *Sociological Focus* 17(2), apr 84 : 157-173.

2831 HERZLICH, Claudine; PIERET, Janine. *Malades d'hier, malades d'aujourd'hui : de la mort collective au devoir de guérison.* Paris : Payot, 1984, 295 p.

2832 HESSE, Hans Albrecht. "Die Berufsunfähigkeit des Arbeiters. Soziologische Anmerkungen zur Berufsunfähigkeitsrente" (Workers' occupational disability. Sociological remarks on occupational disability pension), *Mitteilungen aus der Arbeitsmarkt- und Berufsforchung* 16(1), 1983 : 68-75.

2833 HIMSWORTH, Harold. "Epidemiology, genetics and sociology", *Journal of Biosocial Science* 16(2), apr 84 : 159-176.

2834 JACKSON, Mary E.; TESSLER, Richard C. "Perceived lack of control over life events : antecedents and consequences in a discharged patient sample", *Social Science Research* 13(3), sep 84 : 287-301. [USA]

2835 KING, James A.; [et al.]. "Physical health problems among the mentally ill", *International Social Science Review* 59(2), 1984 : 88-99. [USA]

2836 LAOR, Nathaniel. "The autonomy of the mentally ill : a case-study in individualistic ethics", *Philosophy of the Social Sciences / Philosophie des Sciences Sociales* 14(3), sep 84 : 331-349.

2837 LEFTON, Mark. "Chronic disease and applied sociology : an essay in personalized sociology", *Sociological Inquiry* 54(4), 1984 : 466-476. [USA]

2838 MONTGOMERY, Stuart. "Accounting for the social distribution of mild mental subnormality : determinism, process and structure", *International Journal of Sociology and Social Policy* 3(4), 1983 : 48-63. [UK]

2839 NORIO, Reijo. "The Finnish disease heritage as a product of the population structure", *Yearbook of Population Research in Finland* 22, 1984 : 7-14.

2840 PLAUCHU, Henri; BIDEAU, Alain. "Epidémiologie et constitution d'un registre de population à propos d'une concentration géographique d'une maladie héréditaire rare", *Population* 39(4-5), jul-oct 84 : 765-785. [France]

2841 STASINOS, Demetrios P. "Attitudes of parents toward the educable mentally retarded Greek child as influenced by their socio-economic status and the sex of this child", *Études Helléniques* 1(1), spr 83 : 41-52.

2842 TAGUCHI, Hiroaki. "Byoin-ka sareta kanjya yakuwari" (Hospitalized patient role and terminally ill patients), *Kumamoto Journal of Culture and Humanities* 12, 1984 : 1-24.

2843 TEPLIN, Linda A. "Criminalizing mental disorder : the comparative arrest rate of the mentally ill", *American Psychologist* 39(7), jul 84 : 794-803. [USA]

2844 VILLEVAL, Marie-Claire. "L'insertion professionnelle des personnes handicapées", *Sociologie du Travail* 26(1), mar 84 : 92-104.

2845 ZUCMAN, Elizabeth. *Famille et handicap dans le monde : analyse critique de travaux de la dernière décennie.* Paris : Centre Technique National d'Études et de Recherches sur les Handicaps et les Inadaptations, 1983, 181 p. bibl.

15330 Mortality
Mortalité

2846 "Révolution (Une) au profit de la survie et du développement des enfants", *Carnets de l'Enfance* (61-62), 1983 : 11-298. [With contributions by James P. GRANT, Jon E. ROHDE]

2847 ARRIANGA, Eduardo E. "Measuring and explaining the change in life expectancies", *Demography* 21(1), feb 84 : 83-96.

2848 BENNETT, Neil G.; HORIUCHI, Shiro. "Mortality estimation from registered deaths in less developed countries", *Demography* 21(2), mai 84 : 217-234.

2849 BERTOLI, Fernando; RENT, Clyda S.; RENT, George S. "Infant mortality by socio-economic status for Blacks, Indians and Whites : a longitudinal analysis of North Carolina, 1968-1977", *Sociology and Social Research* 68(3), apr 84 : 364-377. [USA]

2850 BOLANDER, Ann-Marie. "A halandóság svédországban" (Mortality in Sweden), *Demográfia* 27(1), 1984 : 13-50.

2851   BOURGUIGNON, Odile. "La famille et la mort des enfants", _Social Science Information /_
Information sur les Sciences Sociales 23(2), 1984 : 325-339.

2852   BOUVIER COLLE, Marie-Hélène. "Activité et espérance de vie féminine", _Revue Française_
des Affaires Sociales 38(suppl.), jun 84 : 31-47.

2853   CAMPBELL, Eugene K. "Mortality levels in Liberia and policy implications : an
application of the census survival ratio method", _Genus_ 40(3-4), jul-dec 84 : 97-116.

2854   CASELLI, Graziella. "Les causes de décès en France : III. Un effort d'interprétation des
différences géographiques : application à la période 1974-76", _Population_ 39(6),
nov-dec 84 : 1011-1044.

2855   CHIANG, Chin Long. _The life table and its application._ Malabar, FL : Robert E. Krieger
Publishing Co., 1984, xix-316 p.

2856   COMPTON. P. A. "Rising mortality in Hungary", _Population Studies_ 39(1), mar 85 : 71-86.

2857   COURGEAU, Daniel. "Relations entre cycle de vie et migrations", _Population_ 39(3), mai-jun
84 : 483-513. [France]

2858   DAMIANI, Paul; [et al.]. "Analyse de la mortalité générale par âge, suivant le sexe : mise
en évidence de deux types de mortalité", _Journal de la Société de Statistique de Paris_ 125(3),
trim. 3, 84 : 158-163. [France]

2859   DASVARMA, G. L. "Infant and child deaths in Indonesia : how many can be prevented?",
Majalah Demografi Indonesia 11(21), jun 84 : 1-13.

2860   DESPLANQUES, Guy. "L'inégalité sociale devant la mort", _Économie et Statistique_ 162,
jan 84 : 29-50. [France]

2861   DINKEL, R. H. "The seeming paradox of increasing mortality in a highly industrialized
nation : the example of the Soviet Union", _Population Studies_ 39(1), mar 85 : 87-97.

2862   DINKEL, Reiner. "Sterblichkeit in Perioden und Kohortenbetrachtung : zugleich eine
ansatzweise Berechnung der Kohortensterbetafel für Deutschland" (Mortality as observed
by periods and cohorts : and a tentative computation of a cohort life table for Germany),
Zeitschrift für Bevölkerungswissenschaft 10(4), 1984 : 477-500. [German DR; Germany FR]

2863   EBERSTEIN, Isaac W.; PARKER, Jan Reese. "Racial differences in infant mortality
by cause of death : the impact of birth weight and maternal age", _Demography_ 21(3),
aug 84 : 309-321. [USA]

2864   EGIDI, Viviana. "Trent'anni di evoluzione della mortalita' degli adulti in Italia" (Thirty
years of adult mortality evolution in Italy), _Genus_ 40(1-2), jan-jun 84 : 71-106.

2865   EKANEM, Ita I.; SOM, Ranjan K. "The problem of choosing model life tables for African
countries", _Genus_ 40(1-2), jan-jun 84 : 57-70.

2866   FARGUES, Philippe. "Âges au décès et niveaux de mortalité : évaluer le taux d'enregistre-
ment des décès à partir de leur structure par âge : application à la Tunisie", _Population_
39(1), jan-feb 84 : 47-76.

2867   FROMAGET, Michel. "L'imaginaire adulte de la mort comme fonction de l'âge et du
sexe. Essai de psychothanatologie différentielle", _Année Sociologique_ 34, 1984 : 203-224.

2868   GOLDBERG, H. I.; [et al.]. "Infant mortality and breast-feeding in North-Eastern Brazil",
Population Studies 38(1), mar 84 : 105-115.

2869   HANSLUWKA, Harald. "Zur Politik der Säuglinsgssterblichkeit" (On the politics of infant
mortality), _Zeitschrift für Bevölkerungswissenschaft_ 10(2), 1984 : 133-152.

2870   HILL, Allan; RANDALL, Sara. "Différences géographiques et sociales dans la mortalité
infantile et juvénile au Mali", _Population_ 39(6), nov-dec 84 : 921-946.

2871   HOBCRAFT, J. N.; MCDONALD, J. W.; RUTSTEIN, S. O. "Socio-economic factors
in infant and child mortality : a cross-national comparison", _Population Studies_ 38(2),
jul 84 : 193-223.

2872   JUÁREZ, Fátima. "Examen crítico de la técnica de tablas de vida en las tendencias sobre
fecundidad : el caso de México" (Critical examination of life tables technique in fertility
trends : the case of Mexico), _Demografía y Economía_ 18(3), 1984 : 287-333.

2873   KRISTANTO, Bambang. "Some socio-economic factors affecting infant and child
mortality with special reference to Indonesia", _Majalah Demografi Indonesia_ 10(19),
jun 83 : 19-32.

2874   LANGFORD, C. M. "Sex differentials in mortality in Sri Lanka : changes since the 1920s",
Journal of Biosocial Science 16(3), jul 84 : 399-410.

2875   LANTOINE, Catherine; PRESSAT, Roland. "Nouveaux aspects de la mortalité infantile",
Population 39(2), mar-apr 84 : 253-264. [France]

2876   LUTZ, Wofgang. "The changing nature of the link between infant mortality and fertility
in Finland 1776-1978", _Yearbook of Population Research in Finland_ 22, 1984 : 26-45.

2877   MARI BHAT, P. N.; PRESTON, Samuel; DYSON, Tim. _Vital rates in India, 1961-1981._
Washington, DC : National Academy Press, 1984, xvi-173 p. ill., bibl.

2878   MYERS, George C. "Sterblichkeitsrückgang, Lebensverlängerung und Alter der Bevölkerung" (Mortality declines, life extension and population aging), *Zeitschrift für Bevölkerungswissenschaft* 10(4), 1984 : 463-475. [USA]

2879   NATHANSON, C. A. "Sex differences in mortality", *Annual Review of Sociology* 10, 1984 : 191-213. [DC; LDC]

2880   NATIONS UNIES. DÉPARTEMENT DES AFFAIRES ÉCONOMIQUES ET SOCIALES INTERNATIONALES. *Tables types de mortalité pour les pays en développement.* New York, NY : NU, 1984, vii-351 p.

2881   NAYAR, P. K. B. "Ecology, social welfare and mortality behaviour. The case of Kerala, India", *Revue Internationale de Sociologie / International Review of Sociology* 19(1-2-3), apr-aug-dec 83 : 115-136.

2882   OCHSMANN, Randolph. "Belief in afterlife as a moderator of fear of death?", *European Journal of Social Psychology* 14(1), jan-mar 84 : 53-67.

2883   OKUDA, Kazuhiko. "Seikatsu kouzou kenkyu no konnichi teki shiten" (Contemporary research on life structure), *Review of Contemporary Sociology* 18, 1984 : 50-77.

2884   PALLONI, A. "Estimation of adult mortality using forward and backward projection", *Population Studies* 38(3), nov 84 : 479-493.

2885   PAMUK, Elsie R. "Social class inequality in mortality from 1921 to 1972 in England and Wales", *Population Studies* 39(1), mar 85 : 17-31.

2886   PARANT, Alain. "L'inégalité sociale devant la mort", *Futuribles* (79), aug 84 : 69-81. [France]

2887   POST, Jerrold M. "Dreams of glory and the life cycle : reflections on the life course of narcissistic leaders", *Journal of Military Sociology* 12(1), 1984 : 49-60.

2888   PRAŽÁKOVÁ, Jana. "Kojenecká úmrtnost ve smečenské farnosti v letech 1730-1779 (na základě matrik)" (Infant mortality in the parish of Smečno during 1730-1770 (according to parish register)), *Demografie* 26(3), 1984 : 229-236. [Czechoslovakia]

2889   PREISWERK, Yvonne. "Mort, culture populaire et pouvoir", *Schweizerische Zeitschrift für Soziologie / Revue Suisse de Sociologie* 10(1), 1984 : 85-96. [Suisse]

2890   RADKOVSKÝ, Josef; VITKOVSKÝ, Karel. "Vývoj úmrtnosti a nemocnosti na zhoubné novotvary v ČSSR" (Mortality and morbidity development on neoplasms in Czechoslovakia), *Demografie* 26(2), 1984 : 123-141.

2891   RAVENHOLT, R. T. "Addiction mortality in the United States, 1980 : tobacco, alcohol, and other substances", *Population and Development Review* 10(4), dec 84 : 697-724.

2892   ROBINE, J. M.; COLVEZ, A. "L'espérance de vie sans incapacité et ses composantes : de nouveaux indicateurs pour mesurer la santé et les besoins de la population", *Population* 39(1), jan-feb 84 : 27-46.

2893   SALHI, Mohamed. *L'évolution récente de la mortalité en Algérie (1965-1981).* Louvain-la-Neuve : Cabay, 1984, 52 p. ill., bibl.

2894   SMITH, David P. "Robustness of 5qx estimators under nonstationarity", *Demography* 21(4), nov 84 : 613-622.

2895   SUCHINDRAN, C. M.; ADLAKHA, A. L. "Effect of infant mortality on subsequent fertility of women in Jordan : a life table analysis", *Journal of Biosocial Science* 16(2), apr 84 : 219-229.

2896   SYROVÁTKA, A.; RYCHTARÍKOVÁ, J. "Naissances vivantes et décès de moins d'un an selon le poids à la naissance en République socialiste tchèque entre 1950 et 1980", *Population* 39(3), mai-jun 84 : 515-539. [Czechoslovakia]

2897   UEDA, Kōzō. *Recent trends of mortality in Asian countries.* Tokyo : Southeast Asian Medical Information Center, 1983, ix-158 p. ill., bibl.

2898   UNITED NATIONS. SECRETARIAT. "Mortality and health policy : main issues for the 1980s", *Population Bulletin of the United Nations* 16, 1984 : 40-61.

2899   VIELROSE, Egon. "Niektóre standaryzowane współczynniki zgonów niemowląt" (Some standardized infant death rates), *Studia Demograficzne* 21(4), 1983 : 21-27.

2900   YAMAMOTO, Kenji. "Shakaigaku to seikatsu kouzou" (Sociology and life structure), *Kagoshima Keizai Daigaku Shakaigakubu Ronshu* 3(1), 1984 : 101-120.

15340   Fertility. Natality
Fécondité. Natalité

2901   ANANTA, Aris. "A sequential economic model of fertility behaviour in developing countries", *Majalah Demografi Indonesia* 10(19), jun 83 : 1-17.

2902   ANDERSON, John E.; CLELAND, John G. "The World Fertility Survey and contraceptive prevalence surveys : a comparison of substantive results", *Studies in Family Planning* 15(1), jan 84 : 1-13.

2903   ATOH, Makoto. "Shussei-ritsu teika no geiin to kongo no mitooshi" (The causes for the recent decline in Japanese fertility and its prospect), *Journal of Population Problems* 171, 1984 : 22-35.

2904   BABADZAN, Alain. "Une perspective pour deux passages : notes sur la représentation traditionnelle de la naissance et de la mort en Polynésie", *Homme* 23(3), sept 83 : 81-99.

2905   BASAVARAJAPPA, K. G. "Ethnic fertility differences in Canada, 1926-1971 : an examination of assimilation hypothesis", *Journal of Biosocial Science* 16(1), jan 84 : 45-54.

2906   BECKER, Stan. "Les causes de la tendance saisonnière des naissances au Bangladesh rural", *Population* 39(2), mar-apr 84 : 265-280.

2907   BLAKE, Judith. "Catholicism and fertility : on attitudes of young Americans", *Population and Development Review* 10(2), jun 84 : 329-340.

2908   BLOOM, David E. "Delayed child-bearing in the United States", *Population Research and Policy Review* 3(2), jun 84 : 103-139.

2909   BLOOM, David E.; TRUSSELL, James. "What are the determinants of delayed child-bearing and permanent childlessness in the United States?", *Demography* 21(4), nov 84 : 591-611.

2910   BOERMA, J. T.; VAN VIANEN, H. A. W. "Birth interval, mortality and growth of children in a rural area in Kenya", *Journal of Biosocial Science* 16(4), oct 84 : 475-486.

2911   BOOTH, Heather. "Transforming Gompertz' function for fertility analysis : the development of a standard for the Relational Gompertz Function", *Population Studies* 38(3), nov 84 : 495-506.

2912   BOYMAN, Elsa. "De l'enfantement. Les vicissitudes d'une notion primordiale", *Cahiers Internationaux de Sociologie* 77, 1984 : 303-321.

2913   CAIN, M. "On the relationship between landholding and fertility", *Population Studies* 39(1), mar 85 : 5-15.

2914   CALDWELL, J. C. "Fertility trends and prospects in Australia and other industrialized countries", *Australian and New Zealand Journal of Sociology* 20(1), mar 84 : 3-22.

2915   CARLSON, Elwood D. "Social determinants of low birth weight in a high-risk population", *Demography* 21(2), mai 84 : 207-216. [USA]

2916   CHERNICHOVSKY, Dov. "Socio-economic correlates of fertility behavior in rural Botswana", *Genus* 40(3-4), jul-dec 84 : 129-146.

2917   COALE, Ansley J. "Fertility in prerevolutionary rural China : in defense of a reassessment", *Population and Development Review* 10(3), sep 84 : 471-480.

2918   DAY, Lincoln H. "Minority-group status and fertility : a more detailed test of the hypothesis", *Sociological Quarterly* 25(4), 1984 : 456-472. [Australia]

2919   DAY, Lincoln H.; DAY, Alice Taylor. "Fertility and 'life chances' — a comparison among 19 countries of controlled fertility", *International Journal of Comparative Sociology* 25(3-4), sep-dec 84 : 197-225. [Developing countries]

2920   FEENEY, G.; ROSS, J. A. "Analyzing open birth interval distributions", *Population Studies* 38(3), nov 84 : 473-478. [Indonesia]

2921   GENNE, Marcelle. "Les facteurs stratégiques du déclin de la fécondité", *Tiers-Monde* 25(98), jun 84 : 329-349.

2922   GRÜNEWALD, Werner. "Ein methodischer und empirischer Vergleich ausgewählter Konzepte zur Fruchtbarkeitsmessung" (A methodological and empirical comparison of selected concepts of fertility measurement), *Zeitschrift für Bevölkerungswissenschaft* 10(2), 1984 : 209-230.

2923   GUILLON, M. "Natalité des étrangers et renforcement de la pluri-ethni. Le cas de la France", *Espace, Populations, Sociétés* (2), 1983 : 103-116.

2924   GUPTA, Prithwis das. "Contributions of other socio-economic factors to the fertility differentials of women by education : a multivariate approach", *Genus* 40(3-4), jul-dec 84 : 117-127.

2925   HINDE, P. R. A.; WOODS, R. I. "Variations in historical natural fertility patterns and the measurement of fertility control", *Journal of Biosocial Science* 16(3), jul 84 : 309-321.

2926   HOBCRAFT, J. "Fertility exposure analysis : a new method for assessing the contribution of proximate determinants to fertility differentials", *Population Studies* 38(1), mar 84 : 21-45. [Dominican Republic]

2927   HOLLERBACH, Paula E.; DIAZ-BRIQUETS, Sergio. *Fertility determinants in Cuba.* Washington, DC : National Academy Press, 1983, xx-242 p. ill., bibl.

2928   KALULE-SABITI, I. "Bongaarts' proximate determinants of fertility applied to group data from the Kenya Fertility Survey 1977-78", *Journal of Biosocial Science* 16(2), apr 84 : 205-218.

2929   KELLY, William R.; CUTRIGHT, Philipps. "Economic and other determinants of annual change in US fertility : 1917-1976", *Social Science Research* 13(3), sep 84 : 250-267.

2930   KNODEL, John; HAVANON, Napaporn; PRAMUALRATANA, Anthony. "Fertility transition in Thailand : a qualitative analysis", *Population and Development Review* 10(2), jun 84 : 297-328.

2931   LAVELY, W. R. "The rural Chinese fertility transition : a report from Shifang Xian, Sichuan", *Population Studies* 38(3), nov 84 : 365-384.

2932   LEE, B. S.; FARBER, S. C. "Fertility adaptation by rural-urban migrants in developing countries : the case of Korea", *Population Studies* 38(1), mar 84 : 141-155.

2933   LEHRER, Evelyn. "The impact of child mortality on spacing by parity : a Cox-Regression analysis", *Demography* 21(3), aug 84 : 323-337. [Malaysia]

2934   LEHRER, Evelyn; NERLOVE, Marc. "The impact of expected child survival on husbands' and wives' desired fertility in Malaysia : a log-linear probability model", *Social Science Research* 13(3), sep 84 : 236-249.

2935   LEUNG, Angela Kiche. "Autour de la naissance : la mère et l'enfant en Chine aux XVIᶜ et XVIIᶜ siècles", *Cahiers Internationaux de Sociologie* 76, 1984 : 51-69. [Rôle du Confucianisme]

2936   LEVY, Diane E.; MILLER, Robert K. Jr.; WILLIS, Cecil L. "Social and economic structural antecedents of fertility", *Sociological Inquiry* 54(1), 1984 : 26-43. [USA]

2937   LINDGREN, Jarl. "The fertility increase in Finland in 1982", *Yearbook of Population Research in Finland* 22, 1984 : 77-83.

2938   LOCOH, Thérèse. *Fécondité et famille en Afrique de l'Ouest : le Togo méridional contemporain.* Paris : Presses Universitaires de France, 1984, xiii-182 p. bibl.

2939   LWECHUNGURA KAMUZORA, C. "High fertility and the demand for labour in peasant economies : the case of Bukala district, Tanzania", *Development and Change* 15(1), jan 84 : 105-124.

2940   MATHEWS, Georges. *Le choc démographique : le déclin du Québec est-il inévitable?* Montréal, PQ : Boréal Express, 1984, 204 p. bibl.

2941   MORGAN, S. Philip; RINDFUSS, Ronald R.; PARNELL, Allan. "Modern fertility patterns : contrasts between the United States and Japan", *Population and Development Review* 10(1), mar 84 : 19-40.

2942   MURPHY, M. J. "Fertility, birth timing and marital breakdown : a reinterpretation of the evidence", *Journal of Biosocial Science* 16(4), oct 84 : 487-500.

2943   NEWMAN, James L.; LURA, Russell P. "Fertility control in Africa", *Geographical Review* 73(4), oct 83 : 396-406.

2944   PONGRÁCZ, T. *Fiatalkori terhességek társadalmi-demográfiai vizsgálata* (Socio-demographic examination of juvenile pregnancies). Budapest : Központi Statisztikai Hivatal, Népességkutató Intézet, 1983, 58 p.

2945   PRESTON, Samuel H.; BHAT, P. N. Mari. "New evidence on fertility and mortality trends in India", *Population and Development Review* 10(3), sep 84 : 481-503.

2946   RETHERFORD, Robert D.; CHO, Lee-Jay; KIM, Nam-Il. "Census-derived estimates of fertility by duration since first marriage in the Republic of Korea", *Demography* 21(4), nov 84 : 537-558.

2947   SINGH, Susheela; CASTERLINE, B.; CLELAND, J. G. "The proximate determinants of fertility : sub-national variations", *Population Studies* 39(1), mar 85 : 113-135.

2948   SLESINGER, Doris P.; OKADA, Yoshitaka. "Fertility patterns of Hispanic migrant farm women : testing the effect of assimilation", *Rural Sociology* 49(3), 1984 : 430-440. [USA]

2949   SMITHERS, A. G.; COOPER, H. J. "Social class and season of birth", *Journal of Social Psychology* 124(1), oct 84 : 79-84.

2950   SPIESS, Erika; [et al.]. "Wertwandel und generatives Verhalten : Ergebnisse einer Längsschnittstudie an jungen Ehepaaren" (Changing values and reproductive behaviour : results of a longitudinal study performed on young married couples), *Zeitschrift für Bevölkerungswissenschaft* 10(2), 1984 : 153-168. [Germany FR]

2951   STOKES, C. Shannon; SCHUTJER, Wayne A. "A cautionary note on public policies in conflict : land reform and human fertility in rural Egypt", *Comparative Politics* 16(1), oct 83 : 97-104.

2952   SWICEGOOD, C. Gray; RINDFUSS, Ronald R.; MORGAN, S. Philip. "Measurement and replication : evaluating the consistency of eight U.S. fertility surveys", *Demography* 21(1), feb 84 : 19-34.

2953   TABUTIN, Dominique. "La fécondité et la mortalité dans les recensements africains des 25 dernières années", *Population* 39(2), mar-apr 84 : 295-312.

2954   TAWIAH, E. O. "Determinants of cumulative fertility in Ghana", *Demography* 21(1), feb 84 : 1-8.

2955   TOLNAY, Stewart E.; CHRISTENSON, R. L. "The effects of social setting and family planning programs on recent fertility declines in developing countries : a reassessment", *Sociology and Social Research* 69(1), oct 84 : 72-89.

2956   TUNG, Shui-Liang. "The rapid fertility decline in Guam natives", *Journal of Biosocial Science* 16(2), apr 84 : 231-239.

2957   UNITED NATIONS. SECRETARIAT. "The contribution of the world fertility survey data to our understanding of fertility levels and trends in selected developing countries", *Population Bulletin of the United Nations* 16, 1984 : 62-76.

2958   VAN LOO, M. Frances; BAGOZZI, Richard P. "Labor force participation and fertility : a social analysis of their antecedents and simultaneity", *Human Relations* 37(11), nov 84 : 941-967.

2959   WOLF, Arthur P. "Fertility in prerevolutionary rural China", *Population and Development Review* 10(3), sep 84 : 443-470.

2960   YANO, Kazue. "Shussei kohdoh to ishiki ni kansuru shinsei-shi teki kohsatsu" (Fertility decline and attitudinal change : studies on 'histoire des mentalités'), *Toyo University Bulletin of the Graduate School* 20, 1984 : 73-82.

15350   **Family planning**
          Planification de la famille

2961   "Evolución y políticas de la población en América latina" (Population evolution and policies in Latin America), *Notas de población* 11(33), dec 83 : 9-140.

2962   "Die Mütter" (The mothers), *Kursbuch* (76), jun 84 : 1-166. [With contributions by Hortense von HEPPE, Marie MUHLENAU, Marina MOELLER-GAMBAROFF, Eva DANE, Catherine HAYES]

2963   "Políticas de población en América Latina : experiencia de 10 anos" (Population policies in Latin America : ten year experience), *Notas de Población* 11(33), dec 83 : 67-140.

2964   BACHRACH, Christine A. "Contraceptive practice among American women, 1973-1982", *Family Planning Perspectives* 16(6), nov-dec 84 : 253-259.

2965   BONGAARTS, John. "Implications of future fetility trends for future contraceptive practice", *Population and Development Review* 10(2), jun 84 : 341-352.

2966   CALLAN, Victor J.; GALLOIS, Cynthia. "Perceptions of contraceptive methods : a multidimensional scaling analysis", *Journal of Biosocial Science* 16(2), apr 84 : 277-286. [Australia]

2967   CALLAN, Victor J.; HEE, Raymond W. Que. "The choice of sterilization : voluntary childless couples, mothers of one child by choice, and males seeking reversal of vasectomy", *Journal of Biosocial Science* 16(2), apr 84 : 241-248. [Australia]

2968   CHAYOVAN, Napaporn; HERMALIN, Albert I.; KNODEL, John. "Measuring accessibility to family planning services in rural Thailand", *Studies in Family Planning* 15(5), sep-oct 84 : 201-211.

2969   CHEN, Chao-nan. *An experiment about family planning attitude change.* Nankang; Taipei : Institute of Economics, Academia Sinica, 1983, xv-154 p. ill., bibl. [China]

2970   DANDA, Ajit K. *Family planning : an adaptive strategy : a case study from West Bengal.* New Delhi : Inter-India Publications, 1984, xiii-138 p. bibl., ind.

2971   DAVIS, Nancy. "Abortion and self-defence", *Philosophy and Public Affairs* 13(3), sum 84 : 175-207.

2972   DÍEZ MEDRANO, Juan. "Reflexiones teóricas sobre la evolución de la ilegitimidad en Europa (1945-1984)" (Theoretical reflections on the evolution of illegitimacy in Europe (1945-1984)), *Revista Española de Investigaciones Sociológicas* 27, jul-sep 84 : 79-106.

2973   DINKEL, Reiner. "Haben die geburtenfördernden Massnahmen der DDR Erfolg? Eine vergleichende Darstellung der Fertilitätsentwicklung in beiden deutschen Staaten" (Are birth policy measures successful in the German Democratic Republic? A comparative study of the evolution of fertility in the two German states), *IFO-Studien* 30(2), 1984 : 139-162.

2974   DOH, Rainer. "Antikonzeptiva in der Türkei. Methoden und sozio-ökonomische Hintergründe : eine Darstellung aufgrund neuester daten" (Contraception in Turkey. Methods and socio-economic background : a presentation based on the most recent data available), *Zeitschrift für Bevölkerungswissenschaft* 10(1), 1984 : 75-87.

2975   ENTWISLE, Barbara; [et al.]. "A multilevel model of family planning availability and contraceptive use in rural Thailand", *Demography* 21(4), nov 84 : 559-574.

2976   FURSTENBERG, Frank F. Jr.; [et al.]. "Family communication and teenagers' contraceptive use", *Family Planning Perspectives* 16(4), jul-aug 84 : 163-170. [USA]

2977   GERARD, Hubert. "Types of intervention available to a demographic policy : a theoretical approach", *Population Bulletin of the United Nations* 16, 1984 : 16-25.

2978   GOLDSTEIN, Michael S. "Creating and controlling a medical market : abortion in Los Angeles after liberalization", *Social Problems* 31(5), jun 84 : 514-529.

2979   HAFFEY, Joan; ZIMMERMAN, Margot L.; PERKIN, Gordon W. "Communicating Contraception", *Populi* 11(2), 1984 : 31-39.

2980   HARTMAN, Moshe. "Pronatalistic tendencies and religiosity in Israël", *Sociology and Social Research* 68(2), jan 84 : 247-258.

2981   HENSHAW, Stanley K.; WALLISCH, Lynn S. "The Medicaid cutoff and abortion services for the poor", *Family Planning Perspectives* 16(4), jul-aug 84 : 170-181. [USA]

2982   HERNÁNDEZ, Donald J. "Fertility reduction policies and poverty in Third World countries : ethical issues", *Journal of Applied Behavioral Science* 20(4), 1984 : 343-362.

2983   HÖPFLINGER, F.; KÜHNE, F. "Contraception : answers of wives and husbands compared in a survey of Swiss couples", *Journal of Biosocial Science* 16(2), apr 84 : 259-268.

2984   INSTITUTO MEXICANO DEL SEGURO SOCIAL. *Planeación familiar y cambio demográfico* (Family planning and demographic change). Mexico, DF : IMSS, 1983, 554 p. ill., bibl.

2985   JABLENSKY, A.; [et al.]. "Mental health and female sterilization", *Journal of Biosocial Science* 16(1), jan 84 : 1-21.

2986   KHAN, A. R. "Risks and costs of illegally induced abortion in Bangladesh", *Journal of Biosocial Science* 16(1), jan 84 : 89-98.

2987   KOENING, M. A.; SIMMONS, G. B.; MISRA, B. D. "Husband-wife inconsistencies in contraceptive use responses", *Population Studies* 38(2), jul 84 : 281-298.

2988   LAING, John E. "Natural family planning in the Philippines", *Studies in Family Planning* 15(2), mar 84 : 49-61.

2989   LEDBETTER, Rosanna. "Thirty years of family planning in India", *Asian Survey* 24(7), jul 84 : 736-758.

2990   LEGGE, Jerome S. "The unintended consequences of policy change : the effect of a restrictive abortion policy", *Administration and Society* 15(2), aug 83 : 243-256. [Romania]

2991   LOZA, Sara. "African strategies", *Populi* 11(1), 1984 : 42-50. [Kenya; Egypt; Tunisia]

2992   MARQUES PEREIRA, Bérengère. "L'idéologie de l'intérêt général et l'enjeu législatif en matière d'interruption volontaire de grossesse", *Revue de l'Institut de Sociologie* (1-2), 1984 : 239-256.

2993   MOSHER, William D.; GOLDSCHEIDER, Calvin. "Contraceptive patterns of religious and racial groups in the United States, 1955-76 : convergence and distinctiveness", *Studies in Family Planning* 15(3), mai-jun 84 : 101-111.

2994   MÜNKEL, Wilma. "Geburtenrückgang als Folge veränderten generativen Handelns des Mannes" (Decline of the birth rate as a result of changes in the reproductive behaviour of the male), *Zeitschrift für Bevölkerungswissenschaft* 10(2), 1984 : 193-207. [Germany FR]

2995   MUSTAFA, Mutasim Abu Bakr. "Male attitudes towards family planning in Khartoum, Sudan", *Journal of Biosocial Science* 16(4), oct 84 : 437-449.

2996   NAGHMA-E., Rehan; MCFARLANE, H. P.; SANI, Sule. "Profile of contraceptive clients in Katsina, Northern Nigeria", *Journal of Biosocial Science* 16(4), oct 84 : 427-436.

2997   NESS, Gayl De Forest; ANDO, Hirofumi. *The land is shrinking : population planning in Asia.* Baltimore, MD : Johns Hopkins University Press, 1984, xxii-225 p. bibl., ind.

2998   NEWMAN, John L.; MCCULLOCH, Charles E. "A hazard rate approach to the timing of births", *Econometrica* 52(4), jul 84 : 939-961. [Costa Rica]

2999   OGAWA, Naohiro; HODGE, Robert William. *Fertility and the locus of family control in contemporary Japan.* Bangkok : Population Division, Economic and Social Commission for Asia and the Pacific, 1983, 28 p. bibl.

3000   OLEDZKI, Michał. "Polityka demograficzna jako spojrzenie na człowieka" (Population policy as an outlook on mankind), *Studia Demograficzne* 22(4), 1984 : 19-33.

3001   PATHAK, K. B.; MURTHY, P. K. "On the acceptability of different methods of family planning in India : 1971-1980", *Indian Journal of Social Work* 44(4), jan 84 : 393-403.

3002   PETERSEN, K. A. "The public funding of abortion services : comparative developments in the United States and Australia", *International and Comparative Law Quarterly* 33(1), jan 84 : 158-180.

3003   PORTER, Elaine G. "Birth control discontinuance as a diffusion process", *Studies in Family Planning* 15(1), jan 84 : 20-29. [Dominican Republic]

3004   RINDFUSS, Ronald R.; MORGAN, S. Philip; SWICEGOOD, C. Gray. "The transition to motherhood : the intersection of structural and temporal dimensions", *American Sociological Review* 49(3), jun 84 : 359-372. [USA]

3005   ROSSI, Alice S. "Gender and parenthood", *American Sociological Review* 49(1), feb 84 : 1-19. [USA]

3006   SAITH, Ashwani. "China's new population policies : rationale and some implications", *Development and Change* 15(3), jul 84 : 321-358.

3007   SCHELLSTEDE, William P.; CISZEWSKI, Robert L. "Social marketing of contraceptives in Bangladesh", *Studies in Family Planning* 15(1), jan 84 : 30-39.

3008   SESHACHALAM, P. *Decision-making in family welfare planning : perceptions of programme personnel on policy, programme design, organisation and management systems, and decision-making behaviour and norms.* New Delhi : Marwah, 1984, xxvi-444 p. bibl., ind. [India]

3009   SHALEV, Carmel. "A man's right to be equal : the abortion issue", *Israel Law Review* 18(3-4), aut 83 : 381-430.

3010   SITZLER, Kathrin. "Der Schatten Herders ... Bevölkerungspolitik in Ungarn" (Herder's shadow ... demographic policy in Hungary), *Südosteuropa — Zeitschrift für Gegenwartsforschung* 33(11-12), 1984 : 641-651.

3011   SRINIVASAN, K.; [et al.]. "Factors affecting fertility control in India : a cross-sectional study", *Population and Development Review* 10(2), jun 84 : 273-296.

3012   STUART, Martha. "Le changement social par l'échange : femmes, vidéo et planification familiale à Java", *Tiers-Monde* 24(95), sep 83 : 567-572.

3013   SWEEMER, Cécile de. "The influence of child spacing on child survival", *Population Studies* 38(1), mar 84 : 47-72. [India]

3014   TOMLINSON, Richard. "Social policy in Europe : the French population debate", *Public Interest* (76), sum 84 : 111-120.

3015   TORRES, Aida. "The effects of federal funding cuts on family planning services, 1980-1983", *Family Planning Perspectives* 16(3), mai-jun 84 : 134-138. [USA]

3016   UTOMO, Budi; ALIMOESO, Sudibyo; CHAI, Bin Park. "Factors affecting the use and non use of contraception", *Majalah Demografi Indonesia* 10(20), dec 83 : 19-48.

3017   WEARING, Betsy. *The ideology of motherhood : a study of Sydney suburban mothers.* Sydney; Boston, MA : G. Allen and Unwin, 1984, 242 p. ill., bibl., ind.

3018   WONG, Siu-Lun. "Consequences of China's new population policy", *China Quarterly* (98), jun 84 : 220-240.

3019   WORLD HEALTH ORGANIZATION. REGIONAL OFFICE FOR EUROPE. *Family planning and sex education of young people.* Copenhagen : WHO, 1984, 41 p.

15400   MARRIAGE. FAMILY
MARIAGE. FAMILLE

15410   Sexual behaviour
Comportement sexuel

3020   "Féminisme international : réseau contre l'esclavage sexuel. Rapport de l'atelier féministe international contre la traite des femmes. Rotterdam (Pays Bas) 6-15 avril 1983", *Nouvelles Questions Féministes* (8), wint 84 : 5-151.

3021   "Prostitutes", *Sage Annual Review of Studies in Deviance* 7, 1983 : 77-146. [USA]

3022   BENKHEIRA, Mohammed Hocine. "Allah, ses hommes et leurs femmes : notes sur le dispositif de sexualité en Islam", *Peuples Méditerranéens / Mediterranean Peoples* (25), dec 83 : 35-45.

3023   BÉRARD, Pierre. "Le sexe entre tradition et modernité, XVIe-XVIIIe siècle", *Cahiers Internationaux de Sociologie* 76, 1984 : 135-160.

3024   BILLY, John O. G.; RODGERS, Joseph Lee; UDRY, J. Richard. "Adolescent sexual behavior and friendship choice", *Social Forces* 62(3), mar 84 : 653-678.

3025   BOUHDIBA, Abdelwahab. "La société maghrébine face à la question sexuelle", *Cahiers Internationaux de Sociologie* 76, 1984 : 91-110.

3026   CAVAILHES, Jean; DUTEY, Pierre; BACH-IGNASSE, Gérard. *Rapport gai : enquête sur les modes de vie homosexuels en France.* Paris : Persona, 1984, 277 p. bibl.

3027   CLARK, Samuel D. Jr.; ZABIN, Laurie S.; HARDY, Janet B. "Sex, contraception and parenthood : experience and attitudes among urban black young men", *Family Planning Perspectives* 16(2), mar-apr 84 : 77-82. [USA]

3028   COHN, Steven F.; GALLAGHER, James E. "Gay movements and legal change : some aspects of the dynamics of a social problem", *Social Problems* 32(1), oct 84 : 72-86. [USA]

3029   DUMAS, Claude; KIROUAC, Gilles. "Analyse critique des fondements empiriques de l'interprétation sociobiologique de l'évitement de l'inceste chez l'humain", *Social Science Information / Information sur les Sciences Sociales* 23(6), 1984 : 895-919.

3030   FERGUSON, Ann; [et al.]. "Forum : the feminist sexuality debates", *Signs* 10(1), aut 84 : 104-135. [USA]

3031   FOSSE-POLIAK, C. "La notion de prostitution : une 'définition préalable'", *Déviance et Société* 8(3), sep 84 : 251-266.

3032   GIRTLER, Roland. "Die Prostituirte und ihre Kunden" (The prostitute and her clients), *Kölner Zeitschrift für Soziologie und Sozialpsychologie* 36(2), jun 82 : 323-341. [Austria; Germany FR]

3033 GREENBERG, David F.; BYSTRYN, Marcia H. "Capitalism, bureaucracy, and male homosexuality", *Contemporary Crises* 8(1), jan 84 : 33-56.

3034 GROARKE, Lee. "Pornography : from liberalism to censorship", *Queen's Quarterly* 90(4), wint 83 : 1108-1120. [Canada]

3035 HEROLD, Edward Stephen. *Sexual behaviour of Canadian young people.* Markham, ON : Fitzhenry and Whiteside, 1984, 183 p. ill., bibl.

3036 JOARDAR, Biswanath. *Prostitution : a bibliographical synthesis.* New Delhi : Inter-India Publications, 1984, xii-135 p.

3037 JOARDAR, Biswanath. *Prostitution in historical and modern perspectives.* New Delhi : Inter-India Publications, 1984, 304 p.

3038 KING, Dave. "Condition, orientation, role or false consciousness? Models of homosexuality and transsexualism", *Sociological Review* 32(1), feb 84 : 38-56.

3039 KIRKPATRICK, George R.; ZURCHER, Louis A. Jr. "Women against pornography : feminist anti-pornography crusades in American society", *International Journal of Sociology and Social Policy* 3(4), 1983 : 1-30.

3040 LE PAPE, Marc; VIDAL, Claudine. "Libéralisme et vécus sexuels à Abidjan", *Cahiers Internationaux de Sociologie* 76, 1984 : 111-118. [Côte d'Ivoire]

3041 LOY, Pamela Hewitt; STEWART, Lea P. "The extent and effects of the sexual harassment of working women", *Sociological Focus* 17(1), jan 84 : 31-43. [USA]

3042 MAFFESOLI, Michel. "La prostitution comme 'forme' de socialité", *Cahiers Internationaux de Sociologie* 76, 1984 : 119-133.

3043 MAGHAN, Jess; SAGARIN, Edward. "Homosexuals as victimizers and victims", *Sage Annual Review of Studies in Deviance* 7, 1983 : 147-162. [USA]

3044 O'CONNELL, Martin; ROGERS, Carolyn C. "Out-of-wedlock births, premarital pregnancies and their effect of family formation and marital dissolution", *Family Planning Perspectives* 16(4), jul-aug 84 : 157-162.

3045 PERROT, Philippe. "La vérité des apparences ou le drame du corps bourgeois (XVIIIᶜ-XIXᶜ siècles)", *Cahiers Internationaux de Sociologie* 76, 1984 : 185-199. [France]

3046 SIKKA, K. D. "Prostitution : Indian perspectives and realities", *Indian Journal of Social Work* 45(2), jul 84 : 213-231.

3047 SPRINGER DE FREITAS, Renan. "Prostitutas, caftinas e policias : a dialéctica das ordens opostas" (Prostitutes, madams and cops : the dialectics of opposed orders), *Dados* 27(2), 1984 : 199-214.

3048 TEACHMAN, Jay D.; POLONKO, Karen A. "Out of sequence : the timing of marriage following a premarital birth", *Social Forces* 63(1), sep 84 : 245-260. [USA]

3049 TIRYAKIAN, Edward A. "L'anomie sexuelle en France avant la Révolution", *Cahiers Internationaux de Sociologie* 76, 1984 : 161-184.

3050 TRUONG, Thanh-Dam. "The dynamics of sex tourism : the case of Southeast Asia", *Development and Change* 14(4), oct 83 : 533-553.

3051 UTAUMI, Yoichi. "Fukuoka-shi no baishun" (Prostitution in Fukuoka city), *Study Reports of Fukuoka Junior College of Social Work and Child Education* 17, 1984 : 1-21.

3052 WOOD, Michael; HUGHES, Michael. "The moral basis of moral reform : status discontent vs. culture and socialization as explanations of anti-pornography social movement adherence", *American Sociological Review* 49(1), feb 84 : 86-99. [USA]

3053 ZABIN, Laurie S.; [et al.]. "Adolescent sexual attitudes and behavior : are they consistent?", *Family Planning Perspectives* 16(4), jul-aug 84 : 181-185. [USA]

15420 Marriage. Nuptiality
Mariage. Nuptialité

3054 ATKINSON, Jean; HUSTON, Ted L. "Sex role orientation and division of labor early in marriage", *Journal of Personality and Social Psychology* 46(2), feb 84 : 330-345. [USA]

3055 BAILEY, Caroline. *Loving conspiracy : marriage in the 1980s.* London; New York, NY : Quartet Books, 1984, xiv-240 p. bibl.

3056 BARNES, Howard L.; [et al.]. "Marital satisfaction : positive regard versus effective communications as explanatory variables", *Journal of Social Psychology* 123(1), jun 84 : 71-78.

3057 BHAT, M.; KANBARGI, R. "Estimating the incidence of widow and widower re-marriages in India from census data", *Population Studies* 38(1), mar 84 : 89-103.

3058 BOULIER, Bryan L.; ROSENZWEIG, Mark R. "Schooling, search, and spouse selection : testing economic theories of marriage and household behavior", *Journal of Political Economy* 92(4), aug 84 : 712-732. [Philippines]

3059 BRABIN, Loretta. "Polygamy : an indicator of nutritional stress in African agricultural societies?", *Africa (London)* 54(1), 1984 : 31-45.

3060 BRETON, Albert. *Le mariage, la population et le taux d'activité des femmes.* Ottawa : Centre d'Édition du Gouvernement du Canada, 1983, x-36 p.

3061 BUBA, Hans-Peter; [et al.]. "Gemischt-nationale Ehen in der Bundesrepublik Deutschland" (Inter-marriages in the Federal Republic of Germany), *Zeitschrift für Bevölkerungswissenschaft* 10(4), 1984 : 421-448.

3062 BUMPASS, Larry L. "Children and marital disruption : a replication and update", *Demography* 21(1), feb 84 : 71-82. [USA]

3063 CALDWELL, John C.; SRINIVASAN, K. "New data on nuptiality and fertility in China", *Population and Development Review* 10(1), mar 84 : 71-80.

3064 CHARLE, Christophe. "Le beau mariage d'Émile Durkheim", *Actes de la Recherche en Sciences Sociales* 55, nov 84 : 45-49.

3065 COOKINGHAM, Mary E. "Bluestockings, spinsters and pedagogues, 1865 to 1910", *Population Studies* 38(3), nov 84 : 349-364. [USA]

3066 CSEH-SZOMBATHY, László. "A válások társadalmi okai" (Social causes of divorces), *Valóság* 27(5), 1984 : 74-81.

3067 DAVIDSON, Bernard. "A test of equity theory for marital adjustment", *Social Psychology Quarterly* 47(1), mar 84 : 36-42.

3068 DIWAN, Paras; KUMAR, Virendra; [eds.]. *Law towards stable marriages.* Delhi : Seema, 1984, 437 p.

3069 GARLICK, Patricia. "Judicial separation : a research study", *Modern Law Review* 46(6), nov 83 : 719-737. [UK]

3070 GOLDMAN, Noreen. "Changes in widowhood and divorce and expected durations of marriage", *Demography* 21(3), aug 84 : 297-307.

3071 HASKEY, J. "Social class and socio-economic differentials in divorce in England and Wales", *Population Studies* 38(3), nov 84 : 419-438.

3072 HEUSCH, Luc de. "Du bon usage des femmes et des boeufs : les transformations du mariage en Afrique australe", *Homme* 23(4), dec 83 : 5-32. [See also pp. 33-54 by Adam KUPER]

3073 HOEM, Jan M.; SELMER, Randi. "Negligible influence of premarital cohabitation on marital fertility in current Danish cohorts, 1975", *Demography* 21(2), mai 84 : 193-206.

3074 HÖPFLINGER, François. "Heirais und Geburtenhäufigkeit bei Teenagern : ein inter-europäischer Vergleich" (Nuptiality and natality of teenagers : an inter-European comparison), *Zeitschrift für Bevölkerungswissenschaft* 10(2), 1984 : 169-191.

3075 HUNTER, Kevin A. "Marital dissolution : an economic analysis", *American Economist* 28(1), 1984 : 63-68. [USA]

3076 JAAKKOLA, Risto; AROMAA, Kauko; CANTELL, Ilkka. "The diffusion of consensual unions in Finland in the 1970s", *Yearbook of Population Research in Finland* 22, 1984 : 15-25.

3077 KAMARÁS, Ferenc; OROSZI, Zsuzsanna. *Házasság és család az 1970-es években. Az 1966-ban és 1974-ben kötött házasságok longitudinális vizsgálata 1980-ig* (Marriage and family in the 70ies. Longitudinal investigation of marriages contracted in 1966 and in 1977 until 1980). Budapest : Statisztikai Kiadó, 1983, 93 p.

3078 KLAT, Myriam; KHUDR, Adèle. "Cousin marriages in Beirut, Lebanon : is the pattern changing?", *Journal of Biosocial Science* 16(3), jul 84 : 369-373.

3079 KLIMAS BLANC, Ann. "Nonmarital cohabitation and fertility in the United States and Western Europe", *Population Research and Policy Review* 3(2), jun 84 : 181-193.

3080 KOO, Helen P.; GRIFFITH, Janet D.; SUCHINDRAN, C. M. "The effects of children on divorce and re-marriage : a multivariate analysis of life table probabilities", *Population Studies* 38(3), nov 84 : 451-471. [USA]

3081 KOO, Ja-Soon. "Support systems of Korean widows", *Korea Journal* 24(1), jan 84 : 38-50.

3082 KUBIK, Włodzimierz. "Rozwody i dezintegracja rodziny : próba typologii czynników" (Divorces and disintegration of the family : attempt at a typology of determinants), *Studia Socjologiczne* 93(2), 1984 : 127-150.

3083 LESNÝ, Ivan. "Vliv Véku při rozvodu na sňatečnost rozvodových kohort" (The influence of age at the time of divorce on the rate of remarriage of divorcees), *Demografie* 26(3), 1984 : 201-208. [Czechoslovakia]

3084 LUCKE, Doris; BERGHAHN, Sabine. "Die Praxis des neuen Scheidungsrechts in der Bundesrepublik" (Practice of the new law on divorce in the Federal Republic), *Leviathan* 11(4), 1983 : 537-563.

3085 MUÑOZ-PEREZ, Francisco; TRIBALAT, Michèle. "Mariages d'étrangers et mariages mixtes en France : evolution depuis la Première Guerre", *Population* 39(3), mai-jun 84 : 427-462.

3086 NAVAJTIS, G. A. "Opyt psihologičeskogo konsul'tirovanija supružeskih konfliktov" (An essay of psychological consultation on marital conflicts), *Psihologičeskij Žurnal* (4), 1983 : 70-72.

3087 NONOYAMA, Hisaya. "Sai-kon oyobi sai-kon kazoku no soshiki-ka" (Organization of the remarriage and the reconstituted family), *St. Andrew's University Sociological Review* 17(2), 1984 : 29-58. [Continued in ibid. : 18(1), 1984 : 61-100]

3088 NUSS, Shirley. "Family maintenance activities : husbands' participation in centrally-planned and market-oriented countries", *Insurgent Sociologist* 12(1-2), 1984 : 13-24.

3089 PROKOPEC, Jiří; SCHÜLLER, Vratislav; DYTRYCH, Zdeněk. "Rozvody pražských manželství — situace tři roky po rozvodu" (Divorces and marriages in Prague — situation three years after the divorce), *Demografie* 26(4), 1984 : 297-304.

3090 REYNOLDS, Robert S. Jr.; [et al.]. "An exploratory analysis of county divorce rates", *Sociology and Social Research* 69(1), oct 84 : 109-121.

3091 RICO LARA, Manuel. "Divorcio y matrimonio civil en España" (Divorce and civil marriage in Spain), *Sistema* (58), jan 84 : 121-132.

3092 RYCHTARÍKOVÁ, Jitka. "Tabulky sňatečnosti a metody jejich konstrukce" (Nuptiality tables and methods of their construction), *Demografie* 26(2), 1984 : 110-122. [Czechoslovakia]

3093 SANDERS, A. J. G. M. "Ten years of the Botswana Matrimonial Causes Act : further proposals for divorce reform", *Journal of African Law* 26(2), aut 82 : 163-176.

3094 SCHOEN, Robert; BAJ, John; WOODROW, Karen. "Marriage and divorce in twentieth century Belgian cohorts", *Journal of Family History* 9(1), 1984 : 88-103.

3095 SCHULTZ, Martin. "Divorce in early America : origins and patterns in three north central states", *Sociological Quarterly* 25(4), 1984 : 511-525.

3096 SMITH, A. Wade; MEITZ, June E. G. "Life-course effects on marital disruption", *Social Indicators Research* 13(4), nov 83 : 395-417. [USA]

3097 SRINIVAS, M. V. *Some reflections on dowry.* Delhi : Oxford University Press, 1984, 32 p.

3098 SRIVASTAVA, J. N. "Determinants of female age at marriage in rural Uttar Pradesh", *Indian Journal of Economics* 64(254), jan 84 : 327-344.

3099 STOLIN, V.; ROMANOVA, T. "Gotovnost' k braku i supruženskie konflikty" (Readiness for marriage and marital conflicts), *in : Čelovek v aktivnom vozraste* Moskva, 1984 : 56-62.

3100 THOMAS, Philip. "African marriage-by numbers", *Contemporary Review* 245(1423), aug 84 : 64-67.

3101 VARRO, Gabrielle. *La femme transplantée : une étude du mariage franco-américain en France et le bilinguisme des enfants.* Lille : Presses Universitaires de Lille, 1984, 184 p. bibl.

3102 WONG, Aline K.; KUO, Eddie C. Y. *Divorce in Singapore.* Singapore : G. Brash, 1983, 113 p. ill., bibl.

15430 Family
Famille

3103 "Famiglia e salute" (Family and health), *Difesa Sociale* 63(1), feb 84 : 7-96. [Italy] [With contributions by Franco FOSCHI, Pierpaolo DONATI, Carlo VETERE, Antonietta RAVASIO]

3104 "Familia en Colombia" (Family in Colombia), *Revista Javeriana* 102(506), jul 84 : 3-45. [With contributions by Cecilia RESTREPO DE URIBE, Nelly ROJAS DE GONZALEZ, María Teresa GNECCO DE RUIZ, Jorge Humberto PELAEZ]

3105 "Masculinités aujourd'hui. Pères et fils", *Autrement. Série Mutations* (61), jun 84 : 1-232. [With contributions by Dominique COURTIER, François HERAN, Bernard SCHNAPPER]

3106 "Recherches et famille", *Revue Française des Affaires Sociales* 37(4), dec 83 : 3-254. [France] [With contributions by Daniel BERTAUX, Nadine LEFAUCHEUR, Alice BARTHEZ]

3107 "Strains on household roles and relations", *Social Problems* 31(3), feb 84 : 273-310. [USA] [With contributions by Sharon K. HOUSEKNECHT, Gilly WEST, Danileen R. LOSEKE, Spencer E. CAHILL]

3108 "Vie (La) de famille", *Autrement. Série Monde* (9), oct 84 : 200-231. [Southern Africa] [With contributions by Philippe HAERINGER, Yves MARGUERAT, Brigitte TALLON, Kinsinga BITONDO]

3109 ACOCK, Alan C. "Parents and their children : the study of inter-generational influence", *Sociology and Social Research* 68(2), jan 84 : 151-171. [USA]

3110 ACOCK, Alan C.; FULLER, Theodore. "The attitude-behavior relationship and parental influence · circular mobility in Thailand", *Social Forces* 62(4), jun 84 : 973-994.

3111 ADAMEK, Raymond J.; KOLLER, Marvin E. "Size of family of orientation and family size preference : a replication", *Sociological Focus* 17(3), aug 84 : 201-210. [USA]

3112 ALBERDI, Inés; ESCARIO, Pilar; HAIMOVICH, Perla. "Actitudes de las mujeres hacia el cambio familiar" (Female attitudes towards family change), *Revista Española de Investigaciones Sociológicas* 27, jul-sep 84 : 41-59. [Spain]

3113   AUDIBERT, Agnès. *Le matriarcat breton.* Paris : Presses Universitaires de France, 1984,
        160 p. bibl. [France]
3114   BALBO, Laura. "Famiglia e stato nella societa contemporanea" (Family and state in
        contemporary society), *Stato e Mercato* 10, apr 84 : 3-33.
3115   BANGO, Jenö. "Ergebnisse ungarischer Familiensoziologie" (Conclusions on Hungarian
        family sociology), *Osteuropa* 34(5), mai 84 : 344-351.
3116   BAUHAIN, Claude; TOKITSU, Kenji. "Structures familiales et sexualité au Japon à
        l'époque moderne", *Cahiers Internationaux de Sociologie* 76, 1984 : 71-90.
3117   BEN-RAFAEL, Eliezer; WEITMAN, Sasha. "The reconstitution of the family in the
        kibbutz", *Archives Européennes de Sociologie* 25(1), 1984 : 1-27.
3118   BINNS, David; MARS, Gerald. "Family, community and unemployment : a study in
        change", *Sociological Review* 32(4), nov 84 : 662-695. [UK]
3119   BOHOLM, Asa. *Swedish kinship. An exploration into cultural processes of belonging and continuity.*
        Göteborg : Acta Universitatis Gothoburgensis, 1983, 252 p. ill.
3120   BREMOND, Claude. "La famille séparée", *Communications (Paris)* 39, 1984 : 5-45.
3121   BUSLOV, K. P.; ČIGIR', A. É.; [eds.]. *Trudovye i nravstvennye osnovy sovetskoj sem'i* (Labour
        and mutual bases of the Soviet family). Minsk : Nauka i Tehnika, 1982, 112 p.
3122   CERNESCU, Traila. "Familia tinără si serviciile sociale specifice" (The young family and
        special social services), *Viitorul Social* 76(5), oct 83 : 416-423. [Romania]
3123   CHAKRABORTY, Prafulla; BHOWMICK, Samita. "Some aspects of household
        organization and family structures in Calcutta", *Eastern Anthropologist* 36(1), mar 83 : 31-44.
3124   CONZE, Werner. "Neue Literatur zur Sozialgeschichte der Familie" (New literature on
        social history of the family), *Vierteljahrschrift für Sozial- und Wirtschaftsgeschichte* 71(1),
        1984 : 59-72.
3125   CROUTER, Ann C. "Spillover from family to work : the neglected side of the work-family
        interface", *Human Relations* 37(6), jun 84 : 425-442.
3126   CSEH-SZOMBATHY, László. "Változások a család társadalmi és gazdasági szerepében"
        (Changes in the social and economic role of the family), *Társadalomkutatás* 2(3-4),
        1984 : 53-63. [Hungary]
3127   ČULINOVIĆ-KONSTANTINOVIĆ, Vesna. "Promjene seoske porodice i običajnog
        ponašanja pri sklapanju braka" (Changes in the rural family and in wedding customs),
        Sociologija Sela (82), 1983 : 183-197. [Yugoslavia]
3128   DAMIEN, André. "Evolution ou révolution dans la famille", *Revue des Sciences Morales et
        Politiques* 138(4), 1983 : 693-712. [France]
3129   DARITY, William A.; MYERS, Samuel L. Jr. "Does welfare dependency cause female
        headship? The case of Black family", *Journal of Marriage and the Family* 46(4), nov
        84 : 765-779. [USA] [See also ibid. : pp. 781-790 by Glenna SPITZE]
3130   DEGIOVANNI, Patrick; DEVILLE, Jean-Claude; GUBIAN, Alain. "Répartition des
        familles selon le nombre d'enfants : un modèle et son application à la fécondité
        différentielle", *Population* 39(3), mai-jun 84 : 563-586. [France]
3131   DENZIN, Norman K. "Toward a phenomenology of domestic, family violence", *American
        Journal of Sociology* 90(3), nov 84 : 483-513. [USA]
3132   DORNBUSCH, Sanford M.; [et al.]. "Black control of adolescent dating", *Sociological
        Perspectives* 27(3), jul 84 : 301-323. [USA]
3133   DOUMANIS, Mariella. *Mothering in Greece : from collectivism to individualism.* London; New
        York, NY : Academic Press, 1983, viii-146 p. bibl., ind.
3134   DOYLE, Anna-Beth; GOLD, Dolores; MOSKOWITZ, Debbie S.; [eds.]. *Children in families
        under stress.* San Francisco, CA : Jossey-Bass, 1984, 120 p. ill., bibl., ind.
3135   ELIASH, Ben Zion. "Ethnic pluralism or melting pot ? The dilemma of rabbinical
        adjudication in Israeli Family Law", *Israel Law Review* 18(3-4), aut 83 : 348-380.
3136   FOSTER, Herbert J. "African patterns in the Afro-American family", *Journal of Black Studies*
        14(2), dec 83 : 201-232. [USA]
3137   FRYZLEWICZ, Zofia. "Struktura pokoleniowa rodzin rolniczych" (A generation structure
        of farming families), *Wieś i Rolnictwo* 44(3), 1984 : 109-132.
3138   GAVAKI, Efie. "Cultural changes in the Greek family in Montreal : an intra and inter-
        generational analysis", *Études Helléniques* 1(2), 1983 : 5-11.
3139   GOODY, Jack. *The development of the family and marriage in Europe.* Cambridge : University
        Press, 1983, xii-308 p. ill., tabl., bibl.
3140   GYÖRGYI, Márta. "A home-leltár hazai alkalmazásának tapasztalatai, módszer a családi
        környezet hatásának mérésére" (Results of the Hungarian application of home inventory.
        A research method for measuring the effect of family environment), *Pszichológia* 4(4),
        1984 : 577-595.

3141   HAMILTON, Gary G. "Patriarchalism in imperial China and Western Europe. A revision of Weber's sociology domination", *Theory and Society* 13(3), mai 84 : 393-425.

3142   HATANAKA, Munekazu. "Okinawa no boshi-setai ni kansuru kiso teki kenkyu" (Study of a fatherless family in Okinawa), *Journal of Okinawa Christian Junior College* 12, 1984 : 83-111.

3143   HILDEBRANDT, Hans-Jürgen. *Der Evolutionismus in der Familienforschung des XIX. Jahrhunderts* (The evolutionism in the family research in the XIXth century). Berlin : D. Reimer, 1983, iii-496 p. bibl.

3144   HORNA, Jarmilla; LUPRI, Eugen; MILLS, Donald L. "Dilemmas in researching family work roles", *International Journal of Comparative Sociology* 25(3-4), sep-dec 84 : 189-196. [Canada]

3145   HUMPHREYS, S. C. *Women and death; comparative studies.* London; Boston, MA... Routledge and Kegan Paul, 1983, xiv-210 p. bibl., ind., tabl., ill.

3146   INKELES, Alex. "The responsiveness of family patterns to economic change in the United States", *Tocqueville Review* 6(1), sum 84 : 5-50.

3147   JAROSZ, Maria. "Dezorganizacja rodziny" (Disorganization of family), *Człowiek i Światopogląd* 4, 1984 : 26-37.

3148   KAWASAKI, Sumio; YAMANAKA, Miyuki; SOMEYA, Yoshiko. "Kaigai dekasegi sha no kazoku to seikatsu" (Family life of oversea workers : the case of T and N villages in Kagoshima prefecture in Japan), *Kagoshima Keizai Daigaku Shakaigakubu Ronshu* 3(3), 1984 : 25-69.

3149   KAYONGO-MALE, Diane; ONYANGO, Philista. *The sociology of the African family.* London; New York, NY... Longman, 1984, 176 p. bibl., ind.

3150   KOBRIN, Frances E.; WAITE, Linda J. "Effects of childhood family structure on the transition to marriage", *Journal of Marriage and the Family* 46(4), nov 84 : 807-816. [USA]

3151   KOMOROWSKA, Jadwiga. *Świąteczne zwyczaje domowe w wielkim mieście. Studium na przykładzie Warszawy* (Family feast-day customs in a big city. An example study in Warsaw). Warszawa : Państwowe Wydawnictwo Naukowe, 1984, 585 p.

3152   KOSTEN, M.; MITCHELL, R. J. "Family size and social class in nineteenth century Tasmania, Australia", *Journal of Biosocial Science* 16(1), jan 84 : 55-63.

3153   KRATCOSKI, Peter C. "Perspectives on intrafamily violence", *Human Relations* 37(6), jun 84 : 443-453. [USA]

3154   KULIKOWSKA, Wanda; KULIKOWSKI, Roman. "Analiza dzietności rodzin i aktywności zawodowej rodziców" (An analysis of the number of children in families and economic activity of the parents), *Studia Demograficzne* 22(3), 1984 : 3-16. [Poland]

3155   KUROSU, Nobuyuki. "Kazoku no musubitsuki : sono suryo teki haaku no kanousei ni tsuite" (The connections of family members : about possibility of its quantity grasp), *Sociologicus* 7, 1984 : 39-78.

3156   LA ROSSA, Ralph. "Teaching family sociology through case studies", *Teaching Sociology* 11(3), apr 84 : 315-322. [USA]

3157   LAPIERRE-ADAMCYK, Evelyne. "Le cycle de vie familiale au Québec : vues comparaties, XVIIᵉ-XXᵉ siècles", *Cahiers Québécois de Démographie* 13(1), apr 84 : 59-78.

3158   LAUTMAN, Jacques. "Famille et activité professionnelle : incidences réciproques (France 1950-1980)", *Année Sociologique* 34, 1984 : 43-59.

3159   LEMIEUX, Claude. *La Chine : une histoire de famille.* Montréal, PQ : Éditions Saint-Martin; Ville Saint-Laurent : Diffusion Prologue, 1984, 180 p. bibl.

3160   MATULENIS, A.; [et al.]. *Aktual'nye voprosy sem'i i vospitanija* (Topical questions on family and education). Vil'njus : Institut Filosofii, Sociologii i Prava Akademija Nauk Lit. SSR, 1983, 219 p.

3161   MBUINGA, Vubu. "Les nouveaux régimes matrimoniaux zaïrois. Étude comparative avec les systèmes éthiopien et sénégalais", *Zaïre-Afrique* 28(181), jan 84 : 7-22.

3162   MCDANIEL, C. K.; HAMMEL, E. A. "A kin-based measure of 'r' and an evaluation of its effectiveness", *Demography* 21(1), feb 84 : 41-52.

3163   MCDANIEL, Susan A. "Family size expectations among selected Edmonton women : three explanatory frameworks compared", *Canadian Review of Sociology and Anthropology / Revue Canadienne de Sociologie et d'Anthropologie* 21(1), feb 84 : 75-91. [Canada]

3164   MEHRYAR, Amir H.; TASHAKKORI, Abbas. "A father's education as a determinant of socioeconomic and cultural characteristics of families in a sample of Iranian adolescents", *Sociological Inquiry* 54(1), wint 84 : 62-71.

3165   MICHNA, Karol. "Społeczno-zawodowa struktura rodzin chłopskich : na przykładzie pięciu regionów" (Socio-occupational structure of peasant families : based on the example of five regions), *Wieś Współczesna* 4, 1984 : 75-82.

3166   MILLER, Karen A. "The effects of industrialization of men's attitudes towards the extended family and women's rights : a cross national study", *Journal of Marriage and the Family* 46(1), feb 84 : 153-160.

3167   MOŽNÝ, Ivo; NERUDOVÁ, Liliana. "Opakovaná a neúplná rodina z hlediska kvality
        sociální reprodukce" (Families of a second marriage and one-parent families from the
        point of view of the children's successful integration into society), *Demografie* 26(3),
        1984 : 209-216. [Czechoslovakia]

3168   PIERCE, Jennifer. "The implications of functionalism for Chicano family research", *Berkeley
        Journal of Sociology* 29, 1984 : 93-117. [USA]

3169   PODEDWORNA, Hanna. "Rodzina pracownika PGR jako jedenz typów rodziny wiejskiej
        w Polsce" (State farmhand's family as one of the rural family types in Poland), *Roczniki
        Socjologii Wsi* 18, 80-81 : 57-68.

3170   POLLOCK, Linda A. *Forgotten children : parent-child relations from 1500 to 1900*. New York, NY :
        Cambridge University Press, 1984, 334 p. bibl., ind.

3171   PORST, Rolf. "Haushalte und Familien 1982. Zur Erfassung und Beschreibung von
        Haushalts- und Familienstrukturen mit Hilfe repräsentativer Bevölkerungsumfragen"
        (Households and families in 1982. On the comprehension and description of houshold
        and family structures using surveys of representative population), *Zeitschrift für Soziologie*
        13(2), apr 84 : 165-175.

3172   RAMU, G. N. "Family background and perceived marital happiness : a comparison of
        voluntary childless couples and parents", *Canadian Journal of Sociology / Cahiers Canadiens
        de Sociologie* 9(1), 1984 : 47-67. [Canada]

3173   REEDER, Amy L.; CONGER, Rand D. "Differential mother and father influences on
        the educational attainment of Black and White women", *Sociological Quarterly* 25(2),
        spr 84 : 239-250.

3174   ROBBINS, James M. "Out-of-wedlock abortion and delivery : the importance of male
        partner", *Social Problems* 31(3), feb 84 : 334-350. [USA]

3175   ROSSI, Giovanna. "Famiglia, servizi socio-sanitari e nuove forme di volontariato" (Family,
        social service and new forms of voluntary action), *Studi di Sociologia* 22(3), jul-sep 84 : 289-300.

3176   RUGH, Andrea B. *Family in contemporary Egypt*. Syracuse, NY : Syracuse University Press,
        1984, xi-305 p. bibl., ind.

3177   SAKSENA, D. N.; SRIVASTAVA, J. B. "Impact of child mortality and sociodemographic
        attributes on family size desire : some data from urban India", *Journal of Biosocial Science*
        16(1), jan 84 : 119-126.

3178   SCHÄFERS, Bernhard. "Familie im Wandel" (Changing family), *Gegenwartskunde* 33(3),
        1984 : 277-288. [Germany FR]

3179   SCHWARZ, Karl. "Eltern und Kinder in unvollständigen Familien" (Parents and children
        in incomplete families), *Zeitschrift für Bevölkerungswissenschaft* 10(1), 1984 : 3-36. [Germany FR]

3180   SGRITTA, Giovanni B. "Recherches et familles dans la crise de l'État-Providence (le cas
        italien)", *Revue Française des Affaires Sociales* 37(4), dec 83 : 167-172.

3181   SHIMIZU, Yoshifumi. "Chu-bu Thai nouson ni okeru kazoku kouzou no ichi kosatsu"
        (A study of family structure in a Central Thai rural community), *Study Reports of Baika
        Junior College* 32, 1984 : 133-174.

3182   SMITH, Raymond T.; [ed.]. *Kinship ideology and practice in Latin America*. Chapel Hill, NC :
        University of North Carolina Press, 1984, viii-341 p.

3183   STEELMAN, Lala Carr; DOBY, John T. "Family size and birth order as factors on the
        IQ performance of black and white children", *Sociology of Education* 56(2), apr 83 : 101-109.

3184   SUGAYA, Yoshiko. "Kazoku ishiki no sedai, cohort bunseki" (Intergenerational and
        intercohort variability in normative family solidarity), *Miyagi Gakuin Kenkyu Ronbunshu*
        61, 1984 : 23-50.

3185   TAMURA, Kenji. "Nihon no shorai to katei" (The future of Japan and the Japanese
        family), *Toyo University Bulletin of Faculty of Sociology* 21, 1984 : 1-16.

3186   THOMPSON, Paul. "The family and child-rearing as forces for economic change : towards
        fresh research approaches", *Sociology (London)* 18(4), nov 84 : 515-530. [UK]

3187   TITAMIES, Marketta. "The realization of ideals concerning family size", *Yearbook of
        Population Research in Finland* 22, 1984 : 60-76.

3188   TRAWIŃSKA, Maria. "Rodzina — procesy ludnościowe" (Family — population
        processes), *Człowiek i Światopogląd* 4, 1984 : 11-25.

3189   TRINCAZ, Jacqueline; TRINCAZ, Pierre. "L'éclatement de la famille africaine : religions
        et migrations, dot et polygamie", *Cahiers ORSTOM. Série Sciences Humaines* 19(2),
        1983 : 195-202.

3190   TYSZKA, Zbigniew. "Mikro- i makrospołeczne uwarunkowania procesów socjalizacyjno-
        wychowawczych w rodzinie" (Micro- and macro-social conditions of socializational-
        educational processes in the family), *Kwartalnik Pedagogiczny* 3, 1984 : 3-14.

3191   TYSZKA, Zbigniew; [ed.]. *Rodzina a struktura społeczna* (Family and social structure).
        Bydgoszcz : Pomorze, 1984, 317 p.

3192   VAN DORP, P. Patricia. *Algunos aspectos de la familia chilena* (Some aspects of the Chilean family). Santiago de Chile : Centro Bellarmino, Departamento de Investigaciones Sociológicas, 1984, 129 p. bibl.

3193   VILLAC, Michel. "Structures familiales et milieux sociaux", *Économie et Statistique* (171-172), nov-dec 84 : 135-151. [France]

3194   VUCHINICH, Samuel. "Sequencing and social structure in family conflict", *Social Psychology Quarterly* 47(3), sep 84 : 217-234.

3195   VYTLAČIL, Josef. "Struktura týdenního časového fondu manželů a manželek v rodinách se závislými détmi ČSR" (Structure of weekly time fund of husbands and wives in families with dependent children in the Czechoslovak Socialist Republic), *Demografie* 26(1), 1984 : 33-39.

3196   WATANABE, Yoshio. "Okinawa no shinzoku kankei o arawasu kotoba to minzoku gainen" (Folk concepts concerning the kinship terminology in Okinawan people), *Gaifu* 10-11, 1984 : 138-152.

3197   WEIL, Richard H. "International adoptions : the quiet migration", *International Migration Review* 18(66), sum 84 : 276-293.

3198   WINKLER, Robin; VAN KEPPEL, Margaret. *Relinquishing mothers in adoption : their long-term adjustment.* Melbourne : Institute of Family Studies, 1984, ix-100 p. bibl.

3199   WOLF, Douglas A. "Kin availability and the living arrangements of older women", *Social Science Research* 13(1), mar 84 : 72-89. [USA]

3200   YUZAWA, Yasuhiko; [ed.]. *1983 nen no kazoku mondai* (Family problems in 1983). Tokyo : Kasei Kyoikusha, 1984, 200 p. [Japan]

3201   ZAJCEV, A. N. "Aktual'nye problemy sem'i pri socializme" (Topical problems of family under socialism), *Naučnye Doklady Vysšej Školy. Naučnyj Kommunizm* (3), 1983 : 68-76.

15440   Women's status
Statut de la femme

3202   "Agriculture et condition des femmes", *Études Rurales* 92, oct-dec 83 : 9-56. [France]

3203   *Bibliographic guide to studies on the status of women : development and population trends.* Paris : UNESCO; New York, NY : Unipub, Bowker..., 1983, 292 p. ind.

3204   "Federal (The) government considers the status of women", *Sage Yearbooks in Women's Policy Studies* 7, 1984 : 17-44. [USA] [With contributions by Esther PETERSON and Catherine EAST]

3205   "Feminism and the media", *Mass Communication Review Yearbook* 4, 1983 : 211-283. [USA] [With contributions by Maryann YODELIS SMITH, Gertrude JOCH ROBINSON, Angela McROBBIE, Thelma McCORMACK]

3206   "Femmes (Les) et l'État", *Nouvelles Questions Féministes* (6-7), spr 84 : 5-176. [With contributions by Christine DELPHY, Judith FRIEDLANDER, Ti-Grace ATKINSON, Rosalind POLLOCK PETCHEVSKY, Hilary LAND]

3207   "Femmes et mouvements de sociétés", *Pensée* (238), apr 84 : 5-113. [France] [With contributions by G. DUBY, D. BLEITRACH, F. HURSTEL, E. GUIBERT-SLEDZIEWSKI]

3208   "Femmes et pouvoir", *Politique* (5), wint 84 : 170 p. [Canada] [With contributions by N. BOILY, C. SIMARD, C. DUGUAY, M. de SEVE, M. LAMONT]

3209   "Socialist feminism today", *Socialist Review* 14(1), feb 84 : 33-57. [USA] [With contributions by Meredith TAX, Wendy LUTTRELL]

3210   "United Nations decade for women world conference", *Women and Politics* 4(1), spr 84 : 93 p. [With contributions by Naomi B. LYNN, Rita Mae KELLY, Carol A. CHRISTY, Sandra DANFORTH]

3211   "Women in Southern Africa", *Journal of Southern African Studies* 10(1), oct 83 : 1-143. [With contributions by Julia C. WELLS, Marcia WRIGHT, David HIRSCHMANN, Megan VAUGHAN]

3212   "Women, oppression and liberation", *Review of African Political Economy* (27-28), 1983 : 1-184. [Africa] [With contributions by Stephanie URDANG, Susie JACOBS, Kate CREHAN, Rayad FELDMAN, Deborah GAITSKELL]

3213   BABB, Lawrence A. "Indegenous feminism in a modern Hindu sect", *Signs* 9(3), spr 84 : 399-416.

3214   BADOWSKA, Elżbieta. "Społeczna pozycja kobiet w Szwecji" (The social status of women in Sweden), *Polityka Społeczna* 10(11-12), 1983 : 25-27.

3215   BANDARAGE, Asoka. "Women in development : liberalism, Marxism and Marxist-feminism", *Development and Change* 15(4), oct 84 : 495-515.

3216   BETHKE ELSHTAIN, Jean. "Toward a reflective feminist theory", *Women and Politics* 3(4), wint 83 : 7-26. [See also Sandra HARDING, 'Common cause : toward a reflective feminist theory']

3217   BOCK, Ulla; BRASZEIL, Anne; SCHMERL, Christian; [eds.]. *Frauen an den Universitäten : zur Situation von Studentinnen und Hochschullehrerinnen in der männlichen Wissenschaftshierarchie* (Women in the universities : on the situation of women students and women university teachers in the male scientific hierarchy). Frankfurt-am-Main; New York, NY : Campus, 1983, 262 p. bibl.

3218   BOUCHIER, David. *The feminist challenge : the movement for women's liberation in Britain and the USA.* London : Macmillan Press, 1983, xi-252 p. bibl., ind.

3219   BRAHIMI, Denise. *Femmes arabes et soeurs musulmanes.* Paris : Tierce, 1984, 318 p. bibl.

3220   CANIOU, Juliette. "Les fonctions sociales de l'enseignement agricole féminin", *Études Rurales* 92, oct-dec 83 : 41-56. [France]

3221   CARDIN, Michèle; HOME, Alice. "La pratique du service social avec les groupes de femmes", *Service Social* 32(1-2), jun 83 : 170-185. [Canada]

3222   CARROLL, Susan J. "Women candidates and support feminist concerns : the closet feminist syndrome", *Western Political Quarterly* 37(2), jun 84 : 307-323. [USA]

3223   CASTRO, Ginette. *Radioscopie du féminisme américain.* Paris : Presses de la Fondation Nationale des Sciences Politiques, 1984, viii-303 p. bibl., ind. [Brazil]

3224   CHAKI-SIRCAS, Manjusri. *Feminism in a traditional society : women of the Manipur Valley.* Delhi : Shakti, 1984, 247 p.

3225   CLARK, Janet M.; [ed.]. "Women in state and local politics", *Social Science Journal (Fort Collins)* 21(1), jan 84 : 1-107. [USA]

3226   COCKS, Joan. "Wordless emotions : some critical reflections on radical feminism", *Politics and Society* 13(1), 84 : 27-57. [USA]

3227   COHEN, Yolande. "Femmes et histoire", *Recherches Sociographiques* 25(3), sep-dec 84 : 467-477. [Canada]

3228   DAHL, Tove Stang. "Women's rights to money", *International Journal of the Sociology of Law* 12(2), mai 84 : 137-152. [Norway]

3229   DE PINA CABRAL, João. "As mulheres, a maternidade e a posse da terra no Alto Minho" (Women, motherhood and land ownership in the Alto Minho), *Análise Social* 20(1), 1984 : 97-112. [Portugal]

3230   DIXON, Ruth B. "Women and human rights", *Populi* 11(1), 1984 : 5-23.

3231   ECKLEIN, Joan. "Obstacles to understanding the changing role of women in socialist countries", *Insurgent Sociologist* 12(1-2), 1984 : 7-12. [German DR]

3232   FARGE, Arlette; KLAPISCH-ZUBER, Christiane; [eds.]. *Madame ou Mademoiselle? Itinéraires de la solitude féminine : XVIIIe-XXe siècles.* Paris : Montalba, 1984, 301 p. bibl.

3233   FENNEMA, Elizabeth; AUER, M. Jane; [eds.]. *Women and education : equity or equality?* Berkeley, CA : McCutchan Publishing Corporation, 1984, xiii-266 p. ill., bibl., ind.

3234   FLAMANT-PAPARATTI, Danielle. *Bien pensantes, cocodettes et bas-bleus : la femme bourgeoise à travers la presse féminine et familiale : 1873-1887.* Paris : Denoël, 1984, 205 p. bibl., ill.

3235   FLORA, Cornelia Butler. "Socialist feminism in Latin America", *Women and Politics* 4(1), spr 84 : 69-93.

3236   FORTMANN, Louise. "Economic status and women's participation in agriculture : a Botswana case study", *Rural Sociology* 49(3), 1984 : 452-464.

3237   FRIEDLANDER, Judith. "La question féministe juive", *Nouvelles Questions Féministes* (6-7), spr 84 : 21-34.

3238   GOTTLIEB, Roger. "Mothering and the reproduction of power", *Socialist Review* 14(77), oct 84 : 93-119.

3239   GRANIEWSKA, Danuta. "Awans społeczno-zawodowy kobiet" (The socio-professional promotion of woman), *Nowe Drogi* (3), 1984 : 18-26. [Poland]

3240   GRANIEWSKA, Danuta. "Awans społeczno-zawodowy kobiet" (Socio-occupational advancement of women), *Nowe Drogi* 3, 1984 : 18-26.

3241   HAILE, Daniel. "Rural women's legal status in Ethiopia", *Verfassung und Recht in Übersee* 17(3), trim. 3, 84 : 289-310.

3242   HARTMAN, Harriet; HARTMAN, Moshe. "The effect of migration on women's roles in various countries", *International Journal of Sociology and Social Policy* 3(3), 1983 : 86-103.

3243   HOLTER, Harriet; [ed.]. *Patriarchy in a welfare society.* Oslo : Universitetsforlaget; Irvington-Hudson, NY : Columbia University Press, 1984, 235 p. ill., bibl.

3244   HOOPER, Beverly. "China's modernization : are young women going to lose out?", *Modern China* 10(3), jul 84 : 317-343.

3245   HOSHINO ALTBACH, Edith. "The new German women's movement", *Signs* 9(3), spr 84 : 454-469.

3246 HUNTER, Alfred A.; DENTON, Margaret A. "Do female candidates 'lose votes'? The experience of female candidates in the 1979 and 1980 Canadian general elections", *Canadian Review of Sociology and Anthropology / Revue Canadienne de Sociologie et d'Anthropologie* 21(4), nov 84 : 395-406.

3247 KATZENSTEIN, Mary Fainsod. "Feminism and the meaning of the vote", *Signs* 10(1), aut 84 : 5-26. [USA]

3248 KAUFMAN, McCall. "Politics of difference : the women's movement in France from May 1968 to Mitterrand", *Signs* 9(2), wint 83 : 282-293.

3249 KIRKWOOD, Julieta. "El feminismo como negación del autoritarismo" (Feminism as authoritarianism negation), *Nueva Sociedad* (71), feb 84 : 114-121. [Chile]

3250 LADJ-TEICHMANN, Dagmar. *Erziehung zur Weiblichkeit durch Textilarbeiten : ein Beitrag zur Sozialgeschichte der Frauenbildung im 19. Jahrhundert* (Women's education through textile work : a contribution to the social history of women's training in the 19th century). Weinheim : Beltz, 1983, 250 p. ill., bibl.

3251 LEBRA, Takie Sugiyama. *Japanese women : constraint and fulfilment.* Honolulu, HI : University of Hawaii Press, 1984, xii-345 p. bibl.

3252 LÉVY, Marie-Françoise. *De mères en filles : l'éducation des Françaises, 1850-1880.* Paris : Calmann-Lévy, 1984, 190 p. bibl.

3253 MAN RHIM, Soon. "The status of women in China : yesterday and today", *Asian Studies* 20, dec 82 : 1-44.

3254 MARONEY, Heather Jon. "Feminism at work", *New Left Review* (141), oct 83 : 51-71. [Canada]

3255 MARSHALL, Susan E. "Politics and female status in North Africa : a reconsideration of development theory", *Economic Development and Cultural Change* 32(3), apr 84 : 499-524.

3256 MASCIA-LEES, Frances E. *Toward a model of women's status.* New York, NY : P. Lang, 1984, 138 p. ill., bibl.

3257 MASTERS, Roger D. "Explaining 'male chauvinism' and 'feminism' : cultural differences in male and female reproductive strategies", *Women and Politics* 3(2-3), aut 83 : 165-210.

3258 MAXWELL, Mary Percival; MAXWELL, James D. "Women and the elite : educational and occupational aspirations of private school females 1966-76", *Canadian Review of Sociology and Anthropology / Revue Canadienne de Sociologie et d'Anthropologie* 21(4), nov 84 : 371-394. [Canada]

3259 MIKELL, Gwendolyn. "Filiation, economic crisis and the status of women in rural Ghana", *Canadian Journal of African Studies* 18(1), 1984 : 195-218.

3260 MITCHELL, Juliet. *Women, the longest revolution : essays on feminism, literature, and psychoanalysis.* London : Virago, 1984, xiii-335 p. bibl., ind.

3261 MITTER, Dwarka Nath. *The position of women in Hindu law.* Delhi : Inter-India, 1984, 707 p.

3262 MOATASSIME, Ahmed. "Femmes musulmanes entre 'l'état sauvage' et les 'cultures civilisées' ", *Tiers-Monde* 25(97), mar 84 : 139-154.

3263 MOROKVAŠIĆ, Mirjana. "Institutionalised equality and women's conditions in Yugoslavia", *Equal Opportunities International* 2(4), 1983 : 9-17.

3264 MUECKE, Marjorie A. "Make money not babies : changing status markers of Northern Thai women", *Asian Survey* 24(4), apr 84 : 459-470.

3265 MULLANEY, Marie Marmo. "Women and the theory of the 'revolutionary personality' : comments, criticisms, and suggestions for further study", *Social Science Journal (Fort Collins)* 21(2), apr 84 : 49-70.

3266 NAZZARI, Muriel. "The 'woman question' in Cuba : an analysis of material constraints on its solution", *Signs* 9(2), wint 83 : 246-263.

3267 OCHIAI, Emiko. "Feminism riron ni okeru 'kanai-sei' to 'kindai' -Marx-shugi, Ortner-ha jyosei jinruigaku, jyosei no shakai-shi" ('Modernization' and 'domesticity' in theories of feminism-Marxist feminism, Ortner's anthropology and social history of women), *Annual Report of Women's Studies Society* 5, 1984 : 1-11.

3268 PELZER WHITE, Christine. "Collectives and the status of women : the Vietnamese experience", *Convergence* 17(1), 1984 : 46-54.

3269 PITCH, Tamar. "Il movimento delle donne e la legge sulla violenza sessuale" (Women's movement and the law on sexual violence), *Problemi del Socialismo* (27-28), dec 83 : 192-214. [Italy]

3270 POLLOCK PETCHEVSKY, Rosalind. "L'anti-féminisme et la montée de la Nouvelle Droite aux États-Unis", *Nouvelles Questions Féministes* (6-7), spr 84 : 55-104.

3271 POOL, John J. *Woman's influence in the East.* Delhi : Inter-India, 1984, 284 p. [India]

3272 PUST, Carola; [et al.]. *Frauen in der BRD : Beruf, Familie, Gewerkschaften, Frauenbewegung* (Women in the FRG : occupation, family, trade unions, feminist movement). Hamburg : VSA-Verlag, 1983, 223 p. ill., bibl.

3273   ROTHSCHILD, Thomas. "Antifeministisches" (Antifeminism), *Frankfurter Hefte* 39(9), sep 84 : 36-43.
3274   SACHCHIDANANDA; SINHA, Ramesh P. *Women's rights : myth and reality.* Jaipur : Printwell, 1984, 126 p. [India]
3275   SHAH, Kalpana. *Women's liberation and voluntary action.* Delhi : Ajanta, 1984, 155 p. [India]
3276   SKARD, Torild; HAAVIO-MANNILA, Elina. "Equality between the sexes : myth or reality in Norden?", *Daedalus* 113(1), wint 84 : 141-167.
3277   UENO, Chizuko. "Renai, kekkon ideology to bosei ideology -feminism, sono kojin shugi to kyodo-tai shugi" (Romantic love ideology and maternalist ideology : individualist and communist in feminism), *Annual Report for Women's Studies* 5, 1984 : 102-110.
3278   WEIR, Angela; WILSON, Elisabeth. "The British women's movement", *New Left Review* (148), dec 84 : 74-103.
3279   YORGUN, Pembenaz. "The women's question and difficulties of feminism in Turkey", *Khamsin* 11, 1984 : 70-85.
3280   YOUNG, Gay. "Women, development, and human rights : issues in integrated trans-national production", *Journal of Applied Behavioral Science* 20(4), 1984 : 383-401. [Mexico]

15500   ETHNIC GROUPS
        GROUPES ETHNIQUES

15510   Ethnicity. Tribes
        Ethnicité. Tribus

3281   "Autre (L'), l'étranger : présence et exclusion dans le discours", *Mots* (8), mar 84 : 5-227. [With contributions by Gill SEIDEL, Pierre FIALA, Colette GUILLAUMIN, Jacqueline AUTHIER-REVUZ, Lidia ROMEU]
3282   "Blacks in America", *Wilson Quarterly* 8(2), spr 84 : 48-103. [With contributions by Harvard SITKOFF, Terry EASTLAND, Gary PUCKREIN, William Julius WILSON]
3283   "Estudios sobre los Indios de Costa Rica : sociología antropología, língiustia, historia" (Studies on Costa Rica's Indians : sociology, anthropology, linguistics, history), *América Indígena* 43(1), mar 83 : 5-227. [With contributions by Carmen MURILLO CHAVARRI, Omar HERNANDEZ CRUZ, Gerardo Octavio SUAREZ GARCES, M. María Eugenia MURILLO, Carlos BORGE CARVAJAL]
3284   "Etnos, narod, nacija" (Ethnic groups, population, nation), *Gledišta* 24(1-2), feb 83 : 5-241. [Yugoslavia] [With a contribution by Branisla BRBORIC]
3285   "Identité ethnique et culturelle", *Recherches Sociologiques* 15(2-3), 1984 : 155-372.
3286   "Identité ethnique et culturelle", *Recherches Sociologiques* 15(2-3), 1984 : 155-372.
3287   "Mexican (The) origin experience in the United States", *Social Science Quarterly* 65(2), jun 84 : 241-679. [A special issue. With contributions by Karen O'CONNOR, Lee EPSTEIN, Malcolm D. HOLMES, Howard C. DAUDISTEL, Rodolfo O. DE LA GARZA, David VAUGHAN]
3288   *Nacional'nye men'sinstva i immigranty v sovremennom kapitalisticeskom mire* (National minorities and immigrants in the contemporary capitalist world). Kiev : Naukova Dumka, 1984, 293 p.
3289   "Pueblos (Los) indios y el desarrollo" (Indian people and development), *América Indígena* 43(2), jun 83 : 241-395. [Latin America] [With contributions by Larissa LOMNITZ, Philippe DESCOLA, Sílvio Coelho dos SANTOS]
3290   "Pueblos indios de la Amazonia" (Indian people of Amazonia), *América Indígena* 43(3), sept 83 : 435-682. [With contributions by Alcida Rita RAMOS, Audrey BUTT COLSON, Nelly ARVELO-JIMENEZ, Abel PEROZO]
3291   AGUIRRE, Adalberto Jr.; MARTÍNEZ, Ruben. "Hispanics and the US occupational structure : a focus on vocational education", *International Journal of Sociology and Social Policy* 4(2), 1984 : 50-59.
3292   ALEXANDER, Christian. "Aboriginals in capitalist Australia : what it means to become civilised", *Australian and New Zealand Journal of Sociology* 20(2), jul 84 : 233-242.
3293   ALLARD, Joseph. "Racial and ethnic definition as reflections of public policy", *Journal of American Studies* 17(3), dec 83 : 417-435. [USA]
3294   ANCTIL, Pierre. "Double majorité et multiplicité ethnoculturelle à Montréal", *Recherches Sociographiques* 25(3), sep-dec 84 : 441-456.
3295   BELOTE, Linda Smith; BELOTE, Jim. "Drain from the bottom : individual ethnic identity change in Southern Ecuador", *Social Forces* 63(1), sep 84 : 24-50.
3296   BEOZZO, José Oscar. "Situação do negro na sociedade brasileira" (Black population situation in Brazilian society), *Vozes* 77(7), sep 83 : 5-17.

3297   BHAT, Chandrashekhar. *Ethnicity and mobility : emerging ethnic identity in social mobility among the Waddars of South India.* Delhi : Concept, 1984, xii-213 p.

3298   BODY-GENDROT, Sophie; MASLOW-ARMAND, Laura; STEWART, Danièle. *Les noirs américains aujourd'hui.* Paris : Armand Colin, 1984, 173 p. bibl., ind.

3299   BOSTOCK, W. "L'influence de la présence française sur la politique ethnique au Canada dans une perspective comparative avec l'Australie", *Recherches Sociologiques* 15(2-3), 1984 : 359-368.

3300   CAHALI, Yussef Said. *Estatuto de estrangeiro* (Foreigner's status). São Paulo, SP : Editora Saraiva, 1983, xvii-587 p. bibl. [Brazil]

3301   CAIRNS, Ed; MERCER, G. W. "Social identity in Northern Ireland", *Human Relations* 37(12), dec 84 : 1095-1102.

3302   CENTRE DE RELATIONS INTERNATIONALES ET DE SCIENCES POLITIQUES D'AMIENS. *La France au pluriel?* Paris : L'Harmattan, 1984, 255 p. ill., bibl.

3303   COHEN, Erik. "Ethnicity and legitimation in contemporary Israel", *Jerusalem Quarterly* (28), sum 83 : 111-124.

3304   DILLON, M. C. "'A terrible hiding...' Western Australia's aboriginal heritage policy", *Australian Journal of Public Administration* 42(4), dec 83 : 486-502.

3305   DRAGOSAVAC, Dušan. *Aktualni aspekti nacionalnog pitanja u Jugoslaviji* (Present aspects of the national situation in Yugoslavia). Zagreb : Globus, 1984, 319 p. bibl., ind.

3306   DUTTER, Lee E. "The political relevance of ethnicity among Israeli Jews", *Plural Societies* 14(1-2), sum 83 : 17-31.

3307   ELKLIT, Jorgen; TONS GAARD, Ole. "The policies of majority groups towards national minorities in the Danish-German border region : why the differences?", *Ethnic and Racial Studies* 6(4), oct 83 : 477-491.

3308   ENDICOTT, Kirk. "The economy of the Batek of Malaysia : annual and historical perspectives", *Research in Economic Anthropology* 6, 1984 : 29-52.

3309   FOLDS, Ralph. "Education and the development of rural Australian aborigene communities", *Community Development Journal* 19(3), jul 84 : 151-157.

3310   GERBER, Linda M. "Community characteristics and out-migration from Canadian Indian reserves : path analyses", *Canadian Review of Sociology and Anthropology / Revue Canadienne de Sociologie et d'Anthropologie* 21(2), mai 84 : 145-165.

3311   GLOWCZEWSKI, Barbara. "Au pays du dreamland et de la terre rouge : les aborigènes", *Autrement. Série Monde* (7), apr 84 : 133-183.

3312   HAINES, Herbert H. "Black radicalization and the funding of civil rights : 1957-1970", *Social Problems* 32(1), oct 84 : 31-43. [USA]

3313   HILL, Paul Bernhard. "Räumliche Nähe und soziale Distanz zu ethnischen Minderheiten" (Spatial proximity and social distance to ethnic minorities), *Zeitschrift für Soziologie* 13(4), oct 84 : 363-370.

3314   HOLZKAMP-OSTERKAMP, Ute. "'Auslanderfeindlichkeit'" (Hostility toward foreigners), *Blätter für Deutsche und Internationale Politik* 29(8), aug 84 : 973-982. [Germany FR]

3315   HUMPHREY, Ronald; SCHUMAN, Howard. "The portrayal of blacks in magazine advertisements : 1950-1982", *Public Opinion Quarterly* 48(3), 1984 : 551-563. [USA]

3316   JABBRA, Nancy W. "Community politics and ethnicity among Lebanese in Nova Scotia", *Canadian Review of Sociology and Anthropology / Revue Canadienne de Sociologie et d'Anthropologie* 21(4), nov 84 : 449-465.

3317   JACOBSON, Cardell K. "Internal colonialism and native Americans : Indian labor in the United States from 1871 to World War II", *Social Science Quarterly* 65(1), mar 84 : 158-171.

3318   JARDEL, J. P. "Identité et idéologies aux Antilles françaises. Négrisme, négritude et antillanité", *Recherches Sociologiques* 15(2-3), 1984 : 209-231.

3319   JUREIDINI, Paul A.; MCLAURIN, R. D. *Jordan : the impact of social change on the role of the tribes.* New York, NY : Praeger, 1984, 98 p. bibl.

3320   KASHIOKA, Tomihide. "Shakai hatten ni okeru 'minzoku' no ichi : gainen no kento" (Ethnicity in social development : a conceptual stocktaking), *Kansai Gaikokugo Daigaku Kenkyu Ronshu* 39, 1984 : 209-225.

3321   KÖNIG, Karin; STAUBE, Hanne. *Kalte Heimat : junge Ausländer in der Bundesrepublik* (A cold country : young foreigners in the Federal Republic). Reinbek : Rowohlt Taschenbuch Verlag, 1984, 220 p. ill.

3322   LABROUSSE, Alain. *Le réveil en Amérique andine.* Lausanne : Favre, 1984, 218 p. bibl.

3323   LE BORGNE, Louis. "Les questions dites 'ethniques'", *Recherches Sociographiques* 25(3), sep-dec 84 : 421-439. [Canada]

3324   LECHNER, Frank J. "Ethnicity and revitalization in the modern world system", *Sociological Focus* 17(3), aug 84 : 243-256.

3325   LEWIS, Herbert S. "Yemenite ethnicity in Israel", *Jewish Journal of Sociology* 26(1), jun 84 : 5-24.

3326   LIM, Linda Y. C.; GOSLING, L. A. Peter; [eds.]. _The Chinese in Southeast Asia. I. Ethnicity and economic activity._ Singapore : Maruzen Asia, 1983, viii-335 p.

3327   LIPMAN, Jonathan N. "Ethnicity and politics in Republican China : the Ma family warlords of Gansu", _Modern China_ 10(3), jul 84 : 285-316.

3328   MALENGREAU, Jacques. "Identifications et classifications socio-ethniques dans deux aires villageoises des Andes péruviennes", _Civilisations_ 33(2), 1983 : 187-226.

3329   MARGER, Martin N. "Social movement organizations and response to environmental change : the NAACP, 1960-1973", _Social Problems_ 32(1), oct 84 : 16-30. [USA] [National Association for the Advancement of Coloured Persons]

3330   MATEJKO, A. "Le changement d'identité ethnique : l'impact des nouveaux arrivants sur les Canadiens-Polonais", _Recherches Sociologiques_ 15(2-3), 1984 : 241-266.

3331   MEIER, Kenneth J.; ENGLAND, Robert E. "Black representation and educational policy : are they related?", _American Political Science Review_ 78(2), jun 84 : 392-403.

3332   NAGEL, Joane. "The ethnic revolution : the emergence of ethnic nationalism in modern states", _Sociology and Social Research_ 68(4), jul 84 : 417-434.

3333   NAIR, K. S. "Structural pluralism and ethnic boundaries : an empirical analysis in an Indian city", _Ethnic and Racial Studies_ 6(4), oct 83 : 410-437.

3334   PAQUETTE, Lyne; PERREAULT, Jeannine. "Un demi-million d'Indiens inscrits au Canada en l'an 2000?", _Cahiers Québécois de Démographie_ 13(1), apr 84 : 101-116.

3335   PENNINX, R. "Research and policy with regard to ethnic minorities in the Netherlands : an historical outline and the state of affairs", _International Migration / Migrations Internationales_ 22(4), 1984 : 345-366.

3336   PIEKE, Frank N. "De Chinese gemeenschap in verstarring" (The Chinese community in crisis), _Sociologische Gids_ 31(5), 1984 : 427-441. [Netherlands]

3337   PORTES, Alejandro. "The rise of ethnicity : determinants of ethnic perceptions among Cuban exiles in Miami", _American Sociological Review_ 49(3), jun 84 : 383-397.

3338   RAIZADA, Ajit. _Tribal development in Madhya Pradesh : a planning perspective._ Delhi : Inter-India, 1984, 220 p. [India]

3339   SHARMA, Brahm Dev. _Planning for tribal development._ Delhi : Prachi, 1984, xv-398 p. [India]

3340   SIMON, Sherry. "Écrire la différence. La perspective minoritaire", _Recherches Sociographiques_ 25(3), sep-dec 84 : 457-465. [Canada]

3341   SMITH, Anthony D. "Ethnic myths and ethnic revivals", _Archives Européennes de Sociologie_ 25(2), 1984 : 283-305.

3342   SMITH, Anthony D. "Ethnic persistence and national transformation", _British Journal of Sociology_ 35(3), sep 84 : 452-461. [Review article]

3343   SMOLICZ, J. J. "Social systems in multicultural societies", _International Journal of Sociology and Social Policy_ 3(3), 1983 : 1-15.

3344   STARR, Paul D.; STRAITS, Bruce C. "Status inconsistency and marginality in Malaysia", _Sociological Perspectives_ 27(1), jan 84 : 53-83.

3345   STEINBERG, Bernard. "The present era in Jewish education : a global comparative perspective", _Jewish Journal of Sociology_ 26(2), dec 84 : 93-109.

3346   SUNDBERG, Jan. "Ethnic maintenance in an integrated mass democracy", _West European Politics_ 7(3), jul 84 : 91-108. [Finland]

3347   TATZ, Colin. "Aborigines and the age of atonement", _Australian Quarterly_ 55(3), spr 83 : 291-306. [Australia]

3348   THOMAS, Curlew O. "Blacks, socio-economic status and the civil rights movements decline, 1970-1979 : an examination of some hypotheses", _Phylon_ 45(1), mar 84 : 40-51. [USA]

3349   TOMLINSON, Sally; TOMES, Hilary. _Ethnic minorities in British schools : a review of the literature, 1960-82._ London; Exeter, NH : Heinemann Educational, 1983, 154 p. bibl.

3350   TOSHIYUKI, Tamura. "Korean minority in Japan : an overview", _Asian Economies_ (46), sep 83 : 5-21.

3351   VAN HORNE, Winston A.; TONNESEN, Thomas V.; [eds.]. _Ethnicity and war._ Milwaukee, WI : University of Wisconsin System, American Ethnic Studies Co-ordinating Committee/Urban Corridor Consortium, 1984, xiii-173 p. bibl.

3352   VILLEMEZ, Wayne J.; BEGGS, John J. "Black capitalism and black inequality : some sociological considerations", _Social Forces_ 63(1), sep 84 : 117-144.

3353   WACKER, R. Fred. _Ethnicity, pluralism and race : race relations theory in America before Myrdal._ Westport, CT : Greenwood, 1983, 114 p.

3354   WARSHOFSKY LAPIDUS, Gail. "Ethnonationalism and political stability : the Soviet case", _World Politics_ 36(4), jul 84 : 555-580.

3355   WILLHEM, Sidney M. "Black/white equality : the socioeconomic conditions of Blacks in America", _Journal of Black Studies_ 14(2), dec 83 : 151-184.

3356   YISHAI, Yael. "Responsiveness to ethnic demands : the case of Israël", *Ethnic and Racial Studies* 7(2), apr 84 : 283-300.
3357   YOSHINO, Kohsaku. "Race, racism and nationalism", *Sophia University Studies in Sociology* 6-7, 1984 : 124-135.

15520   Interethnic relations. Racism
Relations interethniques. Racisme

3358   "British racism : the road to 1984", *Race and Class* 25(2), aut 83 : 1-107. [With contributions by A. SIVANANDAN, Cecil GUTZMORE, Lee BRIDGES, Chris SEARLE]
3359   "Sri Lanka : racism and the authoritarian State", *Race and Class* 26(1), sum 84 : 1-193. [With contributions by A. SIVANANDAN, Kumari JARDENA, Rachel KURIAN]
3360   ADAM, Heribert. "Racist capitalism versus capitalist non-racialism in South Africa", *Ethnic and Racial Studies* 7(2), apr 84 : 269-282.
3361   ADAM, Michel. "Racisme et catégories du genre humain", *Homme* 24(2), jun 84 : 77-96.
3362   BARRETT, Stanley R. "Racism, ethics and the subversive nature of anthropological inquiry", *Philosophy of the Social Sciences / Philosophie des Sciences Sociales* 14(1), mar 84 : 1-25.
3363   BLUM, Terry C. "Racial inequality and salience : an examination of Blau's theory of social structure", *Social Forces* 62(3), mar 84 : 607-617.
3364   BOSTOCK, W. "L'influence de la présence française sur la politique ethnique au Canada dans une perspective comparative avec l'Australie", *Recherches Sociologiques* 15(2-3), 1984 : 359-368.
3365   BREWER, John D. "Competing understanding of common sense understanding : a brief comment on 'common sense racism'", *British Journal of Sociology* 35(1), mar 84 : 66-74. [UK]
3366   BRITTAN, Arthur; MAYNARD, Mary. *Racism, sexism and oppression.* Oxford : Basil Blackwell, 1984, 236 p.
3367   BUTLER, John Sibley; HOLMES, Malcolm D. "Race, separatist ideology, and organizational commitment", *Social Science Quarterly* 65(1), mar 84 : 138-149.
3368   CAMPBELL, Everett J. "Discrimination : market or societal?", *International Journal of Social Economics* 11(1-2), 1984 : 14-23. [USA]
3369   CASHMORE, Ernes Ellis; TROYNA, Barry. *Introduction to race relations.* London : Routledge and Kegan Paul, 1983, vi-272 p. bibl., ind.
3370   CASTLES, Stephen. "Racism and politics in West Germany", *Race and Class* 25(3), wint 84 : 37-51.
3371   CLEMENT, R. "Aspects socio-psychologiques de la communication inter-ethnique et de l'identité sociale", *Recherches Sociologiques* 15(2-3), 1984 : 293-312. [Canada]
3372   CORNELL, Stephen. "Crisis and response in Indian-white relations : 1960-1984", *Social Problems* 32(1), oct 84 : 44-59. [USA]
3373   CROSS, Theodore L. *The Black power imperative : racial inequality and the politics of nonviolence.* New York, NY : Faulkner, 1984, xv-907 p. ill., bibl., ind.
3374   DARAGAN, N. Ja. "Scotnošenie etničeskih i konfessional'nyh obščnostej v SŠA" (Relations between religions and ethnic groups in the USA), *Sovetskaja Étnografija* (1), feb 84 : 60-72.
3375   DELACAMPAGNE, Christian. *L'invention du racisme : Antiquité et Moyen-Âge.* Paris : Payot, 1983, 353 p. bibl.
3376   DRIEDGER, Leo; CLIFTON, Rodney A. "Ethnic stereotypes : images of ethnocentrism, reciprocity or dissimilarity?", *Canadian Review of Sociology and Anthropology / Revue Canadienne de Sociologie et d'Anthropologie* 21(3), aug 84 : 287-301. [Canada]
3377   EPSTEIN, Simon. *L'antisémitisme français : aujourd'hui et demain.* Paris : Belfond, 1984, 255 p.
3378   FRANCO, Juan N.; MALLOY, Thomas; GONZALEZ, Roberto. "Ethnic and acculturation differences in self-disclosure", *Journal of Social Psychology* 122(1), feb 84 : 21-32.
3379   FREDMAN, Sandra; NELL, Marian; RANDALL, Peter. *The narrow margin : how black and white South Africans view change. Comp. by the Human Awareness Programme from the research of the Arnold Bergstraesser Institute of Socio-Political Research.* Cape Town : D. Philip, 1983, 127 p. ill.
3380   FRIEDGUT, Theodore H. "Soviet anti-zionism and antisemitism : another cycle", *Soviet Jewish Affairs* 14(1), feb 84 : 3-22.
3381   FRIEDMAN, Jean-Pierre. *Au coeur du racisme.* Paris : Favre, 1984, 255 p.
3382   GEORGE, Herman Jr. *American race relations theory : a review of four models.* Lanham, MD : University Press of America, 1984, 272 p. bibl., ind.
3383   GIRAUD, Michel. "Le regard égaré : ethnocentrisme, xénophobie ou racisme?", *Temps Modernes* 41(459), oct 84 : 737-750. [France]

3384   GOSWAMI, Subir. "Apartheid : its legal framework and political repercussions", *Journal of Political Studies* 16(2), sep 83 : 69-80.

3385   GREIVE, Hermann. *Geschichte des modernen Antisemitismus in Deutschland* (History of modern antisemitism in Germany). Darmstadt : Wissenschaftliche Buchgesellschaft, 1983, ix-224 p. bibl., ind.

3386   HANÁK, Péter; [ed.]. *Zsidókérdés, asszimiláció, antiszemitizmus. Tanulmányok a zsidókérdésről a huszadik századi Magyarországon* (Jewish problem, assimilation, antisemitism. Studies on the Jewish problem in the XXth century Hungary). Budapest : Gondolat, 1984, 378 p.

3387   HASHIM, Wan. *Race relations in Malaysia.* Kuala Lumpur : Heinemann Educational Books (Asia), 1983, xvii-127 p. bibl., ind.

3388   ICKES, William. "Composition in black and white : determinants of interaction in interracial dyads", *Journal of Personality and Social Psychology* 47(2), aug 84 : 330-341. [USA]

3389   JACOBSON, Cardell K. "The Bakke decision : white reactions to the US Supreme Court's test of affirmative action programs", *Journal of Conflict Resolution* 27(4), dec 83 : 587-705.

3390   JAYEWARDENE, C. H. S.; JAYEWARDENE, Hilda. *Tea for two : ethnic violence in Sri Lanka.* Ottawa : Crimcare, 1984, xii-157 p. map, bibl., ind.

3391   JEANNIERE, Abel. "Dans le maquis des racismes", *Études*, oct 84 : 293-307. [France]

3392   JONES, Ellen; GRUPP, Fred W. "Modernisation and ethnic equalisation in the USSR", *Soviet Studies* 36(2), apr 84 : 159-184.

3393   KARKLINS, Rasma. "Ethnic politics and access to higher education : the Soviet case", *Comparative Politics* 16(3), apr 84 : 277-294.

3394   KENDE, Péter. "Zsidóság antiszemitizmus nélkül? Antiszemitizmus zsidóság nélkül?" (Jews without antisemitism? Antisemitism without Jews?), *Valóság* 27(8), 1984 : 69-88. [Hungary]

3395   KHLEIF, Bud B. "The ethnic crisis in Lebanon : towards a socio-cultural analysis", *Sociologus* 34(2), 1984 : 121-139.

3396   KINCAID, D. Lawrence; [et al.]. "The cultural convergence of Korean immigrants in Hawaii. An empirical test of a mathematical theory", *Quality and Quantity* 18(1), dec 83 : 59-70.

3397   KINGSTON, Paul J. *Anti-Semitism in France during the 1930s : organisations, personalities, and propaganda.* Hull, PQ : University of Hull Press, 1983, ix-152 p. bibl., ind.

3398   KINLOCH, Graham Charles. *Race and ethnic relations : an annotated bibliography.* New York, NY : Garland, 1984, 250 p. ind. [USA]

3399   KIRSCHENBAUM, Alan. "Segregated integration : a research note on the fallacy of misplaced numbers", *Social Forces* 62(3), mar 84 : 784-793. [USA]

3400   LODGE, Tom. *Black politics in South Africa since 1945.* Harlow, Essex; New York, NY : Longman, 1983, x-389 p. ind.

3401   LOGAN, John R.; SCHNEIDER, Mark. "Racial segregation and racial change in American suburbs, 1970-1980", *American Journal of Sociology* 89(4), jan 84 : 874-888.

3402   MANOR, Yohanan. "L'antisionisme", *Revue Française de Science Politique* 34(2), apr 84 : 295-323.

3403   MARE, Robert D.; WINSHIP, Christopher. "The paradox of lessening racial inequality and joblessness among black youth : enrollment, enlistment, and employment, 1964-1981", *American Sociological Review* 49(1), feb 84 : 39-55. [USA]

3404   MARTIRE, Gregory; CLARK, Ruth. *Anti-Semitism in the United States : a study of American prejudice in the 1980s.* New York, NY : Praeger, 1983, 188 p. bibl., ind.

3405   MARUS, Michael R. "Are the French antisemitic ?", *Jerusalem Quarterly* (32), sum 84 : 81-97.

3406   MASSEY, Douglas S.; MULLAN, Brendan P. "Processes of Hispanic and Black spatial assimilation", *American Journal of Sociology* 89(4), jan 84 : 836-873. [USA]

3407   MATTHEWS, Bruce. "The situation in Jaffna and how it came about", *Round Table* (290), apr 84 : 188-204. [Sri Lanka]

3408   MEHLMAN, Jeffrey. *Legacies of anti-Semitism in France.* Minneapolis, MN : University of Minnesota Press, 1983, 159 p. bibl., ind.

3409   MERRIMAN, W. Richard; PARENT, T. Wayne. "Sources of citizen attitudes toward government race policy", *Polity* 16(1), aut 83 : 30-47. [USA]

3410   MILES, Robert. "Marxism versus the sociology of 'race relations'?", *Ethnic and Racial Studies* 7(2), apr 84 : 217-237. [UK]

3411   MILES, Robert. "The riots of 1958 : the ideological construction of 'race relations' as a political issue in Britain", *Immigrants and Minorities* 3(3), nov 84 : 252-275.

3412   MOTLHABI, Mokgethi Buti George. *The theory and practice of black resistance to apartheid : a social-ethical analysis.* Johannesburg : Skotaville Publishers, 1984, xxvii-326 p. ill., bibl., ind.

3413   OKOLO, Chukwudum Barnabas. "Apartheid as unfreedom", *Présence Africaine* (129), trim. 1, 84 : 20-37.

3414   OLDER, Jules. "Reducing racial imbalance in New Zealand universities and professions", *Australian and New Zealand Journal of Sociology* 20(2), jul 84 : 243-256.
3415   PORTER, Richard C. "Apartheid, the job ladder, and the evolutionary hypothesis : empirical evidence from South African manufacturing, 1960-1977", *Economic Development and Cultural Change* 33(1), oct 84 : 117-141.
3416   RAGIN, Charles C.; MAYER, Susan E.; DRASS, Kriss A. "Assessing discrimination : a Boolean approach", *American Sociological Review* 49(2), apr 84 : 221-234. [USA]
3417   REID, James J. *Tribalism and society in Islamic Iran, 1500-1629.* Malibu, CA : Undena Publications, 1983, xiii-220 p. ill., bibl., ind.
3418   RICH, Paul. "The long Victorian sunset : anthropology, eugenics and race in Britain : 1900-1948", *Patterns of Prejudice* 18(3), jul 84 : 3-17.
3419   RICH, Paul B. "Philanthropic racism in Britain : the Liverpool University Settlement, the anti-slavery society and the issue of 'half-caste' children 1919-51", *Immigrants and Minorities* 3(1), mar 84 : 69-88.
3420   SCOTT, Joseph W. "1984 : the public and private governance of race relations", *Sociological Focus* 17(3), aug 84 : 175-187. [USA]
3421   SHAFIR, Michael. "From Eminescu to Goga via Corneliu Vadim Tudor : a new round of antisemitism in Romanian cultural life", *Soviet Jewish Affairs* 14(3), nov 84 : 3-14.
3422   SHAH, Ghanshyam. *Economic differentiations and tribal identity.* Delhi : Ajanta, 1984, 152 p. [India]
3423   SHAIN, Milton. "From pariah to parvenu : the anti-Jewish stereotype in South Africa, 1880-1910", *Jewish Journal of Sociology* 26(2), dec 84 : 111-127.
3424   SHANGI, Lennard M. "Racial stratification, sex, and mental ability : a comparison of five groups in Trinidad", *Journal of Black Studies* 14(1), sep 83 : 69-82.
3425   SINGH, Ajit K. *Tribal development in India.* Delhi : Amar, 1984, 160 p.
3426   TUCH, Steven A. "A multivariate analysis of response structure : race attitudes, 1972-1977", *Social Science Research* 13(1), mar 84 : 55-71. [USA]
3427   VIARD, Philippe. "Les crimes racistes en France (1973-1983)", *Temps Modernes* 40(452-453-454), mai 84 : 1942-1952.
3428   WEISS, Hilde. *Antisemitische Vorurteile in Österreich : theoretische und empirische Analysen* (Antisemitic prejudices in Austria : theoretical and empirical analyses). Wien : Braumüller, 1984, vi-155 p. bibl.
3429   WIEVIORKA, Michel. *Les Juifs, la Pologne et Solidarność.* Paris : Denoël, 1984, 210 p. ill., bibl.
3430   WILSON, Anne. " 'Mixed race' children in British society : some theoretical considerations", *British Journal of Sociology* 35(1), mar 84 : 42-65.
3431   YAMAMOTO, Noboru. *Buraku sabetsu no shakaigaku teki kenkyu* (Buraku-discrimination : a sociological study). Tokyo : Akashi Shoten, 1984, 486 p. [Japan]
3432   YÜAN, Chung-ming. *Awakening conscience : racism in Australia.* Hong Kong : Lung Men Press, 1983, 221 p. bibl., ind.

15600   MIGRATION
MIGRATION

15610   Migrants. Migration policy
Migrants. Politique migratoire

3433   ARAGON, Luis E. "El problema migratorio en la Panamazonia : una aproximación teórica y una alternativa metodológica" (Migration problem in Amazonia : a theoretical approximation and a methodological alternative), *Revista Geográfica* (97), jun 83 : 44-55.
3434   BANERJEE, Biswajit. "Social networks in the migration process : empirical evidence on chain migration in India", *Journal of Developing Areas* 17(2), jan 83 : 185-196.
3435   BIRRELL, R. "A new era in Australian migration policy", *International Migration Review* 18(65), 1984 : 65-84.
3436   BOLEDA, Mario. "Les migrations au Canada sous le régime français (1608-1760)", *Cahiers Québécois de Démographie* 13(1), apr 84 : 23-40.
3437   COX, D. "Peut-on améliorer l'organisation des services sociaux pour migrants?" (Welfare services for migrants : can they be better planned?), *International Migration / Migrations Internationales* 23(1), 1985 : 73-95.
3438   EAGLSTEIN, A. Solomon; BERMAN, Yitzhak. "Long-term multivariate prediction of migration patterns", *Social Indicators Research* 15(3), oct 84 : 281-288. [Israel]
3439   GIORDANO, Christian. "Zwischen Mirabella und Sindelfingen. Zur Verflechtung von Uniformierungs- und Differenzierungsprozessen bei Migrationsphänomenen" (Between

Mirabella and Sindelfingen. Homogenization and differentiation as interlocking processes in migration phenomena), *Schweizerische Zeitschrift für Soziologie / Revue Suisse de Sociologie* 10(2)(Spec. No), 1984 : 437-464. [Italy; Germany FR]

3440 HAOUR-KNIPE, Mary. "Les paradoxes de la migration volontaire : migrantes occasionnelles et migrantes professionnelles", *Schweizerische Zeitschrift für Soziologie / Revue Suisse de Sociologie* 10(2)(Spec. No), 1984 : 517-538.

3441 KNABE, Bernd. "Mobilität in der Sowjetunion. Zur Frage Planwidriger Bevölkerungs- und Arbeitskräfteverlagerungen" (Mobility in Soviet Union. Population movements and manpower migration contrary to the plan), *Osteuropa* 33(11-12), dec 83 : 849-859.

3442 MAINGOT, A. P. "Caribbean migration as a structural reality", *Annales des Pays d'Amérique Centrale et des Cariaïbes* 4, 1983 : 125-139.

3443 MARSHALL, Dawn. "Migration and development in the Eastern Caribbean", *in : Conference : migration and development in the Caribbean* S.l. : s.n., 1984, 29 p.

3444 MARYAŃSKI, Andrzej. *Migracje w świecie* (Migration in the world). Warszawa : Państwowe Wydawnictwo Naukowe, 1984, 205 p.

3445 MCNEILL, William H. "Human migration in historical perspectives", *Population and Development Review* 10(1), mar 84 : 1-18.

3446 MOLHO, Ian. "Distance deterrence relationships in multistream migration models", *Manchester School of Economic and Social Studies* 52(1), mar 84 : 49-69. [UK]

3447 MOROKVAŠIĆ, Mirjana; [ed.]. "Migration in Europe : trends in research and sociological approaches : perspectives from the countries of origin and destination (1960-1983)", *Current Sociology / Sociologie Contemporaine* 32(2), 1984 : vii-x-1-198. [See for the second part, ibid. : 32(3), 1984 : 199-362]

3448 MYERS, George C.; MUSCHKIN, Clara G. "Demographic consequences of migration trends in Puerto Rico : 1950-1980", *International Migration / Migrations Internationales* 22(3), 1984 : 214-227.

3449 PACHECO, Angel M.; LUCCA-IRIZARRY, Nydia; WAPNER, Seymour. "El estudio de la migración : retos para la psicología social y la psicología ambiental" (Migration study : challenge to social psychology and environmental psychology), *Revista Latino-americana de Psicología* 16(2), 1984 : 253-276.

3450 SAGAZA, Haruo. "Tokyo-to no jinko idou no jittai ni tsuite" (Some comments on the 'Special survey on migration in Tokyo metropolitan area'), *Shakaigaku Nenshi* 25, 1984 : 85-100.

3451 SCHLOTTMANN ALAN M.; HERZOG, Henry W. Jr. "Career and geographic mobility interactions : implications for the age selectivity of migration", *Journal of Human Resources* 19(1), wint 84 : 72-86. [USA]

3452 SINGH, S. N.; [et al.]. "Migration expectancy in rural areas of Eastern Uttar Pradesh", *Indian Journal of Social Work* 45(2), jul 84 : 155-166. [India]

3453 TIRTOSUDARMO, Riwanto. "Migration decision making : a review of literature", *Majalah Demografi Indonesia* 10(20), dec 83 : 1-18.

**15620   External migration
           Migration externe**

3454 "Illegal immigration", *International Migration Review* 18(67), 1984 : 409-813. [A special issue]

3455 "Immigration (L') étrangère en Europe occidentale", *Espace, Populations, Sociétés* (2), 1983 : 9-116. [With contributions by M. POULAIN, Ch. WATTELAR, J. R. BERTRAND, N. BOUMAZA]

3456 "Immigration (L') maghrébine en France : les faits et les mythes", *Temps Modernes* 40(452-453), mai 84 : 1557-2192. [With contributions by Bruno ÉTIENNE, Jean-Yves GUERIN, René GALISSOT, Yves BENOT]

3457 "Migration of women", *International Migration Review* 18(68), 1984 : 908-1314. [A special issue]

3458 "Migration. World trends, localized flows and their absorption", *International Social Science Journal / Revue Internationale des Sciences Sociales* 36(3), 1984 : 409-536.

3459 ALPHEIS, Hannes. "Integration von rückkehrenden Migranten in Joannina, Griechenland" (Integration of returning migrants to Ioannina, Greece), *Zeitschrift für Soziologie* 13(4), oct 84 : 371-376. [From Germany FR]

3460 ALTMAN, Yochanan; MARS, Gerald. "The emigration of Soviet Georgian Jews to Israel", *Jewish Journal of Sociology* 26(1), jun 84 : 35-45.

3461 ANCTIL, Pierre; CALDWELL, Gary; [eds.]. "Immigrants", *Recherches Sociographiques* 25(3), sep-dec 84 : 335-465. [Canada]

3462   APPLEYARD, R. T. "International migrations in a changing world", *International Migration / Migrations Internationales* 22(3), 1984 : 169-177.

3463   ARDITIS, Solon. "L'immigration illégale et les sanctions à l'encontre des employeurs aux États-Unis : l'anti-modèle des lois d'État", *Studi Emigrazione* 21(74), jun 84 : 153-174.

3464   ARONOWITZ, Michael. "The social and emotional adjustment of immigrant children : a review of the literature", *International Migration Review* 18(66), sum 84 : 237-257.

3465   ATCHISON, John. "Patterns of Australian and Canadian immigration 1900-1983", *International Migration / Migrations Internationales* 22(1), 1984 : 4-32.

3466   AYUBI, Nazih. "The Egyptian 'brain drain' : a multi-dimensional problem", *International Journal of Middle East Studies* 15(4), nov 83 : 431-450.

3467   BACHELLERIE, Patrick. "Immigrés et réfugiés : la responsabilité de l'Occident", *Politique Internationale* (25), aut 84 : 279-288.

3468   BASAVARAJAPPA, K. G.; VERMA, Ravi B. P. "Les immigrants asiens au Canada : quelques résultats du recensement de 1981" (Asian immigrants in Canada : some findings from 1981 census), *International Migration / Migrations Internationales* 23(1), 1985 : 97-121.

3469   BEGAG, Azouz. *L'immigré et sa ville.* Lyon : Presses Universitaires de Lyon, 1984, 189 p. bibl. [France]

3470   CACOPARDO, Maria Cristina; MORENO, José Luis. "Caracteristicas demograficas y ocupacionales de los migrantes italianos hacia Argentina (1880-1930)" (Demographic and occupational characteristics of Italian migrants to Argentina, 1880-1930), *Studi Emigrazione* 21(75), sep 84 : 277-293.

3471   CATSIAPIS, Jean. "Les Grecs de France", *Études Helléniques* 1(1), spr 83 : 33-40.

3472   CONDÉ, J. "A socio-economic survey of Malian, Mauritanian and Senegalese immigrants resident in France", *International Migrations* 22(2), 1984 : 144-151.

3473   COSTA-LASCOUX, J. "L'espace migratoire institutionnel : un espace clos et contrôlé?", *Espace, Populations, Sociétés* (2), 1983 : 69-87. [France]

3474   CROPLEY, A. J. *The education of immigrant children : a social-psychological introduction.* London : Croom Helm, 1983, 206 p. ill., bibl., ind.

3475   DANZIGER, Nira. "The contagion effect, an additional aspect in the dynamics of emigration : the case of Israel", *International Migration / Migrations Internationales* 22(1), 1984 : 33-44.

3476   DEAKIN, Stephen. "Immigration control : the Liberal Party and the West Midlands liberals 1950-1970", *Immigrants and Minorities* 3(3), nov 84 : 297-311.

3477   DIAZ-BRIQUETS, Sergio; FREDERICK, Melinda J. . "Colombian emigration : a research note on its probable quantitative extent", *International Migration Review* 18(65), 1984 : 99-110.

3478   FREUND, Wolfgang Slim. "Travailleurs immigrés : retour? oui... mais! À la lumière du cas tunisien", *Schweizerische Zeitschrift für Soziologie / Revue Suisse de Sociologie* 10(2)(Spec. No), 1984 : 595-612.

3479   GAMBINO, Ferruccio. "L'Italie, pays d'immigration : rapports sociaux et formes juridiques", *Peuples Méditerranéens / Mediterranean Peoples* (27-28), sep 84 : 173-185.

3480   GOSSELIN, Jean-Pierre. "Une immigration de la onzième heure : les Latino-Américains", *Recherches Sociographiques* 25(3), sep-dec 84 : 393-420. [Canada]

3481   GRASMUCK, Sherri. "The impact of emigration on national development : three sending communities in the Dominican Republic", *Development and Change* 15(3), jul 84 : 381-403.

3482   GUTTMACHER, Sally. "Immigrant workers : health, law and public policy", *Journal of Health, Politics Policy and Law* 9(3), aut 84 : 503-514. [USA]

3483   HELLENCOURT, Bernard d'. "Les partis du gouvernement et l'immigration depuis la guerre : la définition d'un enjeu", *Revue Française de Civilisation Britannique* 3(1), dec 84 : 57-67. [UK]

3484   HELLY, Denise. "Les buandiers chinois de Montréal au tournant du siècle", *Recherches Sociographiques* 25(3), sep-dec 84 : 343-365.

3485   HUDSON, James L. "The ethics of immigration restriction", *Social Theory and Practice* 10(2), sum 84 : 201-239.

3486   HURH, Won Moo; KIM, Kwang Chung. "Adhesive sociocultural adaptation of Korean immigrants in the US : an alternative strategy of minority adaptation", *International Migration Review* 18(66), sum 84 : 188-216.

3487   JOHNSTON, William J. "La pensée mitte européenne dans l'émigration autrichienne 1930-1960", *Cadmos* 6(23-24), wint 83 : 87-106.

3488   KARADAWI, Ahmed. "Constraints on assistance to refugees : some observations from the Sudan", *AWR Bulletin* 21(4), 1983 : 189-200.

3489   KELLEY, Jonathan; MCALLISTER, Ian. "Immigrants, socio-economic attainment, and politics in Australia", *British Journal of Sociology* 35(3), sep 84 : 387-405.

3490   KHANDRICHE, Mohamed. "Les enfants d'émigrés algériens en France : éléments d'analyse", *Revue Algérienne des Sciences Juridiques, Économiques et Politiques* 20(4), dec 83 : 456-490.

3491   KIBREAB, Gaim. *Reflections on the African refugee problem : a critical analysis of some basic assumptions.* Uppsala : Scandinavian Institute of African Studies, 1983, 154 p.

3492   KNUDSEN, John C. "Resettlement patterns and socio-cultural adaptation among Vietnamese refugees in Norway", *Asian Profile* 12(1), feb 84 : 79-90.

3493   KOMAI, Hiroshi. "Canada no hi-hakujin-kei imin -kokusai imin no shakaigaku teki kenkyu no tame no sozai to shite" (Non-white immigrants in Canada : as a case for the sociology of international migration), *in : Ohashi, Kaoru;* [ed.], Urbanization problem in welfare countries Tokyo : Kakiuchi Shuppan, 1984, 261-279 p.

3494   KOURVETARIS, George. "The early and late Greek immigrant : a comparative sociological and socio-psychological profile", *Études Helléniques* 1(1), spr 83 : 23-32.

3495   KREISEL, Werner. "Die kleineren Einwanderungsbewegungen nach Hawaii" (Minor waves of immigration to Hawaii), *Sociologus* 34(1), 1984 : 2-29.

3496   LACHENMANN, Gudrun. "Das Dilemma der Industrieländer angesichts der Flüchtlingsproblematik in Asien" (Industrialized countries dilemma towards Asian refugees), *Verfassung und Recht in Übersee* 17(3), trim. 3, 84 : 331-347.

3497   LEBON, André. "L'Europe et les migrations internationales. La situation en 1983", *Studi Emigrazione* 21(73), mar 84 : 2-42.

3498   LEE, Mun-Woong. "Ethnic art activities of Soviet Koreans in Central Asia", *Korea Journal* 24(2), feb 84 : 4-16.

3499   LLAUMETT, Maria. *Les jeunes d'origine étrangère : de la marginalisation à la participation.* Paris : CIEM, Éditions L'Harmattan, 1984, 150 p. ill., bibl. [France]

3500   MATEJKO, A. "Le changement d'identité ethnique : l'impact des nouveaux arrivants sur les Canadiens-Polonais", *Recherches Sociologiques* 15(2-3), 1984 : 241-266.

3501   MCKEE, David L. "Some specifics on the loss of professional personnel from the Commonwealth Caribbean", *Inter-American Economic Affairs* 37(3), wint 83 : 57-76.

3502   MIN, Pyong Gap. "From white-collar occupations to small business : Korean immigrants' occupational adjustment", *Sociological Quarterly* 25(3), sum 84 : 333-352.

3503   MOROKVAŠIĆ, Mirjana. "Emigration féminine et femmes immigrées : discussion de quelques tendances dans la recherche", *Pluriel* (36), 1983 : 20-51.

3504   NOIRIEL, Gérard. "L'histoire de l'immigration en France. Note sur un enjeu", *Actes de la Recherche en Sciences Sociales* 54, sep 84 : 72-76.

3505   NOIRIEL, Gérard. *Longwy : immigrés et prolétaires, 1880-1980.* Paris : Presses Universitaires de France, 1984, 396 p.

3506   NOWAK, Margaret. *Tibetan refugees. Youth and the new generation of meaning.* New Brunswick, NJ : Rutgers University Press, 1984, 220 p. ind., map.

3507   OKAMURA, Jonathan Y. "Filipino hometown associations in Hawaii", *Ethnology* 22(4), oct 83 : 341-353.

3508   ORIOL, Michel. "L'effet Antée ou les paradoxes de l'identité périodique", *Peuples Méditerranéens / Mediterranean Peoples* (24), sep 83 : 45-60.

3509   ORIOL, Michel. "L'émigré portugais ou l'homme multidimensionnel", *Schweizerische Zeitschrift für Soziologie / Revue Suisse de Sociologie* 10(2)(Spec. No), 1984 : 541-562. [France]

3510   PAPADEMETRIOU, Demetrios G. "Immigration reform, American style", *International Migration / Migrations Internationales* 22(4), 1984 : 265-270.

3511   PERESSINI, Mauro. "Stratégies migratoires et pratiques communautaires : les Italiens du Frioul", *Recherches Sociographiques* 25(3), sep-dec 84 : 367-391. [Canada]

3512   PEROTTI, Antonio. "La France et ses immigrés depuis 1945", *Regards sur l'Actualité* (102), jun 84 : 31-44.

3513   POINARD, M.; HILY, M.-A. "Réseaux informels et officiels dans la communauté portugaise en France", *Espace, Populations, Sociétés* (2), 1983 : 57-68.

3514   PRIETO ESCUDERO, Germán. "Motivaciones etiológico-sociológicas de la emigración" (Emigration etiologico-sociological motivations), *Revista de Política Social* (142), jun 82 : 111-131. [Spain]

3515   RAMELLA, Susana T. de Jefferies. "Las ideas sobre inmigración durante la primer postguerra" (Ideas on immigration during the first postwar), *SOCIOLOGICA — Revista Argentina de Ciencias Sociales* 9, 1984 : 81-113. [Argentina]

3516   REGNAUT-LABORD, Caroline. "Naissance et fin d'une émigration soviétique?", *Revue d'Études Comparatives Est-Ouest* 15(3), sep 84 : 125-134.

3517   REIMERS, David. "South and East-Asian immigration into the United-States : from exclusion to inclusion", *Immigrants and Minorities* 3(1), mar 84 : 30-48.

3518   ROSE, Peter I. "The harbor masters : American politics and refugee policy", *Research in Social Problems and Public Policy* 3, 1984 : 273-312.

3519   ROSKIN, Michael; EDLESON, Jeffrey L. "A research note on the emotional health of English-speaking immigrants in Israel", *Jewish Journal of Sociology* 26(2), dec 84 : 139-144.

3520   RUILE, A. "L'intégration des étrangers dans les grandes villes allemandes : bases théoriques, observations empiriques et évaluation d'une situation", *Espace, Populations, Sociétés* (2), 1983 : 89-102.

3521   SALVATORI, Franco. "Giovani emigrati della seconda generazione" (Young emigrants of the second generation), *Affari Sociali Internazionali* 12(2), 1984 : 57-67. [Italy]

3522   SAPIRO, Virginia. "Women, citizenship and nationality : immigration and naturalization policies in the United States", *Politics and Society* 13(1), 84 : 1-26. [USA]

3523   SAYAD, Abdelmalek. "État, nation et immigration : l'ordre national à l'épreuve de l'immigration", *Peuples Méditerranéens / Mediterranean Peoples* (27-28), sep 84 : 187-205.

3524   SCHMITTER, Barbara. "Sending States and immigrant minorities : the case of Italy", *Comparative Studies in Society and History* 26(2), apr 84 : 325-334.

3525   SCHULTZ, T. Paul. "The schooling and health of children of U.S. immigrants and natives", *Research in Population Economics* 5, 1984 : 251-288.

3526   SEGAL, Aaron. "The half-open door", *Wilson Quarterly* 7(1), 1983 : 116-129. [USA]

3527   ŠLEPAKOV, A. N.; ŠAMŠUR, O. V. "Immigracionnaja problema : novye tendencii" (Immigration problem : new trends), *SŠA* 14(3), mar 84 : 29-40. [USA]

3528   STARE, Franci. "Demografski in ekonomski poloji za vrnitev delavcev iz tujine v Jugoslavijo s posebnim ozirom na Slovenijo", (Demographic and economic conditions of the return of workers from abroad to Yugoslavia with special regard to Slovenia), *Ekonomska Revija* 35(2-3), mar 84 : 333-335.

3529   STARK, Oded. "Discontinuity and the theory of international migration", *Kyklos* 37(2), 1984 : 206-222.

3530   STEFANSKI, Valentina-Maria. *Zum Prozess der Emanzipation und Integration von Aussenseitern : polnische Arbeitsmigranten im Ruhrgebiet* (On the process of emancipation and integration of marginal peoples : Polish labour migrants in the Ruhr region). Dortmund : Rheinisch-Westfälische Auslandsgesellschaft e.V., Forschungsstelle Ostmitteleuropa, 1984, x-327 p. ill., bibl.

3531   SZÁNTÓ, Miklós. "Bevándorlás és kettős azonosságtudat" (Immigration and dual identity), *Szociológia* 12(3), 1983 : 289-298.

3532   TASSELLO, Graziano; [ed.]. "Religione ed emigrazione : una selezione bibliografica" (Religion and emigration : a bibliographical selection), *Studi Emigrazione / Études Migrations* (76), 1984 : 439-523.

3533   TRAN, Quang Ba. "L'accueil canadien aux réfugiés d'Asie du sud-est", *Recherches Sociologiques* 15(2-3), 1984 : 267-290.

3534   WIHTOL DE WENDEN, Catherine. "The evolution of French immigration policy after May 1981", *International Migrations* 22(3), 1984 : 199-213.

3535   WOON, Yuen-fong. "The voluntary sojourner among the overseas Chinese : myth or reality?", *Pacific Affairs* 56(4), wint 84 : 673-690.

3536   ZASLAVSKY, Victor; BRYM, Robert J. *Soviet-Jewish emigration and Soviet nationality policy.* New York, NY : St. Martin's Press; London : Macmillan, 1983, viii-185 p.

15630   Internal migration
Migration interne

3537   "Mouvements de population en URSS", *Soviet Geography* 24(8), oct 83 : 547-619. [With contributions by Roland J. FUCHS, George J. DEMKO, G. A. GOLTS, B. S. KHOREV, V. N. LIKHODED, I. M. TABORIS-SKAYA]

3538   ADEPOJU, Aderanti. "Migration et développement rural au Nigéria", *Travail et Société* 9(1), mar 84 : 33-55.

3539   BANERJEE, Biswajit. "Information flow, expectations and job search. Rural-to-urban migration process in India", *Journal of Development Economics* 15(1-2-3), mai-jun-aug 84 : 239-257.

3540   BANERJEE, Biswajit. "Rural-to-urban migration and conjugal separation : an Indian case study", *Economic Development and Cultural Change* 34(4), jul 84 : 767-780.

3541   BERMAN, Yitzhak; KAGLSTEIN, A. Solomon. "Social factors as predictors of internal migration patterns in Israel", *Social Indicators Research* 13(4), nov 83 : 419-424.

3542   BERNARD, René. "Les gitans dans la nation", *Études*, jan 84 : 33-41. [France]

3543   BERTALAN, János; BERTI, Béla. "A budapesti agglomeráció ingavándor-forgalma" (Commuting within the Budapest agglomeration), *Demográfia* 27(1), 1984 : 77-97.

3544   BOLEDA, Mario. "Un caso de emigración agraria o el fin de una era agrícola" (A case of agrarian emigration or the end of an agricultural age), _SOCIOLOGICA — Revista Argentina de Ciencias Sociales_ 9, 1984 : 55-78.

3545   CAMPBELL, Rex R.; GURKOVICH, Lorraine. "Turnaround migration as an episode of collective behavior", _Rural Sociology_ 49(1), 1984 : 89-105. [USA]

3546   CARVAJAL, A. Guillermo. "Les migrations intérieures à Costa Rica" (Internal migrations in Costa Rica), _Revista Geográfica_ (98), dec 83 : 91-114.

3547   CHRISTIANSEN, Robert. "The pattern of internal migration in response to structural change in the economy of Malawi 1966-77", _Development and Change_ 15(1), jan 84 : 125-151.

3548   FARBER, Stephen C.; LEE, Bun Song. "Fertility adaptations of rural-to-urban migrant women : a method of estimation applied to Korean women", _Demography_ 21(3), aug 84 : 339-345.

3549   FULLER, Theodore D.; [et al.]. _Migration and development in modern Thailand._ Bangkok : Social Science Association of Thailand, 1983, xxv-244 p. ill., maps, bibl.

3550   GRAVEREAU, Jacques. "Chine : l'exode de 500 millions de paysans?", _Afrique et Asie Modernes_ (139), wint 84 : 35-42.

3551   GUPTA, Surendra K. "Role of migration in the urbanisation process of Assam", _Social Action_ 34(1), jan-mar 84 : 67-76.

3552   HUMEAU, Jean-Baptiste. "Les comportements de travail et de loisir : facteurs de mobilité des populations tsiganes. Observation de groupes familiaux manouches dans les campagnes angevines", _Norois_ 30(120), dec 83 : 571-582. [France]

3553   KHAN, Najma. _Studies in human migration._ New Delhi : Rajesh Publications, 1983, vi-275 p. bibl., ind.

3554   KIM, Joochul. "Factors affecting urban to rural migration", _Growth and Change_ 14(3), jul 83 : 38-43. [USA]

3555   MARKS, Shula; RICHARDSON, Peter; [eds.]. _International labour migration : historical perspectives._ Hounslow, Middlesex : M. Temple Smith, 1984, viii-280 p. bibl., ind.

3556   MORRISON, Peter A.; [ed.]. _Population movements : their forms and functions in urbanization and development._ Liege : Ordina, 1983, iv-351 p. ill., bibl., ind.

3557   O'LOUGHLIN, John; GLEBE, Günther. "Intraurban migration in West German cities", _Geographical Review_ 74(1), jan 84 : 1-23.

3558   OLIVEIRA-ROCA, Maria. "Migracija radnika iz neurbanih naselja SR Hrvatske — regionalne razlike" (Population migrations out of non-urban settlements in the Socialist Republic of Croatia — regional differences), _Sociologija Sela_ 21(79-81), 1983 : 71-82.

3559   PÁL, László. "Az ingázó dolgozók életformájáról, életmódjának sajátosságairól" (Characteristics of the way of life of commuting workers), _Társadalomtudományi Közlemények_ 14(3), 1984 : 373-385.

3560   PLANE, David A.; ISSERMAN, Andrew. "U.S. interstate labor force migration : an analysis of trends, net exchanges and migration subsystems", _Socio-Economic Planning Sciences_ 17(5-6), 1983 : 251-266.

3561   PREMI, Mahendra K. "Internal migration in India 1961-1981", _Social Action_ 34(3), jul-sep 84 : 272-285.

3562   RASILA, Viljo. _Teollistumiskauden muuttoliikkeet : mikrohistoriallinen tutkimus Tampereen seudulta = Migrations in Finland during the period of industrialisation : a microhistorical study._ Tampere : Tampereen Yliopisto, 1983, 323 p. ill.

3563   SCHLEE, Günther. "Nomaden und Staat. Das Beispiel Nordkenia" (Nomads and the State. The example of Northern Kenya), _Sociologus_ 34(2), 1984 : 140-161.

3564   SOFRANKO, Andrew J.; FLIEGEL, Frederick C. "Dissatisfaction with satisfaction", _Rural Sociology_ 49(3), 1984 : 353-373. [USA] [Community satisfaction of migrants to 75 non-metropolitan counties in the North Central Region]

3565   SPITZE, Glenna. "The effect of family migration on wives' employment : how long does it last?", _Social Science Quarterly_ 65(1), mar 84 : 21-36. [USA]

3566   STARK, Oded. "A note on modelling labour migration in LDCs", _Journal of Development Studies_ 20(4), jul 84 : 318-321.

3567   STARK, Oded. "Rural-to-urban migration in LCD's : a relative deprivation approach", _Economic Development and Cultural Change_ 32(3), apr 84 : 475-486.

3568   TANADA, Hirofumi. "Eygpt ni okeru jinko idou to toshi idou yoin, idou ruikei, tekioh" (Internal migration and urban society in Egypt), _Shakaigaku Nenshi_ 25, 1984 : 121-140.

3569   TANI, Katsuhide; TAGAMI, Yoshimi. "Manila dai toshi-ken eno jinko ryushutsu chiiki ni okeru ryushutsu yoin no bunseki" (A study of out-migration and its factors in Eastern Samar, an out-migration province to metropolitan Manila), _Tohoku Fukushi Kiyo_ 8(1), 1984 : 43-63.

3570   ZASLAVSKAYA, T. I.; KOREL, L. V. "Rural-urban migration in the USSR : problems and prospects", *Sociologia Ruralis* 24(3-4), 1984 : 229-241.
3571   ZIROTTI, Jean Pierre. "Les tsiganes ou l'identité sans frontières", *Peuples Méditerranéens / Mediterranean Peoples* (24), sep 83 : 61-70.

16100   ECOLOGY. GEOGRAPHY. HUMAN SETTLEMENTS
         ÉCOLOGIE. GÉOGRAPHIE. ÉTABLISSEMENTS HUMAINS

16110   Human geography
         Géographie humaine

3572   BAILLY, Antoine S.; [ed.]. *Les concepts de la géographie humaine.* Paris : Masson, 1984, 204 p. bibl., ind.

3573   BUSLOV, K. P. *Social'nye aspekty ēkologii* (Social aspects of ecology). Minsk : Nauka i Tehnika, 1983, 232 p.

3574   CARROLL, Glenn R. "Organizational ecology", *Annual Review of Sociology* 10, 1984 : 71-93.

3575   COUGHENOUR, C. Milton. "Social ecology and agriculture", *Rural Sociology* 49(1), 1984 : 1-22.

3576   DUPUPET, Michel. *Comprendre l'écologie.* Lyon : Chronique Sociale, 1984, 302 p. bibl., ill.

3577   GARKOVENKO, R. V. "Obščaja teorija otnošenij obščestva s prirodoj i global'naja ēkologija" (The general theory of the society relations with nature : the aggregate ecology), *in : Filosofskie problemy global'noj ēkologii* Moskva, 1983 : 59-79.

3578   GIRUSOV, É. V. "Ēkologičeskoe soznanie kak uslovie optimizacii vzaimodejstvija obščestva i prirody" (Ecological consciousness as a condition of optimization of interaction between society and nature), *in : Filosofskie problemy global'noj ēkologii* Moskva, 1983 : 105-120.

3579   GOLUBEC, M. A. *Aktual'nye voprosy ēkologii* (Topical questions on ecology). Kiev : Naukova Dumka, 1982, 157 p.

3580   HAMM, Bernd. "Aktuelle Probleme sozialökologischer Analyse" (Topical problems of socioecological analyses), *Kölner Zeitschrift für Soziologie und Sozialpsychologie* 36(2), jun 82 : 277-292.

3581   HITZLER, Ronald; HONER, Anne. "Lebenswelt — Milieu — Situation. Terminologische Vorschläge zur theoretischen Verständigung" (Life-world — milieu — situation. Terminological suggestions for theoretical understanding), *Kölner Zeitschrift für Soziologie und Sozialpsychologie* 36(1), mar 84 : 56-74.

3582   ILLARIONOVA, N. V. "O metodologičeskih podhodah k global'noj ēkologii" (On the methodological approach to aggregate ecology), *in : Nekotorye filosofskie problemy sovremennogo estestvoznanija* Kišinev, 1984 : 48-59.

3583   KITSCHELT, Herbert. *Der ökologische Diskurs : eine Analyse von Gesellschaftskonzeption in der Energiedebatte* (The ecological discourse : an analysis of society concepts in the energy debate). Frankfurt-am-Main; New York, NY : Campus, 1984, 263 p. bibl.

3584   KRYLOV, A. I.; [et al.]. "Filosofija i problema zaščity ēkologičeskih osnov žizni obščestva" (Philosophy and defence problems of the ecological bases of society life), *in : Dialektika v naukah o prirode i čeloveke : trudy III Vsesojuznogo Soveščanija po filosofskim voprosam sovremennogo estestvoznanija. IV. Čelovek, obščestvo i priroda v vek NTR* Moskva, 1983 : 224-229.

3585   LOS', V. A. "Otnošenie čelovek-prirodnaja sreda kak global'no-kompleksnaja problema" (The man natural environment relation as a global and complex problem), *in : Dialektika v naukah o prirode i čeloveke : trudy III Vsesojuznogo Soveščanija po filosofskim voprosam sovremennogo estestvoznanija. IV. Čelovek, obščestvo i priroda v vek NTR* Moskva, 1983 : 230-235.

3586   MICKLIN, Michael; CHOLDIN, Harvey M.; [eds.]. *Sociological human ecology : contemporary issues and applications.* Boulder, CO : Westview Press, 1984, xiv-454 p. ill., bibl., ind.

3587   MURTON, Brian J. "L'approche humaniste des lieux en Nouvelle-Zélande", *Espace Géographique* 12(4), dec 83 : 253-262.

3588   NOIN, Daniel; [ed.]. *Géographie sociale : actes du Colloque de Lyon, 14-16 octobre 1982.* Paris : Groupe Universitaire d'Études sur la Population et l'Espace Social, 1983, 513 p. bibl., cartes.

3589   PEARSON, Roger; [ed.]. *Ecology and evolution.* Washington, DC : Institute for the Study of Man, Inc., 1984, 92 p.

3590   PIRAGES, Dennis. "The ecological perspective and the social sciences", *International Studies Quarterly* 27(3), sep 83 : 243-255.

3591   POWELL, Joseph Michaël. "Les pionniers de la géographie australienne", *Espace Géographique* 12(4), dec 83 : 279-292.

3592 RUDEL, Thomas K. "The human ecology of rural land use planning", *Rural Sociology* 49(4), 1984 : 491-504. [USA]
3593 SANTOS, Milton. "Geography in the late twentieth century : new roles for a threatened discipline", *International Social Science Journal / Revue Internationale des Sciences Sociales* 36(4), 1984 : 657-672.
3594 STAROSTIN, A. M. "Problemy nabljudenija i experimenta v global'noj ekologii" (Problems of observation and experiment in global ecology), *in : Filosofskie problemy global'noj ekologii* Moskva, 1983 : 196-215.
3595 WHYTE, Robert Orr; [ed.]. *The evolution of the east Asian environment. 2 vols.* Hong Kong : Centre of Asian Studies, 1984.

16120   Nature. Soils. Water
Nature. Sols. Eau

3596 "Hommes (Les) et l'eau", *Études Rurales* 93-94, jan-jun 84 : 7-238.
3597 ERKOMAIŠVILI, V. "O cennostnom otnošenii k prirode" (On the valuable relation to nature), *Kommunist Gruzii* (12), 1983 : 63-69.
3598 GIRENOK, F. I. "Nekotorye problemy issledovanija svjazej prirody i obščestva" (Some problems of research on the relations between nature and society), *in : Dialektika v naukah o prirode i čeloveke : trudy III Vsesojuznogo Soveščanija po filosofskim voprosam sovremennogo estestvoznanija. IV. Čelovek, obščestvo i priroda v vek NTR* Moskva, 1983 : 270-273.
3599 KOBYLJANSKIJ, V. A. "K probleme razgraničenija i vyjavlenija vzaimnoj svjazi prirody i obščestva" (Problems of the delimitation and exposure of the mutual relation between nature and society), *in : Filosofskie problemy global'noj ekologii* Moskva, 1983 : 31-59.
3600 LEGRAIN, Dominique. "Un sondage sur la protection du littoral : cinq Français sur dix", *Revue Politique et Parlementaire* 85(906), oct 83 : 66-79. [France]
3601 LOPATA, P. P.; TIHONOVA, N. E. "Nekotorye social'no-političeskie problemy vzaimodejstvija obščestva i prirody" (Some socio-political problems of the interaction between society and nature), *Naučnye Doklady Vysšej Školy. Naučnyj Kommunizm* (5), 1983 : 31-38.
3602 MAMEDOV, N. M. "Tehničeskoe osvoenie prirody" (Technical exploitation of nature), *in : Filosofskie problemy global'noj ekologii* Moskva, 1983 : 161-178.
3603 MUSATOVA, L. Ja. "Kompleksnyj podhod k probleme ohrany okružajuščej sredy" (Complex approach to the protection of environment problem), *Filosofskie Voprosy Mediciny i Biologii* 15, 1983 : 105-108.
3604 OLEJNIKOV, Ju. V.; ŠATALOV, A. T. "Problemy issledovanija vzaimodejstvia obščestva i prirody" (Problems of research on the interaction between society and nature), *in : Mirovozzrenčeskie i metodologičeskie problemy naučnogo poznanija. Filosofskie voprosy konkretno-naučnogo znanıja* Moskva, 1983 : 18-41.
3605 PEGOV, S. A.; VOROŠUK, A. N. "Sistema modelirovanija processov biosfery" (System of elaboration models of the biosphere processes), *in : Filosofsko-metodologičeskie osnovanija sistemnyh issledovanij : sistemnyj analiz i sistemnoe modelirovanie* Moskva, 1983 : 260-273.
3606 RATHJE, William; RITENBAUGH, Cheryl K.; [eds.]. "Household refuse analysis : theory, method, and applications in social science", *American Behavioral Scientist* 28(1), sep-oct 84 : 3-153.
3607 REJMERS, N. F. "Sistemnye osnovy prirodopol'zovanija" (Systemic bases of the nature utilization), *in : Filosofskie problemy global'noj ekologii* Moskva, 1983 : 121-160.
3608 TASALOV, V. I. "Priroda kak vnutrennij faktor kul'tury" (Nature as an inherent factor of culture), *Priroda* (12), 1983 : 91-97.

16130   Citizens. Inhabitants
Citoyens. Habitants

3609 ANDERSEN SARTI, Ingrid; BARBOSA FILHO, Rubem. "Desafios e desafinos nos caminhos da cidadania" (Challenges and dissonant notes in the route to citizenship), *Dados* 26(3), 1983 : 315-334. [Brazil]
3610 ISAEV, K. I. "Social'nye problemy sel'skogo rasselenija na sovremennom etape : na materialah Kirgizskoj SSR" (Social problems of rural settlement in the contemporary era : with Kirghiz SSR materials), *Naučnye Doklady Vysšej Školy. Naučnyj Kommunizm* (5), 1983 : 38-46.
3611 JOSEPH, Isaac. *Le passant considérable : essai sur la dispersion de l'espace public.* Paris : Méridiens, 1984, 146 p. bibl.

3612   MUSIL, Jiří. "Problémy osídlení a migrace" (Problems of settlement and migration), *Demografie* 26(1), 1984 : 13-18.

3613   PAZIENTI, Massimo. "Alcune ipotesi sulle modificazioni recenti della struttura insediativa in Italia" (Some hypothesis on the recent modifications of habitat structure in Italy), *Rassegna Economica (Napoli)* 48(2), mar-apr 84 : 401-421.

3614   SMIDOVIČ, S. "Politika rasselenija v SSSR : k probleme vybora cely" (The settlement policy in the USSR : problem of the objectives choice), *Rasselenie i Demografičeskie Processy* (41), 1983 : 3-17.

3615   WERNECK VIANNA, Luis. "O problema da cidadania na hora da transição democrática" (The problem of citizenship in the process of transition to democracy), *Dados* 26(3), 1983 : 243-264. [Brazil]

16200   COMMUNITY
         COMMUNAUTÉ

3616   "Community development and the role of the change agent", *Community Development Journal* 19(4), oct 84 : 214-265. [With contributions by Sidney JACOBS, Trudy BREKELBAUM, Bridget DILLON, Bidum KAYUNSA]

3617   "Labor-community coalition-building : case examples", *Social Policy* 13(4), spr 83 : 15-60. [USA] [With contributions by Gary DELGADO, Richard KAZIS, Richard GROSSMAN, Craig KAPLAN, Bogdan DENITCH, Charles KADUSHIN]

3618   BARDO, J. W.; HUGHEY, J. B. "The structure of community satisfaction in a British and an American community", *Journal of Social Psychology* 124(2), dec 84 : 151-157. [Hemel Hempstead, UK; Knoxville, USA]

3619   BARDO, John W. "Sociospatial predictors of community satisfaction", *Journal of Social Psychology* 122(2), apr 84 : 189-198. [Hemel Hempstead, UK]

3620   BŐHM, Antal; PÁL, László; [eds.]. *Helyi társadalom. I. Hipotézisek — kutatási módszerek* (Local society. I. Hypotheses — research methods). Budapest : Magyar Szocialista Munkáspárt Társadalomtudományi Intézete, 1983, 197 p. [Hungary]

3621   CHRISTENSON, James A. "Gemeinschaft and Gesellschaft : testing the spatial and communal hypotheses", *Social Forces* 63(1), sep 84 : 160-168.

3622   EKPENYONG, Stephen. "The effects of mining activities on a peasant community : a case study", *Development and Change* 15(2), apr 84 : 251-273.

3623   ELLIS, Carolyn. "Change and ambivalence on the periphery", *Rural Sociology* 49(4), 1984 : 505-516. [USA]

3624   FAISON, Barbara H. *The development of community organization practice theory, 1956-1983 : an annotated bibliography.* Monticello, IL : Vance Bibliographies, 1984, 10 p.

3625   FARRELL, B.; [ed.]. *Communications and community in Ireland.* Dublin : Mercier Press, 1984, 133 p.

3626   FITZGERALD, Kath; THORNS, David. *Locality studies : a bibliography and index.* Monticello, IL : Vance Bibliographies, 1984, 171 p. bibl., ind.

3627   GALASKIEWICZ, Joseph; KROHN, Karl R. "Positions, roles, and dependencies in a community interorganization system", *Sociological Quarterly* 25(4), 1984 : 527-550. [USA]

3628   GILBERT, Alan; WARD, Peter. "Community action by the urban poor : democratic involvement, community self-help or a means of social control?", *World Development* 12(8), aug 84 : 769-782. [Latin America]

3629   HILLERY, George A. Jr. "Gemeinschaft Verstehen : a theory of the middle range", *Social Forces* 63(2), dec 84 : 307-334. [Community comprehension — in cloistered monastery]

3630   JOHNSON, William C. "Government on the ground community power and locational politics", *International Social Science Review* 59(4), 1984 : 3-11. [USA]

3631   KATANO, Takashi; YAGASAKI, Seiji. " 'Chiiki community no seijyuku' towa nanika" (What does 'Maturation of local community' mean?), *Chuo-gakuin University Bulletin of the Research Institute* 1(1), 1984 : 77-86. [Japan]

3632   KRANNICH, Richard S. K.; GREIDER, Thomas. "Personal well-being in rapid growth and stable communities : multiple indicators and contrasting results", *Rural Sociology* 49(4), 1984 : 541-552. [USA]

3633   KUMADA, Toshio; TANAKA, Shigeyoshi. "Shudan kan network ni yoru chiiki shakai kenkyu no kokoromi : dai toshi kohgai no chonai-kai o jirei to shite" (Interassociation networks in local communities : an empirical study), *Hogaku Kenkyu* 57(8), 1984 : 56-77.

3634   MARTIN, Kenneth E.; WILKINSON, Kenneth P. "Local participation in the federal grant system : effects of community action", *Rural Sociology* 49(3), 1984 : 374-388. [USA]

3635   MILLER, Michael K.; VOTH, Donald E.; CHAPMAN, Diana Danforth. "Estimating the effects of community resource development efforts on country quality of life", *Rural Sociology* 49(1), spr 84 : 37-66.
3636   MORIYA, Takahiko; FURUKI, Toshiaki; [eds.]. *Chiiki shakai to seiji bunka* (Community and political culture : toward a development of civil autonomy). Tokyo : Yushindo, 1984, 275 p. [Japan]
3637   OSBORNE, J. Grayson; BOYLE, William; BORG, Walter R. "Rapid community growth and the problems of elementary and secondary students", *Rural Sociology* 49(4), 1984 : 553-567. [USA]
3638   PAPPI, Franz Urban; KAPPELHOFF, Peter. "Abhängigkeit, Tausch und kollektive Entscheidung in einer Gemeinde-elite" (Dependence, exchange, and collective decision among a community elite), *Zeitschrift für Soziologie* 13(2), apr 84 : 87-117. [Germany FR]
3639   PAPPI, Franz Urban; MELBECK, Christian. "Das Machtpotential von Organisationen in der Gemeindepolitik" (The power potential of organizations in community policy), *Kölner Zeitschrift für Soziologie und Sozialpsychologie* 36(3), sep 84 : 557-584.
3640   PETERSEN, Larry R.; TAKAYAMA, K. Peter. "Community and commitment among Catholics : a test of local-cosmopolitan theory", *Sociological Quarterly* 25(1), wint 84 : 97-112. [USA]
3641   ROZEN, P.; [ed.]. *Introduction of innovations through community development : report of the main lectures.* Marcinelle : International Association for Community Development, 1983, 385 p. bibl.
3642   SHINOHARA, Takahiro. "Chiiki shakai hendo to chiiki seikatsu shudan -rito community no baai" (Social change and locality groups in an island community), *Keizaigaku-ronshu of Kagoshima University* 22, 1984 : 99-133. [Japan]
3643   SILAVWE, Geoffrey. "Community development programmes in Zambia : an evaluation and assessment of events", *Community Development Journal* 19(3), jul 84 : 167-175.
3644   STINNER, William F.; KAN, Stephen H. "Newcomer-returnee differences in non-metropolitan Utah communities", *Social Science Journal (Fort Collins)* 21(2), apr 84 : 135-149.
3645   TAKAHASHI, Hidehiro. "Gendai shihon shugi ni okeru kyodo-sei to sono saihen" (Community life and its reorganization in capitalist society), *Soshioroji* 29(2), 1984 : 129-142.
3646   VASOO, S. "Reviewing the direction of community development in Singapore", *Community Development Journal* 19(1), jan 84 : 7-19.

16300   **RURAL. URBAN**
         RURAL. URBAIN

16310   **Rural sociology**
         Sociologie rurale

3647   "Changing the rural part of human settlement systems", *Ekistics* 50(303), dec 83 : 428-507. [With contributions by Jean-Claude GROSBUSCH, Vassilis KARAPOSTOLIS, Avinoam MEIR, Franklyn R. KALOKO, P. A. OKUNEYE, Mohammad KAMIAR; continued in ibid. 51(304), feb 84 : 4-74]
3648   "Chinese rural development : the great transformation", *International Journal of Sociology* 14(4), 1984-85 : 3-100.
3649   "Peasants, the administration and rural development", *Sociologia Ruralis* 24(1), 1984 : 5-78. [With contributions by P. GESCHIERE, S. L. SAMPSON, B. HANISCH]
3650   "Politics (The) of rural development in Latin America", *Boletín de Estudios Latinoamericanos y del Caribe* (35), dec 83 : 3-116. [With contributions by Gerrit HUIZER]
3651   *Social'nye processy v sovremennoj derevne* (Social processes in contemporary villages). Baku : s.n., 1982, 167 p. [USSR]
3652   AZIZ, Sartaj. "Réflexions sur les conditions du développement rural", *Revue Internationale du Travail* 123(3), mai-jun 84 : 297-307.
3653   BADOURÈS, Anne-Marie; BOUYOU, Maurice. *La paysannerie en Périgord : 1940-1950.* Bordeaux : Éditions Le Mascaret, 1983, 165-8 p. ill.
3654   BADY, Abamby Zentho. "Les villages communautaires : bases du pouvoir populaire mozambicain", *Mois en Afrique* 19(215-216), jan 84 : 18-31.
3655   BEJARANO GONZÁLEZ, Fernando. "La irregularidad de la tenencia de la tierra en las colonias populares (1976-1982)" (Orregularity of land tenure in the popular colonies (1976-1982)), *Revista Mexicana de Sociología* 45(3), jul-sep 83 : 797-827. [Mexico]
3656   BELL, Peter D. *Peasants in socialist transition : life in a collectivized Hungarian village.* Berkeley, CA : University of California Press, 1984, ix-322 p. ill., bibl., ind.

3657   BERGMAN, Theodor. *Agrarian reform in India, with special reference to Kerala, Karnataka, Andhra Pradesh and West Bengal.* Delhi : Agricole, 1984, viii-216 p.

3658   BILLAZ, René; [et al.]. *Actions de développement et sociétés rurales.* Douala : Institut Panafricain pour le Développement, 1983, 194 p. ill., bibl. [Burkina-Faso]

3659   BOIS, Paul. *Paysans de l'Ouest : des structures économiques et sociales aux options politiques depuis l'époque révolutionnaire dans la Sarthe.* Paris : Éditions de l'École des Hautes Études en Sciences Sociales, 1984, rev., xix-716 p. bibl., ind.

3660   BONNAMOUR, Jacqueline; [et al.]. *Paysages agraires et sociétés.* Paris : CDU-SEDES, 1984, 380 p. bibl.

3661   BOSE, Pradip Kumar. *Classes in rural society : a sociological study of some Bengal villages.* Delhi : Ajanta, 1984, 272 p.

3662   BOURIN, Monique; DURAND, Robert. *Vivre au village au Moyen Âge : les solidarités paysannes du XIᵉ au XIIIᵉ siècles.* Paris : Messidor / Temps Actuels, 1984, 258 p. bibl., ill., cartes.

3663   BRUCKMÜLLER, Ernst. "Strukturwandel der österreichischen Landwirtschaftsgesellschaften im 19. Jahrhundert" (Structural change of Austrian agricultural societies in the nineteenth century), *Zeitschrift für Agrargeschichte und Agrarsoziologie* 32(1), 1984 : 1-30.

3664   BUREAU INTERNATIONAL DU TRAVAIL. *Le développement rural et la femme en Afrique.* Genève : BIT, 1984, x-169 p. bibl.

3665   BURGAT, François; NANCY, Michel. *Les villages socialistes de la révolution agraire algérienne : 1972-1982.* Paris : Éditions du Centre National de la Recherche Scientifique, 1984, 288 p. bibl.

3666   CERNEA, Michael M. "The role of sociological knowledge in planned rural development", *Sociologia Ruralis* 24(3-4), 1984 : 185-201.

3667   CHANG, Yun Shik. "A better community : changing aspects of hamlet solidarity in Korea", *Asian and Pacific Quarterly of Cultural and Social Affairs* 16(2), sum 84 : 1-18.

3668   DAS, Arvind N. *Agrarian unrest and socio-economic change in Bihar, 1900-1980.* New Delhi : Manohar, 1983, xvi-354 p. bibl., ind.

3669   DAVIS, Marvin. *Rank and rivalty : the politics of inequality in rural west Bengal.* Cambridge : University Press, 1983, x-239 p. map; tabl., bibl.

3670   ELEGOET, Fanch. *Révoltes paysannes en Bretagne à l'origine de l'organisation des marchés.* Plobennec, Finistère : Éditions du Léon, 1984, 504 p. bibl., cartes.

3671   FARRELL, Gilda. *El acceso a la tierra del campesino ecuatoriano* (Access to land property for the Ecuadorian peasant). Quito : Mundo Andino, Fundación Ecuatoriana Populorum Progressio, 1983, 132 p. ill., bibl.

3672   FIRST-DILIĆ, Ruža. "O pokazateljima za planiranje seoskog razvitka" (On indicators for planning rural development), *Sociologija Sela* 21(79-81), 1983 : 151-165. [Yugoslavia]

3673   FLEURY, Marie-France. "Un village Diakhanke du Sénégal oriental : Missirah", *Cahiers d'Outre-Mer* 37(145), mar 84 : 63-85.

3674   GAŁAJ, Dyzma. "O nie docenianej sprzeczności w przeobrażeniach społeczności chłopskiej" (On an underestimated inconsistency in transformations of peasants' community), *Wieś i Rolnictwo* 42(1), 1984 : 7-18.

3675   GOLDSTEIN, Alice. "Aspects of change in a nineteenth-century German village", *Journal of Family History* 9(2), 1984 : 145-157.

3676   GORIACHENKO, E. E. "Programmes for spatial organization of rural areas in the USSR", *Sociologia Ruralis* 24(3-4), 1984 : 242-254.

3677   GORLACH, Krzysztof; SEREGA, Zygmunt. "Chłostwo jako kategoria społeczna : dwa ujęcia" (Peasantry as social category : two approaches), *Studia Socjologiczne* 94(3), 1984 : 89-103.

3678   GRABOWSKA, Urszula. "Ewolucja społeczno-ekonomicznej struktury wsi podmiejskich" (Evolution of socio-economic structure of suburban villages), *Zagadnienia Ekonomiki Rolnej* (5), 1983 : 17-34. [Poland]

3679   GRAY, John N. "Domestic entreprise and social relations in a Nepalese village", *Contributions to Indian Sociology* 17(2), jul-dec 83 : 245-274.

3680   HAHULINA, L. A.; [ed.]. *Sovremennoe razvitie sibirskogo sela : opyt sociologičeskogo izučenija* (Contemporary development of Siberian villages : an essay of sociological research). Novosibirsk : Institut Ėkonomiki i Organizacii Promyšlennogo Proizvodstva, 1983, 151 p.

3681   HARCSA, István. "Mezőgazdasági kistermelés, életkörülmények, életmód" (Small scale agricultural production, life conditions, way of life), *Társadalomkutatás* 2(3-4), 1984 : 134-153. [Hungary]

3682   HAUBERT, Maxime. "Réforme agraire, coopératives et pouvoir paysan dans la Sierra équatorienne", *Communautés* (66), dec 83 : 76-91.

3683   HEINS POTTER, Sulamith. "The position of peasants in modern China's social order", *Modern China* 9(4), oct 83 : 465-499.

3684 HERBON, Dietmar. "Politische Strukturen eines Dorfes in Bangladesh" (Political structures of a village in Bangladesh), *Verfassung und Recht in Übersee* 17(4), trim. 4, 84 : 475-491.

3685 IBRAHIM, Zawawi. "Malay peasants and proletarian consciousmess", *Bulletin of Concerned Asian Scholars* 15(4), dec 83 : 39-55.

3686 JOHANSEN, Harley E.; FUGUITT, Glenn V. *The changing rural village in America : demographic and economic trends since 1950*. Cambridge, MA : Ballinger Publishing Co., 1984, xix-259 p. ill., bibl., ind.

3687 JOSE, A. V. "Agrarian reforms in Kerala : the role of peasant organisations", *Journal of Contemporary Asia* 14(1), 84 : 48-61. [India]

3688 JOSHI, S. C.; [ed.]. *Rural development in the Himalaya : problems and prospects*. Naini Tal : Gyanodaya, 1984, 384 p.

3689 JULIEN-LABRUYÈRE, François. *Paysans charentais : histoire des campagnes d'Aunis, Saintonge, et bas Angoumois*. 2 vols. La Rochelle : Rupella, 1983, 524; 429 p. bibl., ind.

3690 KAEWTHEP, Kanoksak. *Les transformations structurelles et les conflits de classes dans la société rurale thaïlandaise d'après l'étude d'un cas : la Fédération de la paysannerie thaïlandaise/Farmer Federation of Thailand, 1973-76*. S.l. : s.n., 1984, 416 p. bibl., carte.

3691 KAMIKUBO, Tatsuo. "Inkyo-sei no mura no chiiki hikaku kenkyu -Mie-ken Shima-chiho, Kokufu, Funakoshi chiku no baai" (A study on the territorial comparison of two typical rural communities famous for their practices of retiring), *Chukyo Junior College Ronso* 15(1), 1984 : 310-326. [Japan]

3692 KANNO, Masashi; TAHARA, Otoyori; HOSOYA, Takashi. *Tohoku nohmin no shiso to koudo* (Thought and behavior of peasant in Tohoku district). Tokyo : Ochanomizu Shobo, 1984, 932 p.

3693 KATZIR, Yael. "Yemenite Jewish women in Israeli rural development : female power versus male authority", *Economic Development and Cultural Change* 32(1), oct 83 : 45-61.

3694 KEYDER, Çağlar. "Paths of rural transformation in Turkey", *Journal of Peasant Studies* 11(1), oct 83 : 34-49.

3695 KÜNG, Emil. "Ländliche Entwicklung in der Dritten Welt" (Rural development in the Third World), *Universitas* 39(2), 1984 : 137-147.

3696 ŁAPIŃSKI-TYSZKA, Krystyna. *Czynniki zróznicowania standardu materialnego rodzin chłopskich* (Differentiating factors of economic standard of peasant families). Wrocław : Ossolineum, 1984, 228 p.

3697 LUXARDO, Hervé. *Rase campagne : la fin des communautés paysannes, 1830-1914*. Paris : Aubier, 1984, 253 p. bibl.

3698 MADAN, Gurmukh Ram. *Village development in India : a sociological approach*. New Delhi : Allied Publishers, 1983, xvi-390 p. bibl., ind.

3699 MARTINELLI, Bruno. *Une communauté rurale de Provence face au changement : Pourrières et ses environs dans la haute vallée de l'Arc*. Paris : Éditions du Centre National de la Recherche Scientifique, 1983, 254 p. bibl.

3700 MÁTYUS, Aliz. "Pusztafalu — fejlődés — és leépüléstörténet" (Growth and decline of a village named Pusztafalu), *Kultúra és Közösség* 11(4), 1984 : 70-78. [Hungary]

3701 MÁTYUS, Aliz; TAUSZ, Katalin. *Maga-urak parasztok és uradalmi cselédek : szociográfia* (Self-managing peasants and landlord agricultural workers : sociography). Budapest : Magvető, 1984, 217 p.

3702 MEHTA, Shirin. *The peasantry and nationalism : a study of the Bardoli satyagraha*. New Delhi : Manohar, 1984, x-215 p. bibl., ind.

3703 MEHTA, Shiv R. *Rural development policies and programmes : a sociological perspective*. Delhi : Sage, 1984, 192 p. [India]

3704 MENCHER, Joan P.; [ed.]. *Social anthropology of peasantry*. Bombay : Somaiya, 1983, xii-351 p. bibl.

3705 MENDRAS, Henri. *La fin des paysans; suivi d'une réflexion sur 'La fin des paysans', vingt ans après*. Le Paradou : Actes Sud, 1984, 370 p. bibl., ind.

3706 MORMONT, Marc. "The emergence of rural struggles and their ideological effects", *International Journal of Urban and Regional Research* 7(4), dec 83 : 559-575. [Europe] [FRE; GER; SPA]

3707 N'KALOULOU, Bernard. *Dynamique paysanne et développement rural au Congo*. Paris : L'Harmattan, 1984, 260 p. bibl.

3708 NARAYAN, B. K.; VASUDEVA RAO, D. *Integrated rural development : an approach to command areas*. Bangalore : IBH Prakashana, 1983, xvi-175 p. bibl. [India]

3709 NEŠIĆ, Dragoljub. "Indijska seoska zajednica" (The Indian village community), *Sociologija Sela* (82), 1983 : 233-243.

3710   NOWAKOWA, Irena. "Rolnicy z wykształceniem. Praca, gospodarstwo, środowisko społeczne" (Educated farmers : work, farm, social environment), *Wieś i Rolnictwo* 42(1), 1984 : 67-84.

3711   NÚÑEZ SOTO, Orlando. *Avances en materia de desarrollo rural en Nicaragua* (Rural development progresses in Nicaragua). Roma : Oficina Regional de la FAO para América Latina y el Caribe; División de Recursos Humanos, Instituciones y Reforma Agraria, FAO, 1984, iv-59 p.

3712   NZEZA, Bilakila. "Mythes et réalités du collectivisme agraire : le cas des Kongos du Bas-Zaïre", *Revue Canadienne d'Études du Développement* 4(2), 1983 : 364-371.

3713   O'BRIEN, Jay. "The social reproduction of tenant cultivators and class formation in the Gezira scheme, Sudan", *Research in Economic Anthropology* 6, 1984 : 217-241.

3714   OMAR LERDA, Francisco. "La diferenciación social en los ejidos y comunidades agrarias" (Social differentiation in 'ejidos' and agrarian communities), *Investigación Económica* (170), oct-dec 84 : 161-185. [Mexico]

3715   OOMEN, T. K. *Social transformation in rural India : mobilization and state intervention.* Delhi : Vikas, 1984, 326 p.

3716   PATEL, M. L. *Planning strategy for tribal development.* Delhi : Inter-India, 1984, 191 p.

3717   PATHY, Jaganath. *Tribal peasantry and dynamics of development.* Delhi : Inter-India, 1984, xiii-233 p.

3718   PERKINS, Dwight Heald; YUSUF, Shahid. *Rural development in China.* Baltimore, MD : Johns Hopkins University Press, 1984, x-235 p. bibl., ind.

3719   PHILLIPS, David R.; WILLIAMS, Allan M. *Rural Britain : a social geography.* Oxford, Oxfordshire : Basil Blackwell, 1984, viii-274 p. ill., bibl., ind.

3720   PILICHOWSKI, Andrzej. "Zespoły rolników indywidualnych : stymulatory i bariery" (Groups of individual farmers : stimulators and barriers), *Roczniki Socjologii Wsi* 18, 1980-81 : 129-136.

3721   PLATTEAU, Jean-Philippe. "The drive towards mechanization of small-scale fisheries in Kerala : a study of the transformation process of traditional village societies", *Development and Change* 15(1), jan 84 : 65-103.

3722   RYSZKOWSKI, Lech. "Ekologiczne zasady kształtowania obszarów wiejskich" (Ecological rules for development of rural areas), *Zagadnienia Ekonomiki Rolnej* (1), 1984 : 16-22.

3723   SETH, A. N. *Peasant organizations in India.* Delhi : B. R. Publishers, 1984, 174 p.

3724   SEVILLA GUZMAN, E. "El campesinado : elementos para su reconstrucción teórica en el pensamiento social" (Peasantry : elements for a theoretical reconstruction in social thought), *Agricultura y Sociedad* 27(4-6), 1983 : 33-79.

3725   SICKING, Thom. *Religion et développement : étude comparée de deux villages libanais.* Beyrouth : Dar El-Machreq, 1984, 230 p. bibl.

3726   SIMUŠ, P. I. "Nekotorye problemy izučenija obraza žizni sovetskoj derevni" (Some problems of study on the way of life in Soviet villages), *Istorija SSSR* 26(3), jun 83 : 3-19.

3727   SMITH, Richard M.; [ed.]. *Land, kinship and life cycle.* Cambridge : University Press, 1984, xiv-547 p. maps, tabl., bibl.

3728   STAROVEROV, V. I.; [ed.]. *Évoljucija krest'janstva socialističeskih stran v poslevoennyj period* (Evolution of the socialist countries peasantry in the post-war period). Moskva : Institut Sociologičeskih Issledovanij Akademija Nauk SSSR, 1984, 180 p.

3729   STRAUCH, Judith. "Community and kinship in Southeastern China : the view of the multilineage villages of Hong-Kong", *Journal of Asian Studies* 43(1), nov 83 : 21-50.

3730   SUAUD, Charles. "Le mythe de la base. Les états généraux du développement agricole et la production d'une parole paysanne", *Actes de la Recherche en Sciences Sociales* 52-53, jun 84 : 56-79. [France]

3731   SUNDARAN, I. S. *Anti-poverty rural development in India.* Delhi : D. K. Publishers, 1984, xviii-297 p.

3732   SZLAJFER, Henryk. "Chłopstwo w strukturze kapitalizmu państwowego : przykład Tanzanii" (Peasantry in the structure of State capitalism : the case of Tanzania), *Roczniki Socjologii Wsi* 18, 1980-81 : 215-238.

3733   SZOBOSZLAI, György. "Az aprófalvak érdekképviselete" (Interest representation of small villages), *Társadalomtudományi Közlemények* 14(2), 1984 : 205-215.

3734   THEKKAMALAI, S. S. *Rural development and social change in India.* Delhi; New Delhi : D. K. Publications, 1983, xv-280 p. bibl., ind.

3735   THOMPSON, Stuart E. "Taiwan : rural society", *China Quarterly* (99), sep 84 : 553-568.

3736   TOLNAY, Stewart E. "Black family formation and tenancy in the farm south, 1900'", *American Journal of Sociology* 90(2), sep 84 : 305-325. [USA]

3737   TÓTH, Pál Péter; [ed.]. *Agrárszociológiai írások Magyarországon, 1900-1945* (Rural sociological writings in Hungary, 1900-1945). Budapest : Kossuth Kiadó, 1984, 35 p.

3738 TROUILLOT, Michel-Rolph. "Caribbean peasantries and world capitalism : an approach to micro-level studies", *Nieuwe West-Indische Gids* 58(1-2), 1984 : 37-59.

3739 TSUCHIDA, Hideo. "Nohson chiiki shakai no hendo" (The transformation of the rural community), *Memoirs of Osaka Kyoiku University* 32(2/3), 1984 : 89-117. [Japan]

3740 WERTH, Nicolas. *La vie quotidienne des paysans russes de la Révolution à la collectivisation : 1917-1939.* Paris : Hachette Littérature, 1984, 410 p. bibl.

3741 WILKINSON, Kenneth P. "Rurality and patterns of social disruption", *Rural Sociology* 49(1), 1984 : 23-36. [USA]

3742 ZASLAVSKAYA, T. I.; MUCHNIK, I. B.; MUCHNIK, M. B. "Problems of zonal differentiation of specific rural development programmes", *Social Indicators Research* 14(3), apr 84 : 351-362. [USSR]

3743 ZOTOVA, O. I.; [et al.]. *Osobennosti psihologii krest'janstva : prošloe i nastojašče* (Features of peasantry psychology : past and present). Moskva : Nauka, 1983, 168 p.

16320 Urban sociology
Sociologie urbaine

3744 "Capitales de la couleur", *Autrement. Série Monde* (9), oct 84 : 1-316. [Southern Africa] [With contributions by Jean-François LANTERI, Alain MARIE]

3745 "Cities in transformation, class, capital, and the State", *Urban Affairs Annual Reviews* 26, 1984 : 1-263. [USA] [With contributions by Michael Peter SMITH, Robert A. BEAUREGARD, Michael D. KENNEDY, Saskia SASSEN-KOOB]

3746 "Droit (Le) au logement (Journées mexicaines)", *Travaux de l'Association Henri Capitant* 33, 1982 : 1-724. [With contributions by Jacques STASSEN, Fernand BOUYSSOU, David PUGSLEY]

3747 "Green belts", *Planning Outlook* 25(2), 1982 : 41-80. [UK] [With contributions by Richard MUNTON, Patrick LAVERY, Ken WILLIS, Abdul KHAKEE]

3748 "Habitat et développement : des politiques à l'épreuve des résultats", *Économie et Humanisme* (276), apr 84 : 5-50. [With contributions by Isabelle MILBERT, Mahieddine HEDLI, Jean-Pierre FREY]

3749 "Londres", *Autrement. Série Monde* (6), mar 84 : 1-266.

3750 "New hope for cities?", *Urban Affairs Quarterly* 19(4), jun 84 : 429-510. [USA] [With contributions by Stephen L. PERCY, Robert WARREN, Jeffrey L. BRUDNEY]

3751 "Political (The) economy of urbanization in Asia : a special issue", *Comparative Urban Research* 10(1), 83 : 5-107. [With contributions by Martin KING WHYTE, Roger J. NEMETH, David A. SMITH, Mike DOUGLASS]

3752 "Politiques (Les) urbaines françaises depuis 1945 : table ronde 17-18 juin 1982", *Bulletin de l'Institut d'Histoire du Temps Présent* (5), 1984 : 3-137. [Supplément : série histoire urbaine. With contributions by Marie Geneviève DEZES, Antoine PROST]

3753 "Pour une démocratie urbaine", *Parole et Société* 91(5-6), 1983 : 297-396. [With contributions by Xavier OUSSET, Bernadette HUGER, Maurice IMBERT, Christian CARSEN, Jacques CHAUVIN]

3754 "Soviet cities", *Soviet Geography* 25(7), sep 84 : 481-502. [With contributions by G. A. GORNOSTAYEVA, G. L. VASIL'YEV, O. L. PRIVALOVA, I. V. NIKOL'SKIY]

3755 "Tokyo", *Autrement. Série Monde* (8), sep 84 : 1-344.

3756 "Urban ecology", *Social Forces* 62(4), jun 84 : 905-940. [USA] [With contributions by Barry EDMONSTON, Thomas M. GUTERBOCK, Isaac W. EBERSTEIN, Omer R. GALLE]

3757 "Urban policy problems", *Policy Studies Review* 3(1), aug 83 : 41-119. [USA] [With contributions by Harry RICHARDSON, Donald L. FAIRCHILD, John D. HUTCHESON JR.]

3758 "Urban theory and national urban policy", *Urban Affairs Quarterly* 19(1), sep 83 : 3-132. [USA] [With contributions by John D. KASARDA, Roger FRIEDLAND, Terry Nichols CLARK, John R. LOGAN, Elinor OSTROM]

3759 ADENIJI, Kunle. "Local planning authorities and the crisis of urban growth management in Nigeria : the Oyo State experience", *Planning and Administration* 11(1), spr 84 : 24-29.

3760 AIT-AMARA, Hamid. "Le développement urbain et industriel en Algérie et les mutations de la société rurale", *Revue Algérienne des Sciences Juridiques, Économiques et Politiques* 20(3), sep 83 : 169-179.

3761 AITOV, N. A.; KAMAEV, R. B. "O metodologii izučenija social'nyh različij goroda i derevni" (On the methodology of study on social differences between towns and villages), *Sociologičeskie Issledovanija (Moskva)* (2), 1983 : 136-140.

3762 ALALUF, Mateo. "Ville-objet et vils sujets", *Annales de l'Institut de Sociologie*, 1983 : 21-34.

3763   ALTHADE, Gérard; LÉGÉ, Bernard; SÉLIM, Monique. *Urbanisme et réhabilitation symbolique : Ivry, Boulogne, Amiens.* Paris : Anthropos, 1984, 297 p. [France]

3764   AMIS, Philip. "Squatters of tenants : the commercialization of unauthorized housing in Nairobi", *World Development* 12(1), jan 84 : 87-96. [Kenya]

3765   ANDRLE, Alois; SRB, Vladimír. "Bydlení rodin ve svétle údajů sčítání lidu, domů a bytů 1980" (Housing of families in light of 1980 population and housing census data), *Demografie* 26(2), 1984 : 99-109. [Czechoslovakia]

3766   ANKERL, Guy. "Sur-urbanisation dans le Tiers-Monde?", *Futuribles* (73), jan 84 : 25-48.

3767   ASIANA, Setle Opumi. "The land factor in housing for low income urban settlers : the example of Nadina, Ghana", *Third World Planning Review* 6(2), mai 84 : 171-184.

3768   BAHR, Jürgen; MERTINS, Günter. "Un modelo de diferenciación socio-espacial de las metropolis de América latina" (A model of socio-spatial differentiation of Latin America's metropolis), *Revista Geográfica* (98), dec 83 : 23-29.

3769   BARDO, John W. "A reexamination of the neighborhood as a socio-spatial schema", *Sociological Inquiry* 54(3), 1984 : 346-358. [Hemel Hempstead, UK]

3770   BAUDELLE, Guy. *Villeneuve d'Ascq, ville nouvelle : un exemple d'urbanisme concerté.* Paris : Éditions du 'Moniteur', 1984, 198 p. ill., cartes.

3771   BENTHAM, C. G. "Urban problems and public dissatisfaction in the metropolitan areas of England", *Regional Studies* 17(5), oct 83 : 339-346.

3772   BEREY, Katalin. "A lakáspolitikai stratégiák típusai. Nyugat-európai és egyesült államokbeli tapasztalatok" (Types of strategy of housing policy. Experiences in Western Europe and in the United States), *Szociológia* 12(3), 1983 : 319-325.

3773   BERTRAND, Michel-Jean. "Une approche de la forme urbaine et de la centralité", *Annales de Géographie* 93(520), dec 84 : 666-686.

3774   BLUM, Terry C.; KINGSTON, Paul William. "Home ownership and social attachment", *Sociological Perspectives* 27(2), apr 84 : 159-180. [USA]

3775   BOND, Andrew R. "Urban planning and design in the Soviet North : the Noril'sk experience", *Soviet Geography* 25(3), mar 84 : 145-165.

3776   BONVALET, Catherine. "Évolutions démographiques et logement", *Revue Française des Affaires Sociales* 38(suppl.), jun 84 : 187-204. [France]

3777   BOURNE, Larry S. "Urban Canada in transition. Recent patterns of social and demo-graphic change", *Zeitschrift der Gesellschaft für Kanada-Studien* 4(2), 1984 : 65-84.

3778   BOZON, Michel. *Vie quotidienne et rapports sociaux dans une petite ville de province : la mise en scène des différences.* Lyon : Presses Universitaires de Lyon, 1984, 300 p. bibl., ind.

3779   BRADNOCK, Robert W. *Urbanisation in India.* London : J. Murray, 1984, vi-58 p. ill., bibl., ind.

3780   BRAMBILA, Carlos; SALAZAR, Héctor. "Concentración y distribución de los tamaños de ciudades en México 1940 a 1980" (Urban concentration and distribution by size in Mexico, 1940-1980), *Demografía y Economía* 18(1), jan-mar 84 : 48-85.

3781   BURSIK, Robert J. Jr. "Urban dynamics and ecological studies of delinquency", *Social Forces* 63(2), dec 84 : 393-413.

3782   ČALDAROVIĆ, Ognjen. "Bibliografija radova o čikaškoj sociološkoj školi dvadesetih i tridesetih godina ovog stoljeća" (Bibliography of works of the Chicago School of Sociology), *Revija za Sociologiju* 13(1-4), 1983 : 115-125.

3783   CELA, Jorge. "El estudio de la ciudad. Notas bibliográficas sobre sociología urbana" (Urban study. Bibliography on urban sociology), *Estudios Sociales* 16(53), nov 83 : 55-66. [Dominican Republic]

3784   CHABBI, Morched. "Urbanisation spontanée et acteurs fonciers : le cas des lotisseurs clandestins à Tunis", *Genève-Afrique* 22(1), 1984 : 123-137.

3785   CHATTERJEE, Lata; NIJKAMP, Peter; [eds.]. *Urban and regional policy analysis in developing countries.* Aldershot, Hants; Brookfield, VT : Gower, 1983, vii-270 p. ill., bibl.

3786   COHEN, Erik. "The social transformation of a market township in Southern Thailand", *Pacific Viewpoint* 24(2), oct 83 : 167-188.

3787   COURADE, Georges; BRUNEAU, Michel. "Développement rural et processus d'urbanisation dans le Tiers-Monde", *Cahiers ORSTOM. Série Sciences Humaines* 19(1), 1983 : 59-92.

3788   DAHMANN, Donald C. "Racial differences in housing consumption during the 1970s : insights from a components of inventory change analysis", *Urban Geography* 4(3), sep 83 : 203-222. [USA]

3789   DAIDO, Yasujiro; OKUDA, Noriaki. *Henbo suru shuhen toshi -Takarazuka-shi no case study* (Suburban community in transition : a case study in Takarazuka city). Tokyo : Koseisha Koseikaku, 1984, 292 p. [Japan]

3790   DÁNIEL, Zsuzsa; TEMESI, József. "A lakáselosztás hatása a társadalmi egyenlőtlenségre, 1976-1980" (Effect of dwelling distribution on social inequality, 1976-1980), *Statisztikai Szemle* 62(7), jul 84 : 687-701. [Hungary]

3791   DARMAU, Frédéric; HEGIN, Patrick. "Le logement social depuis 1820", *Regards sur l'Actualité* (97), jan 84 : 24-35. [France]

3792   DE CASTRO, Iná Elias. "Housing projects : widening the controversy surrounding the removal of 'favelas' ", *Revista Geográfica* (97), jun 83 : 56-69. [Brazil]

3793   DE PINA CABRAL, João. "Comentários críticos sobre a casa e a família no Alto Minho rural" (Critical comment about home and family in the rural Alto Minho), *Análise Social* 20(2-3), 1984 : 263-284. [Portugal]

3794   DEL ACEBO IBAÑEZ, Enrique; [ed.]. *La ciudad. Su esencia, su historia, sus patologías* (The city. Its essence, history and pathologies). Buenos Aires : Ediciones FADES, 1984, 393 p.

3795   DELLE DONNE, Marcella. "Roma marginale : analisi di una realtà fisiologica della città" (Marginale Rome : analysis of a physiological reality of the city), *Critica Sociologica* 69, spr 84 : 93-117.

3796   DEN BOON, A. K.; DE RUITER, Bob. "Amsterdam en zijn krakers, een ondersoeksnotitie" (Amsterdam and the squatters' riots, a research note), *Sociologische Gids* 31(2), 1984 : 184-189.

3797   DOH, Rainer. "Urbanisierung und Bevölkerungsentwicklung in den türkischen Regionen" (Urbanization and demographic evolution in Turkish regions), *Orient* 24(3), sep 83 : 486-500.

3798   DREIER, Peter. "The tenants' movement in the United States", *International Journal of Urban and Regional Research* 8(2), 84 : 255-279. [FRE; GER; SPA]

3799   DUPREZ, Dominique. "Les squatters : les genèses sociales d'un mouvement urbain localisé", *Contradictions* (38), wint 84 : 103-123. [France]

3800   DUREZ-DEMAL, Martine. *La politique du logement social.* Bruxelles : Centre de Recherche et d'Information Socio-Politiques, 1983, 38 p. ill., bibl., tabl. [Belgium]

3801   EBERSTEIN, Isaac W.; GALLE, Omer R. "The metropolitan system in the South : functional differentiation and trade patterns", *Social Forces* 62(4), jun 84 : 926-94O. [USA]

3802   EDMONSTON, Barry; GUTERBOCK, Thomas M. "Is suburbanization slowing down? Recent trends in population deconcentration in US metropolitan areas", *Social Forces* 62(4), jun 84 : 905-925.

3803   ENGLAND, J. Lynn; ALBRECHTS, Stan L. "Boomtowns and social disruption", *Rural Sociology* 49(2), 1984 : 230-246. [USA]

3804   ENOSH, Nava; LESLAU, Abraham; SHACHAM, Josef. "Residential quality assessment : a conceptual model and empirical test", *Social Indicators Research* 14(4), mai 84 : 453-476. [Israel]

3805   ENYEDI, György. *Az urbanizációs ciklus és a magyar településhálózat átalakulása* (The urbanization cycle and the transformation of the Hungarian settlement network). Budapest : Akadémiai Kiadó, 1984, 37 p.

3806   ERCOLE, Enrico. "Politica urbana e consumi culturali" (Urban policy and cultural consumption), *Quaderni di Sociologia* 30(2-3-4), 1982 : 456-482. [Italy]

3807   ERDMANN, Claudia. "Emtwicklungsphasen der New Towns in Schottland. Von der Gartenstadt zum Regionalzentrum" (Stages of development of the New Towns in Scotland. From the garden town to the regional centre), *Geographische Rundschau* 35(9), 1983 : 434-458.

3808   ERVIN, Delbert J. "Correlates of urban residential structure", *Sociological Focus* 17(1), jan 84 : 59-75. [USA]

3809   FINDLAY, Allan; [et al.]. "Maintaining the status quo : an analysis of social space in post-colonial Rabat", *Urban Studies* 21(1), feb 84 : 41-51. [Morocco]

3810   FIREBAUGH, Glenn. "Urbanization of the nonfarm population : a research note on the convergence of rich and poor nations", *Social Forces* 62(3), mar 84 : 775-783.

3811   FISHER, David Hackett; [ed.]. *Concord : the social history of a New England town, 1750-1850.* Waltham : Brandeis University, 1983, 400 p. bibl.

3812   FOURNIER, Serge. "La dynamique de la croissance urbaine d'une ville moyenne française : le modèle CARPE", *Revue d'Économie Régionale et Urbaine* (1), 1984 : 67-94.

3813   FRACKIEWICZ, Lucyna. "Społeczne aspekty urbanizacji" (Social aspects of urbanization), *Polityka Społeczna* 11(8), 1984 : 1-4. [Poland]

3814   FRANCE. SECRÉTARIAT GÉNÉRAL DU GROUPE CENTRAL DES VILLES NOUVELLES, *Villes nouvelles de France.* Paris : le Secrétariat, 1983, 48 p. ill., cartes.

3815   FRIEDLAND, Roger; PALMER, Donald. "Park place and main street : business and the urban power structure", *Annual Review of Sociology* 10, 1984 : 393-416.

3816   FUJITA, Hiroo. "Toshi to kokka no kankei ni tsuite -urban sociology ni kansuru ichi kohsatsu" (Study of urban sociology), *Shakaigaku Hyoron* 34(4), 1984 : 421-436.

3817   GILBERT, Alan. "Planning, invasions and land speculation : the role of the State in
        Venezuela", *Third World Planning Review* 6(3), aug 84 : 225-238.
3818   GOLDSTONE, Jack A. "Urbanization and inflation : lessons from the English price
        revolution of the sixteenth and seventeenth centuries", *American Journal of Sociology* 89(5),
        mar 84 : 1122-1160.
3819   GRANT, Jonathan S.; KWOK, Yin-Wang. "Planning and development in China and
        Hong-Kong", *Third World Planning Review* 6(1), feb 84 : 1-115. [With contributions by
        David D. BUCK, Léon HOA, Xue-Quiang XU, K. S. PUN, Alexander CUTHBERT]
3820   GREENHALGH, Susan. "Networks and their modes : urban society on Taiwan", *China
        Quarterly* (99), sep 84 : 529-552.
3821   GRIGAS, R. S. "Gorod kak ob'ekt kompleksnogo sociologičeskogo issledovanija" (Town
        as an object of complex sociological research), *Trudy Akademii Nauk Litovskoj SSR. Serija
        Obščestvennye Nauki* (3), 1983 : 51-60.
3822   GUEST, Avery M. "Robert Park and the natural area : a sentimental review", *Sociology
        and Social Research* 69(1), oct 84 : 1-21.
3823   GUEST, Avery M.; LEE, Barrett A. "The social organization of local areas", *Urban Affairs
        Quarterly* 19(2), dec 83 : 217-240. [USA]
3824   GULIĆ, Andrej. "Stambena problematika radnika doseljenih u Ljubljanu" (Housing
        problems of migrant workers in Ljubljana), *Sociologija Sela* (82), 1983 : 199-209.
        [Yugoslavia]
3825   HAAR, Charles M.; HOROWITZ, Steven. "A perspective on planning in Jerusalem",
        Urban Law and Policy 6(3), jun 84 : 279-292.
3826   HAMNETT, Chris. "Housing the two nations : socio-tenurial polarization in England
        and Wales, 1961-81", *Urban Studies* 21(4), nov 84 : 389-405.
3827   HARDOY, J. E.; PORTES, A.; [comps.]. *Ciudades y sistemas urbanos* (Cities and urban
        systems). Buenos Aires : Consejo Latinoamericano de Ciencias Sociales, 1984, 258 p.
3828   HAUSLADEN, Gary. "The satellite city in Soviet urban development", *Soviet Geography*
        25(4), apr 84 : 229-247.
3829   HEGEDÜS, József; TOSICS, Iván. "Lakásreform a nyolcvanas években" (Reform of the
        housing policy in the eighties in Hungary), *Medvetánc* 2-3(4-1), 1983-84 : 177-200.
3830   HENDERSON, Jeff; KARN, Valerie. "Race, class and the allocation of public housing
        in Britain", *Urban Studies* 21(2), mai 84 : 115-128.
3831   HERBERT, D. T.; HIJAZI, Naila B. "Urban deprivation in the developing world : the
        case of Khartoum/Omdurman", *Third World Planning Review* 6(3), aug 84 : 263-281.
        [Sudan]
3832   HERDOIZA, Wilson. "Autogestion urbaine en Equateur", *Études Foncières* (21),
        aut 83 : 23-28.
3833   HESSE, Joachim Jens; WOLLMANN, Hellmut; [eds.]. *Probleme der Stadtpolitik in den 80er
        Jahren* (Problems of urban policy in the eighties). Frankfurt-am-Main; New York, NY :
        Campus, 1983, 438 p. ill., bibl.
3834   HODŽIĆ, Alija. "Urbanizacija kao element kulturne transformacije sela" (Urbanisation
        as an element of cultural transformation), *Sociologija Sela* 21(79-81), 1983 : 127-138.
        [Yugoslavia]
3835   HOFMEISTER, Burkhard. "Die südafrikanische Stadt. Versuch eines Strukturschemas
        der Städte in der Republik Südafrika" (The South-African town. Looking at a structure
        pattern of towns in the Republic of South Africa), *Erde* 114(4), 1983 : 256-274.
3836   HOHM, Charles F. "Housing aspirations and fertility", *Sociology and Social Research* 68(3),
        apr 84 : 350-363. [USA]
3837   HOLTON, R. J. "Cities and transitions to capitalism and socialism", *International Journal of
        Urban and Regional Research* 8(1), mar 84 : 13-37. [FRE; GER; SPA]
3838   IBAROLLA, Jesus. *Se loger au XXᵉ siècle : le logement ouvrier à l'époque contemporaine*. Grenoble :
        Université des Sciences Sociales, Centre de Recherche d'Histoire Économique Sociale
        et Institutionnelle, 1984, xvi-123 p.
3839   IBARRA, Valentín; PUENTE, Sergio; SCHTEINGART, Martha. "La ciudad y el medio
        ambiente" (City and its environment), *Demografía y Economía* 18(1), jan-mar 84 : 110-143.
3840   ISLAMI, Hivzi. "Problemi urbanizacija i standarda ruralnih naselja Kosova" (Problems of
        urbanization and of the standard of living of Kosovo rural settlements), *Sociologija* 26(3-4),
        jul-dec 84 : 317-324.
3841   ISOMURA, Ei'ichi. *Sumai no shakaigaku 20 no sho* (Sociolog of urban dwellings). Tokyo :
        Mainichi-shinbun-sha, 1984, 269 p. [Japan]
3842   IVANOV, Ju M. "Razvivajuščiesja strany : problemy kapitalističeskoj ėvoljucii otnošenij
        garoda : derevni" (Developing countries : urban-rural relationship development
        problems), *Voprosy Istorii* 58(8), aug 84 : 51-66.

3843   IWASAKI, Nobuhiko; YOSHIHARA, Naoki. "Chiiki shakai kenkyu no tohtatsu ten to kadai" (Tasks facing urban sociology in Japan), *For New Sociology* 10(2/3), 1984 : 43-65.
3844   JACQUEMET, Gérard. *Belleville au XIXe siècle : du faubourg à la ville*. Paris : Éditions de l'École des Hautes Études en Sciences Sociales, Touzot, 1984, 452 p. cartes, bibl.
3845   JAŁOWIECKI, Bohdan. "Wartości nowoczesnej urbanistyki" (Values of modern town planning), *Studia Socjologiczne* 92(1), 1984 : 193-207.
3846   JANICKIJ, O. N. "Socialistčeskij gorod : razvitie prirodoohrannoj dejatel'nosti naselenija" (The socialist town : environment protection development), *Rabočij Klass i Sovremennyj Mir* (3), jun 84 : 47-60.
3847   JENKINS, S. P.; MAYNARD, A. K. "Intergenerational continuities in housing", *Urban Studies* 20(4), nov 83 : 431-438.
3848   JOHNSON, Nan E. "Housing quality and child mortality in the rural Philippines", *Journal of Biosocial Science* 16(4), oct 84 : 531-540.
3849   KELEN, András. "A synoikismostól a városig" (From the synoikismos to the city), *Szociológia* 12(1-2), 1983 : 17-26.
3850   KENNEDY, Leslie W. *The urban kaleidoscope : Canadian perspectives*. Toronto, ON; New York, NY... McGraw-Hill Ryerson, 1983, xv-184 p. bibl., ind., ill.
3851   KJAER JENSEN, Mogens. *Unges boligsituation* (Youth housing situation). København : Teknisk Forlag, 1983, 139 p. ill., bibl. [Denmark]
3852   KOMAI, Hiroshi. "Jyumin sanka to bunsan-gata toshi keikaku -Tronto no jikken" (Citizen participation and decentralized city planning : an experiment in Toronto), *in : Ohashi, Kaoru;* [ed.], Urbanization problem in welfare countries Tokyo : Kakiuchi Shuppan, 1984, 296-310 p.
3853   KRAUS, Vered. "Social segregation in Israel as a function of objective and subjective attributes of the ethnic groups", *Sociology and Social Research* 69(1), oct 84 : 50-71.
3854   LAKE, Robert W.; [ed.]. *Readings in urban analysis : perspectives on urban form and structure*. New Brunswick, NJ : Rutgers University, Center for Urban Policy Research, 1983, xxv-316 p.
3855   LEAVITT, Jacqueline; SAEGERT, Susan. "Women and abandoned buildings : a feminist approach to housing", *Social Policy* 15(1), sum 84 : 32-39. [USA]
3856   LEE, Barrett A.; [et al.]. "Testing the decline-of-community thesis : neighborhood organizations in Seattle, 1929 and 1979", *American Journal of Sociology* 89(5), mar 84 : 1161-1188. [USA]
3857   LENNARD, Suzanne H. Crowhurst; LENNARD, Henry L. *Public life in urban places : social and architectural characteristics conducive to public life in European cities*. Southampton, NY : Gondolier Press, 1984, 74 p. ill., bibl.
3858   LINN, Johannes F. *Cities in the developing world : policies for their equitable and efficient growth*. New York, NY; Oxford... Oxford University Press, 1983, xxi-230 p.
3859   LOGAN, John R. "The disappearance of communities from national urban policy", *Urban Affairs Quarterly* 19(1), sep 83 : 75-90. [USA]
3860   MADHAVA RAO, A. G.; [et al.]; [eds.]. *Modern trends in housing in developing countries*. Delhi : Oxford & I.B.H., 1984, 380 p.
3861   MAGLIONE, Jean. "Quartiers dégradés : des espaces à rétablir ou une histoire à réhabiliter? Que font les techniciens du cadre de vie?", *Annales de la Recherche Urbaine* (21), jan 84 : 106-122. [France]
3862   MALDONADO, Victor Alfonso. "Fenómenos de maldesarrollo urbano en México" (Phenomena of urban misdevelopment in Mexico), *Rivista di Studi Politici Internazionali* 50(4), dec 83 : 583-588.
3863   MALIĆ, Adolf. "Urbanizacija i infrastrukturna opremljenost sela u SR Hrvatskoj" (The urbanization and infrastructural development of villages in the Socialist Republic of Croatia), *Sociologija Sela* 21(79-81), 1983 : 139-150.
3864   MALIKOWSKI, Marian. "Obiektywne aspekty więzi mieszkańców z miastem : na przykładzie Rzeszowa" (Objective aspects of the ties between the town-dwellers and their town : an example of Rzeszów), *Studia Socjologiczne* 92(1), 1984 : 211-230.
3865   MALIKOWSKI, Marian. *Więź mieszkańców z miastem. Studium socjologiczne na przykładzie społeczeństwa miasta Rzeczowa* (Bond of inhabitants with their city. Sociological study based on the example of the community of the city of Rzeszów). Rzeszów : Towarzystwo Naukowe w Rzeszowie, 1984, 156 p.
3866   MANN, Susan. "Urbanization and historical change in China", *Modern China* 10(1), jan 84 : 79-114.
3867   MCLEAY, E. M. "Housing as a political issue : a comparative study", *Comparative Politics* 17(1), oct 84 : 85-105. [UK; New Zealand]
3868   MERRETT, Stephen. "The assessment of housing consumption requirements in developing countries", *Third World Planning Review* 6(4), nov 84 : 319-329.

3869   MERTINS, Günter. "Marginalsiedlungen in Grossstädten der Dritten Welt" (Marginal
         settlements in the big cities of the third world), *Geographische Rundschau* 36(9), 1984 : 434-442.
3870   MEYER, David R. "Control and coordination links in the metropolitan system of cities : the
         South as case study", *Social Forces* 63(2), dec 84 : 349-362. [USA]
3871   MIRLOUP, Joël. "Tourisme et loisirs en milieux urbain et péri-urbain en France",
         Annales de Géographie 93(520), dec 84 : 704-718.
3872   MIROWSKI, Włodzimierz; MLINAR, Zdravko; [eds.]. *Urban social processes in Poland and
         Yugoslavia : theoretical and methodological issues.* Warszawa : Polska Akademia Nauk Instytut
         Filozofii i Socjologii, 1984, 174 p.
3873   MISHRA, G. N. *Urban politics in India.* Meerut : Anu Books, 1984, 164-xii p.
3874   MÖLLER, Hans-Georg. "Elat. Stadtplanung und Stadtentwicklung" (Elat. Town planning
         and town development), *Erde* 114(4), 1983 : 275-288.
3875   MOLOTCH, Harvey; LOGAN, John. "Tensions in the growth machine : overcoming
         resistance to value free development", *Social Problems* 31(5), jun 84 : 483-499. [USA]
3876   MORTON, Henry W. "La ville soviétique contemporaine", *Revue d'Études Comparatives
         Est-Ouest* 15(2), jun 84 : 5-28.
3877   MUOGHALU, Leonard N. "Subjective indices of housing satisfaction as social indicators
         for planning public housing in Nigeria", *Social Indicators Research* 15(2), aug 84 : 145-164.
3878   MUSIL, Siri; RYSAVY, Zdenek. "Urban and regional processes under capitalism and
         socialism : a case study from Czechoslovakia", *International Journal of Urban and Regional
         Research* 7(4), dec 83 : 495-527. [FRE; GER; SPA]
3879   NIITSU, Koichi. "Hatten tojyo koku 4 toshi ni okeru suramu jyumin no ishiki" (Types of
         attitude of slum dwellers in four selected cities of developing countries : overall and com-
         parative view), *Ajia Keizai* 25(4), 1984 : 18-39.
3880   NIITSU, Koichi. "Hatten tojyo koku no toshi-ka to suramu" (Urbanization and slum
         dwellers in developing countries), *Ajia Keizai* 25(4), 1984 : 5-17.
3881   NORRIS, William P. "Patron-client relationships in the urban social structure : a Brazilian
         case study", *Human Organization* 43(1), spr 84 : 16-26.
3882   NOSCHIS, Kaj. *Signification affective du quartier.* Paris : Méridiens, 1984, 170 p.
3883   O'NEILL, Maria Monica. "Segregaçaõ residencial" (Residential segregation), *Revista
         Geográfica* (97), jun 83 : 36-43. [Brazil]
3884   PADDISON, R.; [et al.]. "Restructuring the urban planning machine : a comparison of
         two North African cities", *Third World Planning Review* 6(3), aug 84 : 283-298.
3885   PAUL-LÉVY, Françoise. *La ville en croix : de la Révolution de 1848 à la rénovation haussmannienne :
         éléments pour une problématique générale.* Paris : Méridiens, 1984, 239 p. bibl. [France]
3886   PEIL, Margaret; SADA, Pius O. *African urban society.* Chichester : Wiley, 1984, xi-391 p.
3887   PLETSCH, Alfred. "Die 'Villes Nouvelles' in Frankreich" (The 'Villes Nouvelles' in
         France), *Geographische Rundschau* 35(9), 1983 : 425-432.
3888   POLYAN, P. M. "The support frame of settlement in the Caucasus", *Soviet Geography*
         25(8), oct 84 : 559-571.
3889   POPOVSKI, Vesna. "Čikaška škola u urbanoj sociologiji" (The Chicago School of Urban
         Sociology), *Revija za Sociologiju* 13(1-4), 1983 : 103-113.
3890   PRUVOT, Michel; WEBER-KLEIN, Christiane. "Écologie urbaine factorielle comparée :
         essai méthodologique et application à Strasbourg", *Espace Géographique* 13(2), jun
         84 : 136-150. [France]
3891   RANGA RAO, K. *Cities and slums : a study of a squattor's settlement in the city of Vijayawada.*
         Delhi : Concept, 1984, 117 p. [India]
3892   RICH, Jonathan M. "Municipal boundaries in a discriminatory housing market : an
         example of racial leap-frogging", *Urban Studies* 21(1), feb 84 : 31-40. [USA]
3893   RIVIERE D'ARC, Hélène; SCHNEIER, Graciela. "Activités informelles et espace : le
         cas Guyana (Venezuela) et Camaçari (Brésil)", *Tiers-Monde* 24(95), sep 83 : 653-668.
3894   RONNÅS, Per. *Urbanization in Romania : a geography of social and economic change since
         independence.* Stockholm : Economic Research Institute, Stockholm School of Economics,
         1984, xvi-398 p. bibl.
3895   ROWLAND, Richard H. "The growth of large cities in the USSR : policies and trends
         1959-1979", *Urban Geography* 4(3), sep 83 : 258-279.
3896   RUDDER, Véronique de. "Le logement des Maghrébins : racisme et habitat", *Temps
         Modernes* 40(452-453-454), mai 84 : 1956-1974.
3897   RYU, Jai Poong. *Residential segregation of blacks in metropolitan America.* Seoul : American Studies
         Institute, Seoul National University, 1983, 281 p. ill., bibl., ind.
3898   SACHS, Ignacy. "Les grandes villes face à la crise : travail, nourriture et énergie dans
         l'éco-développement urbain", *Amérique Latine* (18), jun 84 : 30-43. [Latin America]

3899   SÁNCHEZ LEÓN, Abelardo; OLIVERA C., Luis; [eds.]. *Lima, una metrópoli : 7 debates*
        (Lima, a metropolis : 7 debates). Lima : Desco, 1983, 274 p. ill., bibl.
3900   ŠATALIN, S.; PČELINCEV, O. "Urbanizacija v uslovijah NTR" (Urbanization under
        conditions of the scientific and technical revolution), *Obščestvennye Nauki (Moskva)* (4),
        1984 : 26-39.
3901   SCHABERT, Tilo. "Planen für die Renaissance der Stadt : die neue Stadtentwicklungspolitik
        in Frankreich" (Plans for urban renewal : the new policy for urban development in
        France), *Archiv für Kommunalwissenschaften* 22(1), 1983 : 74-90.
3902   SHARMA, Krishna Datta. *Urban development in the metropolitan shadow : a case study from
        Haryana*. Delhi : Inter-India, 1984, 200 p.
3903   SIQUEIRA, Lêda; SOUZA, Aída L. F. de. "The evolution of metropolitan spaces in
        Brazil'', *Revista Geográfica* (97), jun 83 : 10-28. [See also ibid. : pp. 29-30 by Nice Lecocq
        MULLER]
3904   SMITH, W. Randy; SELWOOD, David F. "Office location and the density-distance
        relationship", *Urban Geography* 4(4), dec 83 : 302-316. [USA]
3905   ST. JOHN, Craig; CLARK, Frieda. "Race and social class conferences in the characteristics
        desired in residential neighborhoods", *Social Science Quarterly* 65(3), sep 84 : 803-813.
        [USA]
3906   ST. JOHN, Craig; CLARK, Frieda. "Racial differences in dimensions of neighborhood
        satisfaction", *Social Indicators Research* 15(1), jul 84 : 43-60. [USA]
3907   STAHURA, John M. "A research note on the metropolitan determinants of suburban
        persistence", *Social Forces* 62(3), mar 84 : 767-774. [USA]
3908   STERNSTEIN, Larry. "The growth of the population of the world's preeminent 'primate
        city' : Bangkok at its bicentenary", *Journal of Southeast Asian Studies* 15(1), mar 84 : 43-68.
3909   STUCLIFFE, Anthony; [ed.]. *Metropolis, 1890-1940*. Chicago, IL : University of Chicago
        Press, 1984, viii-458 p. ill., bibl., ind.
3910   SULLIVAN, O.; MURPHY, M. J. "Housing pathways and stratification : some evidence
        from a British national survey", *Journal of Social Policy* 13(2), apr 84 : 147-165.
3911   SUTTLES, Gerald D. "The cumulative texture of local urban culture", *American Journal of
        Sociology* 90(2), sep 84 : 283-304. [USA]
3912   SWEDNER, Harald. *Human welfare and action research in urban settings : essays on the implementation
        of social change*. Stockholm : Delegation for Social Research; Swedish Council for Building
        Research, 1983, 276 p. bibl., ind., ill.
3913   SZIRMAI, Viktória. "Várostervezés, új városok, urbanisztikai problémák a szocialista
        társadalomban" (Town-planning, new towns, problems of urbanism in the socialist
        society), *Társadalomtudományi Közlemények* 14(1), 1984 : 122-137.
3914   TACCHI, Enrico Maria. "La sociologia del territorio" (Urban sociology), *Studi di Sociologia*
        22(3), jul-sep 84 : 317-326.
3915   TUCKER, S. N. "An analysis of housing subsidy schemes in Australia", *Urban Studies*
        20(4), nov 83 : 439-453.
3916   URANO, Masaki. "Chiiki jyumin soshiki to jishin bohsai -chiiki boshai eno torikumi no
        jittai to kadai o meggute" (Neighborhood organizations and earthquake disaster preven-
        tion), *Shakaikagaku Tokyu* 29, 1984 : 99-151.
3917   URANO, Masaki. "Toshi-ka ronso to gendai toshi-shakaigaku -Ohmi riron o megutte"
        (Symposium on urbanization and urban sociology of today), *Shakaigaku Nenshi* 25,
        1984 : 101-120.
3918   VIRTANEN, Pekka V. "Urban land policy in developing countries : congresses and
        reality", *Planning and Administration* 11(1), spr 84 : 7-14.
3919   WALLIS, Aleksander. "Struktury społeczne wobec urbanizacyjnej hipertrofii" (Social
        structures facing urban hipertrophy), *Kultura i Społeczeństwo* 28(3), 1984 : 3-8.
3920   WALSH, A. Crosbie. "The search for an appropriate housing policy in Fiji", *Third World
        Planning Review* 6(2), mai 84 : 185-199.
3921   WEBBER, Michael John. *Explanation, prediction, and planning : the Lowry model*. London : Pion,
        1984, 214 p. ill., bibl., ind.
3922   WELFELD, Irving; CARMEL, Joseph. "A new wave housing program : respecting the
        intelligence of the poor", *Urban Law and Policy* 6(3), jun 84 : 293-302. [USA]
3923   WHYTE, Martin Kind; PARISH, William L. *Urban life in contemporary China*. Chicago, IL :
        University of Chicago Press, 1984, viii-408 p. ind., map, ill
3924   WILSON, Franklin D. "Urban ecology : urbanization and systems of cities", *Annual Review
        of Sociology* 10, 1984 : 283-307.
3925   YANITSKI, Oleg. "Connaissance écologique et théorie de l'urbanisation", *Sciences Sociales
        — Académie des Sciences de l'URSS* (2), 1984 : 141-160.

3926   YOSHIHARA, Naoki. "Toshi-shakaigaku no atarashii choryu -oboegaki" (A new trend
        in urban sociology — a memorandum), _For New Sociology_ 10(1), 1984 : 1-15.
3927   ZIMMERMANN, Janos J. "Neue Städte in Ägypten" (New towns in Egypt), _Geographische
        Rundschau_ 36(5), 1984 : 230-235.
3928   ZIÓŁKOWSKI, Marian. "Zmiany w sytuacji mieszkaniowej ludności w latach 1978-1982"
        (Changes in housing situation of population in 1978-1982), _Wiadomości Statystyczne_ 29(1),
        1984 : 5-7. [Poland]
3929   ZITOUNI, Françoise. "Le mal-habiter : exclusion et précarisation par l'habitat", _Projet_
        (182), feb 84 : 203-213. [France]
3930   ZONN, Leo E. "Decision-making within a constrained population : residential choice by
        Black urban households", _Journal of Black Studies_ 14(3), mar 84 : 327-340. [USA]

17100   ECONOMIC SOCIOLOGY
SOCIOLOGIE ÉCONOMIQUE

3931   DEVINE, T. M.; DICKSON, David; [eds.]. *Ireland and Scotland, 1600-1850 : parallels and contrasts in economic and social development*. Edinburgh : Donald; Atlantic Highlands, NJ : Humanities Press, 1983, 283 p.

17200   ECONOMIC SYSTEMS
SYSTÈMES ÉCONOMIQUES

17210   Economic doctrines
Doctrines économiques

3932   "Current problems in copyright", *Library Trends* 32(2), aut 83 : 161-248. [USA] [With contributions by Roger D. BILLINGS, Jerome K. MILLER, Linda M. MATTHEWS]
3933   ABRAMS, Howard B. "Copyright, misappropriation, and preemption : constituional and statutory limits of state law protection", *Supreme Court Review*, 1983 : 509-581. [USA]
3934   BENCHENEB, Ali. "Les contrats et le droit d'auteur en Algérie", *Revue Algérienne des Sciences Juridiques, Économiques et Politiques* 20(3), sep 83 : 183-240.
3935   HRYNIEWICZ, Janusz T. "Stan badań nad stosunkami własności w Polsce" (The state of research on the property relations in Poland), *Studia Socjologiczne* 94(3), 1984 : 70-88.
3936   KOZYR-KOWALSKI, Stanisław. "Klasy społeczeństwa a ekonomiczno-socjologiczne pojmowanie własności" (Social classes and the socio-economic conception of property), *Kultura i Społeczeństwo* 28(1), 1984 : 15-30. [Continued in ibid. : 28(2), 1984 : 129-153]
3937   MADJARIAN, Grégoire. "Le jeu sémantique du concept de propriété et le matérialisme économique de Marx", *Revue Européenne des Sciences Sociales. Cahiers Vilfredo Pareto* 22(66), 1984 : 111-122.
3938   RYAN, Alan. *Property and political theory*. Oxford : B. Blackwell, 1984, viii-198 p.
3939   VAVER, David. "Authors' moral rights in Canada", *International Review of Industrial Property and Copyright Law* 14(2), 1983 : 329-371.

17220   Capitalism. Collectivism
Capitalisme. Collectivisme

3940   "Gesellschaftsstrategie des realen Sozialismus" (The social strategy of real socialism), *Einheit* 38(12), 1983 : 1091-1167. [German DR] [With contributions by Günter KALEX, Werner SCHELER, Gerhard WEISS, KRÖMKE]
3941   AMINZADE, Ronald. "Capitalist industrialization and patterns of industrial protest : a comparative urban study of nineteenth-century France", *American Sociological Review* 49(4), aug 84 : 437-453.
3942   BAVISKAR, B. S.; ATTWOOD, D. W. "Rural co-operatives in India : a comparative analysis of their economic survival and social impact", *Contributions to Indian Sociology* 17(1), jan-jul 84 : 85-107.
3943   BERMAN, Bruce. "Structure and process in the bureaucratic states of colonial Africa", *Development and Change* 15(2), apr 84 : 161-202.
3944   BURAWOY, Michael. "Karl Marx and the Satanic mills : factory politics under early capitalism in England, the United States, and Russia", *American Journal of Sociology* 90(2), sep 84 : 247-282.
3945   COOPER, Mark N. "State capitalism, class structure and social transformation in the Third World : the case of Egypt", *International Journal of Middle East Studies* 15(4), nov 83 : 451-469.
3946   FREUND, Julien. "Luther et le capitalisme selon Max Weber", *Revue Européenne des Sciences Sociales. Cahiers Vilfredo Pareto* 22(66), 1984 : 129-149.
3947   HIRSCHFELD, André; VERDIER, Roger. *Le secteur coopératif en France*. Paris : La Documentation Française, 1984, 144 p. bibl.
3948   KLEMENT'EV, D. S. *Ličnost' razvitogo socialističeskogo obščestva : metodologičeskij analiz* (Personality of the developed socialist society : a methodological analysis). Moskva : Izdatel'stvo Moskovskogo Universiteta, 1984, 144 p.

3949 KOZLOVSKIJ, V. E. "Protivorečija v nslovijah socializma" (Contradictions under socialism), _Voprosy Filosofii_ 37(8), 1984 : 11-20.
3950 KULIKOV, V. V. "K. Marks ob istoričeskih ětapah razvitija kommunističeskogo obščestva" (K. Marx on historical stages of the communist society development), _Izvestija Akademii Nauk SSSR. Serija Ěkonomičeskaja_ (6), 1983 : 5-11.
3951 LEW, Roland. "La nature sociale des pays du 'socialisme réel : note pour une recherche'', _Revue des Pays de l'Est_ 24(1-2), 1983 : 233-248.
3952 LISLE-WILLIAMS, Michael. "Beyond the market : the survival of family capitalism in the English merchant banks", _British Journal of Sociology_ 35(2), jun 84 : 241-271.
3953 OLIVER, Nick. "An examination of organizational commitment in six workers cooperatives in Scotland", _Human Relations_ 37(1), jan 84 : 29-45.
3954 PERKINS, Robert L. "Kierkegaard's critique of the 'bourgeois' state", _Inquiry_ 27(2-3), jul 84 : 207-218.
3955 PRUTSCHER, Pius M. "Was macht den Markt sozial?" (What makes the market social?), _International Journal of Social Economics_ 11(1-2), 1984 : 117-126. [Austria]
3956 ROJEK, Chris. "Time and socialist construction", _International Journal of Sociology and Social Policy_ 4(2), 1984 : 42-49.
3957 SOMMER, Robert; [et al.]. "Consumer cooperatives and worker collectives : a comparison", _Sociological Perspectives_ 27(2), apr 84 : 139-157. [USA]
3958 VASIL'EVA, I. V. "Potrebitel'stvo kak harakternaja čerta buržuaznogo obraza žizni" (Consumption as an essential character of the bourgeois way of life), _Voprosy Naučnogo Kommunizma (Kiev)_ (54), 1983 : 73-79.
3959 YADAV, Sohan Ram. _Nepal : feudalism and rural formation._ Delhi : Cosmo, 1984, 249 p.
3960 ZINN, Karl Georg. " 'Sättigung' im gesamtwirtschaftlichen Zusammenhang. Anmerkungen zu einer umstrittenen Sache" ('Satiety' in a national economic context. Remarks on a controverse), _Jahrbuch für Sozialwissenschaft_ 35(1), 1984 : 1-24.

17300 ECONOMIC SITUATION. STANDARD OF LIVING
SITUATION ÉCONOMIQUE. NIVEAU DE VIE

17310 Economy. Economic development
Économie. Développement économique

3961 "Psychological and sociological foundations of economic behaviour", _American Economic Review_ 74(2), mai 84 Papers and Proceedings : 79-96. [With contributions by George A. AKERLOF, James S. COLEMAN, and Albert O. HIRSCHMAN]
3962 GEREFFI, Gary. "Power and dependency in an interdependent world : a guide to understanding the contemporary global crisis", _International Journal of Comparative Sociology_ 25(1-2), apr 84 : 91-113.
3963 GUNDER FRANK, André. "Global crisis and transformation", _Development and Change_ 14(3), jul 83 : 323-346.
3964 NIKOLIĆ, Tomislav Z. "Socijalizam i ekonomska kriza" (Socialism and economic crisis), _Sociologija_ 26(3-4), jul-dec 84 : 359-372.
3965 TRELOGGEN PETERSON, Jean. "Cash, consumerism, and savings : economic change among the Agta foragers of Luzon, Philippines", _Research in Economic Anthropology_ 6, 1984 : 53-73.
3966 YAMAMURA, Etsuo. "Keizai hatten ni okeru model kihan tekioh ni kansuru kenkyu" (A study on model reference adaptive control in economic development), _Hokkaido University Journal of the Graduate School of Environmental Science_ 7(1), 1984 : 1-13.

17320 Income. Living conditions
Revenu. Conditions de vie

3967 BABEAU, André; LEBART, Ludovic. "Les conditions de vie et les aspirations des Français", _Futuribles_ (76), apr 84 : 37-51.
3968 BESKID, Lidia; [ed.]. _Warunki życia i potrzeby społeczeństwa polskiego 1982_ (Living conditions and requirements of Polish society in 1982). Warszawa : Polska Akademia Nauk Instytut Filozofii i Socjologii, 1984, 232 p.
3969 FARKAS, Katalin; PATAKI, Judit. _Az életszínvonal tényei és tükröződése a közvéleményben. Összefoglaló a Tömegkommunikációs Kutatóközpontban készült vizsgálatok alapján_ (The facts of the living standard and its repercussion in the public opinion. Summary on the basis of studies made in the Mass Communication Research Centre). Budapest : MRT Tömegkommunikációs Kutatóközpont, 1983, 23 p. [Hungary]

3970   GALLAND, Olivier. "Précarité et entrées dans la vie", *Revue Française de Sociologie* 25(1), jan-mar 84 : 49-66. [France]

3971   GILBERT, Neil. "Welfare for profit : moral, empirical and theoretical perspectives", *Journal of Social Policy* 13(1), jan 84 : 63-74. [USA]

3972   GLATZER, Wolfgang; ZAPF, Wolfgang; [eds.]. *Lebensqualität in der Bundesrepublik : objektive Lebensbedingungen und subjektive Wohlbefinden* (Quality of life in the Federal Republic : objective living conditions ans subjective well-being). Frankfurt-am-Main : Campus-Verlag, 1984, 443 p. bibl.

3973   GRENIER, Gilles. "The effects of language characteristecs on the wages of Hispanic-American males", *Journal of Human Resources* 19(1), wint 84 : 35-52.

3974   HANSEN, Arvid; ANDERSEN, Arne S. *Barns levekår / Children's level of living*. Oslo : Statistisk Sentralbyrå, H. Aschehoug og Universitetsforlaget, 1984, 122 p. ill. [Norway]

3975   HARING, Marilyn J.; STOCK, William A.; OKUN, Morris A. "A research synthesis of gender and social class as correlates of subjective well-being", *Human Relations* 37(8), aug 84 : 645-657.

3976   LEVINE, Mark F.; TAYLOR, James C. "Defining quality of working life", *Human Relations* 37(1), jan 84 : 81-104.

3977   MASTEKAASA, Arne; MOUM, Torbjørn. "The perceived quality of life in Norway : regional variations and contextual effects", *Social Indicators Research* 14(4), mai 84 : 385-419.

3978   MCLANAHAN SARA S.; SØRENSEN, Aage B. "Life events and psychological well-being : a reexamination of theoretical and methodological issues", *Social Science Research* 13(2), jun 84 : 111-128. [USA]

3979   MIECZKOWSKI, Bogdan; ZINAM, Oleg. *Bureaucracy, ideology, technology : quality of life East and West*. Charleston, IL : Association for the Study of the Nationalities (USSR and East Europe), 1984, xiii-463 p. ill., bibl., ind.

3980   MORRIS, Lydia D. "Redundancy and patterns of household finance", *Sociological Review* 32(3), aug 84 : 492-523.

3981   REIMERS, Cordelia W. "Sources of family income differentials among Hispanics, Blacks, and White non-Hispanics", *American Journal of Sociology* 89(4), jan 84 : 889-903.

3982   STANGELAND, Per. "Getting rich slowly. The social impact of oil activities", *Acta Sociologica* 27(3), 1984 : 215-237. [Norway]

3983   STAPLETON, David C.; YOUNG, Douglas J. "The effects of demographic change on the distribution of wages, 1967-1990", *Journal of Human Resources* 19(2), spr 84 : 175-201. [USA]

3984   STAROSTA, Paweł. "Zróżnicowanie położenia materialnego rodzin wiejskich" (Rural population's income disparities), *Roczniki Socjologii Wsi* 18, 1980-81 : 105-121.

3985   UTAGAWA, Tkuo. "Chiho toshi no seikatsu no shitsu to community leader" (Attitudinal quality of life and community leaders), *Jinmonronkyu* 44, 1984 : 1-14.

3986   VAJDA, Ágnes; [et al.]; [eds.]. *Életkörülmények, lakásviszonyok, lakásmobilitás. Adatgyűjtemény az 1978. évi életmód-, életkörülmények felvétel adataiból* (Life conditions, dwelling conditions, dwelling mobility. Data selection of the 1978 census on the way of life and life conditions). Budapest : Központi Statisztikai Hivatal, 1984, 350 p. [Hungary]

3987   WILLIAMS, Robert E.; KESSLER, Lorence L. *A closer look at comparable worth : a study of the basic questions to be addressed in approaching pay equity*. Washington, DC : National Foundation for the Study of Equal Employment Policy, 1984, ix-84 p. bibl. [USA]

3988   ZAMFIR, Catalin. "La qualité de la vie et la 'philosophie du sac' ", *Revue Roumaine* 37(7), 1983 : 53-61.

3989   ZWICKY, H. "L'inégalité des revenus et les ressources du contrôle social. Un test de la thèse de menace : l'exemple des cantons suisses", *Déviance et Société* 8(4), dec 84 : 357-375.

17400   ENTERPRISES. PRODUCTION
ENTREPRISES, PRODUCTION

17410   Business economics. Management
Économie de l'entreprise. Gestion

3990   ADEJUGBE, Michael. "The myths and realities of Nigeria's business indigenization", *Development and Change* 15(4), oct 84 : 577-592.

3991   BELLACE, Janice R.; LATTA, Geoffrey W. "Making the corporation transparent : prelude to multinational bargaining", *Columbia Journal of World Business* 18(2), sum 83 : 73-80.

3992   BENNELL, Paul. "Industrial class formation in Ghana : some empirical observations", *Development and Change* 15(4), oct 84 : 593-612.

3993   BRAEHMER, Uwe. "Kommunikationsforschung in Industrieunternehmen — ein
        Interessenkonflikt?" (Communication researches in industrial enterprises — a conflict
        of interests), *Communications (Sankt Augustin)* 9(2-3), 1983 : 299-314. [Switzerland]
3994   BUTERA, Federico. *L'orologio e l'organismo; il cambiamento organizzativo nella grande impresa in
        Italia : cultura industriale, conflitto, adattamento e nuove tecnologie* (Orology and organism;
        organizational change of the big enterprise in Italy : industrial culture, conflict, and
        adjustment of new technologies). Milano : Franco Angeli, 1984, 312 p. bibl.
3995   DANZIGER, Raymond. *Le bilan social, outil d'information et de gestion.* Paris : Dunod,
        1983, x-189 p. ill., bibl., ind.
3996   GHOSH, Pradip K. *Business and society : a study of business environment interface.* Delhi : Sultan
        Chand, 1984, 268 p.
3997   GRANOVETTER, Mark. "Small is beautiful : labor markets and establishment size",
        American Sociological Review 49(3), jun 84 : 323-334. [USA]
3998   JACHER, Władysław; [ed.]. *Socjologiczne problemy kierowania i zarzadzania przedsiębiorstwem
        w Polsce* (Sociological problems of directing, and managing the enterprise in Poland).
        Katowice : Uniwersytet Śląski, 1983, 149 p.
3999   LABORDE, Genie Z. *Influencing with integrity : management skills for communication and negotiation.*
        Palo Alto, CA : Science and Behavior Books, Syntony Publishing Co., 1983, xix-231 p.
4000   LITTLEJOHN, Virginia. "Women's business enterprises", *Sage Yearbooks in Women's Policy
        Studies* 7, 1983 : 286-301. [USA]
4001   MATENAAR, Dieter. *Organisationskultur und organisatorische Gestaltung : die Gestaltungsrelevanz
        der Kultur des Organisationssystems der Unternehmung* (Organization culture and organizational
        formation : the formation relevance of culture of the organization system of the enter-
        prise). Berlin : Duncker und Humblot, 1983, 160 p. ill., bibl.
4002   MOK, A. L.; [ed.]. "Het midden- en kleinbedrijf" (The small and medium enterprise),
        Sociologische Gids 30(3-4), mai-jun/jul-aug 83 : 167-275.
4003   ORNSTEIN, Michael. "Interlocking directorates in Canada : intercorporate or class
        alliance?", *Administrative Science Quarterly* 29(2), jun 84 : 210-231.
4004   PERSING, Bobbye Sorrels. *Business communication fundamentals.* Columbus, OH : C. E.
        Merrill, 1984, xx-584 p. ill., bibl., ind.
4005   RAVEYRE, Marie-Françoise; SAGLIO, Jean. "Les systèmes industriels localisés : éléments
        pour une analyse sociologique des ensembles de P.M.E. industriels", *Sociologie du Travail*
        26(2), jun 84 : 157-176.
4006   ROSARIO-BRAID, Florangel. *Communication strategies for productivity improvement.* Tokyo :
        Asian Productivity Organization, 1983, rev., iv-300 p. ill., bibl., ind.
4007   ROVATI, Giancarlo. "Stili di leadership aziendale ed orientamenti politico-sociali degli
        imprenditori delle piccole aziende" (Entrepreneurs of small firms : leadership style and
        socio-political attitudes), *Studi di Sociologia* 22(4), oct-dec 84 : 394-421. [Italy]
4008   ROVATI, Giancarlo. " 'Vecchi' e 'nuovi' imprenditori delle piccole aziende : formazione,
        mobilità, autostima" ('Former' and 'later' entrepreneurs of small firms : formation,
        mobility, value), *Studi di Sociologia* 22(2), apr-jun 84 : 191-208. [Italy]
4009   SAINSAULIEU, Renaud. "Renouveau des cultures d'entreprises?", *Projet* (183),
        mar 84 : 294-304.
4010   SHAPIRO, Irving S. "Managerial communication : the view from inside", *California
        Management Review* 27(1), 1984 : 157-172.
4011   TOMLINSON, J. D. "Economic and sociological theories of the enterprise and industrial
        democracy", *British Journal of Sociology* 35(4), dec 84 : 591-605.
4012   WATASE, Hiroshi. *Keiei soshiki to kazoku shudan — soshiki ron o koete* (Industrial organization
        and family — beyond organization theory). Osaka : Chuokeizaisha, 1984, 202 p.
4013   ZIEGLER, Rolf. "Das Netz der Personen- und Kapitalverflechtungen deutscher und
        österreichischer Wirtschaftsunternehmen" (The network of personal and financial inter-
        lacings of German and Austrian economic enterprises), *Kölner Zeitschrift für Soziologie und
        Sozialpsychologie* 36(3), sep 84 : 585-614.

17420   Productivity. Technology
        Productivité. Technologie

4014   "Forces (Les) productives dans la France d'aujourd'hui", *Pensée* (241), oct 84 : 5-87. [With
        contributions by C. GINDIN, Y. BOUCHUT, H. JACOT, P. BOCCARA]
4015   "Héros (Les) de l'économie", *Autrement. Série Mutations* (59), apr 84 : 1-251. [France]
4016   "New technology and the information age", *Mass Communication Review Yearbook* 4,
        1983 : 521-607. [USA] [With contributions by Charles FOMBRON, W. Graham
        ASTLEY, Herbert I. SCHILLER, Philip ELLIOTT, David H. WEAVER]

4017 "Potentiel (Le) scientifique et technique de l'URSS", *Commerce et Coopération* (109), dec 83 : 19-64. [With contributions by V. DISSON, A. I. MIKHAÏLOV, Y. A. TCHERNYCHEV]

4018 "Progrès, croissance, emploi", *Reflets et Perspectives de la Vie Économique* 23(1-2), feb 84 : 3-125. [With contributions by Raymond ARON, Georges GORIELY, Guy HAARSCHER]

4019 "Sciences humaines et bureautique", *BRISES* (5), oct 84 : 3-99. [With contributions by Francis PAVE, Ghislaine PELLAT, Jean-Jacques ROUBIERE, Jacques TRAHAND]

4020 ALARCON, Reynaldo. "La investigación en la universidad peruana" (Research in the Peruvian university), *Socialismo y Participación* (22), jun 83 : 155-164.

4021 BAILEY, Conner. *The sociology of production in rural Malay society.* Kuala Lumpur : Oxford University Press, 1983, xiv-226 p. ind., bibl., maps.

4022 BAYART, Denis; BERRY, Michel. "De la controverse à la recherche : les enjeux de la mise en oeuvre des automatismes dans l'industrie", *Sociologie du Travail* 26(4), oct-dec 84 : 500-509. [France]

4023 BAYEN, Marcel. "Enjeux technologiques : la formation en priorité", *Futuribles* (73), jan 84 : 49-64.

4024 BERTOLOTTI, David S. Jr. *Culture and technology.* Bowling Green, OH : Bowling Green State University Popular Press, 1984, 153 p.

4025 BHALLA, A. S. "Le dilemme technologique du tiers monde", *Travail et Société* 9(4), oct-dec 84 : 345-354.

4026 BLANCHARD, Francis. "La technologie, le travail et la société : quelques indices tirés des recherches du BIT", *Revue Internationale du Travail* 123(3), mai-jun 84 : 287-296.

4027 BOSSIO, Juan Carlos. "Les technologies avancées et leur enjeu pour les pays en développement", *Travail et Société* 9(4), oct-dec 84 : 367-384.

4028 BRINKERHOFF, Merlin B.; JACOB, Jeffrey C. "Alternative technology and quality of life : an exploration survey of British Columbia smallholders", *Social Indicators Research* 14(2), feb 84 : 177-194. [Canada]

4029 CARPENTIER, Renée. *Les nouvelles technologies et le travail salarié des femmes.* Québec : Gouvernement du Québec, 1983, 116 p. bibl.

4030 CASAS, Rosalba. "Ciencia y tecnología en México. Antecedentes y características actuales" (Science and technology in Mexico. Antecedentes and present characteristics), *Revista Mexicana de Sociología* 45(4), oct-dec 83 : 1323-1334.

4031 CAVESTRO, William. "Automatisation, organisation du travail et qualification dans les PME : le cas des machines-outils à commande numérique", *Sociologie du Travail* 26(4), oct-dec 84 : 434-446. [France] [Petites et Moyennes Entreprises]

4032 CHAUMONT, Roselyne; RASSE, Paul. "Nouvelles technologies et nouveaux droits des travailleurs", *Sociologie du Travail* 26(4), oct-dec 84 : 528-534. [France]

4033 COOLAHAN, John. "Science and technology as elements of educational and socio-economic changes in Ireland 1958-1983", *Administration (Dublin)* 32(1), 1984 : 89-99.

4034 COPPOCK, Rob. *Social constraints on technological progress.* Aldershot, Hampshire; Brookfield, VT... Gower, 1984, vii-291 p. ill., bibl.

4035 FABBRINI, Sergio. "Nuove tecnologie, potere e cambiamento sociale" (New technology, power and social change), *Studi di Sociologia* 22(2), apr-jun 84 : 127-143.

4036 FRIDERES, J. S.; [et al.]. "Technophobia : incidence and potential causal factors", *Social Indicators Research* 13(4), nov 83 : 381-393.

4037 FRISBIE, W. Parker; [et al.]. "A measurement of technological change : an ecological perspective", *Social Forces* 62(3), mar 84 : 750-766.

4038 GALITZ, Wilbert O. *Humanizing office automation : the impact of ergonomics on productivity.* Wellesley, MA : QED Information Sciences, 1984, xi-276 p. ill., bibl.

4039 GRUHN, Werner. "Soziale Folgeprobleme der Automatisierung in der DDR" (The social consequences of automation in GDR), *Deutsche Studien* 22(86), jun 84 : 136-147.

4040 HETHERINGTON, Robert W. "Response to innovation : the problem-oriented system in a mental health setting", *Canadian Review of Sociology and Anthropology / Revue Canadienne de Sociologie et d'Anthropologie* 21(2), mai 84 : 202-230. [Canada]

4041 ILJUŠEČKIN, V. P.; [et al.]. "Obmen mnenijami : aktual'nye problemy analiza proizvoditel'nyh sil dokapitalističeskih klassovyh obščestv" (Exchange of views : topical problems of the analysis of productive forces of the pre-capitalist class societies), *Filosofskie Nauki* (6), 1983 : 12-34.

4042 JOHNSON, Knowlton W.; FRAZIER, William D.; RIDDICK, Major F. Jr. "A change strategy for linking the worlds of academia and practice", *Journal of Applied Behavioral Science* 19(4), 1983 : 439-451. [Followed by a comment by Mark VAN DE VALL, (ibid. : 452-454) and Carl A. BRAMLETTE Jr., (ibid. : 455-457) and a reply by the author, (ibid. : 457-460)]

4043 KAPLINSKY, Raphael. *Automation : the technology and society.* Harlow, Essex : Longman, 1984, xvii-197 p. ill., bibl., ind.

4044 KROKER, Arthur. "Processed world : technology and culture in the thought of Marshall McLuhan", *Philosophy of the Social Sciences / Philosophie des Sciences Sociales* 14(4), dec 84 : 433-459.

4045 KUL'KIN, A. M. "Naučnaja dejatel'nost' v sisteme sovremennogo kapitalizma" (Scientific activity in the contemporary capitalist system), *Voprosy Filosofii* (1), 1984 : 104-112.

4046 MARIÉ, Michel. "Pour une anthropologie des grands ouvrages : le canal de Provence", *Annales de la Recherche Urbaine* (21), jan 84 : 5-35. [France]

4047 MCQUILLAN, Kevin. "Modes of production and demographic patterns in nineteenth-century France", *American Journal of Sociology* 89(6), mai 84 : 1324-1346.

4048 MERCIER, Pierre-Alain; PLASSARD, François; SCARDIGLI, Victor. *La société digitale : les nouvelles technologies au futur quotidien.* Paris : Éditions du Seuil, 1984, 213 p. bibl.

4049 MULDUR, U.; DRAY, J.; CORCOS, E. *La bureaucratique : quelle politique sociale pour quelle technologie?* Paris : La Documentation Française, 1983, 190 p. ill., bibl.

4050 OVČINNIKOV, Ju. A. "Marksizm-leninizm i naučno-tehničeskij progress" (Marxism-Leninism and the scientific and technical progress), *Voprosy Filosofii* (5), 1983 : 24-33.

4051 PIOTET, Françoise. "Nouvelles technologies, nouveaux droits. Positions, propositions et actions de la CFDT", *Sociologie du Travail* 26(4), oct-dec 84 : 535-540. [France]

4052 POLITIS, Michel. *Techniques de la bureautique.* Paris : Masson, 1984, 155 p. bibl.

4053 RAMO, Simon. *What's wrong with our technological society — and how to fix it.* New York, NY; London... McGraw-Hill, 1983, 280 p.

4054 ROY, Pierre André. *Impact économique et sociologique de la robotique industrielle en France.* Lille : CNDP, CRDP Lille, 1983, 116 p. ill., bibl.

4055 RYBCZYNSKI, W. *Paper heroes, un regard sur la technologie appropriée.* Paris : Parenthèses, 1983, 158 p.

4056 SARKISIAN, Sarkis. *Sotsialna dialektika i tekhnicheski progres* (Social dialectics and technical progress). Sofia : Dŭrzh. izd-vo Nauka i Izkustvo, 1983, 215 p. bibl. [Bulgaria]

4057 SCHWARTZ, Gail Garfield; NEIKIRK, William. *The work revolution.* New York, NY : Rawson Associates, 1984, 255 p. bibl., ind. [USA]

4058 SINGH, Hira. *The Asiatic mode of production : a critical analysis.* Toronto, ON : Department of Sociology, University of Toronto, 1983, 24 p. bibl.

4059 SOLO, Robert. "The logic of technology in-transfer", *International Social Science Review* 59(3), 1984 : 150-161.

4060 STANKIEWICZ, Janina; WALKOWIAK, Jerzy. "Socjologiczne problemy kształtowania aktywności innowacyjnej w przemysłowych zakładach pracy" (Sociological aspects of forming innovational activity in industrial plants), *Ruch Prawniczy, Ekonomiczny i Socjologiczny* 1, 1984 : 255-277.

4061 STARR, S. Frederick. "High tech in the USSR. Technology and freedom in the Soviet Union", *Current* 265, sep 84 : 22-28.

4062 TALLARD, Michèle. "La prise en compte des nouvelles technologies dans la négociation collective : le cas de la RFA", *Sociologie du Travail* 26(4), oct-dec 84 : 510-521.

4063 TREU, Tiziano. "L'incidence des nouvelles technologies sur l'emploi, les conditions de travail et les relations professionnelles", *Travail et Société* 9(2), jun 84 : 122-141. [Suivi d'une postface par Pierre F. GONOD concernant la prospective du travail et la maîtrise sociale de la technologie, pp. 141-150]

4064 UNIVERSITÉ DE NICE. CENTRE DE LA MÉDITERRANÉE MODERNE ET CONTEMPORAINE. *Innovations et technologies dans les pays méditerranéens : XVIᵉ-XXᵉ siècles; journées d'études organisées à Bendor, 22-24 avril 1982.* Nice : le Centre, 1984, 208 p. bibl.

4065 WANG, In Keun. "Communication strategies for interchange of technologies", *Asian Economies* (44), mar 83 : 5-27.

17430   Agriculture. Trade. Industry
Agriculture. Commerce. Industrie

4066 "Artisianats (Les) urbains en Afrique", *Genève-Afrique* 22(1), 1984 : 34-137. [With contributions by Angelo BARAMPAMA, Olatunji Y. OYENEYE, Guy LE BOTERF, Philibert RANSONI]

4067 "Family (The) farm; corporatism, the State and survival strategies", *Sociologia Ruralis* 24(2), 1984 : 103-156.

4068 "Household (The) and the large scale agricultural unit", *Review (F. Braudel Center)* 7(2), aut 83 : 181-360. [Developing countries] [With contributions by Petra ULSHOFER, Albert MEYERS, Georg STAUTH]

4069 ALBRECHT, Don E.; MURDOCK, Steve H. "Toward a human ecological perspective on part-time farming", *Rural Sociology* 49(3), 1984 : 389-411. [USA]

4070 BERARDI, Gigi M.; GEISLER, Charles C. *The social consequences and challenges of new agricultural technologies*. Boulder, CO : Westview Press, 1984, xxi-376 p. ill., bibl.

4071 CHINN, David; NAVARRO, Peter. "Capture and ideology in American farm policy", *Rural Sociology* 49(4), 1984 : 517-529.

4072 CORLAY, Jean-Pierre. "Le conflit des pêches françaises en 1980 : essai de socio-géographie halieutique", *Norois* 31(121), mar 84 : 155-169.

4073 FABIANI, Jean-Louis. "L'opposition à la chasse et l'affrontement des représentations de la nature", *Actes de la Recherche en Sciences Sociales* 54, sep 84 : 81-84.

4074 FRYŻLEWICZ, Zofia. "Przyszłość indywidualnych gospodarstw rolnych w opinii ich właścicieli" (The future of privately-owned farms in the opinion of their owners), *Wieś i Rolnictwo* 42(1), 1984 : 227-244.

4075 GAŁAJ, Dyzma. "Socjologiczne aspekty prywatnej własności ziemi w Polsce" (Sociological aspects of the private ownership of land in Poland), *Wieś i Rolnictwo* 43(2), 1984 : 123-132.

4076 GARRETT, Patricia. "The relevance of structural variables for farming systems research", *Rural Sociology* 49(4), 1984 : 580-589.

4077 HARUVI, Nava; KISLEV, Yoav. "Cooperation in the moshav", *Journal of Comparative Economics* 8(1), mar 84 : 54-73.

4078 ISTITUTO NAZIONALE DI SOCIOLOGIA RURALE. *Gastronomia e società* (Gastronomy and society). Milano : Franco Angeli, 1984, 675 p. ill., bibl.

4079 KŁODZIŃSKI, Marek. "Rozwój prostych form kooperacji w polskim rolnictwie" (Development of simple forms of cooperation in Polish farming), *Roczniki Socjologii Wsi* 18, 80-81 : 41-55.

4080 KOBAYASHI, Koichiro. "Tei seicho keizai eno iko to jyu-ko kigyo no soshiki fuudo no henka katei" (Changes in organizational climate of heavy-industrial enterprises in the changing environments), *Toyo University Bulletin of Faculty of Sociology* 21, 1984 : 57-110. [Japan]

4081 LEVIATAN, Uri. "Research note. The Kibbutz as a situation for cross-cultural research", *Organization Studies* 5(1), 1984 : 67-75. [In collaboration with the European Group for Organizational Studies, Berlin, New York]

4082 LOVATT, David; HAM, Brian. "The distributional implications of de-industrialization", *British Journal of Sociology* 35(4), dec 84 : 498-521.

4083 LULOFF, A. E.; CHITTENDEN, Wendy H. "Rural industrialization : a logit analysis", *Rural Sociology* 49(1), 1984 : 67-88. [USA]

4084 MANN, Susan A. "Sharecropping in the cotton South : a case of uneven development in agriculture", *Rural Sociology* 49(3), 1984 : 412-429. [USA]

4085 MARSDEN, Terry. "Capitalist farming and the farm family : a case study", *Sociology (London)* 18(2), mai 84 : 205-224.

4086 MEIER, Peter C. "Continuity and change in peasant household production : the spinners and knitters of Carabuela, Northern Ecuador", *Canadian Review of Sociology and Anthropology / Revue Canadienne de Sociologie et d'Anthropologie* 21(4), nov 84 : 431-448.

4087 PIPAT-GIRAUDEL, Catherine. "L'exploitation agricole et la condition de la femme; les silences de la loi d'orientation agricole du 4 juillet 1980", *Revue de Droit Rural* (120), jan 84 : 1-17. [France]

4088 REIMER, Bill. "Farm mechanization : the impact on labour at the level of the farm household", *Canadian Journal of Sociology / Cahiers Canadiens de Sociologie* 9(4), 1984 : 429-443. [Quebec, Canada]

4089 ROSNER, Menachem; TANNENBAUM, Arnold S. *Ownership and alienation in kibbutz factories*. Haifa : University of Haifa, the University Center of the Kibbutz, Institute for Study and Research of the Kibbutz and the Cooperative Idea, 1983, 37 p. ill., bibl.

4090 RUS, Veljko. "Protuslovije između industriajalizacije i profesionalizacije rada" (The opposition between the industrialization and professionalization of work), *Revija za Sociologiju* 14(1-2), 1984 : 47-58.

4091 SHEPHER, Israel. *The kibbutz : an anthropological study*. Norwood, PA : Norwood Editions, 1983, x-208 p. bibl.

4092 SPYBEY, Tony. "Traditional and professional frames of meaning in management", *Sociology (London)* 18(4), nov 84 : 550-562. [UK]

4093 USUI, Takashi. "Sanken model ni yoru nokyo no ishi kettei bunseki -soshiki no ishi kettei kouzou" (The decision-making system of the Japanese agricultural cooperative society), *Kinjyo Gakuin University Bulletin Social Sciences Series* 26, 1984 : 1-44.

4094 WALOSIK, Jerzy. "Współdziałanie sektorów polskiego rolnictwa" (An interaction between sectors in Polish farming. Sociological studies on the countryside), *Wieś i Rolnictwo* 44(3), 1984 : 133-144.

4095   WELLS, Miriam J. "The resurgence of sharecropping : historical anomaly or political strategy?", *American Journal of Sociology* 90(1), jul 84 : 1-19. [USA]
4096   WILLIAMS, Karel; WILLIAMS, John; THOMAS, Dennis. *Why are the British bad at manufacturing?* London; Boston, MA : Routledge and Kegan Paul, 1983, xiii-288 p. bibl., ind.
4097   YONNET, Paul. "La société automobile", *Débat* (31), sep 84 : 128-148.
4098   ŽUPANČIČ, Milan. "Uključivanje individualne poljoprivrede u društvenu podjelu rada" (Including private farming in the social division of labour), *Sociologija Sela* 21(79-81), 1983 : 113-126. [Yugoslavia]

17500   CONSUMPTION. MARKET. PRICES
CONSOMMATION. MARCHÉ. PRIX

17510   Consumer behaviour
Comportement du consommateur

4099   BIHL, Luc; WILLETTE, Luc. *Une histoire du mouvement consommateur : mille ans de luttes.* Paris : Aubier, 1984, 253 p. bibl. [France]
4100   DARDIS, Rachel. "Consumer risk response and consumer protection : an economic analysis of seat belt usage", *Journal of Consumer Affairs* 17(2), wint 83 : 245-261. [USA]
4101   FOXALL, Gordon R. *Consumer choice.* New York, NY : St. Martin's Press, 1983, viii-149 p.
4102   KALWANI, Manohar U.; WEVENBERGH, Marcel. *Entropy models of consumer behavior : similarities and differences.* West Lafayette, IN : Institute for Research in the Behavioral, Economic and Management Sciences, Krannert Graduate School of Management, Purdue University, 1984, 38 various p. bibl.
4103   MILIC-CZERNIAK, Róża. "Specyfika potrzeb konsumpcyjnych i sposobów ich zaspokajania w górnośląskich gospodarstwach domowych" (Specification of consumption requirements and ways of their gratification in the households of the Upper Silesia region), *Studia nad Ekonomiką Regionu* 14, 1984 : 257-271.
4104   MULLEN, Brian. "Social psychological models of impression formation among consumers", *Journal of Social Psychology* 124(1), oct 84 : 65-77.
4105   OKUDA, Kazuhiko. *Shohi kodo paradigm no shin tenkai* (A new development of consumption behavior paradigm). Tokyo : Hakuto Shobo, 1984, 322 p.
4106   POTTER, Robert B. "Consumer behavior and spatial cognition in relation to the extraversion-introversion dimension of personality", *Journal of Social Psychology* 123(1), jun 84 : 29-34.
4107   UUSITALO, Liisa; [ed.]. *Consumer behavior and environmental quality : trends and prospects in the ways of life : proceedings of a symposium organized by the International Institute for Environment and Society of the Science Center of Berlin, November 1980.* New York, NY : St. Martin's Press, 1983, 142 p.
4108   WARLAND, Rex H.; [et al.]. "Consumer complaining and community involvement : an exploration of their theoretical and empirical linkages", *Journal of Consumer Affairs* 18(1), sum 84 : 64-78. [USA]
4109   WAY, Wendy L. "Using content analysis to examine consumer behaviors portrayed on television : a pilot study in a consumer education context", *Journal of Consumer Affairs* 18(1), sum 84 : 79-91. [USA]

17520   Demand. Supply
Demande. Offre

4110   BUSS, Eugen. *Markt und Gesellschaft : eine soziologische Untersuchung zum Strukturwandel der Wirtschaft* (Market and society : a sociological research on the structural change of economy). Berlin : Duncker und Humblot, 1983, 174 p. bibl.
4111   GRAY, John N. "Lamb auctions on the borders", *Archives Européennes de Sociologie* 25(1), 1984 : 54-82. [UK]
4112   KAMIŃSKI, Antoni Zdzisław. *Monopol i konkurencja : socjologiczna analiza instytucji polityczno-gospodarczych* (Monopoly and competition : a sociological analysis of politico-economic institutions). Warszawa : Państwowe Wydawnictwo Naukowa, 1984, 241 p.
4113   MAL'CEV, V. A. *Sorevnovanie i ličnost' : opyt sociologičeskogo analiza* (Competition and personality : an essay of sociological analysis). Moskva : Mysl', 1983, 157 p.
4114   ŠOROHOVA, É. V.; [et al.]. "Social'no-psihologičeskoe issledovanie dejatel'nosti sorevnujuščihsja kollektivov" (Socio-psychological research on the activity of competing collectivities), *in : Prikladnye problemy social'noj psihologii* Moskva, 1983 : 68-87.

17600 CREDIT. FINANCING. MONEY
CRÉDIT. FINANCEMENT. MONNAIE

4115 BURNS, Tom R.; BAUMGARTNER, Thomas; DEVILLÉ, Philippe. "Inflation, politics and social change : institutional and theoretical crisis in contemporary economy-and-society", *International Journal of Comparative Sociology* 25(1-2), apr 84 : 73-90.

4116 CAUET, Sylvie. "La monnaie électronique", *Bulletin du Crédit national* 10(42), trim. 1, 84 : 72-102. [France]

4117 CAVALLI, Alessandro; PERUCCHI, Lucio. "La filosofia del denaro di Georg Simmel" (Georg Simmel's philosophy of money), *Critica Sociologica* 69, 1984 : 122-164.

4118 FURNHAM, Adrian. "Determinants of attitudes toward taxation in Britain", *Human Relations* 37(7), jul 84 : 535-546.

4119 LAKSACI, Mohammed. "Monnaie et banque dans une économie planifiée", *Reflets et Perspectives de la Vie Économique* 23(3), jun 84 : 159-184.

4120 MAREC, Yannick. *Le 'clou' rouennais : des origines à nos jours (1778-1982) : du Mont de piété au Crédit municipal : contribution à l'histoire de la pauvreté en province.* Rouen : Éditions du P'tit Normand, 1983, 232 p. ill., bibl., ind.

4121 SPROULE-JONES, Mark; [ed.]. "Methodological individualism and public choice", *American Behavioral Scientist* 28(2), nov-dec 84 : 163-288.

4122 VINOT, Pierre. "Aspects socio-économiques des prélèvements obligatoires", *Journal de la Société de Statistique de Paris* 125(4), trim. 4, 84 : 203-220. [France]

4123 WILLIAMS, Numan A. *Insurance : an introduction to personal risk management.* Cincinatti, OH : South-Western Publishing Co., 1984, x-310 p. ill., bibl., ind.

17700 ECONOMIC POLICY. PLANNING
POLITIQUE ÉCONOMIQUE, PLANIFICATION

4124 "Desarrollo, estilos de vida, población y medio ambiente en América Latina" (Development, life styles, population and environment in Latin America), *Notas de Población* 22(36), dec 84 : 9-57.

4125 "Regional development in Australia and New Zealand", *Australian and New Zealand Journal of Sociology* 20(3), nov 84 : 299-404.

4126 BARRENECHEA LERCARI, Carlos; [ed.]. *El problema regional hoy* (Regional problem today). Lima : Centro Nacional de Estudios y Asesoría Popular, 1983, 315 p.

4127 BENKO, G. B. "Regional science : evolution over thirty years", *International Social Science Journal / Revue Internationale des Sciences Sociales* 36(4), 1984 : 699-712.

4128 BINET, Jacques. "Développement. Transfert de technologie. Transfert de culture", *Diogène* 126, apr-jun 84 : 22-42.

4129 BURSZTYN, Marcel. *O poder dos donos : planejamento e clientelismo no Nordeste* (The power of gifts : planning and clientelism in the Northeast). Petrópolis : Vozes-CNPq, 1984, 178 p. ill., bibl. [Brazil]

4130 DAMROSZ, Jerzy. "Determinanty podziałów regionalnych : tendencje unifikacyjne e tendencje dyferencjacyjne" (Determinants of regional divisions : tendencies to unify vs. tendencies to differentiate), *Roczniki Socjologii Wsi* 18, 80-81 : 9-22.

4131 ELCOCK, Howard; [ed.]. *What sort of society? Economic and social policy in modern Britain.* Oxford : Robertson; Totowa, NJ : Biblio Distribution Centre, 1982, vi-248 p.

4132 HAMM, Bernd. "Sozialraumanalyse" (Social space analysis), *Gegenwartskunde* 33(1), trim. 1, 84 : 49-60.

4133 KITOH, Tsuneo. "Okinawa no chiiki fukko no mondai ten to jyumin ishiki" (Problems of regional advancement and inhabitant's consciousness in Okinawa), *Nihon University Journal of Sociology* 90, 1984 : 37-51.

4134 TANAKA, Toyoji. "Chiiki shakai to chiho jichi-tai : chiiki kankyo jyoken no henka" (Regional society and local government : changing conditions in regional social environment and organizational reform of administrative bureaucracy), *Soshioroji* 29(2), 1984 : 27-44. [Japan]

4135 VELLINGA, Menno; KRUIJT, Dirk. "Estado, desarrollo regional y burguesía regional" (State, regional development and regional bourgeoisie), *Revista Interamericana de Planificación* 18(70), jun 84 : 89-108. [Peru; Colombia]

4136 WILLIAMS, Alan. "La loi néo zélandaise sur les rémunérations, 1979-80. Une analyse descriptive de l'intervention du gouvernement", *Travail et Société* 9(1), mar 84 : 57-81.

18100 INDUSTRIAL SOCIOLOGY. SOCIOLOGY OF WORK
SOCIOLOGIE INDUSTRIELLE. SOCIOLOGIE DU TRAVAIL

4137 "Sociología industrial" (Industrial sociology), *Revista Internacional de Sociología* 42(49), mar 84 : 5-306. [Spain] [With contributions by Manuel NAVARRO LOPEZ, José A. GARMENDIA, Francisco PARRA LUNA, Manuel GARCIA FERRANDO, Manuel MARTIN SERRANO]

4138 BOLTE, Karl Martin; TREUTNER, Erhard; [eds.]. *Subjektorientierte Arbeits- und Berufssoziologie* (Subject-oriented sociology of work and occupational sociology). Frankfurt-am-Main; New York, NY : Campus, 1983, 415 p. bibl.

4139 CORTELLAZZI, Silvia. "La sociologia del lavoro e dell'organizzazione" (Sociology of work and of organization), *Studi di Sociologia* 22(3), jul-sep 84 : 237-260.

4140 KAWANISHI, Hirosuke. "Dai san ki rodo-shakaigaku no seika" (Review of the results and tasks of labour sociology in Japan today), *Labour Annual 1984*, 1984 : 233-245.

4141 KUZ'MIN, É. S.; SVENCICKIJ, A. L.; [eds.]. *Promyšlennaja social'naja psihologija* (The industrial social psychology). Leningrad : Izdatel'stvo Leningradskogo Universiteta, 1982, 205 p.

4142 LELLI, Marcello. "Sull'oggetto della sociologia del lavoro" (On the subject of the sociology of work), *Studi di Sociologia* 22(2), apr-jun 84 : 164-175.

4143 MILLER, Delbert C. "Whatever will happen to industrial sociology", *Sociological Quarterly* 25(2), 1984 : 251-256. [With a commentary by Curt TAUSKY, ibid. : 257-260, and Eugene V. SCHNEIDER, ibid. : 261-265]

4144 NOVARA, Francesco; ROZZI, Renato A.; SARCHIELLI, Guido. *Psicologia del lavoro* (Psychology of labour). Bologna : Mulino, 1983, 304 p. ill., bibl.

4145 SCHMALE, Hugo. *Psychologie der Arbeit* (Psychology of work). Stuttgart : Klett-Cotta, 1983, 265 p. ill., bibl., ind.

4146 SCHUMM-GARLING, Ursula. *Soziologie des Industriebetriebes* (Sociology of the industrial enterprise). Stuttgart : Kohlhammer, 1983, 123 p. bibl.

4147 STAHL, Thomas. *Betriebssoziologie und Moral : zur Kritik der soziologischen Sichtweise* (Industrial sociology and morals : on the critique of the sociological point of view). Frankfurt-am-Main; New York, NY : Campus, 1984, 318 p. ill., bibl.

4148 TAUSKY, Curt. *Work and society : an introduction to industrial sociology*. Itasca, IL : F. E. Peacock, 1984, viii-163 p. bibl., ind.

18200 EMPLOYMENT. LABOUR MARKET
EMPLOI. MARCHÉ DU TRAVAIL

18210 Labour. Manpower
Travail. Main-d'oeuvre

4149 "Population active — emploi — groupes sociaux", *Économie et Statistique* (171-172), nov-dec 84 : 1-181. [France]

4150 "Travail et famille", *Tocqueville Review* 5(2), wint 83 : 279-428. [With contributions by Christopher C. HARRIS, Louis ROUSSEL, Catherine GOKALP; continued in ibid. 6(1), sum 84 : 5-168]

4151 APPLEBAUM, H. *Work in non-market and transitional societies*. Albany, NY : State University of New York Press, 1984, xv-398 p. bibl.

4152 BAUER, Leonhard. "Arbeit ist nicht gleich Arbeit. Die gesellschaftliche 'erzwungene' Bewertung von Tätigkeiten" (Labour is not like labour. The social 'extorted' evaluation of activities), *Jahrbuch für Sozialwissenschaft* 35(1), 1984 : 66-91.

4153 BEARDSWORTH, Alan D.; [et al.]; [eds.]. "Employers and recruitment : explorations in labour demand", *International Journal of Social Economics* 11(7), 1984 : 3-120. [UK; USA]

4154 BEDIN, Jean-Marie. "Modélisation prévisionnelle de l'emploi et mobilité du travail", *Cahiers du Centre d'Études de l'Emploi* (27), 1984 : 107-188.

4155 BERGQUIST, Charles; [ed.]. *Labor in the capitalist world-economy*. London; Beverly Hills, CA : Sage Publications, 1984, 309 p.

4156 BROWAEYS, Xavier; CHATELAIN, Paul. *La France du travail*. Paris : Presses Universitaires de France, 1984, 267 p. ill., cartes, bibl.

4157 DEMIN, V. M. "Trud kak vid čelovečeskoj dejatel'nosti" (Labour as an aspect of human activity), *Filosofskie Nauki* (1), 1984 : 10-18.

4158 DOMAŃSKI, Henryk. "Rola segmentacji rynku pracy w procesie społecznej strukturalizacji" (The role of segmentation of labour market in the process of social structuralization), *Studia Socjologiczne* 92(1), 1984 : 161-178.

4159 GODSCHALK, J. J. "Wordt het geen tijd 'arbeid' breder te omschrijven?" (An extensive definition of 'labor'?), *Sociologische Gids* 31(6), 1984 : 507-517.

4160 HUMPHRIES, Jane; RUBERY, Jill. "The reconstitution of the supply side of the labour market : the relative autonomy of social reproduction", *Cambridge Journal of Economics* 8(4), dec 84 : 331-346.

4161 JAROSIŃSKA, Maria. *Rynek siły roboczej w opinii publiczne. Raport z badań maj 1982* (The labour market in public opinion. A research report, May 1982). Warszawa : Polska Akademia Nauk, Instytut Filozofii i Sociologii, 1984, 144 p. [Poland]

4162 JOLL, Caroline; [et al.]. *Developments in labour market analysis.* Boston, MA; London... Allen and Unwin, 1983, xii-398 p.

4163 KORDASZEWSKI, Jan; [ed.]. *Przemiany systemu pracy w PRL w latach 1962-2000* (Changes of the labour system in the PPR over the period 1962-2000). Wrocław : Zakład Narodowy im. Ossolińskich, 1984, 505 p.

4164 LAURITO, Clemente R. *Influencia de los recursos humanos en el desarrollo económico y social, con un método de racionalización de tareas* (Influence of human resources in the economic and social development, with a method of tasks rationalization). Buenos Aires : Eficiencia, 1984, 95 p.

4165 LEMON, Anthony. "State control over the labor market in South Africa", *International Political Science Review* 5(2), 84 : 189-208. [FRE]

4166 LINHART, Daniel. "Crise et travail", *Temps Modernes* 40(450), jan 84 : 1284-1315. [France]

4167 MALAČIČ, Janez. "Kritika teorije 'čeloveškega kapitala'" (Criticism of the 'human capital theory'), *Ekonomska Revija* 35(4), mar 84 : 419-345.

4168 MALAČIČ, Janez. "Teorija 'čeloveškega kapitala'" (Theory of 'human capital'), *Ekonomska Revija* 35(2-3), mar 84 : 271-288.

4169 MILKOVICH, George; [ed.]. "Human resource strategy and evaluation", *Industrial Relations* 23(2), 1984 : 151-217. [USA]

4170 MORRIS, L. D. "Patterns of social activity and post-redundancy labour-market experience", *Sociology (London)* 18(2), mai 84 : 339-352. [UK]

4171 PEDERSEN, Peder J. "Dynamiske processer på arbejdsmarkedet" (Dynamic processes in labour market), *Økonomi og Politik* 57(2), 1983 : 140-156. [Denmark]

4172 PEREZ SAINZ, J. P. "Industrialización y fuerza de trabajo en Ecuador" (Industrialization and labour force in Ecuador), *Boletín de Estudios Latinoamericanos y del Caribe* (37), dec 84 : 19-43.

4173 RAULT, Daniel. "Secteurs d'activité : l'évolution des structures de la main-d'oeuvre", *Économie et Statistique* (171-172), nov-dec 84 : 35-47. [France]

4174 SCHMIDT, Klaus-Dieter. *Arbeitsmarkt und Bildungspolitik* (Labour market and educational policy). Tübingen : J. C. B. Mohr, 1984, xii-149 p. bibl., ind.

4175 VARGA, Károly. "Az emberi erőforrás sorsa az erőforrás-korlátos gazdaságban" (The fate of human resource in the economy of limited resources), *Szociológia* 12(3), 1983 : 237-252.

4176 WHITE, Robert W.; ALTHAUSER, Robert P. "Internal labor markets, promotions, and worker skill : an indirect test of skill ILMs", *Social Science Research* 13(4), dec 84 : 373-392. [USA]

4177 ZIMMERMAN-TANSELLA, Christa. "Considerazioni sullo sviluppo della psicologia del lavoro" (Thoughts on labour psychology development), *Difesa Sociale* 62(6), dec 83 : 80-89.

18220   Employment. Unemployment
Emploi. Chômage

4178 BAGELLA, Michele. "Note sul concetto di disoccupazione involontaria" (Notes on the concept of involuntary unemployment), *Giornale degli Economisti e Annali di Economia* 43(3-4), mar-apr 84 : 213-236.

4179 BLOCK, Bernhard. "Psycho-soziale Folgen von Arbeitslosigkeit" (Psychologic and social consequences of unemployment), *Frankfurter Hefte* 39(8), 1984 : 24-32.

4180 BÖSEKE, Harry; SPITZNER, Albert; [eds.]. *Jugend ohne Arbeit* (Youth without work). Bornheim-Merten : Lamuv, 1983, 205 p. ill., bibl.

4181 BOUTINET, J. P.; DELALEU, A. "L'école face au projet d'insertion professionnelle des jeunes", *Bulletin de Psychologie* 37(367), oct 84 : 957-983. [France]

4182 BREEN, Richard. "Status attainment or job attainment? The effects of sex and class on youth unemployment", *British Journal of Sociology* 35(3), sep 84 : 363-386. [Ireland]

4183   BREMICKER, Burckhardt; KLEMMER, P.; ORTMEYER, A. *Analyse der Arbeitslosigkeit in den Regionen Nordrhein-Westfalens* (Analysis of the unemployment in the North Rhine-Westphaly regions). Bochum : N. Brockmeyer, 1984, xx-381 p. ill., bibl.

4184   BRUN, François; BRYGOO, Angélina. "Situation et comportement des chômeurs vis-à-vis des emplois offerts", *Cahiers du Centre d'Études de l'Emploi* 28(2), 1984 : 99-199. [France]

4185   BÜCHTEMANN, Christoph F.; ROSENBLADT, Bernhard von. "Kumulative Arbeitslosigkeit. Wiedereingliederungsprobleme Arbeitsloser bei anhaltend ungünstiger Beschäftigungslage" (Cumulative unemployment. The rehabilitation problem of unemployed in a continuous unfavourable situation), *Mitteilungen aus der Arbeitsmarkt- und Berufsforschung* 16(3), 1983 : 262-275.

4186   DEMERS, Marie. "Chômage chez les jeunes : conséquences psychologiques et sociales", *Relations Industrielles* 38(4), 1983 : 785-814.

4187   EPEMA, J. M.; VALKENBURG, F. C. "Werkloosheid in oude stadswijken" (Unemployment in old city neighborhoods), *Sociologische Gids* 31(1), 1984 : 24-47. [Netherlands]

4188   FESTY, Patrick. "Le chômage et les familles aux Etats-Unis", *Population* 39(3), mai-jun 84 : 614-617.

4189   FORNI, Floreal H.; BENENCIA, Roberto; NEIMAN, Guillermo. *Notas sobre la situación y el estado del conocimiento del empleo rural* (Notes on the situation and the state of knowledge about rural employment). Buenos Aires : Centro de Estudios e Investigaciones Laborales, 1984, 30 p.

4190   FREYSSINET, Jacques. *Le chômage.* Paris : La Découverte, 1984, 128 p. bibl.

4191   GAUDEMAR, Jean-Paul de. "L'usine éclatée : les stratégies d'emploi à distance face à la crise du travail", *Mouvement Social* (125), dec 83 : 113-124. [France]

4192   GERSUNY, Carl. "From contract to status : perspectives on employment seniority", *Sociological Inquiry* 54(1), wint 84 : 44-61.

4193   GHIBUȚIU, Aurel. "La jeunesse et l'univers du travail", *Revue Roumaine* 37(7), 1983 : 43-53.

4194   GNOSS, Roland. *Das Problem der Arbeitslosigkeit in der Bundesrepublik Deutschland : eine quantitative und qualitative Globalanalyse auf der Basis aggregierter Daten* (Unemployment problem in the Federal Republic of Germany : a quantitative and qualitative global analysis on the basis of aggregated data). Frankfurt-am-Main : Haag + Herchen, 1983, xvi-154 p. ill., bibl.

4195   HARTEN, Hans-Christian. *Jugendarbeitslosigkeit in der EG* (Youth unemployment in the EEC). Frankfurt-am-Main; New York, NY : Campus, 1983, 360 p. ill., bibl.

4196   HORNER, Wolfgang. "L'école et l'insertion professionnelle en France et en URSS", *Orientation Scolaire et Professionnelle* 13(3), 1984 : 203-212.

4197   ISHUMI, Abel G. M. *The urban jobless in eastern Africa : a study of the unemployed population in the growing urban centres, with special reference to Tanzania.* Uppsala : Scandinavian Institute of African Studies, 1984, 112 p. ill., bibl.

4198   KAHN, Laurence M.; LOW, Stuart A. "An empirical model of employed search, unemployed search and non-search", *Journal of Human Resources* 19(1), wint 84 : 104-117. [USA]

4199   KASARDA, John D. "Entry-level jobs, mobility and urban minority unemployment", *Urban Affairs Quarterly* 19(1), sep 83 : 21-40. [USA]

4200   KEROVEC, Nada. "Promjene u strukturi nezaposlenosti u SR Hrvatskoj" (Changes in the unemployment structure of the Socialist Republic of Croatia), *Sociologija Sela* 21(79-81), 1983 : 101-111.

4201   KUMAR, Krishna. "Unemployment as a problem in the development of industrial societies : the English experience", *Sociological Review* 32(2), mai 84 : 185-233.

4202   LYNCH, Lisa M.; RICHARDSON, Ray. "Unemployment of young workers in Britain", *British Journal of Industrial Relations* 20(3), nov 82 : 362-372.

4203   MARE, Robert D.; WINSHIP, Christopher; KUBITSCHEK, Warren N. "The transition from youth to adult : understanding the age pattern of employment", *American Journal of Sociology* 90(2), sep 84 : 326-358. [USA]

4204   MCNABB, Robert; WOODWARD, Nicholas. "The effect of recurrent spells upon unemployment duration", *British Journal of Industrial Relations* 20(1), mar 82 : 105-108. [UK]

4205   NELSON, Hal; FIEDLER, Fred P. "Welfare for the unemployed : the rise and fall of a social experiment", *Human Organization* 43(2), 1984 : 168-177. [USA]

4206   ORGANISATION DE COOPÉRATION ET DE DÉVELOPPEMENT ÉCONOMIQUE. *Faciliter l'emploi des jeunes : politiques pour l'Irlande et le Portugal.* Paris : OCDE, 1984, 201 p. bibl.

4207   ORGANISATION DE COOPÉRATION ET DE DÉVELOPPEMENT ÉCONOMIQUE. *La nature du chômage des jeunes : analyse à l'attention des pouvoirs publics.* Paris : OCDE, 1984, 263 p. bibl.

4208   PARADEISE, Catherine. "La marine marchande française : un marché du travail fermé?", *Revue Française de Sociologie* 25(3), jul-sep 84 : 352-375.

4209   RACIONERO, Luis. *Del paro al ocio* (From unemployment to leisure). Barcelona : Anagrama, 1983, 150 p.

4210   SCHWARTZ, Bertrand. "La inserción profesional y social de los jovenes" (Youth occupational and social insertion), *Revista de Estudios de Juventud* (14), jun 84 : 30-221.

4211   SENIOR, Barbara; NAYLOR, John B. "A skills exchange for unemployed people", *Human Relations* 37(8), aug 84 : 589-602.

4212   SEXTON, J. J. *Recent trends in youth unemployment.* Dublin : Economic and Social Research Institute, 1983, viii-87 p. ill., bibl. [Ireland]

4213   SOUTH, Scott J. "Unemployment and social problems in the post-war United States", *Social Indicators Research* 15(4), nov 84 : 389-416.

4214   SPRUIT, I. P. "Definities van werkloosheid en analyseproblemen" (Definition of unemployment and analysis problems), *Sociologische Gids* 31(1), 1984 : 80-95. [Netherlands]

4215   STACK, Steven. "The effect of unemployment duration on national suicide rates : a time series analysis, 1948-1982", *Sociological Focus* 17(1), jan 84 : 17-29. [USA]

4216   STANDING, Guy. "La notion de chômage technologique", *Revue Internationale du Travail* 123(2), mar-apr 84 : 137-161.

4217   TAZELAAR, Frits; SPRENGERS, Maarten. "Werkloosheid en sociaal isolement" (Unemployment and social isolation), *Sociologische Gids* 31(1), 1984 : 48-79.

4218   VAN DER WERF, Dirk. *Crisis en maatschappelijke keuze : een visie op de crisis en de werkloosheid in het licht van de lange gold* (Crisis and social choice : an overview of crisis and unemployment in a long-wave approach). Leeuwarden : Eisma, 1983, xvi-299 p. ill., bibl., ind. [Netherlands]

4219   VAN HOUWELINGEN, Jeannet; TAZELAAR, Frits; VERBEEK, Albert. "Werkloosheid, gezondheid en sterfte in naoorlogs Nederland. Een macro-analyse op basis van ambtelijk statistische bronnenmateriaal" (Unemployment, health and death in postwar Netherlands : a macro-analysis based on statistical sources), *Sociologische Gids* 31(1), 1984 : 6-23.

18230   Employment services. Job evaluation
Services d'emploi. Évaluation des emplois

4220   CIPRESSI, Pierpaolo. *I comportamenti antisindicali del datore di lavoro* (The anti-trade union behaviour of the employer). Milano : A. Giuffrè, 1983, 225 p. bibl., ind.

4221   DANDURAND, P. "Crise, État et politiques de main-d'oeuvre", *Revue Internationale d'Action Communautaire* (10), aut 83 : 101-115. [Canada]

4222   GASTWIRTH, Joseph L. "Statistical methods for analyzing claims of employment discrimination", *Industrial and Labor Relations Review* 38(1), oct 84 : 75-86. [USA]

4223   GINSBERG, Helen. *Full employment and public policy : the United States and Sweden.* Lexington, MA; Toronto, ON : Heath, Lexington Books, 1983, xix-235 p.

4224   JENNESS, Robert A. *Positive adjustment in manpower and social policies.* Paris : OECD Publications and Information Center, 1984, 88 p. bibl.

4225   MAARSE, J. A. M. "Arbeidsmarktbeleid : enkele trends en effecten" (Labour market policy : some trends and effects), *Sociologische Gids* 31(1), 1984 : 96-120. [Netherlands]

4226   PARVATHAMMA, C. *Employment problems of university graduates.* New Delhi : Ashish, 1984, xv-163 p. bibl., ind. [India]

4227   SEMYONOV, Moshe; HOYT, Danny R.; SCOTT, Richard I. "Place, race and differential occupational opportunities", *Demography* 21(2), mai 84 : 258-270. [USA]

4228   SOFER, Catherine. "Emplois 'féminins' et emplois 'masculins' : mesure de la ségrégation et évolution de la féminisation des emplois", *Annales de l'INSEE* (52), dec 83 : 55-84. [France]

4229   YAMAGUCHI, Kazuo. "Inequality of occupational opportunity : an analysis of components and trends using information theoretic measures", *in : Treiman, D. J.; Robinson, R. V.;* [eds.], Research in social stratification and mobility. III. Greenwich, CT : JAI Press, 1984, 93-121 p.

18240   Women workers. Young workers
Travailleuses. Jeunes travailleurs

4230   "Entre-deux-mondes des travailleurs immigrés / Zwischenwelten der Gastarbeiter", *Schweizerische Zeitschrift für Soziologie / Revue Suisse de Sociologie* 10(2)(Spec. No), 1984 : 329-611.

4231   "Inländer / Ausländer" (Native people / foreign people), *Vorgänge* 23(6), 1984 : 20-106. [Germany FR]

4232 "Limites et frontières", *Espace, Populations, Sociétés* (1), 1984 : 4-154. [EEC countries] [With contributions by Bernhard MOHR, Noel CRAMER, Robert SEVRIN]

4233 "Participation (La) des femmes dans le marché du travail", *Demography* 21(2), mai 84 : 157-183. [USA] [With contributions by Ross M. STOLZENBERG, Linda J. WAITE, Diane H. FELMLEE]

4234 "Travail des femmes et famille", *Sociologie du Travail* 26(3), sep 84 : 241-375. [With contributions by M. A. BARRERE-MAURISSON, A. BARTHEZ, M. HAICAULT, M. HIRATA, I. HUMPHREY]

4235 "Women and work", *South African Labour Bulletin* 9(3), dec 83 : 1-93. [With contributions by Barbara KLUGMAN, Amanda ARMSTRONG, Paul ARENSON, Inga MOLZEN, Joanne YANITCH]

4236 "Women workers : gender inequalities and social justice", *Social Action* 34(4), oct-dec 84 : 325-405. [India]

4237 "Work and family role for women", *Journal of Marriage and the Family* 46(2), mai 84 : 357-447. [USA] [With contributions by Elizabeth MARET, Barbara FINLAY, Suzanne M. ALLEN, Richard A. KALISH, Judy CORDER, Ellen HOCK]

4238 AHMAD, Mohiuddin. *Working women in rural Bangladesh : a case study.* Dhaka : Community Development Library, 1983, 50 p.

4239 AHMAD, Zubeida. "Les femmes des régions rurales et leur travail : comment les tirer de leur dépendance?", *Revue Internationale du Travail* 123(1), jan-feb 84 : 77-93.

4240 ALCOBENDAS TIRADO, María Pilar. *Datos sobre el trabajo de la mujer en España* (Data on women's work in Spain). Madrid : Centro de Investigaciones Sociológicas, 1983, 217 p. bibl.

4241 ARMSTRONG, Pat. *Labour pains : women's work in crisis.* Toronto, ON : Women's Press, 1984, 273 p. bibl.

4242 AUGUST, Jochen. "Die Entwicklung des Arbeitsmarkts in Deutschland in den 30er Jahren und der Masseneinsatz ausländischer Arbeitskräfte während des Zweiten Weltkriegs. Das Fallbeispiel der polnischen zivilen Arbeitskräfte und Kriegsgefangenen 1939/40" (The development of the labour market in Germany in the thirties and the mass utilization of foreign manpower during the second World War. The case of the Polish civil manpower and war prisoners in 1939/40), *Archiv für Sozialgeschichte* 24, 1984 : 305-353.

4243 BARHOUM, Mohammed Ima. "Attitudes of university students towards women's work : the case of Jordan", *International Journal of Middle East Studies* 15(3), aug 83 : 369-376.

4244 BENENSON, Harold. "Women's occupational and family achievement in the US class system : a critique of the dual-career family analysis", *British Journal of Sociology* 35(1), mar 84 : 19-41.

4245 BENNETT, Laura. "Legal intervention and the female workforce : the Australian Conciliation and Arbitration Court, 1907-1921", *International Journal of the Sociology of Law* 12(1), feb 84 : 23-36.

4246 BETZ, Ellen L. "A study of career patterns of women college graduates", *Journal of Vocational Behavior* 24(3), jun 84 : 249-263. [USA]

4247 BIELEFELD, Uli. "Sozialerfahrung und ihre Verarbeitung. Arbeit, Arbeitslosigkeit und Nichtarbeit junger Ausländer" (Social experience and its elaboration. Work, unemployment and not working of young foreigners), *Schweizerische Zeitschrift für Soziologie / Revue Suisse de Sociologie* 10(2)(Spec. No), 1984 : 563-594. [Turk workers in Germany FR]

4248 BOOTH, Alan; [et al.]. "Women, outside employmlent, and marital instability", *American Journal of Sociology* 90(3), nov 84 : 567-583. [USA]

4249 BOSE, Christine E. "Household resources and US women's work : factors affecting gainful employment at the turn of the century", *American Sociological Review* 49(4), aug 84 : 474-490.

4250 CASPER, Dale E. *Women in the labor force : recent research, 1980-1983.* Monticello, IL : Vance Bibliographies, 1984, 18 p. bibl. [USA]

4251 CHAUDHURY, Rafiqul Huda. "The effect of mother's work on child care, dietary intake, and dietary adequacy of pre-school children", *Bangladesh Development Studies* 10(4), dec 82 : 33-61. [Bangladesh]

4252 CLERMONT, Louise. *Les femmes et l'aménagement du temps de travail salarié.* Québec : Gouvernement du Québec, Conseil du Statut de la Femme, 1983, vi-94 p. bibl.

4253 COYLE, A. *Redundant women.* London : Women's Press, 1984, vi-154 p. [UK]

4254 DAVIS, Kingsley. "Wives and work : the sex role revolution and its consequences", *Population and Development Review* 10(3), sep 84 : 397-417.

4255 DE OLIVEIRA, Zuleica Lopes Cavalcanti; [et al.]. "Aspectos sócio-demográficos do trabalho feminino nas áreas urbanas do Estado de São Paulo, 1970-1976" (Sociodemographic aspects of women's work in urban areas of Sao Paulo State, 1970-1976), *Revista Geográfica* (97), jun 83 : 70-82. [Brazil]

4256 DEBERDT, Michel. "Situation des travailleurs migrants à l'heure de la retraite : approche sanitaire", *Gérontologie et Société* 28, apr-mai 84 : 161-168.

4257 DEL VENTO BIELBY, Denise; BIELBY, William T. "Work commitment, sex-role attitudes, and women's employment", *American Sociological Review* 49(2), apr 84 : 234-247. [USA]

4258 DENNIS, Carolyne. "Capitalist development and women's work : a Nigerian case study", *Review of African Political Economy* (27-28), 1983 : 109-119.

4259 DEX, Shirley. "Work history analysis, women and large scale data sets", *Sociological Review* 32(4), nov 84 : 637-661. [UK]

4260 DOHSE, Knuth. "Foreign workers and work force management in West Germany", *Economic and Industrial Democracy* 5(4), nov 84 : 495-509.

4261 FENDRICH, Michael. "Wives' employment and husbands' distress : a meta-analysis and a replication", *Journal of Marriage and the Family* 46(4), nov 84 : 871-879. [USA]

4262 FLEMING, Jane P. "Wider opportunities for women : the search for equal employment", *Sage Yearbooks in Women's Policy Studies* 7, 1983 : 79-89. [USA]

4263 FOX, Mary Frank; HESSE-BIBER, Sharlene. *Women at work.* Palo Alto, CA : Mayfield Publishing Co., 1984, xiv-276 p. ill., bibl., ind. [USA]

4264 FUENTES, Annette; EHRENREICH, Barbara. *Women in the global factory.* New York, NY : Institute for New Communications; Boston, MA : South End Press, 1983, rev., 64 p. ill., bibl.

4265 GALLAND, Olivier; LOUIS, Marie-Victoire. *Jeunes en transit : l'aventure ambiguë des foyers de jeunes travailleurs.* Paris : Économie et Humanisme, Éditions Ouvrières, 1984, 236 p. bibl. [France]

4266 GALLIN, Rita S. "The entry of Chinese women into the rural labor force : a case study from Taiwan", *Signs* 9(3), spr 84 : 383-398.

4267 GARCÍA, Philip. "Dual language characteristics and earnings : male Mexican workers in the United States", *Social Science Research* 13(3), sep 84 : 221-235.

4268 GASPARD, Françoise; SERVAN-SCHREIBER, Claude. *La fin des immigrés.* Paris : Éditions du Seuil, 1984, 213 p. bibl.

4269 GRANIEWSKA, Danuta. "Awans społeczno-zawodowy kobiet" (Women's social and occupational promotion), *Nowe Drogi* 417(3), mar 84 : 18-26. [Poland]

4270 GRASSO, Jean C. *Pregnancy and work.* New York, NY : Avon, 1984, xiv-239 p.

4271 GREENSPAN, Miriam. "The fear of being alone : female psychology and women's work", *Socialist Review* 14(1), feb 84 : 93-112. [USA]

4272 GROMOVA, I. V.; DANILOVA, È. Z. "Vlijanie ėkonomičeskih i social'nyh faktorov truda ženščiny na razvitie eě kak ličnosti v razvitom socialističeskom obščestve" (Influence of economic and social factors of the woman's labour on her development as a personality in the developed socialist society), *in : Vzaimodejstvie ėkonomičeskoj i social'noj storon žizni obščestva v uslovijah razvitogo socializma* Smolensk, 1983 : 63-73.

4273 GUPTA, R. N. "Correlates of female participation in economic activity", *Indian Labour Journal* 25(3), mar 84 : 345-356.

4274 HANSON, Sandra L.; [et al.]. "Consequences of involuntary low parity for women's perceptions of homemaker and work roles : findings from a 24-year longitudinal study", *Sociology and Social Research* 68(3), apr 84 : 326-349. [USA]

4275 HERBERT, Ulrich. "Zwangsarbeit als Lernprozess. Zur Beschäftigung ausländischer Arbeiter in der westdeutschen Industrie im Ersten Weltkrieg" (Hard labour as a learning process. On the occupation of foreign workers in the West German industry during World War I), *Archiv für Sozialgeschichte* 24, 1984 : 285-304.

4276 HERZIG, Arno. "Kinderarbeit in Deutschland in Manufaktur und Protofabrik (1750-1850)" (Children's work in Germany in manufactures and proto-factories (1750-1850)), *Archiv für Sozialgeschichte* 23, 1983 : 311-375.

4277 HETTLAGE, Robert. "Unerhörte Eintragungen in ein Gästebuch — à propos der 'Gastarbeiter'" (Incredible entries in a guests book — about 'Foreign workers'), *Schweizerische Zeitschrift für Soziologie / Revue Suisse de Sociologie* 10(2)(Spec. No), 1984 : 331-354. [Switzerland]

4278 HETTLAGE-VARJAS, Andrea; HETTLAGE, Robert. "Kulturelle Zwischenwelten. Fremdarbeiter — eine Ethnie?" (Cultural transitional worlds. Foreign workers — an ethnic entity?), *Schweizerische Zeitschrift für Soziologie / Revue Suisse de Sociologie* 10(2)(Spec. No), 1984 : 357-404.

4279 HILY, Marie-Antoinette; POINARD, Michel. "À propos des associations portugaises en France ou l'identité condensée", *Schweizerische Zeitschrift für Soziologie / Revue Suisse de Sociologie* 10(2)(Spec. No), 1984 : 465-484.

4280 HONG, Sawon. "Korean women at work", *Korea Journal* 24(1), jan 84 : 4-37.

4281   HUMPHREY, John. "The growth of female employment in Brazilian manufacturing industry in the 1970s", *Journal of Development Studies* 20(4), jul 84 : 224-247.

4282   JOSEPH, George. *Women at work : the British experience.* Oxford : Allan; Atlantic Highlands, NJ : Humanities Press, 1983, x-278 p.

4283   JURIK, Nancy C.; HALEMBA, Gregory J. "Gender, working conditions and the job satisfaction of women in a non-traditional occupation : female correctional officers in men's prisons", *Sociological Quarterly* 25(4), 1984 : 551-566. [USA]

4284   KONCZ, Katalin. "A nők foglalkoztatásának demográfiai, gazdasági körülményei Magyarországon az ipari forradalom kibontakozásától az első világháborúig" (Demographic and economic conditions of female occupation from the beginnings of the industrial revolution to the first World War in Hungary), *Demográfia* 27(2-3), 1984 : 275-293.

4285   KONTOS, Maria. *Verbandsstrategien zur Ausländerbeschäftigung in der Bundesrepublik : eine Analyse der Integrationsstrategien der Unternehmerverbände und der Gewerkschaften gegenüber den ausländischen Arbeitern* (Unions' strategies for the employment of foreign workers in West Germany : an analysis of the integration strategies of the employers' associations and of trade unions concerning immigrant workers). Königstein-im-Taunus : Hanstein, 1983, viii-235 p. bibl.

4286   KREBSBACH-GNATH, Camilla; [et al.]. *Frauenbeschäftigung und neue Technologien* (Women's employment and new technologies). München : R. Oldenbourg, 1983, ix-327 p. bibl., ill.

4287   KRELL, Gertraude. *Das Bild der Frau in der Arbeitswissenschaft* (Woman's image in labour science). Frankfurt-am-Main; New York, NY : Campus, 1984, 234 p. ill., bibl.

4288   LAGRAVE, Rose-Marie. "Bilan critique des recherches sur les agricultrices en France", *Études Rurales* 92, oct-dec 83 : 9-40.

4289   LAMMING, G. N. *Women in agricultural cooperatives : constraints and limitation to full participation.* Rome : Human Resources, Institutions, and Agrarian Reform Division, Food and Agriculture Organization of the United Nations, 1983, vi-51 p. bibl. [Developing countries]

4290   LANDAU, C. E. "La CE et l'égalité entre hommes et femmes en matière d'emploi : législation et jurisprudence récentes", *Revue Internationale du Travail* 123(1), jan-feb 84 : 57-76.

4291   LEITNER, Helga. *Gastarbeiter in der städtischen Gesellschaft : Segregation, Integration und Assimilation von Arbeitsmigranten; am Beispiel jugoslawischer Gastarbeiter in Wien* (Immigrated workers in urban society : segregation, integration and assimilation of labour migrants; by the example of Yugoslav migrant workers in Vienna). Frankfurt-am-Main; New York, NY : Campus, 1983, 328 p. ill., bibl.

4292   LHIJUMBA, Beat J. "Attitudes of Tanzanian husbands towards the employment of their wives", *Africa Development* 8(2), jun 83 : 74-85.

4293   LIMAGE, Leslie J. "Young migrants of the second generation in Europe : education and labor market insertion prospects", *International Migrations* 22(4), 1984 : 367-388.

4294   LIPPOLD, M. "Lebensbedingungen, Organisiertheit und Wertorientierungen von Arbeiterinnen in der beginnenden Weltwirtschaftskrise" (Living conditions, organization and value orientation of women workers at the beginning of the world economic crisis), *Jahrbuch für Volkskunde und Kulturgeschichte* 11, 1983 : 90-122.

4295   LOLLIVIER, Stéfan. "Revenu offert, prétentions salariales et activité des femmes mariées : un modèle d'analyse", *Économie et Statistique* 167, jun 84 : 3-15. [France]

4296   MARSHALL, Gordon. "On the sociology of women's unemployment, its neglect and significance", *Sociological Review* 32(2), mai 84 : 234-259.

4297   MASUR, Jenny. "Women's work in rural Andalusia", *Ethnology* 23(1), jan 84 : 25-38. [Spain]

4298   MATHER, Celia E. "Industrialization in the Tangerang regency of West Java : women workers and the Islamic patriarchy", *Bulletin of Concerned Asian Scholars* 15(2), 1983 : 2-17.

4299   MATTHAEI, Julie A. *An economic history of women in America : women's work, the sexual division of labor, and the development of capitalism.* Brighton : Harvester Press, 1982, xiv-381 p.

4300   MOLNÁRNÉ VENYIGE, Júlia. "A női munka és a társadalmi munkaszervezet" (Female labour and social organization of work), *Magyar Tudomány* 29(2), 1984 : 137-144. [Hungary]

4301   NAMIHIRA, Isao; HIGA, Teruyuki; KYAN, Shiichi. "Jyoshi rodo-ryoku no dohko to sono shakai keizai teki eikyo ni kansuru chosa houkoku" (A report on the trend of women's labor force and its socio-economic effects), *Okinawa L + E* 13, 1984 : 1-67.

4302   NASH, June; KELLY, Maria Patricia Fernandez. *Women, men, and the international division of labor.* Albany, NY : State University of New York Press, 1983, 400 p. bibl., ind.

4303   NEMITZ, Barbara. "Die arbeitsschutzbedürftige Frau" (Women workers' protection), *Argument* 26(147), oct 84 : 699-718. [Germany FR]

4304 ODENDAHL, Teresa; GRIFFEN, Joyce; [eds.]. "Women and work", *Social Science Journal (Fort Collins)* 21(4), oct 84 : 3-107.

4305 PAPANEK, Hanna. "Geschlechts-und Klassendifferenzierung. Frauenarbeit und soziale Ungleichheit im internationalen Vergleich" (Sex and class differentiation. Women's work and social inequality : an international comparison), *Soziale Welt* 35(1-2), 1984 : 190-214.

4306 PAUKERT, Liba. *The employment and unemployment of women in OECD countries.* Paris : Organisation for Economic Co-operation and Development; Washington, DC : OECD Publications and Information Center, 1984, 88 p. ill., bibl. [Abstract USA]

4307 PITROU, Agnès; [et al.]. "De l'indivisibilité à la reconnaissance : travail de la femme et stratégies familiales", *Tocqueville Review* 6(1), sum 84 : 85-96. [France]

4308 PITTIN, Renée. "Le travail occulté des femmes invisibles : collecte et analyse d'informations au Nigeria", *Revue Internationale du Travail* 123(4), jul-aug 84 : 515-534.

4309 RAMANAMMA, A.; BAMBAWALE, Usha. "Transitory status images of working women in modern India", *Indian Journal of Social Work* 45(2), jul 84 : 189-202.

4310 RAMET, Pedro. "Women, work and self-management in Yugoslavia", *East European Quarterly* 17(4), jan 84 : 459-468.

4311 REXROAT, Cynthia; SHEHAN, Constance. "Expected versus actual work roles of women", *American Sociological Review* 49(3), jun 84 : 349-358. [USA]

4312 RUGHÖFT, Sigrid. "Frauen in Familie und Beruf" (Women in family and profession), *Hauswirtschaft und Wissenschaft* 32(1), 1984 : 25-32.

4313 SABOURIN, Annie. *Le travail des femmes dans la CEE : les conditions juridiques.* Paris : Economica, 1984, viii-149 p. bibl.

4314 SALOWSKY, Heinz. *Sozialpolitische Aspekte der Ausländerbeschäftigung* (Socio-political aspects of foreigners' employment). Köln : Deutscher Instituts-Verlag, 1983, 40 p. bibl. [Germany FR]

4315 SANGER, Mary Bryna. "Generating employment for AFDC mothers", *Social Service Review* 58(1), mar 84 : 28-48. [USA] [Aid to Families with Dependent Children]

4316 SCHIFFAUER, Werner. "Religion und Identität. Eine Fallstudie zum Problem der Reislamisierung bei Arbeitsemigranten" (Religion and identity. A case study of the problem of the return to Islam among migrant workers), *Schweizerische Zeitschrift für Soziologie / Revue Suisse de Sociologie* 10(2)(Spec. No), 1984 : 485-516. [Turkish migrants in Germany FR]

4317 SELVA, Beatriz. *Modalidades del trabajo femenino en San Felipe del Agua, Oaxaca* (Modalities of the women's work in San Felipe del Agua, Oaxaca). México : FLACSO, 1984, 112 p.

4318 SMART, John E.; TEODOSIO, Virginia A.; JIMENEZ, Carol J. "Les travailleurs philippins au Moyen-Orient : profil social et incidences sur la politique d'immigration" (Filipino Workers in the Middle East : social profile and policy implications), *International Migration / Migrations Internationales* 23(1), 1985 : 29-43.

4319 STOLZENBERG, Ross M.; WAITE, Linda J. "Local labor markets, children and labor force participation of wives", *Demography* 21(2), mai 84 : 157-170. [USA]

4320 TALWAR, Usha. *Social profile of working women.* Jodhpur : Jain Brothers, 1984, 252 p. [India]

4321 UGALDE, Antonio. "La mujer en la fuerza laboral en Santo Domingo : un estudio socio-demográfico" (Women in Santo Domingo labour force : a socio-demographic study), *Estudios Sociales (Santo Domingo)* 17(55), mar 84 : 85-102.

4322 VALETTE, Aline; CAPY, Marcelle. *Femmes et travail au XIXe siècle.* Paris : Syros, 1984, 150 p.

4323 WOLF-GRAAF, Anke. *Die verborgene Geschichte der Frauenarbeit* (The hidden history of women's work). Weinheim : Beltz, 1983, 160 p. ill., bibl.

18300 PERSONNEL MANAGEMENT. WORKING CONDITIONS
ADMINISTRATION DU PERSONNEL. CONDITIONS DE TRAVAIL

18310 Work standards. Work study
Normes de travail. Étude du travail

4324 BARON, James N.; BIELBY, William T. "The organization of work in a segmented economy", *American Sociological Review* 49(4), aug 84 : 454-473. [USA]

4325 BHATIA, S. K. *Personnel management and industrial relations : new ideas, trends and experiences.* New Delhi : Deep and Deep, 1983, viii-238 p. bibl., ind.

4326 BYARS, Lloyd L.; RUE, Leslie W. *Human resource and personnel management.* Homewood, IL : R. D. Irwin, 1984, xv-501 p. ill., bibl., ind.

4327 CASTILLO, Juan José. "Las 'nuevas formas de organización del trabajo'" (The 'new forms of work organization'), *Revista Española de Investigaciones Sociológicas* 26, apr-jun 84 : 201-212.

4328 DÜRHOLT, Eva; [et al.]. *Qualitative Arbeitsanalyse : neue Verfahren zur Beurteilung von Tätigkeiten* (Qualitative work analysis : new method for activity assessment). Frankfurt-am-Main; New York, NY : Campus, 1983, 352 p.

4329 GUSOV, A. Z. "Social'nye rezervy trudovogo kollektiva i ih učet v upravlenii" (Social reserves of the labour collectivity and their calculation in management), *in : Aktual'nye problemy social'nogo upravlenija* L'vov, 1983 : 117-128.

4330 GUSTAVSEN, Jorn; HÉTHY, Lajos. "Szervezett vagy 'humanizált' ipari munkát? Új munkaszervezeti formák és társadalmi-gazdasági környezetük Európában" (Organized or 'humanized' industrial work? New Forms of work organization and their social-economic surroundings in Europe), *Valóság* 27(10), 1984 : 45-57.

4331 HVINDEN, Bjórn. "Exits and entrances : notes for a theory of socialization and boundary-crossing in work organizations", *Acta Sociologica* 27(3), 1984 : 185-198.

4332 ITO, Minoru. "Développement de la micro-électronique et changements de l'organisation du travail dans les entreprises japonaises", *Sociologie du Travail* 26(4), oct-dec 84 : 457-467.

4333 KELLY, John. "Pratiques patronales de restructuration du travail : procès de travail, marché de l'emploi et débouchés commerciaux", *Sociologie du Travail* 26(1), mar 84 : 26-49.

4334 KOLETNIK, Franc. "Problemi prihodkov in stroškov pri svobodni menjavi dela v okviru delovne organizacije" (Income and expense in the free exchange of labor within the framework of the work organization), *Ekonomska Revija* 35(1), mar 84 : 77-91. [Yugoslavia]

4335 LOUVEL, Denis. *La véritable seconde révolution industrielle; réflexion sur les procédés anciens et actuels de fonctionnement de l'entreprise : Taylor, Ford, sociologie industrielle, cercles de qualité, groupes de travail, etc.* Buchères : D. Louvel, 1983, 244 p. ill.

4336 MAKSIMOV, A. G.; [et al.]. "Trudovoj kollektiv i formirovanie social'noj otvetstvennosti ličnosti" (The labour collectivity and formation of social responsibility of the personality), *Nekotorye Filosofskie Problemy Gosudarstva i Prava* (4), 1983 : 118-127.

4337 MALLE, Silvana. "Nuova forme di organizzazione del lavoro in URSS : le brigate di lavoro" (New forms of work organization in the USSR : the working brigades), *Rivista Internazionale di Scienze Sociali* 92(4), oct-dec 84 : 509-528.

4338 MEIKSINS, Peter F. "Scientific management and class relations : a dissenting view", *Theory and Society* 13(2), mar 84 : 177-209.

4339 MOROZOV, M. V. "Rol' trudovogo kollektiva v formirovanii ličnosti rabotnika sel'sko-hozjajstvennogo proizvodstva" (Role of the labour collectivity in the formation of a worker's personality in the agricultural production), *in : Trudovoj kollektiv i formirovanie ličnosti* Moskva, 1983 : 105-119.

4340 RUFFIER, Jean. "Industrialiser sans tayloriser", *Sociologie du Travail* 26(4), oct-dec 84 : 522-527.

4341 ŠEPEL', V. M.; [ed.]. *Social'noe upravlenie i ĕffektivnost' proizvodstva : opyt sociologičeskogo issledovanija problemy* (Social management and efficiency of production : an essay of sociological research on the problem). Moskva : Ĕkonomika, 1982, 183 p.

4342 ŠOROHOVA, Ĕ. V.; [et al.]. *Social'no-psihologičeskie problemy proizvodstvennogo kollektiva* (Socio-psychological problems of a production collectivity). Moskva : s.n., 1983, 283 p.

4343 STAUDT, Erich. "Wachsende Freiräume in der Gestaltung von Arbeitsorganisationen" (Growing leisure spaces in the work organization pattern), *Mitteilungen aus der Arbeitsmarkt- und Berufsforschung* 17(1), 1984 : 94-104.

4344 STEPANJUK, V. P. "Trudovoj kollektiv v social'no-klassovoj strukture razvitogo socializma" (The labour collectivity in the socio-class structure of developed socialism), *in : XXVI s'ezd KPSS o dostiženii social'noj odnorodnosti sovetskogo obščestva* Moskva, 1983 : 124-132.

4345 STOREY, John. *Managerial prerogative and the question of control.* London; Boston, MA... Routledge and Kegan Paul, 1983, viii-243 p.

4346 TERSSAC, Gilbert de; CORIAT, Benjamin. "Micro-électronique et travail ouvrier dans les industries de process", *Sociologie du Travail* 26(4), oct-dec 84 : 384-397.

4347 TOURÉ, Oussouby. "Le refus du travail forcé au Sénégal oriental", *Cahiers d'Études Africaines* 24(1), 1984 : 25-38.

18320 Working conditions
Conditions du travail

4348 "Histoire des fabriques", *Études Rurales* 93-94, jan-jun 84 : 241-291. [France]

4349 AGNEW, Robert. "The work ethic and delinquency", *Sociological Focus* 17(4), oct 84 : 337-346. [USA]

4350 ANDORKA, Rudolf. "Elements of private welfare production in Hungary (from time budget data)", *Social Indicators Research* 14(3), apr 84 : 235-239. [1976-77]

4351 ANDORKA, Rudolf; HARCSA, István; NIEMI, Iiris. "Az időfelhasználás Magyarországon és Finnországban" (Time budget in Hungary and in Finland), *Statisztikai Szemle* 62(6), jun 84 : 621-637.

4352 ANDORKA, Rudolf; HARCSA, István; NIEMI, Iiris. *Use of time in Hungary and in Finland : comparison of results of time budget surveys by the Central Statistical Offices of Finland and Hungary.* Helsinki : Central Statistical Office of Finland, 1983, 62 p.

4353 BÄCKER, Gerhard. "Lebensbedürfnisse und Arbeitszeitverkürzung. Ein Schritt zur Versöhnung von Arbeit und Leben?" (The living necessitities and the reduction of work working time. A step to the reconciliation of labour and life?), *Mitarbeit (Die)* 32(4), 1983 : 294-309.

4354 BAGNARA, Sebastiano; VETRONE, Giuseppe. "Osservazioni sui rapporti fra caratteristiche della communicazione nell'ambiente di lavoro e disturbi psichici degli addetti ai calcolatori elettronici" (On the relations between communications characteristics in the work environment and computer workers' psychical disturbances), *Difesa Sociale* 62(5), oct 83 : 28-40. [Italy]

4355 BARAN, Józef. "Określenie klimatu społecznego w środowisku pracy" (Qualification of social climate in working environment), *Humanizacja Pracy* 3, 1984 : 58-66.

4356 BOGUN, Manfred. *Berufseinstellungen von Verwaltungsbeamten : ein empirischer Vergleich zwischen Anwärtern und berufserfahrenen Beamten* (Professional attitudes of administrative employees : an empirical comparison between candidates and experienced employees). Freiburg-im-Breisgau : Hochschulverlag, 1983, ix-367 p. ill., bibl. [Germany FR]

4357 BOISARD, Pierre; VENNAT-DEBAYE, Marie-Madeleine. "Réduction de la durée du travail et attitudes temporelles", *Cahiers du Centre d'Études de l'Emploi* (27), 1984 : 3-101. [France]

4358 BRUNET, Luc. *Le climat de travail dans l'organisation : définition, diagnostic et conséquences.* Montréal, PQ : Agence d'ARC, 1983, 141 p. bibl.

4359 BURGDORFF, Stephan; MEYER-LARSEN, Werner; [eds.]. *Weniger Arbeit : Überlebenchance der Industriegesellschaft* (Less work : survival opportunity for the industrial society). Reinbek-bei-Hamburg : Rowohlt, 1984, 188 p. ill. [Germany FR]

4360 CARMIGNANI, Fabrizo. *Assenteismo e presenteismo : due strategie del comportamento operaio* (Absenteeism and presentism : two strategies of the worker's behaviour). Milano : Franco Angeli, 1984, 211 p. bibl.

4361 CLOSE, Paul; COLLINS, Rosie. "Domestic labour and patriarchy : the implications of a study in the North-East of England", *International Journal of Sociology and Social Policy* 3(4), 1983 : 31-47.

4362 CUNNINGHAM, J. Barton; WHITE, T. H.; [eds.]. *Quality of working life : contemporary cases.* Ottawa : Canadian Government Publishing Centre, Supply and Services, Canada, 1984, xiv-484 p. ill., bibl.

4363 CZAJKA, Stanisław. *Człowiek i jego potrzeby w procesie pracy* (Man and his requirements in the work process). Warszawa : Państwowe Wudawnictwo Ekonomiczne, 1984, 199 p.

4364 D'ARCY, Carl; SYROTUIK, John; SIDDIQUE, C. M. "Perceived job attributes, job satisfaction, and psychological distress : a comparison of working men and women", *Human Relations* 37(8), 1984 : 603-611. [Canada]

4365 DELAMOTTE, Yves; TAKEZAWA, Sin-ichi. *Quality of working life in international perspective.* Geneva : International Labour Office, 1984, ix-89 p. ill., bibl.

4366 DELEY, Warren W. "American and Danish police 'drop-out' rates : Denmark's force as a case study in high job satisfaction, low stress and low turnover", *Journal of Vocational Behavior* 25(1), aug 84 : 58-69.

4367 DELLI CARPINI, Michael X.; [et al.]. "Does it make any difference how you feel about your job? An exploratory study of the relationship between job satisfaction and political orientations", *Micropolitics* 3(2), 1983 : 227-251. [USA]

4368 DOBROWOLSKA, Danuta. *Wartość pracy dla jednostki w środowisku przemysłowym* (Employment as value for an individual in industrial environment). Wrocław : Ossolineum, 1984, 427 p.

4369 DRANCOURT, Michel. *La fin du travail.* Paris : Hachette, 1984, 329 p. ill., bibl. [France]

4370 DUCLOS, Denis. "La santé au travail comme thème d'action militante : l'expérience des groupes COSH aux États-Unis", *Sociologie du Travail* 26(2), jun 84 : 177-194.

4371 DUGGER, William M. "Human liberation : workplace reform as the next step in social evolution", *International Journal of Social Economics* 11(5), 1984 : 29-39.

4372 DWORKIN, James B.; [et al.]. "How German workers view their jobs", *Columbia Journal of World Business* 18(2), sum 83 : 48-54.

4373 ERALY, Alain. "À propos de la satisfaction au travail. Nouvelles perspectives", *Annales de l'Institut de Sociologie,* 1983 : 61-79.

4374   FRASER, Thomas Morris. *Human stress, work, and job satisfaction : a critical approach.*
        Geneva : International Labour Office, 1983, 72 p. ill., bibl.
4375   GERMANN, Richard; BLUMENSON, Diane; ARNOLD, Peter. *Working and liking it.*
        New York, NY : Fawcett Columbine, 1984, xii-191 p.
4376   GLAUBRECHT, Helmut; WAGNER, Dieter; ZANDER, Ernst. *Arbeitszeit im Wandel : neue
        Formen der Arbeitszeitgestaltung* (Working time in change : new forms of working time
        arrangement). Freiburg-im-Breisgau : R. Huafe, 1984, 273 p. ill., bibl., ind.
4377   GOETCHEUS, Vernon M. "Voluntarism... and Reagan", *Journal of the Institute for
        Socioeconomic Studies* 9(2), sum 84 : 36-48.
4378   GORDON, Michael E.; BEAUVAIS, Laura L.; LADD, Robert T. "The job satisfaction
        and union commitment of unionized engineers", *Industrial and Labor Relations Review*
        37(3), apr 84 : 359-370. [USA]
4379   GRAY, David E. "Job satisfaction among Australian nurses", *Human Relations* 37(12),
        dec 84 : 1063-1077.
4380   GROSSIN, William. "Temps de travail et temps libres", *Revue Française des Affaires Sociales*
        38(2), jun 84 : 9-20.
4381   GUEST, Robert H. "Organizational democracy and the quality of work life : the man on
        the assembly line", *International Yearbook of Organizational Democracy* 1, 83 : 139-153. [USA]
4382   GUSTAVSEN, Bjørn. "The Norwegian work environment reform : the transition from
        general principles to workplace action", *International Yearbook of Organizational Democracy*,
        83 : 545-563.
4383   HABUDA, Ludwik. "Niektóre elementy systemu wartości pracy urzędników terenowej
        administracji państwowej" (Some elements of the work quality values system of regional
        civil servants), *Humanizacja Pracy* 3, 1984 : 3-16.
4384   HART, Robert A. *Shorter working time : a dilemma for collective bargaining.* Paris : Organisation
        for Economic Co-operation and Development; Washington, DC : OECD Publications
        and Information Center, 1984, 92 p. ill., bibl.
4385   HETTLAGE, Robert. "Humanisierung der Arbeit. Über einige Zusammenhänge zwischen
        Wirklichkeitsbildern und Wirklichkeit" (Humanization of work. About some relations
        between images of reality and reality), *Betriebswirtschaft (Die)* 43(3), 1983 : 395-406.
        [Germany FR]
4386   HIRDINA, H. "Rationalisierte Hausarbeit : die Küche im Neuen Bauen" (Rationalized
        housework : the kitchen in the new building), *Jahrbuch für Volkskunde und Kulturgeschichte*
        11, 1983 : 44-80. [German DR]
4387   HOLLER, Manfred J. "Humanisierung der Arbeit als Managementstrategie" (The
        humanization of work as management strategy), *Mitarbeit (Die)* 32(2), 1983 : 110-124.
4388   HOLMSTRÖM, Mark. *Industry and inequality : the social anthropology of Indian labour.*
        Cambridge, Cambridgeshire; New York, NY : Cambridge University Press, 1984, x-342 p.
        bibl., ind.
4389   HOPKINS, Andrew. "Blood money? The effect of bonus pay on safety in coal mines",
        Australian and New Zealand Journal of Sociology 20(1), mar 84 : 23-46.
4390   HOPKINS, Andrew; PARNELL, Nina. "Why coal mine safety regulations in Australia
        are not enforced", *International Journal of the Sociology of Law* 12(2), mai 84 : 179-194.
4391   HUDSON, Randy. "Corporate structure and job satisfaction : a focus on employer
        characteristics", *Sociology and Social Research* 69(1), oct 84 : 22-49.
4392   IVANCEVICH, John M.; MATTESON, Michael T. "A type A-B person-work environ-
        ment interaction model for examinig occupational stress and consequences", *Human
        Relations* 37(7), jul 84 : 491-513.
4393   IWASAKI, Nobuhiko. "Jidosha sangyo rodo-sha ni okeru rodo seikatsu to sogai" (Labour
        and alienation of automobile workers), *Kobe University Bulletin of the Faculty of Letters* 11,
        1984 : 1-57. [Japan]
4394   JEDRZYCKI, Wiesław; [ed.]. *Człowiek, praca, postęp społeczny* (Man, labour, social progress).
        Warszawa : Państwowe Wydawnictwo Ekonomiczne, 1984, 295 p. [Poland]
4395   JOIN-LAMBERT, M. T.; [ed.]. *Aménagement et réduction du temps de travail.* Paris : la
        Documentation Française, 1984, 282 p.
4396   KAIJAGE, Fred J. *Labor conditions in the Tanzanian mining industry, 1930-1960.* Boston, MA :
        African Studies Center, Boston University, 1983, 23 p. bibl.
4397   KERN, Horst; SCHUMANN, Michael. "Work and social character : old and new
        contours", *Economic and Industrial Democracy* 5(1), feb 84 : 51-71.
4398   KESSLER, Francis. "La durée du travail en Allemagne 150 ans d'histoire législative et
        conventionnelle", *Allemagnes d'Aujourd'hui* (90), dec 84 : 6-25.
4399   KRAU, Edgar. "The attitudes toward work in career transitions", *Journal of Vocational Behavior*
        23(3), dec 83 : 270-285. [Israel]

4400 KRAU, Edgar. "Commitment to work in immigrants : its functions and peculiarities", *Journal of Vocational Behavior* 24(3), jun 84 : 329-339. [USA]

4401 KRUPINSKI, Jerzy. "Psychological disturbances and work fulfilment", *Australian and New Zealand Journal of Sociology* 20(1), mar 84 : 56-65. [Australia; USA; New Zealand]

4402 KURTZ, Marie France D. "Les budgets-temps : réflexion épistémologique", *Année Sociologique* 34, 1984 : 9-27. [France]

4403 LEIPERT, Christian. "Humanisierung der Lebens- und Arbeitswelt als Herausforderung an die ökonomische Theorie" (The humanization of life and labour world as a challenge to economic theory), *Zeitschrift für Sozialökonomie* 21(60), 1984 : 23-28.

4404 LEMEL, Yannick. "Emplois du temps et activités ménagères : un bilan et des perspectives", *Année Sociologique* 34, 1984 : 29-42. [France]

4405 LIMA CAMARGO, Luis Octavio de. "Temps libre et culture des aires urbaines dans les sociétés en voie de développement : le cas du Brésil", *Tiers-Monde* 25(97), mar 84 : 125-138.

4406 LINGSOM, Susan; ELLINGSAETER, Anne Lise. *Arbeid, fritid og samvaer : endringer i tidsbruk i 70-årene = Work, leisure, and time spent with others : changes in time use in the 70's.* Oslo : Statistisk Sentralbyrå, 1983, 124 p. ill., bibl.

4407 LOOS, Jocelyne. "Le syndicalisme à l'épreuve des expériences d'aménagement du temps de travail", *Revue Française des Affaires Sociales* 38(2), jun 84 : 21-38. [France]

4408 LÜDTKE, Hartmut. "Gleichförmigkeiten im alltäglichen Freizeitverhalten : eine Analyse von Zeitbudget-Daten aus zwei norddeutschen Grossstädten" (Similarities in weekday free time behaviour : time budget-data analysis from two big cities of northern Germany), *Zeitschrift für Soziologie* 13(4), oct 84 : 346-362.

4409 MAIER, Walter. *Kriterien humaner Arbeit : Persönlichkeitsentwicklung durch humane Arbeitssysteme* (The criteria of human work : personality development through the human working system). Stuttgart : F. Engke, 1983, 417 p. ill., bibl., ind.

4410 MANSELL, Jacquelynne; RANKIN, Tom. *Changing organizations : the quality of working life process.* Toronto, ON : Ontario Ministry of Labour, Ontario Quality of Working Life Centre, 1983, 56 p. bibl.

4411 MASTEKAASA, Arne. "Multiplicative and additive models of job and life satisfaction", *Social Indicators Research* 14(2), feb 84 : 141-163. [USA]

4412 MEHRENBERGER, Gabriel. "Le travail, arme secrète des Japonais", *Études*, apr 84 : 463-476.

4413 MEIER, Gretl S. *Worker learning and worktime flexibility.* Kalamazoo, MI : Upjohn Institute for Employement Research, 1983, ix-64 p.

4414 MEURANT, Jacques. *Le service volontaire de la Croix-Rouge dans la société d'aujourd'hui.* Genève : Institut Henry-Dunant, 1984, x-201-8 p. ill., bibl.

4415 MITTLER, Hans. *Humanisierung der Industriearbeit durch Organisationsentwicklung* (Humanization of the industrial work through organizational development). Frankfurt-am-Main : R. G. Fischer, 1984, 242 p. ill., bibl.

4416 MOTTAZ, Clifford. "Education and work satisfaction", *Human Relations* 37(11), nov 84 : 985-1004.

4417 NACHREINER, Friedhelm. "Psychologische Probleme der Arbeitszeit. Schichtarbeit und ihre psychosozialen Konsequenzen" (The psychological problems of the working time. Shift work and its psychosocial consequences), *Universitas* 39(4), 1984 : 349-356.

4418 NEAR, Janet P. "Relationships between job satisfaction and life satisfaction : test of a causal model", *Social Indicators Research* 15(4), nov 84 : 351-367. [USA]

4419 ORGANISATION INTERNATIONALE DU TRAVAIL. *Les conditions et le milieu de travail.* Genève : BIT, 1984, vii-91 p.

4420 PAUL, Jean-Jacques. "Comportement en cours d'étude et emploi", *Consommation* 31(1), mar 84 : 89-106. [France] [ENG]

4421 PAVLOV, O. "URSS. Organización y trabajo voluntario" (USSR. Organization and voluntary work), *Revista de Estudios de Juventud* (13), mar 84 : 159-170.

4422 PIETRUCHA, Jerzy. "Humanistyczne uwarunkowania środowiska pracy" (Humanistic determinants of work environment), *Humanizacja Pracy* (3), 1984 : 17-25.

4423 PIOTET, Françoise; MABILE, Jacques. *Conditions de travail, mode d'emploi. 2 vols.* Montrouge, Hauts-de-Seine : Édition de l'ANACT, 1984, 214, [40] p. bibl.

4424 POLSKA AKADEMIA NAUK KOMITET BADAŃ I PROGNOZ 'POLSKA 2000'. *Ewolucje polskiego systemu pracy w latach 1981-2000. Konferencja w Jabłonnie, 10-11 grudnia 1981 r.* (Evolution of the Polish labour system in the years 1981-2000. Conference in Jablonna, December 10-11th, 1981). Wrocław : Ossolineum, 1984, 490 p.

4425 PRESSER, Harriet B. "Job characteristics of spouses and their work shifts", *Demography* 21(4), nov 84 : 575-589. [USA]

4426 PRIETO ESCUDERO, Germán. "Seguro de accidentes de trabajo agricola e industrial : significación sociológica" (Agricultural and industrial occupational accidents : sociological significance), _Revista de Política Social_ (140), dec 83 : 73-95.

4427 RIPON, Albert. _La qualité de la vie de travail._ Paris : Presses Universitaires de France, 1983, 268 p. ill., bibl. [France]

4428 RONEN, Simcha. _Alternative work schedules : selecting — implementing — and evaluating._ Homewood, IL : D. Jones-Irwin, 1984, xiii-255 p. ill., bibl., ind.

4429 SAPIR, Jacques. _Travail et travailleurs en URSS._ Paris : La Découverte, 1984, 126 p. bibl.

4430 SCHNEIDER, Michael. _Streit um Arbeitszeit : Geschichte des Kampfes um Arbeitszeitverkürzung in Deutschland_ (Fight for working time : history of the disputes for working-time shortening in Germany. Ed. by Hans Mayr and Hans Janssen). Köln : Bund-Verlag, 1984, 286-4 p. ill., bibl.

4431 SCHOOLER, Carmi; [et al.]. "Work for the household : its nature and consequences for husbands and wives", _American Journal of Sociology_ 90(1), jul 84 : 97-124. [USA]

4432 SCHWERIN, Hans-Alexander von. "Humanisierung der Arbeit und Betriebsverfassung : Anmerkungen zur Funktion des Betriebsrats im Kontext von Strategien der Beeinflussung technisch-organisatorischen Wandels im Betrieb" (Humanization of work and plant constitution : the function of the works committee in the context of strategies foe influencing techno-organizational change in plant), _Klner Zeitschrift für Soziologie und Sozialpsychologie_ 36(1), mar 84 : 107-125.

4433 SEILLAN, Hubert. "L'entreprise et la sécurité du travail", _Revue Française des Affaires Sociales_ 38(1), mar 84 : 77-102. [France]

4434 SOBCZAK-RUSTECKA, Janina. "Społeczno-ekonomiczne skutki wypadków przy pracy i chorób zawodowych" (Social and economic consequences of occupational accidents and diseases), _Praca i Zabezpieczenie Społeczne_ 26(11), 1984 : 9-16. [Poland]

4435 SPERLING, Hans Joachim. _Pause als soziale Arbeitszeit : theoretische und praktische Aspekte einer gewerkschaftlichen Arbeits- und Zeitpolitik_ (Pause as social working time : theoretical and practical aspects of trade unions' work and time policy). Berlin : Verlag Die Arbeitswelt, 1983, 200 p. [Germany FR]

4436 SPYROPOULOS, Georges. "Les conditions de travail dans les pays industriels : quel avenir?", _Revue Internationale du Travail_ 123(4), jul-aug 84 : 429-444.

4437 STACHOWICZ, Andrzej. "Budżet czasu dziecka wiejskiego a uczestnictwo w kulturze" (A time budget of a countryside child and participation in culture), _Wieś Współczesna_ 12, 1984 : 78-85.

4438 VALADEZ, Joseph J.; CLIGNET, Rémi. "Housework as an ordeal : culture of standards versus standardization of culture", _American Journal of Sociology_ 89(4), jan 84 : 812-835.

4439 WILSON, Mark. "Family, urban and regional influences on giving behaviour", _Papers of the Regional Science Association_ 53, 1983 : 189-197. [USA]

4440 YANKELOVICH, Daniel; IMMERWAHR, John. "Putting the work ethic to work", _Society_ 21(2), feb 84 : 58-76.

4441 ZAMPETTI, Pier Luigi. _L'uomo e il lavoro nella nuova società : dai sindicati ai computers?_ (Man and work in the new society : from trade unions to computers?). Milano : Rusconi, 1984, 203 p.

4442 ZBIEGIEŃ-MACIĄG, Lidia. _Motywacyjne uwarunkowania społecznej aktywności załogi przemysłowej a satysfakcja z pracy_ (Motivational conditions of social activity of industrial staff and work satisfaction). Kraków : Akademia Górniczo-Hutnicza, 1984, 184 p.

18330 Labour turnover
Renouvellement de la main-d'oeuvre

4443 ALLEN, P. T. "Size of workforce, morale and absenteeism : a re-examination", _British Journal of Industrial Relations_ 20(1), mar 82 : 83-100.

4444 ALLEN, Steven G. "Trade unions, absenteeism, and exit voice", _Industrial and Labor Relations Review_ 37(3), apr 84 : 331-345. [USA]

4445 CROCKER, Jennifer; [ed.]. "After affirmative action : barriers to occupational advancement for women and minorities", _American Behavioral Scientist_ 27(3), feb 84 : 283-407. [With contributions by Kay DEAUX, William H. EXUM]

4446 EDWARDS, Paul; SCULLION, Hugh. "Absenteeism and the control of work", _Sociological Review_ 32(3), aug 84 : 547-572. [UK]

4447 FARRELL, Dan; PETERSEN, James C. "Commitment, absenteeism, and turnover of new employees : a longitudinal study", _Human Relations_ 37(8), aug 84 : 681-692.

4448 GUSTMAN, Alan L.; STEINMEIER, Thomas L. "Partial retirement and the analysis of retirement behavior", _Industrial and Labor Relations Review_ 37(3), apr 84 : 403-415. [USA]

4449   KRUIDENIER, H. "Over de voorspelbaarheid van de hoogte van het ziekteverzuim m.b.v. werkloosheidscijfers : een analyse over de periode 1965-1982" (Sick leave forecasting according to unemployment rates : an analysis over the 1965-1982 period), *Mens en Maatschappij* 59(1), feb 84 : 68-81. [Netherlands]
4450   PARNES, Herbert S.; [ed.]. *Policy issues in work and retirement.* Kalamazoo, MI : W. E. Upjohn Institute for Employment Research, 1983, vii-286 p.
4451   REGNIER, Claude. "Les migrations de retraite et le déracinement géographique", *Gérontologie et Société* 27, jan 84 : 11-31. [France]

18400   OCCUPATIONS. VOCATIONAL TRAINING
PROFESSIONS. FORMATION PROFESSIONNELLE

18410   Occupational sociology
Sociologie de la profession

4452   AKIYAMA, Kenji. "Profession gainen ni kansuru sho-mondai" (Problems of the concept of 'professions'), *Shakaigaku Nenshi* 25, 1984 : 181-196.
4453   BAUER, Leonhard. "Arbeit ist nicht gleich Arbeit. Die gesellschaftliche (erzwungene) Bewertung von Tätigkeiten" (Work is not similar work. The social (forced) valuation of occupations), *Jahrbuch für Sozialwissenschaft* 35(1), 1984 : 66-91.
4454   BENNELL, Paul; GODFREY, Martin. "The professions in Africa : some interactions between local and international markets", *Development and Change* 14(3), jul 83 : 373-402.
4455   CLOGG, Clifford C.; SHOCKEY, James W. "Mismatch between occupation and schooling : a prevalence measure, recent trends and demographic analysis", *Demography* 21(2), mai 84 : 235-247. [USA]
4456   KERN, Horst; SCHUMANN, Michael. "Vers une professionnalisation du travail industriel", *Sociologie du Travail* 26(4), oct-dec 84 : 398-406. [Allemagne RF]
4457   SPORER, Željka. "Selektiva bibliografija radova iz područja sociologije profesije" (Selected bibliography on works concerning the sociology of professions), *Revija za Sociologiju* 14(1-2), 1984 : 59-67.
4458   SZRETER, Simon R. S. "The genesis of the Registrar-General's social classification of occupations", *British Journal of Sociology* 35(4), dec 84 : 522-546. [UK]

18420   Occupational life. Vocational guidance
Vie professionnelle. Orientation professionnelle

4459   AGARWAL, A.; TRIPATHI, K. K. "Influence of prolonged deprivation, age and culture on the development of future orientation", *European Journal of Social Psychology* 14(4), oct dec 84 : 451 453. [Among Indian and Nepalese students]
4460   BENAVOT, Aaron. "Rise and decline of vocational education", *Sociology of Education* 56(2), apr 83 : 63-76.
4461   BENNELL, Paul. "Occupational transfer : a case study of craft-training policies in Kenya : 1945-1980", *Comparative Education Review* 28(1), feb 84 : 28-51.
4462   BLOSSFELD, Hans-Peter. "Die Entwicklung der qualifikationsspezifischer Verdienst-relationen von Berufsanfängern zwischen 1970 und 1982. Regressionsanalytische Unter-suchungen auf der Basis von Volkszählungs- und Mikrozensusdaten" (The development of qualification-specific earning relations of career-beginners between 1970 and 1982. Regression-analytical studies based on census- and microcensus data), *Kölner Zeitschrift für Soziologie und Sozialpsychologie* 36(2), jun 82 : 291-322. [Germany FR]
4463   BORJAS, George J. "Race, turnover, and male earnings", *Industrial Relations* 23(1), wint. 84 : 73-89. [USA]
4464   BRAUN, Frank; HARTMANN, Elfriede. *Jugendliche in der Berufswahl : eine Bibliographie* (Youth in occupational choice : a bibliography). München : Verlag Deutsches Jugend-institut, 1984, 236 p. bibl., ind. [Germany FR]
4465   CACIOPPE, Ron; MOCK, Philip. "A comparison of the quality of work experience in government and private organizations", *Human Relations* 37(11), nov 84 : 923-940.
4466   CHANG A., Ligia. *La formación de trabajadores en América Latina* (Vocational training in Latin America). Santiago de Chile : Oficina Regional de la UNESCO para América Latina y el Caribe, 1983, 48 p. bibl.
4467   CHÁVEZ PÉREZ, Guillermo. *Programa experimental de educación y formación de 'obreros profesionales'* (The experimental curriculum of vocational education and training). Santiago de Chile : Oficina Regional de Educación de la UNESCO para América Latina y el Caribe, 1983, 121 p. ill. [Chile]

4468   DOMAŃSKI, Henryk; SAWIŃSKI, Zbigniew. "Prestiż i pozycja społeczna jako wymiary ruchliwości zawodowej" (Prestige and social position as dimensions of occupational structure in Poland), *Studia Socjologiczne* 93(2), 1984 : 107-125.

4469   DUBAR, C. "Les fonctions de la formation continue en France : interprétations et confrontations théoriques", *Recherches Sociologiques* 15(1), 1984 : 29-36.

4470   EYRAUD, François; [et al.]. "Développement des qualifications et apprentissage par l'entreprise des nouvelles technologies : le cas des MOCN dans l'industrie française", *Sociologie du Travail* 26(4), oct-dec 84 : 482-499. [France] [Machines-Outils à Commande Numérique]

4471   FAIVRE, Denise. "La réinsertion professionnelle des femmes : mobilité professionnelle et accès à l'emploi", *Formation Emploi* (5), mar 84 : 29-38. [France]

4472   FREYSSENET, Michel. "La requalification des opérateurs et la forme sociale actuelle d'automatisation", *Sociologie du Travail* 26(4), oct-dec 84 : 422-433. [France]

4473   GEURTS, P. A. T. M.; BRAAM, G. P. A. "Changes in occupational stratification in the Netherlands; an exploration of the influence of cultural factors", *Netherlands' Journal of Sociology* 20(2), oct 84 : 150-167.

4474   GUPPY, L. Neil. "Dissensus or consensus : a cross-national comparison of occupational prestige scales", *Canadian Journal of Sociology / Cahiers Canadiens de Sociologie* 9(1), 1984 : 69-83. [USA; Canada]

4475   GUPPY, Neil; GOYDER, John C. "Consensus on occupational prestige : a reassessment of the evidence", *Social Forces* 62(3), mar 84 : 709-725.

4476   HAUSER, Robert M. "Some cross-population comparisons of family bias in the effects of schooling on occupational status", *Social Science Research* 13(2), jun 84 : 159-187. [USA]

4477   HEIMER, Carol A. "Organizational and individual control of career development in engineering project work", *Acta Sociologica* 27(4), 1984 : 283-310.

4478   HOLBAN, Ion. "Modele de calificare profesională" (Occupational qualification models), *Viitorul Social* 76(2), apr 83 : 126-134. [Romania]

4479   HOPE, Keith. "Intergenerational and career mobility in Britain : an integrated analysis", *Social Science Research* 13(1), mar 84 : 20-37.

4480   HOUT, Michael. "Occupational mobility of Black men : 1962 to 1973", *American Sociological Review* 49(3), jun 84 : 308-322. [USA]

4481   HOUT, Michael. "Status, autonomy, and training in occupational mobility", *American Journal of Sociology* 89(6), mai 84 : 1379-1409. [USA]

4482   JONES, Bryn; WOOD, Stephen. "Qualifications tacites, division du travail et nouvelles technologies", *Sociologie du Travail* 26(4), oct-dec 84 : 407-421.

4483   KUTAS, János; VÁMOS, Dóra. "Foglalkozási csoportok és a foglalkoztatás" (Occupational groups and employment), *Közgazdasági Szemle* 31(3), mar 84 : 269-280. [Hungary]

4484   LATREILLE, Geneviève. *Les chemins de l'orientation professionnelle : 30 années de luttes et de recherches.* Lyon : Presses Universitaires de Lyon, 1984, xvi-211 p. bibl.

4485   LŐRINCZ, Lajos. "Career system in public administration", *Acta Juridica* 25(3-4), 1983 : 371-385. [Hungary]

4486   MACDONALD, Keith M. "Professional formation : the case of Scottish accountants", *British Journal of Sociology* 35(2), jun 84 : 174-189.

4487   MURGATROYD, Linda. "Women, men and the social grading of occupations", *British Journal of Sociology* 35(4), dec 84 : 473-497.

4488   NEVADOMSKY, Joseph. "Perceptions of occupational prestige and income among secondary school students in Nigeria", *Sociologus* 34(1), 1984 : 74-87.

4489   NOVIKOV, V. V.; FETISOV, E. N. *Social'nye problemy podgotovki molodeži k trudu* (Social problems of the youth preparation for labour). Moskva : Mysl', 1984, 215 p.

4490   PLESSIS, Jean-Claude. *Concevoir et gérer la formation dans l'entreprise.* Paris : Éditions d'Organisation, 1984, 162 p.

4491   POITOU, Jean-Pierre. "L'évolution des qualifications et des savoir-faire dans les bureaux d'études face à la conception assistée par ordinateur", *Sociologie du Travail* 26(4), oct-dec 84 : 468-481. [France]

4492   POLLAK, Michael. "Projet scientifique, carrière professionnelle et stratégie politique", *Actes de la Recherche en Sciences Sociales* 55, nov 84 : 54-63.

4493   POMPE, J. H.; RUTGES, A. "Het meten van beroepsprestige. Enige kannttekeningen bij een beroepsprestigeschaal voor de jaren tachtig" (Measuring occupational prestige. Comments on the occupational prestige scale for the eighties), *Mens en Maatschappij* 59(3), aug 84 : 292-300. [Netherlands]

4494   RESZKE, Irena. *Prestiż społeczny a płeć. Kryteria prestiżu zawodów i osób* (Social prestige and the sex. Prestige criteria of occupations and persons). Wrocław : Ossolineum, 1984, 224 p.

4495   ROBB, Roberta Edgecome. "Occupational segregation and equal pay for work of equal value", *Relations Industrielles* 39(1), 1984 : 146-166. [Canada]

4496   ROSANVALLON, A.; TROUSSIER, J. F. *Formation aux changements et qualification ouvrière.* Paris : Commissariat Général du Plan; Grenoble : Université des Sciences Sociales, Institut de Recherche Économique et de Planification, 1983, ii-174 p. bibl.

4497   SCHES, Christian. "La qualification des emplois : connaissance statistique et évaluation politique", *CLES* (2), sem. 2, 83 : 53-70. [France]

4498   SILVESTRE, Jean-Jacques. "Professionalisation (La). L'exemple allemand", *Pouvoirs* (30), 1984 : 39-46.

4499   SINGH, Kalam. "Occupational mobility in the rural setting", *Indian Journal of Social Research* 25(2), aug 84 : 210-225. [India]

4500   SKVORETZ, John. "Career mobility as a Poisson process. An application to the career dynamics of men and women in the US Office of the Comptroller of the Currency from the Civil War to World War II", *Social Science Research* 13(2), jun 84 : 198-220.

4501   WEIERMAIR, Klaus. *Apprenticeship training in Canada : a theoretical and empirical analysis.* Ottawa : Economic Council of Canada, 1984, 244 p. bibl., ill.

4502   WILKINSON, Barry. "Technologie, compétence et formation : une étude de cas sur les machines à commande numérique", *Sociologie du Travail* 26(4), oct-dec 84 : 447-456. [Royaume-Uni]

4503   WINCHELL, Anne E. "Conceptual systems and Holland's theory of vocational choice", *Journal of Personality and Social Psychology* 46(2), feb 84 : 376-383. [USA]

4504   WINDOLF, Paul. "L'expansion de l'enseignement et la surqualification sur le marché du travail", *Archives Européennes de Sociologie* 25(1), 1984 : 101-143.

4505   WOJCIECHOWSKA-RATAJCZAK, Bogumiła. "Struktura społeczno-zawodowa ludności wiejskiej w Polsce" (Socio-occupational structure of the countrymen in Poland), *Wieś Współczesna* 1, 1984 : 24-32.

18500   EMPLOYEES. TECHNICIANS. WORKERS
EMPLOYÉS. TECHNICIENS. TRAVAILLEURS

18510   Workers
Travailleurs

4506   BOURQUELOT, Françoise. "Les travailleurs agricoles en Amérique latine", *Nouvelles Campagnes* (26), dec 83 : 24-32.

4507   CRISP, Jeff. *The story of an African working class : Ghanaian miners' struggles, 1870-1980.* London : Zed Books; Totowa, NJ : Biblio Distributor Center, 1984, xviii-200 p. ill., map, bibl., ind.

4508   DAS, Arvind N.; NILAKANT, V.; DUBEY, P. S., [eds.]. *The worker and the working class : a labour studies anthology.* New Delhi : Public Enterprises Centre for Continuing Education; Delhi : Bookwell Publication, 1984, 274 p. bibl.

4509   DIXON, Ruth. "Land, labour, and the sex composition of the agricultural labour force : an international comparison", *Development and Change* 14(3), jul 83 : 347-372.

4510   DZUN, Włodzimierz; WAJDA, Augustyn. "Pracownicy PGR w społecznej strukturze wsi" (State farm employees in the social structure of rural areas), *Ideologia i Polityka* 9, 1984 : 114-125.

4511   FARKAS, Zoltán. "Munkások érdek- és érdekeltségi viszonyai" (Interest relations of workers), *Szociológia* 12(1-2), 1983 : 27-52.

4512   JANISZEWSKI, Ludwik; SOSNOWSKI, Adam. *Socjologia morska. Wybór zagadnień* (Maritime sociology. Selection of problems). Wroław : Ossolineum, 1984, 215 p.

4513   KADA, Yukiko. "Evolution of joint fishers' rights and village community structure on Lake Biwa", *Senri Ethnological Studies* 17, 1984 : 137-158. [Japan]

4514   KOVÁCS, Ferenc; [ed.]. *Az ipari dolgozók rétegződése; magyar-lengyel összehasonlítás. Műhelytanulmány* (Industrial workers' stratification : a Hungarian-Polish comparison. A workshop study). Budapest : Magyar Szocialista Munkáspárt KB Társadalomtudományi Intézete, 1984, 210 p.

4515   MALANOWSKI, Jan. "Polish workers", *International Journal of Sociology* 14(3), 1984 : 1-116.

4516   MAZARS, Lucien. *Terre de mine : bassin d'Aubin-Decazeville.* Paris : l'Auteur, 1984, 259-64 p. bibl., ill.

4517   PANJWANI, Narendra. "Living with capitalism : class, caste and paternalism among industrial workers in Bombay", *Contributions to Indian Sociology* 18(2), jul-dec 84 : 267-292.

4518   ROMAGNOLI, Guido; SARCHIELLI, Guido. *Immagini del lavoro : una ricerca tra il lavoratori manuali* (Images of labour : a research among manual workers). Bari : De Donato, 1983, 291 p. bibl. [Italy]

4519   ROUILLÉ, André. "Les images photographiques du monde du travail sous le Second Empire", *Actes de la Recherche en Sciences Sociales* 54, sep 84 : 31-43. [France; XIXth century]

4520   SOSNOWSKI, Adam. *Środowisko społeczno-zawodowe marynarzy* (Socio-occupational environment of seamen). Warszawa : Państwowe Wydawnictwo Naukowe, 1984, 247 p.

4521   SZAKÁCS, Sándor. "Az állami gazdaságok dolgozóinak helyzete és helye a társadalomban 1945-1975" (State farm workers and their social status in Hungary between 1945 and 1975), *Agrártörténeti Szemle* 25(1-2), 1983 : 56-74.

4522   TANNER, Julian. "Skill levels of manual workers and beliefs about work, management, and industry : a comparison of craft and non-craft workers in Edmonton", *Canadian Journal of Sociology / Cahiers Canadiens de Sociologie* 9(3), 1984 : 303-318. [Canada]

18520   Employees
Employés

4523   GAITSKELL, Deborah; [et al.]. "Class, race and gender : domestic workers in South Africa", *Review of African Political Economy* (27-28); 1983 : 86-108.

4524   KOLOSI, Tamás; TUCEK, Milan. "Differenciálódás és közeledés. Az ipari dolgozók belső rétegződése hat szocialista országban" (Differentiation and approach. Internal stratification of industrial employees in six socialist countries), *Szociológia* 12(1-2), 1983 : 1-15.

4525   KŐMUVES, Márta. "Foglalkozása : takarítónő. Tanulmány takarítónőkről húsz interjú alapján" (Occupation : cleaning woman. Research on cleaning women on the basis of twenty interviews), *Valóság* 27(9), 1984 : 65-74.

4526   RUBBO, Anna; TAUSSIG, Michael. "Up off their knees : servanthood in South-West Colombia", *Latin American Perspectives* 10(4), aut 83 : 5-23.

18530   Managers. Technicians
Cadres. Techniciens

4527   BOLTANSKI, Luc. "How a social group objectified itself : 'cadres' in France, 1936-45", *Social Science Information / Information sur les Sciences Sociales* 23(3), 1984 : 469-491.

4528   BOUWEN, René; VAN RENSBERGEN, Johan. "Bedrijfsgebondenheid herontdekt? Een onderzoek naar de motivatiestructuur van kaderleden" (Unveiled business management? A survey on the motivation structure of managers), *Economisch en Sociaal Tijdschrift* 38(3), jun 84 : 303-313. [Belgium]

4529   CESAREO, Vincenzo; BOVONE, Laura; ROVATI, Giancarlo. *Dirigere la piccola impresa negli anni '80 : ricerca sull'immagine e sul ruolo del dirigente* (To manage the small business in the eighties : research on manager's image and role). Milano : Franco Angeli, 1983, 182 p. ill., bibl. [Italy]

4530   EVERETT, J. E.; STENING, B. W. "Japanese and British managerial colleagues. How they view each other", *Journal of Management Studies* 20(4), oct 80 : 467-475.

4531   MATIĆ, Milan. "La démocratisation de la politique des cadres", *Questions Actuelles du Socialisme* 34(3), mar 84 : 50-57. [Yugoslavia]

4532   SCHMIDT, Stuart M.; KIPNIS, David. "Managers' pursuit of individual and organizational goals", *Human Relations* 37(10), oct 84 : 781-794.

4533   VAN LARE, James. *Supervisory leadership.* New York, NY : Training By Design, 1984, vii-151 p. bibl.

4534   VILLETTE, Michel. "Une technologie sociale d'ingénieur-conseil", *Actes de la Recherche en Sciences Sociales* 54, sep 84 : 45-56. [France]

18540   Liberal professions
Professions libérales

4535   BARBICHON, Guy. "Sociologie de l'acteur et psychologie sociale", *Connexions* 42, 1983 : 27-39. [France]

4536   SMITH, Carol A. "Does a commodity economy enrich the few while ruining the masses? Differentiation among petty commodity producers in Guatemala", *Journal of Peasant Studies* 11(3), apr 84 : 60-95.

4537   ZVEKIĆ, Uglješa. "Kosmopolitizam i lokalizam u sudijskoj profesiji" (Cosmopolitan and local orientation in judicial profession), *Sociologija* 26(1-2), jan-jun 84 : 139-157.

18600 LABOUR RELATIONS
RELATIONS DU TRAVAIL

4538 "Communication et travail", *Psychologie Française* 28(3-4), dec 83 : 226-302. [With contributions by M. LACOSTE, V. de KEYSER, A. SAVOYANT, J. LEPLAT, J. THEYREAU, L. PINSKE, Y. QUEINNEC]

4539 "Industrial relations in India", *Social Action* 34(1), jan-mar 84 : 1-66.

4540 "Relations (Les) du travail au Japon", *Cahier — Centre de Recherche sur les Mutations des Sociétés Industrielles* (3), dec 83 : 5-98. [With contributions by Ichiro SAGA, Koichi SATO, Jean-Louis MOYNOT]

4541 AHIAUZU, Augustine I. "Methods of job regulation in Nigeria workplaces : a study of cultural influences in industrial relations", *Genève-Afrique* 22(1), 1984 : 107-122.

4542 BENNETT, John; [et al.]. "Bibliography 1982", *British Journal of industrial Relations* 22(2), jul 84 : 218-264. [Industrial relations in the UK]

4543 CONSOLI, Francesco. "Concetti e dati nelle comparazioni internazionali delle relazioni di lavoro. Considerazioni in margine ai problemi teorici posti dalle connessioni internazionali di banche dati" (Concepts and data in international comparison of work relations. Marginal considerations of the theoretical problems posed by international connexions of data banks), *Studi di Sociologia* 22(1), jan-mar 84 : 22-36.

4544 COROUGES, Christian; PIALOUX, Michel. "Chronique Peugeot", *Actes de la Recherche en Sciences Sociales* 52-53, jun 84 : 88-95. [France] [Continued in ibid. : 54, sep 84 : 57-69]

4545 DALTON, Dan R.; TODOR, William D. "Unanticipated consequences of union-management cooperation : an interrupted time series analysis", *Journal of Applied Behavioral Science* 20(3), 1984 : 253-264. [USA]

4546 DE LA VILLA, Luis Enrique. *Panorama de las relaciones laborales en España* (Panorama of the industrial relations in Spain). Madrid : Tecnos, 1983, 284 p. ind.

4547 GARBARINO, Joseph W. "Unionism without unions : the new industrial relations?", *Industrial Relations* 23(1), 1984 : 40-51. [USA]

4548 GOODMAN, J. F. R. *Employment relations in industrial society.* Deddington; Oxford : P. Allan, 1984, ix-244 p. ill., bibl., ind.

4549 HELBURN, I. B.; SHEARER, John C. "Human resources and industrial relations in China : a time of ferment", *Industrial and Labor Relations Review* 38(1), oct 84 : 3-15.

4550 JAIN, Anand Prasad. "Industrial relations in a changing economy", *Indian Journal of Social Research* 25(2), aug 84 : 171-180. [India]

4551 KOCHAN, Thomas A.; MCKERSIE, Robert B.; CAPPELLI, Peter. "Strategic choice and industrial relations theory", *Industrial Relations* 23(1), 1984 : 16-39. [USA]

4552 LOWITT, Thomas. "Political power and industrial relations in Eastern Europe : normal times and crises", *International Yearbook of Organizational Democracy* 1, 83 : 505-529.

4553 MAMORIA, C. B.; MAMORIA, Satish. *Labour welfare, social security, and industrial peace in India.* Allahabad : Kitab Mahal, 1983, viii-430 p. bibl.

4554 MARGINSON, Paul. "The districtive effects of plant and company size on workplace industrial relations", *British Journal of Industrial Relations* 22(1), mar 84 : 1-14.

4555 MAURICE, M.; SELLIER, F.; SILVESTRE, J. J. "Rules, contexts and actors observations based on a comparison between France and Germany", *British Journal of industrial Relations* 22(3), nov 84 : 346-363.

4556 MILLER, Doug. "Social partnership and the determinants of workplace independence in West Germany", *British Journal of Industrial Relations* 20(1), mar 82 : 44-66.

4557 MROCZKOWSKI, Tomasz. "Is the American labour-management relationship changing?", *British Journal of Industrial Relations* 22(1), mar 84 : 47-62.

4558 OGDEN, S. G. "Bargaining structure and the control of industrial relations", *British Journal of Industrial Relations* 20(2), jul 82 : 170-185. [UK]

4559 PALMER, Gill. *British industrial relations.* London; Boston, MA... Allen and Unwin, 1983, x-259 p.

4560 POOLE, Michael; [et al.]. "Managerial attitudes and behaviour in industrial relations : evidence from a national survey", *British Journal of Industrial Relations* 20(3), nov 82 : 285-307.

4561 RAMASWAMY, E. A. *Power and justice : the state in industrial relations.* Delhi : Oxford University Press, 1984, x-218 p. [India]

4562 REGINI, Marino. "I tentativi italiani di 'patto sociale' a cavallo degli anni '80" (Italian 'social pact' attempts in between the eighties), *Mulino* 33(2), apr 84 : 291-304.

4563 SARKIS, Bassam. *El sistema de relaciones industriales en Colombia* (The industrial relations system in Colombia). Bogotá : Universidad de los Andes, Facultad de Administración, Sarkis Consultores, 1983, 286 p. ill., bibl.

4564 SCHUSTER, Michael. "The Scanlon Plan : a longitudinal analysis", *Journal of Applied Behavioral Science* 20(1), 1984 : 23-38. [USA]

4565 STRAUSS, George. "Industrial relations : time of change", *Industrial Relations* 23(1), 1984 : 1-15. [USA]

4566 THOMPSON, Mark; PONAK, Allen. "Les relations professionnelles dans les entreprises publiques canadiennes", *Revue Internationale du Travail* 123(5), sep-oct 84 : 699-718.

4567 WEISS, Dimitri. "Du concept de 'professionnalité' dans les relations industrielles italiennes", *Relations Industrielles* 38(2), 1983 : 369-379.

18610 Labour law
Droit du travail

4568 CARROLL, Thomas M. "Right to work laws do matter", *Southern Economic Journal* 50(2), oct 83 : 494-509. [USA]

4569 EL BORAT, Ahmad. "Evolutions et permanences à travers le Code du travail égyptien de 1981", *Bulletin du Centre de Documentation et d'Études Juridiques, Économiques et Sociales* 12(15), dec 83 : 11-49.

4570 FRANCO ZAPATA, Ramón. *Apuntes de derecho del trabajo* (Labour law topics). Caracas : Editorial Bicentenario, 1983, 257 p. bibl. [Venezuela]

4571 JOŃCZYK, Jan. *Prawo pracy* (Labour law). Warszawa : Państwowe Wydawnictwo Naukowe, 1984, 593 p. [Poland]

4572 MONTT BALMACEDA, Manuel. *Principios de derecho internacional del trabajo* (Principles of international labour law). Santiago de Chile : Editorial Jurídica de Chile, 1984, 196 p. bibl.

4573 PÉREZ, Benito. *Derecho del trabajo* (Labour law). Buenos Aires : Editorial Astrea, 1983, xxiv-520 p. bibl. [Argentina]

4574 SMITH, Robert Ellis. *Workrights.* New York, NY : Dutton; Toronto, ON : Clark, Irwin, 1983, xvii-267 p.

4575 SUPIOT, Alain. "Délégalisation, normalisation et droit du travail", *Droit Social* (5), mai 84 : 296-307. [France]

4576 VACCA, Michele. *Il diritto di sciopero e le sue limitazioni nelle organizzazioni e nei paesi europei* (The right to strike and its restrictions in the European organizations and countries). Milano : A. Giuffrè, 1983, 255 p. bibl.

4577 VAN DROOGHENBROECK, Jacques. "Le juge et le travail : entre l'économique et le social", *Revue Nouvelle* 80(10), oct 84 : 253-264. [Belgium]

18620 Employers' organizations
Organisations patronales

4578 ILLUMINATI, Augusto. "Figure del produttore" (producer types), *Critica Sociologica* 70, 1984 : 94-99.

18630 Trade unions
Syndicats

4579 "Gli anni settanta nel sindicato" (Trade unionism in the seventies), *Rassegna Sindacale. Quaderni* 20(100), feb 83 : 3-257. [Italy]

4580 "Neokorporatistische Politikentwicklung in Westeuropa" (Neo corporatist political evolution in Western Europe), *Journal für Sozialforschung* 23(4), 83 : 407-459. [With contributions by Gerhard LEHMBRUCH, Roland CZADA]

4581 "Syndicats (Les) dans l'entreprise après les lois Auroux", *Droit Social* (1), jan 84 : 1-89. [France] [With contributions by Gérard LYON-CAEN, Raymond SOUBIE, Hugues BLASSEL, Claire SUTTER]

4582 ABÓS, Alvaro. *Las organizaciones sindicales y el poder militar, 1976-1983* (Trade unions organizations and military power, 1976-1983). Buenos Aires : Centro Editor de América Latina, 1984, 150 p. bibl., ill. [Argentina]

4583 ADDISON, John T.; BURTON, John. *Trade unions and society : some lessons of the British experience.* Vancouver, BC : Fraser Institute, 1984, xxviii-190 p. bibl., ind.

4584 BAIN, George Sayers; ELSHEIKH, Farouk. "Union growth and the business cycle : a disaggregated study", *British Journal of Industrial Relations* 20(1), mar 82 : 34-43. [UK]

4585 BARKER, Allan; LEWIS, Paul; MCCANN, Michael. "Trade unions and the organisation of the unemployed", *British Journal of industrial Relations* 22(3), nov 84 : 391-404. [UK]

4586 BARRETO, António. "Classe e Estado : os sindicatos na reforma agrária" (Class and State : trade unions in the agrarian reform), *Análise Social* 20(1), 1984 : 41-95. [Portugal]

4587 BASTIAS, Alberto; HENRIQUEZ, Helia. "El movimiento sindical en el Estado autoritario. La experiencia chilena" (Trade union movement in an authoritarian State. Chilean example), *Nueva Sociedad* (70), feb 84 : 101-111.

4588 BEAUMONT, P. B. "The future for trade union recognition in Britain", *Columbia Journal of World Business* 18(2), sum 83 : 87-94.

4589 BEAUMONT, P. B. "Trade union recognition in Northern Ireland", *British Journal of industrial Relations* 22(3), nov 84 : 364-371.

4590 BLYTON, Paul; URSELL, Gill. "Vertical recruitment in white-collar trade unions : some causes and consequences", *British Journal of Industrial Relations* 20(2), jul 82 : 186-194.

4591 BUKSTI, Jacob A. "Organisationer og offentlig politik" (Trade unions and public policy), *Nordisk Administrativt Tidsskrift* 64(2), 1983 : 191-212. [Denmark]

4592 CAMPERO, Guillermo. *Los gremios empresariales en el período 1970-1983 : comportamiento sociopolítico y orientaciones ideológicas* (The business trade unions during the period 1970-1983 : social-political behaviour and ideological trends). Santiago de Chile : Instituto Latinoamericano de Estudios Transnacionales, 1984, 327 p. bibl. [Chile]

4593 CHARNEY, Craig. "La renaissance syndicale noire en Afrique du Sud, 1973-1983", *Politique Africaine* (15), sep 84 : 97-113.

4594 CHHACHHI, Amrita; PALET, Ravi; KURIAN, Paul. "Control of workers' control : workers and economic development in Poland", *Insurgent Sociologist* 12(1-2), 1984 : 143-161.

4595 CHRISTOFFERSEN, Hans Rohr. *Fremdsprachige Literatur über die dänische Arbeiterbewegung : eine Bibliographie = Foreign language literature on the Danish labour movement : a bibliography.* København : Arbejderbevaegelsens Bibliotek og Arkiv, 1983, 29 p.

4596 CIANCAGLINI, Michelangelo. *Etica sociale e azione sindacale* (Social ethics and trade union action). Milano : Franco Angeli, 1983, 190 p. [Italy]

4597 CRAFT, James A.; ABBOUSHI, Suhail. "The Union image : concept, programs and analysis", *Journal of Labor Research* 4(4), aut 83 : 299-314. [USA]

4598 DEPPE, Frank. *Ende oder Zukunft der Arbeiterbewegung? Gewerkschaftspolitik nach der Wende : eine kritische Bestandsaufnahme* (End or future of the labour movement? Trade union policy towards change : a critical inventory). Köln : Pahl-Rugenstein, 1984, 314 p. bibl.

4599 DEPRETTO, Jean-Paul; SCHWEITZER, Sylvie V. *Le communisme à l'usine : vie ouvrière et mouvement ouvrier chez Renault, 1920-1939.* Roubaix : EDIRES, 1984, 284 p. bibl. [France]

4600 DETTLING, Warnfried. *Demokratie in Gewerkschaften, Gewerkschaften in der Demokratie : die Verteilung der Macht zwischen Mitgliedern und Funktionären* (Democracy in trade unions, trade unions in the democracy : power distribution between members and officers). München : Olzog, 1983, 150 p. bibl.

4601 DEUTSCHMANN, Christoph. "Industrial and enterprise unionism : organizational structures of unions and labour market sources of union power in West Germany and Japan in an historical perspective", *East Asia* 2, 1984 : 51-64.

4602 DOMMERGUES, Pierre; GROUX, Guy; MASON, John. *Les syndicats français et américains face aux mutations technologiques.* Paris : Anthropos-Encrages, 1984, 382 p. bibl.

4603 EBBINGHAUSEN, Rolf; THIEMANN, Friedrich; [eds.]. *Das Ende der Arbeiterbewegung in Deutschland?* (The end of the labour movement in Germany?). Opladen : Westdeutscher Verlag, 1984, 605 p.

4604 FALL, Mar. "Le mouvement syndical sénégalais à la veille de l'indépendance", *Peuples Noirs — Peuples Africains* 7(38), apr 84 : 5-17.

4605 FAVILLI, Paolo. *Riformismo e sindacalismo : una teoria economica del movimento operaio, tra Turati e Graziadei* (Reformis and trade unionism : an economic theory of the labour movement post Turati and Graziadei). Roma : Fondazione G. Brondolini; Milano : Franco Angeli, 1984, 366 p. bibl.

4606 FERMAN, Louis A.; [ed.]. "The future of American unionism", *Annals of the American Academy of Political and Social Science* 473, mai 84 : 9-189.

4607 FINA, Lluis; HAWKESWORTH, Richard I. "Syndicalisme et négociation collective en Espagne postfranquiste", *Travail et Société* 9(1), mar 84 : 3-31.

4608 FISHMAN, Robert. "El movimiento obrero en la transición : objetivos políticos y organizativos" (Labour movement in transition : political and organizational objectives), *Revista Española de Investigaciones Sociológicas* 26, apr-jun 84 : 61-112. [Spain]

4609 FURNHAM, Adrian. "The Protestant work ethic, voting behaviour and attitudes to the trade unions", *Political Studies* 32(3), sep 84 : 420-436. [UK]

4610 GAUTIER, Maurice Paul. "Le syndicalisme à l'américaine : conciliation ou conflit", *Revue Française d'Études Américaines* 9(21-22), nov 84 : 473-480.

4611   GULLETT, C. Ray; WHISENHUNT, Donald W. "Industrial representation or 'company union' : the contribution of W. L. Mackenzie King", *International Social Science Review* 59(2), 1984 : 82-87. [USA]

4612   HAGUE, Rod. "Confrontation, incorporation and exclusion : British trade unions in collectivist and post-collectivist politics", *West European Politics* 6(4), oct 83 : 130-162.

4613   HINTON, James. *Labour and socialism : a history of the British labour movement, 1867-1974.* Amherst, MA : University of Massachusetts Press, 1983, ix-212 p.

4614   ISHIKAWA, Akihiro. "Japanese trade-unionism in a changing environment", *International Social Science Journal / Revue Internationale des Sciences Sociales* 36(2), 1984 : 271-283.

4615   ISMACIL, Muhammad Ahmad. "Le principe de la liberté syndicale dans le droit égyptien", *Bulletin du Centre de Documentation et d'Études Juridiques, Économiques et Sociales* 12(15), dec 83 : 75-87.

4616   IZRAELI, Dafna N. "The attitudinal effects of gender mix in union committees", *Industrial and Labor Relations Review* 37(2), jan 84 : 212-221. [Israel]

4617   JAUCH, Susanne. *Gewerkschaftsbewegung in Frankreich und Deutschland : ein kontrastiver Vergleich ihrer zentralen Merkmale bis zum Ersten Weltkrieg* (Labour movements in France and Germany : a contrastive comparison of their central characteristics until the First World War). Frankfurt-am-Main : Campus-Verlag, 1984, 189 p. bibl.

4618   KANNONIER, Reinhard. *Zentralismus oder Demokratie : zur Organisationsfrage in der Arbeiterbewegung* (Centralism or democracy : on organization problem of the labour movement). Wien : Europaverlag, 1983, vi-188 p. bibl.

4619   KESSELMAN, Mark; GROUX, Guy; [eds.]. *1968-1982 : le mouvement ouvrier français; crise économique et changement politique.* Paris : Éditions Ouvrières, 1984, 382 p. bibl.

4620   KRAHN, Harvey; LOWE, Graham S. "Public attitudes towards unions : some Canadian evidence", *Journal of Labor Research* 5(2), spr 84 : 149-164.

4621   LANGE, Peter. "Politiche dei redditi e democrazia sindacale in Europa occidentale" (Income policy and trade unions' democracy in Western Europe), *Stato e Mercato* 9, dec 83 : 425-474.

4622   LAPORTE, Jean-Pierre. *Les syndicats et la gestion participative.* Montréal, PQ : Éditions Agence d'ARC, 1983, xii-155 p. bibl.

4623   LIPPE, Angelika. *Gewerkschaftliche Frauenarbeit : Parallelität ihrer Probleme in Frankreich und in der Bundesrepublik Deutschland (1949-1979)* (Trade-union women's work : a parallel of its problems in France and in the Federal Republic of Germany (1949-1979)). Frankfurt-am-Main; New York, NY : Campus, 1983, 271 p. ill., bibl.

4624   LÓPEZ VILLEGAS-MANJARREZ, Virginia. *La CTM vs. las organizaciones obreras* (The CTM against worker's organizations). México, DF : Ediciones El Caballito, 1983, 126 p. bibl. [Confederación de Trabajadores de México]

4625   LOWITT, Thomas. "The working class and union structures in Eastern Europe", *British Journal of Industrial Relations* 20(1), mar 82 : 67-75.

4626   LUCAS, Erhard. *Vom Scheitern der deutschen Arbeiterbewegung* (From the failures of the German labour movement). Basel : Stroemfeld; Frankfurt-am-Main : Roter Stern, 1983, 202 p. ill., bibl.

4627   MALANOWSKI, Andrzej. "Du principe de la liberté syndicale dans le cadre de la législation actuelle en Pologne", *Droit Social* (9-10), oct 84 : 567-572.

4628   MAREE, Johann. "Democracy and oligarchy in trade unions : the independent trade unions in the Transvaal and the Western province General Workers' Union in the 1970s", *Social Dynamics* 8(1), jun 82 : 41-52. [South Africa]

4629   MAZYRIN, V. M. "Profsojuzy SRV v bor'be zapovyšenie social'noj aktivnosti i ulučšenie žizni trudjaščihsja" (Trade unions in the Socialist Republic of Vietnam), *Rabočij Klass i Sovremennyj Mir* 12(5), oct 83 : 76-84.

4630   MCDONALD, Joseph A.; CLELLAND, Donald A. "Textile workers and union sentiment", *Social Forces* 63(2), dec 84 : 502-521. [USA]

4631   METCALF, David. "Unions and the distribution of earnings", *British Journal of Industrial Relations* 20(2), jul 82 : 163-169. [UK]

4632   MIHAJLOVA, L. V. "Gollandskie profsojuzy" (Dutch trade unions), *Rabočij Klass i Sovremennyj Mir* (1), 1984 : 67-74.

4633   NYDEN, Philip W. "Evolution of black political influence in American trade unions", *Journal of Black Studies* 13(4), jun 83 : 379-398.

4634   ORGANISATION INTERNATIONALE DU TRAVAIL. *La situation syndicale et les relations professionnelles en Norvège.* Genève : BIT, 1984, xii-97 p. bibl.

4635   ORGANISATION INTERNATIONALE DU TRAVAIL. *La situation syndicale et les relations professionnelles en Hongrie.* Genève : BIT, 1984, xii-103 p. bibl.

4636   ORTLIEB, Heinz-Dietrich. "Gewerkschaften- in Verwirrung oder auf Abwegen?" (Trade unions in disarray or ruined?), *Hamburger Jahrbuch für Wirtschafts- und Gesellschaftspolitik* 29, 1984 : 98-111. [Germany FR]

4637   PERRET, Daniel. "Les syndicats européens et la politique contractuelle", *Humanisme et Entreprise* (145), jun 84 : 53-67.

4638   PHELPS BROWN, Henry. *The origin of trade unions power.* London : Oxford University Press; New York, NY... Clarendon Press, 1983, vi-320 p. [UK]

4639   PRAVDA, Alex. "Gewerkschaften in kommunistischen Staaten. Die Sonderefälle Polen und Ungarn" (Trade unions in communist countries. Poland and Hungary), *Journal für Sozialforschung* 24(1), 84 : 47-75.

4640   PREVOST, Gary. "Change and continuity in the Spanish labour movement", *West European Politics* 7(1), jan 84 : 80-94.

4641   RAMBAUD, Placide. "Syndicalisme agricole et crise de la société polonaise", *Revue Économique et Sociale* 42(1), jan 84 : 66-75.

4642   RATZ, Ursula. "Arbeiterbewegung zwischen Protest und Reform" (Labour movement between protest and reform), *Neue Politische Literatur* 29(2), 1984 : 205-220.

4643   RAVIER, Jean-Pierre. "Le mouvement syndical britannique depuis 1945", *Revue Française de Civilisation Britannique* 3(1), dec 84 : 43-55.

4644   RIOSA, Alceo. *Il movimento operaio tra società e Stato : il caso italiano nell'epoca della II Internazionale* (The labour movement between society and State : the Italian case in the age of the IInd International). Milano : Franco Angeli, 1984, 222 p. bibl.

4645   RUIZ-TAGLE P., Jaime. *El sindicalismo chileno más allá de la crisis* (The Chilean trade-unionism beyond the crisis). Santiago de Chile : Programa de Economía del Trabajo, Academia de Humanismo Cristiano, 1984, 28 p.

4646   SCALAPINO, Robert A. *The early Japanese labor movement : labor and politics in a developing society.* Berkeley, CA : Institute of East Asian Studies, University of California, Berkeley, Center for Japanese Studies, 1983, x-304 p. ill., bibl., ind.

4647   SCHMITTER, Philippe C. "Teoria della democrazia e pratica neo-corporatista" (Theory of democracy and neo-corporatist practice), *Stato e Mercato* 9, dec 83 : 385-424.

4648   SCREPANTI, Ernesto. "Long economic cycles and recurring proletarian insurgencies", *Review (F. Braudel Center)* 7(3), wint 84 : 509-548.

4649   SEIFERT, Roger V. "Some aspects of factional opposition : Rank and File and the National Union of Teachers 1967-1982", *British Journal of industrial Relations* 22(3), nov 84 : 372-390. [UK]

4650   SELLIER, François. "Du mouvement ouvrier au syndicalisme réel", *Esprit* (6), jun 84 : 29-41. [France]

4651   SHIROM, Azie; SHAVIT, Sara. "Job and union work satisfaction of part time union officers", *Administration and Society* 16(1), mai 84 : 83-96. [Israel]

4652   SINHA, Ramesh P. *Social dimension of trade unionism in India.* New Delhi : Uppal Publishing House, 1984, xiii-193 p. bibl., ind.

4653   SMITH, W. Randy. "Dynamics of plural unionism in France : the CGT, CFDT and industrial conflict", *British Journal of Industrial Relations* 22(1), mar 84 : 15-33.

4654   SOLÉ, Carlota. "El debate corporativismo-neocorporatismo" (The corporativism-neocorporatism debate), *Revista Española de Investigaciones Sociológicas* 26, apr-jun 84 : 9-27.

4655   SOOD, Santosh. *Trade union leadership in India : a case study.* New Delhi : Deep and Deep, 1984, 262 p. bibl., ind.

4656   SPERANZA, Lorenzo. "Le tendenze dell'azione sindacale negli anni '70 e nei primi anni '80 in Italia" (Trade union action trends in the seventies and at the beginning of the eighties in Italy), *Economia e Lavoro* 17(4), dec 83 : 175-185.

4657   TAVARES DE ALMEIDA, Maria Hermínia. "Novas demandas, novos direitos : experiências do sindicalismo paulista na última década" (New claims, new rights : experiences of the São Paulo's union movement in the last decade), *Dados* 26(3), 1983 : 265-290.

4658   TENNSTEDT, Florian. *Vom Proleten zum Industriearbeiter : Arbeiterbewegung und Sozialpolitik in Deutschland, 1800 bis 1914* (From proletarian to industrial worker : labour movement and social policy in Germany, 1800-1914). Köln : Bund-Verlag, 1983, 614-1 p. ill., bibl.

4659   TERRY, Michael. "Organising a fragmented workforce : shop stewards in local government", *British Journal of Industrial Relations* 20(1), mar 82 : 1-19. [UK]

4660   THIKIAN, Alexandre; ARMAND, Monique. *Le mouvement ouvrier bulgare : publications socialistes bulgares, 1882-1918; essai bibliographique.* Paris : Édition de l'École des Hautes Études en Sciences Sociales; Institut d'Études Slaves, 1984, 253 p. ind., bibl.

4661   THOMPSON, Mark; ROXBOROUGH, Ian. "Union elections and democracy in Mexico : a comparative research", *British Journal of Industrial Relations* 20(2), jul 82 : 201-217.

4662 TOURAINE, Alain; WIEVIORKA, Michel; DUBET, François. *Le mouvement ouvrier.* Paris : Fayard, 1984, 438 p. ill., bibl., ind.

4663 VAN DER MERWE, Roux. "Trade unions and the democratic order", *Optima* 31(4), dec 83 : 160-169. [South Africa]

4664 WEBSTER, Eddie. "The International Metalworkers Federation in South Africa (1974-1980)", *South African Labour Bulletin* 9(6), mai 84 : 77-94.

4665 WEHMHORNER, Arnold. "Trade unionism in Thailand : a new dimension in a modernising society", *Journal of Contemporary Asia* 13(4), 83 : 481-496.

4666 WEINSTOCK, Nathan. *Le pain de la misère : histoire du mouvement ouvrier juif en Europe. I. L'Empire russe jusqu'en 1914. II. L'Europe centrale et occidentale jusqu'en 1914.* Paris : La Découverte, 1984.

4667 WILSON, David C.; [et al.]. "The limits of trade union power in organisational decision making", *British Journal of Industrial Relations* 20(3), nov 82 : 322-341.

4668 YCAZA, Patricio. *Historia del movimiento obrero ecuatoriano : de su génesis al Frente Popular* (History of the Ecuadorian labour movement : from its beginning to Popular Front). Quito : Centro de Documentación e Información de los Movimientos Sociales del Ecuador, 1984, 371 p. ill., bibl.

4669 ZORRILLA, Rubén H. *El liderazgo sindical argentino : desde sus origenes hasta 1975* (The Argentine trade unionist leadership : from its beginning to 1975). Buenos Aires : Ediciones Siglo Veinte, 1983, 167 p. ill., bibl.

18640   Labour disputes
Conflits du travail

4670 CHARRIA ANGULO, Pedro. "La huelga legal y la huelga ilegal o paro" (Legal strike or illegal strike or unemployment), *Universitas (Colombia)* (65), nov 83 : 77-93. [Colombia]

4671 ESAIASSON, Peter; GILLJAM, Mikael. "Välharna och de vildastrejkerna" (Swedish voters and wildcat strikes), *Statsvetenskaplig Tidskrift* 86(3), 1983 : 197-207.

4672 FISCHER, Hanna; JACOBSEN, Chanoch. "Unauthorised strikes and slow-downs in Israel : an institutionalised evasion of union rules", *British Journal of Industrial Relations* 20(3), nov 82 : 342-348.

4673 FISHER, E. G.; PERCY, M. B. "The impact of unanticipated output and consumer prices on wildcat strikes", *Relations Industrielles* 38(2), 1983 : 254-276. [Canada]

4674 GOODSTEIN, Phil H. *The theory of the general strike from the French Revolution to Poland.* Boulder, CO : East European Monographs; New York, NY : Columbia University Press, 1984, 337 p. bibl., ind.

4675 HARTLEY, Jean. *Steel strike : a case study in industrial relations.* London : Batsford Academic and Educational, 1983, 209 p. ill., bibl., ind.

4676 JOSEPH, Philip A. "Perfecting the administrative solution to labour disputes : British Columbia experiment", *Relations Industrielles* 38(2), 1983 : 380-414. [Canada]

4677 JOYCE, Paul; WOODS, Adrian. "The management of conflict : a quantitative analysis", *British Journal of Industrial Relations* 22(1), mar 84 : 63-76.

4678 KARLHOFER, Ferdinand. *Wilde Streiks in Österreich : Entstehungs- und Verlaufsbedingungen industrieller Konflikte in der siebziger Jahren* (Wildcat strikes in Austria : origin and evolution conditions of industrial conflicts in the seventies). Wien : Böhlau, 1983, 158 p. bibl.

4679 MILLER, Ronald L. *The resolution of disputes and grievances in New Zealand : analysis, observations, and recommendations.* Wellington : Industrial Relations Centre, Victoria University of Wellington, 1983, vi-76 p. ill., bibl.

4680 NAPOLI, Mario. *Conflitto e consenso : quadro legale e relazioni industriali degli anni ottanta* (Conflict and consensus : legal framework and industrial relations of the eighties). Roma : Lavoro, 1983, 202 p. bibl. [Italy]

4681 PALDAM, Martin; PEDERSEN, Peder J. "The large pattern of industrial conflict — a comparative study of 18 countries, 1919-1979", *International Journal of Social Economics* 11(5), 1984 : 3-28.

4682 PERROT, Michelle. *Jeunesse de la grève : France, 1871-1890.* Paris : Éditions du Seuil, 1984, 324 p. ill.

4683 PRAIS, S. J. "Strike frequencies and plant-size : a comment on Swedish and UK experience", *British Journal of Industrial Relations* 20(1), mar 82 : 101-104.

4684 RICHEZ, Jean-Claude. "Référent national et mouvement gréviste", *Pluriel* (36), 1983 : 52-80. [Western Europe]

4685 RODGERS, Robert C.; STRAUSSMAN, Jeffrey D. "What factors contribute to the duration of strikes by public employees ?", *International Journal of Public Administration* 6(2), 84 : 183-199. [USA]

4686   WAHKAMP, Andy. "Luchas colectives de las obreras peruanas" (Peruvian women workers' labour disputes), *Boletín de Estudios Latinoamericanos y del Caribe* (37), dec 84 : 69-83.

4687   WALSH, Kenneth. *Strikes in Europe and the United States : measurement and incidence.* New York, NY : St. Martin's Press, 1983, xiv-230 p. bibl., ind.

4688   WOLKINSON, Benjamin W.; COHEN, Abraham. "Use of work sanctions in Israeli labour disputes", *British Journal of Industrial Relations* 20(2), jul 82 : 231-246.

4689   ZECHARAIAH, John. *Administration of industrial labour disputes.* Delhi : Ashish, 1984, 224 p. [India]

18650   Arbitration. Mediation
Arbitrage. Médiation

4690   BLANPAIN, Roger. "Les tendances de la négociation collective en Belgique", *Revue Internationale du Travail* 123(3), mai-jun 84 : 347-360.

4691   DABSCHECK, Braham; NILAND, John. "Les tendances récentes de la négociation collective en Australie", *Revue Internationale du Travail* 123(5), sep-oct 84 : 679-697.

4692   DURAND, Michelle. "Dimensions économique des revendications salariales : une analyse de données sectorielles", *Sociologie du Travail* 26(1), mar 84 : 64-91.

4693   FLANAGAN, Robert J. "Wage concessions and long-term union wage flexibility", *Brookings Papers on Economic Activity* (1), 1984 : 183-216. [USA] [Followed by a discussion by Marvin H. KOSTERS, ibid. : 217-221]

4694   FÜRSTENBERG, Friedrich. "Les tendances récentes de la négociation collective en République fédérale d'Allemagne", *Revue Internationale du Travail* 123(5), sep-oct 84 : 661-678.

4695   GIUGNI, Gino. "Les tendances récentes de la négociation collective en Italie", *Revue Internationale du Travail* 123(5), sep-oct 84 : 643-660.

4696   HYDE, Alan. "Democracy in collective bargaining", *Yale Law Journal* 93(5), apr 84 : 793-856. [USA]

4697   IMOISILI, Imonitie C. "La négociation collective dans le secteur privé au Nigéria", *Travail et Société* 9(4), oct-dec 84 : 397-408.

4698   KATZ, Harry C. "The US automobile collective bargaining system in transition", *British Journal of Industrial Relations* 22(2), jul 84 : 205-217.

4699   KELLY, James. "Management strategy and the reform of collective bargaining : case from the British Steel Corporation", *British Journal of Industrial Relations* 22(2), jul 84 : 135-153.

4700   KRISLOV, Joseph. "Supplying mediation services in five countries : some current problems", *Columbia Journal of World Business* 18(2), sum 83 : 55-63.

4701   LESTER, Richard Allen. *Labor arbitration in state and local government : an examination of experience in eight states and New York City.* Princeton, NJ : Industrial Relations Section, Firestone Library, Princeton University, 1984, x-210 p. bibl.

4702   ROBERTS, B. C. "Les tendances récentes de la négociation collective au Royaume-Uni", *Revue Internationale du Travail* 123(3), mai-jun 84 : 309-331.

4703   RUDOLPH, Helmut. "Die Entwicklung der Vermittlungen in Arbeit" (The development of labour mediation), *Mitteilungen aus der Arbeitsmarkt- und Berufsforschung* 17(2), 1984 : 168-182.

4704   SHIRAI, Taishiro. "Les tendances récentes de la négociation collective au Japon", *Revue Internationale du Travail* 123(3), mai-jun 84 : 333-346.

18660   Collective agreements. Workers' participation
Conventions collectives. Participation des travailleurs

4705   "Participation des travailleurs à la gestion : pratiques et perspectives", *Travail et Société* 9(3), sep 84 : 233-284. [With contributions by Alan GLADSTONE, Rose Marie GREVE, Jacob MANKIDY, Tayo FASHOYIN]

4706   ALEXANDER, Kenneth O. "The promise and perils of worker participation in management", *American Journal of Economics and Sociology* 43(2), apr 84 : 197-204. [USA]

4707   BLYTON, Paul. "Some old and new problems in employee participation in decision-making", *International Social Science Journal / Revue Internationale des Sciences Sociales* 36(2), 1984 : 217-232.

4708   BOUFFARTIGUE, Paul; LABRUYERE, Chantal. "La sollicitation de l'initiative ouvrière : quels enjeux?", *Pensée* (240), aug 84 : 93-105. [France]

4709   CHARLTON, Jacqueline H. "The rise and fall of employee participation in British public administration", *Economic and Industrial Democracy* 5(2), mai 84 : 261-272.

4710   DZUN, Włodzimierz. "Uczestnictwo zatóg PGR w zarządzaniu" (Participations of state farm employees in management), *Wieś Współczesna* 3, 1984 : 70-78.

4711   FIRŪȚA, Argentina. "Constientizare și participare în sistemul autoconducerii muncitorești" (Consciousness and participation in workers' self-management system), *Viitorul Social* 76(6), dec 83 : 528-535. [Romania]

4712   GRASMICK, Harold G.; FINLEY, Nancy J.; GLASER, Deborah L. "Labor force participation, sex-role attitudes, and female crime", *Social Science Quarterly* 65(3), sep 84 : 703-718. [USA]

4713   HANSON, Charles; RATHKEY, Paul. "Industrial democracy : a post-Bullock shopfloor view", *British Journal of Industrial Relations* 22(2), jul 84 : 154-168.

4714   KIM, Kyong-Dong. "Socio-economic changes and political selectivity in the development of industrial democracy in the Republic of Korea", *Economic and Industrial Democracy* 5(4), nov 84 : 445-467.

4715   KOPECKI, A. "Politiĉeskaja aktivnost' trudjaŝĉihsja i ih uĉastie v upravlenii socialistiĉeskim obŝĉestvom" (The workers' political activity and their participations to management of the socialist society), *Nauĉnoe Upravlenie Obŝĉestvom* (16), 1983 : 43-53.

4716   LAAKSONEN, Oiva. "Participation down and up the line : comparative industrial democracy trends in China and Europe", *International Social Science Journal / Revue Internationale des Sciences Sociales* 36(2), 1984 : 299-318.

4717   LAFFERTY, William M. "Workplace democratization in Norway : current status and future prospects with special emphasis on the role of public sector", *Acta Sociologica* 27(2), 1984 : 123-138.

4718   LE GOFF, Jacques. "Une nouvelle citoyenneté dans l'entreprise : éléments d'analyse des lois Auroux. I", *Masses Ouvrières* (387), oct 83 : 3-19. [France] [Part II continued in ibid. : (388), dec 83 : 3-28]

4719   LOCKETT, Martin. "Organizational democracy and politics in China", *International Yearbook of Organizational Democracy* 1, 83 : 591-635.

4720   MONGIA, J. N. *Worker's participation in management in India.* Delhi : Neera Enterprises, 1983, 38 p.

4721   OHYAMA, Nobuyoshi. "Worker's participation in management as an ambivalent process : a Japanese case", *Hokkaido Daigaku Jinbunkagakuronshu* 22, 1984 : 1-17.

4722   PERNER, Detlef. *Mitbestimmung im Handwerk? Die politische und soziale Funktion der Handwerkskammern in Geflecht der Unternehmerorganisationen* (Joint management in trade? The political and social function of trade corporations in the light of employers' organizations). Köln : Bund-Verlag, 1983, 569 p. ill., bibl. [Germany FR]

4723   REGALIA, Ida. *Eletti e abbandonati : modelli e stili di rappresentanza in fabbrica* (Elects and waifs : patterns and styles of representation in manufacture). Bologna : Il Mulino, 1984, 355 p. [Italy]

4724   SCHULLER, Tom; HYMAN, Jeffrey. "Forms of ownership and control : decision-making within a financial institution", *Sociology (London)* 18(1), feb 84 : 51-70.

4725   SPINRAD, William. "Work democracy : an overview", *International Social Science Journal / Revue Internationale des Sciences Sociales* 36(2), 1984 : 197-215.

4726   TURCOTTE, Pierre Régis; BERGERON, Jean-Louis. *Les cercles de qualité : nature et stratégie d'implantation.* Paris : Chotard; Montréal, PQ : Agences d'Arc, 1984, xii-219 p. bibl.

4727   VANDAMME, Jacques; [ed.]. *L'information et la consultation des travailleurs dans les entreprises multinationales.* Paris : Presses Universitaires de France; Genève : Institut de Recherche et d'Information sur les Multinationales, 1984, 290 p.

18700   LEISURE
LOISIR

4728   "Approches géographiques des loisirs", *Norois* 30(120), dec 83 : 479-677. [With contributions by Karl RUPPERT, Peter WEBER, Roger G. BENNETT]

4729   "Freizeitforschung und Freizeitplanung" (Leisure research and planning), *Raumforschung und Raumordnung* 41(4), 1983 : 121-168. [Germany FR] [With contributions by Christoph BECKER]

4730   MATEJKO, Alexander J. "The self-defeat of leisure : the macro-social model and its application", *Sociologia Internationalis* 22(2), 1984 : 161-196.

18710   Leisure time
Temps de loisir

4731   BERTRAND, Michèle. *Les vacances des Français en 1981 et 1982.* Paris : Institut National de la Statistique et des Études Économiques, 1984, 148 p.

4732 JAROSIŃSKA, Maria. "Wypoczynek urlopowy pracowników przemysłu w krajach socjalistycznych" (Holiday rest of industrial workers in socialist countries), *Studia Socjologiczne* 93(2), 1984 : 57-86.

4733 LEIF, Joseph. *Temps libre et temps à soi : l'enjeu éducatif et culturel.* Paris : Éditions ESF, 1984, 128 p.

4734 SAMUEL, Nicole; ROMER, Madeleine. *Le temps libre : un temps social.* Paris : Méridiens, 1984, 207 p.

4735 TOMKA, Miklós. *A szabad szombat értéke és felhasználása — néhány közvéleménykutatási adat alapján* (The value and use of free Saturday — on the basis of some public opinion research data). Budapest : MRT Tömegkommunikációs Kutatóközpont, 1983, 57 p.

4736 YAMADA, Kenzo. "Leisure activities of the Japanese", *Studies of Broadcasting* (19), mar 83 : 93-118.

18720 Leisure utilization
Utilisation des loisirs

4737 "Lessons from videogames and media : effects on the young", *Journal of Communication* 34(2), spr 84 : 72-167. [USA] [With contributions by Jerome L. SINGER, Joanne CANTOR, Glenn G. SPARKS, Mark FETLER]

4738 "Panorama du tourisme en France", *Revue de Géographie de Lyon* 59(1-2), 1984 : 5-116. [With contributions by Emile FLAMENT, Joël MIRLOUP, Janine RENUCCI, Bernard BARBIER, Michel BONNEAU]

4739 ASCHER, François. *Tourisme : sociétés transnationales et identités culturelles.* Paris : UNESCO, 1984, 106 p. bibl.

4740 BARUCCI, Piero; [ed.]. "Il turismo nella società e nella cultura postindustriale" (Tourism in society and in postindustrial culture), *Rivista Internazionale di Scienze Economiche e Commerciali* 31(7), jul 84 : 593-695. [With contributions by Brian ARCHER, Paolo COSTA, Manuel FIGUEROLA PALOMO, René BARETZE]

4741 BROHM, Jean-Marie. "La religion sportive", *Actions et Recherches Sociales* (3), nov 83 : 101-117.

4742 COHEN, Erik. "The sociology of tourism : approaches, issues, and findings", *Annual Review of Sociology* 10, 1984 : 373-392.

4743 FREY, James H.; EADINGTON, William R.; [eds.]. "Gambling : views from the social sciences", *Annals of the American Academy of Political and Social Science* 474, jul 84 : 9-177. [With contributions by Robert G. BLAKEY, Peter REUTER]

4744 GRANSOW, Volker. "Der autistische Walkman. Unterhaltungselektronik, Öffentlichkeit und Freizeit" (The Autistic Walkman. Leisure electronics, people and free time), *Blätter für Deutsche und Internationale Politik* 29(8), aug 84 : 963-973. [Germany FR]

4745 JÁNOSI, György. "A szórakozás és a társadalmi előítéletek" (Entertainment and social prejudice), *Kultúra és Közösség* 11(3), 1984 : 83-94.

4746 JHALLY, Sut. "The spectacle of accumulation : material and cultural factors in the evolution of the sports/media complex", *Insurgent Sociologist* 12(3), 1984 : 41-57. [USA] [With a comment by Barry TRUCHIL, ibid. : 59-60 and a reply by the author, ibid. : 60-61]

4747 KNÖTIG, Paul; REICHARDT, Robert. "Videospiele und Freizeitverhalten" (Video games and leisure utilization), *Journal für Sozialforschung* 24(4), 84 : 423-439. [Austria]

4748 LOSEV, M. M. "Ideologiceskij aspekt fiziceskoj kul'tury i sporta" (Ideological aspect of physical culture and sport), *in : Duhovnaja kul'tura i ideologija* Saransk, 1983 : 127-138.

4749 MARSHALL, John M. "Gambles and the shadow price of death", *American Economic Review* 74(1), mar 84 : 73-86.

4750 MIRABILE, Francesco. "Aspects culturels du tourisme dans la Communauté européene", *Rivista di Studi Politici Internazionali* 51(2), jun 84 : 214-230.

4751 RAMOS, Roberto. *Futebol : ideologia do poder* (Football : the ideology of power). Petrópolis : Vozes, 1984, 114 p. bibl. [Brazil]

4752 ROSSEL, Pierre. *Tourisme et Tiers Monde : un mariage blanc.* Lausanne : P.-M. Favre, 1984, 174 p. ill., bibl.

4753 SANSOT, Pierre. "La sociologie des émotions sportives", *Cahiers Internationaux de Sociologie* 77, 1984 : 323-338.

4754 SUŁKOWSKI, Bogusław. *Zabawa. Studium socjologiczne* (Entertainment. Sociological study). Warszawa : Państwowe Wydawnictwo Naukowe, 1984, 277 p.

4755 TATZ, Colin. "Sport in South Africa : the myth of integration", *Australian Quarterly* 55(4), dec 83 : 405-420.

4756 VALLET, Odon. "Le sport entre la politique et le commerce", *Études*, aug 84 : 55-62.

4757   VALLET, Odon. "Sports et jeux ou le corps arbitre", *Projet* (183), mar 84 : 323-330.
        [France]
4758   WEISGERBER, Pierre. "Tourisme, de l'économie au culturel", *Wallonie* 11(4),
        1984 : 255-270. [Belgium]
4759   WOHL, Andrzej. "Sport as a contemporary form of cultural motor activity", *Dialectics
        and Humanism* 1, 1984 : 75-85.

19100   POLITICAL SCIENCE. POLITICAL SOCIOLOGY
SCIENCE POLITIQUE. SOCIOLOGIE POLITIQUE

4760   BOURDIEU, Pierre. "La délégation et la fétichisme politique", *Actes de la Recherche en Sciences Sociales* 52-53, jun 84 : 49-55.

4761   GILENS, Martin. "The gender gap : psychology, social structure, and support for Reagan", *Berkeley Journal of Sociology* 29, 1984 : 35-56. [USA]

4762   IONESCU, Ghita. *Politics and pursuit of happiness.* London : Longman, 1984, x-240 p.

4763   LONG, Samuel. "Psychopolitical orientations of white and black youth : a test of five models", *Journal of Black Studies* 13(4), jun 83 : 439-456. [USA]

4764   OKOTH-OGENDO, H. W. O. "Development and the legal process in Kenya : an analysis of the role of law in rural development administration", *International Journal of the Sociology of Law* 12(1), feb 84 : 59-83.

4765   RHODES, Aaron A. "Material and nonmaterial incentives in political machines", *Archives Européennes de Sociologie* 25(1), 1984 : 28-53. [USA]

4766   RUSCONI, Gian Enrico. *Scambio, minaccia, decisione : elementi di sociologica politica* (Exchange, threat, decision : elements of political sociology). Bologna : Il Mulino, 1984, 284 p. bibl.

4767   SNIDERMAN, Paul M.; [et al.]. "Policy reasoning and political values : the problem of racial equality", *American Journal of Political Science* 28(1), feb 84 : 75-94. [USA]

4768   ZWICKY, Heinrich. "Forschungstendenzen in der politischen Soziologie" (Research trends in political sociology), *Schweizerische Zeitschrift für Soziologie / Revue Suisse de Sociologie* 10(1), 1984 : 97-124. [Switzerland]

19200   POLITICAL DOCTRINES. POLITICAL THOUGHT
DOCTRINES POLITIQUES. PENSÉE POLITIQUE

19210   Political philosophy
Philosophie politique

4769   "Philosophes (Les) et la politique", *Actes de la Recherche en Sciences Sociales* 55, nov 84 : 1-75.

4770   TYGART, Clarence E. "Political liberalism-conservatism among clergy : the question of dimensionality", *Human Relations* 37(10), oct 84 : 853-861. [USA]

19220   Political power
Pouvoir politique

4771   BORSONI, Paolo. "Legitimazione e scambio politico nel dibattito Habermas-Luhmann" (Legitimation and political change in the Habermas-Luhmann debate), *Critica Sociologica* 69, 1984 : 48-63.

19230   Communism. Nationalism
Communisme. Nationalisme

4772   "After the referenda : the future of ethnic nationalism in Britain and Canada", *Ethnic and Racial Studies* 7(1), jan 84 : 1-193. [With contributions by Maurice PINARD, Richard HAMILTON, Gerald L. GOLD, David McCRONE]

4773   "Religions et nationalismes. Canada et Québec", *Social Compass* 31(4), 1984 : 328-438. [With contributions by Jacques LYLBERBERG, François-Pierre GINGRAS, Neil NEVITTE]

4774   "Tending the roots : nationalism and populism", *Archives Européennes de Sociologie* 25(2), 1984 : 245-305.

4775   AHMETOV, K. G. "K voprosu ob ocenke ideologii sovremennogo nacionalizma v osvobodivšihsja stranah" (Question on evaluation of the contemporary nationalism ideology in the liberated countries), *in : Aktual'nye problemy istoričeskogo materializma* Alma-Ata, 1982 : 201-214.

4776   BERNAL, Ignacio. "Patriotisme et vieilles pierres", *Diogène* 125, jan-mar 84 : 3-13. [Mexique]

4777   BREWER, John D. "Looking back at fascism : a phenomenological analysis of BUF membership", *Sociological Review* 32(4), nov 84 : 742-760. [UK] [British Union of Fascists]
4778   BURK, James. "Patriotism and the all-volunteer force", *Journal of Military Sociology* 12(2), 1984 : 229-241. [USA]
4779   CIPKO, A. S. *Nekotorye filosofskie aspekty teorii socializma* (Some philosophical aspects of the theory of socialism). Moskva : Nauka, 1983, 216 p.
4780   FEATHER, H. R. "Conservative thought and the English bourgeoisie", *Sociological Review* 32(2), mai 84 : 260-284.
4781   FELLING, A.; PETERS, J. "Conservatisme in Nederland nader bekeken" (Conservatism in the Netherlands nearer viewed), *Mens en Maatschappij* 59(4), nov 84 : 339-362.
4782   GANE, Mike. "Institutional socialism and the sociological critique of communism (introduction to Durkheim and Mauss)", *Economy and Society* 13(3), 1984 : 304-330.
4783   GERE, Edwin A. Jr. "New England regionalism and Reagan federalism", *International Social Science Review* 59(4), 1984 : 12-18. [USA]
4784   GOLUBOVIĆ, Zagorka. "Kriza socijalizma" (Socialism crisis), *Gledišta* 25(1-2), feb 84 : 85-104.
4785   HAMMOND, John L. "The Portuguese revolution : two models of socialist transition", *Insurgent Sociologist* 12(1-2), 1984 : 83-100. [1974]
4786   HOFFERT, Robert W. "Scripture and the expression of liberalism", *Social Science Journal (Fort Collins)* 21(2), apr 84 : 15-31.
4787   KAMINSKY, Catherine; KRUK, Simon. *Le nationalisme arabe et le nationalisme juif.* Paris : Presses Universitaires de France, 1983, 244 p.
4788   KESSELMAN, Mark. "Dilemmas of socialist transition in France : modernizing the Republic versus democratic socialist transition", *Insurgent Sociologist* 12(1-2), 1984 : 71-82. [1981-1984]
4789   LABIN, Suzanne. *Socialisme : la démagogie du changement.* Paris : Debresse, 1983, 245 p.
4790   LANE, David. "The structure of Soviet socialism : recent Western theoretical approaches", *Insurgent Sociologist* 12(1-2), 1984 : 101-112.
4791   LEATHERS, Charles G. "Liberalism theology, the new religious political right, and Veblen's ambivalent view of Christianity", *Journal of Economic Issues* 18(4), dec 84 : 1155-1175.
4792   LEMIEUX, Pierre. *Du libéralisme à l'anarcho-capitalisme.* Paris : Presses Universitaires de France, 1983, 171 p. bibl.
4793   LICHTENSTEIN, Peter M. "Some theoretical coordinates of radical liberalism", *American Journal of Economics and Sociology* 43(3), jul 84 : 333-339.
4794   MACGREGOR, D. *The communist ideal in Hegel and Marx.* London : Allen and Unwin, 1984, xvi-582 p.
4795   MÁIZ, Ramón. "Raza y mito céltico en los orígenes del nacionalismo gallego : Manuel M. Murguia" (Race and celtic myth in the origins of the Galician nationalism : Manuel M. Murguia), *Revista Española de Investigaciones Sociológicas* 25, jan-mar 84 : 137-180.
4796   MAJEED, Akhtar; [ed.]. *Regionalism : developmental tensions in India.* Delhi : Cosmo, 1984, vii-227 p.
4797   MANGANARO FAVARETTO, Gilda. *Possibilità e limiti nel 'socialismo scientifico' di P. J. Proudhon* (Possibility and limits of the 'scientific socialism' of P. J. Proudhon). Roma : Ateneo, 1983, 230 p. bibl., ind.
4798   MINTZ, Frank. "Anarhizam jučer i anarhizam danas" (Anarchism yesterday and anarchism today), *Revija za Sociologiju* 14(1-2), 1984 : 109-120.
4799   NIKOLIĆ, Radivoj. "Anarhistička kritika marksističkih koncepcija o državi" (Anarchist critique of Marxist concepts of State), *Revija za Sociologiju* 14(1-2), 1984 : 89-98.
4800   OKLOBDŽIJA, Mirjana. "Anarhistička organizacija pokreta i društva" (The anarchist organization of the movement of the State), *Revija za Sociologiju* 14(1-2), 1984 : 99-108.
4801   OSTERFELD, David. *Freedom, society and the state : an investigation into the possibility of society without government.* Lanham, MD; London : University Press of America, 1983, xviii-399 p.
4802   PILIPENKO, N. V. "Dialektika obščego i osobennogo v stanovlenii i razvitii socializma" (Dialectics of the general and the particular in the future and development of socialism), *Sociologičeskie Issledovanija (Moskva)* (2), 1983 : 192-201.
4803   POLIN, Raymond; POLIN, Claude. *Le libéralisme : espoir ou péril.* Paris : Table Ronde, 1984, 370 p.
4804   RAY, John J.; HEAVEN, Patrick C. L. "Conservatism and authoritarianism among urban Afrikaners", *Journal of Social Psychology* 122(2), apr 84 : 163-170.
4805   RELLY, Bavin. "Personal mobility and the South African economy : lifting curbs on opportunity", *South Africa International* 14(3), jan 84 : 476-482.
4806   TADIĆ, Ljubomir. "Anarhizam i socijalna teorija" (Anarchism and social theory), *Revija za Sociologiju* 14(1-2), 1984 : 69-78.

4807   TERADA, Atsuhiro. "E. Burke no hoshu shugi -chishiki shakaigaku teki ni mita ichi shiron" (E. Burke's conservatism : a study in sociology of knowledge), *Nihon University Journal of Sociology* 89, 1984 : 38-53.

19240   Democracy. Dictatorship
Démocratie. Dictature

4808   ARATÓ, Andrew; GOLDFARB, Jeffrey; [eds.]. "Democracy", *Social Research* 50(4), wint 83 : 699-973. [With contributions by Claus OFFE, Peter MURPHY, Arthur J. JACOBSON, Manfred STANLEY, Philippe C. SCHAITTER, José CASANOVA]

4809   BAECHLER, Jean. "Le pouvoir des idées en démocratie", *Connaissance Politique* 2, mai 83 : 141-157.

4810   DEMYK, M. "Ambitions militaires et esprit oligarchique au Guatemala", *Annales des Pays d'Amérique Centrale et des Cariaïbes* 4, 1983 : 7-15.

4811   FONTAINE, Jean-Marc. "A quoi sert le totalitarisme?", *Homme et Société* 71-72, jan-jun 84 : 7-21.

4812   GUGGENBERGER, Bernd; OFFE, Claus; [eds.]. *An der Grenzen der Mehrheitsdemokratie : Politik und Soziologie der Mehrheitsregel* (On the limits of majority democracy : politics and sociology of majority rule). Opladen : Westdeutscher Verlag, 1984, 326 p. bibl.

4813   INDIČ, Trivo. "Fabbrijeva kritika diktature i revolucije (pa i oktobarske)" (Fabbri's critique of dictatorship and revolution (including the October Revolution)), *Revija za Sociologiju* 14(1-2), 1984 : 129-140.

4814   LAMBERT, Angela. *Unquiet souls : the Indian summer of the British aristocracy, 1880-1918.* London : Macmillan, 1984, xxiv-262-48 p. bibl., ind., ill.

4815   OBRADOVIĆ, Daniela. "Totalitarizam kao tendencija" (Totalitarianism as a trend), *Sociologija* 26(3-4), jul-dec 84 : 373-385. [A review article]

4816   SCHMITTER, Philippe C. "Democratic theory and neocorporatist practice", *Social Research* 50(4), 1983 : 885-928.

4817   THOMAS, J. J. R. "Weber and direct democracy", *British Journal of Sociology* 35(2), jun 84 : 216-240.

4818   VALDÉS, G. "La democracia en la Argentina" (Democracy in Argentina), *Ideas en Ciencias Sociales* 1(1), 1984 : 70-81.

4819   VALLIN, Pierre. "Démocratie et religion", *Études*, mar 84 : 449-462.

4820   WALIGORSKI, Conrad P. "Conservative economist critics of democracy", *Social Science Journal (Fort Collins)* 21(2), apr 84 : 99-116.

4821   WIPPLER, R. "Het oligarchieprobleem : Michels' ijzeren wet en latere problemeoplossingen" (Oligarchy problem : Michels' cast-iron law and problem solutions), *Mens en Maatschappij* 59(2), mai 84 : 115-141.

19300   CONSTITUTION. STATE
CONSTITUTION. ÉTAT

19310   Political systems
Systèmes politiques

4822   "État (L') et la Méditerranée", *Peuples Méditerranéens / Mediterranean Peoples* (27-28), sep 84 : 3-299. [With contributions by Paul VIEILLE, Laënnec HURBON, Ali OUMLIL]

4823   AŠIN, G. K. "Amerikanskaja sociologija o haraktere političeskoj sistemy SŠA" (American sociology on the character of the USA political system), *Sociologičeskie Issledovanija (Moskva)* (3), 1983 : 186-192.

4824   AVRAMOVIĆ, Zoran. "Kako institucionalizovati političku vlast" (How to put political power in institutions), *Sociologija* 26(3-4), jul-dec 84 : 343-358.

4825   BIRCH, Anthony H. "Overload, ungovernability and delegitimation : the theories and the British case", *British Journal of Political Science* 14(2), apr 84 : 135-160.

4826   BOOTH, John A.; SELIGSON, Mitchell A. "The political culture of authoritarianism in Mexico : a reexamination", *Latin American Research Review* 19(1), 1984 : 106-124.

4827   BURSTYN, Varda. "Masculine dominance and the State", *Socialist Register*, 1983 : 45-89.

4828   CLAESSEN, Hans; GESCHIERE, Peter; [eds.]. "Staatsvorming in Africa", *Sociologische Gids* 31(4), 1984 : 298-368.

4829   DAVIJAN, A. G. *Političeskaja sistema socialističeskogo tipa* (Political system of the socialist type). Èrevan : Lujs, 1983, 250 p.

4830   GERLAH, A. "Socialističeskaja demokratija kak spravedlivyj politicěskij režim" (The socialist democracy as a just political system), *in : Marksistko-leninskaja koncepcija politicěskoj sistemy socialističeskogo obščestva* Moskva, 1982 : 64-72.

4831   GUPTA, N. K. "Political development and political leadership in village communities",
         Indian Journal of Social Research 25(2), aug 84 : 181-192. [India]
4832   KAVIRAJ, Sudipta. "On the crisis of political institutions in India", *Contributions to Indian
         Sociology* 18(2), jul-dec 84 : 223-243.
4833   KOVÁCS, István. "Változás — átalakulás — az állam társadalmi és gazdasági szerepében"
         (Changes in — transformation of — the State's social and economic roles), *Társadalomkutatás*
         2(3-4), 1984 : 13-21. [Hungary]
4834   LANUZA, Alberto; [et al.]. *Economía y sociedad en la construcción del estado en Nicaragua* (Economy
         and society in the building of state in Nicaragua). San José : ICAP, 1983, 276 p. ill., bibl.
4835   MAHESHWARI, Shriram. *Political development in India.* Delhi : Concept, 1984, 149 p.
4836   MANN, Michael. "The autonomous power of the state : its origins, mechanisms and
         results", *Archives Européennes de Sociologie* 25(2), 1984 : 185-213.
4837   MARČENKO, M. N. "Antagonistićeskaja priroda politićeskoj sistemy buržuaznogo
         obšćestva" (The antagonistic nature of the political system of bourgeois society), *Naučnye
         Doklady Vysšej Školy. Naučnyj Kommunizm* (3), 1983 : 90-97.
4838   OBRADOVIĆ, Marija. "Shvatanja politićkih sistema birokratskih društava S. N. Ajzenštata"
         (Concept of political systems of bureaucratic societies of S. N. Eisenstadt), *Sociologija*
         26(3-4), jul-dec 84 : 386-397.
4839   PALLOIX, Christian. "Les formes contemporaines de la socialisation", *Cahier — Centre de
         Recherche sur les Mutations des Sociétés Industrielles* (1), oct 83 : 28-42.
4840   PIERSON, Christopher. "New theories of state and civil society recent developments in
         post-Marxist analysis of the state", *Sociology (London)* 18(4), nov 84 : 562-579.
4841   RASSOLOV, M. M. "Informacionnyj aspekt funkcionirovanija politićeskoj sistemy"
         (Informational aspect of functioning of the political system), *in : Marksistko-leninskaja
         koncepcija politićeskoj sistemy socialistićeskogo obšćestva* Moskva, 1982 : 50-55.
4842   ROCHON, Thomas R. "The creation of political institutions : two cases from the
         Netherlands", *International Journal of Comparative Sociology* 25(3-4), sep-dec 84 : 173-188.
4843   SOUBIE, Raymond. "Un consensus sur l'État est-il possible?", *Revue Politique et Parlementaire*
         86(908), feb 84 : 9-20. [France]
4844   THOMAS, George M.; MEYER, John W. "The expansion of the state", *Annual Review
         of Sociology* 10, 1984 : 461-482.
4845   VAN DEN BERCKEN, W. "Staat en ideologie in de Sovjetunie" (State and ideology
         in Soviet Union), *Internationale Spectator* 37(10), oct 83 : 630-649.
4846   WEISS, Linda. "The Italian state and small business", *Archives Européennes de Sociologie* 25(2),
         1984 : 214-241.
4847   WOOD, Geof. "State intervention and bureaucratic reproduction : comparative thoughts",
         Development and Change 15(1), jan 84 : 23-41.

         **19320   Human rights
                      Droits de l'homme**

4848   "Content regulation and the dimensions of free expression", *Harvard Law Review* 96(8),
         jun 83 : 1854-1873. [USA] [Abstract 34-789]
4849   "Human Rights", *Daedalus* 112(4), aut 83 : 1-280. [With contributions by Maurice
         CRANSTON, Stanley HOFFMANN, Gaston V. RIMLINGER, Leszek KOLAKOWSKI,
         John Gerard RUGGIE, Merle GOLDMAN]
4850   "Human Rights", *Social Philosophy and Policy* 1(2), spr 84 : 1-175. [With contributions by
         Alan GEWIRTH, Arthur C. DANTO, Allan GIBBARD, James FISHKIN]
4851   "Liberté (La) de la presse en Côte d'Ivoire", *Peuples Noirs — Peuples Africains* 7(41-42),
         dec 84 : 104-140.
4852   "Liberty and equality", *Social Philosophy and Policy* 2(1), aut 84 : 1-173. [With contributions
         by R. M. HARE, James M. BUCHANAN, Loren E. LOMASKY, Allen BUCHANAN,
         Michael LEVIN, David BRAYBROOKE]
4853   "Menschenrechte, Minderheiten und Flüchtlinge in Asien" (Human rights, minorities and
         refugees in Asia), *Internationales Asien Forum* 15(1-2), mai 84 : 5-150. [With contributions
         by Hiroko YAMANE, David J. WESSELS, Gananath OBEYESEKERE, Wolfgang
         S. HEINZ]
4854   ALSTON, Philip. "Conjuring up new human rights : a proposal for quality control",
         American Journal of International Law 78(3), jul 84 : 607-621.
4855   ARNHART, Larry. "Darwin, Aristotle and the biology of human rights", *Social Science
         Information / Information sur les Sciences Sociales* 23(3), 1984 : 493-521.
4856   BARKAN, Steven E. "Legal control of the Southern civil rights movement", *American
         Sociological Review* 49(4), aug 84 : 552-565. [USA] [1955-1965]

4857 BLASER, Arthur W. "The rhetoric, promise, and performance of human rights : Soviet and American perspectives", *Journal of Applied Behavioral Science* 20(4), 1984 : 471-489.

4858 DOPPELT, Gerald. "Conflicting social paradigms of human freedom and the problem of justification", *Inquiry* 27(1), mar 84 : 51-86. [With a response by Carol C. GOULD, ibid. : 87-103 and Mihailo MARKOVIĆ, ibid. : 105-115]

4859 GOLDFARB, Jeffrey C. "1984 : Poland, public freedom, and human rights", *Journal of Applied Behavioral Science* 20(4), 1984 : 455-469.

4860 HICKERSON, Steven R. "Complexity and the meaning of freedom : the instrumentalist view", *American Journal of Economics and Sociology* 43(4), oct 84 : 435-442.

4861 HICKERSON, Steven R. "Complexity and the meaning of freedom : the classical liberal view", *American Journal of Economics and Sociology* 43(1), jan 84 : 91-101.

4862 HUSAK, Douglas N. "Why there are no human rights", *Social Theory and Practice* 10(2), sum 84 : 125-141.

4863 LANE, David. "Human rights under State socialism", *Political Studies* 32(3), sep 84 : 349-368.

4864 MARKOVIĆ, Mihailo. "Human freedom from a democratic socialist point ov view : a reply to Doppelt", *Inquiry* 27(1), mar 84 : 105-115.

4865 PAUL, Ellen Frankel; PAUL, Jeffrey; MILLER, Fred Dycus Jr. *Human rights.* Oxford; New York, NY : Basil Blackwell, 1984, 175 p. bibl.

4866 RODRÍGUEZ-IBAÑEZ, José Enrique. "'De civitate': perspectiva sociológica" ('De civitate' : sociological prospect), *Sistema* (63), nov 84 : 85-108.

4867 SHER, George. "Right violations and injustices : can we always avoid trade-offs?", *Ethics* 94(2), jan 84 : 212-224.

4868 VÖRÖS, Gyula. "Szabadság és társadalom. Marx Grundrisséje nyomán" (Freedom and society. On the basis of Marx's Grundrisse), *Társadalomtudományi Közlemények* (2), 1984 : 279-296.

4869 WELCH, Claude Jr.; MELTZER, Ronald I. *Human rights and development in Africa.* Albany, NY : State University of New York Press, 1984, x-349 p. ind.

4870 WHITEHEAD, John W. *The stealing of America.* Westchester, IL : Crossway Books, 1983, xiii-158 p. bibl., ind.

19330 **Political representation**
Représentation politique

19340 **Government**
Gouvernement

4871 ALLO, Eliane. "Un nouvel art de gouverner : Leibniz et la gestion savante de la société par les assurances", *Actes de la Recherche en Sciences Sociales* 55, nov 84 : 33-40.

4872 BROGDEN, Mike; BROGDEN, Ann. "From Henry III to Liverpool 8 : the unity of police street powers", *International Journal of the Sociology of Law* 12(1), feb 84 : 37-58.

4873 DE LAET, C.; VAN OUTRIVE, L. "Recherches sur la police, 1978-1982", *Déviance et Société* 8(3), sep 84 : 267-294. [Voir pour la 2e partie, ibid. : 8(4), dec 84 : 377-414]

4874 FARAGÓ, Katalin P. "A magyar fiatalok rendőrképének vizsgálata" (Examination of youth's perception of policemen), *Magyar Pszichológiai Szemle* 41(3), 1984 : 214-231. [Hungary]

4875 FIELDING, Nigel. "Police socialization and police competence", *British Journal of Sociology* 35(4), dec 84 : 568-590. [UK]

4876 HOLDAWAY, Simon. *Inside the British police : a force at work.* Oxford : Basil Blackwell, 1983, vi-186 p. bibl., ind.

4877 JEFFERSON, Tony; GRIMSHAW, Roger. "The problem of law enforcement policy in England and Wales : the case of community policy and racial attacks", *International Journal of the Sociology of Law* 12(2), mai 84 : 117-135.

4878 MAINWARING-WHITE, Sarah. *The policing revolution : police technology, democracy, and liberty in Britain.* Totowa, NJ : Barnes and Noble Books; Brighton, Sussex : Harvester Press, 1983, 250 p.

4879 MCCULLAGH, Ciaran. "Police powers and the problem of crime in Ireland : some implications of international research", *Administration (Dublin)* 31(4), 1984 : 412-442.

4880 ROZELL, Mark J. "In defense of executive privilege : historic developments and modern imperatives", *International Social Science Review* 59(2), 1984 : 67-81. [USA]

4881 YADAVA, R. S. "In defence of Indian police", *Radical Humanist* 47(2), mai 83 : 16-19 & 23.

19350   **Parliament**
         Parlement

19360   **Judiciary power**
         Pouvoir judiciaire

4882   "Juger ... de quel droit?", *Revue Nouvelle* 80(10), oct 84 : 237-316. [Belgium] [With
        contributions by Béatrice HAUBERT, Paul MARTENS, Jacques VAN DROOGHEN-
        BROECK, Marie-Françoise RIGAUX]
4883   SALAS, Luis. "The emergence and decline of the Cuban popular tribunals", *Law and
        Society Review* 17(4), 1983 : 587-612.
4884   WILLEN, Richard S. "Religion and the law : the secularization of testimonial procedures",
        Sociological Analysis 44(1), 1983 : 53-64. [UK]

19400   **PUBLIC ADMINISTRATION**
         ADMINISTRATION PUBLIQUE

19410   **Civil service. Technocracy**
         Fonction publique. Technocratie

4885   "Whitehall (The) machine : a discussion", *Political Quarterly* 55(1), mar 84 : 3-28. [With
        contributions by J. HOSKYNS and L. PLIATZKY]
4886   BRENOT-OULDALI, Annie; QUARRÉ, Dominique. "Les effectifs des agents de l'État
        de 1975 à 1982", *Économie et Statistique* 167, jun 84 : 17-33. [France]
4887   COING, Helmut. *Ausbildung von Elitebeamten in Frankreich und Grossbritannien* (Training of
        elite civil servants in France and Great Britain). Berlin : Duncker und Humblot, 1983, 58 p.
        bibl.
4888   DOMETRIUS, Nelson C. "Minorities and women among state agency leaders", *Social
        Science Quarterly* 65(1), mar 84 : 127-137.
4889   GÁTHY, Vera. *A közigazgatás társadalmi problémái a mai Indiában* (The social problems of
        public administration in contemporary India). Budapest : Akadémiai Kiadó, 1984, 278 p.
4890   GUILLEMIN, Jacques. "Chefferie traditionnelle et administration publique au Niger",
        Mois en Afrique 18(213-214), nov 83 : 115-124.
4891   LANGKAU-HERRMANN, Monika; [et al.]. *Frauen im öffentlichen Dienst* (Women in the
        civil service). Bonn : Verlag Neue Gesellschaft, 1983, 161 p. bibl. [Germany FR]
4892   MUSHKAT, Miron. "Social group representation in the Hong Kong administrative class",
        Revue Internationale de Sociologie / International Review of Sociology 19(1-2-3), apr-aug-dec
        83 : 155-176.
4893   RAINEY, Hal G. "Public agencies and private firms : incentive structures, goals, and
        individuals roles", *Administration and Society* 15(2), aug 83 : 207-242. [USA]
4894   SIMIS, Konstantin. "Andropows Kampagne gegen die Korruption" (Andropov's action
        against corruption), *Europäische Rundschau* 12(1), 1984 : 55-68. [USSR]

19420   **Central government. Local government**
         Administration centrale. Administration locale

4895   AIKEN, Michael; MARTINOTTI, Guido. "Sistema urbano, governo della città e giunte
        di sinistra nei grandi comuni italiani" (Urban system, city management and left in the
        great Italian communes), *Quaderni di Sociologia* 30(2-3-4), 1982 : 177-248.
4896   BIGGART, Nicole Woolsey. "A sociological analysis of the presidential staff", *Sociological
        Quarterly* 25(1), wint 84 : 27-43. [USA]
4897   BROSIO, Giorgio; FERRERO, Mario; SANTAGATA, Walter. "Gli amministratori locali
        come politici : un tentativo di verifica empirica dei bilanci comunali italiani" (The local
        managers as political men : an attempt at empirical auditing of Italian municipal
        accounts), *Quaderni di Sociologia* 30(2-3-4), 1982 : 249-284.
4898   CALDERÓN, Fernando; LASERNA, Roberto; [comps.]. *El poder de las regiones* (The power
        of the regions). Cochabamba : Centro de Estudios de la Realidad Económica y Social;
        S.l. : Comité Urbano Regional del Consejo Latino Americano de Ciencias Sociales,
        1983, 271 p. bibl. [Bolivia]
4899   DION, Stéphane. "Les politiques municipales de concertation : néo-corporatisme et
        démocratie", *Sociologie du Travail* 26(2), jun 84 : 121-140.
4900   GÓMEZ NAVAS, Oscar. *Administración municipal y urbanización en Venezuela* (Municipal
        administration and urbanization in Venezuela). Caracas : Editorial Equinoccio,
        1983, 151 p. bibl.

4901   GUILLEMIN, Alain. "Pouvoir de représentation et constitution de l'identité locale", *Actes de la Recherche en Sciences Sociales* 52-53, jun 84 : 15-17.

4902   MIURA, Shigeji. *Gendai gyosei kouho kenkyu jyosetsu* (A study of modern public relations in local government). Tokyo : Gakubunsha, 1984, 252 p. [Japan]

4903   OLÁH, Miklós; VÁGVÖLGYI, B. András. "Egy helyi döntés körülményei" (The circumstances of a local decision), *Valóság* 27(6), 1984 : 42-52. [Hungary]

4904   OSTROWSKI, John W.; [et al.]. "Local government capacity building : a structured group process approach", *Administration and Society* 16(1), mai 84 : 3-26. [USA]

4905   RAJPUT, R. S.; MEGHE, D. R.; [eds.]. *Panchayati raj in India : democracy at grassroots.* Delhi : Deep and Deep, 1984, 286 p.

4906   REBORA, Gianfranco. *Organizzazione e direzione dell'ente locale : teoria e modelli per l'amministrazione pubblica* (Organization and direction of local organism : theory and models for the public administration). Milano : A. Giuffrè, 1983, xvi-275 p. ill., bibl. [Italy]

19500   POLITICAL PARTIES. PRESSURE GROUPS
PARTIS POLITIQUES. GROUPES DE PRESSION

19510   Party systems. Political parties
Systèmes de parti. Partis politiques

4907   "Gouvernement (Le) du parti québécois", *Recherches Sociographiques* 25(1), apr 84 : 7-124. [With contributions by Gilles LESAGE, Vincent LEMIEUX, Louis MASSICOTTE, Réjean PELLETIER, Jean CRETE]

4908   BANERJEE, Kishalay. *Regional political parties in India.* Delhi : B. R. Publishers, 1984, xix-375 p.

4909   DI TELLA, Torcuato. "The popular parties : Brazil and Argentina in a Latin American perspective", *Government and Opposition* 19(2), spr 84 : 250-276.

4910   JANOWSKI, Karol B. "Ujmowanie sprzeczności społecznych w myśli politycznej PZPR" (Approach to the social contradictions in the political thought of the Polish United Workers' Party), *Studia Socjologiczne* 94(3), 1984 : 20-46.

4911   LLERA RAMO, Francisco José. "El sistema de partidos vasco : distancia ideológica y legitimación política" (Party system in Euskadi : ideological distance and political legitimation), *Revista Española de Investigaciones Sociológicas* 28, oct-dec 84 : 171-206. [Spain]

4912   MADAN, N. L. *Congress party and social change.* Delhi : B. R. Publishers, 1984, xi-404 p. [India]

4913   MCALLISTER, Ian; O'CONNELL, Declan. "The political sociology of party support in Ireland", *Comparative Politics* 16(2), jan 84 : 191-204.

4914   OBERST, Timothy. "Chama Cha Mapinduzi and FRELIMO : the party and the transition to socialism", *Insurgent Sociologist* 12(1-2), 1984 : 25-37. [Tanzania; Mozambique]

4915   ROCCA, James V. "Austria's second party. An exercise in electoral frustration?", *International Social Science Review* 59(4), 1984 : 19-26.

4916   SUNDQUIST, James L. *Dynamics of the party system : alignment and realignment of political parties in the United States.* Washington, DC : Brookings Institution, 1983, rev., xiv-466 p.

4917   VINOGRADOV, V. D. *Partija v sisteme socialističeskogo obščestva : filosofsko-metodologičeskie problemy issledovanij* (Party in the socialist society system : philosophical and methodological problems of research). Leningrad : Nauka, 1983, 152 p.

4918   ZORRILLA, R. H. "El sistema de partidos : la otra oportunidad" (The party system : the other opportunity), *Ideas en Ciencias Sociales* 1(1), 1984 : 55-69. [Argentina]

19520   Pressure groups. Protest movements
Groupes de pression. Mouvements contestataires

4919   "Interest groups and public policy : a symposium", *Policy Studies Journal* 11(4), jun 83 : 599-708. [With contributions by A. G. JORDAN, J. J. RICHARDSON, Terry F. BUSS, F. Stevens REDBURN, Kathleen A. STAUDT]

4920   "Révolutions (Les) sociales des années 40 du XXᵉ siècle", *Nouvelle Revue Internationale* 27(7), jul 84 : 148-184. [Eastern Europe]

4921   "Social activists and people's movements", *Social Action* 34(2), apr-jun 84 : 115-215. [India]

4922   AJISAKA, Manabu. "Europe ni okeru toshi shakaiundo no ichi dohkoh" (A trend of urban social movement in Europe with reference to International Journal of Urban and Regional Research), *For New Sociology* 10(1), 1984 : 16-30.

4923   ALSENE, E. "L'alternative au tournant", *Revue Internationale d'Action Communautaire* (10), aut 83 : 49-62. [Canada]

4924 BRAND, Karl-Werner; BÜSSER, Detlef; RUCHT, Dieter. _Aufbruch in eine andere Gesellschaft : neue soziale Bewegungen in der Bundesrepublik_ (Raising towards an other society : new social movements in the Federal Republic). Frankfurt-am-Main; New York, NY : Campus, 1983, 300 p. bibl., ind.

4925 BRÜCKNER, Peter. _Selbstbefeiung : Provokation und soziale Bewegungen_ (Self-liberation : provocation and social movements). Berlin : K. Wagenbach, 1983, 105 p. ill.

4926 CABLE, Sherry. "Professionalization in social movement organization : a case study of Pennsylvanians for Biblical Morality", _Sociological Focus_ 17(4), oct 84 : 287-304. [USA]

4927 EVERS, Tilman. "Identidade : a face oculta dos novos movimentos sociais" (Identity : the new social movements hidden face), _Novos Estudos CEBRAP_ 2(4), apr 84 : 11-23. [Latin America]

4928 EYERMAN, Ron. "Social movements and social theory", _Sociology (London)_ 18(1), feb 84 : 71-82.

4929 FADDA, Giulietta. "Los movimientos sociales urbanos : algunas consideraciones teoricas" (Urban social movements : theoretical considerations), _Socialismo y Participación_ (24), dec 83 : 105-111. [Venezuela]

4930 FEHÉR, Ferenc; HELLER, Agnès. "From red to green", _Telos_ (59), spr 84 : 35-44.

4931 GAIS, Thomas L.; [et al.]. "Interest groups, iron triangles and representative institutions in American national government", _British Journal of Political Science_ 14(2), apr 84 : 161-185.

4932 GIAMMANCO, Rosanna. "Rationality and the peace movement : a Weberian analysis", _Sociologia_ 18(3), sep-dec 84 : 47-59.

4933 HALFMANN, Jost. "Soziale Bewegungen und Staat : Nicht-intendierte Folgen neokorporatistischer Politik" (Social movements and State : unexpected consequences of the neocorporatist policy), _Soziale Welt_ 35(3), 1984 : 294-312.

4934 HANISCH, Rolf; [ed.]. _Soziale Bewegungen in Entwicklungsländern_ (Social movements in developing countries). Baden-Baden : Nomos, 1983, vi-345 p. ill., bibl.

4935 JAPP, Klaus P. "Selbsterzeugung oder Fremdverschulden : Thesen zum Rationalismus in den Theorien sozialer Bewegungen" (Spontaneous generation or external responsibility : theses on rationalism in social movements theories), _Soziale Welt_ 35(3), 1984 : 313-329.

4936 KAJITA, Takamichi. "France sayoku seken-ka no shakai undo" (Social movements in the period of socialists' government in France), _Keizai Hyoron_, jun 84 : 64-77.

4937 KALEKIN-FISHMAN, Devorah. "Agitation and identity : social movements in Israel", _Sociologia Internationalis_ 22(2), 1984 : 141-159.

4938 KAMENS, David M. "Statist' ideology, national political control of education, and youth protest : comparative analysis", _Journal of Conflict Resolution_ 27(4), dec 83 : 563-589.

4939 KASHIOKA, Tomihide. "Kokka to minzoku no fu-icchi : minzoku undo no doutai teki typology" (Incongruence between state and nation : toward a dynamic typology of nationalistic movements), _Kansai Gaikokugo Daigaku Kenkyu Ronshu_ 40, 1984 : 437-450.

4940 KIVISTO, Peter. "Contemporary social movements in advanced industrial societies and sociological intervention : an appraisal of Alain Tourain's 'Pratique'", _Acta Sociologica_ 27(4), 1984 : 355-366.

4941 LAAKKONEN, Vesa. "Die Genossenschaftsbewegung in Finnland" (Cooperative movement in Finland), _Zeitschrift für das Gesamte Genossenschaftswesen_ 34(1), 1984 : 40-44.

4942 LOFLAND, John; JAMISON, Michael. "Social movement locals : modal member structures", _Sociological Analysis_ 45(2), 1984 : 115-129.

4943 MISZTAL, Bronisław. "Socjologiczna teoria ruchów społecznych" (Sociological theory of social movements), _Studia Socjologiczne_ 92(1), 1984 : 113-138.

4944 MURRELL, Peter. "An examination of the factors affecting the formation of interest groups in OECD countries", _Public Choice_ 43(2), 1984 : 151-171.

4945 NEDELMANN, Birgitta. "New political movements and changes in processes of intermediation", _Social Science Information / Information sur les Sciences Sociales_ 23(6), 1984 : 1029-1048.

4946 OHATA, Hiroshi. "'Shugo kodo ron' no shakai undo riron eno shisa" (Some implications of 'the logic of collective action' to the theory of social movements), _Shakaigaku Ronso_ 5, 1984 : 9-36.

4947 PRÄTORIUS, Rainer. _Soziologie der politischen Organisationen : eine Einführung_ (Sociology of political organizations : an introduction). Darmstadt : Wissenschaftliche Buchgesellschaft, 1984, vii-120 p. bibl., ind.

4948 PRIEST, T. B.; SYLVES, Richard T.; SCUDDER, David F. "Corporate advice : large corporations and federal advisory committees", _Social Science Quarterly_ 65(1), mar 84 : 100-111. [USA]

4949 SALISBURY, Robert H. "Interest representation : the dominance of institutions", _American Political Science Review_ 78(1), mar 84 : 64-76. [USA]

4950   SKILLING, H. Gordon. "Interest groups and communist politics revisited", *World Politics* 36(1), oct 83 : 1-27.

4951   STEWART, Charles J.; SMITH, Craig Allen; DENTON, Robert E. Jr. *Persuasion and social movements*. Prospect Heights, IL : Waveland Press, 1984, xi-227 p. ill., bibl., ind.

4952   TAKADA, Akihiko. "America ni okeru kusanone shimin undo no atarashii doko San Francisco wangan chiiki o chushin ni" (A new development of the grass-roots movement in the United States : an interview research in San Francisco bay area), *Seikei University Bulletin of the Faculty of Humanities* 20, 1984 : 62-95.

4953   TORRES, Carlos; TORRES, Lara. *Cooperativismo, el modelo alternativo : estudio sobre su ideología, instituciones y técnicas* (Cooperativism, the alternative pattern : study on its ideology, institutions and techniques). Lima : Universidad de Lima, 1983, xviii-309 p. ill., bibl., ind. [Peru]

4954   TOURAINE, Alain. "Les mouvements sociaux : objet particulier ou problème central de l'analyse sociologique?", *Revue Française de Sociologie* 25(1), jan-mar 84 : 3-19.

4955   VAN SNIPPENBURG, L. B. "Belangengroepen en economische groel : een cross-nationale studie" (Interest groups and economic growth : a cross-national study), *Sociologische Gids* 31(2), 1984 : 164-183.

4956   WILSON, Frank L. "French interest group politics : pluralist or neocorporatist?", *American Political Science Review* 77(4), dec 83 : 895-910.

19530   Political majority. Political opposition
Majorité politique. Opposition politique

4957   CARERES PRENDES, J. "El Salvador revolutionary struggle and the Church's option for the poor", *Social Compass* 30(2-3), 1983 : 261-298.

4958   WIESNER, Joachim. "Die neuen politischen Protest-Bewegung in zeitgeschichtlicher und Demokratie-theoretischer Sicht" (New political protest movements from an historical perspective and from the point of view of the theory of democracy), *Jahrbuch für Christliche Sozialwissenschaften* 25, 1984 : 89-136. [Germany FR]

19600   POLITICAL BEHAVIOUR. ELECTIONS. POLITICS
COMPORTEMENT POLITIQUE. ÉLECTIONS. POLITIQUE

19610   Political leaders. Political society
Leaders politiques. Société politique

4959   HINTZEN, Percy C. "Bases of elite support for a regime : race, ideology, and clientelism as bases for leaders in Guyana and Trinidad", *Comparative Political Studies* 16(3), oct 83 : 363-391.

4960   MURAMATSU, Michio; KRAUSS, Ellis S. "Bureaucrats and politicians in policymaking : the case of Japan", *American Political Science Review* 78(1), mar 84 : 126-146.

4961   WIATR, Jerzy J. "Przywództwo polityczne w Polsce w świetle badań socjologicznych" (Political leadership in Poland in the light of sociological research), *Studia Socjologiczne* 93(2), 1984 : 11-27.

19620   Political attitudes. Political participation
Attitudes politiques. Participation politique

4962   "Biopolitics and gender", *Women and Politics* 3(2-3), aut 83 : 210 p. [With contributions by Denise L. BAER, David A. BOSITIS, Susan Ann KAY, Douglas B. MEIKLE, Glendon SCHUBERT]

4963   "Politische Kultur" (Political culture), *Österreichische Zeitschrift für Politikwissenschaft* 13(1), trim. l. 84 : 1-136. [Austria] [With contributions by Heide GERSTENBERGER, Peter GERLICH, Eva KREISKY]

4964   BELOV, G. A. "Obščestvenno-političeskaja aktivnost'kak projavlenie političeskoj kul'tury" (Socio-political activity as an expression of the political culture), *Sovetskoe Gosudarstvo i Pravo* (6), jun 84 : 3-10. [USSR]

4965   BOGUSLAWSKI, Alexander. "Hinten weit in der Türkei. Zur politischen Kultur der türkischen Landbevölkerung" (Turkey's background. Turkish rural population political culture), *Orient* 24(3), sep 83 : 501-517.

4966   BRAUNGART, Richard G.; BRAUNGART, Margaret M. "Generational politics", *Micropolitics* 3(3), 1984 : 349-415.

4967   BRAUNGART, Richard G.; BRAUNGART, Margaret M.; [eds.]. "Life course and generational politics", *Journal of Political and Military Sociology* 12(1), spr 84 : 1-211.

4968   BRINT, Steven. "'New-class' and cumulative trend explanations of the liberal political attitudes of professionals", *American Journal of Sociology* 90(1), jul 84 : 30-71. [USA]

4969   CHRISTY, Carol A. "Economic development and sex differences in political participation", *Women and Politics* 4(1), spr 84 : 7-34.

4970   CONEN, Gabriele. *Politisches Lernen in der Familienarbeit : ein vernachlässigtes Feld politischer Sozialisation* (Political learning in family work : a neglected field for political socialization). Köln : Pahl Rugenstein, 1983, iii-239 p. ill., bibl.

4971   DAVTJAN, A. G. "Političeskaja kul'tura razvitogo socializma" (The political culture of developed socialism), *Voprosy Naučnogo Kommunizma (Erevan)* (2), 1982 : 104-120.

4972   DI FRANCEISCO, Wayne; GITELMAN, Zvi. "Soviet political culture and 'covert participation' in policy implementation", *American Political Science Review* 78(3), sep 84 : 603-621.

4973   ELSINGA, E. "Vormen van politieke participatie in Nederland" (Formes of political participation in the Netherlands), *Mens en Maatschappij* 59(4), nov 84 : 388-407.

4974   FOWLKES, Diane L. "Developing a theory of countersocialization : gender, race, and politics in the lives of women activists", *Micropolitics* 3(2), 1983 : 181-225. [USA]

4975   FRATCZAK-RUDNICKA, Barbara. "The influence of current political events on the perception of social differentiations among a group of Warsaw teenagers and their parents", *International Journal of Political Education* 6(3), nov 83 : 263-280.

4976   GERBNER, George; [et al.]. "Political conclaves of television viewing", *Public Opinion Quarterly* 48(1b), spr 84 : 283-300. [USA]

4977   GLYNN, Rosalie M. "Political attitudes and religious commitment in New Zealand: two case studies", *Political Science* 35(2), dec 83 : 282-300.

4978   GUBERSKIJ, S. A. "Nekotorye voprosy formirovanija političeskoj kul'tury v razvitom socialističeskom obščestve" (Some questions on the political culture formation in the developed socialist society), *Voprosy Obščestvennyh Nauk (Kiev)* (55), 1983 : 62-65.

4979   HAGNER, Paul R.; PIERCE, John C. "Racial differences in political conceptualization", *Western Political Quarterly* 37(2), jun 84 : 212-235. [USA]

4980   KURKIN, B. A. "Političeskaja kul'tura" (Political culture), *Sovetskoe Gosudarstvo i Pravo* (7), 1983 : 48-55.

4981   LAFFERTY, William M. "Political participation in the social-democratic State : a normative-empirical framework for the analysis of decision-making involvement in Norway", *Scandinavian Political Studies* (4), dec 83 : 281-308.

4982   MILIĆ, Andelka. "Porodica i političko ponašanje" (Family and political behaviour), *Socioloski Pregled* 18(1-2), aug 84 : 67-86. [Yugoslavia]

4983   MININA, L. F. "O političeskoj kul'ture kak filosofsko-sociologičeskoj kategorii" (On political culture as a philosophical and sociological category), *Vestnik Har'kovskogo Univer-siteta* (244), 1983 : 8-12.

4984   MULLER, Edward N.; GODWIN, R. Kenneth. "Democratic and aggressive political participation : estimation of a nonrecursive model", *Political Behavior* 6(2), 1984 : 129-146.

4985   NICE, David C. "Political corruption in the American States", *American Politics Quarterly* 11(4), oct 83 : 507-517.

4986   O'DONNELL, Guillermo. *¿Y a mí, que me importa? Notas sobre sociabilidad y política en Argentina y Brasil* (And so what? Notes on sociability and politics in Argentina and Brazil). Buenos Aires : Centre de Estudios de Estado y Sociedad, 1984, 68 p.

4987   PARRY, Geraint; MOYSER, George. "Political participation in Britain : a research agenda for a new study", *Government and Opposition* 19(1), wint 84 : 68-92.

4988   PASSERON, Jean-Claude; SINGLY, François de. "Différences dans la différence : socialisation de classe et socialisation sexuelle", *Revue Française de Science Politique* 34(1), feb 84 : 48-78. [France]

4989   ROY, W. T. "The political culture of Fijian Indians Rama Rajya in the South Seas", *Plural Societies* 14(3-4), wint 83 : 77-84.

4990   SCHULSTER, Ilsa. "Constraints and opportunities in political participation : the case of Zambian women", *Genève-Afrique* 21(2), 1983 : 7-37.

4991   SMIDT, Corwin. "Partisan affections and change in partisan self-images", *American Politics Quarterly* 12(3), jul 84 : 267-283. [USA]

19630   Elections
Élections

4992   ALDRICH, John H. "A spatial model with party activists : implications for electoral dynamics", *Public Choice* 41(1), 1983 : 63-100. [USA] [See also ibid. : pp. 101-102 by Melvin J. HINICH, ibid. : pp. 103-105, a response by John H. ALDRICH]

4993   ALLUM, Percy; ENDRIGHETTO, Tommasina. "Elezioni ed elettorato a Vicenza nel dopoguerra" (Elections and electorate in Vicenza after the war), *Quaderni di Sociologia* 30(2-3-4), 1982 : 355-398.

4994   ALTSCHULER, Bruce E. "The enigmatic American voter", *Teaching Politics (London)* 13(2), mai 84 : 260-273.

4995   ANDERSEN, Jørgen Goul. "Decline of class voting or change in class voting? : social classes and party choice in Denmark in the 1970's", *European Journal of Political Research* 12(3), sep 84 : 243-259.

4996   BEN-ZADOK, Efraim; GOLDBERG, Giora. "A socio-political change in the Israeli development towns : an analysis of voting patterns of oriental Jews", *Plural Societies* 14(1-2), sum 83 : 49-65.

4997   BLACK, Jerome H. "Revisiting the effects of canvassing on voting behaviour", *Canadian Journal of Political Science* 17(2), jun 84 : 351-374. [Canada]

4998   CAMPBELL, James E. "Candidate image evaluations : influence and rationalization in presidential primaries", *American Politics Quarterly* 11(3), jul 83 : 293-313. [USA]

4999   FENSTER, Mark J. "Approval voting : do moderates gain?", *Political Methodology* 9(4), 1983 : 355-376. [USA]

5000   FISHBURN, Peter C. "Dimensions of election procedures : analysis and comparisons", *Theory and Decision* 15(4), dec 83 : 371-397.

5001   FLOOD, Merrill M. "Effectiveness of dynamic value voting", *Human Systems Management* 4(3), spr 84 : 152-162.

5002   FREDERICK, William C.; MYERS, Mildred S. "Public policy advertising and the 1980 presidential election", *Research in Corporate Social Performance and Policy* 5, 1983 : 59-86.

5003   GANT, Michael M. "Citizen uncertainty and turnout in the 1980 presidential campaign", *Political Behavior* 5(2), 1983 : 257-275. [USA]

5004   GANT, Michael M. "Citizens' evaluations of the 1980 presidential candidates : influence of campaign strategies", *American Politics Quarterly* 11(3), jul 83 : 327-348. [USA]

5005   GLASS, David; [et al.]. "Voter turnout : an international comparison", *Public Opinion* 6(6), jan 84 : 49-55.

5006   GORENEMAN, Sid. "Candidate sex and delegate voting in a pre-primary party endorsement election", *Women and Politics* 3(1), spr 83 : 39-56. [USA]

5007   GRUNBERG, Gérard; SCHWEISGUTH, Étienne. "Las capas medias asalariadas y la evolución de los comportamientos electorales en Francia, 1967 1984" (The middle strata of wage earners and the evolution of electoral behaviour in France, 1967-1984), *Revista Española de Investigaciones Sociológicas* 26, apr-jun 84 : 151-166.

5008   HOLLER, Manfred J.; [ed.]. *Wahlanalyse : Hypothesen, Methoden und Ergebnisse* (Electoral analysis : hypothesis, methods and results). München : Tuduv, 1984, 230 p. bibl.

5009   KROUSE, Richard; MARCUS, George. "Electoral studies and democratic theory reconsidered", *Political Behavior* 6(1), 1984 : 23-39.

5010   LUTTBERG, Norman R. "Differential voting turnout decline in the American States, 1960-82", *Social Science Quarterly* 65(1), mar 84 : 60-73.

5011   MANNHEIMER, Renato; ZAJCZYK, Francesca. "L'astensionismo elettorale. Elementi di analisi a partire dai risultati del referendum 1981" (Electoral abstentionism. Elements of analysis from the results of referendum in 1981), *Quaderni di Sociologia* 30(2-3-4), 1982 : 399-455. [Italy]

5012   MINNS, Daniel Richard. "Voting as an influential behavior : child and adolescent beliefs", *American Politics Quarterly* 12(3), jul 84 : 285-304. [USA]

5013   MONTERO GIBERT, José Ramón. "Niveles, fluctuaciones y tendencias del abstencionismo electoral en España y Europa" (Levels, fluctuations and trends of electoral abstentionism in Spain and Europe), *Revista Española de Investigaciones Sociológicas* 28, oct-dec 84 : 223-242.

5014   NEF, Rolf; ROSENMUND, Moritz. "Das energiepolitische Plebiszit vom 23. September 1984 zwischen Entwicklungserwartung und Wachstumskritik. Ein Beispiel ereignisorientierter, raumbezogener Gesellschaftsanalyse" (The energy policy plebiscite of Sept. 23, 1984 between the expectations of development and critique on growth. An example of event oriented, morphological analysis of society), *Schweizerische Zeitschrift für Soziologie / Revue Suisse de Sociologie* 10(3), 1984 : 689-721.

5015   PALFREY, Thomas R.; ROSENTHAL, Howard. "A strategic calculus of voting", *Public
        Choice* 41(1), 1983 : 7-53. [See also ibid. : pp. 55-61 by Bernard GROFMAN]
5016   REED, Steven; BRUNK, Gregory G. "A test of two theories of economically motivated
        voting : the case of Japan", *Comparative Politics* 17(1), oct 84 : 55-66.
5017   SCHMITT, Karl. "Appartenance confessionnelle et comportement électoral en Allemagne",
        Revue d'Allemagne 16(2), jun 84 : 177-210.
5018   SIGELMAN, Lee; WELCH, Susan. "Race, gender and opinion toward Black and female
        presidential candidates", *Public Opinion Quarterly* 48(2), sum 84 : 467-475. [USA]
5019   WEATHERFORD, M. Stephen. "Reciprocal causation in a model of the vote : replication
        and extension", *Political Behavior* 5(2), 1983 : 191-208. [USA]
5020   WEST, Darrell M. "Cheers and jeers : candidate presentations and audience reactions
        in the 1980 presidential campaign", *American Politics Quarterly* 12(1), jan 84 : 23-50. [USA]
5021   WORRE, Torben. "Vaelgeradfaerd 1971-1981" (Voting behaviour, 1971-1981), *Økonomi
        og Politik* 57(4), 1983 : 263-273. [Denmark]

        **19640   Politics
                   Politique**

5022   CHAFFEE, Wilber A. "The political economy of revolution and democracy : toward a
        theory of Latin American politics", *American Journal of Economics and Sociology* 43(4),
        oct 84 : 385-398.
5023   EDIE, Carlene J. "Jamaican political processes : a system in search of a paradigm", *Journal
        of Development Studies* 20(4), jul 84 : 248-270.
5024   FEDOSEEV, A. A. "Leninskie idei o politike i sovremennost'" (Leninist ideas on politics
        and the contemporary era), *Aktual'nye Problemy Istorii Marksistsko-Leninskoj Filosofii* (1),
        1983 : 6-22.
5025   HANDBERG, Roger. "Creationism, conservatism, and ideology : fringe issues in American
        politics", *Social Science Journal (Fort Collins)* 21(3), jul 84 : 37-51.
5026   HARTMANN, Jürgen. *Politik und Gesellschaft in Japan, USA, Westeuropa. Ein einführender
        Vergleich* (Politics and society in Japan, USA, Western Europe. An introductory
        comparison). Frankfurt-am-Main : Campus, 1983, 221 p. bibl.
5027   SZOBOSZLAI, György; [ed.]. *Politika és társadalom* (Politics and society). Budapest : Kossuth
        Kiadó, 1983, 180 p.

        **19700   ARMY. MILITARY SOCIOLOGY
                   ARMÉE. SOCIOLOGIE MILITAIRE**

5028   "Militarization and society", *Alternatives* 10(1), sum 84 : 1-191. [With contributions by Robin
        LUCKHAM, Tamas SZENTES, Felipe AGUERO, Marek THEE]
5029   BACHMAN, Jerald G. "American high school seniors view the military : 1976-1982",
        Armed Forces and Society 10(1), aut 83 : 86-104.
5030   CARDONA ESCANERO, Gabriel. *Historia del ejército : el peso de un grupo social diferente*
        (History of the army : the impact of a different social group). Barcelona : Editorial
        Humanitas, 1983, 148 p. bibl.
5031   GOMEZ YAÑEZ, José Antonio. "Sobre la sociología del militar español" (On the sociology
        of Spanish military personnel), *Sistema* (59), mar 84 : 103-116.
5032   HOLM, Tom. "Intergenerational rapprochement among American Indians : a study of
        thirty five Indian veterans of the Vietnam war", *Journal of Political and Military Sociology*
        12(1), spr 84 : 161-170.
5033   LANGTON, Kenneth P. "The influence of military service on social consciousness and
        protest behavior : a study of Peruvian mine workers", *Comparative Political Studies* 16(4),
        jan 84 : 479-504.
5034   LISSAK, Moshe; [ed.]. *Israeli society and its defense establishment : the social and political impact
        of a protracted violent conflict.* London : F. Cass, 1984, 152 p. bibl.
5035   MANIGART, Philippe. "Le déclin de l'armée de masse en Belgique", *Revue de l'Institut
        de Sociologie* (1-2), 1984 : 213-237.
5036   MAZUR, Allan; MAZUR, Julie; KEATING, Caroline. "Military rank attainment of a
        West Point class : effects of cadets' physical features", *American Journal of Sociology* 90(1),
        jul 84 : 125-150. [USA]
5037   SPARK, Alasdair. "The soldier at the heart of the war : the myth of the Green Beret in
        the popular culture of the Vietnam era", *Journal of American Studies* 18(1), apr 84 : 29-48.
5038   STRETCH, Robert H.; FIGLEY, Charles R. "Combat and the Vietnam veterans :
        assessment of psycho-social adjustment", *Armed Forces and Society* 10(2), wint 84 : 311-319.

19800 INTERNATIONAL RELATIONS
RELATIONS INTERNATIONALES

19810 International law. International organizations
Droit international. Organisations internationales

5039 "Arbitration", *International Lawyer* 17(4), aut 83 : 661-697. [With contributions by Thomas P. DEVITT, Charles N. BROWER, Georges R. DELAUME]

5040 "Colloque (Le) roumano-français sur le Droit international économique, organisé par l'A.D.I.R.I. à Bucarest, 2-3 décembre 1983", *Revue Roumaine d'Études Internationales* 18(2), apr 84 : 81-175. [With contributions by Claude-Albert COLLIARD, Dominique CARREAU, Thiébaut FLORY]

5041 DRACHE, Daniel; [et al.]. "Beyond dependency", *Canadian Journal of Political and Social Theory* 7(3), aut 83 : 5-24. [With contributions by Arthur KROKER, Marcel RIOUX, Susan CREAN, Daniel LATOUCHE, Nicole LAURIN-FRENETTE, R. T. NAYLOR, Jorge NIOSI] [Abstract 34-2043]

5042 MANNARI, Hiroshi; BEFU, Harumi; [eds.]. *The challenge of Japan's internationalization : organization and culture.* Tokyo : Kodansha, 1984, 308 p.

5043 NOBEL, Peter. "Internationalisierung der Tatbestände und nationalstaatliches Recht" (Phenomenons internationalization and national States law), *Aussenwirtschaft* 39(1-2), mai 84 : 91-118.

5044 UNITED NATIONS LIBRARY, GENEVA. *The Third World and international law : selected bibliography, 1955-1982.* Geneva : UN, 1983, 100 p. bibl.

19820 Foreign policy. Sovereignty
Politique étrangère. Souveraineté

5045 "Impérialisme (L') aujourd'hui", *Espaces et Sociétés* (44), jun 84 : 7-131. [With contributions by René GALLISSOT, André GUNDER FRANK, Serge LATOUCHE, Alain LIPIETZ]

5046 ANDERSON, Paul A. "Foreign policy as a goal directed activity", *Philosophy of the Social Sciences / Philosophie des Sciences Sociales* 14(2), jun 84 : 159-181. [USA]

5047 ROUTLEY, Richard. "On the alleged inconsistency, moral insensitivity and fanaticism of pacifism", *Inquiry* 27(1), mar 84 : 117-148.

5048 VESTUTI, Guido. "Schumpeter e la teoria dell'imperialismo" (Schumpeter and the theory of imperialism), *Studi di Sociologia* 22(1), jan-mar 84 : 99-103.

19830 International cooperation. War
Coopération internationale. Guerre

5049 "Ethical and moral issues of war and peace : role of the Churches", *Bulletin of Peace Proposals* 15(3), 1984 : 193-283. [With contributions by Kjell SKJELSBAEK, Bruce M. RUSSETT, Thomas RISSEKAPPEN, Joachim GARSTECKI]

5050 EBERWEIN, Wolf-Dieter; NIENSTEDT, Heinz-Werner. "Ansteckung, Abschreckung und Zyklen militärischer Konflikte und internationaler Kriege im 20. Jahrhundert" (Contagion, deterrence and cycles of military conflicts and international wars in the XXth century), *Zeitschrift für Soziologie* 13(2), apr 84 : 118-133.

5051 FEDOROV, É. K. "Mir kak uslovie optimizacii otnošenij čeloveka i prirody" (Peace as a condition of optimization of the man-nature relations), *in : Dialektika v naukah o prirode i čeloveke : trudy III Vsesojuznogo Soveščanija po filosofskim voprosam sovremennogo estvoznanija. IV. Čelovek, obščestvo i priroda v vek NTR* Moskva, 1983 : 52-77.

5052 ISARD, Walter; NAGAO, Yoshimi; [eds.]. *International and regional conflict : analytic approaches.* Cambridge, MA : Ballinger, 1983, xv-236 p.

5053 KARABANOV, N. V. "Filosofskie problemy mira" (Philosophical problems of peace), *in : Filosofskie metodologičeskie seminary* Moskva, 1984 : 149-161.

5054 KRIESBERG, Louis. "Social theory and the de-escalation of international conflict", *Sociological Review* 32(3), aug 84 : 471-491.

5055 STOLL, Richard J. "Bloc concentration and dispute escalation among the major powers, 1830 1965", *Social Science Quarterly* 65(1), mar 84 : 48-59.

19840 Disarmament. Weapons
Désarmement. Armes

20100   SOCIAL PROBLEMS
          PROBLÈMES SOCIAUX

20110   Applied sociology
          Sociologie appliquée

5056   "Bürgerliche Gesellschaft und soziale Empirie" (Bourgeois society and empirical social research), *Argument* 26(143), feb 84 : 18-73. [With contributions by Eberhard BRAUN, Immanuel WALLERSTEIN, Judith A. COOK, Mary M. FONOW]

5057   ANDERSON, R. J.; SHARROCK, W. W.; [eds.]. *Applied sociological perspectives*. Delhi : Heritage, 1984, 220 p.

5058   BELL, C.; ROBERTS, H.; [eds.]. *Social researching*. Henley-on-Thames : Routledge and Kegan Paul, 1984, x-230 p.

5059   BUZOV, Željko. "Metodološki problemi istraživanja izvanrednih i kriznih situacija" (Methodological problems in research on extra-ordinary and crisis situations), *Revija za Sociologiju* 13(1-4), 1983 : 95-101.

5060   CHEKKI, Dan A. "American support to social research : the case of India", *Indian Journal of Social Research* 25(1), apr 84 : 58-67.

5061   DUMONT, J. P. "L'information sociale", *Revue Française des Affaires Sociales* 38(1), mar 84 : 7-24. [France]

5062   GOTO, Noriaki. "Chiiki jyumin ni yoru chosa kenkyu katsudo to chiiki shakai keisei -'Ohmiya machizukuri kenkyu kai' no jirei o chushin to shite" (Sociological implication of the social research by regional residents), *Nihon University Journal of Sociology* 90, 1984 : 52-63.

5063   LOSENKOV, V. A. *Social'naja informacija v žizni gorodskogo naselenija i opyt sociologičeskih issledovanij* (Social information in an urban population life : an essay of sociological research). Leningrad : Nauka, 1983, 102 p.

5064   MUSHKAT, Miron. "Transforming social data into social information for policy purposes : some critical observations on the societal accounting movement", *Sociologia Internationalis* 22(1), 1984 : 43-58.

5065   NEJMER, Ju. L. "Informacionnoe obespečenie social'nogo upravlenija" (Informational supply of social management), *in : Aktual'nye problemy social'nogo upravlenija v regione* Vladivostok, 1982 : 76-86.

5066   WOOD, Michael. "Using key-word-in-context concordance programs for qualitative and quantitative social research", *Journal of Applied Behavioral Science* 20(3), 1984 : 289-297.

5067   ŽURAVLEV, G. T.; ŽUKOV, N. N. "Nekotorye problemy vybora metodov i tehničeskih sredstv i preobrazovanija social'noj informacii" (Some problems of choice between methods and technical means in transformation of social information), *in : Social'naja informacija v sisteme naučnyh issledovanij problem molodeži* Moskva, 1983 : 64-75.

20120   Social pathology
          Pathologie sociale

5068   BUROV, V. "Social'no-filosofskie problemy razvivajuščihsja stran" (Socio-philosophical problems of developing countries), *Kommunist (Moskva)* (15), 1983 : 123-126.

5069   COHEN, E. "Problemas sociales, políticas sociales y planificación social" (Social problems, social policies and social designs), *Ideas en Ciencias Sociales* 1(2), 1984 : 65-73. [Argentina]

5070   GALTUNG, Johan. "On the dialectic between crisis and crisis perception", *International Journal of Comparative Sociology* 25(1-2), 1984 : 2-32.

5071   HORWITZ, Allan V. "The economy and social pathology", *Annual Review of Sociology* 10, 1984 : 95-119.

5072   INA, Masato. "Shakai mondai to seikatsu-shi bunseki — C. W. Mills chishiki shakaigaku no houhou ron teki sai-kento" (A theory of social problems and biographical approach — C. W. Mills' sociology of knowledge and sociological realism : methodological reinter-pretation), *Hitotsubashi Journal of Social Sciences* 8(4), 1984 : 1-15.

5073   KORALEWICZ-ZEBIK, Jadwiga. "Lęk a stratyfikacja społeczna : lata siedemdziesiąte w Polsce" (Anxiety and social structure : the seventies in Poland), *Kultura i Społeczeństwo* 28(3), 1984 : 179-190.

5074   LE NET, Michel. "Inclure les exclus. Du concept d'égalité sociale à l'évolution de l'action sociale", *Revue Française des Affaires Sociales* 38(1), mar 84 : 25-58. [France]

5075   MADGE, Nicola; [ed.]. *Families at risk.* London : Heinemann Educational Books, 1983, viii-227 p. bibl., ind. [UK]

5076   QUAH, Stella R. "Social discipline in Singapore : an alternative for the resolution of social problems", *Journal of Southeast Asian Studies* 14(2), sep 83 : 266-289.

5077   RAJKIEWICZ, Antoni. "Badania nad patologią społeczną" (Inquiries about social pathology), *Polityka Społeczna* 10(11-12), 1983 : 14-15.

20130   Disasters
Catastrophes

5078   KREPS, G. A. "Sociological inquiry and disaster research", *Annual Review of Sociology* 10, 1984 : 309-330.

5079   NAGPAUL, Hans. "Sociology of disaster in Indian society : a case study of floods from recovery to rehabilities strategies in rural communities of North India", *Indian Journal of Social Research* 25(1), apr 84 : 68-78. [Harayana State, Northern India] [1977]

5080   NODA, Takashi. "Saigai to soshiki" (Organizations in disaster), *Osaka Daigaku Nenpo Ningenkagaku* 5, 1984 : 79-95.

20140   Poverty
Pauvreté

5081   "Faim (La) dans le Tiers-Monde", *Cahiers Français* (213), dec 83 : 1-80 et 32.

5082   "Homelessness", *Urban and Social Change Review* 17(2), sum 84 : 2-20. [USA] [With contributions by Stephen CRYSTAL, Marjorie HOPE, James YOUNG]

5083   "Pauvreté et action sociale", *Actions et Recherches Sociales* (4), dec 83 : 7-118. [France] [With contributions by Dominique BOULLIER, Brigitte BREBANT, Marie-Annick BARTHE]

5084   "Situación nutricional de la población colombiana" (Colombian population nutrition situation), *Revista de Planeación y Desarrollo* 15(2-3), sep 83 : 107-121.

5085   "Underprivileged (The) in society : studies on Kenya", *Journal of Eastern African Research & Development* 13, 83 : 1-219. [With contributions by Gideon S. WERE, Philista P. M. ONYANGO, Diane KAYONGO-MALE, J. V. N. RIRA]

5086   ARGUELLO, Omar. "Pobreza y fecundidad en Costa Rica" (Poverty and fertility in Costa Rica), *Notas de población* 11(32), aug 83 : 9-54. [See also ibid. : pp. 79-122 by Luis ROSERO BIXBY]

5087   BEEGHLEY, Leonard. *Living poorly in America.* New York, NY : Praeger, 1983, xi-211 p.

5088   BLUNT, Peter. "Conditions for basic need satisfaction in Africa through decentralized forms of decision making", *Journal of Applied Behavioral Science* 20(4), 1984 : 403-421.

5089   BRAMBILLA, Francesco. "Povertà e ricchezza" (Poverty and wealth), *Giornale degli Economisti e Annali di Economia* 43(11-12), nov-dec 84 : 801-850. [Italy]

5090   BREBANT, Brigitte. *La pauvreté, un destin?* Paris : L'Harmattan, 1984, 179 p. bibl.

5091   DOGBÉ, Yves Emmanuel. *Lettre ouverte aux pauvres d'Afrique; suivi de Participation populaire et développement.* Le-Mée-sur-Seine : Éditions Akpagnon, 1983, 140 p. bibl.

5092   ELLIS, G. F. R. "The dimensions of poverty", *Social Indicators Research* 15(3), oct 84 : 229-253. [South Africa]

5093   EZEKIEL, Raphael S. *Voices from the corner : poverty and racism in the inner city.* Philadelphia, PA : Temple University Press, 1984, 232 p.

5094   GAMSON, William A.; SCHMEIDLER, Emilie. "Organizing the poor", *Theory and Society* 13(4), jul 84 : 567-585. [With a rejoinder by Richard A. CLOWARD and Frances Fox PIVEN, ibid. : 587-599]

5095   GARINE, Igor de. "De la perception de la malnutrition dans les sociétés traditionnelles", *Social Science Information / Information sur les Sciences Sociales* 23(4-5), 1984 : 731-754.

5096   GHATAK, Anita. "A demand function for food for India : pooling cross-section and time series data", *Indian Journal of Economics* 65(256), jul 84 : 1-14.

5097   GLARDON, Marie-Jo; [et al.]. *Les pauvres dans la ville : à la recherche des familles sous-prolétariennes à Genève.* Lausanne : Éditions d'En Bas, 1984, 275 p. bibl.

5098   HADIMANI, R. N. *The politics of poverty.* New Delhi : Ashish, 1984, xxi-194 p. ill., bibl., ind. [India]

5100   HERPIN, Nicolas. "Panier et budget : l'alimentation des ouvriers urbains", *Revue Française de Sociologie* 25(1), jan-mar 84 : 20-48. [France]

5101   HUNECKE, Volker. "Überlegungen zur Geschichte der Armut im vorindustriellen Europa" (Considerations on the history of poverty in preindustrial Europe), *Geschichte und Gesellschaft* 9(4), 1983 : 480-512.

5102   HYNES, Thomas J. Jr.; CAMPBELL, William F. *An end to poverty : a critical analysis of the problems involved in decreasing poverty in the United States.* Lincolnwood, IL : National Textbook Company, 1984, ix-250 p. bibl.

5103   JIMENEZ, Pilar R.; FRANCISCO, Josefa S. *The rural poor in Leyte : a social and institutional profile.* Manila : Research Center, De La Salle University, 1984, iv-88 p. ill., bibl.

5104   KEARNS, Kevin C. "Homelessness in Dublin : an Irish urban disorder", *American Journal of Economics and Sociology* 43(2), apr 84 : 217-233.

5105   KRAVITZ, Linda. *Taking stock : rural people and poverty from 1970 to 1983.* Washington, DC : Housing Assistance Council, 1984, vi-120 p.

5106   MANCHANDA, Rajinder Kaur; HANSRA, B. S. "The retention of nutritional knowlege gained by the members of Ladies Charcha Mandals by the use of selected extension teaching methods", *Indian Journal of Social Research* 25(1), apr 84 : 16-23. [India]

5107   MURRAY, Charles. "The war on poverty : 1965-1980", *Wilson Quarterly* 8(4), aut 84 : 94-136. [USA]

5108   NICOLAS, Jean-Pierre. *La pauvreté intolérable : biographie sociale d'une famille assistée.* Toulouse : Erès, 1984, 208 p. bibl.

5109   OOMEN, T. K. "Sources of deprivation and styles of protest : the case of the Dalits in India", *Contributions to Indian Sociology* 17(1), jan-jul 84 : 46-61.

5110   SCHRIJVERS, Joke. "Blueprint for undernutrition : an example from Sri Lanka", *Sociologia Ruralis* 24(3-4), 1984 : 255-273.

5111   SHLONSKY, Hagith R. "Continuity in poverty along family lines : a reexamination of the intergenerational cycle of poverty", *Human Relations* 37(6), jun 84 : 455-472. [Israel]

5112   STONER, Madeleine R. "The plight of homeless women", *Social Service Review* 57(4), dec 84 : 565-581. [USA]

5113   UPPAL, J. N. *Bengal famine of 1943 : a man-made tragedy.* Delhi : Atma Ram, 1984, 269 p.

5114   VÉRIN, Pierre; RAMAMONJISOA, Suzy. "Psychologie de la pauvreté. Deux opinions", *Cahiers d'Études Africaines* 23(4), 1983 : 441-445. [Madagascar]

5115   VILLENEUVE, André. "Construire un indicateur de précarité : les étapes d'une démarche empirique", *Économie et Statistique* 168, jul-aug 84 : 93-105. [France]

5116   WESTERGAARD, Kirsten. *Pauperization and rural women in Bangladesh : a case study.* Comilla : Bangladesh Academy for Rural Development, 1983, ii-127 p. bibl.

5117   WIMBERLEY, Dale W. "Socioeconomic deprivation and religious salience : a cognitive behavioral approach", *Sociological Quarterly* 25(2), spr 84 : 223-238.

20150   Alcoholism. Drugs of abuse
**   Alcoolisme. Drogue**

5118   "Addicts and alcoholics", *Sage Annual Review of Studies in Deviance* 7, 1983 : 33-76. [USA] [With contributions by Charles WINICK, Robert J. KELLY]

5119   "Toxicomanie (La)", *Cahiers d'Anthropologie* 1(2), 1983 : 1-40. [With contributions by Rodolphe INGOLD, Odile PLAISANT]

5120   BACHMAN, Jerald G.; O'MALLEY, Patrick M.; JOHNSTON, Lloyd D. "Drug use among young adults : the impacts of role status and social environment", *Journal of Personality and Social Psychology* 47(3), sep 84 : 629-645.

5121   BOADO, Alicia. "Reseña histórica-antropológica de las drogas en distintas culturas" (Historical and anthropological report of drugs in different cultures), *RS Cuadernos de Realidades Sociales* (23-24), jan 84 : 131-152.

5122   BORGOGNONI, Ezio. "Incomunicabilità e droga" (Incommunicability and drugs), *Difesa Sociale* 62(6), dec 83 : 45-56. [Italy]

5123   BRUNETTA, G. "Giovani e famiglie di fronte alla droga" (Youth and families facing drug addiction), *Aggiornamenti Sociali* 36(1), jan 85 : 69-84. [Italy]

5124   CACERES, Baldomero. "El problema de la coca en el Peru" (Problem of coca in Peru), *Socialismo y Participación* (21), mar 83 : 51-67.

5125   CORDIER, Alain. "Démographie et consommation médicale", *Revue Française des Affaires Sociales* 38(suppl.), jun 84 : 103-125. [France]

5126   DORN, Nicholas. *Alcohol, youth, and the state.* London : Croom Helm, 1983, 280 p. ill., bibl., ind.

5127   FASER, Mark; HAWKINS, J. David. "Social network analysis and drug misuse", *Social Service Review* 58(1), mar 84 : 81-97. [USA]

5128 FILLAUT, Thierry. *L'alcoolisme dans l'ouest de la France pendant la second moitié du XIX$_e$ siècle.* Paris : La Documentation Française, 1983, 247 p. ill., bibl.

5129 FRASER, Mark. "Family, school and peer correlates of adolescent drug abuse", *Social Service Review* 58(3), sep 84 : 434-447. [USA]

5130 GABE, Jonathan; LIPSHITZ-PHILLIPS, Susan. "Tranquillisers as social control?", *Sociological Review* 32(3), aug 84 : 524-546. [UK]

5131 GODARD, Jacques. "L'alcoolisme aujourd'hui", *Études*, mar 84 : 315-328.

5132 HODGINS, Sheilagh; MORISSETTE, Pauline. "L'alcoolisme chez les femmes", *Service Social* 32(1-2), jun 83 : 274-295.

5133 LUBIT, Roy; RUSSETT, Bruce. "The effects of drugs on decision making", *Journal of Conflict Resolution* 28(1), mar 84 : 85-102.

5134 MCALLISTER, Alfred L.; KROSNICK, Jon A.; MILBURN, Michael A. "Causes of adolescent cigarette smoking : tests of a structural equation model", *Social Psychology Quarterly* 47(1), mar 84 : 24-36.

5135 MENENDEZ, Eduardo L. "El problema del alcoholismo y la crisis del modelo médico hegemónico" (The problem of alcoholism and the crisis of the hegemonic medical model), *Cuadernos Médico Sociales* 28, jun 84 : 7-24.

5136 MICHALCZYK, Tadeusz. *Wzory społeczno-kulturowe a zjawisko pijaństwa a alkoholizmu w srodowisku robotniczym* (Socio-cultural patterns and phenomena of drinking and alcoholism in workmen's environment). Opole : Wydawnictwo Instytutu Śląskiego, 1984, 160 p. [Research conducted in Opole Province]

5137 MORNINGSTAR, Patricia Cleckner; CHITWOOD, Dale D. "Cocaine users' view of themselves : implicit behavior theory in context", *Human Organization* 43(4), 1984 : 307-318. [USA]

5138 MOTOMURA, Hiroshi. "Alcohol Izon-sha no inshu pattern : kenjyo-sha tono hikaku ni oite" (A study of alcoholic drinking pattern : a comparison with non-alcoholics), *Osaka-Shiritsu-Daigaku Seikatsukagakubu Kiyo* 30, 1984 : 305-316.

5139 NOREM-HEBEISEN, Ardyth; [et al.]. "Predictors and concomitants of changes in drug use patterns among teenagers", *Journal of Social Psychology* 124(1), oct 84 : 43-50. [USA]

5140 PEYROT, Mark. "Cycles of social problem development : the case of drug abuse", *Sociological Quarterly* 25(1), wint 84 : 83-95. [USA]

5141 THÉVENIN, Guy Faustin. *L'évènement alcool dans le parcours migratoire.* Paris : La Documentation Française, 1983, 167-1 p. ill., bibl. [France]

5142 THOM, D. Rodney. "The demand for alcohol in Ireland", *Economic and Social Review* 15(4), jul 84 : 325-336.

5143 WUNDERER, Hartmann. "Alkohol in der Geschichte" (Alcohol in history), *Neue Politische Literatur* 28(4), dec 83 : 436-458.

20160   Crime. Delinquency
Délit. Délinquance

5144 "Droit (Le) du punir", *Annales Internationales de Criminologie* 21(2), 1983 : 151-357. [With contributions by J. MARTINEZ RINCONCES, J. M. DELGADO OCANDO, E. NOVOA MONREAL, F. VARONA DUQUE]

5145 "Sanctions (Des)", *Archives de Politique Criminelle* (7), 84 : 49-176. [France]

5146 "Three papers on crime and criminal justice?", *Social Problems* 31(1), oct 83 : 1-58. [USA] [With contributions by James BRADY, Eileen B. LEONARD]

5147 ABRAM KOBAN, Linda. "Parents in prison : a comparative analysis of the effects of incarceration on the families of men and women", *Research in Law, Deviance and Social Control* 5, 1983 : 171-183. [USA]

5148 AGNEW, Robert. "Autonomy and delinquency", *Sociological Perspectives* 27(2), apr 84 : 219-240. [USA]

5149 AHLBURG, Dennis A.; SCHAPIRO, Morton Owen. "Socio-economic ramifications of changing cohort size : an analysis of US postwar suicide rates by age and sex", *Demography* 21(1), feb 84 : 97-108.

5150 AUGUSTUS, Somerville. *Crime and religious beliefs in India.* Delhi : Asian, 1984, 216 p.

5151 AVELINE, François; [et al.]. "Suicide et rythmes sociaux", *Économie et Statistique* (168), jul-aug 84 : 71-76.

5152 BABAEV, M. M. "Duhovnaja kul'tura i prestupnost'" (Intellectual culture and criminality), *in : Vlijanie social'nyh uslovij na prestupnost'* Moskva, 1983 : 59-73.

5153 BARTH, Richard P.; BLYTHE, Betty J. "The contribution of stress to child abuse", *Social Service Review* 57(3), sep 83 : 477-489. [USA]

5154   BAUDELOT, Christian; ESTABLET, Roger. "Suicide : l'évolution séculaire d'un fait
         social", *Économie et Statistique* 168, jul-aug 84 : 59-70. [France] [See also ibid. : pp. 71-76
         by François AVELINE]

5155   BELIVEAU, Lionel. "Le traitement en criminologie : revue des programmes d'intervention
         au Canada", *Annales Internationales de Criminologie* 21(1), 1983 : 63-107.

5156   BERK, Richard A.; [et al.]. "Prisons as self-regulating systems : a comparison of historical
         patterns in California for male and female offenders", *Law and Society Review* 17(4),
         1983 : 547-586.

5157   BERNARD, Léonel; LAPIERRE, André. "Loi 24 : délinquance juvénile et pratiques
         préventives", *Revue Internationale d'Action Communautaire* 11(51), spr 84 : 29-34. [Canada]

5158   BESNARD, Philippe. "Modes d'emploi du 'Suicide'. Intégration et régulation dans la
         théorie durkheimienne", *Année Sociologique* 34, 1984 : 127-163.

5159   BISHOP, Donna M.; FRAZIER, Charles E. "The effects of gender on charge reduction",
         Sociological Quarterly 25(3), 1984 : 385-396. [USA]

5160   BOWERS, William J.; PIERCE, Glenn L.; MCDEVITT, John F. *Legal homicide : death
         as punishment in America, 1864-1982.* Boston, MA : Northeastern University Press, 1984,
         rev., xxviii-614 p. ill., bibl., ind.

5161   BRODEUR, J.-P. "La criminologie marxiste : controverses récentes", *Déviance et Société*
         8(1), mar 84 : 43-70.

5162   BRUCKMEIER, Karl; [et al.]. *Jugenddelinquenz in der Wahrnehmung von Sozialarbeitern und
         Polizeibeamten : eine empirische Untersuchung* (Juvenile delinquency in the testimony of social
         workers and policy officials : an empirical research). Weinheim : Beltz, 1984, 188 p. bibl.

5163   BRUNETTA, G. "Il fenomeno del suicidio in Italia nell' ultimo trentennio" (Suicide in
         Italy for the last thirty years), *Aggiornamenti Sociali* 35(6), jun 84 : 465-475.

5164   BUENO ARUS, Francisco. "La delincuencia juvenil en España" (Juvenile delinquency
         in Spain), *Razón y Fe* 209(1025), feb 84 : 125-143.

5165   BULTHE, Bruno; SCREVENS, Christiane. *Les prisons et la contestation collective.* Bruxelles :
         Bruylant, 1984, 222 p. bibl.

5166   BYNUM, Timothy S.; PATERNOSTER, Raymond. "Discrimination revisited : an
         exploration of frontstage and backstage criminal justice decision making", *Sociology and
         Social Research* 69(1), oct 84 : 90-108.

5167   CÉLEM, Rosangela. *As relações sociais em prisão de tipo semi-aberta : uma experiência em seviço
         social* (Social relations in half opened prison : an experience in social service). São Paulo :
         Cortez Editora, 1983, 72 p. ill., bibl. [Brazil]

5168   CIRBA, Laurence. "Juges et délinquants mineurs", *Temps Modernes* 40(452-453-454),
         mai 84 : 2035-2052. [France]

5169   CLARKE, Alan H. "Perception of crime and fear of victimisation among elderly people",
         Ageing and Society 4(3), sep 84 : 327-342.

5170   COOPER, H. H. A. *On assassination.* Boulder, CO : Paladin Press, 1984, v-209 p. bibl.

5171   DAVIS, Michael. "Is the death penalty irrevocable?", *Social Theory and Practice* 10(2),
         sum 84 : 143-156. [USA]

5172   DI CHIARA, Albert; GALLIHER, John F. "Thirty years of deterrence research :
         characteristics, causes and consequences", *Contemporary Crises* 8(3), jul 84 : 243-263.

5173   DI MARIA, F.; [et al.]. "Influenza del sesso, dell'età e del livello di istruzione sulla valutazione
         di atti criminosi di diversa natura" (The influence of sex, age and educational level on the
         evaluation of crimes of various kinds), *Studi di Sociologia* 22(1), jan-mar 84 : 61-73. [Italy]

5174   DILLIG, Peter. *Selbstbild junger Krimineller : eine empirische Untersuchung* (Self-portrait of juvenile
         delinquents : an empirical research). Weinheim : Beltz, 1983, xii-355 p. bibl. [Germany FR]

5175   DORLHAC DE BORNE, Hélène. *Changer la prison.* Paris : Plon, 1984, 183 p.

5176   EKSTEDT, John W.; GRIFFITHS, Curt T. *Corrections in Canada : policy and practice.*
         Toronto, ON; Boston, MA : Butterworths, 1984, xv-407 p. ill., bibl., ind.

5177   ERICKSON, Maynard L.; STAFFORD, Mark C.; GALLIHER, James M. "The
         normative erosion hypothesis : the latent consequences of juvenile justice practices",
         Sociological Quarterly 25(3), 1984 : 373-384. [USA]

5178   FELSON, Richard B.; RIBNER, Stephen A.; SIEGEL, Merryl S. "Age and the effect of
         third parties during criminal violence", *Sociology and Social Research* 68(4), jul 84 : 452-462.
         [USA]

5179   FRIEDLAND, M. L. *A century of criminal justice.* Toronto, ON : Carswell Legal Publications,
         1984, xxii-254 p.

5180   FRÜHLING, Hugo. "Repressive policies and legal dissent in authoritarian regimes : Chile
         1973-1981", *International Journal of the Sociology of Law* 12(4), nov 84 : 351-374.

5181   GARBARINO, James; EBATA, Aaron. "The significance of ethnic and cultural differences
         in child maltreatment", *Journal of Marriage and the Family* 45(4), nov 83 : 773-783. [USA]

5182 GODEFROY, Th.; LAFFARGUE, B. "Crise économique et criminalité. Criminologie de la misère ou misère de la criminologie?", *Déviance et Société* 8(1), mar 84 : 73-100.

5183 GREENBERG, Martin S.; RUBACK, R. Barry; [eds.]. "Criminal victimization", *Journal of Social Issues* 40(1), 1984 : 1-181. [With contributions by R. Lance SHOTLAND, Lynne I. GOODSTEIN, Robert R. KIDD, Ellen F. CHAYET]

5184 GYÖRGYI, Kálmán. *Büntetések és intézkedések* (Punishments and measures). Budapest : Közgazdasági és Jogi Könyvkiadó, 1984, 438 p. [Hungary]

5185 HAGAN, John; STOCK, Chris. "The transformation of trouble : police certification and state compensation of sexual assault claims", *Law and Policy Quarterly* 5(2), apr 83 : 215-236. [USA]

5186 HAKIM, Simon; SPIEGEL, Uriel; WEINBLATT, J. "Substitution, size effects, and the composition of property crime", *Social Science Quarterly* 65(3), sep 84 : 719-734. [USA]

5187 HASSIN, Yael. "Juvenile delinquency in Israel 1948-1977", *Research in Law, Deviance and Social Control* 5, 1983 : 25-50.

5188 HAUSFATER, Glenn; BLAFFER, Hrdy; [eds.]. *Infanticide : comparative and evolutionary perspectives.* New York, NY : Aldine, 1984, 598 p. bibl., ind.

5189 HEPP, Osvaldo T. *Internación de menores y sus problemas sociales* (Internment of minors and its social problems). Buenos Aires : Depalma, 1984, 280 p.

5190 HIROSHI, Iwai. "Japon : délinquance juvénile, causes et remèdes", *Futuribles* (74), feb 84 : 15-24.

5191 HOWARD, Judith A. "The 'normal' victim : the effects of gender stereotypes on reactions to victims", *Social Psychology Quarterly* 47(3), sep 84 : 270-281.

5192 JACKSON, Pamela Irving. "Opportunity and crime : a function of city size", *Sociology and Social Research* 68(2), jan 84 : 172-193. [USA]

5193 JUNGER-TAS, J.; [ed.]. *Jeugddelinquentie* (Juvenile delinquency). 's-Gravenhage : Ministerie van Justitie, Staatsuitgeverij, 1983, 130 p. ill., bibl. [Netherlands]

5194 KARMEN, Andrew. "Deviants as victims", *Sage Annual Review of Studies in Deviance* 7, 1983 : 236-254.

5195 KASAHARA, Masanari; [ed.]. *Rojin mondai no konnichi teki kadai -rojin anraku-shi mondai ni kansuru ronbun to shiryo* (Present subject on the problem of the aged — thesis and data on euthanasia). Tokyo : Surugadai Shippansha, 1984, 135 p.

5196 KENNEDY, Leslie W.; KRAHN, Harvey. "Rural-urban origin and fear of crime : the case for 'rural baggage' ", *Rural Sociology* 49(2), 1984 : 247-260. [Canada]

5197 KIYOTA, Katsuhiko. "Gendai-gata hiko no tokucho to shakai teki haikei" (Characteristics and social backgrounds of the contemporary-type juvenile delinquency), *Japanese Journal of Sociological Criminology* 9, 1984 : 139-160.

5198 KRUTTSCHNITT, Candace; GREEN, Donald E. "The sex-sanctioning issue : is it history?", *American Sociological Review* 49(4), aug 84 : 541-551.

5199 LARSON, Calvin J. *Crime-justice and society.* Bayside, NY : General Hall, Inc., 1984, x-386 p. ill., bibl., ind. [USA]

5200 LEOCATTA, Silvia R. *El fenómeno de la delincuencia en la Argentina : una visión integral desde la perspective psicosociológica* (The delinquency phenomenon in Argentina : an integral study from the psychosociological view). Buenos Aires : Ediciones Fundación FORUM, 1984, 90 p. bibl.

5201 LÉVY, Thierry. *Le crime en toute humanité.* Paris : Grasset, 1984, 245 p.

5202 LOUIS-GÉRIN, Christiane; [et al.]. "Crime et société", *Revue Française de Sociologie* 25(4), oct-dec 84 : 623-683. [France]

5203 MACNAMARA, Donald E. J. "Prisoners as victimizers and victims", *Sage Annual Review of Studies in Deviance* 7, 1983 : 219-236. [USA]

5204 MAWEYA, Mata Lingume. "Structures socioéconomiques et délinquance juvénile à Kisangani", *Zaïre-Afrique* 24(183), mar 84 : 163-174. [Zaire]

5205 MAYSUYAMA, Hiromitsu. "Nihon ni okeru jisatsu no shakaigaku teki kenkyu : jisatsu-ritsu no chiiki ruikei" (Sociological studies of suicide in Japan : regional types of suicide rate), *Sociologicus* 7, 1984 : 21-38.

5206 MCDOWELL, Charles P. *Criminal justice : a community relations approach.* Cincinnati, OH : Pilgrimage, 1984, viii-473 p. bibl., ind.

5207 MENARD, Scott; MORSE, Barbara J. "A structuralist critique of the IQ-delinquency hypothesis : theory and evidence", *American Journal of Sociology* 89(6), mai 84 : 1347-1378. [USA] [Data from San Diego high school youths]

5208 MIR, Mehraj-ud-Din. *Crime and criminal justice system in India.* Delhi : Deep and Deep, 1984, 338 p.

5209 MUGISHIMA, Fumio; HARADA, Yutaka; HOSHINO, Kanehiro. "Kaisan, kaimetsu shita bohryoku-dan no sai-hensei ni kansuru chosa kenkyu" (A study on the reorganization of dissolved and/or destroyed criminal gangs), *Reports of National Institute of Police Science* 25(1), 1984 : 21-33.

5210   MYERS, Samuel L. Jr. "Do better wages reduce crime?", *American Journal of Economics and Sociology* 43(2), apr 84 : 191-195. [USA]

5211   NAKAJIMA, Akinori. "E. Durkheim no taibatsu hihan ron" (On E. Durkheim's critical theory to corporal punishment), *Bulletin of Aichi University of Education* 33, 1984 : 31-40.

5212   NELSON, James F. "Modelling individual and aggregate victimization rates", *Social Science Research* 13(4), dec 84 : 352-372. [USA]

5213   NEUAMN, Elías; IRURZUN, Víctor J. *La sociedad carcelaria; aspectos penológicos y sociológicos* (The prison society : penal and sociological aspects). Buenos Aires : Depalma SRL, 1984, xvi-2-138 p.

5214   NOVÁK, Mária; PÁL, László. "A viszszaeső bűnözés szociológiai megítélése" (Sociological interpretation of recidivous crime), *Szociológia* 12(3), 1983 : 299-305.

5215   PETERSON, Ruth D.; HAGAN, John. "Changing conceptions of race : towards an account of anomalous findings of sentencing research", *American Sociological Review* 49(1), feb 84 : 56-70. [USA]

5216   PORTIGLIATTI-BARBOS, Mario. "Le démarrage éternel : traitement en milieu institutionnel et prévention 'ouverte' en Italie", *Annales Internationales de Criminologie* 21(1), 1983 : 121-128.

5217   PRUITT, Charles R.; RUILSON, James R. "A longitudinal study of the effect of race on sentencing", *Law and Society Review* 17(4), 1983 : 613-635. [USA]

5218   RÁCZ, József; GÖNCZ, Dániel; KÉTHELYI, Judit. "A. Z. téri 'csövesek'. Egy szociológiai vizsgálat tapasztalataiból" (Tramps of a Budapest square. Some conclusions of a sociological investigation), *Világosság* 25(11), 1984 : 674-682.

5219   RAUMA, David. "Going for the gold : prosecutorial decision making in cases of wife assault", *Social Science Research* 13(4), dec 84 : 321-351. [USA]

5220   ROWE, David C.; OSGOOD, D. Wayne. "Heredity and sociological theories of delinquency : a reconsideration", *American Sociological Review* 49(4), aug 84 : 526-540.

5221   SABEAN, David. "La conscience et la peur : qui a tué le pasteur?", *Actes de la Recherche en Sciences Sociales* 51, mar 84 : 41-53.

5222   SANDOVAL HUERTAS, Emiro. "La región más oscura y más transparente del poder estatal : la disciplina carcelaria" (The darkest and the clearest area of state power : discipline in prison), *Sistema* (60-61), jun 84 : 191-207.

5223   SCHULTE, Regina. "Les incendiaires", *Actes de la Recherche en Sciences Sociales* 51, mar 84 : 55-66.

5224   SCULLY, Diana; MAROLLA, Diana. "Convicted rapists' vocabulary of motives : excuses and justifications", *Social Problems* 31(5), jun 84 : 530-544. [USA]

5225   SMITH, D. Randall; SMITH, William R. "Patterns of delinquent careers : an assessment of three perspectives", *Social Science Research* 13(2), jun 84 : 129-158.

5226   SMITH, D. Randall; SMITH, William R.; NOMA, Elliot. "Delinquent career-lines : a conceptual link between theory and juvenile offenses", *Sociological Quarterly* 25(2), 1984 : 155-172. [USA]

5227   SOMERHAUSEN, Colette. "Les enfants maltraités : approche sociologique du phénomène", *Revue de l'Institut de Sociologie* (1-2), 1984 : 199-212.

5228   SOUTH, Scott J. "Racial differences in suicide : the effect of economic convergence", *Social Science Quarterly* 65(1), mar 84 : 172-180. [USA]

5229   SPERGEL, Irving A. "Violent gangs in Chicago : in search of social policy", *Social Service Review* 58(2), jun 84 : 199-226.

5230   STAPLES, William G. "Toward a structural perspective on gender bias in the juvenile court", *Sociological Perspectives* 27(3), jul 84 : 349-367. [USA]

5231   STOLZ, Barbara Ann. "Congress and capital punishment : an exercise in symbolic politics", *Law and Policy Quarterly* 5(2), apr 83 : 157-180. [USA]

5232   STRATENWERTH, Günter; BERNOULLI, Andreas. *Der schweizerische Strafvollzug : Ergebnisse einer empirischen Untersuchung* (The Swiss penal system : results of an empirical research). Aarau : Sauerländer, 1983, xiv-274 p. ill., bibl.

5233   STROGOVIČ, M. S. "Socialističeskaja demokratija, ukreplenie zakonnosti i bor'ba s prestupnost'ju" (Socialist democracy, reinforcement of legality and struggle against criminality), *Voprosy Filosofii* (3), 1984 : 3-17.

5234   SUMIDA, Masaki; WATANABE, Yasuo. "Seito no hiko kohdo ni taisuru kyoshi shudan no shidou-sei to sono koka" (Teachers' group activity for delinquent student guidance and its effect), *Japanese Journal of Sociological Criminology* 9, 1984 : 98-118.

5235   TAYLOR, Ian R. *Crime, capitalism, and community : three essays in socialist criminology.* Toronto, ON : Butterworths, 1983, xi-156 p. bibl. [Canada]

5236 THORNBERRY, Terence P.; CHRISTENSON, R. L. "Juvenile justice decision-making as a longitudinal process", *Social Forces* 63(2), dec 84 : 433-444. [USA]

5237 THORNBERRY, Terence P.; CHRISTENSON, R. L. "Unemployment and criminal involvement : an investigation of reciprocal causal structures", *American Sociological Review* 49(3), jun 84 : 398-411. [USA]

5238 TOKUOKA, Hideo. "Beikoku ni okeru shonen shihou seisaku no douko to kodomo-kan, ningen-kan no henka" (Recent trends of juvenile justice policies in the U.S.A.), *Kyoiku Shakaigaku Kenkyu* 39, 1984 : 18-31.

5239 TSIEN, Tche-hao. "L'évolution récente de la politique criminelle en Chine populaire", *Archives de Politique Criminelle* (7), 84 : 263-285.

5240 VALENTICH, Mary; GRIPTON, James. "Ideological perspectives on the sexual assault of women", *Social Service Review* 58(3), sep 84 : 448-461. [USA]

5241 VERSPIEREN, Patrick. "Sur la pente de l'euthanasie", *Études*, jan 84 : 43-54. [France]

5242 WARR, Mark. "Fear of victimization : why are women and the elderly more afraid?", *Social Science Quarterly* 65(3), sep 84 : 681-702. [USA]

5243 WASSERMAN, Ira M. "A longitudinal analysis between suicide, unemployment and marital dissolution", *Journal of Marriage and the Family* 46(4), nov 84 : 853-859. [USA]

5244 WEBB, David. "More on gender and justice : girls offenders on supervision", *Sociology (London)* 18(3), aug 84 : 367-381. [UK]

5245 WILKINSON, Kenneth P. "A research note on homicide and rurality", *Social Forces* 63(2), dec 84 : 445-452. [USA]

5246 WILKINSON, Kenneth P. "Violent crime in the Western energy-development region", *Sociological Perspectives* 27(2), apr 84 : 241-256. [USA]

5247 WILSON, Colin. *A criminal history of mankind.* London; New York, NY : Granada, 1984, xviii-702 p. bibl., ind.

5248 WITHERS, Glenn. "Crime, punishment and deterrence in Australia : an empirical investigation", *Economic Record* 60(169), jun 84 : 176-185.

5249 YAMAMOTO, Tsutomu. "Jiko honi teki jisatsu ni kansuru meidai no kento -senso to jisatsu tono kankei kara" (Examination on egoistic suicide proposition : from the point of the relation between war and suicide), *Shakaigaku Hyoron* 35(1), 1984 : 77-88.

5250 YOKOYAMA, Minoru. "The juvenile justice system in Japan", *in : Brusten, M.;* [et al.]; [eds.], Youth crime, social control and prevention s.l. : Gesamthochschule Wuppertal, 1984, 102-113 p.

5251 ZERGUINE, Ramdane. "Approche de la délinquance des jeunes en Algérie", *Revue Algérienne des Sciences Juridiques, Économiques et Politiques* 20(1), mar 83 : 145-168.

5252 ZINGRAFF, Matthew; THOMSON, Randall. "Differential sentencing of women and men in the USA", *International Journal of the Sociology of Law* 12(4), nov 84 : 401-413.

20200 SOCIAL POLICY
POLITIQUE SOCIALE

20210 Social action. Social planning
Action sociale. Planification sociale

5253 "Distributional impacts of public policies : a symposium", *Policy Studies Journal* 12(1), sep 83 : 43-168. [USA] [With contributions by Roger PUPP, John MENEFEE, Robert MAYER, John BURTON, Laurie BASSI, Irwin GARFINKEL, Donald T. DELLERICH]

5254 "Social (The) welfare system and social welfare expenditures of the Republic of China", *Industry of Free China* 60(3), sep 83 : 25-35.

5255 "Welfare (The) State, 1883-1983", *Comparative Social Research* 6, 83 : 3-378. [With contributions by John LOGUE, Uriel ROSENTHAL]

5256 "Wohlfahrtstaat (Der)" (Welfare State), *Gewerkschaftliche Monatshefte* 35(8), aug 84 : 453-510. [Germany FR] [With contributions by Egon MATZNER, Georg VOBRUBA, Frank SCHULZ]

5257 ALBER, Jens. "Versorgungsklassen im Wohlfahrtsstaat. Überlegungen und Daten zur Situation in der Bundesrepublik" (Supply classes in welfare state. Considerations and data concerning the situation in the Federal Republic), *Kölner Zeitschrift für Soziologie und Sozialpsychologie* 36(2), jun 84 : 226-251.

5258 ALEHINA, Z. F. "Faktory social'noj aktivnosti" (Factors of the social activity), *Metodologičeskie Voprosy Nauki* (9), 1983 : 132-142.

5259 ANDERSEN, Bent Rold. "Den danske velfaerdsstat" (The Danish welfare state), *Økonomi og Politik* 57(1), 1983 : 24-33.

5260   ANGELUSZ, Róbert; TARDOS, Róbert. "Felfogások a szociálpolitika néhány általános kérdéséről" (Concepts of some general questions of social policy), *Szociológia* 12(1-2), 1983 : 117-134.

5261   BIELENSKI, Harabi; ROSENBLADT, Bernhard von; RUHLAND, Walter. *Herausforderungen der Sozialpolitik* (Social policy challenges). Bonn : Bundesminister für Arbeit und Sozialordnung, 1983, 133 p. ill., bibl. [Germany FR]

5262   BILLIS, David. *Welfare bureaucracies : their design and change in response to social problems.* London : Heinemann, 1984, 252 p. ill., bibl., ind.

5263   BLÜM, Norbert; BRAUN, Hans; WOHLFARTH, Karl Anton. *Leistungsprinzip und soziale Gerechtigkeit* (Performance principle and social justice). Köln : J. P. Bachem, 1983, 63 p. bibl.

5264   BÖPPLE, Arthur. *Sozialpolitik in der DDR : Probleme, Aspekte im Vergleich* (Social policy in the GDR : problems, comparative aspects). Frankfurt-am-Main : Nachrichten-Verlagsgesellschaft, 1983, 82 p.

5265   CARR-HILL, Roy A. "The political choice of social indicators", *Quality and Quantity* 18(2), feb 84 : 173-191. [UK]

5266   CHOWDHURY, Omar Haider. "Measuring social welfare : theory and practice", *Bangladesh Development Studies* 10(2), jun 82 : 1-18.

5267   COUGHLAN, Anthony. "Ireland's Welfare State in time of crisis", *Administration (Dublin)* 32(1), 1984 : 37-54.

5268   DĄBROWSKA, Grażyna. "Wybrane elementy polityki społecznej w świetle danych GUS za 1983 rok" (Selected issues of social policy in the light of official statistical data for 1983), *Praca i Zabezpieczenie Społeczne* 26(5-6), 1984 : 12-17. [Poland]

5269   DEMBINSKI, Pawel H. "Politique économique — politique sociale : un dilemme?", *Travail et Société* 9(2), apr-jun 84 : 205-226.

5270   DI BERNARDO, Giuliano. *Le regole dell'azione sociale* (The rules of social action). Milano : Saggiatore, 1983, 221 p. ill., bibl., ind.

5271   DONATI, Pierpaolo. *Riposte alla crisi dello stato sociale : le nuove politiche sociali in prospettiva sociologica* (Replies to the welfare state crisis : the new social policies in sociological prospect). Milano : Franco Angeli, 1984, 309 p. ill., bibl.

5272   EDNEY, Julian J. "Rationality and social justice", *Human Relations* 37(2), feb 84 : 163-179.

5273   ERDEI, Ferenc. *Történelem és társadalomkutatás.* Ed. by Kálmán Kulcsár (History and social research). Budapest : Akadémiai Kiadó, 1984, 482 p. bibl. [Hungary]

5274   FERGE, Zsuzsa. "Szociálpolitika a gazdaságban és társadalomban" (Social policy in economics and society), *Társadalomkutatás* 2(2), 1984 : 54-70. [Hungary]

5275   FERNÁNDEZ, Arturo; ROZAS, Margarita. *Políticas sociales y trabajo social* (Social policies and social work). Buenos Aires : Humanitas, 1984, 197 p.

5276   FIGASZEWSKA, Iwona; KOZAK, Marek. "Społeczny klimat reformy" (Social climate of the reform), *Studia Socjologiczne* 94(3), 1984 : 223-244.

5277   FILIPPOV, N. T.; [ed.]. *Social'noe planirovanie na promyšlennyh predprijatijah* (Social planning in the industrial enterprises). Moskva : Moskovskij Rabočij, 1983, 143 p. [USSR]

5278   GADŽIEV, A. G. "Narodnoe blagosostojanie kak social'naja i ėkonomičeskaja kategorija" (People's welfare as a social and economic category), *Vestnik Moskovskogo Universiteta. Teorija Naučnogo Kommunizma* (5), 1983 : 41-48.

5279   GÄFGEN, Gérard. "Entstehung und Expansion des Wohlfahrtsstaats" (Formation and expansion of the Welfare State), *Hamburger Jahrbuch für Wirtschafts- und Gesellschaftspolitik* 29, 1984 : 55-72.

5280   GEISSLER, Heiner. "Sozialpolitik als qualitative Aufgabe" (Social policy, Germany FR), *Mitarbeit (Die)* 32(1), 1983 : 36-42. [Germany FR]

5281   GINET, Jean-Christophe. "Protection sociale et développement", *Revue Française des Affaires Sociales* 38(2), jun 84 : 141-155.

5282   GOLINOWSKA, Stanisława. "Podmioty polityki społecznej" (The subjects of social policy), *Polityka Społeczna* 11(8), 1984 : 4-9.

5283   GORE, M. S. "Social policy and the sociologist", *Indian Journal of Social Research* 25(1), apr 84 : 85-93.

5284   GUILLEMARD, Anne-Marie. "Jalons pour une sociologie des politiques sociales. Le cas de la politique française de la vieillesse", *Sociologie et Sociétés* 16(2), oct 84 : 119-128.

5285   INDRA, P. "Social'noe planirovanie i prognozirovanie razvitija socialističeskogo obščestva" (Social planning and forecast of the socialist society development), *Naučnoe Upravlenie Obščestvom* (16) 1983 : 105-120.

5286   IZIGA, Roger. *Perú estructura urbana y proceso histórico social* (Urban structure and historico-social process in Peru). Lima : Ediciones Atusparia, 1983, 212 p. bibl.

5287   JOBERT, Bruno. "The testing of the alternative : two major innovations in Indian social policy", *Social Science Information / Information sur les Sciences Sociales* 23(6), 1984 : 921-954.

5288   JONES, Brian J. "Toward a constructive theory for anti-poverty policy", *American Journal of Economics and Sociology* 43(2), apr 84 : 247-256.

5289   KAHN, Alfred J.; KAMERMAN, Sheila B. "Social assistance : an eight-country overview", *Journal of the Institute for Socioeconomic Studies* 8(4), wint 84 : 93-112.

5290   KLEIN, Rudolf. "La crise internationale des politiques sociales : dilemmes conceptuels et choix politiques possibles", *Politiques et Management Public* 1(3), sum 83 : 3-33.

5291   KUHNLE, Stein. *Velferdsstaten* (Welfare state). Oslo : Tiden, 1983, 140 p. ill., bibl. [Norway]

5292   KUHNLE, Stein. *Velferdsstatens utvikling : Norge i komparativt perspektiv* (Welfare state development : Norway in comparative perspective). Bergen : Universitetsforlaget, 1983, 195 p. ill., bibl., ind.

5293   LADSOUS, Jacques. *Le projet social dans la solidarité nationale : une politique de solidarité à mettre en oeuvre.* Paris : Scarabée, 1984, 159 p. bibl.

5294   LEHNER, Franz. "The vanishing of spontaneity : socio-economic conditions of the Welfare State", *European Journal of Political Research* 11(4), dec 83 : 437-444.

5295   LIEBETRAU, Henrik. *Dansk socialpolitik 1974-1982* (Danish social policy 1974-1982). København : Socialistiske Økonomer, 1983, 240 p. bibl.

5296   LIPSKY, Michael. "Bureaucratic disentitlement in social welfare programs", *Social Service Review* 58(1), mar 84 : 3-27. [USA]

5297   LOFQUIST, William A. *Discovering the meaning of prevention : a practical approach to positive change.* Tucson, AZ : AYD Publications, 1983, ix-151 p. ill., bibl.

5298   LOGUE, John. "Social welfare, equality, and the labor movement in Denmark and Sweden", *Comparative Social Research* 6, 83 : 243-277.

5299   MARTINDALE, Don Albert. *The scope of social theory : essays and sketches. 2 vols.* Houston, TX : Cap and Gown Press, 1984, xiv-597 p. bibl., ind.

5300   MATHUR, Prakash Chand. *Social bases of Indian politics.* Jaipur : Aalekh Publishers, 1984, vii-252 p. bibl., ind.

5301   MICHALSKY, Helga. "Parteien und Sozialpolitik in der Bundesrepublik Deutschland" (Parties and social policy in the Federal Republic of Germany), *Sozialer Fortschritt* 33(6), 1984 : 134-142.

5302   MIDGLEY, James. "Diffusion and the development of social policy : evidence from the Third World", *Journal of Social Policy* 13(2), apr 84 : 167-184.

5303   MIDGLEY, James. "L'assistance sociale : une forme de protection sociale de substitution dans les pays en développement", *Revue Internationale de Sécurité Sociale* 37(3), 1984 : 275-294.

5304   MIENO, Takashi. *Fukushi to shakai keikaku no riron* (Theory on welfare and social planning). Tokyo : Hakuto Shobo, 1984, 276 p.

5305   MILLER, Thomas G. "Goffman, social acting, and social behavior", *Journal for the Theory of Social Behaviour* 14(2), jul 84 : 141-163.

5306   MØRCH, Frede. "Litteratur om de nordiske velfaerdsstater. Den skandinaviske model" (Literature on the Nordic welfare states. The Scandinavian model), *Økonomi og Politik* 57(1), 1983 : 58-63.

5307   MORRIS, Robert. "The future challenge to the past : the case of the American welfare system", *Journal of Social Policy* 13(4), oct 84 : 383-396. [With a comment by D. M. AUSTIN; [et al.], ibid. : 389-414 and a reply by the author, ibid. : 415-416]

5308   MUBYARTO. "Social and Economic justice", *Bulletin of Indonesian Economic Studies* 20(3), dec 84 : 36-54. [Indonesia]

5309   MUNZ, Rainer; WINTERSBERGER, Helmut. "L'État-providence autrichien : politique sociale et programmes de maintien du revenu entre 1970 et 1984", *Revue Internationale de Sécurité Sociale* 37(3), 1984 : 334-350.

5310   MURRAY, Charles A. *Losing ground : American social policy, 1950-1980.* New York, NY : Basic Books, 1984, xii-323 p. ill., bibl., ind.

5311   PAPP, Zsolt. "A 'jóléti állam' problémái — szociológiai nézőpontból" (The problems of the 'welfare State' from a sociological point of view), *Medvetánc* 2-3(4-1), 1983-84 : 142-159.

5312   PINC, Karel. *Sociální politika a socialistické hospodárství* (Social policy and socialist economy). Praha : Univerzita Karlova, 1983, 125 p. bibl.

5313   PIRRO, Federico. *Mezzogiorno fra utopia e realtà : dibattiti, progetti e dinamiche socioeconomiche nel Mezzogiorno degli anni '60 e '70* (Southern Italy between utopia and reality : debates, projects and socioeconomic dynamics in Southern Italy during the sixties and seventies). Bari : Dedalo, 1983, 141 p. bibl. [Italy]

5314   POLLINI, Gabriele. "Classificazione delle azioni e tipologia dell'agire sociale. Pareto e Weber" (Classification of actions and social action typology. Pareto and Weber), *Studi di Sociologia* 22(4), oct-dec 84 : 349-373.

5315   QUANTE, Stefan. "La politique sociale du nouveau gouvernement : changement ou
         continuité?", *Allemagnes d'Aujourd'hui* (86), dec 83 : 18-31. [Germany FR]
5316   QUITO, Emerita S. "Value as a factor in social action", *International Social Science Journal /
         Revue Internationale des Sciences Sociales* 36(4), 1984 : 603-613.
5317   RANKOVIČ, Miodrag; [ed.]. "Savremeno jugoslovensko društvo — sociološko istraživanje
         uzroka krize i mogućnosti izlaska" (Yugoslav contemporary society — sociological study
         of causes of the crisis and ways out of the crisis), *Sociologija* 24(2-3), 1982 : 195-366.
5318   REGT, Ali de. *Arbeidersgezinnen en beschavingsarbeid : ontwikkelingen in Nederland, 1870-1940;
         een historisch-sociologische studie* (Workers' families and cultural work : developments in
         the Netherlands, 1870-1940; an historical-sociological study). Meppel : Boom, 1984, 330 p.
         bibl., ind.
5319   REIN, Martin. *From policy to practice.* Armonk, NY : Sharpe, 1983, xv-256 p.
5320   ROSENTHAL, Uriel. "The Welfare State or state of welfare : repression and welfare in the
         modern State", *Comparative Social Research* 6, 83 : 279-298. [Netherlands]
5321   RUNCIMAN, W. G. *A treatise on social theory. I. The methodology of social theory.* Cambridge :
         University Press, 1983, xii-350 p. ill.
5322   SCHAFER, Robert B.; KEITH, Patricia M.; LORENZ, Frederick O. "Equity/inequity
         and the self-concept : an interactionist analysis", *Social Psychology Quarterly* 47(1),
         mar 84 : 42-49.
5323   SHARMA, P. N.; SHASTRI, C. *Social planning : concepts and techniques.* Lucknow : Print-
         House, 1984, 416 p.
5324   STAHL, Thomas; ZÄNGLE, Michael. *Die Legende von der Krise des Sozialstaates* (The legend
         of the crisis of welfare state). Frankfurt-am-Main; New York, NY : Campus, 1984, 188 p.
         bibl.
5325   STILLER, Pavel. *Sozialpolitik in der UdSSR 1950-80* (Social policy in the USSR 1950-80).
         Baden-Baden : Nomos Verlagsgesellschaft, 1983, 336 p. ill., bibl.
5326   STOESZ, D. "'Corporate welfare' : l'industrie des services sociaux et la réforme du Welfare
         State aux États-Unis", *Revue Internationale d'Action Communautaire* (10), aut 83 : 87-99.
5327   TACHON, Michel. "L'action sociale, un bricolage politique", *Projet* (184), apr 84 : 445-456.
         [France]
5328   TAKEGAWA, Shogo. "Shakai seisaku to shakai teki kachi" (Social policy and social values),
         Quarterly of Social Security Research 19(4), 1984 : 457-466.
5329   TAYLOR-GOOBY, Peter. "The Welfare State and individual freedom : attitudes to
         Welfare spending and to the power of the State", *Political Studies* 31(4), dec 83 : 640-649.
         [UK]
5330   TOINET, Marie-France. "La politique sociale du président Reagan", *Études*, oct 84 : 309-321.
5331   TRAŠNEA, Ovidiu. *Filosofia socialá şi politicá a neoconservatorismului* (Social philosophy and
         neo-conservatism policy). Bucureşti : Editura Politică, 1984, 122 p.
5332   TUOMELA, Saimo. "Social action-functions", *Philosophy of the Social Sciences / Philosophie
         des Sciences Sociales* 14(2), jun 84 : 133-147.
5333   ULRICH, Werner. *Critical heuristics of social planning : a new approach to practical philosophy.*
         Bern : P. Haupt, 1983, 504 p. ill., ind., bibl.
5334   UTTLEY, Stephen. "Reformulating the development theory of welfare", *Journal of Social
         Policy* 13(4), oct 84 : 447-465.
5335   VAN DEN BRINK-BUDGEN, Roy. "Freedom and the welfare state : a multi-dimensional
         problem", *Journal of Social Policy* 13(1), jan 84 : 21-39. [Robert Goodin's suggestions]
5336   VOS, C. J. "Verzorgingsstaat en sociologie; economische crisis en macrosociologische tekort"
         (Welfare state and sociology; economic crisis and macrosociological shortage), *Mens en
         Maatschappij* 59(2), mai 84 : 179-188.
5337   WALKER, Alan. *Social planning : a strategy for socialist welfare.* Oxford, Oxfordshire : Basil
         Blackwell, 1984, xi-276 p. ill., bibl., ind. [UK]
5338   WALZER, Michael Laban. *Spheres of justice : defence of pluralism and equality.* Oxford : Martin
         Robertson, 1983, xviii-345 p. bibl., ind.
5339   WEIGERT, Andrew J. *Life and society : a meditation on the social thought of José Ortega y Gasset.*
         New York, NY : Irvington Publishers, 1983, 250 p. bibl., ind.
5340   ZORILLA RUIZ, Manuel María. *Transformaciones del derecho social* (Transformations of social
         law). Bilbao : Universidad de Deusto, 1984, 163 p. bibl. [Spain]

         20220   Social security
                    Sécurité sociale

5341   "Aide (L') ménagère", *Gérontologie et Société* 31, dec 84-jan 85 : 3-177. [France]

5342   "Développement et tendances de la Sécurité sociale 1981-1983", *Revue Internationale de Sécurité Sociale* 36(4), 1983 : 471-561.

5343   "Du maintien à domicile á l'hébergement", *Gérontologie et Société* 25, jun 83 : 3-101.

5344   "Soutien (Le) à domicile", *Gérontologie et Société* 30, oct 84 : 3-140. [France]

5345   ARTICUS, Stephan. "Themen sozialwissenschaftlicher Forschung im Bereich der Sozialen Sicherung in Entwicklungsländern" (Social science research themes in the field of social insurance in the developing countries), *Vierteljahresschrift für Sozialrecht* 11(1), 1983 : 67-94.

5346   BERLIN, Sharon B.; JONES, Linda E. "Life after welfare : AFDC termination among long-term recipients", *Social Service Review* 57(3), sep 83 : 378-402. [USA] [Aid to Families with Dependent Children]

5347   BHATNAGAR, Depak. *Labour welfare and social security legislation in India.* New Delhi : Deep and Deep, 1984, 302 p.

5348   BROWNELL, Arlene; SHUMAKER, Sally A.; [eds.]. "Social support : new perspectives in theory, research, and intervention. I. Theory and research", *Journal of Social Issues* 40(4), 1984 : 1-134.

5349   CHARLES, Jean-François. "La Sécurité sociale en Suisse : traits essentiels et problèmes actuels", *Revue Internationale de Sécurité Sociale* 37(2), 1984 : 199-215.

5350   CONSEIL DE L'EUROPE. COMITÉ DIRECTEUR POUR LES AFFAIRES SOCIALES. *La protection sociale des personnes très âgées : quatrième âge.* Strasbourg : CE, 1984, 117 p. [Europe]

5351   CORDEIRO, Albano. "La sécurité sociale et les immigrés : rumeurs et vérités", *Temps Modernes* 40(452-453), mai 84 : 2126-2147. [France]

5352   CORIN, Ellen; [et al.]. "Entre les services professionnels et les réseaux sociaux : les stratégies d'existence des personnes âgées", *Sociologie et Sociétés* 16(2), oct 84 : 89-104. [Canada]

5353   DRBOHLAV, Vlastimil. "Protection et Sécurité sociale des mères exerçant une activité professionnelle en Tchécoslovaquie", *Revue Internationale de Sécurité Sociale* 37(2), 1984 : 192-198.

5354   EKERT, Olivia. "Prestations familiales, fiscalité et redistribution", *Revue Française des Affaires Sociales* 38(suppl.), jun 84 : 127-149. [France]

5355   ENGO, Pierre-Désiré. "La protection sociale en République unie du Cameroun", *Revue Internationale de Sécurité Sociale* 37(3), 1984 : 295-309.

5356   ESENWEIN-ROTHE, Ingeborg. "Demo-ökonomische Aspekte einer staatlichen Familienpolitik" (Demo-economic aspects of a State family policy), *Jahrbuch für Sozialwissenschaft* 35(2-3), 1984 : 265-281. [Germany FR]

5357   FLEURY TEIXEIRA, Sonia Maria. "Previdência 'versus' assistência na politica social brasileira" (Health care 'versus' welfare assistance in Brazilian social policy), *Dados* 27(3), 1984 : 321-345.

5358   GRANT, Karen R. "The inverse care law in the context of universal free health insurance in Canada : toward meeting health needs through social policy", *Sociological Focus* 17(2), apr 84 : 137 155.

5359   GRUAT, J. V. "L'extension de la protection sociale en République gabonaise : consolidation du développement", *Revue Internationale du Travail* 123(4), jul-aug 84 : 499-514.

5360   HANSON, Russell L. "The 'content' of welfare policy : the States and aid to families with dependent children", *Journal of Politics* 45(3), aug 83 : 771-785. [USA]

5361   ISUANI, Ernesto A. "Previdência e assistência social na América Latina : limites estructurais e mudanças necessárias" (Social security and public assistance in Latin America : structural limits and the need for change), *Dados* 27(3), 1984 : 307-320.

5362   KAMERMAN, Sheila B.; KAHN, Alfred I. "Income transfers and mother-only families in eight countries", *Social Service Review* 57(3), sep 83 : 448-464.

5363   KÖHLER, Peter A.; ZACHER, Hans F.; [eds.]. *Beiträge zu Geshichte und aktueller Situation der Sozialversicherung* (Contributions to the history and the present situation of social insurance). Berlin : Duncker und Humblot, 1983, 737 p. bibl. [Colloquium of the Max-Planck Institut für Ausländisches und Internationales Sozialrecht]

5364   LAMBERT, Denis-Clair. "Les limites de la protection sociale", *Contrepoint* (49), trim. 3, 84 : 114-132. [France]

5365   LAND, Hilary; PARKER, Roy. "La politique de la famille en Grande-Bretagne et sa dimension idéologique", *Nouvelles Questions Féministes* (6-7), spr 84 : 107-154.

5366   O'HIGGINS, Michael. "Privatisation and social security", *Political Quarterly* 55(2), jun 84 : 129-139. [UK]

5367   ORGANISATION INTERNATIONALE DU TRAVAIL. *La sécurité sociale à l'horizon 2000 : la sécurité sociale face à l'évolution économique et sociale des pays industrialisés : rapport.* Genève : BIT, 1984, xix-131 p.

5368 PARTSCH, Manfred. *Prinzipien und Formen sozialer Sicherung in nicht-industriellen Gesellschaften* (Principles and forms of social insurance in non-industrial societies). Berlin : Duncker und Humblot, 1983, 168 p. bibl.

5369 PASSANANTE, María I. "Sugerencias para una política social de ancianidad" (Suggestions for a social policy for old age), *SOCIOLOGICA — Revista Argentina de Ciencias Sociales* 9, 1984 : 155-176. [Argentina]

5370 PERRIN, Guy. "Cent ans d'assurance sociale", *Revue Belge de Sécurité Sociale* 25(8-9), sep 83 : 837-873.

5371 PERRIN, Guy. "Cent ans d'assurance sociale", *Travail et Société* 9(2), apr-jun 84 : 195-208. [Voir les 2e et 3e parties ibid. : 9(3), jul-sep 84 : 319-330 et 9(4), oct-dec 84 : 421-433]

5372 ROSENBERG, Mark. *Las luchas por el seguro social en Costa Rica* (The fights for the social security in Costa Rica). San José : Editorial Costa Rica, 1983, 210 p. bibl.

5373 STINCHCOMBE, Arthur L. "Third party buying : the trend and the consequences", *Social Forces* 62(4), jun 84 : 861-884.

5374 TAMURA, Kenji. "Tsu-sho houhou ni yoru chihou-sei rojin oyobi sono kazoku ni taisuru case work teki approach no kenkyu" (A study of a casework approach for senile day-care clients and their families), *Toyo University Bulletin of Faculty of Sociology* 22(1), 1984 : 23-164. [Japan]

5375 TANABE, Yoshiaki. "Rodo hoken : gendai chugoku no shakai hosho seido" (The labour insurance : social security systems in China), *Kaigai Shakaihosho* 69, 1984 : 2-15.

5376 WASSERSTROM, Jeffrey. "Resistance to the one-child family", *Modern China* 10(3), jul 84 : 345-374. [China]

5377 WILLIAMSON, John B. "Old age relief policy prior to 1900 : the trend toward restrictive-ness", *American Journal of Economics and Sociology* 43(3), jul 84 : 369-384. [USA]

5378 ZAY, Nicolas. "Analyse critique des politiques et des institutions québécoises concernant les personnes âgées", *Sociologie et Sociétés* 16(2), oct 84 : 105-118.

5379 ZEILIGER, Jean. "Un centre de prévention pour les retraités", *Gérontologie et Société* 28, apr-mai 84 : 169-174. [France]

20300 SOCIAL WORK
TRAVAIL SOCIAL

5380 "Travail social : modèles d'analyse", *Actions et Recherches Sociales* (2), sep 84 : 1-113. [France] [With contributions by Dominique BOULLIER, Jacques BEAUCHARD, Bruno BORDAGE]

5381 ALAYON, Norberto. *Perspectivas del trabajo social* (Social work perspectives). Buenos Aires : Humanitas, 1984, 91 p. [Argentina]

5382 ANDER EGG, Ezequiel. *Evaluación de programas de trabajo social* (Evaluation of social work programmes). Buenos Aires : Humanitas, 1984, 86 p.

5383 BRANDT, Eberhard. *Sozialarbeit in antagonistischer Gesellschaft : ein Beitrag zur Theorie der Sozialarbeit* (Social work in conflictual society : a contribution to the theory of social work). Köln : Pahl-Rugenstein, 1983, 172 p. bibl.

5384 DEPNER, Rolf; LINDEN, Hans; MENZEL, Elmar. *Chaos im System der Behindertenhilfe? Eine empirische Untersuchung zur Professionalisierung sozialer Berufe* (Disorder in the system of aid to disabled persons? An empirical analysis of professionalization of the social work). Weinheim : Beltz, 1983, 227 p. ill., bibl. [Germany FR]

5385 DU RANQUET, Mathilde. *Recherches en casework : l'efficacité et sa mesure en service social.* St. Hyacinthe, PQ : Edisem; Toulouse : Privat, 1983, 2e rev., 208 p. bibl.

5386 JORDAN, Bill. *Invitation to social work.* Oxford : M. Robertson, 1984, 198 p. bibl., ind. [UK]

5387 JORDAN, Bill; PARTON, Nigel; [eds.]. *The political dimensions of social work.* Oxford : B. Blackwell, 1983, vi-205 p. [UK]

5388 KAGLE, Jill Doner. *Social work records.* Homewood, IL : Dorsey Press, 1984, xiii-161 p. ill., bibl., ind.

5389 OHTA, Yoshihiro; SATO, Toyomichi; [eds.]. *Sohsharu wahku : katei to sono tenkai* (Introduction to social work practice : processes and their development). Tokyo : Kaiseisha, 1984, 149 p. [Japan]

5390 RONNBY, Alf. *Socialarbetets förklaringsmodeller* (Explanatory models for social work). Malmö : LiberFörlag, 1983, 234 p. ill., bibl., ind. [Sweden]

5391 ROVERE, Ana María; ALLENDE, Cecilia; CORNEJO, María del Carmen. *Propuestas metodológicas para el trabajo social* (Methodological proposals for social work). Buenos Aires : Editorial Humanitas, 1984, 69 p. bibl.

5392 SIDDIQUI, H. Y. *Social work and social action.* Delhi : Harnan, 1984, 184 p.

20400 SOCIAL SERVICES
SERVICES SOCIAUX

20410 Medical sociology. Medicine
Sociologie médicale. Médecine

5393   "Médecines du futur", *Projet* (190), dec 84 : 1099-1114. [With contributions by P. M. GALETTI, H. PLAUCHU]

5394   BOUGEROL, Christiane. "Les représentations raciales du corps dans la médecine populaire en Guadeloupe", *Cahiers Internationaux de Sociologie* 77, 1984 : 287-302.

5395   CAREGORODCEV, G. I.; ĔROHIN, V. G. "Predmet i problematika sociologičeskih issledovanij v medicine" (Objectives and problematics of sociological research in medicine), *Vestnik Akademii Medicinskih Nauk* (6), 1984 : 13-25.

5396   COLLIGNON, René. "Les conditions de développement d'une psychiatrie sociale au Sénégal", *Présence Africaine* (129), trim. 1, 84 : 3-19.

5397   GERSHMAN, Carl. "Psychiatric abuse in the Soviet Union", *Society* 21(5), aug 84 : 54-59.

5398   LOYOLA, Maria Andréa. *Médicos e curandeiros : conflicto social e saúde* (Physicians and healers : social conflict and health). São Paulo-SP : Difel, 1983, viii-198 p. ill., bibl. [Brazil]

5399   MORGAN, John H.; [ed.]. *Third world medicine and social change : a reader in social science and medicine.* Lanham, MD : University Press of America, 1983, x-317 p. bibl.

5400   RESTAK, Richard M. "Psychiatry in America", *Wilson Quarterly* 7(4), aut 83 : 94-112.

5401   UNDERHILL, Paul K. "Verso una comprensione sociologica della medicina intensa come sistema di conoscenza" (Toward a sociological understanding of medicine as a system of knowledge), *Rassegna Italiana di Sociologia* 25(4), oct-dec 84 : 573-606.

5402   VAILLE, Charles. "L'expérimentation animale", *Revue Française des Affaires Sociales* 38(2), jun 84 : 103-113. [France]

20420 Public health
Santé publique

5403   "Health and stratification", *Sociological Focus* 17(2), apr 84 : 87-174. [USA]

5404   "Health in development", *Research in Human Capital and Development* 3, 1983 : 217-358. [With contributions by Robert N. GROSSE, Barbara H. PERRY, Wilfried MALENBAUM, Ronald J. VOGEL, Nancy T. GREENSPAN, N. D. MCGRATH, T. FÜLÖP, W. A. REINKE]

5405   "Health in human capital formation", *Research in Human Capital and Development* 3, 1983 : 77-214. [USA] [With contributions by Linda N. EDWARDS, Michael GROSSMAN, Don CHERNICHOVSKY, Douglas COATE, Eugene LEWIT]

5406   "Health, society and politics", *IDS Bulletin* 14(4), oct 83 : 1-78. [Developing countries] [With contributions by Alastair Md. GRAY, Carlyle DE MACÊDO, Caesar A. de B. VIEIRA, Malcolm SEGALL, Oscar GISH, Ramón VALDIVIESO]

5407   "Política (A) e administração da saúde pública no Brasil e na América latina" (Public health policy and administration in Brazil and Latin America), *Revista de Administração Pública* 17(3), sep 83 : 4-149. [With contributions by Antônio Sergio da Silva AROUCA, Hésio CORDEIRO, Cornelis Johannes VAN STRALEN, Roberto Passos NOGUEIRA, Antônio GUERRA]

5408   BARRIENTOS, Gustavo. "La salud de las trabajadoras de la salud" (Health service women workers' health), *Revista Mexicana de Sociología* 45(3), jul-sep 83 : 877-914. [Mexico]

5409   CALNAN, Michael. "The politics of health : the case of smoking control", *Journal of Social Policy* 13(3), jul 84 : 279-296.

5410   CHARRAUD, Alain. "Formes et évolution de la consommation médicale aux différents âges de la vie", *Économie et Statistique* 163, feb 84 : 47-66. [France]

5411   DE LEONARDIS, Ota. "Il sistema sanitario" (Health system), *Problemi del Socialismo* (27-28), dec 83 : 152-174. [Italy]

5412   DE MIGUEL, Jesús M. *Estructura del sector sanitario* (Structure of the health sector). Madrid : Tecnos, 1983, 159 p. ill., bibl.

5413   DUBE, S.; SACHDEV, P. S.; [eds.]. *Mental health problems of the socially disadvantaged.* New Delhi : Tata McGraw-Hill, 1983, xvi-198 p. bibl., ind. [India]

5414   GILLIOZ, Lucienne. "La prévention comme normalisation culturelle", *Schweizerische Zeitschrift für Soziologie / Revue Suisse de Sociologie* 10(1), 1984 : 37-84. [Suisse]

5415   GOBIN, Corinne. "Les maisons médicales francophones. Déprofessionnalisation de la médecine ou promotion d'un nouveau mode d'intervention illimitée du médical?", *Revue de l'Institut de Sociologie* (1-2), 1984 : 257-273. [Belgique]

5416   GRAHAM LEAR, Julia. "Women's health and public policy : 1976-1982", *Sage Yearbooks in Women's Policy Studies* 7, 1983 : 148-162. [USA]
5417   HOGAN, Roseann R. "The stress role : a conceptual development", *Sociological Quarterly* 25(4), 1984 : 567-579.
5418   HORN, James J. "The Mexican revolution and health care, or the health of the Mexican revolution", *Latin American Perspectives* 10(4), aut 83 : 24-39.
5419   ITYAVYAR, Dennis A. "The political economy of health care problems in Nigeria", *Ufahamu* 13(1), aut 83 : 45-63.
5420   KLEIN, Rudolf. "The politics of ideology vs. the reality of politics : the case of Britain's national health service in 1980s", *Milbank Memorial Fund Quarterly* 62(1), wint 84 : 82-109.
5421   KOHLER RIESSMAN, Catherine. "Women and medicalization : a new perspective", *Social Policy* 14(1), sum 83 : 3-18. [USA]
5422   LISICYN, Ju. P.; SAHNO, A. V. "Metodologičeskij analiz ponjatija 'obščestvennoe zdorov'e'" (Methodological analysis of the 'social health' concept), *Vestnik Akademii Medicinskih Nauk* (6), 1984 : 25-40.
5423   LOSONCZI, Ágnes. "Társadalmi ártalom, társadalmi védelem. Egészség-szociológiai kutatás tapasztalataiból" (Social harm, social protection. Some consequences of a sociological research on health), *Társadalomkutatás* 2(1), 1984 : 70-87.
5424   NICOLAS ORTIZ, Carlos. *El derecho a la salud y los derechos de los enfermos : apuntes sobre la sanidad española* (Right to health and patients' rights : notes on Spanish public health). Madrid : Editorial Encuentro, 1983, 206 p.
5425   POLTON, Dominique. "La décentralisation du système de santé. Analyse de l'expérience britannique", *Revue Française des Affaires Sociales* 38(1), mar 84 : 131-162.
5426   POSTAL, P. "Un système de santé pris au piège du mal développement : le cas du Brésil", *Cahiers de Sociologie et de Démographie Médicales* 24(1), mar 84 : 5-42.
5427   RAO, P. S. S.; RICHARD, J. "Socioeconomic and demographic correlates of medical care and health practices", *Journal of Biosocial Science* 16(3), jul 84 : 343-355. [India]
5428   RIBEIRO, Lucia. "Movimento popular e saúde : a participação da Igreja" (Popular movement and health : the Church's participation), *Vozes* 78(5), jul 84 : 5-22. [Brazil]
5429   ROCHEFORT, David A. "Origins of the 'Third psychiatric revolution' : the Community Mental Health Centers Act of 1963", *Journal of Health, Politics Policy and Law* 9(1), spr 84 : 1-30. [USA]
5430   SCHWARTZMAN, Helen B.; [et al.]. "Children, families, and mental health service organizations : cultures in conflict", *Human Organization* 43(4), 1984 : 297-306. [USA]
5431   SEARLE, C. Maureen; GALLAGHER, Eugene B. "Manpower issues in Saudi health development", *Milbank Memorial Fund Quarterly* 61(4), aut 83 : 659-686.
5432   SEJMAN, I. M. "Rejganomika i zdravoohranenie" ('Reaganomics' and public health), *SSA* 14(3), mar 84 : 41-49.
5433   SOURNIA, Jean-Charles. "Que signifient libéralisme et socialisme en médecine?", *Revue des Sciences Morales et Politiques* 139(2), 1984 : 201-212. [France]
5434   THOITS, Peggy A. "Explaining distribution of psychological vulnerability : lack of social support in the face of life stress", *Social Forces* 63(2), dec 84 : 453-481. [USA]
5435   VENTURINI, Ernesto; ATTI, Stefania. "Per una politica di salute mentale : il ruolo svolto dall' Organizzazione mondiale della sanita in Africa" (For a mental health policy : World Health Organization's role in Africa), *Africa (Roma)* 39(3), sep 84 : 375-390.
5436   WAITZKIN, Howard. "Health policy and social change : a comparative history of Chile and Cuba", *Social Problems* 31(2), dec 83 : 235-248.

          20430   Hospitals
          Hôpitaux

5437   "10e Assises nationales de l'hospitalisation publique", *Revue Hospitalière de France* 48(369), mar 84 : 209-258. [France]
5438   ABADIE, Juan P. "Sistema Nacional de Salud. Bases para su discusión y elaboración" (National Health System. Bases for discussion and elaboration), *Cuadernos Médico Sociales* 29-30, nov 84 : 77-86.
5439   ANGEL, Ronald; CLEARY, Paul D. "The effects of social structure and culture on reported health", *Social Science Quarterly* 65(3), sep 84 : 814-828. [USA]
5440   COHRAN, Daniel S.; [et al.]. "Effect of organizational size on conflict frequency and location in hospitals", *Journal of Management Studies* 20(4), oct 83 : 441-451. [USA]
5441   DEHAENE, J. L. "L'offre médicale et para-médicale en Belgique", *Revue Belge de Sécurité Sociale* 26(1-2), feb 84 : 3-157.

5442   DUCKETT, S. J. "Assuring hospital standards : the introduction of hospital accreditation in Australia", *Australian Journal of Public Administration* 42(3), sep 83 : 385-402.

5443   EVE, Susan Brown. "Age strata differences in utilization of health care services among adults in the United States", *Sociological Focus* 17(2), apr 84 : 105-120.

5444   FEDER, Judith; [et al.]. "Poor people and poor hospitals : implications for public policy", *Journal of Health, Politics Policy and Law* 9(2), sum 84 : 237-250. [USA]

5445   FERLIE, Ewan; PAHL, Jan; QUINE, Lyn. "Professional collaboration in services for mentally handicapped people", *Journal of Social Policy* 13(2), apr 84 : 185-202.

5446   HENDERSON, Gail E.; COHEN, Myron S. *The Chinese hospital : a socialist work unit.* New Haven, CT : Yale University Press, 1984, xvi-183 p.

5447   KOHLER RIESSMAN, Catherine. "The use of health services by the poor : are there any promising models", *Social Policy* 14(4), spr 84 : 30-40. [USA]

5448   LALIBERTY, Rene; CHRISTOPHER, W. I. *Enhancing productivity in health care facilities.* Owing Mills, MD : National Health Publishing, 1984, xviii-184 p. ill., bibl., ind.

5449   LAVOIE, Francine. "Citizen participation in health care", *Social Service Delivery Systems* 6, 1983 : 225-238. [Canada]

5450   MARTIN, John Powell; EVANS, Debbie. *Hospitals in trouble.* Oxford : Basil Blackwell, 1984, xiv-273 p. bibl., ind.

5451   MARTINELLI, Alberto. "I sistemi sanitari delle società industriali avanzate" (Health systems in advanced industrial societies), *Giornale degli Economisti e Annali di Economia* 43(11-12), nov-dec 84 : 763-781.

5452   MILLER, Dean F. *Dimensions of community health.* Dubuque, IA : W. C. Brown Publishers, 1984, xvii-398 p. ill., bibl., ind.

5453   PHILLIPS, James F.; [et al.]. "Transferring health and family planning service innovations to the public sector : an experiment in organization development in Bangladesh", *Studies in Family Planning* 15(2), mar 84 : 62-73.

5454   RICHARD, Michel P. "Asylums revisited : 1957-1982", *International Social Science Review* 59(3), 1984 : 171-178. [USA]

5455   RIDDER, Paul. "Humanität im Krankenhaus. Einige Schlussfolgerungen für die Praxis" (Humanity in hospital. Some conclusions for praxis), *Sociologia Internationalis* 22(1), 1984 : 111-133. [Germany FR]

5456   SILVERMAN, David. "Going private : ceremonial forms in a private oncology clinic", *Sociology (London)* 18(2), mai 84 : 191-204. [UK]

5457   VERONELLI, Juan Carlos. "Los proyectos de transformación del sistema nacional de servicios de salud en América Latina" (The transformation projects of the National System of Health Services in Latin-America), *Cuadernos Médico Sociales* 27, mar 84 : 31-46.

5458   WALT, Gillian; MELAMED, Angela; [eds.]. *Mozambique : towards a people's health service.* London : Zed Books; Totowa, NJ : Biblio Distribution Center, 1984, x-150 p. ill., bibl.

20440   Social workers
Travailleurs sociaux

5459   "Action (L') de la Sécurité sociale dans le domaine des services sociaux : tendances récentes et problémes actuels", *Revue Internationale de Sécurité Sociale* 36(4), 1983 : 562-583.

5460   ALVAREZ, Elena; [et al.]. *Organización y administración de servicios sociales* (Organization and administration of social services). Buenos Aires : Humanitas, 1984, 144 p.

5461   BOUCHAYER, Françoise. "Médecine et puéricultrices de Protection maternelle et infantile. La recherche d'une identité et d'une légitimité professionnelles", *Revue Française de Sociologie* 25(1), jan-mar 84 : 67-90. [France]

5462   BRENNA, A. "Les conditons de l'exercice des médecins italiens dans les années 80", *Cahiers de Sociologie et de Démographie Médicales* 24(3), sep 84 : 187-207.

5463   CLIMENT DE ZAJELENCZYC, Graciela; MENDES DIZ DE CABO, Ana María. "Médicos para la comunidad, su socialización" (Physicians for community, its socialization), *Cuadernos Médico Sociales* 29-30, nov 84 : 87-93.

5464   COHEN, Lawrence H.; [ed.]. "Quality assurance in the human services", *American Behavioral Scientist* 27(5), jun 84 : 547-672. [With contributions by Kathleen LOHR, Robert H. BROOK, William R. TASH, Gerald M. STAHLER]

5465   COOLEN, J. A.; KRUSE, H. J. "Onderlinge hulp naast overheidszorg. Een empirische verkenning in relatie tot gemeentelijke sociale dienstverlening" (Social support systems. An empirical study concerning public social service provision), *Sociologische Gids* 31(5), 1984 : 412-426. [Netherlands]

5466   DARVEAU-FOURNIER, Lise; HOME, Alice. "Les groupes de service social à Québec. Recherche des rapports entre théorie et pratique", *Service Social* 32(1-2), jun 83 : 129-155.

5467   DAVEY, Judith A.; DWYER, Máire. *Meeting needs in the community : a discussion paper on social services.* Wellington : New Zealand Planning Council, 1984, viii-66 p. ill., bibl.
5468   DAVIS, Leonard. *Sex and the social worker.* London : Heinemann Educational Books, 1983, 115 p. bibl., ind.
5469   DIMITRIJEVIĆ, Dušan. "Physicians", *Yugoslav Survey* 25(1), feb 84 : 131-140. [Yugoslavia]
5470   DUBEY, Sumati Narain; MURDIA, Ratna; [eds.]. *Organizational designs and management methods for human service organizations.* Bombay : Himalay Publishing House, 1983, ix-363 p. bibl. [India]
5471   EGELUND, Tine; HALSKOV, Therese. *Praksis i socialt arbejde* (Praxis and social work). København : Munksgaard, 1984, 222 p. bibl.
5472   GRANT, Linda; DUROSS, Daniel J. "Expected rewards of practice and personal life priorities of men and women medical students", *Sociological Focus* 17(2), apr 84 : 87-104. [USA]
5473   GUILLET, Pierre. "Le médecin généraliste et la santé des personnes âgées", *Gérontologie et Société* 28, apr-mai 84 : 44-49. [France]
5474   ION, Jacques; TRICART, Jean-Paul. *Les travailleurs sociaux.* Paris : La Découverte, 1984, 125 p. bibl.
5475   LEROY, X. "Densité et activité des médecins en Belgique. Situation actuelle, évolution et perspectives", *Cahiers de Sociologie et de Démographie Médicales* 24(2), jun 84 : 157-181.
5476   MATTIONI, Angelo. "Servizi alla persona e pluralismo sociale" (Social services and social pluralism), *Vita e Pensiero* 67(10), oct 84 : 8-17. [Italy]
5477   MUEL-DREYFUS, Francine. "Le fantôme du médecin de famille", *Actes de la Recherche en Sciences Sociales* 54, sep 84 : 70-71. [France]
5478   PERLADO, Fernando. *Servicios sociales para la vejez* (Social services for the aged). Zaragoza : Caja de Ahorros de la Inmaculada, 1983, 74 p. [Spain]
5479   ROCHEFORT, R.; DEVEVEY, J. "Les jeunes médecins libéraux. Évolution de 1979 à 1982", *Cahiers de Sociologie et de Démographie Médicales* 24(2), jun 84 : 97-123. [France]
5480   RUBIN, Allen; THORELLI, Irene M. "Egoistic motives and longevity of participation by social service volunteers", *Journal of Applied Behavioral Science* 20(3), 1984 : 223-235. [USA]
5481   SCHIRRMACHER, Gerd. *Sozialwesen und Sozialarbeit in der Türkei* (Social services and social work in Turkey). Köln : Pahl-Rugenstein, 1983, 783 p. ill., bibl.
5482   TIWARI, A. S. "Society and allopathy in India", *Indian Journal of Social Research* 25(1), apr 84 : 94-98.

AUTHOR INDEX
INDEX DES AUTEURS

Abadie, Juan P., 5438
Abboushi, Suhail, 4597
Abbruzzese, Salvatore, 1277
Abell, Peter, 537
Abercrombie, Nicholas, 166
Abós, Alvaro, 4582
Abram Koban, Linda, 5147
Abrams, Howard B., 3933
Abse, D. Wilfred, 703
Abu-Laban, Sharon McIrvin, 2714
Abuhamdia, Zakaria A., 1586
Ackermann, Werner, 409
Acock, Alan C., 3109, 3110
Adair, Philippe, 1587
Adam, Barry D., 2368
Adam, Heribert, 3360
Adam, Michel, 3361
Adamek, Raymond J., 3111
Adamek, Wojciech, 270
Adams, David Robert, 144
Adams, Gerald R., 485, 2670
Adamson, David, 2246
Addison, John T., 4583
Adejugbe, Michael, 3990
Adeniji, Kunle, 3759
Adepoju, Aderanti, 3538
Adimorah, E. N. O., 154
Adlakha, A. L., 2895
Adler, Jonathan E., 2581
Adler, Terry, 545
Aebischer, Verena, 682
Agarwal, A., 4459
Agarwal, G. K., 1275
Agnew, Robert, 538, 4349, 5148
Agrawala, Vasudeva Sharana, 900
Aguirre, Adalberto Jr., 3291
Aguirre, B. E., 861
Agulla, J. C., 3, 901
Ahiauzu, Augustine I., 4541
Ahlburg, Dennis A., 5149
Ahmad, Aqueil, 1503
Ahmad, Imtiaz, 1327
Ahmad, Mohiuddin, 4238
Ahmad, Zubeida, 4239
Ahmed, Akbar S., 1328
Ahmetov, K. G., 4775
Aiken, Michael, 4895
Aird, John S., 2768
Ait-Amara, Hamid, 3760
Ait-Sahalia, Rachid, 456
Aitchison, Jean, 167
Aitken, Robert, 1329
Aitov, N., 1089
Aitov, N. A., 2156, 3761
Ajisaka, Manabu, 4922
Akers, Ronald L., 1132
Akimoto, Ritsuo, 4, 5, 93, 871

Akiyama, Kenji, 4452
Akiyama, Takashiro, 1654
Akiyama, Toyoko, 1075
Al-Shahi, Ahmed, 1376
Alaluf, Mateo, 3762
Alarcon, Reynaldo, 4020
Alayon, Norberto, 5381
Alber, Jens, 5257
Alberdi, Inés, 3112
Albrecht, Don E., 4069
Albrecht, Richard, 1631
Albrechts, Stan L., 3803
Alcobendas Tirado, María Pilar, 4240
Aldenderfer, Mark S., 297
Aldrich, John H., 4992
Alehina, Z. F., 5258
Aleksandrova, È., 539
Aleksandrowicz, Dariusz, 6
Alexander, Christian, 3292
Alexander, Jeffrey C., 298
Alexander, Karl L., 1990
Alexander, Kenneth O., 4706
Alexander, Peter, 842
Algozzine, Bob, 2112
Alimoeso, Sudibyo, 3016
Allard, Joseph, 3293
Allard, R., 1614
Allardt, Erik, 2671
Allen, C. G., 167
Allen, P. T., 2247, 4443
Allen, Steven G., 4444
Allende, Cecilia, 5391
Allerbeck, Klaus R., 299
Allo, Eliane, 441, 4871
Allum, Percy, 4993
Almeida, Ayi-Francisco d', 1655
Alnol'dov, A. I., 902
Alo, Oladimej I., 7
Alonso Erausquin, Manuel, 1656
Alpheis, Hannes, 3459
Alsene, E., 4923
Alston, Philip, 4854
Altbach, Philip G., 2031
Althade, Gérard, 3763
Althauser, Robert P., 4176
Altheide, David L., 1657
Altman, Yochanan, 3460
Altschuler, Bruce E., 4994
Alvarez, Elena, 5460
Alvarez de Pérez, María Graciela, 150
Alwin, Duane F., 2125
Amano, Masako, 2562
Amatya, Saphalya, 1010
Ambert, Anne-Marie, 2114
Ambrester, Marcus L., 1541
Amburgey, Terry L., 410
Aminzade, Ronald, 3941

Amiot, Michel, 8
Amis, Philip, 3764
Amuta, Chidi, 1798
Ananta, Aris, 2901
Anctil, Pierre, 3294, 3461
Anděl, Jiří, 2769
Ander Egg, Ezequiel, 5382
Andersen, Arne S., 3974
Andersen, Bent Rold, 5259
Andersen, Jørgen Goul, 4995
Andersen, Susan M., 488
Andersen Sarti, Ingrid, 3609
Anderson, John E., 2902
Anderson, Kathryn H., 2643
Anderson, Paul A., 5046
Anderson, R. J., 9, 5057
Andersson, Lars, 576
Andezian, S., 362
Ando, Hirofumi, 2997
Andorka, Rudolf, 411, 412, 2563, 4350,
    4351, 4352
Andress, Hans-Jürgen, 2369
Andrle, Alois, 3765
Angel, Ronald, 5439
Angelusz, Róbert, 1542, 5260
Anišin, V. A., 2482
Ankerl, Guy, 3766
Anohin, A. M., 2715
Antoine, Jacques, 374
Antonetti, Nicola, 10
Anyang'nyong'o, Pater, 2248
Aoi, Kazuo, 1330
Aparicio, Miriam de Santander, 271
Apfelbaum, Erika, 489
Applebaum, H., 4151
Appleyard, R. T., 3462
Arab-Ogly, E., 2341
Arabie, Phipps, 615
Aragon, Luis E., 3433
Aram, John D., 653
Araragi, Shinzo, 363
Arata, Silvia, 2032, 2329
Arató, Andrew, 4808
Archer, Brian, 4740
Archer, D., 1090
Archetti, Eduardo, 2770
Ardigò, Achille, 1209
Arditis, Solon, 3463
Arguello, Omar, 5086
Arhangel'skij, L. M., 1049
Arias-Godinez, Beatriz, 2133
Arimoto, Akira, 1504, 1891
Arisue, Ken, 364
Arkoun, Mohammed, 1489
Armand, Monique, 4660
Armenakis, Achilles A., 715
Armstrong, Pat, 4241
Arnault, France, 196
Arnhart, Larry, 4855
Arnol'dov, A. O., 1011
Arnold, Odile, 1403
Arnold, Peter, 4375

Aromaa, Kauko, 3076
Aronowitz, Michael, 3464
Aronson, Jonathan D., 1554
Arrianga, Eduardo E., 2847
Arruda, Marcos, 1864
Arthur, W. Brian, 2510
Articus, Stephan, 96, 5345
Asano, Hitoshi, 2762
Asanovic, Sreten, 903
Asch, Susan, 1404
Ascher, François, 4739
Asiana, Setle Opumi, 3767
Ašin, G. K., 4823
Askew, Thomas A., 1405
Asoh, Makoto, 2136
Assiter, Alison, 197
Astilla, Estela, 609
Atchison, John, 3465
Atkinson, Francis D., 2141
Atkinson, Jean, 3054
Atoh, Makoto, 2903
Atoyi, Yoshio, 11
Atti, Stefania, 5435
Attwood, D. W., 3942
Aubery, Pierre, 1406
Audibert, Agnès, 3113
Auer, M. Jane, 3233
Auger, Iván, 1276
August, Jochen, 4242
Augustus, Somerville, 5150
Auster, Donald, 683
Austin, Diane J., 12
Auza, Néstor T., 1331
Avelar, Sonia María, 2309
Aveline, François, 5151, 5154
Avetisjan, É. H., 2033
Avramović, Zoran, 4824
Ayrookuzhiel, A. M. Abraham, 1449
Ayubi, Nazih, 3466
Aziz, Sartaj, 3652
Azovceva, S. G., 1188
Azria, Régine, 1277, 1332

Babadzan, Alain, 2904
Babaev, M. M., 5152
Babb, Lawrence A., 3213
Babeau, André, 3967
Bačškina, T. I., 1505
Bach-Ignasse, Gérard, 3026
Bacharach, Samuel B., 709
Bachellerie, Patrick, 3467
Bachman, Jerald G., 5029, 5120
Bachmann, Christian, 1588
Bachrach, Christine A., 2964
Bäcker, Gerhard, 4353
Bacquet, Alexis, 1658
Baczko, Bronisław, 862
Badeeva, G. V., 2414
Badelt, Christoph, 721
Bădescu, Ilie, 13
Badham, Richard, 2484
Badourès, Anne-Marie, 3653

Badowska, Elżbieta, 3214
Bady, Abamby Zentho, 3654
Baechler, Jean, 4809
Baer, Douglas E., 1050, 2368
Baetens Beardsmore, Hugo, 1589
Baethge, Martin, 2672
Bagella, Michele, 4178
Bages, Robert, 904
Bagnara, Sebastiano, 641, 4354
Bagozzi, Richard P., 2958
Bahr, Jürgen, 3768
Bailey, Caroline, 3055
Bailey, Conner, 4021
Bailey, Kenneth, 198
Bailly, Antoine S., 3572
Bain, George Sayers, 4584
Bainbridge, William Sims, 1278, 1471
Baj, John, 3094
Bajluk, V. V., 540
Balázs, János, 300
Balbo, Laura, 3114
Balevski, Dano, 413
Ball, Stephen J., 2134
Balle, Francis, 1659
Ballhatchet, Kenneth, 2392
Bambawale, Usha, 4309
Bandarage, Asoka, 3215
Bandyopadhyay, Tradas, 863
Banerjee, Biswajit, 3434, 3539, 3540
Banerjee, Kishalay, 4908
Bango, Jenö, 3115
Banister, Judith, 2771
Bankston, William B., 1110
Baño, Rodrigo, 14
Bar-Haim, Gabriel, 94
Baraldi, Claudio, 577
Baran, Józef, 4355
Barbichon, Guy, 1189, 4535
Barboni, E. J., 951
Barbosa Filho, Rubem, 3609
Barbut, Marc, 2186
Bardo, J. W., 3618-19, 3769
Baretze, René, 4740
Barhoum, Mohammed Ima, 4243
Barkan, Steven E., 4856
Barker, Allan, 4585
Barker, Eileen, 1490
Barker, Francis, 1799
Barley, Stephen R., 734
Barling, Julian, 738
Barnes, Howard L., 3056
Barnett, Homer Garner, 15
Baron, James N., 2187, 4324
Barran, José P., 2772
Barrenechea Lercari, Carlos, 4126
Barrère-Maurisson, M.-A., 2564
Barreto, António, 4586
Barrett, Stanley R., 3362
Barrientos, Gustavo, 5408
Barrow, Christine, 375
Barth, Richard P., 5153
Bartmann, Hermann, 638

Bartók, János, 414
Barucci, Piero, 4740
Basavarajappa, K. G., 2905, 3468
Bash, Harry H., 16
Basier, Luc, 1588
Basker, Eileen, 1012
Bastenier, Albert, 1190, 1352
Bastias, Alberto, 4587
Bastid, Marianne, 1922
Bate, Paul, 722
Bateman, N., 301
Bätz, Kurt, 1333
Baubérot, Jean, 1334, 1491
Baudelle, Guy, 3770
Baudelot, Christian, 5154
Bauer, Leonhard, 4152, 4453
Bäuerle, Ferdinand, 1637
Bauhain, Claude, 3116
Baumann, Roland, 2415
Baumgartner, Thomas, 4115
Baviskar, B. S., 3942
Bawin-Legros, Bernadette, 905
Bayart, Denis, 4022
Bayce, Rafaél, 1865
Bayen, Marcel, 4023
Beardsworth, Alan D., 4153
Beaud, Paul, 1091
Beaumont, P. B., 4588, 4589
Beauvais, Laura L., 4378
Becher, Heribert J., 199
Becker, George, 1335
Becker, J. W., 1051
Becker, Stan, 2906
Beckford, James A., 1407
Bedin, Jean-Marie, 4154
Beeghley, Leonard, 5087
Beeker, Carolyn, 617
Beer, Patrice de, 1336
Beer, Ursula, 2188
Befu, Harumi, 5042
Begag, Azouz, 3469
Begaux-Francotte, Colette, 1232
Beggs, John J., 3352
Behrman, Jere R., 1986
Beirne, Piers, 1260
Bejarano González, Fernando, 3655
Béjin, André, 2416, 2565
Béland, François, 2716
Beliveau, Lionel, 5155
Bell, C., 5058
Bell, Peter D., 3656
Bellace, Janice R., 3991
Bellah, Robert N., 1279
Belote, Jim, 3295
Belote, Linda Smith, 3295
Belov, G. A., 4964
Belov, N. I., 2457
Ben Cheikh, Abdelkader, 1800
Ben-Rafael, Eliezer, 3117
Ben-Zadok, Efraim, 4996
Ben-Zeev, Aaron, 541
Benachenhou, A., 117

Benavot, Aaron, 4460
Bencheneb, Ali, 3934
Bendix, Reinhard, 2393
Benediktov, B. A., 1866
Benediktov, N. A., 2417
Benediktov, S. B., 1866
Benencia, Roberto, 4189
Benenson, Harold, 4244
Benguigui, Georges, 764
Bénichou, Pierre, 2090
Benkheira, Mohammed Hocine, 3022
Benko, G. B., 4127
Bennell, Paul, 3992, 4454, 4461
Benner, Jeffrey, 542
Bennett, John, 4542
Bennett, Laura, 4245
Bennett, Neil G., 2848
Bennett, W. Lance, 1660
Benoist, Jean, 2418
Bentham, C. G., 3771
Benyamin, Isabelle, 1543
Beozzo, José Oscar, 3296
Bérard, Pierre, 3023
Berardi, Gigi M., 4070
Berdahl, Robert O., 2071
Berey, Katalin, 3772
Berezina, Ju-I., 2249
Berg, Bruce, 739
Berg, John H., 616
Bergeron, Jean-Louis, 4726
Berghahn, Sabine, 3084
Bergman, Theodor, 3657
Bergquist, Charles, 4155
Berk, Richard A., 5156
Berlin, Sharon B., 5346
Berman, Bruce, 3943
Berman, Yitzhak, 2717, 3438, 3541
Bernal, Ignacio, 4776
Bernard, Léonel, 5157
Bernard, Paul, 2224
Bernard, René, 3542
Berner, Hermann, 365
Berner, Karl-Heinz, 1506
Bernoulli, Andreas, 5232
Bernstein, J. M., 1801
Berque, Jacques, 1337
Berrio, Jordi, 1632
Berry, Colin, 1661
Berry, Michel, 4022
Berry, William Dale, 302
Bertalan, János, 3543
Bertasio, Danila, 132
Bertaux, Daniel, 172
Berthelot, Jean-Michel, 1867
Berthoud, Gérald, 2419
Berti, Béla, 3543
Bertilsson, Margareta, 200
Bertoli, Fernando, 2849
Bertolotti, David S. Jr., 4024
Bertrand, Michel-Jean, 3773
Bertrand, Michèle, 1280, 4731
Beskid, Lidia, 3968

Besnard, Philippe, 5158
Bessonov, B. N., 201
Béteille, A., 2189
Bethke Elshtain, Jean, 3216
Betz, Ellen L., 4246
Beyhaut, Gustavo, 906
Beynier, Dominique, 303
Bezzubov, A. N., 155
Bhachu, Parminder, 684
Bhalla, A. S., 4025
Bhan, Kiran Sumbali, 629
Bhat, Chandrashekhar, 3297
Bhat, M., 3057
Bhat, P. N. Mari, 2945
Bhatia, S. K., 4325
Bhatnagar, Depak, 5347
Bhowmick, Samita, 3123
Biagi, Marta C., 781
Bichot, Jacques, 1092
Bideau, Alain, 2840
Bidou, Catherine, 2250
Bielby, William T., 4257, 4324
Bielefeld, Uli, 4247
Bielenski, Harabi, 5261
Biernacka, Maria, 1013
Bierschenk, Thomas, 1338
Biggart, Nicole Woolsey, 4896
Bihl, Luc, 4099
Bihr, Alain, 2251
Billaz, René, 3658
Billet, Jean, 2511, 2511
Billig, Wilhelm, 2773
Billis, David, 5262
Billy, John O. G., 3024
Binet, Jacques, 4128
Binns, David, 3118
Birch, Anthony H., 4825
Birrell, R., 3435
Bishop, Donna M., 5159
Black, Donald V., 156
Black, Jerome H., 4997
Blaffer, Hardy, 5188
Blake, Judith, 2907
Blakey, Robert G., 4743
Blalock, Hubert Jr., 346
Blalock, Hubert M., 304
Blanchard, Francis, 4026
Blanchot, Maurice, 2342
Blancpain, Robert, 2673
Blankoff-Scarr, G., 1590
Blanpain, Roger, 4690
Blaser, Arthur W., 4857
Blashfield, Roger K., 297
Blass, Thomas, 457
Blau, Peter M., 617
Bleitrach, Danielle, 2343
Blinova, L. N., 843
Bliss, Frank, 2485
Block, A. de, 1923
Block, Bernhard, 4179
Blom, Raimo, 2252
Blondeau, Danielle, 2823

Bloom, David E., 2908, 2909
Blossfeld, Hans-Peter, 1924, 4462
Blüm, Norbert, 5263
Blum, Terry C., 3363, 3774
Blumberg, Melvin, 110
Blumenson, Diane, 4375
Blunt, Peter, 5088
Blythe, Betty J., 5153
Blyton, Paul, 4590, 4707
Boado, Alicia, 5121
Boalt Boëthius, Siv, 674
Boasso, Camilo A., 1233
Bociurkiw, Bohdan R., 1339
Bock, Ulla, 3217
Bodalev, A. A., 514
Boden, Margaret A., 133
Body-Gendrot, Sophie, 3298
Boemer, Marilyn Laurence, 1662
Boerma, J. T., 2910
Bogart, Leo, 1663
Bogdanov, V. A., 515
Bogun, Manfred, 4356
Boguo, Makeli, 1591
Boguslawski, Alexander, 4965
Bőhm, Antal, 3620
Bohnen, Alfred, 1544
Boholm, Asa, 3119
Bois, Paul, 3659
Bois, Pierre du, 1592
Boisard, Pierre, 4357
Bojko, P. N., 2420
Bokan', Ju. I., 2421
Bokszański, Zbigniew, 490
Bolander, Ann-Marie, 2850
Boldyrev, V. A., 2512
Boleda, Mario, 3436, 3544
Bölling, Rainer, 2126
Bolster, Arthur S. Jr., 1868
Boltanski, Luc, 4527
Bolte, Karl Martin, 4138
Bond, Andrew R., 3775
Bongaarts, John, 2965
Bonjean, Charles M., 762
Bonnamour, Jacqueline, 3660
Bonney, Bill, 1664
Bonvalet, Catherine, 3776
Bookman, John T., 2157
Booth, Alan, 4248
Booth, Alison, 864
Booth, David B., 95
Booth, Heather, 2911
Booth, John A., 4826
Böpple, Arthur, 5264
Borchorst, Anette, 2566
Bordenave, Juan E. Díaz, 1545
Borev, V. Ju., 1546
Borg, Walter R., 3637
Borggrefe, Friedhelm, 1340
Borgognoni, Ezio, 5122
Borillo, Mario, 134
Borjas, George J., 4463
Bornschier, Volker, 2190

Borowicz, Ryszard, 2674
Borsoni, Paolo, 4771
Borstow, B., 2083
Bortaz, V., 305
Bose, Christine E., 4249
Bose, Pradip Kumar, 3661
Böseke, Harry, 4180
Bossio, Juan Carlos, 4027
Bostock, W., 3299, 3364
Bosworth, Edmund, 2394
Botoas, B. P., 1925
Bottomore, T., 17
Bouchayer, Françoise, 5461
Bouchier, David, 3218
Boudon, Raymond, 202, 844, 2422
Bouffartigue, Paul, 4708
Bougerol, Christiane, 5394
Bouhdiba, Abdelwahab, 3025
Bouillin-Dartevelle, Roselyne, 2675
Boulier, Bryan L., 3058
Boulot, Serge, 2115
Bourdelais, Patrice, 2718
Bourdieu, Pierre, 2127, 2253, 4760
Bourguignon, Odile, 2851
Bourhis, Richard Y., 693
Bourin, Monique, 3662
Bourne, Larry S., 3777
Bourquelot, Françoise, 4506
Bourricaud, François, 202
Boutin, André, 2128
Boutinet, J. P., 4181
Bouvier Colle, Marie-Hélène, 2852
Bouwen, René, 4528
Bouyou, Maurice, 3653
Bova, Vincenzo, 639
Bovone, Laura, 184, 4529
Bowen, Kurt Derek, 1341
Bowers, William J., 5160
Boyle, Harry J., 1665
Boyle, William, 3637
Boyman, Elsa, 2912
Boyson-Fradet, Danielle, 2115
Bozon, Michel, 3778
Braam, G. P. A., 2719, 4473
Brabin, Loretta, 3059
Bradnock, Robert W., 3779
Braehmer, Uwe, 3993
Braga de Cruz, Manuel, 2676
Brahimi, Denise, 3219
Brainerd, Gordon R. Jr., 1119
Brambila, Carlos, 3780
Brambilla, Francesco, 5089
Bramlette, Carl A. Jr., 4042
Branch, Kristi, 2423, 2476
Brand, Karl-Werner, 4924
Brandt, Eberhard, 5383
Braszeil, Anne, 3217
Braun, Frank, 4464
Braun, Hans, 96, 5263
Braungart, Margaret M., 2720, 4966, 4967
Braungart, Richard G., 2635, 4966, 4967
Bravo, Héctor Félix, 1926

Brebant, Brigitte, 5090
Brechon, Pierre, 1342
Breckler, Steven J., 806
Breen, Richard, 272, 4182
Bremicker, Burckhardt, 4183
Bremond, Claude, 3120
Brenna, A., 5462
Brennan, Jerry, 916
Brenot-Ouldali, Annie, 4886
Breton, Albert, 3060
Breton, Raymond, 1547
Breuer, Stefan, 1234
Brewer, John D., 3365, 4777
Briand, Jean-Pierre, 2191
Brick, Barbara, 248
Briggs, Stephen R., 1094
Brinkerhoff, Merlin B., 4028
Brint, Steven, 4968
Brischetto, Robert, 714
Brittan, Arthur, 3366
Britten, Nicky, 2254, 2620
Broadhead, Robert S., 97
Brodeur, J.-P., 5161
Brogden, Ann, 4872
Brogden, Mike, 4872
Brohm, Jean-Marie, 4741
Bromlej, Ju. V., 872, 2486
Bromlej, N. Ta., 907
Bronfman, Mario, 2192
Bronsztejn, Szyja, 2774
Brook, Robert H., 5464
Brosio, Giorgio, 4897
Broughton, John M., 1210, 2605
Brow, Phil, 2824
Browaeys, Xavier, 4156
Brown, Harold I., 203
Brown, Rupert, 704
Browne, Eric C., 908
Browne, Ray B., 794
Brownell, Arlene, 5348
Bruce, Steve, 1314
Bruchis, Michael, 1593
Bruckmeier, Karl, 5162
Bruckmüller, Ernst, 3663
Brückner, Peter, 4925
Brun, François, 4184
Bruneau, Michel, 2255, 3787
Brunet, Luc, 4358
Brunetta, G., 5123, 5163
Brunk, Gregory G., 5016
Brunner, José Joaquín, 18, 19, 833, 909,
  1507, 1508, 1869, 2034
Brusten, M., 5250
Brůžek, Miloslav, 910
Bryant, Christopher G. A., 20
Brygoo, Angélina, 4184
Brym, Robert J., 3536
Bryman, Alan, 98
Brzezinski, Jerzy, 480
Buba, Hans-Peter, 3061
Bubis, Gerald B., 1343
Bubnovič, A. V., 1093

Buchmann, Marlis, 173
Buchner-Jeziorska, Anna, 2193
Büchtemann, Christoph F., 4185
Buck, David D., 3819
Buckland, Peter, 1870
Buckley, Anthony D., 1344
Budd, Richard J., 204
Buechler, Steve, 2567
Bueno Arus, Francisco, 5164
Bueva, L., 516
Bühl, Walter L., 640, 2424
Bujra, Janet M., 2568
Buksti, Jacob A., 4591
Bullinger, Martin, 1666
Bullivant, Brian Milton, 911
Bulmer, Martin, 21
Bulthe, Bruno, 5165
Bumgarner, George William, 1408
Bumpass, Larry L., 3062
Bunker, Stephen G., 2487
Burakowski, Stanisław, 912
Burawoy, Michael, 3944
Burgalassi, Silvano, 1281, 2721
Burgat, François, 3665
Burgdorff, Stephan, 4359
Burgess, Robert G., 1871
Burghart, Richard, 1345
Burk, James, 4778
Burke, Edmund III, 22
Burkett, Steven R,, 1074
Burnham, Ly, 2806
Burns, Tom R., 998, 4115
Burov, V., 5068
Bursik, Robert J. Jr., 3781
Burstyn, Varda, 4827
Bursztyn, Marcel, 4129
Burt, Ronald S., 661
Burton, John, 4583
Burton, Michael G., 2344
Busino, Giovanni, 23, 2419
Buslov, K. P., 3121, 3573
Buss, Arnold H., 1094
Buss, Eugen, 4110
Büsser, Detlef, 4924
Butera, Federico, 3994
Butler, John Sibley, 3367
Buttel, Frederick H., 2569
Buturlov, R. V., 2425
Buzov, Željko, 5059
Byars, Lloyd L., 4326
Bynum, Timothy S., 5166
Bystryn, Marcia H., 3033

Cable, Sherry, 4926
Cabral, Nelson E., 1594
Cacaly, Serge, 157
Caceres, Baldomero, 5124
Cacioppe, Ron, 4465
Cacopardo, Maria Cristina, 3470
Caesar, Michael, 1802
Cahali, Yussef Said, 3300
Cahn, Dudley D., 1551

Cain, Glen G., 1991
Cain, M., 2913
Cairns, Ed, 3301
Cal, A. Victoria, 814
Čaldarović, Ognjen, 3782
Calder, Bobby J., 1162
Calderón, Fernando, 4898
Caldwell, Gary, 3461
Caldwell, J. C., 2914, 3063
Calinescu, Matei, 913
Calista, Donald J., 1052
Callan, Victor J., 2644, 2966, 2967
Calnan, Michael, 5409
Calot, Gérard, 2513, 2636, 2775
Cámara, Gabriel, 2084
Camargo, Aspásia, 174
Camilleri, C., 914, 1053, 2035
Campbell, Colin, 826
Campbell, Eugene K., 2853
Campbell, Everett J., 3368
Campbell, J. Gabriel, 379
Campbell, James E., 4998
Campbell, Jennifer, 626
Campbell, Karen E., 1141
Campbell, Rex R., 3545
Campbell, Richard T., 2370
Campbell, Susan M., 2426
Campbell, William F., 5102
Campero, Guillermo, 4592
Campos Manzo, José Maria, 1633
Caniou, Juliette, 3220
Cannon, Lynn Weber, 2256
Canovas Sanchez, Francisco, 2677
Cantell, Ilkka, 3076
Caplow, Theodore, 1054
Cappelli, Peter, 4551
Caprara, G. V., 630
Capy, Marcelle, 4322
Carboni, Carlo, 2257
Cardin, Michèle, 3221
Cardona Escanero, Gabriel, 5030
Carduner, Jean, 915
Caregorodcev, G. I., 5395
Careres Prendes, J., 4957
Caride, José Antonio, 1872
Carlson, Elwood, 1409
Carlson, Elwood D., 2915
Carlton, Eric, 845
Carmel, Joseph, 3922
Carmignani, Fabrizo, 4360
Caro, Jean-Yves, 74
Carpentier, Renée, 4029
Carr-Hill, Roy A., 5265
Carroll, Glenn R., 410, 1667, 3574
Carroll, James Elwood, 1408
Carroll, Lucy, 1346
Carroll, Michael P., 1803
Carroll, Susan J., 3222
Carroll, Terrance G., 1282
Carroll, Thomas M., 4568
Carroll, William K., 481
Carter, P., 1459

Cartier, Michel, 2514
Cartocci, Roberto, 1055
Carvajal, A. Guillermo, 3546
Casanova, José, 1492, 4808
Casas, Rosalba, 4030
Caselli, Graziella, 2854
Casey, Neil, 740
Cashmore, Ernes Ellis, 3369
Caspard, Pierre, 1873
Casper, Dale E., 4250
Casterline, B., 2947
Castiglione, Laurence V., 1927
Castillo, Juan José, 4327
Castles, Stephen, 3370
Castro, Ginette, 3223
Castro de Salmerón, Alicia, 150
Catanzaro, Raimondo, 2258
Catsiapis, Jean, 2515, 3471
Cattell, Raymond B., 916
Cauet, Sylvie, 4116
Cavailhes, Jean, 3026
Cavalli, Alessandro, 2678, 4117
Cavestro, William, 4031
Čeharin, É. M., 517, 917
Cela, Jorge, 3783
Célem, Rosangela, 5167
Cernea, Michael M., 3666
Černega, V. N., 2345
Cernescu, Traila, 3122
Cerulo, Karen A., 1842
Cesareo, Giovanni, 1668
Cesareo, Vincenzo, 2427, 4529
Chabaud, Danielle, 2570
Chabbi, Morched, 3784
Chabry, Annie, 685
Chabry, Laurent, 685
Chaffee, Wilber A., 5022
Chai, Bin Park, 3016
Chaigneau, Pascal, 1669
Chaki-Sircas, Manjusri, 3224
Chakraborty, Prafulla, 3123
Cham, Mbye Baboucar, 1670
Chamberlin, John R., 865
Champagne, Patrick, 866
Champion, Françoise, 1450
Chandler, G., 158
Chandon-Moet, Bernard, 1347
Chang, A. Ligia, 4466
Chang, Ming-Cheng, 2641
Chang, Yun Shik, 3667
Chapman, Diana Danforth, 3635
Chapoulie, Jean-Michel, 366
Charbonneau, Hubert, 2776
Charle, Christophe, 3064
Charles, Jean-François, 5349
Charlton, Jacqueline H., 4709
Charney, Craig, 4593
Charraud, Alain, 5410
Charria Angulo, Pedro, 1670
Chassaing, Françoise, 2001
Chassin, Laurie, 491
Chatelain, Paul, 4156

Chatterjee, Lata, 3785
Chatterji, Probhat Chandra, 1014
Chaudhry, Kiren Aziz, 834
Chaudhuri, Buddhadeb, 2002
Chaudhuri, K. K., 1095
Chaudhuri, P. N., 2807
Chaudhury, Rafiqul Huda, 4251
Chaumont, Roselyne, 4032
Chávez Pérez, Guillermo, 4467
Chayet, Ellen F., 5183
Chayovan, Napaporn, 2968
Chebel, Malek, 1548
Chekki, Dan A., 5060
Chen, Chao-nan, 2969
Cheng, Joseph L. C., 741
Cherki, Eddy, 1671
Cherni, Zeineb, 1804
Chernichovsky, Dov, 2916
Chhachhi, Amrita, 4594
Chiang, Chin Long, 2855
Chiba, Masashi, 118
Chichilnisky, Graciela, 442
Chinn, David, 4071
Chittenden, Wendy H., 4083
Chitwood, Dale D., 5137
Chlewiński, Zdzisław, 1472
Cho, Lee-Jay, 2946
Choldin, Harvey M., 3586
Chowdhury, Omar Haider, 5266
Christenson, James A., 1056, 3621
Christenson, R. L., 2955, 5236, 5237
Christiansen, Robert, 3547
Christoffersen, Hans Rohr, 4595
Christopher, W. I., 5448
Christy, Carol A., 4969
Ciancaglini, Michelangelo, 4596
Ciano, Jane, 2019
Cibois, Philippe, 306
Ciborra, C., 742
Ciechocińska, Maria, 415
Cigir', A. É., 3121
Cipko, A. S., 4779
Cipressi, Pierpaolo, 4220
Cipriani, Roberto, 1348, 1509
Cirba, Laurence, 5168
Ciria, Alberto, 2036
Ciszewski, Robert L., 3007
Ciupak, Edward, 1473
Civikly, Jean M., 1549
Claessen, Hans, 4828
Clapier-Valladon, S., 918
Claramunt, Ana N., 1992
Clark, Alfred W., 807
Clark, Frieda, 3905, 3906
Clark, Janet M., 3225
Clark, Malcolm, 1235
Clark, Ruth, 3404
Clark, Samuel D. Jr., 3027
Clarke, Alan H., 5169
Clarke, Alex M., 2037
Clarke, Chris, 2096
Clausen, John A., 458

Clausse, Arnould, 1874
Clavaud, Richard, 1671
Clavel, Maïté, 846
Cleary, Paul D., 5439
Cleland, J. G., 2902, 2947
Clelland, Donald A., 4630
Clement, Jérôme, 1672
Clement, R., 3371
Clermont, Louise, 4252
Clifton, Rodney A., 3376
Clignet, Rémi, 4438
Climent de Zajelenczyc, Graciela, 5463
Clogg, Clifford C., 4455
Close, Paul, 4361
Cloward, Richard A., 5094
Clune, William H. III, 2022
Cluzel, Jean, 1015
Coale, Ansley J., 2777, 2917
Cobalti, Antonio, 1875
Cobbe, James H., 1876
Cochran, Larry, 518
Cocks, Joan, 3226
Code, Lorraine B., 2571
Coenen-Huther, Jacques, 367
Coffy, Robert, 1410
Cogges-Hall, Porter E., 125
Cohen, Abraham, 4688
Cohen, Ayala, 307
Cohen, E., 3303, 3786, 4742, 5069
Cohen, Lawrence H., 5464
Cohen, Myron S., 5446
Cohen, Yolande, 2038, 3227
Cohn, Steven F., 3028
Cohran, Daniel S., 5440
Coing, Helmut, 4887
Coleman, Hyvel, 1595
Coleman, James S., 1991, 2006, 2018
Collignon, René, 5396
Collins, Randall, 1096
Collins, Rosie, 4361
Colliot-Thélène, Catherine, 205
Collot, Claudette, 2722
Colombis, Alessio, 2158
Colomer, Fernando, 1283
Colorni, Vittore, 1349
Colvez, A., 2892
Combessie, Jean-Claude, 2194
Combs, James E., 1191
Compton. P. A., 2856
Condé, J., 3472
Condé, Maryse, 1805
Condran, Gretchen A., 2516
Conen, Gabriele, 4970
Conger, Rand D., 3173
Conlisk, John, 1928
Connel, R. W., 2259
Consoli, Francesco, 4543
Conze, Werner, 3124
Cook, Judith A., 99
Cookingham, Mary E., 3065
Coolahan, John, 4033
Coolen, J. A., 5465

Cooper, Bruce S., 1929
Cooper, H. H. A., 5170
Cooper, H. J., 2949
Cooper, Joel, 707
Cooper, Mark N., 3945
Cooper, Robert L., 1596
Coppock, Rob, 4034
Corcos, E., 4049
Cordeiro, Albano, 5351
Corder, Judy, 762
Cordier, Alain, 5125
Coriat, Benjamin, 4346
Corin, Ellen, 5352
Corke, Michael, 1993
Corlay, Jean-Pierre, 4072
Cormack, Ian R. N., 2428
Cornejo, María del Carmen, 5391
Cornell, Stephen, 3372
Cornes, Paul, 2825
Corouges, Christian, 4544
Corraze, Jacques, 1597
Cortellazzi, Silvia, 4139
Cortese, Anthony J., 273
Corvalan, Graziella, 1598
Costa, Paolo, 4740
Costa-Lascoux, J., 3473
Costin, Lela B., 1930
Coughenour, C. Milton, 3575
Coughlan, Anthony, 5267
Courade, Georges, 3787
Courgeau, Daniel, 2857
Cox, D., 3437
Coyle, A., 4253
Coyne, Margaret Urban, 800
Crabb, Edward G., 2195
Craft, James A., 4597
Craib, Ian, 206
Crandall, James E., 543
Craven, B. M., 2039
Crean, Susan, 5041
Creemers, Bert P. M., 1931
Crespi, Pietro, 1550
Crimmins, Eileen M., 2778
Crisp, Jeff, 4507
Crocker, Jennifer, 4445
Croix, Alain, 1451
Crombie, Alastair D., 2085
Crook, Anne, 308
Cropley, A. J., 3474
Cross, Kathryn Patricia, 2086
Cross, Theodore L., 3373
Crosson, Patricia H., 2040
Crouse, James, 2376
Crouter, Ann C., 3125
Crozier, Michel, 2020
Cseh-Szombathy, László, 919, 3066, 3126
Cuatrecasas, Juan, 631
Cuban, Larry, 1994
Čulinović-Konstantinović, Vesna, 3127
Cummings, Scott, 119
Cuneo, Carl J., 2260
Cunningham, J. Barton, 4362

Curien, Nicolas, 1673
Curry, Evans W., 404
Curtis, Bruce, 1932
Curtis, James, 2261
Curtis, James E., 1050
Cushman, Donald P., 1551
Cuthbert, Alexander, 3819
Cutright, Phillips, 416, 2929
Cutrona, Carolyn E., 593
Czajka, Stanisław, 4363
Czerwiński, Marcin, 873

D'Arcy, Carl, 4364
Da Silva, José Ariovaldo, 1440
Dąbrowska, Grażyna, 5268
Dabscheck, Braham, 4691
Dahl, Tove Stang, 3228
Dahmann, Donald C., 3788
Dähn, Horst, 1411
Daido, Yasujiro, 3789
Daix, Pierre, 1767
Dalessio, Anthony, 380
Daley, Dennis, 743
Dalton, Dan R., 4545
Daly, Kathleen, 1183
Damiani, Paul, 2858
Damien, André, 3128
Damrosz, Jerzy, 4130
Damus, Martin, 1834
Danda, Ajit K., 2970
Dandurand, P., 4221
Dániel, Zsuzsa, 3790
Daniels Shepard, Marietta, 159
Danilova, É. Z., 4272
Dannefer, Dale, 2708
Danon-Boileau, Henri, 2116
Danziger, Nira, 3475
Danziger, Raymond, 3995
Daragan, N. Ja, 3374
Darczewska, Krystyna, 1350
Dardis, Rachel, 4100
Darity, William A., 3129
Darkenwald, Gordon G., 2087
Darmau, Frédéric, 3791
Darré, Jean-Pierre, 1057
Darveau-Fournier, Lise, 5466
Das, Arvind N., 3668, 4508
Das, Veena, 1351
Das Gupta, Amitabha, 1526
Dašdamirov, A. F., 519
Dasgupta, Hoimanti, 1097
Dassetto, Felice, 1352
Dasvarma, G. L., 2859
Datler, Wilfried, 1877
Davey, Judith A., 5467
David, Marie-Gabrielle, 2645
Davidson, Andrew R., 815
Davidson, Bernard, 3067
Davis, Charles H., 120
Davis, James A., 376, 417
Davis, Kingsley, 4254
Davis, Leonard, 5468

Davis, Marvin, 3669
Davis, Michael, 5171
Davis, Nancy, 2971
Davis, Tim R., 795
Davtjan, A. G., 4829, 4971
Day, Alice Taylor, 2919
Day, Lincoln H., 2918, 2919
De Barros, José Tavares, 1674
De Castro, Iná Elias, 3792
De Cola, Lee, 2779
De Friedemann, Nina S., 1192
De la Villa, Luis Enrique, 4546
De Laet, C., 4873
De Leeuw, E. D., 384
De Leonardis, Ota, 5411
De Martini, Joseph R., 2041
De Mesquita Samara, Eni, 2517
De Miguel, Jesús M., 5412
De Moura Castro, Cláudio, 2088
De Oliveira, Zuleica Lopes Cavalcanti, 2518, 4255
De Paulo, Bella M., 605
De Pina Cabral, João, 3229, 3793
De Rivera, Joseph, 544
De Ruiter, Bob, 3796
De Tezanos, Araceli, 1933
Deakin, Stephen, 3476
Dean, E., 1878
Dean, John, 1316
Deaux, Kay, 820, 4445
Deberdt, Michel, 4256
Debray, Quentin, 1193
Decleve, H., 1098
Deconchy, Jean-Pierre, 808, 1431
Degiovanni, Patrick, 3130
Dehaene, J. L., 5441
Dejemeppe, Benôit, 1099
Del Acebo Ibañez, Enrique, 3794
Del Aguila, Rafael, 847
Del Nero Da Costa, Iraci, 2517
Del Vento Bielby, Denise, 4257
Delacampagne, Christian, 3375
Delaleu, A., 4181
Delamotte, Yves, 4365
Delcourt, J., 1879, 1880
Deldime, Roger, 1851
Deley, Warren W., 4366
Deliens, L., 381
Della Selva, Patricia C., 2679
Delle Donne, Marcella, 3795
Delli Carpini, Michael X., 4367
Dembinski, Pawel H., 5269
Demeny, Paul, 2780
Demers, Marie, 4186
Demin, V. M., 4157
Demyk, M., 4810
Den Boon, A. K., 3796
Denni, Bernard, 1342
Dennis, Carolyne, 4258
Dent, Owen, 2658
Denton, Margaret A., 3246
Denton, Robert E. Jr., 4951

Denzin, Norman K., 175, 3131
Denzler, Georg, 1412
Depner, Rolf, 5384
Deppe, Frank, 4598
Depretto, Jean-Paul, 4599
Deprez, K., 1599
Dermutz, Susanne, 1934
Des Harnais, Gaston, 735
Des Pres, T., 1814
Desheriev, Yunus D., 2429
Desjardins, Bertrand, 2723
Desplanques, Guy, 2860
Dettling, Warnfried, 4600
Deutschmann, Christoph, 4601
Dev, Bimal J., 2233
Devadoss, Mudiappasamy, 2042
Devevey, J., 5479
Deville, Jean-Claude, 3130
Devillé, Philippe, 4115
Devine, T. M., 3931
Dews, Peter, 76
Dex, Shirley, 4259
Dhavernas, Marie-Jo, 2572
Di Bernardo, Giuliano, 5270
Di Chiara, Albert, 5172
Di Franceisco, Wayne, 4972
Di Giorgi, Piero, 2681
Di Maria, F., 5173
Di Stefano, Thomas, 642
Di Tella, Torcuato, 4909
Diani, Maro, 641
Diaz-Briquets, Sergio, 2927, 3477
Dickie-Clarke, H. F., 309
Dickson, David, 3931
Dienelt, Karl, 207
Díez Hochleitner, Ricardo, 1935
Díez Medrano, Juan, 2972
Dilchev, Konstantin, 2346
Diligenskij, G. G., 2262
Dillig, Peter, 5174
Dillon, M. C., 3304
Dillon, Michele, 2682
Dimitrijević, Dušan, 5469
Dinitto, Diana, 418
Dinkel, R. H., 2861-62, 2973
Dino, Gusine, 1806
Dion, Stéphane, 4899
Dirn, Louis, 2724
Dissanayake, Wimal, 15ᶜ '
Diwan, Paras, 3068
Dixon, Ruth, 4509
Dixon, Ruth B., 3230
Djaït, Hichem, 1058
Djiwandono, A. Sudiharto, 2430
Djorkjević, Živorad, 2347
Dobles, Ricardo R., 1936
Dobratz, Betty A., 2263
Dobrianov, Velichko, 419
Dobrowolska, Danuta, 4368
Dobson, William R., 485
Doby, John T., 3183
Dodge, Peter, 1937

Dogalov, A. G., 1100
Dogbé, Yves Emmanuel, 5091
Doh, Rainer, 2974, 3797
Dohse, Knuth, 4260
Doise, Willem, 459
Dokučaeva, T. N., 2725
Dolton, Peter J., 2573
Domański, Henryk, 4158, 4468
Domenach, Jean-Marie, 274
Dometrius, Nelson C., 4888
Dominguez, Virginia R., 1012
Dommergues, Pierre, 4602
Don-Yehiya, Eliezer, 1299
Donati, Paolo R., 744
Donati, Pierpaolo, 578, 5271
Donegani, Jean-Marie, 1353
Doppelt, Gerald, 4858
Dorđević, Dragoljub B., 1452
Doreian, Patrick, 310, 314
Dorlhac de Borne, Hélène, 5175
Dorn, Nicholas, 5126
Dornbusch, Sanford M., 3132
Doskač, A. G., 311
Doumanis, Mariella, 3133
Dove, Janine, 1317
Dow, Gwyneth, 2129
Dow, Malcolm M., 312
Doyle, Anna-Beth, 3134
Dozier, Carol, 1755
Drache, Daniel, 5041
Dragosavac, Dušan, 3305
Drake, Richard, 1101
Drancourt, Michel, 4369
Drass, Kriss A., 3416
Dray, J., 4049
Drbohlav, Vlastimil, 5353
Dreier, Peter, 3798
Dreifelds, Juris, 2519
Dric, V. I., 2159
Driedger, Leo, 3376
Droge, Ulfert, 315
Drouard, Alain, 24
Drudy, Sheelagh, 2160
Drüke, Helmut, 1675
Du Pasquier, Roger, 1354
Du Ranquet, Mathilde, 5385
Du Ross, Daniel J., 5472
Dubar, C., 2089, 4469
Dube, S., 5413
Dubet, François, 4662
Dubey, P. S., 4508
Dubey, Sumati Narain, 5470
Duborgel, Bruno, 2130
Dubost, J., 111, 460
Duckett, S. J., 5442
Duckworth, Derek, 2826
Duclos, Denis, 4370
Ducret, Jean-Jacques, 461
Duczkowska-Malysz, Katarzyna, 1059
Dudley, Edward J., 1600
Dugger, William M., 4371
Duijx, A. W. M., 384

Dumais, Alfred, 1284
Dumas, Claude, 3029
Dumazedier, Joffre, 176
Dumont, Gérard-François, 2520
Dumont, J. P., 5061
Dumont, Louis, 618
Dumont, Martine, 2634
Dumont, Paul, 1355
Duncan, Otis Dudley, 462
Dunde, Siegfried Rudolf, 632
Dunham, Randall B., 745
Dupâquier, Jacques, 2521
Dupâquier, Michel, 2522
Dupont, Véronique, 2523
Duprez, Dominique, 3799
Dupupet, Michel, 3576
Duran Heras, María Angeles, 2196
Durand, Jacques, 1676
Durand, Michelle, 4692
Durand, Robert, 3662
Durand, Yves, 1938
Durez-Demal, Martine, 3800
Durham, Eunice R., 920
Dürholt, Eva, 4328
Dusek, Jerome B., 2679
Dussault, Georges, 2524
Dutey, Pierre, 3026
Dutter, Lee E., 3306
Dworkin, James B., 4372
Dwyer, Máire, 5467
Dynes, Russell R., 121
Dyson, Tim, 2877
Dytrych, Zdeněk, 3089
Dziewulski, Henryk, 208
Dzinic, Firdus, 1677-78
Džioev, O. I., 209
Dzun, Włodzimierz, 4510, 4710
Džunusov, M. S., 2431

Eadington, William R., 4743
Eaglstein, A. Solomon, 3438
Eagly, Alice H., 801
Earhart, H. Byron, 1285
Earnhardt, Kent C., 2525
Ebata, Aaron, 5181
Ebbinghausen, Rolf, 4603
Eberstein, Isaac W., 2863, 3801
Eberts, Randall W., 2131
Eberwein, Wolf-Dieter, 5050
Eccles (Parsons), Jacqueline, 545
Ecklein, Joan, 3231
Edebiri, U., 1852
Eder, Donna, 567, 705
Edgar, Patricia, 1552
Edie, Carlene J., 5023
Edleson, Jeffrey L., 3519
Edmonston, Barry, 3802
Edney, Julian J., 5272
Edwards, David J., 579
Edwards, Paul, 4446
Effler, Manfred, 594
Efimova, N. Ju., 546

Egan, Kieran, 1102
Egashira, Seigo, 782
Egelund, Tine, 5471
Egidi, Viviana, 2864
Eglite, P., 2526
Egorov, A. G., 921
Ehara, Takekazu, 2043
Ehara, Yumiko, 2574
Ehrenreich, Barbara, 4264
Ehrlich, Konrad, 1553
Eickelman, Christine, 2575
Ejima, Shusaku, 1103, 1441
Ekanem, Ita I., 2865
Ekert, Olivia, 5354
Ekerwald, Hedvig, 2117
Ekpenyong, Stephen, 3622
Ekstedt, John W., 5176
El Borat, Ahmad, 4569
Elboudrari, Hassan, 1356, 1357
Elcock, Howard, 4131
Elegoet, Fanch, 3670
Eliash, Ben Zion, 3135
Elklit, Jorgen, 3307
Ellingsaeter, Anne Lise, 4406
Ellis, Carolyn, 3623
Ellis, G. F. R., 5092
Elsheikh, Farouk, 4584
Elsinga, E., 4973
Elzinga, Aant, 1516
Emna, Ben-Miled, 2683
Enderwitz, Herbert, 1939
Endicott, Kirk, 3308
Endrighetto, Tommasina, 4993
Engineer, Asghar Ali, 1104
England, J. Lynn, 3803
England, Paula, 2576
England, Robert E., 3331
Engo, Pierre-Désiré, 5355
Enomoto, Kazuko, 2726
Enosh, Nava, 3804
Enriquez, Eugène, 463, 746, 1105
Entwisle, Barbara, 2975
Enyedi, György, 3805
Epema, J. M., 4187
Epskamp, Kees, 1853
Epstein, Simon, 3377
Eraly, Alain, 4373
Ercole, Enrico, 3806
Erdei, Ferenc, 5273
Erdmann, Claudia, 3807
Eremenko, V. A., 520
Erfurt, U., 848
Erickson, Maynard L., 5177
Erikson, Robert, 2264
Erina, É. B., 275
Erkomaišvili, V., 3597
Ermisch, J. F., 2577
Erohin, V. G., 5395
Ervin, Delbert, 2578
Ervin, Delbert J., 3808
Esaiasson, Peter, 4671
Escala, Alberto, 2044

Escario, Pilar, 3112
Escotet, Miguel Angel, 1940
Esenwein-Rothe, Ingeborg, 5356
Esler, Anthony, 2637, 2638
Espérandieu, Véronique, 2090
Esposito, Elena, 492
Esser, Hartmut, 313
Establet, Roger, 5154
Eth, Spencer, 2646
Evangelisti, Valerio, 2197
Evans, Arthur S., 77
Evans, Debbie, 5450
Evans, Jeremy, 2781
Eve, Susan Brown, 5443
Evêquoz, Grégoire, 2021
Everett, J. E., 4530
Evers, Tilman, 4927
Exum, William H., 4445
Eyerman, Ron, 4928
Eyraud, François, 4470
Eyre, L. Alan, 1106
Ezekiel, Raphael S., 5093
Ezrahi, Yarom, 1516

Fabbrini, Sergio, 4035
Fabiani, Jean-Louis, 4073
Fabre-Rosane, Gilles, 1679
Fabricius, Volker, 1412
Fadda, Giulietta, 4929
Faison, Barbara H., 3624
Faivre, Denise, 4471
Falk, Gerhard, 1107
Fall, Mar, 4604
Fallding, Harold, 1358
Fallenstein, Klaus, 2091
Fandiño, Graciela, 1941
Faragó, Katalin P., 4874
Fararo, Thomas J., 276, 314, 391, 662, 1060
Farber, S. C., 2932, 3548
Farge, Arlette, 3232
Fargues, Philippe, 2866
Faria, José Eduardo, 1236
Farkas, Katalin, 3969
Farkas, Zoltán, 4511
Farrell, B., 3625
Farrell, Dan, 4447
Farrell, Gilda, 3671
Farry, Marcelle, 557
Faser, Mark, 5127
Fassin, Didier, 464
Faugeron, Claude, 1237
Faunce, William A., 2118
Favilli, Paolo, 4605
Fazio, Russell H., 493
Feather, H. R., 4780
Feather, N. T., 1474
Fecteau, J. M., 1108
Feder, Judith, 5444
Fedorik, V. M., 835
Fedorov, É. K., 5051
Fedorovskaja, É., 539
Fedoseev, A. A., 5024

Fedotova, V. G., 100
Feeney, G., 2920
Feger, Hubert, 315
Fehér, Ferenc, 4930
Feketekuty, Geza, 1554
Feldman, Lauren S., 612
Felling, A., 922, 4781
Felmlee, Diane, 705
Felson, Richard B., 5178
Fendrich, Michael, 4261
Fennema, Elizabeth, 3233
Fenster, Mark J., 4999
Fenton, Steve, 210
Fenyö, Stefano, 277
Feragus, Jacques, 2827
Ferge, Zsuzsa, 1109, 2579, 5274
Ferguson, Ann, 3030
Ferguson, Douglas W., 1442
Ferguson, Kathy E., 747
Ferlie, Ewan, 5445
Ferman, Louis A., 4606
Fernández, Arturo, 5275
Fernández, Marta E., 781, 2032, 2329
Ferra, Coloma, 1992
Ferrand, Dominique J., 2432
Ferrand-Bechmann, Dan, 723
Ferrarotti, Franco, 1453, 1493, 1680
Ferreira de Almeida, João, 2198
Ferrer, Julio, 2684
Ferrero, Mario, 4897
Festy, Patrick, 2527, 4188
Fetisov, É. N., 4489
Fetisov, V. Ja., 211
Fichter, Joseph H., 25
Fiedler, Fred P., 4205
Fielding, Nigel, 4875
Figaszewska, Iwona, 5276
Figley, Charles R., 5038
Figueroa Navarro, Alfredo, 26
Figuerola Palomo, Manuel, 4740
Fileni, Franco, 136
Filgueira, Nea, 2580
Filipović, Mileva, 212
Filippov, F. R., 2161
Filippov, N. T., 5277
Fillaut, Thierry, 5128
Filonov, G. N., 1942
Fina, Lluis, 4607
Finch, Janet, 1995
Finckenstein, Christiane, 1061
Findlay, Allan, 3809
Fine, Gary Alan, 748
Finestein, Israel, 1359
Finley, Nancy J., 4712
Finnis, John, 1211
Firebaugh, Glenn, 3810
First-Dilič, Ruža, 3672
Firūṭa, Argentina, 4711
Fischer, Hanna, 4672
Fischer, Lucy Rose, 2727
Fischer, Werner, 185
Fishburn, Peter C., 5000

Fisher, D. V., 494
Fisher, David Hackett, 3811
Fisher, E. G., 4673
Fisher, Peter S., 2531
Fishman, Joshua A., 1527, 1528, 1601, 1602
Fishman, Robert, 4608
Fishwick, Marshall W., 794
Fitzgerald, Kath, 3626
Fitzpatrick, Kevin M., 617
FitzRoy, Felix R., 749
Flacks, Richard, 1181
Flamant-Paparatti, Danielle, 3234
Flanagan, Owen J. Jr., 2581
Flanagan, Robert J., 4693
Fleck, James, 137, 1516
Fleming, Jane P., 4262
Flere, Sergej, 2371
Fleury, Marie-France, 3673
Fleury Teixeira, Sonia Maria, 5357
Fliegel, Frederick C., 3564
Fligstein, Neil, 2333
Flis, Andrzej, 213
Flis, Janusz, 214
Flis, Mariola, 316
Flood, Merrill M., 5001
Flora, Cornelia Butler, 3235
Florens, Jean-Pierre, 2199
Flowers, Ronald Bruce, 1286
Foddy, W. H., 1555
Fojgel', A. M., 1287
Földesi-Szabó, Györgyi, 2330
Folds, Ralph, 3309
Foley, Mary Ann, 2646
Fombrun, Charles J., 750
Fomin, A. V., 1681
Foner, Nancy, 2639
Fonow, Mary M., 99
Føns-Jørgensen, Eva, 1556
Fonseca, Claudia, 1212
Fontaine, Jean-Marc, 4811
Fordham, Paul, 2092
Forge, Simon, 1682
Forni, Floreal H., 4189
Forquin, Jean-Claude, 2132
Forrester, John, 465
Forsé, Michel, 724, 2452
Forsyth, Craig J., 1110
Forsyth, Donelson R., 466
Fortes, Meyer, 1062
Fortin, Nina E., 1827
Fortmann, Louise, 3236
Fosse-Poliak, C., 3031
Foster, Herbert J., 3136
Foster, Thomas W., 1413
Fouquier, Éric, 1529
Fourie, David P., 495
Fournier, Serge, 3812
Fowlkes, Diane L., 4974
Fox, James Alan, 317
Fox, John, 318
Fox, Mary Frank, 4263
Foxall, Gordon R., 4101

Frąckiewicz, Lucyna, 3813
Fraile, Eduardo A., 2045
Francisco, Josefa S., 5103
Franco, Juan N., 3378
Franco, R., 2433
Franco Arbelaez, Augusto, 1881
Franco Zapata, Ramón, 4570
Frank, J. A., 867
Franklin, Richard K., 1943
Fraser, Mark, 5129
Fraser, Nancy, 215
Fraser, Thomas Morris, 4374
Frątczak, Ewa, 2528, 2782
Fratczak-Rudnicka, Barbara, 4975
Frazier, Charles E., 5159
Frazier, William D., 4042
Frédéric, Louis, 923
Frederick, Melinda J. , 3477
Frederick, William C., 5002
Fredholm, Eva M., 627
Fredman, Sandra, 3379
Fredriksen, Birger, 2046
Freedman, Ann E., 2582
Freeman, John, 753
Freeman, Linton C., 392, 663
Freese, Lee, 2338
Freidson, Eliot, 1063
Frend, W. H. C., 1360
Freund, Julien, 216, 3946
Freund, Wolfgang Slim, 1016, 3478
Frey, James H., 4743
Freyssenet, Michel, 4472
Freyssinet, Jacques, 4190
Frideres, J. S., 4036
Friedgut, Theodore H., 3380
Friedkin, Noah E., 699
Friedland, M. L., 5179
Friedland, Roger, 3815
Friedlander, Judith, 3237
Friedman, Jean-Pierre, 3381
Frisbie, W. Parker, 4037
Frisby, David, 217
Frith, Simon, 2685
Froese, Leonhard, 1882
Frolov, I. T., 1006
Fromaget, Michel, 2867
Froomkin, Joseph, 2047
Frühling, Hugo, 5180
Fry, C. George, 1361
Fryżlewicz, Zofia, 3137, 4074
Fuchs, Victor R., 924
Fuentes, Annette, 4264
Fuguitt, Glenn V., 3686
Fuhrman, Ellsworth R., 1510
Fujii, Masao, 1362
Fujita, Hiroo, 3816
Fujita, Kunihiko, 619
Fukada, Hiroshi, 1288
Fukaya, Masashi, 477
Fukuoka, Yasunori, 821
Fullat Genís, Octavio, 1944
Fuller, Theodore, 3110, 3549

Fumuni, Bikuri, 1213
Funatsu, Mamoru, 278
Fung, Margaret C., 156
Fürer-Haimendorf, Christoph von, 2434
Furnham, A., 1475-76, 4118, 4609
Furstenberg, Frank F. Jr., 2976
Fürstenberg, Friedrich, 4694
Furter, Pierre, 925
Furuki, Toshiaki, 2435, 3636
Füstös, László, 393

Gabás Pallás, Raúl, 1768
Gabe, Jonathan, 5130
Gabel, Joseph, 1111
Gabuzjan, K. S., 521
Gadžiev, A. G., 5278
Gäfgen, Gérard, 5279
Gaft, L. G., 2163
Gaillard, Jean-Michel, 2436
Gais, Thomas L., 4931
Gaitskell, Deborah, 4523
Gałaj, Dyzma, 3674, 4075
Galaskiewicz, Joseph, 358, 3627
Galavotti, Maria Carla, 279
Galenson, Walter, 1414
Galeski, Boguslaw, 643
Galitz, Wilbert O., 4038
Gallagher, Eugene B., 5431
Gallagher, James E., 3028
Galland, Olivier, 3970, 4265
Gallant, Clifford J., 2622
Galle, Omer R., 3801
Galliher, James M., 5177
Galliher, John F., 5172
Gallin, Rita S., 4266
Gallois, Cynthia, 2966
Galtung, Johan, 998, 5070
Gambetta, Diego, 547
Gambetta, Guido, 279
Gambino, Ferruccio, 3479
Gamson, William A., 5094
Gane, Mike, 4782
Gant, Michael M., 5003, 5004
Garai, L., 496
Garbarino, James, 5181
Garbarino, Joseph W., 4547
García, Philip, 4267
García Cuerpo, Marcelino, 1935
García Guadilla, Carmen, 1883
García Guadilla, Naty, 2565
Gardes, Jean-Claude, 1683
Gareau, Frederick H., 27, 28
Garelli, Franco, 1454, 2686
Garine, Igor de, 5095
Garkovenko, R. V., 3577
Garlick, Patricia, 3069
Garrett, Patricia, 4076
Garron, Robert, 2265
Gartner, R., 1090
Gaspard, Françoise, 4268
Gasparini, Giovanni, 184
Gasperini, Lavinia, 1884

Gasson, Ruth, 2783
Gast, David L., 2110
Gastwirth, Joseph L., 4222
Gáthy, Vera, 4889
Gauchet, Marcel, 1289
Gaudemar, Jean-Paul de, 4191
Gautier, Maurice Paul, 4610
Gavaki, Efie, 3138
Gazar'jan, V. G., 926
Geddert, Heinrich, 1238
Geddes, Patric, 29
Gede, A., 218
Geibel, Karl, 1684
Geisler, Charles C., 4070
Geissler, Heiner, 5280
Gelašvili, N. M., 368
Gellner, Ernest, 30
Gelpi, Ettore, 2093
Genne, Marcelle, 2921
Gensollen, Michel, 1673
George, Herman Jr., 3382
George, Vincent, 1854
Georgeon, François, 1945
Gerard, Hubert, 2977
Gerber, Linda M., 3310
Gerbner, George, 4976
Gerčikov, V. I., 78
Gere, Edwin A. Jr., 4783
Gereben, Ferenc, 548
Gereffi, Gary, 998, 3962
Gerlah, A., 4830
Germann, Richard, 4375
Gershman, Carl, 5397
Gersuny, Carl, 4192
Geschiere, Peter, 4828
Geurts, P. A. T. M., 4473
Ghatak, Anita, 5096
Gheorghe, Elena, 927
Gheorghiu, Mihai Dinu, 31
Ghibuțiu, Aurel, 4193
Ghosh, Pradip K., 2529, 3996
Ghosh, S. K., 2583
Giammanco, Rosanna, 4932
Gibian, G., 1814
Gibson, Roland, 394
Giddings, Paula, 2584
Gifreu, Josep, 1685
Gilbert, Alan, 3628, 3817
Gilbert, Neil, 3971
Gilens, Martin, 4761
Giles, Howard, 1603
Gillen, Otto, 1455
Gillespie, Gilbert W. Jr., 2569
Gilli, Roger, 842
Gillioz, Lucienne, 5414
Gilljam, Mikael, 4671
Ginet, Jean-Christophe, 5281
Gingerich, Wallace J., 420
Gingras, Yves, 1604
Ginsberg, Helen, 4223
Ginsburg, Mark B., 2133
Giordano, Christian, 3439

Giori, Danilo, 2728
Girard, Alain, 2784
Giraud, Michel, 3383
Girenko, N., 1017
Girenok, F. I., 3598
Giroux, Henry A., 1885, 1886
Girtler, Roland, 3032
Girusov, É. V., 3578
Gitelman, Zvi, 4972
Gitworth, Jacques, 1456
Giugni, Gino, 4695
Giuzzardi, Gustavo, 1281
Gizatov, K. T., 928
Gladwyn, Christina H., 549
Glardon, Marie-Jo, 5097
Glaser, Deborah L., 4712
Glaser, S., 439
Glasman, Monique, 1686
Glass, David, 5005
Glassman, Robert B., 751
Glatzer, Wolfgang, 3972
Glaubrecht, Helmut, 4376
Glauser, Michael J., 725
Glebe, Günther, 3557
Glenday, Daniel, 2266
Glenn, Norval D., 32, 2585
Glezerman, G. É., 929
Glick, Paul C., 2586, 2587
Gloeckner, Edward, 2348
Glover, David, 1687
Glowczewski, Barbara, 3311
Glucklich, Ariel, 1363
Glynn, Carroll J., 836
Glynn, Rosalie M., 4977
Gnoss, Roland, 4194
Goban-Klas, Tomasz, 1557
Gobin, Corinne, 5415
Goćkowski, Janusz, 79
Godard, Jacques, 5131
Godefroy, Th., 5182
Godfrey, Martin, 4454
Godschalk, J. J., 4159
Godwin, R. Kenneth, 4984
Goetcheus, Vernon M., 4377
Gojowy, Detlef, 1843
Gokalp, Catherine, 2645
Gold, Dolores, 3134
Goldberg, Albert I., 122
Goldberg, Giora, 4996
Goldberg, H. I., 2868
Goldberg, Harvey E., 2687
Goldberger, Arthur S., 1991
Goldfarb, Jeffrey, 4808, 4859
Goldin, Carol S., 2828
Goldman, Noreen, 3070
Goldman, Robert, 2372
Goldscheider, Calvin, 2993
Goldstein, Alice, 3675
Goldstein, Jan, 33
Goldstein, Michael S., 2978
Goldstone, Jack A., 3818
Goldthorpe, John H., 2620

Gołębiowski, Bronisław, 930, 931, 1112, 2267
Golenkova, Z., 2437
Golinowska, Stanisława, 5282
Golubec, M. A., 3579
Golubović, Zagorka, 4784
Gómez Navas, Oscar, 4900
Gómez Yañez, José Antonio, 5031
Gončarenko, N. V., 932
Göncz, Dániel, 5218
Gonod, Pierre F., 4063
Gonsales, R. F., 1558
Gontard, Maurice, 1996
Gontarev, G. A., 2200
Gonzalez, Luis, 2395
Gonzalez, Roberto, 3378
Good, Anthony, 1559
Goodman, Gail S., 2646
Goodman, J. F. R., 4548
Goodson, Ivor F., 2134
Goodstein, Lynne I., 5183
Goodstein, Phil H., 4674
Goody, Jack, 3139
Göpel-Gruner, Dagmar, 752
Gopinathan, S., 2070
Gordon, David F., 1477
Gordon, L. A., 2268
Gordon, Michael E., 644, 4378
Gordon, Pierre, 1194
Gordon, Robert J., 1239
Gore, M. S., 5283
Goreneman, Sid, 5006
Goriachenko, E. E., 3676
Goriely, Georges, 2438
Gorlach, Krzysztof, 3677
Gosal, Gurdev Singh, 2785
Gosen, Sylvia, 582
Gosling, L. A. Peter, 3326
Gosselin, Jean-Pierre, 3480
Goswami, Subir, 3384
Goto, Kazuhiko, 1688
Goto, Noriaki, 5062
Gottlieb, Roger, 3238
Goudsblom, J., 933
Gould, Carol C., 522, 4858
Gourou, Pierre, 934
Gouveia, J. L., 1946, 1947
Govaerts, France, 2729
Goyder, John C., 4475
Grabowska, Urszula, 3678
Gradev, Doncho, 802
Graham Lear, Julia, 5416
Grajek, Susan, 625
Granero, Mirta, 467
Graniewska, Danuta, 3239, 3240, 4269
Granovetter, Mark, 3997
Gransow, Volker, 4744
Grant, Jonathan S., 3819
Grant, Karen R., 5358
Grant, Linda, 5472
Gras, Alain, 319
Grasmick, Harold G., 4712
Grasmuck, Sherri, 3481

Grasso, Jean C., 4270
Grathoff, Richard, 219
Gravereau, Jacques, 3550
Gray, David E., 4379
Gray, John N., 3679, 4111
Gray, Louis N., 550
Grečin, A. S., 1240
Greeley, Andrew M., 1415
Green, Donald E., 5198
Green, Samuel B., 715
Greenbaum, Joseph, 186
Greenberg, David F., 3033
Greenberg, Martin S., 5183
Greene, Les R., 602
Greenfeld, Liah, 1769
Greenhalgh, Susan, 2201, 3820
Greenspan, Miriam, 4271
Greer, G. Brian, 556
Greer, J. E., 1214
Gregoire, Robert, 1018
Greider, Thomas, 3632
Greil, Arthur L., 726
Greive, Hermann, 3385
Grémy, Jean-Paul, 421
Grenier, Gilles, 1605, 3973
Griffen, Joyce, 4304
Griffith, Janet D., 3080
Griffiths, Curt T., 5176
Griffiths, J., 1241
Grigas, R. S., 3821
Grimshaw, Roger, 4877
Gripton, James, 5240
Grize, Jean-Blaise, 1606
Groarke, Lee, 3034
Grofman, Bernard, 5015
Gromova, I. V., 4272
Grosperrin, Bernard, 1887
Grossin, William, 4380
Groux, Guy, 4602, 4619
Groves, Robert M., 382
Gruat, J. V., 5359
Gruenfeld, Leopold W., 700
Gruhn, Werner, 4039
Grunberg, Gérard, 5007
Grundelach, Peter, 727
Grundhöfer, Horst, 383
Gruner, Roger, 1019
Grünewald, Werner, 2922
Grunow, Dieter, 710
Grupp, Fred W., 3392
Grusky, David B., 2373
Gruson, Pascale, 2048
Guberskij, S. A., 4978
Gubian, Alain, 3130
Gudymenko, A. V., 482
Guest, Avery M., 2551, 3822, 3823
Guest, Robert H., 4381
Guggenberger, Bernd, 4812
Guibourdenche, Henri, 2511
Guillé-Escuret, Georges, 34
Guillemard, Anne-Marie, 5284
Guillemin, Alain, 1113, 4901

Guillemin, Jacques, 4890
Guillet, Pierre, 5473
Guillon, M., 2923
Gulič, Andrej, 3824
Gullett, C. Ray, 4611
Gunder Frank, André, 3963
Guppy, Neil, 4474-75
Gupta, A. R., 2234
Gupta, K. C., 1114
Gupta, Kuntesh, 2829
Gupta, N. K., 4831
Gupta, Prithwis das, 2924
Gupta, R. N., 4273
Gupta, Shiva K., 2202
Gupta, Surendra K., 3551
Gurkovich, Lorraine, 3545
Gurny, Ruth, 173
Gusfield, Joseph R., 1560
Gusov, A. Z., 4329
Gusso, Divonzir Arthur, 2088
Gustafsson, Karl Erik, 1689
Gustavsen, Bjørn, 4330, 4382
Gustman, Alan L., 4448
Guterbock, Thomas M., 3802
Gutiérrez, Francisco, 1690
Gutiérrez Estévez, Manuel, 1364
Guttmacher, Sally, 3482
Güzel, Sehmus, 2269
Guzman Garcia, Luis, 1416
Gvišiani, D. M., 320, 321
Györgyi, Márta, 3140
Györgyi, Kálmán, 5184

Haar, Charles M., 3825
Haarmann, Harold, 1607, 1691
Haavio-Mannila, Elina, 3276
Habuda, Ludwik, 4383
Hadden, Jeffrey K., 1290
Hadlmanl, R. N., 5098
Haferkamp, Hans, 220
Haffey, Joan, 2979
Haga, Hiroshi, 2757
Hagan, John, 5185, 5215
Hagendijk, R. P., 935, 1530
Hagner, Paul R., 4979
Hague, Rod, 4612
Hahulina, L. A., 3680
Haile, Daniel, 3241
Haimovich, Perla, 3112
Haines, Herbert H., 3312
Hainsworth, Peter, 1802
Hakim, Simon, 5186
Hale, Ronald J., 2830
Halemba, Gregory J., 4283
Halevi, Ran, 1417
Halfmann, Jost, 4933
Hall, J. A., 2349
Hall, Robert L., 1123
Hallen, G. C., 35
Haller, Max, 2270
Halsey, A. H., 177
Halskov, Therese, 5471

Ham, Brian, 4082
Hamaguchi, Haruhiko, 36, 101
Hamana, Atsushi, 2271
Hamann, Rudolf, 1020
Hamel, Rainer Enrique, 2094
Hamilton, Gary G., 3141
Hamm, Bernd, 3580, 4132
Hammel, E. A., 3162
Hammer, Muriel, 664
Hammersley, Martyn, 1888
Hammond, John L., 4785
Hamnett, Chris, 3826
Hampson, Robert B., 1115
Hanák, Katalin, 1692, 2588
Hanák, Péter, 3386
Hand, Carl M., 1291
Handberg, Roger, 5025
Handimani, R. N., 5099
Handl, Johann, 2203
Hanisch, Rolf, 4934
Hankiss, Elemér, 936
Hannan, Damian, 1997
Hannan, Michael T., 753
Hanova, O. V., 937
Hansell, Stephen, 675
Hansen, Arvid, 3974
Hansen, Erik Jørgen, 665
Hansen, Miriam, 1830
Hansen, Pierre, 551
Hansluwka, Harald, 2869
Hanson, Charles, 4713
Hanson, Russell L., 5360
Hanson, Sandra L., 4274
Hansra, B. S., 5106
Haour-Knipe, Mary, 3440
Hara, Junsuke, 187
Harada, Yutaka, 5209
Harayama, Tetsu, 1561
Harcsa, István, 938, 2374, 2439, 3681, 4351, 4352
Harding, Robert R., 1948
Harding, Sandra, 3216
Hardoy, J. E., 3827
Hardy, Janet B., 3027
Hargens, Lowell, 416
Haring, Marilyn J., 3975
Harlow, Barbara, 1807
Harman, Chris, 1693
Harman, Grant, 2049
Harms, John B., 1511
Harouel, Jean-Louis, 2204
Harper, Charles L., 1494
Harris, Barry C., 754
Harris, Peter Richard, 1531
Harris, Richard J., 714
Harrison-Mattley, Peter, 1949
Hart, Robert A., 4384
Harten, Hans-Christian, 4195
Hartley, Jean, 4675
Hartman, G., 1814
Hartman, Harriet, 3242
Hartman, Moshe, 2980, 3242

Hartmann, Elfriede, 4464
Hartmann, Jürgen, 5026
Hartmann, P., 1878
Hartung, Wolfdietrich, 1608
Haru, Terry T., 1215
Haruvi, Nava, 4077
Harvey, Edward B., 2050
Hashim, Wan, 3387
Hashimoto, Kazuta, 939
Hashizume, Daisaburo, 322
Haskey, J., 3071
Hassin, Yael, 5187
Hastie, Reid, 595
Hatanaka, Munekazu, 3142
Hattori, Toru, 552
Haubert, Maxime, 3682
Häuselmann, Erich, 2673
Hauser, Robert M., 2205, 2373, 2375, 4476
Hausfater, Glenn, 5188
Hausladen, Gary, 3828
Havanon, Napaporn, 2930
Havelka, J., 2688
Hawkes, Glenn R., 2331
Hawkesworth, Richard I., 4607
Hawkins, J. David, 5127
Hawkins, M. J., 2119
Hawley, Willis, 1116
Hay, Henry F., 1021
Hay, Margaret Jean, 2589
Hayami, Yujiro, 1080
Hayashi, Masataka, 369
Hayes, Adrian C., 395
Hayes, Louis D., 1365
Hazan, Haim, 2730
Heal, Geoffrey, 442
Healy, Sheila, 623
Heath, Anthony, 2620
Heath, Shirley Brice, 1808
Heaven, Patrick C. L., 4804
Hechter, Michael, 1064, 2162
Heckathorn, Douglas D., 396
Hee, Raymond W. Que., 2967
Hegar, Rebecca L., 2647
Hegedüs, József, 3829
Hegin, Patrick, 3791
Hegland, Mary, 1443
Heimer, Carol A., 4477
Heinrich, Nathalie, 1809
Heins Potter, Sulamith, 3683
Heisel, Marsel A., 2731
Hekman, Susan, 553
Helburn, I. B., 4549
Held, Thomas, 2590
Helin, E., 1216
Hellencourt, Bernard d', 3483
Heller, Agnès, 4930
Heller, Peter, 1600
Helly, Denise, 3484
Helson, Ravenna, 1117
Helwig, Gisela, 2689
Hembroff, Larry A., 2332
Hempton, David, 1418

Hendershot, Gerry E., 1304
Henderson, Gail E., 5446
Henderson, Jeff, 3830
Henningham, J. P., 1694
Hennis, Wilhelm, 523
Henriquez, Helia, 4587
Henry, Louis, 2530
Henshaw, Stanley K., 2981
Hepburn, Mary A., 1950
Hepp, Osvaldo T., 5189
Héran, François, 422
Herbert, D. T., 3831
Herbert, Ulrich, 4275
Herbison, Peter, 557
Herbon, Dietmar, 3684
Herdoiza, Wilson, 3832
Hermalin, Albert I., 2968
Hernández, Donald J., 2982
Hernández Díaz, José María, 1889
Herold, Edward Stephen, 3035
Herpin, Nicolas, 5100
Herr, Paul M., 493
Herrero Castro, Santos, 2010
Herries-Jenkins, Gwyn, 2085
Herriman, Michael, 1951
Hervieu-Leger, Danièle, 1292
Hervin, Jacky, 2511
Herzberg, Irene, 2135
Herzberg, Max John, 1457
Herzig, Arno, 4276
Herzlich, Claudine, 2831
Herzog, Felix, 1242
Herzog, Henry W. Jr., 3451
Hesse, Hans Albrecht, 2832
Hesse, Joachim Jens, 3833
Hesse-Biber, Sharlene, 4263
Hetherington, Robert W., 4040
Héthy, Lajos, 4330
Hettlage, Robert, 4277, 4278, 4385
Hettlage-Varjas, Andrea, 4278
Heusch, Luc de, 3072
Hewstone, Miles, 596, 682
Heyderbrand, Wolf V., 755
Hickerson, Steven R., 4860, 4861
Hickman, Carol A., 1074
Hickox, M. S., 37
Hicks, Alexander, 2333
Hicks, Lou E., 280
Higa, Teruyuki, 4301
Hijazi, Naila B., 3831
Hildebrandt, Hans-Jürgen, 3143
Hildreth, W. Bartley, 760
Hill, Allan, 2870
Hill, Paul Bernhard, 3313
Hill, Stephen, 166
Hillenbrand, Carole, 2394
Hillery, George A. Jr., 3629
Hily, M.-A., 3513, 4279
Himmelstein, Jerome L., 123
Himsworth, Harold, 2833
Hinde, P. R. A., 2925
Hindess, Barry, 554

Hinich, Melvin J., 4992
Hinnels, John R., 1293
Hinton, James, 4613
Hintzen, Percy C., 4959
Hinz, Eike, 1458
Hiraoka, Koichi, 2747
Hirdina, H., 4386
Hiroshi, Iwai, 5190
Hirsch, Helga, 1695
Hirschfeld, André, 3947
Hirschman, Charles, 2334
Hishimura, Yukihiko, 2008
Hitt, Michael A., 221
Hitzler, Ronald, 323, 3581
Hizaoui, Abdelkrim, 1696
Hlebnikov, I. B., 524
Ho, D. Y. F., 2073
Hoa, Léon, 3819
Hoag, Lisbeth J., 500
Hoag, Wendy J., 299
Hobcraft, J., 2926
Hobcraft, J. N., 2871
Hobsbawm, Eric, 1195
Hodge, Robert William, 2999
Hodgins, Sheilagh, 5132
Hodžić, Alija, 3834
Hoeben, W., 1931
Hoelter, Jon W., 497
Hoem, Jan M., 3073
Hoffer, Thomas, 1991, 2006, 2018
Hoffert, Robert W., 4786
Hoffman, Bruce, 1118, 1119
Hoffman, Carol, 2727
Hoffman, O., 2440
Hoffmann, Stanley, 2350
Hofmeister, Burkhard, 3835
Hofstetter, C. Richard, 1697
Hogan, Roseann R., 5417
Hoge, Dean R., 498, 1065
Hoge, Jann L., 1065
Hohm, Charles F., 3836
Holban, Ion, 4478
Hołda-Róziewicz, Henryka, 483
Holdaway, Simon, 4876
Holler, Manfred J., 4387, 5008
Hollerbach, Paula E., 2927
Hollingsworth, Ellen Jane, 2022
Holm, Tom, 5032
Holmberg, David, 1318
Holmes, Malcolm D., 3367
Holmström, Mark, 4388
Holter, Harriet, 3243
Holtmann, Dieter, 324
Holton, R. J., 3837
Holzkamp-Osterkamp, Ute, 3314
Homans, Margaret, 1810
Home, Alice, 3221, 5466
Homenko, A. I., 940
Honer, Anne, 3581
Hong, Sawon, 4280
Honneth, Axel, 874
Hooper, Beverly, 3244

Hope, Christine A., 1464
Hope, Keith, 1998, 4479
Höpflinger, F., 2983, 3074
Hopkins, Andrew, 4389, 4390
Hopkins, Frances L., 875
Horiuchi, Shiro, 2848
Horn, James J., 5418
Horna, Jarmilla, 3144
Horner, Wolfgang, 4196
Hornsby-Smith, M. P., 1366
Horowitz, Steven, 3825
Horwitz, Allan V., 5071
Hoshino, Kanehiro, 5209
Hoshino Altbach, Edith, 3245
Hosoya, Takashi, 3692
Hotchkiss, H. Lawrence, 404
Hough, George C. Jr., 2795
Hout, Michael, 4480, 4481
Howard, Judith A., 5191
Hox, J. J., 384
Hoyt, Danny R., 4227
Hryniewicz, Janusz T., 2272, 3935
Huber, Wolfgang, 141
Huberman, A. Michael, 338
Hudson, James L., 3485
Hudson, Randy, 4391
Huffman, Sandra L., 2648
Hughes, J. A., 9
Hughes, Michael, 3052
Hughey, J. B., 3618
Hull, Terence H., 2786
Hull, Valerie J., 2786
Humbert, Geneviève, 1811
Humblet, Jean-E., 1609
Humeau, Jean-Baptiste, 3552
Hummel, Hans J., 325
Humphrey, John, 4281
Humphrey, Ronald, 3315
Humphreys, S. C., 3145
Humphries, Jane, 4160
Hund, John, 1243
Hunecke, Volker, 5101
Hunt, Jennifer, 2591
Hunter, Alfred A., 3246
Hunter, Ian, 1610
Hunter, Kevin A., 3075
Hurh, Won Moo, 3486
Husak, Douglas N., 4862
Hussain, Donna, 142
Huston, Ted L., 3054
Hutchison, Ray, 2787
Huyssen, Andreas, 2441
Hvinden, Bjørn, 4331
Hyde, Alan, 4696
Hyman, Jeffrey, 4724
Hynes, Thomas J. Jr., 5102

Ibarolla, Jesus, 3838
Ibarra, Valentín, 3839
Ibragimov, R. I., 1022
Ibrahim, Zawawi, 3685
Ickes, William, 3388

Igarashi, Yoshio, 190
Igithanjan, É. D., 2163
Iglesias de Ussel, Julio, 2649
Igonet-Fastinger, P., 499, 509
Ikeda, Hideo, 2136
Ikeda, Kanji, 2273
Ikonnikova, S. N., 876
Ikor, Roger, 1419
Iljušečkin, V. P., 4041
Illarionova, N. V., 3582
Illner, M., 423
Illuminati, Augusto, 4578
Imada, Andrew S., 380
Imaizumi, Reisuke, 941
Imazu, Kohjiro, 2707
Immerwahr, John, 4440
Imoisili, Imonitie C., 4697
Ina, Masato, 5072
Indič, Trivo, 4813
Indra, P., 5285
Infestas Gil, Angel, 2010
Inglehart, Ronald, 555
Inkeles, Alex, 3146
Inoue, Jun'ichi, 1120
Inoue, Shun, 877, 1121
Inoue, Teruko, 1698
Ioffe, S. F., 524
Ion, Jacques, 5474
Iončar, Ana, 2788
Ionescu, Ghita, 4762
Ireland, P. W., 1244
Irigary, Luce, 2592
Irurzun, Víctor J., 5213
Irving, Thomas Ballantine, 1367
Isaev, K. I., 3610
Isambert-Jamati, Viviane, 1999
Isard, Walter, 5052
Ishikawa, Akihiro, 2206, 4614
Ishumi, Abel G. M., 4197
Islam, Rizwanul, 2274
Islami, Hivzi, 3840
Ismacil, Muhammad Ahmad, 4615
Isomura, Ei'ichi, 821, 3841
Isserman, Andrew, 3560
Isserman, Andrew M., 2531
Isuani, Ernesto A., 5361
Itō, Minoru, 4332
Ityavyar, Dennis A., 5419
Iupin, A. A., 2409
Ivancevich, John M., 4392
Ivanov, Ju M., 3842
Ivanov, V. N., 1634
Iwama, Tsuyoshi, 2690
Iwami, Kazuhiko, 1122, 2691
Iwaniszek, John, 647
Iwasaki, Nobuhiko, 3843, 4393
Iziga, Roger, 5286
Izraeli, Dafna N., 4616

Jaakkola, Risto, 3076
Jabbra, Nancy W., 3316
Jablensky, A., 2985

Jacenko, A. I., 942
Jacher, Władysław, 1023, 3998
Jackson, John B., 340
Jackson, Mary E., 2834
Jackson, N. V., 1459
Jackson, Pamela Irving, 5192
Jacob, Jeffrey C., 4028
Jacobs, Jerry, 789
Jacobsen, Chanoch, 4672
Jacobson, Arthur J., 4808
Jacobson, Cardell K., 3317, 3389
Jacoby, Joseph E., 38
Jacquemet, Gérard, 1495, 3844
Jacques, Jeffrey M., 1123
Jadykina, N. V., 540
Jaffé, A. J., 434
Jagielski, Andrzej, 2789
Jagodzinski, Wolfgang, 326, 943, 1066
Jaguaribe, Hélio, 1124
Jain, Anand Prasad, 4550
Jain, Uday, 597
Jairath, Vinod K., 124
Jakubowicz, Patrick, 1237
Jałowiecki, Bohdan, 3845
James, David R., 2018
Jamison, Andrew, 1516
Jamison, Michael, 4942
Janickij, O. N., 3846
Janiszewski, Ludwik, 4512
Janman, Karen, 2593
Jánosi, György, 4745
Janowski, Karol B., 4910
Jansen, Torben Bo, 143
Janssen, Hans, 4430
Japp, Klaus P., 4935
Jarausch, Konrad Hugo, 2051
Jardel, J. P., 3318
Jarosińska, Maria, 4161, 4732
Jarosz, Maria, 2207, 3147
Jarousse, Jean-Pierre, 2052
Jasper, James M., 1770
Jauch, Susanne, 4617
Javeau, Claude, 944
Jay, Salim, 1812
Jayadeva Das, D., 2275
Jayewardene, C. H. S. , 3390
Jayewardene, Hilda, 3390
Jeanniere, Abel, 3391
Jędrzycki, Wiesław, 4394
Jeeves, Malcolm A., 556
Jefferson, Tony, 4877
Jeffery, Ina A., 809
Jencks, Christopher, 2376
Jendoubi, Mehdi, 1699, 1700
Jenkins, S. P., 3847
Jenkinson, Sally, 2062
Jenness, Robert A., 4224
Jensen, Stefan, 1701
Jerrome, Dorothy, 620
Jhally, Sut, 4746
Jilek, Miroslav, 281
Jimenez, Carol J., 4318

Jimenez, Marc, 1771
Jimenez, Pilar R., 5103
Joardar, Biswanath, 3036, 3037
Joas, Hans, 222
Jobber, David, 385
Jobert, Bruno, 5287
Jobes, Patrick C., 55
Joe, Victor C., 447
Johansen, Harley E., 3686
John, Klaus-Dieter, 638
John, Robert, 282
Johnson, David W., 645, 680
Johnson, Knowlton W., 4042
Johnson, M. Bruce, 1252
Johnson, Marcia K., 2646
Johnson, Nan E., 3848
Johnson, Roger T., 645, 680
Johnson, Roland H. III, 90
Johnson, William C., 3630
Johnsson-Smaragdi, Ulla, 1702
Johnston, Les, 223
Johnston, Lloyd D., 5120
Johnston, W. Lee, 2692
Johnston, William J., 3487
Join-Lambert, M. T., 4395
Joll, Caroline, 4162
Jończyk, Jan, 4571
Jones, Brian J., 5288
Jones, Bryn, 4482
Jones, Ellen, 3392
Jones, F. L., 666
Jones, J. H., 1110
Jones, Linda E., 5346
Jones, Lyle V., 125
Jones, R. Dallas, 593
Jones, Sue, 598
Jonsson, Britta, 945
Joó, Rudolf, 2208
Joossens, Luc, 1703
Jordan, Bill, 5386, 5387
Jørgensen, Per Schultz, 580
Jose, A. V., 3687
Joseph, George, 4282
Joseph, Isaac, 3611
Joseph, Philip A., 4676
Joshi, S. C., 3688
Jowett, A. J., 2532
Joyce, Paul, 4677
Juárez, Fátima, 2872
Judd, Charles M., 283
Juhász, Júlia, 946
Julien-Labruyère, François, 3689
Jungbluth, Paul, 1953
Junger-Tas, J., 5193
Junusov, A. M., 1067
Jureidini, Paul A., 3319
Jurich, Joan, 2594
Juričić, Živka, 2276
Jurik, Nancy C., 4283

Kačajnova, N. B., 284
Kačanovskij, Ju. V., 2410

Kaci, Djamel, 947
Kada, Yukiko, 4513
Kaelble, Hartmut, 2377
Kaes, René, 1125
Kaewthep, Kanoksak, 3690
Kagle, Jill Doner, 5388
Kaglstein, A. Solomon, 3541
Kahn, Alfred I., 5362
Kahn, Alfred J., 5289
Kahn, Laurence M., 4198
Kaijage, Fred J., 4396
Kain, Roger, 1835
Kajita, Takamichi, 4936
Kaldate, Sudha, 2488
Kalekin-Fishman, Devorah, 4937
Kaleta, Andrzej, 80
Kalia, Narendra Nath, 151
Kalina, V. F., 948
Kalliopuska, Mirja, 621
Kalomalos, Thanassis, 224
Kalule-Sabiti, I., 2928
Kalwani, Manohar U., 4102
Kamaev, R. B., 3761
Kamarás, Ferenc, 3077
Kamens, David M., 4938
Kamerman, Sheila B., 5289, 5362
Kamikubo, Tatsuo, 3691
Kamiński, Antoni Zdzisław, 4112
Kaminsky, Catherine, 4787
Kamler, Howard, 949
Kamman, Richard, 557
Kan, Stephen H., 3644
Kanbargi, R., 3057
Kanehisa, Tching, 1635
Kanerko, Isamu, 2732
Kanno, Masashi, 3692
Kannonier, Reinhard, 4618
Kanomata, Nobuo, 2378
Kantor, K. M., 225
Kantowsky, D., 39
Kaplan, A. B., 2442
Kaplan, Morton A., 1512
Kaplan, Steven L., 1196
Kaplinsky, Raphael, 4043
Kappelhoff, Peter, 327, 3638
Karabanov, N. V., 5053
Karadawi, Ahmed, 3488
Karakseev, T. D., 2443
Karasawa, Kazuyoshi, 711
Karklins, Rasma, 3393
Karlhofer, Ferdinand, 4678
Karmen, Andrew, 5194
Karn, Valerie, 3830
Karson, Marvin J., 328
Karunatilake, H. N. S., 424
Kasahara, Masanari, 2733, 5195
Kasarda, John D., 4199
Kashioka, Tomihide, 3320, 4939
Katano, Takashi, 3631
Katase, Kazuo, 1217
Kats, Rachel, 122
Katunarić, Vjeran, 2164

Katz, Harry C., 4698
Katzen, M., 1878
Katzenstein, Mary Fainsod, 3247
Katzir, Yael, 3693
Kaufman, McCall, 3248
Kaviraj, Sudipta, 4832
Kawai, Takao, 2379
Kawamura, Nozomu, 40, 822
Kawanishi, Hirosuke, 4140
Kawasaki, Sumio, 3148
Kay, Geoffrey, 1245
Kay, Susan Ann, 41
Kayongo-Male, Diane, 3149
Kazin, A. L., 1704
Kearl, Michael C., 500
Kearney, Mary-Louise, 1532
Kearns, Kevin C., 5104
Keating, Caroline, 5036
Keats, Barbara W., 221
Keckeisen, Wolfgang, 1890
Kędelski, Mieczysław, 1218
Kedourie, Elie, 686
Keenum, Deborah G., 1980
Keith, Patricia M., 5322
Kejing, Li, 2367
Kelen, András, 3849
Kellens, G., 1216
Keller, Thomas, 1420
Kelley, Allen C., 2790
Kelley, David, 558
Kelley, Jonathan, 666, 1421, 3489
Kelly, I. W., 475
Kelly, James, 4699
Kelly, James R., 1368
Kelly, John, 4333
Kelly, Maria Patricia Fernandez, 4302
Kelly, Robert F., 226
Kelly, William R., 2929
Kemerov, V. E., 329
Kende, Péter, 3394
Kende, Pierre, 2209
Kendillen, Leila, 947
Kennedy, Leslie W., 3850, 5196
Kennedy, Richard, 1294
Kent, Stephen A., 1478
Kepel, Gilles, 1369
Kerber, Kenneth W., 803
Kerckhoff, Alan, 2380
Keremeckij, Ja. N., 2277
Kern, Horst, 4397, 4456
Kerovec, Nada, 4200
Kerstholt, Frans, 2278
Kešelava, V., 1126
Kesselman, Mark, 4619, 4788
Kessler, Francis, 4398
Kessler, Lorence L., 3987
Kéthelyi, Judit, 5218
Kethudov, R. G., 1127
Kets de Vries, Manfred F. R., 756
Kettler, David, 2396
Keyder, Çağlar, 3694
Keyfitz, Nathan, 2533, 2534

Khakhulina, L. A., 425
Khan, A. R., 2986
Khan, M. H., 160
Khan, Najma, 3553
Khandriche, Mohamed, 3490
Khanna, Durga Prasad Singh, 81
Khleif, Bud B., 3395
Khoury, Joseph, 285
Khubchandani, Lachman M., 1611
Khudr, Adèle, 3078
Kibreab, Gaim, 3491
Kidd, Robert R., 5183
Kidd, Ross, 1855
Kiefl, Walter, 828
Kiersch, Gerhard, 950
Kieser, Alfred, 757
Kilbourne, Brock K., 1068
Kilbourne, Maria T., 1068
Kilgore, Sally B., 1990
Kilmurray, Avila, 2096
Kim, Jae-On, 102
Kim, Joochul, 3554
Kim, Kwang Chung, 3486
Kim, Kyong-Dong, 4714
Kim, Nam-Il, 2946
Kim, Young J., 2535
Kimura, Kiyoshi, 712
Kimura, Kunihiro, 783
Kincaid, D. Lawrence, 3396
King, Dave, 3038
King, James A., 2835
Kingston, Paul J., 3397
Kingston, Paul William, 3774
Kinloch, Graham Charles, 3398
Kipnis, David, 4532
Kiratsov, P., 161
Kirk, H. David, 2650
Kirk, Maurice, 2536
Kirkland, James Ray, 687
Kirkpatrick, George R., 3039
Kirkwood, Julieta, 3249
Kirouac, Gilles, 3029
Kirschenbaum, Alan, 3399
Kislev, Yoav, 4077
Kississou-Boma, J. R., 2279
Kissler, Leo, 1246, 1247
Kitamura, Kazuo, 1069
Kitazawa, Yutaka, 878
Kitoh, Tsuneo, 4133
Kitschelt, Herbert, 3583
Kittsteiner, Heinz-Dieter, 581
Kivisto, Peter, 4940
Kiyota, Katsuhiko, 5197
Kjaer Jensen, Mogens, 3851
Klapisch-Zuber, Christiane, 3232
Klat, Myriam, 3078
Klein, Rudolf, 5290, 5420
Kleinke, Chris L., 810
Klement'ev, D. S., 3948
Klemmer, P., 4183
Klepov, V. N., 155
Klevorick, Alvin K., 676

Klimas Blanc, Ann, 3079
Klimov, V. A., 1070
Klockars, Carl B., 1071
Kłodziński, Marek, 2791, 4079
Kłoskowska, Antonina, 951
Klüver, Hartmut, 1128
Knabe, Bernd, 3441
Knapp, Martin, 2734
Knapp, Peter, 227
Knight, Stephen, 1813
Knilli, Friedrich, 1705
Knodel, John, 2930, 2968
Knoke, David, 728
Knopp, András, 2351
Knötig, Paul, 4747
Knox, Alan Boyd, 2087
Knudsen, John C., 3492
Kobayashi, Kazuho, 228
Kobayashi, Koichiro, 4080
Kobrin, Frances E., 3150
Kobyljanskij, V. A., 3599
Kochan, Thomas A., 4551
Kodjo, Edem, 2444
Koening, M. A., 2987
Koffler, Judith S., 1814
Kogan, David, 2053
Kogan, Maurice, 2053
Kőhegyi, Kálmán, 758
Köhler, Peter A., 5363
Kohler Riessman, Catherine, 5421, 5447
Kohli, Martin, 172
Kohn, Rachael L. E., 1422
Kojima, Masaru, 2000
Kolack, Shirley, 1370
Kolenda, Pauline, 2235
Koletnik, Franc, 4334
Koller, Karl, 582
Koller, Marvin E., 3111
Kolm, Serge-Christophe, 229
Kolosi, Tamás, 2165, 2210, 2211, 2212, 4524
Komai, Hiroshi, 3493, 3852
Komarovsky, Mirra, 2595
Komorowska, Jadwiga, 3151
Kőműves, Márta, 4525
Kon, I., 952
Koncz, Katalin, 4284
Kondo, Motoo, 1891
Konev, V. A., 953
König, Karin, 3321
König, René, 42, 178
Konstantinov, F. R., 2397
Kontos, Maria, 4285
Koo, Helen P., 3080
Koo, Ja-Soon, 2735, 3081
Koops, K., 1931
Kopecki, A., 4715
Köpeczi, Bela, 954
Kopelman, Richard E., 1820
Koralewicz-Zębik, Jadwiga, 2213, 5073
Kordaszewski, Jan, 4163
Korel, L. V., 3570
Kornienko, É. V., 1072

Korte, Elke, 1954
Kościański, Tadeusz, 2792
Kosolapov, N. A., 468
Kosolapov, R. I., 2280
Kostecki, Marian, 622
Kosten, M., 3152
Kosters, Marvin H., 4693
Kourvetaris, George, 3494
Kourvetaris, George A., 2263
Kovács, Ferenc, 4514
Kovács, István, 4833
Kovacsics, Jozsef, 426
Kowalewicz, Kazimierz, 1856
Kowalski, Mieczysław, 2793
Koyano, Wataru, 2736, 2757
Kozak, Marek, 5276
Kozakiewicz, Mikołaj, 1129, 2054, 2693
Kozlovskij, V. E., 3949
Kožurin, Ja. Ja., 1295
Kozyr-Kowalski, Stanisław, 230, 2281, 3936
Kozyrev, Ju. N., 2352
Krahé, Barbara, 817
Krahn, Harvey, 4620, 5196
Kramar, Robin, 2596
Kramarae, Cheris, 1612
Kramer, Fred, 1423
Krannich, Richard S. K., 3632
Krasin, Ju., 1130
Kraśko, Nina, 43
Kratcoski, Peter C., 3153
Krau, Edgar, 4399, 4400
Kraus, Vered, 3853
Krause, Steven, 623
Krauss, Ellis S., 646, 4960
Kravitz, David A., 647
Kravitz, Linda, 5105
Krawietz, Werner, 1248
Krebsbach-Gnath, Camilla, 4286
Kreisel, Werner, 3495
Krell, Gertraude, 4287
Kreps, G. A., 5078
Kriegel, Annie, 1371
Kriesberg, Louis, 5054
Krishna, Shyam, 469
Krishna Iyer, V. R., 2214
Krislov, Joseph, 4700
Kristanto, Bambang, 2873
Krjažkov, P. É., 1131
Krohn, Karl R., 3627
Krohn, Marvin D., 1132
Kroker, Arthur, 4044, 5041
Krosnick, Jon A., 5134
Krouse, Richard, 5009
Krueger, Janet, 558
Kruglanski, Arie W., 594
Kruidenier, H., 4449
Kruijt, Dirk, 4135
Kruk, Simon, 4787
Krupiński, Jerzy, 4401
Kruse, H. J., 5465
Kruttschnitt, Candace, 5198
Krylov, A. I., 3584

Krysinski, Wladimir, 2445
Krzemień-Ojak, Sław, 955
Krzepkowski, Stanisław, 1296
Kubik, Włodzimierz, 3082
Kubitschek, Warren N., 4203
Kučenko, V. I., 525
Kučera, Milan, 2794
Kuczi, Tibor, 2137
Kudrin, V., 2215
Kühne, F., 2983
Kuhnle, Stein, 5291, 5292
Kuipers, Theo. A. F., 44
Kuji, Toshitake, 330, 501
Kul'kin, A. M., 4045
Kulcsár, Kálmán, 956, 2446, 2537, 5273
Kuličenko, M. I., 957
Kulich, Jindra, 2095
Kulikov, V. V., 3950
Kulikowska, Wanda, 3154
Kulikowski, Roman, 3154
Kumada, Toshio, 3633
Kumar, Krishna, 4201
Kumar, Ravinder, 2398
Kumar, Vijay, 2236
Kumar, Virendra, 3068
Kumar Ghosh, Suniti, 2282
Kunczik, Michael, 1706
Küng, Emil, 3695
Kuo, Eddie C. Y., 1613, 1707, 3102
Kuper, Adam, 3072
Kurian, Paul, 4594
Kurkin, B. A., 4980
Kurmanbaeva, N. M., 559
Kurosu, Nobuyuki, 3155
Kurtz, Marie France D., 4402
Kutas, János, 4483
Kutrzeba-Pojnarowa, Anna, 958
Kuz'min, É. S., 4141
Kuz'mina, L., 872
Kužel'naja, I. P., 1133
Kwaśniewski, Krzysztof, 1772
Kwok, Yin-Wang, 3819
Kyan, Shiichi, 4301
Kyntäjä, Timo, 1249

La Garanderie, Antoine de, 2138
La Haye, Yves de, 1562
La Rossa, Ralph, 3156
Laakkonen, Vesa, 4941
Laaksonen, Oiva, 4716
Labin, Suzanne, 4789
Labkovskaja, G. S., 1773
Laborde, Genie Z., 3999
Labourdette, Sergio Daniel, 784
Labrousse, Alain, 3322
Labruyere, Chantal, 4708
Lachenmann, Gudrun, 3496
Lachiver, Marcel, 2538
Lacroix, Jean-Michel, 688
Ladd, Robert T., 4378
Ladj-Teichmann, Dagmar, 3250
Ladner, Benjamin, 2108

Lador-Lederer, Joseph, 1372
Ladrière, Paul, 1460
Ladsous, Jacques, 5293
Laeyendecker, L., 2447
Lafarge, Claude, 1815
Laffargue, B., 5182
Lafferty, William M., 4717, 4981
Lagrange, H., 1134-35
Lagrave, Rose-Marie, 4288
Laing, John E., 2988
Laitin, David D., 1424
Lajeunesse-Pillard, Nicole, 2651
Lake, Robert W., 3854
Laksaci, Mohammed, 4119
Laliberty, Rene, 5448
Lallement, J., 1513
Lamberechts, Luc, 1816
Lambert, Angela, 4814
Lambert, Denis-Clair, 5364
Lambert, Wallace E., 2652
Lamming, G. N., 4289
Lancelot, Alain, 377
Land, Hilary, 5365
Land, Kenneth C., 2795
Landau, C. E., 4290
Landau, Simha F., 1136
Landes, David S., 331
Landry, R., 1614
Lane, David, 4790, 4863
Lane, Dermot A., 1297
Lane, Jan-Erik, 2055
Langaney, André, 231
Lange, Norbert de, 2796
Lange, Peter, 4621
Langford, C. M., 2874
Langkau-Herrmann, Monika, 4891
Langlois, Claude, 1373, 1425
Langton, Kenneth P., 5033
Lantoine, Catherine, 2875
Lantz, Herman R., 45
Lanuza, Alberto, 4834
Lanza-Kaduce, Lonn, 1132
Lanzetti, Clemente, 1298
Laor, Nathaniel, 2836
Lapierre, André, 5157
Lapierre, J. W., 502
Lapierre-Adamcyk, Evelyne, 3157
Łapiński-Tyszka, Krystyna, 3696
Laponce, Jean, 2489
Laporte, Jean-Pierre, 4622
Laprévote, Gilles, 2139
Larionescu, Maria, 1514
Larose, André, 2539
Larson, Calvin J., 5199
Laserna, Roberto, 4898
Lash, Scott, 868
Lasker, G. W., 505
Lassman, Peter, 2166
Latouche, Daniel, 5041
Latouche, Serge, 286, 879
Latreille, Geneviève, 4484
Latta, Geoffrey W., 3991

Lau, Richard R., 599
Laubier, Patrick de, 583, 1426
Lauderdale, Pat, 1137
Laumann, Edward O., 397
Laurent, Philippe, 2490
Laurin-Frenette, Nicole, 5041
Laurito, Clemente R., 4164
Lautard, E. Hugh, 2216
Lautman, Jacques, 179, 959, 3158
Lavely, W. R., 2931
Lavoie, Francine, 5449
Lawson, William D., 2335
Le Borgne, Louis, 3323
Le Breton, David, 2597
Le Doeuff, Michelle, 82
Le Gall, Didier, 303
Le Goff, Jacques, 4718
Le Net, Michel, 5074
Le Pape, Marc, 3040
Le Roy, Étienne, 1250
Lean, R., 2016
Leathers, Charles G., 4791
Leavitt, Jacqueline, 3855
Lebart, Ludovic, 3967
Lebel, Pierre, 648
Leblici, Huseyin, 759
Lebon, André, 3497
Lebra, Takie Sugiyama, 3251
Lechner, Frank J., 3324
Lechner, Norbert, 960
Leclercq, Jean Michel, 1955
Ledbetter, Rosanna, 2989
Ledoux, Yves, 332
Ledrut, Raymond, 333
Ledvinka, James, 760
Lee, B. S., 2932
Lee, Barrett A., 3823, 3856
Lee, Bun Song, 3548
Lee, Clive Howard, 2399
Lee, Gary R., 2742
Lee, Jung-Sokk, 1740
Lee, Mun-Woong, 3498
Lee, Raymond N., 1366
Lee, Shun-shin, 2631
Lefton, Mark, 2837
Légaré, Jacques, 2723
Legault, Albert, 1138
Légé, Bernard, 3763
Leger, Alain, 2140
Legge, Jerome S., 2990
Legge, Karen, 761
Legowicz, Jan, 1139
Legrain, Dominique, 3600
Lehner, Franz, 5294
Lehrer, Evelyn, 2933, 2934
Leicht, Kevin, 1494
Leif, Joseph, 4733
Leipert, Christian, 4403
Leiter, Jeffrey, 706
Leitner, Helga, 4291
Lejbzon, B., 1130
Lelli, Marcello, 4142

Lemel, Yannick, 961, 4404
Lemieux, Claude, 3159
Lemieux, Pierre, 4792
Lemke, Christiane, 2694
Lemon, Anthony, 4165
Lenk, Peter J., 667
Lennard, Henry L., 3857
Lennard, Suzanne H. Crowhurst, 3857
Lenoir, N., 1579
Lenoir, Rémi, 2737
Lenski, Gerhard, 2491
Leocatta, Silvia R., 5200
Leonard, Peter, 484
Leonard, Wilbert M. II, 2830
Leonard-Barton, Dorothy, 1563
Lepehin, A. V., 46
Lepper, Mark R., 813
Lequin, Yves-Claude, 2381
Leroy, X., 5475
Leslau, Abraham, 3804
Lesný, Ivan, 3083
Lester, Richard Allen, 4701
Leung, Angela K., 1817, 2935
Levasseur, Jacqueline, 2001
Levi, Michael, 1251
Leviatan, Uri, 4081
Levin, Henry M., 1956
Levin, Nora, 1374
Levine, Mark F., 3976
Levine, Robert A., 990
Levinsen, Jørn, 287
Levitt, Cyril, 2056
Lévy, Diane E., 2936
Lévy, Marie-Françoise, 3252
Lévy, René, 180
Lévy, Thierry, 5201
Lew, Roland, 3951
Lewicki, Pawel, 600
Lewis, Bernard, 1375
Lewis, Glen, 1140
Lewis, Herbert S., 3325
Lewis, Laurie L., 820
Lewis, Paul, 4585
Lhijumba, Beat J., 4292
Li, K. T., 2797
Lichtenstein, Heinz, 503
Lichtenstein, Peter M., 4793
Liebetrau, Henrik, 5295
Liebman, Charles S., 1299
Liebrand, Wim B. G., 443
Liehm, Antonin J., 1818
Lilge, Hans-Georg, 584
Lim, Hy-Sop, 2167
Lim, Linda Y. C., 3326
Lima Camargo, Luis Octavio de, 4405
Limage, Leslie J., 4293
Lin, Thung-Rung, 700
Linares Valdivia, Edmundo, 2057
Lincoln, James R., 689
Linden, Hans, 5384
Lindgren, Jarl, 2937
Lindzey, Gardner, 125

Ling, Peter, 1892
Lingsom, Susan, 4406
Linhart, Daniel, 4166
Linn, Johannes F., 3858
Linneweber, Volker, 633, 636
Lion, Antoine, 2090
Lipman, Jonathan N., 3327
Lippe, Angelika, 4623
Lippold, M., 4294
Lipset, Seymour Martin, 837
Lipshitz-Phillips, Susan, 5130
Lipsitz, George, 1300
Lipsky, Michael, 5296
Lisicyn, Ju. P., 5422
Liska, Allen E., 811, 812
Lisle, Edmond, 103
Lisle-Williams, Michael, 2283, 3952
Lisón, Carmelo, 504
Liss, L. F., 334
Lissak, Moshe, 5034
Lissowski, Grzegorz, 427
Listhaug, Ola, 1073
Listvin, V. F., 1070
Lisý, Ján, 2492
Littlejohn, Virginia, 4000
Livada, Svetozar, 2798
Liveanu, Vasile, 335
Livingstone, D. W., 2284
Livšic, Ju., 962
Ljancev, P. P., 526
Llaumett, Maria, 3499
Llera Ramo, Francisco José, 4911
Lloyd, Genevieve, 232
Locatis, Craig, 2141
Lockett, Betty A., 2738
Lockett, Martin, 4719
Locoh, Thérèse, 2938
Lodge, Tom, 3400
Lofland, John, 4942
Lofquist, William A., 5297
Logan, John, 3875
Logan, John R., 3401, 3859
Logue, John, 5298
Lohr, Kathleen, 5464
Lojkine, Jean, 2285
Lokombe Kitete, Ndew'Okongo, 1615
Lollivier, Stéfan, 4295
Lombard, Jacques, 1197
Lomov, B. F., 470
Long, J. Scott, 288
Long, Norman, 2493
Long, Samuel, 4763
Long, Susan, 701
Long, Theodore E., 1290
Longuenesse, Elisabeth, 2286
Lönnroth, Lars, 2353
Loos, Jocelyne, 4407
Lopata, P. P., 3601
López Villegas-Manjarrez, Virginia, 4624
Loptson, P. J., 475
Lord, Charles G., 813
Loree, Donald J., 2216

Lorenz, Frederick O., 5322
Lőrincz, Lajos, 4485
Los', V. A., 3585
Löschper, Gabi, 634, 636
Losenkov, V. A., 5063
Losev, M. M., 4748
Losonczi, Ágnes, 5423
Louis, Marie-Victoire, 4265
Louis-Gérin, Christiane, 5202
Louvel, Denis, 4335
Lovatt, David, 4082
Lovejoy, F. H., 2612
Lovejoy, Paul E., 2237
Lovett, Tom, 2096
Low, Stuart A., 4198
Lowe, Graham S., 4620
Lowe, Philip, 1708
Lowitt, Thomas, 4552, 4625
Löwy, Michaël, 1461
Loy, Pamela Hewitt, 3041
Loyola, Maria Andréa, 5398
Loza, Sara, 2991
Lubit, Roy, 5133
Lucas, Erhard, 4626
Lucas, Madeleine, 1957
Lucca-Irizarry, Nydia, 3449
Lučinva, S. M., 2287
Lucke, Doris, 3084
Luckmann, Thomas, 1616
Lüdtke, Hartmut, 4408
Lufler, Henry S. Jr., 2022
Luger, Kurt, 1709
Luhmann, Niklas, 963
Luloff, A. E., 4083
Lundu, Maurice C., 162
Lupri, Eugen, 3144
Luque, Enrique, 880
Lura, Russell P., 2943
Lusk, Cynthia M., 283
Luthans, Fred, 795
Luttberg, Norman R., 5010
Lutyńska, Krystyna, 386
Lutz, Wofgang, 2876
Luxardo, Hervé, 3697
Lwechungura Kamuzora, C., 2939
Lykken, David T., 1071
Lynch, Frederick R., 112
Lynch, Lisa M., 4202
Lyon, David, 47
Lyons, David, 1219
Lysenko, A. A., 2448
Lyson, Thomas A., 83

Maarse, J. A. M., 4225
Mabile, Jacques, 4423
MacDonald, Keith M., 4486
MacEoin, Denis, 1376
MacGregor, D., 4794
Machado Pais, José, 964
Machalek, Richard, 2474
Machan, Tibor R., 1252
Machin, Howard, 103

Mack, Arien, 186
Mackerras, Colin, 1198
Mackie, Diane, 707, 813
MacNamara, Donald E. J., 5203
Madan, Gurmukh Ram, 3698
Madan, N. L., 4912
Madge, Nicola, 5075
Madhava Rao, A. G., 3860
Madjarian, Grégoire, 3937
Mador, Ju. P., 2288
Maeda, Daisaku, 2762
Maeda, Yutaka, 233
Maffesoli, Michel, 3042
Maghan, Jess, 3043
Maglione, Jean, 3861
Maguire, Patricia, 2598
Magun, V. S., 527
Maharov, V. G., 2449
Maheshwari, Shriram, 4835
Maier, Walter, 4409
Maingot, A. P., 3442
Mainwaring, Scott, 1427
Mainwaring-White, Sarah, 4878
Mair, Nathan H., 1428
Maire, Jean-Claude, 1515
Máiz, Ramón, 4795
Majeed, Akhtar, 4796
Majer, Andrzej, 2799
Majumdar, Prabhat Kumara, 2002
Maki, Masahide, 2739
Maksimov, A. G., 4336
Mal, Suraj., 597
Mal'cev, V. A., 4113
Malačič, Janez, 4167, 4168
Malanowski, Andrzej, 4627
Malanowski, Jan, 4515
Maldonado, Victor Alfonso, 3862
Malengreau, Jacques, 3328
Mall, M. G., 2097
Malić, Adolf, 3863
Malikowski, Marian, 3864, 3865
Malinin, V., 234
Malle, Silvana, 4337
Malloy, Thomas, 3378
Malyško, L. N., 2450
Mamedov, N. M., 3602
Mamoria, C. B., 4553
Mamoria, Satish, 4553
Man Rhim, Soon, 3253
Manchanda, Rajinder Kaur, 5106
Mandell, Myrna, 336
Manderson, Lenore, 2599
Manganaro Favaretto, Gilda, 4797
Mani, A., 560
Manigart, Philippe, 5035
Mann, M., 168
Mann, Michael, 4836
Mann, Ram Singh, 235
Mann, Susan, 3866
Mann, Susan A., 4084
Mannari, Hiroshi, 5042
Mannheimer, Renato, 5011

Manor, Yohanan, 3402
Mansell, Jacquelynne, 4410
Manz, Charles C., 708
Marçais, Dominique, 1317
Marcel, Odile, 1893
Marčenko, M. N., 4837
Marcus, George, 5009
Mare, Robert D., 438, 3403, 4203
Marec, Yannick, 4120
Maree, Johann, 4628
Margalit, Baruch A., 635
Marger, Martin N., 3329
Marginson, Paul, 4554
Margolis, Joseph, 337
Marhuenda, Jean-Pierre, 1564
Mari Bhat, P. N., 2877
Marianelli, Alessandro, 2289
Mariański, Janusz, 1479
Marié, Michel, 4046
Marini, Margaret Mooney, 2058, 2709
Marion, Marie-Odile, 2217
Markham, William T., 762
Markiewicz-Lagneau, Janina, 2048
Marković, Mihailo, 4858, 4864
Marks, Shula, 3555
Mármora, Leopoldo, 965
Marolla, Diana, 5224
Maroney, Heather Jon, 3254
Marques Pereira, Bérengère, 2992
Marra, Ezio, 2168
Mars, Gerald, 3118, 3460
Marsden, Peter V., 397, 1141
Marsden, Terry, 4085
Marshall, Dawn, 3443
Marshall, Gordon, 4296
Marshall, John M., 4749
Marshall, Susan E., 3255
Marshner, Connaught, 1958
Marta Sosa, Joaquin, 2059
Martens, Bernd, 398
Martens, L., 1923
Martin, John Powell, 5450
Martin, Kenneth E., 3634
Martin, Thomas N., 804
Martindale, Don Albert, 5299
Martinelli, Alberto, 5451
Martinelli, Bruno, 3699
Martínez, Ruben, 3291
Martinotti, Guido, 4895
Martire, Gregory, 3404
Martorelli, Horacio, 2800
Marus, Michael R., 3405
Maruyama, Tetsuo, 2060
Maryański, Andrzej, 3444
Mascarenhas, Ophelia, 2600
Maschino, Maurice Tarik, 1959
Mascia-Lees, Frances E., 3256
Mascie-Taylor, C. G. N., 505, 561
Maslow-Armand, Laura, 3290
Mason, David, 690
Mason, John, 4602
Massard, Josiane, 2653

Massé, Jacqueline, 2740
Massey, David, 2290
Massey, Douglas S., 3406
Mastekaasa, Arne, 3977, 4411
Masters, Roger D., 1142, 3257
Masuch, Michael, 713
Masur, Jenny, 4297
Matejko, A., 3330, 3500
Matejko, Alexander J., 729, 966, 4730
Matenaar, Dieter, 4001
Mather, Celia E., 4298
Mathews, Georges, 2940
Mathiowetz, Nancy A., 382
Mathur, Prakash Chand, 5300
Matić, Milan, 4531
Matjaš, T. P., 848
Matsumoto, Kazuyoshi, 967
Matteson, Michael T., 4392
Matthaei, Julie A., 4299
Matthews, Bruce, 3407
Matthews, P. W., 1960
Matthiessen, P. C., 2540
Mattick, P. Jr., 48
Mattioni, Angelo, 5476
Matulenis, A., 3160
Mátyus, Aliz, 3700, 3701
Mauger, Paul A., 635
Maupas, Didier, 2003
Maurer, John G., 719
Maurice, M., 4555
Mauskopf, Joséphine, 444
Mauss, Armand L., 1429
Maweya, Mata Lingume, 5204
Maxwell, James D., 3258
Maxwell, Mary Percival, 3258
Mayer, Ellen R., 2595
Mayer, Lawrence, 2072
Mayer, Susan E., 3416
Mayer, Thomas F., 668
Mayhew, Bruce H., 399
Mayhew, Leon, 2451
Maynard, A. K., 3847
Maynard, Douglas W., 1143
Maynard, Mary, 3366
Mayr, Hans, 4430
Mayrl, William W., 49
Maysuyama, Hiromitsu, 5205
Mazars, Lucien, 4516
Mazepa, V. I., 1774
Mazur, Allan, 5036
Mazur, Julie, 5036
Mazyrin, V. M., 4629
Mbilinyi, Marjorie J., 2600
Mbuinga, Vubu, 3161
Mbunda, D., 1024
McAdams, Dan P., 623
McAllister, Alfred L., 5134
McAllister, Ian, 1421, 3489, 4913
McAndrew, Francis T., 823
McCall, George J., 370
McCann, Michael, 4585
McCartan, Anne-Marie, 2086

McCarthy, C. M., 163
McCarthy, John D., 498
McCarthy, Thomas A., 236
McCartney, James L., 104
McClure, John, 289
McConnell, Scott, 2354
McCormack, Thelma, 1025
McCrig, Robert, 2074
McCullagh, Ciaran, 4879
McCulloch, Charles E., 2998
McDaniel, C. K., 3162
McDaniel, Susan A., 2650, 3163
McDevitt, John F., 5160
McDonald, J. W., 2871
McDonald, Joseph A., 4630
McDonough, Peter, 834
McDowell, Charles P., 5206
Mčedlov, M. P., 1301
McFarlane, H. P., 2996
McFate, Patricia A., 968
McGlamery, C. Donald, 1147
McKee, David L., 3501
McKeganey, Neil, 677
McKersie, Robert B., 4551
McKirnan, David J., 1617
McLanahan Sara S., 3978
McLaurin, R. D., 3319
McLeay, E. M., 3867
McLeod, Jack M., 836
McMahon, A. M., 471
McMillan, Marilyn M., 2795
McNabb, Robert, 4204
McNall, Scott G., 237
McNeill, William H., 3445
McNicoll, Geoffrey, 2801
McQuarie, Donald, 2313
McQuillan, Kevin, 4047
Mechling, Jay, 1819
Meece, Judith L., 545
Meeker, Barbara F., 585
Meertens, Roel W., 387
Meggitt, Mervyn J., 1239
Meghe, D. R., 4905
Meheu, Louis, 126
Mehlman, Jeffrey, 3408
Mehrenberger, Gabriel, 4412
Mehryar, Amir H., 3164
Mehta, Shirin, 3702
Mehta, Shiv R., 3703
Meier, Gretl S., 4413
Meier, Kenneth J., 3331
Meier, Peter C., 4086
Meier, Robert F., 1074
Meikle, Douglas B., 41
Meiksins, Peter F., 4338
Meillassoux, Claude, 2169
Meitz, June E. G., 3096
Meja, Volker, 2396
Melamed, Angela, 5458
Melbeck, Christian, 3639
Melburg, Valerie, 601
Meltzer, Ronald I., 4869

Melucci, Alberto, 763
Menard, Scott, 5207
Mencher, Joan P., 3704
Mendelsohn, Everett, 1516
Mendes Diz de Cabo, Ana María, 5463
Méndez Dominguez, Alfredo, 1026
Mendras, Henri, 2452, 3705
Menendez, Eduardo L., 5135
Menger, Pierre-Michel, 1844
Menoras, Henri, 2724
Mensah, Ebow, 2654
Menzel, Elmar, 5384
Mercer, G. W., 3301
Mercier, Pierre-Alain, 4048
Mereminskij, G. M., 2288
Merler, Alberto, 371
Merrett, Stephen, 3868
Merriman, W. Richard, 3409
Mertins, Günter, 3768, 3869
Merton, Robert K., 1377
Metcalf, David, 4631
Metcalf, William J., 969
Meurant, Jacques, 4414
Meyer, David R., 3870
Meyer, John W., 4844
Meyer, Manfred, 1710
Meyer, Philip, 1711
Meyer-Larsen, Werner, 4359
Meyrowitz, Joshua, 2655
Meyzenq, Claude, 2511
Mežvev, V., 970
Miccoli, Paolo, 238
Miceli, Sergio, 1027
Michalczyk, Tadeusz, 5136
Michalowicz, Jerzy, 1560
Michalsky, Helga, 5301
Michna, Karol, 3165
Micklin, Michael, 3586
Midgley, James, 5302, 5303
Midwinter, Eric, 2741
Mieczkowski, Bogdan, 3979
Mielke, James H., 2541
Mieno, Takashi, 5304
Miethe, Terance D., 2742
Migliarese, P., 742
Mignon, Jean-Marie, 2695
Miguens, José Enrique, 1144
Mihajlova, L. V., 4632
Miheev, A. I., 528
Mikami, Takeshi, 849
Mikell, Gwendolyn, 3259
Mikov, É. G., 2802
Milburn, Michael A., 5134
Miles, Matthew B., 338
Miles, Robert, 3410, 3411
Milić, Andelka, 4982
Milić, Vojin, 1517
Milic-Czerniak, Róża, 4103
Milkovich, George, 4169
Miller, Arthur H., 1480
Miller, Danny, 756
Miller, Dean F., 5452

Miller, Delbert C., 4143
Miller, Doug, 4556
Miller, Errol, 1894
Miller, Fred Dycus Jr., 4865
Miller, Jack, 1378
Miller, Joan G., 971
Miller, Karen A., 3166
Miller, Lawrence M., 972
Miller, Michael K., 3635
Miller, Peter V., 448
Miller, R. W., 239
Miller, Robert K. Jr., 2936
Miller, Ronald L., 4679
Miller, Thomas G., 5305
Miller, William C., 973
Mills, Donald L., 3144
Mills, Edgar, 714
Mills, Harlan D., 144
Millsap, Mary Ann, 2601
Milner, Jean Claude, 2004
Milo, Daniel, 1712
Milogolov, S. V., 974
Min, Pyong Gap, 3502
Minault, Gail, 1379
Minerbi Belgrado, Anna, 1302
Minina, L. F., 4983
Minns, Daniel Richard, 5012
Minor, W. William, 2453
Mintz, Frank, 4798
Miquel, Pierre, 1713
Mir, Mehraj-ud-Din, 5208
Mirabile, Francesco, 4750
Miracle, Andrew W. Jr., 1618, 2121
Mirescu, Adriana, 1462
Mirloup, Joël, 3871
Mirowski, Włodzimierz, 3872
Miscol, Oltea, 927
Mishra, G. N., 3873
Mishra, L. N., 1145
Misra, B. D., 2987
Misztal, Barbara A., 240
Misztal, Bronisław, 240, 4943
Misztal, Maria, 1961
Mitchell, Juliet, 3260
Mitchell, R. J., 3152
Mitchell, Richard G. Jr., 1146
Mitchell, Valory, 1117
Mitropoulos, Mit, 1714
Mitter, Dwarka Nath, 3261
Mittler, Hans, 4415
Miura, Shigeji, 1715, 4902
Miyamoto, Kohji, 785, 786
Mleczko, Franciszek Wiktor, 2170
Mlinar, Zdravko, 3872
Mlonek, Krystyna, 2696
Moane, Geraldine, 1117
Moatassime, Ahmed, 3262
Mobe-Fansiama, Anicet, 2005
Mock, Philip, 4465
Moen, Elizabeth W., 2531
Moitel, Pierre, 1962
Mok, A. L., 4002

Mokrzycki, Edmind, 50
Mokyr, Joel, 2803
Molho, Ian, 3446
Möller, Hans-Georg, 3874
Molnar, Joseph J., 2335
Molnárné Venyige, Júlia, 4300
Molotch, Harvey, 3875
Moltmann, Jürgen, 1303
Moncada, Alberto, 1895
Monchambert, Sabine, 1963
Mongia, J. N., 4720
Monjardet, Dominique, 850
Montanino, Fred, 1071
Montero García, Feliciano, 1380
Montero Gibert, José Ramón, 5013
Montgomery, Stuart, 2838
Montjardet, Dominique, 764
Montt Balmaceda, Manuel, 4572
Moore Johnson, Susan, 2142
Moorhouse, H. F., 975
Mooser, Josef, 2291
Moragas Spa, Miguel de, 1716
Mørch, Frede, 5306
Moreno, José Luis, 3470
Morgan, Gareth, 2454
Morgan, John H., 5399
Morgan, S. P., 2602, 2941, 2952, 3004
Morgan, William R., 2006
Morgon, A., 1570
Mori, Mototaka, 51
Morin, Edgar, 188
Morin, Violette, 1717
Morinis, E. Allan, 1444
Morissette, Pauline, 5132
Morita, Yohji, 2707
Moriya, Takahiko, 3636
Mormont, Marc, 3706
Morningstar, Patricia Cleckner, 5137
Morokvašić, Mirjana, 3263, 3447, 3503
Morot-Sir, Edouard, 1028
Morozov, B. M., 1718
Morozov, M. V., 4339
Morris, L. D., 4170
Morris, Lydia D., 3980
Morris, Raymond N., 976
Morris, Robert, 5307
Morrison, David, 1708
Morrison, Peter H., 3556
Morrison, Thomas J., 602, 796
Morse, Barbara J., 5207
Morton, Henry W., 3876
Moscovici, Serge, 189
Mosher, William D., 1304, 2993
Moskowitz, Debbie S., 3134
Mosley, Paul, 1719
Motlhabi, Mokgethi Buti George, 3412
Motomura, Hiroshi, 5138
Motrič, É. L., 2802
Mott, Frank L., 977
Mott, James, 1245
Mott, Susan H., 977
Mottaz, Clifford, 4416

Motwani, Kewal, 52
Moum, Torbjørn, 3977
Mouzelis, Nicos, 241
Moya, Carlos, 506
Moyser, George, 4987
Možný, Ivo, 3167
Mrela, Krzysztof, 622
Mroczkowski, Tomasz, 4557
Mubyarto, 5308
Muchnik, I. B., 3742
Muchnik, M. B., 3742
Muecke, Marjorie A., 3264
Muel-Dreyfus, Francine, 2143, 5477
Mueller, Dennis C., 749
Mueser, Peter, 2376
Mugishima, Fumio, 5209
Muhić, Fuad, 1381
Muhiudeen, Clare, 1476
Muir, Donald E., 1147
Mukherjee, S. N., 1813
Mukhopadhyay, Carol Chapnick, 2603
Muldur, U., 4049
Mulkay, Michael, 339
Mullan, Brendan P., 3406
Mullaney, Marie Marmo, 3265
Mullen, Brian, 4104
Muller, Edward N., 4984
Müller, Karl, 2500
Muller, Nice Lecocq, 3903
Mulligan, James G., 1964
Mullins, Lynn S., 1820
Mummendey, Amélie, 636, 637
Munizaga, Giselle, 1565
Münkel, Wilma, 2994
Münkler, Herfried, 2400
Munnichs, J. M. A., 2743
Muñoz, Guillermo, 1933
Muñoz-Perez, Francisco, 3085
Munslow, Barry, 2292
Münster, Arno, 1319
Muntean, George, 1821
Munz, Rainer, 5309
Muoghalu, Leonard N., 3877
Muramatsu, Michio, 4960
Muramatsu, Yasuko, 1075, 1720
Murav'ev, V. I., 851
Murdia, Ratna, 5470
Murdock, Steve H., 4069
Murgatroyd, Linda, 4487
Murillo Ferrol, Francisco, 2455
Murniek, É., 2171
Murphy, M. J., 2942, 3910
Murphy, Peter, 1220, 4808
Murphy, Raymond, 787
Murray, Barbara, 2590
Murray, Charles, 5107
Murray, Charles A., 5310
Murray, Linda A., 105
Murrell, Peter, 4944
Murthy, P. K., 3001
Murthy, Sheela, 2355
Murton, Brian J., 3587

Musatova, L. Ja., 3603
Muschkin, Clara G., 3448
Musgrave, P. W., 1221
Mushaben, Joyce Marie, 1965, 2697
Mushkat, Miron, 4892, 5064
Musil, Jiří, 3612
Musil, Siri, 3878
Mustafa, Mutasim Abu Bakr, 2995
Mutran, Elizabeth, 2744
Myers, David E., 2332
Myers, George C., 2878, 3448
Myers, Mildred S., 5002
Myers, Samuel L. Jr., 3129, 5210

N'Kaloulou, Bernard, 3707
Nacer, Bourenane, 2494
Nachreiner, Friedhelm, 4417
Nagai, Michio, 1566
Nagao, Yoshimi, 5052
Nagata, Eriko, 586
Nagel, Joane, 3332
Naghma-E., Rehan, 2996
Nagla, B. K., 2172
Nagpaul, Hans, 5079
Nagy, Attila, 548
Nagy, Endre, 1775
Nagy, Katalin S., 978
Nahoum-Grappe, Véronique, 1836
Nails, Debra, 2604, 2605
Naimark, N. M., 1814
Nair, K. S., 3333
Nakagawa, Hideki, 1199
Nakajima, Akinori, 5211
Nakajima, Michio, 1076
Nakamura, Masato, 2293
Namihira, Isao, 2456, 4301
Nancy, Michel, 3665
Nandy, Santosh K., 59
Nap, Charles B., 2336
Napoli, Mario, 4680
Narayan, B. K., 3708
Narayan, V. K., 702
Nash, June, 4302
Natale, Marcello, 2804
Nath, Raghu, 702
Nathanson, C. A., 2879
Nauta, A. P. N., 1051
Navajtis, G. A., 3086
Navarro, Peter, 4071
Navlakha, Suren, 2061
Nayar, P. K. B., 2881
Naylor, John B., 4211
Naylor, R. T., 5041
Nazareth, J. Manuel, 2805
Nazimova, A. K., 2268
Nazir-Ali, Michael, 1382
Nazzari, Muriel, 3266
Ndoma, Ungina, 1619
Near, Janet P., 4418
Neave, Guy R., 2062
Nedelcovych, Mima, 2064
Nedelmann, Birgitta, 4945

Nef, Rolf, 5014
Negi, Akira, 2060
Neidert, Lisa J., 1966
Neikirk, William, 4057
Neiman, Guillermo, 4189
Nejmer, Ju. L., 5065
Nelde, Peter Hans, 1620
Nell, Marian, 3379
Nelson, G. K., 1445
Nelson, Hal, 4205
Nelson, James F., 5212
Nelson, William, 2218
Némedi, Dénes, 1077
Németh, Károly, 2698
Nemitz, Barbara, 4303
Nerlove, Marc, 2934
Nerudová, Liliana, 3167
Nešić, Dragoljub, 3709
Ness, Gayl De Forest, 2997
Netter, Jeffry M., 1636
Neuamn, Elías, 5213
Neuman, Carole A., 389
Nevadomsky, Joseph, 4488
Nevesely, Karel, 2294
Newman, James L., 2943
Newman, John L., 2998
Ng'ang'a, James Mwangi, 1896
Nice, David C., 4985
Nichols, Keith R., 823
Nicholson, Linda J., 2605, 2606
Nicholson, Michael, 106
Nickolaus, Barbara, 1705
Nicolas, Jean-Pierre, 5108
Nicolas Ortiz, Carlos, 5424
Nielsen, François, 2225
Nielsen, Greg N., 340
Nielsen, Kurt Aagaard, 1148
Niemi, Iiris, 4351, 4352
Nienstedt, Heinz-Werner, 5050
Niitsu, Koichi, 3879, 3880
Nijkamp, Peter, 3785
Nikol'skij, L. B., 1305
Nikolić, Radivoj, 4799
Nikolić, Tomislav Ž., 3964
Nilakant, V., 4508
Niland, John, 4691
Niosi, Jorge, 2295, 5041
Nishihara, Kazuhisa, 242
Nishine, Kazuo, 1897
Nishishita, Akitoshi, 2745, 2762
Nishiyama, Misako, 669
Nishiyama, Toshihiko, 1481
Nissen, Ursula, 2135
Nizet, J., 2023, 2144
Nizet, Jean, 2145
Nobel, Peter, 5043
Noda, Takashi, 5080
Noin, Daniel, 2543, 3588
Noiriel, Gérard, 3504, 3505
Nolan, Patrick D., 2491
Noma, Elliot, 5226
Nonoyama, Hisaya, 3087

Norem-Hebeisen, Ardyth, 5139
Norio, Reijo, 2839
Norris, William P., 797, 3881
North, Derek, 204
Noschis, Kaj, 3882
Novák, Mária, 5214
Novara, Francesco, 4144
Novikov, A. I., 2296
Novikov, V. V., 4489
Nowacki, Grzegorz, 2007
Nowak, Leszek, 480
Nowak, Margaret, 3506
Nowakowa, Irena, 3710
Nowakowski, Stefan, 2297
Nowicka, Ewa, 1463
Nowotny, Helga, 1516
Ntanombaye, P., 507
Numan, K. B., 351
Numata, Kenya, 788, 1222
Núñez Soto, Orlando, 3711
Nuss, Shirley, 3088
Nyden, Philip W., 4633
Nyquist, Thomas E., 2356
Nystrom, Paul C., 765
Nzeza, Bilakila, 3712

O'Barr, William M., 1612
O'Brien, Denise, 2607
O'Brien, Jay, 3713
O'Connell, Declan, 4913
O'Connell, Martin, 3044
O'Connor, Charles J., 608
O'Donnell, Guillermo, 4986
O'Higgins, Michael, 5366
O'Keefe, Daniel Lawrence, 1320
O'Loughlin, John, 3557
O'Loughlin, Mary-Ann, 2605
O'Malley, Michael N., 587
O'Malley, Pat, 1253
O'Malley, Patrick M., 5120
O'Neill, Maria Monica, 3883
O'Toole, Roger, 1306
Oberst, Timothy, 4914
Obidziński, Stanisław, 2746
Obradović, Daniela, 4815
Obradović, Marija, 4838
Ochi, Noboru, 1715
Ochiai, Emiko, 2173, 3267
Ochsmann, Randolph, 2882
Odendahl, Teresa, 4304
Odeye, Michèle, 730
Oepen, Manfred, 1721
Offe, Claus, 4808, 4812
Ogawa, Naohiro, 2999
Ogden, S. G., 4558
Ogryzko-Wiewiórski, Henryk, 378
Ohashi, Kaoru, 3493, 3852
Ohashi, Terue, 1722
Ohata, Hiroshi, 2747, 4946
Ohta, Yoshihiro, 5389
Ohyama, Nobuyoshi, 181, 4721
Ojima, Fumiaki, 1967

Okada, Naoyuki, 1723
Okada, Yoshitaka, 2948
Okaji, Toshio, 2298, 2299
Okamura, Jonathan Y., 3507
Oklobdžija, Mirjana, 4800
Okolo, Chukwudum Barnabas, 3413
Okoth-Ogendo, H. W. O., 4764
Okrent, Mark B., 243
Okuda, Kazuhiko, 341, 2883, 4105
Okuda, Noriaki, 3789
Okuda, Shinjo, 2008
Okun, Morris A., 3975
Okwesa, B. A., 1567
Ol'šanskij, D. V., 979
Oláh, Miklós, 4903
Older, Jules, 3414
Olędzki, Michał, 3000
Olejnikov, Ju. V., 3604
Oleničeva, G. V., 1149
Olesen Larsen, Peder, 2063
Oliveira-Roca, Maria, 3558
Oliver, Ivan, 1496
Oliver, Nick, 3953
Olivera C., Luis, 3899
Ollman, Bertell, 1968
Olney, Timothy J., 493
Ologoudou, Emile, 2300
Olson, James M., 814
Omar Lerda, Francisco, 3714
Ono, Michikuni, 244, 1568
Onushkin, Victor G., 2098
Onyango, Philista, 3149
Oomen, T. K., 3715, 5109
Oosten, Jarich, 245
Opp, Karl-Dieter, 824, 1078
Oriol, M., 508, 509
Oriol, Michel, 3508, 3509
Orleans, Leo A., 2806
Orlova, É. A., 902
Orlow, D., 1814
Ornstein, Michael, 4003
Oroszi, Zsuzsanna, 3077
Ortlieb, Heinz-Dietrich, 4636
Ortmeyer, A., 4183
Ory, Pascal, 1725
Osborne, J. Grayson, 3637
Osborne, Robert D., 1898
Oschlies, Wolf, 1383
Osgood, D. Wayne, 5220
Osiel, Mark, 1200-01
Osipov, N. É., 2457
Osipov, V., 1970
Ossowski, Stanisław, 980
Ostapenko, I. P., 2301
Osterfeld, David, 4801
Ostrowski, John W., 4904
Oswald, Hans, 182
Otomo, Atsushi, 2813
Ottomanský, J., 2688
Oudot, J., 1570
Ovalle, Nestor K. II, 766
Ovčinnikov, Ju. A., 4050

Overton, Elizabeth, 2577
Ovsjannikov, M. F., 1776
Owen, David R., 2661
Owens, Robert E. Jr., 1621
Owsley, Heidi H., 388
Ozawa, Takahiro, 1578

Pace, Enzo, 107
Pacewicz, Piotr, 2458
Pacheco, Angel M., 3449
Paddison, R., 3884
Padoux, André, 2608
Pagel, Mark D., 815
Pahl, Jan, 5445
Pahl, R. E., 2219
Pai Panandiker, V. A., 2807
Paillat, Paul, 2748, 2749
Pál, László, 981, 3559, 3620, 5214
Paldam, Martin, 4681
Palet, Ravi, 4594
Palfrey, Thomas R., 5015
Paliwal, M. R., 2459
Pallas, Aaron M., 1990
Palloix, Christian, 4839
Palloni, A., 2884
Pallottini, Michele, 982
Palmer, Donald, 3815
Palmer, Gill, 4559
Palmer, Michael Beaussenat, 1726
Palmer, Monte, 2064
Paloheimo, Heikki, 649
Pamuk, Elsie R., 2885
Pandolfi, Alessandro, 440
Pandy, Riajendra, 2220
Panjwani, Narendra, 4517
Papademetriou, Demetrios G., 3510
Papadopoulos, Jean, 1518
Papanek, Hanna, 4305
Papozjan, S. S., 400
Papp, Zsolt, 5311
Pappi, Franz Urban, 2357, 3638, 3639
Paquette, Lyne, 3334
Paradeise, Catherine, 4208
Parant, Alain, 2886
Pardo, Isaac J., 852
Parent, T. Wayne, 3409
Parish, William L., 3923
Park, Han S., 983
Parker, Jan Reese, 2863
Parker, Roy, 5365
Parnell, Allan, 2941
Parnell, Nina, 4390
Parnes, Herbert S., 4450
Parpart, Jane L., 2302
Parry, Geraint, 4987
Parthasarathi, J., 2808
Parton, Nigel, 5387
Partsch, Manfred, 5368
Parvathamma, C., 2238, 2239, 4226
Pascallon, Pierre, 1029
Paškov, A. S., 2460
Passanante, María I., 5369

Passaris, Solange, 731
Passeron, Jean-Claude, 4988
Passow, A. Harry, 2656
Pataki, Judit, 3969
Patel, M. L., 3716
Pateria, A. K., 767
Paternoster, Raymond, 5166
Pathak, K. B., 3001
Pathy, Jaganath, 3717
Patiño Avila, J. Ernesto, 53
Paty, D., 2009, 2020
Pauchet, Catherine, 1254
Paukert, Liba, 4306
Paul, Ellen Frankel, 4865
Paul, Jean-Jacques, 4420
Paul, Jean-Louis, 246
Paul, Jeffrey, 4865
Paul-Lévy, Françoise, 3885
Pavlov, O., 4421
Pazienti, Massimo, 3613
Pčelincev, O., 3900
Pearson, Judy Cornelia, 1569
Pearson, Roger, 3589
Peces-Barba Martínez, Gregorio, 1255
Pedan, V. P., 1072
Pedersen, Peder J., 4171, 4681
Pegov, S. A., 3605
Peil, Margaret, 562, 3886
Peled, Elad, 1971
Peloille, Bernard, 984
Pelzer White, Christine, 3268
Pendleton, Brian F., 428
Peneff, Jean, 429
Penninx, R., 3335
Pepitone, Albert, 296
Percy, M. B., 4673
Peressini, Mauro, 3511
Pérez, Benito, 4573
Pérez, Lisandro, 2009
Pérez, María, 1728
Pérez de Zapata, Amarilis, 2013
Pérez Gomez, Angel A., 1727
Pérez Sainz, J. P., 4172
Perkin, Gordon W., 2979
Perkins, Dwight Heald, 3718
Perkins, Robert L., 3954
Perlado, Fernando, 5478
Perner, Detlef, 4722
Perotti, Antonio, 3512
Perreault, Jeannine, 3334
Perret, Daniel, 4637
Perrin, G., 5370-71
Perrot, Michelle, 4682
Perrot, Philippe, 3045
Perry, Charles S., 430
Perry, Elizabeth, 1150
Persell, Caroline Hodges, 54
Persing, Bobbye Sorrels, 4004
Perucchi, Lucio, 4117
Peters, Heinz, 1972
Peters, J., 922, 4781
Peters, Michael, 113

Petersen, James C., 4447
Petersen, K. A., 3002
Petersen, Larry R., 1482, 3640
Petersen, Trond, 2303
Peterson, Abby, 2609
Peterson, Ruth D., 5215
Petit, François, 472
Petrov, L. V., 1729
Petruska, Richard, 574
Pétrusson, Pétur, 1497
Peukert, Reinhard, 1622
Peyrot, Mark, 5140
Pfetsch, Frank R., 128
Pflaum, Dieter, 1637
Phares, E. Jerry, 529
Phelps Brown, Henry, 4638
Philibert, Michel, 2750
Phillips, David R., 3719
Phillips, James F., 5453
Pialoux, Michel, 4544
Piazolo, Paul Harro, 1030
Piazzi, Giuliano, 510
Pieke, Frank N., 3336
Pierce, Glenn L., 5160
Pierce, Jennifer, 3168
Pierce, John C., 4979
Pieret, Janine, 2831
Pierrard, Pierre, 1430
Pierson, Christopher, 4840
Pietrucha, Jerzy, 4422
Pijnenburg, Bert, 1384
Pilichowski, Andrzej, 3720
Pilipenko, N. V., 4802
Pinc, Karel, 5312
Pineda Arroyo, José María, 2010
Pinkus, Benjamin, 1385
Pinto, Louis, 2358
Pinto, Marina, 2065
Piotet, Françoise, 4051, 4423
Piotrowski, Marcin, 1202
Pipat-Giraudel, Catherine, 4087
Pipping, Knut, 247
Pirages, Dennis, 3590
Pires, José Maria, 1498
Piret, Jean-Marc, 1431
Pirro, Federico, 5313
Pištora, Ladislav, 164
Pitch, Tamar, 3269
Pitrou, Agnès, 4307
Pittendrigh, Adele S., 55
Pittin, Renée, 4308
Piven, Frances Fox, 5094
Piveteau, Jacques, 1730
Piwowarski, Władysław, 1483
Place, Helen, 2221
Plane, David A., 3560
Plassard, François, 4048
Platkovskij, V. V., 985
Platteau, Jean-Philippe, 3721
Plauchu, Henri, 2840
Plessis, Jean-Claude, 4490
Pletnev, É., 2304

Pletsch, Alfred, 3887
Plimak, É. G., 2461
Poche, Bernard, 290
Podedworna, Hanna, 3169
Podgornyh, N. I., 1151
Poglia, Edo, 1973
Pohoski, Michał, 2337
Poinard, M., 3513, 4279
Poitevin, Guy, 1152
Poitou, Jean-Pierre, 4491
Pole, D. Graham, 2462
Polin, Claude, 4803
Polin, Raymond, 4803
Politis, Michel, 4052
Pollak, Michael, 4492
Pollak-Eltz, Angelina, 1203
Pollini, Gabriele, 5314
Pollock, Linda A., 3170
Pollock Petchevsky, Rosalind, 3270
Polonko, Karen A., 3048
Polton, Dominique, 5425
Polyan, P. M., 3888
Pompe, J. H., 4493
Ponak, Allen, 4566
Pond, Samuel B. III, 715
Pongrácz, T., 2944
Ponting, J. Rick, 691
Pool, John J., 3271
Poole, Michael, 4560
Pope, William Ray, 466
Popkewitz, Thomas S., 2024
Popov, Nebojša, 2066
Popović, Mihailo V., 2222
Popovski, Vesna, 3889
Pörn, Ingmar, 511
Porro, Renato, 1731
Porst, Rolf, 3171
Porter, Elaine G., 3003
Porter, Richard C., 3415
Portes, A., 3827
Portes, Alejandro, 3337
Portigliatti-Barbos, Mario, 5216
Portnjagin, A. P., 342
Porto, A. J., 1974
Posner, Barry Z., 2610
Post, Jerrold M., 2887
Postal, P., 5426
Postone, Moishe, 248
Potter, Jonathan, 249
Potter, Robert B., 4106
Poulalion, Gabriel, 2544
Poulat, Émile, 1432
Poulsen, Jørgen, 1556
Poupeye, Camille, 1857
Pousset, André, 678
Powell, Brian, 789
Powell, Fred, 2657
Powell, Gary N., 2610
Powell, Joseph Michaël, 3591
Powell, Robert J., 807
Power, Richard, 588
Powers, Mary G., 2336

Powers, Michael J., 144
Powers, Richard H., 1899
Prais, S. J., 4683
Pramling, Ingrid, 563
Pramualratana, Anthony, 2930
Prandi, Carlo, 1386
Prätorius, Rainer, 4947
Pravda, Alex, 4639
Pražáková, Jana, 2888
Preiswerk, Roy A., 1031
Preiswerk, Yvonne, 2889
Premfors, Rune, 2067
Premi, Mahendra K., 3561
Prensky, David, 728
Pressat, Roland, 2545, 2810, 2875
Presser, Harriet B., 4425
Preston, Samuel, 2877, 2945
Prevost, Gary, 4640
Pridatkina, L. P., 2359
Priest, T. B., 2360, 4948
Prieto Escudero, Germán, 3514, 4426
Prigožin, A. I., 768
Pringle, Charles D., 110
Prins, A. A. M., 1530
Prokopec, Jiří, 3089
Prudhomme, Claude, 1307
Pruitt, Charles R., 5217
Prutscher, Pius M., 3955
Pruvot, Michel, 3890
Puente, Sergio, 3839
Puente de Guzman, Maria Alicia, 1416
Pullega, Paolo, 1777
Pun, K. S., 3819
Purkait, Biswa Ranjan, 2011
Pushka, Asllan, 2546
Puškin, V. G., 343
Pust, Carola, 3272
Pynoos, Robert S., 2646

Qaysī, Māhir, 1900
Quah, Stella R., 5076
Quante, Stefan, 5315
Quarré, Dominique, 4886
Quere, Mireille, 1732
Quester, George H., 1733
Quine, Lyn, 5445
Quito, Emerita S., 5316

Raab, Erich, 1930
Rabier, Jacques-René, 555
Rabow, Jerome, 389
Raboy, Marc, 1734
Racionero, Luis, 4209
Rácz, Attila, 1256
Rácz, József, 5218
Radics, Katalin, 2351
Radkovský, Josef, 2890
Radnitzky, Gerard, 986
Radovanovic, Milorad, 1533
Radu, Michael S., 1153
Radway, Janice, 1822
Rafferty, Ellen, 1623

Raffi, Guy, 731
Raghuvanshi, M. S., 2699
Ragin, Charles C., 3416
Rahim, Syed A., 1552
Rai, Ramesh Chandra, 2236
Raillon, François, 2068
Raillon, Louis, 1901
Rainey, Hal G., 4893
Raiser, Harald, 716
Raizada, Ajit, 3338
Raj, Lajpat, 1446, 1902
Rajkiewicz, Antoni, 5077
Rajput, R. S., 4905
Ralic, Prvoslav, 2700
Rama, Germán W., 1975
Ramamonjisoa, Suzy, 5114
Ramanamma, A., 4309
Ramaswamy, E. A., 4561
Rambaud, Placide, 4641
Rambaudi, Daniele, 838
Ramella, Susana T. de Jefferies, 3515
Ramet, Pedro, 4310
Ramírez, Rafael, 2454
Ramírez Goicoechea, Eugenia, 987
Ramo, Simon, 4053
Ramos, Roberto, 4751
Ramu, G. N., 3172
Rančić, Miroljub, 2812
Rancic, Miroljub, 2811
Randall, Peter, 3379
Randall, Sara, 2870
Ranga Rao, K., 3891
Rangari, A. D., 2240
Ranger, Terence, 1195
Ranjard, Patrice, 2146
Rankin, Tom, 4410
Rankovič, Miodrag, 5317
Rao, P. S. S., 5427
Rapoport, Ammon, 445
Rapping, Elayne, 1735
Rashid, Mamunur, 1855
Rasila, Viljo, 3562
Rasinski, Kenneth, 606
Raškova, R. T., 988
Rasmussen, Erik, 2223
Rasse, Paul, 4032
Rassolov, M. M., 4841
Rathje, William, 3606
Rathkey, Paul, 4713
Ratz, Ursula, 4642
Raulet, Gérard, 2463
Rault, Daniel, 4173
Rauma, David, 5219
Ravenholt, R. T., 2891
Raveyre, Marie-Françoise, 4005
Ravier, Jean-Pierre, 4643
Rawalt, Marguerite, 2611
Ray, J. J., 816, 564, 827, 828, 2612, 4804
Re, Anna da, 56
Read, Doris, 485
Read, Stephen J., 603
Rebora, Gianfranco, 4906

Reed, Steven, 5016
Reeder, Amy L., 3173
Rees, C. Roger, 624
Regalia, Ida, 4723
Regini, Marino, 4562
Regnaut-Labord, Caroline, 3516
Regnier, Claude, 4451
Regt, Ali de, 5318
Rehbein, Jochen, 1553
Reher, David-Sven, 2547
Reichardt, Robert, 4747
Reicher, S. D., 1154, 1155
Reid, James J., 3417
Reilly, Charles A., 1032
Reilly, Peter A., 1366
Reimer, Bill, 4088
Reimers, Cordelia W., 3981
Reimers, David, 3517
Rein, Martin, 5319
Reitzes, Donald G., 2744
Rejmers, N. F., 3607
Relly, Bavin, 4805
Remmer, Johannes, 2511
Renaud, Jean, 2224
Renckstorf, Karsten, 1736
Rent, Clyda S., 2849
Rent, George S., 2849
Rentschler, Eric, 1737
Requena y Díez de Revenga, Miguel, 825
Restak, Richard M., 5400
Reszke, Irena, 4494
Retherford, Robert D., 2946
Reuillard, J. P., 1570
Reulecke, Jürgen, 2401
Reuter, Peter, 4743
Rexing, Heinz-Peter, 1903
Rexroat, Cynthia, 4311
Reyer, Jürgen, 2012
Reyes, Román, 108
Reykowski, Janusz, 650
Reyna, S. P., 2305
Reynolds, Robert S. Jr., 3090
Reznikov, V. B., 651
Rhodes, Aaron A., 4765
Ribeiro, Lucia, 5428
Ribner, Stephen A., 5178
Ribolzi, Luisa, 1156, 1904
Ricci, Giacomo, 1837
Rich, Jonathan M., 3892
Rich, Paul, 3418-19
Richard, J., 5427
Richard, Michel P., 5454
Richard, Pablo, 1433
Richards, D. A. J., 1814
Richards, J. M., 84
Richardson, Peter, 3555
Richardson, Ray, 4202
Richardson, T. E., 105
Richer, Stephen, 2613
Richez, Jean-Claude, 4684
Richtand, Carol, 431
Rico Lara, Manuel, 3091

Ridder, Paul, 5455
Riddick, Major F. Jr., 4042
Riedle, Klaus, 1519
Rieffel, Rémy, 1738
Rigaux, Marie-Françoise, 1099
Rigby, K., 829
Rindfuss, R. R., 2602, 2941, 2952, 3004
Rindskopf, David, 401
Riordan, Catherine A., 1157
Riosa, Alceo, 4644
Rioux, Marcel, 2495, 5041
Ripon, Albert, 4427
Ritenbaugh, Cheryl K., 3606
Ritter, Robert L., 2069
Rivera, Anny, 1565
Riviere d'Arc, Hélène, 3893
Ro'i, Yaacov, 1387
Robb, Roberta Edgecome, 4495
Robbins, James M., 3174
Robbins, Thomas, 1499
Robert, Philippe, 1257
Roberts, B. C., 4702
Roberts, Fred S., 372
Roberts, H., 5058
Roberts, Keith A., 1308
Roberts, Michael, 2241
Robertson, Claire C., 2614
Robin, Régine, 1823
Robine, J. M., 2892
Robinson, Francis, 1388
Robinson, R. V., 4229
Robinson, Robert V., 2306, 2382
Robinson, Viviane, 113
Rocca, James V., 4915
Rochefort, David A., 5429
Rochefort, R., 5479
Rochon, Thomas R., 4842
Rodgers, Joseph Lee, 3024
Rodgers, Robert C., 4685
Rodríguez-Ibañez, José Enrique, 4866
Rogers, Carolyn C., 3044
Rohlen, Thomas P., 646
Rohrmoser, Günter, 1158
Roiz Célix, Miguel, 2464
Rojek, Chris, 3956
Romagnoli, Guido, 4518
Romano, P., 742
Romanova, T., 3099
Romanow, Allyn L., 565
Romer, Madeleine, 4734
Romero, Emiliano, 1933
Romilly, Jacqueline de, 1976
Romney, A. Kimball, 145
Ronen, Simcha, 4428
Ronnås, Per, 3894
Ronnby, Alf, 5390
Rook, Karen S., 1159
Root, Laurence S., 2751
Ros i Garcia, María, 1534
Rosanvallon, A., 4496
Rosario, Fe María, 2013
Rosario-Braid, Florangel, 4006

Rose, Peter I., 3518
Rosen, Lawrence, 1389
Rosenberg, Mark, 5372
Rosenberger, David S., 1979
Rosenbladt, Bernhard von, 4185, 5261
Rosenfeld, Gerry, 2120
Rosenfeld, Rachel A., 2225
Rosenfield, Denis L., 1258
Rosenmayr, Leopold, 2752
Rosenmund, Moritz, 5014
Rosenthal, Howard, 5015
Rosenthal, Uriel, 5320
Rosenzweig, Mark R., 3058
Rosero Bixby, Luis, 5086
Rosiecki, Wojciech, 1160
Roška, S., 2701
Roskin, Michael, 3519
Rosner, Menachem, 4089
Ross, H. Laurence, 1079
Ross, J. A., 2920
Ross, Lee, 488
Ross, Robert, 2242
Rossel, Pierre, 4752
Rossi, Alice S., 3005
Rossi, Giovanna, 2753, 3175
Rossi, Peter H., 1183
Roth, Guenther, 1223
Rothschild, Michael, 676
Rothschild, Thomas, 3273
Rouch, Jean-Louis, 2402
Rougier, Henri, 2511
Rouillé, André, 4519
Routley, Richard, 5047
Rovati, Giancarlo, 2465, 4007, 4008, 4529
Rovere, Ana María, 5391
Rowan, Brian, 2121
Rowe, David C., 5220
Rowland, D. T., 2754
Rowland, Richard H., 3895
Roxborough, Ian, 4661
Roy, Pierre André, 4054
Roy, W. T., 692, 4989
Roy, William G., 2307
Rozas, Margarita, 5275
Rozell, Mark J., 4880
Rozen, P., 3641
Rožko, K. G., 566
Rozzi, Renato A., 4144
Ruback, R. Barry, 5183
Rubbo, Anna, 4526
Rubel, M., 1161
Rubery, Jill, 4160
Rubin, Allen, 5480
Rubin, Jeffrey Z., 652, 657
Rubinstein, David, 717
Rubio Carracedo, José, 250
Rucht, Dieter, 4924
Rudder, Véronique de, 3896
Rudel, Thomas K., 3592
Rudolph, Helmut, 4703
Rudy, David R., 726
Rue, Leslie W., 4326

Ruffier, Jean, 4340
Rugh, Andrea B., 3176
Rughöft, Sigrid, 4312
Ruhland, Walter, 5261
Ruijter, Arie de, 245
Ruile, A., 3520
Ruilson, James R., 5217
Ruiz-Tagle P., Jaime, 4645
Rule, James B., 1259
Runciman, W. G., 5321
Rürup, Reinhard, 1390
Rus, Veljko, 4090
Rusconi, Gian Enrico, 4766
Russell, Dan, 589, 593
Russell, Peter A., 2383
Russett, Bruce, 5133
Ruszkowski, Paweł, 2308
Rutges, A., 4493
Ruthven, Malise, 1391
Rutstein, S. O., 2871
Ruttan, Vernon W., 1080
Rutte, C. G., 798
Ryan, Alan, 3938
Ryan, Judy, 2658
Rybczynski, W., 4055
Rychtaříková, J., 2896, 3092
Rysavy, Zdenek, 3878
Ryszkowski, Lech, 3722
Ryu, Jai Poong, 3897

Sabean, David, 5221
Saberwal, Satish, 57, 2466
Sabour, M'hammed, 2361
Sabourin, Annie, 4313
Sachchidananda, 3274
Sachdev, Itesh, 693
Sachdev, P. S., 5413
Sachs, Ignacy, 3898
Sachs, Viola, 1321
Sada, Pius O., 3886
Sadykov, M. B., 530
Saegert, Susan, 3855
Saez, José Luis, 1739
Sagarin, Edward, 3043
Sagaza, Haruo, 2813, 3450
Saglio, Jean, 4005
Šagulidze, T. G., 839
Sahli, Anne Marie, 2814, 2548
Sahno, A. V., 5422
Sainsaulieu, Renaud, 4009
Saint-Arnaud, Pierre, 58
Saint-Georges, P. de, 2147
Saint-Ouen, François, 1624
Saint-Sernin, Bertrand, 85, 86
Saith, Ashwani, 3006
Saito, Yoshio, 190
Sajó, András, 2467
Saksena, D. N., 3177
Sakuta, Kel'Ichl, 1824
Salas, Luis, 4883
Salazar, Héctor, 3780
Salhi, Mohamed, 2893

Salipante, Paul F., 653
Salisbury, Robert H., 4949
Salmon, Charles T., 1740
Salomé, Bernard, 1905
Salowsky, Heinz, 4314
Salvadori, Mario, 138
Salvatori, Franco, 3521
Samaha, Khalil, 735
Samarajiwa, Rohan, 1741
Sampson, Robert J., 694
Šamšur, O. V., 3527
Samuel, Nicole, 4734
Sánchez León, Abelardo, 3899
Sandelands, Lloyd E., 1162
Sanders, A. J. G. M., 3093
Sanders, Ivan, 1825
Sanderson, Stuart, 385
Sandis, Eva, 695
Sandler, Todd, 679
Sandoval, Salvador Antonio M., 2309
Sandoval Huertas, Emiro, 5222
Sanford, Stephanie, 567
Sanger, Mary Bryna, 4315
Sangren, P. Steven, 1447
Sanguinetti, Horacio J., 2036
Sani, Sule, 2996
Sano, Masahiko, 604
Sanson, Henri, 1033
Sansot, Pierre, 4753
Santagata, Walter, 4897
Santalainen, Timo, 773
Santos, Milton, 3593
Santos Hernández, Roberto, 1977
Sapir, Jacques, 4429
Šapiro, V. D., 2755
Sapiro, Virginia, 3522
Saqib, Ghulam Nabi, 1978
Saraceno, Chiara, 2710
Sarchielli, Guido, 4144, 4518
Saris, W. E., 1628
Sarkar, Benoy Kumar, 59
Sarkar, J., 2243
Sarkis, Bassam, 4563
Sarkisıan, Sarkis, 4056
Sas, Judit H., 2615
Sassoon, Joseph, 769
Šatalin, S., 3900
Šatalov, A. T., 3604
Šatalova, O. A., 344
Sathyamurthy, T. V., 2496
Sato, Naoyoshi, 1520
Sato, Takeshi, 1742, 1743
Sato, Tomio, 1163
Sato, Toyomichi, 5389
Sato, Yasuyuki, 251, 2174
Sato, Yoshiyuki, 732, 1571
Satyanarayanan, 2239
Sauber, Mariana, 1823
Saucedo Lugo, María Elena, 150
Saucier, Jean-François, 2114
Saul, Mahir, 2014
Saurma, Adalbert, 989

Sauś, Jan, 2310
Savčenko, T. M., 528
Savin-Williams, Ritch C., 1186
Savoy-Clot, Isabelle, 2616
Sawiński, Zbigniew, 4468
Saxe, Richard W., 1979
Sayad, Abdelmalek, 3523
Sayles, Marnie L., 568
Scaff, Lawrence A., 252
Scalapino, Robert A., 4646
Scardigli, Victor, 4048
Schabert, Tilo, 3901
Schafer, Robert B., 5322
Schäfers, Bernhard, 3178
Schaitter, Philippe C., 4808
Schapiro, Morton Owen, 5149
Scheirer, Mary Ann, 2617
Schellstede, William P., 3007
Schenk, Michael, 670, 1572
Sches, Christian, 4497
Schiffauer, Werner, 4316
Schirmacher, Wolfgang, 2468
Schirrmacher, Gerd, 5481
Schizzerotto, Antonio, 1906
Schlee, Günther, 3563
Schlegel, Jean-Louis, 512
Schlott, Wolfgang, 1826
Schlottmann Alan M., 3451
Schmale, Hugo, 4145
Schmeidler, Emilie, 5094
Schmerl, Christian, 3217
Schmid, Josef, 2549
Schmida, Leslie C., 1980
Schmidt, Burghart, 2469
Schmidt, Klaus-Dieter, 4174
Schmidt, Stuart M., 4532
Schmidt, Warren H., 2610
Schmitt, Karl, 5017
Schmitt, Neal, 644
Schmitt, Raymon L., 2830
Schmitter, Barbara, 3524
Schmitter, Philippe C., 4647, 4816
Schmutz, Georges, 402
Schneider, Eugene V., 4143
Schneider, Mark, 3401
Schneider, Michael, 4430
Schneider, Susan, 718
Schneider, Walter G., 644
Schneider, William, 837
Schneier, Graciela, 3893
Schoen, Robert, 3094
Schoenberg, Ronald, 431
Schofield, Norman, 2175
Schomburg, Harald, 2672
Schooler, Carmi, 4431
Schramm, Wilbur, 183
Schreuder, Osmund, 922
Schrijvers, Joke, 5110
Schrodt, Philip A., 345
Schroyer, Trent, 1521
Schteingart, Martha, 3839
Schubarth, Glena, 587

Schudson, Michael, 1744
Schuetz, Janice E., 1549
Schuller, Tom, 4724
Schüller, Vratislav, 3089
Schulman, Michael D., 2328
Schulster, Ilsa, 4990
Schulte, Joachim, 1230
Schulte, Regina, 5223
Schultz, Martin, 3095
Schultz, T. Paul, 3525
Schulz, Muriel, 1612
Schuman, Howard, 3315
Schumann, Michael, 4397, 4456
Schumm-Garling, Ursula, 4146
Schuster, Michael, 4564
Schutjer, Wayne A., 2951
Schutt, Russell K., 346
Schuwer, Philippe, 1745
Schwartz, Bertrand, 4210
Schwartz, Gail Garfield, 4057
Schwartz, Joseph E., 347
Schwartz, Michael, 1392
Schwartzman, Helen B., 5430
Schwarz, Karl, 3179
Schweder, Richard A., 990
Schweisguth, Étienne, 5007
Schweitzer, Sylvie V., 4599
Schwerin, Hans-Alexander von, 4432
Sciulli, David, 1164
Scott, Joseph W., 3420
Scott, Richard I., 4227
Scott, William A., 1165
Scotton, Carol Myers, 388
Screpanti, Ernesto, 4648
Screvens, Christiane, 5165
Scudder, David F., 4948
Scullion, Hugh, 4446
Scully, Diana, 5224
Scurrah, Martin J., 770
Searle, C. Maureen, 5431
Secretan, Philibert, 2470
Segal, Aaron, 3526
Segal, Mady Wechsler, 624
Segundo, Juan-Luis, 1309
Segura, Denise, 696
Séguy, Jean, 790, 1310, 1434
Seidman, Steven, 253, 2471
Seifert, Roger V., 4649
Seiguerman, Osvaldo, 1778
Seillan, Hubert, 4433
Šejman, I. M., 5432
Šejnis, V. L., 1166, 2472
Seligson, Mitchell A., 4826
Seliktar, Ofira, 697
Sélim, Monique, 3763
Sell, Jane, 2338
Sellier, F., 4555
Sellier, François, 2311, 4650
Selmer, Randi, 3073
Selva, Beatriz, 4317
Selvaratnam, V., 2070
Selvin, Hanan C., 87, 569

Selwood, David F., 3904
Semyonov, Moshe, 4227
Senior, Barbara, 4211
Seoane Pascual, Luis, 1034
Šepel', V. M., 4341
Seręga, Zygmunt, 3677
Seri, Dedy, 1845
Serino, Vinicio, 791
Servaes, Jan, 1573
Servan-Schreiber, Claude, 4268
Seshachalam, P., 3008
Seth, A. N., 3723
Ševčenko, V., 254
Sève, Lucien, 255
Sevilla Guzman, E., 3724
Sewart, John J., 256
Sewell, William H., 2205
Sexton, J. J., 4212
Sgritta, Giovanni B., 3180
Shacham, Josef, 3804
Shadish, William R. Jr., 717
Shafir, Michael, 3421
Shah, Ghanshyam, 3422
Shah, Kalpana, 3275
Shain, Milton, 3423
Shalev, Carmel, 3009
Shamir, Michal, 830
Shand, Nancy, 2659
Shangi, Lennard M., 3424
Shankari, Uma, 1393
Shapiro, Irving S., 4010
Sharlet, Robert, 1260
Sharma, Brahm Dev, 3339
Sharma, Krishna Datta, 3902
Sharma, P. N., 5323
Sharma, Ram Avtar, 1261
Sharrock, W. W., 9, 390, 5057
Shastri, C., 5323
Shattuck, Michael L., 2071
Shavit, Sara, 4651
Shavit, Yossi, 2015
Shaw, Timothy M., 2302
Shearer, John C., 4549
Shearman, Peter, 1625
Shehan, Constance, 4311
Sheingold, Karen, 2148
Shekhawat, Virenda, 1522
Shen, Cynthia H., 432
Shenkar, Oded, 771
Shepher, Israel, 4091
Sher, Ada Elizabeth, 2756
Sher, George, 4867
Sherman, Lawrence W., 1167
Sherman Swing, Elizabeth, 2099
Shernock, Stanley Kent, 831
Shibata, Hiroshi, 2757
Shibata, Singo, 1779
Shida, Kiyoshi, 322, 348
Shimizu, Mikio, 1746
Shimizu, Yoshifumi, 3181
Shin, Eui-Hang, 513
Shinar, Pessah, 1394

Shinohara, Takahiro, 3642
Shiobara, Tsutomu, 257, 869
Shirai, Taishiro, 4704
Shirom, Azie, 4651
Shlonsky, Hagith R., 5111
Shockey, James W., 4455
Shoji, Kohkichi, 60
Sholk, Richard, 2312
Shorish, M. Mobin, 1626
Shorter, Edward, 473
Shotland, R. Lance, 5183
Shrivastava, Paul, 718
Shumaker, Sally A., 5348
Sicking, Thom, 3725
Siddique, C. M., 4364
Siddiqui, H. Y., 5392
Siebert, R. J., 258
Siegel, Merryl S., 5178
Siegers, Jacques, 2618
Sierra Alvarez, José, 853
Sierra Pop, Oscar Rolando, 654
Sigal, Silvia, 1627
Sigelman, Lee, 5018
Šihiriev, P. N., 474
Siim, Birte, 2566
Sikka, K. D., 3046
Silavwe, Geoffrey, 3643
Silbermann, Alphons, 1395
Siltanen, Janet, 2619
Silver, Charles, 1168
Silverman, David, 5456
Silvestre, J. J., 4498, 4555
Simich, J. L., 66
Simis, Konstantin, 4894
Simkus, Albert, 2384
Simmons, G. B., 2987
Simms, L. Moody Jr., 1838
Simon, Rita J., 698
Simon, Sherry, 3340
Simonds, A. P., 146
Simonton, Dean Keith, 1780
Sims, Henry P. Jr., 708
Simuš, P. I., 3726
Sinda, Martial, 1435
Singh, Ajit K., 3425
Singh, Bhudev, 1169
Singh, Hira, 4058
Singh, Kalam, 4499
Singh, S. N., 3452
Singh, Susheela, 2947
Singh, Yogendra, 61
Singleton, Royce Jr., 803
Singly, François de, 349, 433, 4988
Sinha, R. K., 1170
Sinha, Ramesh P., 3274, 4652
Siqueira, Lêda, 3903
Sirianni, Carmen J., 2226
Sirinelli, Jean-François, 2362
Sitzler, Kathrin, 3010
Six, Bernd, 817
Sjoberg, Andrée F., 1224, 1225
Sjoberg, Gideon, 772, 776, 1224, 1225

Sjöström, Margareta, 2100
Sjöström, Rolf, 2100
Skard, Torild, 3276
Skilling, H. Gordon, 4950
Skot-Hansen, Dorte, 1035
Skvorcov, L. V., 2403
Skvoretz, John, 662, 1060, 2385, 4500
Slaby, Andrew Edmund, 1171
Slavin, B. F., 2425
Šlepakov, A. N., 3527
Slesinger, Doris P., 2948
Słomińska, Janina, 2109
Small, Stephen A., 1186
Smart, John E., 4318
Smidovič, S., 3614
Smidt, Corwin, 4991
Smirnov, G. L., 2473
Smith, A. Anthony, 259
Smith, A. Wade, 3096
Smith, Anthony D., 3341, 3342
Smith, Brian H., 840
Smith, Carol A., 4536
Smith, Craig Allen, 4951
Smith, D. Randall, 5225, 5226
Smith, David P., 2894
Smith, Dennis, 991, 1226
Smith, Dorothy E., 2176
Smith, Karl A., 680
Smith, Leslie, 475
Smith, Michael E., 1311
Smith, Monte, 626
Smith, Raymond T., 3182
Smith, Richard M., 3727
Smith, Robert Ellis, 4574
Smith, Robert J., 992
Smith, Thomas Ewin, 2149
Smith, Tom William, 376
Smith, W. Randy, 3904, 4653
Smith, William R., 5225, 5226
Smithers, A. G., 2949
Smolicz, J. J., 2016, 3343
Snellen, I. T. M., 129
Sniderman, Paul M., 4767
Snizek, W. E., 1747, 2072
Snow, David A., 2474
Snyder, Eldon E., 2150
Sobczak-Rustecka, Janina, 4434
Sodeur, Wolfgang, 325
Sofer, Catherine, 4228
Sofranko, Andrew J., 3564
Sogrine, Vladimir, 2404
Sokolova, É. I., 531
Sokolova, M. N., 2405
Sokólska, Joanna, 1981
Solé, Carlota, 4654
Soles, Deborah Hansen, 570
Solo, Robert, 4059
Sołoma, Luba, 2151
Solomonescu, Olimpia, 2815
Solopov, É. F., 2475
Som, Ranjan K., 2865
Somerhausen, Colette, 5227

Someya, Yoshiko, 3148
Sommer, Carl, 2017
Sommer, Robert, 114, 3957
Sommerville, Joseph C., 1979
Sondhi, Krishan, 1574
Sood, Santosh, 4655
Sørensen, Aage B., 3978
Soriano, Lawrence J., 656
Šorohova, È. V., 4114, 4342
Sosa, Nicolás M., 1227
Sosnowski, Adam, 4512, 4520
Soubie, Raymond, 4843
Sournia, Jean-Charles, 5433
South, Scott J., 4213, 5228
Souza, Aída L. F. de, 3903
Spano, Ivano, 486
Spark, Alasdair, 5037
Spaulding, Marc, 2313
Specht, Walter, 2702
Spellman, Peter W., 1405
Spencer, Christopher, 204
Spencer, Martin E., 2411
Speranza, Lorenzo, 4656
Spergel, Irving A., 5229
Sperling, Hans Joachim, 4435
Spiegel, Uriel, 5186
Spiess, Erika, 2950
Špiljuk, V. A., 993
Spinks, J. A., 2073
Spinrad, William, 4725
Spirer, Herbert F., 434
Spitze, Glenna, 3129, 3565
Spitzner, Albert, 4180
Šporer, Željka, 91, 4457
Spread, Patrick, 655
Spreitzer, Elmer, 2150
Sprengers, Maarten, 4217
Springer de Freitas, Renan, 3047
Sprinzen, Merle, 347
Sproule-Jones, Mark, 4121
Spruit, I. P., 4214
Spybey, Tony, 1575, 4092
Spyropoulos, Georges, 4436
Squires, Gregory D., 83
Srb, Vladimír, 1982, 3765
Srinivas, M. N., 2244
Srinivas, M. V., 3097
Srinivasan, K., 3011, 3063
Srivastava, J. B., 3177
Srivastava, J. N., 3098
Srivastava, K. C., 2386
Srivastava, R. N., 350
St. John, Craig, 3905, 3906
St. John, Edward P., 2074
Stachowicz, Andrzej, 4437
Stack, Steven, 4215
Stafford, Mark C., 5177
Stager, Susan F., 491
Stahl, Thomas, 4147, 5324
Stahler, Gerald M., 5464
Stahura, John M., 3907
Štambuk, Maja, 2816

Stănciulescu, Traian Dinorel, 1839
Standing, Guy, 4216
Stangeland, Per, 3982
Stankiewicz, Janina, 4060
Stanley, Manfred, 4808
Stanley-Baker, Joan, 1781
Stanworth, Michelle, 2619, 2620
Staples, William G., 5230
Stapleton, David C., 3983
Starbuck, William H., 765
Stare, Franci, 3528
Stark, Oded, 3529, 3566, 3567
Stark, Rodney, 1278, 1484
Starosta, Paweł, 3984
Starostin, A. M., 3594
Starostin, B. S., 482
Staroverov, V. I., 3728
Starr, Paul D., 3344
Starr, S. Frederick, 1846, 4061
Stasinos, Demetrios P., 2841
Staube, Hanne, 3321
Staudt, Erich, 4343
Steelman, Lala Carr, 3183
Steeman, Théodore M., 1396
Stefănescu, Ion T., 1036
Stefanski, Valentina-Maria, 3530
Steffen, Valerie J., 801
Stehlík, Jiří, 2817
Stehr, Nico, 2396
Steinberg, Bernard, 3345
Steiner, H., 2177
Steinhoff, Patricia G., 646
Steinkraus, Warren E., 1782
Steinmeier, Thomas L., 4448
Stening, B. W., 4530
Stepanjan, C. A., 2363
Stepanjuk, V. P., 4344
Stephan, G. Edward, 2818
Stephan, Karen H., 2818
Stephen, Timothy D., 1576
Ster, Joze, 1228
Sternberg, Robert J., 625, 656
Sternstein, Larry, 3908
Stevenson, John, 994
Stewart, Charles J., 4951
Stewart, Danièle, 3298
Stewart, Lea P., 3041
Stichter, Sharon, 2589
Stiller, Pavel, 5325
Stinchcombe, Arthur L., 5373
Stinner, William F., 3644
Stock, Chris, 5185
Stock, William A., 3975
Stockhammer, Helmut, 1172
Stoesz, D., 5326
Stokes, C. Shannon, 2951
Stokes, Randall, 191
Stolin, V., 3099
Stoljarov, V. V., 201
Stoll, Richard J., 5055
Stolz, Barbara Ann, 5231
Stolzenberg, Ross M., 4319

Stone, Linda, 379
Stoner, Madeleine R., 5112
Storey, John, 4345
Stover, Ronald G., 1464
Strahl, Danuta, 435
Straits, Bruce C., 3344
Strand, Paul J., 1697
Stratenwerth, Günter, 5232
Strathman, Terry, 2660
Strauch, Judith, 3729
Strause, Glynis Holm, 1541
Strauss, George, 4565
Straussman, Jeffrey D., 4685
Street, Brian V., 2101
Streeter, Thomas, 1748
Strelec, S. N., 520
Stretch, Robert H., 5038
Strobino, Donna M., 2535
Strogovič, M. S., 5233
Strubell i Trueta, Miquel, 1534
Stuart, Martha, 3012
Stucliffe, Anthony, 3909
Studer, K. E., 351
Stump, Roger W., 1500
Stumpf, John, 1165
Suaud, Charles, 3730
Šubrtová, Alena, 2550
Suchindran, C. M., 2895, 3080
Sudama, Trevor, 2314
Sugaya, Yoshiko, 2640, 3184
Suhodob, T. D., 995
Šul'govskij, A. F., 854
Sulimov, E. F., 1173
Sułkowski, Bogusław, 1783, 4754
Sullivan, John, 830
Sullivan, O., 3910
Sumida, Masaki, 5234
Summers, Gene F., 2476
Sun, Te-Hsiung, 2641
Sundaran, I. S., 3731
Sundberg, Jan, 3346
Sundquist, James L., 4916
Sunesson, June, 2178
Supek, Rudi, 88
Supiot, Alain, 4575
Susato, Shigeru, 2179
Susskind, Lawrence, 657
Sutter, Jacques, 1501
Suttles, Gerald D., 3911
Suzuki, Masataka, 1448
Svencickij, A. L., 4141
Swanborn, P. G., 1577
Swanson, David A., 436
Swarup, Anand, 1174
Swatos, William H. Jr., 62, 1312
Swedner, Harald, 3912
Sweemer, Cécile de, 3013
Sweet, James A., 2621
Świątkiewicz, Wojciech, 2227
Swicegood, C. Gray, 2952, 3004
Swingewood, Alan, 63
Sylves, Richard T., 4948

Syrotuik, John, 4364
Syrovátka, A., 2896
Szabó, Márton, 449
Szakács, Sándor, 4521
Szántó, Miklós, 3531
Szántó, Tibor, 64
Szczepański, Jan, 1907
Szczupaczyński, Jerzy, 2315
Szecskő, Tamás, 1749
Szegő, Andrea, 2228
Szekfü, András, 1750
Szirmai, Viktória, 3913
Szlajfer, Henryk, 3732
Szmatka, Jacek, 352
Szoboszlai, György, 3733, 5027
Szocki, Józef, 571
Szostak, Władysław, 147
Szreter, Simon R. S., 4458
Sztompka, Piotr, 65, 2180
Sztumski, Janusz, 658
Szulkin, R., 1814
Szwarc, Halina, 2758
Szymanski, Albert, 2316, 2317

T.-Brault, Marie-Marthe, 2740
Tabačkovskij, V. G., 572
Tabah, Léon, 2819
Tabard, Nicole, 2387
Tabutin, Dominique, 2953
Tacchi, Enrico Maria, 3914
Tacenko, A. I., 572
Tachon, Michel, 5327
Tacq, J. J. A., 291
Tacussel, Patrick, 1175
Tadao Tsukashima, Ronald, 659
Tadej, Perla, 373
Tadić, Ljubomir, 4806
Taeuber, Karl E., 2018
Tagami, Yoshimi, 3569
Taguchi, Hiroaki, 2842
Tahara, Otoyori, 3692
Tainio, Risto, 773
Takada, Akihiko, 4952
Takahashi, Hidehiro, 3645
Takahashi, Hiroshi, 2747
Takasaki, Nozomu, 1578
Takashima, Hideki, 792
Takashina, Susumu, 1751
Takayama, K. Peter, 1482, 3640
Takegawa, Shogo, 2747, 5328
Takeshita, Toshio, 1752
Takezawa, Sin-ichi, 4365
Tallard, Michèle, 4062
Tallman, Irving, 550
Talwar, Usha, 4320
Tamamizu, Toshiaki, 590
Tamura, Kenji, 3185, 5374
Tamura, Norio, 1715, 1753, 1754
Tanabe, Yoshiaki, 5375
Tanada, Hirofumi, 3568
Tanaka, Hidetaka, 2318
Tanaka, Shigeyoshi, 3633

Tanaka, Toyoji, 4134
Tanaka, Yasumasa, 996
Tanalski, Dionizy, 1397
Tancredi, Laurence R., 1171
Tani, Katsuhide, 3569
Tannenbaum, Arnold S., 4089
Tanner, Julian, 4522
Tardos, Róbert, 5260
Tasalov, V. I., 3608
Tash, William R., 5464
Tashakkori, Abbas, 3164
Tassello, Graziano, 3532
Tate, Richard L., 403
Tatsumoto, Yoshifumi, 2691
Tatz, Colin, 3347, 4755
Tausky, Curt, 4143, 4148
Taussig, Michael, 4526
Tausz, Katalin, 3701
Tavares de Almeida, Maria Hermínia, 4657
Tavel, David, 1908
Tawiah, E. O., 2954
Tawney, James W., 2110
Taylor, Colin, 607
Taylor, Gerald D., 1909
Taylor, Henry, 1755
Taylor, Ian R., 5235
Taylor, James C., 3976
Taylor, Patricia Ann, 2585
Taylor, W. H., 1910
Taylor-Gooby, Peter, 5329
Tazelaar, Frits, 4217, 4219
Teachman, Jay D., 3048
Teasdale, T. W., 2661
Tedeschi, Piero, 2319
Tedrow, Lucky M., 436
Teitelboim, Volodia, 2364
Temesi, József, 3790
Ten Napel, Henk, 2320
Tena Artigas, Joaquin, 1935
Tennstedt, Florian, 4658
Teodosio, Virginia A., 4318
Teplin, Linda A., 2843
Teplov, F., 260
Ter-Akopjan, N. B., 2497
Terada, Atsuhiro, 4807
Terestyéni, Tamás, 2703
Terrail, Jean-Paul, 1983
Terrot, Noël, 2102
Terry, Michael, 4659
Terssac, Gilbert de, 4346
Terwey, Michael, 2321
Tesser, Abraham, 626
Tessler, Richard C., 2834
Teubner, Gunther, 1262
Teuter, Klaus, 310
Tewari, Vishwa Nath, 1037
Tezanos, José Félix, 2477
Thadden, Rudolf von, 1436
Thass-Thienemann, Theodore, 1535
Thekkamalai, S. S., 3734
Thélot, Claude, 2388
Thévenin, Guy Faustin, 5141

Thévenot, Laurent, 1081
Thiemann, Friedrich 4603
Thierauf, Robert J., 148
Thiessen, Elmer J., 2111
Thikian, Alexandre, 4660
Thoden Van Velzen, H. U. E., 997
Thoits, Peggy A., 5434
Thom, D. Rodney, 5142
Thomas, Barbara J., 2578
Thomas, Curlew O., 3348
Thomas, Dennis, 4096
Thomas, George M., 4844
Thomas, J. J. R., 4817
Thomas, Philip, 3100
Thompson, John B., 855, 856
Thompson, Mark, 4566, 4661
Thompson, Paul, 3186
Thompson, Stuart E., 3735
Thomson, Randall, 5252
Thorelli, Irene M., 5480
Thornberry, Terence P., 5236, 5237
Thorns, David, 3626
Thornton, Arland, 2641
Thrysøe, Willy, 476
Thumerelle, P. J., 2642
Tibori, Timea, 1847
Tickamyer, Ann, 2372
Tienda, Marta, 1966
Tier, Akolda M., 1485
Tierney, Joan D., 1756
Tietgens, Hans, 2103
Tiffany, Sharon W., 2607
Tihonova, N. E., 3601
Tihun, S. V., 1176
Tilly, Charles, 870
Tilman, Rick, 66
Timberlake, Michael, 2230
Timpanaro, Daniela, 2258
Tirtosudarmo, Riwanto, 3453
Tiryakian, Edward A., 998, 2478, 3049
Tischler, Nancy G., 602
Titamies, Marketta, 3187
Titarenko, L. G., 532
Titkow, Anna, 2662
Tittenbrun, Jacek, 261
Tiwari, A. S., 5482
Tjosvodl, Dean, 733
Tjulin, I. G., 353
Todor, William D., 4545
Todorov, Tzvetan, 292
Toht, A., 948
Toinet, Marie-France, 5330
Tokei, Ferenc, 2498
Tokitsu, Kenji, 3116
Tokuoka, Hideo, 5238
Tolnay, Stewart E., 2551, 2955, 3736
Tomasetta, Leonardo, 149
Tomeh, Aida K., 2622
Tomes, Hilary, 3349
Tominaga, Ken'ichi, 262
Tominaga, Shigeki, 1824
Tomka, Miklós, 1398, 4735

Tomlinson, J. D., 4011
Tomlinson, Richard, 3014
Tomlinson, Sally, 3349
Tonkonogaya, E. P., 2098
Tonnesen, Thomas V., 3351
Tonnon, Philippe, 1757
Tons Gaard, Ole, 3307
Toren, Nina, 89
Toris, Carol, 605
Törnblom, Kjell Y., 627
Torres, Aida, 3015
Torres, Carlos, 4953
Torres, Carlos A., 2104
Torres, Félix, 999
Torres, Lara, 4953
Toščenko, Ž. T., 857, 858
Toshiyuki, Tamura, 3350
Tosics, Iván, 3829
Tóth, Pál Péter, 2365, 3737
Touraine, Alain, 998, 1177, 4662, 4954
Touré, Oussouby, 4347
Toussaint, Nadine, 1758
Touster, S., 1814
Tracy, Paul E., 317
Tran, Quang Ba, 3533
Trąsnea, Ovidiu, 5331
Trawińska, Maria, 3188
Treiman, D. J., 4229
Treloggen Peterson, Jean, 3965
Treu, Tiziano, 4063
Treutner, Erhard, 4138
Triandis, Harry C., 1178
Triaud, Jean-Louis, 1399
Tribalat, Michèle, 3085
Tricart, Jean-Paul, 5474
Trigueiro Mendes, Durmeval, 1911
Trincaz, Jacqueline, 3189
Trincaz, Pierre, 3189
Tripathi, K. K., 4459
Tropman, John E., 2751
Trouillot, Michel-Rolph, 3738
Troussier, J. F., 4496
Troyna, Barry, 3369
Trubnikov, M., 1523
Trudgill, Peter, 1536
Truong, Thanh-Dam, 3050
Trussell, James, 2909
Tryfan, Barbara, 2704, 2759
Tsai, Shu-Ling, 2205
Tschirhart, John T., 679
Tsien, Tche-hao, 5239
Tsuchida, Hideo, 3739
Tsuda, Masumi, 2322
Tsunematsu, Naoyuki, 322
Tsutsui, Kiyotada, 2181
Tucek, Milan, 4524
Tuch, Steven A., 3426
Tuchman, Gaye, 1827
Tucker, S. N., 3915
Tudor, Gheorghe, 2182
Tuiran, Rodolfo A., 2192
Tumarkin, N., 1814

Tung, Shui-Liang, 2956
Tuomela, Saimo, 5332
Turcotte, Paul-André, 1437
Turcotte, Pierre Régis, 4726
Turiel, Elliot, 109
Turner, Bryan S., 166, 2499
Turner, Frederick C., 840
Turner, Jonathan H., 399
Turner, Stephen P., 354
Turpeinen, Oiva, 2552
Turuk, G. P., 355
Twenhöfel, Ralf, 1038
Tygart, C. E., 2075
Tygart, Clarence E., 4770
Tyler, Tom R., 606
Tyszka, Zbigniew, 3190, 3191
Tzuriel, David, 2623

Udry, J. Richard, 3024
Ueda, Kōzō, 2897
Ueno, Chizuko, 1828, 2624, 3277
Uesugi, Takamichi, 477
Ugalde, Antonio, 4321
Uleman, James S., 610
Ulin, Robert C., 1000
Ulman, Richard Barrett, 703
Ulrich, Dave, 774
Ulrich, Werner, 5333
Umino, Michio, 187
Underhill, Paul K., 5401
Ungureanu, Ion, 2479
Unruh, Adolph, 2152
Unruh, Glenys G., 2152
Uppal, J. N., 5113
Urano, Masaki, 3916, 3917
Urry, John, 868
Ursell, Gill, 4590
Usui, Takashi, 4093
Utagawa, Tkuo, 3985
Utasi, Ágnes, 1001
Utaumi, Yoichi, 3051
Utomo, Budi, 3016
Utsunomiya, Teruo, 1313
Uttley, Stephen, 5334
Uusitalo, Liisa, 4107
Uusitalo, Ritva, 2671

Vacca, Michele, 4576
Vaccarini, Italo, 263, 1040, 2406
Vaculik, Jaroslav, 2407
Vágvölgyi, B. András, 4903
Vaille, Charles, 5402
Vajda, Ágnes, 3986
Valadez, Joseph J., 4438
Valadier, Paul, 1179
Valdés, G., 4818
Valentich, Mary, 5240
Valette, Aline, 4322
Valkenburg, F. C., 4187
Vallet, Odon, 4756, 4757
Vallin, Pierre, 4819
Vámos, Dóra, 4483

Van de Vall, Mark, 4042
Van den Bercken, W., 4845
Van den Brink-Budgen, Roy, 5335
Van den Eeden, P., 1628
Van der Burgh, C., 2760
Van der Linden, Harry, 1229
Van der Merwe, Roux, 4663
Van der Pligt, Joop, 607
Van der Werf, Dirk, 4218
Van Dijk, Jan, 264
Van Doorne-Huiskes, J., 2626
Van Dorp, P. Patricia, 3192
Van Drooghenbroeck, Jacques, 4577
Van Goor, H., 381
Van Haecht, Anne, 1912
Van Horne, Winston A., 3351
Van Houwelingen, Jeannet, 4219
Van Keppel, Margaret, 3198
Van Lare, James, 4533
Van Lier, Leo A. W., 1629
Van Liere, Kent D., 1291
Van Loo, M. Frances, 2958
Van Maanen, John, 734
Van Nieuwenhuijze, C. A. O., 1041
Van Nuland, J., 1579
Van Outrive, L., 1579, 4873
Van Ree, Erik, 2480
Van Rensbergen, Johan, 4528
Van Slype, Georges, 1914
Van Snippenburg, L. B., 4955
Van Vianen, H. A. W., 2910
Van Zandt Winn, Stephen, 2323
Van Zijl, P. J. M., 1577
Vance, Charles M., 775
Vandamme, Jacques, 4727
Varacalli, Joseph A., 1438
Varet, Gilbert, 152
Varga, Károly, 4175
Varro, Gabrielle, 3101
Vasil'eva, I. V., 3958
Vasoo, S., 3646
Vasquez, Ana, 489
Vasudeva Rao, D., 3708
Vaughan, Ted R., 772, 776, 1224, 1225
Vaver, David, 3939
Veen, P., 478
Veith, Richard H., 1759
Velázquez Guzmán, María Guadalupe, 1984
Velikij, P. P., 533
Veling, Kars, 356
Vellinga, Menno, 4135
Vennat-Debaye, Marie-Madeleine, 4357
Venturini, Ernesto, 5435
Venuti, Maria Caterina, 293
Verbeek, Albert, 4219
Verdier, R., 591
Verdier, Roger, 3947
Vérin, Pierre, 5114
Verma, G. C., 1913
Verma, Ravi B. P., 3468
Veronelli, Juan Carlos, 5457
Verquerre, Régis, 592

Verret, Michel, 1002
Verspieren, Patrick, 5241
Vertz, Laura L., 908
Verwayen, Henri, 437
Vestuti, Guido, 5048
Vetrone, Giuseppe, 4354
Viard, Philippe, 3427
Vidal, Claudine, 3040
Vidal, Daniel, 1465
Viehoff, Ludger, 67
Vielrose, Egon, 2899
Viet, Jean, 1914
Viet-Depaule, Nathalie, 2285
Viktorin, V. M., 1205
Vil'čko, Ja. A., 534
Villac, Michel, 3193
Villemez, Wayne J., 3352
Villeneuve, André, 5115
Villette, Michel, 4534
Villeval, Marie-Claire, 2844
Vinck, Dominique, 68
Vinogradov, V. A., 1580
Vinogradov, V. D., 4917
Vinot, Pierre, 4122
Virtanen, Pekka V., 3918
Viscusi, W. Kip, 608
Vitkovský, Karel, 2890
Vivan, Itala, 1322
Vladislavlev, A. P., 2105
Vlasova, V. B., 1206
Vogel, Lise, 265
Vogler, Richard, 1263
Volgyes, Ivan, 2821
Voroncov, B. N., 535
Voronov, A. A., 357
Voronovič, B. A., 294
Voropaev, Ju. F., 859
Vörös, Gizella B., 1829
Vörös, Gyula, 1868
Vorošuk, A. N., 3605
Vos, C. J., 5336
Voskamp, Ulrich, 2672
Voth, Donald E., 3635
Voydanoff, Patricia, 2627
Vredenburgh, Donald J., 719
Vuchinich, Samuel, 3194
Vukovich, György, 2554
Vytlačil, Josef, 3195

Waardenburg, Jean-Jacques, 2153
Wacker, R. Fred, 3353
Wagenaar, Theodore C., 346
Wagner, Dieter, 4376
Wagner de Reyna, Alberto, 1003
Wahkamp, Andy, 4686
Waismann, Friedrich, 1230
Waite, Linda J., 3150, 4319
Waitzkin, Howard, 5436
Wajda, Augustyn, 4510
Waldauer, Charles, 2628
Waldenfels, Bernhard, 219
Waligorski, Conrad P., 4820

Walker, Alan, 5337
Walker, James C., 2605
Walkowiak, Jerzy, 4060
Wallace, T. Dudley, 444
Walling, Derald, 404
Wallis, Aleksander, 3919
Wallis, Roy, 1314, 1466
Wallisch, Lynn S., 2981
Walosik, Jerzy, 2229, 4094
Walsh, A. Crosbie, 3920
Walsh, Kenneth, 4687
Walt, Gillian, 5458
Walter, Gordon A., 777
Waltz, Susan E., 1400
Walzer, Michael Laban, 5338
Wanderley, Luiz Eduardo W., 2106
Wandruszka, Mario, 1630
Wang, Chi-Hsien, 310
Wang, Georgette, 1581
Wang, In Keun, 4065
Wapner, Seymour, 3449
Ward, Daniel Franklin, 1784
Ward, Peter, 3628
Warland, Rex H., 4108
Warnier, Jean-Dominique, 139
Warr, Mark, 5242
Warren, Mark, 860
Warshofsky Lapidus, Gail, 3354
Wasserman, Ira M., 5243
Wasserman, Stanley, 358
Wasserstrom, Jeffrey, 5376
Watanabe, Hideki, 805
Watanabe, Hiroshi, 2107
Watanabe, Yasuo, 5234
Watanabe, Yoshio, 3196
Watanabe, Yuko, 2761
Watari, Akeshi, 1760
Watase, Hiroshi, 4012
Watkins, David, 609
Watson, D. R., 390
Watson, James L., 2324
Wattenberg, Martin P., 1480
Watts, W. David, 90
Way, Wendy L., 4109
Wearden, Stanley T., 1711
Wearing, Betsy, 3017
Weatherford, M. Stephen, 5019
Webb, David, 5244
Webber, Michael John, 3921
Weber, Silke, 1207
Weber-Klein, Christiane, 3890
Webster, Eddie, 4664
Weeks, Dudley, 660
Wegner, Daniel M., 573
Wehmhorner, Arnold, 4665
Weiermair, Klaus, 4501
Weigel, Sigrid, 1830
Weigert, Andrew J., 5339
Weil, Richard H., 3197
Weiler, Antonius Gerardus, 2629
Weinblatt, J., 5186
Weinert, Ansfried B., 720

Weinstock, Nathan, 4666
Weir, Angela, 3278
Weisberg, R., 1814
Weisgerber, Pierre, 4758
Weiss, Dimitri, 4567
Weiss, Hilde, 3428
Weiss, Johannes, 628
Weiss, Linda, 4846
Weitman, Sasha, 3117
Wejland, Andrzej P., 793
Welch, Claude Jr., 4869
Welch, Susan, 5018
Welfeld, Irving, 3922
Weller, Susan C., 145
Wells, Miriam J., 4095
Welz, Rainer, 1180
Werneck Vianna, Luis, 3615
Werth, Nicolas, 3740
West, Darrell M., 5020
Westergaard, Kirsten, 5116
Westergård-Nielsen, N., 1985
Westlander, Gunnela, 2630
Westley, Frances, 1467
Westrum, Ron, 735
Wetherall, Charles F., 2663
Wevenbergh, Marcel, 4102
Wexley, Kenneth N., 778
Weyer, Johannes, 69
Whalen, Jack, 1181
Whaling, Frank, 1315, 1486
Whetten, David A., 759
Whisenhunt, Donald W., 4611
White, F. C., 1915
White, Karl R., 2122
White, Lawrence J., 165
White, Merry I., 1916
White, Robert W., 4176
White, T. H., 4362
Whitehead, John W., 4870
Whitley, Richard, 779
Whyte, Martin Kind, 3923
Whyte, Robert Orr, 3595
Wiatr, Jerzy J., 4961
Wiedemann, Paul, 2500
Wieruszewska, Maria, 1004, 1042
Wiesner, Joachim, 4958
Wieviorka, Michel, 3429, 4662
Wihtol de Wenden, Catherine, 3534
Wilbert, Gerd, 1005
Wiley, Richard E., 1761
Wilke, H. A. M., 478, 798
Wilkes, K. V., 266
Wilkinson, Barry, 4502
Wilkinson, Kenneth P., 3634, 3741, 5245, 5246
Wilks, Jeffrey, 2644
Willen, Richard S., 4884
Willener, Alfred, 2706
Willer, David, 405
Willette, Luc, 4099
Willhem, Sidney M., 3355
Williams, Alan, 4136

Williams, Allan M., 3719
Williams, Jennifer, 704
Williams, John, 4096
Williams, Karel, 4096
Williams, Kirk R., 2230
Williams, Norma, 772
Williams, Numan A., 4123
Williams, Patricia E., 1762
Williams, Raymond, 1043
Williams, Robert E., 3987
Williamson, J. G., 2555, 2790
Williamson, John B., 5377
Williamson, Oliver E., 749
Willis, Cecil L., 2936
Willot, Didier, 1763
Wilpert, Bernhard, 736
Wilson, Anne, 3430
Wilson, Brian, 2076
Wilson, Colin, 5247
Wilson, David C., 4667
Wilson, Elisabeth, 3278
Wilson, Everett K., 87, 569
Wilson, Frank L., 4956
Wilson, Franklin D., 3924
Wilson, John P., 574
Wilson, Mark, 4439
Wilson, Stephen, 1401, 1468
Wilson, Thomas P., 406
Wilson, Timothy D., 818
Wimberley, Dale W., 5117
Win, Kanwza, 1917
Winchell, Anne E., 4503
Winclawski, Włodzimierz, 1918
Windolf, Paul, 2077, 4504
Winkin, Yves, 115, 881
Winkler, Donald R., 2078
Winkler, G., 2177
Winkler, Robin, 3198
Winock, Michel, 2366
Winship, Christopher, 438, 676, 3403, 4203
Winter, Laraine, 610
Wintersberger, Helmut, 5309
Wippler, R., 4821
Withers, Glenn, 5248
Wixman, Ronald, 1402
Wnuk-Lipiński, Edmund, 2210, 2211
Wódz, Jacek, 658
Wodz, Jacek, 1182
Wohl, Andrzej, 4759
Wohlfahrth, Norbert, 710
Wohlfarth, Karl Anton, 2501, 5263
Wojciechowska-Ratajczak, Bogumiła, 4505
Wojnar, Irena, 1785
Wolf, Arthur P., 2959
Wolf, Douglas A., 3199
Wolf-Graaf, Anke, 4323
Wolfe, Barbara L., 1986
Wolkinson, Benjamin W., 4688
Wollmann, Hellmut, 3833
Wondji, Christophe, 1044
Wong, Aline K., 3102
Wong, Morrison G., 2334

Wong, Siu-Lun, 3018
Wood, Geof, 4847
Wood, James R., 799
Wood, Michael, 3052, 5066
Wood, Stephen, 4482
Woodman, Richard W., 717
Woodrow, Karen, 3094
Woodrum, Eric, 359
Woods, Adrian, 4677
Woods, R. I., 2925
Woodward, Nicholas, 4204
Woon, Yuen-fong, 3535
Worre, Torben, 5021
Wozniak, Paul R., 70
Woźniak, Robert, 2231
Wright, James D., 1183
Wrobel, Vera, 1987
Wunderer, Hartmann, 5143
Wunsch, Guillaume J., 2556
Wyckoff, James H., 1988, 1989

Xu, Xue-Quiang, 3819

Yadav, Sohan Ram, 3959
Yadava, R. S., 4881
Yagasaki, Seiji, 3631
Yaguchi, Kazue, 2762
Yamada, Kenzo, 4736
Yamagishi, Toshio, 681
Yamaguchi, Kazuo, 4229
Yamaguchi, Tohru, 2707
Yamamoto, Kenji, 2900
Yamamoto, Noboru, 2232, 2325, 3431
Yamamoto, Tsutomu, 5249
Yamamura, Etsuo, 3966
Yamanaka, Miyuki, 3148
Yamasaki, Keiichi, 2574
Yanitski, Oleg, 3925
Yaniv, Avner, 2079
Yankelovich, Daniel, 4440
Yano, Kazue, 2960
Yao, Esther, 2631
Yasin, Sy, 103
Yasukawa, Hazime, 487
Yates, Gayle Graham, 1487
Yazawa, Shujiro, 71
Ycaza, Patricio, 4668
Yen, Ch'ing-huang, 2326
Yishai, Yael, 3356
Ymonet, Marie, 267
Yokoyama, Minoru, 5250
Yokoyama, Shigeru, 1075
Yokoyama, Yasuo, 268
Yonnet, Paul, 4097
Yorgun, Pembenaz, 3279
Yoshihara, Naoki, 3843, 3926
Yoshii, Hiroaki, 2574
Yoshino, Kohsaku, 3357
Yoshitani, Hiroya, 1439, 1469
Yoshizawa, Natsuko, 295
Young, Douglas J., 3983
Young, Frank W., 432

Young, Gay, 3280
Youxin, Cheng, 2367
Ysseldyke, James E., 2112
Yu, Eui-Young, 513
Yu, Shiao-Ling, 1831
Yüan, Chung-ming, 3432
Yukl, Gary A., 778
Yunker, James A., 611
Yusuf, Shahid, 3718
Yuzawa, Yasuhiko, 3200

Zabin, Laurie S., 3027, 3053
Zachary, Wayne W., 671
Zacher, Hans F., 5363
Zagare, Frank C., 446
Zaghal, Ali S., 2481
Zagladin, V. V., 1006
Zaika, N. F., 546
Zajcev, A. N., 3201
Zajczyk, Francesca, 5011
Zakrzewska, Elżbieta, 269
Zald, Mayer, 123
Zambelli, Franco, 1919
Zamfir, Catalin, 3988
Zamogil'nyj, S. I., 2327
Zampetti, Pier Luigi, 4441
Zanardo, Aldo, 1184
Zander, Ernst, 4376
Zängle, Michael, 5324
Zanker, Karin, 1524
Zapf, Wolfgang, 3972
Žarnikov, A. É., 1007
Zaslavskaya, T. I., 3570, 3742
Zaslavsky, Victor, 3536
Zay, Nicolas, 5378
Zbiegień-Maciąg, Lidia, 4442
Zecharaiah, John, 4689
Zeigarnik, B. V., 479
Zeiliger, Jean, 5379
Zeitlin, June H., 1185
Zeitz, Gerald, 780
Zeldin, R. Shepherd, 1186
Zelditch, Morris Jr., 1060
Zent, Michael R., 2632
Zerguine, Ramdane, 5251

Zeugin, Peter, 2673
Zey-Ferrell, Mary, 2578
Zhongshen, Zhang, 2557
Zhordania, Josif, 1848
Ziegler, Rolf, 360, 1082, 4013
Ziemilski, Andrzej, 1045
Zijderveld, Anton C., 882
Zimmerman, Don H., 1143
Zimmerman, Margot L., 2979
Zimmerman-Tansella, Christa, 4177
Zimmermann, Janos J., 3927
Zinam, Oleg, 3979
Zingraff, Matthew, 5252
Zingraff, Rhonda, 2328
Zinn, Karl Georg, 3960
Ziółkowski, Marian, 3928
Zipes, Jack David, 1832
Zirotti, Jean Pierre, 3571
Zis', A. Ja., 1786
Zito, George V., 1470
Zitouni, Françoise, 3929
Zoc, V. A., 1208
Zolberg, Vera L., 1787
Zoller, Michael, 1582
Zonn, Leo E., 3930
Zorilla Ruiz, Manuel María, 5340
Zorrilla, R. H., 4669, 4918
Zotova, O. I., 3743
Zsigmond, László, 72
Zsolnai, László, 64
Zubenko, L. A., 2633
Zubkov, M. F., 2482
Zuckerman, Miron, 612
Zucman, Elizabeth, 2845
Zuiches, James J., 130
Zukier, Henri, 296
Žukov, N. N., 5067
Župančič, Milan, 4098
Zupanov, Josip, 91
Žuravlev, G. T., 5067
Žuravlev, V. V., 1008
Zurcher, Louis A. Jr., 3039
Zvekić, Uglješa, 4537
Zwicky, H., 3989

SUBJECT INDEX

Abandoned children, 2651
Ability grouping, 705, 2121
Abortion, 2971, 3009
    Australia, 816, 3002
    Bangladesh, 2986
    Belgium, 2992
    Los Angeles, 2978
    Romania, 2990
    USA, 2981, 3002, 3174
Abramowski, Edward, 213
Absenteeism, 4360, 4447
    Netherlands, 4449
    United Kingdom, 4443, 4446
    USA, 4444
Academic achievement, *use* Academic success
Academic freedom
    Australia, 1951
    Canada, 2027
    France, 1963
    USA, 1968
Academic success, 1762, 2113, 2118, 2121-22
    Canada, 2114
    Sweden, 2117
    USA, 3173
Access to education
    Germany FR, 1954
    USSR, 3393
Acculturation
    Israel, 1012
    USA, 3378
Achievement, 545
Achievement motivation, 538, 564, 706
    Germany FR, 828
Action, 487, 537, 540, 553, 566, 570, 572-73, 800, 1701
Action research, 111-13, 3912
    Canada, 114
    USA, 110
Action theory, 204, 220-21, 233, 1230
Activists
    India, 4921
Actors, 4535
Administration, *use* Public administration
Administrative control, 653, 740, 750, 762, 766, 780
Administrative corruption
    USSR, 4894
Administrative law
    Kenya, 4764
Administrative reforms
    Japan, 4134
Adolescence, 1702, 2670, 2679, 2681
    USA, 2709
Adolescents, 567, 1186, 1756, 2675, 3024, 5134
    Australia, 1221
    France, 2020

Israel, 2623
    USA, 977, 1115, 5139
Adopted children, 2661
    Australia, 3198
    Malaysia, 2653
    North America, 2650
    Northern Ireland, 2657
    United Kingdom, 2650
    USA, 2647
Adorno, Theodor W., 1771
Adult education, 2081, 2083, 2107
    Europe, 2095
    France, 2102
    Germany FR, 2091, 2103
    India, 2097
    Mexico, 2104
    United Kingdom, 2085, 2092, 2096
    USA, 2086, 2087
    USSR, 2098
Adulthood, 2710
    USA, 2708, 2709
Adults
    Italy, 2864
Advanced technology, *use* High technology
Advertising, 1637, 1703, 3315
    Brazil, 1633
    France, 349
    Japan, 1635
    USA, 1636, 5002
Aesthetics, 1768, 1771, 1773-74, 1777, 1836
    Hungary, 1775
Affiliation, 617
Affinity
    Australia, 618
    India, 618
Affluent society
    Israel, 3960
Africa
    Basic needs, 5088
    Cinema, 1642, 1655, 1670
    Colonialism, 3943
    Cooperatives, 614
    Cultural history, 1044
    Decision making, 5088
    Economic development, 4869
    Elite, 2356
    Emigrants, 3472
    Family, 3149, 3189
    Fertility, 2943, 2953
    Handicrafts, 4066
    Human rights, 4869
    Language, 1852
    Languages, 1591
    Life tables, 2865
    Literature, 1788, 1795
    Mental health, 5435
    Middle class, 2356

Minority groups, 690
Mortality, 2953
Occupations, 4454
Polygamy, 3059, 3100
Poor, 5091
Refugees, 3491
Religious communities, 1435
Rural development, 3664, 5091
Sex roles, 2568
Slavery, 2237
Social classes, 2248
Social conditions, 5091
Social development, 2444
Solidarity, 614
Theatre, 1852
Urban society, 3886
Women's role, 3664
Women's status, 3212
Women's work, 2568
Africa South of the Sahara
    Law, 1250
    Science policy, 120
    Women, 2589
Age, 2830
    USA, 5178
Age at marriage
    India, 3098
Age distribution
    Europe, 2642
Age groups, 2636
Aged, 576, 2045, 2713-14, 2726, 2729, 2733,
        2742, 2750, 2753, 2761, 5169, 5195
    Australia, 2754
    Canada, 2716
    China, 2756
    France, 1085, 2724, 2737, 2749
    Israel, 2717, 2730
    Japan, 2732, 2745, 2747, 2757, 2762
    Korea R, 2735
    Netherlands, 2719
    Poland, 2758
    South Africa : Pretoria, 2760
    United Kingdom, 2734, 2741
    USA, 2727, 2744, 2751, 3199
    USSR, 2755
Ageing, 2736, 2740
    Developing countries, 2731
    Japan, 2739
    USA, 2711, 2720
Aggression, 631, 636, 1136
Aggressiveness, 629-30, 633-35, 637
Agrarian reforms
    Algeria, 3665
    Ecuador, 3682
    India, 3657, 3687
    Portugal, 4586
Agrarian relations
    India, 3669
Agrarian structure
    Mexico, 1984
Agricultural cooperation
    Poland, 4079

Agricultural cooperatives
    Developing countries, 4289
    Ecuador, 3682
    Israel, 4077
    Japan, 4093
Agricultural education
    France, 3220
Agricultural employment
    Asia, 2274
Agricultural market
    France, 3670
Agricultural mechanization
    Canada, 4088
    India, 3721
    USA, 4070
Agricultural policy
    USA, 4071
Agricultural production
    Morocco, 1128
    Tunisia, 1128
Agricultural workers, 4506, 4509
    France, 4288
    Hungary, 3701, 4521
    Poland, 4510, 4710
Agriculture, 3575
    France, 3202
Albania
    Penal law, 1254
Alcoholism, 1079, 5131-32, 5135, 5138, 5143
    France, 5128, 5141
    Germany FR, 1180
    Ireland, 5142
    Poland, 5136
    United Kingdom, 5126
    USA, 2891, 5118
Algeria
    Agrarian reforms, 3665
    Child psychology, 456
    Christianity, 1033
    Copyright, 3934
    Cultural interaction, 1033
    Emigrants, 3490
    Everyday life, 947
    Islam, 1033, 1338
    Juvenile delinquency, 5251
    Life tables, 2893
    Mortality, 2893
    Political systems, 1338
    Population movement, 2814
    Society, 894
    Urban development, 3760
    Villages, 3665
Alienation, 1096, 1111, 1126-27, 1146, 1163,
        1164
    India, 1169, 1170, 1174
    Israel, 4089
    Japan, 4393
Alternative technology
    Canada, 4028
Althusser, Louis, 197, 212
Altman, Irwin, 1555
Amazonia

Indigenous population, 3290
  Linguistics, 1525
America
  Media, 1753
Amusement, *use* Entertainment
Anarchism, 4798-4801, 4806, 4813
Ancestor cult, 1441
Andean Region
  Ethnic groups, 3322
Androgyny
  Australia, 2612
Animal domestication, 2572
Animals
  France, 2558
Anomie, 3049
Anthologies
  India, 4508
Anthropogeography, *use* Human geography
Anthropological methodology, 234
Anthropological research, 3362
Anthropology, 1000
  Costa Rica, 3283
Anticlericalism
  France, 1495
Anticommunism, 2215
Antisemitism, 3402
  Austria, 3428
  France, 3377, 3397, 3405, 3408
  Germany, 3385
  Hungary, 3386, 3394
  Poland, 3429
  Romania, 3421
  South Africa, 3423
  USA, 3404
  USSR, 3380
Antisocial behaviour
  USSR, 1232
Anxiety, 543
Apartheid
  South Africa, 3384, 3412-13, 3415
Applied arts, *use* Handicrafts
Applied research, 1225
Applied sociology, 83, 5057
  USA, 2837
Apprenticeship
  Canada, 4501
Appropriate technology, 4055
Arab countries
  Cultural alienation, 2361
  Cultural identity, 2361
  Educational systems, 1980
  Foreign languages, 1586
  Intelligentsia, 2361
  Nationalism, 4787
  Publishing, 1800
  Social mobility, 2381
  Teaching, 2153
  Women, 2625
  Working class, 2381
  Writers, 1800
Arrangement of working time, *use* Working
    time arrangement

Arbitration
  USA, 4701
Architecture
  Italy, 1837
  Romania, 1839
  United Kingdom, 1835
  USA, 1833
Area studies
  Brazil, 371
Argentina
  Care of the aged, 5369
  Catholics, 1331
  Delinquency, 5200
  Democracy, 4818
  Educational output, 1992
  Educational policy, 1974
  Health services, 5438
  Higher education, 1974
  Immigration, 3515
  Labour law, 4573
  Old age policy, 5369
  Party systems, 4918
  Political socialization, 4986
  Political speech, 1627
  Primary education, 1992
  Private education, 1926
  Rural employment, 4189
  Social policy, 5069
  Social problems, 5069
  Social stratification, 2032
  Social work, 5381
  Society, 901
  Sociology, 3
  Speech analysis, 1627
  Students, 2032
  Trade unions, 4582, 4669
  Universities, 2044
  University reforms, 2036
Aristocracy
  United Kingdom, 4814
Aristotle, 4855
Armed forces, 5028, 5030
  Belgium, 5035
  Israel, 5034
  USA, 3367, 4778
Army
  USA, 5037
Aron, Raymond, 86, 171, 178-79, 2341,
    2349-50, 2354, 2362
Art, 1008, 1766, 1770, 1778 1785-86
  Israel, 1769
  Japan, 1781
  Southern Africa, 1764
  USA, 1765
  USSR, 3498
Art museums
  USA, 1787
Art objects, *use* Works of art
Art theories, 1767
Artificial intelligence, 132-33, 137, 139
Artisans, *use* Craftsmen
Artistic creation, 1776, 1779-80

ASEAN countries
  Higher education, 2070
Asia
  Agricultural employment, 2274
  Business communication, 4006
  Emigrants, 3496
  Family planning, 2997
  Human rights, 4853
  Languages, 1305
  Modes of production, 4058
  Mortality, 2897
  Proletariat, 2274
  Religion, 1305
  Urban population, 2813
  Urbanization, 3751
Asiatic religions, 1361
Aspirations
  Indonesia, 560
Assassination, *use* Homicide
Associations, 731, 732, 2713, 3633, 4279
  Congo, 730
  France, 724
  Senegal, 730
Asylums, 5454
Atheism
  USSR, 1387
Attitude change, 2960
  China, 2969
Attitude scales, 448
Attitude to work, 4349, 4360, 4397, 4401,
    4442
  Canada, 4364
  France, 4420
  Germany FR, 4356, 4372
  Israel, 4399
  Japan, 4412
  USA, 4400
Attitudes, 607, 806-07, 810-12, 814, 817-18,
    4007
  Australia, 816
  Poland, 2007, 2799
  Spain, 3112
  USA, 813
Attorneys, *use* Lawyers
Attribution, 495, 593-97, 599, 601, 607, 609,
    612, 803
Audience, 1720
Audiovisual aids
  Java, 3012
Australia
  Abortion, 816, 3002
  Academic freedom, 1951
  Adolescents, 1221
  Adopted children, 3198
  Affinity, 618
  Aged, 2754
  Androgyny, 2612
  Attitudes, 816
  Bonuses, 4389
  Broadcasting, 1664
  Catholicism, 816
  Civilization, 884

Collective bargaining, 4691
Conservatism, 816
Contraception, 2967
Contraceptive methods, 2966
Crime prevention, 5248
Cultural pluralism, 889, 911
Demographic transition, 2754
Education, 3309
Educational policy, 1892
Educational reforms, 1949
Ethnic policy, 3364
Ethnicity, 3299
Family size, 3152
Female labour, 4245
Fertility, 2914, 2918
Geography, 3591
History of education, 1892
Hospitals, 5442
Housing policy, 3915
Immigrants, 1165, 1326, 3489
Immigration, 3465
Indigenous population, 3292, 3304, 3309,
    3311, 3347
Jews, 1326
Journalists, 1694
Labour market, 2596
Legal aspects, 4245
Marriage, 618
Mental health, 2612
Migration policy, 3435
Minority groups, 687, 2918
Morality, 1221
Multicultural education, 1960
Myths, 2612
Nurses, 4379
Occupational safety, 4389, 4390
Private schools, 2016
Protestant ethics, 1474
Racism, 3432
Regional development, 4125
Sex discrimination, 2596
Sex roles, 2612
Social adaptation, 1165
Sociology, 12
Sociology of law, 1253
Universities, 2037
University management, 2074
Unmarried mothers, 3198
Value systems, 1221
Violence, 1140
Australia : Sydney
  Motherhood, 3017
Austria
  Antisemitism, 3428
  Business communities, 4013
  Educational policy, 1934
  Educational reforms, 1934
  Emigration, 3487
  Farmers, 3663
  Games, 4747
  History of sociology, 51
  Intellectuals, 3487

Leisure utilization, 4747
Market economy, 3955
Mass media, 1709
Political culture, 4963
Political parties, 4915
Prostitution, 3032
Social control, 1048
Social history, 3663
Social policy, 5309
Wildcat strikes, 4678
Austria : Vienna
Migrant workers, 4291
Authoritarianism, 564, 827, 829
Germany FR, 828
Mexico, 4826
South Africa, 4804
USSR, 831
Authority, 781, 792
Automation, 4043
France, 4022, 4031, 4472, 4491
German DR, 4039
Latin America, 159
USA, 4057
Automobile industry
Japan, 4393
USA, 4698
Automobiles, 4097

Balance theory, 824
Bangladesh
Abortion, 2986
Birth, 2906
Child rearing, 4251
Contraception, 3007
Family planning, 5453
Health services, 5453
Libraries, 160
Rural poverty, 5116
Rural women, 5116
Theatre, 1855
Villages, 3684
Women workers, 4238
Working mothers, 4251
Bankers
United Kingdom, 2283
Bargaining, 644, 648, 652, 657
Bargaining power, 652
Bargaining theory, 652
Barristers, *use* Lawyers
Basic education
Brazil, 2088, 2106
Mexico, 2084
Basic needs
Africa, 5088
Basic rights, 1252
Behaviour, 808-12, 815, 817
Belgium
Abortion, 2992
Armed forces, 5035
Bilingual education, 2099
Bilingualism, 1599
Books, 1757

Collective bargaining, 4690
Divorce, 3094
Education, 1912
Health services, 5441
Housing policy, 3800
Islam, 1352
Judges, 4882
Labour law, 4577
Language teaching, 1599
Managers, 4528
Marriage, 3094
Medical care, 5415
Medical occupations, 5415
Military service, 5035
Physicians, 5475
Religious minorities, 1352
School administration, 2023
Secondary schools, 2023
Social housing, 3800
Theatre, 1851
Tourism, 4758
Training, 2128
Violence, 1099
Belief, 765, 1294
Pakistan, 834
Bell, Daniel, 66
Benin
Social classes, 2300
Berger, Peter L., 1819
Bible, 581
Bibliographies, 152, 263, 1156, 1277, 1298,
2465, 2600, 2637, 3036, 3175, 3203,
3532, 3624, 3626, 3782, 3914, 4139,
4457, 4464, 4542
Brazil, 2517
Bulgaria, 4660
Denmark, 4595
Developing countries, 5044
Europe, 2095
Latin America, 150
Maghreb, 1394
USA, 3398
Bilingual education
Belgium, 2099
Mexico, 2094
USA, 2099
Bilingualism, 1585, 1618
Belgium, 1599
Canada, 1614
France, 3101
Paraguay, 1598
USA, 4267
USSR, 1590
Biographies, 172-75, 180-81, 5072
Biosphere, 3605
Birth, 2912, 2949
Bangladesh, 2906
China, 2935
Polynesia, 2904
USA, 2915
Birth control
Dominican Republic, 3003

Poland, 3188
Birth intervals
  Indonesia, 2920
  Kenya, 2910
  Malaysia, 2933
Birth order, 600, 3183
Birth spacing
  Costa Rica, 2998
  India, 3013
Blacks
  Brazil, 3296
  USA, 1805, 2256, 2335, 2584, 3129, 3136,
    3282, 3298, 3312, 3315, 3331, 3348,
    3352, 3355, 3373, 3403, 3736, 3897,
    4480, 4633
Blau, Peter M., 655, 662, 694, 2155, 3363
Blindness
  USA, 2828
Bloch, Ernest, 1319
Body language, *use* Non-verbal communication
Body symbolism
  Maghreb, 1548
Bolivia
  Local power, 4898
  Student movements, 2057
Bonuses
  Australia, 4389
Book reviews, 151
Books
  Belgium, 1757
Botswana
  Divorce, 3093
  Fertility, 2916
  Women's participation, 3236
  Women's status, 3236
Bourdieu, Pierre, 874
Bourgeois society, 3954, 4837, 5056
Bourgeoisie, 2296
  Canada, 2260, 2295
  Colombia, 4135
  France, 3045
  India, 2282
  Nicaragua, 2312
  Peru, 4135
  United Kingdom, 4780
Brahmanism
  India, 1393
Brain drain
  Caribbean, 3501
  Egypt, 3466
Brazil
  Advertising, 1633
  Area studies, 371
  Basic education, 2088, 2106
  Bibliographies, 2517
  Blacks, 3296
  Breast-feeding, 2868
  Catholic Church, 1427, 1440, 2106
  Church and State, 1498
  Cinema, 1674
  Citizenship, 3609, 3615
  Class consciousness, 2309

Clientelism, 797, 4129
Collective bargaining, 2309
Communication, 1545
Cultural policy, 1027
Delinquent rehabilitation, 5167
Educational opportunities, 1956
Educational philosophy, 1911
Female labour, 4281
Fertility, 444
Folk culture, 1200, 1201, 1207
Foreigners, 3300
Health, 5426, 5428
Historical demography, 2517
Honour, 1212
Housing policy, 3792
Infant mortality, 2868
Intellectuals, 1201
Leisure time, 4405
Libraries, 163
Liturgy, 1440
Metropolitan areas, 3903
New towns, 3893
Political socialization, 4986
Poverty, 797
Prison, 5167
Private education, 1987
Public education, 1987
Public health, 5407
Regional planning, 4129
Residential segregation, 3883
Resource exploitation, 2487
Slums, 1212, 3792
Social conditions, 371
Social conflicts, 651
Social development, 2420
Social inequality, 1956
Social security, 5357
Social work, 5167
Sport, 4751
Stochastic models, 444
Time budgets, 4405
Trade unions, 4657
Traditional medicine, 5398
Underdevelopment, 2487
Urban structure, 3881
Women's work, 4255
Breast-feeding, 2658
  Brazil, 2868
  Developing countries, 2648
  Japan, 2659
  Malaysia, 2643
  USA, 2659
Broadcasting, 1713
  Australia, 1664
  Japan, 1688, 1751
  USA, 1748
Brotherhoods
  USA, 1414
Buddhism, 229, 1329, 1362
  Nepal, 2434
Buildings
  Poland, 2799

Bulgaria
    Bibliographies, 4660
    Information services, 161
    Jews, 1383
    Labour movements, 4660
    Ruling class, 2346
    Socialism, 4660
    Statistics, 413
    Technological change, 4056
Bureaucracy, 739, 772, 776
    China, 771
    India, 767
    USA, 743, 747
Bureaucratic control, *use* Administrative control
Bureaucratic organization, *use* Bureaucracy
Burotics, *use* Office automation
Burke, Edmund, 4807
Burkina-Faso
    Class formation, 2305
    Rural development, 3658
    Rural schools, 2014
Burma
    Education, 1917
Burundi
    Names, 507
Business communication, 3995, 3999, 4004, 4010
    Asia, 4006
    Switzerland, 3993
Business communities, 3996
    Austria, 4013
    Germany FR, 4013
    Ghana, 3992
    Nigeria, 3990
Business cycles, 4648
    United Kingdom, 4584
Business management
    Canada, 481
    Poland, 3998
Business organization, 4001, 4012
    Italy, 3994
    Japan, 711, 4080

California
    Prison, 5156
Cameroon
    Social security, 5355
Canada
    Academic freedom, 2027
    Academic success, 2114
    Action research, 114
    Aged, 2716
    Agricultural mechanization, 4088
    Alternative technology, 4028
    Apprenticeship, 4501
    Attitude to work, 4364
    Bilingualism, 1614
    Bourgeoisie, 2260, 2295
    Business management, 481
    Care of the aged, 5352, 5378
    Citizens, 5449
    Class formation, 2266
    Copyright, 3939

Crime, 5196
Criminology, 5155, 5235
Cultural policy, 1025
Democratization, 1947
Demonstrations, 867
Dependence relationships, 5041
Deviance, 1108
Division of labour, 2224
Divorce, 2114
Educational opportunities, 3258
Educational provision, 1946
Educational systems, 1947
Elections, 3246
Elite, 3258
Emigration, 3477
Employment policy, 4221
Entrepreneurship, 4003
Ethnic groups, 1050, 2216, 3294, 3323
Ethnic minorities, 3340
Ethnic policy, 3364
Ethnicity, 3299, 3330, 3316, 3371
Ethnocentrism, 3376
Family, 3138
Family life, 3144, 3157, 3172
Family size, 3163, 3172
Feminism, 3254
Fertility, 2905
Health insurance, 5358
Health services, 5449
Historical demography, 2539, 3157, 3436
Immigrant assimilation, 3330, 3533
Immigrants, 3138, 3461, 3468, 3480,
    3484, 3493, 3500, 3511
Immigration, 3465
Indigenous population, 3310, 3334
Individuals, 481
Innovations, 4040
Interethnic communication, 3371
Juvenile delinquency, 5157
Labour disputes, 4676
Labour relations, 4566
Languages, 1604
Lawyers, 2368
Life cycle, 3157
Linguistic minorities, 1605
Local politics, 3316
Manual workers, 4522
Marital satisfaction, 3172
Marriage, 3060
Mental health, 4040
Migration, 3436
Minority groups, 688, 691, 1605
Nation building, 2489
National identity, 976
Nationalism, 4772
Occupational choice, 3258
Occupational prestige, 4474
Occupational qualification, 4522
Occupational segregation, 4495
Political parties, 4907
Population, 2539
Population movement, 2776

Pornography, 3034
Public enterprises, 4566
Punishment, 5176
Quality of life, 4028, 4362
Racial stereotypes, 3376
Refugees, 3533
Role, 3144
Rural areas, 5196
Science policy, 126
Scientific community, 126
Sexual behaviour, 3035
Social change, 3777
Social classes, 481, 2261
Social mobility, 2368, 2383
Social movements, 4923
Social services, 5466
Social stratification, 2216, 2261
Social structure, 340
Student movements, 2056
Symbols, 1547
Theatre, 1850
Towns, 3850
Trade unions, 4620
Universities, 2027
Urban areas, 3777
Urban population, 3777
Urbanization, 3850
Value systems, 1050
Voting behaviour, 4997
Wildcat strikes, 4673
Women's organizations, 3221
Women's participation, 3208, 3227
Women's status, 3246, 3258
Women's work, 3060, 4241
Working conditions, 4362, 4410
Youth, 3035
Canada — USA
   International relations, 5041
Canada : Quebec
   Catholic Church, 1437
   Fertility decline, 2940
   Nationalism, 1428, 1437, 4773
   New technologies, 4029
   Protestant Churches, 1428
   Religion, 4773
   Women workers, 4252
   Women's employment, 4029
   Working time arrangement, 4252
Canada : Toronto
   Decentralization, 3852
   Local government, 3852
   Urban planning, 3852
Capital, 1245
Capital cities
   Japan, 3755
   Southern Africa, 3744
   Thailand, 3908
   United Kingdom, 3749
Capital interest, *use* Interest
Capital punishment
   USA, 5160, 5171, 5231
Capitalism, 223, 1776, 2293, 3946, 4045

United Kingdom, 3952
Capitalist countries
   Immigrants, 3288
   Labour, 4155
   National minorities, 3288
   Social mobility, 2382
   Structural change, 2382
   Working class, 2262
Capitalist development, 1932
Capitalist society, 822, 2315, 3645
Care of the aged
   Argentina, 5369
   Canada, 5352, 5378
   Europe, 5350
   France, 5341, 5343, 5344, 5379, 5473
   Japan, 2732, 5374
   Spain, 5478
   USA, 5377
Career choice, *use* Occupational choice
Career development, 2225, 4477, 4492
   Hungary, 4485
   United Kingdom, 4479
   USA, 4500
Careers, *use* Occupations
Caribbean
   Brain drain, 3501
   Communication, 1567
   Educational research, 1894
   Migration, 3442, 3443
   Peasantry, 3738
   Social surveys, 375
Carnivals
   Colombia, 1192
   France, 1197
Cars, *use* Automobiles
Cartoons, 1639, 1728
   France, 1725
Case studies, 3156
Casework, 5385
Castes
   India, 1170, 2202, 2234-36, 2238-40,
      2243-44, 2386
   India : Assam, 2233
   Sri Lanka, 2241
Catastrophe theory, 640
Catholic Church, 1410, 1426
   Brazil, 1427, 1440, 2106
   Canada : Quebec, 1437
   Central America, 1433
   El Salvador, 4957
   France, 1425, 1430
   Guatemala, 654
   Nicaragua, 1416
   USA, 1406, 1415, 1438
Catholicism, 988, 1364
   Australia, 816
   France, 1353, 1373
   Hungary, 1398
   Italy, 1348, 1386
   Korea R, 1323
   Mexico, 1364
   Peru, 1364

Poland, 1350, 1397
Spain, 1364, 1380
USA, 1368, 1392, 2907
Catholics
Argentina, 1331
France, 1342
Netherlands, 1384
Northern Ireland, 1214
United Kingdom, 1366
USA, 3640
Causal analysis, 302
Causal explanation, 240
Causal inference, 597, 609
Causality, 279, 291
Censuses
Germany FR, 361
Central Africa
Ideology, 2279
Social classes, 2279
Central America
Catholic Church, 1433
Central government
USA, 4896
Ceremonials, *use* Rites
Certeau, Michel de, 1450, 1465
Chałasiński, Józef, 80, 930, 1918, 2297
Charisma, 782, 788, 790
Chicago School of Sociology, 21
Child abuse, 5153, 5227
USA, 5181
Child adoption, 3197
Child care
France, 5461
Child development, 1731, 2652
Child labour
Germany, 4276
Child mortality, 2851, 2871
Developing countries, 2846
France, 2875
India, 3177
Indonesia, 2859, 2873
Malaysia, 2643, 2933
Mali, 2870
Philippines, 3848
USA, 2863
Child psychology, 469, 477
Algeria, 456
Child rearing, 3186
Bangladesh, 4251
USA, 2660
Child-parent relations, *use* Parent-child relations
Childhood, 2655
Spain, 2649
Children, 1703, 1710, 2646, 2662
France, 2645
Nigeria, 2654
Norway, 3974
Papua New Guinea, 2644
Philippines, 609
Chile
Communication research, 1565
Everyday life, 960

Family, 3192
Feminism, 3249
Health policy, 5436
Higher education, 2034
Public opinion, 833
Repression, 5180
Self-management, 770
Social sciences, 14
Sociology, 18, 19
Trade unionism, 4587, 4645
Trade unions, 4592
Vocational education, 4467
Vocational training, 4467
China
Aged, 2756
Attitude change, 2969
Birth, 2935
Bureaucracy, 771
Class structure, 2324
Collective behaviour, 1150
Criminal justice, 5239
Cults, 1446
Demography, 2557
Education, 1902
Educational policy, 1922, 1943
Emigrants, 3535
Ethnic groups, 3327
Family, 3159
Family planning, 2969
Family policy, 5376
Fertility, 2917, 2931, 2959, 3063
Folklore, 1198
Historical demography, 2931
Hospitals, 5446
Industrial democracy, 4716
Information services, 156
Intellectuals, 2355, 2367
Labour relations, 4549
Literature, 1817
Love, 613
Marriage, 613, 3159
Nuptiality, 3063
Patriarchy, 3141
Peasants, 3683
Poetry, 1831
Political protest, 1831
Population, 2508, 2514, 2532, 2534
Population censuses, 2768, 2775
Population movement, 2771, 2777
Population policy, 3006, 3018
Rural areas, 2917, 2959
Rural development, 3648, 3718
Rural-urban migration, 3550
Sexuality, 1817
Sociability, 1817
Social security, 5375
Social stratification, 2324
Students, 2073
Theatre, 1857
Urban life, 3923
Urban planning, 3819
Urban population, 2806

Urbanization, 3866
Value systems, 1061
Violence, 1150
Women, 2631
Women's status, 3244, 3253
Workers' participation, 4719
Working class, 2245
Chinese
Economic life, 3326
Ethnicity, 3326
Choice models, *use* Decision models
Choice theory, *use* Decision theory
Christian Churches
Iceland, 1497
Christianity, 47, 1358, 1360, 1658
Algeria, 1033
Madagascar, 1347
USA, 62, 1396
Church and State
Brazil, 1498
United Kingdom, 1418
Church attendance, *use* Religious practice
Church history
France, 1430
Germany FR, 1412
Churches, 1436
German DR, 1411
USA, 1405
Zaire, 1404
Cinema, 1647, 1681
Africa, 1642, 1655, 1670
Brazil, 1674
France, 1641
Germany FR, 1737
Spain, 1727
USSR, 1704
Cities, *use* Towns
Citizens
Canada, 5449
Citizenship
Brazil, 3609, 3615
Civil religion
Israel, 1299
USA, 1276, 1279
Civil rights, 4866
South Africa, 3400
USA, 4856, 4870
Civil servants
France, 4886, 4887
Poland, 4383
United Kingdom, 4590, 4887
USA, 4888
Civil service
Germany FR, 4891
Civil society, 10, 4840
Scotland, 2499
Civilization, 912, 933, 934, 974, 985, 991,
999, 1006
Australia, 884
India, 900
Surinam, 997
Civilization crisis

Western countries, 966
Class conflicts, 2307
Thailand, 3690
Class consciousness
Brazil, 2309
Greece, 2263
Japan, 2322
United Kingdom, 2254
USA, 2256, 2328
Class differentiation, 2321, 4305
Germany FR, 2203
Class domination, 2303
Class formation, 2253, 2259, 2270, 2273,
2303, 2318
Burkina-Faso, 2305
Canada, 2266
Ghana, 3992
Nicaragua, 1416
Thailand, 2255
Class relations, 2306, 2315, 4338
Class structure, 2293, 2298-99, 2310, 2316
China, 2324
Czechoslovakia, 2294
Developed countries, 2257
Egypt, 3945
Malaysia, 2326
Singapore, 2326
United Kingdom, 2283
Class struggle, 2251, 2288
France, 2311
Poland, 2317
South Africa, 2290
Class theory, 2278
Class values, 2284
Classification, 916, 4458
Classrooms, 705, 706
Clergy
USA, 4770
Clientelism
Brazil, 797, 4129
Clinical psychology, 454
Clubs, 620, 679
Cluster analysis, 297
CMEA countries
Social indicators, 411
Coal mines
France, 4516
Coalitions, 445, 647
Cognitive development, 2692
Cohort analysis, 326
Germany, 2862
Hungary, 919
USA, 5149
Collective action, 868, 4946
France, 870
United Kingdom, 870
Collective bargaining, 4384
Australia, 4691
Belgium, 4690
Brazil, 2309
Germany FR, 4062, 4694
Italy, 4695

Japan, 4704
Nigeria, 4697
Spain, 4607
United Kingdom, 4558, 4699, 4702
USA, 4696, 4698
Collective behaviour, 568, 869, 2344
China, 1150
Cuba, 861
Poland, 622
Collective choice, *use* Public choice
Collective consciousness, 502, 862
Collective decision, *use* Public choice
Collective farms
USSR, 3740
College women, *use* Women students
Collins, Randall, 787
Colombia
Bourgeoisie, 4135
Carnivals, 1192
Domestic workers, 4526
Education, 1881
Educational systems, 1941
Family, 3104
Labour law, 4670
Labour relations, 4563
Nutrition, 5084
Regional development, 4135
School-community relationship, 1933
Strikes, 4670
Colonialism
Africa, 3943
Coloured persons
USA, 3329
Commercial banks, 3952
Communication, 514, 670, 1091, 1538, 1546,
      1549, 1558, 1569-70, 1572, 2483, 4538
Brazil, 1545
Caribbean, 1567
Developing countries, 1573
France, 1543, 1562
Hungary, 1542
India, 1574
Ireland, 3625
Italy, 4354
Japan, 1566
Communication in management, *use*
      Business communication
Communication media, *use* Media
Communication network
Japan, 1578
Communication policy
Developed countries, 1552
Poland, 1557
USA, 1582
Communication research, 1539, 1553
Chile, 1565
Denmark, 1556
France, 1564
United Kingdom, 1742
USA, 1537
Communication systems, 1581
Communication technology, 1540

Communication theory, 220, 1544, 1571
Communism, 211, 4782, 4794
Community, 967, 3621
Community development, 2426, 3616, 3641
France, 2285
Japan, 3642
New Zealand, 5467
Nigeria, 3622
Singapore, 3646
USA, 3623, 3632, 3634-35, 3637
Zambia, 3643
Community life, 3629
Ireland, 3625
United Kingdom, 3118
Community membership, 3644
USA, 1132, 3564, 3640
Community organization, 3624, 3627, 3645
Germany FR, 3638
Community participation
Latin America, 3628
USA, 3617
Community power, 3630, 3639
Community satisfaction
United Kingdom, 3618, 3619
USA, 3618
Community study, 363, 364
Japan, 369
Commuting, 3559
Hungary, 3543
Company unions, 4611
Comparative education, 1882
Iraq — Egypt, 1900
Competition, 4112-14
Complex organizations, 729, 735
Computer science, 134-36
Computerization, 152, 663, 4048
Computers, 131, 138, 2123
USA, 382
Comte, Auguste, 72, 183, 1568, 2110
Conceptualization, 367, 558
Conflict management, *use* Dispute settlement
Conflict resolution, *use* Dispute settlement
Conflicts, 649, 3194
Germany FR, 638
Japan, 646
Northern Ireland, 1421
USA, 5440
Conflicts of generations, *use* Generation conflicts
Confucianism, 2935
Congo
Associations, 730
Rural development, 3707
Towns, 730
Congregations
France, 1425
Congresses
Netherlands, 245
Consanguineous marriage
Lebanon, 3078
Consensual union
Denmark, 3073
Finland, 3076

USA, 3079
Western Europe, 3079
Consensus, 838
USA, 611
Conservatism, 447, 564, 4807, 5025
Australia, 816
Netherlands, 4781
South Africa, 4804
United Kingdom, 4780
USA, 1482
Consumer behaviour, 826, 4101-02, 4104-07
Poland, 4103
USA, 4100, 4108, 4109
Consumer demand
Poland, 4103
Consumer movements
France, 4099
Consumer society, 3958
Consumption, 1001
Content analysis, 317, 339, 340, 349, 359, 1577
Contextual analysis, 304
Continuing education, 2093
France, 2089
USA, 2086
USSR, 2105
Contraception, 815, 2902, 2979, 2987, 3016
Australia, 2967
Bangladesh, 3007
Nigeria, 2996
Switzerland, 2983
Turkey, 2974
USA, 2964, 2976, 2993
Contraceptive methods, 2985
Australia, 2966
Cooking, 4078
Cooperative farms, *use* Agricultural
    cooperatives
Cooperative movements
Finland, 4941
Peru, 4953
Cooperative sector
France, 3947
Cooperatives
Africa, 614
India, 3942
United Kingdom, 3953
USA, 3957
Copyright
Algeria, 3934
Canada, 3939
USA, 3932, 3933
Corporate culture
USA, 972
Corporate management, *use* Business management
Corporatism, 4647, 4654, 4816
Western Europe, 4580
Correlation, 407, 428
Cosmology
Japan, 1448
Costa Rica
Anthropology, 3283
Birth spacing, 2998

Fertility, 5086
Indigenous population, 3283
Internal migration, 3546
Poverty, 5086
Radio, 1690
School-community relationship, 1936
Social security, 5372
Counterculture, 2441
Latin America, 885
Cox, Harvey, 1272
Craftsmen
Guatemala, 4536
Creativity, 1172, 1790, 2130, 2663, 5025
Crime, 2742, 5201
Canada, 5196
France, 5202
India, 5150, 5208
Ireland, 4879
USA, 5146, 5186, 5246
Crime prevention
Australia, 5248
USA, 5210
Criminal justice, 5177, 5179, 5201
China, 5239
India, 5208
Japan, 5250
Switzerland, 5232
USA, 1071, 5159, 5166, 5199, 5206
Criminal law, *use* Penal law
Criminal sentencing
USA, 5198, 5252
Criminal sociology, 5223, 5247
Criminality, *use* Delinquency
Criminals, *use* Offenders
Criminology, 2453, 5161, 5182
Canada, 5155, 5235
Critical path analysis, 435
Critical theory, 250, 256, 258
Criticism, 1856
Cross-cultural analysis, 1581
Cross-national analysis, 4474
Crowd, 1155
Cuba
Collective behaviour, 861
Fertility, 2927
Health policy, 5436
Judiciary power, 4883
Population censuses, 2809
Women's status, 3266
Cults, 1362, 1442, 1445, 1468
China, 1446
Taiwan, 1447
Cultural alienation
Arab countries, 2361
Cultural attitudes, 2471
Cultural behaviour, 1045, 2227
Cultural change, 2426
Guatemala, 1026
Poland, 2267
Yugoslavia, 3834
Cultural conflicts, 1039
Switzerland, 1038

Cultural consumption
   Italy, 3806
Cultural contacts, *use* Cultural interaction
Cultural cooperation
   Germany FR, 1016
   Maghreb, 1016
Cultural development, 1011, 1022
   Developing countries, 1029
   Europe, 1030
   Indonesia, 2430
   Poland, 1013
Cultural differentiation, *use* Cultural pluralism
Cultural dimension of development, 1041
Cultural dissemination
   France, 1015
Cultural dynamics, 1017
Cultural evolution, *use* Cultural change
Cultural history
   Africa, 1044
   Italy, 2400
   United Kingdom, 1043
Cultural identity, 362, 3285, 3286, 4739
   Arab countries, 2361
   Developing countries, 1020
   India, 1152
   Latin America, 2364
   North Africa, 1019
   Poland, 1042
   Spain, 1034
Cultural implications
   Poland, 4437
Cultural integration
   Poland, 1023
Cultural interaction
   Algeria, 1033
   USA, 1600
Cultural life
   Latin America, 1032
   United Kingdom, 1043
Cultural norms
   Switzerland, 5414
Cultural patterns, 916
Cultural pluralism
   Australia, 889, 911
Cultural policy, 1040
   Brazil, 1027
   Canada, 1025
   EEC countries, 1018
   France, 1009, 1015, 1028
   Nepal, 1010
   Norway, 1035
   Romania, 1036
Cultural practices
   France, 915
Cultural progress, *use* Cultural development
Cultural relations
   Japan, 5042
   USA — Europe, 1021
Cultural specificity
   India : Punjab, 1037
Cultural systems, 1000
Cultural tradition, 4128

Cultural transmission, *use* Cultural tradition
Cultural values, 1024
   India, 1014
Culture, 136, 192, 201, 225, 510, 572, 893,
      909-10, 920, 930, 932, 937, 942,
      951-53, 970-71, 979, 988, 995-96,
      1008, 1124, 1206, 1546, 2288, 3608,
      4024, 4044, 5152
   Developing countries, 886
   France, 1267
   Hungary, 978
   Italy, 887
   Japan, 2435
   Latin America, 906, 1003
   Netherlands, 935, 4473
   Poland, 895, 1004
   Romania, 913, 927
   Spain, 982
   USA, 968, 5439
   USSR, 1005, 1378
   Yugoslavia, 903
Culture and development, *use* Cultural
      dimension of development
Culture change, *use* Cultural change
Curaçao
   Working class, 2320
Curriculum
   United Kingdom, 2132
   USA, 775
Curriculum development, 2134, 2152
Customary law
   Papua New Guinea, 1239
Customs, 1205
Cybernetics, 343
Czechoslovakia
   Class structure, 2294
   Divorce, 3083, 3089
   Family, 3167, 3195
   Historiography, 2407
   Housing, 3765
   Human settlements, 3612
   Infant mortality, 2888, 2896
   Levels of education, 1982
   Libraries, 164
   Maternity benefits, 5353
   Migration, 3612
   Mortality, 2890
   Population composition, 2769
   Population growth, 2794
   Regional disparities, 2769
   Social development, 2439
   Social indicators, 423
   Social planning, 423
   Urbanization, 3878
   Youth, 2688

Daily life, *use* Everyday life
Darwin, Charles, 4855
Darwinism, 2416
Das, Bhagwan, 81
Data analysis, 300-01, 306-07, 318, 338, 389
Data archives, *use* Data banks

Data banks, 157
USSR, 155
Data collecting, 429
Data protection
United Kingdom, 308
Death, 2830, 2867, 2882, 3145
France, 2886
France : Brittany, 1451
Polynesia, 2904
Switzerland, 2889
Death penalty, *use* Capital punishment
Decentralization
Canada : Toronto, 3852
Dechristianization
France, 1495
Decision making, 287, 372, 542, 547, 550,
551, 676, 4093, 5133
Africa, 5088
United Kingdom, 4667
Decision models, 549, 565, 2603
Decision theory, 554
Decorative arts, *use* Fine arts
Defence policy
Israel, 5034
Deindustrialization
United Kingdom, 4082
Delinquency, 538, 1090, 1231, 5152, 5169,
5183, 5207, 5223, 5233
Argentina, 5200
Italy, 5173
USA, 3781, 5178, 5192, 5220, 5225, 5237,
5242
Delinquent rehabilitation
Brazil, 5167
Delinquents
USA, 2843
Demand for labour, 4153
Tanzania, 2939
Democracy, 1209, 4647, 4808-09, 4812,
4816-17, 4819-20
Argentina, 4818
Democratic centralism, 4618
Democratization
Canada, 1947
Demographic indicators, 2513
Demographic research, 2530, 2535
Spain, 2547
Demographic transition
Australia, 2754
India, 2778
India : Goa, 2807
Latin America, 416
Demography, 2504, 2526, 2544, 2550, 2556
China, 2557
United Kingdom, 2522
USSR, 2519
Demonstrations, 866, 1113
Canada, 867
Denmark
Bibliographies, 4595
Communication research, 1556
Consensual union, 3073

Fertility, 3073
Groups, 665
Higher education, 2063
Housing, 3851
Job satisfaction, 4366
Labour market, 4171
Labour movements, 4595
Mass media, 1556
National minorities, 3307
Police, 4366
Social policy, 5295
Social services, 5471
Social welfare, 5298
Trade unions, 4591
Voluntary organizations, 727
Voting behaviour, 4995, 5021
Welfare State, 5259
Women, 2566
Youth, 3851
Deontology
Malaysia, 1476
United Kingdom, 1476
Dependence relationships, 388
Canada, 5041
Deprivation, 597
India, 5109
USA, 5117
Derrida, Jacques, 215
Desegregation
USA, 1116, 1123, 1147
Determinism, 289
Developed countries
Class structure, 2257
Communication policy, 1552
Health services, 5451
Social security, 5367
Urban population, 3810
Working conditions, 4436
Developing countries, 2490, 2498
Ageing, 2731
Agricultural cooperatives, 4289
Bibliographies, 5044
Breast-feeding, 2648
Child mortality, 2846
Communication, 1573
Cultural development, 1029
Cultural identity, 1020
Culture, 886
Economic and social development, 2500
Educational development, 1921
Educational research, 1859
Ethics, 2982
Family farms, 4068
Family planning, 2955, 2982
Fertility, 2901, 2957
Fertility decline, 2955
Food, 2080
Health, 2080, 5404
Health policy, 5406
High technology, 4027
Housing, 3860, 3868
Housing policy, 3748

Hunger, 5081
International law, 5044
Labour migration, 3566
Life tables, 2880
Literacy, 2080
Mass media, 1638
Mortality, 2848
Oral tradition, 1808
Peasantry, 3704
Population, 2529
Population projections, 2553
Poverty, 2982
Press, 1741
Proletariat, 2292
Regional policy, 3785
Religion, 1282
Rural development, 3695
Rural sociology, 3704
Rural-urban migration, 3567
Slums, 3869, 3879, 3880
Social action, 5303
Social anthropology, 3704
Social change, 2440
Social movements, 4934
Social policy, 5281, 5302
Social problems, 5068
Social security, 5345, 5368
Student movements, 2031
Suburban areas, 3869
Technological change, 4025
Tourist trade, 4752
Towns, 3842
Traditional theatre, 1853
Urban growth, 3858
Urban policy, 3785, 3918
Urban population, 3810
Urbanization, 3766, 3787, 3880
Women workers, 4289
Women's role, 2598
Development planning, 2553
Development policy, 3215, 4128
  Haiti, 1905
Development potential
  Poland, 2789
Development research
  India, 2496
Development styles
  Latin America, 4124
Development theory, 2491, 2494, 3255
Deviance, 1074, 1137, 1146, 1157, 1182
  Canada, 1108
  Germany FR, 1180
  Japan, 1103
  USA, 1084, 1132
Dialectical materialism, 246
Dialectics, 212, 255, 2469, 4802
Dialects
  Switzerland, 1592
  Western Africa, 1594
Dictatorship, 4813
Dictionaries, 166, 167, 1293, 1294, 1310, 1637

Diplomas
  Western Europe, 2077
Disability
  United Kingdom, 2826
Disabled persons, 2845
  France, 2827, 2844
  Greece, 2841
  India, 2829
  USA, 2822
Disabled workers, 2832
  United Kingdom, 2825
Disasters, 5078, 5080
  India, 5079
  Japan, 3916
Discrimination, 666, 822
  Japan, 821
Discussion groups, 680
Diseases, 2196, 3134
  Finland, 2839
  USA, 2837
Dispute settlement, 652, 653, 656, 660
  India, 4689
  New Zealand, 4679
Divination
  Guatemala, 1458
Division of labour, 2183, 2188, 2219, 2226, 4098, 4482
  Canada, 2224
  USA, 3054
Divorce, 2942, 3066, 3070, 3082
  Belgium, 3094
  Botswana, 3093
  Canada, 2114
  Czechoslovakia, 3083, 3089
  Germany FR, 3084
  Singapore, 3102
  Spain, 3091
  United Kingdom, 3069, 3071
  USA, 3062, 3075, 3080, 3090, 3095, 5243
Documentation centres, *use* Information services
Dohen, G. A., 259
Domestic workers, 4525
  Colombia, 4526
  South Africa, 4523
Domination, 781, 787
Dominican Republic
  Birth control, 3003
  Educational systems, 1977
  Emigration, 3481
  Fertility, 2926
  Mass media, 1739
  Preschool education, 2013
  Urban sociology, 3783
  Women's work, 4321
Dommanget, Maurice, 2402
Dowry
  India, 3097
Drawing, 1836
Dropout
  Kenya : Nairobi, 2019
Drug addiction, 5119, 5133
  Italy, 5122, 5123

USA, 1074, 2891, 5118, 5127, 5129, 5137,
   5139, 5140
Drugs
   France, 5125
   United Kingdom, 5130
Drugs of abuse, 5121
   Germany FR, 1180
   Peru, 5124
   USA, 5120
Dumont, Louis, 2419
Duration of unemployment, *use*
   Unemployment duration
Durkheim, Émile, 210, 222, 354, 1076, 1111,
   1296, 1467, 2226, 3064, 4782, 5158,
   5211
Dwelling, *use* Housing
Dyad, 683, 689

Eastern Asia
   Environment, 3595
Eastern Europe
   Economic inequality, 2209
   Labour relations, 4552
   Literature, 1818
   Quality of life, 3979
   Social change, 4920
   Social inequality, 2209
   Social movements, 4920
   Television, 1733
   Trade unions, 4625
   Working class, 4625
Ecological analysis, 3580
Ecology, 3573-79, 3582, 3584-85, 3589-90,
   3594, 3598-99, 4073, 5051
Econometric models, 4154
Economic and social development, 2533, 4164
   Developing countries, 2500
   India, 767
   Latin America, 2506
Economic behaviour
   USA, 3961
Economic change, 3963
   Philippines, 3965
Economic control, 1252
Economic crisis, *use* Economic recession
Economic development, 2476, 3186, 3966
   Africa, 4869
   India, 1275
   Poland, 4594
Economic disturbances, *use* Business cycles
Economic fluctuations, *use* Business cycles
Economic growth, 4955
Economic history
   Hungary, 4284
   Ireland, 3931
   Scotland, 3931
Economic inequality
   Eastern Europe, 2209
Economic justice, 5308
Economic life
   Chinese, 3326
   Southeastern Asia, 3326

Economic policy
   United Kingdom, 4131
Economic recession, 3962-64, 5182
Economic regulation, *use* Economic control
Economic sociology, 1587
Ecuador
   Agrarian reforms, 3682
   Agricultural cooperatives, 3682
   Ethnicity, 3295
   Handicrafts, 4086
   Industrialization, 4172
   Labour movements, 4668
   Land tenure, 3671
   Manpower, 4172
   Urban policy, 3832
Education, 792, 1102, 1553, 1785, 1872,
   1907, 1914, 4416
   Australia, 3309
   Belgium, 1912
   Burma, 1917
   China, 1902
   Colombia, 1881
   France, 1858
   Germany FR, 1903
   Haiti, 1905
   India, 2240, 2459
   Japan, 1916
   Kenya, 1896
   Lesotho, 1876
   Mozambique, 1884
   Nicaragua, 1864
   Northern Ireland, 1898
   Pakistan, 1365
   Poland, 1013
   South Africa, 1870
   Spain, 1895
   Sweden, 2323
   USA, 1862, 1863, 1908, 1909, 2601
Education of women, *use* Women's education
Educational development
   Developing countries, 1921
   Ireland, 4033
Educational guidance
   Italy, 547
Educational history, *use* History of education
Educational innovations, 2136
   Spain, 2010
Educational levels, *use* Levels of education
Educational materials, *use* Teaching aids
Educational needs, 1981
Educational objectives, 1915, 1938, 2284
   France, 1962
   India, 2699
Educational opportunities, 2186, 2337
   Brazil, 1956
   Canada, 3258
   France, 1983, 2194, 2199
   Germany, 2377
Educational output, 1584, 1964, 2116
   Argentina, 1992
   France, 2048
   Poland, 2048

USA, 1937, 2048
USSR, 2048
Educational philosophy, 293, 1890, 1915
  Brazil, 1911
  USA, 1899
Educational planning, 1952, 2136
  Latin America, 1940
  Switzerland, 1973
Educational policy, 117, 4174, 4938
  Argentina, 1974
  Australia, 1892
  Austria, 1934
  China, 1922, 1943
  Israel, 1971
  Mexico, 1984
  Portugal, 1969
  Switzerland, 1973
  Turkey, 1945
  United Kingdom, 3474
  USA, 1927, 3331
  Venezuela, 2059
Educational provision
  Canada, 1946
  France, 2194
  United Kingdom, 2132
Educational psychology, 1877
  USSR, 1866
Educational reforms, 1932, 1939, 2024
  Australia, 1949
  Austria, 1934
  Egypt, 1978
  Germany FR, 1924, 1965
  Japan, 1967
  Latin America, 1975
  Pakistan, 1978
  Spain, 1935
  Turkey, 1978
  USA, 1958
Educational research, 1065, 1060, 1919
  Caribbean, 1894
  Developing countries, 1859
  Latin America, 1869, 1883
Educational sciences, *use* Sciences of education
Educational sociology, 1156, 1861, 1871,
    1875, 1879-80, 1885, 1888, 1891, 1897,
    1904, 1918
  France, 1867
  Italy, 1906
Educational systems, 1923, 1942, 1970
  Arab countries, 1980
  Canada, 1947
  Colombia, 1941
  Dominican Republic, 1977
  France, 1959, 1976
  Japan, 1955
  Netherlands, 1953
  Paraguay, 1972
  Poland, 1961
  USSR, 1925
Educational technology, 2141
Educational theory, *use* Theory of education
EEC

Women's work, 4290
EEC countries
  Cultural policy, 1018
  Frontier workers, 4232
  Tourism, 4750
  Trade unions, 4637
  Women, 2560
  Women's work, 4313
  Youth unemployment, 4195
Egalitarianism, 2231
Ego, 485, 487
  Israel, 2623
Egocentrism, 512
Egypt
  Brain drain, 3466
  Class structure, 3945
  Educational reforms, 1978
  Family, 3176
  Fertility, 2951
  Internal migration, 3568
  Islam, 1369
  Labour law, 4569, 4615
  Land reforms, 2951
  New towns, 3927
  Population policy, 2991
  Regional development, 2485
  State capitalism, 3945
  Trade unions, 4615
  Traditional society, 2485
  Urban society, 3568
Eisenstadt, S. N., 4838
El Salvador
  Catholic Church, 4957
  Political protest, 4957
Elderly, *use* Aged
Elections
  Canada, 3246
  Italy, 4993
Electoral abstentionism
  Europe, 5013
  Italy, 5011
  Spain, 5013
Electoral behaviour, *use* Voting behaviour
Electoral campaigning
  USA, 5002, 5004, 5020
Electoral sociology, 5009
Elementary groups, *use* Small groups
Elementary schools, *use* Primary schools
Eliade, Mircea, 1462
Elias, Norbert, 313, 991
Elite, 79, 2344, 2357
  Africa, 2356
  Canada, 3258
  France, 2345
  United Kingdom, 2339
  USA, 2360
Emigrants
  Africa, 3472
  Algeria, 3490
  Asia, 3496
  China, 3535
  Italy, 3470, 3521

Korea R, 3486, 3498
Mexico, 3287
Portugal, 3508, 3509
Spain, 1034
Turkey, 4247
USA, 3440
USSR, 1326, 1374
Yugoslavia, 4291
Emigration, 3503, 3532
Austria, 3487
Canada, 3477
Dominican Republic, 3481
Hungary, 3531
Israel, 3475
Italy, 3524
North Africa, 3456
Spain, 3514
USSR, 3460, 3516, 3536
Emotion, 544, 4753
Empathy, 621
Empirical research, 365, 368
Empiricism, 106, 203
Employees
Germany FR, 4356
Socialist countries, 4524
Employment, 38, 90, 4063
France, 4149, 4191
Germany FR, 1903
Employment creation, 4026
Employment discrimination
France, 4228
Italy, 4220
USA, 2576, 4222
Employment opportunities, 2337, 4229
India, 4226
USA, 4227
Employment policy, 4224, 4450
Canada, 4221
Netherlands, 4225
Sweden, 4223
USA, 4223
Encyclopedias, 168, 1310
Engineers
France, 4534
Enterprises, 1244, 4009, 4011
Entertainment, 4745, 4754
Entrepreneurs
Italy, 4007, 4008
USA, 4000
Entrepreneurship
Canada, 4003
Entry to working life, 4210
France, 2844, 4181, 4196
USA, 4203
USSR, 4196
Western Europe, 2077
Environment, 311, 1291, 3581, 3583
Eastern Asia, 3595
India, 2881
Latin America, 4124
Environmental protection, 3603
France, 3600

United Kingdom, 1708
Environmental quality, 4107
Epidemiology, 2833
France, 2840
Epistemology, 271, 274, 277, 282, 286, 292,
293, 461, 594
Equal opportunity, 2218, 4290
Germany, 2377
Germany FR, 2203
New Zealand, 2221
Equal pay
USA, 3987
Equity, 3067, 5322
Ergonomics, 4038
Establishment, *use* Ruling class
Ethics, 97, 826, 1209, 1211, 1215, 1219,
1222-24, 1227, 1230, 1238, 1252, 1268,
1303, 1329, 2592, 2836, 3362, 5049
Developing countries, 2982
Ethiopia
Literacy, 2100
Women's status, 3241
Ethnic conflicts, *use* Racial conflicts
Ethnic consciousness, *use* Ethnicity
Ethnic discrimination, *use* Racial
discrimination
Ethnic groups
Andean Region, 3322
Canada, 1050, 2216, 3294, 3323
China, 3327
France, 2923
India, 3333
Israel, 3325, 3356, 3853
Malaysia, 3308, 3344
Netherlands, 3336
USA, 2334, 3291, 3293, 3317, 4481
USSR, 3498
Yugoslavia, 3284
Ethnic identity, *use* Ethnicity
Ethnic minorities
Canada, 3340
France, 3552
Germany FR, 3313
Japan, 3350
Mexico, 2217
Netherlands, 3335
United Kingdom, 3349
USA, 3287
Ethnic pluralism, 3343
France, 3302
Italy, 1349
USA, 3353
Yugoslavia, 3305
Ethnic policy
Australia, 3364
Canada, 3364
USSR, 3392
Ethnic segregation, *use* Racial segregation
Ethnic separatism, *use* Apartheid
Ethnicity, 3285-86, 3320, 3324, 3332, 3341,
3342, 3345, 3351
Australia, 3299

Canada, 3299, 3316, 3330, 3371
    Chinese, 3326
    Ecuador, 3295
    Finland, 3346
    India, 3297
    Israel, 3303, 3306
    Northern Ireland, 3301
    Portugal, 4279
    Southeastern Asia, 3326
    Spain, 987
    United Kingdom, 2246
    USA, 1601, 3337, 3353
    USSR, 3354
    West Indies, 3318
Ethnocentrism
    Canada, 3376
Ethnography, 881
Ethnolinguistics, 1614, 1617
Ethnology, 872
    USA, 513
Ethnomethodology, 875, 878, 2574
Ethnopsychology, 990
Ethos, 2501
Europe
    Adult education, 2095
    Age distribution, 2642
    Bibliographies, 2095
    Care of the aged, 5350
    Cultural development, 1030
    Electoral abstentionism, 5013
    Family, 3139
    Illegitimacy, 2972
    Immigrants, 4293
    Industrial democracy, 4716
    International migration, 3497
    Jews, 4666
    Labour market, 4293
    Labour movements, 4662, 4666
    Life satisfaction, 555
    Marriage, 3139
    Migration, 3447
    Nationalist movements, 4684
    Nuptiality, 3074
    Population, 2520, 2540
    Poverty, 5101
    Right to strike, 4576
    Rural environment, 3706
    Rural women, 2783
    Social history, 5101
    Social movements, 4922
    Sociology of religion, 1296
    Strikes, 4687
    Terrorism, 1119
    Urban areas, 4922
    Urban life, 3857
    Urban planning, 3857
    Women workers, 2783
    Work organization, 4330
    Young workers, 4293
Euthanasia, 5195
    France, 5241
Evaluation techniques, 2423

Everyday life, 269, 944, 961, 964, 971, 989, 1182
    Algeria, 947
    Chile, 960
    France, 918, 3778
    Hungary, 978
    Japan, 923, 2757
    USSR, 3740
Evolutionism, 231
Exchange, 655
Executive power, 4880
Experimental games, 443, 445
Explanation, 289

F scale, 827
Fabbri, Luigi, 4813
Factor analysis, 414, 431, 447
Factories
    France, 4348
    Japan, 669
    USSR, 78
Factory size, *use* Size of enterprise
Factory workers, *use* Industrial workers
Failure, 597
Fairy tales, 1832
Family, 1222, 1343, 2845, 2851, 3088, 3114, 3120, 3124-25, 3145, 3166, 3175, 3186, 3191, 4150, 4234
    Africa, 3149, 3189
    Canada, 3138
    Chile, 3192
    China, 3159
    Colombia, 3104
    Czechoslovakia, 3167, 3195
    Egypt, 3176
    Europe, 3139
    France, 3106, 3128, 4307
    German DR, 2689
    Germany FR, 3171, 3178, 4970
    Hungary, 3077, 3126
    India, 3123
    Israel, 3117
    Italy, 3103, 3180
    Japan, 3116, 3185
    Netherlands, 5318
    Poland, 3137, 3165, 3169, 3188
    Romania, 3122
    Socialist countries, 3201
    Spain, 2649
    Taiwan, 2641
    Togo, 2938
    United Kingdom, 3118, 5075
    USA, 3107, 3129, 3136, 3146, 3168, 4244
    USSR, 3121
    Yugoslavia, 3127, 4982
Family allowances, 5362
    USA, 5346
Family budgets
    France, 5100
    USA, 4249
Family disintegration, 3082
    Poland, 3147

Family education, 3160, 3190
Family environment
  Hungary, 3140
  Taiwan, 2201
  USA, 3153, 4476
Family farms, 4067
  Developing countries, 4068
  France, 4087
  Poland, 4074
  United Kingdom, 4085
  USA, 2569
Family group
  USA, 3199
Family integration, 3155, 3184
Family law
  India, 3068
  Israel, 3135
  Zaire, 3161
Family life, 2173, 2627, 4012
  Canada, 3144, 3157, 3172
  France, 1983, 3158
  Japan, 3148
  Southern Africa, 3108
  Spain, 3112
  USA, 1065, 3131
Family planning, 2594, 2965, 3019
  Asia, 2997
  Bangladesh, 5453
  China, 2969
  Developing countries, 2955, 2982
  India, 2970, 2989, 3001, 3008, 3011
  Japan, 2999
  Java, 3012
  Mexico, 2984
  Philippines, 2988
  Sudan, 2995
  Thailand, 2968, 2975
  USA, 2551, 3015
Family policy
  China, 5376
  France, 5354
  Germany FR, 5356
  United Kingdom, 5365
  USA, 5360
Family relations, 3194
  India, 2829
  Japan, 3200
  United Kingdom, 4085
Family rites
  Poland : Warsaw, 3151
Family size, 3183
  Australia, 3152
  Canada, 3163, 3172
  Finland, 3187
  France, 3130
  India, 3177
  Poland, 3154
  USA, 3111
Family structure, 2564, 3181
  France, 1495, 3193
  USA, 3736
Famine

India : Bengal, 5113
Farm cooperatives, *use* Agricultural cooperatives
Farmers
  Austria, 3663
  France, 1057
  Poland, 1059, 2746, 3137, 3710, 3720
Farming
  Poland, 4079, 4094
Farming methods
  USA, 4070
Farming systems
  United Kingdom, 4085
  USA, 4076
Farr, William, 2522
Fascism
  United Kingdom, 4777
Fashion, 1187, 1199
Father, 3105
  Iran, 3164
Fatherhood, 2994
Fatherland, 980
Fear, 2742, 2882
Feast-days
  Poland : Warsaw, 3151
Feasts, *use* Festivals
Federalism
  India, 2065
  USA, 4783
Female labour
  Australia, 4245
  Brazil, 4281
  Japan, 4301
Female offenders
  United Kingdom, 5244
  USA, 4712
Female workers *use,* Women workers
Feminine press
  Japan, 1698
Feminism, 3206, 3216, 3237, 3257, 3260,
    3267, 3273, 3277
  Canada, 3254
  Chile, 3249
  Germany FR, 3272
  India, 3213
  India : Manipur Valley, 3224
  Latin America, 3235
  United Kingdom, 3218
  USA, 41, 99, 2584, 3205, 3209, 3218,
    3222-23, 3226, 3247, 3270, 5240
Fertility, 2902, 2911, 2913, 2919, 2922,
    2924-25, 2942, 2947, 2950, 2958
  Africa, 2943, 2953
  Australia, 2914, 2918
  Botswana, 2916
  Brazil, 444
  Canada, 2905
  China, 2917, 2931, 2959, 3063
  Costa Rica, 5086
  Cuba, 2927
  Denmark, 3073
  Developing countries, 2901, 2957
  Dominican Republic, 2926

Egypt, 2951
Finland, 2876, 2937
France, 2527
German DR, 2973
Germany FR, 2973
Ghana, 2954
Guam, 2956
India, 2945
Japan, 2903, 2941
Kenya, 2928
Korea R, 2932, 3548
Malaysia, 2934
Mexico, 2872
Nepal, 379
Tanzania, 2939
Togo, 2938
USA, 977, 1304, 2907, 2909, 2929, 2936,
    2941, 2948, 2952, 3836
Fertility decline, 2921, 2960
Canada : Quebec, 2940
Developing countries, 2955
Thailand, 2930
Yugoslavia, 2798
Fertility rate
Guatemala, 1026
Korea R, 2946
Festivals, 1194
France, 1197
Fetishism, 4760
Feudalism
Nepal, 3959
Field observation, *use* Field work
Field work, 366, 370
Fiji
Housing policy, 3920
Political culture, 4989
Fine arts
USA, 1838
Finland
Consensual union, 3076
Cooperative movements, 4941
Diseases, 2839
Ethnicity, 3346
Family size, 3187
Fertility, 2876, 2937
Historical demography, 2541, 2552, 2876
Industrialization, 3562
Infant mortality, 2552, 2876
Internal migration, 3562
Morbidity, 2541
Smallpox, 2541
Time budgets, 4351, 4352
Voting behaviour, 3346
Firm management, *use* Business management
Firms, *use* Enterprises
Fishermen
Japan, 4513
Fishery
France, 4072
Fishery management
India, 3721
Fishing villages

Japan, 4513
Folk art
USA, 1784
Folk culture, 1189, 1190, 1196, 1204
Brazil, 1200, 1201, 1207
Norway, 1035
Poland, 1202
Switzerland, 2889
USA, 1191
Folk medicine, *use* Traditional medicine
Folk religion, *use* Popular religion
Folk songs
USSR, 1848
Folklore
China, 1198
Venezuela, 1203
Food
Developing countries, 2080
Food consumption
France, 5100
India, 5096
Forced labour
Senegal, 4347
Forecasting techniques, 133, 270, 281, 2810
Forecasts, 275, 284, 2409, 2410
USA, 296
Foreign labour, *use* Foreign workers
Foreign languages
Arab countries, 1586
Japan, 1607
USA, 1600
Foreign policy, 5046
Foreign policy making
India, 542
Foreign students, 2025
France, 2035
USA, 2078
Foreign workers
France, 3896, 4279
Germany, 4242, 4275
Germany FR, 3439, 4231, 4247, 4260,
    4285, 4314, 4316
Switzerland, 1038, 4230, 4277, 4278
USA, 1966, 4267
Western Asia, 4318
Foreigners, 3281
Brazil, 3300
France, 489, 3499
Germany FR, 3314, 3321
Switzerland, 3440
Formalization, 134, 276
Foucault, Michel, 33, 76
France
Academic freedom, 1963
Adolescents, 2020
Adult education, 2102
Advertising, 349
Aged, 1085, 2724, 2737, 2749
Agricultural education, 3220
Agricultural market, 3670
Agricultural workers, 4288
Agriculture, 3202

Alcoholism, 5128, 5141
Animals, 2558
Anticlericalism, 1495
Antisemitism, 3377, 3397, 3405, 3408
Associations, 724
Attitude to work, 4420
Automation, 4022, 4031, 4472, 4491
Bilingualism, 3101
Bourgeoisie, 3045
Care of the aged, 5341, 5343, 5344, 5379,
    5473
Carnivals, 1197
Cartoons, 1725
Catholic Church, 1425, 1430
Catholicism, 1353, 1373
Catholics, 1342
Child care, 5461
Child mortality, 2875
Children, 2645
Church history, 1430
Cinema, 1641
Civil servants, 4886, 4887
Class struggle, 2311
Coal mines, 4516
Collective action, 870
Communication, 1543, 1562
Communication research, 1564
Community development, 2285
Congregations, 1425
Consumer movements, 4099
Continuing education, 2089
Cooperative sector, 3947
Crime, 5202
Cultural dissemination, 1015
Cultural policy, 1009, 1015, 1028
Cultural practices, 915
Culture, 1267
Death, 2886
Dechristianization, 1495
Disabled persons, 2827, 2844
Drugs, 5125
Education, 1858
Educational objectives, 1962
Educational opportunities, 1983, 2194, 2199
Educational output, 2048
Educational provision, 2194
Educational sociology, 1867
Educational systems, 1959, 1976
Elite, 2345
Employment, 4149, 4191
Employment discrimination, 4228
Engineers, 4534
Entry to working life, 2844, 4181, 4196
Environmental protection, 3600
Epidemiology, 2840
Ethnic groups, 2923
Ethnic minorities, 3552
Ethnic pluralism, 3302
Euthanasia, 5241
Everyday life, 918, 3778
Factories, 4348
Family, 3106, 3128, 4307

Family budgets, 5100
Family farms, 4087
Family life, 1983, 3158
Family policy, 5354
Family size, 3130
Family structure, 1495, 3193
Farmers, 1057
Fertility, 2527
Festivals, 1197
Fishery, 4072
Food consumption, 5100
Foreign students, 2035
Foreign workers, 3896, 4279
Foreigners, 489, 3499
Freemasonry, 1417
Geography, 2502
Gerontology, 2718
Groups, 4149
Health, 2712, 5433
Health policy, 4256
Higher education, 2048
Historical demography, 2527, 2538
History, 2405
History of capitalism, 3941
History of education, 1887, 1996, 2143
Holidays, 4731
Homosexuality, 3026
Hospitals, 5437
Housework, 4404
Housing, 3776, 3896
Identity, 489
Illiteracy, 2090
Immigrant assimilation, 3499, 3513
Immigrants, 3469, 3471, 3472, 3490,
    3505, 3508, 3512, 5141
Immigration, 3456, 3504
Immigration policy, 3473, 3534
Industrial management, 4335
Industrial revolution, 4335
Industrialization, 3941
Innovations, 4015
Intellectuals, 2340-43, 2349-50, 2354,
    2362, 2366
Interest groups, 4956
Internal migration, 2857
Interpersonal relations, 592
Job requirements, 4497
Judicial process, 1237
Juvenile delinquency, 5168
Labour, 4156, 4166
Labour disputes, 3941
Labour law, 4032, 4051, 4575
Labour movements, 4599, 4617, 4619, 4662
Labour relations, 4544, 4555
Labour structure, 4173
Language, 1588
Leisure, 4738
Leisure time, 4369
Leisure utilization, 3552, 4731
Life cycle, 2857
Life expectancy, 2852, 2892
Life styles, 883, 904

Linguistics, 1717
Living conditions, 3967
Local government, 2285, 4899
Loneliness, 2722, 2748, 3232
Managers, 4527
Manpower, 4149, 4156
Market regulation, 3670
Marriage, 349
Married women, 4295
Marxism, 267
Mass education, 2052
Mass media, 1734, 1763
Matriarchy, 3113
Medical care, 5410
Medical research, 5402
Merchant marine, 4208
Middle class, 764, 2250, 2265, 5007
Middle-sized towns, 3812
Migrant workers, 3509, 4256, 4268
Migration, 4451
Miners, 4516
Mixed marriage, 3085, 3101
Modes of production, 4047
Monasticism, 1403
Money, 4116
Mortality, 2854, 2858, 2860
Music, 1841
Natality, 2923
Nation, 984
New technologies, 4032, 4051, 4470
New towns, 3770, 3814, 3887
Nomads, 3542, 3552
Nuns, 1425
Occupational life, 3158
Occupational qualification, 4031, 4470, 4472, 4491, 4496
Occupational safety, 4433
Occupational status, 1809, 5461
Office automation, 4049
Old age, 2712, 2722, 2748
Old age policy, 5284
Older workers, 4256
Parish, 1432
Peasant society, 3662
Peasantry, 3653
Peasants, 3689, 3705, 3730
Pediatricians, 5461
Penal law, 1237
Philosophers, 76, 82, 85, 86
Photography, 4519
Physicians, 5461, 5473, 5477, 5479
Political attitudes, 1342
Political culture, 1267
Political socialization, 4988
Polls, 374, 377
Population, 2502, 2509, 2523, 2543, 5125
Population movement, 4047
Population policy, 3014
Poverty, 5083, 5115
Press, 1672, 1758, 3234
Primary education, 1999, 2001, 2003
Private schools, 2004

Production, 4014
Proletariat, 3505
Protestantism, 1334
Public opinion, 377, 832, 1135
Public opinion polls, 1501
Punishment, 5145
Quality circles, 4335
Quality of life, 4369
Quality of work, 4427
Race relations, 4268
Racism, 3383, 3391, 3427
Radio, 1679
Regional analysis, 2285
Regional development, 1543
Religion, 1267
Religious attitudes, 1342
Religious history, 1403
Religious practice, 1488, 1501
Retired persons, 2737
Retirement, 4451
Robotics, 4054
Rural areas, 904
Rural communities, 3697
Rural history, 3697
School administration, 2020
School environment, 2021
School failure, 2115
Schooling, 1957
Sciences of education, 1860
Secondary education, 1996, 2009
Sects, 1419
Sex roles, 2622
Sexual behaviour, 3045, 3049
Small and medium enterprises, 4005
Sociability, 575, 1417
Social action, 5327
Social change, 724, 2436
Social conditions, 2452
Social disadvantage, 5074
Social environment, 3193
Social history, 1417, 1983, 3049, 3232, 3234, 3252, 3662, 5128
Social housing, 3791, 3929
Social inequality, 2194, 2199, 2886
Social information, 5061
Social isolation, 1085
Social mobility, 2375, 2387, 2388
Social movements, 4936
Social norms, 1057
Social participation, 1092
Social policy, 4049
Social relations, 3778
Social science research, 103
Social sciences, 24
Social security, 5351, 5364
Social stratification, 2191
Social structure, 2179
Social work, 5380
Socialism, 4788, 4797
Socialization, 2020
Society, 888
Sociologists, 171

Sociology, 22, 33
Sociology of religion, 1292
Sociology of work, 2285
Speech analysis, 1624
Sport, 4757
State, 4843
Strikes, 4682
Student movements, 2038
Suicide, 5154
Taxation, 4122
Teacher training, 2139
Teacher-student relationship, 2140
Teachers, 2143, 2146
Teaching of sociology, 8
Technological change, 4046, 4496, 4602
Television, 1679, 1717
Textile industry, 3941
Theory of education, 1893
Time budgets, 904, 3158, 4402, 4404
Tourism, 3871, 4738
Trade unionism, 4650
Trade unions, 4581, 4602, 4623, 4653
Translation, 1809
Unemployed, 4184
Unemployment, 4208
Universities, 1959, 2052
Urban areas, 904, 5100
Urban environment, 3890
Urban life, 3778, 3871
Urban planning, 3770
Urban policy, 3752, 3901
Urban population, 3469
Urban renewal, 3763, 3861, 3885, 3901
Urban society, 3753
Urban sociology, 3799, 3885
Urbanism, 3763
Villages, 3662
Violence, 1134, 1135
Vocational rehabilitation, 4471
Vocational training, 4469
Voluntary organizations, 723
Voting behaviour, 5007
Wage negotiations, 4692
Women, 1373
Women workers, 4288
Women's education, 3220, 3252
Women's employment, 4228, 4295, 4471
Women's liberation movements, 3248
Women's participation, 4623
Women's status, 3202, 3207, 3232, 3234
Women's work, 2852, 4307
Work organization, 4031, 4335
Work standards, 1057
Workers, 4519
Workers' participation, 4708
Workers' representation, 4718
Working class, 1430, 1983, 2285, 5100
Working class culture, 1002
Working conditions, 4369
Working time, 4357
Working time arrangement, 4395, 4407
Writers, 1809

Young workers, 4265
Youth, 2665, 3499
France : Brittany
    Death, 1451
    Peasant movements, 3670
    Religious beliefs, 1451
France : Paris
    Suburban areas, 3844
    Urbanization, 3844
France : Provence
    Rural communities, 3699
France : Rouen
    Pawnbroking, 4120
    Poverty, 4120
France : Sarthe
    Peasantry, 3659
Frankfurt School, *use* Critical theory
Freedom, 891, 892, 4852, 4858, 4860, 4861,
    4864, 4868
Freedom of education, *use* Academic freedom
Freedom of expression, *use* Freedom of speech
Freedom of speech
    USA, 4848
Freedom of the press
    Ivory Coast, 4851
Freemasonry, 1431
    France, 1417
French Speaking Africa
    Youth organizations, 2695
French Speaking countries
    Law, 1250
Friendship, 616, 620, 623, 626, 627, 675, 3024
Frontier workers
    EEC countries, 4232
Functionalism, 198, 261
Future, 2411
Future society, 855
Futurology, 2408, 2409, 2410

Gabon
    Social security, 5359
Gadamer, Hans-Georg, 553
Galligan, Carol, 1210, 2604
Gambling, 4743, 4749
Game theory, 446
Games
    Austria, 4747
    Germany FR, 4744
    USA, 4737
Gangs, 5209
    Sweden, 2684
    USA, 5229
Gastronomy, 4078
Gender, *use* Sex
General systems theory, 439, 440
Generation conflicts, 2637, 2639
Generation differences, 2640, 3184
    Japan, 943
    United Kingdom, 4479
    Yugoslavia, 2371
Generations, 2635, 2638
Genetic psychology, 461, 475, 631

Genetics, 2833
Geography, 3593, 4728
    Australia, 3591
    France, 2502
German DR
    Automation, 4039
    Churches, 1411
    Family, 2689
    Fertility, 2973
    Housework, 4386
    Leisure policy, 2694
    Literature, 1792, 1811
    National consciousness, 950
    Painting, 1834
    Poetry, 1797
    Population policy, 2973
    Social policy, 5264
    Socialist society, 3940
    Way of life, 898
    Writers, 1791
    Youth, 2689
    Youth policy, 2694
Germany
    Antisemitism, 3385
    Child labour, 4276
    Cohort analysis, 2862
    Educational opportunities, 2377
    Equal opportunity, 2377
    Foreign workers, 4242, 4275
    Hours of work, 4430
    Industrial revolution, 2401
    Labour market, 4242
    Labour movements, 4598, 4617, 4626, 4658
    Language, 1620
    Life tables, 2862
    Political attitudes, 2697
    Press, 1683
    Science policy, 128
    Social history, 2126, 2401, 3675, 4242,
        4275, 4276, 4658
    Social mobility, 2377
    Sociological theory, 217
    Sociology, 6
    Students, 2051
    Teachers, 2126
    Textile industry, 3250
    Villages, 3675
    Women's education, 3250
    Women's work, 3250
    Working class, 2291, 2401
    Working conditions, 4275
    Working time, 4398
    Youth, 2697
Germany FR
    Access to education, 1954
    Achievement motivation, 828
    Adult education, 2091, 2103
    Alcoholism, 1180
    Attitude to work, 4356, 4372
    Authoritarianism, 828
    Business communities, 4013
    Censuses, 361

    Church history, 1412
    Cinema, 1737
    Civil service, 4891
    Class differentiation, 2203
    Collective bargaining, 4062, 4694
    Community organization, 3638
    Conflicts, 638
    Cultural cooperation, 1016
    Deviance, 1180
    Divorce, 3084
    Drugs of abuse, 1180
    Education, 1903
    Educational reforms, 1924, 1965
    Employees, 4356
    Employment, 1903
    Equal opportunity, 2203
    Ethnic minorities, 3313
    Family, 3171, 3178, 4970
    Family policy, 5356
    Feminism, 3272
    Fertility, 2973
    Foreign workers, 3439, 4231, 4247, 4260,
        4285, 4314, 4316
    Foreigners, 3314, 3321
    Games, 4744
    Higher education, 2030
    Hospitals, 5455
    Households, 3171
    Humanization of work, 4385, 4432
    Immigrant assimilation, 3520, 3530
    Industrial workers, 4456
    Jews, 1390
    Journalism, 1675
    Juvenile delinquency, 5162, 5174
    Labour law, 4303
    Labour movements, 4603
    Labour relations, 4555, 4556
    Leisure, 4729
    Leisure time, 4408
    Libraries, 158
    Literature, 1792, 1830
    Local government, 3638
    Marginality, 1721
    Mass media, 1684, 1721
    Migrants, 1721
    Migration, 3439
    Mixed marriage, 3061
    National consciousness, 908, 950
    National minorities, 3307
    New technologies, 4062
    Novels, 1816
    Occupational choice, 4464
    Occupational qualification, 4462
    One-parent family, 3179
    Peace movements, 1223
    Penal law, 1242
    Political parties, 5301
    Political protest, 4958
    Political socialization, 4970
    Population, 2549
    Population policy, 2973
    Press, 1649

Professionalization, 4456, 5384
Prostitution, 3032
Quality of life, 3972
Racism, 3370
Readers, 1631
Schools, 2012
Sects, 1420
Self-perception, 5174
Social change, 299
Social distance, 3313
Social mobility, 2369
Social movements, 4924, 4925
Social policy, 5261, 5280, 5301, 5315
Social science research, 96
Social work, 5384, 5384
Sociology, 42, 69
Student movements, 2038, 2056
Suicide, 1180
Teaching of sociology, 67
Terrorism, 1107, 1158
Time budgets, 4408
Trade unionism, 1675
Trade unions, 4601, 4623, 4636
Unemployment, 4183, 4194
Universities, 3217
Urban life, 4408
Urban policy, 3833
Urban-urban migration, 3557
Vocational training, 4498
Voting behaviour, 5017
Welfare State, 5256, 5257
Women workers, 4303
Women's employment, 3272, 4286, 4891
Women's liberation movements, 3245
Women's participation, 4623
Women's status, 3217, 3272
Workers' participation, 4722
Working time, 4435
Working time arrangement, 4359
Young workers, 3321, 4462
Youth, 299, 2680
Youth employment, 1924
Youth unemployment, 4180, 4247
Gerontology, 2715, 2736, 2752
   France, 2718
   Netherlands, 2743
   USA, 2738
Ghana
   Business communities, 3992
   Class formation, 3992
   Fertility, 2954
   Housing, 3767
   Labour movements, 4507
   Miners, 4507
   Women's status, 3259
Ghana : Accra
   Social classes, 2614
   Women's role, 2614
Giddens, Anthony, 309, 786
Gift, 1054
Gifted children, 2656, 2663
Glass-workers

Italy, 2289
Goethe, Johann W., 1478
Goffman, Erving, 170, 182, 194, 783, 5305
Gouldner, Alvin, 169, 256, 1510
Government, 4871
Government policy, 147
Graduates, 2045
   India, 4226
Gramsci, Antonio, 955
Graph theory, 315
Greece
   Class consciousness, 2263
   Disabled persons, 2841
   Mother, 3133
   Political attitudes, 2263
   Population, 2515
   Return migration, 3459
   Science policy, 127
   Women's role, 3133
Group affiliation, *use* Group membership
Group analysis, 666, 669
   USA, 4904
Group behaviour
   Guyana, 703
Group cohesiveness, 699, 700, 702
Group consciousness, 4527
Group effectiveness, *use* Group performance
Group functioning, 708
Group identification, 704
Group influence, 682, 705, 706, 726, 807
Group integration, 701
Group membership, 602
   USA, 707
Group performance, 741
Group pressure, 702
Group size, 443, 602, 694
Group solidarity, 590
Groups
   France, 4149
Guadeloupe
   Traditional medicine, 5394
Guam
   Fertility, 2956
Guatemala
   Catholic Church, 654
   Craftsmen, 4536
   Cultural change, 1026
   Divination, 1458
   Fertility rate, 1026
   Oligarchy, 4810
   Social conflicts, 654
Guyana
   Group behaviour, 703
   Political leaders, 4959
   Sects, 703

Habermas, Jürgen, 220, 236, 259, 1544,
   1571, 4771
Habitat
   Italy, 3613
Haiti
   Development policy, 1905

Education, 1905
Handbooks, *use* Textbooks
Handicapped persons, *use* Disabled persons
Handicrafts
  Africa, 4066
  Ecuador, 4086
Happiness, 4762
Hawaii
  Immigrants, 3507
  Immigration, 3495
  Interethnic communication, 3396
Hayek, Friedrich von, 986
Health, 5422, 5423
  Brazil, 5426, 5428
  Developing countries, 2080, 5404
  France, 2712, 5433
  Italy, 3103
  Japan, 2206
  Latin America, 2185
  Mexico, 5408
  Netherlands, 4219
  Saudi Arabia, 5431
  United Kingdom, 5425
  USA, 3482, 5405
Health care, *use* Medical care
Health insurance, 2832
  Canada, 5358
  USA, 5373
Health management
  Switzerland, 5414
Health policy, 2898
  Chile, 5436
  Cuba, 5436
  Developing countries, 5406
  France, 4256
  Italy, 5411
  Mexico, 5418
  United Kingdom, 5409, 5420
  USA, 5416, 5432
Health services, 5399, 5430, 5452
  Argentina, 5438
  Bangladesh, 5453
  Belgium, 5441
  Canada, 5449
  Developed countries, 5451
  Latin America, 5457
  Mexico, 5408
  Mozambique, 5458
  United Kingdom, 5456
  USA, 5439, 5443, 5447
Hegel, Georg Wilhelm Friedrich, 1258, 4794
Hegetology, *use* Political leadership
Heresies, 1470
Hermeneutics, 243, 250, 553, 1622, 5270
Heroes, 1756
  USA, 794
Heuristics, 5333
Hierarchical scale, 449
High schools, *use* Secondary schools
High technology, 996
  Developing countries, 4027

Higher education, 2040, 2042, 2050, 2069, 2127
  Argentina, 1974
  ASEAN countries, 2070
  Chile, 2034
  Denmark, 2063
  France, 2048
  Germany FR, 2030
  India, 2061, 2065
  Japan, 2043, 2060
  Korea R, 2028
  Latin America, 150
  Norway, 2046
  Poland, 2048, 2054
  Sweden, 2055, 2062, 2067
  United Kingdom, 2026, 2039, 2053
  USA, 775, 1123, 2047, 2048, 2578
  USSR, 2048
  Venezuela, 2059
Hindess, Barry, 785
Hinduism, 1363, 1444
  India, 1345, 1449
Historical analysis, 335
Historical demography, 2521
  Brazil, 2517
  Canada, 2539, 3157, 3436
  China, 2931
  Finland, 2541, 2552, 2876
  France, 2527, 2538
  United Kingdom, 2555
  USA, 2516, 2551, 3065
  USSR, 2545
Historical materialism, *use* Marxism
Historicism, 218, 234
Historiography
  Czechoslovakia, 2407
  Mexico, 2395
  USA, 2404
History, 2389-90, 2396-97, 2403, 2410, 2463, 2606
  France, 2405
  Southern Asia, 2392
History of capitalism, 3944
  France, 3941
History of education, 1873, 1878
  Australia, 1892
  France, 1887, 1996, 2143
  India : Rajasthan, 1913
  Nigeria, 1910
  Spain, 1889
History of ideas, 1513
History of sociology, 10, 29, 63, 72, 2327
  Austria, 51
  India, 59
  Japan, 36, 40
  Poland, 43
  United Kingdom, 37
  USA, 4, 5, 21, 58, 62, 71
Holbach, Paul Henry Thiry d', 1302
Holidays
  France, 4731
  Socialist countries, 4732
Holland, J. L., 4503

Holy places
  Japan, 1469
Home ownership
  USA, 3774
Homeless people
  Ireland, 5104
  USA, 5082, 5112
Homicide, 5170
  USA, 5245
Homosexuality, 3033, 3038
  France, 3026
  USA, 3028, 3043
Hong Kong
  Kinship, 3729
  Public administration, 4892
  Urban planning, 3819
  Villages, 3729
Honour
  Brazil, 1212
Hospital administration, *use*
    Hospital management
Hospital management, 5448
  USA, 653
Hospitals
  Australia, 5442
  China, 5446
  France, 5437
  Germany FR, 5455
  Japan, 2842
  United Kingdom, 5450
  USA, 5440, 5444
Hours of work
  Germany, 4430
  USA, 4425
Household budgets
  United Kingdom, 3980
Household income
  USA, 2585
Households, 2577, 2602, 2621, 3606
  Germany FR, 3171
  Hungary, 2563
  USA, 2586, 2587, 2617
Housewives
  Japan, 2562
Housework, 4438
  France, 4404
  German DR, 4386
  United Kingdom, 4361
  USA, 4431
Housing, 3746, 3838, 3847
  Czechoslovakia, 3765
  Denmark, 3851
  Developing countries, 3860, 3868
  France, 3776, 3896
  Ghana, 3767
  Hungary, 3790, 3986
  Philippines, 3848
  Poland, 3928
  United Kingdom, 3826, 3910
  USA, 3788, 3855
Housing needs
  USA, 3836

Yugoslavia, 3824
Housing policy
  Australia, 3915
  Belgium, 3800
  Brazil, 3792
  Developing countries, 3748
  Fiji, 3920
  Hungary, 3829
  New Zealand, 3867
  Nigeria, 3877
  United Kingdom, 3830, 3867
  USA, 3772, 3922
  Western Europe, 3772
Hughes, Everett C., 366
Human body, 2559, 2597, 3045
Human capital, *use* Human resources
Human ecology, 3586, 3592
Human geography, 3572, 3588
  New Zealand, 3587
Human physiology
  Switzerland, 2634
Human resources, 4164, 4167, 4168, 4175
  USA, 4169
Human rights, 97, 1224, 4849-50, 4854-55,
    4857, 4862, 4865, 4867
  Africa, 4869
  Asia, 4853
  Poland, 4859
  Socialist countries, 4863
Human settlements, 3610
  Czechoslovakia, 3612
  USSR, 3614
Humanities
  USA, 2108
Humanization of work, 4038, 4363, 4387,
    4403, 4415
  Germany FR, 4385, 4432
  Poland, 4394
Humour, 567
Hungary
  Aesthetics, 1775
  Agricultural workers, 3701, 4521
  Antisemitism, 3386, 3394
  Career development, 4485
  Catholicism, 1398
  Cohort analysis, 919
  Communication, 1542
  Commuting, 3543
  Culture, 978
  Economic history, 4284
  Emigration, 3531
  Everyday life, 978
  Family, 3077, 3126
  Family environment, 3140
  Households, 2563
  Housing, 3790, 3986
  Housing policy, 3829
  Industrial workers, 4514
  Intellectuals, 2351, 2365
  Jews, 1825
  Labour relations, 4635
  Life styles, 938

Literature, 1825
Living conditions, 3969, 3986
Local communities, 3620
Local power, 4903
Marriage, 3077
Modernization, 2446
Mortality, 2856
Music, 1847
National identity, 954
Occupational groups, 4483
Peasants, 3656, 3681, 3701
Police, 4874
Popular literature, 1829
Population, 2537, 2554
Population policy, 2537, 3010
Press, 2703
Public administration, 4485
Public opinion, 3969
Punishment, 5184
Religious history, 1273
Rural areas, 5273
Rural population, 2821
Rural sociology, 3737
Social change, 2446
Social conditions, 5273
Social development, 2439
Social inequality, 2211, 3790
Social mobility, 2374, 2384
Social policy, 5274
Social relations, 1109
Social status, 2330
Social stratification, 2212, 2228, 4514
Social structure, 2165
Society, 956
Sociology of family, 3115
Sportsmen, 2330
State, 4833
Statistics, 426
Television, 1692
Time budgets, 4350, 4351, 4352
Trade unions, 4635, 4639
Tramps, 5218
Urban sociology, 5218
Urbanization, 2554, 3805
Villages, 2563, 3700
Way of life, 919, 946
Welfare, 4350
Women's employment, 4284, 4300
Young workers, 938
Youth, 2703
Youth policy, 2698
Hunger, 1215
Developing countries, 5081
Hunting, 4073
Husband, 3088
Husserl, Edmund, 238

Iceland
Christian Churches, 1497
Secularization, 1497
Social history, 3931
Idealism, 262

Identification, 628
Identity, 496, 499-503, 506, 508-10, 726,
2150, 2729
France, 489
Latin America, 4927
Spain, 504
Ideology, 228, 484, 769, 841, 844-45, 848,
851, 855-60, 920, 1127, 1778, 2296,
2442, 5025
Central Africa, 2279
Latin America, 854
Illegal immigration, 3454
USA, 3463
Illegitimacy
Europe, 2972
Illiteracy
France, 2090
Illness, *use* Diseases
Imagination, 862, 1175, 1790, 2867
Immigrant adaptation
USA, 3486
Immigrant assimilation, 3464
Canada, 3330, 3533
France, 3499, 3513
Germany FR, 3520, 3530
Switzerland, 1038
United Kingdom, 3474
USA, 3287, 3502
Immigrants, 3242
Australia, 1165, 1326, 3489
Canada, 3138, 3461, 3468, 3480, 3484,
3493, 3500, 3511
Capitalist countries, 3288
Europe, 4293
France, 3469, 3471, 3472, 3490, 3505,
3508, 3512, 5141
Hawaii, 3507
Industrialized countries, 3496
Israel, 89, 1012, 3519
Korea, 3396
USA, 1374, 2948, 3482, 3494, 3525
Immigration, 3523
Argentina, 3515
Australia, 3465
Canada, 3465
France, 3456, 3504
Hawaii, 3495
Israel, 3460
Italy, 3479
North America, 3531
Western Europe, 3455
Immigration policy, 3485
France, 3473, 3534
United Kingdom, 3476, 3483
USA, 3510, 3517, 3522, 3526, 3527
Western Asia, 4318
Imperialism, 5045, 5048
In-service training, 4490
Incest taboo, 3029
Income, 285
Income distribution
Norway, 3982

Taiwan, 2201
United Kingdom, 4082, 4631
Income inequality, 2321
  Poland, 3984
  Sweden, 2323
  Switzerland, 3989
  USA, 3981
Incomes policy
  New Zealand, 4136
India
  Activists, 4921
  Adult education, 2097
  Affinity, 618
  Age at marriage, 3098
  Agrarian reforms, 3657, 3687
  Agrarian relations, 3669
  Agricultural mechanization, 3721
  Alienation, 1169, 1170, 1174
  Anthologies, 4508
  Birth spacing, 3013
  Bourgeoisie, 2282
  Brahmanism, 1393
  Bureaucracy, 767
  Castes, 1170, 2202, 2234-36, 2238-40,
    2243-44, 2386
  Child mortality, 3177
  Civilization, 900
  Communication, 1574
  Cooperatives, 3942
  Crime, 5150, 5208
  Criminal justice, 5208
  Cultural identity, 1152
  Cultural values, 1014
  Demographic transition, 2778
  Deprivation, 5109
  Development research, 2496
  Disabled persons, 2829
  Disasters, 5079
  Dispute settlement, 4689
  Dowry, 3097
  Economic and social development, 767
  Economic development, 1275
  Education, 2240, 2459
  Educational objectives, 2699
  Employment opportunities, 4226
  Environment, 2881
  Ethnic groups, 3333
  Ethnicity, 3297
  Family, 3123
  Family law, 3068
  Family planning, 2970, 2989, 3001, 3008,
    3011
  Family relations, 2829
  Family size, 3177
  Federalism, 2065
  Feminism, 3213
  Fertility, 2945
  Fishery management, 3721
  Food consumption, 5096
  Foreign policy making, 542
  Graduates, 4226
  Higher education, 2061, 2065

Hinduism, 1345, 1449
History of sociology, 59
Industrial workers, 1169, 4517
Institutions, 1047
Internal migration, 3553, 3561
Islam, 1346, 1351, 1379
Justice, 1261
Labour disputes, 4689
Labour policy, 4561
Labour relations, 4539, 4550, 4553, 4561
Language, 1611
Life tables, 2877
Local government, 4905
Marginal people, 1152
Marriage, 618, 3068
Mass media, 1652
Medical care, 5427
Medical occupations, 5482
Mental health, 5413
Migration, 3434, 3452
Mortality, 2881, 2945
Moslems, 1327
Nationalism, 3702
Nutrition, 5106
Occupational groups, 1145
Occupational mobility, 4499
Peasant organizations, 3723
Peasantry, 3702, 3717
Pilgrimages, 1444
Police, 4881
Political alienation, 1114, 1145
Political development, 4831, 4835
Political institutions, 4832
Political leadership, 4831
Political parties, 4908, 4912
Politics, 2172, 3873, 5300
Population, 2507
Population growth, 2785
Poverty, 1152, 5099
Prostitution, 3046
Public administration, 4889
Regionalism, 4796
Religion, 1275
Religious beliefs, 5150
Religious revival, 1379
Religious traditions, 1014
Remarriage, 3057
Riots, 1104
Rural areas, 3942, 4499
Rural development, 3688, 3698, 3703,
  3708, 3715-17, 3721, 3731, 3734
Rural population, 2808
Rural poverty, 5098
Rural youth, 2699
Rural-urban migration, 3539, 3540, 3551
Sacred, 1449
Science, 1503
Scientific community, 124
Sects, 3213
Sex, 2608
Sex discrimination, 4236
Slums, 3891

Social change, 2234, 2243, 2459, 2462, 2466, 3715, 3734, 4912
Social conditions, 2398, 5300
Social distance, 1097
Social history, 2398
Social inequality, 5413
Social justice, 4236
Social mobility, 2386, 3297
Social movements, 4921
Social order, 1261
Social participation, 1095
Social policy, 5287
Social problems, 4889
Social protest, 5109
Social research, 5060
Social security, 4553, 5347
Social services, 5470
Social stratification, 2202
Social structure, 2172
Social welfare, 2881
Sociological theory, 235
Sociologists, 81
Sociology, 35, 39, 57, 61
Sociology of development, 2488
Squatters, 3891
Students, 1152, 1174
Symbolism, 1559
Towns, 3891
Trade unions, 4652, 4655
Traditionalism, 1014
Tribal society, 3339
Tribalism, 3422, 3425
Tribes, 2238, 3716, 3717
Urban development, 3902
Urban life, 3873
Urbanization, 3551, 3779
Villages, 3698, 3709, 3721, 4831
Women workers, 4236, 4273, 4309, 4320
Women's liberation movements, 3275
Women's rights, 3274
Women's status, 3261, 3271
Workers, 4508
Workers' participation, 4720
Working class, 4508
Working conditions, 4388
India : Assam
Castes, 2233
Social mobility, 2233
India : Bengal
Famine, 5113
Rural society, 3661
Social classes, 3661
Social inequality, 2214, 3669
Villages, 3661
India : Bihar
Peasantry, 3668
India : Goa
Demographic transition, 2807
India : Kerala
Politics, 2275
Working class, 2275
India : Madhya Pradesh

Tribal society, 3338
India : Manipur Valley
Feminism, 3224
Women's status, 3224
India : Punjab
Cultural specificity, 1037
India : Rajasthan
History of education, 1913
India : West Bengal
Primary education, 2002, 2011
Sex discrimination, 2002
Indigenous population
Amazonia, 3290
Australia, 3292, 3304, 3309, 3311, 3347
Canada, 3310, 3334
Costa Rica, 3283
Latin America, 3289
Peru, 3328
Individual and society, 480, 482, 486
Individual farms, *use* Private farms
Individual rights, 777
Individualism, 313, 501, 4121
Individuality, 480, 1760
Individuals, 483, 484, 776
Canada, 481
Indonesia
Aspirations, 560
Birth intervals, 2920
Child mortality, 2859, 2873
Cultural development, 2430
Infant mortality, 2859, 2873
Islam, 1325
Migration, 3453
Population dynamics, 2786
Social development, 2430
Student movements, 2068
Students, 560
Women's role, 2599
Industrial conflicts, *use* Labour disputes
Industrial democracy, 4011, 4725
China, 4716
Europe, 4716
Korea R, 4714
United Kingdom, 4713
Industrial employment
South Africa, 3415
Industrial enterprises
Japan, 4080
USSR, 5277
Industrial innovations, 4060
Industrial management
France, 4335
United Kingdom, 4092, 4096
Industrial participation, *use* Workers' participation
Industrial plants, *use* Factories
Industrial psychology, 4141, 4144
Industrial relations, *use* Labour relations
Industrial revolution, 2790
France, 4335
Germany, 2401
Industrial society, 583, 2484, 2495, 2501
United Kingdom, 4548

Industrial sociology, 4143, 4146, 4147, 4148
  Spain, 4137
Industrial workers
  Germany FR, 4456
  Hungary, 4514
  India, 1169, 4517
  Israel, 307
  Poland, 4514
  Socialist countries, 4732
Industrialization, 3166, 4090
  Ecuador, 4172
  Finland, 3562
  France, 3941
  Java, 4298
  Poland, 2773
  USA, 4083
Industrialized countries
  Immigrants, 3496
Infant mortality, 2192, 2869, 2899
  Brazil, 2868
  Czechoslovakia, 2888, 2896
  Finland, 2552, 2876
  Indonesia, 2859, 2873
  Malaysia, 2934
  Mali, 2870
  USA, 2849
Infanticide, 5188
Inflation, 4115
  United Kingdom, 3818
Information, 141, 146, 611, 4841
Information dissemination, 140
Information exchange, 145, 725
Information processing, 142, 676, 1914
Information services
  Bulgaria, 161
  China, 156
  Japan, 156
Information systems, 147
Information technology, 143, 149
Information transfer, *use* Information exchange
Innovation policy, 4060
Innovations, 755, 1080
  Canada, 4040
  France, 4015
  Mediterranean countries, 4064
Institutionalization, 1080
Institutions, 10, 744, 1060, 1076
  India, 1047
  Norway, 1073
Insurance, 4123
Intellectual ability, 5207
Intellectual development, 2119
Intellectuals, 2358
  Austria, 3487
  Brazil, 1201
  China, 2355, 2367
  France, 2340-43, 2349-50, 2354, 2362, 2366
  Hungary, 2351, 2365
  Latin America, 2364
  Romania, 3421
  Scandinavia, 2353
  Yugoslavia, 2347

Intelligence, 536, 561, 3183
Intelligentsia, 2352
  Arab countries, 2361
  USSR, 2348, 2359, 2363
Intercultural communication, 1031
Interdisciplinary research
  USA, 115
Interest, 559
Interest groups, 4919, 4944, 4955
  France, 4956
  Socialist countries, 4950
  USA, 4931, 4948, 4949
Interethnic communication
  Canada, 3371
  Hawaii, 3396
Interethnic relations
  Lebanon, 3395
  USA, 3372, 3374
Intergenerational relations
  Taiwan, 2641
Intergroup relations, 642, 645, 694
  USA, 659
Interindividual relations, *use* Interpersonal relations
Internal migration
  Costa Rica, 3546
  Egypt, 3568
  Finland, 3562
  France, 2857
  India, 3553, 3561
  Israel, 3541
  Malawi, 3547
  Nigeria, 3538
  USA, 3560, 3565
  USSR, 3537
International business enterprises, *use*
  · Multinational enterprises
International conflicts, 5050, 5052, 5054, 5055
International division of labour, 4302
International law, 5039, 5040, 5043
  Developing countries, 5044
International migration, 2820, 3457-58, 3462,
    3493, 3529, 3555
  Europe, 3497
International relations, 353, 468
  Canada — USA, 5041
  USA — Canada, 5041
Internationalization
  Japan, 5042
Interpersonal attraction, 624
Interpersonal communication, 1541, 1551, 1563
Interpersonal conflicts, 660
Interpersonal perception, 605
Interpersonal relations, 325, 383, 577-81,
    584-85, 587-88, 591, 674, 1576, 1780
  France, 592
Interpretation, 278
Interviewers, 388
  USA, 382
Interviews, 380, 381, 383, 386, 389, 448, 664
Intragroup relations, 758
Iran
  Father, 3164

Islam, 3417
Levels of education, 3164
Political anthropology, 1443
Rites, 1443
Social history, 2394, 3417
Social mobility, 3164
Tribalism, 3417
Iraq — Egypt
Comparative education, 1900
Ireland
Alcoholism, 5142
Communication, 3625
Community life, 3625
Crime, 4879
Economic history, 3931
Educational development, 4033
Homeless people, 5104
Police, 4879
Political parties, 4913
Protestants, 1341
Secondary education, 1997
Sex roles, 1997
Technology, 4033
Welfare State, 5267
Youth, 2682
Youth employment, 4206
Youth unemployment, 4182, 4212
Islam, 1058, 1324, 1328, 1337, 1354, 1367,
      1375-76, 1382, 1391, 1399, 1978, 3022,
      3219, 4316
Algeria, 1033, 1338
Belgium, 1352
Egypt, 1369
India, 1346, 1351, 1379
Indonesia, 1325
Iran, 3417
Maghreb, 1394
Malaysia, 1336
North Africa, 1356, 1357
Oman, 1338
Pakistan, 1365
Southern Asia, 1388
Tunisia, 1400
Turkey, 1355, 1489
USSR, 1339, 1387
Israel
Acculturation, 1012
Adolescents, 2623
Affluent society, 3960
Aged, 2717, 2730
Agricultural cooperatives, 4077
Alienation, 4089
Armed forces, 5034
Art, 1769
Attitude to work, 4399
Civil religion, 1299
Defence policy, 5034
Educational policy, 1971
Ego, 2623
Emigration, 3475
Ethnic groups, 3325, 3356, 3853
Ethnicity, 3303, 3306

Family, 3117
Family law, 3135
Immigrants, 89, 1012, 3519
Immigration, 3460
Industrial workers, 307
Internal migration, 3541
Job satisfaction, 4651
Juvenile delinquency, 5187
Kibbutz, 4081, 4089, 4091
Labour disputes, 4688
Migration, 3438
Militarization, 5034
Minority groups, 697
Nationalism, 4787
Population, 2524
Population movement, 2774
Poverty, 5111
Pronatalist policy, 2980
Property, 4089
Quality of life, 3804
Religion, 2730
Religiosity, 2980
Resident satisfaction, 3804
Residential segregation, 3853
Rural development, 3693
Scientific community, 122
Scientists, 89
Secondary education, 2015
Sex roles, 2623
Slowdowns, 4672
Social movements, 4937
Strikes, 4672
Students, 2079
Tolerance, 830
Trade unions, 4616, 4651, 4688
Urban development, 3874
Urban planning, 3825, 3874
Urban youth, 2687
Voting behaviour, 4996
Women's status, 3693
Italy
Adults, 2864
Architecture, 1837
Business organization, 3994
Catholicism, 1348, 1386
Collective bargaining, 4695
Communication, 4354
Cultural consumption, 3806
Cultural history, 2400
Culture, 887
Delinquency, 5173
Drug addiction, 5122, 5123
Educational guidance, 547
Educational sociology, 1906
Elections, 4993
Electoral abstentionism, 5011
Emigrants, 3470, 3521
Emigration, 3524
Employment discrimination, 4220
Entrepreneurs, 4007, 4008
Ethnic pluralism, 1349
Family, 3103, 3180

Glass-workers, 2289
Habitat, 3613
Health, 3103
Health policy, 5411
Immigration, 3479
Jews, 1349
Labour disputes, 4680
Labour law, 4220, 4680
Labour movements, 4644
Labour relations, 4562, 4567
Local government, 4895, 4897, 4906
Manual workers, 4518
Middle class, 2258
Migration, 3439
Mortality, 2864
Periodicals, 184
Physicians, 5462
Population dynamics, 2804
Press, 641
Prison, 5216
Proletariat, 2289
Religious life, 1454
Sacred, 1454
Slums, 3795
Small and medium enterprises, 4007,
    4008, 4529, 4846
Social conflicts, 641
Social history, 2400, 4644
Social order, 2158
Social services, 5476
Social structure, 2168
Society, 897
Sociology, 56
State, 4846
Suburban areas, 3795
Suicide, 5163
Terrorism, 1101, 1138
Trade union action, 4596
Trade unionism, 4579
Trade unions, 2289, 4220, 4605, 4656
Urban growth, 3795
Urban policy, 3806
Villages, 2158
Violence, 1184
Voting behaviour, 2168
Women's liberation movements, 3269
Work environment, 4354
Workers' representation, 4723
Writers, 1802
Italy : Southern
Social policy, 5313
Ivory Coast
Freedom of the press, 4851
Mass media, 1686
Music, 1845
Sexual behaviour, 3040

Jamaica
Politics, 5023
Rural development, 1854
Theatre, 1854
Violence, 1106

Japan
Administrative reforms, 4134
Advertising, 1635
Aged, 2732, 2745, 2747, 2757, 2762
Ageing, 2739
Agricultural cooperatives, 4093
Alienation, 4393
Art, 1781
Attitude to work, 4412
Automobile industry, 4393
Breast-feeding, 2659
Broadcasting, 1688, 1751
Business organization, 711, 4080
Capital cities, 3755
Care of the aged, 2732, 5374
Class consciousness, 2322
Collective bargaining, 4704
Communication, 1566
Communication network, 1578
Community development, 3642
Community study, 369
Conflicts, 646
Cosmology, 1448
Criminal justice, 5250
Cultural relations, 5042
Culture, 2435
Deviance, 1103
Disasters, 3916
Discrimination, 821
Education, 1916
Educational reforms, 1967
Educational systems, 1955
Ethnic minorities, 3350
Everyday life, 923, 2757
Factories, 669
Family, 3116, 3185
Family life, 3148
Family planning, 2999
Family relations, 3200
Female labour, 4301
Feminine press, 1698
Fertility, 2903, 2941
Fishermen, 4513
Fishing villages, 4513
Foreign languages, 1607
Generation differences, 943
Health, 2206
Higher education, 2043, 2060
History of sociology, 36, 40
Holy places, 1469
Hospitals, 2842
Housewives, 2562
Industrial enterprises, 4080
Information services, 156
Internationalization, 5042
Journalism, 821
Juvenile delinquency, 5190, 5250
Kinship, 3196
Knowledge, 1520
Labour movements, 4646
Labour relations, 181, 4540
Language, 1691

Leisure time, 4736
Life styles, 899, 2271
Local communities, 3631, 3636
Local government, 4134, 4902
Mass media, 1691
Metropolitan areas, 2232
Microelectronics, 4332
Migrant workers, 3148
Migration, 3450
Modernization, 2456
National character, 943
National stereotypes, 1607
Neighbourhood, 3916
Occupations, 2739
One-parent family, 3142
Patients, 2842
Peasants, 3692
Political culture, 3636
Political men, 4960
Politics, 5026
Prostitution, 3051
Racial discrimination, 3431
Regional development, 4133, 4134
Religion, 1285
Retirement, 3691
Retirement, 2747
Rites, 1448
Rural communities, 3691, 3739
Secondary education, 2008
Secondary schools, 1103, 1967
Sects, 1439
Sexuality, 3116
Social classes, 2271, 2325
Social consciousness, 2691, 4133
Social development, 2435
Social history, 923, 2181
Social indicators, 432
Social life, 369
Social mobility, 2232, 2379
Social order, 992
Social research, 5062
Social stratification, 2206, 2232, 2325
Social structure, 369, 2181, 2456
Social work, 5389
Society, 992
Sociology of culture, 877
Sociology of organizations, 711
Sociology of work, 4140
Structural analysis, 322
Suicide, 5205
Teachers, 1967
Television, 1654, 1746
Trade unionism, 4614
Trade unions, 4601
Traditional society, 1439
Traditions, 992
Urban areas, 3450
Urban housing, 3841
Urban sociology, 3843
Value, 1052
Value systems, 1075
Voting behaviour, 5016

Women, 2745
Women's status, 3251
Work organization, 4332
Workers' self-management, 4721
Working class, 2249
Working conditions, 4393
Youth, 2691
Japan — United Kingdom
Managers, 4530
Perception of others, 4530
Japan : Takarazuka
Social change, 3789
Suburban areas, 3789
Java
Audiovisual aids, 3012
Family planning, 3012
Industrialization, 4298
Languages, 1623
Urban population, 2781
Women workers, 4298
Jealousy, 632
Jews, 1343, 1371, 1372, 1395, 3237, 3345
Australia, 1326
Bulgaria, 1383
Europe, 4666
Germany FR, 1390
Hungary, 1825
Italy, 1349
Poland, 3429
United Kingdom, 1359
USA, 1374
USSR, 1370, 1378, 1385, 1823, 3460, 3536
Job creation, *use* Employment creation
Job enrichment
USA, 4381
Job mobility, *use* Occupational mobility
Job opportunities, *use* Employment opportunities
Job requirements
France, 4497
Job satisfaction, 2331, 4368, 4373-75, 4379,
4391, 4409, 4416, 4442
Denmark, 4366
Israel, 4651
United Kingdom, 4443
USA, 4283, 4366, 4367, 4378, 4411, 4418
Job seekers
USA, 4198
Joint management, *use* Workers' participation
Jordan
Life tables, 2895
Social change, 2481, 3319
Tribes, 3319
Women workers, 4243
Journalism, 1700, 1726
Germany FR, 1675
Japan, 821
Journalists, 1699, 1724, 1738
Australia, 1694
USA, 1694
Venezuela, 1645
Journals, *use* Periodicals
Journey to work, *use* Commuting

Judaism, 1319, 1332-33, 1375, 1442, 1461
Judges
    Belgium, 4882
Judgment, 273
    USA, 283
Judicial process
    France, 1237
    United Kingdom, 4884
Judiciary power
    Cuba, 4883
Jury
    USA, 676
Justice, 1231
    India, 1261
Juvenile courts
    USA, 5236, 5238
Juvenile delinquency, 469, 5177, 5189, 5197,
    5234
    Algeria, 5251
    Canada, 5157
    France, 5168
    Germany FR, 5162, 5174
    Israel, 5187
    Japan, 5190, 5250
    Netherlands, 5193
    Spain, 5164
    United Kingdom, 2685
    USA, 2702, 4349, 5148, 5226
    Zaire, 5204

Kant, Emmanuel, 53, 226, 541
Kenya
    Administrative law, 4764
    Birth intervals, 2910
    Education, 1896
    Fertility, 2928
    Nomads, 3563
    Population policy, 2991
    Poverty, 5085
    Squatters, 3764
    Vocational training, 4461
Kenya : Nairobi
    Dropout, 2019
    Secondary schools, 2019
Keynes, J. M., 1
Kibbutz
    Israel, 4081, 4089, 4091
Kierkegaard, S., 511, 3954
Kinship, 3162, 3727
    Hong Kong, 3729
    Japan, 3196
    Latin America, 3182
    Sweden, 3119
Knowledge, 1523, 5401
    Japan, 1520
    USA, 283
Korea
    Immigrants, 3396
    National identity, 983
Korea R
    Aged, 2735
    Catholicism, 1323

Emigrants, 3486, 3498
Fertility, 2932, 3548
Fertility rate, 2946
Higher education, 2028
Industrial democracy, 4714
Rural life, 3667
Rural-urban migration, 3548
Social structure, 2167
Solidarity, 3667
Villages, 3667
Widow, 3081
Women workers, 4280
Korsch, Karl, 552
Kuhn, T., 1508

Labelling, 604, 608
Labour, 2460, 4150-52, 4157, 4159, 4177
    Capitalist countries, 4155
    France, 4156, 4166
    Poland, 4163
Labour collectivity, 528, 4329, 4336, 4339,
    4342, 4344
Labour conditions, *use* Working conditions
Labour demand, *use* Demand for labour
Labour disputes, 639, 4681, 4703
    Canada, 4676
    France, 3941
    India, 4689
    Israel, 4688
    Italy, 4680
    New Zealand, 4679
    Peru, 4686
    United Kingdom, 4677
    USA, 4701
Labour force, *use* Manpower
Labour law, 4572, 4574
    Argentina, 4573
    Belgium, 4577
    Colombia, 4670
    Egypt, 4569, 4615
    France, 4032, 4051, 4575
    Germany FR, 4303
    Italy, 4220, 4680
    Poland, 4571, 4627
    Venezuela, 4570
Labour market, 4158, 4162, 4174, 4333
    Australia, 2596
    Denmark, 4171
    Europe, 4293
    Germany, 4242
    Netherlands, 4225
    Poland, 4161
    South Africa, 4165
    United Kingdom, 4170
    USA, 696, 4176
Labour market policy, *use* Employment policy
Labour migration, 3555
    Developing countries, 3566
    Poland, 3530
Labour mobility, 4154
Labour movements, 4618, 4642, 4648
    Bulgaria, 4660

Denmark, 4595
Ecuador, 4668
Europe, 4662, 4666
France, 4599, 4617, 4619, 4662
Germany, 4598, 4617, 4626, 4658
Germany FR, 4603
Ghana, 4507
Italy, 4644
Japan, 4646
Poland, 3429, 4594
Spain, 4608
United Kingdom, 4613
Labour policy
India, 4561
Labour relations, 4325, 4538, 4543
Canada, 4566
China, 4549
Colombia, 4563
Eastern Europe, 4552
France, 4544, 4555
Germany FR, 4555, 4556
Hungary, 4635
India, 4539, 4550, 4553, 4561
Italy, 4562, 4567
Japan, 181, 4540
Nigeria, 4541
Norway, 4634
Spain, 4546
United Kingdom, 4542, 4548, 4554, 4558-60
USA, 4545, 4547, 4551, 4557, 4564-65
Labour self-management, *use*
    Workers' self-management
Labour standards, *use* Work standards
Labour structure
France, 4173
Labour supply, 4160
Labour turnover, 4447
Labour unions, *use* Trade Unions
Labour-managed firms, *use*
    Workers' self-management
Labour-management relations, *use* Labour relations
Land property
Poland, 1059, 4074, 4075
Portugal, 3229
Land reforms
Egypt, 2951
Land tenure, 3727
Ecuador, 3671
Mexico, 3655
Land use
USA, 3592
Language, 1321, 1512, 1587, 1589, 1595-96,
    1602, 1608-10, 1612, 1616, 1630, 3281
Africa, 1852
France, 1588
Germany, 1620
India, 1611
Japan, 1691
Language acquisition, 1621
Language minorities, *use* Linguistic minorities
Language planning
Singapore, 1613

Language policy
Singapore, 1707
USSR, 1593, 1625, 1626
Zaire, 1619
Language teaching, 1532
Belgium, 1599
Zaire, 1615
Languages, 1583, 1606
Africa, 1591
Asia, 1305
Canada, 1604
Java, 1623
Latin America
Automation, 159
Bibliographies, 150
Community participation, 3628
Counterculture, 885
Cultural identity, 2364
Cultural life, 1032
Culture, 906, 1003
Demographic transition, 416
Development styles, 4124
Economic and social development, 2506
Educational planning, 1940
Educational reforms, 1975
Educational research, 1869, 1883
Environment, 4124
Feminism, 3235
Health, 2185
Health services, 5457
Higher education, 150
Identity, 4927
Ideology, 854
Indigenous population, 3289
Intellectuals, 2364
Kinship, 3182
Libraries, 159
Life styles, 4124
Literature, 1796
Male-female relationships, 2565
Metropolis, 3768
Migration, 3433
Political participation, 1032
Political parties, 4909
Politics, 5022
Population, 2506, 2518, 4124
Population distribution, 2764
Population movement, 2766
Population policy, 2961, 2963
Population projections, 2766
Poverty, 1003
Public health, 5407
Public opinion, 840
Regression analysis, 416
Revolution, 2482
Rural development, 3650
Rural population, 2770
Social movements, 4927
Social security, 5361
Social stratification, 2185
Society, 1796
Terrorism, 1153

Theology, 1309
Urbanization, 3898
Vocational training, 4466
Lavater, Johann Kaspar, 2634
Law, 1233, 1238, 1244-45, 1248, 1262-63, 1814
    Africa South of the Sahara, 1250
    French Speaking countries, 1250
    Socialist countries, 1256
    South Africa, 1243
    USSR, 1260
Lawyers, 4537
    Canada, 2368
Lazarsfeld, Paul, 176
Le Play, Frédéric, 196
Leaders, 799, 2887
Leadership, 708, 795, 796, 798, 1572, 3985,
    4533
Learning, 556, 563, 680
Lebanon
    Consanguineous marriage, 3078
    Interethnic relations, 3395
    Religion, 3725
    Rural development, 3725
    Villages, 3725
Legal aspects
    Australia, 4245
Legal philosophy, *use* Philosophy of law
Legends, 1803, 1828
Legislation, 1079
Legitimacy, 4771
Leibniz, Gottfried Wilhelm, 4871
Leisure, 4209, 4343, 4728, 4730
    France, 4738
    Germany FR, 4729
Leisure policy
    German DR, 2694
Leisure time, 4380, 4733-35
    Brazil, 4405
    France, 4369
    Germany FR, 4408
    Japan, 4736
Leisure utilization
    Austria, 4747
    France, 3552, 4731
Lenin, V. I., 2231, 2296, 5024
Leninism, *use* Marxism-Leninism
Lesotho
    Education, 1876
Levels of education, 1931, 2924
    Czechoslovakia, 1982
    Iran, 3164
    USA, 1966, 4481
Levi-Strauss, Claude, 2174
Levinas, E., 1283
Lewin, Kurt, 479
Liberalism, 4786, 4791-93, 4803, 4861
    South Africa, 4805
Liberia
    Mortality, 2853
Liberty, *use* Freedom
Libraries
    Bangladesh, 160

Brazil, 163
Czechoslovakia, 164
Germany FR, 158
Latin America, 159
Nigeria, 154
USA, 153, 165
Zambia, 162
Life cycle, 500, 2640, 2883, 2887, 2900, 3096,
    3727
    Canada, 3157
    France, 2857
Life expectancy
    France, 2852, 2892
    Poland, 1218
    USA, 2847
Life satisfaction
    Europe, 555
    New Zealand, 557
    Norway, 3977
    Sierra Leone, 562
    USA, 4411, 4418
Life styles, 523, 905, 949, 969, 973, 1001, 2900
    France, 883, 904
    Hungary, 938
    Japan, 899, 2271
    Latin America, 4124
    USA, 977
    USSR, 425
Life tables, 428, 2855
    Africa, 2865
    Algeria, 2893
    Developing countries, 2880
    Germany, 2862
    India, 2877
    Jordan, 2895
    México, 2872
Life-long education, *use* Continuing education
Linear models, 272, 288
Linguistic anthropology, *use* Ethnolinguistics
Linguistic minorities
    Canada, 1605
Linguistics, 1526
    Amazonia, 1525
    France, 1717
    Yugoslavia, 1533
Literacy, 2101
    Developing countries, 2080
    Ethiopia, 2100
    United Kingdom, 2082
Literature, 1316, 1322, 1610, 1789-90, 1794,
    1810, 1814-15
    Africa, 1788, 1795
    China, 1817
    Eastern Europe, 1818
    German DR, 1792, 1811
    Germany FR, 1792, 1830
    Hungary, 1825
    Latin America, 1796
    Maghreb, 1812
    Nigeria, 1798
    Romania, 1821
    Tunisia, 1804

Turkey, 1793, 1806
United Kingdom, 1827
USA, 1820, 2660
USSR, 1823, 1826
Western Asia, 1807
Liturgy
    Brazil, 1440
Living conditions, 3696, 3970
    France, 3967
    Hungary, 3969, 3986
    Norway, 3974
    Poland, 2674, 3968
    South Africa : Pretoria, 2760
    United Kingdom, 3980
Lobbies, *use* Interest groups
Local communities, 981, 3626, 3633
    Hungary, 3620
    Japan, 3631, 3636
    USA, 3640
Local culture
    USA, 3911
Local government, 1754, 4901
    Canada : Toronto, 3852
    France, 2285, 4899
    Germany FR, 3638
    India, 4905
    Italy, 4895, 4897, 4906
    Japan, 4134, 4902
    United Kingdom, 4659
    USA, 4701, 4904
    Venezuela, 4900
Local politics
    Canada, 3316
Local power
    Bolivia, 4898
    Hungary, 4903
Locke, John, 2157
Logic, 394, 402, 475
Loneliness, 576, 582, 583, 590
    France, 2722, 2748, 3232
    USA, 589
Los Angeles
    Abortion, 2978
Love, 619, 625, 3277
    China, 613
Luhmann, Niklas, 492, 4771
Lukács, György, 1777, 1801

Machonin, P., 2294
Madagascar
    Christianity, 1347
    Poverty, 5114
    Press, 1669
    Racial differentiation, 1347
Magazines, *use* Periodicals
Maghreb
    Bibliographies, 1394
    Body symbolism, 1548
    Cultural cooperation, 1016
    Islam, 1394
    Literature, 1812
    Sexuality, 3025

Value systems, 1053
Magic, 841, 1316, 1320
Mail surveys, 384
    United Kingdom, 385
Majority groups, 693
    Middle East, 686
Majority rules, 4812
Malawi
    Internal migration, 3547
Malaysia
    Adopted children, 2653
    Birth intervals, 2933
    Breast-feeding, 2643
    Child mortality, 2643, 2933
    Class structure, 2326
    Deontology, 1476
    Ethnic groups, 3308, 3344
    Fertility, 2934
    Infant mortality, 2934
    Islam, 1336
    Peasants, 3685
    Production, 4021
    Protestant ethics, 1476
    Race relations, 3387
    Social mobility, 2326
    Society, 4021
    Women's role, 2599
Male-female relationships
    Latin America, 2565
Mali
    Child mortality, 2870
    Infant mortality, 2870
Malnutrition, 5095
    Sri Lanka, 5110
Malthus, T. R., 2416
Management, 737, 751, 764
    USA, 779
Management information systems, 144, 148
Managers, 2610, 4529, 4532
    Belgium, 4528
    France, 4527
    Japan — United Kingdom, 4530
    United Kingdom, 4560
    USA, 3352
    Yugoslavia, 4531
Mannheim, Karl, 1511, 2308, 2396
Manpower
    Ecuador, 4172
    France, 4149, 4156
Manpower policy, *use* Employment policy
Manpower utilization
    USA, 4169
Manual workers
    Canada, 4522
    Italy, 4518
Marginal people
    India, 1152
    Sweden, 2684
Marginality, 1110
    Germany FR, 1721
Marital conflict, 3086, 3099
Marital disruption, *use* Marital separation

Marital interaction, 3067
Marital satisfaction, 3056
    Canada, 3172
Marital separation, 3096
Marital stability
    USA, 4248
Market, 4110
    United Kingdom, 4111
Market economy
    Austria, 3955
Market regulation
    France, 3670
Marriage, 3055, 3064
    Australia, 618
    Belgium, 3094
    Canada, 3060
    China, 613, 3159
    Europe, 3139
    France, 349
    Hungary, 3077
    India, 618, 3068
    Philippines, 3058
    South Africa, 3072
    USA, 3048, 3054
Married persons
    USA, 4425
Married women
    France, 4295
Marshall, T. H., 177
Martinique
    Youth, 2668
    Youth employment, 2668
Marx, Karl, 1, 48, 193, 216, 239, 246, 260,
        320, 394, 859, 1007, 1111, 1161, 1229,
        2177, 2304, 2431, 2497, 3937, 3944,
        3950, 4794, 4868
Marxism, 193, 205, 207, 223, 228-30, 237,
        239, 241, 248, 254, 259, 261, 264-65,
        476, 486, 868, 965, 988, 1126, 1164,
        2278, 2313, 3410, 3937, 4799
    France, 267
    Poland, 2229
Marxism-Leninism, 4050
Mass communication, 1648, 1706, 1720, 1723,
        1729, 1742, 1749, 1750, 1752
Mass education
    France, 2052
Mass media, 606, 1040, 1091, 1529, 1650,
        1657-58, 1666, 1687, 1697, 1718,
        1722-23, 1731, 1743, 1760
    Austria, 1709
    Denmark, 1556
    Developing countries, 1638
    Dominican Republic, 1739
    France, 1734, 1763
    Germany FR, 1684, 1721
    India, 1652
    Ivory Coast, 1686
    Japan, 1691
    Spain, 1716
    Spain : Catalonia, 1685
    Sweden, 1689

    United Kingdom, 1708
    USA, 1651, 1660, 1662, 3205, 4016, 4746
    Yugoslavia, 1677, 1678
Mass society, 941
Mate selection, 617
    Philippines, 3058
Material culture, 3606
Materialism, 224
Maternity benefits
    Czechoslovakia, 5353
Mathematical analysis, 391, 393, 397, 405
Mathematical methods, 400
Mathematical models, 302, 310, 395, 398-99,
        401, 403-04
Mathematics, 335, 392, 396, 406
Matriarchy
    France, 3113
Mauss, Marcel, 4782
McLuhan, Marshall, 4044
Mead, G. H., 487
Meaning, 333, 1317, 1575, 2471
Measurement, 372
Meat market
    United Kingdom, 4111
Media, 1653, 1659, 1676, 1701, 1715, 1736,
        1754
    America, 1753
    North America, 1671
    USA, 1744, 4737
Mediation, 652, 4700, 4703
Medical care, 2831, 5448
    Belgium, 5415
    France, 5410
    India, 5427
    Mozambique, 5458
    Nigeria, 5419
    United Kingdom, 5450
    USA, 5403, 5421
Medical occupations
    Belgium, 5415
    India, 5482
    USA, 5472
Medical research
    France, 5402
Medical sociology, 5395
Medicinal drugs, *use* Drugs
Medicine, 5393, 5401
Mediterranean countries
    Innovations, 4064
    Population, 2548
    Population dynamics, 2763
    State, 4822
    Technological change, 4064
Men, 3105
Mental deficiency
    United Kingdom, 2838
Mental diseases, 2632, 2823, 2835
    USA, 2824, 2843
Mental health, 804, 5430
    Africa, 5435
    Australia, 2612
    Canada, 4040

India, 5413
USA, 5429, 5434
Mental hospitals
United Kingdom, 5445
Mental hygiene, 5417
Mental retardation
Trinidad and Tobago, 3424
Mental stress, 973
Mentally disabled, 2836
United Kingdom, 5445
Merchant marine
France, 4208
Merton, Robert K., 54, 66, 1335, 1504,
1507
Messianism, 1319
Mestizos
United Kingdom, 3430
Metropolis, 3919
Latin America, 3768
Peru, 3899
Metropolitan areas
Brazil, 3903
Japan, 2232
USA, 3756, 3801, 3870
Mexico
Adult education, 2104
Agrarian structure, 1984
Authoritarianism, 4826
Basic education, 2084
Bilingual education, 2094
Educational policy, 1984
Emigrants, 3287
Ethnic minorities, 2217
Family planning, 2984
Fertility, 2872
Health, 5408
Health policy, 5418
Health services, 5408
Historiography, 2395
Land tenure, 3655
Life tables, 2872
Patriotism, 4776
Political systems, 4826
Rural communities, 3714
Social differentiation, 3714
Social inequality, 2217
Social reproduction, 2133
Teaching aids, 2133
Towns, 3780
Trade unions, 4624, 4661
Urban concentration, 3780
Urban development, 3862
Women workers, 5408
Women's rights, 3280
Women's work, 4317
Microanalysis, 345
Microcomputers
USA, 2148
Microelectronics, 4346
Japan, 4332
Middle class, 850, 2287, 2313
Africa, 2356

France, 764, 5007
France, 2250, 2265
Italy, 2258
Sweden, 2117
Middle East
Majority groups, 686
Minorities, 686
Middle range theory, 3629
Middle-sized towns
France, 3812
Migrant workers
Austria : Vienna, 4291
France, 3509, 4256, 4268
Japan, 3148
Portugal, 4279
South Africa, 2290
Turkey, 4316
Yugoslavia, 3824
Migrants, 3437
Germany FR, 1721
Switzerland, 3440
Migration, 3444-46, 3449
Canada, 3436
Caribbean, 3442, 3443
Czechoslovakia, 3612
Europe, 3447
France, 4451
Germany FR, 3439
India, 3434, 3452
Indonesia, 3453
Israel, 3438
Italy, 3439
Japan, 3450
Latin America, 3433
Puerto Rico, 3448
USA, 3451
USSR, 3441
Migration policy
Australia, 3435
Militarization
Israel, 5034
Military
USA, 5029
Military personnel
USA, 5036
Military service
Belgium, 5035
Peru, 5033
Military sociology, 5031
Mill, John Stuart, 1288
Millenarianism, 849
Mills, C. W., 66, 5072
Miners
France, 4516
Ghana, 4507
Mining
Tanzania, 4396
Minorities
Middle East, 686
Near East, 685
Minority culture
Western Europe, 925

Minority groups, 682, 693
    Africa, 690
    Australia, 687, 2918
    Canada, 688, 691, 1605
    Israel, 697
    New Zealand, 692
    United Kingdom, 684
    USA, 695, 696, 698, 3168, 3973, 4888
Minority rights, 2208
Missionaries
    Nigeria, 1910
Mixed bloods, *use* Mestizos
Mixed marriage
    France, 3085, 3101
    Germany FR, 3061
Models, 285
Modernity, 782, 1312, 1450, 2419, 2441,
    2445, 2451, 2463, 2468-71, 2478
Modernization
    Hungary, 2446
    Japan, 2456
    Spain, 2464, 2477
Modes of production, 4041
    Asia, 4058
    France, 4047
Monasticism
    France, 1403
Money, 4117
    France, 4116
    Socialist countries, 4119
Monopolies, 4112
Monotheism, 1464
Moore, Barrington, 1226
Moral crisis
    Yugoslavia, 1228
Moral development, 1210, 1217, 2605
Morality, 232, 1220, 1226, 1229, 2581,
    2605, 2606
    Australia, 1221
    Northern Ireland, 1214
    Poland, 1218
Morals, 273, 1216, 1225, 2762, 4147
    USSR, 3121
    Zaire, 1213
Morbidity
    Finland, 2541
Mores, 1193
Morocco
    Agricultural production, 1128
    Revolt, 1128
    Students, 2064
    Urban space, 3809
Mortality, 2879, 2884, 2894, 2898
    Africa, 2953
    Algeria, 2893
    Asia, 2897
    Czechoslovakia, 2890
    Developing countries, 2848
    France, 2854, 2858, 2860
    Hungary, 2856
    India, 2881, 2945
    Italy, 2864

    Liberia, 2853
    Netherlands, 4219
    Sri Lanka, 2874
    Sweden, 2850
    Tunisia, 2866
    United Kingdom, 2885
    USA, 2516, 2891
    USSR, 2861
Mortality decline, 2878
Moslems, 1389, 3262
    India, 1327
    Southern Asia, 1388
    USSR, 1402
    Yugoslavia, 1381
Mother
    Greece, 3133
Mother tongue, 1584
    USA, 1601
Motherhood, 2962
    Australia : Sydney, 3017
    Portugal, 3229
    USA, 2058, 3004
Motivation, 574, 1157
Motivational analysis, 390, 443
Mozambique
    Education, 1884
    Health services, 5458
    Medical care, 5458
    Political parties, 4914
    Villages, 3654
Multicultural education
    Australia, 1960
Multidisciplinary research, *use*
        Interdisciplinary research
Multilingualism, 1589
Multinational enterprises, 3991, 4727
Multivariate analysis, 324, 328, 3426
Municipal administration, *use*
        Local government
Murder, *use* Homicide
Murderers, 5221
Music, 682, 1842, 1844
    France, 1841
    Hungary, 1847
    Ivory Coast, 1845
    USA, 1840
    USSR, 1843
Muslims, *use* Moslems
Myrdal, Gunnar, 3353
Mysticism, 1450, 1455, 1461, 1465
Myths, 1457, 1459, 1462, 1463, 3341
    Australia, 2612

Names
    Burundi, 507
    United Kingdom, 505
    USA, 513
Natality
    France, 2923
    USA, 2908
Nation, 890-92, 930, 957, 965, 980, 1007
    France, 984

Nation building, 2483
  Canada, 2489
National character
  Japan, 943
National consciousness
  German DR, 950
  Germany FR, 908, 950
National development, 3342
  Scotland, 2499
National identity
  Canada, 976
  Hungary, 954
  Korea, 983
  Netherlands, 922
  North Africa, 914
  Portugal, 4279
  Spain, 987
  Turkey, 4316
National minorities
  Capitalist countries, 3288
  Denmark, 3307
  Germany FR, 3307
  Yugoslavia, 3305
National stereotypes, 825
  Japan, 1607
Nationalism, 3332, 3357, 4774, 4775, 4939
  Arab countries, 4787
  Canada, 4772
  Canada : Quebec, 1428, 1437, 4773
  India, 3702
  Israel, 4787
  Spain, 4795
  United Kingdom, 4772
Nationalist movements
  Europe, 4684
Nationalities policy
  USSR, 3536
Nationality, 2171
Natives, *use* Indigenous population
Natural law, 1234
Nature, 3578, 3597-99, 3601-02, 3604,
    3607-08
Near East
  Minorities, 685
Needs, 527, 532, 539, 546, 559
  Poland, 3968
Negotiation, *use* Bargaining
Negroes, *use* Blacks
Neighbourhood, 3882
  Japan, 3916
  Netherlands, 4187
  United Kingdom, 3769
  USA, 3856
Neoconservatism, 2441, 5331
Nepal
  Buddhism, 2434
  Cultural policy, 1010
  Fertility, 379
  Feudalism, 3959
  Rural society, 3959
  Shamanism, 1318
  Social change, 2434

  Surveys, 379
  Villages, 3679
Netherlands
  Absenteeism, 4449
  Aged, 2719
  Catholics, 1384
  Congresses, 245
  Conservatism, 4781
  Culture, 935, 4473
  Educational systems, 1953
  Employment policy, 4225
  Ethnic groups, 3336
  Ethnic minorities, 3335
  Family, 5318
  Gerontology, 2743
  Health, 4219
  Juvenile delinquency, 5193
  Labour market, 4225
  Mortality, 4219
  National identity, 922
  Neighbourhood, 4187
  Occupational prestige, 4493
  Occupational stratification, 4473
  Political institutions, 4842
  Political participation, 4973
  Protestants, 1384
  Religion, 1269
  Science policy, 129
  Sex discrimination, 2618
  Sex roles, 1953
  Slums, 4187
  Social conditions, 5318
  Social history, 5318
  Social networks, 1530
  Social services, 5465
  Social stratification, 2719
  Sociolinguistics, 1530
  Sociology of religion, 1264
  Squatters, 3796
  Students, 935
  Trade unions, 4632
  Unemployment, 4187, 4214, 4218, 4219
  Unemployment level, 4449
  Welfare State, 1269, 5320
  Women's education, 1953
  Women's work, 2618
  Workers, 5318
Network analysis, 310, 312, 314, 315, 325,
    327, 336, 347, 358, 360
Neuroses
  Poland, 1472
New international information order, 1554,
    1580
New technologies, 4026, 4035, 4048, 4063,
    4286, 4482
  Canada : Quebec, 4029
  France, 4032, 4051, 4470
  Germany FR, 4062
  USA, 4016, 4070
New towns
  Brazil, 3893
  Egypt, 3927

France, 3770, 3814, 3887
United Kingdom, 3769, 3807
Venezuela, 3893
New Zealand
    Community development, 5467
    Dispute settlement, 4679
    Equal opportunity, 2221
    Housing policy, 3867
    Human geography, 3587
    Incomes policy, 4136
    Labour disputes, 4679
    Life satisfaction, 557
    Minority groups, 692
    Political behaviour, 4977
    Population, 2542
    Racial discrimination, 3414
    Regional development, 4125
    Religious groups, 4977
    Social services, 5467
    State intervention, 4136
Newspapers, *use* Press
Nicaragua
    Bourgeoisie, 2312
    Catholic Church, 1416
    Class formation, 1416
    Education, 1864
    Rural development, 3711
    Schooling, 1986
    State building, 4834
Nietzsche, Friedrich, 860, 1478
Niger
    Public administration, 4890
Nigeria
    Business communities, 3990
    Children, 2654
    Collective bargaining, 4697
    Community development, 3622
    Contraception, 2996
    History of education, 1910
    Housing policy, 3877
    Internal migration, 3538
    Labour relations, 4541
    Libraries, 154
    Literature, 1798
    Medical care, 5419
    Missionaries, 1910
    Occupational prestige, 4488
    Peasant society, 3622
    Poverty, 2654
    Private sector, 4697
    Religious groups, 1424
    Resident satisfaction, 3877
    Rural development, 3538
    Sociology, 7
    Urban planning, 3759
    Vocational guidance, 4488
    Women's work, 4258, 4308
Nomads, 3571
    France, 3542, 3552
    Kenya, 3563
Non-verbal communication, 1597
Non-violence

USA, 3373
North Africa
    Cultural identity, 1019
    Emigration, 3456
    Islam, 1356, 1357
    National identity, 914
    Politics, 3255
    Urban planning, 3884
    Women's status, 3255
North America
    Adopted children, 2650
    Immigration, 3531
    Media, 1671
    Television, 1665
Northern Ireland
    Adopted children, 2657
    Catholics, 1214
    Conflicts, 1421
    Education, 1898
    Ethnicity, 3301
    Morality, 1214
    Protestants, 1214, 1344
    Religious communities, 1421
    Status attainment, 1421
Norway
    Children, 3974
    Cultural policy, 1035
    Folk culture, 1035
    Higher education, 2046
    Income distribution, 3982
    Institutions, 1073
    Labour relations, 4634
    Life satisfaction, 3977
    Living conditions, 3974
    Petroleum resources, 894
    Political participation, 4981
    Quality of life, 3977
    Refugees, 3492
    Society, 894
    Time budgets, 4406
    Trade unions, 4634
    Welfare State, 5291, 5292
    Women's status, 3228
    Work environment, 4382
    Workers' participation, 4717
Novels, 1801, 1819, 2445
    Germany FR, 1816
    USA, 1822
Nuclear energy, 1519
Nuclear power, *use* Nuclear energy
Nuns
    France, 1425
Nuptiality, 3092
    China, 3063
    Europe, 3074
    USA, 3065
Nurses
    Australia, 4379
Nutrition
    Colombia, 5084
    India, 5106

Obituaries, 169-71, 176-79, 182-83
Objectivity, 6, 294
Observation, 367, 881
Occultism, 1317, 1321, 1322
Occupational accidents
   Poland, 4434
   Spain, 4426
Occupational achievement, 2593
Occupational choice, 4459
   Canada, 3258
   Germany FR, 4464
   USA, 4503
Occupational diseases
   Poland, 4434
Occupational environment, 4520
Occupational ethics, *use* Deontology
Occupational groups, 734
   Hungary, 4483
   India, 1145
Occupational life, 1110
   France, 3158
Occupational mobility
   India, 4499
   United Kingdom, 4479
   USA, 4463, 4480, 4481, 4500
Occupational prestige, 4475, 4487, 4494
   Canada, 4474
   Netherlands, 4493
   Nigeria, 4488
   Poland, 4468
   USA, 4474
Occupational promotion
   USA, 4445
Occupational qualification, 4211, 4482, 4504
   Canada, 4522
   France, 4031, 4470, 4472, 4491, 4496
   Germany FR, 4462
   Romania, 4478
   United Kingdom, 4502
Occupational ranking, *use* Occupational
   stratification
Occupational safety
   Australia, 4389, 4390
   France, 4433
   USA, 4370
Occupational segregation
   Canada, 4495
Occupational sociology, 4138, 4457
Occupational status, 4487
   France, 1809, 5461
   Poland, 3154
   USA, 4192, 4476
Occupational stratification
   Netherlands, 4473
Occupational structure
   Poland, 3165, 4468, 4505
Occupations, 1063, 4452, 4453, 4455, 4458
   Africa, 4454
   Japan, 2739
   Poland, 2791
Oceania
   Women's role, 2607

OECD countries
   Women's employment, 4306
Offenders, 5194, 5209
Office automation, 4019, 4038, 4052
   France, 4049
Old age, 2721, 2723, 2728
   France, 2712, 2722, 2748
   Poland, 2746, 2759
Old age policy
   Argentina, 5369
   France, 5284
Older people, *use* Aged
Older workers
   France, 4256
Oligarchy, 4821
   Guatemala, 4810
Oman
   Islam, 1338
   Political systems, 1338
   Women's role, 2575
   Women's status, 2575
One-parent family
   Germany FR, 3179
   Japan, 3142
   USA, 3150
Opinion, 1572
Oral tradition
   Developing countries, 1808
Organization theory, 712, 717, 720, 728, 4012
Organizational analysis, 713-15, 718-19, 893
Organizational behaviour, 741, 745, 748-49,
     754-56, 765, 774-75, 778
   South Africa, 738
Organizational change, 727, 744, 752-53, 758,
     760-61, 763, 769, 773, 777, 3994, 4415
Organizational dysfunctions, 742, 1110
Organizational goal, 768, 4532
Organizational research, 689, 710, 716, 3574
Organizational structure, 740, 746, 757, 759
Organizations, 722, 725-26, 733-34, 736,
     2432, 3639, 5080
Ortega y Gasset, José, 5339
Ossowski, Stanislaw, 2310
Ouchi, William, 751
Owners, 223

Pacifism, 5047
Paganism, 1456
Painting
   German DR, 1834
Pakistan
   Belief, 834
   Education, 1365
   Educational reforms, 1978
   Islam, 1365
   Students, 834
Panama
   Social sciences, 26
Papua New Guinea
   Children, 2644
   Customary law, 1239
Paradigm, 290, 1507

Paraguay
  Bilingualism, 1598
  Educational systems, 1972
Parent-child relations, 3105, 3134, 3170
  Spain, 2649
  Thailand, 3110
  USA, 3109, 3132, 3173
Parenthood
  USA, 3005, 3027
Parents' education
  USA, 2125
Pareto, Vilfredo, 844, 5314
Parish
  France, 1432
  United Kingdom, 1366
Park, Robert E., 871, 3822
Parkin, Frank, 787
Parsons, Talcott, 226, 261, 878, 1164, 2451
Part-time employment, 4428
Part-time farming
  USA, 4069
Participant observation, 362, 373
Party systems
  Argentina, 4918
  Spain, 4911
  USA, 4916
Patients, 578, 2830, 2831, 2834
  Japan, 2842
Patriarchy
  China, 3141
  Western Europe, 3141
Patriotism
  Mexico, 4776
  USA, 4778
Patron-client relations, *use* Clientelism
Pawnbroking
  France : Rouen, 4120
Peace, 5049, 5051, 5053
Peace movements, 1263, 4932
  Germany FR, 1223
Peasant culture
  Poland, 958
Peasant movements, 1113
  France : Brittany, 3670
Peasant organizations
  India, 3723
Peasant society, 3660, 3696
  France, 3662
  Nigeria, 3622
Peasantry, 3677, 3724, 3743
  Caribbean, 3738
  Developing countries, 3704
  France, 3653
  France : Sarthe, 3659
  India, 3702, 3717
  India : Bihar, 3668
  Poland, 3165, 3674
  Socialist countries, 3728
  Tanzania, 3732
  Thailand, 2255, 3690
  Turkey, 3694
  USSR, 3740

Peasants, 3649
  China, 3683
  France, 3689, 3705, 3730
  Hungary, 3656, 3681, 3701
  Japan, 3692
  Malaysia, 3685
Pedagogy, *use* Sciences of education
Pediatricians
  France, 5461
Peer groups, 567, 675, 807
Penal law, 1251, 1257
  Albania, 1254
  France, 1237
  Germany FR, 1242
  USSR, 1232
Penitentiary system, 5175
Pension funds
  United Kingdom, 4724
Pension schemes
  USA, 5373
Perception, 541, 2646
Perception of others, 598, 600
  Japan — United Kingdom, 4530
Performance, 5263
Periodicals, 1527
  Italy, 184
  Switzerland, 185
  USA, 186
Person, Yves, 1044
Personality, 484, 514-15, 519-21, 523, 525,
    527, 529-30, 532-35, 802, 1558, 4113
  USA, 1117
Personality development, 516, 517, 522, 524,
    526, 528, 531, 1072, 4272, 4336, 4409
Personality traits, 518, 4106
Personnel management, 778, 4325, 4326,
    4341, 4345
Personnel supervision, *use* Personnel
management
Persuasion, 1632, 4951
Peru
  Bourgeoisie, 4135
  Catholicism, 1364
  Cooperative movements, 4953
  Drugs of abuse, 5124
  Indigenous population, 3328
  Labour disputes, 4686
  Metropolis, 3899
  Military service, 5033
  Regional development, 4135
  Regional planning, 4126
  Scientific research, 4020
  Self-management, 770
  Social conditions, 5286
  Social consciousness, 5033
  Urban structure, 5286
  Women workers, 4686
Peru : Lima
  Urban economics, 3899
Petroleum resources
  Norway, 894
Phenomenology, 219, 238, 242, 1120, 1313

Philippines
    Child mortality, 3848
    Children, 609
    Economic change, 3965
    Family planning, 2988
    Housing, 3848
    Marriage, 3058
    Mate selection, 3058
    Primary schools, 2000
    Rural-urban migration, 3569
Philippines : Leyte
    Rural poverty, 5103
Philosophers
    France, 76, 82, 85, 86
Philosophical thought, 209
Philosophy, 192, 195, 201, 225, 226, 232,
        243, 552, 2468
Philosophy of art, 1782
Philosophy of law, 1219, 1235, 1255, 1258
Philosophy of science, 1522
Photography
    France, 4519
Physicians, 578, 5463
    Belgium, 5475
    France, 5461, 5473, 5477, 5479
    Italy, 5462
    Yugoslavia, 5469
Piaget, Jean, 461
Pilgrimages
    India, 1444
Planned parenthood, *use* Family planning
Plant size
    Sweden, 4683
    United Kingdom, 4554, 4683
Playing activities, 2613
Plebiscite
    Switzerland, 5014
Plural society, *use* Social pluralism
Poetry
    China, 1831
    German DR, 1797
Poland
    Aged, 2758
    Agricultural cooperation, 4079
    Agricultural workers, 4510, 4710
    Alcoholism, 5136
    Antisemitism, 3429
    Attitudes, 2007, 2799
    Birth control, 3188
    Buildings, 2799
    Business management, 3998
    Catholicism, 1350, 1397
    Civil servants, 4383
    Class struggle, 2317
    Collective behaviour, 622
    Communication policy, 1557
    Consumer behaviour, 4103
    Consumer demand, 4103
    Cultural change, 2267
    Cultural development, 1013
    Cultural identity, 1042
    Cultural implications, 4437

Cultural integration, 1023
Culture, 895, 1004
Development potential, 2789
Economic development, 4594
Education, 1013
Educational output, 2048
Educational systems, 1961
Family, 3137, 3165, 3169, 3188
Family disintegration, 3147
Family farms, 4074
Family size, 3154
Farmers, 1059, 2746, 3137, 3710, 3720
Farming, 4079, 4094
Folk culture, 1202
Higher education, 2048, 2054
History of sociology, 43
Housing, 3928
Human rights, 4859
Humanization of work, 4394
Income inequality, 3984
Industrial workers, 4514
Industrialization, 2773
Jews, 3429
Labour, 4163
Labour law, 4571, 4627
Labour market, 4161
Labour migration, 3530
Labour movements, 3429, 4594
Land property, 1059, 4074, 4075
Life expectancy, 1218
Living conditions, 2674, 3968
Marxism, 2229
Morality, 1218
Needs, 3968
Neuroses, 1472
Occupational accidents, 4434
Occupational diseases, 4434
Occupational prestige, 4468
Occupational status, 3154
Occupational structure, 3165, 4468,
    4505
Occupations, 2791
Old age, 2746, 2759
Peasant culture, 958
Peasantry, 3165, 3674
Political ideologies, 4910
Political leadership, 4961
Political parties, 4910
Political socialization, 4975
Population distribution, 2789
Population forecasts, 2528
Population movement, 2773
Property, 3935
Protestants, 1340
Public opinion, 4161
Publishing, 1695
Pupils, 2007
Reading habits, 571
Regional policy, 4130
Religiosity, 1472, 1473
Religious education, 2109
Rural areas, 1013, 2759, 4510

Rural population, 571, 1004, 1042, 1112, 1202, 1472, 2170, 2791-93, 2799, 3984, 4505
Rural youth, 2704, 4437
Social behaviour, 1139
Social classes, 2272
Social conflicts, 643, 650, 658
Social consciousness, 1112, 2213
Social disorganization, 658
Social environment, 1218
Social equality, 2210
Social indicators, 415
Social inequality, 2210, 2211, 2213
Social judgment, 2229
Social mobility, 2272
Social perception, 2213
Social planning, 415
Social policy, 2696, 5268
Social reforms, 5276
Social reproduction, 1961
Social status, 4468
Social stratification, 4514
Social structure, 2170, 5073
Social unrest, 5073
Socialism, 2007
Socialization, 1129
Sociological theory, 240
Sociologists, 80
Sociology, 65
Solidarity, 622
State farms, 3169, 4510, 4710
Time budgets, 4437
Trade unions, 4627, 4639, 4641
Urban life, 3864
Urban planning, 3845
Urban population, 2782
Urbanization, 3813, 3872
Value systems, 1059, 4383
Villages, 2792, 3678
Women's status, 3239
Women's work, 4269
Workers, 4515, 5136
Workers' participation, 4710
Working class, 2267
Working conditions, 4394, 4424
Youth, 1129, 1473, 2674, 2693, 2696
Poland : Rzeszów
  Urban communities, 3865
Poland : Warsaw
  Family rites, 3151
  Feast-days, 3151
Police, 3047, 4873
  Denmark, 4366
  Hungary, 4874
  India, 4881
  Ireland, 4879
  United Kingdom, 4872, 4875, 4876-78
  USA, 2591, 4366
Political action, 554
Political affiliation
  USA, 4976
Political alienation, 1161

India, 1114, 1145
Political anthropology, 880
  Iran, 1443
Political attitudes
  France, 1342
  Germany, 2697
  Greece, 2263
  USA, 2692, 4968, 4979, 4991
Political behaviour, 4962, 4967
  New Zealand, 4977
  USA, 4367
  Yugoslavia, 4982
Political change, 4771
Political contestation, *use* Political protest
Political corruption
  USA, 4985
Political culture, 4971, 4978, 4980, 4983
  Austria, 4963
  Fiji, 4989
  France, 1267
  Japan, 3636
  Turkey, 4965
  USSR, 4964, 4972
Political development
  India, 4831, 4835
Political elite, 174
Political ideologies
  Poland, 4910
  USA, 4770
Political institutions, 4824
  India, 4832
  Netherlands, 4842
Political leaders
  Guyana, 4959
  Trinidad, 4959
Political leadership
  India, 4831
  Poland, 4961
Political men
  Japan, 4960
Political movements, 4945, 4947
  United Kingdom, 4777
Political participation, 4969, 4984
  Latin America, 1032
  Netherlands, 4973
  Norway, 4981
  United Kingdom, 4987
  Zambia, 4990
Political parties, 4917
  Austria, 4915
  Canada, 4907
  Germany FR, 5301
  India, 4908, 4912
  Ireland, 4913
  Latin America, 4909
  Mozambique, 4914
  Poland, 4910
  Tanzania, 4914
Political philosophy, 4769
Political protest
  China, 1831
  El Salvador, 4957

Germany FR, 4958
Political psychology, 4762
  USA, 4761, 4763
Political socialization, 4966
  Argentina, 4986
  Brazil, 4986
  France, 4988
  Germany FR, 4970
  Poland, 4975
  USA, 4974
Political sociology, 4760, 4766
  Switzerland, 4768
  USA, 4765, 4767
Political speech
  Argentina, 1627
Political systems, 892, 4829-30, 4837-38, 4841
  Algeria, 1338
  Mexico, 4826
  Oman, 1338
  USA, 4823
Political theory, 3938
Politicians, *use* Political men
Politics, 1303, 1794, 2465, 4762, 5024, 5027
  India, 2172, 3873, 5300
  India : Kerala, 2275
  Jamaica, 5023
  Japan, 5026
  Latin America, 5022
  North Africa, 3255
  Sweden, 2609
  USA, 1636, 2720, 5025, 5026
  Western Europe, 5026
Polls
  France, 374, 377
Polygamy
  Africa, 3059, 3100
Polynesia
  Birth, 2904
  Death, 2904
Poor
  Africa, 5091
Popper, Karl Raimund, 1518
Popular culture, *use* Folk culture
Popular literature
  Hungary, 1829
Popular religion, 790, 1483
Population, 4132
  Canada, 2539
  China, 2508, 2514, 2532, 2534
  Developing countries, 2529
  Europe, 2520, 2540
  France, 2502, 2509, 2523, 2543, 5125
  Germany FR, 2549
  Greece, 2515
  Hungary, 2537, 2554
  India, 2507
  Israel, 2524
  Latin America, 2506, 2518, 4124
  Mediterranean countries, 2548
  New Zealand, 2542
  Puerto Rico, 2525
  Socialist countries, 2512

Western Europe, 2511
Population ageing, 2878, 4450
Population censuses
  China, 2768, 2775
  Cuba, 2809
  USA, 2787, 2795
Population composition
  Czechoslovakia, 2769
Population distribution, 2818, 2820
  Latin America, 2764
  Poland, 2789
  Taiwan, 2797
  Yugoslavia, 2546
Population dynamics
  Indonesia, 2786
  Italy, 2804
  Mediterranean countries, 2763
  Romania, 2815
Population forecasts, 2503, 2536
  Poland, 2528
  USA, 2531
Population growth, 2767, 2780, 2790, 2801
  Czechoslovakia, 2794
  India, 2785
  USA, 2796
Population movement, 2784, 2802
  Algeria, 2814
  Canada, 2776
  China, 2771, 2777
  France, 4047
  Israel, 2774
  Latin America, 2766
  Poland, 2773
  Portugal, 2805
  United Kingdom, 2803
  Yugoslavia, 2788
Population optimum, 2817
Population policy, 2784, 2977, 3000
  China, 3006, 3018
  Egypt, 2991
  France, 3014
  German DR, 2973
  Germany FR, 2973
  Hungary, 2537, 3010
  Kenya, 2991
  Latin America, 2961, 2963
  Tunisia, 2991
Population projections, 2505, 2533, 2780, 2884
  Developing countries, 2553
  Latin America, 2766
Population theory, 436, 2510
Populism, 4774
Pornography
  Canada, 3034
  USA, 3039, 3052
Portugal
  Agrarian reforms, 4586
  Educational policy, 1969
  Emigrants, 3508, 3509
  Ethnicity, 4279
  Land property, 3229
  Migrant workers, 4279

Motherhood, 3229
National identity, 4279
Population movement, 2805
Rural housing, 3793
Socialism, 4785
Trade unions, 4586
Women's status, 3229
Youth, 2676
Youth employment, 4206
Positivism, 250, 262
Post-industrial society, 1736, 2484, 2492
Poulantzas, N., 2298
Poverty, 5089, 5090, 5094, 5108, 5288
Brazil, 797
Costa Rica, 5086
Developing countries, 2982
Europe, 5101
France, 5083, 5115
France : Rouen, 4120
India, 1152, 5099
Israel, 5111
Kenya, 5085
Latin America, 1003
Madagascar, 5114
Nigeria, 2654
South Africa, 5092
Sudan, 3831
Switzerland : Geneva, 5097
USA, 5087, 5093, 5102, 5107
Power, 442, 783-86, 791, 1612, 2889
Practice, 290, 552
Pragmatism, 222, 266
Predictions, *use* Forecasts
Pregnancy, 2944, 4270
Premarital intercourse
USA, 3044, 3048
Preschool education
Dominican Republic, 2013
Spain, 2010
United Kingdom, 1995
Press, 1693, 1747, 1873
Developing countries, 1741
France, 1672, 1758, 3234
Germany, 1683
Germany FR, 1649
Hungary, 2703
Italy, 641
Madagascar, 1669
Tunisia, 1696
United Kingdom, 1719, 1732
USA, 1663, 1667, 1711, 1740
Prestige, 789, 793
Price rise
United Kingdom, 3818
Primary education
Argentina, 1992
France, 1999, 2001, 2003
India : West Bengal, 2002, 2011
Primary schools
Philippines, 2000
Primitive society, 2486, 2497
Prison, 5165, 5213, 5222

Brazil, 5167
California, 5156
Italy, 5216
USA, 4283
Prisoners, 491
USA, 5147, 5203
Privacy, 1555
Privacy protection, 1579
Private education
Argentina, 1926
Brazil, 1987
Spain, 1944
USA, 1920, 1929
Private farms
Yugoslavia, 4098
Private schools
Australia, 2016
France, 2004
South Africa, 1993
USA, 1990, 1991, 2006, 2018
Private sector, 4465
Nigeria, 4697
Probability calculus, 441
Probability models, *use* Stochastic models
Problem solving, 678
Producers, 4578
Production
France, 4014
Malaysia, 4021
Production collectivities, 2425
Production efficiency, *use* Productivity
Production functions, 1964
Production systems, 2564
Productivity, 4341
Professional ethics, *use* Deontology
Professionalization, 19, 4090
Germany FR, 4456, 5384
USA, 4926
Professions, *use* Occupations
Programme evaluation, 5382
Proletarian internationalism, 2431
Proletariat
Asia, 2274
Developing countries, 2292
France, 3505
Italy, 2289
United Kingdom, 2247
Pronatalist policy
Israel, 2980
Propaganda, 1634, 1718
Property, 2281, 3936-38, 5186
Israel, 4089
Poland, 3935
Prophecy, 790
Prostitution, 3020, 3031, 3036, 3037, 3042, 3047
Austria, 3032
Germany FR, 3032
India, 3046
Japan, 3051
Southeastern Asia, 3050
USA, 3021
Protest movements, 4938

Protestant Churches
  Canada : Quebec, 1428
  United Kingdom, 1418
  USA, 1408
Protestant ethics, 1475, 3946
  Australia, 1474
  Malaysia, 1476
  United Kingdom, 1476
Protestantism, 1335, 1377, 3946
  France, 1334
Protestants
  Ireland, 1341
  Netherlands, 1384
  Northern Ireland, 1214, 1344
  Poland, 1340
Proudhon, Pierre Joseph, 4797
Psychiatry
  Senegal, 5396
  USA, 5400
  USSR, 5397
Psychoanalysis, 207, 451, 454, 465, 476,
    1105, 1125, 1280, 1803, 1877
Psycholinguistics, 1531, 1535
Psychological anthropology, *use*
    Ethnopsychology
Psychological factors, 4401
Psychology, 467, 470, 4177
  USA, 452, 455
  USSR, 450
Psychology of education, *use*
    Educational psychology
Psychopathology, 464, 473
Psychosociology, 460, 463, 472
Psychotherapy, 672
Public administration, 3649
  Hong Kong, 4892
  Hungary, 4485
  India, 4889
  Niger, 4890
  United Kingdom, 4885
  USA, 4893
Public choice, 863, 864
  USA, 865
Public corporations, *use* Public enterprises
Public education
  Brazil, 1987
  Spain, 1944
  USA, 1988, 1989, 1990, 1991, 2006,
    2018
Public enterprises
  Canada, 4566
Public finance, 4121
Public health
  Brazil, 5407
  Latin America, 5407
  Spain, 5412, 5424
Public opinion, 835, 836, 839, 1666
  Chile, 833
  France, 377, 832, 1135
  Hungary, 3969
  Latin America, 840
  Poland, 4161

Public opinion polls, 837, 4735
  France, 1501
Public ownership
  USA, 1711
Public schools, *use* Secondary schools
Public sector, 4465
Public services, 2040
Publishing, 1668, 1680, 1712, 1745
  Arab countries, 1800
  Poland, 1695
Puerto Rico
  Migration, 3448
  Population, 2525
Punishment, 5144, 5172, 5189, 5211
  Canada, 5176
  France, 5145
  Hungary, 5184
  USA, 5215, 5217, 5230
Pupils
  Poland, 2007
Puritanism, 1478

Qualitative analysis, 338
Quality circles, 4726
  France, 4335
Quality of life, 2753, 3976, 3985, 3988
  Canada, 4028, 4362
  Eastern Europe, 3979
  France, 4369
  Germany FR, 3972
  Israel, 3804
  Norway, 3977
  USA, 3635
  Western countries, 3979
Quality of work, 4383
  France, 4427
Quantitative analysis, 365
Questionnaires, 386, 387
Quételet, Adolphe, 1216

Race, 871, 1124, 3357
Race relations, 3369, 3410
  France, 4268
  Malaysia, 3387
  South Africa, 3379, 3400
  Trinidad and Tobago, 2314
  USA, 2584, 3353, 3382, 3388, 3389, 3398,
    3406, 3420
Racial attitudes
  USA, 3409, 3426, 4767
Racial conflicts
  Sri Lanka, 3390, 3407
  United Kingdom, 3411, 4877
Racial differentiation, 5228
  Madagascar, 1347
  USA, 273, 3378, 4979
Racial discrimination
  Japan, 3431
  New Zealand, 3414
  United Kingdom, 3830
  USA, 3368, 3416, 3892, 4445, 5166, 5215
  USSR, 3393

Racial inequality, 3363
　　Trinidad and Tobago, 3424
　　USA, 3373, 3403
Racial prejudice
　　USA, 5018
Racial segregation, 3399
　　USA, 2018, 3367, 3401
Racial stereotypes
　　Canada, 3376
Racism, 564, 3281, 3357, 3361, 3362, 3366,
　　3375, 3381
　　Australia, 3432
　　France, 3383, 3391, 3427
　　Germany FR, 3370
　　South Africa, 3360
　　Sri Lanka, 3359
　　United Kingdom, 3358, 3365, 3418, 3419
　　USA, 5093
Radio, 1644
　　Costa Rica, 1690
　　France, 1679
Rape
　　USA, 5185, 5224, 5240
Rationalism, 4935
Rationality, 6, 287, 800, 1575, 2463, 2823,
　　4932, 5272
Rationalization, 2432
Rawls, John, 226
Readers
　　Germany FR, 1631
Reading habits, 548
　　Poland, 571
Reason, 232
Recidivism, 5214
Reciprocity, 586
Recruitment, 4153
Refugees
　　Africa, 3491
　　Canada, 3533
　　Norway, 3492
　　Sudan, 3488
　　Tibet, 3506
　　USA, 3518
　　Western countries, 3467
Regional analysis, 4127, 4132
　　France, 2285
Regional development, 2802
　　Australia, 4125
　　Colombia, 4135
　　Egypt, 2485
　　France, 1543
　　Japan, 4133, 4134
　　New Zealand, 4125
　　Peru, 4135
Regional disparities
　　Czechoslovakia, 2769
Regional imbalances, *use* Regional disparities
Regional planning
　　Brazil, 4129
　　Peru, 4126
Regional policy
　　Developing countries, 3785

Poland, 4130
Regionalism
　　India, 4796
　　USA, 4783
Regression analysis, 436, 438
　　Latin America, 416
Regulation, 1081, 1205, 1252
Relative deprivation, 568
Religion, 258, 841, 1222, 1265, 1274, 1278,
　　1281, 1283-84, 1287-89, 1291, 1293-95,
　　1301-02, 1312-14, 2406, 3532, 4819,
　　4884
　　Asia, 1305
　　Canada : Quebec, 4773
　　Developing countries, 1282
　　France, 1267
　　India, 1275
　　Israel, 2730
　　Japan, 1285
　　Lebanon, 3725
　　Netherlands, 1269
　　United Kingdom, 1269
　　USA, 1266, 1269, 1286, 1290, 1300, 1304,
　　1311
Religiosity, 1479, 1483
　　Israel, 2980
　　Poland, 1472, 1473
　　USA, 1290, 1480, 1487, 5117
Religious affiliation
　　USA, 1500
Religious attitudes, 1344, 1479
　　France, 1342
Religious behaviour, 1477, 1481, 1484
　　USA, 1471, 1482
Religious beliefs, 2882
　　France : Brittany, 1451
　　India, 5150
　　USA, 1413
Religious change
　　United Kingdom, 1366
Religious communities
　　Africa, 1435
　　Northern Ireland, 1421
Religious discrimination
　　United Kingdom, 1490
Religious education, 2111
　　Poland, 2109
Religious experience, 1455
Religious freedom
　　Sudan, 1485
Religious groups, 1422, 1477
　　New Zealand, 4977
　　Nigeria, 1424
　　USA, 1056
Religious history
　　France, 1403
　　Hungary, 1273
　　Reunion Island, 1307
Religious ideas, 1486
Religious institutions, 1407
　　USA, 1409
Religious liberty, *use* Religious freedom

Religious life, 1466, 1467
  Italy, 1454
Religious minorities
  Belgium, 1352
Religious movements, 1467
  USA, 1499
Religious orders, 1434
Religious practice, 1399
  France, 1488, 1501
Religious revival, 1445, 1492, 1496, 4316
  India, 1379
  USA, 1494
Religious symbolism
  Yugoslavia, 1452
Religious traditions, 1486
  India, 1014
Remarriage, 3087
  India, 3057
Representation, 819
Repression
  Chile, 5180
Research, 98, 1583
Research coordination, 118
Research financing
  USA, 116, 119, 121, 123, 130
Research foundations
  USA, 5060
Research methods, 346, 353, 533
Research policy
  USA, 104
Research programmes
  USA, 125
Research techniques, 5066
Research trends
  Switzerland, 4768
Resident satisfaction, 3905
  Israel, 3804
  Nigeria, 3877
  USA, 3906, 3930
Residential areas
  USA, 3808
Residential segregation
  Brazil, 3883
  Israel, 3853
  USA, 3897
Resistance movements
  South Africa, 2242
Resource exploitation, 2533
  Brazil, 2487
Responsibility, 4336
Retired persons
  France, 2737
  USSR, 2725
Retirement, 4450
  France, 4451
  Japan, 2747
  Japan, 3691
  USA, 4448
Return migration
  Greece, 3459
  Tunisia, 3478
  Yugoslavia, 3528

Reunion Island
  Religious history, 1307
  Social change, 2418
  Social development, 2418
  Theatre, 1849
  Youth, 2668
  Youth employment, 2668
Reviews, *use* Periodicals
Revolt
  Morocco, 1128
  Tunisia, 1128
Revolution, 216, 2287, 2438, 2458, 2461,
    2480, 4813
  Latin America, 2482
Revolutionaries, 3265
Revolutionary movements, 2458
Rice, 934
Right to strike
  Europe, 4576
Right to work, 4568
Riots
  India, 1104
  United Kingdom, 1154, 1155
Rites, 769, 1208, 2597
  Iran, 1443
  Japan, 1448
Ritual, *use* Rites
Robotics
  France, 4054
Robots, 137
Rock music
  USA, 1846
Roemer, John, 2303
Role, 800, 801, 802, 803, 804, 1082
  Canada, 3144
Role differentiation, 3627
Role playing, 2150
Role theory, 805
Romania
  Abortion, 2990
  Antisemitism, 3421
  Architecture, 1839
  Cultural policy, 1036
  Culture, 913, 927
  Family, 3122
  Intellectuals, 3421
  Literature, 1821
  Occupational qualification, 4478
  Population dynamics, 2815
  Social structure, 2182
  Sociological research, 101
  Sociology, 13, 31
  Sociology of knowledge, 1514
  Urbanization, 3894
  Workers' self-management, 4711
Romanticism, 619, 826, 3277, 3324
Rules, *use* Social norms
Ruling class, 10
  Bulgaria, 2346
Rural areas, 1483, 3610, 4239
  Canada, 5196
  China, 2917, 2959

France, 904
Hungary, 5273
India, 3942, 4499
Poland, 1013, 2759, 4510
USA, 430, 2335, 3741, 4083, 5245
USSR, 3676
Yugoslavia, 3127
Rural communities, 3181
France, 3697
France : Provence, 3699
Japan, 3691, 3739
Mexico, 3714
Zaire, 3712
Rural development, 2415, 3649, 3652,
3666, 3722
Africa, 3664, 5091
Burkina-Faso, 3658
China, 3648, 3718
Congo, 3707
Developing countries, 3695
India, 3688, 3698, 3703, 3708, 3715-17,
3721, 3731, 3734
Israel, 3693
Jamaica, 1854
Latin America, 3650
Lebanon, 3725
Nicaragua, 3711
Nigeria, 3538
Socialist countries, 3728
USA, 3635
USSR, 3742
Yugoslavia, 3672
Rural dwellings, *use* Rural housing
Rural employment
Argentina, 4189
Rural environment
Europe, 3706
Rural exodus, *use* Rural-urban migration
Rural history
France, 3697
Rural housing
Portugal, 3793
Rural life
Korea R, 3667
United Kingdom, 3719
USSR, 3726, 3740
Rural population
Hungary, 2821
India, 2808
Latin America, 2770
Poland, 571, 1004, 1042, 1112, 1202,
1472, 2170, 2791-93, 2799, 3984, 4505
Turkey, 4965
Yugoslavia, 2798, 2816
Rural poverty
Bangladesh, 5116
India, 5098
Philippines : Leyte, 5103
USA, 5105
Rural schools
Burkina-Faso, 2014
Rural society, 3647

India : Bengal, 3661
Nepal, 3959
Taiwan, 3735
Thailand, 3690
Rural sociology
Developing countries, 3704
Hungary, 3737
Rural women, 2765
Bangladesh, 5116
Europe, 2783
Uruguay, 2800
Rural youth, 1981
India, 2699
Poland, 2704, 4437
Rural-urban migration, 3544, 3556
China, 3550
Developing countries, 3567
India, 3539, 3540, 3551
Korea R, 3548
Philippines, 3569
Thailand, 3549
USSR, 3570
Yugoslavia, 3558

Sacred, 1453, 1460
India, 1449
Italy, 1454
Sacrifice, 1442
Safety devices, 204
Sailors, *use* Seafarers
Saint-Simon, Claude-Henri de, 2318
Saints, 1468
Sanctions, 1082
Sartre, Jean-Paul, 82, 2083
Satellite towns
USSR, 3828
Saudi Arabia
Health, 5431
Scale analysis, 447
Scalogram analysis, *use* Hierarchical scale
Scandinavia
Intellectuals, 2353
Welfare State, 5306
Women's status, 3276
Scanlon, Joseph, 4564
School achievement, *use* Academic success
School administration, 2024
Belgium, 2023
France, 2020
School children, *use* Pupils
School desegregation
USA, 1948
School discipline
USA, 2022
School environment
France, 2021
School failure, 2116
France, 2115
USA, 2120
School management, *use* School administration
School segregation
United Kingdom, 3349

School-community relationship
  Colombia, 1933
  Costa Rica, 1936
  USA, 1930, 1979
Schooling, 4455
  France, 1957
  Nicaragua, 1986
  USA, 1928, 1950, 2585, 4476
Schools, 633
  Germany FR, 2012
  USA, 1994, 2017
  Zaire, 2005
Schumpeter, J., 5048
Schütz, Alfred, 208, 233
Science, 1227, 1335, 1377, 1504, 1512, 1515,
    1516, 1521, 1524, 2475
  India, 1503
  USA, 1502
Science policy, 117
  Africa South of the Sahara, 120
  Canada, 126
  Germany, 128
  Greece, 127
  Netherlands, 129
Sciences of education, 1890
  France, 1860
Sciences of man, *use* Social sciences
Scientific and technical progress, 3900, 4030,
    4050
  USSR, 4017
Scientific community, 74, 2571
  Canada, 126
  India, 124
  Israel, 122
Scientific research, 4045
  Peru, 4020
  USA, 4042
Scientists, 73, 74, 79
  Israel, 89
  USA, 84
Scotland
  Civil society, 2499
  Economic history, 3931
  National development, 2499
  Social history, 3931
  State, 2499
Seafarers, 4512, 4520
  USA, 1110
Seasons, 2949
Secondary education, 2144
  France, 1996, 2009
  Ireland, 1997
  Israel, 2015
  Japan, 2008
  USSR, 1866
Secondary groups, *use* Complex organizations
Secondary schools, 1998
  Belgium, 2023
  Japan, 1103, 1967
  Kenya : Nairobi, 2019
Sects, 1423, 1429
  France, 1419

Germany FR, 1420
Guyana, 703
India, 3213
Japan, 1439
USA, 1413
Secularization, 1491, 1493
  Iceland, 1497
  Turkey, 1489
Self-assessment, *use* Self-evaluation
Self-concept, 94, 488, 490, 492, 511, 5322
Self-esteem, 491, 495, 498, 2118
Self-evaluation, 497
Self-expression, 494
Self-management, 708
  Chile, 770
  Peru, 770
Self-perception, 493
  Germany FR, 5174
Self-reliance
  Zimbabwe, 2428
Semiology, 1529
Senegal
  Associations, 730
  Forced labour, 4347
  Psychiatry, 5396
  Towns, 730
  Trade unionism, 4604
  Villages, 3673
Seniority
  USA, 4192
Serres, Michel, 85
Sex, 232, 2561, 5468
  India, 2608
Sex differentiation, 545, 789, 1464, 2188,
    2570, 2592, 2610, 2613, 2632, 2762,
    2879, 3975, 4305, 5191
  Sweden, 2609
  USA, 2585, 5159, 5252
Sex discrimination, 2573, 2628, 4287
  Australia, 2596
  India, 4236
  India : West Bengal, 2002
  Netherlands, 2618
  Switzerland, 2616
  United Kingdom, 4253, 5244
  USA, 2576, 2578, 3987, 4445
Sex distribution, 4509
Sex equality, 2579
  Sweden, 2630
  USA, 2582, 2601, 2611
Sex roles, 801, 1210, 1569, 2564, 2567, 2590,
    2593, 2594, 2603, 2615, 2619, 2624,
    2627, 3088, 4254
  Africa, 2568
  Australia, 2612
  France, 2622
  Ireland, 1997
  Israel, 2623
  Netherlands, 1953
  USA, 820, 2569, 2591, 3054, 4299,
    4712
Sexism, 2574, 2604, 3366

Sexual behaviour, 3023, 3024
    Canada, 3035
    France, 3045, 3049
    Ivory Coast, 3040
    USA, 3027, 3053
Sexual harassment
    USA, 3041
Sexual union, *use* Consensual union
Sexuality, 3022
    China, 1817
    Japan, 3116
    Maghreb, 3025
    USA, 3030
Shamanism
    Nepal, 1318
Sharecropping, 4095
    USA, 4084
Shift work, 4417
Shipbuilding
    United Kingdom, 740
Shop stewards
    United Kingdom, 4659
Sick persons, *use* Patients
Sierra Leone
    Life satisfaction, 562
Signs, 1568
Simmel, Georg, 199, 217, 4117
Simulation techniques, 760
Singapore
    Class structure, 2326
    Community development, 3646
    Divorce, 3102
    Language planning, 1613
    Language policy, 1707
    Social mobility, 2326
    Social problems, 5076
    Television, 1707
    Women's role, 2599
Single-parent family, *use* One-parent family
Size of enterprise, 4391
    USA, 3997
Skill demands, *use* Job requirements
Skills
    USA, 4176
Slavery
    Africa, 2237
    South Africa, 2242
Slowdowns
    Israel, 4672
Slums
    Brazil, 1212, 3792
    Developing countries, 3869, 3879, 3880
    India, 3891
    Italy, 3795
    Netherlands, 4187
    USA, 2120
Small and medium enterprises, 4002
    France, 4005
    Italy, 4007, 4008, 4529, 4846
Small groups, 669, 673, 674, 678, 681
Smallpox
    Finland, 2541

Smith, Wilfried Cantwell, 1486
Smoking, 5134
    United Kingdom, 5409
    USA, 2891
Sociability
    China, 1817
    France, 575, 1417
Social action, 5258, 5270, 5289, 5297, 5305,
        5314, 5316, 5332, 5392
    Developing countries, 5303
    France, 5327
Social adaptation
    Australia, 1165
    USA, 1117
Social anthropology, 879
    Developing countries, 3704
    United Kingdom, 214
Social behaviour, 106, 574, 1125, 1157, 1178,
        1186, 1193, 5305
    Poland, 1139
    USA, 1115
Social biology, 34, 68, 70, 751
    USA, 41
Social casework, *use* Casework
Social change, 799, 1051, 1209, 2156, 2161,
        2307, 2413-15, 2421-24, 2426-27, 2442,
        2447, 2452-54, 2465, 2467, 2474, 2476,
        2478-79, 2583, 2705, 3642, 3912, 3963,
        4035, 5285, 5297, 5399
    Canada, 3777
    Developing countries, 2440
    Eastern Europe, 4920
    France, 724, 2436
    Germany FR, 299
    Hungary, 2446
    India, 2234, 2243, 2459, 2462, 2466,
        3715, 3734, 4912
    Japan : Takarazuka, 3789
    Jordan, 2481, 3319
    Nepal, 2434
    Reunion Island, 2418
    Spain, 2455, 2477
    Thailand, 3786
Social classes, 1091, 1124, 2192, 2252, 2281,
        2308, 2319, 2327, 2567, 3936, 3975
    Africa, 2248
    Benin, 2300
    Canada, 481, 2261
    Central Africa, 2279
    Ghana : Accra, 2614
    India : Bengal, 3661
    Japan, 2271, 2325
    Poland, 2272
    Sweden, 2264, 2323
    Trinidad and Tobago, 2314
    United Kingdom, 2246, 2620, 2949
    Western Asia, 2286
    Yugoslavia, 2222
    Zambia, 2302
Social communication, *use* Communication
Social conditions
    Africa, 5091

Brazil, 371
France, 2452
Hungary, 5273
India, 2398, 5300
Netherlands, 5318
Peru, 5286
United Kingdom, 994
Yugoslavia, 5317
Social conflicts, 639, 640, 2230, 4700
Brazil, 651
Guatemala, 654
Italy, 641
Poland, 643, 650, 658
Social conformity, 1171
Social consciousness, 480, 1093, 1100, 1120,
1122, 1131, 1133, 1149, 1151, 1160,
1722, 2403
Japan, 2691, 4133
Peru, 5033
Poland, 1112, 2213
Social contract, 2157
Social control, 746, 839, 1063, 1064, 1070,
1074, 1079, 1171, 1252, 2162, 2230
Austria, 1048
United Kingdom, 5130
USA, 1071, 1755
Social data, *use* Social information
Social development, 294, 516, 957, 1166,
2200, 2397, 2412, 2417, 2425, 2431,
2433, 2437, 2448, 2449, 2450, 2457,
2460, 2472, 2475, 3320, 4034
Africa, 2444
Brazil, 2420
Czechoslovakia, 2439
Hungary, 2439
Indonesia, 2430
Japan, 2435
Reunion Island, 2418
USSR, 2163, 2429, 2443, 2473
Zimbabwe, 2428
Social differentiation, 2184, 2200, 2227
Mexico, 3714
United Kingdom, 2197
Social disadvantage
France, 5074
Social disorganization, 1842, 2422
Poland, 658
USA, 3741, 3803
Social distance
Germany FR, 3313
India, 1097
Social doctrines, 1426
Spain, 1380
Social dynamics, 2406
Social environment, 3575
France, 3193
Poland, 1218
Social equality, 2193, 2208, 2223, 2231
Hungary, 2210
Poland, 2210
Social equilibrium, 2175
Social evolution, *use* Social change

Social exchange, 2174
Social factors, 926
Social groups, *use* Groups
Social hierarchy, *use* Social stratification
Social history, 1234, 1436, 2391, 2393, 2402,
2406, 3124, 3445, 5255
Austria, 3663
Europe, 5101
France, 1417, 1983, 3049, 3232, 3234,
3252, 3662, 5128
Germany, 2126, 2401, 3675, 4242, 4275,
4276, 4658
India, 2398
Iran, 2394, 3417
Ireland, 3931
Italy, 2400, 4644
Japan, 923, 2181
Netherlands, 5318
Scotland, 3931
Spain, 504
United Kingdom, 2246, 2399, 2803, 3818,
4814
USA, 3095, 3736, 3811
Social housing
Belgium, 3800
France, 3791, 3929
Social indicators, 300, 419, 430, 437, 2186
CMEA countries, 411
Czechoslovakia, 423
Japan, 432
Poland, 415
United Kingdom, 5265
USSR, 425
Social inequality, 2186, 2189, 2192-93,
2195-96, 2204, 2207, 2225, 2229-30,
4229, 4305
Brazil, 1956
Eastern Europe, 2209
France, 2194, 2199, 2886
Hungary, 2210-11, 3790
India, 5413
India : Bengal, 2214, 3669
Mexico, 2217
Poland, 2210, 2211, 2213
Taiwan, 2201
United Kingdom, 2885
Yugoslavia, 2222
Social influence, 485, 1199
Social information, 5063, 5064, 5065, 5067
France, 5061
Social infrastructure, 2159
Social insurance, *use* Social security
Social integration, 699, 1089, 1105, 1124,
2171, 3439
Yugoslavia, 1088
Social interaction, 580, 1094, 1159, 1162,
1175, 1702
Social isolation, 582, 4217
France, 1085
Social judgment, 603, 610, 3724
Poland, 2229
USA, 611

Social justice, 5263, 5272, 5308, 5338
  India, 4236
  USA, 1928
Social legislation
  Spain, 5340
Social life, 52, 858, 1166, 1176, 1177
  Japan, 369
  USSR, 1173
Social medicine, 5399
Social mobility, 2050, 2215, 2373, 2380, 2626,
    2661, 3110
  Arab countries, 2381
  Canada, 2368, 2383
  Capitalist countries, 2382
  France, 2375, 2387, 2388
  Germany, 2377
  Germany FR, 2369
  Hungary, 2374, 2384
  India, 2386, 3297
  India : Assam, 2233
  Iran, 3164
  Japan, 2232, 2379
  Malaysia, 2326
  Poland, 2272
  Singapore, 2326
  Sweden, 2375
  United Kingdom, 1366, 2375
  USA, 2385
  Yugoslavia, 2371
Social movements, 744, 763, 769, 869, 4928,
    4930, 4933, 4935, 4939-40, 4942-43,
    4946, 4951, 4954
  Canada, 4923
  Developing countries, 4934
  Eastern Europe, 4920
  Europe, 4922
  France, 4936
  Germany FR, 4924, 4925
  India, 4921
  Israel, 4937
  Latin America, 4927
  United Kingdom, 2096
  USA, 4926, 4952
  Venezuela, 4929
Social networks, 360, 392, 615, 662-63,
    667-68, 670-71, 759
  Netherlands, 1530
  USA, 661, 664
Social norms, 1051, 1054, 1062, 1068, 1076,
    1078, 1081, 1082
  France, 1057
  USA, 2709, 3048
Social order, 1064, 2162, 2176, 2178
  India, 1261
  Italy, 2158
  Japan, 992
Social origin, 2329, 2337
  Sweden, 2117
  USA, 5439
Social participation, 1142, 1168
  France, 1092
  India, 1095

Social pathology, 5071, 5077
Social perception, 490, 602, 606, 5095
  Poland, 2213
Social philosophy, 5331
Social planning, 5285, 5304, 5323, 5333
  Czechoslovakia, 423
  Poland, 415
  United Kingdom, 5337
  USSR, 5277
Social pluralism, 2208, 5338
Social policy, 46, 418-19, 2433, 2678, 4224,
    5260, 5269, 5271, 5275, 5282-84, 5288,
    5290, 5293, 5312, 5319, 5324, 5328
  Argentina, 5069
  Austria, 5309
  Denmark, 5295
  Developing countries, 5281, 5302
  France, 4049
  German DR, 5264
  Germany FR, 5261, 5280, 5301, 5315
  Hungary, 5274
  India, 5287
  Italy : Southern, 5313
  Poland, 2696, 5268
  United Kingdom, 4131, 5265
  USA, 5253, 5296, 5310, 5330
  USSR, 5325
Social power, *use* Social control
Social pressure, *use* Social control
Social problems, 5072, 5262
  Argentina, 5069
  Developing countries, 5068
  India, 4889
  Singapore, 5076
  United Kingdom, 5075
  USA, 4213
Social progress, *use* Social development
Social protest, 568, 1130, 5165
  India, 5109
  USA, 1181
Social psychology, 189, 400, 453, 457, 459,
    460, 468, 471, 478, 824, 3449, 4114,
    4535
  USA, 458, 466
  USSR, 479
  Western Europe, 474
Social reforms
  Poland, 5276
Social relations, 74, 530, 1091, 1141, 1143, 1389
  France, 3778
  Hungary, 1109
Social reproduction, 2161, 2169, 2173, 4160
  Mexico, 2133
  Poland, 1961
  United Kingdom, 2160
Social research, 187, 5056, 5058, 5059, 5066
  India, 5060
  Japan, 5062
  USA, 186
Social role, *use* Role
Social science research, 97, 100, 106, 108,
    109, 157, 365, 2625

France, 103
Germany FR, 96
United Kingdom, 103, 105
USA, 92, 104
Social sciences, 1, 15, 30, 48, 53, 64, 134,
    243, 406, 2389
Chile, 14
France, 24
Panama, 26
USA, 27, 28, 32, 119, 121, 123, 130
Social security, 5342, 5348, 5363, 5370, 5371
Brazil, 5357
Cameroon, 5355
China, 5375
Costa Rica, 5372
Developed countries, 5367
Developing countries, 5345, 5368
France, 5351, 5364
Gabon, 5359
India, 4553, 5347
Latin America, 5361
Switzerland, 5349
United Kingdom, 5366
Social services, 3175, 3624, 5459, 5460
Canada, 5466
Denmark, 5471
India, 5470
Italy, 5476
Netherlands, 5465
New Zealand, 5467
Spain, 5478
Turkey, 5481
USA, 5464
Social status, 2118, 2122, 2151, 2331, 2332,
    2338, 3627, 4494
Hungary, 2330
Poland, 4468
USA, 2333, 2334, 2335, 2336, 4481
Social stereotypes, 2613
Social stratification, 1561, 2187, 2198, 2215,
    2220, 2270, 2329, 2626
Argentina, 2032
Canada, 2216, 2261
China, 2324
France, 2191
Hungary, 2212, 2228, 4514
India, 2202
Japan, 2206, 2232, 2325
Latin America, 2185
Netherlands, 2719
Poland, 4514
Switzerland, 2190
United Kingdom, 3910
USA, 2205, 5403
Social structure, 228, 244, 316, 344, 662, 699,
    787, 2155, 2156, 2164, 2166, 2171,
    2177, 3191, 3194, 3363, 4158
Canada, 340
France, 2179
Hungary, 2165
India, 2172
Italy, 2168

Japan, 369, 2181, 2456
Korea R, 2167
Poland, 2170, 5073
Romania, 2182
Spain, 2464
USSR, 2163, 2725
Social success, 597
Social surveys, 301
Caribbean, 375
USA, 376
Social system, 198, 2180
Yugoslavia, 2154
Social theory, 206, 268, 786, 1000, 4806,
    4928, 5054, 5299, 5321, 5339
Social unrest, 963, 2478, 5070
Poland, 5073
USA, 2041, 5434
Social values, 799, 973
Social welfare, 5266, 5278
Denmark, 5298
India, 2881
Sweden, 5298
Taiwan, 5254
Social work, 5275, 5382, 5383, 5388, 5391, 5392
Argentina, 5381
Brazil, 5167
France, 5380
Germany FR, 5384, 5384
Japan, 5389
Sweden, 5390
Turkey, 5481
United Kingdom, 5386, 5387
USA, 1930
Social workers, 5468, 5474
United Kingdom, 5445
USA, 5480
Socialism, 17, 517, 3964, 4779, 4782, 4784,
    4789, 4802, 4829
Bulgaria, 4660
France, 4788, 4797
Poland, 2007
Portugal, 4785
USSR, 4790
Socialist countries, 3956
Employees, 4524
Family, 3201
Holidays, 4732
Human rights, 4863
Industrial workers, 4732
Interest groups, 4950
Law, 1256
Money, 4119
Peasantry, 3728
Population, 2512
Rural development, 3728
Urban environment, 3846
Urban planning, 3913
Way of life, 948
Women's role, 3231
Women's status, 3231
Socialist culture, 928
Socialist economy, 5312

Socialist society, 147, 835, 902, 907, 1070,
2437, 2460, 3948, 3949, 3950, 3951,
4715, 4917, 4978, 5285
German DR, 3940
Socialist way of life, 929, 940, 962, 993, 1786,
2159
Socialization, 510, 1102, 1148, 1156, 1172,
1217, 1904, 2728, 3190, 4331, 5463
France, 2020
Poland, 1129
United Kingdom, 4875
Society, 872, 936, 963, 967, 970, 981, 986,
998, 2427, 3578, 3598, 3599, 3601,
3604, 3621, 4868
Algeria, 894
Argentina, 901
France, 888
Hungary, 956
Italy, 897
Japan, 992
Latin America, 1796
Malaysia, 4021
Norway, 894
United Kingdom, 994
USSR, 917, 921
Sociobiology, *use* Social biology
Sociolinguistics, 1527, 1528, 1532, 1536
Netherlands, 1530
Spain, 1534
USSR, 2429
Yugoslavia, 1533
Sociological analysis, 303, 371, 1505
Sociological associations
United Kingdom, 177
Sociological education, *use* Teaching of sociology
Sociological methodology, 106, 303, 305, 313,
323, 329-30, 334, 337, 342, 350,
354-56
Sociological research, 94, 95, 107, 291
Romania, 101
USA, 93, 99, 102
USSR, 2163
Sociological theory, 194, 196, 199, 202, 206,
208, 210-11, 213, 216, 226-27, 236,
247, 251-53, 257, 260, 263, 268-69,
391, 963
Germany, 217
India, 235
Poland, 240
Sociologists, 38, 75, 87, 88, 90, 1460
France, 171
India, 81
Poland, 80
USA, 77, 83
USSR, 78
Yugoslavia, 91
Sociology, 9, 11, 17, 23, 25, 44, 46, 47, 50,
52, 60, 75
Argentina, 3
Australia, 12
Chile, 18, 19
France, 22, 33

Germany, 6
Germany FR, 42, 69
India, 35, 39, 57, 61
Italy, 56
Nigeria, 7
Poland, 65
Romania, 13, 31
USA, 16, 20, 45, 66, 4823
Yugoslavia, 2
Sociology of art, 951, 1772
Sociology of culture, 871, 873, 874, 876, 882,
1000
Japan, 877
Sociology of development, 2493, 3666
India, 2488
Sociology of education, *use* Educational
sociology
Sociology of family, 2570, 3143, 3149, 3156
Hungary, 3115
Sociology of knowledge, 286, 1505-11,
1517-19, 4807, 5072
Romania, 1514
Sociology of law, 1236, 1240-41, 1246-47,
1249, 1259
Australia, 1253
Sociology of literature, 340, 1799, 1801, 1813,
1824
Sociology of occupations, *use* Occupational
sociology
Sociology of organizations, 709, 4139
Japan, 711
Sociology of religion, 1268, 1270, 1277,
1280-81, 1298, 1306, 1308, 1310, 1315,
1467, 1484
Europe, 1296
France, 1292
Netherlands, 1264
USA, 1271, 1272
Sociology of science, *use* Sociology of
knowledge 1514
Sociology of sport, 4753
Sociology of work, 2570, 4138, 4139, 4142,
4145
France, 2285
Japan, 4140
Sociometric relations, 347, 615
Sociometry, 462
Sola Pool, Ithiel de, 183
Solidarity, 5293
Africa, 614
Korea R, 3667
Poland, 622
Soldiers, *use* Military personnel
Sorel, Georges, 2438
South Africa
Antisemitism, 3423
Apartheid, 3384, 3412, 3413, 3415
Authoritarianism, 4804
Civil rights, 3400
Class struggle, 2290
Conservatism, 4804
Domestic workers, 4523

Education, 1870
Industrial employment, 3415
Labour market, 4165
Law, 1243
Liberalism, 4805
Marriage, 3072
Migrant workers, 2290
Organizational behaviour, 738
Poverty, 5092
Private schools, 1993
Race relations, 3379, 3400
Racism, 3360
Resistance movements, 2242
Slavery, 2242
Sport, 4755
Towns, 3835
Trade unionism, 4593
Trade unions, 4628, 4663, 4664
Women's work, 4235
South Africa : Pretoria
Aged, 2760
Living conditions, 2760
Southeastern Asia
Economic life, 3326
Ethnicity, 3326
Prostitution, 3050
Tourist trade, 3050
Southern Africa
Art, 1764
Capital cities, 3744
Family life, 3108
Women's status, 3211
Women's work, 3211
Southern Asia
History, 2392
Islam, 1388
Moslems, 1388
Statistical data, 424
Space, 332
Spain
Attitudes, 3112
Care of the aged, 5478
Catholicism, 1364, 1380
Childhood, 2649
Cinema, 1727
Collective bargaining, 4607
Cultural identity, 1034
Culture, 982
Demographic research, 2547
Divorce, 3091
Education, 1895
Educational innovations, 2010
Educational reforms, 1935
Electoral abstentionism, 5013
Emigrants, 1034
Emigration, 3514
Ethnicity, 987
Family, 2649
Family life, 3112
History of education, 1889
Identity, 504
Industrial sociology, 4137

Juvenile delinquency, 5164
Labour movements, 4608
Labour relations, 4546
Mass media, 1716
Modernization, 2464, 2477
National identity, 987
Nationalism, 4795
Occupational accidents, 4426
Parent-child relations, 2649
Party systems, 4911
Preschool education, 2010
Private education, 1944
Public education, 1944
Public health, 5412, 5424
Social change, 2455, 2477
Social doctrines, 1380
Social history, 504
Social legislation, 5340
Social services, 5478
Social structure, 2464
Sociolinguistics, 1534
Television, 1656
Trade unionism, 4607
Trade unions, 4640
Women, 3112
Women's work, 4240, 4297
Youth, 2667
Youth policy, 2677
Spain : Catalonia
Mass media, 1685
Spatial distribution, 3611
Special education, 2110, 2112
Speech analysis, 1603, 1617, 1622, 1628, 1629
Argentina, 1627
France, 1624
Spencer, Herbert, 202
Spinoza, Baruch, 1161
Sport, 512, 4741, 4748, 4756, 4759
Brazil, 4751
France, 4757
South Africa, 4755
United Kingdom, 975
USA, 4746
Sportsmen
Hungary, 2330
Sprout, Harold, 3590
Sprout, Margaret, 3590
Squatters
India, 3891
Kenya, 3764
Netherlands, 3796
Sri Lanka
Castes, 2241
Malnutrition, 5110
Mortality, 2874
Racial conflicts, 3390, 3407
Racism, 3359
Youth, 2690
Srole's scale, *use* Anomie
Standard of living
USSR, 425
Yugoslavia, 3840

Starvation, *use* Famine
State, 2252, 3206, 3523, 4799, 4800, 4827-28,
    4836, 4840, 4844
  France, 4843
  Hungary, 4833
  Italy, 4846
  Mediterranean countries, 4822
  Scotland, 2499
  USSR, 4845
State building
  Nicaragua, 4834
State capitalism
  Egypt, 3945
  Tanzania, 3732
State farms
  Poland, 3169, 4510, 4710
State intervention, 4839, 4847
  New Zealand, 4136
  United Kingdom, 4825
State monopoly capitalism, *use* State capitalism
Statistical analysis, 417, 421, 422, 427, 433,
    2194, 2779
Statistical data, 429
  Southern Asia, 424
Statistical tables, 3092
Statistics, 408, 409, 412, 434, 1216
  Bulgaria, 413
  Hungary, 426
Status attainment, 2378
  Northern Ireland, 1421
  USA, 2370, 2372, 2376
Stereotypes, 823, 3315, 5191
  USA, 820
Stochastic models, 279
  Brazil, 444
Stoetzel, Jean, 285
Strikes, 4674
  Colombia, 4670
  Europe, 4687
  France, 4682
  Israel, 4672
  Sweden, 4683
  United Kingdom, 4675, 4683
  USA, 4685, 4687
  Western Europe, 4684
Structural analysis, 212, 298, 309, 314, 333,
    340, 348, 351, 352, 397
  Japan, 322
Structural change
  Capitalist countries, 2382
Structuralism, 197, 200, 215, 244, 245, 251,
    255, 261, 1506
  United Kingdom, 214
Student behaviour
  USA, 2029, 2041
Student movements
  Bolivia, 2057
  Canada, 2056
  Developing countries, 2031
  France, 2038
  Germany FR, 2038, 2056
  Indonesia, 2068

  USA, 2056
  Yugoslavia, 2066
Students, 823, 1122, 1133, 2033, 2329
  Argentina, 2032
  China, 2073
  Germany, 2051
  India, 1152, 1174
  Indonesia, 560
  Israel, 2079
  Morocco, 2064
  Netherlands, 935
  Pakistan, 834
  USA, 1181, 2072, 3637, 5472
  Zambia, 2076
Sturzo, Luigi, 10
Subculture, 1429
Subjectivity, 173, 294, 295, 501, 509, 878, 2761
Suburban areas
  Developing countries, 3869
  France : Paris, 3844
  Italy, 3795
  Japan : Takarazuka, 3789
  USA, 3756, 3802, 3907
Sudan
  Family planning, 2995
  Poverty, 3831
  Refugees, 3488
  Religious freedom, 1485
  Tenant farmers, 3713
  Urban development, 3831
Suicide, 5151, 5158, 5228, 5249
  France, 5154
  Germany FR, 1180
  Italy, 5163
  Japan, 5205
  USA, 4215, 5149, 5243
Sumner, William Graham, 58
Superannuation, *use* Retirement
Supervisors, 4533
Surinam
  Civilization, 997
Survey analysis, 299, 341
Surveys, 378
  Nepal, 379
Swanson, Guy E., 1271
Sweden
  Academic success, 2117
  Education, 2323
  Employment policy, 4223
  Gangs, 2684
  Higher education, 2055, 2062, 2067
  Income inequality, 2323
  Kinship, 3119
  Marginal people, 2684
  Mass media, 1689
  Middle class, 2117
  Mortality, 2850
  Plant size, 4683
  Politics, 2609
  Sex differentiation, 2609
  Sex equality, 2630
  Social classes, 2264, 2323

Social mobility, 2375
Social origin, 2117
Social welfare, 5298
Social work, 5390
Strikes, 4683
Way of life, 945
Wildcat strikes, 4671
Women's status, 3214
Youth, 2684
Switzerland
  Business communication, 3993
  Contraception, 2983
  Criminal justice, 5232
  Cultural conflicts, 1038
  Cultural norms, 5414
  Death, 2889
  Dialects, 1592
  Educational planning, 1973
  Educational policy, 1973
  Folk culture, 2889
  Foreign workers, 1038, 4230, 4277, 4278
  Foreigners, 3440
  Health management, 5414
  Human physiology, 2634
  Immigrant assimilation, 1038
  Income inequality, 3989
  Migrants, 3440
  Periodicals, 185
  Plebiscite, 5014
  Political sociology, 4768
  Research trends, 4768
  Sex discrimination, 2616
  Social security, 5349
  Social stratification, 2190
  Women, 3440
  Youth, 2673
  Youth organizations, 2669
Switzerland : Geneva
  Poverty, 5097
Switzerland : Zurich
  Youth organizations, 2706
Syllabus, *use* Curriculum
Symbolic interaction, 1561, 1576, 1577
Symbolism, 769, 1560, 2406
  India, 1559
Symbols, 244, 951
  Canada, 1547
Syndicalism, *use* Trade unionism
Systems analysis, 311, 320, 321, 343, 344,
    357, 716, 2147
Systems of education, *use* Educational systems

Taiwan
  Cults, 1447
  Family, 2641
  Family environment, 2201
  Income distribution, 2201
  Intergenerational relations, 2641
  Population distribution, 2797
  Rural society, 3735
  Social inequality, 2201
  Social welfare, 5254

Urban society, 3820
Women's employment, 4266
Tanzania
  Demand for labour, 2939
  Fertility, 2939
  Mining, 4396
  Peasantry, 3732
  Political parties, 4914
  State capitalism, 3732
  Unemployed, 4197
  Women, 2600
  Women's work, 4292
  Working conditions, 4396
Taxation
  France, 4122
  United Kingdom, 4118
Teacher training, 2129
  France, 2139
  Western Europe, 2135
Teacher-student relationship, 2138, 2144,
    2145, 5234
  France, 2140
Teachers, 2127, 2137, 2150, 2151
  France, 2143, 2146
  Germany, 2126
  Japan, 1967
  United Kingdom, 4649
  USA, 2131, 2142
Teaching, 2147
  Arab countries, 2153
  USA, 2124, 2149
Teaching aids, 2123, 2141
  Mexico, 2133
  USA, 2148
Teaching methods, 2130
Teaching of sociology, 38, 54, 55, 346, 3156
  France, 8
  Germany FR, 67
  USA, 49
Technical progress, *use* Technological change
Technical unemployment, 4216
Technological change, 4018, 4034, 4037,
    4053, 4441
  Bulgaria, 4056
  Developing countries, 4025
  France, 4046, 4496, 4602
  Mediterranean countries, 4064
  USA, 4602
Technology, 4023, 4024, 4036, 4044
  Ireland, 4033
  USSR, 4061
Technology transfer, 4059, 4065, 4128
Telecommunications, 1643, 1673
  USA, 1761
Television, 388, 1589, 1682, 1702, 1703,
    1705, 1710, 1713, 1730, 1756, 1762,
    2588
  Eastern Europe, 1733
  France, 1679, 1717
  Hungary, 1692
  Japan, 1654, 1746
  North America, 1665

Singapore, 1707
Spain, 1656
USA, 1640, 1646, 1661, 1714, 1735, 1755, 4109, 4976
Tenant farmers
   Sudan, 3713
   USA, 3736
Tenants
   USA, 3798
Terror
   USSR, 1260
Terrorism, 1086, 1087, 1144, 1179
   Europe, 1119
   Germany FR, 1107, 1158
   Italy, 1101, 1138
   Latin America, 1153
   Western Europe, 1118
Textbooks, 187, 188, 189, 190, 191
Textile industry, 3944
   France, 3941
   Germany, 3250
   USA, 2328, 4630
Thailand
   Capital cities, 3908
   Class conflicts, 3690
   Class formation, 2255
   Family planning, 2968, 2975
   Fertility decline, 2930
   Parent-child relations, 3110
   Peasantry, 2255, 3690
   Rural society, 3690
   Rural-urban migration, 3549
   Social change, 3786
   Towns, 3786
   Trade unionism, 4665
   Women's status, 3264
Theatre, 1856
   Africa, 1852
   Bangladesh, 1855
   Belgium, 1851
   Canada, 1850
   China, 1857
   Jamaica, 1854
   Reunion Island, 1849
Theology, 1297, 1303
   Latin America, 1309
Theory, 249
Theory of culture, 990
Theory of education, 1874, 1886, 1901
   France, 1893
Theory of games, *use* Game theory
Therapeutic groups, 672, 677
Thesaurus, 167, 1914
Third World, *use* Developing countries
Thomas, W. I., 5
Tibet
   Refugees, 3506
Time, 316, 319, 331, 2729
Time budgets
   Brazil, 4405
   Finland, 4351, 4352
   France, 904, 3158, 4402, 4404

Germany FR, 4408
Hungary, 4350, 4351, 4352
Norway, 4406
Poland, 4437
Time series, 410, 418, 420, 4215, 4545
Time study, *use* Work study
Togo
   Family, 2938
   Fertility, 2938
Tolerance
   Israel, 830
   USA, 830
Tönnies, F., 3621
Totalitarianism, 4811, 4815
Touraine, Alain, 4940
Tourism, 4739, 4740, 4742
   Belgium, 4758
   EEC countries, 4750
   France, 3871, 4738
Tourist trade
   Developing countries, 4752
   Southeastern Asia, 3050
Town centre
   USA, 3892
Town planning, *use* Urban planning
Towns, 3761, 3762, 3773, 3794, 3827, 3837, 3909
   Canada, 3850
   Congo, 730
   Developing countries, 3842
   India, 3891
   Mexico, 3780
   Senegal, 730
   South Africa, 3835
   Thailand, 3786
   USA, 3745, 3750, 3811
   USSR, 3754, 3876, 3895
Trade union action
   Italy, 4596
Trade unionism
   Chile, 4587, 4645
   France, 4650
   Germany FR, 1675
   Italy, 4579
   Japan, 4614
   Senegal, 4604
   South Africa, 4593
   Spain, 4607
   Thailand, 4665
   United Kingdom, 4638, 4643
   USA, 4606
Trade unions, 4600, 4622
   Argentina, 4582, 4669
   Brazil, 4657
   Canada, 4620
   Chile, 4592
   Denmark, 4591
   Eastern Europe, 4625
   EEC countries, 4637
   Egypt, 4615
   France, 4581, 4602, 4623, 4653
   Germany FR, 4601, 4623, 4636

Hungary, 4635, 4639
India, 4652, 4655
Israel, 4616, 4651, 4688
Italy, 2289, 4220, 4605, 4656
Japan, 4601
Mexico, 4624, 4661
Netherlands, 4632
Norway, 4634
Poland, 4627, 4639, 4641
Portugal, 4586
South Africa, 4628, 4663, 4664
Spain, 4640
United Kingdom, 864, 4583-85, 4588-90,
    4609, 4612, 4631, 4649, 4667
USA, 455, 2142, 4444, 4547, 4597, 4602,
    4610, 4630, 4633
Vietnam, 4629
Western Europe, 4621
Traditional medicine
Brazil, 5398
Guadeloupe, 5394
Traditional society, 4151, 5095
Egypt, 2485
Japan, 1439
Traditional theatre
Developing countries, 1853
Traditionalism
India, 1014
Traditions, 1188, 1195, 1206, 1208
Japan, 992
Training
Belgium, 2128
Training groups, 672
Tramps
Hungary, 5218
Transition from school to work, 1985
Translation
France, 1809
Tribal society
India, 3339
India : Madhya Pradesh, 3338
Tribalism
India, 3422, 3425
Iran, 3417
Tribes
India, 2238, 3716, 3717
Jordan, 3319
Trinidad
Political leaders, 4959
Trinidad and Tobago
Mental retardation, 3424
Race relations, 2314
Racial inequality, 3424
Social classes, 2314
Tunisia
Agricultural production, 1128
Islam, 1400
Literature, 1804
Mortality, 2866
Population policy, 2991
Press, 1696
Return migration, 3478

Revolt, 1128
Urbanization, 3784
Youth, 2683
Turkey
Contraception, 2974
Educational policy, 1945
Educational reforms, 1978
Emigrants, 4247
Islam, 1355, 1489
Literature, 1793, 1806
Migrant workers, 4316
National identity, 4316
Peasantry, 3694
Political culture, 4965
Rural population, 4965
Secularization, 1489
Social services, 5481
Social work, 5481
Urban population, 3797
Urbanization, 3797
Women's status, 3279
Working class, 2269
Turnaround migration, *use* Urban-rural
    migration
Two-person games, 442
Typology, 5314
USA, 280

Underdevelopment
Brazil, 2487
Understanding, 282
Unemployed, 4211
France, 4184
Tanzania, 4197
United Kingdom, 4585
USA, 4205
Unemployment, 4178, 4179, 4185, 4190,
    4209, 4217, 4296
France, 4208
Germany FR, 4183, 4194
Netherlands, 4187, 4214, 4218, 4219
United Kingdom, 3118, 4201
USA, 4188, 4213, 5237, 5243
Yugoslavia, 4200
Unemployment duration, 4204
USA, 4215
Unemployment level
Netherlands, 4449
Unequal exchange, 2487
United Kingdom
Absenteeism, 4443, 4446
Adopted children, 2650
Adult education, 2085, 2092, 2096
Aged, 2734, 2741
Alcoholism, 5126
Architecture, 1835
Aristocracy, 4814
Bankers, 2283
Bourgeoisie, 4780
Business cycles, 4584
Capital cities, 3749
Capitalism, 3952

Career development, 4479
Catholics, 1366
Church and State, 1418
Civil servants, 4590, 4887
Class consciousness, 2254
Class structure, 2283
Collective action, 870
Collective bargaining, 4558, 4699, 4702
Communication research, 1742
Community life, 3118
Community satisfaction, 3618, 3619
Conservatism, 4780
Cooperatives, 3953
Cultural history, 1043
Cultural life, 1043
Curriculum, 2132
Data protection, 308
Decision making, 4667
Deindustrialization, 4082
Demography, 2522
Deontology, 1476
Disability, 2826
Disabled workers, 2825
Divorce, 3069, 3071
Drugs, 5130
Economic policy, 4131
Educational policy, 3474
Educational provision, 2132
Elite, 2339
Environmental protection, 1708
Ethnic minorities, 3349
Ethnicity, 2246
Family, 3118, 5075
Family farms, 4085
Family policy, 5365
Family relations, 4085
Farming systems, 4085
Fascism, 4777
Female offenders, 5244
Feminism, 3218
Generation differences, 4479
Health, 5425
Health policy, 5409, 5420
Health services, 5456
Higher education, 2026, 2039, 2053
Historical demography, 2555
History of sociology, 37
Hospitals, 5450
Household budgets, 3980
Housework, 4361
Housing, 3826, 3910
Housing policy, 3830, 3867
Immigrant assimilation, 3474
Immigration policy, 3476, 3483
Income distribution, 4082, 4631
Industrial democracy, 4713
Industrial management, 4092, 4096
Industrial society, 4548
Inflation, 3818
Jews, 1359
Job satisfaction, 4443
Judicial process, 4884

Juvenile delinquency, 2685
Labour disputes, 4677
Labour market, 4170
Labour movements, 4613
Labour relations, 4542, 4548, 4554,
   4558-60
Literacy, 2082
Literature, 1827
Living conditions, 3980
Local government, 4659
Mail surveys, 385
Managers, 4560
Market, 4111
Mass media, 1708
Meat market, 4111
Medical care, 5450
Mental deficiency, 2838
Mental hospitals, 5445
Mentally disabled, 5445
Mestizos, 3430
Minority groups, 684
Mortality, 2885
Names, 505
Nationalism, 4772
Neighbourhood, 3769
New towns, 3769, 3807
Occupational mobility, 4479
Occupational qualification, 4502
Parish, 1366
Pension funds, 4724
Plant size, 4554, 4683
Police, 4872, 4875-78
Political movements, 4777
Political participation, 4987
Population movement, 2803
Preschool education, 1995
Press, 1719, 1732
Price rise, 3818
Proletariat, 2247
Protestant Churches, 1418
Protestant ethics, 1476
Public administration, 4885
Racial conflicts, 3411, 4877
Racial discrimination, 3830
Racism, 3358, 3365, 3418, 3419
Religion, 1269
Religious change, 1366
Religious discrimination, 1490
Riots, 1154, 1155
Rural life, 3719
School segregation, 3349
Sex discrimination, 4253, 5244
Shipbuilding, 740
Shop stewards, 4659
Smoking, 5409
Social anthropology, 214
Social classes, 2246, 2620, 2949
Social conditions, 994
Social control, 5130
Social differentiation, 2197
Social history, 2246, 2399, 2803, 3818, 4814
Social indicators, 5265

Social inequality, 2885
Social mobility, 1366, 2375
Social movements, 2096
Social planning, 5337
Social policy, 4131, 5265
Social problems, 5075
Social reproduction, 2160
Social science research, 103, 105
Social security, 5366
Social stratification, 3910
Social work, 5386, 5387
Social workers, 5445
Socialization, 4875
Society, 994
Sociological associations, 177
Sport, 975
State intervention, 4825
Strikes, 4675, 4683
Structuralism, 214
Taxation, 4118
Teachers, 4649
Trade unionism, 4638, 4643
Trade unions, 864, 4583-85, 4588-90,
    4609, 4612, 4631, 4649, 4667
Unemployed, 4585
Unemployment, 3118, 4201
Universities, 2071, 2085
Urban areas, 3771
Urban planning, 3747
Urbanization, 3818
Vocational rehabilitation, 2825
Vocational training, 4486
Welfare State, 1269, 5329, 5337
Women, 2620
Women's employment, 4253
Women's organizations, 3278
Women's status, 1827
Women's work, 4259, 4282
Workers' participation, 4709, 4724
Working class, 1995
Working class culture, 975
Working mothers, 1995
Young workers, 4202
Youth, 2685
Youth unemployment, 4202
Youth unrest, 5126
Universities, 2049
    Argentina, 2044
    Australia, 2037
    Canada, 2027
    France, 1959, 2052
    Germany FR, 3217
    United Kingdom, 2071, 2085
University campus
    USA, 1147
University management
    Australia, 2074
    USA, 2075
University reforms
    Argentina, 2036
Unmarried mothers, 5362
    Australia, 3198

USA, 3174, 4315
Unwritten law, *use* Customary law
Upper class
    USA, 2360
Urban agglomerations, *use* Towns
Urban areas, 3827
    Canada, 3777
    Europe, 4922
    France, 904, 5100
    Japan, 3450
    United Kingdom, 3771
    USA, 430
Urban communities
    Poland : Rzeszów, 3865
    USA, 3781, 3911
Urban concentration
    Mexico, 3780
Urban development, 2415, 2790, 3919
    Algeria, 3760
    India, 3902
    Israel, 3874
    Mexico, 3862
    Sudan, 3831
    USA, 3803
Urban economics
    Peru : Lima, 3899
Urban employment
    USA, 4199
Urban environment, 3839, 3924
    France, 3890
    Socialist countries, 3846
Urban growth
    Developing countries, 3858
    Italy, 3795
    USA, 3875
Urban housing
    Japan, 3841
Urban life, 1803, 2772, 3912, 5063
    China, 3923
    Europe, 3857
    France, 3778, 3871
    Germany FR, 4408
    India, 3873
    Poland, 3864
    USA, 3856, 5093, 5192
Urban planning, 3909, 3921
    Canada : Toronto, 3852
    China, 3819
    Europe, 3857
    France, 3770
    Hong Kong, 3819
    Israel, 3825, 3874
    Nigeria, 3759
    North Africa, 3884
    Poland, 3845
    Socialist countries, 3913
    United Kingdom, 3747
    USA, 3904
    USSR, 3775
    Venezuela, 3817
Urban policy, 3854
    Developing countries, 3785, 3918

Ecuador, 3832
France, 3752, 3901
Germany FR, 3833
Italy, 3806
USA, 3757, 3758, 3859
Urban population, 2772, 2779, 2810
Asia, 2813
Canada, 3777
China, 2806
Developed countries, 3810
Developing countries, 3810
France, 3469
Java, 2781
Poland, 2782
Turkey, 3797
Yugoslavia, 2811, 2812
Urban renewal
France, 3763, 3861, 3885, 3901
Urban society
Africa, 3886
Egypt, 3568
France, 3753
Taiwan, 3820
Urban sociology, 364, 3816, 3821, 3822,
3849, 3914, 3917, 3926
Dominican Republic, 3783
France, 3799, 3885
Hungary, 5218
Japan, 3843
USA, 3782, 3823, 3889, 5146
Urban space, 3815
Morocco, 3809
Urban structure, 3815, 3854, 3919
Brazil, 3881
Peru, 5286
Urban youth
Israel, 2687
Urban-rural migration
USA, 3545, 3554, 3564
Urban-urban migration
Germany FR, 3557
Urbanism
France, 3763
Urbanization, 3556, 3810, 3900, 3909, 3917,
3924, 3925
Asia, 3751
Canada, 3850
China, 3866
Czechoslovakia, 3878
Developing countries, 3766, 3787, 3880
France : Paris, 3844
Hungary, 2554, 3805
India, 3551, 3779
Latin America, 3898
Poland, 3813, 3872
Romania, 3894
Tunisia, 3784
Turkey, 3797
United Kingdom, 3818
USSR, 3888
Venezuela, 4900
Yugoslavia, 3834, 3840, 3863, 3872

Zimbabwe, 2428
Uruguay
Rural women, 2800
Women, 2580
Women's work, 2800
USA
Abortion, 2981, 3002, 3174
Absenteeism, 4444
Academic freedom, 1968
Academic success, 3173
Acculturation, 3378
Action research, 110
Adolescence, 2709
Adolescents, 977, 1115, 5139
Adopted children, 2647
Adult education, 2086, 2087
Adulthood, 2708, 2709
Advertising, 1636, 5002
Age, 5178
Aged, 2727, 2744, 2751, 3199
Ageing, 2711, 2720
Agricultural mechanization, 4070
Agricultural policy, 4071
Alcoholism, 2891, 5118
Antisemitism, 3404
Applied sociology, 2837
Arbitration, 4701
Architecture, 1833
Armed forces, 3367, 4778
Army, 5037
Art, 1765
Art museums, 1787
Attitude to work, 4400
Attitudes, 813
Automation, 4057
Automobile industry, 4698
Bibliographies, 3398
Bilingual education, 2099
Bilingualism, 4267
Birth, 2915
Blacks, 1805, 2256, 2335, 2584, 3129,
3136, 3298, 3282, 3312, 3315, 3331,
3348, 3352, 3355, 3373, 3736, 3403,
3897, 4480, 4633
Blindness, 2828
Breast-feeding, 2659
Broadcasting, 1748
Brotherhoods, 1414
Bureaucracy, 743, 747
Capital punishment, 5160, 5171, 5231
Care of the aged, 5377
Career development, 4500
Catholic Church, 1406, 1415, 1438
Catholicism, 1368, 1392, 2907
Catholics, 3640
Central government, 4896
Child abuse, 5181
Child mortality, 2863
Child rearing, 2660
Christianity, 62, 1396
Churches, 1405
Civil religion, 1276, 1279

Civil rights, 4856, 4870
Civil servants, 4888
Class consciousness, 2256, 2328
Clergy, 4770
Cohort analysis, 5149
Collective bargaining, 4696, 4698
Coloured persons, 3329
Communication policy, 1582
Communication research, 1537
Community development, 3623, 3632,
    3634, 3635, 3637
Community membership, 1132, 3564, 3640
Community participation, 3617
Community satisfaction, 3618
Computers, 382
Conflicts, 5440
Consensual union, 3079
Consensus, 611
Conservatism, 1482
Consumer behaviour, 4100, 4108, 4109
Continuing education, 2086
Contraception, 2964, 2976, 2993
Cooperatives, 3957
Copyright, 3932, 3933
Corporate culture, 972
Crime, 5146, 5186, 5246
Crime prevention, 5210
Criminal justice, 1071, 5159, 5166, 5199, 5206
Criminal sentencing, 5198, 5252
Cultural interaction, 1600
Culture, 968, 5439
Curriculum, 775
Delinquency, 3781, 5178, 5192, 5220,
    5225, 5237, 5242
Delinquents, 2843
Deprivation, 5117
Desegregation, 1116, 1123, 1147
Deviance, 1084, 1132
Disabled persons, 2822
Diseases, 2837
Division of labour, 3054
Divorce, 3062, 3075, 3080, 3090, 3095, 5243
Drug addiction, 1074, 2891, 5118, 5127,
    5129, 5137, 5139, 5140
Drugs of abuse, 5120
Economic behaviour, 3961
Education, 1862, 1863, 1908, 1909, 2601
Educational output, 1937, 2048
Educational philosophy, 1899
Educational policy, 1927, 3331
Educational reforms, 1958
Electoral campaigning, 5002, 5004, 5020
Elite, 2360
Emigrants, 3440
Employment discrimination, 2576, 4222
Employment opportunities, 4227
Employment policy, 4223
Entrepreneurs, 4000
Entry to working life, 4203
Equal pay, 3987
Ethnic groups, 2334, 3291, 3293, 3317, 4481
Ethnic minorities, 3287

Ethnic pluralism, 3353
Ethnicity, 1601, 3337, 3353
Ethnology, 513
Family, 3107, 3129, 3136, 3146, 3168, 4244
Family allowances, 5346
Family budgets, 4249
Family environment, 3153, 4476
Family farms, 2569
Family group, 3199
Family life, 1065, 3131
Family planning, 2551, 3015
Family policy, 5360
Family size, 3111
Family structure, 3736
Farming methods, 4070
Farming systems, 4076
Federalism, 4783
Female offenders, 4712
Feminism, 41, 99, 2584, 3205, 3209, 3218,
    3222, 3223, 3226, 3247, 3270, 5240
Fertility, 977, 1304, 2907, 2909, 2929,
    2936, 2941, 2948, 2952, 3836
Fine arts, 1838
Folk art, 1784
Folk culture, 1191
Forecasts, 296
Foreign languages, 1600
Foreign students, 2078
Foreign workers, 1966, 4267
Freedom of speech, 4848
Games, 4737
Gangs, 5229
Gerontology, 2738
Group analysis, 4904
Group membership, 707
Health, 3482, 5405
Health insurance, 5373
Health policy, 5416, 5432
Health services, 5439, 5443, 5447
Heroes, 794
Higher education, 775, 1123, 2047, 2048,
    2578
Historical demography, 2516, 2551, 3065
Historiography, 2404
History of sociology, 4, 5, 21, 58, 62, 71
Home ownership, 3774
Homeless people, 5082, 5112
Homicide, 5245
Homosexuality, 3028, 3043
Hospital management, 653
Hospitals, 5440, 5444
Hours of work, 4425
Household income, 2585
Households, 2586, 2587, 2617
Housework, 4431
Housing, 3788, 3855
Housing needs, 3836
Housing policy, 3772, 3922
Human resources, 4169
Humanities, 2108
Illegal immigration, 3463
Immigrant adaptation, 3486

Immigrant assimilation, 3287, 3502
Immigrants, 1374, 2948, 3482, 3494, 3525
Immigration policy, 3510, 3517, 3522,
	3526, 3527
Income inequality, 3981
Industrialization, 4083
Infant mortality, 2849
Interdisciplinary research, 115
Interest groups, 4931, 4948, 4949
Interethnic relations, 3372, 3374
Intergroup relations, 659
Internal migration, 3560, 3565
Interviewers, 382
Jews, 1374
Job enrichment, 4381
Job satisfaction, 4283, 4366, 4367, 4378,
	4411, 4418
Job seekers, 4198
Journalists, 1694
Judgment, 283
Jury, 676
Juvenile courts, 5236, 5238
Juvenile delinquency, 2702, 4349, 5148, 5226
Knowledge, 283
Labour disputes, 4701
Labour market, 696, 4176
Labour relations, 4545, 4547, 4551, 4557,
	4564-65
Land use, 3592
Levels of education, 1966, 4481
Libraries, 153, 165
Life expectancy, 2847
Life satisfaction, 4411, 4418
Life styles, 977
Literature, 1820, 2660
Local communities, 3640
Local culture, 3911
Local government, 4701, 4904
Loneliness, 589
Management, 779
Managers, 3352
Manpower utilization, 4169
Marital stability, 4248
Marriage, 3048, 3054
Married persons, 4425
Mass media, 1651, 1660, 1662, 3205,
	4016, 4746
Media, 1744, 4737
Medical care, 5403, 5421
Medical occupations, 5472
Mental diseases, 2824, 2843
Mental health, 5429, 5434
Metropolitan areas, 3756, 3801, 3870
Microcomputers, 2148
Migration, 3451
Military, 5029
Military personnel, 5036
Minority groups, 695, 696, 698, 3168,
	3973, 4888
Mortality, 2516, 2891
Mother tongue, 1601
Motherhood, 2058, 3004

Music, 1840
Names, 513
Natality, 2908
Neighbourhood, 3856
New technologies, 4016, 4070
Non-violence, 3373
Novels, 1822
Nuptiality, 3065
Occupational choice, 4503
Occupational mobility, 4463, 4480, 4481, 4500
Occupational prestige, 4474
Occupational promotion, 4445
Occupational safety, 4370
Occupational status, 4192, 4476
One-parent family, 3150
Parent-child relations, 3109, 3132, 3173
Parenthood, 3005, 3027
Parents' education, 2125
Part-time farming, 4069
Party systems, 4916
Patriotism, 4778
Pension schemes, 5373
Periodicals, 186
Personality, 1117
Police, 2591, 4366
Political affiliation, 4976
Political attitudes, 2692, 4968, 4979, 4991
Political behaviour, 4367
Political corruption, 4985
Political ideologies, 4770
Political psychology, 4761, 4763
Political socialization, 4974
Political sociology, 4765, 4767
Political systems, 4823
Politics, 1636, 2720, 5025, 5026
Population censuses, 2787, 2795
Population forecasts, 2531
Population growth, 2796
Pornography, 3039, 3052
Poverty, 5087, 5093, 5102, 5107
Premarital intercourse, 3044, 3048
Press, 1663, 1667, 1711, 1740
Prison, 4283
Prisoners, 5147, 5203
Private education, 1920, 1929
Private schools, 1990, 1991, 2006, 2018
Professionalization, 4926
Prostitution, 3021
Protestant Churches, 1408
Psychiatry, 5400
Psychology, 452, 455
Public administration, 4893
Public choice, 865
Public education, 1988, 1989, 1990, 1991,
	2006, 2018
Public ownership, 1711
Punishment, 5215, 5217, 5230
Quality of life, 3635
Race relations, 2584, 3353, 3382, 3388,
	3389, 3398, 3406, 3420
Racial attitudes, 3409, 3426, 4767
Racial differentiation, 273, 3378, 4979

Racial discrimination, 3368, 3416, 3892, 4445, 5166, 5215
Racial inequality, 3373, 3403
Racial prejudice, 5018
Racial segregation, 2018, 3367, 3401
Racism, 5093
Rape, 5185, 5224, 5240
Refugees, 3518
Regionalism, 4783
Religion, 1266, 1269, 1286, 1290, 1300, 1304, 1311
Religiosity, 1290, 1480, 1487, 5117
Religious affiliation, 1500
Religious behaviour, 1471, 1482
Religious beliefs, 1413
Religious groups, 1056
Religious institutions, 1409
Religious movements, 1499
Religious revival, 1494
Research financing, 116, 119, 121, 123, 130
Research foundations, 5060
Research policy, 104
Research programmes, 125
Resident satisfaction, 3906, 3930
Residential areas, 3808
Residential segregation, 3897
Retirement, 4448
Rock music, 1846
Rural areas, 430, 2335, 3741, 4083, 5245
Rural development, 3635
Rural poverty, 5105
School desegregation, 1948
School discipline, 2022
School failure, 2120
School-community relationship, 1930, 1979
Schooling, 1928, 1950, 2585, 4476
Schools, 1994, 2017
Science, 1502
Scientific research, 1042
Scientists, 84
Seafarers, 1110
Sects, 1413
Seniority, 4192
Sex differentiation, 2585, 5159, 5252
Sex discrimination, 2576, 2578, 3987, 4445
Sex equality, 2582, 2601, 2611
Sex roles, 820, 2569, 2591, 3054, 4299, 4712
Sexual behaviour, 3027, 3053
Sexual harassment, 3041
Sexuality, 3030
Sharecropping, 4084
Size of enterprise, 3997
Skills, 4176
Slums, 2120
Smoking, 2891
Social adaptation, 1117
Social behaviour, 1115
Social biology, 41
Social control, 1071, 1755
Social disorganization, 3741, 3803
Social history, 3095, 3736, 3811
Social judgment, 611

Social justice, 1928
Social mobility, 2385
Social movements, 4926, 4952
Social networks, 661, 664
Social norms, 2709, 3048
Social origin, 5439
Social policy, 5253, 5296, 5310, 5330
Social problems, 4213
Social protest, 1181
Social psychology, 458, 466
Social research, 186
Social science research, 92, 104
Social sciences, 27, 28, 32, 119, 121, 123, 130
Social services, 5464
Social status, 2333, 2334, 2335, 2336, 4481
Social stratification, 2205, 5403
Social surveys, 376
Social unrest, 2041, 5434
Social work, 1930
Social workers, 5480
Sociological research, 93, 99, 102
Sociologists, 77, 83
Sociology, 16, 20, 45, 66, 4823
Sociology of religion, 1271, 1272
Sport, 4746
Status attainment, 2370, 2372, 2376
Stereotypes, 820
Strikes, 4685, 4687
Student behaviour, 2029, 2041
Student movements, 2056
Students, 1181, 2072, 3637, 5472
Suburban areas, 3756, 3802, 3907
Suicide, 4215, 5149, 5243
Teachers, 2131, 2142
Teaching, 2124, 2149
Teaching aids, 2148
Teaching of sociology, 49
Technological change, 4602
Telecommunications, 1761
Television, 1640, 1646, 1661, 1714, 1735, 1755, 4109, 4976
Tenant farmers, 3736
Tenants, 3798
Textile industry, 2328, 4630
Tolerance, 830
Town centre, 3892
Towns, 3745, 3750, 3811
Trade unionism, 4606
Trade unions, 455, 2142, 4444, 4547, 4597, 4602, 4610, 4630, 4633
Typology, 280
Unemployed, 4205
Unemployment, 4188, 4213, 5237, 5243
Unemployment duration, 4215
University campus, 1147
University management, 2075
Unmarried mothers, 3174, 4315
Upper class, 2360
Urban areas, 430
Urban communities, 3781, 3911
Urban development, 3803
Urban employment, 4199

Urban growth, 3875
Urban life, 3856, 5093, 5192
Urban planning, 3904
Urban policy, 3757, 3758, 3859
Urban sociology, 3782, 3823, 3889, 5146
Urban-rural migration, 3545, 3554, 3564
Value orientation, 1056
Value systems, 1065
Veterans, 5032, 5038
Victims, 5212, 5219, 5242
Villages, 3686
Violence, 1167, 1183, 1185, 1662, 3131, 3153, 5229
Vocational training, 3291
Voluntary work, 4377, 4439
Voting, 5019
Voting behaviour, 1480, 4992, 4994, 4998, 4999, 5003, 5006, 5010, 5018
Wage determination, 2333
Wage differentials, 3983, 4463
Wage discrimination, 2576
Wage negotiations, 4693
Wage rate, 1966, 5210
Wages, 3973
Way of life, 924
Welfare, 3978
Welfare policy, 5307
Welfare State, 1269, 5326
Wife, 5219
Women, 1415, 3199, 4888
Women students, 2058, 3065
Women workers, 3041, 4237
Women's education, 3173
Women's employment, 696, 4246, 4248, 4249, 4250, 4257, 4262, 4311, 4315
Women's participation, 3225
Women's role, 977, 2584
Women's status, 3204, 3522, 4274
Women's work, 3565, 4233, 4244, 4261, 4263, 4271, 4274, 4283, 4299, 4319
Work organization, 4324
Workers' participation, 4706, 4712
Working class, 2277
Working conditions, 4057, 4440
Writers, 1805
Youth, 1065, 2692, 2702, 4763
Youth unemployment, 3403
USA — Canada
International relations, 5041
USA — Europe
Cultural relations, 1021
USSR
Access to education, 3393
Administrative corruption, 4894
Adult education, 2098
Aged, 2755
Antisemitism, 3380
Antisocial behaviour, 1232
Art, 3498
Atheism, 1387
Authoritarianism, 831
Bilingualism, 1590

Cinema, 1704
Collective farms, 3740
Continuing education, 2105
Culture, 1005, 1378
Data banks, 155
Demography, 2519
Educational output, 2048
Educational psychology, 1866
Educational systems, 1925
Emigrants, 1326, 1374
Emigration, 3460, 3516, 3536
Entry to working life, 4196
Ethnic groups, 3498
Ethnic policy, 3392
Ethnicity, 3354
Everyday life, 3740
Factories, 78
Family, 3121
Folk songs, 1848
Higher education, 2048
Historical demography, 2545
Human settlements, 3614
Industrial enterprises, 5277
Intelligentsia, 2348, 2359, 2363
Internal migration, 3537
Islam, 1339, 1387
Jews, 1370, 1378, 1385, 1823, 3460, 3536
Language policy, 1593, 1625, 1626
Law, 1260
Life styles, 425
Literature, 1823, 1826
Migration, 3441
Morals, 3121
Mortality, 2861
Moslems, 1402
Music, 1843
Nationalities policy, 3536
Peasantry, 3740
Penal law, 1232
Political culture, 4964, 4972
Psychiatry, 5397
Psychology, 450
Racial discrimination, 3393
Retired persons, 2725
Rural areas, 3676
Rural development, 3742
Rural life, 3726, 3740
Rural-urban migration, 3570
Satellite towns, 3828
Scientific and technical progress, 4017
Secondary education, 1866
Social development, 2163, 2429, 2443, 2473
Social indicators, 425
Social life, 1173
Social planning, 5277
Social policy, 5325
Social psychology, 479
Social structure, 2163, 2725
Socialism, 4790
Society, 917, 921
Sociolinguistics, 2429
Sociological research, 2163

Sociologists, 78
Standard of living, 425
State, 4845
Technology, 4061
Terror, 1260
Towns, 3754, 3876, 3895
Urban planning, 3775
Urbanization, 3888
Value systems, 1067
Villages, 3651, 3680, 3726
Voluntary work, 4421
Women, 2633
Work organization, 4337
Workers, 4429
Workers' participation, 2301
Working class, 2268, 2301
Working conditions, 4429
Youth, 155
Utilitarianism, 2451
Utility measurement, 372
Utopia, 137, 764, 842-43, 846-47, 850,
    852-53, 862, 1516
Utopianism, 66, 849

Value, 1077, 5316
Japan, 1052
Value orientation, 1066, 1072
USA, 1056
Value systems, 1049, 1051, 1055, 1058, 1069,
    1224, 2610, 2662, 2950, 5328
Australia, 1221
Canada, 1050
China, 1061
Japan, 1075
Maghreb, 1053
Poland, 1059, 4383
USA, 1065
USSR, 1067
Zaïre, 1046
Values, *use* Value systems
Veblen, Thorstein, 66, 4791
Venezuela
Educational policy, 2059
Folklore, 1203
Higher education, 2059
Journalists, 1645
Labour law, 4570
Local government, 4900
New towns, 3893
Social movements, 4929
Urban planning, 3817
Urbanization, 4900
Verbal communication, 1550
Veterans
USA, 5032, 5038
Victims, 606, 636, 5183, 5191
USA, 5212, 5219, 5242
Videotex, 1759
Vietnam
Trade unions, 4629
Women's status, 3268
Villages, 3733, 3761

Algeria, 3665
Bangladesh, 3684
France, 3662
Germany, 3675
Hong Kong, 3729
Hungary, 2563, 3700
India, 3698, 3709, 3721, 4831
India : Bengal, 3661
Italy, 2158
Korea R, 3667
Lebanon, 3725
Mozambique, 3654
Nepal, 3679
Poland, 2792, 3678
Senegal, 3673
USA, 3686
USSR, 3651, 3680, 3726
Yugoslavia, 3863
Violence, 1083, 1090, 1098, 1113, 1121, 1122,
    1136
Australia, 1140
Belgium, 1099
China, 1150
France, 1134, 1135
Italy, 1184
Jamaica, 1106
USA, 1167, 1183, 1185, 1662, 3131, 3153,
    5229
Vocational choice, *use* Occupational choice
Vocational education, 4460
Chile, 4467
Vocational guidance, 4484
Nigeria, 4488
Vocational rehabilitation
France, 4471
United Kingdom, 2825
Vocational training, 4489
Chile, 4467
France, 4469
Germany FR, 4498
Kenya, 4461
Latin America, 4466
United Kingdom, 4486
USA, 3291
Voluntary organizations, 721, 728
Denmark, 727
France, 723
Voluntary work, 3175, 4414
USA, 4377, 4439
USSR, 4421
Voting, 5000, 5001, 5012
USA, 5019
Voting abstentionism, *use* Electoral
    abstentionism
Voting behaviour, 5008, 5015
Canada, 4997
Denmark, 4995, 5021
Finland, 3346
France, 5007
Germany FR, 5017
Israel, 4996
Italy, 2168

Japan, 5016
USA, 1480, 4992, 4994, 4998, 4999, 5003, 5006, 5010, 5018
Voting turnout, 5005
Voyer, Jean-Pierre, 246

Wage bargaining, *use* Wage negotiations
Wage determination
USA, 2333
Wage differentials
USA, 3983, 4463
Wage discrimination
USA, 2576
Wage negotiations
France, 4692
USA, 4693
Wage rate
USA, 1966, 5210
Wages
USA, 3973
War, 3351, 5249
Water, 3596
Water resources, 3596
Way of life, 896, 902, 907, 939, 959, 3559, 4107
German DR, 898
Hungary, 919, 946
Socialist countries, 948
Sweden, 945
USA, 924
Wealth, 5089
Weber, Max, 39, 233, 252-53, 282, 523, 781, 787, 791-92, 826, 1223, 1296, 1475, 1478, 1897, 2220, 2471, 3141, 3946, 4817, 4932, 5314
Wedding
Yugoslavia, 3127
Welfare, 2726, 2753, 2761, 3971, 3975
Hungary, 4350
USA, 3978
Welfare criteria, 3979
Welfare measurement, 5266
Welfare policy, 5262, 5304
USA, 5307
Welfare State, 2678, 5255, 5271, 5279, 5294, 5311, 5324, 5334-36
Denmark, 5259
Germany FR, 5256, 5257
Ireland, 5267
Netherlands, 1269, 5320
Norway, 5291, 5292
Scandinavia, 5306
United Kingdom, 1269, 5329, 5337
USA, 1269, 5326
West Indies
Ethnicity, 3318
Westermarck, Edvard, 247
Western Africa
Dialects, 1594
Western Asia
Foreign workers, 4318
Immigration policy, 4318

Literature, 1807
Social classes, 2286
Western countries
Civilization crisis, 966
Quality of life, 3979
Refugees, 3467
Western Europe
Consensual union, 3079
Corporatism, 4580
Diplomas, 2077
Entry to working life, 2077
Housing policy, 3772
Immigration, 3455
Minority culture, 925
Patriarchy, 3141
Politics, 5026
Population, 2511
Social psychology, 474
Strikes, 4684
Teacher training, 2135
Terrorism, 1118
Trade unions, 4621
White collar workers, *use* Employees
Widow
Korea R, 3081
Widowhood, 3070
Wife, 4254
USA, 5219
Wildcat strikes
Austria, 4678
Canada, 4673
Sweden, 4671
Wittgenstein, Ludwig, 9
Women, 576, 1722, 2581, 2588, 2605, 2606, 2626, 2640, 2714, 3145, 3457
Africa South of the Sahara, 2589
Arab countries, 2625
China, 2631
Denmark, 2566
EEC countries, 2560
France, 1373
Japan, 2745
Spain, 3112
Switzerland, 3440
Tanzania, 2600
United Kingdom, 2620
Uruguay, 2580
USA, 1415, 3199, 4888
USSR, 2633
Women homeworkers, *use* Housewives
Women students
USA, 2058, 3065
Women workers, 2958, 4264, 4272, 4294, 4296
Bangladesh, 4238
Canada : Quebec, 4252
Developing countries, 4289
Europe, 2783
France, 4288
Germany FR, 4303
India, 4236, 4273, 4309, 4320
Java, 4298
Jordan, 4243

Korea R, 4280
Mexico, 5408
Peru, 4686
USA, 3041, 4237
Women's education, 3233
  France, 3220, 3252
  Germany, 3250
  Netherlands, 1953
  USA, 3173
Women's employment, 2183, 4234, 4270, 4296
  Canada : Quebec, 4029
  France, 4228, 4295, 4471
  Germany FR, 3272, 4286, 4891
  Hungary, 4284, 4300
  OECD countries, 4306
  Taiwan, 4266
  United Kingdom, 4253
  USA, 696, 4246, 4248-50, 4257, 4262,
    4311, 4315
  Yugoslavia, 4310
Women's liberation movements
  France, 3248
  Germany FR, 3245
  India, 3275
  Italy, 3269
Women's organizations
  Canada, 3221
  United Kingdom, 3278
Women's participation, 2629, 3215, 3265
  Botswana, 3236
  Canada, 3208, 3227
  France, 4623
  Germany FR, 4623
  USA, 3225
Women's promotion, 3240
Women's rights, 3243
  India, 3274
  Mexico, 3280
Women's role, 2571, 2583, 2595, 2629
  Africa, 3664
  Developing countries, 2598
  Ghana : Accra, 2614
  Greece, 3133
  Indonesia, 2599
  Malaysia, 2599
  Oceania, 2607
  Oman, 2575
  Singapore, 2599
  Socialist countries, 3231
  USA, 977, 2584
Women's status, 265, 3203, 3210, 3219, 3230,
    3238, 3242, 3243, 3256, 3262, 4312,
    4494
  Africa, 3212
  Botswana, 3236
  Canada, 3246, 3258
  China, 3244, 3253
  Cuba, 3266
  Ethiopia, 3241
  France, 3202, 3207, 3232, 3234
  Germany FR, 3217, 3272
  Ghana, 3259

India, 3261, 3271
India : Manipur Valley, 3224
Israel, 3693
Japan, 3251
North Africa, 3255
Norway, 3228
Oman, 2575
Poland, 3239
Portugal, 3229
Scandinavia, 3276
Socialist countries, 3231
Southern Africa, 3211
Sweden, 3214
Thailand, 3264
Turkey, 3279
United Kingdom, 1827
USA, 3204, 3522, 4274
Vietnam, 3268
Yugoslavia, 3263
Zambia, 4990
Women's work, 3243, 4234, 4239, 4254,
    4264, 4270, 4287, 4302, 4304, 4305,
    4312, 4322, 4323
  Africa, 2568
  Brazil, 4255
  Canada, 3060, 4241
  Dominican Republic, 4321
  EEC, 4290
  EEC countries, 4313
  France, 2852, 4307
  Germany, 3250
  Mexico, 4317
  Netherlands, 2618
  Nigeria, 4258, 4308
  Poland, 4269
  South Africa, 4235
  Southern Africa, 3211
  Spain, 4240, 4297
  Tanzania, 4292
  United Kingdom, 4259, 4282
  Uruguay, 2800
  USA, 3565, 4233, 4244, 4261, 4263, 4271,
    4274, 4283, 4299, 4319
Work accidents, *use* Occupational accidents
Work environment, 1595, 4358, 4392, 4419, 4422
  Italy, 4354
  Norway, 4382
Work experience, 4465
Work motivation, *use* Attitude to work
Work organization, 4151, 4327, 4331, 4333,
    4338, 4340, 4343, 4346
  Europe, 4330
  France, 4031, 4335
  Japan, 4332
  USA, 4324
  USSR, 4337
  Yugoslavia, 4334
Work place, 4371
Work safety, *use* Occupational safety
Work standards
  France, 1057
Work study, 4328

Workers, 1783, 2304, 3125, 4397, 4511
  France, 4519
  India, 4508
  Netherlands, 5318
  Poland, 4515, 5136
  USSR, 4429
Workers' movements, *use* Labour movements
Workers' participation, 4622, 4705, 4707,
    4715, 4727
  China, 4719
  France, 4708
  Germany FR, 4722
  India, 4720
  Norway, 4717
  Poland, 4710
  United Kingdom, 4709, 4724
  USA, 4706, 4712
  USSR, 2301
Workers' representation
  France, 4718
  Italy, 4723
Workers' self-management
  Japan, 4721
  Romania, 4711
Working class, 196, 2278, 2280, 2288, 2297,
    2304, 2315, 3838
  Arab countries, 2381
  Capitalist countries, 2262
  China, 2245
  Curaçao, 2320
  Eastern Europe, 4625
  France, 1430, 1983, 2285, 5100
  Germany, 2291, 2401
  India, 4508
  India : Kerala, 2275
  Japan, 2249
  Poland, 2267
  Turkey, 2269
  United Kingdom, 1995
  USA, 2277
  USSR, 2268, 2301
  Yugoslavia, 2276
Working class culture, 931, 955
  France, 1002
  United Kingdom, 975
Working conditions, 2299, 3976, 4355, 4363,
    4365, 4374, 4419, 4423, 4441
  Canada, 4362, 4410
  Developed countries, 4436
  France, 4369
  Germany, 4275
  India, 4388
  Japan, 4393
  Poland, 4394, 4424
  Tanzania, 4396
  USA, 4057, 4440
  USSR, 4429
Working mothers
  Bangladesh, 4251
  United Kingdom, 1995
Working time, 4380, 4417
  France, 4357

  Germany, 4398
  Germany FR, 4435
Working time arrangement, 4353, 4376, 4384,
    4413, 4428
  Canada : Quebec, 4252
  France, 4395, 4407
  Germany FR, 4359
Working women, *use* Women workers
Works of art, 1783
World economy, 4155
World population, 2817, 2819
Worship, *use* Cults
Writers
  Arab countries, 1800
  France, 1809
  German DR, 1791
  Italy, 1802
  USA, 1805
Writing, 569

Yoga, 1401
Young workers, 1981
  Europe, 4293
  France, 4265
  Germany FR, 3321, 4462
  Hungary, 938
  United Kingdom, 4202
Youth, 1160, 1681, 2664, 2666, 2671-72,
    2678, 2686, 2701, 2705, 2707, 2944,
    4938
  Canada, 3035
  Czechoslovakia, 2688
  Denmark, 3851
  France, 2665, 3499
  German DR, 2689
  Germany, 2697
  Germany FR, 299, 2680
  Hungary, 2703
  Ireland, 2682
  Japan, 2691
  Martinique, 2668
  Poland, 1129, 1473, 2674, 2693, 2696
  Portugal, 2676
  Reunion Island, 2668
  Spain, 2667
  Sri Lanka, 2690
  Sweden, 2684
  Switzerland, 2673
  Tunisia, 2683
  United Kingdom, 2685
  USA, 1065, 2692, 2702, 4763
  USSR, 155
Youth employment, 4193, 4207
  Germany FR, 1924
  Ireland, 4206
  Martinique, 2668
  Portugal, 4206
  Reunion Island, 2668
Youth organizations, 2635
  French Speaking Africa, 2695
  Switzerland, 2669
  Switzerland : Zurich, 2706

Youth policy
 German DR, 2694
 Hungary, 2698
 Spain, 2677
Youth unemployment, 4186
 EEC countries, 4195
 Germany FR, 4180, 4247
 Ireland, 4182, 4212
 United Kingdom, 4202
 USA, 3403
Youth unrest
 United Kingdom, 5126
Yugoslavia
 Cultural change, 3834
 Culture, 903
 Emigrants, 4291
 Ethnic groups, 3284
 Ethnic pluralism, 3305
 Family, 3127, 4982
 Fertility decline, 2798
 Generation differences, 2371
 Housing needs, 3824
 Intellectuals, 2347
 Linguistics, 1533
 Managers, 4531
 Mass media, 1677, 1678
 Migrant workers, 3824
 Moral crisis, 1228
 Moslems, 1381
 National minorities, 3305
 Physicians, 5469
 Political behaviour, 4982
 Population distribution, 2546
 Population movement, 2788
 Private farms, 4098
 Religious symbolism, 1452
 Return migration, 3528
 Rural areas, 3127
 Rural development, 3672
 Rural population, 2798, 2816
 Rural-urban migration, 3558
 Social classes, 2222
 Social conditions, 5317

 Social inequality, 2222
 Social integration, 1088
 Social mobility, 2371
 Social system, 2154
 Sociolinguistics, 1533
 Sociologists, 91
 Sociology, 2
 Standard of living, 3840
 Student movements, 2066
 Unemployment, 4200
 Urban population, 2811, 2812
 Urbanization, 3834, 3840, 3863, 3872
 Villages, 3863
 Wedding, 3127
 Women's employment, 4310
 Women's status, 3263
 Work organization, 4334
 Working class, 2276

Zaire
 Churches, 1404
 Family law, 3161
 Juvenile delinquency, 5204
 Language policy, 1619
 Language teaching, 1615
 Morals, 1213
 Rural communities, 3712
 Schools, 2005
 Value systems, 1046
Zambia
 Community development, 3643
 Libraries, 162
 Political participation, 4990
 Social classes, 2302
 Students, 2076
 Women's status, 4990
Zen, 1329, 1330
Zimbabwe
 Self-reliance, 2428
 Social development, 2428
 Urbanization, 2428
Znaniecki, Florian, 912

INDEX DES MATIÈRES

Abandon d'études
    Kenya : Nairobi, 2019
Abramowski, Edward, 213
Absentéisme, 4360, 4447
    États-Unis, 4444
    Pays-Bas, 4449
    Royaume-Uni, 4443, 4446
Abstentionnisme électoral
    Espagne, 5013
    Europe, 5013
    Italie, 5011
Accès à l'éducation
    Allemagne RF, 1954
    URSS, 3393
Accidents du travail
    Espagne, 4426
    Pologne, 4434
Accomplissement, 545
Acculturation
    États-Unis, 3378
    Israël, 1012
Acquisition de connaissances, 556, 563, 680
Acquisition du langage, 1621
Acteurs, 4535
Action, 487, 537, 540, 553, 566, 570, 572-73,
    800, 1701
Action collective, 868, 4946
    France, 870
    Royaume-Uni, 870
Action politique, 554
Action sociale, 5258, 5270, 5289, 5297, 5305,
    5314, 5316, 5332, 5392
    France, 5327
    Pays en développement, 5303
Action syndicale
    Italie, 4596
Activistes
    Inde, 4921
Activités ludiques, 2613
Adaptation des immigrants
    États-Unis, 3486
Adaptation sociale
    Australie, 1165
    États-Unis, 1117
Administration centrale
    États-Unis, 4896
Administration locale, 1754, 4901
    Allemagne RF, 3638
    Canada : Toronto, 3852
    États-Unis, 4701, 4904
    France, 2285, 4899
    Inde, 4905
    Italie, 4895, 4897, 4906
    Japon, 4134, 4902
    Royaume-Uni, 4659
    Venezuela, 4900

Administration publique, 3649
    États-Unis, 4893
    Hong Kong, 4892
    Hongrie, 4485
    Inde, 4889
    Niger, 4890
    Royaume-Uni, 4885
Administration scolaire, 2024
    Belgique, 2023
    France, 2020
Adolescence, 1702, 2670, 2679, 2681
    États-Unis, 2709
Adolescents, 567, 1186, 1756, 2675, 3024, 5134
    Australie, 1221
    États-Unis, 977, 1115, 5139
    France, 2020
    Israël, 2623
Adoption d'enfant, 3197
Adorno, Theodor W., 1771
Adultes
    Italie, 2864
Affiliation, 617
Affiliation politique
    États-Unis, 4976
Affiliation religieuse
    États-Unis, 1500
Affinité
    Australie, 618
    Inde, 618
Afrique
    Artisanat, 4066
    Besoins fondamentaux, 5088
    Cinéma, 1642, 1655, 1670
    Classe moyenne, 2356
    Classes sociales, 2248
    Colonialisme, 3943
    Communautés religieuses, 1435
    Conditions sociales, 5091
    Coopératives, 614
    Développement économique, 4869
    Développement rural, 3664, 5091
    Développement social, 2444
    Droits de l'homme, 4869
    Élite, 2356
    Émigrants, 3472
    Esclavage, 2237
    Famille, 3149, 3189
    Fécondité, 2943, 2953
    Groupes minoritaires, 690
    Histoire culturelle, 1044
    Langage, 1852
    Langues, 1591
    Littérature, 1788, 1795
    Mortalité, 2953
    Pauvres, 5091
    Polygamie, 3059, 3100

Prise de décision, 5088
Professions, 4454
Réfugiés, 3491
Rôle des femmes, 3664
Rôles sexuels, 2568
Santé mentale, 5435
Société urbaine, 3886
Solidarité, 614
Statut de la femme, 3212
Tables de mortalité, 2865
Théâtre, 1852
Travail des femmes, 2568
Afrique au Sud du Sahara
 Droit, 1250
 Femmes, 2589
 Politique scientifique, 120
Afrique Centrale
 Classes sociales, 2279
 Idéologie, 2279
Afrique du Nord
 Aménagement urbain, 3884
 Émigration, 3456
 Identité culturelle, 1019
 Identité nationale, 914
 Islam, 1356, 1357
 Politique, 3255
 Statut de la femme, 3255
Afrique du Sud
 Antisémitisme, 3423
 Apartheid, 3384, 3412, 3413, 3415
 Autoritarisme, 4804
 Comportement de l'organisation, 738
 Conservatisme, 4804
 Droit, 1243
 Droits du citoyen, 3400
 Écoles privées, 1993
 Éducation, 1870
 Emploi industriel, 3415
 Esclavage, 2242
 Gens de maison, 4523
 Libéralisme, 4805
 Lutte de classes, 2290
 Marché du travail, 4165
 Mariage, 3072
 Mouvements de résistance, 2242
 Pauvreté, 5092
 Racisme, 3360
 Relations raciales, 3379, 3400
 Sport, 4755
 Syndicalisme, 4593
 Syndicats, 4628, 4663, 4664
 Travail des femmes, 4235
 Travailleurs migrants, 2290
 Villes, 3835
Afrique du Sud : Pretoria
 Conditions de vie, 2760
 Personnes âgées, 2760
Afrique francophone
 Organisations de jeunesse, 2695
Afrique méridionale
 Art, 1764
 Statut de la femme, 3211

Travail des femmes, 3211
 Vie familiale, 3108
 Villes capitales, 3744
Afrique occidentale
 Dialectes, 1594
Âge, 2830
 États-Unis, 5178
Âge adulte, 2710
 États-Unis, 2708, 2709
Âge au mariage
 Inde, 3098
Agression, 631, 636, 1136
Agressivité, 629-30, 633-35, 637
Agriculteurs
 Autriche, 3663
 France, 1057
 Pologne, 1059, 2746, 3137, 3710, 3720
Agriculture, 3575
 France, 3202
Agriculture à temps partiel
 États-Unis, 4069
Agriexploitation
 Pologne, 4079, 4094
Aide à l'enfance
 France, 5461
Aide aux gens âgés
 Argentine, 5369
 Canada, 5352, 5378
 Espagne, 5478
 États-Unis, 5377
 Europe, 5350
 France, 5341, 5343, 5344, 5379, 5473
 Japon, 2732, 5374
Aires métropolitaines
 Brésil, 3903
 États-Unis, 3756, 3801, 3870
 Japon, 2232
Albanie
 Droit penal, 1254
Alcoolisme, 1079, 5131-32, 5135, 5138, 5143
 Allemagne RF, 1180
 États-Unis, 2891, 5118
 France, 5128, 5141
 Irlande, 5142
 Pologne, 5136
 Royaume-Uni, 5126
Algérie
 Christianisme, 1033
 Conjoncture démographique, 2814
 Délinquance juvénile, 5251
 Développement urbain, 3760
 Droit d'auteur, 3934
 Émigrants, 3490
 Interaction culturelle, 1033
 Islam, 1033, 1338
 Mortalité, 2893
 Psychologie de l'enfant, 456
 Réformes agraires, 3665
 Société, 894
 Systèmes politiques, 1338
 Tables de mortalité, 2893
 Vie quotidienne, 947

Villages, 3665
Aliénation, 1096, 1111, 1126-27, 1146, 1163, 1164
    Inde, 1169, 1170, 1174
    Israël, 4089
    Japon, 4393
Aliénation culturelle
    Pays arabes, 2361
Aliénation politique, 1161
    Inde, 1114, 1145
Aliments
    Pays en développement, 2080
Allaitement naturel, 2658
    Brésil, 2868
    États-Unis, 2659
    Japon, 2659
    Malaisie, 2643
    Pays en développement, 2648
Allemagne
    Analyse par cohorte, 2862
    Antisémitisme, 3385
    Attitudes politiques, 2697
    Chances d'éducation, 2377
    Classe ouvrière, 2291, 2401
    Conditions de travail, 4275
    Éducation des femmes, 3250
    Égalité de chances, 2377
    Enseignants, 2126
    Étudiants, 2051
    Heures de travail, 4430
    Histoire sociale, 2126, 2401, 3675, 4242,
        4275, 4276, 4658
    Industrie textile, 3250
    Jeunesse, 2697
    Langage, 1620
    Marché du travail, 4242
    Mobilité sociale, 2377
    Mouvements ouvriers, 4598, 4617, 4626, 4658
    Politique scientifique, 128
    Presse, 1683
    Révolution industrielle, 2401
    Sociologie, 6
    Tables de mortalité, 2862
    Temps de travail, 4398
    Théorie sociologique, 217
    Travail des enfants, 4276
    Travail des femmes, 3250
    Travailleurs étrangers, 4242, 4275
    Villages, 3675
Allemagne RD
    Automation, 4039
    Conscience nationale, 950
    Écrivains, 1791
    Églises, 1411
    Famille, 2689
    Fécondité, 2973
    Genre de vie, 898
    Jeunesse, 2689
    Littérature, 1792, 1811
    Peinture, 1834
    Poésie, 1797
    Politique de la jeunesse, 2694
    Politique démographique, 2973

    Politique des loisirs, 2694
    Politique sociale, 5264
    Société socialiste, 3940
    Travail ménager, 4386
Allemagne RF
    Accès à l'éducation, 1954
    Administration locale, 3638
    Alcoolisme, 1180
    Aménagement du temps de travail, 4359
    Assimilation des immigrants, 3520, 3530
    Attitude envers le travail, 4356, 4372
    Autoritarisme, 828
    Bibliothèques, 158
    Budgets temps, 4408
    Changement social, 299
    Choix d'une profession, 4464
    Chômage, 4183, 4194
    Chômage des jeunes, 4180, 4247
    Cinéma, 1737
    Comportement électoral, 5017
    Conflits, 638
    Conscience nationale, 908, 950
    Contestation politique, 4958
    Coopération culturelle, 1016
    Délinquance juvénile, 5162, 5174
    Déviance, 1180
    Différenciation de classes, 2203
    Distance sociale, 3313
    Divorce, 3084
    Drogue, 1180
    Droit du travail, 4303
    Droit pénal, 1242
    Écoles, 2012
    Éducation, 1903
    Éducation des adultes, 2091, 2103
    Égalité de chances, 2203
    Emploi, 1903
    Emploi des femmes, 3272, 4286, 4891
    Emploi des jeunes, 1924
    Employés, 4356
    Enseignement de la sociologie, 67
    Enseignement supérieur, 2030
    État providence, 5256, 5257
    Étrangers, 3314, 3321
    Famille, 3171, 3178, 4970
    Famille monoparentale, 3179
    Fécondité, 2973
    Féminisme, 3272
    Fonction publique, 4891
    Formation professionnelle, 4498
    Histoire de l'Église, 1412
    Hôpitaux, 5455
    Humanisation du travail, 4385, 4432
    Jeunes travailleurs, 3321, 4462
    Jeunesse, 299, 2680
    Jeux, 4744
    Journalisme, 1675
    Juifs, 1390
    Lecteurs, 1631
    Littérature, 1792, 1830
    Loisir, 4729
    Marginalité, 1721

Mariage mixte, 3061
Ménages, 3171
Migrants, 1721
Migration, 3439
Migration urbaine-urbaine, 3557
Milieux d'affaires, 4013
Minorités ethniques, 3313
Minorités nationales, 3307
Mobilité sociale, 2369
Motivation d'accomplissement, 828
Mouvements de libération de la femme, 3245
Mouvements étudiants, 2038, 2056
Mouvements ouvriers, 4603
Mouvements pacifistes, 1223
Mouvements sociaux, 4924, 4925
Moyens de communication de masse, 1684, 1721
Négociation collective, 4062, 4694
Organisation communautaire, 3638
Ouvriers industriels, 4456
Participation des femmes, 4623
Participation des travailleurs, 4722
Partis politiques, 5301
Perception de soi, 5174
Politique démographique, 2973
Politique familiale, 5356
Politique sociale, 5261, 5280, 5301, 5315
Politique urbaine, 3833
Population, 2549
Presse, 1649
Professionnalisation, 4456, 5384
Prostitution, 3032
Qualification professionnelle, 4462
Qualité de la vie, 3972
Racisme, 3370
Recensements, 361
Recherche en sciences sociales, 96
Réformes de l'enseignement, 1924, 1965
Relations du travail, 4555, 4556
Romans, 1816
Sectes, 1420
Socialisation politique, 4970
Sociologie, 42, 69
Statut de la femme, 3217, 3272
Suicide, 1180
Syndicalisme, 1675
Syndicats, 4601, 4623, 4636
Technologies nouvelles, 4062
Temps de loisir, 4408
Temps de travail, 4435
Terrorisme, 1107, 1158
Travail social, 5384, 5384
Travailleurs étrangers, 3439, 4231, 4247, 4260, 4285, 4314, 4316
Travailleuses, 4303
Universités, 3217
Vie urbaine, 4408
Allocations de maternité
   Tchécoslovaquie, 5353
Allocations familiales, 5362
   États-Unis, 5346
Alphabétisation, 2101

Éthiopie, 2100
Pays en développement, 2080
Royaume-Uni, 2082
Althusser, Louis, 197, 212
Altman, Irwin, 1555
Amazonie
   Linguistique, 1525
   Population indigène, 3290
Aménagement du temps de travail, 4353, 4376, 4384, 4413, 4428
   Allemagne RF, 4359
   Canada : Québec, 4252
   France, 4395, 4407
Aménagement urbain, 3921
   Afrique du Nord, 3884
   Canada : Toronto, 3852
   Chine, 3819
   États-Unis, 3904
   Europe, 3857
   France, 3770
   Hong Kong, 3819
   Israël, 3825, 3874
   Nigeria, 3759
   Pays socialistes, 3913
   Pologne, 3845
   Royaume-Uni, 3747
   URSS, 3775
   Venezuela, 3817
Amérique
   Moyens de communication, 1753
Amérique centrale
   Église catholique, 1433
Amérique du Nord
   Enfants adoptés, 2650
   Immigration, 3531
   Moyens de communication, 1671
   Télévision, 1665
Amérique latine
   Analyse de régression, 416
   Automation, 159
   Bibliographies, 150
   Bibliothèques, 159
   Conjoncture démographique, 2766
   Contre-culture, 885
   Culture, 906, 1003
   Développement économique et social, 2506
   Développement rural, 3650
   Enseignement supérieur, 150
   Environnement, 4124
   Féminisme, 3235
   Formation professionnelle, 4466
   Identité, 4927
   Identité culturelle, 2364
   Idéologie, 854
   Intellectuels, 2364
   Littérature, 1796
   Métropole, 3768
   Migration, 3433
   Modes de vie, 1121
   Mouvements sociaux, 4927
   Opinion publique, 840
   Parenté, 3182

Participation de la collectivité, 3628
Participation politique, 1032
Partis politiques, 4909
Pauvreté, 1003
Planification de l'éducation, 1940
Politique, 5022
Politique démographique, 2961, 2963
Population, 2506, 2518, 4124
Population indigène, 3289
Population rurale, 2770
Projections démographiques, 2766
Recherche pédagogique, 1869, 1883
Réformes de l'enseignement, 1975
Relations hommes-femmes, 2565
Répartition de la population, 2764
Révolution, 2482
Santé, 2185
Santé publique, 5407
Sécurité sociale, 5361
Services de santé, 5457
Société, 1796
Stratification sociale, 2185
Styles de développement, 4124
Terrorisme, 1153
Théologie, 1309
Transition démographique, 416
Urbanisation, 3898
Vie culturelle, 1032
Amitié, 616, 620, 623, 626, 627, 675, 3024
Amour, 619, 625, 3277
    Chine, 613
Analphabétisme
    France, 2090
Analyse causale, 302
Analyse contextuelle, 304
Analyse d'enquête, 299, 341
Analyse de contenu, 317, 339, 340, 349, 359,
    1577
Analyse de groupe, 666, 669
    États-Unis, 4904
Analyse de motivation, 390, 443
Analyse de régression, 436, 438
    Amérique latine, 416
Analyse de réseau, 310, 312, 314, 315, 325,
    327, 336, 347, 358, 360
Analyse de systèmes, 311, 320, 321, 343, 344,
    357, 716, 2147
Analyse des données, 300-01, 306-07, 318,
    338, 389
Analyse du chemin critique, 435
Analyse du discours, 1603, 1617, 1622, 1628,
    1629
    Argentine, 1627
    France, 1624
Analyse écologique, 3580
Analyse factorielle, 414, 431, 447
Analyse hiérarchique, 447
Analyse historique, 335
Analyse mathématique, 391, 393, 397, 405
Analyse multivariée, 324, 328, 3426
Analyse organisationnelle, 713-15, 718-19,
    893

Analyse par cohorte, 326
    Allemagne, 2862
    États-Unis, 5149
    Hongrie, 919
Analyse par grappe, 297
Analyse qualitative, 338
Analyse quantitative, 365
Analyse régionale, 4127, 4132
    France, 2285
Analyse sociologique, 303, 371, 1505
Analyse statistique, 417, 421, 422, 427, 433,
    2194, 2779
Analyse structurale, 212, 298, 309, 314, 333,
    340, 348, 351, 352, 397
    Japon, 322
Analyse transculturelle, 1581
Analyse transnationale, 4474
Anarchisme, 4798-4801, 4806, 4813
Ancienneté
    États-Unis, 4192
Anciens combattants
    États-Unis, 5032, 5038
Androgynie
    Australie, 2612
Angoisse, 543
Animaux
    France, 2558
Anomie, 3049
Anthologies
    Inde, 4508
Anthropologie, 1000
    Costa Rica, 3283
Anthropologie politique, 880
    Iran, 1443
Anthropologie sociale, 879
    Pays en développement, 3704
    Royaume-Uni, 214
Anticléricalisme
    France, 1495
Anticommunisme, 2215
Antilles
    Identité ethnique, 3318
Antisémitisme, 3402
    Afrique du Sud, 3423
    Allemagne, 3385
    Autriche, 3428
    États-Unis, 3404
    France, 3377, 3397, 3405, 3408
    Hongrie, 3386, 3394
    Pologne, 3429
    Roumanie, 3421
    URSS, 3380
Apartheid
    Afrique du Sud, 3384, 3412-13, 3415
Appartenance à la collectivité, 3644
    États-Unis, 1132, 3564, 3640
Appartenance au groupe, 602
    États-Unis, 707
Apprentissage
    Canada, 4501
Arabie saoudite
    Santé, 5431

Arbitrage
  États-Unis, 4701
Architecture
  États-Unis, 1833
  Italie, 1837
  Roumanie, 1839
  Royaume-Uni, 1835
Argent, 4117
  France, 4116
  Pays socialistes, 4119
Argentine
  Aide aux gens âgés, 5369
  Analyse du discours, 1627
  Catholiques, 1331
  Délinquance, 5200
  Démocratie, 4818
  Discours politique, 1627
  Droit du travail, 4573
  Emploi rural, 4189
  Enseignement primaire, 1992
  Enseignement privé, 1926
  Enseignement supérieur, 1974
  Étudiants, 2032
  Immigration, 3515
  Politique de l'éducation, 1974
  Politique de la vieillesse, 5369
  Politique sociale, 5069
  Problèmes sociaux, 5069
  Réformes universitaires, 2036
  Rendement de l'éducation, 1992
  Services de santé, 5438
  Socialisation politique, 4986
  Société, 901
  Sociologie, 3
  Stratification sociale, 2032
  Syndicats, 4582, 4669
  Systèmes de parti, 4918
  Travail social, 5381
  Universités, 2044
Aristocratie
  Royaume-Uni, 4814
Aristotle, 4855
Armée de terre
  États-Unis, 5037
Aron, Raymond, 86, 171, 178-79, 2341,
    2349-50, 2354, 2362
Art, 1008, 1766, 1770, 1778, 1785-86
  Afrique méridionale, 1764
  États-Unis, 1765
  Israël, 1769
  Japon, 1781
  URSS, 3498
Art culinaire, 4078
Art populaire
  États-Unis, 1784
Artisanat
  Afrique, 4066
  Équateur, 4086
Artisans
  Guatémala, 4536
Asie
  Communication dans l'entreprise, 4006

Droits de l'homme, 4853
Émigrants, 3496
Emploi agricole, 2274
Langues, 1305
Modes de production, 4058
Mortalité, 2897
Planification de la famille, 2997
Population urbaine, 2813
Prolétariat, 2274
Religion, 1305
Urbanisation, 3751
Asie du Sud
  Données statistiques, 424
  Histoire, 2392
  Islam, 1388
  Musulmans, 1388
Asie du Sud-Est
  Ethnicité, 3326
  Prostitution, 3050
  Tourisme international, 3050
  Vie économique, 3326
Asie occidentale
  Classes sociales, 2286
  Littérature, 1807
  Politique d'immigration, 4318
  Travailleurs étrangers, 4318
Asie orientale
  Environnement, 3595
Asiles, 5454
Aspects juridiques
  Australie, 4245
Aspirations
  Indonésie, 560
Assimilation des immigrants, 3464
  Allemagne RF, 3520, 3530
  Canada, 3330, 3533
  États-Unis, 3287, 3502
  France, 3499, 3513
  Royaume-Uni, 3474
  Suisse, 1038
Associations, 731, 732, 2713, 3633, 4279
  Congo, 730
  France, 724
  Sénégal, 730
Associations de sociologie
  Royaume-Uni, 177
Assurance maladie, 2832
  Canada, 5358
  États-Unis, 5373
Assurances, 4123
Athéisme
  URSS, 1387
Attitude envers le travail, 4349, 4360, 4397,
    4401, 4442
  Allemagne RF, 4356, 4372
  Canada, 4364
  États-Unis, 4400
  France, 4420
  Israël, 4399
  Japon, 4412
Attitudes, 607, 806-07, 810-12, 814, 817-18,
    4007

Australie, 816
Espagne, 3112
États-Unis, 813
Pologne, 2007, 2799
Attitudes culturelles, 2471
Attitudes politiques
Allemagne, 2697
États-Unis, 2692, 4968, 4979, 4991
France, 1342
Grèce, 2263
Attitudes raciales
États-Unis, 3409, 3426, 4767
Attitudes religieuses, 1344, 1479
France, 1342
Attraction interpersonnelle, 624
Attribution, 495, 593-97, 599, 601, 607, 609, 612, 803
Australie
Adaptation sociale, 1165
Adolescents, 1221
Affinité, 618
Androgynie, 2612
Aspects juridiques, 4245
Attitudes, 816
Avortement, 816, 3002
Catholicisme, 816
Civilisation, 884
Conservatisme, 816
Contraception, 2967
Développement régional, 4125
Dimension de la famille, 3152
Discrimination sexuelle, 2596
Écoles privées, 2016
Éducation, 3309
Enfants adoptés, 3198
Enseignement multiculturel, 1960
Éthique protestante, 1474
Ethnicité, 3299
Fécondité, 2914, 2918
Géographie, 3591
Gestion des universités, 2074
Groupes minoritaires, 687, 2918
Histoire de l'éducation, 1892
Hôpitaux, 5442
Immigrants, 1165, 1326, 3489
Immigration, 3465
Infirmières, 4379
Journalistes, 1694
Juifs, 1326
Liberté de l'enseignement, 1951
Main-d'oeuvre féminine, 4245
Marché du travail, 2596
Mariage, 618
Mères célibataires, 3198
Méthodes contraceptives, 2966
Moralité, 1221
Mythes, 2612
Négociation collective, 4691
Personnes âgées, 2754
Pluralisme culturel, 889, 911
Politique de l'éducation, 1892
Politique du logement, 3915

Politique ethnique, 3364
Politique migratoire, 3435
Population indigène, 3292, 3304, 3309, 3311, 3347
Prévention de la délinquance, 5248
Primes de salaires, 4389
Racisme, 3432
Radiodiffusion, 1664
Réformes de l'enseignement, 1949
Rôles sexuels, 2612
Santé mentale, 2612
Sécurité du travail, 4389, 4390
Sociologie, 12
Sociologie du droit, 1253
Systèmes de valeur, 1221
Transition démographique, 2754
Universités, 2037
Violence, 1140
Australie : Sydney
Maternité, 3017
Autodéveloppement
Zimbabwe, 2428
Autogestion, 708
Chili, 770
Pérou, 770
Autogestion ouvrière
Japon, 4721
Roumanie, 4711
Automation, 4043
Allemagne RD, 4039
Amérique latine, 159
États-Unis, 4057
France, 4022, 4031, 4472, 4491
Automobiles, 4097
Autoritarisme, 564, 827, 829
Afrique du Sud, 4804
Allemagne RF, 828
Mexique, 4826
URSS, 831
Autorité, 781, 792
Autriche
Agriculteurs, 3663
Antisémitisme, 3428
Culture politique, 4963
Économie de marché, 3955
Émigration, 3487
Grèves sauvages, 4678
Histoire de la sociologie, 51
Histoire sociale, 3663
Intellectuels, 3487
Jeux, 4747
Milieux d'affaires, 4013
Moyens de communication de masse, 1709
Partis politiques, 4915
Politique de l'éducation, 1934
Politique sociale, 5309
Prostitution, 3032
Réformes de l'enseignement, 1934
Régulation sociale, 1048
Utilisation des loisirs, 4747
Autriche : Vienne
Travailleurs migrants, 4291

Avortement, 2971, 3009
  Australie, 816, 3002
  Bangladesh, 2986
  Belgique, 2992
  États-Unis, 2981, 3002, 3174
  Los Angeles, 2978
  Roumanie, 2990

Baisse de la fécondité, 2921, 2960
  Canada : Québec, 2940
  Pays en développement, 2955
  Thaïlande, 2930
  Yougoslavie, 2798
Baisse de la mortalité, 2878
Bandes, 5209
  États-Unis, 5229
  Suède, 2684
Bangladesh
  Avortement, 2986
  Bibliothèques, 160
  Contraception, 3007
  Femmes rurales, 5116
  Mères travailleuses, 4251
  Naissance, 2906
  Pauvreté rurale, 5116
  Planification de la famille, 5453
  Puériculture, 4251
  Services de santé, 5453
  Théâtre, 1855
  Travailleuses, 4238
  Villages, 3684
Banque de données, 157
  URSS, 155
Banques commerciales, 3952
Banquiers
  Royaume-Uni, 2283
Bâtiments
  Pologne, 2799
Beaux-arts
  États-Unis, 1838
Belgique
  Administration scolaire, 2023
  Avortement, 2992
  Bilinguisme, 1599
  Cadres, 4528
  Divorce, 3094
  Droit du travail, 4577
  Écoles secondaires, 2023
  Éducation, 1912
  Enseignement bilingue, 2099
  Enseignement des langues, 1599
  Forces armées, 5035
  Formation, 2128
  Islam, 1352
  Juges, 4882
  Livres, 1757
  Logements sociaux, 3800
  Mariage, 3094
  Médecins, 5475
  Minorités religieuses, 1352
  Négociation collective, 4690
  Politique du logement, 3800

Professions médicales, 5415
Service militaire, 5035
Services de santé, 5441
Soins médicaux, 5415
Théâtre, 1851
Tourisme, 4758
Violence, 1099
Bell, Daniel, 66
Bénin
  Classes sociales, 2300
Berger, Peter L., 1819
Besoins, 527, 532, 539, 546, 559
  Pologne, 3968
Besoins d'éducation, 1981
Besoins de logement
  États-Unis, 3836
  Yougoslavie, 3824
Besoins fondamentaux
  Afrique, 5088
Bible, 581
Bibliographies, 152, 263, 1156, 1277, 1298, 2465,
    2600, 2637, 3036, 3175, 3203, 3532, 3624,
    3626, 3782, 3914, 4139, 4457, 4464, 4542
  Amérique latine, 150
  Brésil, 2517
  Bulgarie, 4660
  Danemark, 4595
  États-Unis, 3398
  Europe, 2095
  Maghreb, 1394
  Pays en développement, 5044
Bibliothèques
  Allemagne RF, 158
  Amérique latine, 159
  Bangladesh, 160
  Brésil, 163
  États-Unis, 153, 165
  Nigeria, 154
  Tchécoslovaquie, 161
  Zambie, 162
Bidonvilles
  Brésil, 1212, 3792
  États-Unis, 2120
  Inde, 3891
  Italie, 3795
  Pays en développement, 3869, 3879, 3880
  Pays-Bas, 4187
Bien-être, 2726, 2753, 2761, 3971, 3975
  États-Unis, 3978
  Hongrie, 4350
Bien-être social, 5266, 5278
  Danemark, 5298
  Inde, 2881
  Suède, 5298
  Taïwan, 5254
Bilinguisme, 1585, 1618
  Belgique, 1599
  Canada, 1614
  États-Unis, 4267
  France, 3101
  Paraguay, 1598
  URSS, 1590

Biographies, 172-75, 180-81, 5072
Biologie sociale, 34, 68, 70, 751
    États-Unis, 41
Biosphère, 3605
Birmanie
    Éducation, 1917
Blau, Peter M., 655, 662, 694, 2155, 3363
Bloch, Ernest, 1319
Bolivie
    Mouvements étudiants, 2057
    Pouvoir local, 4898
Bonheur, 4762
Botswana
    Divorce, 3093
    Fécondité, 2916
    Participation des femmes, 3236
    Statut de la femme, 3236
Bouddhisme, 229, 1329, 1362
    Népal, 2434
Bourdieu, Pierre, 874
Bourgeoisie, 2296
    Canada, 2260, 2295
    Colombie, 4135
    France, 3045
    Inde, 2282
    Nicaragua, 2312
    Pérou, 4135
    Royaume-Uni, 4780
Brahmanisme
    Inde, 1393
Brésil
    Aires métropolitaines, 3903
    Allaitement naturel, 2868
    Bibliographies, 2517
    Bibliothèques, 163
    Bidonvilles, 1212, 3792
    Budgets temps, 4405
    Chances d'éducation, 1956
    Cinéma, 1674
    Citoyenneté, 3609, 3615
    Clientélisme, 797, 4129
    Communication, 1545
    Conditions sociales, 371
    Conflits sociaux, 651
    Conscience de classe, 2309
    Culture populaire, 1200, 1201, 1207
    Démographie historique, 2517
    Développement social, 2420
    Éducation de base, 2088, 2106
    Église catholique, 1427, 1440, 2106
    Église et État, 1498
    Enseignement privé, 1987
    Enseignement public, 1987
    Étrangers, 3300
    Études d'aire, 371
    Exploitation des ressources, 2487
    Fécondité, 444
    Honneur, 1212
    Inégalité sociale, 1956
    Intellectuels, 1201
    Liturgie, 1440
    Main-d'oeuvre féminine, 4281

Médecine traditionnelle, 5398
Modèles stochastiques, 444
Mortalité infantile, 2868
Négociation collective, 2309
Noirs, 3296
Pauvreté, 797
Philosophie de l'éducation, 1911
Planification régionale, 4129
Politique culturelle, 1027
Politique du logement, 3792
Prison, 5167
Publicité, 1633
Réadaptation des délinquants, 5167
Santé, 5426, 5428
Santé publique, 5407
Sécurité sociale, 5357
Segrégation résidentielle, 3883
Socialisation politique, 4986
Sous-développement, 2487
Sport, 4751
Structure urbaine, 3881
Syndicats, 4657
Temps de loisir, 4405
Travail des femmes, 4255
Travail social, 5167
Villes nouvelles, 3893
Budgets des ménages
    Royaume-Uni, 3980
Budgets familiaux
    États-Unis, 4249
    France, 5100
Budgets temps
    Allemagne RF, 4408
    Brésil, 4405
    Finlande, 4351, 4352
    France, 904, 3158, 4402, 4404
    Hongrie, 4350, 4351, 4352
    Norvège, 4406
    Pologne, 4437
Bulgarie
    Bibliographies, 4660
    Changement technologique, 4056
    Classe dirigeante, 2346
    Juifs, 1383
    Mouvements ouvriers, 4660
    Services d'information, 161
    Socialisme, 4660
    Statistique, 413
Bureaucratie, 739, 772, 776
    Chine, 771
    États-Unis, 743, 747
    Inde, 767
Bureautique, 4019, 4038, 4052
    France, 4049
Burke, Edmund, 4807
Burkina-Faso
    Développement rural, 3658
    Écoles rurales, 2014
    Formation de classe, 2305
Burundi
    Noms, 507
But de l'organisation, 768, 4532

Cadres, 2610, 4529, 4532
    Belgique, 4528
    États-Unis, 3352
    France, 4527
    Japon — Royaume-Uni, 4530
    Royaume-Uni, 4560
    Yougoslavie, 4531
Caisses de retraite
    Royaume-Uni, 4724
Calcul des probabilités, 441
Californie
    Prison, 5156
Cameroun
    Sécurité sociale, 5355
Campagne électorale
    États-Unis, 5002, 5004, 5020
Campus universitaire
    États-Unis, 1147
Canada
    Aide aux gens âgés, 5352, 5378
    Apprentissage, 4501
    Assimilation des immigrants, 3330, 3533
    Assurance maladie, 5358
    Attitude envers le travail, 4364
    Bilinguisme, 1614
    Bourgeoisie, 2260, 2295
    Chances d'éducation, 3258
    Changement social, 3777
    Châtiment, 5176
    Choix d'une profession, 3258
    Citoyens, 5449
    Classes sociales, 481, 2261
    Communauté scientifique, 126
    Communication interethnique, 3371
    Comportement électoral, 4997
    Comportement sexuel, 3035
    Conditions de travail, 4362, 4410
    Conflits du travail, 4676
    Conjoncture démographique, 2776
    Construction nationale, 2489
    Criminologie, 5155, 5235
    Cycle de vie, 3157
    Délinquance juvénile, 5157
    Délits, 5196
    Démocratisation, 1947
    Démographie historique, 2539, 3157, 3436
    Déviance, 1108
    Dimension de la famille, 3163, 3172
    Direction de l'entreprise, 4003
    Division du travail, 2224
    Divorce, 2114
    Droit d'auteur, 3939
    Élections, 3246
    Élite, 3258
    Émigration, 3477
    Entreprises publiques, 4566
    Ethnicité, 3299, 3316
    Ethnocentrisme, 3376
    Famille, 3138
    Fécondité, 2905
    Féminisme, 3254
    Formation de classe, 2266

Gestion d'entreprises, 481
Grèves sauvages, 4673
Groupes ethniques, 1050, 2216, 3294, 3323
Groupes minoritaires, 688, 691, 1605
Hommes de loi, 2368
Identité ethnique, 3330, 3371
Identité nationale, 976
Immigrants, 3138, 3461, 3468, 3480, 3484, 3493, 3500, 3511
Immigration, 3465
Individus, 481
Innovations, 4040
Jeunesse, 3035
Langues, 1604
Liberté de l'enseignement, 2027
Manifestations, 867
Mariage, 3060
Mécanisation agricole, 4088
Migration, 3436
Minorités ethniques, 3340
Minorités linguistiques, 1605
Mobilité sociale, 2368, 2383
Mouvements étudiants, 2056
Mouvements sociaux, 4923
Nationalisme, 4772
Organisations féminines, 3221
Participation des femmes, 3208, 3227
Partis politiques, 4907
Personnes âgées, 2716
Politique culturelle, 1025
Politique de l'emploi, 4221
Politique ethnique, 3364
Politique locale, 3316
Politique scientifique, 126
Population, 2539
Population indigène, 3310, 3334
Population urbaine, 3777
Pornographie, 3034
Prestige professionnel, 4474
Qualification professionnelle, 4522
Qualité de la vie, 4028, 4362
Recherche action, 114
Réfugiés, 3533
Relations de dépendance, 5041
Relations du travail, 4566
Réussite dans les études, 2114
Rôle, 3144
Santé mentale, 4040
Satisfaction conjugale, 3172
Scolarisation, 1946
Segrégation professionnelle, 4495
Services de santé, 5449
Services sociaux, 5466
Statut de la femme, 3246, 3258
Stéréotypes raciaux, 3376
Stratification sociale, 2216, 2261
Structure sociale, 340
Symboles, 1547
Syndicats, 4620
Systèmes d'enseignement, 1947
Systèmes de valeur, 1050

Technologie alternative, 4028
Théâtre, 1850
Travail des femmes, 3060, 4241
Travailleurs manuels, 4522
Universités, 2027
Urbanisation, 3850
Vie familiale, 3144, 3157, 3172
Villes, 3850
Zones rurales, 5196
Zones urbaines, 3777
Canada — États-Unis
 Relations internationales, 5041
Canada : Québec
 Aménagement du temps de travail, 4252
 Baisse de la fécondité, 2940
 Église catholique, 1437
 Églises protestantes, 1428
 Emploi des femmes, 4029
 Nationalisme, 1428, 1437, 4773
 Religion, 4773
 Technologies nouvelles, 4029
 Travailleuses, 4252
Canada : Toronto
 Administration locale, 3852
 Aménagement urbain, 3852
 Décentralisation, 3852
Capacité intellectuelle, 5207
Capital, 1245
Capitalisme, 223, 1776, 2293, 3946, 4045
 Royaume-Uni, 3952
Capitalisme d'État
 Égypte, 3945
 Tanzanie, 3732
Caractère national
 Japon, 943
Caraïbes
 Communication, 1567
 Enquêtes sociales, 375
 Exode des compétences, 3501
 Migration, 3442, 3443
 Paysannerie, 3738
 Recherche pédagogique, 1894
Carnavals
 Colombie, 1192
 France, 1197
Castes
 Inde, 1170, 2202, 2234-36, 2238-40,
  2243-44, 2386
 Inde : Assam, 2233
 Sri Lanka, 2241
Catholicisme, 988, 1364
 Australie, 816
 Corée R, 1323
 Espagne, 1364, 1380
 États-Unis, 1368, 1392, 2907
 France, 1353, 1373
 Hongrie, 1398
 Italie, 1348, 1386
 Mexique, 1364
 Pérou, 1364
 Pologne, 1350, 1397
Catholiques

Argentine, 1331
 États-Unis, 3640
 France, 1342
 Irlande du Nord, 1214
 Pays-Bas, 1384
 Royaume-Uni, 1366
Causalité, 279, 291
Cécité
 États-Unis, 2828
CEE
 Travail des femmes, 4290
Centralisme démocratique, 4618
Centre ville
 États-Unis, 3892
Cercles de qualité, 4726
 France, 4335
Cérémonie de mariage
 Yougoslavie, 3127
Certeau, Michel de, 1450, 1465
Chałasiński, Józef, 80, 930, 1918, 2297
Chamanisme
 Népal, 1318
Chances d'éducation, 2186, 2337
 Allemagne, 2377
 Brésil, 1956
 Canada, 3258
 France, 1983, 2194, 2199
Chances d'obtenir un emploi, 2337, 4229
 États-Unis, 4227
 Inde, 4226
Changement culturel, 2426
 Guatémala, 1026
 Pologne, 2267
 Yougoslavie, 3834
Changement d'attitude, 2960
 Chine, 2969
Changement d'organisation, 727, 744, 752-53,
  758, 760-61, 763, 769, 773, 777, 3994,
  4415
Changement économique, 3963
 Philippines, 3965
Changement politique, 4771
Changement religieux
 Royaume-Uni, 1366
Changement social, 799, 1051, 1209, 2156,
  2161, 2307, 2413-15, 2421-24, 2426-27,
  2442, 2447, 2452-54, 2465, 2467, 2474,
  2476, 2478-79, 2583, 2705, 3642, 3912,
  3963, 4035, 5285, 5297, 5399
 Allemagne RF, 299
 Canada, 3777
 Espagne, 2455, 2477
 Europe orientale, 4920
 France, 724, 2436
 Hongrie, 2446
 Île de la Réunion, 2418
 Inde, 2234, 2243, 2459, 2462, 2466, 3715,
  3734, 4912
 Japon : Takarazuka, 3789
 Jordanie, 2481, 3319
 Népal, 2434
 Pays en développement, 2440

Thaïlande, 3786
Changement structurel
  Pays capitalistes, 2382
Changement technologique, 4018, 4034, 4037,
    4053, 4441
  Bulgarie, 4056
  États-Unis, 4602
  France, 4046, 4496, 4602
  Pays en développement, 4025
  Pays méditerranéens, 4064
Chansons populaires
  URSS, 1848
Charisme, 782, 788, 790
Chasse, 4073
Châtiment, 5144, 5172, 5189, 5211
  Canada, 5176
  États-Unis, 5215, 5217, 5230
  France, 5145
  Hongrie, 5184
Chefs d'entreprise
  États-Unis, 4000
  Italie, 4007, 4008
Chicago School of Sociology, 21
Chili
  Autogestion, 770
  Enseignement professionnel, 4467
  Enseignement supérieur, 2034
  Famille, 3192
  Féminisme, 3249
  Formation professionnelle, 4467
  Opinion publique, 833
  Politique sanitaire, 5436
  Recherche sur la communication, 1565
  Répression, 5180
  Sciences sociales, 14
  Sociologie, 18, 19
  Syndicalisme, 4587, 4645
  Syndicats, 4592
  Vie quotidienne, 960
Chine
  Aménagement urbain, 3819
  Amour, 613
  Bureaucratie, 771
  Changement d'attitude, 2969
  Classe ouvrière, 2245
  Comportement collectif, 1150
  Conjoncture démographique, 2771, 2777
  Contestation politique, 1831
  Cultes, 1446
  Démocratie industrielle, 4716
  Démographie, 2557
  Démographie historique, 2931
  Développement rural, 3648, 3718
  Éducation, 1902
  Émigrants, 3535
  Étudiants, 2073
  Famille, 3159
  Fécondité, 2917, 2931, 2959, 3063
  Femmes, 2631
  Folklore, 1198
  Groupes ethniques, 3327
  Hôpitaux, 5446

  Intellectuels, 2355, 2367
  Justice criminelle, 5239
  Littérature, 1817
  Mariage, 613, 3159
  Migration rurale-urbaine, 3550
  Naissance, 2935
  Nuptialité, 3063
  Participation des travailleurs, 4719
  Patriarcat, 3141
  Paysans, 3683
  Personnes âgées, 2756
  Planification de la famille, 2969
  Poésie, 1831
  Politique de l'éducation, 1922, 1943
  Politique démographique, 3006, 3018
  Politique familiale, 5376
  Population, 2508, 2514, 2532, 2534
  Population urbaine, 2806
  Recensements de population, 2768, 2775
  Relations du travail, 4549
  Sécurité sociale, 5375
  Services d'information, 156
  Sexualité, 1817
  Sociabilité, 1817
  Statut de la femme, 3244, 3253
  Stratification sociale, 2324
  Structure de classe, 2324
  Systèmes de valeur, 1061
  Théâtre, 1857
  Urbanisation, 3866
  Vie urbaine, 3923
  Violence, 1150
  Zones rurales, 2917, 2959
Chinois
  Ethnicité, 3326
  Vie économique, 3326
Choix collectif, 863, 864
  États-Unis, 865
Choix d'une profession, 4459
  Allemagne RF, 4464
  Canada, 3258
  États-Unis, 4503
Choix du conjoint, 617
  Philippines, 3058
Chômage, 4178, 4179, 4185, 4190, 4209,
    4217, 4296
  Allemagne RF, 4183, 4194
  États-Unis, 4188, 4213, 5237, 5243
  France, 4208
  Pays-Bas, 4187, 4214, 4218, 4219
  Royaume-Uni, 3118, 4201
  Yougoslavie, 4200
Chômage des jeunes, 4186
  Allemagne RF, 4180, 4247
  États-Unis, 3403
  Irlande, 4182, 4212
  Pays de la CEE, 4195
  Royaume-Uni, 4202
Chômage technologique, 4216
Chômeurs, 4211
  États-Unis, 4205
  France, 4184

Royaume-Uni, 4585
Tanzanie, 4197
Christianisme, 47, 1358, 1360, 1658
 Algérie, 1033
 États-Unis, 62, 1396
 Madagascar, 1347
Cinéma, 1647, 1681
 Afrique, 1642, 1655, 1670
 Allemagne RF, 1737
 Brésil, 1674
 Espagne, 1727
 France, 1641
 URSS, 1704
Citoyenneté
 Brésil, 3609, 3615
Citoyens
 Canada, 5449
Civilisation, 912, 933, 934, 974, 985, 991,
  999, 1006
 Australie, 884
 Inde, 900
 Suriname, 997
Classe dirigeante, 10
 Bulgarie, 2346
Classe moyenne, 850, 2287, 2313
 Afrique, 2356
 France, 764, 2250, 2265, 5007
 Italie, 2258
 Suède, 2117
Classe ouvrière, 196, 2278, 2280, 2288, 2297,
  2304, 2315, 3838
 Allemagne, 2291, 2401
 Chine, 2245
 Curaçao, 2320
 États-Unis, 2277
 Europe orientale, 4625
 France, 1430, 1983, 2285, 5100
 Inde, 4508
 Inde : Kerala, 2275
 Japon, 2249
 Pays arabes, 2381
 Pays capitalistes, 2262
 Pologne, 2267
 Royaume-Uni, 1995
 Turquie, 2269
 URSS, 2268, 2301
 Yougoslavie, 2276
Classe supérieure
 États-Unis, 2360
Classes sociales, 1091, 1124, 2192, 2252,
  2281, 2308, 2319, 2327, 2567, 3936,
  3975
 Afrique, 2248
 Afrique centrale, 2279
 Asie occidentale, 2286
 Bénin, 2300
 Canada, 481, 2261
 Ghana : Accra, 2614
 Inde : Bengale, 3661
 Japon, 2271, 2325
 Pologne, 2272
 Royaume-Uni, 2246, 2620, 2949

Suède, 2264, 2323
Trinité-et-Tabago, 2314
Yougoslavie, 2222
Zambie, 2302
Classification, 916, 4458
Clergé
 États-Unis, 4770
Clientélisme
 Brésil, 797, 4129
Clochards
 Hongrie, 5218
Clubs, 620, 679
Coalitions, 445, 647
Cohésion du groupe, 699, 700, 702
Collectifs de production, 2425
Collectivité, 967, 3621
Collectivité de travail, 528, 4329, 4336, 4339,
  4342, 4344
Collectivités locales, 981, 3626, 3633
 États-Unis, 3640
 Hongrie, 3620
 Japon, 3631, 3636
Collectivités rurales, 3181
 France, 3697
 France : Province, 3699
 Japon, 3691, 3739
 Mexique, 3714
 Zaïre, 3712
Collectivités urbaines
 États-Unis, 3781, 3911
 Pologne : Rzeszów, 3865
Collins, Randall, 787
Colombie
 Bourgeoisie, 4135
 Carnavals, 1192
 Développement régional, 4135
 Droit du travail, 4670
 Éducation, 1881
 Famille, 3104
 Gens de maison, 4526
 Grèves, 4670
 Nutrition, 5084
 Relations du travail, 4563
 Relations école-collectivité, 1933
 Systèmes d'enseignement, 1941
Colonialisme
 Afrique, 3943
Communauté scientifique, 74, 2571
 Canada, 126
 Inde, 124
 Israël, 122
Communautés religieuses
 Afrique, 1435
 Irlande du Nord, 1421
Communication, 514, 670, 1091, 1538, 1546,
  1549, 1558, 1569-70, 1572, 2483, 4538
 Brésil, 1545
 Caraïbes, 1567
 France, 1543, 1562
 Hongrie, 1542
 Inde, 1574
 Irlande, 3625

Italie, 4354
Japon, 1566
Pays en développement, 1573
Communication dans l'entreprise, 3995, 3999,
    4004, 4010
  Asie, 4006
  Suisse, 3993
Communication de masse, 1648, 1706, 1720,
    1723, 1729, 1742, 1749, 1750, 1752
Communication interculturelle, 1031
Communication interethnique
  Canada, 3371
  Hawaï, 3396
Communication interpersonnelle, 1541, 1551,
    1563
Communication non-verbale, 1597
Communication verbale, 1550
Communisme, 211, 4782, 4794
Compétences
  États-Unis, 4176
Comportement, 808-12, 815, 817
Comportement antisocial
  URSS, 1232
Comportement collectif, 568, 869, 2344
  Chine, 1150
  Cuba, 861
  Pologne, 622
Comportement culturel, 1045, 2227
Comportement de l'étudiant
  États-Unis, 2029, 2041
Comportement de l'organisation, 741, 745,
    748-49, 754-56, 765, 774-75, 778
  Afrique du Sud, 738
Comportement du consommateur, 826,
    4101-02, 4104-07
  États-Unis, 4100, 4108, 4109
  Pologne, 4103
Comportement du groupe
  Guyana, 703
Comportement économique
  États-Unis, 3961
Comportement électoral, 5008, 5015
  Allemagne RF, 5017
  Canada, 4997
  Danemark, 4995, 5021
  États-Unis, 1480, 4992, 4994, 4998, 4999,
    5003, 5006, 5010, 5018
  Finlande, 3346
  France, 5007
  Israël, 4996
  Italie, 2168
  Japon, 5016
Comportement politique, 4962, 4967
  États-Unis, 4367
  Nouvelle Zélande, 4977
  Yougoslavie, 4982
Comportement religieux, 1477, 1481, 1484
  États-Unis, 1471, 1482
Comportement sexuel, 3023, 3024
  Canada, 3035
  Côte d'Ivoire, 3040
  États-Unis, 3027, 3053

France, 3045, 3049
Comportement social 106, 574, 1125, 1157,
    1178, 1186, 1193, 5305
  États-Unis, 1115
  Pologne, 1139
Composition de la population
  Tchécoslovaquie, 2769
Compréhension, 282
Comptes rendus de livres, 151
Comte, Auguste, 72, 483, 1568, 2119
Concentration urbaine
  Mexique, 3780
Conception de soi, 94, 488, 490, 492, 511,
    5322
Conceptualisation, 367, 558
Concurrence, 4112-14
Condamnation pénale
  États-Unis, 5198, 5252
Conditions de travail, 2299, 3976, 4355, 4363,
    4365, 4374, 4419, 4423, 4441
  Allemagne, 4275
  Canada, 4362, 4410
  États-Unis, 4057, 4440
  France, 4369
  Inde, 4388
  Japon, 4393
  Pays développés, 4436
  Pologne, 4394, 4424
  Tanzanie, 4396
  URSS, 4429
Conditions de vie, 3696, 3970
  Afrique du Sud : Pretoria, 2760
  France, 3967
  Hongrie, 3969, 3986
  Norvège, 3974
  Pologne, 2674, 3968
  Royaume-Uni, 3980
Conditions sociales
  Afrique, 5091
  Brésil, 371
  France, 2452
  Hongrie, 5273
  Inde, 2398, 5300
  Pays-Bas, 5318
  Pérou, 5286
  Royaume-Uni, 994
  Yougoslavie, 5317
Conflit conjugal, 3086, 3099
Conflits, 649, 3194
  Allemagne RF, 638
  États-Unis, 5440
  Irlande du Nord, 1421
  Japon, 646
Conflits culturels, 1039
  Suisse, 1038
Conflits de classe, 2307
  Thaïlande, 3690
Conflits de générations, 2637, 2639
Conflits du travail, 639, 4681, 4709
  Canada, 4676
  États-Unis, 4701
  France, 3941

Inde, 4689
Israël, 4688
Italie, 4680
Nouvelle Zélande, 4679
Pérou, 4686
Royaume-Uni, 4677
Conflits internationaux, 5050, 5052, 5054, 5055
Conflits interpersonnels, 660
Conflits raciaux
Royaume-Uni, 3411, 4877
Sri Lanka, 3390, 3407
Conflits sociaux, 639, 640, 2230, 4700
Brésil, 651
Guatémala, 654
Italie, 641
Pologne, 643, 650, 658
Conformité sociale, 1171
Confréries
États-Unis, 1414
Confucianisme, 2935
Congo
Associations, 730
Développement rural, 3707
Villes, 730
Congrégations
France, 1425
Congrès
Pays-Bas, 245
Conjoncture démographique, 2784, 2802
Algérie, 2814
Amérique latine, 2766
Canada, 2776
Chine, 2771, 2777
France, 4047
Israël, 2774
Pologne, 2773
Portugal, 2805
Royaume-Uni, 2803
Yougoslavie, 2788
Connaissance, 1523, 5401
États-Unis, 283
Japon, 1520
Conscience collective, 502, 862
Conscience de classe
Brésil, 2309
États-Unis, 2256, 2328
Grèce, 2263
Japon, 2322
Royaume-Uni, 2254
Conscience de groupe, 4527
Conscience nationale
Allemagne RD, 950
Allemagne RF, 908, 950
Conscience sociale, 480, 1093, 1100, 1120, 1122, 1131, 1133, 1149, 1151, 1160, 1722, 2403
Japon, 2691, 4133
Pérou, 5033
Pologne, 1112, 2213
Consensus, 838
États-Unis, 611

Conservatisme, 447, 564, 4807, 5025
Afrique du Sud, 4804
Australie, 816
États-Unis, 1482
Pays-Bas, 4781
Royaume-Uni, 4780
Consommation, 1001
Consommation alimentaire
France, 5100
Inde, 5096
Consommation culturelle
Italie, 3806
Construction de l'État
Nicaragua, 4834
Construction nationale, 2483
Canada, 2489
Construction navale
Royaume-Uni, 740
Contes de fées, 1832
Contestation politique
Allemagne RF, 4958
Chine, 1831
El Salvador, 4957
Contestation sociale, 568, 1130, 5165
États-Unis, 1181
Inde, 5109
Contraception, 815, 2902, 2979, 2987, 3016
Australie, 2967
Bangladesh, 3007
États-Unis, 2964, 2976, 2993
Nigeria, 2996
Suisse, 2983
Turquie, 2974
Contrat social, 2157
Contre-culture, 2441
Amérique latine, 885
Contremaîtres, 4533
Contrôle administratif, 653, 740, 750, 762, 766, 780
Contrôle économique, 1252
Coopération agricole
Pologne, 4079
Coopération culturelle
Allemagne RF, 1016
Maghreb, 1016
Coopératives
Afrique, 614
États-Unis, 3957
Inde, 3942
Royaume-Uni, 3953
Coopératives agricoles
Équateur, 3682
Israël, 4077
Japon, 4093
Pays en développement, 4289
Coordination des recherches, 118
Corée
Identité nationale, 983
Immigrants, 3396
Corée R
Catholicisme, 1323
Démocratie industrielle, 4714

Émigrants, 3486, 3498
Enseignement supérieur, 2028
Fécondité, 2932, 3548
Migration rurale-urbaine, 3548
Personnes âgées, 2735
Solidarité, 3667
Structure sociale, 2167
Taux de fécondité, 2946
Travailleuses, 4280
Veuve, 3081
Vie rurale, 3667
Villages, 3667
Corporatisme, 4647, 4654, 4816
Europe occidentale, 4580
Corps humain, 2559, 2597, 3045
Corrélation, 407, 428
Corruption administrative
URSS, 4894
Corruption politique
États-Unis, 4985
Cosmologie
Japon, 1448
Costa Rica
Anthropologie, 3283
Espacement des naissances, 2998
Fécondité, 5086
Migration interne, 3546
Pauvreté, 5086
Population indigène, 3283
Radio, 1690
Relations école-collectivité, 1936
Sécurité sociale, 5372
Côte d'Ivoire
Comportement sexuel, 3040
Liberté de la presse, 4851
Moyens de communication de masse, 1686
Musique, 1845
Coutumes, 1205
Cox, Harvey, 1272
Création artistique, 1776, 1779-80
Création d'emplois, 4026
Créativité, 1172, 1790, 2130, 2663, 5025
Criminologie, 2453, 5161, 5182
Canada, 5155, 5235
Crise de civilisation
Pays occidentaux, 966
Crise morale
Yougoslavie, 1228
Critères du bien-être, 3979
Critique, 1856
Croissance démographique, 2767, 2780, 2790, 2801
États-Unis, 2796
Inde, 2785
Tchécoslovaquie, 2794
Croissance économique, 4955
Croissance urbaine
États-Unis, 3875
Italie, 3795
Pays en développement, 3858
Croyance, 765, 1294
Pakistan, 834

Croyances religieuses, 2882
États-Unis, 1413
France : Bretagne, 1451
Inde, 5150
Cuba
Comportement collectif, 861
Fécondité, 2927
Politique sanitaire, 5436
Pouvoir judiciaire, 4883
Recensement de population, 2809
Statut de la femme, 3266
Culte des ancêtres, 1441
Cultes, 1362, 1442, 1445, 1468
Chine, 1446
Taïwan, 1447
Culture, 136, 192, 201, 225, 510, 572, 893, 909-10,
920, 930, 932, 937, 942, 951-53, 970-71,
979, 988, 995-96, 1008, 1124, 1206,
1546, 2288, 3608, 4024, 4044, 5152
Amérique latine, 906, 1003
Espagne, 982
États-Unis, 968, 5439
France, 1267
Hongrie, 978
Italie, 887
Japon, 2435
Pays en développement, 886
Pays-Bas, 935, 4473
Pologne, 895, 1004
Roumanie, 913, 927
URSS, 1005, 1378
Yougoslavie, 903
Culture d'entreprise
États-Unis, 972
Culture locale
États-Unis, 3911
Culture matérielle, 3606
Culture minoritaire
Europe occidentale, 925
Culture ouvrière, 931, 955
France, 1002
Royaume-Uni, 975
Culture paysanne
Pologne, 958
Culture politique, 4971, 4978, 4980, 4983
Autriche, 4963
Fidji, 4989
France, 1267
Japon, 3636
Turquie, 4965
URSS, 4964, 4972
Culture populaire, 1189, 1190, 1196, 1204
Brésil, 1200, 1201, 1207
États-Unis, 1191
Norvège, 1035
Pologne, 1202
Suisse, 2889
Culture socialiste, 928
Curaçao
Classe ouvrière, 2320
Curriculum
États-Unis, 775

Royaume-Uni, 2132
Cybernétique, 343
Cycle de vie, 500, 2640, 2883, 2887, 2900,
    3096, 3727
    Canada, 3157
    France, 2857
Cycles économiques, 4648
    Royaume-Uni, 4584

Danemark
    Bibliographies, 4595
    Bien-être social, 5298
    Comportement électoral, 4995, 5021
    Enseignement supérieur, 2063
    État providence, 5259
    Fécondité, 3073
    Femmes, 2566
    Groupes sociaux, 665
    Jeunesse, 3851
    Logement, 3851
    Marché du travail, 4171
    Minorités nationales, 3307
    Mouvements ouvriers, 4595
    Moyens de communication de masse, 1556
    Organisations bénévoles, 727
    Police, 4366
    Politique sociale, 5295
    Recherche sur la communication, 1556
    Satisfaction au travail, 4366
    Services sociaux, 5471
    Syndicats, 4591
    Union consensuelle, 3073
Darwin, Charles, 4855
Darwinisme, 2416
Das, Bhagwan, 81
Débilité mentale
    Royaume-Uni, 2838
Décentralisation
    Canada : Toronto, 3852
Déchristianisation
    France, 1495
Délégués du personnel
    Royaume-Uni, 4659
Délinquance, 538, 1090, 1231, 5152, 5169,
    5183, 5207, 5223, 5233
    Argentine, 5200
    États-Unis, 3781, 5178, 5192, 5220, 5225,
    5237, 5242
    Italie, 5173
Délinquance juvénile, 469, 5177, 5189, 5197,
    5234
    Algérie, 5251
    Allemagne RF, 5162, 5174
    Canada, 5157
    Espagne, 5164
    États-Unis, 2702, 4349, 5148, 5226
    France, 5168
    Israël, 5187
    Japon, 5190, 5250
    Pays-Bas, 5193
    Royaume-Uni, 2685
    Zaïre, 5204

Délinquantes
    États-Unis, 4712
    Royaume-Uni, 5244
Délinquants, 5194, 5209
    États-Unis, 2843
Délits, 2742, 5201
    Canada, 5196
    États-Unis, 5146, 5186, 5246
    France, 5202
    Inde, 5150, 5208
    Irlande, 4879
Demande de consommation
    Pologne, 4103
Demande de main d'oeuvre, 4153
    Tanzanie, 2939
Demandeurs d'emploi
    États-Unis, 4198
Démocratie, 1209, 4647, 4808-09, 4812,
    4816-17, 4819-20
    Argentine, 4818
Démocratie industrielle, 4011, 4725
    Chine, 4716
    Corée R, 4714
    Europe, 4716
    Royaume-Uni, 4713
Démocratisation
    .Canada, 1947
Démographie, 2504, 2526, 2544, 2550, 2556
    Chine, 2557
    Royaume-Uni, 2522
    URSS, 2519
Démographie historique, 2521
    Brésil, 2517
    Canada, 2539, 3157, 3436
    Chine, 2931
    États-Unis, 2516, 2551, 3065
    Finlande, 2541, 2552, 2876
    France, 2527, 2538
    Royaume-Uni, 2555
    URSS, 2545
Déontologie
    Malaisie, 1476
    Royaume-Uni, 1476
Déroulement de carrière, 2225, 4477, 4492
    États-Unis, 4500
    Hongrie, 4485
    Royaume-Uni, 4479
Derrida, Jacques, 215
Désastres, 5078, 5080
    Inde, 5079
    Japon, 3916
Déségrégation
    États-Unis, 1116, 1123, 1147
Déségrégation scolaire
    États-Unis, 1948
Désindustrialisation
    Royaume-Uni, 4082
Désintégration de la famille, 3082
    Pologne, 3147
Désorganisation sociale, 1842, 2422
    États-Unis, 3741, 3803
    Pologne, 658

Dessin, 1836
Dessins humoristiques, 1639, 1728
  France, 1725
Déterminisme, 289
Développement capitaliste, 1932
Développement cognitif, 2692
Développement culturel, 1011, 1022
  Europe, 1030
  Indonésie, 2430
  Pays en développement, 1029
  Pologne, 1013
Développement de l'éducation
  Irlande, 4033
  Pays en développement, 1921
Développement de l'enfant, 1731, 2652
Développement de la personnalité, 516, 517,
    522, 524, 526, 528, 531, 1072, 4272,
    4336, 4409
Développement des collectivités, 2426, 3616,
    3641
  États-Unis, 3623, 3632, 3634-35, 3637
  France, 2285
  Japon, 3642
  Nigeria, 3622
  Nouvelle Zélande, 5467
  Singapour, 3646
  Zambie, 3643
Développement du curriculum, 2134, 2152
Développement économique, 2476, 3186, 3966
  Afrique, 4869
  Inde, 1275
  Pologne, 4594
Développement économique et social, 2533,
    4164
  Amérique latine, 2506
  Inde, 767
  Pays en développement, 2500
Développement intellectuel, 2119
Développement moral, 1210, 1217, 2605
Développement national, 3342
  Écosse, 2499
Développement politique
  Inde, 4831, 4835
Développement régional, 2802
  Australie, 4125
  Colombie, 4135
  Égypte, 2485
  France, 1543
  Japon, 4133, 4134
  Nouvelle Zélande, 4125
  Pérou, 4135
Développement rural, 2415, 3649, 3652, 3666,
    3722
  Afrique, 3664, 5091
  Amérique latine, 3650
  Burkina-Faso, 3658
  Chine, 3648, 3718
  Congo, 3707
  États-Unis, 3635
  Inde, 3688, 3698, 3703, 3708, 3715-17,
    3721, 3731, 3734
  Israël, 3693

Jamaïque, 1854
Liban, 3725
Nicaragua, 3711
Nigeria, 3538
Pays en développement, 3695
Pays socialistes, 3728
URSS, 3742
Yougoslavie, 3672
Développement social, 294, 516, 957, 1166,
    2200, 2397, 2412, 2417, 2425, 2431,
    2433, 2437, 2448, 2449, 2450, 2457,
    2460, 2472, 2475, 3320, 4034
  Afrique, 2444
  Brésil, 2420
  Hongrie, 2439
  Île de la Réunion, 2418
  Indonésie, 2430
  Japon, 2435
  Tchécoslovaquie, 2439
  URSS, 2163, 2429, 2443, 2473
  Zimbabwe, 2428
Développement urbain, 2415, 2790, 3919
  Algérie, 3760
  États-Unis, 3803
  Inde, 3902
  Israël, 3874
  Mexique, 3862
  Soudan, 3831
Déviance, 1074, 1137, 1146, 1157, 1182
  Allemagne RF, 1180
  Canada, 1108
  États-Unis, 1084, 1132
  Japon, 1103
Dialectes
  Afrique occidentale, 1594
  Suisse, 1592
Dialectique, 212, 255, 2469, 4802
Dictature, 4813
Dictionnaires, 166, 167, 1293, 1294, 1310,
    1637
Différences de générations, 2640, 3184
  Japon, 943
  Royaume-Uni, 4479
  Yougoslavie, 2371
Différenciation de classes, 2321, 4305
  Allemagne RF, 2203
Différenciation des rôles, 3627
Différenciation raciale, 5228
  États-Unis, 273, 3378, 4979
  Madagascar, 1347
Différenciation sexuelle, 545, 789, 1464, 2188,
    2570, 2592, 2610, 2613, 2632, 2762,
    2879, 3975, 4305, 5191
  États-Unis, 2585, 5159, 5252
  Suède, 2609
Différenciation sociale, 2184, 2200, 2227
  Mexique, 3714
  Royaume-Uni, 2197
Diffusion de l'information, 140
Diffusion de la culture
  France, 1015
Dimension culturelle du développement, 1041

Dimension de l'entreprise, 4391
  États-Unis, 3997
Dimension de l'entreprise industrielle
  Royaume-Uni, 4554, 4683
  Suède, 4683
Dimension de la famille, 3183
  Australie, 3152
  Canada, 3163, 3172
  États-Unis, 3111
  Finlande, 3187
  France, 3130
  Inde, 3177
  Pologne, 3154
Dimension du groupe, 443, 602, 694
Diplômes
  Europe occidentale, 2077
Diplômés d'université, 2045
  Inde, 4226
Direction de l'entreprise
  Canada, 4003
Discipline scolaire
  États-Unis, 2022
Discours politique
  Argentine, 1627
Discrimination, 666, 822
  Japon, 821
Discrimination dans l'emploi
  États-Unis, 2576, 4222
  France, 4228
  Italie, 4220
Discrimination raciale
  États-Unis, 3368, 3416, 3892, 4445, 5166,
    5215
  Japon, 3431
  Nouvelle Zélande, 3414
  Royaume-Uni, 3830
  URSS, 3393
Discrimination religieuse
  Royaume-Uni, 1490
Discrimination salariale
  États-Unis, 2576
Discrimination sexuelle, 2573, 2628, 4287
  Australie, 2596
  États-Unis, 2576, 2578, 3987, 4445
  Inde, 4236
  Inde : Bengale Ouest, 2002
  Pays-Bas, 2618
  Royaume-Uni, 4253, 5244
  Suisse, 2616
Disparités régionales
  Tchécoslovaquie, 2769
Dispositifs de protection, 204
Distance sociale
  Allemagne RF, 3313
  Inde, 1097
Divertissement, 4745, 4754
Divination
  Guatémala, 1458
Division du travail, 2183, 2188, 2219, 2226,
    4098, 4482
  Canada, 2224
  États-Unis, 3054

Division internationale du travail, 4302
Divorce, 2942, 3066, 3070, 3082
  Allemagne RF, 3084
  Belgique, 3094
  Botswana, 3093
  Canada, 2114
  Espagne, 3091
  États-Unis, 3062, 3075, 3080, 3090, 3095,
    5243
  Royaume-Uni, 3069, 3071
  Singapour, 3102
  Tchécoslovaquie, 3083, 3089
Doctrines sociales, 1426
  Espagne, 1380
Dohen, G. A., 259
Domestication animale, 2572
Domination, 781, 787
Domination de classe, 2303
Dommanget, Maurice, 2402
Don, 1054
Données statistiques, 429
  Asie du Sud, 424
Dot
  Inde, 3097
Drogue, 5121
  Allemagne RF, 1180
  États-Unis, 5120
  Pérou, 5124
Droit, 1233, 1238, 1244-45, 1248, 1262-63,
    1814
  Afrique au Sud du Sahara, 1250
  Afrique du Sud, 1243
  Pays francophones, 1250
  Pays socialistes, 1256
  URSS, 1260
Droit administratif
  Kenya, 4764
Droit au travail, 4568
Droit coutumier
  Papouasie Nouvelle Guinée, 1239
Droit d'auteur
  Algérie, 3934
  Canada, 3939
  États-Unis, 3932, 3933
Droit de grève
  Europe, 4576
Droit de la famille
  Inde, 3068
  Israël, 3135
  Zaïre, 3161
Droit du travail, 4572, 4574
  Allemagne RF, 4303
  Argentine, 4573
  Belgique, 4577
  Colombie, 4670
  Égypte, 4569, 4615
  France, 4032, 4051, 4575
  Italie, 4220, 4680
  Pologne, 4571, 4627
  Venezuela, 4570
Droit international, 5039, 5040, 5043
  Pays en développement, 5044

Droit naturel, 1234
Droit pénal, 1251, 1257
    Albanie, 1254
    Allemagne RF, 1242
    France, 1237
    URSS, 1232
Droits de l'homme, 97, 1224, 4849-50,
        4854-55, 4857, 4862, 4865, 4867
    Afrique, 4869
    Asie, 4853
    Pays socialistes, 4863
    Pologne, 4859
Droits de la femme, 3243
    Inde, 3274
    Mexique, 3280
Droits des minorités, 2208
Droits du citoyen, 4866
    Afrique du Sud, 3400
    États-Unis, 4856, 4870
Droits fondamentaux, 1252
Droits individuels, 777
Dumont, Louis, 2419
Durée du chômage, 4204
    États-Unis, 4215
Durkheim, Émile, 210, 222, 354, 1076, 1111,
        1296, 1467, 2226, 3064, 4782, 5158,
        5211
Dyade, 683, 689
Dynamique culturelle, 1017
Dynamique de la population
    Indonésie, 2786
    Italie, 2804
    Pays méditerranéens, 2763
    Roumanie, 2815
Dynamique sociale, 2406
Dysfonctions de l'organisation, 742, 1110

Eau, 3596
Échange, 655
Échange d'information, 145, 725
Échange inégal, 2487
Échange social, 2174
Échec, 597
Échec scolaire, 2116
    États-Unis, 2120
    France, 2115
Échelle F, 827
Échelle hiérarchique, 449
Échelles d'attitude, 448
Écoles, 633
    Allemagne RF, 2012
    États-Unis, 1994, 2017
    Zaïre, 2005
Écoles primaires
    Philippines, 2000
Écoles privées
    Afrique du Sud, 1993
    Australie, 2016
    États-Unis, 1990, 1991, 2006, 2018
    France, 2004
Écoles rurales
    Burkina-Faso, 2014

Écoles secondaires, 1998
    Belgique, 2023
    Japon, 1103, 1967
    Kenya : Nairobi, 2019
Écologie, 3573-79, 3582, 3584-85, 3589-90,
        3594, 3598-99, 4073, 5051
Écologie humaine, 3586, 3592
Économie de marché
    Autriche, 3955
Économie mondiale, 4155
Économie socialiste, 5312
Économie urbaine
    Pérou : Lima, 3899
Écosse
    Développement national, 2499
    État, 2499
    Histoire économique, 3931
    Histoire sociale, 3931
    Société civile, 2499
Écriture, 569
Écrivains
    Allemagne RD, 1791
    États-Unis, 1805
    France, 1809
    Italie, 1802
    Pays arabes, 1800
Édition, 1668, 1680, 1712, 1745
    Pays arabes, 1800
    Pologne, 1695
Éducation, 792, 1102, 1553, 1785, 1872,
        1907, 1914, 4416
    Afrique du Sud, 1870
    Allemagne RF, 1903
    Australie, 3309
    Belgique, 1912
    Birmanie, 1917
    Chine, 1902
    Colombie, 1881
    Espagne, 1895
    États-Unis, 1862, 1863, 1908, 1909, 2601
    France, 1858
    Haïti, 1905
    Inde, 2240, 2459
    Irlande du Nord, 1898
    Japon, 1916
    Kenya, 1896
    Lesotho, 1876
    Mozambique, 1884
    Nicaragua, 1864
    Pakistan, 1365
    Pologne, 1013
    Suède, 2323
Éducation comparée, 1882
    Irak — Égypte, 1900
Éducation de base
    Brésil, 2088, 2106
    Mexique, 2084
Éducation de masse
    France, 2052
Éducation des adultes, 2081, 2083, 2107
    Allemagne RF, 2091, 2103
    États-Unis, 2086, 2087

Europe, 2095
France, 2102
Inde, 2097
Mexique, 2104
Royaume-Uni, 2085, 2092, 2096
URSS, 2098
Éducation des femmes, 3233
Allemagne, 3250
États-Unis, 3173
France, 3220, 3252
Pays-Bas, 1953
Éducation des parents
États-Unis, 2125
Éducation familiale, 3160, 3190
Éducation permanente, 2093
États-Unis, 2086
France, 2089
URSS, 2105
Éducation préscolaire
Espagne, 2010
République dominicaine, 2013
Royaume-Uni, 1995
Éducation religieuse, 2111
Pologne, 2109
Éducation spéciale, 2110, 2112
Égalitarisme, 2231
Égalité de chances, 2218, 4290
Allemagne, 2377
Allemagne RF, 2203
Nouvelle Zélande, 2221
Égalité de rémunération
États-Unis, 3987
Égalité des sexes, 2579
États-Unis, 2582, 2601, 2611
Suède, 2630
Égalité sociale, 2193, 2208, 2223, 2231
Hongrie, 2210
Pologne, 2210
Église catholique, 1410, 1426
Amérique centrale, 1433
Brésil, 1427, 1440, 2106
Canada : Québec, 1437
El Salvador, 4957
États-Unis, 1406, 1415, 1438
France, 1425, 1430
Guatémala, 654
Nicaragua, 1416
Église et État
Brésil, 1498
Royaume-Uni, 1418
Églises, 1436
Allemagne RD, 1411
États-Unis, 1405
Zaïre, 1404
Églises Chrétiennes
Islande, 1497
Églises protestantes
Canada : Québec, 1428
États-Unis, 1408
Royaume-Uni, 1418
Ego, 485, 487
Israël, 2623

Egocentrisme, 512
Égypte
Capitalisme d'État, 3945
Développement régional, 2485
Droit du travail, 4569, 4615
Exode des compétences, 3466
Famille, 3176
Fécondité, 2951
Islam, 1369
Migration interne, 3568
Politique démographique, 2991
Réformes de l'enseignement, 1978
Réformes foncières, 2951
Société traditionnelle, 2485
Société urbaine, 3568
Structure de classe, 3945
Syndicats, 4615
Villes nouvelles, 3927
Eisenstadt, S. N., 4838
El Salvador
Contestation politique, 4957
Église catholique, 4957
Élaboration de la politique étrangère
Inde, 542
Élections
Canada, 3246
Italie, 4993
Élèves
Pologne, 2007
Eliade, Mircea, 1462
Elias, Norbert, 313, 991
Élite, 79, 2344, 2357
Afrique, 2356
Canada, 3258
États-Unis, 2360
France, 2345
Royaume-Uni, 2339
Élite politique, 174
Émeutes
Inde, 1104
Royaume-Uni, 1154, 1155
Émigrants
Afrique, 3472
Algérie, 3490
Asie, 3496
Chine, 3535
Corée R, 3486, 3498
Espagne, 1034
États-Unis, 3440
Italie, 3470, 3521
Mexique, 3287
Portugal, 3508, 3509
Turquie, 4247
URSS, 1326, 1374
Yougoslavie, 4291
Émigration, 3503, 3532
Afrique du Nord, 3456
Autriche, 3487
Canada, 3477
Espagne, 3514
Hongrie, 3531
Israël, 3475

Italie, 3524
République dominicaine, 3481
URSS, 3460, 3516, 3536
Émotion, 544, 4753
Empathie, 621
Empirisme, 106, 203
Emploi, 38, 90, 4063
Allemagne RF, 1903
France, 4149, 4191
Emploi à temps partiel, 4428
Emploi agricole
Asie, 2274
Emploi des femmes, 2183, 4234, 4270, 4296
Allemagne RF, 3272, 4286, 4891
Canada : Québec, 4029
États-Unis, 696, 4246, 4248-50, 4257,
4262, 4311, 4315
France, 4228, 4295, 4471
Hongrie, 4284, 4300
Pays de l'OCDE, 4306
Royaume-Uni, 4253
Taïwan, 4266
Yougoslavie, 4310
Emploi des jeunes, 4193, 4207
Allemagne RF, 1924
Île de la Réunion, 2668
Irlande, 4206
Martinique, 2668
Portugal, 4206
Emploi industriel
Afrique du Sud, 3415
Emploi rural
Argentine, 4189
Emploi urbain
États-Unis, 4199
Employés
Allemagne RF, 4356
Pays socialistes, 4524
Encyclopédies, 168, 1310
Énergie nucléaire, 1519
Enfance, 2655
Espagne, 2649
Enfants, 1703, 1710, 2646, 2662
France, 2645
Nigeria, 2654
Norvège, 3974
Papouasie Nouvelle Guinée, 2644
Philippines, 609
Enfants abandonnés, 2651
Enfants adoptés, 2661
Amérique du Nord, 2650
Australie, 3198
États-Unis, 2647
Irlande du Nord, 2657
Malaisie, 2653
Royaume-Uni, 2650
Enfants doués, 2656, 2663
Enfants martyrs, 5153, 5227
États-Unis, 5181
Enquêtes, 378
Népal, 379
Enquêtes par correspondance, 384

Royaume-Uni, 385
Enquêtes sociales, 301
Caraïbes, 375
États-Unis, 376
Enquêteurs, 388
États-Unis, 382
Enrichissement des tâches
États-Unis, 4381
Enseignants, 2127, 2137, 2150, 2151
Allemagne, 2126
États-Unis, 2131, 2142
France, 2143, 2146
Japon, 1967
Royaume-Uni, 4649
Enseignement, 2147
États-Unis, 2124, 2149
Pays arabes, 2153
Enseignement agricole
France, 3220
Enseignement bilingue
Belgique, 2099
États-Unis, 2099
Mexique,* 2094
Enseignement de la sociologie, 38, 54, 55,
346, 3156
Allemagne RF, 67
États-Unis, 49
France, 8
Enseignement des langues, 1532
Belgique, 1599
Zaïre, 1615
Enseignement multiculturel
Australie, 1960
Enseignement primaire
Argentine, 1992
France, 1999, 2001, 2003
Inde : Bengale Ouest, 2002, 2011
Enseignement privé
Argentine, 1926
Brésil, 1987
Espagne, 1944
États-Unis, 1920, 1929
Enseignement professionnel, 4460
Chili, 4467
Enseignement public
Brésil, 1987
Espagne, 1944
États-Unis, 1988, 1989, 1990, 1991, 2006,
2018
Enseignement secondaire, 2144
France, 1996, 2009
Irlande, 1997
Israël, 2015
Japon, 2008
URSS, 1866
Enseignement supérieur, 2040, 2042, 2050,
2069, 2127
Allemagne RF, 2030
Amérique latine, 150
Argentine, 1974
Chili, 2034
Corée R, 2028

Danemark, 2063
États-Unis, 775, 1123, 2047, 2048, 2578
France, 2048
Inde, 2061, 2065
Japon, 2043, 2060
Norvège, 2046
Pays de l'ASEAN, 2070
Pologne, 2048, 2054
Royaume-Uni, 2026, 2039, 2053
Suède, 2055, 2062, 2067
URSS, 2048
Venezuela, 2059
Entreprises, 1244, 4009, 4011
Entreprises agricoles privées
Yougoslavie, 4098
Entreprises industrielles
Japon, 4080
URSS, 5277
Entreprises multinationales, 3991, 4727
Entreprises publiques
Canada, 4566
Entretiens, 380, 381, 383, 386, 389, 448, 664
Environnement, 311, 1291, 3581, 3583
Amérique latine, 4124
Asie orientale, 3595
Inde, 2881
Epidémiologie, 2833
France, 2840
Épistémologie, 271, 274, 277, 282, 286, 292,
293, 461, 594
Épouse, 4254
États-Unis, 5219
Équateur
Artisanat, 4086
Coopératives agricoles, 3682
Ethnicité, 3295
Industrialisation, 4172
Main-d'oeuvre, 4172
Mouvements ouvriers, 4668
Politique urbaine, 3832
Réformes agraires, 3682
Régimes fonciers, 3671
Équilibre social, 2175
Équité, 3067, 5322
Ergonomie, 4038
Esclavage
Afrique, 2237
Afrique du Sud, 2242
Espace, 332
Espace urbain, 3815
Maroc, 3809
Espacement des naissances
Costa Rica, 2998
Inde, 3013
Espagne
Abstentionnisme électoral, 5013
Accidents du travail, 4426
Aide aux gens âgés, 5478
Attitudes, 3112
Catholicisme, 1364, 1380
Changement social, 2455, 2477
Cinéma, 1727

Culture, 982
Délinquance juvénile, 5164
Divorce, 3091
Doctrines sociales, 1380
Éducation, 1895
Éducation préscolaire, 2010
Émigrants, 1034
Émigration, 3514
Enfance, 2649
Enseignement privé, 1944
Enseignement public, 1944
Ethnicité, 987
Famille, 2649
Femmes, 3112
Histoire de l'éducation, 1889
Histoire sociale, 504
Identité, 504
Identité culturelle, 1034
Identité nationale, 987
Innovations pédogogiques, 2010
Jeunesse, 2667
Législation sociale, 5340
Modernisation, 2464, 2477
Mouvements ouvriers, 4608
Moyens de communication de masse, 1716
Nationalisme, 4795
Négociation collective, 4607
Politique de la jeunesse, 2677
Recherche démographique, 2547
Réformes de l'enseignement, 1935
Relations du travail, 4546
Relations parents-enfants, 2649
Santé publique, 5412, 5424
Services sociaux, 5478
Sociolinguistique, 1534
Sociologie industrielle, 4137
Structure sociale, 2464
Syndicalisme, 4607
Syndicats, 4640
Systèmes de parti, 4911
Télévision, 1656
Travail des femmes, 4240, 4297
Vie familiale, 3112
Espagne : Catalogne
Moyens de communication de masse, 1685
Espérance de vie
États-Unis, 2847
France, 2852, 2892
Pologne, 1218
Esthétique, 1768, 1771, 1773-74, 1777, 1836
Hongrie, 1775
Estime de soi, 491, 495, 498, 2118
Établissements humains, 3610
Tchécoslovaquie, 3612
URSS, 3614
État, 2252, 3206, 3523, 4799, 4800, 4827-28,
4836, 4840, 4844
Écosse, 2499
France, 4843
Hongrie, 4833
Italie, 4846
Pays méditerranéens, 4822

URSS, 4845
État providence, 2678, 5255, 5271, 5279,
	5294, 5311, 5324, 5334-36
	Allemagne RF, 5256, 5257
	Danemark, 5259
	États-Unis, 1269, 5326
	Irlande, 5267
	Norvège, 5291, 5292
	Pays-Bas, 1269, 5320
	Royaume-Uni, 1269, 5329, 5337
	Scandinavie, 5306
États-Unis
	Absentéisme, 4444
	Acculturation, 3378
	Adaptation des immigrants, 3486
	Adaptation sociale, 1117
	Administration centrale, 4896
	Administration locale, 4701, 4904
	Administration publique, 4893
	Adolescence, 2709
	Adolescents, 977, 1115, 5139
	Affiliation politique, 4976
	Affiliation religieuse, 1500
	Âge, 5178
	Âge adulte, 2708, 2709
	Agriculture à temps partiel, 4069
	Aide aux gens âgés, 5377
	Aires métropolitaines, 3756, 3801, 3870
	Alcoolisme, 2891, 5118
	Allaitement naturel, 2659
	Allocations familiales, 5346
	Aménagement urbain, 3904
	Analyse de groupe, 4904
	Analyse par cohorte, 5149
	Ancienneté, 4192
	Anciens combattants, 5032, 5038
	Antisémitisme, 3404
	Appartenance à la collectivité, 1132, 3564,
		3640
	Appartenance au groupe, 707
	Arbitrage, 4701
	Architecture, 1833
	Armée de terre, 5037
	Art, 1765
	Art populaire, 1784
	Assimilation des immigrants, 3287, 3502
	Assurance maladie, 5373
	Attitude envers le travail, 4400
	Attitudes, 813
	Attitudes politiques, 2692, 4968, 4979,
		4991
	Attitudes raciales, 3409, 3426, 4767
	Automation, 4057
	Avortement, 2981, 3002, 3174
	Bandes, 5229
	Beaux-arts, 1838
	Besoins de logement, 3836
	Bibliographies, 3398
	Bibliothèques, 153, 165
	Bidonvilles, 2120
	Bien-être, 3978
	Bilinguisme, 4267

Biologie sociale, 41
Budgets familiaux, 4249
Bureaucratie, 743, 747
Cadres, 3352
Campagne électorale, 5002, 5004, 5020
Campus universitaire, 1147
Catholicisme, 1368, 1392, 2907
Catholiques, 3640
Cécité, 2828
Centre ville, 3892
Chances d'obtenir un emploi, 4227
Changement technologique, 4602
Châtiment, 5215, 5217, 5230
Chefs d'entreprise, 4000
Choix collectif, 865
Choix d'une profession, 4503
Chômage, 4188, 4213, 5237, 5243
Chômage des jeunes, 3403
Chômeurs, 4205
Christianisme, 62, 1396
Classe ouvrière, 2277
Classe supérieure, 2360
Clergé, 4770
Collectivités locales, 3640
Collectivités urbaines, 3781, 3911
Compétences, 4176
Comportement de l'étudiant, 2029, 2041
Comportement du consommateur, 4100,
	4108, 4109
Comportement économique, 3961
Comportement électoral, 1480, 4992, 4994,
	4998, 4999, 5003, 5006, 5010, 5018
Comportement politique, 4367
Comportement religieux, 1471, 1482
Comportement sexuel, 3027, 3053
Comportement social, 1115
Condamnation pénale, 5198, 5252
Conditions de travail, 4057, 4440
Conflits, 5440
Conflits du travail, 4701
Confréries, 1414
Connaissance, 283
Conscience de classe, 2256, 2328
Consensus, 611
Conservatisme, 1482
Contestation sociale, 1181
Contraception, 2964, 2976, 2993
Coopératives, 3957
Corruption politique, 4985
Croissance démographique, 2796
Croissance urbaine, 3875
Croyances religieuses, 1413
Culture, 968, 5439
Culture d'entreprise, 972
Culture locale, 3911
Culture populaire, 1191
Curriculum, 775
Délinquance, 3781, 5178, 5192, 5220,
	5225, 5237, 5242
Délinquance juvénile, 2702, 4349, 5148,
	5226
Délinquantes, 4712

Délinquants, 2843
Délits, 5146, 5186, 5246
Demandeurs d'emploi, 4198
Démographie historique, 2516, 2551, 3065
Déroulement de carrière, 4500
Déségrégation, 1116, 1123, 1147
Déségrégation scolaire, 1948
Désorganisation sociale, 3741, 3803
Développement des collectivités, 3623,
   3632, 3634, 3635, 3637
Développement rural, 3635
Développement urbain, 3803
Déviance, 1084, 1132
Différenciation raciale, 273, 3378, 4979
Différenciation sexuelle, 2585, 5159, 5252
Dimension de l'entreprise, 3997
Dimension de la famille, 3111
Discipline scolaire, 2022
Discrimination dans l'emploi, 2576, 4222
Discrimination raciale, 3368, 3416, 3892,
   4445, 5166, 5215
Discrimination salariale, 2576
Discrimination sexuelle, 2576, 2578, 3987,
   4445
Division du travail, 3054
Divorce, 3062, 3075, 3080, 3090, 3095,
   5243
Drogue, 5120
Droit d'auteur, 3932, 3933
Droits du citoyen, 4856, 4870
Durée du chômage, 4215
Échec scolaire, 2120
Écoles, 1994, 2017
Écoles privées, 1990, 1991, 2006, 2018
Écrivains, 1805
Éducation, 1862, 1863, 1908, 1909, 2601
Éducation des adultes, 2086, 2087
Éducation des femmes, 3173
Éducation des parents, 2125
Éducation permanente, 2086
Égalité de rémunération, 3987
Égalité des sexes, 2582, 2601, 2611
Église catholique, 1406, 1415, 1438
Églises, 1405
Églises protestantes, 1408
Élite, 2360
Émigrants, 3440
Emploi des femmes, 696, 4246, 4248,
   4249, 4250, 4257, 4262, 4311, 4315
Emploi urbain, 4199
Enfants adoptés, 2647
Enfants martyrs, 5181
Enquêtes sociales, 376
Enquêteurs, 382
Enrichissement des tâches, 4381
Enseignants, 2131, 2142
Enseignement, 2124, 2149
Enseignement bilingue, 2099
Enseignement de la sociologie, 49
Enseignement privé, 1920, 1929
Enseignement public, 1988, 1989, 1990,
   1991, 2006, 2018

Enseignement supérieur, 775, 1123, 2047,
   2048, 2578
Épouse, 5219
Espérance de vie, 2847
État providence, 1269, 5326
Ethnicité, 1601, 3337, 3353
Ethnologie, 513
Études littéraires, 2108
Étudiantes, 2058, 3065
Étudiants, 1181, 2072, 3637, 5472
Étudiants étrangers, 2078
Éventail des salaires, 3983, 4463
Famille, 3107, 3129, 3136, 3146, 3168,
   4244
Famille monoparentale, 3150
Fécondité, 977, 1304, 2907, 2909, 2929,
   2936, 2941, 2948, 2952, 3836
Fédéralisme, 4783
Féminisme, 41, 99, 2584, 3205, 3209,
   3218, 3222, 3223, 3226, 3247, 3270,
   5240
Femmes, 1415, 3199, 4888
Fermes familiales, 2569
Fermiers, 3736
Financement de la recherche, 116, 119,
   121, 123, 130
Fixation du salaire, 2333
Fonctionnaires, 4888
Fondations de recherche, 5060
Forces armées, 3367, 4778
Formation professionnelle, 3291
Genre de vie, 924
Gens de couleur, 3329
Gérontologie, 2738
Gestion, 779
Gestion des universités, 2075
Gestion hospitalière, 653
Grèves, 4685, 4687
Groupe familial, 3199
Groupes d'intérêt, 4931, 4948, 4949
Groupes ethniques, 2334, 3291, 3293,
   3317, 4481
Groupes minoritaires, 695, 696, 698, 3168,
   3973, 4888
Groupes religieux, 1056
Handicapés, 2822
Harcèlement sexuel, 3041
Héros, 794
Heures de travail, 4425
Histoire de la sociologie, 4, 5, 21, 58, 62,
   71
Histoire sociale, 3095, 3736, 3811
Historiographie, 2404
Homicide, 5245
Homosexualité, 3028, 3043
Hôpitaux, 5440, 5444
Idéologies politiques, 4770
Immigrants, 1374, 2948, 3482, 3494, 3525
Immigration clandestine, 3463
Industrialisation, 4083
Industrie automobile, 4698
Industrie textile, 2328, 4630

Inégalité de revenu, 3981
Inégalité raciale, 3373, 3403
Insertion professionnelle, 4203
Institutions religieuses, 1409
Interaction culturelle, 1600
Jeunesse, 1065, 2692, 2702, 4763
Jeux, 4737
Journalistes, 1694
Jugement, 283
Jugement social, 611
Juifs, 1374
Jury, 676
Justice criminelle, 1071, 5159, 5166, 5199, 5206
Justice sociale, 1928
Langue maternelle, 1601
Langues étrangères, 1600
Liberté d'expression, 4848
Liberté de l'enseignement, 1968
Littérature, 1820, 2660
Locataires, 3798
Logement, 3788, 3855
Maladies, 2837
Maladies mentales, 2824, 2843
Malaise social, 2041, 5434
Marché du travail, 696, 4176
Mariage, 3048, 3054
Marins, 1110
Maternité, 2058, 3004
Mécanisation agricole, 4070
Ménages, 2586, 2587, 2617
Mères célibataires, 3174, 4315
Métayage, 4084
Méthodes d'exploitation agricole, 4070
Microordinateurs, 2148
Migration, 3451
Migration interne, 3560, 3565
Migration urbaine-rurale, 3545, 3554, 3564
Milieu familial, 3153, 4476
Militaires, 5029, 5036
Minorités ethniques, 3287
Mobilité professionnelle, 4463, 4480, 4481, 4500
Mobilité sociale, 2385
Modes de vie, 977
Mortalité, 2516, 2891
Mortalité des enfants, 2863
Mortalité infantile, 2849
Mouvements étudiants, 2056
Mouvements religieux, 1499
Mouvements sociaux, 4926, 4952
Moyens d'enseignement, 2148
Moyens de communication, 1744, 4737
Moyens de communication de masse, 1651, 1660, 1662, 3205, 4016, 4746
Musées d'art, 1787
Musique, 1840
Musique rock, 1846
Naissance, 2915
Natalité, 2908
Négociation collective, 4696, 4698

Négociations salariales, 4693
Niveaux d'enseignement, 1966, 4481
Noirs, 1805, 2256, 2335, 2584, 3129, 3136, 3282, 3298, 3312, 3315, 3331, 3348, 3352, 3355, 3373, 3403, 3736, 3897, 4480, 4633
Noms, 513
Non-violence, 3373
Normes sociales, 2709, 3048
Nuptialité, 3065
Obtention du statut, 2370, 2372, 2376
Ordinateurs, 382
Organisation du travail, 4324
Orientation aux valeurs, 1056
Origine sociale, 5439
Participation de la collectivité, 3617
Participation des femmes, 3225
Participation des travailleurs, 4706, 4712
Paternité-maternité, 3005, 3027
Patriotisme, 4778
Pauvreté, 5087, 5093, 5102, 5107
Pauvreté rurale, 5105
Peine de mort, 5160, 5171, 5231
Périodiques, 186
Personnalité, 1117
Personnes âgées, 2727, 2744, 2751, 3199
Personnes mariées, 4425
Philosophie de l'éducation, 1899
Planification de la famille, 2551, 3015
Plans de retraite, 5373
Pluralisme ethnique, 3353
Police, 2591, 4366
Politique, 1636, 2720, 5025, 5026
Politique agricole, 4071
Politique d'immigration, 3510, 3517, 3522, 3526, 3527
Politique de bien-être, 5307
Politique de l'éducation, 1927, 3331
Politique de l'emploi, 4223
Politique de la communication, 1582
Politique de la recherche, 104
Politique du logement, 3772, 3922
Politique familiale, 5360
Politique sanitaire, 5416, 5432
Politique sociale, 5253, 5296, 5310, 5330
Politique urbaine, 3757, 3758, 3859
Pornographie, 3039, 3052
Préjugé racial, 5018
Presse, 1663, 1667, 1711, 1740
Prestige professionnel, 4474
Prévention de la délinquance, 5210
Prévisions, 296
Prévisions démographiques, 2531
Prison, 4283
Prisonniers, 5147, 5203
Privation, 5117
Problèmes sociaux, 4213
Professionnalisation, 4926
Professions médicales, 5472
Programmes de recherche, 125
Promotion professionnelle, 4445
Propriété du domicile, 3774

Propriété publique, 1711
Prostitution, 3021
Psychiâtrie, 5400
Psychologie, 452, 455
Psychologie politique, 4761, 4763
Psychologie sociale, 458, 466
Publicité, 1636, 5002
Puériculture, 2660
Qualité de la vie, 3635
Quartier, 3856
Racisme, 5093
Radiodiffusion, 1748
Rapports avant le mariage, 3044, 3048
Recensements de population, 2787, 2795
Recherche action, 110
Recherche en sciences sociales, 92, 104
Recherche interdisciplinaire, 115
Recherche scientifique, 4042
Recherche sociale, 186
Recherche sociologique, 93, 99, 102
Recherche sur la communication, 1537
Réformes de l'enseignement, 1958
Réfugiés, 3518
Régionalisme, 4783
Régulation sociale, 1071, 1755
Relations du travail, 4545, 4547, 4551,
    4557, 4564
Relations école-collectivité, 1930, 1979
Relations industrielles, 4565
Relations interethniques, 3372, 3374
Relations intergroupes, 659
Relations parents-enfants, 3109, 3132,
    3173
Relations raciales, 2584, 3353, 3382, 3388,
    3389, 3398, 3406, 3420
Religion, 1266, 1269, 1286, 1290, 1300,
    1304, 1311
Religion civile, 1276, 1279
Religiosité, 1290, 1480, 1487, 5117
Rendement de l'éducation, 1937, 2048
Réseaux sociaux, 661, 664
Ressources humaines, 4169
Retraite, 4448
Réussite dan les études, 3173
Réveil religieux, 1494
Revenu des ménages, 2585
Rôle des femmes, 977, 2584
Rôles sexuels, 820, 2569, 2591, 3054,
    4299, 4712
Romans, 1822
Salaires, 3973
Sans abri, 5082, 5112
Santé, 3482, 5405
Santé mentale, 5429, 5434
Satisfaction au travail, 4283, 4366, 4367,
    4378, 4411, 4418
Satisfaction de l'existence, 4411, 4418
Satisfaction de vie communautaire, 3618
Satisfaction résidentielle, 3906, 3930
Science, 1502
Sciences sociales, 27, 28, 32, 119, 121,
    123, 130

Scientifiques, 84
Scolarité, 1928, 1950, 2585, 4476
Sectes, 1413
Sécurité du travail, 4370
Ségrégation raciale, 2018, 3367, 3401
Segrégation résidentielle, 3897
Services de santé, 5439, 5443, 5447
Services sociaux, 5464
Sexualité, 3030
Socialisation politique, 4974
Sociologie, 16, 20, 45, 66, 4823
Sociologie appliquée, 2837
Sociologie de la religion, 1271, 1272
Sociologie politique, 4765, 4767
Sociologie urbaine, 3782, 3823, 3889, 5146
Sociologues, 77, 83
Soins médicaux, 5403, 5421
Solitude, 589
Sport, 4746
Stabilité conjugale, 4248
Statut de la femme, 3204, 3522, 4274
Statut professionnel, 4192, 4476
Statut social, 2333, 2334, 2335, 2336, 4481
Stéréotypes, 820
Stratification sociale, 2205, 5403
Structure de la famille, 3736
Suicide, 4215, 5149, 5243
Syndicalisme, 4606
Syndicats, 455, 2142, 4444, 4547, 4597,
    4602, 4610, 4630, 4633
Systèmes d'exploitation, 4076
Systèmes de parti, 4916
Systèmes de valeur, 1065
Systèmes politiques, 4823
Taux de salaire, 1966, 5210
Technologies nouvelles, 4016, 4070
Télécommunications, 1761
Télévision, 1640, 1646, 1661, 1714, 1735,
    1755, 4109, 4976
Tolérance, 830
Toxicomanie, 1074, 2891, 5118, 5127,
    5129, 5137, 5139, 5140
Travail bénévole, 4377, 4439
Travail des femmes, 3565, 4233, 4244,
    4261, 4263, 4271, 4274, 4283, 4299,
    4319
Travail ménager, 4431
Travail social, 1930
Travailleurs étrangers, 1966, 4267
Travailleurs sociaux, 5480
Travailleuses, 3041, 4237
Tribunaux pour enfants, 5236, 5238
Typologie, 280
Union consensuelle, 3079
Usage du tabac, 2891
Utilisation de la main-d'oeuvre, 4169
Utilisation des terres, 3592
Victimes, 5212, 5219, 5242
Vie familiale, 1065, 3131
Vie urbaine, 3856, 5093, 5192
Vieillissement, 2711, 2720
Villages, 3686

Villes, 3745, 3750, 3811
Viol, 5185, 5224, 5240
Violence, 1167, 1183, 1185, 1662, 3131, 3153, 5229
Vote, 5019
Zones résidentielles, 3808
Zones rurales, 430, 2335, 3741, 4083, 5245
Zones suburbaines, 3756, 3802, 3907
Zones urbaines, 430
États-Unis — Canada
  Relations internationales, 5041
États-Unis — Europe
  Relations culturelles, 1021
Éthiopie
  Alphabétisation, 2100
  Statut de la femme, 3241
Éthique, 97, 826, 1209, 1211, 1215, 1219, 1222-24, 1227, 1230, 1238, 1252, 1268, 1303, 1329, 2592, 2836, 3362, 5049
  Pays en développement, 2982
Éthique protestante, 1475, 3946
  Australie, 1474
  Malaisie, 1476
  Royaume-Uni, 1476
Ethnicité, 3285-86, 3320, 3324, 3332, 3341, 3342, 3345, 3351
  Antilles, 3318
  Asie du Sud-Est, 3326
  Australie, 3299
  Canada, 3299, 3316
  Canada, 3330, 3371
  Chinois, 3326
  Équateur, 3295
  Espagne, 987
  États-Unis, 1601, 3337, 3353
  Finlande, 3346
  Inde, 3297
  Irlande du Nord, 3301
  Israël, 3303, 3306
  Portugal, 4279
  Royaume-Uni, 2246
  URSS, 3354
Ethnocentrisme
  Canada, 3376
Ethnographie, 881
Ethnolinguistique, 1614, 1617
Ethnologie, 872
  États-Unis, 513
Ethnométhodologie, 875, 878, 2574
Ethnopsychologie, 990
Éthos, 2501
Étiquetage, 604, 608
Étrangers, 3281
  Allemagne RF, 3314, 3321
  Brésil, 3300
  France, 489, 3499
  Suisse, 3440
Étude de collectivité, 363, 364
  Japon, 369
Étude du travail, 4328
Études d'aire

Brésil, 371
Études de cas, 3156
Études littéraires
  États-Unis, 2108
Étudiantes
  États-Unis, 2058, 3065
Étudiants, 823, 1122, 1133, 2033, 2329
  Allemagne, 2051
  Argentine, 2032
  Chine, 2073
  États-Unis, 1181, 2072, 3637, 5472
  Inde, 1152, 1174
  Indonésie, 560
  Israël, 2079
  Maroc, 2064
  Pakistan, 834
  Pays-Bas, 935
  Zambie, 2076
Étudiants étrangers, 2025
  États-Unis, 2078
  France, 2035
Europe
  Abstentionnisme électoral, 5013
  Aide aux gens âgés, 5350
  Aménagement urbain, 3857
  Bibliographies, 2095
  Démocratie industrielle, 4716
  Développement culturel, 1030
  Droit de grève, 4576
  Éducation des adultes, 2095
  Famille, 3139
  Femmes rurales, 2783
  Grèves, 4687
  Histoire sociale, 5101
  Illégitimité, 2972
  Immigrants, 4293
  Jeunes travailleurs, 4293
  Juifs, 4666
  Marche du travail, 4293
  Mariage, 3139
  Migration, 3447
  Migration internationale, 3497
  Milieu rural, 3706
  Mouvements nationalistes, 4684
  Mouvements ouvriers, 4662, 4666
  Mouvements sociaux, 4922
  Nuptialité, 3074
  Organisation du travail, 4330
  Pauvreté, 5101
  Population, 2520, 2540
  Répartition par âge, 2642
  Satisfaction de l'existence, 555
  Sociologie de la religion, 1296
  Terrorisme, 1119
  Travailleuses, 2783
  Vie urbaine, 3857
  Zones urbaines, 4922
Europe occidentale
  Corporatisme, 4580
  Culture minoritaire, 925
  Diplômes, 2077
  Formation des enseignants, 2135

Grèves, 4684
Immigration, 3455
Insertion professionnelle, 2077
Patriarcat, 3141
Politique, 5026
Politique du logement, 3772
Population, 2511
Psychologie sociale, 474
Syndicats, 4621
Terrorisme, 1118
Union consensuelle, 3079
Europe orientale
   Changement social, 4920
   Classe ouvrière, 4625
   Inégalité économique, 2209
   Inégalité sociale, 2209
   Littérature, 1818
   Mouvements sociaux, 4920
   Qualité de la vie, 3979
   Relations du travail, 4552
   Syndicats, 4625
   Télévision, 1733
Euthanasie, 5195
   France, 5241
Évaluation de programme, 5382
Évaluation de soi, 497
Éventail des salaires
   États-Unis, 3983, 4463
Évolutionnisme, 231
Exode des compétences
   Caraïbes, 3501
   Égypte, 3466
Expérience du travail, 4465
Expérience religieuse, 1455
Explication, 289
Explication causale, 240
Exploitation des ressources, 2533
   Brésil, 2487
Expression de soi, 494

Fabbri, Luigi, 4813
Facteurs psychologiques, 4401
Facteurs sociaux, 926
Faim, 1215
   Pays en développement, 5081
Famille, 1222, 1343, 2845, 2851, 3088, 3114,
      3120, 3124-25, 3145, 3166, 3175, 3186,
      3191, 4150, 4234
   Afrique, 3149, 3189
   Allemagne RD, 2689
   Allemagne RF, 3171, 3178, 4970
   Canada, 3138
   Chili, 3192
   Chine, 3159
   Colombie, 3104
   Égypte, 3176
   Espagne, 2649
   États-Unis, 3107, 3129, 3136, 3146, 3168,
      4244
   Europe, 3139
   France, 3106, 3128, 4307
   Hongrie, 3077, 3126

Inde, 3123
Israël, 3117
Italie, 3103, 3180
Japon, 3116, 3185
Pays socialistes, 3201
Pays-Bas, 5318
Pologne, 3137, 3165, 3169, 3188
Roumanie, 3122
Royaume-Uni, 3118, 5075
Taïwan, 2641
Tchécoslovaquie, 3167, 3195
Togo, 2938
URSS, 3121
Yougoslavie, 3127, 4982
Famille monoparentale
   Allemagne RF, 3179
   États-Unis, 3150
   Japon, 3142
Famine
   Inde : Bengale, 5113
Farr, William, 2522
Fascisme
   Royaume-Uni, 4777
Fécondité, 2902, 2911, 2913, 2919, 2922,
      2924-25, 2942, 2947, 2950, 2958
   Afrique, 2943, 2953
   Allemagne RD, 2973
   Allemagne RF, 2973
   Australie, 2914, 2918
   Botswana, 2916
   Brésil, 444
   Canada, 2905
   Chine, 2917, 2931, 2959, 3063
   Corée R, 2932, 3548
   Costa Rica, 5086
   Cuba, 2927
   Danemark, 3073
   Égypte, 2951
   États-Unis, 977, 1304, 2907, 2909, 2929,
      2936, 2941, 2948, 2952, 3836
   Finlande, 2876, 2937
   France, 2527
   Ghana, 2954
   Guam, 2956
   Inde, 2945
   Japon, 2903, 2941
   Kenya, 2928
   Malaisie, 2934
   Mexique, 2872
   Népal, 379
   Pays en développement, 2901, 2957
   République dominicaine, 2926
   Tanzanie, 2939
   Togo, 2938
Fédéralisme
   États-Unis, 4783
   Inde, 2065
Féminisme, 3206, 3216, 3237, 3257, 3260,
      3267, 3273, 3277
   Allemagne RF, 3272
   Amérique latine, 3235
   Canada, 3254

Chili, 3249
États-Unis, 41, 99, 2584, 3205, 3209,
    3218, 3222-23, 3226, 3247, 3270, 5240
Inde, 3213
Inde : Vallée de Manipur, 3224
Royaume-Uni, 3218
Femmes, 576, 1722, 2581, 2588, 2605, 2606,
    2626, 2640, 2714, 3145, 3457
Afrique au Sud du Sahara, 2589
Chine, 2631
Danemark, 2566
Espagne, 3112
États-Unis, 1415, 3199, 4888
France, 1373
Japon, 2745
Pays arabes, 2625
Pays de la CEE, 2560
Royaume-Uni, 2620
Suisse, 3440
Tanzanie, 2600
URSS, 2633
Uruguay, 2580
Femmes mariées
France, 4295
Femmes rurales, 2765
Bangladesh, 5116
Europe, 2783
Uruguay, 2800
Féodalisme
Népal, 3959
Fermes collectives
URSS, 3740
Fermes d'État
Pologne, 3169, 4510, 4710
Fermes familiales, 4067
États-Unis, 2569
France, 4087
Pays en développement, 4068
Pologne, 4074
Royaume-Uni, 4085
Fermiers
États-Unis, 3736
Soudan, 3713
Fêtes, 1194
France, 1197
Fétichisme, 4760
Fidji
Culture politique, 4989
Politique du logement, 3920
Financement de la recherche
États-Unis, 116, 119, 121, 123, 130
Finances publiques, 4121
Finlande
Budgets temps, 4351, 4352
Comportement électoral, 3346
Démographie historique, 2541, 2552, 2876
Dimension de la famille, 3187
Ethnicité, 3346
Fécondité, 2876, 2937
Industrialisation, 3562
Maladies, 2839
Migration interne, 3562

Morbidité, 2541
Mortalité infantile, 2552, 2876
Mouvements coopératifs, 4941
Union consensuelle, 3076
Variole, 2541
Fiscalité
France, 4122
Royaume-Uni, 4118
Fixation du salaire
États-Unis, 2333
Folklore
Chine, 1198
Venezuela, 1203
Fonction publique
Allemagne RF, 4891
Fonctionnaires
États-Unis, 4888
France, 4886, 4887
Pologne, 4383
Royaume-Uni, 4590, 4887
Fonctionnalisme, 198, 261
Fonctionnement du groupe, 708
Fonctions de production, 1964
Fondations de recherche
États-Unis, 5060
Forces armées, 5028, 5030
Belgique, 5035
États-Unis, 3367, 4778
Israël, 5034
Formalisation, 134, 276
Formation
Belgique, 2128
Formation de classe, 2253, 2259, 2270, 2273,
    2303, 2318
Burkina-Faso, 2305
Canada, 2266
Ghana, 3992
Nicaragua, 1416
Thaïlande, 2255
Formation des enseignants, 2129
Europe occidentale, 2135
France, 2139
Formation en cours d'emploi, 4490
Formation professionnelle, 4489
Allemagne RF, 4498
Amérique latine, 4466
Chili, 4467
États-Unis, 3291
France, 4469
Kenya, 4461
Royaume-Uni, 4486
Foucault, Michel, 33, 76
Foule, 1155
Franc-maçonnerie, 1431
France, 1417
France
Action collective, 870
Action sociale, 5327
Administration locale, 2285, 4899
Administration scolaire, 2020
Adolescents, 2020
Agriculteurs, 1057

Agriculture, 3202
Aide à l'enfance, 5461
Aide aux gens âgés, 5341, 5343, 5344, 5379, 5473
Alcoolisme, 5128, 5141
Aménagement du temps de travail, 4395, 4407
Aménagement urbain, 3770
Analphabétisme, 2090
Analyse du discours, 1624
Analyse régionale, 2285
Animaux, 2558
Anticléricalisme, 1495
Antisémitisme, 3377, 3397, 3405, 3408
Argent, 4116
Assimilation des immigrants, 3499, 3513
Associations, 724
Attitude envers le travail, 4420
Attitudes politiques, 1342
Attitudes religieuses, 1342
Automation, 4022, 4031, 4472, 4491
Bilinguisme, 3101
Bourgeoisie, 3045
Budgets familiaux, 5100
Budgets temps, 904, 3158, 4402, 4404
Bureautique, 4049
Cadres, 4527
Carnavals, 1197
Catholicisme, 1353, 1373
Catholiques, 1342
Cercles de qualité, 4335
Chances d'éducation, 1983, 2194, 2199
Changement social, 724, 2436
Changement technologique, 4046, 4496, 4602
Châtiment, 5145
Chômage, 4208
Chômeurs, 4184
Cinéma, 1641
Classe moyenne, 764, 2250, 2265, 5007
Classe ouvrière, 1430, 1983, 2285, 5100
Collectivités rurales, 3697
Communication, 1543, 1562
Comportement électoral, 5007
Comportement sexuel, 3045, 3049
Conditions de travail, 4369
Conditions de vie, 3967
Conditions sociales, 2452
Conflits du travail, 3941
Congrégations, 1425
Conjoncture démographique, 4047
Consommation alimentaire, 5100
Culture, 1267
Culture ouvrière, 1002
Culture politique, 1267
Cycle de vie, 2857
Déchristianisation, 1495
Délinquance juvénile, 5168
Délits, 5202
Démographie historique, 2527, 2538
Dessins humoristiques, 1725
Développement des collectivités, 2285

Développement régional, 1543
Diffusion de la culture, 1015
Dimension de la famille, 3130
Discrimination dans l'emploi, 4228
Droit du travail, 4032, 4051, 4575
Droit pénal, 1237
Échec scolaire, 2115
Écoles privées, 2004
Écrivains, 1809
Éducation, 1858
Éducation de masse, 2052
Éducation des adultes, 2102
Éducation des femmes, 3220, 3252
Éducation permanente, 2089
Église catholique, 1425, 1430
Élite, 2345
Emploi, 4149, 4191
Emploi des femmes, 4228, 4295, 4471
Enfants, 2645
Enseignants, 2143, 2146
Enseignement agricole, 3220
Enseignement de la sociologie, 8
Enseignement primaire, 1999, 2001, 2003
Enseignement secondaire, 1996, 2009
Enseignement supérieur, 2048
Epidémiologie, 2840
Espérance de vie, 2852, 2892
État, 4843
Étrangers, 489, 3499
Étudiants étrangers, 2035
Euthanasie, 5241
Famille, 3106, 3128, 4307
Fécondité, 2527
Femmes, 1373
Femmes mariées, 4295
Fermes familiales, 4087
Fêtes, 1197
Fiscalité, 4122
Fonctionnaires, 4886, 4887
Formation des enseignants, 2139
Formation professionnelle, 4469
Franc-maçonnerie, 1417
Géographie, 2502
Gérontologie, 2718
Gestion industrielle, 4335
Grèves, 4682
Groupes, 4149
Groupes d'intérêt, 4956
Groupes ethniques, 2923
Handicap social, 5074
Handicapés, 2827, 2844
Histoire, 2405
Histoire de l'éducation, 1887, 1996, 2143
Histoire de l'Église, 1430
Histoire du capitalisme, 3941
Histoire religieuse, 1403
Histoire rurale, 3697
Histoire sociale, 1417, 1983, 3049, 3232, 3234, 3252, 3662, 5128
Homosexualité, 3026
Hôpitaux, 5437
Identité, 489

Immigrants, 3469, 3471, 3472, 3490, 3505, 3508, 3512, 5141
Immigration, 3456, 3504
Industrialisation, 3941
Industrie textile, 3941
Inégalité sociale, 2194, 2199, 2886
Information sociale, 5061
Ingénieurs, 4534
Innovations, 4015
Insertion professionnelle, 2844, 4181, 4196
Intellectuels, 2340-43, 2349-50, 2354, 2362, 2366
Isolement social, 1085
Jeunes travailleurs, 4265
Jeunesse, 2665, 3499
Langage, 1588
Liberté de l'enseignement, 1963
Linguistique, 1717
Logement, 3776, 3896
Logements sociaux, 3791, 3929
Loisir, 4738
Lutte de classes, 2311
Main-d'oeuvre, 4149, 4156
Marché agricole, 3670
Mariage, 349
Mariage mixte, 3085, 3101
Marine marchande, 4208
Marxisme, 267
Matriarcat, 3113
Médecins, 5461, 5473, 5477, 5479
Médicaments, 5125
Migration, 4451
Migration interne, 2857
Milieu scolaire, 2021
Milieu social, 3193
Milieu urbain, 3890
Mines de houille, 4516
Mineurs, 4516
Minorités ethniques, 3552
Mobilité sociale, 2375, 2387, 2388
Modes de production, 4047
Modes de vie, 883, 904
Monachisme, 1403
Mort, 2886
Mortalité, 2854, 2858, 2860
Mortalité des enfants, 2875
Mouvements de consommateurs, 4099
Mouvements de libération de la femme, 3248
Mouvements étudiants, 2038
Mouvements ouvriers, 4599, 4617, 4619, 4662
Mouvements sociaux, 4936
Moyens de communication de masse, 1734, 1763
Musique, 1841
Natalité, 2923
Nation, 984
Négociations salariales, 4692
Nomades, 3542, 3552
Normes de travail, 1057
Normes sociales, 1057

Objectifs de l'éducation, 1962
Opinion publique, 377, 832, 1135
Organisation du travail, 4031, 4335
Organisations bénévoles, 723
Paroisse, 1432
Participation des femmes, 4623
Participation des travailleurs, 4708
Participation sociale, 1092
Pauvreté, 5083, 5115
Paysannerie, 3653
Paysans, 3689, 3705, 3730
Pêche, 4072
Pédiatres, 5461
Personnes âgées, 1085, 2724, 2737, 2749
Petites et moyennes entreprises, 4005
Philosophes, 76, 82, 85, 86
Photographie, 4519
Pluralisme ethnique, 3302
Politique culturelle, 1009, 1015, 1028
Politique d'immigration, 3473, 3534
Politique de la vieillesse, 5284
Politique démographique, 3014
Politique familiale, 5354
Politique sanitaire, 4256
Politique sociale, 4049
Politique urbaine, 3752, 3901
Population, 2502, 2509, 2523, 2543, 5125
Population urbaine, 3469
Pratique religieuse, 1488, 1501
Pratiques culturelles, 915
Presse, 1672, 1758, 3234
Processus judiciaire, 1237
Production, 4014
Prolétariat, 3505
Protection de l'environnement, 3600
Protestantisme, 1334
Publicité, 349
Qualification professionnelle, 4031, 4470, 4472, 4491, 4496
Qualification requise pour l'emploi, 4497
Qualité de la vie, 4369
Qualité du travail, 4427
Racisme, 3383, 3391, 3427
Radio, 1679
Réadaptation professionnelle, 4471
Recherche en sciences sociales, 103
Recherche médicale, 5402
Recherche sur la communication, 1564
Réglementation du marché, 3670
Relations du travail, 4544, 4555
Relations enseignants-enseignés, 2140
Relations interpersonnelles, 592
Relations raciales, 4268
Relations sociales, 3778
Religieuses, 1425
Religion, 1267
Rendement de l'éducation, 2048
Rénovation urbaine, 3763, 3861, 3885, 3901
Représentation des travailleurs, 4718
Retraite, 4451
Retraités, 2737

Révolution industrielle, 4335
Robotique, 4054
Rôles sexuels, 2622
Santé, 2712, 5433
Sciences de l'éducation, 1860
Sciences sociales, 24
Scolarisation, 2194
Scolarité, 1957
Scrutins, 374, 377
Sectes, 1419
Secteur coopératif, 3947
Sécurité du travail, 4433
Sécurité sociale, 5351, 5364
Sociabilité, 575, 1417
Socialisation, 2020
Socialisation politique, 4988
Socialisme, 4788, 4797
Société, 888
Société paysanne, 3662
Société urbaine, 3753
Sociologie, 22, 33
Sociologie de l'éducation, 1867
Sociologie de la religion, 1292
Sociologie du travail, 2285
Sociologie urbaine, 3799, 3885
Sociologues, 171
Soins médicaux, 5410
Solitude, 2722, 2748, 3232
Sondages d'opinion publique, 1501
Sport, 4757
Statut de la femme, 3202, 3207, 3232, 3234
Statut professionnel, 1809, 5461
Stratification sociale, 2191
Structure de la famille, 1495, 3193
Structure de la main d'oeuvre, 4173
Structure sociale, 2179
Suicide, 5154
Syndicalisme, 4650
Syndicats, 4581, 4602, 4623, 4653
Systèmes d'enseignement, 1959, 1976
Technologies nouvelles, 4032, 4051, 4470
Télévision, 1679, 1717
Temps de loisir, 4369
Temps de travail, 4357
Théorie de l'éducation, 1893
Tourisme, 3871, 4738
Traduction, 1809
Travail, 4156, 4166
Travail des femmes, 2852, 4307
Travail ménager, 4404
Travail social, 5380
Travailleurs, 4519
Travailleurs âgés, 4256
Travailleurs agricoles, 4288
Travailleurs étrangers, 3896, 4279
Travailleurs migrants, 3509, 4256, 4268
Travailleuses, 4288
Universités, 1959, 2052
Urbanisme, 3763
Usines, 4348

Utilisation des loisirs, 3552, 4731
Vacances, 4731
Vie familiale, 1983, 3158
Vie professionnelle, 3158
Vie quotidienne, 918, 3778
Vie urbaine, 3778, 3871
Vieillesse, 2712, 2722, 2748
Villages, 3662
Villes moyennes, 3812
Villes nouvelles, 3770, 3814, 3887
Violence, 1134, 1135
Zones rurales, 904
Zones urbaines, 904, 5100
France : Bretagne
    Croyances religieuses, 1451
    Mort, 1451
    Mouvements paysans, 3670
France : Paris
    Urbanisation, 3844
    Zones suburbaines, 3844
France : Province
    Collectivités rurales, 3699
France : Rouen
    Pauvreté, 4120
    Prêt sur gage, 4120
France : Sarthe
    Paysannerie, 3659
Futur, 2411
Futurologie, 2408, 2409, 2410

Gabon
    Sécurité sociale, 5359
Gadamer, Hans-Georg, 553
Galligan, Carol, 1210, 2604
Gastronomie, 4078
Générations, 2635, 2638
Génétique, 2833
Genre de vie, 896, 902, 907, 939, 959, 3559, 4107
    Allemagne RD, 898
    États-Unis, 924
    Hongrie, 919, 946
    Pays socialistes, 948
    Suède, 945
Genre de vie socialiste, 929, 940, 962, 993, 1786, 2159
Gens de couleur
    États-Unis, 3329
Gens de maison, 4525
    Afrique du Sud, 4523
    Colombie, 4526
Géographie, 3593, 4728
    Australie, 3591
    France, 2502
Géographie humaine, 3572, 3588
    Nouvelle Zélande, 3587
Gérontologie, 2715, 2736, 2752
    États-Unis, 2738
    France, 2718
    Pays-Bas, 2743
Gestion, 737, 751, 764
    États-Unis, 779

Gestion d'entreprises
  Canada, 481
  Pologne, 3998
Gestion des pêches
  Inde, 3721
Gestion des universités
  Australie, 2074
  États-Unis, 2075
Gestion du personnel, 778, 4325, 4326, 4341, 4345
Gestion hospitalière, 5448
  États-Unis, 653
Gestion industrielle
  France, 4335
  Royaume-Uni, 4092, 4096
Gestion sanitaire
  Suisse, 5414
Ghana
  Fécondité, 2954
  Formation de classe, 3992
  Logement, 3767
  Milieux d'affaires, 3992
  Mineurs, 4507
  Mouvements ouvriers, 4507
  Statut de la femme, 3259
Ghana : Accra
  Classes sociales, 2614
  Rôle des femmes, 2614
Giddens, Anthony, 309, 786
Goethe, Johann W., 1478
Goffman, Erving, 170, 182, 194, 783, 5305
Gouldner, Alvin, 169, 256, 1510
Gouvernement, 4871
Gramsci, Antonio, 955
Grèce
  Attitudes politiques, 2263
  Conscience de classe, 2263
  Handicapés, 2841
  Mère, 3133
  Migration de retour, 3459
  Politique scientifique, 127
  Population, 2515
  Rôle des femmes, 3133
Grèves, 4674
  Colombie, 4670
  États-Unis, 4685, 4687
  Europe, 4687
  Europe occidentale, 4684
  France, 4682
  Israël, 4672
  Royaume-Uni, 4675, 4683
  Suède, 4683
Grèves perlées
  Israël, 4672
Grèves sauvages
  Autriche, 4678
  Canada, 4673
  Suède, 4671
Grossesse, 2944, 4270
Groupe familial
  États-Unis, 3199
Groupement par aptitudes, 705, 2121

Groupements professionnels, 734
  Hongrie, 4483
  Inde, 1145
Groupes
  Danemark, 665
  France, 4149
Groupes d'âge, 2636
Groupes d'égaux, 567, 675, 807
Groupes d'intérêt, 4919, 4944, 4955
  États-Unis, 4931, 4948, 4949
  France, 4956
  Pays socialistes, 4950
Groupes de discussion, 680
Groupes de formation, 672
Groupes ethniques
  Canada, 1050, 2216, 3294, 3323
  Chine, 3327
  États-Unis, 2334, 3291, 3293, 3317, 4481
  France, 2923
  Inde, 3333
  Israël, 3325, 3356, 3853
  Malaisie, 3308, 3344
  Pays-Bas, 3336
  Région andine, 3322
  URSS, 3498
  Yougoslavie, 3284
Groupes majoritaires, 693
  Moyen-Orient, 686
Groupes minoritaires, 682, 693
  Afrique, 690
  Australie, 687, 2918
  Canada, 688, 691, 1605
  États-Unis, 695, 696, 698, 3168, 3973, 4888
  Israël, 697
  Nouvelle Zélande, 692
  Royaume-Uni, 684
Groupes religieux, 1422, 1477
  États-Unis, 1056
  Nigeria, 1424
  Nouvelle Zélande, 4977
Groupes restreints, 669, 673, 674, 678, 681
Groupes thérapeutiques, 672, 677
Guadeloupe
  Médecine traditionnelle, 5394
Guam
  Fécondité, 2956
Guatémala
  Artisans, 4536
  Changement culturel, 1026
  Conflits sociaux, 654
  Divination, 1458
  Église catholique, 654
  Oligarchie, 4810
  Taux de fécondité, 1026
Guerre, 3351, 5249
Guyana
  Comportement du groupe, 703
  Leaders politiques, 4959
  Sectes, 703

Habermas, Jürgen, 220, 236, 259, 1544, 1571, 4771

Habitat
  Italie, 3613
Habitudes de lecture, 548
  Pologne, 571
Haïti
  Éducation, 1905
  Politique de développement, 1905
Handicap social
  France, 5074
Handicapés, 2845
  États-Unis, 2822
  France, 2827, 2844
  Grèce, 2841
  Inde, 2829
Handicapés mentaux, 2836
  Royaume-Uni, 5445
Harcélement sexuel
  États-Unis, 3041
Hawaï
  Communication interethnique, 3396
  Immigrants, 3507
  Immigration, 3495
Hayek, Friedrich von, 986
Hegel, Georg Wilhelm Friedrich, 1258, 4794
Hérésies, 1470
Herméneutique, 243, 250, 553, 1622, 5270
Héros, 1756
  États-Unis, 794
Heures de travail
  Allemagne, 4430
  États-Unis, 4425
Heuristique, 5333
Hindess, Barry, 785
Hindouisme, 1363, 1444
  Inde, 1345, 1449
Histoire, 2389-90, 2396-97, 2403, 2410, 2463, 2606
  Asie du Sud, 2392
  France, 2405
Histoire culturelle
  Afrique, 1044
  Italie, 2400
  Royaume-Uni, 1043
Histoire de l'éducation, 1873, 1878
  Australie, 1892
  Espagne, 1889
  France, 1887, 1996, 2143
  Inde : Rājasthān, 1913
  Nigeria, 1910
Histoire de l'Église
  Allemagne RF, 1412
  France, 1430
Histoire de la sociologie, 10, 29, 63, 72, 2327
  Autriche, 51
  États-Unis, 4, 5, 21, 58, 62, 71
  Inde, 59
  Japon, 36, 40
  Pologne, 43
  Royaume-Uni, 37
Histoire des idées, 1513
Histoire du capitalisme, 3944
  France, 3941

Histoire économique
  Écosse, 3931
  Hongrie, 4284
  Irlande, 3931
Histoire religieuse
  France, 1403
  Hongrie, 1273
  Île de la Réunion, 1307
Histoire rurale
  France, 3697
Histoire sociale, 1234, 1436, 2391, 2393, 2402, 2406, 3124, 3445, 5255
  Allemagne, 2126, 2401, 3675, 4242, 4275, 4276, 4658
  Autriche, 3663
  Écosse, 3931
  Espagne, 504
  États-Unis, 3095, 3736, 3811
  Europe, 5101
  France, 1417, 1983, 3049, 3232, 3234, 3252, 3662, 5128
  Inde, 2398
  Iran, 2394, 3417
  Irlande, 3931
  Italie, 2400, 4644
  Japon, 923, 2181
  Pays-Bas, 5318
  Royaume-Uni, 2246, 2399, 2803, 3818, 4814
Historicisme, 218, 234
Historiographie
  États-Unis, 2404
  Mexique, 2395
  Tchécoslovaquie, 2407
Holbach, Paul Henry Thiry d', 1302
Holland, J. L., 4503
Homicide, 5170
  États-Unis, 5245
Hommes, 3105
Hommes de loi, 4537
  Canada, 2368
Hommes politiques
  Japon, 4960
Homosexualité, 3033, 3038
  États-Unis, 3028, 3043
  France, 3026
Hong Kong
  Administration publique, 4892
  Aménagement urbain, 3819
  Parenté, 3729
  Villages, 3729
Hongrie
  Administration publique, 4485
  Analyse par cohorte, 919
  Antisémitisme, 3386, 3394
  Bien-être, 4350
  Budgets temps, 4350, 4351, 4352
  Catholicisme, 1398
  Changement social, 2446
  Châtiment, 5184
  Clochards, 5218
  Collectivités locales, 3620

Communication, 1542
Conditions de vie, 3969, 3986
Conditions sociales, 5273
Culture, 978
Déroulement de carrière, 4485
Développement social, 2439
Émigration, 3531
Emploi des femmes, 4284, 4300
Esthétique, 1775
État, 4833
Famille, 3077, 3126
Genre de vie, 919, 946
Groupements professionnels, 4483
Histoire économique, 4284
Histoire religieuse, 1273
Identité nationale, 954
Inégalité sociale, 2211, 3790
Intellectuels, 2351, 2365
Jeunes travailleurs, 938
Jeunesse, 2703
Juifs, 1825
Littérature, 1825
Littérature populaire, 1829
Logement, 3790, 3986
Mariage, 3077
Ménages, 2563
Migrations alternantes, 3543
Milieu familial, 3140
Mobilité sociale, 2374, 2384
Modernisation, 2446
Modes de vie, 938
Mortalité, 2856
Musique, 1847
Opinion publique, 3969
Ouvriers industriels, 4514
Paysans, 3656, 3681, 3701
Police, 4874
Politique de la jeunesse, 2698
Politique démographique, 2537, 3010
Politique du logement, 3829
Politique sociale, 5274
Population, 2537, 2554
Population rurale, 2821
Pouvoir local, 4903
Presse, 2703
Relations du travail, 4635
Relations sociales, 1109
Société, 956
Sociologie de la famille, 3115
Sociologie rurale, 3737
Sociologie urbaine, 5218
Sportifs, 2330
Statistique, 426
Statut social, 2330
Stratification sociale, 2212, 2228, 4514
Structure sociale, 2165
Syndicats, 4635, 4639
Télévision, 1692
Travailleurs agricoles, 3701, 4521
Urbanisation, 2554, 3805
Vie quotidienne, 978
Villages, 2563, 3700

Zones rurales, 5273
Honneur
    Brésil, 1212
Hôpitaux
    Allemagne RF, 5455
    Australie, 5442
    Chine, 5446
    États-Unis, 5440, 5444
    France, 5437
    Japon, 2842
    Royaume-Uni, 5450
Hôpitaux psychiatriques
    Royaume-Uni, 5445
Hughes, Everett C., 366
Humanisation du travail, 4038, 4363, 4387,
        4403, 4415
    Allemagne RF, 4385, 4432
    Pologne, 4394
Humour, 567
Husserl, Edmund, 238
Hygiène mentale, 5417

Idéalisme, 262
Idées religieuses, 1486
Identification, 628
Identification au groupe, 704
Identité, 496, 499-503, 506, 508-10, 726,
        2150, 2729
    Amérique latine, 4927
    Espagne, 504
    France, 489
Identité culturelle, 362, 3285, 3286, 4739
    Afrique du Nord, 1019
    Amérique latine, 2364
    Espagne, 1034
    Inde, 1152
    Pays arabes, 2361
    Pays en développement, 1020
    Pologne, 1042
Identité nationale
    Afrique du Nord, 914
    Canada, 976
    Corée, 983
    Espagne, 987
    Hongrie, 954
    Pays-Bas, 922
    Portugal, 4279
    Turquie, 4316
Idéologie, 228, 484, 769, 841, 844-45, 848,
        851, 855-60, 920, 1127, 1778, 2296,
        2442, 5025
    Afrique Centrale, 2279
    Amérique latine, 854
Idéologies politiques
    États-Unis, 4770
    Pologne, 4910
Île de la Réunion
    Changement social, 2418
    Développement social, 2418
    Emploi des jeunes, 2668
    Histoire religieuse, 1307
    Jeunesse, 2668

Théâtre, 1849
Illégitimité
    Europe, 2972
Imagination, 862, 1175, 1790, 2867
Immigrants, 3242
    Australie, 1165, 1326, 3489
    Canada, 3138, 3461, 3468, 3480, 3484,
        3493, 3500, 3511
    Corée, 3396
    États-Unis, 1374, 2948, 3482, 3494, 3525
    Europe, 4293
    France, 3469, 3471, 3472, 3490, 3505,
        3508, 3512, 5141
    Hawaï, 3507
    Israël, 89, 1012, 3519
    Pays capitalistes, 3288
    Pays industrialisés, 3496
Immigration, 3523
    Amérique du Nord, 3531
    Argentine, 3515
    Australie, 3465
    Canada, 3465
    Europe occidentale, 3455
    France, 3456, 3504
    Hawaï, 3495
    Israël, 3460
    Italie, 3479
Immigration clandestine, 3454
    États-Unis, 3463
Impérialisme, 5045, 5048
Implications culturelles
    Pologne, 4437
Inde
    Activistes, 4921
    Administration locale, 4905
    Administration publique, 4889
    Affinité, 618
    Âge au mariage, 3098
    Aliénation, 1169, 1170, 1174
    Aliénation politique, 1114, 1145
    Anthologies, 4508
    Bidonvilles, 3891
    Bien-être social, 2881
    Bourgeoisie, 2282
    Brahmanisme, 1393
    Bureaucratie, 767
    Castes, 1170, 2202, 2234-36, 2238-40,
        2243-44, 2386
    Chances d'obtenir un emploi, 4226
    Changement social, 2234, 2243, 2459,
        2462, 2466, 3715, 3734, 4912
    Civilisation, 900
    Classe ouvrière, 4508
    Communauté scientifique, 124
    Communication, 1574
    Conditions de travail, 4388
    Conditions sociales, 2398, 5300
    Conflits du travail, 4689
    Consommation alimentaire, 5096
    Contestation sociale, 5109
    Coopératives, 3942
    Croissance démographique, 2785

Croyances religieuses, 5150
Délits, 5150, 5208
Désastres, 5079
Développement économique, 1275
Développement économique et social, 767
Développement politique, 4831, 4835
Développement rural, 3688, 3698, 3703,
    3708, 3715-17, 3721, 3731, 3734
Développement urbain, 3902
Dimension de la famille, 3177
Diplômés d'université, 4226
Discrimination sexuelle, 4236
Distance sociale, 1097
Dot, 3097
Droit de la famille, 3068
Droits de la femme, 3274
Éducation, 2240, 2459
Éducation des adultes, 2097
Élaboration de la politique étrangère, 542
Émeutes, 1104
Enseignement supérieur, 2061, 2065
Environnement, 2881
Espacement des naissances, 3013
Ethnicité, 3297
Étudiants, 1152, 1174
Famille, 3123
Fécondité, 2945
Fédéralisme, 2065
Féminisme, 3213
Gestion des pêches, 3721
Groupements professionnels, 1145
Groupes ethniques, 3333
Handicapés, 2829
Hindouisme, 1345, 1449
Histoire de la sociologie, 59
Histoire sociale, 2398
Identité culturelle, 1152
Inégalité sociale, 5413
Institutions, 1047
Institutions politiques, 4832
Islam, 1346, 1351, 1379
Jeunesse rurale, 2699
Justice, 1261
Justice criminelle, 5208
Justice sociale, 4236
Langage, 1611
Leadership politique, 4831
Marginaux, 1152
Mariage, 618, 3068
Mécanisation agricole, 3721
Migration, 3434, 3452
Migration interne, 3553, 3561
Migration rurale-urbaine, 3539, 3540,
    3551
Mobilité professionnelle, 4499
Mobilité sociale, 2386, 3297
Mortalité, 2881, 2945
Mortalité des enfants, 3177
Mouvements de libération de la femme,
    3275
Mouvements sociaux, 4921
Moyens de communication de masse, 1652

Musulmans, 1327
Nationalisme, 3702
Nutrition, 5106
Objectifs de l'éducation, 2699
Ordre social, 1261
Organisations agricoles, 3723
Ouvriers industriels, 1169, 4517
Participation des travailleurs, 4720
Participation sociale, 1095
Partis politiques, 4908, 4912
Pauvreté, 1152, 5099
Pauvreté rurale, 5098
Paysannerie, 3702, 3717
Pélerinages, 1444
Planification de la famille, 2970, 2989,
    3001, 3008, 3011
Police, 4881
Politique, 2172, 3873, 5300
Politique du travail, 4561
Politique sociale, 5287
Population, 2507
Population rurale, 2808
Privation, 5109
Problèmes sociaux, 4889
Professions médicales, 5482
Prostitution, 3046
Recherche sociale, 5060
Recherche sur le développement, 2496
Réformes agraires, 3657, 3687
Régionalisme, 4796
Règlement de conflits, 4689
Relations agraires, 3669
Relations du travail, 4539, 4550, 4553,
    4561
Relations familiales, 2829
Religion, 1275
Remariage, 3057
Réveil religieux, 1379
Sacré, 1449
Santé mentale, 5413
Science, 1503
Sectes, 3213
Sécurité sociale, 4553, 5347
Services sociaux, 5470
Sexe, 2608
Société tribale, 3339
Sociologie, 35, 39, 57, 61
Sociologie du développement, 2488
Sociologues, 81
Soins médicaux, 5427
Squatters, 3891
Statut de la femme, 3261, 3271
Stratification sociale, 2202
Structure sociale, 2172
Symbolisme, 1559
Syndicats, 4652, 4655
Tables de mortalité, 2877
Théorie sociologique, 235
Traditionalisme, 1014
Traditions religieuses, 1014
Transition démographique, 2778
Travailleurs, 4508

Travailleuses, 4236, 4273, 4309, 4320
Tribalisme, 3422, 3425
Tribus, 2238, 3716, 3717
Urbanisation, 3551, 3779
Valeurs culturelles, 1014
Vie urbaine, 3873
Villages, 3698, 3709, 3721, 4831
Villes, 3891
Zones rurales, 3942, 4499
Inde : Assam
    Castes, 2233
    Mobilité sociale, 2233
Inde : Bengale
    Classes sociales, 3661
    Famine, 5113
    Inégalité sociale, 2214, 3669
    Société rurale, 3661
    Villages, 3661
Inde : Bengale Ouest
    Discrimination sexuelle, 2002
    Enseignement primaire, 2002, 2011
Inde : Bihar
    Paysannerie, 3668
Inde : Goa
    Transition démographique, 2807
Inde : Kerala
    Classe ouvrière, 2275
    Politique, 2275
Inde : Madhya Pradesh
    Société tribale, 3338
Inde : Pendjab
    Spécificité culturelle, 1037
Inde : Rājasthān
    Histoire de l'éducation, 1913
Inde : Vallée de Manipur
    Féminisme, 3224
    Statut de la femme, 3224
Indicateurs démographiques, 2513
Indicateurs sociaux, 300, 419, 430, 437, 2186
    Japon, 432
    Pays du CAEM, 411
    Pologne, 415
    Royaume-Uni, 5265
    Tchécoslovaquie, 423
    URSS, 425
Individu et société, 480, 482, 486
Individualisme, 313, 501, 4121
Individualité, 480, 1760
Individus, 483, 484, 776
    Canada, 481
Indonésie
    Aspirations, 560
    Développement culturel, 2430
    Développement social, 2430
    Dynamique de la population, 2786
    Étudiants, 560
    Intervalles génésiques, 2920
    Islam, 1325
    Migration, 3453
    Mortalité des enfants, 2859, 2873
    Mortalité infantile, 2859, 2873
    Mouvements étudiants, 2068

Rôle des femmes, 2599
Industrialisation, 3166, 4090
    Équateur, 4172
    États-Unis, 4083
    Finlande, 3562
    France, 3941
    Java, 4298
    Pologne, 2773
Industrie automobile
    États-Unis, 4698
    Japon, 4393
Industrie minière
    Tanzanie, 4396
Industrie textile, 3944
    Allemagne, 3250
    États-Unis, 2328, 4630
    France, 3941
Inégalité de revenu, 2321
    États-Unis, 3981
    Pologne, 3984
    Suède, 2323
    Suisse, 3989
Inégalité économique
    Europe orientale, 2209
Inégalité raciale, 3363
    États-Unis, 3373, 3403
    Trinité-et-Tabago, 3424
Inégalité sociale, 2186, 2189, 2192-93,
    2195-96, 2204, 2207, 2225, 2229-30,
    4229, 4305
    Brésil, 1956
    Europe orientale, 2209
    France, 2194, 2199, 2886
    Hongrie, 2211, 3790
    Hongrie, 2210
    Inde, 5413
    Inde : Bengale, 2214, 3669
    Mexique, 2217
    Pologne, 2210, 2211, 2213
    Royaume-Uni, 2885
    Taïwan, 2201
    Yougoslavie, 2222
Infanticide, 5188
Inférence causale, 597, 609
Infirmières
    Australie, 4379
Inflation, 4115
    Royaume-Uni, 3818
Influence du groupe, 682, 705, 706, 726, 807
Influence sociale, 485, 1199
Information, 141, 146, 611, 4841
Information sociale, 5063, 5064, 5065, 5067
    France, 5061
Informatique, 134-36
Informatisation, 152, 663, 4048
Infrastructure sociale, 2159
Ingénieurs
    France, 4534
Innovations, 755, 1080
    Canada, 4040
    France, 4015
    Pays méditerranéens, 4064

Innovations industrielles, 4060
Innovations pédogogiques, 2136
    Espagne, 2010
Insertion professionnelle, 4210
    États-Unis, 4203
    Europe occidentale, 2077
    France, 2844, 4181, 4196
    URSS, 4196
Institutionnalisation, 1080
Institutions, 10, 744, 1060, 1076
    Inde, 1047
    Norvège, 1073
Institutions politiques, 4824
    Inde, 4832
    Pays-Bas, 4842
Institutions religieuses, 1407
    États-Unis, 1409
Intégration culturelle
    Pologne, 1023
Intégration du groupe, 701
Intégration familiale, 3155, 3184
Intégration sociale, 699, 1089, 1105, 1124,
    2171, 3439
    Yougoslavie, 1088
Intellectuels, 2358
    Amérique latine, 2364
    Autriche, 3487
    Brésil, 1201
    Chine, 2355, 2367
    France, 2340-43, 2349-50, 2354, 2362, 2366
    Hongrie, 2351, 2365
    Roumanie, 3421
    Scandinavie, 2353
    Yougoslavie, 2347
Intelligence, 536, 561, 3183
Intelligence artificielle, 132-33, 137, 139
Intelligentsia, 2352
    Pays arabes, 2361
    URSS, 2348, 2359, 2363
Interaction conjugale, 3067
Interaction culturelle
    Algérie, 1033
    États-Unis, 1600
Interaction sociale, 580, 1094, 1159, 1162,
    1175, 1702
Interaction symbolique, 1561, 1576, 1577
Intérêt, 559
Internationalisation
    Japon, 5042
Internationalisme prolétarien, 2431
Interprétation, 278
Intervalles génésiques
    Indonésie, 2920
    Kenya, 2910
    Malaisie, 2933
Intervention de l'État, 4839, 4847
    Nouvelle Zélande, 4136
    Royaume-Uni, 4825
Invalidité
    Royaume-Uni, 2826
Irak — Égypte
    Éducation comparée, 1900

Iran
    Anthropologie politique, 1443
    Histoire sociale, 2394, 3417
    Islam, 3417
    Mobilité sociale, 3164
    Niveaux d'enseignement, 3164
    Père, 3164
    Rites, 1443
    Tribalisme, 3417
Irlande
    Alcoolisme, 5142
    Chômage des jeunes, 4182, 4212
    Communication, 3625
    Délits, 4879
    Développement de l'éducation, 4033
    Emploi des jeunes, 4206
    Enseignement secondaire, 1997
    État providence, 5267
    Histoire économique, 3931
    Jeunesse, 2682
    Partis politiques, 4913
    Police, 4879
    Protestants, 1341
    Rôles sexuels, 1997
    Sans abri, 5104
    Technologie, 4033
    Vie communautaire, 3625
Irlande du Nord
    Catholiques, 1214
    Communautés religieuses, 1421
    Conflits, 1421
    Éducation, 1898
    Enfants adoptés, 2657
    Ethnicité, 3301
    Moralité, 1214
    Obtention du statut, 1421
    Protestants, 1214, 1344
Islam, 1058, 1324, 1328, 1337, 1354, 1367,
    1375-76, 1382, 1391, 1399, 1978, 3022,
    3219, 4316
    Afrique du Nord, 1356, 1357
    Algérie, 1033, 1338
    Asie du Sud, 1388
    Belgique, 1352
    Égypte, 1369
    Inde, 1346, 1351, 1379
    Indonésie, 1325
    Iran, 3417
    Maghreb, 1394
    Malaisie, 1336
    Oman, 1338
    Pakistan, 1365
    Tunisie, 1400
    Turquie, 1355, 1489
    URSS, 1339, 1387
Islande
    Églises Chrétiennes, 1497
    Histoire sociale, 3931
    Sécularisation, 1497
Isolement social, 582, 4217
    France, 1085
Israël

Acculturation, 1012
Adolescents, 2623
Aliénation, 4089
Aménagement urbain, 3825, 3874
Art, 1769
Attitude envers le travail, 4399
Communauté scientifique, 122
Comportement électoral, 4996
Conflits du travail, 4688
Conjoncture démographique, 2774
Coopératives agricoles, 4077
Délinquance juvénile, 5187
Développement rural, 3693
Développement urbain, 3874
Droit de la famille, 3135
Ego, 2623
Émigration, 3475
Enseignement secondaire, 2015
Ethnicité, 3303, 3306
Étudiants, 2079
Famille, 3117
Forces armées, 5034
Grèves, 4672
Grèves perlées, 4672
Groupes ethniques, 3325, 3356, 3853
Groupes minoritaires, 697
Immigrants, 89, 1012, 3519
Immigration, 3460
Jeunesse urbaine, 2687
Kibboutz, 4081, 4089, 4091
Migration, 3438
Migration interne, 3541
Militarisation, 5034
Mouvements sociaux, 4937
Nationalisme, 4787
Ouvriers industriels, 307
Pauvreté, 5111
Personnes âgées, 2717, 2730
Politique de défense, 5034
Politique de l'éducation, 1971
Politique nataliste, 2980
Population, 2524
Propriété, 4089
Qualité de la vie, 3804
Religion, 2730
Religion civile, 1299
Religiosité, 2980
Rôles sexuels, 2623
Satisfaction au travail, 4651
Satisfaction résidentielle, 3804
Scientifiques, 89
Segrégation résidentielle, 3853
Société d'abondance, 3960
Statut de la femme, 3693
Syndicats, 4616, 4651, 4688
Tolérance, 830
Italie
    Abstentionnisme électoral, 5011
    Action syndicale, 4596
    Administration locale, 4895, 4897, 4906
    Adultes, 2864
    Architecture, 1837

Bidonvilles, 3795
Catholicisme, 1348, 1386
Chefs d'entreprise, 4007, 4008
Classe moyenne, 2258
Communication, 4354
Comportement électoral, 2168
Conflits du travail, 4680
Conflits sociaux, 641
Consommation culturelle, 3806
Croissance urbaine, 3795
Culture, 887
Délinquance, 5173
Discrimination dans l'emploi, 4220
Droit du travail, 4220, 4680
Dynamique de la population, 2804
Écrivains, 1802
Élections, 4993
Émigrants, 3470, 3521
Émigration, 3524
État, 4846
Famille, 3103, 3180
Habitat, 3613
Histoire culturelle, 2400
Histoire sociale, 2400, 4644
Immigration, 3479
Juifs, 1349
Médecins, 5462
Migration, 3439
Milieu de travail, 4354
Mortalité, 2864
Mouvements de libération de la femme, 3269
Mouvements ouvriers, 4644
Négociation collective, 4695
Ordre social, 2158
Organisation de l'entreprise, 3994
Orientation pédagogique, 547
Périodiques, 184
Petites et moyennes entreprises, 4007,
    4008, 4529, 4846
Pluralisme ethnique, 1349
Politique sanitaire, 5411
Politique urbaine, 3806
Presse, 641
Prison, 5216
Prolétariat, 2289
Relations du travail, 4562, 4567
Représentation des travailleurs, 4723
Sacré, 1454
Santé, 3103
Services sociaux, 5476
Société, 897
Sociologie, 56
Sociologie de l'éducation, 1906
Structure sociale, 2168
Suicide, 5163
Syndicalisme, 4579
Syndicats, 2289, 4220, 4605, 4656
Terrorisme, 1101, 1138
Toxicomanie, 5122, 5123
Travailleurs manuels, 4518
Verriers, 2289
Vie religieuse, 1454

Villages, 2158
Violence, 1184
Zones suburbaines, 3795
Italie : Méridional
    Politique sociale, 5313

Jalousie, 632
Jamaïque
    Développement rural, 1854
    Politique, 5023
    Théâtre, 1854
    Violence, 1106
Japon
    Administration locale, 4134, 4902
    Aide aux gens âgés, 2732, 5374
    Aires métropolitaines, 2232
    Aliénation, 4393
    Allaitement naturel, 2659
    Analyse structurale, 322
    Art, 1781
    Attitude envers le travail, 4412
    Autogestion ouvrière, 4721
    Caractère national, 943
    Classe ouvrière, 2249
    Classes sociales, 2271, 2325
    Collectivités locales, 3631, 3636
    Collectivités rurales, 3691, 3739
    Communication, 1566
    Comportement électoral, 5016
    Conditions de travail, 4393
    Conflits, 646
    Connaissance, 1520
    Conscience de classe, 2322
    Conscience sociale, 2691, 4133
    Coopératives agricoles, 4093
    Cosmologie, 1448
    Culture, 2435
    Culture politique, 3636
    Délinquance juvénile, 5190, 5250
    Désastres, 3916
    Développement des collectivités, 3642
    Développement régional, 4133, 4134
    Développement social, 2435
    Déviance, 1103
    Différences de generations, 943
    Discrimination, 821
    Discrimination raciale, 3431
    Écoles secondaires, 1103, 1967
    Éducation, 1916
    Enseignants, 1967
    Enseignement secondaire, 2008
    Enseignement supérieur, 2043, 2060
    Entreprises industrielles, 4080
    Étude de collectivité, 369
    Famille, 3116, 3185
    Famille monoparentale, 3142
    Fécondité, 2903, 2941
    Femmes, 2745
    Histoire de la sociologie, 36, 40
    Histoire sociale, 923, 2181
    Hommes politiques, 4960
    Hôpitaux, 2842

Indicateurs sociaux, 432
Industrie automobile, 4393
Internationalisation, 5042
Jeunesse, 2691
Journalisme, 821
Justice criminelle, 5250
Langage, 1691
Langues étrangères, 1607
Lieux saints, 1469
Logement urbain, 3841
Main-d'oeuvre féminine, 4301
Malades, 2842
Ménagères, 2562
Microélectronique, 4332
Migration, 3450
Minorités ethniques, 3350
Mobilité sociale, 2232, 2379
Modernisation, 2456
Modes de vie, 899, 2271
Mouvements ouvriers, 4646
Moyens de communication de masse, 1691
Négociation collective, 4704
Ordre social, 992
Organisation de l'entreprise, 711, 4080
Organisation du travail, 4332
Parenté, 3196
Paysans, 3692
Pêcheurs, 4513
Personnes âgées, 2732, 2745, 2747, 2757, 2762
Planification de la famille, 2999
Politique, 5026
Presse féminine, 1698
Professions, 2739
Prostitution, 3051
Publicité, 1635
Quartier, 3916
Radiodiffusion, 1688, 1751
Recherche sociale, 5062
Réformes administratives, 4134
Réformes de l'enseignement, 1967
Relations culturelles, 5042
Relations du travail, 181, 4540
Relations familiales, 3200
Religion, 1285
Réseau de communication, 1578
Retraite, 2747, 3691
Rites, 1448
Santé, 2206
Sectes, 1439
Services d'information, 156
Sexualité, 3116
Société, 992
Société traditionnelle, 1439
Sociologie de la culture, 877
Sociologie des organisations, 711
Sociologie du travail, 4140
Sociologie urbaine, 3843
Statut de la femme, 3251
Stéréotypes nationaux, 1607
Stratification sociale, 2206, 2232, 2325
Structure sociale, 369, 2181, 2456

Suicide, 5205
Syndicalisme, 4614
Syndicats, 4601
Systèmes d'enseignement, 1955
Systèmes de valeur, 1075
Télévision, 1654, 1746
Temps de loisir, 4736
Traditions, 992
Travail social, 5389
Travailleurs migrants, 3148
Usines, 669
Valeur, 1052
Vie familiale, 3148
Vie quotidienne, 923, 2757
Vie sociale, 369
Vieillissement, 2739
Villages de pêcheurs, 4513
Villes capitales, 3755
Zones urbaines, 3450
Japon — Royaume-Uni
  Cadres, 4530
  Perception d'autrui, 4530
Japon : Takarazuka
  Changement social, 3789
  Zones suburbaines, 3789
Java
  Industrialisation, 4298
  Langues, 1623
  Moyens audiovisuels, 3012
  Planification de la famille, 3012
  Population urbaine, 2781
  Travailleuses, 4298
Jeu de rôle, 2150
Jeunes travailleurs, 1981
  Allemagne RF, 3321, 4462
  Europe, 4293
  France, 4265
  Hongrie, 938
  Royaume-Uni, 4202
Jeunesse, 1160, 1681, 2664, 2666, 2671-72,
    2678, 2686, 2701, 2705, 2707, 2944,
    4938
  Allemagne, 2697
  Allemagne RD, 2689
  Allemagne RF, 299, 2680
  Canada, 3035
  Danemark, 3851
  Espagne, 2667
  États-Unis, 1065, 2692, 2702, 4763
  France, 2665, 3499
  Hongrie, 2703
  Île de la Réunion, 2668
  Irlande, 2682
  Japon, 2691
  Martinique, 2668
  Pologne, 1129, 1473, 2674, 2693, 2696
  Portugal, 2676
  Royaume-Uni, 2685
  Sri Lanka, 2690
  Suède, 2684
  Suisse, 2673
  Tchécoslovaquie, 2688

Tunisie, 2683
URSS, 155
Jeunesse rurale, 1981
    Inde, 2699
    Pologne, 2704, 4437
Jeunesse urbaine
    Israël, 2687
Jeux
    Allemagne RF, 4744
    Autriche, 4747
    États-Unis, 4737
Jeux à deux personnes, 442
Jeux d'argent, 4743, 4749
Jeux expérimentaux, 443, 445
Jordanie
    Changement social, 2481, 3319
    Tables de mortalité, 2895
    Travailleuses, 4243
    Tribus, 3319
Journalisme, 1700, 1726
    Allemagne RF, 1675
    Japon, 821
Journalistes, 1699, 1724, 1738
    Australie, 1694
    États-Unis, 1694
    Venezuela, 1645
Jours de fête
    Pologne : Varsovie, 3151
Judaïsme, 1319, 1332-33, 1375, 1442, 1461
Jugement, 273
    États-Unis, 283
Jugement social, 603, 610, 3724
    États-Unis, 611
    Pologne, 2229
Juges
    Belgique, 4882
Juifs, 1343, 1371, 1372, 1395, 3237, 3345
    Allemagne RF, 1390
    Australie, 1326
    Bulgarie, 1383
    États-Unis, 1374
    Europe, 4666
    Hongrie, 1825
    Italie, 1349
    Pologne, 3429
    Royaume-Uni, 1359
    URSS, 1370, 1378, 1385, 1823, 3460,
        3536
Jury
    États-Unis, 676
Justice, 1231
    Inde, 1261
Justice criminelle, 5177, 5179, 5201
    Chine, 5239
    États-Unis, 1071, 5159, 5166, 5199, 5206
    Inde, 5208
    Japon, 5250
    Suisse, 5232
Justice économique, 5308
Justice sociale, 5263, 5272, 5308, 5338
    États-Unis, 1928
    Inde, 4236

Kant, Emmanuel, 53, 226, 541
Kenya
    Droit administratif, 4764
    Éducation, 1896
    Fécondité, 2928
    Formation professionnelle, 4461
    Intervalles génésiques, 2910
    Nomades, 3563
    Pauvreté, 5085
    Politique démographique, 2991
    Squatters, 3764
Kenya : Nairobi
    Abandon d'études, 2019
    Écoles secondaires, 2019
Keynes, J. M., 1
Kibboutz
    Israël, 4081, 4089, 4091
Kierkegaard, S., 511, 3954
Korsch, Karl, 552
Kuhn, T., 1508

Langage, 1321, 1512, 1587, 1589, 1595-96,
    1602, 1608-10, 1612, 1616, 1630, 3281
    Afrique, 1852
    Allemagne, 1620
    France, 1588
    Inde, 1611
    Japon, 1691
Langue maternelle, 1584
    États-Unis, 1601
Langues, 1583, 1606
    Afrique, 1591
    Asie, 1305
    Canada, 1604
    Java, 1623
Langues étrangères
    États-Unis, 1600
    Japon, 1607
    Pays arabes, 1586
Lavater, Johann Kaspar, 2634
Lazarsfeld, Paul, 176
Le Play, Frédéric, 196
Leaders, 799, 2887
Leaders politiques
    Guyana, 4959
    Trinité, 4959
Leadership, 708, 795, 796, 798, 1572, 3985,
    4533
Leadership politique
    Inde, 4831
    Pologne, 4961
Lecteurs
    Allemagne RF, 1631
Légendes, 1803, 1828
Législation, 1079
Législation sociale
    Espagne, 5340
Légitimité, 4771
Leibniz, Gottfried Wilhelm, 4871
Lenin, V. I., 2231, 2296, 5024
Lesotho
    Éducation, 1876

Levi-Strauss, Claude, 2174
Levinas, E., 1283
Lewin, Kurt, 479
Liban
    Développement rural, 3725
    Mariage consanguin, 3078
    Relations interethniques, 3395
    Religion, 3725
    Villages, 3725
Libéralisme, 4786, 4791-93, 4803, 4861
    Afrique du Sud, 4805
Libéria
    Mortalité, 2853
Liberté, 891, 892, 4852, 4858, 4860, 4861,
    4864, 4868
Liberté d'expression
    États-Unis, 4848
Liberté de l'enseignement
    Australie, 1951
    Canada, 2027
    États-Unis, 1968
    France, 1963
Liberté de la presse
    Côte d'Ivoire, 4851
Liberté religieuse
    Soudan, 1485
Lieu de travail, 4371
Lieux saints
    Japon, 1469
Linguistique, 1526
    Amazonie, 1525
    France, 1717
    Yougoslavie, 1533
Littérature, 1316, 1322, 1610, 1789-90, 1794,
    1810, 1814-15
    Afrique, 1788, 1795
    Allemagne RD, 1792, 1811
    Allemagne RF, 1792, 1830
    Amérique latine, 1796
    Asie occidentale, 1807
    Chine, 1817
    États-Unis, 1820, 2660
    Europe orientale, 1818
    Hongrie, 1825
    Maghreb, 1812
    Nigeria, 1798
    Roumanie, 1821
    Royaume-Uni, 1827
    Tunisie, 1804
    Turquie, 1793, 1806
    URSS, 1823, 1826
Littérature populaire
    Hongrie, 1829
Liturgie
    Brésil, 1440
Livres
    Belgique, 1757
Locataires
    États-Unis, 3798
Locke, John, 2157
Logement, 3746, 3838, 3847
    Danemark, 3851

    États-Unis, 3788, 3855
    France, 3776, 3896
    Ghana, 3767
    Hongrie, 3790, 3986
    Pays en développement, 3860, 3868
    Philippines, 3848
    Pologne, 3928
    Royaume-Uni, 3826, 3910
    Tchécoslovaquie, 3765
Logement rural
    Portugal, 3793
Logement urbain
    Japon, 3841
Logements sociaux
    Belgique, 3800
    France, 3791, 3929
Logique, 394, 402, 475
Loisir, 4209, 4343, 4728, 4730
    Allemagne RF, 4729
    France, 4738
Los Angeles
    Avortement, 2978
Luhmann, Niklas, 492, 4771
Lukács, György, 1777, 1801
Lutte de classes, 2251, 2288
    Afrique du Sud, 2290
    France, 2311
    Pologne, 2317

Machonin, P., 2294
Madagascar
    Christianisme, 1347
    Différenciation raciale, 1347
    Pauvreté, 5114
    Presse, 1669
Maghreb
    Bibliographies, 1394
    Coopération culturelle, 1016
    Islam, 1394
    Littérature, 1812
    Sexualité, 3025
    Symbolisme du corps, 1548
    Systèmes de valeur, 1053
Magie, 841, 1316, 1320
Main-d'oeuvre
    Équateur, 4172
    France, 4149, 4156
Main-d'oeuvre féminine
    Australie, 4245
    Brésil, 4281
    Japon, 4301
Malades, 578, 2830, 2831, 2834
    Japon, 2842
Maladies, 2196, 3134
    États-Unis, 2837
    Finlande, 2839
Maladies mentales, 2632, 2823, 2835
    États-Unis, 2824, 2843
Maladies professionnelles
    Pologne, 4434
Malaise de la jeunesse
    Royaume-Uni, 5126

Malaise social, 963, 2478, 5070
    États-Unis, 2041, 5434
    Pologne, 5073
Malaisie
    Allaitement naturel, 2643
    Déontologie, 1476
    Enfants adoptés, 2653
    Éthique protestante, 1476
    Fécondité, 2934
    Groupes ethniques, 3308, 3344
    Intervalles génésiques, 2933
    Islam, 1336
    Mobilité sociale, 2326
    Mortalité des enfants, 2643, 2933
    Mortalité infantile, 2934
    Paysans, 3685
    Production, 4021
    Relations raciales, 3387
    Rôle des femmes, 2599
    Société, 4021
    Structure de classe, 2326
Malawi
    Migration interne, 3547
Mali
    Mortalité des enfants, 2870
    Mortalité infantile, 2870
Malnutrition, 5095
    Sri Lanka, 5110
Malthus, T. R., 2416
Manifestations, 866, 1113
    Canada, 867
Mannheim, Karl, 1511, 2308, 2396
Manuels, 187, 188, 189, 190, 191
Marché, 4110
    Royaume-Uni, 4111
Marché agricole
    France, 3670
Marché de la viande
    Royaume-Uni, 4111
Marché du travail, 4158, 4162, 4174, 4333
    Afrique du Sud, 4165
    Allemagne, 4242
    Australie, 2596
    Danemark, 4171
    États-Unis, 696, 4176
    Europe, 4293
    Pays-Bas, 4225
    Pologne, 4161
    Royaume-Uni, 4170
Marginalité, 1110
    Allemagne RF, 1721
Marginaux
    Inde, 1152
    Suède, 2684
Mari, 3088
Mariage, 3055, 3064
    Afrique du Sud, 3072
    Australie, 618
    Belgique, 3094
    Canada, 3060
    Chine, 613, 3159
    États-Unis, 3048, 3054

    Europe, 3139
    France, 349
    Hongrie, 3077
    Inde, 618, 3068
    Philippines, 3058
Mariage consanguin
    Liban, 3078
Mariage mixte
    Allemagne RF, 3061
    France, 3085, 3101
Marine marchande
    France, 4208
Marins, 4512, 4520
    États-Unis, 1110
Maroc
    Espace urbain, 3809
    Étudiants, 2064
    Production agricole, 1128
    Révolte, 1128
Marshall, T. H., 177
Martinique
    Emploi des jeunes, 2668
    Jeunesse, 2668
Marx, Karl, 1, 48, 193, 216, 239, 246, 260,
    320, 394, 859, 1007, 1111, 1161, 1229,
    2177, 2304, 2431, 2497, 3937, 3944,
    3950, 4794, 4868
Marxisme, 193, 205, 207, 223, 228-30,
    237, 239, 241, 248, 254, 259, 261,
    264-65, 476, 486, 868, 965, 988,
    1126, 1164, 2278, 2313, 3410, 3937,
    4799
    France, 267
    Pologne, 2229
Marxisme-Léninisme, 4050
Matérialisme, 224
Matérialisme dialectique, 246
Maternité, 2962
    Australie : Sydney, 3017
    États-Unis, 2058, 3004
    Portugal, 3229
Mathématiques, 335, 392, 396, 406
Matriarcat
    France, 3113
Mauss, Marcel, 4782
McLuhan, Marshall, 4044
Mead, G. H., 487
Mécanisation agricole
    Canada, 4088
    États-Unis, 4070
    Inde, 3721
Médecine, 5393, 5401
Médecine sociale, 5399
Médecine traditionnelle
    Brésil, 5398
    Guadeloupe, 5394
Médecins, 578, 5463
    Belgique, 5475
    France, 5461, 5473, 5477, 5479
    Italie, 5462
    Yougoslavie, 5469
Médiation, 652, 4700, 4703

Médicaments
France, 5125
Royaume-Uni, 5130
Ménagères
Japon, 2562
Ménages, 2577, 2602, 2621, 3606
Allemagne RF, 3171
États-Unis, 2586, 2587, 2617
Hongrie, 2563
Mère
Grèce, 3133
Mères célibataires, 5362
Australie, 3198
États-Unis, 3174, 4315
Mères travailleuses
Bangladesh, 4251
Royaume-Uni, 1995
Merton, Robert K., 54, 66, 1335, 1504, 1507
Messianisme, 1319
Mesure, 372
Mesure de l'utilité, 372
Mesure du bien-être, 5266
Métayage, 4095
États-Unis, 4084
Méthodes contraceptives, 2985
Australie, 2966
Méthodes d'exploitation agricole
États-Unis, 4070
Méthodes de recherche, 346, 353, 533
Méthodes pédagogiques, 2130
Méthodologie anthropologique, 234
Méthodologie sociologique, 106, 303, 305,
313, 323, 329-30, 334, 337, 342, 350,
354-56
Métis
Royaume-Uni, 3430
Métropole, 3919
Amérique latine, 3768
Pérou, 3899
Meurtriers, 5221
Mexique
Autoritarisme, 4826
Collectivités rurales, 3714
Concentration urbaine, 3780
Développement urbain, 3862
Différenciation sociale, 3714
Droits de la femme, 3280
Éducation de base, 2084
Éducation des adultes, 2104
Émigrants, 3287
Enseignement bilingue, 2094
Fécondité, 2872
Historiographie, 2395
Inégalité sociale, 2217
Minorités ethniques, 2217
Moyens d'enseignement, 2133
Patriotisme, 4776
Planification de la famille, 2984
Politique de l'éducation, 1984
Politique sanitaire, 5418
Régimes fonciers, 3655
Reproduction sociale, 2133

Santé, 5408
Services de santé, 5408
Structure agraire, 1984
Syndicats, 4624, 4661
Systèmes politiques, 4826
Tables de mortalité, 2872
Travail des femmes, 4317
Travailleuses, 5408
Villes, 3780
Microanalyse, 345
Microélectronique, 4346
Japon, 4332
Microordinateurs
États-Unis, 2148
Migrants, 3437
Allemagne RF, 1721
Suisse, 3440
Migration, 3444-46, 3449
Allemagne RF, 3439
Amérique latine, 3433
Canada, 3436
Caraïbes, 3442, 3443
États-Unis, 3451
Europe, 3447
France, 4451
Inde, 3434, 3452
Indonésie, 3453
Israël, 3438
Italie, 3439
Japon, 3450
Porto Rico, 3448
Tchécoslovaquie, 3612
URSS, 3441
Migration de retour
Grèce, 3459
Tunisie, 3478
Yougoslavie, 3528
Migration de travail, 3555
Pays en développement, 3566
Pologne, 3530
Migration internationale, 2820, 3457-58,
3462, 3493, 3529, 3555
Europe, 3497
Migration interne
Costa Rica, 3546
Égypte, 3568
États-Unis, 3560, 3565
Finlande, 3562
France, 2857
Inde, 3553, 3561
Israël, 3541
Malawi, 3547
Nigeria, 3538
URSS, 3537
Migration rurale-urbaine, 3544, 3556
Chine, 3550
Corée R, 3548
Inde, 3539, 3540, 3551
Pays en développement, 3567
Philippines, 3569
Thaïlande, 3549
URSS, 3570

Yougoslavie, 3558
Migration urbaine-rurale
  États-Unis, 3545, 3554, 3564
Migration urbaine-urbaine
  Allemagne RF, 3557
Migrations alternantes, 3559
  Hongrie, 3543
Milieu de travail, 1595, 4358, 4392, 4419,
  4422
  Italie, 4354
  Norvège, 4382
Milieu familial
  États-Unis, 3153, 4476
  Hongrie, 3140
  Taïwan, 2201
Milieu professionnel, 4520
Milieu rural
  Europe, 3706
Milieu scolaire
  France, 2021
Milieu social, 3575
  France, 3193
  Pologne, 1218
Milieu urbain, 3839, 3924
  France, 3890
  Pays socialistes, 3846
Milieux d'affaires, 3996
  Allemagne RF, 4013
  Autriche, 4013
  Ghana, 3992
  Nigeria, 3990
Militaires
  États-Unis, 5029, 5036
Militarisation
  Israël, 5034
Mill, John Stuart, 1288
Millénarisme, 849
Mills, C. W., 66, 5072
Mines de houille
  France, 4516
Mineurs
  France, 4516
  Ghana, 4507
Minorités
  Moyen-Orient, 686
  Proche Orient, 685
Minorités ethniques
  Allemagne RF, 3313
  Canada, 3340
  États-Unis, 3287
  France, 3552
  Japon, 3350
  Mexique, 2217
  Pays-Bas, 3335
  Royaume-Uni, 3349
Minorités linguistiques
  Canada, 1605
Minorités nationales
  Allemagne RF, 3307
  Danemark, 3307
  Pays capitalistes, 3288
  Yougoslavie, 3305

Minorités religieuses
  Belgique, 1352
Missionnaires
  Nigeria, 1910
Mobilité de la main d'oeuvre, 4154
Mobilité professionnelle
  États-Unis, 4463, 4480, 4481, 4500
  Inde, 4499
  Royaume-Uni, 4479
Mobilité sociale, 2050, 2215, 2373, 2380,
  2626, 2661, 3110
  Allemagne, 2377
  Allemagne RF, 2369
  Canada, 2368, 2383
  États-Unis, 2385
  France, 2375, 2387, 2388
  Hongrie, 2374, 2384
  Inde, 2386, 3297
  Inde : Assam, 2233
  Iran, 3164
  Japon, 2232, 2379
  Malaisie, 2326
  Pays arabes, 2381
  Pays capitalistes, 2382
  Pologne, 2272
  Royaume-Uni, 1366, 2375
  Singapour, 2326
  Suède, 2375
  Yougoslavie, 2371
Mode, 1187, 1199
Modèles, 285
Modèles culturels, 916
Modèles de décision, 549, 565, 2603
Modèles économétriques, 4154
Modèles linéaires, 272, 288
Modèles mathématiques, 302, 310, 395,
  398-401, 403-04
Modèles stochastiques, 279
  Brésil, 444
Modernisation
  Espagne, 2464, 2477
  Hongrie, 2446
  Japon, 2456
Modernité, 782, 1312, 1450, 2419, 2441,
  2445, 2451, 2463, 2468-71, 2478
Modes de production, 4041
  Asie, 4058
  France, 4047
Modes de vie, 523, 905, 949, 969, 973, 1001, 2900
  Amérique latine, 4124
  États-Unis, 977
  France, 883, 904
  Hongrie, 938
  Japon, 899, 2271
  URSS, 425
Moeurs, 1193
Monachisme
  France, 1403
Monopoles, 4112
Monothéisme, 1464
Montée des prix
  Royaume-Uni, 3818

Moore, Barrington, 1226
Morale, 273, 1216, 1225, 2762, 4147
    URSS, 3121
    Zaïre, 1213
Moralité, 232, 1220, 1226, 1229, 2581, 2605,
        2606
    Australie, 1221
    Irlande du Nord, 1214
    Pologne, 1218
Morbidité
    Finlande, 2541
Mort, 2830, 2867, 2882, 3145
    France, 2886
    France : Bretagne, 1451
    Polynésie, 2904
    Suisse, 2889
Mortalité, 2879, 2884, 2894, 2898
    Afrique, 2953
    Algérie, 2893
    Asie, 2897
    États-Unis, 2516, 2891
    France, 2854, 2858, 2860
    Hongrie, 2856
    Inde, 2881, 2945
    Italie, 2864
    Libéria, 2853
    Pays en développement, 2848
    Pays-Bas, 4219
    Royaume-Uni, 2885
    Sri Lanka, 2874
    Suède, 2850
    Tchécoslovaquie, 2890
    Tunisie, 2866
    URSS, 2861
Mortalité des enfants, 2851, 2871
    États-Unis, 2863
    France, 2875
    Inde, 3177
    Indonésie, 2859, 2873
    Malaisie, 2643, 2933
    Mali, 2870
    Pays en développement, 2846
    Philippines, 3848
Mortalité infantile, 2192, 2869, 2899
    Brésil, 2868
    États-Unis, 2849
    Finlande, 2552, 2876
    Indonésie, 2859, 2873
    Malaisie, 2934
    Mali, 2870
    Tchécoslovaquie, 2888, 2896
Motivation, 574, 1157
Motivation d'accomplissement, 538, 564, 706
    Allemagne RF, 828
Mouvements contestaires, 4938
Mouvements coopératifs
    Finlande, 4941
    Pérou, 4953
Mouvements de consommateurs
    France, 4099
Mouvements de libération de la femme
    Allemagne RF, 3245

France, 3248
Inde, 3275
Italie, 3269
Mouvements de résistance
    Afrique du Sud, 2242
Mouvements étudiants
    Allemagne RF, 2038, 2056
    Bolivie, 2057
    Canada, 2056
    États-Unis, 2056
    France, 2038
    Indonésie, 2068
    Pays en développement, 2031
    Yougoslavie, 2066
Mouvements nationalistes
    Europe, 4684
Mouvements ouvriers, 4618, 4642, 4648
    Allemagne, 4598, 4617, 4626, 4658
    Allemagne RF, 4603
    Bulgarie, 4660
    Danemark, 4595
    Équateur, 4668
    Espagne, 4608
    Europe, 4662, 4666
    France, 4599, 4617, 4619, 4662
    Ghana, 4507
    Italie, 4644
    Japon, 4646
    Pologne, 3429, 4594
    Royaume-Uni, 4613
Mouvements pacifistes, 1263, 4932
    Allemagne RF, 1223
Mouvements paysans, 1113
    France : Bretagne, 3670
Mouvements politiques, 4945, 4947
    Royaume-Uni, 4777
Mouvements religieux, 1467
    États-Unis, 1499
Mouvements révolutionnaires, 2458
Mouvements sociaux, 744, 763, 769, 869,
        4928, 4930, 4933, 4935, 4939-40,
        4942-43, 4946, 4951, 4954
    Allemagne RF, 4924, 4925
    Amérique latine, 4927
    Canada, 4923
    États-Unis, 4926, 4952
    Europe, 4922
    Europe orientale, 4920
    France, 4936
    Inde, 4921
    Israël, 4937
    Pays en développement, 4934
    Royaume-Uni, 2096
    Venezuela, 4929
Moyen-Orient
    Groupes majoritaires, 686
    Minorités, 686
Moyens audiovisuels
    Java, 3012
Moyens d'enseignement, 2123, 2141
    États-Unis, 2148
    Mexique, 2133

Moyens de communication, 1653, 1659, 1676, 1701, 1715, 1736, 1754
    Amérique, 1753
    Amérique du Nord, 1671
    États-Unis, 1744, 4737
Moyens de communication de masse, 606, 1040, 1091, 1529, 1650, 1657-58, 1666, 1687, 1697, 1718, 1722-23, 1731, 1743, 1760
    Allemagne RF, 1684, 1721
    Autriche, 1709
    Côte d'Ivoire, 1686
    Danemark, 1556
    Espagne, 1716
    Espagne : Catologne, 1685
    États-Unis, 1651, 1660, 1662, 3205, 4016, 4746
    France, 1734, 1763
    Inde, 1652
    Japon, 1691
    Pays en développement, 1638
    République dominicaine, 1739
    Royaume-Uni, 1708
    Suède, 1689
    Yougoslavie, 1677, 1678
Mozambique
    Éducation, 1884
    Partis politiques, 4914
    Services de santé, 5458
    Soins médicaux, 5458
    Villages, 3654
Multilinguisme, 1589
Musées d'art
    États-Unis, 1787
Musique, 682, 1842, 1844
    Côte d'Ivoire, 1845
    États-Unis, 1840
    France, 1841
    Hongrie, 1847
    URSS, 1843
Musique rock
    États-Unis, 1846
Musulmans, 1389, 3262
    Asie du Sud, 1388
    Inde, 1327
    URSS, 1402
    Yougoslavie, 1381
Myrdal, Gunnar, 3353
Mysticisme, 1450, 1455, 1461, 1465
Mythes, 1457, 1459, 1462, 1463, 3341
    Australie, 2612

Naissance, 2912, 2949
    Bangladesh, 2906
    Chine, 2935
    États-Unis, 2915
    Polynésie, 2904
Natalité
    États-Unis, 2908
    France, 2923
Nation, 890-92, 930, 957, 965, 980, 1007
    France, 984

Nationalisme, 3332, 3357, 4774, 4775, 4939
    Canada, 4772
    Canada : Québec, 1428, 1437, 4773
    Espagne, 4795
    Inde, 3702
    Israël, 4787
    Pays arabes, 4787
    Royaume-Uni, 4772
Nationalité, 2171
Nature, 3578, 3597-99, 3601-02, 3604, 3607-08
Négociation, 644, 648, 652, 657
Négociation collective, 4384
    Allemagne RF, 4062, 4694
    Australie, 4691
    Belgique, 4690
    Brésil, 2309
    Espagne, 4607
    États-Unis, 4696, 4698
    Italie, 4695
    Japon, 4704
    Nigeria, 4697
    Royaume-Uni, 4558, 4699, 4702
Négociations salariales
    États-Unis, 4693
    France, 4692
Néoconservatisme, 2441, 5331
Népal
    Bouddhisme, 2434
    Chamanisme, 1318
    Changement social, 2434
    Enquêtes, 379
    Fécondité, 379
    Féodalisme, 3959
    Politique culturelle, 1010
    Société rurale, 3959
    Villages, 3679
Névroses
    Pologne, 1472
Nicaragua
    Bourgeoisie, 2312
    Construction de l'État, 4834
    Développement rural, 3711
    Éducation, 1864
    Église catholique, 1416
    Formation de classe, 1416
    Scolarité, 1986
Nietzsche, Friedrich, 860, 1478
Niger
    Administration publique, 4890
Nigeria
    Aménagement urbain, 3759
    Bibliothèques, 154
    Contraception, 2996
    Développement des collectivités, 3622
    Développement rural, 3538
    Enfants, 2654
    Groupes religieux, 1424
    Histoire de l'éducation, 1910
    Littérature, 1798
    Migration interne, 3538
    Milieux d'affaires, 3990

Missionnaires, 1910
Négociation collective, 4697
Orientation professionnelle, 4488
Pauvreté, 2654
Politique du logement, 3877
Prestige professionnel, 4488
Relations du travail, 4541
Satisfaction résidentielle, 3877
Secteur privé, 4697
Société paysanne, 3622
Sociologie, 7
Soins médicaux, 5419
Travail des femmes, 4258, 4308
Niveau de vie
    URSS, 425
    Yougoslavie, 3840
Niveau du chômage
    Pays-Bas, 4449
Niveaux d'enseignement, 1931, 2924
    États-Unis, 1966, 4481
    Iran, 3164
    Tchécoslovaquie, 1982
Noirs
    Brésil, 3296
    États-Unis, 1805, 2256, 2335, 2584, 3129,
        3136, 3282, 3312, 3331, 3348, 3352,
        3355, 3373, 3403, 3897, 4480, 4633
    États-Unis, 3298, 3315, 3736
Nomades, 3571
    France, 3542, 3552
    Kenya, 3563
Noms
    Burundi, 507
    États-Unis, 513
    Royaume-Uni, 505
Non-violence
    États-Unis, 3373
Normes culturelles
    Suisse, 5414
Normes de travail
    France, 1057
Normes sociales, 1051, 1054, 1062, 1068,
        1076, 1078, 1081, 1082
    États-Unis, 2709, 3048
    France, 1057
Norvège
    Budgets temps, 4406
    Conditions de vie, 3974
    Culture populaire, 1035
    Enfants, 3974
    Enseignement supérieur, 2046
    État providence, 5291, 5292
    Institutions, 1073
    Milieu de travail, 4382
    Participation des travailleurs, 4717
    Participation politique, 4981
    Politique culturelle, 1035
    Qualité de la vie, 3977
    Réfugiés, 3492
    Relations du travail, 4634
    Répartition du revenu, 3982
    Ressources pétrolières, 894

Satisfaction de l'existence, 3977
Société, 894
Statut de la femme, 3228
Syndicats, 4634
Notices nécrologiques, 169-71, 176-79, 182-83
Nouvel ordre mondial de l'information, 1554, 1580
Nouvelle Zélande
    Comportement politique, 4977
    Conflits du travail, 4679
    Développement des collectivités, 5467
    Développement régional, 4125
    Discrimination raciale, 3414
    Égalité de chances, 2221
    Géographie humaine, 3587
    Groupes minoritaires, 692
    Groupes religieux, 4977
    Intervention de l'État, 4136
    Politique des revenus, 4136
    Politique du logement, 3867
    Population, 2542
    Règlement de conflits, 4679
    Satisfaction de l'existence, 557
    Services sociaux, 5467
Nuptialité, 3092
    Chine, 3063
    États-Unis, 3065
    Europe, 3074
Nutrition
    Colombie, 5084
    Inde, 5106

Objectifs de l'éducation, 1915, 1938, 2284
    France, 1962
    Inde, 2699
Objectivité, 6, 294
Observation, 367, 881
Observation participante, 362, 373
Obtention du statut, 2378
    États-Unis, 2370, 2372, 2376
    Irlande du Nord, 1421
Occultisme, 1317, 1321, 1322
Océanie
    Rôle des femmes, 2607
Oeuvres d'art, 1783
Offre de main d'oeuvre, 4160
Oligarchie, 4821
    Guatémala, 4810
Oman
    Islam, 1338
    Rôle des femmes, 2575
    Statut de la femme, 2575
    Systèmes politiques, 1338
Opinion, 1572
Opinion publique, 835, 836, 839, 1666
    Amérique latine, 840
    Chili, 833
    France, 377, 832, 1135
    Hongrie, 3969
    Pologne, 4161
Optimum de peuplement, 2817
Ordinateurs, 131, 138, 2123
    États-Unis, 382

Ordre social, 1064, 2162, 2176, 2178
 Inde, 1261
 Italie, 2158
 Japon, 992
Ordres religieux, 1434
Organisation communautaire, 3624, 3627,
 3645
 Allemagne RF, 3638
Organisation de l'entreprise, 4001, 4012
 Italie, 3994
 Japon, 711, 4080
Organisation du travail, 4151, 4327, 4331,
 4333, 4338, 4340, 4343, 4346
 États-Unis, 4324
 Europe, 4330
 France, 4031, 4335
 Japon, 4332
 URSS, 4337
 Yougoslavie, 4334
Organisations, 722, 725-26, 733-34, 736,
 2432, 3639, 5080
Organisations agricoles
 Inde, 3723
Organisations bénévoles, 721, 728
 Danemark, 727
 France, 723
Organisations complexes, 729, 735
Organisations de jeunesse, 2635
 Afrique francophone, 2695
 Suisse, 2669
 Suisse : Zurich, 2706
Organisations féminines
 Canada, 3221
 Royaume-Uni, 3278
Orientation aux valeurs, 1066, 1072
 États-Unis, 1056
Orientation pédagogique
 Italie, 547
Orientation professionnelle, 4484
 Nigeria, 4488
Origine sociale, 2329, 2337
 États-Unis, 5439
 Suède, 2117
Ortega y Gasset, José, 5339
Ossowski, Stanislaw, 2310
Ouchi, William, 751
Ouvriers industriels
 Allemagne RF, 4456
 Hongrie, 4514
 Inde, 1169, 4517
 Israël, 307
 Pays socialistes, 4732
 Pologne, 4514

Pacifisme, 5047
Paganisme, 1456
Paix, 5049, 5051, 5053
Pakistan
 Croyance, 834
 Éducation, 1365
 Étudiants, 834
 Islam, 1365

Réformes de l'enseignement, 1978
Panama
 Sciences sociales, 26
Papouasie Nouvelle Guinée
 Droit coutumier, 1239
 Enfants, 2644
Paradigme, 290, 1507
Paraguay
 Bilinguisme, 1598
 Systèmes d'enseignement, 1972
Parenté, 3162, 3727
 Amérique latine, 3182
 Hong Kong, 3729
 Japon, 3196
 Suède, 3119
Pareto, Vilfredo, 844, 5314
Park, Robert E., 871, 3822
Parkin, Frank, 787
Paroisse
 France, 1432
 Royaume-Uni, 1366
Parsons, Talcott, 226, 261, 878, 1164, 2451
Participation de la collectivité
 Amérique latine, 3628
 États-Unis, 3617
Participation des femmes, 2629, 3215, 3265
 Allemagne RF, 4623
 Botswana, 3236
 Canada, 3208, 3227
 États-Unis, 3225
 France, 4623
Participation des travailleurs, 4622, 4705,
 4707, 4715, 4727
 Allemagne RF, 4722
 Chine, 4719
 États-Unis, 4706, 4712
 France, 4708
 Inde, 4720
 Norvège, 4717
 Pologne, 4710
 Royaume-Uni, 4709, 4724
 URSS, 2301
Participation électorale, 5005
Participation politique, 4969, 4984
 Amérique latine, 1032
 Norvège, 4981
 Pays-Bas, 4973
 Royaume-Uni, 4987
 Zambie, 4990
Participation sociale, 1142, 1168
 France, 1092
 Inde, 1095
Partis politiques, 4917
 Allemagne RF, 5301
 Amérique latine, 4909
 Autriche, 4915
 Canada, 4907
 Inde, 4908, 4912
 Irlande, 4913
 Mozambique, 4914
 Pologne, 4910
 Tanzanie, 4914

Passage à la vie active, 1985
Paternité, 2994
Paternité-maternité
    États-Unis, 3005, 3027
Pathologie sociale, 5071, 5077
Patriarcat
    Chine, 3141
    Europe occidentale, 3141
Patrie, 980
Patriotisme
    États-Unis, 4778
    Mexique, 4776
Pauvres
    Afrique, 5091
Pauvreté, 5089, 5090, 5094, 5108, 5288
    Afrique du Sud, 5092
    Amérique latine, 1003
    Brésil, 797
    Costa Rica, 5086
    États-Unis, 5087, 5093, 5102, 5107
    Europe, 5101
    France, 5083, 5115
    France : Rouen, 4120
    Inde, 1152, 5099
    Israël, 5111
    Kenya, 5085
    Madagascar, 5114
    Nigeria, 2654
    Pays en développement, 2982
    Soudan, 3831
    Suisse : Genève, 5097
Pauvreté rurale
    Bangladesh, 5116
    États-Unis, 5105
    Inde, 5098
    Philippines : Leyte, 5103
Pays arabes
    Aliénation culturelle, 2361
    Classe ouvrière, 2381
    Écrivains, 1800
    Édition, 1800
    Enseignement, 2153
    Femmes, 2625
    Identité culturelle, 2361
    Intelligentsia, 2361
    Langues étrangères, 1586
    Mobilité sociale, 2381
    Nationalisme, 4787
    Systèmes d'enseignement, 1980
Pays capitalistes
    Changement structurel, 2382
    Classe ouvrière, 2262
    Immigrants, 3288
    Minorités nationales, 3288
    Mobilité sociale, 2382
    Travail, 4155
Pays de l'ASEAN
    Enseignement supérieur, 2070
Pays de l'OCDE
    Emploi des femmes, 4306
Pays de la CEE
    Chômage des jeunes, 4195

Femmes, 2560
Politique culturelle, 1018
Syndicats, 4637
Tourisme, 4750
Travail des femmes, 4313
Travailleurs frontaliers, 4232
Pays développés
    Conditions de travail, 4436
    Politique de la communication, 1552
    Population urbaine, 3810
    Sécurité sociale, 5367
    Services de santé, 5451
    Structure de classe, 2257
Pays du CAEM
    Indicateurs sociaux, 411
Pays en développement, 2490, 2498
    Action sociale, 5303
    Aliments, 2080
    Allaitement naturel, 2648
    Alphabétisation, 2080
    Anthropologie sociale, 3704
    Baisse de la fécondité, 2955
    Bibliographies, 5044
    Bidonvilles, 3869, 3879, 3880
    Changement social, 2440
    Changement technologique, 4025
    Communication, 1573
    Coopératives agricoles, 4289
    Croissance urbaine, 3858
    Culture, 886
    Développement culturel, 1029
    Développement de l'éducation, 1921
    Développement économique et social, 2500
    Développement rural, 3695
    Droit international, 5044
    Éthique, 2982
    Faim, 5081
    Fécondité, 2901, 2957
    Fermes familiales, 4068
    Identité culturelle, 1020
    Logement, 3860, 3868
    Migration de travail, 3566
    Migration rurale-urbaine, 3567
    Mortalité, 2848
    Mortalité des enfants, 2846
    Mouvements étudiants, 2031
    Mouvements sociaux, 4934
    Moyens de communication de masse, 1638
    Pauvreté, 2982
    Paysannerie, 3704
    Planification de la famille, 2955, 2982
    Politique du logement, 3748
    Politique régionale, 3785
    Politique sanitaire, 5406
    Politique sociale, 5281, 5302
    Politique urbaine, 3785, 3918
    Population, 2529
    Population urbaine, 3810
    Presse, 1741
    Problèmes sociaux, 5068
    Projections démographiques, 2553
    Prolétariat, 2292

Recherche pédagogique, 1859
Religion, 1282
Rôle des femmes, 2598
Santé, 2080, 5404
Sécurité sociale, 5345, 5368
Sociologie rurale, 3704
Tables de mortalité, 2880
Technologie de pointe, 4027
Théâtre traditionnel, 1853
Tourisme international, 4752
Tradition orale, 1808
Travailleuses, 4289
Urbanisation, 3766, 3787, 3880
Vieillissement, 2731
Villes, 3842
Zones suburbaines, 3869
Pays francophones
Droit, 1250
Pays industrialisés
Immigrants, 3496
Pays méditerranéens
Changement technologique, 4064
Dynamique de la population, 2763
État, 4822
Innovations, 4064
Population, 2548
Pays occidentaux
Crise de civilisation, 966
Qualité de la vie, 3979
Réfugiés, 3467
Pays socialistes, 3956
Aménagement urbain, 3913
Argent, 4119
Développement rural, 3728
Droit, 1256
Droits de l'homme, 4863
Employés, 4524
Famille, 3201
Genre de vie, 948
Groupes d'intérêt, 4950
Milieu urbain, 3846
Ouvriers industriels, 4732
Paysannerie, 3728
Population, 2512
Rôle des femmes, 3231
Statut de la femme, 3231
Vacances, 4732
Pays-Bas
Absentéisme, 4449
Bidonvilles, 4187
Catholiques, 1384
Chômage, 4187, 4214, 4218, 4219
Conditions sociales, 5318
Congrès, 245
Conservatisme, 4781
Culture, 935, 4473
Délinquance juvénile, 5193
Discrimination sexuelle, 2618
Éducation des femmes, 1953
État providence, 1269, 5320
Étudiants, 935
Famille, 5318

Gérontologie, 2743
Groupes ethniques, 3336
Histoire sociale, 5318
Identité nationale, 922
Institutions politiques, 4842
Marché du travail, 4225
Minorités ethniques, 3335
Mortalité, 4219
Niveau du chômage, 4449
Participation politique, 4973
Personnes âgées, 2719
Politique de l'emploi, 4225
Politique scientifique, 129
Prestige professionnel, 4493
Protestants, 1384
Quartier, 4187
Religion, 1269
Réseaux sociaux, 1530
Rôles sexuels, 1953
Santé, 4219
Services sociaux, 5465
Sociolinguistique, 1530
Sociologie de la religion, 1264
Squatters, 3796
Stratification professionnelle, 4473
Stratification sociale, 2719
Syndicats, 4632
Systèmes d'enseignement, 1953
Travail des femmes, 2618
Travailleurs, 5318
Paysannerie, 3677, 3724, 3743
Caraïbes, 3738
France, 3653
France : Sarthe, 3659
Inde, 3702, 3717
Inde : Bihar, 3668
Pays en développement, 3704
Pays socialistes, 3728
Pologne, 3165, 3674
Tanzanie, 3732
Thaïlande, 2255, 3690
Turquie, 3694
URSS, 3740
Paysans, 3649
Chine, 3683
France, 3689, 3705, 3730
Hongrie, 3656, 3681, 3701
Japon, 3692
Malaisie, 3685
Pêche
France, 4072
Pêcheurs
Japon, 4513
Pédiatres
France, 5461
Peine de mort
États-Unis, 5160, 5171, 5231
Peinture
Allemagne RD, 1834
Pélerinages
Inde, 1444
Pensée philosophique, 209

Perception, 541, 2646
Perception d'autrui, 598, 600
  Japon — Royaume-Uni, 4530
Perception de soi, 493
  Allemagne RF, 5174
Perception interpersonnelle, 605
Perception sociale, 490, 602, 606, 5095
  Pologne, 2213
Père, 3105
  Iran, 3164
Performance, 5263
Performance du groupe, 741
Périodiques, 1527
  États-Unis, 186
  Italie, 184
  Suisse, 185
Pérou
  Autogestion, 770
  Bourgeoisie, 4135
  Catholicisme, 1364
  Conditions sociales, 5286
  Conflits du travail, 4686
  Conscience sociale, 5033
  Développement régional, 4135
  Drogue, 5124
  Métropole, 3899
  Mouvements coopératifs, 4953
  Planification régionale, 4126
  Population indigène, 3328
  Recherche scientifique, 4020
  Service militaire, 5033
  Structure urbaine, 5286
  Travailleuses, 4686
Pérou : Lima
  Économie urbaine, 3899
Person, Yves, 1044
Personnalité, 484, 514-15, 519-21, 523, 525,
    527, 529-30, 532-35, 802, 1558, 4113
  États-Unis, 1117
Personnes âgées, 576, 2045, 2713-14, 2726,
    2729, 2733, 2742, 2750, 2753, 2761,
    5169, 5195
  Afrique du Sud : Pretoria, 2760
  Australie, 2754
  Canada, 2716
  Chine, 2756
  Corée R, 2735
  États-Unis, 2727, 2744, 2751, 3199
  France, 1085, 2724, 2737, 2749
  Israël, 2717, 2730
  Japon, 2732, 2745, 2747, 2757, 2762
  Pays-Bas, 2719
  Pologne, 2758
  Royaume-Uni, 2734, 2741
  URSS, 2755
Personnes mariées
  États-Unis, 4425
Persuasion, 1632, 4951
Petites et moyennes entreprises, 4002
  France, 4005
  Italie, 4007, 4008, 4529, 4846
Peur, 2742, 2882

Phénoménologie, 219, 238, 242, 1120, 1313
Philippines
  Changement économique, 3965
  Choix du conjoint, 3058
  Écoles primaires, 2000
  Enfants, 609
  Logement, 3848
  Mariage, 3058
  Migration rurale-urbaine, 3569
  Mortalité des enfants, 3848
  Planification de la famille, 2988
Philippines : Leyte
  Pauvreté rurale, 5103
Philosophes
  France, 76, 82, 85, 86
Philosophie, 192, 195, 201, 225, 226, 232,
    243, 552, 2468
Philosophie de l'art, 1782
Philosophie de l'éducation, 293, 1890, 1915
  Brésil, 1911
  États-Unis, 1899
Philosophie de la science, 1522
Philosophie du droit, 1219, 1235, 1255, 1258
Philosophie politique, 4769
Philosophie sociale, 5331
Photographie
  France, 4519
Physiologie humaine
  Suisse, 2634
Piaget, Jean, 461
Planification de l'éducation, 1952, 2136
  Amérique latine, 1940
  Suisse, 1973
Planification de la famille, 2594, 2965, 3019
  Asie, 2997
  Bangladesh, 5453
  Chine, 2969
  États-Unis, 2551, 3015
  Inde, 2970, 2989, 3001, 3008, 3011
  Japon, 2999
  Java, 3012
  Mexique, 2984
  Pays en développement, 2955, 2982
  Philippines, 2988
  Soudan, 2995
  Thaïlande, 2968, 2975
Planification du développement, 2553
Planification linguistique
  Singapour, 1613
Planification régionale
  Brésil, 4129
  Pérou, 4126
Planification sociale, 5285, 5304, 5323, 5333
  Pologne, 415
  Royaume-Uni, 5337
  Tchécoslovaquie, 423
  URSS, 5277
Planification urbaine, 3909
Plans de retraite
  États-Unis, 5373
Plébiscite
  Suisse, 5014

Pluralisme culturel
  Australie, 889, 911
Pluralisme ethnique, 3343
  États-Unis, 3353
  France, 3302
  Italie, 1349
  Yougoslavie, 3305
Pluralisme social, 2208, 5338
Poésie
  Allemagne RD, 1797
  Chine, 1831
Police, 3047, 4873
  Danemark, 4366
  États-Unis, 2591, 4366
  Hongrie, 4874
  Inde, 4881
  Irlande, 4879
  Royaume-Uni, 4872, 4875, 4876-78
Politique, 1303, 1794, 2465, 4762, 5024, 5027
  Afrique du Nord, 3255
  Amérique latine, 5022
  États-Unis, 1636, 2720, 5025, 5026
  Europe occidentale, 5026
  Inde, 2172, 3873, 5300
  Inde : Kerala, 2275
  Jamaïque, 5023
  Japon, 5026
  Suède, 2609
Politique à l'égard des nationalités
  URSS, 3536
Politique agricole
  États-Unis, 4071
Politique culturelle, 1040
  Brésil, 1027
  Canada, 1025
  France, 1009, 1015, 1028
  Népal, 1010
  Norvège, 1035
  Pays de la CEE, 1018
  Roumanie, 1036
Politique d'immigration, 3485
  Asie occidentale, 4318
  États-Unis, 3510, 3517, 3522, 3526, 3527
  France, 3473, 3534
  Royaume-Uni, 3476, 3483
Politique d'innovation, 4060
Politique de bien-être, 5262, 5304
  États-Unis, 5307
Politique de defense
  Israël, 5034
Politique de développement, 3215, 4128
  Haïti, 1905
Politique de l'éducation, 117, 4174, 4938
  Argentine, 1974
  Australie, 1892
  Autriche, 1934
  Chine, 1922, 1943
  États-Unis, 1927, 3331
  Israël, 1971
  Mexique, 1984
  Portugal, 1969
  Royaume-Uni, 3474

  Suisse, 1973
  Turquie, 1945
  Venezuela, 2059
Politique de l'emploi, 4224, 4450
  Canada, 4221
  États-Unis, 4223
  Pays-Bas, 4225
  Suède, 4223
Politique de la communication
  États-Unis, 1582
  Pays développés, 1552
  Pologne, 1557
Politique de la jeunesse
  Allemagne RD, 2694
  Espagne, 2677
  Hongrie, 2698
Politique de la recherche
  États-Unis, 104
Politique de la vieillesse
  Argentine, 5369
  France, 5284
Politique démographique, 2784, 2977, 3000
  Allemagne RD, 2973
  Allemagne RF, 2973
  Amérique latine, 2961, 2963
  Chine, 3006, 3018
  Égypte, 2991
  France, 3014
  Hongrie, 2537, 3010
  Kenya, 2991
  Tunisie, 2991
Politique des loisirs
  Allemagne RD, 2694
Politique des revenus
  Nouvelle Zélande, 4136
Politique du logement
  Australie, 3915
  Belgique, 3800
  Brésil, 3792
  États-Unis, 3772, 3922
  Europe occidentale, 3772
  Fidji, 3920
  Hongrie, 3829
  Nigeria, 3877
  Nouvelle Zélande, 3867
  Pays en développement, 3748
  Royaume-Uni, 3830, 3867
Politique du travail
  Inde, 4561
Politique économique
  Royaume-Uni, 4131
Politique ethnique
  Australie, 3364
  Canada, 3364
  URSS, 3392
Politique étrangère, 5046
Politique familiale
  Allemagne RF, 5356
  Chine, 5376
  États-Unis, 5360
  France, 5354
  Royaume-Uni, 5365

Politique gouvernementale, 147
Politique linguistique
    Singapour, 1707
    URSS, 1593, 1625, 1626
    Zaïre, 1619
Politique locale
    Canada, 3316
Politique migratoire
    Australie, 3435
Politique nataliste
    Israël, 2980
Politique régionale
    Pays en développement, 3785
    Pologne, 4130
Politique sanitaire, 2898
    Chili, 5436
    Cuba, 5436
    États-Unis, 5416, 5432
    France, 4256
    Italie, 5411
    Mexique, 5418
    Pays en développement, 5406
    Royaume-Uni, 5409, 5420
Politique scientifique, 117
    Afrique au Sud du Sahara, 120
    Allemagne, 128
    Canada, 126
    Grèce, 127
    Pays-Bas, 129
Politique sociale, 46, 418-19, 2433, 2678,
    4224, 5260, 5269, 5271, 5275, 5282-84,
    5288, 5290, 5293, 5312, 5319, 5324,
    5328
    Allemagne RD, 5264
    Allemagne RF, 5261, 5280, 5301, 5315
    Argentine, 5069
    Autriche, 5309
    Danemark, 5295
    États-Unis, 5253, 5296, 5310, 5330
    France, 4049
    Hongrie, 5274
    Inde, 5287
    Italie : Méridional, 5313
    Pays en développement, 5281, 5302
    Pologne, 2696, 5268
    Royaume-Uni, 4131, 5265
    URSS, 5325
Politique urbaine, 3854
    Allemagne RF, 3833
    Équateur, 3832
    États-Unis, 3757, 3758, 3859
    France, 3752, 3901
    Italie, 3806
    Pays en développement, 3785, 3918
Pologne
    Accidents du travail, 4434
    Agriculteurs, 1059, 2746, 3137, 3710, 3720
    Agriexploitation, 4079, 4094
    Alcoolisme, 5136
    Aménagement urbain, 3845
    Antisémitisme, 3429
    Attitudes, 2007, 2799

Bâtiments, 2799
Besoins, 3968
Budgets temps, 4437
Catholicisme, 1350, 1397
Changement culturel, 2267
Classe ouvrière, 2267
Classes sociales, 2272
Comportement collectif, 622
Comportement du consommateur, 4103
Comportement social, 1139
Conditions de travail, 4394, 4424
Conditions de vie, 2674, 3968
Conflits sociaux, 643, 650, 658
Conjoncture démographique, 2773
Conscience sociale, 1112, 2213
Coopération agricole, 4079
Culture, 895, 1004
Culture paysanne, 958
Culture populaire, 1202
Demande de consommation, 4103
Désintégration de la famille, 3147
Désorganisation sociale, 658
Développement culturel, 1013
Développement économique, 4594
Dimension de la famille, 3154
Droit du travail, 4571, 4627
Droits de l'homme, 4859
Édition, 1695
Éducation, 1013
Éducation religieuse, 2109
Égalité sociale, 2210
Élèves, 2007
Enseignement supérieur, 2048, 2054
Espérance de vie, 1218
Famille, 3137, 3165, 3169, 3188
Fermes d'État, 3169, 4510, 4710
Fermes familiales, 4074
Fonctionnaires, 4383
Gestion d'entreprises, 3998
Habitudes de lecture, 571
Histoire de la sociologie, 43
Humanisation du travail, 4394
Identité culturelle, 1042
Idéologies politiques, 4910
Implications culturelles, 4437
Indicateurs sociaux, 415
Industrialisation, 2773
Inégalité de revenu, 3984
Inégalité sociale, 2210, 2211, 2213
Intégration culturelle, 1023
Jeunesse, 1129, 1473, 2674, 2693, 2696
Jeunesse rurale, 2704, 4437
Jugement social, 2229
Juifs, 3429
Leadership politique, 4961
Logement, 3928
Lutte de classes, 2317
Maladies professionnelles, 4434
Malaise social, 5073
Marché du travail, 4161
Marxisme, 2229
Migration de travail, 3530

Milieu social, 1218
Mobilité sociale, 2272
Moralité, 1218
Mouvements ouvriers, 3429, 4594
Névroses, 1472
Opinion publique, 4161
Ouvriers industriels, 4514
Participation des travailleurs, 4710
Partis politiques, 4910
Paysannerie, 3165, 3674
Perception sociale, 2213
Personnes âgées, 2758
Planification sociale, 415
Politique de la communication, 1557
Politique régionale, 4130
Politique sociale, 2696, 5268
Population rurale, 571, 1004, 1042, 1112,
    1202, 1472, 2170, 2791-93, 2799, 3984,
    4505
Population urbaine, 2782
Potentiel de développement, 2789
Prestige professionnel, 4468
Prévisions démographiques, 2528
Professions, 2791
Propriété, 3935
Propriété foncière, 1059, 4074, 4075
Protestants, 1340
Réformes sociales, 5276
Régulation des naissances, 3188
Religiosité, 1472, 1473
Rendement de l'éducation, 2048
Répartition de la population, 2789
Reproduction sociale, 1961
Socialisation, 1129
Socialisation politique, 4975
Socialisme, 2007
Sociologie, 65
Sociologues, 80
Solidarité, 622
Statut de la femme, 3239
Statut professionnel, 3154
Statut social, 4468
Stratification sociale, 4514
Structure professionnelle, 3165, 4468, 4505
Structure sociale, 2170, 5073
Syndicats, 4627, 4639, 4641
Systèmes d'enseignement, 1961
Systèmes de valeur, 1059, 4383
Théorie sociologique, 240
Travail, 4163
Travail des femmes, 4269
Travailleurs, 4515, 5136
Travailleurs agricoles, 4510, 4710
Urbanisation, 3813, 3872
Vie urbaine, 3864
Vieillesse, 2746, 2759
Villages, 2792, 3678
Zones rurales, 1013, 2759, 4510
Pologne : Rzeszów
    Collectivités urbaines, 3865
Pologne : Varsovie
    Jours de fête, 3151

Rites familiaux, 3151
Polygamie
    Afrique, 3059, 3100
Polynésie
    Mort, 2904
    Naissance, 2904
Popper, Karl Raimund, 1518
Population, 4132
    Allemagne RF, 2549
    Amérique latine, 2506, 2518, 4124
    Canada, 2539
    Chine, 2508, 2514, 2532, 2534
    Europe, 2520, 2540
    Europe occidentale, 2511
    France, 2502, 2509, 2523, 2543, 5125
    Grèce, 2515
    Hongrie, 2537, 2554
    Inde, 2507
    Israël, 2524
    Nouvelle Zélande, 2542
    Pays en développement, 2529
    Pays méditerranéens, 2548
    Pays socialistes, 2512
    Porto Rico, 2525
Population indigène
    Amazonie, 3290
    Amérique latine, 3289
    Australie, 3292, 3304, 3309, 3311, 3347
    Canada, 3310, 3334
    Costa Rica, 3283
    Pérou, 3328
Population mondiale, 2817, 2819
Population rurale
    Amérique latine, 2770
    Hongrie, 2821
    Inde, 2808
    Pologne, 571, 1004, 1042, 1112, 1202,
        1472, 2170, 2791-93, 2799, 3984, 4505
    Turquie, 4965
    Yougoslavie, 2798, 2816
Population urbaine, 2772, 2779, 2810
    Asie, 2813
    Canada, 3777
    Chine, 2806
    France, 3469
    Java, 2781
    Pays développés, 3810
    Pays en développement, 3810
    Pologne, 2782
    Turquie, 3797
    Yougoslavie, 2811, 2812
Populisme, 4774
Pornographie
    Canada, 3034
    États-Unis, 3039, 3052
Porto Rico
    Migration, 3448
    Population, 2525
Portugal
    Conjoncture démographique, 2805
    Émigrants, 3508, 3509
    Emploi des jeunes, 4206

Ethnicité, 4279
Identité nationale, 4279
Jeunesse, 2676
Logement rural, 3793
Maternité, 3229
Politique de l'éducation, 1969
Propriété foncière, 3229
Réformes agraires, 4586
Socialisme, 4785
Statut de la femme, 3229
Syndicats, 4586
Travailleurs migrants, 4279
Positivisme, 250, 262
Potentiel de développement
Pologne, 2789
Poulantzas, N., 2298
Pouvoir, 442, 783-86, 791, 1612, 2889
Pouvoir de la collectivité, 3630, 3639
Pouvoir de négociation, 652
Pouvoir exécutif, 4880
Pouvoir judiciaire
Cuba, 4883
Pouvoir local
Bolivie, 4898
Hongrie, 4903
Pragmatisme, 222, 266
Pratique, 290, 552
Pratique religieuse, 1399
France, 1488, 1501
Pratiques culturelles
France, 915
Préjugé racial
États-Unis, 5018
Presse, 1693, 1747, 1873
Allemagne, 1683
Allemagne RF, 1649
États-Unis, 1663, 1667, 1711, 1740
France, 1672, 1758, 3234
Hongrie, 2703
Italie, 641
Madagascar, 1669
Pays en développement, 1741
Royaume-Uni, 1719, 1732
Tunisie, 1696
Presse féminine
Japon, 1698
Pression du groupe, 702
Prestige, 789, 793
Prestige professionnel, 4475, 4487, 4494
Canada, 4474
États-Unis, 4474
Nigeria, 4488
Pays-Bas, 4493
Pologne, 4468
Prêt sur gage
France : Rouen, 4120
Prévention de la délinquance
Australie, 5248
États-Unis, 5210
Prévisions, 275, 284, 2409, 2410
États-Unis, 296
Prévisions démographiques, 2503, 2536

États-Unis, 2531
Pologne, 2528
Primes de salaires
Australie, 4389
Prise de décision, 287, 372, 542, 547, 550,
551, 676, 4093, 5133
Afrique, 5088
Royaume-Uni, 4667
Prison, 5165, 5213, 5222
Brésil, 5167
Californie, 5156
États-Unis, 4283
Italie, 5216
Prisonniers, 491
États-Unis, 5147, 5203
Privation, 597
États-Unis, 5117
Inde, 5109
Privation relative, 568
Problèmes sociaux, 5072, 5262
Argentine, 5069
États-Unis, 4213
Inde, 4889
Pays en développement, 5068
Royaume-Uni, 5075
Singapour, 5076
Processus judiciaire
France, 1237
Royaume-Uni, 4884
Proche Orient
Minorités, 685
Producteurs, 4578
Production
France, 4014
Malaisie, 4021
Production agricole
Maroc, 1128
Tunisie, 1128
Productivité, 4341
Professionnalisation, 19, 4090
Allemagne RF, 4456, 5384
États-Unis, 4926
Professions, 1063, 4452, 4453, 4455, 4458
Afrique, 4454
Japon, 2739
Pologne, 2791
Professions médicales
Belgique, 5415
États-Unis, 5472
Inde, 5482
Programmes de recherche
États-Unis, 125
Progrès scientifique et technique, 3900, 4030,
4050
URSS, 4017
Prohibition de l'inceste, 3029
Projections démographiques, 2505, 2533,
2780, 2884
Amérique latine, 2766
Pays en développement, 2553
Prolétariat
Asie, 2274

France, 3505
Italie, 2289
Pays en développement, 2292
Royaume-Uni, 2247
Promotion de la femme, 3240
Promotion professionnelle
  États-Unis, 4445
Propagande, 1634, 1718
Prophétie, 790
Propriétaires, 223
Propriété, 2281, 3936-38, 5186
  Israël, 4089
  Pologne, 3935
Propriété du domicile
  États-Unis, 3774
Propriété foncière
  Pologne, 1059, 4074, 4075
  Portugal, 3229
Propriété publique
  États-Unis, 1711
Prostitution, 3020, 3031, 3036, 3037, 3042, 3047
  Allemagne RF, 3032
  Asie du Sud-Est, 3050
  Autriche, 3032
  États-Unis, 3021
  Inde, 3046
  Japon, 3051
Protection de l'environnement, 3603
  France, 3600
  Royaume-Uni, 1708
Protection de la vie privée, 1579
Protection des données
  Royaume-Uni, 308
Protestantisme, 1335, 1377, 3946
  France, 1334
Protestants
  Irlande, 1341
  Irlande du Nord, 1214, 1344
  Pays-Bas, 1384
  Pologne, 1340
Proudhon, Pierre Joseph, 4797
Psychanalyse, 207, 451, 454, 465, 476, 1105, 1125, 1280, 1803, 1877
Psychiâtrie
  États-Unis, 5400
  Sénégal, 5396
  URSS, 5397
Psycholinguistique, 1531, 1535
Psychologie, 467, 470, 4177
  États-Unis, 452, 455
  URSS, 450
Psychologie clinique, 454
Psychologie de l'éducation, 1877
  URSS, 1866
Psychologie de l'enfant, 469, 477
  Algérie, 456
Psychologie génétique, 461, 475, 631
Psychologie industrielle, 4141, 4144
Psychologie politique, 4762
  États-Unis, 4761, 4763
Psychologie sociale, 189, 400, 453, 457, 459,

460, 468, 471, 478, 824, 3449, 4114, 4535
  États-Unis, 458, 466
  Europe occidentale, 474
  URSS, 479
Psychopathologie, 464, 473
Psychosociologie, 460, 463, 472
Psychothérapie, 672
Public, 1720
Publicité, 1637, 1703, 3315
  Brésil, 1633
  États-Unis, 1636, 5002
  France, 349
  Japon, 1635
Puériculture, 3186
  Bangladesh, 4251
  États-Unis, 2660
Puritanisme, 1478

Qualification professionnelle, 4211, 4482, 4504
  Allemagne RF, 4462
  Canada, 4522
  France, 4031, 4470, 4472, 4491, 4496
  Roumanie, 4478
  Royaume-Uni, 4502
Qualification requise pour l'emploi
  France, 4497
Qualité de l'environnement, 4107
Qualité de la vie, 2753, 3976, 3985, 3988
  Allemagne RF, 3972
  Canada, 4028, 4362
  États-Unis, 3635
  Europe orientale, 3979
  France, 4369
  Israël, 3804
  Norvège, 3977
  Pays occidentaux, 3979
Qualité du travail, 4383
  France, 4427
Quartier, 3882
  États-Unis, 3856
  Japon, 3916
  Pays-Bas, 4187
  Royaume-Uni, 3769
Questionnaires, 386, 387
Quételet, Adolphe, 1216

Race, 871, 1124, 3357
Racisme, 564, 3281, 3357, 3361, 3362, 3366, 3375, 3381
  Afrique du Sud, 3360
  Allemagne RF, 3370
  Australie, 3432
  États-Unis, 5093
  France, 3383, 3391, 3427
  Royaume-Uni, 3358, 3365, 3418, 3419
  Sri Lanka, 3359
Radio, 1644
  Costa Rica, 1690
  France, 1679
Radiodiffusion, 1713
  Australie, 1664

États-Unis, 1748
Japon, 1688, 1751
Raison, 232
Rang de naissance, 600, 3183
Rapports avant le mariage
    États-Unis, 3044, 3048
Rassemblement des données, 429
Rationalisation, 2432
Rationalisme, 4935
Rationalité, 6, 287, 800, 1575, 2463, 2823,
    4932, 5272
Rawls, John, 226
Réadaptation des délinquants
    Brésil, 5167
Réadaptation professionnelle
    France, 4471
    Royaume-Uni, 2825
Recensements
    Allemagne RF, 361
Recensements de population
    Chine, 2768, 2775
    Cuba, 2809
    États-Unis, 2787, 2795
Récession économique, 3962-64, 5182
Recherche, 98, 1583
Recherche action, 111-13, 3912
    Canada, 114
    États-Unis, 110
Recherche anthropologique, 3362
Recherche appliquée, 1225
Recherche démographique, 2530, 2535
    Espagne, 2547
Recherche empirique, 365, 368
Recherche en sciences sociales, 97, 100, 106,
    108, 109, 157, 365, 2625
    Allemagne RF, 96
    États-Unis, 92, 104
    France, 103
    Royaume-Uni, 103, 105
Recherche interdisciplinaire
    États-Unis, 115
Recherche médicale
    France, 5402
Recherche organisationnelle, 689, 710, 716,
    3574
Recherche pédagogique, 1865, 1868, 1919
    Amérique latine, 1869, 1883
    Caraïbes, 1894
    Pays en développement, 1859
Recherche scientifique, 4045
    États-Unis, 4042
    Pérou, 4020
Recherche sociale, 187, 5056, 5058, 5059,
    5066
    États-Unis, 186
    Inde, 5060
    Japon, 5062
Recherche sociologique, 94, 95, 107, 291
    Etats-Unis, 93, 99, 102
    Roumanie, 101
    URSS, 2163
Recherche sur la communication, 1539, 1553

Chili, 1565
Danemark, 1556
États-Unis, 1537
France, 1564
Royaume-Uni, 1742
Recherche sur le développement
    Inde, 2496
Récidivisme, 5214
Réciprocité, 586
Recrutement, 4153
Réformes administratives
    Japon, 4134
Réformes agraires
    Algérie, 3665
    Équateur, 3682
    Inde, 3657, 3687
    Portugal, 4586
Réformes de l'enseignement, 1932, 1939, 2024
    Allemagne RF, 1924, 1965
    Amérique latine, 1975
    Australie, 1949
    Autriche, 1934
    Égypte, 1978
    Espagne, 1935
    États-Unis, 1958
    Japon, 1967
    Pakistan, 1978
    Turquie, 1978
Réformes foncières
    Égypte, 2951
Réformes sociales
    Pologne, 5276
Réformes universitaires
    Argentine, 2036
Réfugiés
    Afrique, 3491
    Canada, 3533
    États-Unis, 3518
    Norvège, 3492
    Pays occidentaux, 3467
    Soudan, 3488
    Tibet, 3506
Régimes fonciers, 3727
    Équateur, 3671
    Mexique, 3655
Région andine
    Groupes ethniques, 3322
Régionalisme
    États-Unis, 4783
    Inde, 4796
Règlement de conflits, 652, 653, 656, 660
    Inde, 4689
    Nouvelle Zélande, 4679
Réglementation, 1081, 1205, 1252
Réglementation du marché
    France, 3670
Règles de la majorité, 4812
Régulation des naissances
    Pologne, 3188
    République dominicaine, 3003
Régulation sociale, 746, 839, 1063, 1064, 1070,
    1074, 1079, 1171, 1252, 2162, 2230

Autriche, 1048
États-Unis, 1071, 1755
Royaume-Uni, 5130
Relations agraires
Inde, 3669
Relations culturelles
États-Unis — Europe, 1021
Japon, 5042
Relations de classes, 2306, 2315, 4338
Relations de dépendance, 388
Canada, 5041
Relations du travail, 4325, 4538, 4543
Allemagne RF, 4555, 4556
Canada, 4566
Chine, 4549
Colombie, 4563
Espagne, 4546
États-Unis, 4545, 4547, 4551, 4557, 4564-65
Europe orientale, 4552
France, 4544, 4555
Hongrie, 4635
Inde, 4539, 4550, 4553, 4561
Italie, 4562, 4567
Japon, 181, 4540
Nigeria, 4541
Norvège, 4634
Royaume-Uni, 4542, 4548, 4554, 4558-60
Relations école-collectivité
Colombie, 1933
Costa Rica, 1936
États-Unis, 1930, 1979
Relations enseignants-enseignés, 2138, 2144, 2145, 5234
France, 2140
Relations entre générations
Taïwan, 2641
Relations familiales, 3194
Inde, 2829
Japon, 3200
Royaume-Uni, 4085
Relations hommes-femmes
Amérique latine, 2565
Relations interethniques
États-Unis, 3372, 3374
Liban, 3395
Relations intergroupes, 642, 645, 694
États-Unis, 659
Relations internationales, 353, 468
Canada — États-Unis, 5041
États-Unis — Canada, 5041
Relations interpersonnelles, 325, 383, 577-81, 584-85, 587-88, 591, 674, 1576, 1780
France, 592
Relations intragroupe, 758
Relations parents-enfants, 3105, 3134, 3170
Espagne, 2649
États-Unis, 3109, 3132, 3173
Thaïlande, 3110
Relations raciales, 3369, 3410
Afrique du Sud, 3379, 3400
États-Unis, 2584, 3353, 3382, 3388, 3389,

3398, 3406, 3420
France, 4268
Malaisie, 3387
Trinité-et-Tabago, 2314
Relations sociales, 74, 530, 1091, 1141, 1143, 1389
France, 3778
Hongrie, 1109
Relations sociométriques, 347, 615
Religieuses
France, 1425
Religion, 258, 841, 1222, 1265, 1274, 1278, 1281, 1283-84, 1287-89, 1291, 1293-95, 1301-02, 1312-14, 2406, 3532, 4819, 4884
Asie, 1305
Canada : Québec, 4773
États-Unis, 1266, 1269, 1286, 1290, 1300, 1304, 1311
France, 1267
Inde, 1275
Israël, 2730
Japon, 1285
Liban, 3725
Pays en développement, 1282
Pays-Bas, 1269
Royaume-Uni, 1269
Religion civile
États-Unis, 1276, 1279
Israël, 1299
Religion populaire, 790, 1483
Religions asiatiques, 1361
Religiosité, 1479, 1483
États-Unis, 1290, 1480, 1487, 5117
Israël, 2980
Pologne, 1472, 1473
Remariage, 3087
Inde, 3057
Rendement de l'éducation, 1584, 1964, 2116
Argentine, 1992
États-Unis, 1937, 2048
France, 2048
Pologne, 2048
URSS, 2048
Rénovation urbaine
France, 3763, 3861, 3885, 3901
Répartition de la population, 2818, 2820
Amérique latine, 2764
Pologne, 2789
Taïwan, 2797
Yougoslavie, 2546
Répartition du revenu
Norvège, 3982
Royaume-Uni, 4082, 4631
Taïwan, 2201
Répartition par âge
Europe, 2642
Répartition par sexe, 4509
Répartition spatiale, 3611
Représentation, 819
Représentation des travailleurs
France, 4718

Italie, 4723
Répression
  Chili, 5180
Reproduction sociale, 2161, 2169, 2173, 4160
  Mexique, 2133
  Pologne, 1961
  Royaume-Uni, 2160
République dominicaine
  Éducation préscolaire, 2013
  Émigration, 3481
  Fécondité, 2926
  Moyens de communication de masse, 1739
  Régulation des naissances, 3003
  Sociologie urbaine, 3783
  Systèmes d'enseignement, 1977
  Travail des femmes, 4321
Réseau de communication
  Japon, 1578
Réseaux sociaux, 360, 392, 615, 662-63,
    667-68, 670-71, 759
  États-Unis, 661, 664
  Pays-Bas, 1530
Résolution de problème, 678
Responsabilité, 4336
Ressources en eau, 3596
Ressources humaines, 4164, 4167, 4168, 4175
  États-Unis, 4169
Ressources pétrolières
  Norvège, 894
Retard intellectuel
  Trinité-et-Tabago, 3424
Retraite, 4450
  États-Unis, 4448
  France, 4451
  Japon, 2747, 3691
Retraités
  France, 2737
  URSS, 2725
Réussite dans les études, 1762, 2113, 2118,
    2121-22
  Canada, 2114
  États-Unis, 3173
  Suède, 2117
Réussite professionnelle, 2593
Réussite sociale, 597
Réveil religieux, 1445, 1492, 1496, 4316
  États-Unis, 1494
  Inde, 1379
Revenu, 285
Revenu des ménages
  États-Unis, 2585
Révolte
  Maroc, 1128
  Tunisie, 1128
Révolution, 216, 2287, 2438, 2458, 2461,
    2480, 4813
  Amérique latine, 2482
Révolution industrielle, 2790
  Allemagne, 2401
  France, 4335
Révolutionnaires, 3265
Richesse, 5089

Rites, 769, 1208, 2597
  Iran, 1443
  Japon, 1448
Rites familiaux
  Pologne : Varsovie, 3151
Riz, 934
Robotique
  France, 4054
Robots, 137
Roemer, John, 2303
Rôle, 800, 801, 802, 803, 804, 1082
  Canada, 3144
Rôle des femmes, 2571, 2583, 2595, 2629
  Afrique, 3664
  États-Unis, 977, 2584
  Ghana : Accra, 2614
  Grèce, 3133
  Indonésie, 2599
  Malaisie, 2599
  Océanie, 2607
  Oman, 2575
  Pays en développement, 2598
  Pays socialistes, 3231
  Singapour, 2599
Rôles sexuels, 801, 1210, 1569, 2564, 2567,
    2590, 2593, 2594, 2603, 2615, 2619,
    2624, 2627, 3088, 4254
  Afrique, 2568
  Australie, 2612
  États-Unis, 820, 2569, 2591, 3054, 4299,
    4712
  France, 2622
  Irlande, 1997
  Israël, 2623
  Pays-Bas, 1953
Romans, 1801, 1819, 2445
  Allemagne RF, 1816
  États-Unis, 1822
Romantisme, 619, 826, 3277, 3324
Rotation de la main-d'oeuvre, 4447
Roumanie
  Antisémitisme, 3421
  Architecture, 1839
  Autogestion ouvrière, 4711
  Avortement, 2990
  Culture, 913, 927
  Dynamique de la population, 2815
  Famille, 3122
  Intellectuels, 3421
  Littérature, 1821
  Politique culturelle, 1036
  Qualification professionnelle, 4478
  Recherche sociologique, 101
  Sociologie, 13, 31
  Sociologie de la science, 1514
  Structure sociale, 2182
  Urbanisation, 3894
Royaume-Uni
  Absentéisme, 4443, 4446
  Action collective, 870
  Administration locale, 4659
  Administration publique, 4885

Alcoolisme, 5126
Alphabétisation, 2082
Aménagement urbain, 3747
Anthropologie sociale, 214
Architecture, 1835
Aristocratie, 4814
Assimilation des immigrants, 3474
Associations de sociologie, 177
Banquiers, 2283
Bourgeoisie, 4780
Budgets des ménages, 3980
Cadres, 4560
Caisses de retraite, 4724
Capitalisme, 3952
Catholiques, 1366
Changement religieux, 1366
Chômage, 3118, 4201
Chômage des jeunes, 4202
Chômeurs, 4585
Classe ouvrière, 1995
Classes sociales, 2246, 2620, 2949
Conditions de vie, 3980
Conditions sociales, 994
Conflits du travail, 4677
Conflits raciaux, 3411, 4877
Conjoncture démographique, 2803
Conscience de classe, 2254
Conservatisme, 4780
Construction navale, 740
Coopératives, 3953
Culture ouvrière, 975
Curriculum, 2132
Cycles économiques, 4584
Débilité mentale, 2838
Délégués du personnel, 4659
Délinquance juvénile, 2685
Délinquantes, 5244
Démocratie industrielle, 4713
Démographie, 2522
Démographie historique, 2555
Déontologie, 1476
Déroulement de carrière, 4479
Désindustrialisation, 4082
Différences de generations, 4479
Différenciation sociale, 2197
Dimension de l'entreprise industrielle,
    4554, 4683
Discrimination raciale, 3830
Discrimination religieuse, 1490
Discrimination sexuelle, 4253, 5244
Divorce, 3069, 3071
Éducation des adultes, 2085, 2092, 2096
Éducation préscolaire, 1995
Église et État, 1418
Églises protestantes, 1418
Élite, 2339
Émeutes, 1154, 1155
Emploi des femmes, 4253
Enfants adoptés, 2650
Enquêtes par correspondance, 385
Enseignants, 4649
Enseignement supérieur, 2026, 2039, 2053

État providence, 1269, 5329, 5337
Éthique protestante, 1476
Ethnicité, 2246
Famille, 3118, 5075
Fascisme, 4777
Féminisme, 3218
Femmes, 2620
Fermes familiales, 4085
Fiscalité, 4118
Fonctionnaires, 4590, 4887
Formation professionnelle, 4486
Gestion industrielle, 4092, 4096
Grèves, 4675, 4683
Groupes minoritaires, 684
Handicapés mentaux, 5445
Histoire culturelle, 1043
Histoire de la sociologie, 37
Histoire sociale, 2246, 2399, 2803, 3818,
    4814
Hôpitaux, 5450
Hôpitaux psychiatriques, 5445
Indicateurs sociaux, 5265
Inégalité sociale, 2885
Inflation, 3818
Intervention de l'État, 4825
Invalidité, 2826
Jeunes travailleurs, 4202
Jeunesse, 2685
Juifs, 1359
Littérature, 1827
Logement, 3826, 3910
Malaise de la jeunesse, 5126
Marché, 4111
Marché de la viande, 4111
Marché du travail, 4170
Médicaments, 5130
Mères travailleuses, 1995
Métis, 3430
Minorités ethniques, 3349
Mobilité professionnelle, 4479
Mobilité sociale, 1366, 2375
Montée des prix, 3818
Mortalité, 2885
Mouvements ouvriers, 4613
Mouvements politiques, 4777
Mouvements sociaux, 2096
Moyens de communication de masse, 1708
Nationalisme, 4772
Négociation collective, 4558, 4699, 4702
Noms, 505
Organisations féminines, 3278
Paroisse, 1366
Participation des travailleurs, 4709, 4724
Participation politique, 4987
Personnes âgées, 2734, 2741
Planification sociale, 5337
Police, 4872, 4875-78
Politique d'immigration, 3476, 3483
Politique de l'éducation, 3474
Politique du logement, 3830, 3867
Politique économique, 4131
Politique familiale, 5365

Politique sanitaire, 5409, 5420
Politique sociale, 4131, 5265
Presse, 1719, 1732
Prise de décision, 4667
Problèmes sociaux, 5075
Processus judiciaire, 4884
Prolétariat, 2247
Protection de l'environnement, 1708
Protection des données, 308
Qualification professionnelle, 4502
Quartier, 3769
Racisme, 3358, 3365, 3418, 3419
Réadaptation professionnelle, 2825
Recherche en sciences sociales, 103, 105
Recherche sur la communication, 1742
Régulation sociale, 5130
Relations du travail, 4542, 4548, 4554,
    4558-60
Relations familiales, 4085
Religion, 1269
Répartition du revenu, 4082, 4631
Reproduction sociale, 2160
Santé, 5425
Satisfaction au travail, 4443
Satisfaction de vie communautaire, 3618,
    3619
Scolarisation, 2132
Sécurité sociale, 5366
Ségrégation scolaire, 3349
Services de santé, 5456
Socialisation, 4875
Société, 994
Société industrielle, 4548
Soins médicaux, 5450
Sport, 975
Statut de la femme, 1827
Stratification sociale, 3910
Structuralisme, 214
Structure de classe, 2283
Syndicalisme, 4638, 4643
Syndicats, 864, 4583-85, 4588-90, 4609,
    4612, 4631, 4649, 4667
Systèmes d'exploitation, 4085
Travail des femmes, 4259, 4282
Travail ménager, 4361
Travail social, 5386, 5387
Travailleurs handicapés, 2825
Travailleurs sociaux, 5445
Universités, 2071, 2085
Urbanisation, 3818
Usage du tabac, 5409
Vie communautaire, 3118
Vie culturelle, 1043
Vie rurale, 3719
Villes capitales, 3749
Villes nouvelles, 3769, 3807
Zones urbaines, 3771

Sacré, 1453, 1460
    Inde, 1449
    Italie, 1454
Sacrifice, 1442

Saint-Simon, Claude-Henri de, 2318
Saints, 1468
Saisons, 2949
Salaires
    États-Unis, 3973
Salles de classe, 705, 706
Sanctions, 1082
Sans abri
    États-Unis, 5082, 5112
    Irlande, 5104
Santé, 5422, 5423
    Amérique latine, 2185
    Arabie saoudite, 5431
    Brésil, 5426, 5428
    États-Unis, 3482, 5405
    France, 2712, 5433
    Italie, 3103
    Japon, 2206
    Mexique, 5408
    Pays en développement, 2080, 5404
    Pays-Bas, 4219
    Royaume-Uni, 5425
Santé mentale, 804, 5430
    Afrique, 5435
    Australie, 2612
    Canada, 4040
    États-Unis, 5429, 5434
    Inde, 5413
Santé publique
    Amérique latine, 5407
    Brésil, 5407
    Espagne, 5412, 5424
Sartre, Jean-Paul, 82, 2083
Satisfaction au travail, 2331, 4368, 4373-75,
    4379, 4391, 4409, 4416, 4442
    Danemark, 4366
    États-Unis, 4283, 4366, 4367, 4378, 4411,
    4418
    Israël, 4651
    Royaume-Uni, 4443
Satisfaction conjugale, 3056
    Canada, 3172
Satisfaction de l'existence
    États-Unis, 4411, 4418
    Europe, 555
    Norvège, 3977
    Nouvelle Zélande, 557
    Sierra Leone, 562
Satisfaction de vie communautaire
    États-Unis, 3618
    Royaume-Uni, 3618, 3619
Satisfaction résidentielle, 3905
    États-Unis, 3906, 3930
    Israël, 3804
    Nigeria, 3877
Scandinavie
    État providence, 5306
    Intellectuels, 2353
    Statut de la femme, 3276
Scanlon, Joseph, 4564
Schumpeter, J., 5048
Schütz, Alfred, 208, 233

Science, 1227, 1335, 1377, 1504, 1512, 1515,
      1516, 1521, 1524, 2475
    États-Unis, 1502
    Inde, 1503
Sciences de l'éducation, 1890
    France, 1860
Sciences sociales, 1, 15, 30, 48, 53, 64, 134,
      243, 406, 2389
    Chili, 14
    États-Unis, 27, 28, 32, 119, 121, 123, 130
    France, 24
    Panama, 26
Scientifiques, 73, 74, 79
    États-Unis, 84
    Israël, 89
Scolarisation
    Canada, 1946
    France, 2194
    Royaume-Uni, 2132
Scolarité, 4455
    États-Unis, 1928, 1950, 2585, 4476
    France, 1957
    Nicaragua, 1986
Scrutins
    France, 374, 377
Sectes, 1423, 1429
    Allemagne RF, 1420
    États-Unis, 1413
    France, 1419
    Guyana, 703
    Inde, 3213
    Japon, 1439
Secteur coopératif
    France, 3947
Secteur privé, 4465
    Nigeria, 4697
Secteur public, 4465
Sécularisation, 1491, 1493
    Islande, 1497
    Turquie, 1489
Sécurité du travail
    Australie, 4389, 4390
    États-Unis, 4370
    France, 4433
Sécurité sociale, 5342, 5348, 5363, 5370, 5371
    Amérique latine, 5361
    Brésil, 5357
    Cameroun, 5355
    Chine, 5375
    Costa Rica, 5372
    France, 5351, 5364
    Gabon, 5359
    Inde, 4553, 5347
    Pays développés, 5367
    Pays en développement, 5345, 5368
    Royaume-Uni, 5366
    Suisse, 5349
Ségrégation professionnelle
    Canada, 4495
Ségrégation raciale, 3399
    États-Unis, 2018, 3367, 3401
Segrégation résidentielle

Brésil, 3883
    États-Unis, 3897
    Israël, 3853
Ségrégation scolaire
    Royaume-Uni, 3349
Sémiologie, 1529
Sénégal
    Associations, 730
    Psychiâtrie, 5396
    Syndicalisme, 4604
    Travail forcé, 4347
    Villages, 3673
    Villes, 730
Séparation maritale, 3096
Séries temporelles, 410, 418, 420, 4215, 4545
Serres, Michel, 85
Service militaire
    Belgique, 5035
    Pérou, 5033
Services d'information
    Bulgarie, 161
    Chine, 156
    Japon, 156
Services de santé, 5399, 5430, 5452
    Amérique latine, 5457
    Argentine, 5438
    Bangladesh, 5453
    Belgique, 5441
    Canada, 5449
    États-Unis, 5439, 5443, 5447
    Mexique, 5408
    Mozambique, 5458
    Pays développés, 5451
    Royaume-Uni, 5456
Services publics, 2040
Services sociaux, 3175, 3624, 5459, 5460
    Canada, 5466
    Danemark, 5471
    Espagne, 5478
    États-Unis, 5464
    Inde, 5470
    Italie, 5476
    Nouvelle Zélande, 5467
    Pays-Bas, 5465
    Turquie, 5481
Sexe, 232, 2561, 5468
    Inde, 2608
Sexisme, 2574, 2604, 3366
Sexualité, 3022
    Chine, 1817
    États-Unis, 3030
    Japon, 3116
    Maghreb, 3025
Sierra Leone
    Satisfaction de l'existence, 562
Signes, 1568
Signification, 333, 1317, 1575, 2471
Simmel, Georg, 199, 217, 4117
Singapour
    Développement des collectivités, 3646
    Divorce, 3102
    Mobilité sociale, 2326

Planification linguistique, 1613
Politique linguistique, 1707
Problèmes sociaux, 5076
Rôle des femmes, 2599
Structure de classe, 2326
Télévision, 1707
Smith, Wilfried Cantwell, 1486
Sociabilité
    Chine, 1817
    France, 575, 1417
Socialisation, 510, 1102, 1148, 1156, 1172,
    1217, 1904, 2728, 3190, 4331, 5463
    France, 2020
    Pologne, 1129
    Royaume-Uni, 4875
Socialisation politique, 4966
    Allemagne RF, 4970
    Argentine, 4986
    Brésil, 4986
    États-Unis, 4974
    France, 4988
    Pologne, 4975
Socialisme, 17, 517, 3964, 4779, 4782, 4784,
    4789, 4802, 4829
    Bulgarie, 4660
    France, 4788, 4797
    Pologne, 2007
    Portugal, 4785
    URSS, 4790
Société, 872, 936, 963, 967, 970, 981, 986,
    998, 2427, 3578, 3598, 3599, 3601,
    3604, 3621, 4868
    Algérie, 894
    Amérique latine, 1796
    Argentine, 901
    France, 888
    Hongrie, 956
    Italie, 897
    Japon, 992
    Malaisie, 4021
    Norvège, 894
    Royaume-Uni, 994
    URSS, 917, 921
Société bourgeoise, 3954, 4837, 5056
Société capitaliste, 822, 2315, 3645
Société civile, 10, 4840
    Écosse, 2499
Société d'abondance
    Israël, 3960
Société de consommation, 3958
Société de masse, 941
Société future, 855
Société industrielle, 583, 2484, 2495, 2501
    Royaume-Uni, 4548
Société paysanne, 3660, 3696
    France, 3662
    Nigeria, 3622
Société post-industrielle, 1736, 2484, 2492
Société primitive, 2486, 2497
Société rurale, 3647
    Inde : Bengale, 3661
    Népal, 3959

Taïwan, 3735
Thaïlande, 3690
Société socialiste, 147, 835, 902, 907, 1070,
    2437, 2460, 3948, 3949, 3950, 3951,
    4715, 4917, 4978, 5285
    Allemagne RD, 3940
Société traditionnelle, 4151, 5095
    Égypte, 2485
    Japon, 1439
Société tribale
    Inde, 3339
    Inde : Madhya Pradesh, 3338
Société urbaine
    Afrique, 3886
    Égypte, 3568
    France, 3753
    Taïwan, 3820
Sociolinguistique, 1527, 1528, 1532, 1536
    Espagne, 1534
    Pays-Bas, 1530
    URSS, 2429
    Yougoslavie, 1533
Sociologie, 9, 11, 17, 23, 25, 44, 46, 47, 50,
    52, 60, 75
    Allemagne, 6
    Allemagne RF, 42, 69
    Argentine, 3
    Australie, 12
    Chili, 18, 19
    États-Unis, 16, 20, 45, 66, 4823
    France, 22, 33
    Inde, 35, 39, 57, 61
    Italie, 56
    Nigeria, 7
    Pologne, 65
    Roumanie, 13, 31
    Yougoslavie, 2
Sociologie appliquée, 83, 5057
    Etats-Unis, 2837
Sociologie criminelle, 5223, 5247
Sociologie de l'art, 951, 1772
Sociologie de l'éducation, 1156, 1861, 1871,
    1875, 1879-80, 1885, 1888, 1891, 1897,
    1904, 1918
    France, 1867
    Italie, 1906
Sociologie de la connaissance, 286, 1505-11,
    1517-19, 4807, 5072
    Roumanie, 1514
Sociologie de la culture, 871, 873, 874, 876,
    882, 1000
    Japon, 877
Sociologie de la famille, 2570, 3143, 3149,
    3156
    Hongrie, 3115
Sociologie de la littérature, 340, 1799, 1801,
    1813, 1824
Sociologie de la profession, 4138, 4457
Sociologie de la religion, 1268, 1270, 1277,
    1280-81, 1298, 1306, 1308, 1310, 1315,
    1467, 1484
    États-Unis, 1271, 1272

Europe, 1296
France, 1292
Pays-Bas, 1264
Sociologie des organisations, 709, 4139
    Japon, 711
Sociologie du développement, 2493, 3666
    Inde, 2488
Sociologie du droit, 1236, 1240-41, 1246-47,
    1249, 1259
    Australie, 1253
Sociologie du sport, 4753
Sociologie du travail, 2570, 4138, 4139, 4142,
    4145
    France, 2285
    Japon, 4140
Sociologie économique, 1587
Sociologie électorale, 5009
Sociologie industrielle, 4143, 4146, 4147, 4148
    Espagne, 4137
Sociologie médicale, 5395
Sociologie militaire, 5031
Sociologie politique, 4760, 4766
    États-Unis, 4765, 4767
    Suisse, 4768
Sociologie rurale
    Hongrie, 3737
    Pays en développement, 3704
Sociologie urbaine, 364, 3816, 3821, 3822,
    3849, 3914, 3917, 3926
    États-Unis, 3782, 3823, 3889, 5146
    France, 3799, 3885
    Hongrie, 5218
    Japon, 3843
    République dominicaine, 3783
Sociologues, 38, 75, 87, 88, 90, 1460
    États-Unis, 77, 83
    France, 171
    Inde, 81
    Pologne, 80
    URSS, 78
    Yougoslavie, 91
Sociométrie, 462
Soins médicaux, 2831, 5448
    Belgique, 5415
    États-Unis, 5403, 5421
    France, 5410
    Inde, 5427
    Mozambique, 5458
    Nigeria, 5419
    Royaume-Uni, 5450
Sola Pool, Ithiel de, 183
Solidarité, 5293
    Afrique, 614
    Corée R, 3667
    Pologne, 622
Solidarité de groupe, 590
Solitude, 576, 582, 583, 590
    États-Unis, 589
    France, 2722, 2748, 3232
Sondages d'opinion publique, 837, 4735
    France, 1501
Sorel, Georges, 2438

Soudan
    Développement urbain, 3831
    Fermiers, 3713
    Liberté religieuse, 1485
    Pauvreté, 3831
    Planification de la famille, 2995
    Réfugiés, 3488
Sous-développement
    Brésil, 2487
Spécificité culturelle
    Inde : Pendjab, 1037
Spencer, Herbert, 202
Spinoza, Baruch, 1161
Sport, 512, 4741, 4748, 4756, 4759
    Afrique du Sud, 4755
    Brésil, 4751
    États-Unis, 4746
    France, 4757
    Royaume-Uni, 975
Sportifs
    Hongrie, 2330
Sprout, Harold, 3590
Sprout, Margaret, 3590
Squatters
    Inde, 3891
    Kenya, 3764
    Pays-Bas, 3796
Sri Lanka
    Castes, 2241
    Conflits raciaux, 3390, 3407
    Jeunesse, 2690
    Malnutrition, 5110
    Mortalité, 2874
    Racisme, 3359
Stabilité conjugale
    États-Unis, 4248
Statistique, 408, 409, 412, 434, 1216
    Bulgarie, 413
    Hongrie, 426
Statut de la femme, 265, 3203, 3210, 3219,
    3230, 3238, 3242, 3243, 3256, 3262,
    4312, 4494
    Afrique, 3212
    Afrique du Nord, 3255
    Afrique méridionale, 3211
    Allemagne RF, 3217, 3272
    Botswana, 3236
    Canada, 3246, 3258
    Chine, 3244, 3253
    Cuba, 3266
    États-Unis, 3204, 3522, 4274
    Éthiopie, 3241
    France, 3202, 3207, 3232, 3234
    Ghana, 3259
    Inde, 3261, 3271
    Inde : Vallée de Manipur, 3224
    Israël, 3693
    Japon, 3251
    Norvège, 3228
    Oman, 2575
    Pays socialistes, 3231
    Pologne, 3239

Portugal, 3229
Royaume-Uni, 1827
Scandinavie, 3276
Suède, 3214
Thaïlande, 3264
Turquie, 3279
Viêt Nam, 3268
Yougoslavie, 3263
Zambie, 4990
Statut professionnel, 4487
États-Unis, 4192, 4476
France, 1809, 5461
Pologne, 3154
Statut social, 2118, 2122, 2151, 2331, 2332,
2338, 3627, 4494
États-Unis, 2333, 2334, 2335, 2336, 4481
Hongrie, 2330
Pologne, 4468
Stéréotypee sociaux, 2615
Stéréotypes, 823, 3315, 5191
États-Unis, 820
Stéréotypes nationaux, 825
Japon, 1607
Stérérotypes raciaux
Canada, 3376
Stoetzel, Jean, 285
Stratification professionnelle
Pays-Bas, 4473
Stratification sociale, 1561, 2187, 2198, 2215,
2220, 2270, 2329, 2626
Amérique latine, 2185
Argentine, 2032
Canada, 2216, 2261
Chine, 2324
États-Unis, 2205, 5403
France, 2191
Hongrie, 2212, 2228, 4514
Inde, 2202
Japon, 2206, 2232, 2325
Pays-Bas, 2719
Pologne, 4514
Royaume-Uni, 3910
Suisse, 2190
Structuralisme, 197, 200, 215, 244, 245, 251,
255, 261, 1506
Royaume-Uni, 214
Structure agraire
Mexique, 1984
Structure de classe, 2293, 2298-99, 2310, 2316
Chine, 2324
Égypte, 3945
Malaisie, 2326
Pays développés, 2257
Royaume-Uni, 2283
Singapour, 2326
Tchécoslovaquie, 2294
Structure de l'organisation, 740, 746, 757, 759
Structure de la famille, 2564, 3181
États-Unis, 3736
France, 1495, 3193
Structure de la main d'oeuvre
France, 4173

Structure professionnelle
Pologne, 3165, 4468, 4505
Structure sociale, 228, 244, 316, 344, 662,
699, 787, 2155, 2156, 2164, 2166,
2171, 2177, 3191, 3194, 3363, 4158
Canada, 340
Corée R, 2167
Espagne, 2464
France, 2179
Hongrie, 2165
Inde, 2172
Italie, 2168
Japon, 369, 2181, 2456
Pologne, 2170, 5073
Roumanie, 2182
URSS, 2163, 2725
Structure urbaine, 3815, 3854, 3919
Brésil, 3881
Pérou, 5286
Sturzo, Luigi, 10
Styles de développement
Amérique latine, 4124
Subculture, 1429
Subjectivité, 173, 294, 295, 501, 509, 878,
2761
Suède
Bandes, 2684
Bien-être social, 5298
Classe moyenne, 2117
Classes sociales, 2264, 2323
Différenciation sexuelle, 2609
Dimension de l'entreprise industrielle, 4683
Éducation, 2323
Égalité des sexes, 2630
Enseignement supérieur, 2055, 2062, 2067
Genre de vie, 945
Grèves, 4683
Grèves sauvages, 4671
Inégalité de revenu, 2323
Jeunesse, 2684
Marginaux, 2684
Mobilité sociale, 2375
Mortalité, 2850
Moyens de communication de masse, 1689
Origine sociale, 2117
Parenté, 3119
Politique, 2609
Politique de l'emploi, 4223
Réussite dans les études, 2117
Statut de la femme, 3214
Travail social, 5390
Suicide, 5151, 5158, 5228, 5249
Allemagne RF, 1180
États-Unis, 4215, 5149, 5243
France, 5154
Italie, 5163
Japon, 5205
Suisse
Assimilation des immigrants, 1038
Communication dans l'entreprise, 3993
Conflits culturels, 1038
Contraception, 2983

Culture populaire, 2889
Dialectes, 1592
Discrimination sexuelle, 2616
Étrangers, 3440
Femmes, 3440
Gestion sanitaire, 5414
Inégalité de revenu, 3989
Jeunesse, 2673
Justice criminelle, 5232
Migrants, 3440
Mort, 2889
Normes culturelles, 5414
Organisations de jeunesse, 2669
Périodiques, 185
Physiologie humaine, 2634
Planification de l'éducation, 1973
Plébiscite, 5014
Politique de l'éducation, 1973
Sécurité sociale, 5349
Sociologie politique, 4768
Stratification sociale, 2190
Tendances de recherche, 4768
Travailleurs étrangers 1038, 4230, 4277, 4278
Suisse : Genève
Pauvreté, 5097
Suisse : Zurich
Organisations de jeunesse, 2706
Sumner, William Graham, 58
Suriname
Civilisation, 997
Swanson, Guy E., 1271
Symboles, 244, 951
Canada, 1547
Symbolisme, 769, 1560, 2406
Inde, 1559
Symbolisme du corps
Maghreb, 1548
Symbolisme religieux
Yougoslavie, 1452
Syndicalisme
Afrique du Sud, 4593
Allemagne RF, 1675
Chili, 4587, 4645
Espagne, 4607
États-Unis, 4606
France, 4650
Italie, 4579
Japon, 4614
Royaume-Uni, 4638, 4643
Sénégal, 4604
Thaïlande, 4665
Syndicats, 4600, 4622
Afrique du Sud, 4628, 4663, 4664
Allemagne RF, 4601, 4623, 4636
Argentine, 4582, 4669
Brésil, 4657
Canada, 4620
Chili, 4592
Danemark, 4591
Égypte, 4615
Espagne, 4640

États-Unis, 455, 2142, 4444, 4547, 4597, 4602, 4610, 4630, 4633
Europe occidentale, 4621
Europe orientale, 4625
France, 4581, 4602, 4623, 4653
Hongrie, 4635, 4639
Inde, 4652, 4655
Israël, 4616, 4651, 4688
Italie, 2289, 4220, 4605, 4656
Japon, 4601
Mexique, 4624, 4661
Norvège, 4634
Pays de la CEE, 4637
Pays-Bas, 4632
Pologne, 4627, 4639, 4641
Portugal, 4586
Royaume-Uni, 864, 4583-85, 4588-90, 4609, 4612, 4631, 4649, 4667
Viêt Nam, 4629
Syndicats d'entreprise, 4611
Système pénitentiaire, 5175
Système social, 198, 2180
Yougoslavie, 2154
Systèmes culturels, 1000
Systèmes d'enseignement, 1923, 1942, 1970
Canada, 1947
Colombie, 1941
France, 1959, 1976
Japon, 1955
Paraguay, 1972
Pays arabes, 1980
Pays-Bas, 1953
Pologne, 1961
République dominicaine, 1977
URSS, 1925
Systèmes d'exploitation
États-Unis, 4076
Royaume-Uni, 4085
Systèmes d'information, 147
Systèmes d'information de gestion, 144, 148
Systèmes de communication, 1581
Systèmes de parti
Argentine, 4918
Espagne, 4911
États-Unis, 4916
Systèmes de production, 2564
Systèmes de valeur, 1049, 1051, 1055, 1058, 1069, 1224, 2610, 2662, 2950, 5328
Australie, 1221
Canada, 1050
Chine, 1061
États-Unis, 1065
Japon, 1075
Maghreb, 1053
Pologne, 1059, 4383
URSS, 1067
Zaïre, 1046
Systèmes politiques, 892, 4829-30, 4837-38, 4841
Algérie, 1338
États-Unis, 4823
Mexique, 4826
Oman, 1338

Tableaux statistiques, 3092
Tables de mortalité, 428, 2855
  Afrique, 2865
  Algérie, 2893
  Allemagne, 2862
  Inde, 2877
  Jordanie, 2895
  Mexique, 2872
  Pays en développement, 2880
Taïwan
  Bien-être social, 5254
  Cultes, 1447
  Emploi des femmes, 4266
  Famille, 2641
  Inégalité sociale, 2201
  Milieu familial, 2201
  Relations entre générations, 2641
  Répartition de la population, 2797
  Répartition du revenu, 2201
  Société rurale, 3735
  Société urbaine, 3820
Tanzanie
  Capitalisme d'État, 3732
  Chômeurs, 4197
  Conditions de travail, 4396
  Demande de main d'oeuvre, 2939
  Fécondité, 2939
  Femmes, 2600
  Industrie minière, 4396
  Partis politiques, 4914
  Paysannerie, 3732
  Travail des femmes, 4292
Taux de fécondité
  Corée R, 2946
  Guatémala, 1026
Taux de salaire
  États-Unis, 1966, 5210
Tchécoslovaquie
  Allocations de maternité, 5353
  Bibliothèques, 164
  Composition de la population, 2769
  Croissance démographique, 2794
  Développement social, 2439
  Disparités régionales, 2769
  Divorce, 3083, 3089
  Établissements humains, 3612
  Famille, 3167, 3195
  Historiographie, 2407
  Indicateurs sociaux, 423
  Jeunesse, 2688
  Logement, 3765
  Migration, 3612
  Mortalité, 2890
  Mortalité infantile, 2888, 2896
  Niveaux d'enseignement, 1982
  Planification sociale, 423
  Structure de classe, 2294
  Urbanisation, 3878
Techniques d'évaluation, 2423
Techniques de prévision, 133, 270, 281, 2810
Techniques de recherche, 5066
Techniques de simulation, 760

Technologie, 4023, 4024, 4036, 4044
  Irlande, 4033
  URSS, 4061
Technologie alternative
  Canada, 4028
Technologie appropriée, 4055
Technologie de l'éducation, 2141
Technologie de l'information, 143, 149
Technologie de pointe, 996
  Pays en développement, 4027
Technologie des communications, 1540
Technologies nouvelles, 4026, 4035, 4048,
    4063, 4286, 4482
  Allemagne RF, 4062
  Canada : Québec, 4029
  États-Unis, 4016, 4070
  France, 4032, 4051, 4470
Télécommunications, 1643, 1673
  États-Unis, 1761
Télévision, 388, 1589, 1682, 1702, 1703,
    1705, 1710, 1713, 1730, 1756, 1762,
    2588
  Amérique du Nord, 1665
  Espagne, 1656
  États-Unis, 1640, 1646, 1661, 1714, 1735,
    1755, 4109, 4976
  Europe orientale, 1733
  France, 1679, 1717
  Hongrie, 1692
  Japon, 1654, 1746
  Singapour, 1707
Temps, 316, 319, 331, 2729
Temps de loisir, 4380, 4733-35
  Allemagne RF, 4408
  Brésil, 4405
  France, 4369
  Japon, 4736
Temps de travail, 4380, 4417
  Allemagne, 4990
  Allemagne RF, 4435
  France, 4357
Tendances de recherche
  Suisse, 4768
Tension mentale, 973
Terreur
  URSS, 1260
Terrorisme, 1086, 1087, 1144, 1179
  Allemagne RF, 1107, 1158
  Amérique latine, 1153
  Europe, 1119
  Europe occidentale, 1118
  Italie, 1101, 1138
Thaïlande
  Baisse de la fécondité, 2930
  Changement social, 3786
  Conflits de classe, 3690
  Formation de classe, 2255
  Migration rurale-urbaine, 3549
  Paysannerie, 2255, 3690
  Planification de la famille, 2968, 2975
  Relations parents-enfants, 3110
  Société rurale, 3690

Statut de la femme, 3264
Syndicalisme, 4665
Villes, 3786
Villes capitales, 3908
Théâtre, 1856
  Afrique, 1852
  Bangladesh, 1855
  Belgique, 1851
  Canada, 1850
  Chine, 1857
  Île de la Réunion, 1849
  Jamaïque, 1854
Théâtre traditionnel
  Pays en développement, 1853
Théologie, 1297, 1303
  Amérique latine, 1309
Théorie, 249
Théorie à moyenne portée, 3629
Théorie critique, 250, 256, 258
Théorie de classe, 2278
Théorie de l'action, 204, 220-21, 233, 1230
Théorie de l'éducation, 1874, 1886, 1901
  France, 1893
Théorie de l'équilibre, 824
Théorie de l'organisation, 712, 717, 720, 728,
    4012
Théorie de la communication, 220, 1544, 1571
Théorie de la culture, 990
Théorie de la décision, 554
Théorie de la négociation, 652
Théorie de la population, 436, 2510
Théorie des catastrophes, 640
Théorie des graphes, 315
Théorie des jeux, 446
Théorie des systèmes généraux, 439, 440
Théorie du développement, 2491, 2494, 3255
Théorie du rôle, 805
Théorie politique, 3938
Théorie sociale, 206, 268, 786, 1000, 4806,
    4928, 5054, 5299, 5321, 5339
Théorie sociologique, 194, 196, 199, 202, 206,
    208, 210-11, 213, 216, 226-27, 236,
    247, 251-53, 257, 260, 263, 268-69,
    391, 963
  Allemagne, 217
  Inde, 235
  Pologne, 240
Théories artistiques, 1767
Thesaurus, 167, 1914
Thomas, W. I., 5
Tibet
  Réfugiés, 3506
Togo
  Famille, 2938
  Fécondité, 2938
Tolérance
  États-Unis, 830
  Israël, 830
Tönnies, F., 3621
Totalitarisme, 4811, 4815
Touraine, Alain, 4940
Tourisme, 4739, 4740, 4742

Belgique, 4758
France, 3871, 4738
Pays de la CEE, 4750
Tourisme international
  Asie du Sud-Est, 3050
  Pays en développement, 4752
Toxicomanie, 5119, 5133
  États-Unis, 1074, 2891, 5118, 5127, 5129,
    5137, 5139, 5140
  Italie, 5122, 5123
Tradition culturelle, 4128
Tradition orale
  Pays en développement, 1808
Traditionalisme
  Inde, 1014
Traditions, 1188, 1195, 1206, 1208
  Japon, 992
Traditions religieuses, 1486
  Inde, 1014
Traduction
  France, 1809
Traitement de l'information, 142, 676, 1914
Traits de personnalité, 518, 4106
Transfert de technologie, 4059, 4065, 4128
Transition démographique
  Amérique latine, 416
  Australie, 2754
  Inde, 2778
  Inde : Goa, 2807
Travail, 2460, 4150-52, 4157, 4159, 4177
  France, 4156, 4166
  Pays capitalistes, 4155
  Pologne, 4163
Travail bénévole, 3175, 4414
  États-Unis, 4377, 4439
  URSS, 4421
Travail des cas individuels, 5385
Travail des enfants
  Allemagne, 4276
Travail des femmes, 3243, 4234, 4239, 4254,
    4264, 4270, 4287, 4302, 4304, 4305,
    4312, 4322, 4323
  Afrique, 2568
  Afrique du Sud, 4235
  Afrique méridionale, 3211
  Allemagne, 3250
  Brésil, 4255
  Canada, 3060, 4241
  CEE, 4290
  Espagne, 4240, 4297
  États-Unis, 3565, 4233, 4244, 4261, 4263,
    4271, 4274, 4283, 4299, 4319
  France, 2852, 4307
  Mexique, 4317
  Nigeria, 4258, 4308
  Pays de la CEE, 4313
  Pays-Bas, 2618
  Pologne, 4269
  République dominicaine, 4321
  Royaume-Uni, 4259, 4282
  Tanzanie, 4292
  Uruguay, 2800

Travail forcé
  Sénégal, 4347
Travail ménager, 4438
  Allemagne RD, 4386
  États-Unis, 4431
  France, 4404
  Royaume-Uni, 4361
Travail par roulement, 4417
Travail social, 5275, 5382, 5383, 5388, 5391,
    5392
  Allemagne RF, 5384, 5384
  Argentine, 5381
  Brésil, 5167
  États-Unis, 1930
  France, 5380
  Japon, 5389
  Royaume-Uni, 5386, 5387
  Suède, 5390
  Turquie, 5481
Travail sur le terrain, 366, 370
Travailleurs, 1783, 2304, 3125, 4397, 4511
  France, 4519
  Inde, 4508
  Pays-Bas, 5318
  Pologne, 4515, 5136
  URSS, 4429
Travailleurs âgés
  France, 4256
Travailleurs agricoles, 4506, 4509
  France, 4288
  Hongrie, 3701, 4521
  Pologne, 4510, 4710
Travailleurs étrangers
  Allemagne, 4242, 4275
  Allemagne RF, 3439, 4231, 4247, 4260,
    4285, 4314, 4316
  Asie occidentale, 4318
  États-Unis, 1966, 4267
  France, 3896, 4279
  Suisse, 1038, 4230, 4277, 4278
Travailleurs frontaliers
  Pays de la CEE, 4232
Travailleurs handicapés, 2832
  Royaume-Uni, 2825
Travailleurs manuels
  Canada, 4522
  Italie, 4518
Travailleurs migrants
  Afrique du Sud, 2290
  Autriche : Vienne, 4291
  France, 3509, 4256, 4268
  Japon, 3148
  Portugal, 4279
  Turquie, 4316
  Yougoslavie, 3824
Travailleurs sociaux, 5468, 5474
  États-Unis, 5480
  Royaume-Uni, 5445
Travailleuses, 2958, 4264, 4272, 4294, 4296
  Allemagne RF, 4303
  Bangladesh, 4238
  Canada : Québec, 4252

Corée R, 4280
États-Unis, 3041, 4237
Europe, 2783
France, 4288
Inde, 4236, 4273, 4309, 4320
Java, 4298
Jordanie, 4243
Mexique, 5408
Pays en développement, 4289
Pérou, 4686
Tribalisme
  Inde, 3422, 3425
  Iran, 3417
Tribunaux pour enfants
  États-Unis, 5236, 5238
Tribus
  Inde, 2238, 3716, 3717
  Jordanie, 3319
Trinité
  Leaders politiques, 4959
Trinité-et-Tabago
  Classes sociales, 2314
  Inégalité raciale, 3424
  Relations raciales, 2314
  Retard intellectuel, 3424
Tunisie
  Islam, 1400
  Jeunesse, 2683
  Littérature, 1804
  Migration de retour, 3478
  Mortalité, 2866
  Politique démographique, 2991
  Presse, 1696
  Production agricole, 1128
  Révolte, 1128
  Urbanisation, 3784
Turquie
  Classe ouvrière, 2269
  Contraception, 2974
  Culture politique, 4965
  Émigrants, 4247
  Identité nationale, 4316
  Islam, 1355, 1489
  Littérature, 1793, 1806
  Paysannerie, 3694
  Politique de l'éducation, 1945
  Population rurale, 4965
  Population urbaine, 3797
  Réformes de l'enseignement, 1978
  Sécularisation, 1489
  Services sociaux, 5481
  Statut de la femme, 3279
  Travail social, 5481
  Travailleurs migrants, 4316
  Urbanisation, 3797
Typologie, 5314
  États-Unis, 280

Union consensuelle
  Danemark, 3073
  États-Unis, 3079
  Europe occidentale, 3079

Finlande, 3076
Universités, 2049
  Allemagne RF, 3217
  Argentine, 2044
  Australie, 2037
  Canada, 2027
  France, 1959, 2052
  Royaume-Uni, 2071, 2085
Urbanisation, 3556, 3810, 3900, 3909, 3917,
  3924, 3925
  Amérique latine, 3898
  Asie, 3751
  Canada, 3850
  Chine, 3866
  France : Paris, 3844
  Hongrie, 2554, 3805
  Inde, 3551, 3779
  Pays en développement, 3766, 3787, 3880
  Pologne, 3813, 3872
  Roumanie, 3894
  Royaume-Uni, 3818
  Tchécoslovaquie, 3878
  Tunisie, 3784
  Turquie, 3797
  URSS, 3888
  Venezuela, 4900
  Yougoslavie, 3834, 3840, 3863, 3872
  Zimbabwe, 2428
Urbanisme
  France, 3763
URSS
  Accès à l'éducation, 3393
  Aménagement urbain, 3775
  Antisémitisme, 3380
  Art, 3498
  Athéisme, 1387
  Autoritarisme, 831
  Banque de données, 155
  Bilinguisme, 1590
  Chansons populaires, 1848
  Cinéma, 1704
  Classe ouvrière, 2268, 2301
  Comportement antisocial, 1232
  Conditions de travail, 4429
  Corruption administrative, 4894
  Culture, 1005, 1378
  Culture politique, 4964, 4972
  Démographie, 2519
  Démographie historique, 2545
  Développement rural, 3742
  Développement social, 2163, 2429, 2443, 2473
  Discrimination raciale, 3393
  Droit, 1260
  Droit pénal, 1232
  Éducation des adultes, 2098
  Éducation permanente, 2105
  Émigrants, 1326, 1374
  Émigration, 3460, 3516, 3536
  Enseignement secondaire, 1866
  Enseignement supérieur, 2048
  Entreprises industrielles, 5277
  Établissements humains, 3614

État, 4845
Ethnicité, 3354
Famille, 3121
Femmes, 2633
Fermes collectives, 3740
Groupes ethniques, 3498
Indicateurs sociaux, 425
Insertion professionnelle, 4196
Intelligentsia, 2348, 2359, 2363
Islam, 1339, 1387
Jeunesse, 155
Juifs, 1370, 1378, 1385, 1823, 3460,
  3536
Littérature, 1823, 1826
Migration, 3441
Migration interne, 3537
Migration rurale-urbaine, 3570
Modes de vie, 425
Morale, 3121
Mortalité, 2861
Musique, 1843
Musulmans, 1402
Niveau de vie, 425
Organisation du travail, 4337
Participation des travailleurs, 2301
Paysannerie, 3740
Personnes âgées, 2755
Planification sociale, 5277
Politique à l'égard des nationalités, 3536
Politique ethnique, 3392
Politique linguistique, 1593, 1625, 1626
Politique sociale, 5325
Progrès scientifique et technique, 4017
Psychiâtrie, 5397
Psychologie, 450
Psychologie de l'éducation, 1866
Psychologie sociale, 479
Recherche sociologique, 2163
Rendement de l'éducation, 2048
Retraités, 2725
Socialisme, 4790
Société, 917, 921
Sociolinguistique, 2429
Sociologues, 78
Structure sociale, 2163, 2725
Systèmes d'enseignement, 1925
Systèmes de valeur, 1067
Technologie, 4061
Terreur, 1260
Travail bénévole, 4421
Travailleurs, 4429
Urbanisation, 3888
Usines, 78
Vie quotidienne, 3740
Vie rurale, 3726, 3740
Vie sociale, 1173
Villages, 3651, 3680, 3726
Villes, 3754, 3876, 3895
Villes satellites, 3828
Zones rurales, 3676
Uruguay
  Femmes, 2580

Femmes rurales, 2800
  Travail des femmes, 2800
Usage du tabac, 5134
  États-Unis, 2891
  Royaume-Uni, 5409
Usines
  France, 4348
  Japon, 669
  URSS, 78
Utilisation de la main-d'oeuvre
  États-Unis, 4169
Utilisation des loisirs
  Autriche, 4747
  France, 3552, 4731
Utilisation des terres
  États-Unis, 3592
Utilitarisme, 2451
Utopie, 137, 764, 842-43, 846-47, 850,
    852-53, 862, 1516
Utopisme, 66, 849

Vacances
  France, 4731
  Pays socialistes, 4732
Valeur, 1077, 5316
  Japon, 1052
Valeurs culturelles, 1024
  Inde, 1014
Valeurs de classe, 2284
Valeurs sociales, 799, 973
Variole
  Finlande, 2541
Veblen, Thorstein, 66, 4791
Venezuela
  Administration locale, 4900
  Aménagement urbain, 3817
  Droit du travail, 4570
  Enseignement supérieur, 2059
  Folklore, 1203
  Journalistes, 1645
  Mouvements sociaux, 4929
  Politique de l'éducation, 2059
  Urbanisation, 4900
  Villes nouvelles, 3893
Verriers
  Italie, 2289
Veuvage, 3070
Veuve
  Corée R, 3081
Victimes, 606, 636, 5183, 5191
  États-Unis, 5212, 5219, 5242
Videotex, 1759
Vie communautaire, 3629
  Irlande, 3625
  Royaume-Uni, 3118
Vie culturelle
  Amérique latine, 1032
  Royaume-Uni, 1043
Vie économique
  Asie du Sud-Est, 3326
  Chinois, 3326
Vie familiale, 2173, 2627, 4012

Afrique méridionale, 3108
  Canada, 3144, 3157, 3172
  Espagne, 3112
  États-Unis, 1065, 3131
  France, 1983, 3158
  Japon, 3148
Vie privée, 1555
Vie professionnelle, 1110
  France, 3158
Vie quotidienne, 269, 944, 961, 964, 971,
    989, 1182
  Algérie, 947
  Chili, 960
  France, 918, 3778
  Hongrie, 978
  Japon, 923, 2757
  URSS, 3740
Vie religieuse, 1466, 1467
  Italie, 1454
Vie rurale
  Corée R, 3667
  Royaume-Uni, 3719
  URSS, 3726, 3740
Vie sociale, 52, 858, 1166, 1176, 1177
  Japon, 369
  URSS, 1173
Vie urbaine, 1803, 2772, 3912, 5063
  Allemagne RF, 4408
  Chine, 3923
  États-Unis, 3856, 5093, 5192
  Europe, 3857
  France, 3778, 3871
  Inde, 3873
  Pologne, 3864
Vieillesse, 2721, 2723, 2728
  France, 2712, 2722, 2748
  Pologne, 2746, 2759
Vieillissement, 2736, 2740
  États-Unis, 2711, 2720
  Japon, 2739
  Pays en développement, 2731
Vieillissement de la population, 2878, 4450
Viêt Nam
  Statut de la femme, 3268
  Syndicats, 4629
Villages, 3733, 3761
  Algérie, 3665
  Allemagne, 3675
  Bangladesh, 3684
  Corée R, 3667
  États-Unis, 3686
  France, 3662
  Hong Kong, 3729
  Hongrie, 2563, 3700
  Inde, 3698, 3709, 3721, 4831
  Inde : Bengale, 3661
  Italie, 2158
  Liban, 3725
  Mozambique, 3654
  Népal, 3679
  Pologne, 2792, 3678
  Sénégal, 3673

URSS, 3651, 3680, 3726
  Yougoslavie, 3863
Villages de pêcheurs
  Japon, 4513
Villes, 3761, 3762, 3773, 3794, 3827, 3837, 3909
  Afrique du Sud, 3835
  Canada, 3850
  Congo, 730
  États-Unis, 3745, 3750, 3811
  Inde, 3891
  Mexique, 3780
  Pays en développement, 3842
  Sénégal, 730
  Thaïlande, 3786
  URSS, 3754, 3876, 3895
Villes capitales
  Afrique méridionale, 3744
  Japon, 3755
  Royaume-Uni, 3749
  Thaïlande, 3908
Villes moyennes
  France, 3812
Villes nouvelles
  Brésil, 3893
  Égypte, 3927
  France, 3770, 3814, 3887
  Royaume-Uni, 3769, 3807
  Venezuela, 3893
Villes satellites
  URSS, 3828
Viol
  États-Unis, 5185, 5224, 5240
Violence, 1083, 1090, 1098, 1113, 1121, 1122, 1136
  Australie, 1140
  Belgique, 1099
  Chine, 1150
  États-Unis, 1167, 1183, 1185, 1662, 3131, 3153, 5229
  France, 1134, 1135
  Italie, 1184
  Jamaïque, 1106
Vote, 5000, 5001, 5012
  États-Unis, 5019
Voyer, Jean-Pierre, 246

Weber, Max, 39, 233, 252-53, 282, 523, 781, 787, 791-92, 826, 1223, 1296, 1475, 1478, 1897, 2220, 2471, 3141, 3946, 4817, 4932, 5314
Westermarck, Edvard, 247
Wittgenstein, Ludwig, 9

Yoga, 1401
Yougoslavie
  Baisse de la fécondité, 2798
  Besoins de logement, 3824
  Cadres, 4531
  Cérémonie de mariage, 3127
  Changement culturel, 3834
  Chômage, 4200
  Classe ouvrière, 2276

Classes sociales, 2222
  Comportement politique, 4982
  Conditions sociales, 5317
  Conjoncture démographique, 2788
  Crise morale, 1228
  Culture, 903
  Développement rural, 3672
  Différences de générations, 2371
  Émigrants, 4291
  Emploi des femmes, 4310
  Entreprises agricoles privées, 4098
  Famille, 3127, 4982
  Groupes ethniques, 3284
  Inégalité sociale, 2222
  Intégration sociale, 1088
  Intellectuels, 2347
  Linguistique, 1533
  Médecins, 5469
  Migration de retour, 3528
  Migration rurale-urbaine, 3558
  Minorités nationales, 3305
  Mobilité sociale, 2371
  Mouvements étudiants, 2066
  Moyens de communication de masse, 1677, 1678
  Musulmans, 1381
  Niveau de vie, 3840
  Organisation du travail, 4334
  Pluralisme ethnique, 3305
  Population rurale, 2798, 2816
  Population urbaine, 2811, 2812
  Répartition de la population, 2546
  Sociolinguistique, 1533
  Sociologie, 2
  Sociologues, 91
  Statut de la femme, 3263
  Symbolisme religieux, 1452
  Système social, 2154
  Travailleurs migrants, 3824
  Urbanisation, 3834, 3840, 3863, 3872
  Villages, 3863
  Zones rurales, 3127

Zaïre
  Collectivités rurales, 3712
  Délinquance juvénile, 5204
  Droit de la famille, 3161
  Écoles, 2005
  Églises, 1404
  Enseignement des langues, 1615
  Morale, 1213
  Politique linguistique, 1619
  Systèmes de valeur, 1046
Zambie
  Bibliothèques, 162
  Classes sociales, 2302
  Développement des collectivités, 3643
  Étudiants, 2076
  Participation politique, 4990
  Statut de la femme, 4990
Zen, 1329, 1330

Zimbabwe
    Autodéveloppement, 2428
    Développement social, 2428
    Urbanisation, 2428
Znaniecki, Florian, 912
Zones résidentielles
    États-Unis, 3808
Zones rurales, 1483, 3610, 4239
    Canada, 5196
    Chine, 2917, 2959
    États-Unis, 430, 2335, 3741, 4083, 5245
    France, 904
    Hongrie, 5273
    Inde, 3942, 4499
    Pologne, 1013, 2759, 4510

URSS, 3676
Yougoslavie, 3127
Zones suburbaines
    États-Unis, 3756, 3802, 3907
    France : Paris, 3844
    Italie, 3795
    Japon : Takarazuka, 3789
    Pays en développement, 3869
Zones urbaines, 3827
    Canada, 3777
    États-Unis, 430
    Europe, 4922
    France, 904, 5100
    Japon, 3450
    Royaume-Uni, 3771